THE ROUTLEDGE COMPANION
TO PHILOSOPHY OF RELIGION

The Routledge Companion to Philosophy of Religion is an outstanding guide and reference source to the major themes, movements, debates and topics in philosophy of religion. A team of renowned international contributors provide sixty-four accessible entries organised into nine clear parts:

- Philosophical Issues in World Religions
- Key Figures in Philosophy of Religion
- Religious Diversity
- The Theistic Conception of God
- Arguments for God's Existence
- Arguments Against God's Existence
- Philosophical Theology
- Christian Theism
- Recent Topics in Philosophy of Religion.

Covering key religions including Hinduism, Buddhism, and Islam, and key figures such as Augustine, Kierkegaard and Nietzsche, the *Companion* also explores central topics in theism such as the ontological, cosmological and teleological arguments for God's existence.

The final three sections consider Catholicism, Protestantism, Eastern Orthodoxy and current debates in philosophy of religion including theology and religious language, phenomenology, reformed epistemology, religious experience, and religion and science. Also included are entries on topics not usually covered in philosophy of religion, such as sin and salvation, heaven and hell, and prayer.

The Routledge Companion to Philosophy of Religion is essential reading for anyone interested in philosophy, religion and related disciplines.

Chad Meister is Associate Professor and Director of Philosophy at Bethel College. He is the author of *Introducing Philosophy of Religion*, co-editor of *Philosophy of Religion: Classic and Contemporary Issues*, with Paul Copan, and editor of *The Philosophy of Religion Reader*, also published by Routledge.

Paul Copan is the Pledger Family Chair of Philosophy and Ethics at Palm Beach Atlantic University. He is the author of *Loving Wisdom: Christian Philosophy of Religion*, and co-editor of *The Rationality of Theism*.

Routledge Philosophy Companions

Routledge Philosophy Companions offer thorough, high quality surveys and assessments of the major topics and periods in philosophy. Covering key problems, themes and thinkers, all entries are specially commissioned for each volume and written by leading scholars in the field. Clear, accessible and carefully edited and organized, *Routledge Philosophy Companions* are indispensable for anyone coming to a major topic or period in philosophy, as well as for the more advanced reader.

The Routledge Companion to Aesthetics, Second Edition
Edited by Berys Gaut and Dominic McIver Lopes

The Routledge Companion to Philosophy of Religion
Edited by Chad Meister and Paul Copan

The Routledge Companion to Twentieth-Century Philosophy
Edited by Dermot Moran

Forthcoming:

The Routledge Companion to Nineteenth-Century Philosophy
Edited by Dean Moyer

The Routledge Companion to the Philosophy of Science
Edited by Stathis Psillos and Martin Curd

The Routledge Companion to Philosophy of Psychology
Edited by John Symons and Francisco Garzon

The Routledge Companion to Philosophy of Film
Edited by Paisley Livingston and Carl Plantinga

The Routledge Companion to Ethics
Edited by John Skorupski

The Routledge Companion to Metaphysics
Edited by Robin Le Poidevin, Peter Simons, Andrew McGonigal, and Ross Cameron

THE
ROUTLEDGE COMPANION
TO PHILOSOPHY OF
RELIGION

Edited by
Chad Meister and
Paul Copan

LONDON AND NEW YORK

First published 2007
by Routledge
2 Park Square, Milton Park, Abingdon, Oxon OX14 4RN

Simultaneously published in the USA and Canada
by Routledge
270 Madison Ave, New York, NY 10016

Routledge is an imprint of the Taylor & Francis Group, an Informa business

© 2007 Chad Meister and Paul Copan

Typeset in Goudy Oldstyle by Fakenham Photosetting Ltd, Fakenham Norfolk
Printed and bound in Great Britain by The Cromwell Press, Trowbridge, Wiltshire

British Library Cataloguing in Publication Data
A catalogue record for this book is available from the British Library

Library of Congress Cataloging-in-Publication Data
A catalog record for this book has been requested

ISBN: 0-415-38038-3
ISBN 13: 978-0-415-38038-6

CONTENTS

CONTRIBUTORS

Paul Abela is Associate Professor at Acadia University, Nova Scotia, Canada. A Kant scholar, he has published a book on Kant's theoretical philosophy, *Kant's Empirical Realism*, as well as articles on Kant's moral philosophy. His most recent anthology contribution is found in *A Companion to Kant*.

Rahim Acar is a research scholar at Marmara University, Divinity School (Marmara Universitesi, Ilahiyat Fakultesi). His publications include *Talking about God and Talking about Creation: Avicenna's and Thomas Aquinas' Positions* and 'Reconsidering Avicenna's position on God's knowledge of particulars,' in *Interpreting Avicenna: Science and Philosophy in Medieval Islam*.

Pamela Sue Anderson is Reader in Philosophy of Religion, University of Oxford, and Tutorial Fellow in Philosophy, Regent's Park College, Oxford. She has published *Ricoeur and Kant: Philosophy of the Will*, *A Feminist Philosophy of Religion: The Rationality and Myths of Religious Belief*, and co-edited with Beverley Clack, *Feminist Philosophy of Religion: Critical Readings*, as well as publishing various articles on feminist philosophy, philosophy of religion and ethics. She is currently completing *A Philosophy of Love: The Heart Has Its Reasons*, and is working on a collection of her own essays on *Goodness, God and Gender: Enlightenment Secularism and Protestant Feminism*.

Michael Beaty is Professor of Philosophy at Baylor University. His publications include *Christian Theism and the Problems of Philosophy*, *Christian Theism and Moral Philosophy*, *Cultivating Citizens: Essays on Soulcraft and Contemporary Citizenship*, *Christianity and the Soul of the University*, *Christianity: Faith as a Foundation for Intellectual Community*, and *The Schooled Heart: Moral Formation in American Higher Education* (forthcoming).

David Burton is Senior Lecturer in Religious Studies at Canterbury Christ Church University. His books include *Emptiness Appraised: A Critical Study of Nagarjuna's Philosophy*, and *Buddhism, Knowledge and Liberation: A Philosophical Study*. He has also published articles in the journals *Contemporary Buddhism* and *Philosophy East and West*.

Peter Byrne is Professor of Ethics and the Philosophy of Religion at King's College London. His books include *Prolegomena to Religious Pluralism: Reference and*

Realism in Religion, The Moral Interpretation of Religion, Philosophical and Ethical Problems in Mental Handicap, God and Realism, and *Kant on God* (forthcoming). He is the editor of *Religious Studies: An International Journal for the Philosophy of Religion.*

Phillip Cary is Professor of Philosophy at Eastern University in St Davids, Pennsylvania, where he is also scholar-in-residence at the Templeton Honors College. He is author of *Augustine's Invention of the Inner Self* and articles in *Augustinian Studies, The Thomist,* and *Faith and Philosophy,* as well as published lecture courses on tape, including *Augustine: Philosopher and Saint* and *Philosophy and Religion in the West* (The Teaching Company).

Ellen T. Charry is Associate Professor of Theology at Princeton Theological Seminary. Her books include *Franz Rosenzweig on the Freedom of God, By the Renewing of Your Minds,* and *Inquiring after God.* She is immediate past editor of *Theology Today* and has published in numerous conference proceedings, handbooks, encyclopedia, and journals including *Theology Today, Quarterly Review, Sewanee Theological Review, Anglican Theological Review, Interpretation,* and *Modern Theology.*

Chung-ying Cheng is Professor of Philosophy at the University of Hawaii. He has written many books and articles, including *Contemporary Chinese Philosophy, Ontology and Interpretation, New Dimensions of Confucian and Neo-Confucian Philosophy,* and *Chinese Philosophy: Its Modernization and Globalization.* He has published over 200 academic articles in English and Chinese. He founded the *Journal of Chinese Philosophy* and continues to serve as Editor-in-Chief, and he is also the Founding President of the *International Society of Chinese Philosophy.*

John B. Cobb, Jr. is Professor Emeritus of Theology at the Claremont School of Theology and the Claremont Graduate School. He is also co-founder with David Griffin of the Center for Process Studies. With Griffin he co-authored *Process Theology: An Introductory Exposition,* with Charles Birch, *The Liberation of Life,* and with Herman Daly, *For the Common Good.* His own books include A *Christian Natural Theology, Process Theology and Political Theology,* and *Postmodernism and Public Policy.*

Robin Collins is Professor of Philosophy at Messiah College, and specializes in science and religion. He has published over twenty-five articles/book chapters including 'An epistemological critique of Bohmian mechanics' and 'A theistic perspective on the multiverse hypothesis.' He is currently completing a book on the evidence for design from physics and cosmology tentatively entitled *The Well-Tempered Universe: God, Cosmic Fine-tuning, and the Laws of Nature.*

Paul Copan is Pledger Family Chair of Philosophy and Ethics at Palm Beach Atlantic University. He has edited with Paul K. Moser, *The Rationality of Theism,* and with Chad V. Meister, *Philosophy of Religion: Classic and Contemporary Issues.* He has co-authored with William Lane Craig, *Creation Out of Nothing: A Biblical, Philosophical, and Scientific Exploration,* and has written works related to the philosophy of religion including *"True for You, But Not for Me"* and *"That's Just Your Interpretation."* He has contributed to various edited works and has also written many articles and book reviews for journals.

William Lane Craig is a Research Professor of Philosophy at the Talbot School of Theology. He has authored or edited over thirty books, including *The Kalam Cosmological Argument, Divine Foreknowledge and Human Freedom, Theism, Atheism, and Big Bang Cosmology,* and *God, Time, and Eternity,* as well as over a hundred articles in professional journals of philosophy and theology, including *The Journal of Philosophy, American Philosophical Quarterly, Philosophical Studies, Philosophy,* and the *British Journal for Philosophy of Science.*

Donald A. Crosby is Professor of Philosophy Emeritus at Colorado State University. His books include *Horace Bushnell's Theory of Language: In the Context of Other 19th Century Philosophies of Language, Interpretive Theories of Religion, The Specter of the Absurd: Sources and Criticisms of Modern Nihilism, A Religion of Nature,* and *Novelty.* He has also published three co-edited volumes, chapters in books, and articles in a number of journals.

Louis Dupré is the T. Lawrason Riggs Professor Emeritus in the Philosophy of Religion at Yale University. His teaching and writing have concentrated mostly on the phenomenology and philosophy of religion and on the philosophy of culture. He has written fifteen books, including *The Philosophical Foundations of Marxism, The Other Dimension, A Dubious Heritage, Marx's Social Critique of Culture, Passage to Modernity,* and *The Enlightenment and the Intellectual Foundations of Modern Culture.*

Craig A. Evans is Payzant Distinguished Professor of New Testament at Acadia Divinity College in Canada. His books include *Jesus and His Contemporaries, Jesus and the Ossuaries, Ancient Texts for New Testament Studies,* and *Fabricating Jesus: How Modern Scholars Distort the Gospels.* He has also published in numerous journals including *Catholic Biblical Quarterly, Journal of Biblical Literature, New Testament Studies,* and *Novum Testamentum.*

Majid Fakhry is Emeritus Professor of Philosophy at the American University of Beirut, Lebanon. His publications include *A History of Islamic Philosophy, Ethical Theories in Islam, Islamic Philosophy, Theology, and Mysticism, An Interpretation of the Qur'an,* and *Averroes: His Life, Work, and Influence.*

Ronald J. Feenstra is Heritage Professor of Systematic and Philosophical Theology and Director of Doctoral Studies at Calvin Theological Seminary. He co-edited, with Cornelius Plantinga, Jr., *Trinity, Incarnation, and Atonement: Philosophical and Theological Essays.* He has published articles in several journals, including *Modern Theology* and *Calvin Theological Journal,* and in *The Routledge Encyclopedia of Philosophy* and several collections of essays.

Richard M. Gale is Professor Emeritus of Philosophy at the University of Pittsburgh.

His books include *The Language of Time, On the Nature and Existence of God, The Divided Self of William James, William James: An Introduction, On the Philosophy of Religion*, and *God and Metaphysics*. He has also published many articles in a variety of journals.

Laura L. Garcia is a member of the philosophy faculty at Boston College, and specializes in the philosophy of religion. Her articles have appeared in such journals as *Faith and Philosophy, Philosophical Quarterly* and the *National Catholic Bioethics Quarterly*, and she is currently editing a volume on *The Philosophical Impact of the Thought of John Paul II*.

Paul L. Gavrilyuk is Associate Professor of Historical Theology at the University of St Thomas. His books include *The Suffering of the Impassible God: The Dialectics of Patristic Thought* and *A History of the Catechumenate in the Early Church*. His articles have appeared in *The Journal of Theological Studies, Scottish Journal of Theology*, and *Vigiliae Christianae*.

R. Douglas Geivett is Professor of Philosophy in the Talbot Department of Philosophy, Biola University. His books include *Evil and the Evidence for God, In Defense of Miracles*, and *Contemporary Perspectives on Religious Epistemology*. Forthcoming books include a co-edited volume on faith, film and philosophy and an introductory text for the philosophy religion.

Jerome Gellman is Professor of Philosophy at Ben-Gurion University of the Negev, Israel. He has published four books: *The Fear, The Trembling, and the Fire, Experience of God and the Rationality of Theistic Belief, Mystical Experience of God*, and *Abraham! Abraham!* He has also published numerous articles in philosophy of religion and Jewish thought in journals such as *Noûs, Review of Metaphysics, Philosophical Studies, Faith and Philosophy, Religious Studies*, and *Modern Judaism*.

Joshua L. Golding is Professor of Philosophy at Bellarmine University in Louisville, Kentucky. He is the author of *Rationality and Religious Theism* as well as articles in *Religious Studies, Faith and Philosophy, The Modern Schoolman*, and *Tradition*.

Gordon Graham is Henry Luce III Professor of Philosophy and the Arts at Princeton Theological Seminary. He has written many books and articles, including *Eight Theories of Ethics, Evil and Christian Ethics, Ethics and International Relations, The Idea of Christian Charity: A Critique of Some Contemporary Conceptions*, and *Living the Good Life: An Introduction to Moral Philosophy*. He has published in numerous journals such as the *British Journal of Aesthetics, Modern Theology, Philosophical Investigations*, and *Bijdragen: International Journal in Philosophy and Theology*.

John Greco is the Leonard and Elizabeth Eslick Chair in Philosophy, Saint Louis University. His books include *Putting Skeptics in Their Place: The Nature of Skeptical Arguments and Their Role in Philosophical Inquiry, Blackwell Guide to Epistemology*, (as co-editor), *Sosa and His Critics*, (as editor), *Oxford Handbook of Skepticism* as editor, (forthcoming). He has also published numerous articles in such journals as

American Philosophical Quarterly, Noûs, Philosophy and Phenomenological Research, Philosophical Quarterly and *Philosophical Studies.*

Gwen Griffith-Dickson is the Director of the Lokahi Foundation, a research institute in London, and Visiting Professor at King's College London. She is the former (and first female) Gresham Professor of Divinity. Her publications include *Johann Georg Hamann's Relational Metacriticism, Human and Divine,* and *Philosophy of Religion.*

Adolf Grünbaum is Andrew Mellon Professor of Philosophy of Science, Research Professor of Psychiatry, and Chairman of the Center for Philosophy of Science, all at the University of Pittsburgh. He is also the 2006–2007 President of the International Union for the History and Philosophy of Science. He has written in the areas of philosophy of physics, philosophy of psychiatry, the theory of scientific rationality, space-time, the critique of psychoanalysis, and the critique of theism. His books include *Modern Science and Zeno's Paradoxes, Philosophical Problems of Space and Time,* and *Foundations of Psychoanalysis: A Philosophical Critique.*

Wayne J. Hankey is Carnegie Professor of Classics and Chair of the Department of Classics at Dalhousie University. He has spent several years conducting research in Rome and Paris and has held research positions at the universities of Oxford, Cambridge, Harvard, and Boston College. He has published four books and edited seven volumes. These include *God in Himself, Aquinas' Doctrine of God as Expounded in the Summa Theologiae, Oxford Theological Monographs,* and *One Hundred Years of Neoplatonism in France: A Brief Philosophical History.* He has published almost one hundred academic articles and reviews, and since 1997 he has been Secretary and Editor of *Dionysius.*

Harriet A. Harris is a Member of the Faculty of Theology in the University of Oxford, Chaplain of Wadham College, Oxford, and an Honorary University Fellow of the University of Exeter. Her books include *Fundamentalism and Evangelicals,* and, as co-editor, *Faith and Philosophical Analysis: The Impact of Analytical Philosophy upon the Philosophy of Religion.* She also co-edited a special issue of *Women's Philosophical Review,* dedicated to the Philosophy of Religion.

John Hick is a Fellow of the Institute for Advanced Research in Arts and Social Sciences, University of Birmingham, UK. His books (translated between them into seventeen languages) include *The New Frontier of Religion and Science: Religious Experience, Neuroscience, and the Transcendent, An Interpretation of Religion, Evil and the God of Love, A Christian Theology of Religions, The Metaphor of God Incarnate, The Fifth Dimension,* and *Problems of Religious Pluralism.* He has also written over a hundred scholarly articles.

Joshua Hoffman is Professor of Philosophy at the University of North Carolina at Greensboro. His books include *Substance Among Other Categories, Substance: Its Nature and Existence,* and *The Divine Attributes.* He has also published articles in numerous journals, including *The Philosophical Review, Philosophical Studies,* and *Ratio.*

John M. Koller is Professor of Asian and Comparative Philosophy at Rensselaer Polytechnic Institute. His books include *The Indian Way: An Introduction to the Philosophies and Religions of India, Asian Philosophies,* and *A Sourcebook in Asian Philosophy.* He has more than fifty book chapters and articles in professional journals, including the lead chapter, 'Religious violence: a philosophical analysis,' in *Comparative Philosophy and Religion in Times of Terror,* edited by Douglas Allen.

Jean-Yves Lacoste is Professor of Philosophy at the College of Blandings (UK). His books include *Note sur le temps, Expérience et absolu, Experience and the Absolute: Disputed Questions on the Humanity of Man, Présence et parousie,* and, as editor, the *Encyclopedia of Christian Theology.*

Michael Levine is Professor of Philosophy at the University of Western Australia. He has published widely in philosophy of religion. His books include *The Philosophical Foundations of Architectural Discourse, Pantheism: A Non-Theistic Concept of Deity,* and *Hume and the Problem of Miracles.* He has also contributed to many edited works, and published in a number of journals including the *International Journal for the Philosophy of Religion, Asian Philosophy, Theoria,* and *Religious Studies.*

E. J. Lowe is Professor of Philosophy at Durham University, UK. His books include *Kinds of Being, Subjects of Experience, The Possibility of Metaphysics, A Survey of Metaphysics, Locke,* and *The Four-Category Ontology.* He has also published widely in philosophy journals.

Ian S. Markham is the Dean of Hartford Seminary and Professor of Theology and Ethics. He is the author of *Plurality and Christian Ethics, Truth and the Reality of God, Theology of Engagement,* and *Do Morals Matter?* He is the editor of *Reviews in Religion and Theology* and *Conversations in Religion and Theology.* He has recently been honored by delivering the Teape Lectures in India (2004) and the Robertson Fellow Lecture (University of Glasgow) for 2006.

Chad Meister is Associate Professor and Director of Philosophy at Bethel College. He is the author of *Introducing Philosophy of Religion,* co-editor of *Philosophy of Religion: Classic and Contemporary Issues,* with Paul Copan, and editor of *The Philosophy of Religion Reader,* also published by Routledge.

J. P. Moreland is Distinguished Professor of Philosophy at Biola University. He has authored, edited or contributed to thirty books, including *Does God Exist?, Philosophy of Religion: Selected Readings, Naturalism: A Critical Analysis, Universals,* and *Philosophy of Religion: A Reader and Guide.* He has also published over sixty articles in professional journals, including *American Philosophical Quarterly, Australasian Journal of Philosophy, MetaPhilosophy, Philosophy and Phenomenological Research, Religious Studies,* and *Faith and Philosophy.*

Paul K. Moser is Professor and Chair of Philosophy at Loyola University of Chicago. He is the author of *Philosophy after Objectivity, Knowledge and Evidence,* and *Empirical Justification.* He is the editor of *The Oxford Handbook of Epistemology, A Priori*

Knowledge, and *Rationality in Action*, among other works. His articles have appeared in the *American Philosophical Quarterly*, *Synthese*, *Erkenntnis*, *Analysis*, and *Noûs*, among other journals. His just-completed book is *God Incognito*.

Michael J. Murray is the Arthur and Katherine Shadek Professor of Humanities and Philosophy, and Chair of the Philosophy Department at Franklin and Marshall College. His books include *Philosophy of Religion* (with Michael Rea), and two edited volumes: *Philosophy of Religion: The Big Questions* (with Eleonore Stump) and *Reason for the Hope Within*. He has also published in numerous journals including *Philosophy and Phenomenological Research* and *American Philosophical Quarterly*.

Harold A. Netland is Professor of Philosophy of Religion and Intercultural Studies at Trinity Evangelical Divinity School in Deerfield, Illinois. Among his publications are *Dissonant Voices: Religious Pluralism and the Question of Truth*, *Encountering Religious Pluralism*, and *Globalizing Theology*, co-edited with Craig Ott.

Kai Nielsen is Professor Emeritus of Philosophy at the University of Calgary and Adjunct Professor of Philosophy at Concordia University in Montreal. He specializes in metaphilosophy, ethics, social and political philosophy, and philosophy of religion. His numerous books include *Wittgensteinian Fideism?*, *Atheism and Philosophy*, *Naturalism and Religion*, *Naturalism Without Foundations*, *Ethics Without God*, and *Skepticism*.

David S. Oderberg is Professor of Philosophy at the University of Reading, UK. He is the author of *The Metaphysics of Identity over Time*, *Moral Theory*, *Applied Ethics*, and the forthcoming *Real Essentialism*. He has also edited or co-edited a number of books, including *Form and Matter* and *The Old New Logic*. He has published extensively in metaphysics and related subjects in numerous journals and collections.

Alan G. Padgett is Professor of Systematic Theology at Luther Seminary in Saint Paul, MN. He is currently editor of the *Journal for Christian Theological Research* (www.jctr.org), and his own work in philosophy and theology has appeared in over seventy-five academic articles and book chapters. He is the author, co-author or editor of eight books, including *God, Eternity and the Nature of Time*, *Reason and the Christian Religion*, *God and Time: Four Views*, *Science and the Study of God*, and *Christianity and Western Thought*, vol. 2 and 3 (vol. 3 forthcoming).

Keith M. Parsons is Professor of Philosophy at the University of Houston-Clear Lake. His books include *God and the Burden of Proof*, *Drawing Out Leviathan: Dinosaurs and the Science Wars*, *The Great Dinosaur Controversy*, *Copernican Questions*, and, as editor, *The Science Wars*. He has also published articles and review essays in such journals as *Philosophy of Science*, *Academic Questions*, *Philo*, and *Philosophia Christi*. He has contributed chapters to books such as *The Cambridge Companion to Atheism*, *Does God Exist?*, and *Scientific Values and Civic Virtues*.

Terence Penelhum is Professor Emeritus of Religious Studies at the University of Calgary, Canada, where he was also formerly Head of the Philosophy Department and Director of the Calgary Institute for the Humanities. He is the author of many books, including *God and Skepticism*, *Butler*, *Reason and Religious Faith* and *Themes in Hume*.

Ruth Anna Putnam is Professor Emerita of Philosophy at Wellesley College. She is the editor of *The Cambridge Companion to William James* and the author of numerous articles. Her most recent publications are 'Democracy and Value Inquiry' in the *Blackwell Companion to Pragmatism* and 'Varieties of Experience and Pluralities of Perspectives' in *William James and The Varieties of Religious Experience*.

Robert C. Roberts is Distinguished Professor of Ethics at Baylor University. His books include *Emotions: An Essay in Aid of Moral Psychology*, *Spiritual Emotions: Reflections in Christian Ethics*, and (with Jay Wood) *Intellectual Virtues: An Essay in Regulative Epistemology*. He has published numerous articles in journals such as *The Philosophical Review*, *American Philosophical Quarterly*, *Philosophical Studies*, *Journal of Religious Ethics*, and *Faith and Philosophy*.

Gary Rosenkrantz is Professor and Head of the Department of Philosophy at the University of North Carolina at Greensboro. His research interests are in the areas of metaphysics, philosophy of religion, epistemology, philosophy of mathematics, philosophy of language, and philosophy of biology. In addition to some fifty published articles on a variety of topics in these areas, he is the author or co-author of four books: *Haecceity: An Ontological Essay*, *Substance Among Other Categories*, *Substance: Its Nature and Existence*, and *The Divine Attributes*.

Bede Rundle is an Emeritus Fellow in Philosophy at Trinity College, Oxford. As well as contributing to numerous journals and collections of essays, he is the author of *Perception, Sensation, and Verification*, *Grammar in Philosophy*, *Wittgenstein and Contemporary Philosophy of Language*, *Facts*, *Mind in Action*, and *Why There Is Something rather than Nothing*.

Michael Ruse is Lucyle T. Werkmeister Professor of Philosophy and Director of the History and Science Program at Florida State University. He is the author of many books on Charles Darwin and more recently on the relationship between science and religion. These include *The Darwinian Revolution: Science Red in Tooth and Claw*, *Can a Darwinian be a Christian? The Relationship between Science and Religion*, and *The Evolution-Creation Struggle*.

Thomas D. Senor is Associate Professor and Chair of the philosophy department at the University of Arkansas. He is the editor of *The Rationality of Belief and the Plurality of Faith*, and has published articles in epistemology, philosophy of religion, political philosophy, and philosophy of mind. He has served on the Executive Committee of the Society of Christian Philosophers and is the President of the Southwest Philosophical Society.

Gary Shapiro is Tucker-Boatwright Professor in the Humanities and Professor of Philosophy at the University of Richmond. His writings include *Archaeologies of*

Vision: Foucault and Nietzsche on Seeing and Saying, Earthwards: Robert Smithson and Art After Babel, Alcyone, and *Nietzschean Narratives.*

Arvind Sharma is Birks Professor of Comparative Religion in the Faculty of Religious Studies at McGill University in Montreal, Canada. His books include *Classical Hindu Thought: An Introduction, Modern Hindu Thought: An Introduction,* and *A Hindu Perspective on the Philosophy of Religion.* He has published over fifty books and more than five hundred articles.

David Shatz is Professor of Philosophy at Yeshiva University and Adjunct Professor of Religion at Columbia University. He has published many articles and reviews on both general and Jewish philosophy. In addition, he has authored, edited, or co-edited eleven books, including *Philosophy and Faith, Peer Review: A Critical Inquiry,* and *Judaism, Science and Moral Responsibility.*

Mikael Stenmark is Professor of Philosophy of Religion at Uppsala University, Sweden. His books include *How to Relate Science and Religion: A Multidimensional Model, Environmental Ethics and Environmental Policy Making, Scientism: Science, Ethics and Religion,* and *Rationality in Science, Religion and Everyday Life.* He has also published articles in journals such as *Religious Studies, Faith and Philosophy, Zygon: Journal of Religion and Science, The Heythrop Journal,* and *Environmental Ethics.*

Charles Taliaferro is Professor of Philosophy at St Olaf College. His books include *Evidence and Faith: Philosophy and Religion since the Seventeenth Century, Contemporary Philosophy of Religion,* and *Consciousness and the Mind of God.* He has published papers in *Religious Studies, Faith and Philosophy,* the *International Journal for Philosophy of Religion, Sophia,* and elsewhere.

David E. Taylor is currently studying at Franklin and Marshall College. His essay with Michael J. Murray is his first publication.

Daniel von Wachter teaches philosophy at the University of Munich. His published works include a book on ontology (*Dinge und Eigenschaften*) as well as articles such as 'Free agents as cause,' 'A world of fields,' 'The ontological turn misunderstood, and 'Why the argument from causal closure against the existence of immaterial things is bad.' His primary areas of research include metaphysics and philosophy of religion.

Jerry L. Walls is Professor of Philosophy of Religion at Asbury Seminary. Among his books are *Hell: The Logic of Damnation* and *Heaven: The Logic of Eternal Joy.* He is also editor of *The Oxford Handbook of Eschatology.*

Merold Westphal is Distinguished Professor of Philosophy at Fordham University. In addition to two books on Hegel and two on Kierkegaard, his publications include *God, Guilt, and Death: An Existential Phenomenology of Religion, Suspicion and Faith: The Religious Uses of Modern Atheism, Overcoming Onto-theology,* and *Transcendence and Self-Transcendence: On God and the Soul.*

Edward Wierenga is Professor of Religion and of Philosophy at the University of Rochester. He is the author of *The Nature of God*. He has published articles on the divine attributes and other topics in the philosophy of religion in *Noûs*, *Philosophy and Phenomenological Research*, *American Philosophical Quarterly*, *Philosophical Studies*, and *Faith and Philosophy*.

Kwasi Wiredu, formerly of the Department of Philosophy, University of Ghana, is Distinguished University Professor of Philosophy at the University of South Florida. He has published articles on African philosophy and logic in *African Philosophical Inquiry*, *Mind*, *Logique et Analyze*, *The Monist*, among other journals. He edited the *Blackwell Companion to African Philosophy* and has written *Philosophy and an African Culture*.

W. Jay Wood is Associate Professor of Philosophy at Wheaton College. He has written a number of journal articles and books, including *Intellectual Virtues: An Essay in Regulative Epistemology* (with Robert C. Roberts) and *Epistemology: Becoming Intellectually Virtuous*.

Keith Yandell is Julius R. Weinberg Professor of Philosophy at the University of Wisconsin-Madison. Besides his extensive journal publications, he is the author of a number of books, including *The Epistemology of Religious Experience*, *Philosophy of Religion*, *The Soul*, and an edited work, *Faith and Narrative*.

Linda Zagzebski is George Lynn Cross Research Professor of Philosophy and Kingfisher College Chair of the Philosophy of Religion and Ethics at the University of Oklahoma. She is the author of *Divine Motivation Theory*, *Virtues of the Mind*, *The Dilemma of Freedom and Foreknowledge*, and *Philosophy of Religion: An Historical Introduction*. She is also the editor or co-editor of several books in philosophy of religion and epistemology and has authored many articles and book chapters in philosophy of religion, epistemology, and value theory. She is President of the Society of Christian Philosophers and past President of the American Catholic Philosophical Association.

ACKNOWLEDGMENTS

We wish to acknowledge a number of individuals who have been instrumental in the development of this volume. First and foremost, our contributors have done an excellent job of capturing the central aspects of their topics in clear and accessible language – something not always easy to achieve. These colleagues are at the top in their respective areas of study, and their contributions are outstanding. Second, we consulted a number of scholars early on who offered insights into the appropriate themes and contributors; to them we offer a hearty thanks. We also wish to thank Tony Bruce, Amanda Lucas, and the entire editorial staff at Routledge for their strong support and encouragement. They have been most helpful and a real joy to work with.

Chad Meister
Paul Copan

INTRODUCTION

Chad Meister and Paul Copan

The field of philosophy of religion is flourishing, and interest in it is growing inter-
nationally. This widespread appeal is manifested in the large and rapidly increasing
number of monographs and articles which engage in the philosophical reflection
of religion and religious ideas. This volume is designed to be a companion and
guide for those interested in this burgeoning field, whether neophytes or students
or even scholars looking for a general overview of the relevant topics. It includes
an international body of contributors who are not only leaders in their respective
areas but also broad in their backgrounds and in their religious and philosophical
perspectives.

We aim to achieve a number of goals through the inclusion of the various themes
and essays. We wish to offer students and scholars a cutting-edge overview of the
central topics in the philosophy of religion among the major world religions. The
religions of the world are multifarious, and significant philosophical issues that
have arisen within them are not limited to the western traditions. Furthermore, as
the plurality of religious beliefs expands globally, the importance of philosophical
reflection on them – both as distinct belief systems in their own right and as each
relates to the other traditions – continues to increase. Part I, then, surveys seven of
the major religious traditions, both eastern and western, and unfolds the broad array
of philosophical topics central to those traditions.

In the next Part, we focus on some of the key figures in the history of philosophy of
religion from the various religious traditions. There have been a number of significant
philosophers throughout the centuries whose insights regarding religion both marked
their own times and have transcended the ages. Part II, then, includes ten such figures
from differing traditions and perspectives.

Most of the world's religions, and the central historical philosophers within the
religious traditions, either imply or affirm that their claims are objectively true – true
in the propositional sense – and thus should be accepted by everyone. But how would
one go about an analysis of religious truth claims? Is such a pursuit even warranted, or
is religion, at least in part, the joint product of the divine as well as culturally created
concepts through which we structure and interpret religious experience, thus being
removed from rational objectification? Furthermore, for many religious adherents,
their conceptions and experiences of the divine are not understood in western,
theistic terms. A more thorough appreciation of religious diversity and pluralism must
take into consideration these global realities. Part III centers on such questions and

issues, for they are fundamental to understanding current discussions in both religious studies and philosophy of religion.

Philosophers of religion have spent centuries reflecting on a variety of religious concepts, but none has been more dominant than the concept of God. So it is important to examine the principal topics relevant to the nature of the divine. Regarding the *theistic* concept, the emphasis has traditionally been upon the divine attributes: properties such as omniscience, omnipotence, and omnipresence. More recently, scholarly exploration has included issues such as God's relation to time, the hiddenness of God, and divine action. Part IV covers these traditional and contemporary discussions, and whether the divine attributes are coherent and mutually compatible.

Historically, philosophers of religion have been interested in knowing not only whether the concept of God is coherent, but also whether such a concept is true, that is, whether God actually exists. In Part V, then, we expound on six of the major arguments for the existence of God, an activity known as 'natural theology.' Although most of them are quite old in nature, none of them is a philosophical relic; each one has undergone much evolution and advancement in recent decades. Not all philosophers of religion, however, are agreed that the arguments for God's existence are persuasive or even that the concept of God makes sense. To the contrary, there is a variety of responses to such claims, and there are also a number of positive arguments against belief in God. So Part VI offers six different challenges to theistic belief.

Theology proper – the study of the nature of God – has greatly benefited from the work of philosophers, and such philosophical reflection has been developing through the centuries about doctrines *within* the various theistic religious traditions (known as 'philosophical theology,' as opposed to the more *general* category of 'philosophy of religion'). Part VII, then, includes six chapters on philosophical theology, the first three on the major Christian traditions and the latter three on recent movements and themes. Much of the work on religion and religious ideas has historically been on theistic concerns broadly construed, but more recently many philosophers of religion have concentrated on Christian theism. It is commonplace, for example, to see feature articles in leading philosophy of religion journals dealing with such themes as the Trinity, the Incarnation, miracles, and prayer. In Part VIII, we focus on these topics, which are the synthesis of recent scholarship on distinctively Christian themes.

Unlike a common caricature of the study of religion, the philosophy of religion is dynamic, and both old and new currents continue to develop and expand in new and interesting directions. In Part IX, the final section of the volume, we offer an overview of some of these recent and important topics and trends.

This *Companion* is comprehensive and up to date, covering a plethora of significant themes in the growing field of philosophy of religion. While there are some topics that simply could not be addressed, we believe that we have captured the essence of current discussions. We have provided further reading sections at the end of each chapter in order to provide some of the most important works on the topics discussed. It is our wish that this volume encourages you in your exploration of these important themes, many of which have spanned the centuries of human reflection and dialogue.

Part I

PHILOSOPHICAL ISSUES IN THE WORLD RELIGIONS

1

HINDUISM

Arvind Sharma

Introduction

A striking question emerges in relation to Hinduism in the context of philosophical issues in world religions: that whether Hindu philosophy can bring anything to the table *itself* becomes a philosophical issue. For it has been denied by some leading western thinkers that Hindu philosophy qualifies as philosophy, and this itself raises a philosophical issue in the context of world religions which may be articulated as follows: 'Is Hindu mathematics "mathematics," is Sanskrit grammar, *vyākaraṇa*, grammar? Here Rorty would concede the point of any such comparison, for in these disciplines all are agreed about *the point* of inquiry' (Mohanty 1993: 318). But Rorty would not concede this point in relation to Hindu philosophy because 'Indian philosophy is so utterly different from Western that we should not call it "philosophy"' (ibid.). The implication is that Hindu philosophy never liberated itself from myth and theology the way western philosophy was able to. This is not quite correct because *ānvīkṣikī*, as understood in the *Arthaśāstra*, clearly involves philosophical inquiry in the sense that 'it is *pramāṇair arthaprakāśanam*, examination by means of *pramāṇas* of all such objects as are known by perception and scriptures' (ibid.: 317).

A similar objection is raised by Heidegger, whose position is summed up by J. L. Mehta as follows: 'Heidegger agrees with Hegel that "philosophy" is in essence Greek-Western, asserting that there is no other, neither Chinese nor Indian, that the phrase "Western-European philosophy" is in truth a tautology' (in Mohanty 1993: 319). Additionally, 'Heidegger believed that with the end of modernity, philosophy has come to an end' (ibid.: 319). It is helpful to remember here that 'Heidegger, in an attempt to think about the totality of Western thought, characterizes it as *metaphysical* beginning with Plato and culminating in Nietzsche – a tradition which has led, in Heidegger's view, to technology as a way of will to power, of objectifying and calculative thinking' (ibid.) which is denied to Indian thought. However, this overlooks the obvious fact that 'if Western philosophical thought has operated with the subject–object distinction, so has a large segment of Indian thought' (ibid.: 320).

This controversy raises two interesting philosophical issues in the study of world religions. The first is to draw attention to the fact that although philosophy as a discipline may be associated with critical rationality, 'a system of philosophy has not merely to put forward a theory of reality, of man and his relations in the world, of experience and cognition, *it has also to ground, validate and legitimize its theory. Philosophers have never agreed as to the norms, the criteria and the sources of such validation'* (Mohanty 1993: 327, emphasis added). This point will become clearer in the latter part of this essay.

The second is to draw attention to what have been called the 'relativist' and 'essentialist' positions. In the usage of these terms in the present context, the 'relativist' position implies that two philosophical systems may be so radically different as to be incommensurable, while the 'essentialist' position implies that all of them might well constitute essentially the same sort of enterprise. J. N. Mohanty argues that both positions are mistaken in the context of the comparison of Indian and western thought. He believes that 'there are enough similarities between Indian *darśanas* and the Western philosophies to justify translating *darśana* as philosophy – enough differences erupting precisely where similarities first showed themselves to justify talk of *Indian* philosophy' (1993: 330).

Whether Indian – or for that matter – Hindu philosophy is philosophy or not thus emerges as a key philosophical issue in itself, compelling us to define the term philosophy itself, this illustrates the problem of comparison both in world religions in particular and in phenomena in general. There is now a manifest tendency in certain circles to include the discussion of Hindu thought on philosophical issues concerned with religion and we shall now review the situation in the light of this development (Hick 1990: chs 9 and 11).

Indian philosophy

I conceive my assignment henceforth as follows: to identify the philosophical issues that have arisen in Hinduism and place them in the larger context of the comparative philosophy of religions. One may begin by clarifying that there are 'Hindu philosophies' rather than a Hindu philosophy, as it is usually said to consist of the six systems (Zimmer 1951: 605–14). These are the schools of (1) Nyāya, often described as one of logical realism; (2) Vaiśeṣika, characterized by the doctrine of atomic pluralism; (3) Sāṅkhya, a school which subscribes to the fundamental dualism of matter (*prakṛti*) and spirit (*puruṣa*); (4) Yoga, a system which shares many assumptions of the previous school and outlines a system of praxis for achieving its goals; (5) Pūrva-mīmāṃsā (or Mīmāṃsā for short) which advocates Vedic ritualism; and (6) Vedānta, the school which ultimately became the most influential. Vedānta consists of several subschools, all of which claim to provide the correct philosophical interpretation of the section of the Vedas known as the Upaniṣads. The Upaniṣads, along with a text called the *Brahmasūtra* and the *Bhagavadgītā*, constitute the three canonical texts of Vedānta. The six systems are sometimes hyphenated in pairs on account of their strong affinities as Nyāya-Vaiśeṣika, Sāṅkhya-Yoga and Mīmāṃsā-Vedānta.

The three non-orthodox schools: Cārvāka (Indian materialism), Buddhism and Jainism, should be mentioned, to complete the picture. These three are considered non-orthodox because they reject Vedic authority, which the others accept in varying degrees. According to S. Radhakrishnan, 'The acceptance of the authority of the

Vedas by the different systems of Hindu thought is an admission that intuitive insight is a greater light in the abstruse problems of philosphy than logical understanding' (in Mohanty 1993: 322).

Philosophical issues of one kind or another arise in all religions. Some arise in almost all religions (such as the existence of God), while some are peculiar to one tradition (like the doctrine of the Trinity in Christianity). Be that as it may, philosophical issues can be broadly classified into four categories when viewed in the context of world religions:

1 Philosophical issues that a tradition shares with other traditions, for instance, the question of the existence of God. Here the interest lies in any new perspectives the tradition may provide.
2 Philosophical issues that are more or less unique to one tradition, for instance, whether the Qur'ān is 'created or uncreated.' Although the issue might be unique to a tradition, this very fact might sometimes make it highly significant in a cross-cultural context, in the sense that 'only as a result of the non-participant arriving on the scene, and making novel claims and asking unanticipated questions, does the so-called authentic Other engage in acts of self-conscious representation' (McCutcheon 2006: 734n).
3 Philosophical issues which play a major role in other traditions but play a minor or negligible role in the tradition under consideration. Here interest centers on why or how the tradition has 'bucked' the trend.
4 Philosophical issues which play a minor role in the tradition but potentially acquire major significance in a comparative context.

Existence of God

To take category (1): one philosophical issue which Hinduism shares with world religions is that of the existence of God. The issue arises in Hinduism in at least three ways: First classical Hinduism had to contend with the presence of three atheistic philosophical schools in ancient India: Indian materialism, which denied the independent existence of spirit per se; Buddhism, which accepted the idea of divinities (unlike Indian materialism) but rejected a creator God; and Jainism, which accepted the idea of perfected spiritual beings but not of God (Radhakrishnan 1923: pt. I). In this it was similar to a fourth school of Hindu thought called Sāṅkhya, which in its classical formulation likewise accepted the presence of perfected spiritual beings but rejected God as one (Chatterjee and Datta 1950: 44).

Second, classical Hinduism believes in a God who promulgates a scripture but according to one school of it, the Vedānta, the text possesses intrinsic validity and does not owe its purchase on us as the word of God (Murty 1959: ch. 2). Another school, the Nyāya, however, maintained that the Hindu scriptures called the Vedas owed their authority to being the word of God (Puligandla 1975: 183–4).

Third, Hindu thought possesses not only an atheistic but also a transtheistic element, in the form of Advaita Vedānta. This system insists on the existence of God at the empirical level, while denying it at the transcendental level. Curiously enough, the Hindu transtheistic schools are as vigorous in their defense of the existence of God as the theistic ones (Smart 1964).

Two philosophical issues which arise in this context will perhaps particularly engage scholars: (1) that it is the sacred scripture whose authority is directly questioned, while that of God is questioned by implication, and (2) the defense offered for scriptural authority in some forms of Hinduism is such as dispenses with God.

Both these points require further explanation. It should be noted regarding the first point that a non-believer is described as a *nāstika* (or one who says no) in both philosophical and popular Hinduism. In philosophical Hinduism it applies to one who does not believe in the authority of the Vedas, while in popular Hinduism it applies to one who does not believe in the existence of God. This highlights the point that, in philosophical Hinduism, acceptance of scriptural authority counts for more than the acceptance of God.

The reason for this development lies in the conclusion reached in the philosophical schools of Vedānta that the existence of God can only be established on the basis of scriptural authority. Reason, however skillfully deployed, cannot yield a decisive verdict on the issue, as for every argument it is possible to adduce a counterargument. If the proof of the existence of God can only be based on scriptural authority, then naturally it is scriptural authority which must be undermined if belief in God is to be attacked.

The counterattack to the challenge to Vedic authority produced the curious outcome that the Hindu tradition in general upheld Vedic authority without upholding the existence of God. This sundering involved a separation of the ontological, the epistemological, and the deontological dimensions of life on the part of Pūrva-mīmāṁsā, this school of thought offered the formulation that the Vedas are without a beginning, like the universe, and therefore are in no need of an author, no more than a beginningless universe is in need of a creator. The school adheres to its position so rigidly that it even compromises the standard Hindu vision of the universe as one which, although eternally existent, periodically undergoes phases of emergence and dissolution.

This pulsating view of cosmic time is replaced in Pūrva-mīmāṁsā with a linear one, according to which the world was forever as it is now and does not undergo cycles. This occultation of the ontological results from the epistemological orientation of the tradition, as it proceeded to defend attacks on Vedic authority by the Buddhists, the Jains and the Indian materialists. The Mīmāṁsā school argued that the scriptures of the Buddhists and the Jains have been produced by persons, who are liable to error. Therefore their texts too are open to error. By contrast, the Vedas have no authors as such, whose shortcomings could impugn its authority. The Buddhists and the Jains had also attacked Vedic ritual so the Pūrva-mīmāṁsā school, as upholder of the Vedic ritualism, also defended the performance of ritual laid down in the Vedas. With the Vedas thus being impeccable on account of their impersonal character, the validity of the rituals laid down by them was also no longer open to question. They were to be followed not because God had ordained them but because Vedic scriptures had ordained them.

The philosophical defense of God in the transtheistic school of Advaita Vedānta (Deutsch and Dalvi 2004) is intriguing. This school of Advaita Vedānta believes in the sole spiritual reality of an Absolute, which is beyond God. Even God in this system represents a penultimate and ultimately false reality, speaking metaphysically. To use the idiom of this school, God falls in the domain of *māyā*, or that which is less than ultimately real. Only *nirguṇa brahman* is ultimately real in this system. The creation of the world through the working of *māyā* is described in such a way in this philosophical school that it is possible to derive the whole universe without necessarily invoking God. It has thus baffled scholars why this system insists on maintaining the (penultimate) reality of God. Here again the answer may lie in the epistemological rather than the ontological sphere. There can be no knowledge without a knower and a known being involved, according to this school. This is obvious in the case of perception *in* the world. But what of the perception *of* the world? Unless God is conceived as its knower, the world would not qualify as knowable. So once again epistemology has a direct bearing on the ontology of a system.

Verbal testimony

Taking category (2): a philosophical issue perhaps unique to Hindu philosophy is that of verbal testimony as an independent means of knowledge (Hiriyanna 1949: 44–6). The point needs to be elaborated. Most schools of philosophy tend to accept two main ways of knowing: perception and reason (inference). Students are familiar with the debates between empiricism and rationalism so that their relative merits as means of knowledge could provide a point of contention, but few would deny that these could be counted as the two main ways of knowing (Hick 1990: 68–71). Hindu philosophy differs in this respect in offering no fewer than six ways of knowing, which should at least be listed: (1) *pratyakṣa* (perception); (2) *anumāna* (inference); (3) *upamāna* (comparison); (4) *śabda* (verbal authority); (5) *arthāpatti* (postulation) and (6) *abhāva* (non-cognition), although any detailed discussion might run the risk of becoming esoteric (Datta 1932).

Of special interest to us in the present context is *śabda* or verbal testimony, which should be clearly distinguished from *pratyakṣa* (perception) and *anumāna* (inference) as follows. It could be argued that verbal testimony should *not* constitute a special and independent way of knowing because it can be successfully subsumed under *pratyakṣa* or *anumāna*. Words are heard; so they could be placed in the category of perception. Moreover, their truth is to be inferred from the reliability of the speaker; so their validity could also be considered as being based on inference. To understand the Hindu position, one must distinguish clearly between words, and the knowledge conveyed by words. Let us suppose that someone comes and tells us: 'It is raining in the part of the town I am from.' Now these words constitute perception and I may believe them to be true on account of the reliability of the speaker, but the *content* of knowledge conveyed by them is independent of the words and the speaker. *New* knowledge has been conveyed through this act of verbal testimony which is *not* derived either by perception or inference on the part of the person who acquired it.

The contribution of verbal testimony to epistemology is gaining increasing recognition. It is also possible to associate it with two other ideas: the view that the justification for verbal testimony must be sought within words themselves and the further view that its acceptance on its own is a subtle repudiation of the genetic fallacy.

There has been a positive reappraisal of *śabda* or verbal testimony in recent times. Mohanty writes that the theory of *śabda* as *pramāṇa* or verbal and Vedic testimony as a particular feature of Hindu philosophy

> has been criticized as having excluded from the reaches of the Indian thinker a truly critical spirit. I myself used to think so and have not been excused by my colleagues for the severity with which I attacked the theory of *śabdapramāṇa*. Reading Gadamer's *Truth and Method* made me see that while in many details, my criticism was valid, I had not perceived the true nature of *śabda* vis-à-vis critical reason. If Gadamer is right, authentic thinking takes place from within a tradition. The theory of *śabdapramāṇa* raises this insight into a self-conscious epistemological theory. (1993: 328)

Elsewhere he expresses himself on this point as follows:

> Earlier in this essay I had asked two questions: first, can utterances of a speaker cause us to know something which we could have possibly known, given suitable circumstances, by perception (or by inference)? The second question was: is there some unique sort of object which can be known only by cognitions generated by utterances (or texts)? I have dealt with the first question in some detail in order to cast doubt on the claim that such word-generated knowledge of perceptible things is a mode of knowing *sui generis*. Even if this question is answered in the negative, the thesis of *śabdapramāṇa* is not thereby shown to be worthless. On the contrary, the main strength of the theory, and perhaps its original purpose, was to make room for a distinctive way of knowing about a domain of objects which cannot be known otherwise. There are rather two such domains: the alleged supersensible objects such as God, afterlife, soul, karma which are all allegedly real. The other domain consists of ethical duties (*dharma*). An issue far more decisive than the first question for Indian thought was: how do we know about such matters? Here the thesis of *śabdapramāṇa*, already established in the familiar cases of ordinary discourse, is found ready at hand. (Mohanty 2001: 54)

Another speciality of Hindu thought is best related anecdotally, although this does not make it any less significant. Huston Smith writes:

> In 1970, while conducting thirty students around the world for an academic year to study cultures on location, I availed myself of my professional friendship with a distinguished philosopher at the University of Madras,

T. M. P. Mahadevan, to ask him to speak to my students. I felt awkward about the invitation for I assigned him an impossible topic, to explain to neophytes in one short morning how Indian philosophy differs from Western philosophy. I needn't have been concerned, for he rose to the occasion effortlessly. Beginning with a sentence that I remember verbatim for the scope it covered, he said, matter-of-factly: 'Indian philosophy differs from Western in that Western philosophers philosophize from a single state of consciousness, the waking state, whereas India philosophizes from them all.' From that arresting beginning, he went on to explain that India sees waking conscious as one state among four, the other three being the dream state, the state of dreamless sleep, and a final state that is so far from our waking consciousness that it is referred to simply as 'the fourth.'

I pass over the fact that it is only in the last fifty years that the West has taken serious notice of the difference between dream and dreamless sleep, which difference yogis have worked with for millennia. What is important is not the time scale, but the different ways the two civilizations characterize dreamless sleep. The West does not assume that it includes awareness, whereas India holds that we are then more intensely aware than we are when we are awake or dreaming. (Smith 2000: 69–70)

A third feature somewhat unique to the Hindu tradition is its claim that memory, while it constitutes a form of knowledge, may not be considered an independent source of knowledge (Datta 1932: 24–8). This position does not seem to possess a broader philosophical significance, unlike the previous examples, although modern Hindu thinkers are beginning to question it (Olson 2006: 436).

A fourth feature of Hindu thought, however, may possess a special significance in the context of world religions. It is a remarkable feature of Hindu thought that almost all of its schools of thought possess a theory of error (*khyāti*). Thus while theories of truth are not ignored, the extent to which theories of error have evolved in the history of Hindu thought is truly remarkable (Hiriyanna 1957: chs 1–6). This may be in part due to the fact that the various schools of Hindu philosophy evolved side by side in constant debate, instead of the successive replacement of one philosophical school by another, which characterizes the history of western thought (Chatterjee and Datta 1950: 9–10). The question arises: 'If truth is self-evident and every knowledge claims truth, how does error arise? The problem of error has been discussed threadbare by every Indian school' (ibid.: 337). According to the Nyāya-Vaiśeṣika school 'error always has an objective basis, and ... its erroneous character lies in transferring to what is actually presented some feature which does not belong to it' (Hiriyanna 1949: 98). This happens when a rope is mistaken for a snake that has been seen elsewhere, and is technically called *anyathākhyāti*. According to Sāṅkhya-Yoga, error 'is partial knowledge of the thing or things in question which leads to a misconception about them' (Hiriyanna 1957: 29). When we mistake a rope for a snake, according to this account, we have 'stopped short at grasping its features which are common to both' (ibid.: 28); according to one school of Mīmāṃsā, error is due to 'losing sight that two things are unrelated,' namely the rope and the snake, while according to another school it is to be 'ascribed to a wrong synthesis of them' (ibid.: 34), namely that the rope and the snake have been confused (Rao 1998).

Yet another feature of Hindu thought may prove to be of special relevance to the study of world religions. This consists of its identification of comparison (*upamāna*) as a distinct way of knowing, a claim which should not surprise comparative religionists. Jonathan Z. Smith is only refining it as a means when he suggests that it might be more sophisticated to say that A is more like B than C, instead of saying that A, B, and C are alike. The way the significance of comparison is elaborated in Mīmāṃsā (Chatterjee and Datta 1950: 325–6) may be of particular interest; it is argued there that if we come to know that a wild cow (*gavaya*) is a cow because it is comparable to a cow, the essence of the matter consists not of the realization that a *gavaya* is like a cow but that the cow is like a *gavaya*. Thus when in the study of religion we exclaim that tradition A is like tradition B, the point to bear in mind is that this implies that tradition B is like tradition A.

Faith and theodicy

The issue of reason and revelation has been a major philosophical one in the history of other religious systems, but in Hinduism the contest between them never acquired the sharp contours it did in the Abrahamic religions. This might even seem odd given the epistemological significance accorded to scriptural authority or verbal testimony (*śabda*) in Hinduism. To understand the low threshold of conflict between the two in Hinduism, one needs to appreciate the architectonics of the tradition which has consistently emphasized experience and practice (*vijñāna*) over knowledge and dogma (*jñāna*). The primacy that the tradition as a whole accords to actual realization or experience of religious truth has had its effect on the philosophical component of the tradition. One way in which this effect has manifested is the notion of *jīvamukti* or 'living liberation,' which makes philosophical truths not merely academic abstractions but realizable insights into the nature of reality. While it is true that not all schools of Hindu philosophy subscribe to the idea of 'living liberation,' many do, and even those who do not have close analogues to it. This ultimately experiential orientation of Vedantic philosophy, especially, subordinated other merely philosophical – as distinguished from experiential – means of knowing to the latter. When revelation and reason are thus combined with experience, their dyadic opposition yields to the reconciliation that while revelation may be above reason, it cannot be opposed to it (Hiriyanna 1932: 181).

Another issue which has played a major role in the history of religious thought is theodicy. The historian and philosopher Huston Smith says, for instance: 'Evil provides the primary challenge to every religious view of life and the world. Philosophies have no explanation – evil is the rock of Gibraltar on which all rational systems eventually founder and end up in splinters' (Smith 2003: 145). Hindu philosophy, however, is imbued with the notion that we live in not just a universe but in a just universe on account of the pervasive influence of the doctrine of karma within it. Karma virtually insulates God, as it were, from having to answer for evil in the world. The following account is noteworthy in this respect:

> Deussen refers thus to the case of a blind man whom he once met during his Indian tour: 'Not knowing that he had been blind from birth, I sympathized with him and asked by what unfortunate accident the loss of sight had come upon him. Immediately and without showing any sign of bitterness, the answer was ready on his lips, "by some crime committed in a former birth." ' (Hiriyanna 1949: 48–9).

Meaningful scripture

An issue which has played a minor role in the Hindu tradition, which has major importance for modern philosophy, is its view regarding what is meaningful in scripture. The point is best introduced with the help of the following citation from K. Satchidanada Murty (1959: 312–13):

> In this context the principle accepted by the Mīmāṁsā and the Vedānta schools, namely, that a religious scripture is not meant for giving us knowledge of perceptible, or inferable things, is to be borne in mind. This would mean that in a religious scripture it is in vain to seek science or history, and that (as Śaṅkara says clearly) where a scriptural passage contradicts an evident truth of perception, or inference, it is not really a scriptural passage but an *arthavāda* to be discarded. Had European theologians followed this principle, much of the conflict between science and religion could have been avoided. Centuries ago Pseudo-Dionysius said that scriptures are intelligible only to those who can free themselves from 'puerile myths.' Kumārila and Śaṅkara recognized this, and put it into practice. This, again, does not mean there can be no history, or science at all in a scripture; but that it is not what is *important* in a scripture; though, it may, for instance, tell how at a particular time in the past certain people reacted to certain historical events, and saw in them a more direct disclosure of God's activity than in other events; or, in other words, a scripture may provide us with an evaluation of history, based on faith (*Heilsgeschichte*), but not objective history (for that cannot be *saving* history).
>
> It is a great tribute to the ancient Hindu thinkers that principles of scriptural exegesis somewhat similar to theirs are now being advocated by some of the foremost Christian theologians; to wit, the powerful movement of *Entmythologisierung* [demythologizing] inaugurated by Prof. Bultmann.

This context also provides the scope for exploring another key issue: the relationship between religion and science, which has been a highly contentious one in the history of the West, while India has by and large escaped this tension. Huston Smith notes that Alfred North Whitehead called science and religion 'the two most powerful forces in Western history, and he went on to say that the future of humanity will depend on how these two forces settle down into relationship. For five hundred years, the relationship has been a nightmare. For several centuries the Christian Church abused its power, trying to strangle science in its cradle. Once science gained the upper hand in this century, it went on the attack, trying to retire beliefs to the old folks homes!' (Smith 2003: 240). The history of Hinduism has been spared this titanic contest.

Theory and practice

An important philosophical issue raised by Hinduism in the context of the world religions is the relation of philosophy to life. Hindu thinkers have often accused western thought of being too theoretical and academic and not sufficiently connected with the spiritual life. Marx famously declared that traditional philosophers had missed the point of philosophizing: the goal is not merely to *interpret* the world, but to *change* it. Hindu thinkers would have sympathized with this orientation, even while differing from Marxism as such, as being too closely tied to only one dimension of life, namely *artha* or political economy, which counts as only one of the four goals of human existence in Hindu axiology. The other three goals of human life accepted in Hinduism are the pursuit of righteousness (*dharma*) as well as pleasure (*kāma*). To these then is added *mokṣa* (liberation or salvation) as the goal of the spiritual life. This may be an extraordinary norm as opposed to the others but is listed with them – its extraordinariness perhaps not unconnected with the 'leap philosophies' – or philosophies which emphasize a stark discontinuity between conventional and metaphysical truths – found in India (Potter 1965: chs 1 and 11).

Two interesting points emerge from this thrust of the discussion. The first is the close alliance between theory and practice which has been advocated in Hindu thought. Almost all systems of Hindu thought lay down a method for achieving the practical results which follow from the theory. This does not mean that theoretical consistency is not valued for its own sake, and that theory is sacrificed in the interest of practice. But it does mean that the theory is supplemented with a spiritual regimen. The second point emerges when Hindu philosophy is viewed in the light of Hindu axiology. This indicates the cheerful acceptance of the fact that there is more to life than logic, or metaphysics, and that religion is properly the response of the whole of life to the whole of reality.

See also Shankara (Chapter 9), Truth in religion (Chapter 18), Religious pluralism (Chapter 20), Non-theistic conceptions of God (Chapter 22), Mysticism among the world's religions (Chapter 23), The problem of evil (Chapter 37), Theology and religious language (Chapter 48), Religious experience (Chapter 63).

References

Chatterjee, S. and D. Datta (1950) *An Introduction to Indian Philosophy*, Calcutta: University of Calcutta.
Datta, D. M. (1932) *The Six Ways of Knowing*, Calcutta: University of Calcutta. Repr. 1960.

Deutsch, E. and R. Dalvi (2004) *The Essential Vedānta: A New Source Book of Advaita Vedānta*, Bloomington, IN: World Wisdom.

Hick, J. H. (1990) *Philosophy of Religion*, Englewood Cliffs, NJ: Prentice-Hall.

Hiriyanna, M. (1932) *Outlines of Indian Philosophy*, London: Allen & Unwin.

—— (1949) *The Essentials of Indian Philosophy*, London: Allen & Unwin.

—— (1957) *Indian Philosophical Studies*, Mysore: Kavyalaya Publishers.

McCutcheon, R. T. (2006) 'It's a lie. There's no truth in it. It's a sin: on the limits of the humanistic study of religion and the costs of saving others from themselves,' *Journal of the American Academy of Religion* 74/3: 720–50.

Mohanty, J. N. (1993) *Essays on Indian Philosophy: Traditional and Modern*, New Delhi: Oxford University Press.

—— (2001) *Explorations in Philosophy: Indian Philosophy*, vol. 1, ed. B. Gupta, New Delhi: Oxford University Press.

Murty, K. Satchidanada (1959) *Revelation and Reason in Advaita Vedānta*, Waltair: Andhra University, New York: Columbia University Press.

Olson, C. (2006) Review of *Explorations in Philosophy: Indian Philosophy* by J. N. Mohanty, *Journal of Asian Studies* 65/2: 435–7.

Potter, K. H. (1965) *Presuppositions of India's Philosophies*, New Delhi: Prentice-Hall of India.

Puligandla, R. (1975) *Fundamentals of Indian Philosophy*, Nashville, TN: Abingdon Press.

Radhakrishnan, S. (1923) *Indian Philosophy*, vol. 2, London: Allen & Unwin.

Rao, S. (1998) *Perceptual Error: The Indian Theories*, Honolulu: University of Hawaii.

Smart, N. (1964) *Doctrine and Argument in Indian Philosophy*, London: Allen & Unwin.

Smith, H. (2000) *Cleansing the Doors of Perception: The Religious Significance of Entheogenic Plants and Chemicals*, New York: Penguin Putnam.

—— (2003) *The Way Things Are: Conversations with Huston Smith on the Spiritual Life*, ed. P. Cousineau, Berkeley: University of California Press.

Zimmer, H. (1951) *Philosophies of India*, ed. J. Campbell, Princeton, NJ: Princeton University Press.

Further reading

Matilal, B. K. (1971) *Epistemology, Logic, and Grammar in Indian Philosophical Analysis*, The Hague: Mouton. (An attempt to present an analytical and critical tradition which is not western in a western garb, to dispel the notion that analytical critical philosophy is only of western provenance.)

—— (1985) *Logic, Language and Reality: An Introduction to Indian Philosophical Studies*, Delhi: Motilal Banarsidass. (A study of logic and dialectic in ancient and medieval India, including a discussion of problems of philosophic logic in Navyanyāya, and the interaction of grammar and philosophy. Other themes covered are the rival ontologies of Nyāya, Buddhist and Jain schools and moral enigmas of karma.)

—— (1986) *Perception: An Essay on Classical Indian Theories of Knowledge*, Oxford: Clarendon Press. (A comprehensive treatment of perception in Indian philosophy.)

—— (1998) *The Character of Logic in India*, ed. J. Ganeri and H. Tiwari, Albany, NY: State University of New York Press. (The concept of logic as found in the Nyāya, Navyanyāya and Jain schools, and in the thought of Dignāga and Dharmakīrti.)

Matilal, B. K. and A. Chakrabarti (eds) (1994) *Knowing From Words: Western and Indian Philosophical Analysis of Understanding and Testimony*, Dordrecht: Kluwer. (An analysis of understanding and testimony in western and Indian philosophical analysis.)

Mohanty, J. N. (1992) *Reason and Tradition in Indian Thought: An Essay on the Nature of Indian Philosophical Thinking*, Oxford: Clarendon Press. (An essay on *āgama* and *tarka* in Indian thought.)

—— (2000) *The Self and Its Other: Philosophical Essays*, New Delhi: Oxford University Press. (Philosophical reflections on truth, beauty and the sacred, and on the self and the others.)

2
BUDDHISM
David Burton

Buddhist thought has a complex and venerable history, beginning in northern India about 2,500 years ago with its founder, Siddhartha Gautama, and spreading throughout Asia to cultures as diverse as Tibet, Thailand, China, and Japan. A common Buddhist teaching is that things have no unchanging essence, a point that can be applied to Buddhism itself, given that it has been subject to a wide variety of socio-historical transformations. Indeed, Buddhism is so internally diverse that it is difficult to generalize about its philosophical concerns. And there is a vast wealth of scriptural and commentarial literature, much of which has not yet been translated into western languages or subjected to academic study; thus our knowledge of Buddhism is incomplete.

Furthermore, there is a challenging hermeneutical issue, since Buddhist ideas are in many cases open to a range of interpretations. Moreover, the philosophy of religion has developed principally as a Judeo-Christian inquiry and so within a monotheistic rubric that does not apply to Buddhism. The very terms 'philosophy' and 'religion' are problematic as they are of western provenance, with no precise equivalents in Asian languages. With these provisos, what follows is a discussion of a number of key themes in what might be termed the Buddhist philosophy of religion.

No-self

Buddhism is a process ontology according to which the world is a complex web of interconnected events in a state of flux; all phenomena are impermanent and arise by dependent origination (*pratitya-samutpada*), meaning that they are caused rather than autonomous. Consequently, one of its most distinctive teachings is the rejection of the Hindu belief that there is an eternal self (Atman) underlying the many changes that the body and mind undergo. The Buddhists explain the person as a conglomeration of physical and mental events that perpetually change – sometimes subtly and at other times dramatically – with no fixed essence around which these alterations coalesce. In one account, the self is likened to a chariot, which is nothing more than a 'convenient designation' applied to its constituent parts, all of which are impermanent (Horner 1990: 25–8). We are easily beguiled by language into believing that terms such as 'I' and 'chariot' have referents that exist in addition to the flow of events to which these labels are applied.

The Buddhists do not deny that the person exists as a complex bundle of interactive forces that can be distinguished from other persons; they do reject, however, any unchanging substratum underlying the empirical personality. Early Buddhist sources undertake a reduction of the human being into lists of constituent processes, most famously the five aggregates (*skandhas*) of physical form, feelings, perceptions, volitional forces, and consciousness (Nanamoli and Bodhi 1995: 232). Elaborating on the no-self teaching, the Abhidharma texts developed detailed taxonomies of impermanent mental and physical atomic events (dharmas) – such as greed, alertness, tangibility, color, etc. – out of which all people, and other things, are constituted. They also provided complex explanations of the causal relations that govern these dharmas (Bodhi 1993) and their claim that the dharmas are instantaneous led to sophisticated discussions about the nature and duration of a moment (Williams and Tribe 2000: 118–22).

Buddhist texts list the ways in which a hypothetical self might conceivably be related to the observable, impermanent individual – as 'the same as,' 'different from,' or 'the possessor of experience,' etc. – and these relations are all demonstrated to be untenable (Huntington 1989: 175–9). Another frequent argument supporting the no-self doctrine relies on introspection. If one watches the content of one's mind, the Buddhists claim, one observes only transient mental states: ideas, memories, emotions, and so forth. One never perceives a stable 'I' that is having the changing experiences. However, it might be objected that the self cannot be observed but is a necessary condition for the possibility of coherent experience, because there needs to be an enduring subject as a locus for the varied experiences one has. The Buddhists reply by applying a principle similar to Ockham's Razor; the coherence of one's experience is the result of concatenations of mental and material phenomena bound together by causal laws, so that the self construed as a metaphysical entity lurking behind the empirical individual is an unnecessary postulate.

An important implication of the no-self doctrine is that, because people have no fixed essence, they can change morally, developing virtues such as generosity and mindfulness or vices such as selfishness and unawareness. Ultimately, the lack of an unchanging self means that people can transform ignorance into enlightenment (*bodhi*). However, debates arose over whether some sentient beings were incapable of enlightenment, with the consequence that they would remain forever trapped within the cycle of rebirth (*samsara*), and whether the achievements of those who were very advanced on the Buddhist path become irreversible or regression would still be possible (Dutt 1978: 106–8; Williams 1989: 98). There were also disagreements about whether women were capable of enlightenment, some Buddhists answering in the affirmative, others claiming that at best women could act virtuously in this life in order to be reborn as men and then gain enlightenment (Paul 1985).

Another controversy concerned the Pudgalavadins, an Indian Buddhist sect that asserted the existence of the person (*pudgala*) that is ultimately real and not simply a convenient label. Neither identical to, nor entirely distinct from, its impermanent constituents, it is the subject and agent of experiences that undergoes rebirth and attains enlightenment. Furthermore, they claimed scriptural backing for their position. Their opponents accused them of virtually ceasing to be Buddhists, although the Pudgalavadins denied that the 'person' was a 'self' (Williams and Tribe 2000: 124–8). In the Mahayana traditions, some texts contradict the no-self teaching by equating the Buddha nature with the Atman, considering it to be an eternal essence possessed by all living things (Williams 1989: 98–102).

Emptiness and mind only

A very different Mahayana development was the Madhyamaka teaching of emptiness (sunyata), which challenged the Abhidharma dharma theory. The Abhidharma ontology was a two-tier affair, with the dharmas alone having ultimate reality. All other entities, such as mountains, selves and chariots, exist only conventionally; they are constructed by the mind on the basis of the really existing dharmas. By contrast, the Madhyamikas claimed that all entities, including even the dharmas, are empty of ultimate reality and thus exist only conventionally. They employ various arguments to demonstrate that all attempts to categorize reality into identifiable, discrete entities result in incoherence. All things are merely convenient designations used to organize experience and navigate the world. Perhaps paradoxically, the Madhyamikas make this claim self-referential, so that even emptiness itself is proclaimed to be only a convention (Huntington 1989; Inada 1993: esp. 148). The implications of the Madhyamaka emptiness concept have been a matter of considerable debate; there have been numerous interpretations, including mystical absolutism, skepticism, and nihilism (Tuck 1990).

Another major division of Mahayana philosophy is the Yogacara tradition – or set of traditions – according to which the world is 'mind only.' Many Yogacara texts explain that the world is like a shared hallucination and there are no real external objects. What really exists is consciousness, described as a non-dual stream of transient mental events. As if a dream, we experience spatio-temporal entities, but they are not really there. The Yogacarins bolster their position by attacking the intelligibility of the Abhidharma notion of physical atoms as partless, spatio-temporal building blocks of the world of matter. And they claim to give a coherent account of human experience without appealing to the supposedly problematic notion that there are objects independent of our minds. However, it can be countered that this Yogacarin denial of the material world has its own difficulties, most notably the problem of giving a plausible explanation of the experience of an intersubjective world. Here the Yogacarins frequently rely on the theory that our shared experiences occur because of the maturation of similar karma (Anacker 1984: 161–75). It has been common to identify Yogacara as a form of ontological idealism, although this reading has been contested (Luthaus 2002).

Suffering

The Buddhist explanation of the human condition focuses on suffering (duhkha). Given that the world is made up fleeting events, no thing can yield lasting happiness, and attachment inevitably causes unhappiness. Cognitive error and inappropriate affective responses to the world are mutually supporting. The ignorant belief that there are discrete and lasting substances encourages craving for them, but the craving itself clouds one's awareness, prompting one to overlook the facts of impermanence and no-self. Together ignorance and craving are the cause of suffering and the overcoming of them both lies at the heart of the Buddhist soteriological project.

This analysis is open to important objections. It arguably neglects other causes of suffering, such as oppressive social and economic conditions. Moreover, the Carvakas – the materialists and hedonists of ancient India – claimed that the Buddhists were foolishly throwing away the metaphorical grain of pleasure because of the husk of pain. Certainly, attachment to things can cause suffering, but the pleasures that they yield can sometimes make the unhappiness worthwhile (King 1999a: 18). However, a plausible Buddhist response is that the eradication of craving is compatible with a non-appropriative appreciation and valuing of transient things evident, for example, in Zen aesthetics.

It is true that renunciation has been a common feature of Buddhist teaching, especially in connection with monasticism, but Buddhism teaches an ethical middle way between the extremes of self-indulgence and asceticism that need not be world-denying. Furthermore, although Buddhists seek to eradicate craving, this does not mean that desire per se is to be abandoned. For instance, the altruistic desire to help others achieve enlightenment has been widely condoned in Buddhism, most obviously in the Mahayana ideal of the Bodhisattva, the exemplar of compassion who vows not to enter the final nirvana until all have attained liberation. Indeed, Buddhism sees ethical selflessness as a corollary of the no-self teaching; the realization that one does not have an autonomous being encourages one to affirm one's interconnectedness and solidarity with others. In recent times, this has provided the philosophical justification for 'socially engaged Buddhism' (Queen et al. 2003).

Karma and rebirth

Like many other Indian traditions, Buddhism accepts that there is rebirth. For Buddhists, the set of habitual tendencies created by one's deeds passes over to the next life, but there is not reincarnation in a new body of a permanently unchanging essential core of the person. Rebirth is a causally connected process in which the being reborn is not the same as, nor unconnected with, the one who died. Ontologically, Buddhism is a middle way between the extreme views that death is annihilation and that an eternal soul transmigrates.

Rebirths are governed by the law of karma, i.e., good intentional actions have good consequences and morally bad intentional actions have bad results for the perpetrator. These consequences can occur in this or in subsequent lives and are proportionate to the seriousness of the deeds. This provides an explanation of why the virtuous sometimes suffer apparently unjustly – because of bad actions in previous lives – and those who act badly can prosper – because they are enjoying the rewards of good actions in previous lives. Buddhist ethics is thus a version of natural law theory that sees moral recompense and retribution as woven into the fabric of the universe. There is no separation of 'ought' from 'is' and – if the law of karma is strictly construed – no moral luck. Indeed, Buddhist thinkers devote considerable resources to mapping the mechanics of karma, explaining the relative weights of various types of good and bad action and the repercussions of particular deeds (Bodhi 1993: ch. 5).

However, there are philosophical difficulties with this account. The person in the subsequent life is not the same as the person I am now and is only connected to me by shared habitual tendencies created by karma. This future person has a different body and also will probably not remember the past lives. When the link between us seems so tenuous, why should I be particularly concerned about how my actions impact on this future person? Furthermore, the law of karma can be used – or misused – to justify social inequalities and discrimination on the basis of disability, for it explains such disadvantages as the just results of previous bad actions.

There are also important questions about the extent and power of karma. For instance, the Yogacarins consider the material world itself to be simply a product of karmic forces. Alternatively, karma is sometimes construed as dependent origination functioning on the moral plane alongside other laws of causality governing inorganic and organic matter (Nanamoli 1991: 634–9). In addition, Abhidharma thinkers were much exercised by the puzzle of how karma can exert an influence in future lives, given that, like all other events, intentional actions are momentary. Elaborate competing theories were developed to solve this conundrum (Williams and Tribe 2000: 112–24). Another controversial matter is the unbending law of karma. In its most rigid formulation, karmic causality means that each individual is inalienably responsible for her own actions; there can be no escape from the deleterious effects of one's morally bad behavior because one inevitably reaps what one sows. However, some Buddhists maintain that the merit (punya) accrued by good actions can be transferred to others – a practice that is part of the Mahayana Bodhisattva path, for example. The implication is that those to whom merit is transferred can experience happiness that they have not earned by their own deeds, and the law of karma becomes less strict (Williams 1989: 208).

Finally, it seems unlikely that scientific evidence can provide conclusive proof or disproof of karma and rebirth. Many Buddhists ultimately rely on the scriptural testimony concerning the Buddha's own enlightenment, when he is said to have had a direct perception of his and others' past rebirths and the law of karma that governed them (Nanamoli and Bodhi 1995: 276). But ascertaining the reliability of religious experience is, of course, fraught with difficulties. Thus, some recent Buddhists have been agnostic about the traditional teaching of rebirth, often seeking to reinterpret the theory of karma to mean that our good and bad actions have positive and negative consequences respectively on ourselves in this life, our friends and family, our wider society and environment, as well as on future generations (Batchelor 1997: 34–8).

Nirvana

The *summum bonum* for many Buddhists is nirvana, the nature of which has been the subject of long-standing debates, both in Buddhism and in modern scholarship (Welbon 1968). 'Nirvana' literally means 'blown out'; Buddhists describe nirvana in this life as the extinguishing of greed, hatred, and delusion. It is the equanimous condition of the enlightened person who, having eradicated craving and ignorance, will no longer be subject to rebirth. When asked to explain nirvana after death – i.e., the postmortem state of the enlightened being – the Buddha refused to answer, claiming that the investigation of this question is not conducive to the cessation of suffering (Nanamoli and Bodhi 1995: 533-6). But it is unclear whether the Buddha did not know the answer or knew the answer but did not reveal it to his disciples. Another possibility is that the question is inherently unanswerable because the condition of the enlightened being after death does not conform to concepts and words. Indeed, many Buddhist texts depict nirvana as free from conceptualization, indescribable, and as an unconditioned reality that transcends the spatio-temporal world (Collins 1998: ch. 1). Here there is a clear apophatic tendency; the ontological status of the unconditioned remains undetermined, presumably because the categories of existence and nonexistence – like all other designations – apply only to the world of conditioned things. Nirvana is accessible only to a special gnosis beyond language, with all the philosophical quandaries that accompany such assertions of ineffability.

A common point of debate is whether desire for nirvana itself needs to be relinquished or such an aspiration can be distinguished from craving and is thus not an obstacle to enlightenment (Collins 1998: 186–8). In addition, there have been controversies about whether the attainment of nirvana is a sudden realization or a gradual process with identifiable stages (Gregory 1988). And some Mahayana texts equate nirvana with *samsara* (Inada 1993: 158), a claim that might be construed as a quasi-mystical assertion that the unconditioned reality is not transcendent but underlies the world of conditioned things. Alternatively, it might mean that nirvana is not an unconditioned reality at all but is simply the correct understanding of the conditioned world as impermanent and without self, together with the state of calm and happiness that accompanies this realization. A closely related Mahayana teaching is that the Bodhisattvas do not aspire to leave the cycle of birth and death but to achieve nirvana in the midst of *samsara*; motivated by compassion, they vow to help all suffering beings and thus intend, once enlightened, to continue to be reborn though without being subject to craving and ignorance. Given the vast number of sentient beings, and the depths of their suffering, this will be an extremely long and possibly endless task (Williams 1989: 181–4). Here we have a vision of nirvana not as an escape from this world but as an insight into its true nature, coupled with selfless service to others.

Buddha

Buddhism rejects the idea that there is an omnipotent, omniscient, and omni-benevolent creator divinity that stands outside of the universe and is responsible for its existence. An early Buddhist scripture contains a parody of Hindu creation myths, describing Brahma as mistakenly imagining that he has created the universe and all the beings in it (Walshe 1995: 75–7). Later Buddhist thinkers, such as Shantaraksita and Kamalashila, present arguments to refute the claim made by some Hindu thinkers that the cosmos originates from God as its first cause and designer (Jha 1986: ch. 2). Belief in a savior God is often considered deleterious because it discourages one from taking full responsibility for one's own actions and liberation.

However, this is not to say that Buddhism is an atheistic religion. On the contrary, Buddhist texts are replete with many types of gods (*devas*), commonly borrowed and adapted from Hindu cosmology. Most famously, the god Brahma is represented as convincing the newly enlightened Buddha to teach others the path to nirvana (Walshe 1995: 213–15). However, these gods are subject to delusion and craving, and are thus not enlightened. As the result of the accumulation of past good karma, they have extremely long lives but will eventually die and lose their god-status, being reborn lower in the cosmic hierarchy as humans, animals, or supernatural beings such as ghosts and inhabitants of various hells. Indeed, the Buddhists developed an elaborate cosmology depicting a vast universe with many physical and immaterial planes of existence, but its compatibility with modern science is a moot point (Gethin 1998: ch. 5).

The Buddhist attitude to divine beings is further complicated by the varied and complex ways in which the nature of the Buddha has been understood. The early scriptures often depict the Buddha as an exemplary person who has perfected all intellectual and moral virtues. Although he embodies wisdom, he does not claim to know everything, but promises only that he has eradicated his selfish craving and thus understands how to cut off the source of suffering. He will live out the remainder of his natural life and then, unlike the unenlightened, will not be reborn again.

The Buddha is a trailblazer; he is unique in achieving enlightenment without the aid of an enlightened teacher. This attainment is said to be the culmination of long efforts in numerous previous lives. As the primary enlightened teacher, the Buddha is worthy of respect and reverence, but as a guide rather than a savior; individuals must by their own efforts tread the path to enlightenment laid out by him. However, the Buddha is also described as having remarkable psychic powers and the ability to work extraordinary miracles. A stock phrase refers to him as the 'teacher of gods and humans' and he is described as neither a god nor a man, knowing the secrets of the universe that even the highest divinities cannot access (Walshe 1995: 175–80, 193). Unsurprisingly, early records reveal debates about the precise nature of the Buddha, with some Buddhist sects emphasizing Siddhartha Gautama's supramundane character more than others, claiming, for instance, that he did not really need to sleep, eat, bathe, etc. but appeared to do so in order to conform to the ways of the world (Dutt 1978: 71–6).

The belief that the Buddha has supramundane dimensions was developed in subsequent centuries in elaborate ways. In particular, many Mahayana Buddhists worship transcendent Buddhas who are thought to exist in celestial planes and have extraordinary powers such as omniscience. They are able to make compassionate interventions in the universe, even disrupting the laws of karma for the sake of suffering beings. However, those Mahayana Buddhists influenced by the Madhyamaka teaching of universal emptiness warn against a literal understanding of these Buddhas because even they are empty. They are conventionally true, having pragmatic value rather than ultimate reality.

Another strand of the Mahayana tradition advocates that the Buddha nature exists in all sentient beings, either as a potential or as an actuality that has become obscured by adventitious defilements. Some proponents of this idea regard the Buddha as a universal consciousness of which all individual minds are aspects. Others go so far as to claim that all beings – not just those with sentience – *are* the Buddha nature, which appears to mean that all the transient things of this world exist in an enlightened state just as they are already, rather than that the Buddha nature is an essence which they possess concealed behind their impermanent façade (Williams 1989: esp. ch. 5). Despite the aforementioned Buddhist refutations of the existence of God, some of these concepts of Buddhahood will sound familiar to theologians.

Experience, reason and faith

The Buddha encourages individuals to test his teaching for themselves rather than assuming that it is true (Thera and Bodhi 1999: 64–7). The ultimate proof of Buddhist ideas is the enlightenment experience itself, and Buddhists generally place great emphasis on the direct perception of reality, often said to be the product of altered states of consciousness achieved by meditation techniques. Buddhist epistemology devotes much attention to the nature of perception, identifying various types and exploring the mechanics of the perceptual process (Matilal 1986). What is most significant from the point of view of the philosophy of religion is that Buddhists commonly accept the possibility of an unmediated apprehension of the way things really are, and that such an encounter is given ultimate epistemic authority. Of course, the problem of self-deception is acute here.

Furthermore, in contemporary epistemology, the Kantian-influenced trend has been to deny the possibility of an unmediated cognition of reality. The human subject is thought to be always active in formulating the experiences that he or she has, influenced by social and biological conditioning. This means that, like other experiences, the Buddhist enlightenment must itself be constructed according to the culture, beliefs, and expectations of the Buddhist who has the experience. The Buddhists offer an alternative to this 'constructivist epistemology.' Although they acknowledge that the superimposition of concepts and prejudices is typical in ordinary experience, this intervention can be halted so that a pure apprehension of reality is possible (King 1999b: ch. 8).

Although Buddhists usually contend that religious experience is of paramount authority, we have already seen that reason also plays an important role; for instance, there are arguments refuting the self, God, and – in Yogacara Buddhism – the existence of the physical world. Operating in a cultural context that took seriously philosophical debate between rival traditions, Buddhist epistemology developed sophisticated rules for correct reasoning (King 1999a: 130–7). Arguments were advanced in order to refute the opinions of philosophical opponents. In addition, reflection on these arguments has been regarded as an important step on the path to direct perception of reality, as the practitioner trains the mind to internalize Buddhist truths.

Other Buddhists have apparently stressed the discontinuity between reason and ultimate reality. For instance, some Madhyamikas employ arguments only to refute the views of others by showing their inherent contradictions rather than to defend any philosophical thesis of their own. Even the claim that all things are empty must finally be relinquished. However, this 'no views' strategy has been contentious, with opponents claiming that the assertion that one has no philosophical views is itself a view and thus self-refuting. Less radical Madhyamikas refute philosophical doctrines that contradict the teaching of emptiness but do hold the view that all entities are empty, and, they contend, arguments should be advanced in order to establish the truth of this position (King 1999a: 139). Another example of anti-rationalism arguably occurs in Zen Buddhism, which uses meditation on enigmatic utterances (koan) to break through our ordinary dualistic modes of thinking to an insight into reality that transcends reason. However, this interpretation is disputed, with some arguing that koans and the enlightenment they foster have a rational content (Heine and Wright 2000: esp. ch. 11).

What significance, then, do Buddhists attribute to faith? In one sense, faith can be construed as equivalent to a belief that one has only until insight replaces it. That is, one has mere belief in lieu of knowledge. Faith in the efficacy of the Buddhist teaching is something one has when enlightenment has yet to be achieved. Buddhist texts describe faith as a necessary prerequisite that motivates practitioners to undertake and persist with the Buddhist training, and it is said to be especially important at the initial stages of the Buddhist path. However, Buddhists also write about faith as the affective state of confidence or trust that is perfected rather than replaced by the direct perceptual knowledge achieved at enlightenment. Confidence in the possibility of enlightenment and the Buddhist path becomes total because enlightenment by way of the Buddhist training has been attested in one's personal experience (Williams 1989: 215–17; Gethin 2001: 106–12).

Finally, faith functions differently in forms of Buddhism that focus on a celestial Buddha or Buddhas whose grace can save one from *samsara*. Here faith replaces knowledge as the primary means to overcome suffering. The dependence on a transcendent, compassionate Buddha is especially pronounced for Japanese Pure Land Buddhists, who claim that we live in a degenerate age in which selfishness corrupts any attempts to gain enlightenment by our own efforts. Thus, devotion to the eternal Amida Buddha, who has vowed to save all sentient beings, is now thought to be the only realistic way to achieve emancipation (Williams 1989: 264–76). This spectrum of views about faith demonstrates again that we should be sensitive to diversity in the Buddhist philosophy of religion.

See also Hinduism (Chapter 1), Chinese religion (Chapter 4), Non-theistic conceptions of God (Chapter 22), Mysticism among the world's religions (Chapter 23), Religious experience (Chapter 63).

References

Anacker, S. (1984) *Seven Works of Vasubandhu, the Buddhist Psychological Doctor*, Delhi: Motilal Banarsidass.

Batchelor, S. (1997) *Buddhism without Beliefs: A Contemporary Guide to Awakening*, London: Bloomsbury.

Bodhi, Bh. (1993) *A Comprehensive Manual of Abhidhamma: The Abhidhammattha Sangaha*, Kandy: Buddhist Publication Society.

Collins, S. (1998) *Nirvana and Other Buddhist Felicities*, Cambridge: Cambridge University Press.

Dutt, N. (1978) *Buddhist Sects in India*, Delhi: Motilal Banarsidass.

Gethin, R. (1998) *The Foundations of Buddhism*, Oxford: Oxford University Press.

—— (2001) *The Buddhist Path to Awakening*, Oxford: One World.

Gregory, P. N. (1988) *Sudden and Gradual: Approaches to Enlightenment in Chinese Thought*, Honolulu: University of Hawaii Press.

Heine, S. and D. S. Wright (2000) *The Koan: Texts and Contexts in Zen Buddhism*, Oxford: Oxford University Press.

Horner, I. B. (1990) *Milinda's Questions*, Oxford: Pali Text Society.

Huntington, C. W. (1989) *The Emptiness of Emptiness: An Introduction to Early Indian Madhyamika*, Honolulu: University of Hawaii Press.

Inada, K. K. (1993) *Nagarjuna: A Translation of his Mulamadhyamakakarika with an Introductory Essay*, Delhi: Sri Satguru Publications.

Jha, G. (1986) *The Tattvasangraha of Shantaraksita with the Commentary of Kamalashila*, Delhi: Motilal Banarsidass.

King, R. (1999a) *Indian Philosophy: An Introduction to Hindu and Buddhist Thought*, Washington, DC: Georgetown University Press.

—— (1999b) *Orientalism and Religion: Postcolonial Theory, India and 'The Mystic East,'* London: Routledge.

Luthaus, D. (2002) *Buddhist Phenomenology: A Philosophical Investigation of Yogacara Buddhism and the Ch'eng Wei-shih Lun*, London: RoutledgeCurzon.

Matilal, B. K. (1986) *Perception: An Essay on Classical Indian Theories of Knowledge*, Oxford: Clarendon Press.

Nanamoli, Bh. (1991) *The Path of Purification (Visuddhimagga) by Bhadantacariya Buddhaghosa*, Kandy: Buddhist Publication Society.

Nanamoli, Bh. and Bh. Bodhi (1995) *The Middle Length Discourses of the Buddha: A New Translation of the Majjhima Nikaya*, Boston: Wisdom Publications.

Paul, D. Y. (1985) *Women in Buddhism: Images of the Feminine in the Mahayana Tradition*, Berkeley and Los Angeles: University of California Press.

Queen, C., C. Prebish, and D. Keown (2003) *Action Dharma: New Studies in Engaged Buddhism*, London: RoutledgeCurzon.

Thera, N. and Bh. Bodhi (1999) *Numerical Discourses of the Buddha: An Anthology of Suttas from the Anguttara Nikaya*, Kandy: Buddhist Publication Society.

Tuck, A. P. (1990) *Comparative Philosophy and the Philosophy of Scholarship: On the Western Interpretation of Nagarjuna*, Oxford: Oxford University Press.

Walshe, M. (1995) *The Long Discourses of the Buddha: A Translation of the Digha Nikaya*, Somerville, MA: Wisdom Publications.

Welbon, G. (1968) *The Buddhist Nirvana and its Western Interpreters*, Chicago: University of Chicago Press.

Williams, P. (1989) *Mahayana Buddhism: The Doctrinal Foundations*, London: Routledge.

Williams, P. and A. Tribe (2000) *Buddhist Thought: A Complete Introduction to the Indian Tradition*, London: Routledge.

Further reading

Gowans, C. (2003) *Philosophy of the Buddha: An Introduction*, London: Routledge. (Philosophically aware study of early Buddhism.)

Griffiths, P. (1994) *On Being Buddha: The Classical Doctrine of Buddhahood*, Albany, NY: State University of New York Press. (Detailed examination of Mahayana Buddhology.)

Dreyfus, G. B. (1996) *Recognizing Reality: Dharmakirti's Philosophy and its Tibetan Interpretations*, Albany, NY: State University of New York Press. (Sophisticated analysis of an important strand of Buddhist epistemology and ontology.)

Siderits, M. (2003) *Empty Persons: Personal Identity and Buddhist Philosophy*, Aldershot: Ashgate. (Considers the no-self doctrine using concepts and tools from western philosophy.)

3

AFRICAN RELIGIONS

Kwasi Wiredu

Time was when the African mind was considered too elementary for so sublime a
conception as that of a Supreme Being to whom the cosmos is due. Not any longer.
African peoples now have a reputation for religiosity barely short of spirit-intoxic-
ation. Conceptual issues are deeply implicated in this evolution of perception. But let
us start with the basic essentials of the worldview entertained in *most* parts of Africa.

The African worldview: conceptions and misconceptions

Typically, in African thought, there is belief in a hierarchy of beings and entities at the
top of which is a Supreme Being. All the beings on the lower rungs of the hierarchy
down to the bottom are direct or indirect outcomes of the creative activity of the
Supreme Being. Of these, the ones next to the Supreme Being – for terminological
convenience, let us call this being God – are an assortment of spirits, some good, some
bad, others indifferent, with, roughly speaking, a corresponding unevenness of ability.
Especially important among these spirits are those that are associated with physical
objects, such as remarkable trees, mountains, or rivers and those that are thought of
as our ancestors. Then comes the category of human beings, conceived as embodied
spirits, and, below them, non-human animals, vegetation, and inanimate objects.

The obvious question is, 'What elements of this ontology have a religious significance?' The conventional answer is, in effect, 'Every one of them.' Or one might,
following John Mbiti to the same effect, characterize the entire ontology as 'a religious
ontology' (Mbiti 1990: 15). A certain way of seeing the relations between human
beings and the extra-human spirits of the second rung of the hierarchy accounts for
this characterization. The more exalted among the spirits are seen by both African
and foreign students of African culture as objects of worship. People address suppli-
cations to these spirits in the expectation that they will be protected against evil
spirits and other dangers. The spirits are numerous, and their preoccupations various.
Some are cultivated in the interests of just a single household, but others may have
spiritual sway over a whole people. These latter have been called lesser deities or gods
(small 'g'). There are many procedures in African life, often called 'rituals' in English-
speaking accounts, which are aimed at establishing or sustaining good relations
with these spirits. Earlier European visitors to Africa called them 'fetishes' and their

functionaries 'fetish priests.' Many of these 'gods' are thought to reside in various parts of our environment or are patrons thereof.

Of equal importance in African life is the role of the spirits of the departed ancestors in the pursuit of human well-being. In Africa in general what death means is the departure of the animating spirit from the bodily frame. To the spirit itself, therefore, the death of a person, by definition, has no terrors. It leaves the body and betakes itself to a territory adjacent to the earth or underneath it where, in the capacity of an ancestor, it dedicates itself to a single objective, namely, the promotion of the well-being of the living.

Perhaps, the use of 'it' in reference to the ancestors here is somewhat of an affront to their dignity, for in African discourse they are not only spoken of as 'persons,' but also as beings possessed of a moral maturity and spiritual power superior to that of mortals. Their manner of interacting with the living betokens these moral and spiritual qualities: they are widely believed to reward good conduct and punish bad conduct. Punishment may take the form of illness resistant to all the best medicines known in the culture and may require the remedial services of spiritual 'specialists.' But whether they bless or punish, the ancestors, as a rule, retain the reverence of the living. In the eyes of a great many students of African religions, this revering of the ancestors has all the marks of religious devotion. Indeed, the early foreign students of African religions called this attitude 'ancestor worship,' and saw it as the essence of African religion. Nor is that all. The presumed likes and dislikes of the ancestors were taken to constitute the foundation of morals in African thought.

Clarifications must now begin. Traditional Africans do, indeed, believe in a whole host of spirits. But these 'spirits' are not conceived of as *spiritual* entities in the Cartesian sense. By this last phrase is meant here an entity that is non-extended, non-spatial, immaterial, as opposed to extended, spatial, material. This was, perhaps, the most fundamental distinction in Descartes's ontology. Mind, soul, or spirit is an entity that belongs to the first category, body to the second. The point now is that this distinction does not cohere with the conceptual framework of any well-known African system of thought. The fundamental reason for this conceptual dissonance is that in these thought systems existence is spatial: to exist is to be in space.

According to Alexis Kagame, the late Rwandan philosopher, poet, priest, and scientific linguist, existence is expressed in the Bantu languages, which are spoken in a great many areas of south and central Africa, as *liho* or *baho*, each of which means 'is there, at some place' (1976). The Akans, a West African people, express the notion of existence in the same manner, almost to the word. To exist, for them, is to *wo ho*, to be there at some place. Note the identical adverb of spatiality *ho* in both cases.

The afterlife

The consequences of the spatial conception of existence are widespread in African thinking. One major consequence is that notions of Cartesian spirituality fail in meaning or, at least in consistency: if to exist is to be in space, a non-spatial entity, such as a Cartesian spirit, is a nullity. What, then, do we have in mind when we ascribe belief in great numbers of spirits to Africans? This will emerge from a short examination of the African idea of the afterlife. Consider its location. As hinted above, some say it is besides our earth; some that it is beneath it. What, next, of its inhabitants? By all accounts, they are thought to be very much like ourselves. Thus Okot p'Bitek, also a philosopher and a creative writer, speaking of the conception of the ancestors held by his ethnic group, the Luo of Uganda, insists that

> they were not spirits but the ancestors as they were known before death; their voices could be 'recognised' as they spoke through the diviner, they 'felt' hungry and cold, and 'understood' and 'enjoyed' jokes and being teased, etc. They were thought of as whole beings, not dismembered parts of man, i.e., spirits divorced from bodies. (p'Bitek 1971: 104)

Note that the sense of 'spirits' in which p'Bitek is denying that the ancestors are spirits is the Cartesian one.

This similarity between the afterlife, as conceived by Africans, and the present life, as lived by them, seems striking to some foreign students of African culture. The British anthropologist Kenneth Little notes that in the afterlife as conceived by the Mende of Sierra Leone,

> the conditions of this world are apparently continued in the hereafter, and the life led by the ancestral spirits seems to be similar in many respects to that of the people on earth. Some informants described them as cultivating rice farms, building towns, &c. It also seems that the spirits retain an anthropo-morphic character and much of their earthly temperament and disposition. (Little 1954: 116)

In the belief of some African peoples, such as the Akans of West Africa, the ancestors are more staid than those described by p'Bitek, and there is far less detail on their careers than Little seems to have learned from his 'informants.' But the empirical nature of the descriptions is constant. However, though constant, it is not complete. The ancestors are, in terms of imagery, like mortal persons, but they are not perceivable to the naked eye and are conceived to be exempt from the ordinary laws of motion.

Ontologically, all the entities or forces referred to above as spirits are of this kind: they are physical in image, but not subject to all the laws of the ordinary world. Let us call them, for convenience, quasi-physical. Then it would follow from our earlier considerations that spirits are admissible in an African ontology only in a quasi-physical sense. The place of the dead would thus be a quasi-physical environment.

The idea of quasi-physical entities, let it be noted, is not peculiar to African thought. Orthodox Christian discourse is full of references to such entities. Angels, for example, are a privileged class of such entities. Again, the resurrection of the dead is anticipated as a quasi-physical process in which Cartesian souls will be combined with the quasi-physically reconstructed remains of bodies, long united with earth, to form persons exempt from the constraints of physical law. The difference between African traditional thought and that of some very influential modes of thought in the West, such as Christian teaching, is that spiritual entities in both the Cartesian and the quasi-physical senses are accommodated on the Christian side while, on the African side, spirits are countenanced only in the quasi-physical sense. The slight touch of paradox in the notion that some spirits are not spiritual (in the Cartesian sense) is, perhaps, responsible for the neglect of the underlying distinction. Whatever the cause, its neglect has led to an exaggerated view of African religiosity.

As noted earlier on, the whole point of the African afterlife is the pursuit of the well-being of the living. The other world is thus a this-worldly institution. This is in deep contrast with the deliverances of some 'world' religions according to which this world is only a preparation for the next, which will be a scene of eternal bliss or blight, depending on a candidate's merits or demerits. The contrasting this-worldliness of the African afterlife is of a piece with its quasi-physicality and suggests doubts regarding the religious significance of the afterlife.

Actually, the idea of an afterlife does not, in itself, have any religious implications. This is illustrated in western philosophy by the example of the British philosopher John Ellis McTaggart (1866–1925), who both believed in immortality and disbelieved in God. In the African context the point is even clearer. There is no such thing as salvific eschatology in African thought about the postmortem destiny of humankind. Thus the work of the ancestors looks rather like 'business as usual,' the business being the promotion of the well-being of their living lineages of which they remain members and the enforcement of their morals. This qualification is important. The ancestors are not the enforcers of general morality. That is left to reason and persuasion. What are supposed to engage the ancestors, as well as the living elders, are the norms of behavior that are directly relevant to the fortunes of their lineages.

The ancestors, then, are a species of elders, and everybody hopes to become an ancestor in due time. If the ancestors were routinely seen as gods and as beings to be worshiped, that would bespeak a general hankering after self-apotheosis difficult to imagine.

This trend of thought must induce skepticism regarding the notion that the African mind is given to ancestor worship, and that African morality derives from the will of the ancestors. It should already be apparent that ancestor worship is a misnomer for ancestor veneration. But the ascription of an ancestor-command conception of morals to Africans requires more comment. What needs to be noted is not just that the concern of the ancestors is limited to the affairs of their lineages. Indeed, if an ancestor is a ruler, his concerns extend to all the lineages in his town or kingdom. The important consideration is that the rules of conduct that the ancestors are believed to help in enforcing are the same rules that the ancestors themselves lived by, or were expected to live by, when they lived. The justification of those rules must therefore transcend the transitory likes and dislikes of particular ancestors.

Meanwhile, similar doubts emerge concerning the religious status of the variety of spirits spoken of in African ontologies besides the ancestors. It should be easy now to understand that these beings are as creaturely as any creature walking the earth. It is true that some of them are reputed to have extra-human powers that can be tapped for the benefit of human beings. But the procedures that have been called rituals and worship in connection with these 'gods' are, in fact, ways of establishing good relations with them with an eye to their services. These include protection against bad spirits, as hinted above, and the promotion of their more ordinary interests.

Of particular importance is the fact that, although these 'gods' are approached with respect and circumspection, they are not venerated in blind faith. The reference to bad 'gods,' for example, should alert one to the fact that the 'gods' are open to moral review. Their efficiency too is not taken for granted. Danquah (1952: 6) and Busia (1954: 205) made this last point very categorically. The former remarks that 'the general tendency is to sneer at and ridicule the fetish and its priest.' And the latter explains, 'The gods are treated with respect if they deliver the goods, and with contempt, if they fail. ... Attitudes to the [gods] depend upon their success, and vary from healthy respect to sneering contempt.' A worse fate can overtake an under-achieving 'god'; he can be killed. The total withholding of respect from such 'gods,' still more, the directing of scornful attention, can drain them of all vitality. Nor are all the causes of death human-made. For example, if a river dries up, the river 'god' is no more. This is not to say that all the 'gods' end up this way, but ontologically, they can. If the 'gods' can be at all vulnerable, they can hardly be made the foundation of a religion.

The attributes of the African God: an Akan example

So what remains of African religions? The answer is simple: belief and trust in God. But its interpretation is complex. The following many-faceted question immediately arises. Is the being we are calling God here, like the Christian God, the omnipotent, omniscient, omnibenevolent, transcendent creator of the universe out of nothing? This is a deeply conceptual question. To answer it I will take into particularistic account the language of the Akans, an African language of which I have a native, first-hand, understanding.

That the Akans ascribe omniscience to their God is reasonably clear. The similarity between this attribute and the corresponding Christian one is also equally clear. God is described as *Brekyirihunuade*, and this strongly affirms that he knows everything. Similarity shrinks, however, when we come to omnipotence. In the Akan language, or more simply, Akan, the word *Otumfuor* is used in reference to the Supreme Being to indicate that his powers are limitless. He can do all things. But does this include creating a figure which is at the same time a triangle and not a triangle? Although most Christian philosophers would say no, some, such as Descartes, have said yes. On the other hand, even at the level of popular discourse, the Akan response is decidedly negative. The alleged project involves a contradiction, and, according to a communal saying, truths do not conflict (*Nokware mu nni abra*). Hence no well-defined project has been cited that the Supreme Being is unable to accomplish. From this standpoint, then, God's omnipotence consists in his ability to accomplish any well-defined project.

What sorts of projects, then, are or are not considered well-defined? The easiest approach will be by examples, and a most instructive example is the following.

Consider the question whether a law of nature can be violated. At least one Akan answer is that since the law was established by an omniscient being, it does not make sense to suggest that it might need changing. Violating a law of nature therefore is not a well-defined enterprise. Therefore, God cannot be said to be capable of doing it, and yet this implies no diminution of his omnipotence.

Some of the deepest metaphysical reflections of the Akans are in the form of riddles rendered on 'talking' drums. One such riddle, in my interpretation, expresses just the consideration rehearsed in the last paragraph. It says, 'The creator created death, and death killed him.' Not even the creator can evade the cosmic dialectic of life and death. The metaphor – a riddle is a metaphor – does not only affirm the primacy of law in the workings of phenomena; it also insists on its indefeasibility. It might be of interest to note that this thought excludes the possibility of miracles, if a miracle is conceived as involving the *violation* of a law of 'nature.' The idea of the supernatural is similarly excluded, which is why I have encumbered 'nature,' its complementary, with quotation marks. If the idea of the supernatural is faulty, then so is that of nature, since the latter presupposes the intelligibility of the former.

Indefeasible law is what defines cosmic order for the Akan metaphysician or metaphysicians responsible for the drum text discussed above. In another drum text, when an Akan metaphysician inquires what the creator created, his answer is that the creator created order, knowledge, and death (Danquah 1968: 70). Order comes first. Omnipotence inaugurates order; but it cannot displace it.

On this account, the Akan notion of omnipotence has some similarities and some differences with Christian doctrine. However, when we come to transcendence, not even basic intelligibility is to hand. The transcendent is that which transcends space and time. In ontologies such as African ones, in which to exist is to be in space, nothing existent can transcend space and time. The Akan God, therefore, cannot be called transcendent. The contrary has been supposed on the strength of a famous myth probably shared by all African peoples. Here is a simplified form of one Akan version: in very, very, ancient times God lived accessibly close above us. But an old woman, hard of correction, kept pelting him with the butt of the pestle with which she pounded plantain to prepare a favorite Akan dish. In disgust God moved himself up inaccessibly high in the sky and has remained there ever since.

This inaccessibility is what has been interpreted as transcendence. But this interpretation is not unavoidable. Nor is it in consonance with the locative conception of existence embedded in Akan and many African languages. If God exists, He will be in space, and therefore not transcendent, but he could still be quasi-physically inaccessible. In any case, a more plausible interpretation is available. The distance that is held now to separate us from God might be interpreted morally. Then the idea would be that it is our wrong-headedness that separates us from God.

The question of creation

By far the most interesting issue in the interpretation of the Akan concept of God is whether he is conceived as the *ex nihilo* creator of the universe. What has already been said suggests a negative answer. Not unexpectedly, the ground of this rejection is the locative conception of existence. From this premise, we can easily see that 'nothing' presupposes 'something'; it presupposes, in fact, a whole world. The idea of nothing here is that of there not being anything of the sort defined by a given universe of discourse at some particular place. Suppose someone asks another, 'What is there?' and the latter replies, 'Nothing.' The conversation will have to have been about some items of interest. They are, perhaps, talking about furniture, and the remark informs of the absence of any such items in the given location. This conceptualization of nothingness is in terms of the epistemic and other interests of beings in this world. Such a relative notion could not possibly underpin a doctrine of creation from (absolute) nothingness.

Relevant here is an Akan aphorism, which, like the drum texts, speaks in riddles and paradoxes. In it the creator is likened unto a bagworm, and it is queried whether he wove the bag before getting into it or got into it before weaving it. I have argued elsewhere that the 'corresponding cosmogonic paradox is this: Either the creator was somewhere before creating everywhere or he was nowhere while creating everywhere' (Wiredu 1996: 121). That either disjunct is contradictory goes without saying, given a locative conception of existence.

To return to the talking drums, we have a drum text that takes aim at the assumption that creation can be conceived on the model of a motivated action. It runs as follows:

> Who gave word?
> Who gave word?
> Who gave word?
> Who gave word to Hearing?
> For Hearing to have told the Spider,
> For the Spider to have told the Creator,
> For the Creator to have created things?
> (Danquah 1968: 44)

'Hearing' here stands for the understanding and the Spider for creative ingenuity. The Akans are extremely intrigued by the creative genius of the spider as evidenced in the artistry of the spider's web effortlessly woven. In fact, one of the Akan descriptions for God is *Ananse Kokroko*, the Stupendous Spider. Now, then, what is the message? It seems to be the following. A motivated action is one with reasons. But a reason already presupposes the interplay of facts, events, ideas and intentions. If the reason concerns the origin of the entire universe, then, since it cannot have any basis in fact or even fiction, it could itself be met with a request for the reason of that reason and so on *ad infinitum*.

The African mind, as shown in the Akan instance, has been occupied with logical and conceptual issues regarding creation. It has been concerned also with narratives of creation. A most dramatic such narrative comes from the Yoruba. In one version creation is said to have begun in what is now the city of Ile-Ife in Nigeria. The place was then a watery marsh and God (*Olodumare*) sent an agent called *Orisa-nla* to go and spray some dry soil upon the area to firm it up for human habitation. Coming, before all else, upon some palm wine and being thirsty, he drank of it, became drunk and fell asleep *re infecta*. Then God sent another agent, *Oduduwa*, who accomplished the task (Idowu 1962: 22). Contrary to the usual practice of interpreting this story as a message of *ex nihilo* creation, it is transparently a demiurgic metaphor.

A remarkable aspect of this account of the 'beginning' is the bringing into play of human foibles in the cosmological process itself. This is even more glaring in Dogon cosmology, possibly the most sophisticated in Africa, in which the world is the result of the precipitate breaking of a primordial egg by its male component (Griaule and Dieterlen 1954). On this showing, the history of the world is the process of remedying the consequences of this act of willfulness.

The problem of evil

One can detect no doctrine of original sin in traditional African theology, but this portrayal of the cosmos suggests the notion that the interplay of good and evil forces is intrinsic to the world order. This brings us to one approach to what in western philosophy is called the problem of evil. The problem is, 'How is it that a creator who is omnipotent, omniscient and omnibenevolent seems to have created a world containing evil?' It seems to be suggested that if evil is intrinsic to reality, then no one is to blame except the specific perpetrator of a specific act of mischief. However, neither in this nor in any other attempted solution to the problem of evil has there been any consensus among African peoples or their thinkers.

Among the Akans alone quite a few different proposals are known, although almost all of them are related in subtle ways. The first is identical with the cosmologically oriented one just noted (Minkus 1984: 116) to the effect that good and evil are both intrinsic to reality. Closely related to it is the popular Akan saying that if something does not go wrong, something does not go right. There is also the contention that evil is to be blamed not on God, but on the 'gods,' that is, the refractory ones (Busia 1965: 20). Even more interestingly, there is the argument that God cannot be said to have created evil, because it is the result of the free choices of human beings. God created human beings and gave them freedom of choice. For him to *guarantee* that they will make only the right choices would be to take away that incomparably precious gift (Gyekye 1995: 127–8). Behold a free will defense, or, if you like, a free will excuse!

In a favorite Akan literary device in which wise sayings are credited to animals, we have: 'The Hawk says, "All that God created is good."' The thought underlying this saying is one that would have warmed the heart of Leibniz. Close to this is also the saying that if God gives the disease, he gives the cure. But, throwing all theodicy to the winds, Danquah (1968: 88–9) claimed that the Akan view (which he seems to have supported) is that, far from God being omnipotent, he, as the 'Nana,' is himself a participant in the struggle to overcome 'physical pain and evil.' All these ideas about evil require evaluation in the appropriate place (see Wiredu 1996). But here let us take up the question of the basis of the distinction itself between good and evil.

African communalism and morality

Because of the communalistic character of African society, there are widespread affinities in African attitudes to morality. African communalism is a kind of social formation in which kinship relations are of the last consequence. Everyone is brought up to develop a sense of solidarity with large groups of kith and kin. What this bonding means in practice is that one understands that one has obligations to a large number of people on grounds of kinship. Since this applies to everybody, it follows mathematically that each individual is the recipient of a corresponding multitude of rights coming to him as the converse of his obligations. Amid this reciprocity, it becomes clear that the principle of these social relations is the adjustment of the interests of the individual to that of the kinship group and vice versa. This, then, is a principle of the harmonization of interests to the advantage of all the individuals of the kinship group. But since one does not live in this world with relatives alone, it becomes clear also that there is need for a principle for harmonizing interests based not on the kinship standing of the other but simply on his humanity. This is the supreme principle of morality recognized in African society. Among the Akans it says, 'If you don't want it to be done to you, don't do it to others,' which is, recognizably, the contrapositive of what in Christian discourse is called the Golden Rule.

This last is the principle to which a traditional Akan would appeal in moral discussion concerning the rightness or wrongness of an action. Moral justification in terms of the will of authorities, human or divine, is left to children and infantile adults. One of the things most often said about God in Akan society is that God dislikes evil. If the Akans *defined* good and evil as what God likes and what he dislikes, this saying would reduce to the unenlightening tautology that God dislikes what he dislikes.

The African mind has been exercised by more problems about the nature of God and his relations with humankind than we have mentioned. A particularly difficult one concerns predestination and human freedom or responsibility. Questions raised are familiar in other cultures. For example, if every choice and act of ours is predestined, in what sense are we free? Are some given good destinies and others bad ones? And what would be the justice of that? Can a bad destiny be changed? (See Abraham 1962: ch. 2; Idowu 1962: ch. 13; Gyekye 1995: ch. 7; Wiredu 2001.)

On the above showing, African religions begin and end with belief and trust in God. This mind-set is not joined to any institution of God-worship or moral exhortation. There is nothing like a church of which one may or may not be a member, and so there are no *dogmas*. In consequence, in traditional Africa there was no drive to proselytism. Moreover, the trust in God is not in expectation of any special dispensation in the afterlife. This is enough to show that traditional African religions are religions only in the minimal sense of a habitual state of mind linked to the idea of a super human being or power or principle having control over human destiny. In this regard, more may not necessarily mean better.

See also Christianity (Chapter 6), Truth in religion (Chapter 18), Non-theistic conceptions of God (Chapter 22), Omniscience (Chapter 24), Omnipotence (Chapter 25), Omnipresence (Chapter 26), Creation and divine action (Chapter 30), The problem of evil (Chapter 37), Phenomenology of religion (Chapter 61), Religious experience (Chapter 63).

References

Abraham, W. E. (1962) *The Mind of Africa*, Chicago: University of Chicago Press.

Busia, K. A. (1954) 'The Ashanti,' in C. D. Forde (ed.) *African Worlds: Studies in the Cosmological Ideas and Social Values of African Peoples*, Oxford: Oxford University Press.

—— (1965) 'The African world view,' *Presence Africaine* 4: 16–23.

Danquah, J. B. (1952) 'Obligation in Akan society,' *West African Affairs*, 8.

—— (1968) [1944] *The Akan Doctrine of God: A Fragment of Gold Coast Ethics and Religion*, 2nd edn, London: Frank Cass.

Griaule, M. and G. Dieterlen (1954) 'The Dogon of the French Sudan,' in C. D. Forde (ed.) *African Worlds: Studies in the Cosmological Ideas and Social Values of African Peoples*, Oxford: Oxford University Press.

Gyekye, K. (1995) *An Essay on African Philosophical Thought*, 2nd edn, Philadelphia: Temple University Press.

Idowu, E. B. (1962) *Olodumare: God in Yoruba Belief*, London: Longman.

Kagame, A. (1976) 'The empirical acceptation of time and the conception of history in Bantu thought,' in L. Gardet et al. (eds) *Cultures and Time*, Paris: UNESCO.

Little, K. (1954) 'The Mende in Sierra Leone,' in C. D. Forde (ed.), *African Worlds: Studies in the Cosmological Ideas and Social Values of African Peoples*, Oxford: Oxford University Press.

Mbiti, J. (1990) *African Religions and Philosophy*, 2nd edn, London: Heinemann.

Minkus, H. (1984) 'Causal theory in Akwapim Akan philosophy,' in R. A. Wright (ed.) *African Philosophy: An Introduction*, 3rd edn, Lanham, MD: University of America Press.

p'Bitek, O. (1971) *Religion of the Central Luo*, Nairobi, Kenya: East African Literature Bureau.

Wiredu, K. (1996) *Cultural Universals and Particulars: An African Perspective*, Bloomington, IN: Indiana University Press.

—— (2001) 'Determinism and human destiny in an African philosophy,' *The Hamline Review* 25.

Further reading

Idowu, E. B. (1973) *African Traditional Religion: A Definition*, Maryknoll, NY: Orbis Books. (A more orthodox view of African religions than the present essay.)

Mbiti, J. (1970) *Concepts of God in Africa*, New York: Praeger. (A collection of the conceptions of God entertained by a great many African peoples.)

Oladipo, O. (2004) 'Religion in African culture: some conceptual issues,' in K. Wiredu (ed.) *A Companion to Philosophy*, Malden, MA: Blackwell. (Criticism of the assimilation of African religious concepts to western ones.)

p'Bitek, O. (1971) *African Religions in Western Scholarship*, Nairobi, Kenya: East African Literature Bureau. (A classic critique of the transcendentalizing, so to speak, of African religious ideas in western accounts of African religions.)

Sawyerr, H. (1970) *God: Ancestor or Creator?* London: Longman. (A discussion by a Sierra Leonian of Danquah's claim in his *Akan Doctrine of God* (1968) that, for the Akans, God is not an omnipotent being but rather a participant, as 'Nana,' in the struggle against evil.)

Wiredu, K. (1992) 'Death and the afterlife in African culture,' in K. Wiredu and K. Gyekye (eds) *Person and Community: Ghanaian Philosophical Studies*, Washington, DC: Council for Research in Values and Philosophy.

—— (1995) 'On decolonizing African religions,' in J. Malherbe (ed.) *Decolonizing the Mind: Proceedings of the Colloquium held at UNISA*, Pretoria: Research Unit for African Philosophy.

4

CHINESE RELIGIONS

Chung-ying Cheng

Consideration of defining conditions of religion

Although there are many definitions and descriptions of what a religion is, we can project the following five conditions for defining an ideal form of religion or religious spirit; they are based on a reflection on all existing world religions:

1 Such a form of religion must provide an understanding and sometimes an explanation of how the world came into being, how life and human life began, what the purpose/end of human life is and what human death represents.
2 It must provide an idea of a good life or an ideal form of life for a human person to strive for or to rest his or her mind or heart on in ultimate peace and ultimate tranquility.
3 It must provide a way or a system of practice for achieving this good form of life so that a community of people, not just an individual, could follow and incorporate it in their lives.
4 It must provide a central authority for maintaining this system of practice which allows justified and regulated changes and improvements.
5 It must actually establish a following or a community who embody the practice and thus demonstrate and testify to the authenticity of the practice.

(Based on my survey of world religions in Bowker 1997)

The first two requirements provide a theoretical profile of a religion, while the third requires a religion to be practical. The fourth says that it must be a project or enterprise to be promoted or carried out. The last indicates an existential presupposition: a religion must not be an empty class even though a class of one member should be allowed.

These five conditions or requirements allow a system of graded realization of religion in the world's religions as we have come to know them today. A world religion must be a robust and bona fide manifestation of the spirit of religion as stipulated in these five conditions. When it meets all the conditions explicitly, we can speak of such a religion as 'explicit religion' rather than 'implicit religion,' or as 'formal religion' rather than 'informal religion.' We can also speak of a living religion which is presently practiced as a form of life and a past religion which no longer exists today. We can even speak of a formalized religion versus a latent or virtual religion which may not have the explicit form and the organization that supports a practice for a community of believers. We may further distinguish religion as behavior observed from outside a given society versus religion as belief experienced inside an individual.

These distinctions are important as they allow us to speak of religion in a collective (or mass) sense as well as in a highly individualized sense of experience of faith, trust, liberation, delivery, and awakening. It is in light of such a framework of five conditions and multiple analysis of religion that we may undertake to characterize and analyze any religion in the world. This framework obviously recognizes a pluralistic approach to religions in the world even though the position of religious pluralism may not yet be recognized in many established world religions. Theoretically, we can see that each condition above allows a pluralistic approach. In practice many religions seek to maintain a doctrinal unity while giving up unified control and management. But it is interesting to note that when religions become highly individualized and privatized in a postmodern age, even doctrinal unity can be fluid and open to change and variation. It is in light of these factors that we come to view and analyze Chinese religion as a form of life and as a system of basic beliefs with its intrinsic philosophy.

Chinese religion must therefore be considered a plurality, with overlapping identities and shared origin from a remote and yet very basic origin of human experience and reflection on the world and the human self (Cheng 2005).

We shall hold that Chinese religion as a general term denotes a whole set of systems of religious beliefs, which range from explicit, formal or formalized structures to forms of life and practice containing implicit, informal, and latent beliefs rooted in Chinese tradition and Chinese history. They are related to a common origin of experience and understanding which are built on various overlapping perceptions and conceptions representing systematic configurations of ontological and eschatological reinterpretations. Whether Confucianism, Daoism, or later Chinese Buddhism, they all fall into this pattern of thinking and organizing and in this sense remain religious, even though individually and intellectually they also assume forms of philosophy and practical wisdom.

The Confucian classic *Zhong Yong* can be seen as holding a religion as a teaching (*jiao*) of the way that comes from the cultivation of human nature. It is significant to see that for Confucianism human nature is mandated by heaven, and hence a Confucian teaching of the way is a teaching of the way derived from reflection on and development of human nature. But for Daoism (or Taoism), as heaven (*tian*) could be also approached from observation and meditation, the teaching of the way (*dao*) can also include the way of heaven independently of human nature. Both approaches are founded on the tradition of the Yijing. This can be said to be the first characteristic of Chinese religion (Cheng 2002).

A second characteristic of Chinese religion as a whole is that even though Confucianism, Daoism, and Buddhism have been historically at odds, they are also involved in a process of attempting to find harmonization and convergence among themselves, so that we can speak of a 'unity of three religious teachings' (*sanjiao heyi*). But this unity is not regarded as a homogeneous unity, but as a unity individually or severally exhibited in different modes of respective absorption and reinterpretation of the other two from each school of teachings. Each mode of teaching would result in a more compatible and harmonious co-existence with the other two schools of teachings. This is unity by harmonization of diversity from which respective new developments for each school are allowed and anticipated. It is an attitude of mutual inclusion, not mutual exclusion, in the spirit of a high degree of interpretive tolerance and relatedness. Hence I shall speak of Chinese religion as a multifaceted experience and a behavior-belief pattern which has an open ultimate reference as a source of decision and evaluation, and which at the same time strives for the ultimate harmony with other bona fide faiths and practices in a changing world.

Outstanding characteristics of Chinese religion as a whole

In light of these two basic characterizations of Chinese religion, we have to see Chinese religion as a holistic experience of the ultimate which is both severally and collectively significantly different from western religions. For many religionists in the West, Confucianism may not quite qualify as a religious faith but only sustains itself as a socio-political ethic. This is mistaken insofar as a deepened and widened view of Confucianism would reveal more than what socio-political ethic provides. The Confucian socio-political ethic is rooted in an onto-cosmological vision of the ultimate which justifies the value of both life and death and which provides a faith as a spiritual guide of life in such a justification (Ching 1989).

In such a sense, Confucianism is not merely philosophy, but a common faith and common practice for many (including most intellectuals) in the tradition. Many modern Chinese intellectuals may still subscribe to such an understanding and experience of Confucianism as a core system of values and a basic form of practice of life, particularly in a context of family and community. As a consequence of implicit Confucian sentiment and believed values, people would make life sacrifices for their parents, or for their children or their leaders or followers, and take satisfaction in a faithful commitment and trust in human nature (*xing*) or destiny (*ming*) by heaven.

Similarly, for Daoism there is also a religious aspect and a philosophical aspect insofar as we see Daoism as both a form of thinking embodied or leading to a form of life in deep harmony with the nature of reality which is the ultimate *dao*, and as a collective practice centered in a body of basic beliefs catering to the public and community. In this latter connection Daoism as philosophy becomes Daoism as religion, and even a highly formalized religion, as history has demonstrated. The link between Daoism as philosophy (philosophic Daoism, *daojia*) and Daoism as religion (religious Daoism, *daojiao*) is an intricate one, which has recently commanded intense scholarly attention (Fushen and Xishen 2004).

The fact is that Daoism as a classic philosophy could be linked to an even earlier understanding of the relation between man and nature and the relation between beliefs and actions which would motivate one toward realization of a desirable eternal form of life called the *xian* (immortal person). Hence individually Daoism developed into individual schools of philosophical wisdom of the *dao*, while collectively Daoism became a basis for a religious movement which has often had political connotations in times of historical crisis when a wide range of life goals is threatened. For the present purpose, it is useful to note that in the Daoist case we have a good example of how a philosophy could transform itself into a religion in the formal and objective sense of the word (in contrast with the transformation of the Confucian philosophy into a political system of ideological rule). Perhaps the crucial point of the transformation is the introduction of practical methods of life-nourishing and the naming of personal deities or divinities which command popular belief and inspire personal faith (Kohn 1998).

It must also be noted that Daoism in its early forms comes from understanding and experience of the *dao*. Experience of the *dao* is an irreducible element of the formation and transformation of Chinese experience of the ultimate. It has transformed the early Chinese experience of personalized divinity such as *di* and *tian* into open, undefined and indefinable reality which encompasses different forms and various possibilities of self-transcendence and self-transformation.

It is on the basis of Daoism and Confucianism that Chinese Buddhism as a formal religion was molded into individualized sects of elevated philosophical thinking and meditation. As such, Chinese Chan Buddhism is an anti-religion as much as a religion in the sense that adherents make an ardent endeavor to be liberated from any histori-cally ritualized form of life, even religious life; they seek freely to express their creative spirit so that it transcends and yet encompasses the whole of reality. Nevertheless it has retained a historical lineage and a traditional openness and hence appeals to a community of aspirants and practitioners (Cheng 1973).

We need to understand how Confucianism, Daoism, and Buddhism are regarded as systems of religious teachings. But to say that they are unified in some doctrines, as held by the Mind-School scholar and thinker Jiao Hong (1541–1620) in the late Ming dynasty, is not to say that these systems could not have radically different conceptions of reality, the supreme power, and the destiny of human beings. On the other hand, it may become a central and most challenging issue as to whether and how their convergent unity is to be argued or sustained. Nevertheless, the emergence of such a theory of unity of three religions bespeaks a unique nature of Chinese religion, which may prove to have a modern appeal and may challenge the western religions intro-duced into China, such as Christianity and Islam.

Historical evolution of Chinese religion and its implication

There are three foundational concepts related to the origin and beginning of Chinese religion in the broad sense. These are the concept of *di* (ruler), the concept of *tian* (heaven), and the concept of *dao* (the way). Among the three, the concept of *tian* stands for a primary experience of an overarching power in the world of things and people which is also the source of life and the ultimate reality of providence and sustenance (Cheng 1997). This understanding of the *tian* reflects a human

consciousness and understanding of social and political organization and its mainte-
nance. Apparently, the concept of *tian* in the beginning was vague and ambiguous and
acquired more clear reference and definite content over time.

On the basis of the texts of *Shujing* (Book of Documents) and *Shijing* (Book of
Poetry), one can see that *tian* is referred to as the *haotian* (profound heaven) (in the
Yaodian chapter of the Book of Documents). Human beings experience *tian* in the
natural forms and events that they have come to know and sort out by observation.
Hence the first thing the reputed sage-king Yao (c.2600 BCE) did as a ruler was to
ask Xihe to organize a calendar of seasons and natural periods of the time according
to the movements of the sun, moon, and planets, and then to let people know how
to cultivate their lands accordingly. The natural events and times of *tian* are not, of
course, the spiritual *tian* that one naturally comes to revere. For the ancient sage-
kings, nature or *tian* is not simply the visible forms but the invisible spirit, which is
also referred to as the supreme ruler or ruler on high (*shangdi*), or ruler of the heaven
(*tiandi*).

It is possible that by the time of Yao, or even earlier by the time of Huangdi (c.3000
BCE), the idea of a ruling power (*di*) was introduced. In this idea of *tian* there are a will
and a plan for the ruling of the people, since people are now organized into societies
and communities. Those who acquired the political position of ruling would be called
the *di* (emperor) or *wang* (king). It is again possible that the human ruler was called
the *di* or *wang* first and then this notion of ruler was applied to the invisible organizing
and creating force of all the things and life-forms in the world. This force becomes
personalized and referred to as the *shangdi* or ruler on high.

As *di* is often considered the common ancestor of a people, *di* and hence *shangdi*
are also often regarded as the source of life and communal values, and as the people's
moral authority. Having *shangdi* as the moral authority was useful, even necessary, for
maintaining social order and the status of the human ruler. Hence the idea of *tianming*
(mandate of heaven) becomes the basis for political authority and also the ultimate
justification for the overthrow of a corrupt rulership and the subsequent founding of
a new form of political rulership. It is said in the *Shijing* (Book of Poetry) that 'The
command (*ming*) of the *tian* is beautiful and without end' (Poem 267). Political power
hence tends to be founded on the implementation of the mandate of heaven (*tianming*)
as one can see in the *Tangshi* (Oath of Tang) in the *Shujing* (Book of Documents).

However, one still needs to see how the relation between heaven as invisible power
of ordering and human political authority is to be maintained. For this we have two
observations:

(1) The invisible heaven commands reverence which leads to self-watchfulness
over oneself so that one would develop one's virtues in relating to others and in
establishing harmony and productiveness of life and prosperity of life. This motive is
how Confucianism could be said to originate: to revere heaven is to discipline oneself
for harmonious communal living. One comes to an effective awareness of the interrelatedness between heaven and man through reverence for heaven, self-cultivation
of virtues (care for others) in a person and the resulting harmony from family and clan
to community and society. Hence it is said in the Record of Gaotao in the Yuxiashu

Chapter of the Book of Documents that '[The purpose of ruling] consists in knowing the human beings and pacifying the people.'

(2) To show reverence for heaven or *shangdi*, one needs to make sacrifices to heaven as a sign of reverence. Therefore, as early as the time of Yao, and maybe even earlier, special sacrificial rites (called *leiji*) were performed. In fact, what is referred to as the 'three rites' (*sanli*) in the Yuxiashu covers rites to heaven-divinities, rites to earth-deities, and rites to human spirits.

The reverence for heaven is extremely important for the rise of the Daoist religion, for it is in performance of relevant rites that the Daoist priests are empowered to do many services for believers to help them achieve a happy and peaceful life and death.

In connection with the rise of the notion of the *dao*, a third aspect of the natural belief in heaven as invisible ruler on high should be mentioned. This is to do with the use of divination (*pu*) in conducting national affairs. A good example is how Pangeng, the nineteenth ruler of the Shang, appealed to divination by tortoise bones to implement his command to move his people to a new capital (see the Record of Pangeng in *Shangshu*, the Book of Documents). In the Hongfan chapter we also read how large doubts can be resolved and decisions supported by appealing to divination: 'Select and install a diviner by tortoise and a diviner by milfoil and ask them to do divination after informing them of problems at hand' (Hongfan chapter in the Book of Documents). According to this record, the results of divination have to be considered together with consultations from people and ministers and should not on their own be obeyed by the ruler. This shows how divination was used as only one means of understanding of a given situation and hence one source of information for the ruler in ultimately making a decision.

It is also important to note that the symbolic results of divination had to be interpreted by a trusted diviner who would articulate what they signified. Although no precise rules for interpretation were prescribed, natural associations learned from past experience were no doubt essential for correct interpretation. Different shapes of the cracks on the burned bones may have suggested to experienced eyes an association of natural states which offered clues for understanding a possible consequence of taking an appropriate action. The question for the ruler was to see whether these interpretations fitted with perceptions of others, including his own intuitions before deciding on an appropriate action. This suggests a rather rational and reasonable procedure for making decisions and paves the way for the emergence of the system of divination based on a cosmic map known as the *Zhouyi* or *Yijing* (Book of Changes) (Cheng 1994 and 1997).

One can conjecture that for the ancient sage-kings such as Yao, Shun, Yu and Tang, although the decision-making procedure by divination could be formally linked to the ritualistic belief in an invisible ruler on high, the actual decisions to be reached must have admitted human deliberation and considerations of consequences of actions by reflection and historical lessons.

It is against such a background of divination and general belief in a dynamic inter-active relation between the invisible power of heaven (*tian*) and the human potential for virtuous transformation that the idea of the *dao* rises above all, and becomes the central guiding principle for all major philosophical and religious thinking in the Chinese tradition.

Creative development of Confucianism: is Confucianism a religion?

I believe that Confucianism arises from the concern with development of a humane and ordered society that will provide peace and harmony for humanity as a whole race (Cheng 1997). It was Confucius (551–479 BCE) who started the teaching of the way of being human and becoming more human. He developed a system of virtues which has its unity in *ren* (love, care, and benevolence) and *yi* (righteousness and justice) and *li* (respectfulness and property). He further inherited the idea of the *dao* as the source of value in human life and the foundation for organizing human society and government. In this sense he continued a tradition from the time of the sage-kings Yao and Shun including in particular the tradition of *li* from the Zhou. His gradual commitment to the learning and vision of the Yijing (Zhouyi) enabled him and his disciples to articulate the insights of the Yijing in the classic commentaries on the Yi Text.

In doing so, Confucius can be said to be both a renovator and an innovator with his ideas solidly rooted in the ancient Chinese experience of heaven, nature, and man. But Confucius did not wish to found a formal religion, even though with his moral authority and fame and with his large group of disciples and followers he was better equipped than any person in ancient world history to establish himself as a founder of a formal religion. But why, then, did Confucius choose not to found a religion? The answer is that he developed a faith in human self-edification and self-enlightenment for human self-realization in which any authority apart from moral practice and virtues would be a harm and obstacle to the universal enlightenment of humanity.

In this sense Confucius remains a philosopher of religion (rather than a religionist) and a philosopher of humanity (with faith in humanity) with a heart open to learning and a moral readiness to practice and act. Thus Confucianism can be regarded as a universal morality which could be embraced by all human beings, past, present, and future. Confucianism can be seen as embodying both philosophy and religion without a religious form, but with a profound philosophy by which it can function as a human and humane religion for each person. Confucius has left a heritage which has enriched the tradition of the *yi* (change and creativity) in the *Yijing* and the tradition of the *dao* (Cheng 1997: pt. 1; Cheng 2000: ch. 1). Classical Confucianism is a tradition that has influenced Daoism and Buddhism, and that has been enriched by later Confucians, including Zisi, Mencius, and Xunzi.

Julia Ching, in her dialogue with Hans Küng, considers herself both a Catholic and a Confucian in religious beliefs (Ching 1989). She tries to bridge the two traditions in terms of the relationship of human beings to the transcendent dimension of human existence. Apparently she wants the Christian religion to learn from the Confucian concern with humanity and practice of moral cultivation in order to be more humanized, whereas she also wants the Confucian ethics to continue its original openness to the transcendently divine for its spiritual enrichment. Granted that

Christianity and Confucianism represent two systems of values for living the human life and fulfilling its potentiality, the question remains as to which approach captures the ideal form of life. There is also the question of how the two value-systems could learn from each other to form a more open and creative way of understanding life and world.

It might be pointed out that Confucius was the first philosopher to bring out most clearly how any ideal form of life could be cultivated from one's reflections on one's pursuits and actions in life. In his own reflections Confucius stresses learning, social participation, intellectual autonomy, knowledge of heaven and destiny, compassionate understanding, and spiritual freedom. One can see that there are many dimensions of life to be realized and that all dimensions are also steps toward higher levels of life on which eventually one can be said to be one with the ultimate reality called the heaven (*tianren heyi*) (Cheng 1997).

Confucius referred to *tian* in a transcendent way, in a sense in which *tian* is above us and beyond our control, and *tian* plays the role of ordering, ordaining and determining (*ming*) many limiting aspects of our life. Yet it is the same *tian* which is manifested in a life-generating process of cosmos and nature. To be above all things and yet to relate to life in the world is the way of heaven. It is a way for transcending and yet descending, since it is an order which is immanent in things and life, and which has its independent meaning and end as the ultimate ground of life. To stress this sense of transcendence is a special feature of Confucianism, as we see in the Analects. In this sense, what is important is not the existence of heaven but the way heaven performs and presents itself in the world and hence it is the Dao of Heaven which makes heaven heaven.

We must recognize that there are different senses of the word 'transcendence' (Chinese: *chaoyue*). I shall distinguish two such senses, the dynamic one and the static one. In the dynamic sense of transcendence the transcendent is simply the rising and expanding power of transcending beyond a given state of being. In transcending it is both encompassing and detaching. On the other hand, it is not separate or separable from all things which it transcends, and hence all things could be said to be part of the transcending power which also creates, sustains and transforms. This is the transcending power of the *dao* as described by both Confucians and Daoists.

In the static sense of transcendence there is the transcendent object which remains separate and separable from the transcended even though the transcendent object has the power of creation, destruction, and delivery in the same way as Christians conceive of the Christian God. This distinction would save us from the endless disputes over whether there is transcendence in Chinese philosophy and Chinese religion. Overall, one can easily see how the *dao* is transcendent in the dynamic sense, but not in the static sense.

Tian as *tiandao* is eventually realized as nature (*xing*) and human mind (*xin*) in the human person and becomes the essential defining character of humanity; it gives human beings dignity and value and a goal to pursue and reach – namely to develop and cultivate one's nature in fulfilling the functions of life as an individual and as a social unit. One may consider this nature as constituted by the way of heaven and dictated by the power of heaven, which forms the spiritual life and spirituality of the human self. The central function and goal of human life is to become aware and awakened to this inner spirituality of human existence, which can be said to transcend human life and yet is inseparable from human life because it is also the power to enable human life to be fulfilled.

This Confucian transcendence is important to understand by itself as it contrasts with the Christian transcendence. The latter is defined by faith in God and is derived from the conceptualization of God as an entity rather than as a process, as a transcendent divine, powerful personal being who is distinct from the universe and humanity. The biblical story portrays the human fall and sin which lead to a broken relationship between humans and God; it takes the unique sacrifice of Jesus Christ to restore this friendship between God and humans. This is unlike the Confucian view of human destiny, in which an awakening to a general understanding of the human person's inner nature as capable of self-fulfillment.

Daoism from philosophical naturalism to religious naturalism

With the philosophical Daoist, the transformation of the human person is more a matter of returning to nature conceived as the ultimate void, so that one can enjoy the eternal union with nature and eternal renewal of nature in a creative process of the *dao*. But in religious Daoism, there is a mixture of ritualist beliefs that can be traced to the original concept of the invisible nature as the supreme ruler; semi-scientific beliefs that one could achieve a better and rejuvenated life through alchemical, and now bio-medical, treatment and spiritual exercises such as *qigong*, and diet; and finally the philosophical understanding of reality as the void and the vital force (*qi*). I shall explain these in the following few paragraphs.

I take the position that Daoism as religion, or religious Daoism (*daojiao*), is a natural development of some underlying beliefs about the *dao* and *tian* which are rooted in ancient experience of nature and humanity. It also gives rise to the philosophical Daoism (*daojiao*) of Laozi (late sixth century BCE) and Zhuangzi (c.399–295 BCE). In fact, the underlying conception of *tian* has provided an outlet and a foundation for the development of religious Daoism, while philosophical Daoism provides a philosophical sophistication in the concept of the *dao* for justifying and supporting beliefs about the *tian* (Cheng 2004; Wagner 2004).

We may also ask how philosophical Daoism becomes ideologically related to religious Daoism. The answer could be made on two fronts. On the first front, one can see that in both Daodejing and Zhuangzi there are aspects and messages which suggest practical measures for achieving identity with the *dao* such as breath control and meditation. On the second front, one may also see that the ideas of *tian* and *di* and other natural forces gradually came to be personified and to be conceived as mythological figures. Perhaps the Buddhist tradition in naming Buddhas has also inspired the Daoists to follow suit. Hence the power of the beginning of the world is called the Primal Respected One (*yuanshi zengjun*), the power of development of *dao* is called the Supreme One of the *Dao* (*taishang daojun*), and Laozi the person was then simply called the Supreme Old One (*daode laojun*) (Kohn 1998). The generation of Daoist divinities and their relations follows a logical structure and at the same time integrates legendary local human figures who achieved the status of immortal deity by Daoist practices.

We may thus come to see the essence of the Daoist religion as a practice aimed at the immortalization of life so that the living state can be extended indefinitely and death can be avoided. One may indeed inquire into the theoretical basis of this practice. It is often described as consisting of four steps: exercise of the *jing* (essence) into the *qi* (vital force), then exercise of the *qi* into *shen* (spirit), then exercise of the *shen* into *xu* (void), and finally exercise of the *xu* to fit with the *dao*. One may regard *jing, qi, shen*, and *xu* as different grades of *qi*, which contains the seeds of life and which is eternally regenerated as physical life in the dao – the ultimate source of life and spirituality (Fushen and Xishen 2004: ch. 2). For the religious Daoists this is a theory which can be put into action by following certain practices that affect the formative elements of human existence: essence, vital force, and spirit. As a *dao*-cosmic life-genetic theory is assumed to explain the rise of the human being, it is believed that by exercising the inner medicine of self-transformation one can reverse the *dao*-cosmic life-genetic process, so that a new embryo of the human self can be created (Xitai and Shichuang 1999).

Religious Daoism in contrast with Christianity

At this point it may be interesting to ask how religious Daoism (*daojiao*) compares or contrasts with Christianity as a religion. It is obvious that for Daoism the most important belief is that, because of his understanding of the Dao, a human person could transform himself into an existentially individualized state of the *dao* (the state is called *xian*, the immortal) where his own identity as an individual person would also endure forever. The *xian* state of the person would enable the human person to wander, to explore and to live permanently in freedom and happiness. In this sense the limit and finitude of human life would be transcended and death overcome by one's immortality, which was achieved in one's own self-formed inner transformation (transformation by inner medicine or *neidan* which one develops in one's own body) (Fushen and Xishen 2004: divisions 4 and 5; see also Tianshi 2000: pts 1 and 2).

By contrast Christianity affirms strongly the separation between the human and the divine: the human has no power of his own to overcome his finitude and limitation, experienced ultimately as death. He has to rely on God to save his soul and to give him new life in eternity. While people can put faith in God or Jesus Christ, who is believed to be born to save humanity, essentially one could not know God as he knows himself or others like him. It is also interesting to see that although before the modern period Christianity adopted a fixed cosmology and view of the physical world, now some Christian theology would separate science from faith. Thus, no matter how much people have come to know the physical world or how capable they are of transforming their lives or prolonging life by bio-genetic medicine, there is an aspect of the human person which requires God and depends on God for salvation and perfection. And this is the spirit and spiritual life; however, broadly speaking, the Christian Scriptures do emphasize a transformed physicality of redeemed humans (bodily resurrection) and of the entire creation (new heaven and earth) that is rooted in the redemptive work of Jesus.

In this sense God is transcendent and separate and human spirituality is also transcendent and separate, in Christianity. By contrast, the religious Daoist would hold that human existence starts as an original unity of essence (body), vitality, and spirit like the *dao*, but becomes organically differentiated in birth and actual life. The Daoist would also believe that it is humanly possible to re-unite the body, vitality, and spirit into a creative oneness of voidness in *dao*. There is no absolute dualism or dichotomy of soul and body because there is an underlying force in a person; through this one could raise oneself – one's body and soul – to the level of the divine or to full creativity by one's own efforts and exercise of one's native power. However, if one cannot achieve such status, one must be reconciled to merging with the *dao* without continued individualization of one's life. The difference between religious Daoism and Christian theology is one between religious naturalism and religious transcendentalism.

Religious Daoism provided the initial impulse for pursuing knowledge of things and biologic life, but failed to maintain it in an objective pursuit for scientific knowledge. It was known that after many deaths due to alchemical poisoning during the pre-Tang period, latter-day religious Daoists tended to stress a more inner medicinal approach so that a person's transformation became a full spiritual exercise of *qi* and *shen*. In this regard the religious Daoists have reverted to classical Daoist philosophy except that they are more practically minded and better trained in body and mental exercises. The great difference between Christianity and Daoism still remains: instead of a transcendent God there is the immense and profound *dao*, which the Daoist could appropriate and approach, whereas for the Christian there is always a God to rely on whether one masters transformation of one's life by the exercise of science or not (Cheng 2001: 34–7). For the Daoist, one's ability to master one's own life leads to supreme harmony in Dao, which will preserve what is natural among other things. But for the Christian, successful scientific mastery of oneself and others could overturn the belief in God and lead one to play the role of an arbitrary God at the expense of the Dao of nature and life.

Chinese Buddhism as *Dao* interpretation of the *Dharma*

We come to Chinese Buddhism as the last of the three major traditional ethical-religious teachings. Although Buddhism was not native to the Chinese tradition, it has become acculturated by way of intense and active interaction and engagement. Before we could have a clear understanding of Chinese Buddhism as a religion, we must ask how Buddhism contrasts with Christianity and Confucianism and how this contrast reveals the close proximity between Buddhism and Daoism as seen from the perspective of Confucianism. In the first place, Buddhism comes from a deep reflection on the essence of human life after seeing its phases from birth to death.

Like in Daoism, the problem of death is to be confronted and overcome. But unlike Daoism, the Buddhist solution to the problem of death is not to prolong and transform life but (at least according certain versions of Buddhism) to reduce life to illusion and emptiness so that death does not function as a real problem.

In this regard Buddhism is also radically different from Christianity in that it takes life in the common sense seriously and in that it would require the individual to transcend life and death by his or her own understanding and insight into the nature of human existence. No external God is presupposed or deemed necessary. On the contrary, a conception of God and the like would pose an obstacle to, rather than a help for, the final salvation in the form of *nirvana* (Mitchell 2002). The way toward salvation is therefore a matter of training or disciplining one's mind and body into understanding the empty nature of all things and thus the emptiness of the human life and human mind. The mind which realizes the emptiness of all things would eventually empty itself into emptiness.

By such mental and spiritual disciplining one is better prepared to bear the vulgar and secular life and to render death not an object to fear but a state to transcend and jump over. It is clear that there is no transcendent object recognized nor transcendent subject recognized, but an inner or innate nature which is described as the Buddha nature and which is capable of being realized through one's awakening to nothingness. Although as a popular religion Buddhism would allow images of Buddha and Bodhisattava in organized and individual worship, these images must be regarded as means and aids for awakening one's true nature and reminders of one's efforts to transcend into emptiness.

In the actual historical development of Chinese Buddhism, one can see how once Indian Mahayana Buddhism was introduced it was open to the Chinese interpretation in the context of philosophical Daoism (Xianzong 2003). Hence we see how the Sanskrit word *sunyata* was first translated as *wu* (void) in Chinese and how *dharma* was conceived as the *dao*. But the Buddhists strove to assert their distinctiveness by identifying *sunyata* as nothingness and non-clinging-ness from the void, which carries a certain onto-cosmological meaning. As far as the term *dharma* is concerned, it was eventually translated into Chinese as *fa*, which stands for both law and entity (Chan 1963: ch. 20; also Cheng 2006a).

Whereas Daoism stresses self-cultivation of one's mind and nature, body and form, Buddhism would reject the Daoist outer medicine as irrelevant and its inner medicine as impure. Instead, for the Buddhist the important thing is to engage in a deep meditation (*samadhi*) in order to be free from images and passions of world. It is by means of such practice that one would come to break down one's conception of life and death and reach a state of complete extinction known as *nirvana*.

There are six schools of Chinese Buddhism which need to be mentioned and identified according to their respective religious significance (Cheng 2006c; also Mitchell 2002: ch. 7). In the first place there is the Sanlun School which duplicates the Indian Madyamika of Nargajuna (100–200 CE) in stressing the ultimate emptiness of all things. But this school did not last for the reason that to the Chinese mind it is perhaps too negative and provides no justification for any human effort and human achievement. Then there is also the Indian School of Yogacara of Asanga (410–500 CE) and Vasubandhu (420–500 CE) which was introduced into China through the efforts of the famous monk Xuanzhuang (596–664 CE). But again this school did not last, for it is known to be too subjectivist in that it went against the commonsensical and practical sense of reality which Confucianism and Daoism would share and converge in agreement.

Hence we come to four well-known positivist schools of Chinese Buddhism, which were formed and developed by the Chinese scholar-monks on their native soil. I refer to the Tiantai School, the Huayan School, the Chan School, and the Jingtu (Pure Land) School. The Jingtu School was founded by Hui Yuan (333–416 CE) in the Jin Period in the year of 402, while the other three Chinese Buddhist schools were founded and flourished in the Tang Period (618–907 CE).

After the Tang Period, both Tiantai and Huayan declined. In their place Chan Buddhism and the Jingtu School have continued to expand. In modern times in China, Taiwan, and Japan, one can see how Chan (Zen in Japan) and Jingtu (Jodo in Japan) are still very alive among Buddhist communities and large masses of people. There is a tendency in Chinese Buddhism to revive itself because of the impact of Christianity and at the same time to exert its influence on Christianity through the practice of meditation and self-development.

I offer some very brief statements on the position of each Chinese Buddhist School. Beginning with the Tiantai School, the following insight has developed: every individual being has a nature which is germane to salvation in becoming a Buddha or in becoming enlightened and liberated from this world of *samsara* (impermanence) (Zongsan 1982). For the Huayan School, a human individual could come to perceive and realize harmony and peace among all things by showing how we could conceive that different things could be integrated in a whole with each other and with the underlying principles (*li*). The highest understanding and thus awakened intuition leads to the state of harmony of harmonies, which exhibits itself in the free existence of things, free existence of principles, and harmony among all free things and among principles.

Coming to Chan Buddhism, its development and growth are rooted in the realization of mind and the nature of human existence, which is regarded as an embodiment of the ultimate truth and the ultimate good. It takes a resolute mind and a persistent spirit of pursuit to reach the point where total enlightenment becomes possible. The total enlightenment is also a creative act of self-understanding that is not hindered or helped by anything else, although mental preparation and concentration are often required. What is presented as important is the inner creativity of human existence which can be conceived as the Buddha nature or the nature which is the seed of enlightenment (Cheng 1994).

This philosophy of total and sudden enlightenment as stressed by Hui Neng in his Platform Sutra (Tanjing) gives a person a definite direction of pursuit and a clear sense of achievement. It is also interesting to note that for the Chan Buddhist enlightenment is not once and for all but requires constant attentiveness and unceasing practice (Cheng 2000). This also means that once enlightened one can live a meaningful robust life of activity while enabled and empowered by a holistic vision of dynamic comprehension and understanding. This sense of life and vitality of decision-making toward action boosts one's sense of reality and sense of destiny, so that for once mind could be said to be set free from fears and the anxieties about mundane matters and death.

Finally, I must mention the Jingtu School, which is more closely tied to the idea of a personal God or heaven than any other sects of Chinese Buddhist religion. In a sense it has revived the ancient belief in heaven as an all-comprehensive and all-benefiting power of creation and salvation. But it no doubt goes beyond it and has thoroughly explored the power of belief and faith as a way of salvation. It has been pointed out that whereas other sects of Chinese Buddhism have relied on self-efforts of intelligent reflection and meditation for transcendence and achieving the wisdom or insight (*bodhi*) of freedom, the Jingtu, on the other hand, speaks directly of the power of faith in Amitahba Buddha as a universal savior.

Of course even here the Jingtu School also speaks of the importance of one's own strong and sincere desire to become reborn in the World of Supreme Bliss (*jileshijie*) that is the Pure Land (*jingtu*). This means that it takes a synergy of self-reliance and reliance on the merciful power of the Buddha to make it possible that every person, even an evil person, could be redeemed and reborn in the Pure Land. Certainly this belief is not incompatible with the ancient Chinese belief in heaven as a creator and a ruler over all things in the world. This shows that for common people the intellectual intuition and efforts of meditation of the other schools may not be feasible or available. However, with a strong and living faith, combined with the practice of compassion and kind action, one could reach the soteriological end of a religion.

The question has been raised whether the Pure Land School as a religion approximates a theistic position like Christianity. Although there is no definite answer because of different historical contexts, one can see that to have faith, to strongly desire and to act for compassion, is closely comparable to the Christian belief in powers of faith, hope, and charity. On the other hand, it may also appear that the Pure Land School seems to concentrate on the desire for rebirth in a land of bliss, whereas Christianity takes faith in eternal life as a support for living a valuable present-day life. Yet there is no reason why the Pure Land School may not be activated to become a more positive and activist religion for engaging with modern life and the modern world. What needs to be done is often an effort to reform and to put reform into action, as Christianity has done, historically.

All in all, we may come to see how various Buddhist schools enliven the native sense of religion and life which one finds in both Confucianism and Daoism under the auspices of the spirit of *Yijing*: the spirit of creativity, seeking oneness and indefiniteness, going beyond without absolute transcendence, transformation without abandonment of one's true nature, and achieving the universal being in oneself without separating heaven or God from the human person – or the human person from heaven or God.

Concluding remarks

One can see that a philosophy of Chinese religion begins with a historical and empirical understanding of the rise of Chinese systems of religious thought and belief and ends with becoming a Chinese re-interpretation of what a religious belief is. This transformation may be regarded as a Chinese model for religious experience and religious belief. What is involved here is that the nature of religious concepts based on a philosophical reflection and interpretation determines what they refer to and what they signify, and what they offer to meet the ultimate concern of the human person. To explicate and analyze what those beliefs and notions are and how they are applied is to understand them in a comparative framework of other religions. Philosophy of Chinese religion becomes Chinese philosophy of religion insofar as the religious experience of the Chinese is philosophically understood.

Historically, it is the Chinese religion that is philosophically explicated, but philosophically it is the religious values and references which are historically experienced by the Chinese. The question is whether we have a universal framework in which we could speak of Chinese experience of religion together with other traditions such as the Jewish, Christian, or Hindu experience of religion. As humanity shares a common basis for its problems and concerns and anxiety, perhaps we could speak of different experiences and different interpretations of religion as a shared horizon of human nature, human finitude, and human aspiration to fulfill human nature and overcome its finitude. On the other hand, there could not be one single set of historical concepts which could serve as the ultimate universal reference for all historical experiences of relativity; there are only general concepts of the ultimate needs and modes of satisfaction and achievement which could be said to define human life and human values.

In this sense we could no doubt speak of a general religious language or universal religious framework for fulfilling a pluralist function. What is obvious in such a religious framework is not the Christian God or the Daoist Dao or the Hindu Brahman which would dominate either semantically or epistemologically or ontologically. There must be an underlying recognition of a general background of religious ambiguity and creativity which can be seen behind all different forms of religions, and which would come out one way or another in different religious or cultural traditions. How each tradition appropriates this source of religious ambiguity and religious creativity could be seen as the most significant problem in a philosophy of religion.

In conclusion, an inquiry into the philosophy of Chinese religion has to become a Chinese philosophy of religious experience, which in turn has to become a philosophy of both Chinese and non-Chinese religious experiences. The interaction and eventual interfusion between the two signifies how theory and action must be unified dynamically as two aspects of the same thing, namely the dynamic humanity which is experienced as limited and yet profound, ambiguous and yet creative.

See also Buddhism (Chapter 2), Christianity (Chapter 6), Religious pluralism (Chapter 20), Non-theistic conceptions of God (Chapter 22), The problem of evil (Chapter

37), Theology and religious language (Chapter 48), The Incarnation (Chapter 51), Sin and salvation (Chapter 53), Heaven and hell (Chapter 54), Faith (Chapter 56), Phenomenology of religion (Chapter 61), Religious naturalism (Chapter 62), Religious experience (Chapter 63).

References

Five Confucian Classics: Book of Changes (*Yijing*), Book of Poetry (*Shijing*), Book of Documents (*Shujing*), Records of Rites (*Liji*), Spring and Autumn (*Chunjiu*) (note helpful translations by James Legge), in J. Legge (trans.) (1960) *The Chinese Classics*, vols. 1–4, with exegetical notes, Hong Kong: Hong Kong University Press.

Bowker, J. (ed.) (1997) *The Oxford Dictionary of World Religions*, Oxford: Oxford University Press.

Chan W.-t. (1963) *A Source Book in Chinese Philosophy*, Princeton, NJ: Princeton University Press.

Cheng C.-y. (1973) 'On Zen (Chan) language and Zen paradoxes,' *Journal of Chinese Philosophy* 1/1: 77–102.

—— (1994) 'Congchanwu de guandian lun Haidege, Daoyuan yu Hui Neng' (On Heidegger, Dogen and Hui Neng, from the Enlightenmental point of view), in *Chinese Buddhist Study Bulletin* (Taiwan) 7: 263–86.

—— (1997) 'Reality and divinity in Chinese philosophy,' in E. Deutsch and R. Bontekoe (eds) *A Companion to World Philosophies*, Oxford: Blackwell.

—— (2000) 'Onto-epistemology of sudden Enlightenment in Chan Buddhism,' *Chung-Hwa Buddhist Journal* 13/2 (May): 585–611.

—— (2001) 'Zi Zhumu Zhujian Laozi fenxi daojia guandian' (Analyzing the point of view of Daoism from the Bomboo inscriptions of the Zhu tomb), in *Quanshi yu Jiangou*, Peking: Peking Univeristy Press.

—— (2002) 'Ultimate origin, ultimate reality, and the human destiny in Leibniz,' *Journal of Chinese Philosophy* 29/1: 93–118.

—— (2004) 'Dimensions of the Dao and Onto-Ethics in DDJ,' *Journal of Chinese Philosophy* 31/2: 143–82.

—— (2005) 'Toward an integrative pluralism in religion: embodying Whitehead, Cobb and the Yijing,' in D. Griffin (ed.) *Deep Religious Pluralism*, Louisville, KY: Westminster John Knox Press.

—— (2006a) 'Dharma as Dao in Chinese Buddhism: a study of transformation,' in the *Proceedings of International Conference on Dhama and Abidharma in Buddhism*, Mumbai, India.

Ching, J. (with H. Küng) (1989) *Christianity and Chinese Religions*, New York: Doubleday.

Fushen, H. and L. Xishen (2004) *Daoxue Tonglun* (Introduction to Daoism), Beijing: Social Sciences Texts Publisher.

Kohn, L. (1998) *God of the Dao*, Ann Arbor, MI: University of Michigan Press.

Mitchell, D. W. (2002) *Buddhism: Introducing the Buddhist Experience*, Oxford: Oxford University Press.

Tianshi, X. (2000) *Daojia Yangshengxue Gaiyao* (Essentials of Daoist Study of Nurturing Life), Taipei: Free Press.

Wagner, R. G. (2004) *A Chinese Reading of the Daodejing*, Albany, NY: State University of New York Press.

Xianzong, L. (2003) *Fojiao Quanshixue* (Buddhist Hermeneutics), Taipei: New Wenfeng Publishing Company.

Xitai, Q. and Z. Shichuang (eds) (1999) *Daojiao Wenhua Xindian, Jindanpian* (New Classic on Daoist Culture), 'Inner medicine' ch., Shanghai: Literature and Arts Publisher.

Zongsan, M. (1982) *Foxing yu Banru* (Buddha Nature and Bodhi), 2 vols., Taipei: Student Book Company.

Further reading

Cheng C.-y. (1991) *New Dimensions of Confucian/ Neo-Confucian Philosophy*, Albany, NY: State University of New York Press.

—— (1997) 'Reality and divinity in Chinese philosophy,' in E. Deutsch and R. Bontekoe (eds) *A Companion to World Philosophies*, Oxford and Malden, MA: Blackwell. (Dominant features of Chinese notions of reality and the divine are seen as revealed in the main schools and texts of Chinese philosophy.)

—— (2005) 'Toward an integrative pluralism in Religion: Embodying Whitehead, Cobb and the Yijing,' in D. Griffin (ed.) *Deep Religious Pluralism*, Louisville, KY: Westminster John Knox Press. (Pluralism in religion is analyzed and argued in the philosophy of Whitehead and Cobb. It is also shown to be rooted in the dynamic unity of one and many in the onto-cosmology of the Yijing.)

—— (2006b) *Cheng Chung-ying Wenji II: Rujia yu Xinrujia* (The Collected Papers of Chung-ying Cheng, II: Confucianism and Neo-Confucianism), Wuhan: Hubei People's Publishing.

—— (2006c) *Yixue Bentilun* (Ontology in the Study of the Change), Beijing: Peking University Press.

Ching, J. (with H. Küng) (1989) *Christianity and Chinese Religions*, New York: Doubleday. (Convergence and divergence of concepts of the divine in Christianity and Chinese religions are suggested and discussed in a dialogue between two religious thinkers representing Christian and Confucian traditions.)

Kohn, L. (2004) *Daoism and Chinese Culture*, Magdalena, NM: Three Pines Press. (This is a general introduction to Daoism in Chinese culture which explains how Daoism contributes to the development of the culture.)

5

JUDAISM

David Shatz

In many respects, the contributions of Judaism and Jewish philosophers to the philosophy of religion parallel the contributions made by Christianity and Islam. The concepts and problems addressed by thinkers in the three religions are largely identical: for example, the existence of God, the problem of evil, foreknowledge and free will, the status of divine command morality, creation, and providence. Furthermore, the responses promulgated by Jewish philosophers often converge with responses propounded by Muslim and Christian counterparts. This is hardly surprising, since in the tenth through twelfth centuries it was exposure to Islamic thought that gave rise to the whole Jewish enterprise, and subsequently, in the later Middle Ages, Christian scholasticism exerted significant impact on Jewish philosophy (Berger 1997; Rudavsky 2003).

Yet, despite the overlap just described, ancient Jewish texts and later Jewish philosophers sometimes contributed incisive ideas, arguments, and approaches that advance discussion and which it would be unfair to label redundant. In addition, certain issues that Jewish philosophers addressed, primarily in the modern period – for example, the meaning of 'chosenness,' the bindingness of Sinaitic imperatives, Jewish identity, and Zionism – were endemic to Jewish thought. Notwithstanding the salience in modern times of these more particularistic topics, in what follows the emphasis is on a highly select group of issues that occupy a place in all the theistic religions and are the stuff of analytic philosophy of religion.

Talk about God

The Bible, as is well known, speaks in anthropomorphic and anthropopathic language. God walks through the garden of Eden, descends on to Mount Sinai, stretches out his arm; he also becomes angry and sad and the like. The rabbis or sages of the talmudic period added to the stock of anthropomorphic and anthropopathic descriptions, by, for example, speaking of God as wearing phylacteries, shedding tears and suffering as Israel goes into exile. Such depictions of God challenged the philosophical sensibilities of medieval philosophers. They found anthropomorphism problematic because all bodies are divisible while God is metaphysically one. Anthropopathism was objectionable because it contradicted the doctrine of divine immutability. In response to the conflict between the Bible and philosophy, medieval philosophers generally maintained that the biblical language is meant for the masses only – quoting the Talmud (and investing the phrase with new meaning): 'the Torah speaks in the language of humans.' Sometimes, however, Jewish philosophers maintained that the biblical terms had multiple meanings and the correct one in the problematic contexts carried no anthropomorphic or anthropopathic implications.

As with many other issues, discussion of God talk revolves around Moses Maimonides (1135/8–1204), the most prominent of all Jewish philosophers. A fierce opponent of anthropomorphism, anthropopathism, and univocal predication (the thesis that terms as applied to God mean the same as terms when applied to human beings), Maimonides divides the attributes of God into two groups: attributes of action, and attributes of essence. The attributes of action actually are psychological attributes like being compassionate, gracious, and vengeful. In these cases, owing to concerns about immutability, Maimonides – like Anselm, Aquinas and others – interprets the attribution as follows:

God is compassionate $=_{df}$ God does actions such that if a human being were to do those actions we would ascribe to that person the feeling of compassion and call the individual compassionate.

Though he does the action, God does not have the 'inner' emotion. Hence the psychological predicates really refer to divine actions alone (Maimonides' examples of which are workings of nature), not mental states. God is impassible (Maimonides 1963: 123–8).

Attributes of essence include knowing, existent, powerful, eternal, one, incorporeal, living, and willing. Maimonides argues that to ascribe all of these, in fact any of these, to God in the normal way is to introduce multiplicity into a being who is a metaphysical unity. Not only can he not have a plurality of attributes; he cannot have even a single attribute because subject–predicate compositionality introduces multiplicity. Because of this objection to a univocal construal of the attributes, Maimonides subscribes to negative theology (Maimonides 1963: 111–47). That is, to say that God is knowing is to say that he is not not-knowing, and so forth for the other attributes. But – and this is a critical clarification – this negation is to be understood like the negation in 'the wall does not see.' What is being negated is the entire determinable, the general category of knowing/being ignorant. The true upshot of negative theology, then, is that God lies beyond our conceptual repertoire, and 'Silence is praise unto Thee' (Ps. 65: 2). We are left with no way of describing God.

Levi ben Gershom (Gersonides, 1288–1344) saw grave difficulties in Maimonides' negative theology (via negativa). First, if the meaning of the attribution of P to God is ultimately that the entire category P/not-P does not apply to God, what difference does it make where we start? 'God is ignorant' is just as good a starting point as 'God is knowing.' Second, our ability to draw inferences from or to truths about God is impaired. For example, 'God is incorporeal' can no longer be used to prove that 'God cannot be divided into parts,' for we can draw this inference only if we assume that 'incorporeal' means the same when applied to God as when applied to humans, a contention Maimonides emphatically denies. (Indeed, Maimonides' argument that since God is One, no multiplicity exists in Him would be invalid given the equivocity of 'One.') Given these problems for the *via negativa*, Gersonides denies that predicates ascribed to God are completely equivocal. For Gersonides, there is commonality between what the predicates mean in the case of humans and in the case of God – albeit God possesses, say, knowledge and power to a higher, more eminent degree than humans do (Gersonides 1987: 107–15). Also, 'God is P' can mean that God causes P in humans. Aquinas's assessment of negative theology and his alternative proposal is strongly similar to Gersonides'. (Maimonides' view is problematic for other reasons: how could people worship a God of whom they have no concept? What is the point of saying 'God exists'?)

In Christian and Jewish theology today it has become fairly common to question the medieval thesis that God is immutable and its alleged consequence that God has no emotions (Berkovits 1959; Heschel 1962; Wolterstorff 1988). *Inter alia*, an immutable God could not be affected by prayer. Many quest for a new, dynamic understanding of God. People seeking such an understanding might turn to Kabbalah (Jewish mystical teaching) as a resource.

To round out the picture, it should be noted that recent Jewish thought encompasses other approaches, such as the naturalism of the Reconstructionist rabbi Mordecai Kaplan (Kaplan 1934) and the non-cognitivism of Isaiah Leibowitz (Leibowitz 1992).

Evil

Any discussion of Jewish perspectives on the problem of evil must begin with the Bible. Not only the book of Job, but also Psalms, Ecclesiastes, and several prophetic books (Jeremiah, Isaiah, Habakuk) raise the problem. Unlike modern philosophical challenges, the 'objections' raised in these texts do not seek to show that God does not *exist*. Rather they cast doubt on his goodness or justice. And these texts also differ from modern discussions in that instead of asking why any evil exists, they ask why the righteous suffer and the wicked prosper: a formulation which presupposes that a true theodicy would have to be cast in terms of reward and punishment.

For the most part, the biblical books raise the question without providing an answer. Nevertheless, one message of the book of Job is, arguably, that suffering can improve a person spiritually and morally. For (a) Job comes to see God only at the end of the book – intimating a sharpened religious perception created by suffering – and (b) at the end of the book he prays for his friends, and does not (as previously) act for his family alone. On this approach, which may well be criticized for viewing the book as interested in theodicy rather than phenomenology (see Carmy 2004), the book expresses a claim that is integral to the 'soul-making theodicy': suffering promotes virtue. The Bible's version of soul-making, however, if it indeed exists, sees God as sometimes actively inflicting suffering on select individuals, whereas most forms of the soul-making theodicy today posit a universe in which God (passively) lets natural law operate for the sake of giving all people chances to improve their characters. Some philosophers would resist the modern version because it portrays God as leaving his creation alone, contrary to the doctrine of individual providence.

In the Talmud we find an almost bewildering array of approaches to evil. It is interesting that when one sage explicitly states that 'there is no death without sin, and no suffering without transgression,' his view is rejected (Babylonian Talmud, *Shabbat* 55a–b). Various sages propose other theodicies. For instance, at the time of a plague an innocent person might die along with the guilty. There is also the idea that the death of the righteous atones for sin. Especially interesting is the idea of 'tribulations of love' (*Berakhot* 5a), most often taken to mean that God allows the righteous to suffer in this world to increase their reward in the next. But 'tribulations of love' could also mean that the righteous are given the opportunity to exemplify virtue of the highest order. This in turn could mean either that by remaining faithful through suffering, the person is privileged to *exemplify* the virtue of faith and not merely possess it dispositionally; or that when people are righteous, God imposes suffering so that they can improve their character by bringing their dispositions to a new level.

Rabbi Joseph B. Soloveitchik made an important and interesting point about the entire enterprise of theodicy (Soloveitchik 2003: 86–115). The problem with asking why God allows evil is not simply that we don't know (though in fact we don't). The problem is that the better the explanation we have of evil – the more beautifully evil is thought to fit into and contribute to a whole that is good – the less reason we have to engage in moral and social action to fight evil or react to it negatively. Theodicy and moral responsiveness (behavioral or attitudinal) are in conflict.

The Holocaust (often referred to as the *Shoah*) deserves separate mention in this discussion of theodicy. Even though theoretically the horror that was the *Shoah* could be subsumed under the general heading of evil, its scope and horrific character lead many to find all theodicies unsatisfying. Post-Holocaust theology ranges from 'Death of God' theories to 'limited God' accounts, to theories which see *hester panim* (the hiding of the Divine face/presence as integral to Jewish experience), to free will theodicies (Katz 2005).

Divine command and reasons for the commandments

The question of whether God's commands conform to an independent standard of rationality and ethics can be traced back to Plato's *Euthyphro*. Judaism needed to consider not only whether 'ethical' laws were commanded because they are independently right, but also whether ritual laws were independently rational or were instead unrationalizable divine fiats.

A classic text found in the Talmud and Midrash (e.g., Babylonian Talmud, Tractate *Yoma*, 67b) distinguishes two categories of laws or *mitzvot* ('commandments'; singular, *mitzvah*). The commandments in one class are such that 'had they not been written, they ought to have been written.' These laws are called *mishpatim* and they include prohibitions against idolatry, blasphemy, theft, murder, and adultery. The sages' characterization of *mishpatim* as 'had they not been written, they ought to have been written' clearly implies that these commandments have merit independently of their having been commanded. How different this sounds from Dostoevsky's Ivan Karamazov, who declared that 'if there is no God, everything is permitted!' The sages clearly accepted the idea that certain precepts are binding without divine decree, or, at least, are rational in the sense of having social utility. To be sure, the text does not make clear whether we could have arrived at these precepts on our own. Perhaps we appreciate their wisdom or utility or ethical force only once presented with them (just as one might appreciate the brilliance and cogency of a mathematical proof or scientific theory without being able to arrive at it on one's own). But the drift of the passage at least is to establish a non-revelational grounding for certain revealed commands.

According to an important study (Sagi and Statman 1995) Jewish thinkers did not accept 'divine command theories' in an ontological form, but only an epistemological one. Almost universally, Sagi and Statman claim, Jewish thinkers denied that 'right' means commanded by God and 'wrong' means prohibited by God. Rather, they held that an act is commanded by God because it is (independently) right and is prohibited by God because it is (independently) wrong. Nevertheless, the authors of the study argue, Jewish tradition has its share of epistemological divine command theorists, that is, of theorists who maintain that without divine revelation we cannot *know* of certain actions that they are right (or alternatively wrong).

Saadia Gaon (882–942), the father of medieval Jewish philosophy, offers an interesting middle ground between those who say we can know ethical truths without revelation and those who say we cannot (Saadia Gaon 1948: 145–7). For Saadia, the general ethical truth that it is wrong to steal is known to reason, but to apply this precept we need to know what constitutes acquisition of property. Given that several criteria are possible, divine guidance is needed to furnish this knowledge. Similarly, although 'adultery is wrong' is known to reason, we need divine guidance as to what constitutes marriage, or else we cannot apply the law. It is not clear whether for Saadia the details that supply the guidance are backed up by some logical argument, albeit one we cannot come to on our own, or whether the details as to what constitutes ownership or marriage are arbitrarily selected; social cohesion requires that some choice be made, but not that a *particular* choice be made. Interestingly, Maimonides, a great champion of the law's rationality, maintained at least in the case of certain rituals that details of the law might be picked arbitrarily because there is no good reason to prefer one alternative to the other – a Buridan's ass situation, in which a donkey starves to death because he can't decide between two equally appetizing bales of hay. He asserted that rationality requires at times selecting a particular alternative with no reason (Maimonides 1963: 508–10).

So much for *mishpatim*, the first category of *mitzvot* considered by the sages. The second category is *hukkim* (generally translated as 'statutes, decrees'), defined alternatively as laws such that 'Satan challenges them,' or 'the evil inclination challenges them,' or 'the nations of the world challenge them.' Examples include the laws against wearing garments containing both wool and linen, the law of the red heifer used in ancient times to purify those who had come into contact with the dead, and the law of the goat sent (in the times of the Temple) to the wilderness on Yom Kippur to carry the Israelites' sins.

The aforementioned definitions of *hok* are ambiguous. The nations, Satan, or the evil inclination challenge these commandments because they seem to lack rhyme or reason. Are they right that the commandments have no reason? Or do they have a reason we cannot fathom? Or, perhaps, a reason that most people cannot fathom but a select few can?

The great medieval biblical and talmudic commentator Rashi (1040–1105) held that *hukkim* have no reasons and are simply 'decrees.' But among the giants who resisted this view were Moses Maimonides and Moses Nahmanides (1194–1270). The latter insisted that to the extent the sages called certain laws (the *hukkim*) 'decrees,' they did so not in the sense of 'arbitrary fiat,' but in the sense that a king may issue a decree to his subjects *for a reason* even though his subjects do not understand and appreciate the reason (Nahmanides 1971–6, II: 294–5 [Lev. 19: 19]). Maimonides' rejection of the 'no reason for *hukkim*' view was based, *inter alia*, on a Plato-like argument that God, on the view in question, seems to be acting arbitrarily and irrationally. Divine command theorists might think that this state of affairs elevates God (it celebrates his power and liberty), but Maimonides thinks it demotes God by portraying him as irrational and having no purpose behind his commands (Maimonides 1963: 523–4). This argument assumes that wisdom rather than will is the key attribute of God; classical divine command theorists, in contrast, have made will and power central (Idziak 1979: 8–10).

Some Jewish philosophers held that all *hukkim*, while rational, have reasons that are inaccessible to the human mind, others that the reasons were knowable at least by the elite. Numerous explanations have been constructed for ritual laws: these laws place God before one always and lead to a life of holiness; they bring one closer to God in a mystical sense; they and all their particulars symbolically convey metaphysical or ethical truths (see Hirsch 1981; Stern 1987); they – this is a theurgic Kabbalistic explanation – improve the cosmos by uniting different aspects of the Godhead; they force you to learn discipline, thereby making you more fit to observe the ethical laws. Some of these explanations imply that only a particular set of ritual laws can effect the desired end. Others suggest that any set of laws will do. There is a difference, then, between explaining why there are any commandments at all, and explaining why *these*.

The explanations canvassed so far have in common the fact that they are intended to provide the true or real reason behind the commandment: to pinpoint what God had in mind. In the twentieth century, Rabbi Joseph Soloveitchik questioned the feasibility of this task. According to Soloveitchik, we cannot know 'why' God issued a certain command, or 'how' commandments like purification rites work, but we can answer 'what': what moral I can extract for myself, what meaning the commandment has for me. Advocates of Soloveitchik's approach might wish to refine it by placing limits on what can count as an appropriate subjective reason (Soloveitchik 1986: 91–9; 1989: 91–9).

Returning to 'ethical' laws, the reader may have noticed that I conducted my discussion without reference to the most famous argument that God might issue immoral commands. I refer to the evidence of the narrative of the *akedah*, the episode in which God commands Abraham to sacrifice his son Isaac (Gen. 22). In *Fear and Trembling*, Søren Kierkegaard understood the story as affirming that God might command the immoral, though Kierkegaard was not a divine command theorist (he couldn't be, since he sees Abraham as experiencing a *conflict* between religion and morality). Kierkegaard's understanding of the narrative as a conflict between divine command and human morality, however, confronts certain problems. One is that at the end of the story Abraham is commanded not to go through with the sacrifice. The other is that Abraham may not have seen a moral conflict: child sacrifice was common at the time, and the practice makes a certain sense: to be devoted to God is to be ready to sacrifice your most precious 'possession.' Hence the *akedah* text does not support Kierkegaard's reading. The point of the narrative may well be, precisely, that God does not want child sacrifice – because it is immoral (Levenson 1998).

Free will

The challenges to belief in free will and responsibility boil down to four, two emanating from religious teaching and two emanating from secular considerations. The four are: divine foreknowledge; divine planning (preordaining); environmental causes of behavior; and biological causes of behavior. The Bible seems indifferent to such conundra, but philosophers are not.

With regard to divine foreknowledge – the question of how S can act freely if God knows in advance how S will act – Jewish philosophy presents, as is to be expected, a range of theories, including, for example, the idea that God is outside of time and the thesis that rather than God's knowledge determining our actions, God knows what he knows *because* of our actions. Maimonides held that divine knowledge is different in kind from human knowledge, dissolving the problem. Levi Gersonides, as we saw earlier, objected to the doctrine of equivocal predication. Instead, Gersonides proposed a bold solution that God does not (fore)know 'future contingents,' statements about future human free choices; indeed they are unknowable, even lack a truth value in the present. God is still omniscient because he knows all that is know*able* (Feldman 1987: 80–5; Gersonides 1987: 89–137). (For a different and carefully argued reading of Gersonides, see Manekin 1998; for a modified use of Gersonides' view, see Cahn 1967.)

With regard to divine planning, a locus classicus is the story of Joseph and his brothers. Since God had foretold to Abraham that 'your posterity will be strangers in another land' and would be afflicted there (Gen. 15), God's plan required that Jacob's sons descend to Egypt. The brothers meet up with Joseph; they throw Joseph in a pit; eventually he falls into the hands of Egyptians; then, through a series of seeming coincidences, Joseph becomes viceroy of Egypt and his brothers come down to Egypt to procure food during a famine. After Joseph reveals his identity, the entire family ends up in Egypt, the eventual result being the realization of the prediction revealed to Abraham. Now given there was a divine plan, it would appear that the brothers were influenced by God to throw Joseph into the pit and to cause his being sold, exonerating them from responsibility. Likewise, other choices in the plot might appear orchestrated. While some may insist that indeed there is no evidence of the brothers being punished, the more common approach is to assign them responsibility but to declare 'God has many messengers.' In other words: the brothers made their choice freely, but had they not exercised their choice in a way that conformed to the divine plan, the plan would have been realized another way, perhaps by others' free choices. Only if no free human choices would have resulted in the brothers' descent would God have interfered and influenced some people's motivations or realized the plan without human action. Interestingly, Jewish thinkers do not seem to have put forward the approach known as Molinism. According to Molinism, God freely creates exactly those people whose free choices will result in the realization of his plan. Molinism would allow for both divine planning and human free choice.

As in other instances, Kabbalistic views take a radical stance. In particular, some eighteenth- and nineteenth-century Hasidic thinkers held that all is in the hands of heaven, including human thoughts and actions. Divine planning and control excludes human free will. The sole exception is the freedom to think that human beings have no power and free choice. Here, and only here, is there room for freedom (see Gellman 1997).

A particularly perplexing instance of divine meddling with volitions is the deity's hardening of the heart of Pharoah, preventing the Egyptian monarch from releasing the Israelites in the face of the plagues. Maimonides develops a particularly interesting account in which the hardening is really a punishment for Pharoah's earlier, self-induced hardenings. Actually, 'God hardens' may mean here that there is a law of nature, ordained by God, according to which people who have done certain acts repeatedly eventually lose their ability to do otherwise and their ability to do good – an apt punishment. Joseph Albo (d. 1444) suggests that in removing Pharoah's fear of the plagues, God is removing an impediment to Pharoah's exercise of free will (what he most wants to do) and hence restoring Pharoah's free will (Albo 1929, IV: 25; Shatz 1997a). This view anticipates the contemporary proposal by Eleonore Stump that the hardening was meant to realize Pharoah's 'higher-level' will, leaving him free when he keeps the Israelites enslaved (Stump 1988). Others reject this solution and argue that the Bible simply did not place free will as high on its scale of values as we do today (Shatz 1997b).

Turning now to environmental and biological causes, medieval rationalist Jewish philosophers believed – Gersonides and Maimonides are most important – that free will consists in following the rule of reason or intellect, as opposed to the bodily inclinations set by the astral causes (Gersonides) or the influence of matter (Maimonides; he rejected astrology). There are affinities with recent secular approaches, namely, those which (a) view freedom as the ability to respond to reason rather than the ability to do otherwise simpliciter and (b) draw a compatibilist conclusion (Wolf 1990). Since in the medieval theories no constraints are placed on whether intellectual ideas and decisions are caused, from our twenty-first-century point-of-view these theories might be labelled compatibilist, whether or not their proponents would have pondered the possibility of external influences like brainwashing and hypnotism that mold the intellect. Some Jewish philosophers, notably Hasdai Crescas (c.1340–1410/11), are determinists. It can be debated whether his determinism is hard or soft.

Mention must be made, too, of the theory propounded by Rabbi Eliyahu Dessler (d. 1953), a member of the 'Musar' movement which stressed ethical preaching. Dessler maintained that owing to the near ubiquity of environmental influences, the vast majority of human choices are not choices for which the agent is responsible. A person is inculcated with certain values. Nevertheless, each person has a 'point of choice,' a narrow area in which he or she has genuine alternatives to choose from. Herein lies the potential for responsibility (Dessler 1985: 49-64). The point of choice can change over time, owing to our previous choices. There are problems with Dessler's approach: for example, it does not explain how we can justify punishing most criminals, and it seems to ignore the possibility both of repentance and of backsliding (phenomena Dessler affirms). Still, the approach takes what many will regard as a realistic view of character formation. Dessler's approach anticipates the account given by the analytic philosopher Peter van Inwagen. Like Dessler, van Inwagen restricts the scope of human free choice. His key point is not that character is formed by environmental influences but that people act in character, limiting their free will – a point Dessler makes as well (van Inwagen 1989).

Conclusion

As mentioned at the outset, my agenda has been limited; many other topics could have been discussed. Further, except for a few references, I have not pointed to parallels in Christian and Islamic thought. What is before you, however, I believe substantiates the proposition that both ancient and later Jewish texts contribute variety and richness to the exploration of topics in the philosophy of religion.

See also Christianity (Chapter 6), Islam (Chapter 7), Moses Maimonides/Rambam (Chapter 11), Thomas Aquinas (Chapter 12), Søren Kierkegaard (Chapter 15), Omniscience (Chapter 24), Omnipotence (Chapter 25), Omnipresence (Chapter 26), Goodness (Chapter 28), Hiddenness (Chapter 29), The problem of evil (Chapter 37), The problem of religious language (Chapter 39).

References

Albo, J. (1929) *The Book of Roots*, trans. I. Husik, Philadelphia: Jewish Publication Society.

Berger, D. (1997) 'Judaism and general culture in medieval and Early Modern times,' in G. Blidstein, D. Berger, S. Z. Leiman, and A. Lichtenstein, *Judaism's Encounter With Other Cultures: Rejection or Integration?*, ed. J. J. Schacter, Northvale, NJ: Jason Aronson.

Berkovits, E. (1959) *God, Man and History: A Jewish Interpretation*, New York: Jonathan David.

Cahn, S. M. (1967) *Fate, Logic and Time*, New Haven, CT: Yale University Press.

Carmy, S. (2004) 'God is distant, incomprehensible: a literary-theological approach to Zophar's first speech,' *Tradition* 38: 49–63.

Dessler, E. (1985) *Strive for Truth*, vol. 2, ed. A. Carmell, New York: Feldheim.

Feldman, S. (1987) 'Synopsis of Book Three,' in Gersonides (Levi ben Gershom), *The Wars of the Lord*, vol. 2, trans. S. Feldman. Philadelphia: Jewish Publication Society.

Gellman, J. (1997) 'The denial of free will in Hasidic thought,' in C. Manekin and M. Kellner (eds) *Freedom and Moral Responsibility: General and Jewish Perspectives*, College Park, MD: University of Maryland Press.

Gersonides (Levi ben Gershom) (1987) *The Wars of the Lord*, vol. 2, trans. S. Feldman, Philadelphia: Jewish Publication Society.

Heschel, A. J. (1962) *The Prophets: An Introduction*, New York: Harper & Row.

Hirsch, S. R. (1981) *Horeb*, trans. I. Grunfeld, London: Soncino.

Idziak, J. M. (1979) *Divine Command Morality*, New York: Edwin Mellen.

Kaplan, M. (1934) *Judaism as a Civilization*, New York: Macmillan.

Katz, S. (ed.) (2005) *The Impact of the Holocaust on Jewish Theology*, New York: New York University Press.

Leibowitz, I. (1992) *Judaism, Human Values and the State*, ed. E. Goldman, Cambridge, MA: Harvard University Press.

Levenson, J. (1998) 'Abusing Abraham: traditions, religious histories, and modern misinterpretations,' *Judaism* 47: 259–77.

Maimonides, M. (1963) *Guide of the Perplexed*, trans. S. Pines, Chicago: University of Chicago Press.

Manekin, C. (1998) 'On the limited-omniscience interpretation of Gersonides' theory of divine knowledge,' in A. Ivry, E. Wolfson and A. Arkush (eds) *Perspectives on Jewish Thought and Mysticism*, Amsterdam: Harwood Academic Publishers.

Nahmanides, M. (1971–6) *Commentary on the Torah*, trans. C. B. Chavel, New York: Shilo.

Rudavsky, T. (2003) 'The impact of Scholasticism upon Jewish philosophy in the fourteenth and fifteenth centuries,' in D. H. Frank and O. Leaman (eds) *The Cambridge Companion to Medieval Jewish Philosophy*, Cambridge, Cambridge University Press.

Saadia Gaon (1948) *The Book of Beliefs and Opinions*, trans. Samuel Rosenblatt, New Haven, CT: Yale University Press.

Sagi, A. and D. Statman (1995) 'Divine command morality and Jewish tradition,' *Journal of Religious Ethics* 23: 39–67.

Shatz, D. (1997a) 'Freedom, repentance and the hardening of hearts: Albo vs. Maimonides,' *Faith and Philosophy* 14: 478-509.

—— (1997b) 'Heierarchical theories of freedom and the hardening of hearts,' in P. French, T. E. Ueling, Jr. and H. Wettstein (eds) *Midwest Studies in Philosophy* 21, Notre Dame, IN: University of Notre Dame Press.

Soloveitchik, J. B. (1986) *The Halakhic Mind*, New York: Seth Press.

—— (1989) 'May we interpret Hukim?', in *Man of Faith in the Modern World: Reflections of the Rav*, adapted by A. R. Besdin, Hoboken, NJ: Ktav.

—— (2003) *Out of the Whirlwind*, ed. D. Shatz, J. B. Wolowelsky, and R. Ziegler, New York: Toras HoRav Foundation.

Stern, J. (1987) 'Gesture and symbol,' in A. A. Cohen and P. Mendes-Flohr (eds) *Contemporary Jewish Religious Thought*, New York: Free Press.

Stump, E. (1988) 'Sanctification, hardening of the heart, and Frankfurt's concept of free will,' *Journal of Philosophy* 85: 395–420.

van Inwagen, P. (1989) 'When is the will free?', *Philosophical Perspectives* 3: 399–422.

Wolf, S. (1990) *Freedom Within Reason*, New York: Oxford.

Wolterstorff, N. (1988) 'Suffering love,' in T. V. Morris (ed.) *Philosophy and the Christian Faith*, Notre Dame, IN: University of Notre Dame Press.

Further reading

Bleich, J. D (ed.) (1983) *With Perfect Faith: Foundations of Jewish Belief*, New York: Ktav. (A collection of predominantly medieval texts on each of Maimonides' thirteen principles of faith.)

Cohen, A. A. and P. Mendes-Flohr (eds) (1987) *Contemporary Jewish Religious Thought*, New York: Free Press. (Original essays on many concepts in Jewish thought.)

Frank, D. and O. Leaman (eds) (1997) *History of Jewish Philosophy*, London: Routledge. (A multi-authored history of Jewish philosophy from the Bible to contemporary times.)

Frank, D., O. Leaman, and C. H. Manekin (eds) *The Jewish Philosophy Reader*, London: Routledge. (Concise selections from all periods on a wide range of topics.)

6

CHRISTIANITY

Paul K. Moser

According to Acts 11: 26, the disciples of the crucified Jesus of Nazareth were first called 'Christians' at the church in Syrian Antioch. 'Christianity' was something believed and even lived, if imperfectly, by these first-century Christians. The disciples at Antioch serve as an historical anchor for what has come to be called 'Christianity.' They were called 'Christians,' because they were followers of Jesus the 'Christ,' God's 'Messiah' (the Hebrew term, meaning 'specially anointed one,' that underlies the Greek term 'Christ') for Israel and thereby for the world. If we want to understand 'Christians' and 'Christianity,' then we must consider Jesus of Nazareth, even though Christians and Christianity have moved somewhat beyond what the earthly Jesus himself taught.

Jesus, according to Mark 1: 14–15, came preaching the good news of the kingdom of God, saying: the kingdom of God has come near; repent and believe (i.e., trust) in the good news. The 'good news' preached by Jesus was that God's kingdom has come near to Israel. Controversy arose with Jesus' suggestion that God's kingdom has come near *in himself, Jesus.* Accordingly, Jesus announces: 'If, by the finger of God, I cast out demons, then the kingdom of God has come upon you' (Luke 11: 20; cf. Matt. 12: 28). So, Jesus thought of himself as integral to the coming of God's kingdom to Israel. New Testament scholars debate the ways in which Jesus deemed himself integral, but some features identified below seem clear. The more we understand Jesus, in any case, the better we understand the heart of Christianity. Indeed, understanding Jesus is necessary for understanding Christianity. He is its founder and sustainer.

Jesus and Christianity

Jesus tells a man that the way to get everlasting life is to follow him (Mark 10: 17–22). He suggests that the man's obedience to the Mosaic Law lacks the kind of self-giving commitment to God found in following Jesus. Jesus thus remarks that acceptance (or rejection) of him amounts to acceptance (or rejection) of God (Matt. 10: 40; cf. Mark 9: 37; John 13: 20). Jesus also claims authority to forgive sins even when not in God's temple (Mark 2: 1–12) and to arrange for the final judgment as God's king (Luke 22: 29–30; cf. Matt. 7: 21–2; Mark 14: 62). Likewise, Jesus symbolically presents himself as king of Israel, after Zechariah 9: 9, in his humble entry into Jerusalem on a colt

(Mark 11: 1–10; cf. John 12: 12–19), and he suggests that he is even King David's Lord (Mark 12: 35–7).

Jesus claims to be greater than King Solomon and even than God's temple (Luke 11: 31; Matt. 12: 6). In reply to a question from John the Baptist (Luke 7: 18–23), he alludes to Isaiah 61: 1–2 and 35: 5–6 to suggest that he is God's Messiah. This adds credibility to Mark 14: 61–4, where before the chief priests Jesus makes astonishing claims about his status in relation to God. These claims elicit the charge that Jesus is guilty of blasphemy (slandering God's name). Indeed, in all four gospels Jesus elicits the charge of blasphemy from his critics.

In the parable of the wicked tenants (Mark 12: 1–12), Jesus suggests that he is God's beloved Son who, though rejected by humans, is heir to the things of God. He finds support for the lesson of this parable in Psalm 118: 22–3. In addition, at his Last Supper, Jesus claims that his impending death will supply the blood of the (new) covenant poured out for many people (Mark 14: 24; cf. John 6: 53; 1 Cor. 11: 23–6). He thus suggests that his death has special redemptive significance for others. Some ancient Jewish literature acknowledges that suffering can atone for the sins of others (4 Macc. 6: 27–30, 9: 23–5). The surprise, however, is that Jesus regarded his death, the death of a Galilean outcast, as the means of God's new *covenant* of redemption, quite independently of the temple establishment in Jerusalem. The Last Supper is thus crucial to understanding Jesus and Christianity.

Given Jesus' striking remarks and actions concerning himself, E. P. Sanders has concluded that Jesus 'shared the evangelists' view that he fulfilled the hopes of the prophets,' and that 'Jesus' actual claim may have been … not only spokesman for, but viceroy of, God; and not just in a political kingdom but in the kingdom of God' (Sanders 1993: 168, 242; cf. Sanders 1985: 319–27). The previous summary of Jesus' actions and remarks suggests that Jesus regarded himself as God's unique Priest, Judge, King, Messiah, Son, and Redeemer, as the one sent by God to fulfill the hopes of Israel and thus of all other nations as well. No other human could make such authoritative claims with plausibility. Jesus transcends the bounds of human authority. He is either insane or God's unique Son and viceroy, and, despite Mark 3: 21, no evidence of his insanity is forthcoming. As Sanders observes, 'He was not a madman' (1992: 78). People sensitive to personal and moral excellence can come to see that Jesus was not insane.

Just as God is the perfect personal manifestation of wisdom, Jesus is the perfect human manifestation of God's wisdom. Jesus spoke of himself as the representative of God's wisdom (Matt. 11: 16–19; cf. Matt. 23: 34–6). If we acknowledge the authority of Jesus as God's Son and viceroy, the fact that Jesus was fully committed to God as righteously loving Father offers us a good reason to follow suit, volitionally and intellectually.

In one of the most revealing passages in the gospels, Jesus prays:

> I thank you, Father, Lord of heaven and earth, because you have hidden these things [regarding his person and ministry] from the wise and the intelligent and have revealed them to infants; yes, Father, for such was your gracious will.

All things have been handed over to me by my Father; and no one knows who the Son is except the Father, or who the Father is except the Son and anyone to whom the Son chooses to reveal him. (Luke 10: 21–2, NRSV; cf. Matt. 11: 25–7; John 3: 35).

Jesus claims in this prayer that he is the unique son and sole revealer of God and therefore has unequaled authority among humans ('all things have been given to him,' *the* Son, by his Father). Jesus is speaking of a kind of knowledge different from mere justified true belief that God exists. He is speaking of knowing God *as authoritative Father*. Knowing God as First Cause, Designer, or Ground of Being does not amount to, or even serve as a prerequisite for, knowing God as the Lord who is my righteously gracious Father. Consumed by the latter kind of knowing, Jesus addressed God as 'Abba,' best translated as 'Father.' The retention of the Aramaic term in the Greek New Testament (cf. Mark 14: 36; Gal. 4: 5; Rom. 8: 15) offers warrant for treating 'Abba' as a term from Jesus himself.

The basis of proper knowledge of God, according to Jesus, is consciousness of one's standing in a child–parent, or *filial*, relationship to God as a righteously gracious Father. This theme is widely neglected by contemporary philosophy of religion, including Christian approaches to knowledge of God. The relevant kind of knowledge cannot be reduced to justified true belief that God exists. It includes the yielding of one's will to God as supreme Father. Jesus's experience of knowing God as Father finds manifestation in his prayers (cf. Mark 14: 36; Matt. 11: 25–7, 26: 42; Luke 23: 34,46; John 11: 41). Indeed, Jesus seems to have regarded prayer as an ideal avenue to filial knowledge of God.

Distinctively Christian knowledge of God depends on a filial relationship of the sort exemplified by Jesus. It thus relies on a trusting personal relationship with God as Father. Accordingly, Jesus used children to illustrate the humble attitude of trust suitable to entering God's kingdom (Mark 10: 13–16). Our properly knowing the Jewish/Christian God is thus not a matter of passive observation or even rigorous argument. Knowing God properly requires our entering into an active personal relationship with God as Father. God as righteously gracious Father promotes active loving relationships, not mere knowledge that he exists. We come to know God by a kind of personal interaction whereby we yield our will to God. By way of analogy, you could not recognize the genuineness of your parents' love for you if you avoided a sincere personal relationship with them. Filial knowledge of God is thus not just knowledge that another object in the universe exists. Enlightenment conceptions of knowledge as a kind of spectator's observation do not apply here. They are foreign to Jesus' conception of personal knowledge of God as Father, whereby one knows God not as a mere object but as the supreme subject who is Lord of all, including oneself.

Good news about Jesus

Christianity marks a dramatic shift between the time of the earthly Jesus and the time after the crucifixion and resurrection of Jesus. Somehow Jesus as the preacher of the goods news about God became *the object of focus* in the preaching of the good news. The preacher became the preached. In one of the earliest statements of the good news in the New Testament, Paul writes: 'what I received I passed on to you as of first importance: that Christ died for our sins according to the Scriptures, that he was buried, that he was raised on the third day according to the Scriptures, and that he appeared to Peter, and then to the Twelve' (1 Cor. 15: 3–5, NIV). The goods news of Christianity is that Christ died for our sins and was raised from the dead. Why the new focus on Jesus?

As foreshadowed at the Last Supper, Jesus became, in his crucifixion and resurrection, the one who atones for sin and reconciles sinners to God. This changed everything, and it is the heart of the good news of Christianity. At the Last Supper, Jesus announced that he will die 'for the forgiveness of sins' (Matt. 26: 28). The atoning sacrifice of Jesus as God's sinless offering for humans is at the center of God's redemptive work. It sets Jesus apart from Abraham, Moses, Confucius, Krishna, Gautama the Buddha, Muhammad, the Dalai Lama, and every other religious leader. Only Jesus offers himself as God's atoning sacrifice for humans. Only Jesus, therefore, figures in the center of the good news of Christianity needed by humans.

Many people share the apostle Peter's initial denial that the death of Jesus is central to God's plan of reconciliation for humans (Mark 8: 31–2). They doubt that the crucifixion of the Son of God is compatible with God's merciful love. The apostle Paul faced similar doubts about the cross of Jesus among Christians in Corinth. His response: 'I resolved to know nothing while I was with you except Jesus Christ *and him crucified*' (1 Cor. 2: 2). The obedient death of Jesus is no less important than his resurrection. We need to see why, in order to understand Christianity.

The crucifixion seems to brand Jesus as a dismal failure, even as one 'cursed' before God (Gal. 3: 13; Deut. 21: 23). Nonetheless, the cross of Jesus is the place of God's atoning sacrifice and turnaround victory. Out of the apparent defeat of Jesus, God brings proof of his love and forgiveness toward humans, his enemies. The crucifixion of Jesus is God's grand reversal of the darkest human tragedy. As Paul says:

> the message of the cross is foolishness to those who are perishing, but to us who are being saved it is the power of God. Jews demand miraculous signs and Greeks look for wisdom, but we preach Christ crucified: a stumbling block to Jews and foolishness to Gentiles, but to those whom God has called, both Jews and Greeks, Christ the power of God and the wisdom of God. For the foolishness of God is wiser than man's wisdom, and the weakness of God is stronger than man's strength. (1 Cor. 1: 18, 22–5, NIV)

The power of God's self-giving love is demonstrated in the crucified Jesus, whom God approvingly raised from his death on the cross. The invincible power of divine merciful love overcomes even death, thereby surpassing any human power. The resurrection of Jesus is God's indelible signature of approval on his obedient, crucified Son, his atoning sacrifice. The resurrection gets significance from the cross, where Jesus gave full obedience to his Father to reconcile us to his Father. In his full obedience,

Jesus proves his Father's worthiness and pre-eminence. The Son, Jesus, ratifies his Father with full, life-giving obedience.

God sent his Son, Jesus, to live and to die for a definite purpose: to demonstrate God's merciful love for all people, even his enemies (Rom. 5: 6–8). Jesus came to identify with us humans in our weakness and trouble, while he represented his Father in faithful, self-giving love. He thus represents, and serves as a bridge between, God *and* humans, by seeking to reconcile humans to his Father via his gift of merciful love. His obedient death on the cross shows how far he and his Father will go, even to gruesome death, to try to bring humans to God. Jesus gives us all he has, out of his and his Father's love, to demonstrate that God loves us without limit and offers us the gift of unearned membership in God's everlasting family (cf. John 3: 16–17; Rom. 8: 31–2).

God uses the cross of Jesus as the place where our selfish rebellion against God is mercifully judged and forgiven by God. This does not mean that God himself punished Jesus. The New Testament writers do not teach this, contrary to some theologians. God sent Jesus into our troubled, rebellious world to undergo suffering and death that God would deem adequate for dealing justly, under divine righteousness, with our rebellion against God. Jesus thus pays the price on our behalf for righteous divine reconciliation of sinners, and thereby removes any need for fear, condemnation, shame, guilt, and punishment among us in relation to God (Rom. 8: 1).

Jesus, in dying 'for our sins,' reconciles us to his righteous Father as he becomes our Lord and Redeemer. This message of atonement as reconciliation through Jesus defines New Testament Christianity. If we omit it, we have no good news and hence no Christianity. The cross of Jesus is the indispensable focal point of divine–human reconciliation. It is the very heart of the good news of God's amazing gift of gracious love (see 1 Cor. 2: 2). The self-giving, crucified Jesus is the manifest power and mirror image of the all-loving God. The atoning sacrifice of the cross, in all its gruesome horror, is essential to understanding Jesus and Christianity.

The ultimate motive for the crucifixion of Jesus is his Father's *holy, righteous love* for humans, identified by Paul as follows:

> now a righteousness from God, apart from law, has been made known, to which the Law and the Prophets testify. This righteousness from God comes through faith in Jesus Christ to all who believe. There is no difference, for all have sinned and fall short of the glory of God, and are justified freely by his grace through the redemption that came by Christ Jesus. God presented him as a sacrifice of atonement, through faith in his blood. He did this to demonstrate his justice, because in his forbearance he had left the sins committed beforehand unpunished – he did it to demonstrate his justice at the present time, so as to be just and the one who justifies those who have faith in Jesus. (Rom. 3: 21–6, NIV)

The talk of 'justice' here is talk of God's 'righteousness'; the two terms are synonymous. Paul links God's justice/righteousness with his love: 'God proves his own love for us in that while we were still sinners, Christ died for us. … Since we have now been justified by his blood, how much more shall we be saved by him from the wrath [of God]! … [W]hen we were enemies [of God], we were reconciled to him through the death of his Son …' (Rom. 5: 8–10, my own translation). God thus takes the initiative and the crucial means, through Jesus, in divine–human reconciliation. God offers the needed unmerited gift in Jesus, 'by grace.' We are to receive the gracious gift via trust, or faith, in God and Jesus. The needed gift could never be earned by human 'works.'

The living God of perfect love, the Father of Jesus, is also a God of *righteous wrath and judgment* (Rom. 1: 18). *Because* God loves all sinners, he has wrath and judgment toward sin, which leads to death rather than life. God seeks to reconcile us to relationship with himself in a way that exceeds mere forgiveness and satisfies his holy standard of righteous love. Through the loving self-sacrifice of Jesus, *God* meets this standard *for us*, when we could not, would not, and did not. Through Jesus, God welcomes us to himself as our righteous loving Father. As Paul says, 'God was in Christ reconciling the world to himself,' not counting our sins against us (2 Cor. 5: 19). This is the heart of the good news of Jesus Christ and Christianity. This is God's scandalous holy love. It should shake us to our core. We typically hold a different, less demanding standard of love, and we thereby domesticate God and the good news of Jesus. In exalting our preferred standard over God's, we pretend to be God. God meets our selfish pretension with scandalous love that is righteous and merciful. The image of a suffering self-giving God is scandalous, a stumbling-block to prideful humans. God's self-giving love in Jesus, as an alternative to coercive power, makes no sense to us in the terms we ordinarily use to understand ourselves and the world.

The heart of the cross *for Jesus* is his perfectly loving obedience to his Father on our behalf, and not his physical suffering. Jesus expresses the central place of obedience in Gethsemane (Mark 14: 35–6). Likewise, Paul vividly identifies the crucial role of Jesus' obedience. He refers to

> Christ Jesus, who, being in the form of God, did not consider equality with God something to be grasped, but he emptied himself, taking the form of a servant, being made in human likeness. Being found in appearance as a man, he humbled himself and became obedient to death, even death on a cross. (Phil. 2: 6–8, my own translation; cf. Rom. 5: 19).

Jesus can be and is our 'Passover lamb' (1 Cor. 5: 7), our 'sacrifice of atonement' (Rom. 3: 25), because he is perfectly obedient, fully righteous, in the eyes of his holy Father. He became 'a curse for us' to save us from the law's curse on our disobedience to God (Gal. 3: 13). Jesus' perfectly obedient life toward God is an acceptable sacrifice to God for us. Gethsemane and the Last Supper manifest these crucial lessons. Gethsemane shows Jesus passionately resolving to put his Father's will first even in the face of death, and the Last Supper shows Jesus portraying, with the bread and the wine as his body and his blood, the ultimate self-sacrifice pleasing to his Father on our behalf.

Given God's righteousness and our sin, we desperately need a perfect atoning sacrifice. Only the perfectly obedient Jesus can and does provide the needed sacrifice for us, at the command of his Father. God's unique power of sacrificial love is made perfect in Jesus' obedient weakness on the cross (cf. 2 Cor. 12: 9). Without Jesus, we have no reconciler to bring us to the holy God. Jesus alone voluntarily pays the price of our selfish rebellion against God by obediently meeting God's standard of righteous, sacrificial love. Jesus alone, then, is Lord and Savior who takes away the sin of the world (John 1: 29; cf. 1 John 2: 2). This message about Jesus is central to the good news of Christianity.

The Spirit of God and Jesus

At the heart of the good news of Jesus, we find a recurring theme: Jesus is the one who would dispatch the very Spirit of God to humans (Mark 1: 8). In John's Gospel (1: 29–33), Jesus as God's atoning sacrifice is identified directly with the one who would pour out God's Spirit on people. The outpouring of God's Spirit at Pentecost (Acts 2: 1–4), then, is central to the good news of Jesus and Christianity. God's atonement in Jesus includes the means of realizing this atonement in humans: the sending of God's Spirit through Jesus to enable people to commune and live with a holy God. This echoes the prophecy of Ezekiel:

> I will give you a new heart and put a new spirit in you; I will remove from you your heart of stone and give you a heart of flesh. And I will put my Spirit in you and move you to follow my decrees and be careful to keep my laws. (Ezek. 36: 26–7 NIV)

The cross and resurrection of Jesus provide the avenue for a holy God to impart his very Spirit to people unable on their own to commune with God, given that they are unable to love as God loves. God's Spirit enables people to enter into the redemption and communion provided by God himself in Jesus. This is an integral part of the good news of Christianity.

Let's consider the evidence for the good news. Jesus himself, as the human image of God, serves as distinctive evidence of God's reality. He is a living demonstration of God's reality, including God's unsurpassable love. We need to look for the right kind of evidence of God as supplied by God himself. So, we must set aside our misleading preconceptions of such evidence.

The evidence of the good news is supplied and ratified by God's Holy Spirit, whom Paul identifies with the Spirit of Christ (Rom. 8: 9–11). In John's Gospel, Jesus identifies the cognitive and moral role of God's Spirit:

> When [the Spirit] comes, he will convict the world of guilt in regard to sin and righteousness and judgment. ... [W]hen he, the Spirit of truth, comes, he will guide you into all truth. He will not speak on his own; he will speak only what he hears, and he will tell you what is yet to come. He will bring glory to me by taking from what is mine and making it known to you. (John 16: 8, 13–14, NIV)

71

God's Spirit has the cognitive role of making things known regarding Jesus. Jesus is God's unique revealer (Matt. 11: 25–7). He calls us (a) to receive God's Spirit of redemption through trust (that is, faith) in God and (b) thereby to live as God's dependent children. This theme emerges at various places in the New Testament, including 1 Cor. 2: 11–12 and Rom. 8: 14–16; cf. Matt. 16: 16–17. It has important, widely neglected cognitive implications.

God's Spirit seeks to 'lead' people to Jesus and his Father as their Lord and their God. This experience of 'being led' is cognitively significant. It includes the authoritative call to relinquish our selfish willfulness for God's unselfish will exemplified in Jesus. This call works through conscience (see Forsyth 1913), and it comes with moral challenge and conviction, even if we are inclined to dismiss it. Human failure to hear this call is typically the result of our not wanting to hear it on God's terms of unselfish love. We prefer not to have to forgive or to love our enemies in the way God does. It seems preferable to ignore God's call for us to live as dependent children of God who reflect their holy Father.

Skeptics will object that evidence from the presence of God's Spirit does not include an argument for God's reality. This, however, is no real problem, because the reality of evidence does not depend on an argument. Most of our evidence, including evidence from sensory and perceptual experience, does not rely on any argument; this applies, too, to our evidence regarding our psychological states. Likewise, God can have his Spirit call people to turn to himself without his providing them with an argument for God's existence.

Paul writes: '[Christian] hope does not disappoint us, because God has poured out his love into our hearts by the Holy Spirit, whom he has given us' (Rom. 5: 5, NIV). He is making a cognitive point, regarding evidence from God's Spirit, but he does not identify any role for an argument. Paul characterizes the Spirit further: 'those who are led by the Spirit of God are sons of God. For you did not receive a spirit that makes you a slave again to fear, but you received the Spirit of sonship. And by him we cry, 'Abba, Father.' The Spirit himself testifies with our spirit that we are God's children' (Rom. 8: 14–16, NIV; cf. 1 Cor. 2: 10–14). Paul thus agrees with the aforementioned quotation from John's Gospel: God's Spirit has cognitive significance, but no argument is needed. In particular, people can receive testimony directly from God's Spirit that they are God's children. Paul thus comments:

> Where is the wise man? Where is the scholar? Where is the philosopher of this age? Has not God made foolish the wisdom of the world? For since in the wisdom of God the world through its wisdom did not know him, God was pleased through the foolishness of what was preached to save those who believe. (1 Cor. 1: 20–1, NIV)

God provides his own means for humans to know him: the good news of Jesus coupled with the ratifying testimony of God's own Spirit.

Any assessment of evidence for the good news of Christianity must attend to the cognitive role of God's Spirit (Moser 2002, 2003, 2007). Philosophers of religion, including Christian philosophers, have overlooked this important message. As a result, the distinctive evidence underlying Christianity has been widely neglected. We now see that Christianity is no abstract philosophical system. It is, rather, good news from God that is intended to save us from death and bring us into everlasting life with God as our holy, all-loving Father, through the sacrificial life of Jesus. As Paul says: '[Jesus] died for us so that, whether we are awake or asleep, we may live together with him' (1 Thess. 5: 10). The heart of Christianity, then, is: living together with God, thanks to Jesus the Christ.

See also Religious traditions and rational assessments (Chapter 19), Inclusivism and exclusivism (Chapter 21), Hiddenness (Chapter 29), The Incarnation (Chapter 51), Resurrection (Chapter 52), Sin and salvation (Chapter 53), Faith (Chapter 56), Prayer (Chapter 57).

References

Forsyth, P. T. (1913) *The Principle of Authority*, London: Hodder & Stoughton.

Moser, P. K. (2002) 'Cognitive idolatry and divine hiding,' in D. Howard-Snyder and P. Moser (eds) *Divine Hiddenness*, New York: Cambridge University Press.

—— (2003) 'Cognitive inspiration and knowledge of God,' in P. Copan and P. Moser (eds) *The Rationality of Theism*, London: Routledge.

—— (2007) 'Religious skepticism,' forthcoming in J. Greco (ed.) *The Oxford Handbook of Skepticism*, New York: Oxford University Press.

Sanders, E. P. (1985) *Jesus and Judaism*, Philadelphia: Fortress Press.

—— (1992) 'The life of Jesus,' in H. Shanks (ed.) *Christianity and Rabbinic Judaism*, Washington, DC: Biblical Archeology Society.

—— (1993) *The Historical Figure of Jesus*, London: Lane.

Further reading

Copan, P. and P. K. Moser (eds) (2003) *The Rationality of Theism*, London: Routledge. (Presents a wide range of evidence for Christian theism.)

Hunter, A. M. (1967) *The Gospel according to St. Paul*, Philadelphia: Westminster. (Shows that the good news from Jesus and the good news from Paul are at heart the same.)

Johnson, L. T. (1999) *Living Jesus: Learning the Heart of the Gospel*, San Francisco, CA: Harper. (Identifies the cruciform pattern set by Jesus as the core of the good news.)

Minear, P. S. (2002) *The Bible and the Historian*, Nashville, TN: Abingdon. (Makes a case for restoring the reality of God to the study of the Bible.)

Moser, P. K. (2008) *The Elusive God: Reorienting Religious Epistemology*, New York/Cambridge: Cambridge University Press, forthcoming.

—— (2002) 'Cognitive idolatry and divine hiding,' in D. Howard-Snyder and P. Moser (eds) *Divine Hiddenness*, New York: Cambridge University Press. (Presents the kind of evidence to be expected of the Jewish-Christian God.)

Taylor, J. V. (1972) *The Go-Between God: The Holy Spirit and the Christian Mission*, London: SCM. (Identifies the workings of the Holy Spirit in the expansion of Christianity.)

7
ISLAM
Majid Fakhry

Introduction

Islam, as the last of the three monotheistic religions to emanate from the Near East, may be said to have passed through the same stages of development through which Judaism, and to a larger extent Christianity, passed with respect to the interaction of reason and faith.

The story of this interaction, where Islam is concerned, starts systematically in the eighth century, which witnessed the gradual assimilation of Greek philosophical concepts and methods. This interaction came in the wake of the translation of the works of Aristotle, epitomes of Plato's *Dialogues*, Plotinus' *Enneads*, and excerpts from the philosophical works of Galen and Aristotle's commentators, including Alexander of Aphrodesias, Theophrastus, Simplicius, and Philoponus. To this list should be added Proclus' *Liber de Causis* or the *Pure Good*, which, like Plotinus' *Enneads*, referred to in the Arabic sources as the *Athulugia* and ascribed mistakenly to Aristotle, played a decisive role in the rise and development of Islamic Neoplatonism (Fakhry 2004: 4–33).

In general, the reception of Greek philosophy in intellectual and theological Islamic circles was rather mixed. There were first the philosophical enthusiasts, as we may call them, such as al-Kindi (d. *c*.866 CE), whose admiration of philosophy and its Greek masters, especially Plato and Aristotle, was unbounded. However, the reception in theological circles was on the whole hostile, despite the fact that the first theological school, known as the Mu'tazilite, founded by Wasil Ibn 'Ata (d. 748), was grounded in Greek rationalism and reflected the unmistakable impact of Greek philosophy in a modified manner. This school (noted below) was met with undisguised animosity by the traditionalist theologians, especially the followers of one of the leading anti-rationalist scholars in the ninth century, Ahmad Ibn Hanbal (d. 855). However, this anti-rationalism was later moderated somewhat in the wake of the rise of the most influential theological school in Islam, known as Ash'arism after its founder Abu'l-Hasan al-Ash'ari (d. 935), a century later. In modern times, Muslim theologians continued to adhere to the same moderate anti-rationalism of that school.

It is to be noted that the Qur'ān itself abounds in calls to 'the people of understanding' or 'perception' to 'take stock' of the works of creation and the calamities which shall befall the non-Muslim unbelievers (Q. 59; 2; 39: 21, etc.). It also speaks of 'people of reason' who obey God or worship him consciously. In fact, the expression 'they reason' or 'you reason' occurs forty-six times in the Qur'ān.

More significant, perhaps, is the fact that the Qur'ān repeatedly uses the term *hikmah*, the Arabic equivalent of the Greek *sophia* (wisdom), to denote the revelation to the Prophet Muhammad (Q 4: 113; 54: 113) or his predecessors, such as Luqman (Q. 31: 121), David (Q. 28: 20) or Jesus (3: 48; 5: 110). In the latter two verses, Jesus is said to have been taught the Torah by God, the Gospels, as well as 'the wisdom,' which probably refers to the 'sapiential' books of the Old Testament, generally attributed to Solomon. In one verse (Q. 43: 63), Jesus is reported to have said, 'I have come to you with wisdom and to make clear to you part of that whereon you are in disagreement,' probably in reference to the Christological controversies of the time, of which Muhammad must have learned during his travels in Syria and Abyssinia.

The basic theological issues which split the Muslim ranks or exercised the more original scholars from the eighth century on were: (1) the existence of God and his attributes; (2) the nature of revelation and the manner in which God has 'spoken' to the prophets or apostles; (3) the immortality of the soul and the resurrection of the body in the afterlife; (4) the major ethical themes and their grounds in reason or scripture.

God's existence and his attributes

We might begin with the existence of God and the proofs offered by Muslim philosophers or theologians in the demonstration of his existence and the way in which he can be characterized as Creator and Lord.

The overwhelming impression the Qur'ān leaves on its reader is that of God's utter uniqueness, his omnipotence, and his omniscience. Thus, in the opening chapter (*Fatihah*), God is described as the 'Lord of the Worlds ... Master of the Day of Judgment' (Q. 1: 24), and in the near-final chapter (*sura*), he is said to be 'the only one, the everlasting, who did not beget and is not begotten. None is his equal.' (Q. 112: 1–4). Elsewhere, he is described in these words: 'nothing is like unto him' (Q. 42: 11).

All the major Muslim philosophical and theological sects have dwelt on the existence of God, which, to the Sufis, was intuitively certain, God being known directly through the mystical experience of which the Sufis claimed to partake. The arguments given by their rivals may be divided into three categories: (1) The argument from temporal creation (*huduth*), known in Latin as the argument *a novitate mundi*; (2) the argument from contingency or possibility (*imkan*); and (3) the argument from design or the teleological argument. The ontological argument, which does not appear to have had many expositors, will be mentioned briefly below.

The theologians or *mutakallimun*, whether Mu'tazilite or Ash'arite, believed the world to consist of atoms and accidents, which do not endure for two instants of time but are continually created and recreated by God. It followed, according to them, that the world was by definition temporal (*muhdath*) or created in time by its Creator (*muhdith*) or Maker, who will also bring it to an end. This argument was first developed by the philosopher al-Kindi, who was committed to the total agreement of philosophy and religion and diverged radically from his Neoplatonic successors who rejected the concept of creation being *ex nihilo* and in time as philosophically untenable.

Some of the philosophers, led by the great Neoplatonist Ibn Sina, or Avicenna (d. 1037), opted for an argument which had certain similarities to the above-mentioned argument but stemmed from the more rarefied notion of contingency or possibility. According to the exponents of this argument, which is essentially cosmological, the world, which consists of a series of contingent or possible entities, depends ultimately upon a Being who is necessary or non-contingent, labeled by Ibn Sina the Necessary Being. For him and the other exponents of this argument, the world is an eternal emanation from the Necessary Being, rather than a creation *ex nihilo* and in time as their predecessors among the theologians had argued. For them, in other words, the concept of the temporal creation was to be replaced by that of eternal emanation or overflowing (*sudur fayd*) from the Necessary Being, which they sometimes described in Aristotelian fashion as thought thinking itself.

Al-Farabi (d. 950), Ibn Sina's predecessor and founder of Islamic Neoplatonism, accepted the notion of the contingency of the world, and drew from it the same conclusion that Ibn Sina was to draw. In a little-known treatise, he argues that the series of possible or contingent entities necessarily terminates in a Being who is necessary or uncaused, but appears to have inclined to the more subtle ontological argument, which had few supporters in Islam. Thus in one of his major works, *Ihsa' al-'Ulum* (Classification of the sciences), al-Farabi gives an account of the Aristotelian subdivision of existing entities into material and immaterial substance; he proceeds to argue that 'despite their multiplicity, [the immaterial substances] rise from the lowest to the higher and then the highest, until they terminate in a perfect being, nothing more perfect than whom can exist; nor can anything be of equal rank in point of being with Him' (al-Farabi 1949: 89).

Ibn Rushd (Averroes; d. 1198), the great Aristotelian philosopher and commentator, favored the teleological argument, or as he calls it the argument from providence. That argument he believed to be the most accordant with the Qur'an. It rests on the premise that the world and everything in it is necessarily ordered in accordance with the dictates of divine wisdom, so as to subserve the existence and well-being of humankind. He supports these claims by quoting Qur'anic verses 80: 24–32: 'Let humankind consider its nourishment. We have caused the water to flow abundantly; then split the earth wide open; then caused the grain to grow therein; together with vines and green vegetation ... for your enjoyment and that of your cattle' (Ibd Rushd/ Averroes 1964: 152). Ibd Rushd is emphatic that the Qur'an is full of exhortations to the faithful to ponder the wonders of creation, which exhibit God's sovereignty and power, and reproaches those who have failed to do so. As Qur'an 7: 185 puts it, 'Have they not considered the kingdoms of heaven and earth as well as all the things God has created, and how their appointed term may have drawn near,' which is an explicit affirmation of the argument for providence, Ibd Rushd asserts.

With respect to the divine attributes, the Qur'ān, as already mentioned, stresses the attributes of God's uniqueness, deemed as the most fundamental tenet of the Islamic creed known in Arabic as *tawhid*. That tenet was particularly favored by the Muslim Neoplatonists insofar as it chimed in well with Plotinus' concept of the Supreme Being or the One (*To hen*) as he has it, and that of his successor Proclus, or the First (*To proton*). Thus, the founder of Islamic Neoplatonism, al-Farabi, opens his major treatise, *The Virtuous City*, with a detailed discourse on this First who is the cause of all existing entities and is free from all imperfection, is entirely unique and has no partner – a clear critical allusion to the Christian Trinitarian doctrine which was repudiated by all believing Muslims, including philosophers and commoners. God's uniqueness is regarded by al-Farabi as synonymous with his existence, which he regarded as identical with his essence (al-Farabi 1960: 30). From this thesis as a premise, he proceeds to assert that God or the First is entirely indivisible, and as such indefinable insofar as the causes of the existence of the *definiendum* are reducible ultimately to the causes of its existence or that of its components, which in the case of God is entirely excluded.

Ibd Sina, the other great Muslim Neoplatonist, agreed with al-Farabi that the First, or as he calls him the Necessary Being, is one, indivisible, and indefinable. To these attributes Ibd Sina adds those of simplicity, perfection, good will, and truthfulness, but holds the strange view that this Necessary Being has no essence, since the necessity of his existence is independent of any other factor or consideration (Ibn Sina 1986: 270), including that of essence or property.

The other attributes of God, known collectively as the seven attributes of perfection, consisted of knowledge, life, power, will, speech, hearing, and sight. These attributes were regarded by the philosophers and the rationalist theologians as identical with God's essence. The most heated controversies in these circles centered on the attributes of hearing and sight, which the theologians interpreted in a variety of literal ways, but which the philosophers, as a rule, regarded as incompatible with God's simplicity; they held that they should in fact be understood as purely figurative qualifications of the Supreme Being. More specifically, such philosophers as al-Kindi and Ibn Rushd held that the two attributes of hearing and sight should be interpreted as predicates of God, in the sense that his knowledge encompasses all modes of cognition whether intelligible or perceptible.

The origination of the world: creation versus emanation

The Qur'ān speaks of God's creative power underlying the creation and the management of the world in the most dramatic terms. The world is said to have been created in six days by an act of divine fiat (*amr*) following which God sat upon the Throne (Q. 7: 54; 10: 3, etc.). It adds that the world was created 'in truth' rather than 'in sport' (Q. 44: 38) or 'in vain' (Q. 51: 56), but leaves the purpose of creation undefined, except where humans and jinnies (or angels), who are said to have been created by God so as to worship him (Q. 51: 56) are concerned.

For the theologians/*Mutakallimun*, almost without exception, the world was created *ex nihilo* and in time, which the philosophers, with few exceptions, questioned. To begin with, the philosophers tended to steer clear of the use of the term Creator, or rather its Arabic equivalent *khaliq*, substituting for it such terms as Maker (*sani'*), Bringer into Being (*mujid*), or Originator (*bari'*). Al-Kindi went so far as to coin two original terms, *mu'ayyis* and *muhawwi* (from *aysa* or 'to be,' and *huwa* or 'it/he,' to denote the act of creation out of nothing).

The Neoplatonists in particular subscribed to the view of emanation (*fayd, sudur*) as an alternative to that of creation, in order to highlight their notion of the world as the necessary, global entity overflowing eternally from the One or First Being, which is free of willing or temporality. Like Plotinus, they argued that the Supreme Being generates by an eternal act of emanation the first intellect (*noûs*), followed by a series of nine intellects, which terminate in the active intellect, which lies at the periphery of the physical world, followed by the soul (*psyche*), and finally matter (*hyle*), as Plotinus called them. Some philosophers, like Ibn Rushd, were critical of the concept of emanation, but attempted to reconcile the Qur'ānic concept of creation and the Aristotelian concept of eternity by subscribing to that of eternal generation or production (*ihdath da'im*). Ibn Rushd argued that this is implicit in such Qur'ānic verses as Q. 11: 7, which reads: 'It is He who created the heavens and the earth in six days and His throne was upon the water.' This implies, according to Ibn Rushd, the eternity of water, the throne and the time that measures their duration. Similarly, verse Q. 41: 11, which states that 'He arose unto heaven, while it was smoke' implies, according to him, that the heaven was created out of pre-existing matter, which is smoke, rather than out of nothing, as the *mutakallimun* claimed.

With respect to the duration of the world, most philosophers adhered to the concept of post-eternity (*abadiyyah*), or the fact that the world, having existed since all time, will endure forever by reason of the eternity of matter and time. The two major exceptions were al-Kindi and al-Razi, the former adhering to the Qur'ānic view of creation in time, as we have seen; the latter subscribed to a picturesque view of creation whose origins are unknown. The world, he held, was created out of three co-eternal principles of space, time, and matter, to serve as the stage upon which the infatuation of the soul (the fourth co-eternal principle) with matter is destined to be eternally requited in consequence of its union with matter. Whereupon the soul will discover, through the therapeutic function of philosophy, its original essence as a citizen of the intelligible world. Then, the material world will cease to exist and the soul will regain, in Platonic fashion, its original abode in the higher world (al-Razi 1939: 290f.).

Divine revelation and conjunction (*ittisal*) with the active intellect

Man's contact with the divine world was predicated, in the Semitic tradition generally, on the notion of God addressing humankind through his prophets or apostles in humanly intelligible speech, and eventually becoming embodied in the divine logos (word) or Christ. Thus Yahweh spoke to Moses on Mount Sinai and manifested himself in Jesus and finally revealed the Qur'ān, originally embedded in the eternal Tablet (Q. 85: 22), in pure Arabic, to Prophet Muhammad, the 'last of the prophets.'

In more specific terms, the Qur'ān was 'dictated' to Muhammad by the angel Gabriel (*Jibril*), and was then transmitted by Muhammad himself to the so-called 'secretaries of revelation.' It was eventually codified in the authorized version of 'Uthman, the third Caliph, who died in 656. The literal revelation of the Qur'ān as the divine word gave rise in due course to a heated controversy regarding the nature of this revelation and whether it was eternal or created in time.

The Mu'tazilite or rationalist theologians adhered, from the ninth century on, to the thesis of the 'created Qur'ān,' which they rationalized in a way the traditionalists found entirely unacceptable. The meanings or connotations of the verses of the Qur'ān, the Mu'tazilites held, are eternal and uncreated, but the words or letters, recited or written, being accidents, could not be eternal, but are created in time. This view was challenged by Imam Ahmad ibn Hanbal (d. 855), who was jailed and humiliated by order of the pro-Mu'taziltite Caliph al-Ma'mun (813–33). However, he continued to adhere to his notion of the Qur'ān as 'the eternal and uncreated word of God.'

In general, the philosophers as a whole could not reconcile themselves to the thesis of the verbal revelation, and while they paid lip service to the dogma of the revelation of the Qur'ān, they tended to substitute for it the already mentioned concept of conjunction or contact with the active intellect. As interpreted by al-Farabi and his successors, 'conjunction' or contact with the active intellect, the tenth emanation from the Supreme Being or the First, is the token of man's ultimate philosophical enlightenment. That intellect was for al-Farabi and other Neoplatonists such as Ibn Sina the 'storehouse' of all intelligibles accessible to the human mind. As interpreted by the latter, the human mind passes through the four stages of potential, habitual, actual, and acquired intellection before it is ready to receive the 'illumination' of the active intellect. He describes this as a supermundane agency, conjunction, or contact (*ittisal*) which marks the highest stage in man's intellectual journey and is the token of the soul's intellectual self-fulfillment. At that point, Ibn Sina writes,

> the rational soul, whose proper perfection is to become a rational world in which the form of the whole, and the rational order of that whole, as well as the good overflowing in the whole … will be converted into an intelligible world, parallel to the whole existing world, contemplating the absolute truth, and the true beauty, and is united to it and imprinted with its model and shape. (1986: 328)

It is to be noted that despite its idealistic ring, this concept of 'conjunction' with the active intellect stopped short of an even more rarefied concept, that was upheld by the Sufis, who sought to achieve the almost superhuman mystical condition of union or identification with God. Aristotelian philosophers, like Ibn Rushd, accepted the fourfold tabulation of the intellect, but rejected the notion of the active intellect as a supermundane agency with which the human intellect aspires to be united. They argued instead that the active intellect is simply a faculty of the soul, which has to the material (human) intellect the same relation of form to matter. Accordingly, its function consists in actualizing that material intellect, which is pure potentiality, as St Thomas Aquinas (d. 1274) and Aristotelians in the late Middle Ages actually held.

Bodily resurrection and the immortality of the soul

For the Muslim philosophers, the resurrection of the body, so graphically depicted in the Qur'ān, raised the most acute problems. The only exception was al-Kindi, who is known to have been sympathetic to the Mu'tazilite version of Islamic theology (*kalam*). He adhered to the thesis of bodily resurrection and the attendant pleasures of heaven or tortures of hell, as depicted in the Qur'ān, which speaks of God's supreme power 'to bring the bones back to life once they have withered,' thus causing life to come out of death, just as he causes fire to come out of green trees when they turn into wood (Q. 36: 78 f.), as al-Kindi argues (al-Kindi 1850–3).

The Neoplatonist philosophers, with al-Farabi at their head, found the thesis of bodily resurrection unacceptable and adhered with some qualifications to the thesis of the immortality of the soul, so eloquently portrayed in Plato's Dialogues, especially the *Symposium*. This Islamic Neoplatonist, who is also known to have written a political utopia analogous to Plato's *Republic* (entitled 'Opinions of the inhabitants of the virtuous city'), held that individual souls upon departing the body will partake of a growing measure of happiness as they join the successive throngs of kindred souls in the intelligible world. However, those souls which cannot be weaned from bodily pleasure will continue to pass from one body to the other endlessly. Wicked souls will be resuscitated in lower bodily forms until they have finally degenerated down to the bestial level, whereupon they will simply perish. The virtuous souls, by contrast, are assured, according to al-Farabi, of eternal happiness in the higher world (al-Farabi 1960: 118).

Ibn Sina, the other leading Neoplatonist, believed, as we have seen, that the soul, or rather the intellect, attains its perfection upon 'conjunction' with the active intellect. Once the intellect has achieved that condition, it would have achieved its supreme vocation as a replica of the intelligible world to which it belonged prior to its 'descent' into the body. Those souls which fall short of that condition will suffer the misery attendant upon separation from the body. But once they have overcome this misery they will be able to partake of that intellectual pleasure which is 'analogous to that blissful condition proper to the pure, living entities (i.e. spiritual substances) and is greater than any other pleasure' (Ibn Sina 1986: 330).

However, Ibn Sina recognized, in addition to that intellectual condition of which the soul will partake upon separation from the body, a 'scriptural' one consisting of bodily resurrection which is 'warranted by scripture [*shar'*] and can only be demonstrated by recourse to the wholly law [Islamic *shari'ah*] and assent to prophetic records' (1986: 326). That law which 'Muhammad our prophet has brought us,' he writes, 'sets forth for us the nature of the happiness and misery which are in store for the body' (ibid.), an obvious concession to the official Islamic view of resurrection. Ibn Sina is emphatic, however, that the higher intellectual happiness which the 'metaphysical philosophers' are engaged in seeking is higher and consists of that 'proximity to God' which the mystics (Sufis) are intent on seeking and is confirmed by the 'true holy law of Islam.'

The same view was imagined by the Aristotelian philosopher Ibn Rushd, who diverged from Ibn Sina's position on a variety of metaphysical points. For him, 'all the religious laws or creeds are in agreement with the demonstrations of the philosophers' regarding the fate of the soul after death. He believed, however, that the gross corporal resurrection entertained by the vulgar is untenable. For, according to that view, the soul is destined upon resurrection to be reunited to the same body from which it was separated upon death. But how is it possible, Ibn Rushd asks, for the same body which was reduced to dust, has changed into a vegetable, upon which another person has fed, to enter into the makeup of a resurrected body?

It is more reasonable to assume, he argues, that the resurrected soul will be united on the last day to a body which is analogous, but not identical, to its own original body (Ibn Rushd 1930: 586). Nevertheless, Ibn Rushd goes on to explain, the different religious creeds are in agreement regarding the fact of survival after death (ma'ad), despite their disagreement regarding its modality. Some creeds, by which he probably meant the Christians, regard it as spiritual, whereas others, by which he meant Islam, regard it as doubly corporal and spiritual. He then proceeds to explain that the intent of the latter creed is purely instrumental in ensuring a greater receptivity by the masses at large. Thus it appears, he writes, 'that the (corporal) representation found in this our religion [i.e., Islam] is more effective in conducing to the comprehension of the majority of humankind and moving their souls ... whereas spiritual resurrection is less effective in moving these souls' (1964: 244). On this account, Ibn Rushd was accused of heresy by his countrymen while he lived; but when his works were translated into Latin in the thirteenth century, he and his Latin followers, the so-called Latin Averroists, were accused of a certain duplicity known as the double truth.

Historically speaking, it was the view of Ibn Sina that was accepted by later generations of Ishraqi philosophers, such as al-Shirazi (d. 1641), who recognized the harmony of philosophy and mysticism for the first time in Muslim history.

Ethical theories: religious, philosophical and mystical

Ethical controversies in theological and philosophical circles began to raise their heads as early as the eighth century, which witnessed the first contacts with Greek philosophy, as we have seen. Thus the Mu'tazilite or rationalist theologians were moved to raise the fundamental questions of right and wrong, divine justice, and the justification of God's ways, around which controversy turned from the ninth century on. Contrary to the claims of their traditionalist rivals, man is able, according to the Mu'tazilites, to discriminate rationally between right and wrong and to chose freely, by virtue of his God-given reason and free will. Being fully responsible for his actions, man will be punished or rewarded in the hereafter by God, whose justice is absolute and whose decrees are irreversible and unquestionable.

Both on rational and on scriptural grounds, stemming from the Qur'ān, the Mu'tazilites argued that actions are right or wrong in themselves and are not dependent in that respect on what their traditionalist rivals maintained are God's commands and prohibitions. Their rivals, especially the so-called Determinists (*jabriyah*), held that right and wrong are thoroughly determined by God, who is at liberty to punish or reward his servants as he pleases, their fates being pre-determined since all time by the divine decree. For, they held, as the Qur'ān has put it, 'He is not questioned about what He does, but they [i.e., humans] are questioned' (Q. 21: 23).

Islamic philosophical ethics reflects in many ways the Socratic-Platonic influence on the one hand and that of Aristotle on the other. The character of the former influence tended to be eclectic, as the writings of al-Kindi and al-Razi, the greatest admirer of Plato in Islam, illustrate. More systematic or coherent was the impact of Aristotle's *Nicomachean Ethics* translated by Ishaq Ibn Hunain (d. 911) or his father, as commented on by Ibn Rushd and others.

The foremost and best-known writer on ethics in Islam was Ahmad Miskawayh (d. 1030), who is the author of a short psychological treatise, *Al-Fawz al-Asghar* (The Smaller Gain), which serves as a prelude to his major ethical treatise entitled 'The Cultivation of Morals' (*Tahdhib al-Akhlaq*), to which his treatise 'The Essence of Justice' (*Mahiyat al-'Adl*) should be added. In the first treatise, Miskawayh defines justice as the perfection or fulfillment of the three Platonic virtues of wisdom, courage, and temperance, and their equilibrium or proportion. This perfection is then identified in Pythagorean fashion with unity, which for him is synonymous with perfect goodness. In the second treatise he identifies this unity with equality, which is the basis of natural justice, according to him. However, Miskawayh refers to a counterpart of this natural justice, which he labels as 'divine justice' and which exists in the realm of 'metaphysical or everlasting entities' (1964: 20).

The other divisions of justice are then given as conventional and human justice; the former is divided into general and particular and appears to refer to political justice. Human justice, on the other hand, is described as the manner in which the faculties of the soul are at peace with each other and is to the soul what health is to the body. Like Aristotle, he argues that the truly just individual is not one who achieves harmony or equilibrium within himself, as Plato had held in the *Republic*, but rather one who achieves that harmony in the fields of distribution of goods and honors, that of voluntary transactions or that of involuntary transactions involving violence or oppression.

The other two ethical virtues which Miskawayh discusses at some length are friendship and happiness. The bond of friendship is described by him as the primary principle of social association or cohesion. Owing to human imperfection and insufficiency, the individual cannot fulfill his essential needs without the cooperation of his fellow men, hence his need for that association with which friendship is bound up.

The aims of friendship are then given as goodness or virtues, utility or self-interest and a combination of both. But, like Aristotle, he regards the friendship grounded in virtue as truly durable and praiseworthy, unlike utility or pleasure, which are evanescent. He regards intellectual pleasure as entirely different from corporal pleasure and argues that it can reach in some cases the pitch 'of passionate love, is analogous with mystical rapture and is identical to that divine love which some divine men claim to have experienced' (Miskawayh 1966: 138).

Friendship is then described along essentially Aristotelian lines as a means to man's ultimate good or happiness. Like Aristotle, Miskawayh argues that the exercise of man's virtues requires the possession of certain goods or means, such as money or the assistance of associates or friends. But the happiness accruing from such exercise is inferior to that higher happiness which consists of the fulfillment of man's intellectual perfection; this is bound up with that condition of conjunction (*ittisal*) with the Active Intellect, and which the Neoplatonists regarded as the ultimate good of human endeavor and the token of man's ultimate happiness (1966: 41). Miskawayh is extravagant in characterizing this happiness. For him, once man has attained this condition, he will become immune to suffering,

> fully pleased with himself and content with his estate and the emanations he receives from the light of the One. He will derive no other pleasure save from these conditions, is delighted with nothing save these beauties and is not jubilant save at the prospect of revealing that wisdom (he has acquired) to those who are worthy of it. (1966: 85)

As one might expect, this mystical account of happiness is not confined to the philosophers. Some theologians, like al-Ghazālī (d. 1111), or Sufis, like Ibn 'Arabi (d. 1240) without excluding inferior or worldly modes of happiness, have insisted that only mystical contemplation or union with God is the true warrant of ultimate happiness. Thus, al-Ghazālī holds in his ethical treatise *Mizen al-'Amal* (The criterion of action), that by happiness we should understand that otherworldly condition of unadulterated pleasure, unbounded riches, and undiminished perfection lasting for all time. It surpasses that condition of intellectual pleasure which the 'metaphysical philosophers' and even some Sufis have proposed as an alternative to it.

The ultimate goal of human endeavor, for al-Ghazālī, is the relentless quest for God. Apart from shunning all worldly goods or pursuits, the true seeker of God, having apprehended his beauty and majesty, will strive to come closer to him or achieve a spiritual affinity to him, similar to that of the disciple to his master, causing him to seek continually to achieve the perfection of that master. The stages through which the true seeker of God may pass are those of desiring or acquisition of knowledge, saintly conduct, prophetic inspiration, and finally angelic sanctity. Once he has attained that final stage, al-Ghazālī writes: 'The God-seekers will be wholly divested of human traits and will turn into angels in human shape' (al-Ghazālī 1342: 160).

Muhyi al-Din Ibn 'Arabi (d. 1240), one of the two main figures in the history of Sufism, even places mankind in a higher category than the angels by reason of the fact that humans, unlike angels, are able to know God in the spiritual sense as the Truth and in the material sense as the manifestation of that Truth in the form of physical reality.

The human soul for Ibn 'Arabi is a spiritual essence entirely distinct from the body and, as such, capable of attaining the ultimate stage of union with the divine reality. When the soul has attained that stage, he goes on to argue, it would have achieved the condition of self-annihilation and is able thereupon to perceive visually and existentially the unity of all things, the Creator and the created, the visible and the invisible, the temporal and the eternal. At that point, it may be said that the pantheistic cycle is finally closed and all things are reduced to a condition of total ontological unity or identity (Ibn 'Arabi 1949: 381). That, of course, was the climactic point in the Sufi search for self-fulfillment, which did not stop short, in some cases, of self-deification, as the cases of earlier Sufis such as al-Hallaj (d. 922) and al-Bistani (d. 875) clearly show.

See also Ibn Sina/Avicenna (Chapter 10), Mysticism among the world's religions (Chapter 23), Omniscience (Chapter 24), Omnipotence (Chapter 25), Goodness (Chapter 28), Creation and divine action (Chapter 30), The ontological argument (Chapter 31), The cosmological argument (Chapter 32), The teleological argument (Chapter 33), Problems with the concept of God (Chapter 38), Naturalistic rejoinders to theistic arguments (Chapter 40), Theology and religious language (Chapter 48), Heaven and hell (Chapter 54), Religious experience (Chapter 63).

References

Al-Farabi (1949) *Ihsa' al-'Ulum*, Cairo.
—— (1960), *Al-Madinah al-Fadilah*, Beirut.
al-Ghazālī, A.H. (1342 H.), *Mizan al-'Amal*, Cairo.
Al-Kindi, A.Y. (1850-3), *Rasa'il al-Kindi al-Falsafiyeh*, Cairo.
Al-Razi, A. B. (1939) *Opera Metaphysica*, Cairo.
Fakhry, M. (2004) *History of Islamic Philosophy*, New York: Columbia Press.
Ibn 'Arabi, M. D. (1949) *Fusus al-Hikam*, Cairo.
Ibn Rushd (Averroes), A. W. (1930) *Tahafut al-Tahafut*, Beirut.
—— (1964) *Al-Kashf 'an Manahij al-Adillah*, Cairo.
Ibn Sina (Avicenna), A. H. (1986) *Kitab al-Najat*, Beirut.
Miskawayh, A. 'A. (1964) *Mahiyat al-'Adl*, Leiden: Brill.
—— (1966) *Tahdhib al-Akhlaq*, Beirut.

Further reading

Al-Ghazālī, A. H. (1997) *The Incoherence of the Philosophers*, trans M. Marmura, Provo, Utah: Brighham Young University Press. (The most virulent attack on the philosophers, both Arab and Greek, by the leading theologian of his day. It was later criticized by Averroes, who attempted to show the coherence of philosophy and Islam rather than their incoherence or incompatibility, in a work entitled *The Incoherence of the Incoherence*.)
Averroes (2001) *Faith and Reason in Islam*, trans. I. Najjar, Oxford: Oneworld. (An English version of his famous treatise, *The Interrelation of Philosophy and Religion*. Ibn Rushd (Averroes) was the greatest Aristotelian in the Arabic tradition who contributed greatly to the controversy between the philosophers and the theologians, especially al-Ghazali.)
Fakhry, M. (1997) *Islamic Philosophy, Theology, and Mysticism*, Oxford: Oneworld. Reprinted 2000. (A short introduction to the three closely interrelated aspects of Islamic thought and the controversies that surrounded them.)

Part II

KEY FIGURES
IN PHILOSOPHY
OF RELIGION

8
AUGUSTINE
Phillip Cary

Augustine of Hippo (354–430) is the author of the single most influential body of religious writings in the West outside the Bible. As bishop of the city of Hippo in Roman North Africa, he wrote voluminously on theology and church affairs, becoming known for his formulations of the Christian doctrines of grace, original sin, the sacraments, the Church and the holy Trinity. As a philosopher of religion, his importance lies less in the specific arguments found in his works than in a stock of themes, concepts, and images that become integral to western thought through him. Augustine is a Christian Platonist who incorporates classical philosophical ideas into Christian thought and thereby changes the history of both Christianity and philosophy. His most important philosophical debt is to the Neoplatonism of Plotinus (c.205–70), whose profound philosophical spirituality he appropriates and develops into a piety of the heart, intellect, and will, which becomes essential to what the word 'religion' ends up meaning in western thought.

Philosophical writings

Four of Augustine's works are frequent topics of philosophical discussion to this day. First, the *Confessions* (*Conf.*) is a spiritual autobiography containing important discussions of the nature of God and the soul (bk. 7), love and friendship (bk. 4), the divided will (bk. 8), memory (bk. 10), evil and creation (bk. 7), and the relation of eternity and time (bk. 11). Second, the *City of God* (CG) is a huge work designed to refute pagan accusations that Christianity was at fault for the fall of Rome; it contains Augustine's most elaborate treatment of the nature of religion (bk. 10), the relation of Christianity and philosophy (bk. 8), the creation of the world and the origin of evil (bks. 11–14), the meaning of history (bks. 15–18), political theory (bk. 19), and life after death (bks. 20–2). Third, *On Free Choice* (FC), which is the first treatise ever written on the concept of will, also contains a distinctively Augustinian approach to showing the soul how to perceive the existence of God (bk. 2) – it is not really accurate to call it a 'proof' for God's existence – as well as an extended discussion of love and evil, the overall message of which is that the origin of evil must not be blamed on God but on the free will of beings God creates, who fail to love what would make them truly happy. Fourth, the treatise *On the Teacher* develops a philosophy of language in which words are signs that admonish us to look for the intelligible thing they signify but cannot give us an understanding of it.

Other works important for understanding Augustine's philosophy of religion include *Of True Religion* (TR), containing Augustine's most detailed effort to synthesize Christianity and Platonism; *The Nature of the Good* (NG), his fullest elaboration of the theory that evil is a privation of being; *The Usefulness of Belief* (UB), an important statement on the relation of authority and reason; and *On Christian Doctrine* (CD) containing his fullest and most influential discussion of the ethics of love (bk. 1) together with his most systematic treatment of semiotics and philosophy of culture (bk. 2), hermeneutics (bks. 2–3), and rhetoric (bk. 4).

One can see Augustine's metaphysics under construction in his earliest works, which include a series of philosophical dialogues written before he was a bishop, focusing primarily on the ontology of the soul and its relation to God through reason: *On Order* (OO), on the nature of evil and the proper order of studies in the liberal arts needed for the soul to see God; the *Soliloquies* (Sol.), an inner dialogue between Augustine and Reason on the nature of God and the immortality of the soul; *On the Immortality of the Soul* (IS), the rough draft of a sequel to *Soliloquies*; *On the Quantity of the Soul* (QS), which uses the soul's innate knowledge of geometry as a clue to the non-spatial nature of the soul; and *On Music* (OM), a long textbook on poetic meter culminating in the sixth and final book with a neo-Pythagorean meditation on immutable numbers as Reason's clue to the nature of God.

Being and love

For Augustine, God is true Being, the immutable Truth, the supreme Good and eternal Beauty, the source of all being, truth, goodness, and beauty in the world he creates. He is the goal as well as origin of his creatures: as Being he is the source of the soul's life for all eternity; as Truth he is the ultimate object of all the mind's inquiries; as Beauty the ultimate object of all our loves; as Good the source of our ultimate happiness. Platonism, for Augustine, meant above all a way of conceiving God in these terms, transcending all created being, free from the spatial limitations of bodily things and the mutability of the soul. Hence two key attributes of God are his integral omnipresence, which means he is present as a whole everywhere precisely because his being is not dependent on space, and his eternity, which means he is immutable and present as a whole at every point in time precisely because his being is not dependent on time. Behind both attributes is the ontology of divine simplicity (CG 8: 7; 11: 10) which means God is not divisible into parts, so that his omnipresence does not cause him to be spread out part-by-part in space and his eternity does not cause him to live part of his life at one time and part at another. His presence in space and time transcends space and time precisely because it is always presence as an indivisible whole.

In consequence, God has an inviolable integrity and immutability of being to which all creatures – especially the rational soul, which is created in his image – inevitably aspire. Augustine's most famous saying, 'Our hearts are restless until they find rest in Thee' (*Conf.* 1:1), means that in the very incompleteness and dividedness of our changeable being, we desire God in his unchangeable wholeness. The name for this desire is love, and when it is rightly ordered (so that love for God is put before all other loves), it is called 'charity,' Augustine's preferred term for the fulfillment of the biblical command to love God with one's whole heart, soul, and mind. Charity seeks God above all things, and in finding him finds an ultimate happiness in which it may rest eternally. Outside of God, all our loving, seeking, and desiring find only partial and temporary satisfaction, which is why we are restless until we find rest in him.

For Augustine, love is fundamentally a desire for union with what is loved, as a drunk desires to take wine into himself, as a miser desires to possess money, as lovers desire to embrace one another, as philosophers desire to embrace wisdom, and as souls that love God seek eternal union with him. In another famous saying, Augustine therefore pictures love as a kind of gravitational force of attraction which moves us in the direction of what we love, 'My love is my weight' (*Conf.* 13: 9). As in ancient physics weight may not only move a body downward like a stone to join the earth but upward like fire to join the stars in heaven, so in Augustine our carnal desires, called concupiscence or cupidity, weigh us down with attraction to things of the earth, while charity means the heart is afire with desire to be joined with God so that our love is a force bearing us metaphorically upward toward heaven. Moreover, the earthly things we love are not only perishable but multifarious, with the result that our attraction to them pulls us in many different directions and causes in our restless souls an agonizing fragmentation and incoherence that is vividly portrayed in the *Confessions*.

For Augustine, therefore, sin is not an external act but an inner movement of the soul toward anything it finds more attractive than God. Sin is fundamentally its own punishment, for ontological reasons. For love is a desire for union that not only attracts but unites the soul to what it loves, like a kind of glue, as Augustine says (*FC* 1: 15, *Conf.* 4: 10 – not all translations actually render the word for 'glue' literally). Hence to love any temporal being is to unite one's soul with something perishable which it will inevitably lose, causing a grief that is like having part of one's soul torn away (*Conf.* 4: 6–7) – a grief that is all the greater the nobler the thing is that one loves, as grief for a friend involves a deeper sense of loss than a drunkard's hangover. Hence one should love one's friends, but not more than one loves God, and indeed one should love them in God and for God's sake (*Conf.* 4: 9, *CD* 1: 26–34), seeking them not for their own sake, as if they could make one eternally happy, but seeking to enjoy them in God, joined with them in the love of God forever. This is the famous Augustinian distinction between use and enjoyment: the multifarious temporal goods should all be used (*uti*) in order to come to enjoy (*frui*) the one eternal Good, which is God (*CD* 1: 3–5). To love one's neighbors means to assist other souls in coming to share in this same ultimate happiness (*CD* 1: 29) so that they too may belong to 'the fellowship of those who enjoy God and each other in God' (*CG* 19: 13), which is a description of the blessedness of the community that Augustine calls 'the City of God.'

Augustine thus tightly links Platonist ontology with a eudaimonist ethics of love. Other themes of importance for western philosophy of religion can be situated within this framework.

Free will and evil

For Augustine it is evil to love anything more than God, but this does not mean we should not love other things or that any of these things are evil. Quite the contrary: since all things derive their being from God, all being is inherently good. Hence Augustine can say, quite flatly, 'everything that is, is good' (*Conf.* 7: 12). Evil is simply the absence or privation of some good that ought to be present. (Here it is important to bear in mind that Latin has only one word for both 'evil' and 'bad,' which means Augustine's ontology of evil covers bad shirts and bad health as well as moral evil.) There can be evil things only in the sense that there are 'evil goods' (*Ench.* 12) which is to say, good things partially corrupted, damaged, or disordered. There is therefore no such thing as pure evil, because where there is no good at all there is no being at all. Evil is to that extent something like a hole in a shirt – it is bad for the shirt, as a result of which we call it a 'bad shirt' – but pure evil is as impossible as a hole with no shirt to be in. This does not mean that evil is an illusion (for there really are shirts with holes in them), but rather that evil has no substance or being of its own. It always has the character of an absence or privation, as a hole is a disorder in a shirt, as cold is lack of heat and shadow is an absence of light.

Moral evil is therefore a corruption and disorder of the soul, and specifically of the will, which is the power of the soul whose act is to love. Augustine seems to have been the first thinker to conceive of the will as a distinct faculty or power of the soul (Dihle 1982; Kahn 1988; Sorabji 2004). Love is the distinctive act of this power, which is to say, love is what the will does, as seeing is what the eye does and understanding is what the mind does. But as an unhealthy eye can see badly and an ignorant mind can misunderstand, so the will can fail to love what is best. This failure lies at the origin of all moral evil and thus is Augustine's fundamental answer to the question of theodicy. Since, like all evil, it is a privation and a lack rather than a form of being, moral evil does not originate from some positive cause but from a failure of causality, i.e., from the will acting as 'deficient cause' rather than efficient cause (CG 12: 7). From this original failure of the will stem all the sin and suffering in the world, beginning with the devil, who was created as a good angel but fell from God when he sinned by his own free will (CG 12: 1–9), and then spreading to the visible world through the Fall of Adam and Eve, again by their own free will, but aided by the deceit of the devil (CG 14: 10–28).

The crucial move in Augustine's theodicy is therefore the claim that God created rational beings (angels and humans) with free will which was not designed for sin, any more than the eye was designed for blindness. The will is free not in the sense of a liberty of indifference, as if it were equally inclined to good and to evil (that would be like saying the eye is equally inclined to vision and blindness) but in the sense that no external force can coerce it, in contrast to the multitude of forces that can coerce our bodies. On the other hand, a will corrupted by sin is not so free as before, because it is too attached to things it can lose, finds it hard to part with them, and therefore is often compelled by desires that make it unhappy (FC 1: 7–11). Thus in the narrative leading to his famous conversion scene, Augustine pictures his soul as divided between his old desires, which were still powerful in him though he did not want them to be, and his new desire to devote himself wholly to the love of God, which was not yet strong enough to overcome the desires of his old self, which the Bible calls 'the flesh' (*Conf.* 8: 5, 7–10). This state of conflict and division, where one cannot will fully what one wants to will – willing to will but not succeeding! – is thus a kind of bondage in the will itself. Just as only the eye can be blind, only a will created free can suffer this kind of bondage.

Sin therefore undermines freedom of will, while grace restores it. Grace is an inner gift of God, freeing the soul to take delight in what will make it truly happy rather than being captive to desires that afford only temporary pleasure (*SL* 5). It is like a kind of medicine which weakens unhealthy desires and strengthens longing and delight in what is eternally Good for us. Over the course of his career Augustine becomes gradually more explicit that in giving the gift of grace God not only strengthens our good desires but causes the direction of our love to change, 'turning' or 'inclining' the will, in Augustine's language (*GFC* 41). Augustine insists that this does not undermine free will but restores and strengthens it. Like healing blind eyes, it restores a human capacity rather than impairs it. Phenomenologically, we could say, grace takes the form of an overwhelming delight rather than external coercion. To receive the gift of grace is for eternal Beauty to cause us to fall in love with itself (i.e., God), which is of course the love we were made for, leading to the enjoyment of eternal happiness.

Reason and authority

Grace and free will interact in an inner dimension of the soul which is also the location of memory and intellect. Memory is like a inner treasury containing images of the outside world, but also like a great inner palace whose courtyards are open to the sun above, the shining of the light of divine Truth (*Conf.* 10: 8–27). Intellect is like an inner eye created to gaze at this Truth in happy contemplation, or what the later Christian tradition calls beatific vision. The rational soul (in contrast to the irrational souls of the beasts) has a kind of inward nearness to God because of this capacity to see the Truth and love its splendid intelligible Beauty, which is to say because it has Intellect and Will. Souls are superior to bodies because of this inward closeness to God and also because their mode of being is non-spatial. Their journey to God or separation from him takes place not in the external dimension of space but in the psychological dimension of Reason and Will, as the soul is enlightened by inward vision or darkened by ignorance, lifted up by ardent charity or weighed down by earthly concupiscence (*Conf.* 1: 18). However, ontologically, souls always occupy a middle place in the scale of being, above bodies but below God. Hence they turn inward to see God (turning from the lowest, most external dimension of being, that of the bodily world, to the higher, more inward dimension of the soul) but also look ontologically 'upward,' above the soul to the light of Truth (*Conf.* 7: 10).

To understand is always to see for oneself, but in our fallen state this requires arduous effort and submission to external authorities, the way recovering health requires both exercise and following the doctor's orders. Hence, where later western writers contrast reason and faith, Augustine typically contrasts reason and authority (e.g., *OO* 2: 9, *UB* 1, *TR* 24, *Conf.* 6: 5). For Augustine the latter is always a pedagogical rather than political concept. Kings have sovereignty (*imperium*) or power (*potestas*) but only teachers have authority (*auctoritas*), as when we say that a scholar is an authority on her subject. Epistemologically, authority is closely connected with faith, because what an authority teaches ought to be believed so long as our reason is not yet healed and strengthened so as to see the point and understand it for ourselves (*FC* 1: 2, 2: 2, *OT* 11). This is why Augustine speaks specifically of the *usefulness* of faith coming before understanding. Faith does not see more deeply than reason, but it is all we have when reason is too weak and diseased to see what it was created to see. So faith is to understanding as authority is to reason, an incomplete stage on our journey toward the fullness of inner vision, which is our ultimate goal.

On this account, much of what looks like rationalism in other thinkers must count as mere faith from an Augustinian perspective. To believe God exists because you are persuaded by a philosophical proof, for instance, is not the same as to understand God or see him as intelligible Truth with the mind's eye, which for Augustine is the highest and indeed the proper work of reason. Think of the difference between confirming the validity of a proof in geometry and actually 'getting it,' the moment when you say, 'Aha! Now I see it!' For Augustine, beatific vision means 'getting' the eternal Truth which contains all unchanging truths, including the truths of mathematics as well as the Forms of Plato and the divine Wisdom sought by every true philosopher (*FC* 2: 7–13). So long as we are still on the road to this vision, we are like students who occasionally catch glimpses of the Truth we aim to understand, but who for the most part must take our teacher's word for it.

In Augustine's early philosophical dialogues the road to beatitude is a course of studies in the liberal arts, designed to train the mind's eye to ascend from shadowy things of this earth to the brightness of divine Truth (*OO* 2: 11–19). Later, the proper education for seeing God is Christian doctrine, understood as something like the doctor's orders for healing the disease and cleansing the impurity of our inner eye, which is impaired by our habit of gazing with love at external things (*Sol.* 1: 6, *UB* 13). What both programs of education have in common is the Platonist conviction that external things (i.e., bodily things which can be perceived by the senses) are inherently obscure and unintelligible by comparison to the light of Truth within, which is perceived not by the senses but by the intellect. Still, in their very obscurity external things are easier and more attractive to sick eyes, while the inner light is hard to see precisely because it is so bright that it dazzles our weakened powers of intellectual vision, compromised by our impure attachments to the shadowy things of this earth (*Sol.* 1: 13–14). Faith in the authority of external teaching therefore serves to purify the heart and the mind's eye until it is clean and healthy enough to see God.

Instead of inner vision, what faith has is external signs to believe in. Hence Augustine develops a comprehensive theory of signs or semiotics to undergird his epistemology of faith. Any external thing which directs our minds to see some other thing is a sign, as, for example, smoke is a sign of fire and words are signs meant to express and communicate some inner understanding of the mind (CD 2: 1–2). Augustine thus uses semiotics as the framework of his philosophy of language, classifying words as a species of signs, and then uses his philosophy of language to explain the nature of education in *On the Teacher* and to ground a hermeneutics of Scripture in *On Christian Doctrine*. The key contention of *On the Teacher* is that we learn nothing from signs, because we must already understand the thing signified before we can understand the significance of the sign (a contention applied to the words of Scripture in *Conf.* 11: 5; 12: 23–6). The key contention of *On Christian Doctrine* is that in the very act of seeking to understand an obscure passage of Scripture, we are strengthening Christian charity (CD 2: 6). For the right way to use a sacred sign is to heed its admonition to look beyond the external sign itself and seek the inner truth it signifies, a seeking which is a kind of longing and love.

Another religiously important form of sign is what Augustine calls a mystery or sacrament (the latter, *sacramentum*, is the standard Latin translation of the former, the Greek *mysterion*). Like other church fathers, Augustine uses these terms to describe anything that has a hidden meaning, such as an obscure passage of Scripture or the Christian rituals of baptism, anointing (now called confirmation), and Eucharist. Augustine contrasts the latter with pagan rituals and sacrifices which are offered not to the one eternal God but to demons presenting themselves as mediators. The Christian Eucharist, on the other hand, is a sacrifice of praise and thanksgiving outwardly signifying the inner offering of our love to God on the altars of our hearts (CG 10: 4–6). Hence for later western theories of religion, 'sacrament' comes to mean an outward sign of something inward, including the inward gift of grace which makes true Christian love possible.

Controversies

Augustine's Platonism causes some problems for his Christianity, and even more for his Christian readers. This, combined with his vast influence in western Christianity, results in a rich legacy of thinkers appropriating some parts of Augustine's thought rather than others, sometimes misappropriating and misunderstanding, and often generating controversies. Protestant–Catholic controversies in the sixteenth century, for instance, were often as much about the legacy of Augustine as of the Bible, which is why the points at issue were often quite alien to Eastern Orthodoxy. Controversies that are of specifically philosophical interest can be grouped into those concerning free will, those concerning the power of the intellect, those concerning the nature of God, and those concerning Augustine and modernity.

Augustine has been accused of undermining free will in two ways. First, his doctrine of divine eternity implies a very strong doctrine of divine foreknowledge, where God does not merely foresee the future but beholds it as present in an eternal now (*Conf.* 11: 10–13, CG 11: 21). This implies a kind of determinism about the future, but Augustine thinks this does no more to undermine free will than when we see what happens determinately in the present, for the seeing does not make it so (CG 5: 10). What God sees as happening contingently in the future will, without fail, happen contingently in the future. This inaugurates a long tradition of argument, continued by Boethius (*The Consolation of Philosophy* 5.3–4) and Aquinas (*Summa Theologica* I.14.13), but not convincing to everyone.

Second, Augustine has not convinced everyone about the compatibility of free will and grace. Many theologians in the wake of Augustine prefer to conceive of grace as an offer that is up to us to accept, rather than a gift of delight that sovereignly causes our will to change its basic direction. In his later works Augustine is quite explicit that the human decision to accept grace or come to faith is itself caused in us by the gift of grace, without undermining free will. The same critics become especially worried when very late in his career he picks up on biblical language about hardening Pharaoh's heart, as well as a number of related passages, to argue that God can justly turn evil hearts toward specific sins (GFC 41–3). It is worth noting that these critics are found both among Catholics (e.g., the Jesuit tradition stemming from Molina) and Protestants (e.g., the Arminian and Wesleyan traditions), whereas supporters of a stricter Augustinian view of grace are found also both among Catholics (e.g., the Dominican tradition stemming from Aquinas) and Protestants (e.g., both Luther and Calvin).

Augustine's robust Platonist view of the power of the intellect leads to a different set of controversies. Among Catholics, a straightforward reading of Augustine's Platonism is usually resisted because it implies that beatific vision is natural to us, which means that grace heals and strengthens human nature but is not needed to elevate it supernaturally to a vision beyond its natural capacity (Cary 2002). Most Catholic interpreters also want to defend Augustine from charges of 'ontologism,' a technical term referring to a nineteenth-entury movement of Catholic thought, censured by the Vatican, which argued that the intellect always perceives the light of divine Being whenever it perceives the truth of any being (Gilson 1960: 77–111). Among Protestants, on the other hand, the legacy of Augustinian inwardness has led to controversies about the power of the external word and whether it can effectively give what it signifies, as Luther insists, or whether it is merely the occasion for God to work inwardly in the heart, as in most Calvinist theology (Cary 2005). Augustine's strong preference for the latter view leads one Lutheran scholar to describe his position as one of *Sprachfeindschaft* or 'hostility to language' (Duchrow 1965: 241).

Around the end of the twentieth century advocates of open theism and the passibility of God have often taken Augustine as a target (e.g., Boyd 2001) because he is one of the most articulate advocates in the Christian tradition of the thesis that God is immutable and therefore beyond all possibility of passion or suffering. Augustine provides a rationale for reading biblical passages about God's feelings as anthropomorphisms deliberately used by the Scriptures to accommodate human weakness and stir human feelings (e.g., CG 15: 25). He also deploys an interesting hermeneutical principle according to which, when God is said to change in some way (for example, to rest from his work on the seventh day of creation), this means he causes this change in his creatures, as when he gives them rest on the Sabbath day or causes them to find ultimate rest in himself (the principle is first developed in GM 1: 9.15; 1: 22.34, and used frequently in CG 11: 8; 22: 2; 22: 30; etc.).

Finally, while there is no disagreement that Augustine is a founding father of medieval thought, his relation to modernity has been diversely interpreted. Scholars interested in his ontology of God and the soul tend to see him as a founding figure of modernity as well (Menn 1998; Cary 2000) while those interested in Augustine's arguments against the possibility of signs delivering what they signify see him as a precursor of postmodernism and its deconstructive semiotics (Mackey 1982; Williams 1989; Lyotard 2000; Caputo and Scanlon 2005).

See also Thomas Aquinas (Chapter 12), Omniscience (Chapter 24), Omnipresence (Chapter 26), Eternity (Chapter 27), Goodness (Chapter 28), The moral argument (Chapter 34), The problem of evil (Chapter 37), Sin and salvation (Chapter 53), Continental philosophy (Chapter 60).

References

Aquinas, T. (1981) *Summa Theologica*, 5 vols., Westminster, MD: Christian Classics.

Augustine (1947) *The Immortality of the Soul (IS), The Magnitude of the Soul (QS), On Music (OM), The Advantage of Believing (UB), On Faith in Things Unseen*, trans. L. Schopp, et al., Washington, DC: Catholic University of America Press.

—— (1948) *The Happy Life, Answer to the Skeptics, Divine Providence and the Problem of Evil (OO), Soliloquies (Sol.)*, trans. L. Schopp, et al., Washington, DC: Catholic University of America Press.

—— (1953) *The Nature of the Good (NG)* in J. H. S. Burleigh (ed. and trans.) *Augustine: Earlier Writings*, Philadelphia: The Westminster Press.

—— (1953) *Of True Religion (TR)* in J. H. S. Burleigh (ed. and trans.) *Augustine: Earlier Writings*, Philadelphia: Westminster Press.

—— (1953) *The Usefulness of Belief (UB)* in J. H. S. Burleigh (ed. and trans.) *Augustine: Earlier Writings*, Philadelphia: Westminster Press.

—— (1984) *City of God (CG)*, trans. H. Bettenson, New York: Penguin.

—— (1991) *On Genesis against the Manichees (GM)*, trans. R. J. Teske in *Saint Augustine on Genesis*, Washington, DC: Catholic University of America Press.

—— (1993) *Confessions (Conf.)*, trans. F. Sheed, Indianapolis, IN: Hackett.

—— (1993) *On Free Choice of the Will (FC)*, trans. T. Williams, Indianapolis, IN: Hackett.

—— (1995) *On the Teacher (OT)* in P. King (ed. and trans.) *Against the Academicians and The Teacher*, Indianapolis, IN: Hackett.

—— (1997) *The Spirit and the Letter (SL)* in R. J. Teske (ed. and trans.) *Answer to the Pelagians*, I, Hyde Park, NY: New City Press.

—— (1999) *On Christian Teaching (CD)*, trans. R. P. H. Green, New York: Oxford University Press.

—— (1999) *Grace and Free Choice (GFC)* in R. J. Teske (ed. and trans.) *Answer to the Pelagians*, IV, Hyde Park, NY: New City Press.

—— (2006) *Enchiridion (Ench.)* in A. C. Outler (ed. and trans.) *Augustine: Confessions and Enchiridion*, Philadelphia: Westminster John Knox.

Boethius (1999) *The Consolation of Philosophy*, trans. P. G. Walsh, New York: Oxford University Press.

Boyd, G. (2001) *Satan and the Problem of Evil*, Downers Grove, IL: InterVarsity Press.

Caputo, J. and M. Scanlon (2005) *Augustine and Postmodernism: Confessions and Circumfession*, Bloomington, IN: Indiana University Press.

Cary, P. (2000) *Augustine's Invention of the Inner Self: The Legacy of a Christian Platonist*, New York: Oxford University Press.

—— (2002) 'The incomprehensibility of God and the origin of the Thomistic concept of the supernatural,' *Pro Ecclesia* 9: 340–55.

—— (2005) 'Why Luther is not quite Protestant,' *Pro Ecclesia* 14: 447–86.

Dihle, A. (1982) *The Theory of Will in Classical Antiquity*, Berkeley and Los Angeles: University of California Press.

Duchrow, U. (1965) *Sprachverständnis und Biblisches Hören bei Augustin*, Tübingen: J. C. B. Mohr.

Gilson, E. (1960) *The Christian Philosophy of Saint Augustine*, trans. L. E. M. Lynch, New York: Random House.

Kahn, C. (1988) 'Discovering the will: from Aristotle to Augustine,' in J. M. Dillon and A. A. Long (eds) *The Question of 'Eclecticism': Studies in Later Greek Philosophy*, Berkeley and Los Angeles: University of California Press.

Lyotard, J. F. (2000) *The Confession of Augustine*, Stanford, CA: Stanford University Press.

Mackey, L. (1982) 'The mediator mediated: faith and reason in Augustine's De Magistro,' *Franciscan Studies* 42: 135–55.

Menn, S. (1998) *Descartes and Augustine*, Cambridge: Cambridge University Press.

Sorabji, R. (2004) 'The concept of the will from Plato to Maximus the Confessor,' in T. Pink and M. W. F. Stone (eds) *The Will and Human Action: From Antiquity to the Present Day*, London: Routledge.

Williams, R. (1989) 'Language, reality and desire in Augustine's De Doctrina,' *Journal of Literature and Theology* 3: 138–50.

Further reading

Brown, P. (2000) *Augustine of Hippo*, 2nd edn, Berkeley and Los Angeles: University of California Press. (A superb biography that in its original edition in 1967 revolutionized the study of Augustine and late antiquity.)

Burnaby, J. (1938) *Amor Dei: A Study in the Religion of St. Augustine*, London: Hodder & Stoughton. (A classic study of Augustine's concept of love, and still the most comprehensive and balanced treatment of the subject.)

Cary, P. (2000) *Augustine's Invention of the Inner Self: The Legacy of a Christian Platonist*, New York: Oxford University Press. (Examines the link between Augustine's theory of the soul and his Platonist ontology.)

Fitzgerald, A. (ed.) (1999) *Augustine through the Ages: An Encyclopedia*, Grand Rapids, MI: Eerdmans. (An encyclopedia dedicated solely to Augustine and his influence, with fine coverage of philosophical topics.)

O'Connell, R. J. (1969) *St. Augustine's Confessions*, Cambridge, MA: Harvard University Press. (Fascinating and controversial investigation of the Plotinian themes in Augustine's masterpiece.)

O'Daly, G. P. (1987) *Augustine's Philosophy of Mind*, London: Duckworth. (A comprehensive discussion of Augustine's psychology.)

——(1999) *Augustine's* City of God: *A Reader's Guide*, New York: Oxford University Press. (The best one-volume introduction to Augustine's great work.)

Stump, E. and N. Kretzmann (2001) *The Cambridge Companion to Augustine*, Cambridge: Cambridge University Press. (Articles on key philosophical themes by leading scholars.)

9
SHANKARA
John M. Koller

Shankara's place in history

Shankara is widely regarded as one of India's greatest thinkers. Although there is considerable controversy concerning his dates, the best recent scholarship argues that he was born in 700 and died in 750 CE. This was a time of political instability, coming after the fall of the glorious Gupta dynasty and the short-lived peace established by King Harsha in the seventh century. It was also a time of great social and cultural change, which witnessed a decline of both Buddhism and Jainism and a powerful resurgence of Hinduism, a resurgence to which Shankara made significant contributions. His transformations of the ancient and venerable Vedanta tradition were largely responsible for it becoming India's most important spiritual tradition for more than a thousand years.

The Vedanta tradition is rooted in the Vedic quest of more than 3,000 years ago, for the ultimate reality that is the ground of all existence. In the Upanishads, the culminating portions of the Vedas, composed more than 2,500 years ago, this ultimate reality is called Brahman and is frequently said to be identical with the innermost self, the Atman. Although religious ritual continued to be important, increasingly in the Vedanta tradition – as the Upanishads, the concluding (*anta*) parts of the Veda, were called – it was knowledge of Brahman, not action, that was seen as the means of final release and immortality.

But the various Upanishads did not speak with a single voice. While some taught that Brahman is the only true reality and is identical with Atman, others taught that Brahman and the world are both real, and that Atman is a part of Brahman. The *Brahmasutra*, attributed to Badarayana (first century BCE), became a foundational text for Vedanta because it summarized and unified the diverse and sometimes conflicting teachings of the Upanishads. To reconcile the Upanishadic view that Atman and Brahman are identical with the somewhat older Upanishadic view that the individual Atman is different from Brahman, the *Brahmasutra* argues that Brahman and Atman are, in some respects, different, but, at the deepest level, non-different (*advaita*), being identical. In adopting this realistic monism of the *Brahmasutra*, the Vedanta tradition was able to counter both the pluralistic realism of the Nyaya-Vaiseshika tradition and the dualism of the Sankhya-Yoga tradition, establishing itself as Hinduism's most powerful spiritual tradition.

During the approximately 700 years between the establishment of Badarayana's Vedanta tradition and Shankara's reforms of this tradition, Buddhism had come to play a powerful role in India's spiritual and philosophical life. Shankara wrote important commentaries on the *Brahmasutra*, the major Upanishads, the *Bhagavad Gita*, and other texts important to the Vedanta tradition. In all of his writings he sought to overcome the Buddhist influences that threatened the Vedanta insistence on Brahman/Atman as the fundamental, unchanging reality. He also attempted to refute various other Vedantic interpretations as he sought to establish his view that Brahman and Atman are identical, eternal, unchanging, and, ultimately, the only reality. How Shankara argued for his Advaita (non-dual) Vedanta is the subject of the rest of this essay.

Shankara's Advaita Vedanta

All the Vedanta traditions accept the Vedas as the highest truth and the authority on how life should be lived. But the Vedanta traditions, unlike the Mimamsa tradition, regard the knowledge claims, not the injunctions to action, as the crucial part of the Vedas. There are three principal schools of Vedantic thought, all rooted in the Upanishads, differing from each other in the way they account for the relations between persons, things, and ultimate reality (Brahman). The Advaita, championed by Shankara, is a strict non-dualism. The Vishistadvaita, championed by Ramanuja, is a qualified non-dualism, while the third school, Dvaita Vedanta, championed by Madhva, is frankly dualistic.

According to Shankara, Brahman alone is real, the world being mere appearance. Ramanuja claims that the world is real, but is not ultimately different from Brahman, since Brahman is the unity of differences that constitute the world. Madhva argues that the world and Brahman are eternally distinct, that reality is of the dual nature of Brahman plus the world, with Brahman always remaining distinct and different from the world of selves and things.

Looking at Shankara's entire body of work, it is clear that his primary objective was to explain how *moksa*, final release from the suffering of *samsara*, is possible. The *Upadesasahasri*, Shankara's most important non-commentarial work, begins by proclaiming that because the Self, the Atman, is truly Brahman, only knowledge of Brahman can destroy ignorance and end the transmigratory existence that ignorance produces (*Upadesasahasri* I.1.25; Mayeda, 1992: 211, translated from the Sanskrit by J. Koller, here and throughout). The second part of this work, addressed to teachers, opens with the words: 'Now we shall explain how to teach the means to *moksa*, final release' (*Upadesasahasri* II.1.1; Mayeda 1992: 211).

Throughout his writings Shankara expounds the advaitic teaching that Atman, which is identical to Brahman, is ultimately the only reality and that the appearance of plurality is entirely the work of ignorance. It is this conviction that underlies the central project of the *Upadesasahasri*, namely, to show what this ignorance is, how it arises, and how it can be removed. That the self is ultimately of the nature of Atman/

Brahman is never doubted by Shankara, who repeatedly cites the evidence of revelation (*sruti*) for its truth. Significant portions of Shankara's writings are devoted to analyses of the great sayings (*mahavakya*) of the Veda, such as: 'All this is *Atman*' (*Chandogya* 7.25.2); '*Atman* being known … everything is known' (*Brhadaranyaka* 4.5.6); 'There was only Being at the beginning, it was one without a second' (*Chandogya* 6.2.1); 'All this is *Brahman*' (*Mundaka* 2.2.11 and *Chandogya* 3.14.1); and 'This Self is the *Brahman*' (*Brhadaranyaka* 2.5.19). Indeed, almost one fifth of the *Upadesasahasri* is dedicated to analyses of the two great sayings, 'You are That' ('*tat tvam asi*') (*Chandogya*, 6. 8–16) and 'I am Brahman' ('*ahambrahmasmi*') (*Brhadaranyaka*, 1.4.10).

The very fact that the ultimacy of Brahman/Atman was taught in the Upanishads was sufficient for the tradition to accept it as true, for the Upanishads were regarded as errorless revealed truth. Nevertheless, for the critical mind it is important to show that this teaching does not conflict with reason or experience. A significant step in this direction could be taken by showing that opposing claims about reality are self-contradictory and implausible. Consequently the critical examination of the other systems became an important part of the Vedanta agenda and Shankara missed no opportunity to criticize competing thinkers and systems.

Showing that other views were unsatisfactory was not sufficient, however. It was also necessary to show that the view of reality claimed by the Vedantic interpretation of the Upanishads was in accord with the Upanishads themselves and that this view was not subject to the same kinds of criticisms aimed at the other systems. Therefore the Vedanta philosophies came to provide rational criticisms of the other philosophies and also to provide rational defenses of their own interpretations and systems, showing that they did not conflict with either reason or experience.

According to Shankara, Brahman alone is ultimately real. It is the reality that underlies the appearances that constitute the empirical world. Brahman, however, should not be confused with these appearances, for it goes beyond these appearances, not being limited by them. From the empirical and conceptual point of view, Brahman is in the world as its foundation. From the absolute point of view, however, Brahman is beyond the empirical reality that can be known through the senses or by the mind.

This means that the nature and existence of Brahman cannot be proved from perception or reasoning, but is to be taken either on the basis of scriptural testimony (the Upanishads) or by direct and intuitive experience of the kind made possible by yogic concentration. Nevertheless, reason has a useful role in justifying these means of knowing Brahman. It is also important to use reason to show the incoherence and inadequacy of alternative views.

Criticism of other views

Historically, we can see Shankara's advaitic view of the self and consciousness against the four competing views that he singled out for criticism. The first of these is the Mimamsa view that sees the self as an agent and that sees actions – both moral and ritual – as the principal means of achieving the highest goal. Against this view Shankara argues that the true Self, the Atman, cannot be an agent, for agency necessarily involves change and the Atman is changeless. That the Atman is seen as an agent is, according to Shankara, the result of ignorance, an ignorance that mistakes the modifications and agencies of ordinary, embodied, consciousness, for the pure consciousness that is the Atman.

The second competing view is the pluralistic realism of the Nyaya-Vaisheshika tradition. This tradition holds that the world is caused by the combination of atoms. But how can unconscious atoms produce out of their combinations the order that makes possible the moral law claimed by the Vaisheshika philosophers? Further, how or why should unconscious atoms first begin to move around and join together to produce the world? If atoms were incessantly in motion and joining together because of their very nature, then neither the beginning of the world nor its dissolution would be explicable. Since the Vaisheshika philosophers claim that the world is both produced and destroyed, their view is inconsistent, and therefore unsatisfactory, according to Shankara's analysis.

The third competing view is the Buddhist teaching of no-self (*anatmanvada*) that rejects all claims for an eternal, permanent Self. This view, which denies the claims of *Sruti* that Atman, which is identical to Brahman, is the true Self, Shankara rejects as nihilistic. Shankara begins and ends with the reality of Atman. In its identity with Brahman, he regards Atman as the only thing which is ultimately real. As we have noted, his primary concern is to clarify what Atman is and how it can be realized, releasing a person from the suffering of transmigratory existence. In arguing against Buddhist views, Shankara frequently uses one of their favorite forms of arguments, namely, the *reductio ad absurdum*.

The fourth competing view that Shankara seeks to discredit is the Sankhya dualism of spirit and matter, the dualism of *purusa* and *prakrti*. According to Sankhya, the world is the result of the spontaneous evolution of unconscious matter, or *prakrti*, which is composed of the three *gunas: sattva, rajas,* and *tamas.* But how, asks Shankara, can one suppose that the world is the accidental result of an unconscious cause, when it is experienced as a harmonious system of related objects and ordered events? Furthermore, the ultimate purpose of this world, according to Sankhya, is to enable re-born selves to be liberated from their bondage to *samsara,* the cycle of suffering and repeated deaths. Against this view, Shankara argues that because it is unintelligible to attribute purpose to unconscious nature, it makes no sense to claim that the purpose of this world is to make liberation possible.

Analysis of causality

Through his analysis of causality, Shankara launches a powerful attack against all the competing philosophical traditions. Nyaya, Vaisheshika, Sankhya, Buddhism, and Mimamsa all accept that various real changes occur in the world and that these changes are caused. How, asks Shankara, do these traditions view causality? Are their theories of causality, on which their views depend, coherent?

Concerning the relation between cause and effect, logically only two views are possible. Either the effect pre-exists in the cause or it does not. If the effect does not pre-exist in the cause, then the effect is something totally new. This view is called *asatkaryavada* (nonexistence of the effect). If, on the other hand, the claim is that the effect does pre-exist in the cause (*satkaryavada*), then two alternative explanations are possible, neither of which recognizes the effect as a new reality. According to the first alternative, causal change can be explained as a matter of making explicit what was already implicit in the cause. According to the second alternative, there is no difference between cause and effect.

Nyaya and Vaisheshika held the *asatkaryavada* view of causality, as did some of the Mimamsa philosophers. They argued that effects are experienced as something totally new and that this experience is valid. Some Mimamsa philosophers and all Sankhya philosophers held the *satkaryavada* view, admitting change in the sense of making explicit what was implicit in the cause, but denying that effects were new realities.

Shankara, in critically examining these two views of causation, found them both logically unacceptable. Nothing, he argued, can show an effect to be different from its material cause. Clay pots are clay, gold rings are gold, and so forth. Furthermore, the clay pot cannot exist apart from the clay, nor the gold ring apart from the gold. Consequently it is incorrect to say that an effect is something new that has been produced and that it did not exist before. In terms of its material cause, it has always been there. Furthermore, we have no experience of things coming into being out of nothing. Our experience of change is always of something being transformed into something else. To conceive of something coming into existence out of nothing is impossible; all we can think is the transformation of something into something else.

Sankhya also argues vigorously against *asatkaryavada*, pointing out that if the effect were something totally new, without prior existence in any form, then we would have to admit that existence is produced from nonexistence. But if this is possible, why can't nonexistence produce everything? Since curds are nonexistent in water, why can't water produce curds? Since gold is nonexistent in clay, why can't gold rings be produced out of clay? The reason water cannot produce curds, and clay cannot produce gold rings, is because curds have no prior existence in water and gold has no prior existence in clay. On the other hand, curds can be produced from milk because they pre-exist in milk, and gold rings can be produced from bars of gold because they pre-exist in the bars of gold. Clearly, nonexistence does not produce effects; only the pre-existent produces effects, concludes Sankhya.

Shankara accepts these arguments of Sankhya against *asatkaryavada* but goes on to argue against the Sankhya view that the effect actually pre-exists in the cause. If the effect actually pre-exists, he asks, how can there be genuine change? If the effect already exists, then it is impossible for the material to become the effect. It makes no sense to talk of the coming to be of that which already exists. Shankara considers the Sankhya reply: that although matter does not come into existence, the form does. But if the new form comes into existence, it must be admitted that something new, something not pre-existing, comes into being – namely, the new form. But this view, says Shankara, is just another form of *asatkaryavada*, which claims the effect as something new that did not previously exist. This, however, contradicts Sankhya's own rejection of *asatkaryavada*.

Because the Sankhya position is self-contradictory, it is unacceptable to Shankara. The challenge he faces is to set out a consistent view of causality based on the pre-existence of effects in their causes. In meeting this challenge he must be sure that, unlike Sankhya, he does not implicitly assume the *asatkaryavada* view. Since it cannot be denied that changes in form are perceived, the crucial question for Shankara is, 'Is a change in form a *real* change?'

Arguments for non-dualism

Shankara's solution is to show that although changes in form are perceived, this does not imply a change in reality unless a form has reality of its own. But, of course, form has existence only in dependence upon matter, for there is no form except in formed matter. For example, there is no form of a cup except the cup made of clay (or other matter). If a change in form were a change in reality, a person sitting down would be a different reality from a person standing up, since the form is different. But, of course, a person standing up or sitting down is the same person. Therefore, form has no independent reality.

Shankara also argues that if substances are distinct from their forms, then it is impossible to explain the relation between the form and the substance. If the form is distinct from the substance, it cannot be related to the substance except in terms of a third reality which relates them. But then, in order to relate this third reality to the other two, another distinct reality is needed. And to relate this reality to the others, still another is needed.

Because the Sankhya view of bondage and liberation, despite being dualistic, is relatively close to Shankara's own view, it was especially important for him to show how the Sankhya explanation fails. The Sankhya dualism claims the reality of both pure consciousness, *purusa*, and the experienced world, *prakrti*. It hopes, thereby, to provide an explanation of the bondage of *purusa* by *prakrti* and its liberation from this bondage by the knowledge achieved through yoga. However, the Sankhya theory of prakrtic existence seems irrelevant to its theory of the self as *purusa* when it comes to the problem of explaining how *purusa* can be bound by *prakrti* and how it can liberate itself from this bondage. Indeed, Sankhya ultimately is forced to claim that there is no real interaction between *purusa* and *prakrti* and that bondage is only illusory; that in reality, the *purusa* is eternally free.

It is just this problem of explaining how genuine interaction between the dual realities of *purusa* and *prakrti* can occur that Shankara hopes to avoid with his non-dual stance. Shankara's view is that the pure consciousness (*cidatman*) alone is ultimately real; everything else is only appearance. The Self (Atman) that I truly am, he says, in *Upadesasahasri* I.13.3, is 'ever free, pure, transcendentally changeless, invariable, immortal, imperishable, and thus always bodiless' (Mayeda 1992: 132). Further, being bodiless means that the true self neither experiences nor acts. In Shankara's words, 'The false belief that Atman is a doer is due to the belief that the body is Atman' (ibid.: 130). Thus, when a student approached his teacher, a knower of Brahman, and asked how he could obtain release from the suffering of this transmigratory existence, the teacher advised him that he must overcome the ignorance through which he mistakenly thinks that he is an agent, an experiencer and a transmigrator, when in fact he is none of these, but the highest Atman (ibid.: 235).

The mistake of bodily identification

But if all the experiences of the embodied self are ultimately unreal, the result of ignorance, how can this embodied self ever achieve *moksa* by realizing its true nature as Atman? What is this embodied self, and how does its consciousness function? It might seem that Shankara cannot be expected to have a philosophy of empirical or embodied consciousness because whatever is embodied is, like the body, unreal. After all, from his perspective, although I frequently identify with this body, this identification (*adhyasa*) is a mistake, the result of ignorance, for the truth is that I am pure consciousness, Atman, eternal and unchanging, having nothing to do with body or mind. But if taking my embodied consciousness to be real is a mistake, how is this mistake to be explained? What is this ignorance wherein I identify with the body and regard myself as actor and experiencer?

Indeed, it is precisely for the sake of showing that this identification is a mistake, that it results from ignorance, that Shankara needs to develop a philosophy of the empirical self and explain ordinary consciousness. To support his claim that the experiencing, acting self is not the true self, he needs to explain what the embodied mind is and how it comes to be falsely imposed on Atman. Thus, he says, in *Upadesasahasri* II.1.12–13, that if the student seeking the sacred knowledge which brings release from *samsara* says, 'I am eternal and different from the body. The bodies come and go like a person's garment,' the teacher should say, 'You are right,' and then should explain how the body is different from the Self' (Mayeda 1992: 215).

Unmanifest name-and-form

There follows a remarkable passage in which Shankara explains what the body is and how it comes to be. In a highly creative move, he posits an unmanifest name-and-form (*avyakrte namarupa*) as the source of ordinary consciousness and the world of objects. He describes how this unmanifest *namarupa* evolved into the world of name and form as we know it through an evolutionary process according to which it first became manifest as ether, air, fire, water, and earth, in that order. As each of these elements became impregnated with the previous elements, finally earth appeared, as a combination of all five elements. He goes on to say,

> And from earth, rice, barley, and other plants consisting of the five elements are produced. From them, when they are eaten, blood and sperm are produced, related respectively to the bodies of women and men. Both blood and sperm, produced by churning with the churning stick of sexual passion driven by ignorance (*avidya*) and sanctified with sacred formulas, are poured into the womb at the proper time. Through the penetration of fluid from

the womb, they become an embryo and it is delivered in the ninth or tenth month. (Mayeda 1992: 217)

He then explains how this body is named at birth, how it gets its student name, its householder name, and also the name of the forest dweller and *sannyasin*. Repeating that 'the body is different from you (Atman),' Shankara says that the teacher should remind the student that the mind and the sense organs consist only of name-and-form, and quotes passages from the Chandogya Upanishad (VI. 5.4; 6,5; and 7.6) which declare that the mind consists of food (Mayeda 1992: 217).

Like the prakrtic self of Sankhya, this self of name-and-form is said to be unconscious ('like food'), but nonetheless constituted by an awareness enabling it to experience, act, and to identify itself (mistakenly) as a transmigrating, experiencing, acting self. Thus, according to Shankara, a person consists of a physical body, made up of material substances; the senses (eye, ear, etc.); mind; agencies of speech, movement, sex, excretion, and grasping; sense-of-self (*ahamkara*); as well as the internal embodied consciousness (*antahkarana*), all of which are disposed and conditioned according to previous experiences.

The distinction between physical and subtle bodies (*sthulasarira* and *suksmasarira*) is very important, for it recognizes a distinction between mere physicality and humanly embodied physicality. It is a way of insisting on the bodily character of what we think of as mental functions, for the *suksmasarira*, constituted by the five vital airs, the *buddhi* and *manas* through which the *antahkarana* functions, as well as the ten organs (five cognitive-sensory; five conative-motor), is not only itself viewed as a body, but is itself further embodied in the *sthulasarira*. Only for the embodied self are the knowledge and action needed for liberation possible (or necessary). The senses are seen as instruments of the mind, linking mind with the outside world, just as mind links senses with reflective consciousness, and reflective consciousness links up with self. But senses, vital force, mind, and reflective consciousness can function only when embodied; ultimately, the inner organ (*antahkarana*) cannot function except through the bodily self – through its *indriya* or senses.

How the Atman is linked to reflective consciousness, and through consciousness to the mind, and thence to the external world through the *antahkarana* and the senses, is a serious and difficult problem for Shankara. The senses, *antahkarana*, and *buddhi* are ultimately all of the nature of body, whereas Atman is not. But what is of the nature of body is unconscious and unknown, unless known by another, for example, the Atman. Furthermore, Atman is said to be transcendentally changeless (*kutashtha*) and constant (*nitya*), whereas the instruments of knowledge (*antahkarana*), particularly consciousness and its forms (*pratayas*) of intelligible objects, necessarily undergo change in coming to know the changing world. Thus, if as knower of the world, the Atman pervades and illumines consciousness, it will be subject to all the changes of consciousness involved in coming to know something. Since, because of his view of the changelessness of Atman, this is unacceptable to Shankara, he must find some other way of explaining how Atman illumines consciousness.

The role of abhasa

Shankara's innovative solution to this problem is the concept of *abhasa*, a term that means 'reflection,' but that is used by Shankara to refer to a reflection that produces a false appearance, that deludes people, inducing them to mistake embodied consciousness for the pure consciousness of Atman. He says, 'When [ordinary] consciousness is pervaded by the reflection (*abhasa*) of the pure consciousness of Atman (*caitanya*), knowledge arises in it. In this way sound and the other [objects of knowledge] appear. By this people are deluded' (Mayeda 1992: 114). The delusion is that ordinary consciousness appears to be the knower, because of Atman's reflection in it, when in reality it is by nature unconscious. Thus ordinary consciousness falsely appears as knower, when in reality only the Atman knows.

But if no link between Atman consciousness and ordinary consciousness can be established, then none of the valid means of knowledge by which ordinary consciousness operates can provide any knowledge of Atman. This Shankara readily acknowledges, quite surprisingly to the modern, secular mind, saying, 'Just as a dream is true until awakening, so would the identity of the body with Atman be [true, as well as] the authoritativeness of sense-perception and the other [means of knowledge] and the waking state until [the attainment of] knowledge of Atman' (ibid.: 126). In other words, only while we are ignorant of Atman does the world appear real and the means of knowledge of ordinary consciousness appear valid.

How, then, in the final analysis, can Atman be known? Only through faith, only through revelation, the *Sruti*, in which Shankara appears to have unshakable faith. But whose faith? For the embodied self the experience of faith is no more real than the experience of knowledge. For the Atman it is totally unnecessary. The validity of *Sruti* is, for Shankara, as for almost all of the Vedantins, beyond the need of argument or justification, but unless it is valid for the embodied self, it would seem to be irrelevant to achieving *moksa*.

It is in order to explain the appearance of the body and the world while at the same time insisting that Atman/Brahman alone is real that Shankara posits an 'unmanifest name-and-form' (*avyakrte namarupa*) as the source of consciousness and the world. Recall that in order to avoid the problems of dualism, Shankara denies that name-and-form is ultimately real or that it really embodies the Self. For him this account functions to explain only the *appearance* of experience and the world, the reality of which is never admitted.

Shankara introduces an analogy to explain this evolution of *namarupa* from Atman: 'In this manner this element named "ether" arose from the highest Atman as dirty foam from clear water. Foam is neither water nor absolutely different from water, since it is not seen without water. But water is clear and different from foam, which is of the nature of dirt. Likewise, the highest Atman is different from *namarupa*, which corresponds to foam; Atman is pure, clear, and different in essence from it' (Mayeda 1992: 216).

How effective is this analogy? Some critics charge that the analogy breaks down, claiming that since *namarupa* is different from Atman, it cannot possibly be caused by or derived from Atman. Other critics say that even if the analogy holds, it is too weak to support the burden of the Advaita claim that all reality is ultimately the one, undifferentiated Atman. The Advaitin reply to these critics is that because the ultimate reality, Atman, goes beyond all conceptual distinctions, logical analysis and argument cannot establish its reality. Only faith and direct experience can reveal the ultimate, and analogies are necessary to illumine the Atman and clarify how it exists.

See also Hinduism (Chapter 1), Buddhism (Chapter 2), Religious traditions and rational assessments (Chapter 19), Non-theistic conceptions of God (Chapter 22), Mysticism among the world's religions (Chapter 23), Religious experience (Chapter 63).

References

Mayeda, S. (1992) *A Thousand Teachings: The* Upadesasahasri *of Shankara*, Albany, NY: State University of New York Press.
Radhakrishnan, S. (1953) *The Principal Upanishads: Edited with Introduction, Text, Translation and Notes*, London: Allen & Unwin.
—— (1960) *The Brahma Sutra of Badarayana: The Philosophy of Spiritual Life*, London: Allen & Unwin.

Further reading

Comans, M. (2002) *The Method of Early Advaita Vedanta: A Study of Gaudapada, Shankara, Suresvara and Padmapada*, Delhi: Motilal Banarsidass. (The spiritual tradition of Shankara's Vedanta, including his teacher and his two most illustrious students.)
Deutsch, E. (1966) *Advaita Vedanta: A Philosophical Reconstruction*, Honolulu: East-West Center Press. (An excellent introduction to Shankara's views and arguments.)
Isayeva, N. (1992) *Shankara and Indian Philosophy*, Albany, NY: State University of New York Press. (Historical study of Shankara's life and thought.)
Mayeda, S. (1992) *A Thousand Teachings: The Upadesasahasri of Shankara*, Albany, NY: State University of New York Press. (An excellent introduction to the life and thought of Shankara.)

10
IBN SINA/AVICENNA
Rahim Acar

Ibn Sina (c. 980–1037), who is best known in the West as Avicenna, was born in Afshana near Bukhara in Central Asia. His formulation of various philosophical and theological problems had a lasting influence upon Muslim and western thinkers, despite the heavy criticism his theories received. Regarding his philosophy of religion, four major topics may be underlined: (1) his argument for God's existence, (2) his understanding of God's properties and theological language, (3) divine providence, and (4) prophecy. His discussions concerning these topics indicate his efforts to provide a philosophical basis for monotheistic (Islamic) beliefs.

God's existence

For Avicenna God's existence is proven in metaphysics, which investigates existent *qua* existent (Avicenna 1960: 6–9). Avicenna's argument is based on his understanding of what he calls primary concepts and the division of being into that which is necessary by itself and that which is necessary by another. Primary concepts are concepts that are imprinted in the mind and known immediately. These include 'existent,' 'thing,' 'necessary,' 'possible,' and 'impossible.' They cannot be defined or traced back to anything better known (1960: 29, 35). But they can be indicated by a term or a sign so that we may have a better grasp of what they are. For Avicenna, necessity and actual existence imply each other. The notion of necessity is conceived before possibility and impossibility, because 'it signifies certainty of existence' (1960: 36; Davidson 1987: 290). To say that 'something is necessary,' means 'confirmation of its existence.' Thus everything that exists is necessary.

Avicenna argues that existents can be divided into two kinds in the mind: (1) self-necessary and (2) possible in itself but necessary by another. These may be rendered as necessary being and contingent being. These two kinds are distinguished by the applicability of the distinction between essence and existence. For him the essence and existence of things differ from each other. An essence might exist *in re* as the essence of some particular thing, or it might exist in the mind with peculiar mental conditions. However, the essence of something, considered in itself, does not require its existence (Avicenna 1952: 15; Marmura 2005: 23). The distinction is not applicable to the self-necessary being because necessity and existence mutually imply each other, i.e., that which is self-necessary exists by itself. The distinction is applicable to contingent beings. Their essence is not identical to their existence and does not require that they exist. Their existence *in re* adds something to their essence as such. Without reference to anything else, it is simply possible for essences of contingent beings to exist. They cannot be impossible to exist, if considered in themselves; otherwise they would not exist – as contingent beings – at all. They exist on account of their cause (Avicenna 1960: 37–9; 1985: 262–4).

Avicenna's argument for God's existence is an attempt to prove that there is an uncaused cause of contingent beings. His argument in the *Metaphysics* part of the *Shifā'* differs from his argument in some other works. In the *Metaphysics* part of the *Shifā'*, underlining the nature of causation, he argues that an ordered series of causes without a first cause is impossible (1960: 327–8). His reasoning essentially conforms to Aristotle's argument for the first cause (Davidson 1987: 339). Avicenna's argument in the *Ishārāt* (1892: 160–2) and the *Najāt* (1985: 271–6) are more elaborate and conform to each other.

In the *Najāt*, Avicenna begins his argument for the existence of God by reminding readers that there is existence. Existents are either necessary or contingent. Consider anything you want. If it is necessary, the existence of the necessary being is established. Then there is no need to argue further. If it is a contingent being, it exists on account of something else. Contingent beings may be divided into those that simply remain in existence without beginning to exist, and those that begin to exist and continue to exist thereafter. Neither of these two kinds may exist without the causal activity of a necessary being. Hence the existence of a contingent being requires the existence of the necessary being.

Granting the existence of contingent beings, and his division of being into contingent and necessary, might have been sufficient to infer the existence of a necessary being. However, Avicenna adds two further premises before concluding that there is a necessary being. He argues that (1) no contingent being may have an infinite number of contingent causes (existing simultaneously), and (2) a circular causal regress is impossible.

No contingent being may have an infinite number of contingent causes, because no contingent cause may exist without being necessitated. An infinite number of causes are possible only if all causes exist simultaneously. Suppose all causes of some contingent being exist together and none of them is necessary. Whether it is finite or infinite, the set of causes is then either necessary by itself, or contingent by itself. As a whole it must be contingent, since all its members are contingent. Then the whole set needs to have a cause in order to exist. The cause that makes the set exist must be outside the set and necessary by itself, since we included all contingent causes in the set of causes in question. Thus the existence of contingent beings is traced to a necessary being.

The existence of contingent beings cannot be explained by a set of contingent beings causing each other in a circular manner either. In a circular causal regress of a finite number of causes, all members exist together and maintain each other in existence. Even though each member is contingent by itself, the circle of causes as a whole is necessary. Avicenna deems this impossible by *reductio ad absurdum*. In such a circle of causes, each member must be the distant cause of itself as well as the distant effect of itself and so on.

Avicenna's argument may be summarized as following: (1) there are existents, which are presumably contingent; (2) contingent beings, which are possible in themselves but necessary on account of their causes, need a cause necessary by itself; (3) infinite linear causal regress is impossible; (4) circular causal regress is impossible; (5) therefore there is a necessary being, the uncaused cause of contingent beings.

Whether Avicenna's argument for the existence of God is an ontological argument or a cosmological one is a debated issue among scholars. One might consider it as a cosmological argument highlighting Avicenna's cosmological premise, i.e., the existence of contingent beings (Davidson 1987: 298-304). Or one might consider it as an ontological argument, highlighting the a priori character of Avicenna's primary concepts, such as existence and necessity, and the paralleling 'self-evident propositional logical truths,' e.g., an existent is either necessary by itself or only possible (Marmura 2005: 25–6). Although one might devise an ontological argument using Avicenna's data, his argument is a cosmological one. This is because the division of being into necessary and contingent is made in the process of the investigation into existent *qua* existent, the necessity of the necessary being in the division is not logical necessity (Davidson 1987: 293), and it is inferred from the existence of contingent beings.

Knowing God and talking about God

Knowledge of God in himself falls beyond human capacity since metaphysics, the highest science, falls short of having God as its subject matter. Just as the existence of God is established on the basis of *contingents qua existents*, his properties are established insofar as God is the cause of contingent beings. Perfections found in the universe are the effects of God's properties. Since God is the source of everything, the existence of things and the manner in which they exist follows the divine being and perfection (Avicenna 1353: 3–15; 1960: 343–55; 1985: 263–71, 286–8). For Avicenna, the fact that God is the creator of everything requires a relation of similarity as well as a relation of dissimilarity. Many properties are negated of him and many other are affirmed of him on the basis of his negative and positive relations to creatures. Avicenna's emphasis on the relative character of divine properties may not be taken to imply that for Avicenna God is devoid of perfection properties (Rosheger 2000), because he unequivocally states that the perfections found in creation belong first and foremost to God and creaturely perfections are acquired from God.

Avicenna's conception of divine properties as divided into negations and relations might be better understood as divine formal properties and perfection properties. Among the divine formal properties one might include necessity and simplicity (Burrell 1986: 46–7). Unlike divine perfection properties such as knowledge and will, these do not say what God is, but rather indicate the manner in which God is or has perfection properties.

Necessity is the first and foremost divine formal property, which sets God apart from all else. Avicenna frequently remarks that God is necessary in all respects. For him divine necessity implies his simplicity, goodness, self-subsistence, immutability, as well as his being the creator of all contingent things. Since God is self-necessary, he does not owe his being and perfections to anything else and does not acquire or lose his perfection properties. Combined with and *in relation to* the existence of contingent beings, God's necessity implies that he is the cause of other things.

Divine necessity requires unity and simplicity. If there were more than one necessary being, each of them would differ from others, not with regard to the necessity of being but with regard to something additional, such as a substratum or time. But anything additional eliminates the identity of the essence and existence in the necessary being and makes it in need of a cause (Avicenna 1985: 266–7). Hence divine necessity requires that God must be one and simple. It separates God from the rest of beings with regard to the manner of having the perfections proper to him. God lacks the composition of distinct perfection properties. All are identical to God's being.

Perfection properties are attributed to God as relating to creation in positive terms. The perfect, regular, and lasting order in creation, Avicenna argues, indicates that its cause has perfect being and the perfections necessary for this perfect order to happen in the world. Since the kind of properties found in creation are normally traced to voluntary agents, as opposed to natural agents, God must have will, power, and so on (Avicenna 1353: 10; 1960: 368). Attributing perfection properties to God says something about God, yet they do not give a comprehensive knowledge of God. Lest creaturely perfection properties be attributed to God, Avicenna prefers to call them relations and to modify their meaning in accordance with divine formal properties.

He does not systematically treat the issue of predicating perfections of God and creation. Yet he is very much concerned about divine simplicity and unity; he rejects even a verbal composition in God. He denies that God can be composed of constitutive parts, like parts of a statement, which explain the meaning of his name (Avicenna 1985: 264). Nevertheless he also attributes many properties taken from human experience to God and never implies that his statements about God in human terms are equivocations, or unsuitable for philosophical examination. He goes back and forth between predicating properties of God and qualifying them as negative and positive relations to creatures.

His discussion of priority and posteriority may indicate how the difference between the way things have their properties and God has them is observed in language. Properties may be found in different subjects in different manners and may be attributed to them on the basis of a priority-posteriority scale ambiguously or analogically (Avicenna 1960: 163). On this account, God must be prior to everything else with regard to being and perfection properties appropriate to him. Although Avicenna refers to God frequently as 'The First,' his account serves only to remind us that perfection properties cannot be attributed to God and to creation in the same way.

Avicenna prefers to take divine perfection properties insofar as they are modified in light of divine formal properties so that the philosophical value of talking about a simple God in human terms may be respected. To solve the tension between divine simplicity and the creaturely manner of human knowledge and expression, Avicenna attempts to show that perfection properties are ultimately reducible to divine pure being. They are ontologically identical to divine being and they are conceptually reducible to it as well, since they are properties attributed to God *in relation to* creation but not in himself (Avicenna 1960: 366–7; 1985: 287). As a result, perfection properties are predicated of God insofar as they are modified by the divine formal properties. For example, divine will to create cannot be understood and used in arguments without taking its necessity and simplicity into account.

Divine providence and the existence of evil

God, who is the unique self-necessary being, is the creator of the whole universe. The complex structure of beings in the universe indicates that the universe does not exist randomly. God is the cause of the goodness and perfection inasmuch as it is possible. The things making up the universe, their internal structure, and they way they are ordered are included in the divine providence (Avicenna 1892: 185; 1960: 415; 1985: 320). Out of his generosity, God creates the whole universe out of nothing. Things owe to God not only their form, not only their matter, but everything that constitutes them (1960: 266, 342–3).

There is only one universe, and it is a good one. It is a good universe in the sense that it is the work of the creator who has all perfections proper to him. It may also be described as the best universe in the sense that there cannot be any other universe better than it. This is because divine knowledge and will are perfect, necessary, and eternal, and because God is generous and does not withhold any perfection that creatures can have. However, it is not the best of all possible universes, since there is not a set of possibilities out of which God actualizes some. Since God is perfect and necessary in every respect (Avicenna 1892: 158; 1960: 355, 373), divine will and creative action are also necessary. Although Avicenna affirms divine will, he strictly denies that God has the property of choice on the ground that it implies that there is a realm of possibilities independent of God. Since God is the creator of everything, there cannot be anything, even possibility in the true sense, independent of creation (Avicenna 1892: 159–60). Possibility is found within the universe, not above or beyond the universe.

Despite the fact that the creator is pure good, and created the world absolutely freely, without any internal or external restriction, the universe contains evil. Three kinds of evil may be identified: (1) metaphysical, (2) natural, and (3) ethical. Explaining the evil in the metaphysical sense, Avicenna identifies goodness with being and perfection. Evil, in contrast, is defined as the nonexistence of the substance of something or its lack of some perfection proper to it. Metaphysical evil sets other things apart from God. Only God, the self-necessary being, is pure good because he cannot be nonexistent and he does not lack any perfection proper to him. All other beings contain metaphysical evil since they are nonexistent in themselves (Avicenna 1960: 355–6). It is not the metaphysical evil but the natural one which requires justification *vis-à-vis* divine providence inclusive of knowledge, will, and power regarding the universe.

Avicenna maintains that natural evil is an essential part of the structure of the sublunar part of the universe, which is subject to generation and corruption. Natural evil is privation of some perfection resulting from the nature of material things. He divides two kinds of natural evil, one being due to the action of natural causes, such as fires and floods, and the other being due to the failure of natural causes, such as animals born with disabilities. Simply because of their constitution, material beings have their natural properties and have potency to receive opposite qualities. Their actions and passions serve for good for the most part. Fire, for example, burns naturally, and it is useful for the most part. It may also happen that it causes disasters. However, the evil caused by the action of natural agents, or by their failure, happens in fewer cases. Of course there are many cases of evil of these two kinds. But cases where natural agents provide good results and function properly are more than cases of evil where they either serve to unwanted results or function improperly (Avicenna 1892: 185–7; 1985: 324–5). Natural agents would not have good results unless they also had the potency to lead to unwanted evil results. Thus natural evil is virtually a part of the realm of generation and corruption.

Avicenna argues that creation of natural evil is necessary. It is found only in a small portion of the whole creation, and it could not be eliminated without also eliminating more good in the universe. The part that is not subject to generation and corruption does not contain either natural or moral evil. Only the sublunar part of the universe contains natural evil. However, the evil is part of the very constitution of the order in the material realm. Evil in this part of the universe cannot be eliminated unless the whole order of the universe, which is good, for the most part, is also eliminated. In order to eliminate the evil, this part needs to be left nonexistent. Since good is predominant in this part, if God were to leave this part nonexistent, then more good would have been left because of fewer instances of evil. Avicenna deems this more evil. Since there is an unalterable causal relation between supernal and sublunar realms, in order to leave the sublunar realm nonexistent, the supernal realm must be left nonexistent as well. Thus elimination of evil is not possible without leaving the universe nonexistent. And this would be more evil.

Prophecy and revelation

Avicenna's discussion concerning prophecy reflects an Islamic conception of prophecy, even though it was not popular among Muslim theologians, and its constituent elements may be traced to the legacy of ancient Greek and Hellenistic philosophy (Rahman 1958: 63–4). The general structure and basic concepts of Avicenna's theory are traceable to al-Farabi, who was the first to formulate a philosophical theory of prophecy in Islamic culture. However, unlike al-Farabi, Avicenna deliberately tries to establish a philosophical basis for Muslim institutions, including prophecy (Marmura 2005: 202). For Avicenna, divine providence requires the emergence of prophets. Prophets possess three prophetic characteristics: cognitive prophecy at the level of intellect, cognitive prophecy at the level of imagination, and prophecy concerning miraculous events.

The prophecy Avicenna deems necessary refers to the prophecy in a rather technical sense. In this sense a prophet, who institutes a religion and prescribes laws on the basis of divine revelations, is a messenger of God to humanity. The survival and perfection of human beings necessitate the coming forth of prophets. Individual human beings must cooperate with each other in a society to survive and live a proper life. Living in society requires reciprocal transactions, laws, and justice. The need to insure community life and justice is more important than the need of some of the bodily parts, which are useful but not necessary, such as eyelashes.

Justice and laws require a lawgiver. Since laws are meant to address human conditions, the lawgiver must be a human being. But ordinary people cannot identify justice and injustice independently of personal interests. It is impossible that divine providence bestows humanity with useful organs and properties but fails to provide it with something essential and necessary for its survival and proper life. Thus on account of divine providence, there must be prophets. They must be human. They must have specific properties distinguishing them from other men so that prophets have the proper authority in their eyes (Avicenna 1960: 441–2; 1985: 338–9).

Prophets are human beings, but they surpass other people with regard to their abilities concerning reason, imagination, and working out miracles. The prophetic knowledge is intellectually grounded and comes from the same source as rational, philosophical, knowledge. The human soul is an immaterial substance, and it is generated as a potential intellect. Its generation and later actualization as an intellect is due to the active intellect, which stands as the last member of cosmic intelligences emanating from God. The human soul acquires knowledge of secondary intelligible forms from the active intellect by establishing conjunction with the active intellect that possesses all intellectual knowledge. The ability to acquire intellectual knowledge is not uniform in all human beings. Some people have such a strong ability to acquire rational knowledge that they do not require external teaching and preparation. Such a strong ability is called 'holy reason,' which is the cognitive prophetic quality at the intellectual level. Through holy reason, prophets acquire rational knowledge, receiving the inspiration of the active intellect concerning all things, either at once or nearly so. Their ability is so powerful that they seem to know all things by themselves. While ordinary people, including philosophers, need to prepare themselves by studying and reflection, prophets do not. Their knowledge is not classified as imitation, but is strictly rational and based on middle terms, even complete syllogisms (Avicenna 1959: 248–50; 1985: 205–6).

If a person has the cognitive prophetic quality at the intellectual level and has a powerful imaginative faculty, such a person is capable of receiving revelation from the active intellect as well as from heavenly souls through his imaginative faculty. He may get into contact with supernal beings through the imaginative faculty while he is awake. The result of such a contact may contain rational knowledge, or knowledge of things which cannot be known under normal circumstances. It may indicate things as they are in reality, or it may consist of images to be interpreted. During this contact, such a person may perceive an apparition that speaks to him by audible sounds. Either direct or indirect, the knowledge he acquires is reliable because of the strength of his soul (Avicenna 1959: 173–7). In addition to receiving revelation at the imaginative level, the prophetic imaginative faculty also renders 'a figurative depiction of the scientific and philosophical truths obtained' through the intellectual faculty (1959: 248–9; Davidson 1992: 120).

Religious teachings do not always convey truth literally, but they contain symbols, analogies, and parables. When a prophet appears on the historical scene, he is in charge of teaching people about God and establishing laws 'with the permission and command of God, through his revelation and his sending forth of the angel of revelation to him' (Avicenna 1960: 442). Prophets have to include in their message the bare truth in a concise manner, such as the unity of God, his omnipotence, his omniscience, and belief in the hereafter. This much will persuade people to listen to and obey the teaching 'revealed via the mouth of the prophet by God and the angels' (Avicenna 1960: 442). Prophets do not need to teach complicated theological precisions about the nature of God. It is difficult for ordinary people to understand these complicated issues and teaching them to people as they exactly are harms them, rather than benefits them. This is why prophets must let ordinary people know of God's greatness, unity, and uniqueness through symbols and analogies drawn from their experience, so that they understand and accept the message. The fact that prophetic teachings include symbols and analogies is not objectionable, as long as it urges talented people to philosophical investigation (Avicenna 1960: 442–3, 1985: 339–40). The content of the revelation as related by prophets is not precisely eternal divine words. It is the prophetic soul who puts them into words and expresses divine revelation in figurative images and symbols.

What, then, exactly is the role of prophetic souls in the makeup of the sacred teachings? Is the revelation received through the imaginative faculty a purely mental phenomenon, or does it have a veritable ground? One may consider the whole prophetic revelation through imagination as a mental phenomenon by emphasizing the function of the imaginative faculty of the prophet in producing the revealed knowledge (Rahman 1958: 38; Davidson 1992: 120). The experiences of prophets, involving, say, sounds and visions, are not accessible to others. In this sense, they are not objective realities. However, conjunction with the active intellect and other metaphysically real beings is the necessary condition of such prophetic experiences. In this sense, there is an external veritable ground for such prophetic experiences.

Even though Avicenna is criticized for leaving no room for miracles (Al-Ghazâlî 1997: 170–81), he does in fact identify the working of miracles as one of the prophetic properties. Prophets are endowed with the power to work miracles. Adopting the Neoplatonic hierarchy of being, Avicenna maintains that the human soul has a higher place in the ontological hierarchy than the body. It is of the same kind as the supernatural principles which cause matter to assume the variety of forms through which it subsists. Ordinarily, the soul of a human being has the power to shape, govern, and influence simply its own body without being influenced by it. It influences its body via images that its faculty of imagination produces. These images, perceived in the estimative power of the human soul, cause the relevant changes in the body by initiating natural processes. For example, if a really sick man firmly believes that he will be cured, this idea may cause his body to recover (Avicenna 1959: 198–200).

The scope of influence belonging to images in the soul concerning the natural realm depends on the power and nobility of the soul. To the extent that a human soul becomes similar to its principle, the active intellect, the natural realm submits to it in the manner it is governed and affected by the active intellect and other supernal beings. A powerful human soul can work miracles, may heal a sick person or transform basic elements through the images it produces in particular cases, just as the universal heavenly soul exerts influences on the universal nature applicable to all natural things through the images it has (Avicenna 1959: 200–1).

Avicenna's conception of prophecy may be understood as religious experience, in general. It is certainly not limited to prophets in the technical sense but allows for a variety of people to participate in it. His account might even be religiously neutral and broader than religious experience, since it refers to having contact with the supernatural realm, which may produce non-religious results such as fortune-telling. In any case, the cognitive prophetic experiences at the imaginative level and some miraculous acts may safely be included in religious experience. Various people may have, to varying degrees, such prophetic properties. Prophets in the technical sense, i.e., messengers of God, represent the peak of humanity with regard to all three of the prophetic properties based on the strength of rational and imaginative faculties (Avicenna 1960: 435–6; 1984: 116–21; 1985: 334). However, prophets are not the only people with strong rational and imaginative faculties. Although Avicenna's texts do not draw precise boundaries between types of religious experience, they certainly do not limit religious experience to prophets in the technical sense. Indeed, he acknowledges the value of Sufi experience and miracles worked out by Sufis (Avicenna 1892: 219–21).

Avicenna's argument for God's existence has been quite influential on subsequent Muslim, Jewish, and Christian thinkers, such as Maimonides and Thomas Aquinas. Even the arguments presented by Descartes and Leibniz show some affinity to Avicenna's version of the argument (Davidson 1987: 385–406). His distinction between essence and existence is considered to play a crucial role in distinguishing the creator from creation (Burrell 1986: 19–34). It has a part in arguments for God's existence as well as in the doctrine of divine simplicity, which might be the hallmark of the classical theistic conception of God. Avicenna's explanation of divine providence and the existence of evil pretty much reflect a Neoplatonic explanation that is shared by many medieval thinkers. His theory of prophecy sets an example of how a philosopher attempts to account for a religious institution purely on rational grounds.

See also, Islam (Chapter 7), Moses Maimonides/Rambam (Chapter 11), Thomas Aquinas (Chapter 12), The cosmological argument (Chapter 32), The problem of evil (Chapter 37), Naturalistic rejoinders to theistic arguments (Chapter 40), Revelation (Chapter 50), Miracles (Chapter 55), Religious experience (Chapter 63).

References

Al-Ghazālī (1997) *The Incoherence of the Philosophers*, ed. M. Marmura, Provo, UT: Brigham Young University.

Avicenna (AH 1353), *Al-Risâla al-'Arshiyya*, Hyderabad.

—— (1892) *Al-Ishârât wa al-Tanbîhât*, ed. J. Forget, Leiden: Brill.

—— (1952) *Kitâb al-Shifâ', al-Mantiq, al-Madkhal*, ed. Mahmûd al-Khudayrî Fu'âd al-Ihwânî and G. Anawati, Cairo: Organisation Générale des Imprimeries Gouvernamentales.

—— (1959) *Avicenna's De Anima (Arabic Text), being the Psychological Part of* Kitâb al-Shifâ', ed. F. Rahman, London: Oxford University Press.

—— (1960) *Kitâb al-Shifâ', al-Ilâhiyyât*, ed. G. C. Anawati and Sa'îd Zâyd (vol. 1) and M.Y. Mûsâ, Sulaymân Dunyâ and Sa'îd Zâyd (eds.) (vol. 2), Cairo: Organisation Générale des Imprimeries Gouvernamentales.

—— (1984) *Al-Mabda' wa al-Ma'âd*, ed. A. Nûrânî, Tehran: Institute of Islamic Studies, McGill Unviersity.

—— (1985) *Kitâb al-Najâh fî al-Hikmah al-Mantiqiyyah wa-al-Tabî'iyyah wa-al–Ilâhiyyah*, ed. M. Fakhry, Beirut: Dâru'l-Âfâqi'l-Jadîda.

Burrell, D. B. (1986) *Knowing the Unknowable God: Ibn Sînâ, Maimonides, Aquinas*, Notre Dame, IN: University of Notre Dame Press.

Davidson, H. A. (1987) *Proofs for Eternity, Creation and the Existence of God in Medieval Islamic and Jewish Philosophy*, Oxford: Oxford University Press.

—— (1992) *Alfarabi, Avicenna, and Averroes on Intellect: Their Cosmologies, Theories of the Active Intellect, and Theories of Human Intellect*, New York: Oxford University Press.

Marmura, M. E. (2005) *Probing in Islamic Philosophy: Studies in the Philosophies of Ibn Sina, al-Ghazālī and Other Major Muslim Thinkers*, New York: Global Academic Publishing.

Rahman, F. (1958) *Prophecy in Islam: Philosophy and Orthodoxy*, London: Allen and Unwin.

Rosheger, J. P. (2000) 'A note on Avicenna and the divine attributes,' *The Modern Schoolman* 87: 169–77.

Further reading

al-Akiti, M. A. (2004) 'The three properties of prophethood in certain works of Avicenna and al-Gazālī,' in J. McGinnis (ed.) *Interpreting Avicenna: Science and Philosophy in Medieval Islam*, Leiden: Brill. (Explores Avicenna's conception of prophecy and its influence on al-Ghazālī's position.)

Fakhry M. (1984) 'The subject-matter of metaphysics: Aristotle and Ibn Sina (Avicenna),' in M. E. Marmura (ed.) *Islamic Theology and Philosophy: Studies in Honor of George F. Hourani*, Albany, NY: State University of New York. (Traces how Avicenna's conception of metaphysics diverges from that of Aristotle.)

Goodman, L. (1992) *Avicenna*, New York: Routledge. (Provides an overview of Avicenna's thought.)

Mayer, T. (2001) 'Ibn Sina's Burhan al-Siddiqin,' *Journal of Islamic Studies* 12: 18–39. (Discusses Avicenna's argument for God's existence in the *Ishârât*.)

Rahman, F. (1981) 'Essence and existence in Ibn Sina: the myth and the reality,' *Hamdard Islamicus* 4: 3–14. (Discusses Avicenna's distinction between essence and existence.)

11
MOSES
MAIMONIDES / RAMBAM
Jerome Gellman

Rabbi Moshe ben Maimon (Moses son of Maimon), known to us as 'Maimonides,' was born in Cordoba, Spain in 1135/8 and died in 1204. At a young age he wrote a treatise on logic and an innovative commentary to the *Mishnah*, the core corpus of Jewish law. Later he wrote the *Book of Commandments* listing and explaining the proverbial 613 commandments of the Jewish religion. His most important works were his *Mishneh Torah*, an unprecedented, monumental compendium of Jewish law, and his philosophical magnum opus, *The Guide of the Perplexed*, written for the philosophically sophisticated who were perplexed by the apparently non-rational character of Rabbinic Judaism. He also wrote a number of epistles on such topics as the resurrection of the dead (ostensibly 'for') and astrology (soundly 'against'). As a physician, he wrote various medical treatises as well. His stature and influence in Judaism have been immense. A dominant issue in Jewish philosophy after Maimonides was whether one agreed or disagreed with Maimonides on one point or another. And Jewish mystical *Kabbalah* incorporated ideas, and even language, from Maimonides, as well as consciously departed from some of his teachings. Among the Jews there is a saying: 'From Moses to Moses there has been none like Moses.'

Maimonides had a strong influence on Christian thought, for example as 'Rabbi Moses' to Aquinas and Dun Scotus (see Burrell 1986), on Christian mysticism, as in Meister Eckhart, and on modern thought, especially with Leibniz and Spinoza (see Wolfson 1969; Goodman 1980).

When presenting Maimonides' philosophy of religion, we come up against two obstacles. The first pertains to medieval thinkers in general and relates to the difficulty of teasing out Maimonides' philosophy of religion from his theology. Of course, he made no such distinction and his theology and philosophy of religion are intertwined throughout. The second obstacle is more formidable. Maimonides' writing is far from Aquinas's masterful, architectural philosophizing. Maimonides' *Guide of the Perplexed* is a convoluted record of his thought, which goes off into long tangents, doubles back on itself, scatters topics to different locations, and seems to contain several inconsistencies. Indeed, in the 'Introduction,' Maimonides tells the reader that the work contains contradictions. Furthermore, Maimonides sprinkled philosophical ideas into frameworks intended for purposes other than philosophy. Thus, some of his important philosophizing, including one of his central discussions of free will, appears in his commentary to the *Mishnah*, almost exclusively a legal work. Maimonides' views on prophecy, for another, are spread throughout his writings (see Kreisel 2001). His monumental codification of Jewish law, the *Mishneh Torah*, contains many philosophical observations, some consistent with, yet others ostensibly contravening, the *Guide*. Differences exist between what Maimonides wrote in different works, evidencing that during his lifetime he changed his mind on various issues. For example, early on he seemed to be much more opposed to a supernatural interpretation of miracles than later in life (Langerman 2003).

Already in medieval times Jewish thinkers argued vociferously over how to understand the 'Great Eagle,' as he later came to be known, and what were his true views. In modern scholarship, Maimonidean experts are divided between the 'esoterists,' who believe Maimonides presented both an exoteric and an esoteric philosophy (Strauss 1952: 38–94) and the 'harmonizers,' who discern a unified, though admittedly hard to get clear, philosopher (Hartman 1976; Manekin 2005). Others think that Maimonides simply wrote at different philosophical levels for different audiences, with no hidden doctrines. Thus, Oliver Leaman writes, 'Maimonides intends to present clear and decisive arguments in favor of his theses. ... We must address ourselves fully to Maimonides' arguments and not to any putative hidden doctrines which owe far more to the imagination of most commentators than to anything we can find in the text' (Leaman 1990: 17).

Regarding many of Maimonides' key views, scholars are widely divided over how to understand him and whether he was expressing his true view in any given passage. The extraordinary difficulty in pinning Maimonides down has led one scholar to quip: 'There are many "Maimonides" – There is *my*-monides, *your*-monides, and *their*-monides!' Here are some examples. Maimonidean scholars are divided over Maimonides' true view of creation, being at odds over whether he believed in creation *ex nihilo*, in the eternity of a fixed world, as did Aristotle, or an eternal world that God arranged from chaos, as did Plato (for the various views, see Samuelson 1991: 249–71). Likewise, scholars disagree over whether Maimonides believed in libertarian free will or accepted that determinism was compatible with free will (see Gellman 1989: 139–50). Scholars argue over whether Maimonides thought prophecy was a natural phenomenon, or that God had to grant prophecy, or that while God did not have to grant prophecy, he could prevent a person from becoming a prophet (Altmann 1978: 1–19; Kreisel 2001).

Finally, Maimonides' concept of God is a morass of contention between scholars. On the one hand, Maimonides proclaims a severe negative theology according to which we can know only what God is not, not what God is (more about this later). On the other hand, Maimonides qualifies this severe philosophical stance, especially pertaining to God's knowledge. For example, in *Guide* 3: 21, although careful to say that God's knowledge is nothing like ours, nevertheless Maimonides gives us many details about God's knowledge, including that God knows all particulars through knowing God's own essence. And in *Guide* 1: 68 Maimonides seems to say that God's knowledge and human knowledge are one in being knowledge. This situation has led to an array of intricate interpretations of Maimonides' concept of God (for an especially elegant version, see Manekin 2005).

In light of the above, we would do best not to present Maimonides' philosophy of religion by way of very specific views he held about God, creation, free will, and the like, since these have been so variously understood, even in medieval times. We would do better to concentrate on Maimonides' unique approach to the status and meaning of the elements of religious life. This approach consists in the following twofold Maimonidean project:

> demarcating a radical distinction between philosophical religion and popular religion (that is, the religion of the 'multitudes');

and

> determining which elements of popular religion must be replaced by philosophical religion and which elements should remain.

In what follows I will portray this dual Maimonidean project in three areas of the religious life: (1) *semantics*: the meaning assigned to statements about God; (2) *dogmatics*: the meaning and truth value of religious dogmas; and (3) *pragmatics*: understanding the reasons for mandated religious behavior.

Semantics

The distinction between a philosophical and a popular conception of God, of course, predates Maimonides. However, prior to Maimonides, and subsequently as in Aquinas, the leading position on the distinction, with variations – for example, in the Arabic philosopher Ibn Rushd (Averroes) – was this: that the masses used terms of God and creatures univocally, with the same meaning, yielding an 'imaginative' idea of God. Philosophers, in contrast, used terms of God by what is called *pros hen* analogical equivocation, which means that God is the unitary exemplar of an attribute in a perfect, transcendent mode, which creatures then receive in a multiple, creaturely mode from God. So while the attribute might be the 'same' in God and creatures, it 'looks' quite different in the two. Thus, Ibn Rushd, for example, had such a philosophical conception of God, as opposed to the imaginative one of the masses, and he also held that it was dangerous to teach the philosophical concept to the masses (see Averroes 1976). Hence, the divide between the philosophers and the masses stays thoroughly intact on the ground.

Maimonides, especially in *Guide* 1: 51–60, taught a far more radical, 'negative theology' about the concept of God. As I have already noted, there is some question on how to interpret this doctrine and to what extent Maimonides might have compromised it along the way (as with his comments on divine knowledge), but there is no doubt that it had a central role in his thinking even if he may not have followed it out consistently. On Maimonides' negative theology there are no attributes common to God and creatures. All terms used of both are out-and-out equivocal.

Maimonides offers the following kind of analysis of sentences of the form 'God is A,' where A is an attribute: 'It is not the case that God has the complement of A.' For example, to say that 'God is powerful,' is to say, 'It is not the case that God is weak,' where 'weak' is understood in its ordinary, creaturely sense. Such translations apply to any property whatsoever that applies to creatures (including existence!). Thus, in principle it would be legitimate to say, for example, 'God is stupid,' to be translated, 'It is not the case that God is wise,' where 'wise' connotes creaturely wisdom. Since God does not have creaturely wisdom, with this translation the original sentence turns out to be true. Nonetheless, such sentences are banned from religious discourse because permitted positive sentences assigning an attribute to God (like 'God is wise') must serve the purpose of denying of God what is a weakness for creatures (like, 'It is not the case that God is stupid.'). The point of positive attribute-assertions about God is not simply to ascribe an attribute to God, but to deny that God possesses what is an imperfection in creatures.

The only permissible positive sentences about God with predicates carrying their ordinary meanings are those that describe God's 'actions,' which Maimonides then translates into sentences minimally about the effects God has on creation – we know not how. Thus, 'God acts kindly in the production of living embryos,' means that the production of embryos is an effect of God's activity, which we call 'kindness' because were such an effect to come from *our* activity it would typically do so from our 'feelings of affection and compassion' (1963: 125; 1: 54). The translation leaves us with no ascription of any attribute to God, or with any idea about the nature of God's activity.

Allowing for possible moderating moves to his negative theology, it is clear that a major element of Maimonides' philosophical semantics of 'God' pulled in a direction more radical than that of his relevant predecessors. And this philosophical concept of God stood in stark contrast to the imaginative picture of God held by the masses.

On the other hand, Maimonides was adamant that from the very start of their religious education, all must be taught that God has no body. In the *Guide*, Maimonides required teaching the masses 'on traditional authority the belief that God is not a body; and that there is absolutely no likeness in any respect whatever between Him and the things created by Him' (1963: 81; 1: 35). This includes the 'ascription of affectations,' which includes emotions (1963: 80, 84; 1: 35 and 36). Indeed, for Maimonides, in some texts at least, believing that God had a body or had 'affections,' was *worse* than idol worship (1963 1: 36). There is no excuse for a person who is not capable of philosophical contemplation not accepting the authority of the philosopher on the matter of God's incorporeality.

Maimonides does not seem to have been consistent in applying all facets of this requirement for the masses, since elsewhere in the *Guide* (see below) he allows some attributions of emotions to God to remain in popular discourse, with their ordinary, creaturely meaning. And when in his legal work, *Mishneh Torah*, Maimonides comes to list those who have no portion in the World to Come, he includes in the list, 'One who says that there is one Master but He is corporeal and has [physical] form' (1949 and on: Laws of Repentance 3: 6). Pointedly, he does not say that a belief in God's having emotions excludes one from the World to Come. Although Maimonides maintained that emotions were dependent on the body (so that if God had emotions, God would also have to possess a body), he could not expect the masses to know this and to make the same inference. I suggest that in his legal work Maimonides compromised on the stricter demand he elsewhere makes on the 'multitude.'

In the *Guide*, Maimonides provides an extensive translation manual for translating biblical statements prima facie attributing a body to God into statements with no such implications (1963: chs 1–47, *inter alia*, chs 64–71). For example, whenever God is said to 'see' something, the reference is to intellectual apprehension (1963 1: 4), not requiring a body, God's 'sitting' refers to God's unchanging stability, and God's 'place' refers only to what Maimonides calls God's 'ranking' (1963 1: 8).

In contrast to his position on God's incorporeality, Maimonides explicitly prohibits revealing his negative analysis of discourse about God to the multitudes (1963 1: 35). Apparently, the bald belief that God is incorporeal would suffice to inculcate in the multitude the idea of God's perfection, without confusing them with philosophy. Likewise, Maimonides advises keeping the philosophical understanding of prophecy, creation, God's will and knowledge, and the details of providence, from non-philosophers. With regard to these, the masses may be left with their imaginative ideas to guide them.

To summarize Maimonides on philosophical and popular semantics for 'God': he held – more or less – that the true analysis of positive attributes of God was radically different from their ordinary, imaginative meaning. At the same time, this negative theology was to be kept from the masses. Yet, one fundamental negative fact about God, that 'It is not the case that God has a body,' must be taught to all, philosophers and non-philosophers alike.

Dogmatics

Maimonides was the first to formulate a list of Jewish dogmas. In his commentary to the *Mishnah*, Maimonides listed thirteen beliefs that are necessary for a Jew in order to receive a share in the World to Come. These are: the existence of God, the unity of God, God's incorporeality, God's eternity, that God alone is worthy of worship, the existence of prophecy, the superior prophecy of Moses, the divinity of the Torah (Pentateuch), the eternity of the Torah, God's knowing human actions, reward and punishment, the coming of the Messiah, and resurrection of the dead. Although elsewhere Maimonides lists these dogmas somewhat differently, this list has become known as 'Maimonides' Thirteen Principles of Faith.' Important Jewish philosophers differed with Maimonides on whether there should be a list of dogmas at all (e.g., Abarbanel 1982), while others disagreed with his choice (notably, Crescas 1929; Albo 1946). To this day, argument continues over whether a Jew has obligations to dogmatic beliefs and if so what they might be (see Kellner 1999; Shapiro 2004). Nonetheless, Maimonides' innovation became widely popular, and his principles of faith have found their way into the traditional Jewish liturgy (for the history of Jewish dogmatics, see Kellner 1986).

So, on the one hand, Maimonides was responsible for thrusting the category of dogma into the center of Jewish philosophy and also for the most famous and influential formulation ever of Jewish dogma.

On the other hand, for Maimonides, the philosopher and non-philosopher will not necessarily understand the content of a dogma in the same way. To be sure, as we have seen, Maimonides requires the masses to be taught at least a minimally philosophical concept of God, so that everyone must understand his first five principles about God in at least a minimally philosophical way. However, when we come to the principle of prophecy, matters shift. As we have seen, in *Guide* 1: 35 Maimonides includes the philosophical understanding of prophecy in the 'mysteries' and 'secrets' of the Torah, which are not to be spoken of except in 'chapter headings' (Maimonides 1963: 80-1). Significantly, then, after stating the principle of prophecy in his Thirteen Principles, Maimonides writes,

> Explaining this principle would be very lengthy, and our purpose is not to give every detail ... because that belongs to the sciences. So we are only stating this principle. (1995/6, II: 143; my translation from the Hebrew)

This indicates that the masses and the philosopher will understand this dogma in disparate ways. (Only a few have access to the sciences.) I would claim the same for the dogma of the superiority of the prophecy of Moses and for the tenth dogma, concerning God's knowledge of the world, placed at a distance from the opening five dogmas about God that the multitude must understand in a minimally philosophical way.

Not only are there principles of faith that the philosopher and non-philosopher understand differently. More than that, that a belief is a Maimonidean *dogma* may not necessarily imply that Maimonides endorsed its truth. Here's why. In *Guide* 3: 28, Maimonides states a distinction between *true* and religiously *useful* belief. Through true beliefs 'the ultimate perfection may be obtained'; thus

> the Law has communicated only their end and made a call to believe in them in a summary way – that is, to believe in the existence of the deity, may He be exalted, His unity, His knowledge, His power, His will, and His eternity. (3: 28)

Then there are necessary – but not necessarily true – beliefs:

> The Law also makes a call to adopt certain beliefs, belief in which is necessary for the sake of political welfare. (3: 28)

'Political welfare' includes all matters relevant to the welfare of society. As Arthur Hyman has shown, this distinction between true and necessary beliefs continues the medieval distinction between 'apodictic' and 'persuasive' statements (Hyman 1967: 141.)

In that same chapter of the *Guide*, Maimonides' gives but two examples of 'necessary beliefs,' as follows:

> Such, for instance, is our belief that He, may He be exalted, is violently angry with those who disobey Him and that it is therefore necessary to fear Him and to dread Him and to take care not to disobey. (3: 28)

And:

> The belief that He, may He be exalted, responds instantaneously to the prayer of someone wronged or deceived. (3: 28)

Both of these are beliefs that Maimonides strongly rejects. They are false. Yet these beliefs are necessary for the masses to live correctly within the body politic. Why is that? Because while the philosopher lives in accordance with truth, and the love and awe of God, the multitudes can be motivated only by *fear* of God (thus the usefulness of believing in God's anger) and by *hope* in God (thus the necessity of thinking God will straight away right wrongs done to the person who prays). 'Necessary beliefs' will thus motivate the masses to proper behavior in accordance with the divine legislation.

Now let's go on. After a lengthy discussion of creation in the *Guide*, Maimonides concludes that, lacking a proof for creation of the world 'from nothing,' he cannot disprove Aristotle's view of the eternity of the world. Rather, he rejects it in favor of creation from nothing because

> Belief in eternity the way Aristotle sees it … destroys the Law in its principle, necessarily gives the lie to every miracle, and *reduces to inanity all the hopes and threats that the Law has held out*, unless – by God – one interprets the miracles figuratively. … This, however, would result in some sort of crazy imaginings. (2: 25, my emphasis)

This sentiment is echoed in Maimonides' later work, the *Treatise on Resurrection*, where he says that Aristotle's view of the eternity of the world implies 'that everything in the universe is the result of fixed laws, that nature does not change and that there is nothing supernatural.' Therefore, accepting Aristotle, we would have to disbelieve all miracles and 'certainly reject all *hopes* and *fears* derived from scripture, unless miracles are to be explained figuratively' (Maimonides 1952: 25, my emphasis). Not so regarding creation from nothing. Note in both texts the references to 'hope' and 'fear,' which exactly parallel Maimonides' two examples of beliefs that are necessary to motivate the multitude, though not true. For Maimonides, belief in creation from nothing was plausibly a necessary belief, necessary, that is, for grounding the masses' relationship of hope and fear to God. Maimonides does not necessarily endorse its truth.

Nonetheless, in a manuscript in Maimonides' own handwriting, the following is added to the fourth belief in Maimonides' list concerning God's eternity:

> Know that a great foundation of the Torah of Moses is creation of the world. God created it from absolute nothingness. (Maimonides 1995/6, II: 142)

Maimonides inserted this addition after the writing of the *Guide*; so the possibility exists that he changed his mind about the status of creation as only a necessary belief. Yet, in his *Treatise on Resurrection*, written after the *Guide*, Maimonides still writes of creation in the same vein that he did previously. Thus Maimonides may very well have included within his list of dogmas a belief that is necessary only, but not necessarily true, as far as he himself has been able to establish.

To summarize, while Maimonides was the father of popular Jewish dogmatics, he very likely had a decidedly philosophical approach to the status and the purposes of the dogmas he endorsed.

Pragmatics

Prior to Maimonides, Christian theology had developed the notion of 'divine accommodation' or 'divine concession' (see Benin 1993). This notion, alas, was wielded as a weapon against Judaism on behalf of Christianity's supersessionist claims. The Jews were like infants to whom God had to make concessions in order to train them up to a new, adult order, brought to the world by Jesus the Savior. The old ritual order could henceforth be abandoned in favor of the religion of the New Israel. Maimonides embraced the notion of divine accommodation. Maimonides' adoption of this concept was, then, a daring and dangerous move for a Jew to have made, for it plays right into the hands of the Christian theology of Jewish ritual having been a pre-figuration of Christ. Indeed, in the *Guide*, Maimonides dares to introduce this concept in connection with the Temple and animal sacrifices, which Christianity explicitly deemed to have been fulfilled by the new Temple in Christ and the supreme blood sacrifice. Here is what Maimonides says:

> A sudden transition from one opposite to another is impossible. And therefore man, according to his nature, is not capable of abandoning suddenly all to which he was accustomed. ... As at that time the way of life generally accepted and customary in the whole world and the universal service upon which we were brought up consisted in offering various species of living beings in the temples in which images were set up, in worshipping the latter, and in burning incense before them, His wisdom, may He be exalted, and His gracious ruse, which is manifest in regard to all His creatures, did not require that He give us a Law prescribing the rejection, abandonment, and abolition of all these kinds of worship. For one could not then conceive the acceptance of [such a Law], considering the nature of man, which always likes that to which it is accustomed.

Therefore He, may He be exalted, suffered the above-mentioned kinds of worship to remain, but transferred them from created or imaginary and unreal things to His own name, may He be exalted, commanding us to practice them with regard to Him, may He be exalted. (1963: 3: 32)

Maimonides says that this principle of God's concession to human nature in the face of pagan practices applies to 'many things in our Law.' As he later explains, this includes all the commandments of sacrifices and the Temple, the laws of purity and impurity, and many of the laws of agriculture. Maimonides explains these as concessions to be understood in light of idolatrous practices from which the Israelites had to be slowly weaned. Religiously mandated behavior need not reflect what Maimonides calls God's 'first intention,' that is, behavior God commands for the end of producing common welfare and human perfection. It may reflect God's 'second intention' only, that is, what God commands so as to bring people to the point where they are capable of implementing God's first intention.

Maimonides applied this reasoning to what rabbinic literature calls biblical *hukkim* (statutes) as opposed to *mishpatim* (judgments). In rabbinic literature, the former were laws the reasons for which were beyond human ken, and the latter, laws of a rational character whose reasons were accessible to human inquiry. The *hukkim* (statutes) included such biblical laws as the prohibition on eating pig meat and on wearing flax and wool together. Maimonides makes the distinction along entirely different lines: 'Those commandments whose utility is clear to the multitude are called *mishpatim* [judgments], and those whose utility is not clear to the multitude are called *hukkim* [statutes]' (1963: 507; 3: 26). The *hukkim* have reasons. It is only the masses who do not know them. Why do the masses not know the reasons for the *hukkim*? Because they are ignorant of the historical conditions which determined the types and degrees of divine accommodation God found necessary to enact.

In connection with the pragmatic aspects of the religious life, Maimonides had to determine whether the masses should be taught the reasons for the *hukkim*. Joseph Stern has shown conclusively that Maimonides forbade divulging to the masses the reasons for the *hukkim* (Stern 1998: ch. 6). First, when the relevant pagan practices were extant, people would not be weaned away from such practices knowing that was the whole point of the statutes. For the ruse to work, they had to believe that what they were called upon to do was God's absolute will. Secondly, when the relevant pagan practices no longer exist, Maimonides feared the antinomian consequences of concluding that the *hukkim* were now also obsolete. Only the philosopher could be trusted with such knowledge of the reasons for God's laws. (Why the *hukkim* should not become obsolete in such circumstances is a question to which it is not apparent that Maimonides has a clear answer; see Stern 1998: 127.) So once again, we see Maimonides withholding elements of philosophical religion from the non-philosophers.

Conclusion

Maimonides' distinction between philosophical and popular religion and his nuanced view of the relationship between them bear upon contemporary philosophy of religion. He begs us to consider more closely than we often do the meaning of 'having a belief' in religious contexts. There are wide differences between believers on how they understand the semantics, dogmatics, and pragmatics of the very same religion. In what sense does a sophisticated believer *share* a religious belief with an unsophisticated one? In what sense do they have different beliefs? Can we identify a religion with a set of dogmas, or are matters much more subtle than that? Maimonides' philosophy of religion suggests a distinction, perhaps, between *individual* and *collective* belief, where the latter pertains to a level of shared belief that just might diverge on an individual level (see Gellman 2007).

See also Judaism (Chapter 5), Ibn Sina/Avicenna (Chapter 10), Thomas Aquinas (Chapter 12), Truth in religion (Chapter 18), Hiddenness (Chapter 29), Creation and divine action (Chapter 30), Problems with the concept of God (Chapter 38), The problem of religious language (Chapter 39), Theology and religious language (Chapter 48).

References

Abarbanel, I. (1982) *Principles of Faith – Rosh Amanah*, trans. M. Kellner, Oxford: Littman Library of Jewish Civilization.

Albo, J. (1946) *Sefer Ha-Ikkarim (Book of Principles)*, trans. I. Husik, Philadelphia: Jewish Publication Society of America.

Altmann, A. (1978) 'Maimonides and Thomas Aquinas: natural or divine prophecy?' *AJS Review* 3: 1–19.

Averroes (1976) *On the Harmony of Religion and Philosophy*, trans. G. F. Hourani, London: Luzac & Company.

Benin, S. D. (1993) *The Footprints of God: Divine Accommodation in Jewish and Christian Thought*, Albany, NY: State University of New York Press.

Burrell, D. (1986) *Knowing the Unknowable God: Ibn-Sina, Maimonides, Aquinas*, Notre Dame, IN: University of Notre Dame Press.

Crescas, H. (1929) *Crescas' Critique of Aristotle: Or Adonai*, ed. H. A. Wolfson, Cambridge, MA: Harvard University Press.

Gellman, J. (1989) 'Freedom and determinism in the philosophy of Maimonides,' in E. Ormsby (ed.) *Maimonides and his Time*, Washington, DC: Catholic University of America.

—— (2007) 'Beyond belief: on the uses of creedal confession,' *Faith and Philosophy*, 23: 299–313.

Goodman, L. (1980) 'Maimonides and Leibniz,' *Journal of Jewish Studies* 31: 214–25.

Hartman, D. (1976) *Maimonides: Torah and Philosophic Quest*, Philadelphia: Jewish Publications Society of America.

Hyman, A. (1967) 'Maimonides' "Thirteen Principles," in A. Altmann (ed.) *Jewish Medieval and Renaissance Studies*, Cambridge, MA: Harvard University Press.

Kellner, M. (1986) *Dogma in Medieval Jewish Thought from Maimonides to Abravanel*, Oxford: Littman Library of Jewish Civilization by Oxford University.

—— (1999) *Must a Jew Believe Anything?*, London: Littman Library of Jewish Civilization.

Kreisel, H. (2001) *Prophecy: The History of an Idea in Medieval Jewish Philosophy*, Dordrecht: Kluwer.

Langerman, T. (2003) 'Maimonides and the sciences,' in D. F. Frank and O. Leaman (eds) *The Cambridge Companion to Medieval Jewish Philosophy*, Cambridge: Cambridge University Press.

Leaman, O. (1990) *Moses Maimonides*, London: Routledge.

Maimonides (1949 and on) *Mishneh Torah (The Code of Maimonides)*, New Haven, CT: Yale University Press.

—— (1952) *Treatise on Resurrection*, ed. J. Finkel, New York: American Academy for Jewish Research.

—— (1963) *The Guide of the Perplexed*, trans. S. Pines, Chicago: University of Chicago.

—— (1995/6) *Mishnah with the Commentary of Moses son of Maimon*, 2 vols., trans. Y. Kapach, Jerusalem: Mosad Harav Kook.

Manekin, C. H. (2005) *On Maimonides*, Belmont, CA: Wadsworth Publishing.

Samuelson, N. (1991) 'Maimonides' doctrine of creation,' *Harvard Theological Review* 84: 249–71.

Shapiro, M. B. (2004) *The Limits of Orthodox Theology: Maimonides' Thirteen Principles Reappraised*, Oxford: Littman Library of Jewish Civilization.

Stern, J. (1998) *Problems and Parables of Law, Maimonides and Nachmanides on Reasons for the Commandments (Ta'amei Ha-Mitzvot)*, Albany, NY: State University of New York Press.

Strauss, L. (1952) *Persecution and the Art of Writing*, Glencoe, IL: Free Press.

Wolfson, H. A. (1969) *The Philosophy of Spinoza: Unfolding the Latent Processes of his Reasoning*, New York: Schocken Books.

Further reading

Davidson, H. A. (2005) *Moses Maimonides: The Man and his Works*, New York: Oxford University. (A book by one of the leading Maimonides scholars of our time.)

Putnam, H. (1997) 'On negative theology,' *Faith and Philosophy* 14: 407–22. (A sympathetic analysis by an outstanding analytic philosopher.)

Seeskin, K. (1991) *Maimonides: A Guide for Today's Perplexed*, West Orange, NJ: Behram House. (A somewhat popular, sound presentation of Maimonides' central views.)

Twersky, A. (1980) *Introduction to the Code of Maimonides*, New Haven, CT: Yale University Press. (The definitive study of Maimonides' code.)

12
THOMAS AQUINAS
Wayne J. Hankey

The necessity of revealed knowledge questioned

Aquinas' *Summa Theologiae* opens with a question stunning in its revolutionary character which he was the first to ask, displays the fundamental interpenetration of philosophy and religion in his thought, and forces him to adjust their relations in a way which would have the greatest consequences both for the future of philosophy and religion and for the anachronistic representation of their past (Kerr 2002: 12–14). The first article of the first question of the first part of Aquinas' most influential work, the one where he was able for the first time to give theology what he conceived to be its proper order, is 'Whether it is necessary besides the philosophical disciplines to have another teaching.' The question assumes a true knowledge based in the natural powers of reason, asks whether this is all humans should and can know, and whether there is need and room for any other kind of knowledge than the philosophical 'disciplines.'

Sacred doctrine sets herself the task of finding a place and a necessity for herself relative to an assumed natural human knowledge and powers that enable humans to construct a world aiming for, and in an important sense achieving, knowledge even of God. The arguments in the objections used to set up the problem establish what might be called a secular humanism provided by philosophy; this 'secular' world would include God as the necessary foundation to and conclusion of right reason. Revealed doctrine must justify herself in the face of an assumed philosophically constructed world. This paradigm Aquinas thus established for the relations between philosophy and supernaturally revealed knowledge is so influential that it has become normal to look at what preceded him through it, an anachronistic distortion.

Because we generally assume a world constructed by what at present corresponds to these theoretical and practical disciplines, it is almost impossible for us to appreciate the shocking character of Thomas' question to a western Christian in the thirteenth century. The Latin West was still dominated by Augustine and by those self-consciously in his tradition who would successfully oppose Aquinas' innovations during his life (1224/5–74) and immediately afterwards, with the result that positions he maintained were officially condemned by the ecclesiastical authorities during and following the last years of his life (Hankey 2005: 43–5). For the Augustinians philosophy served the quest of faith and love for intellection. When intellection is achieved, faith is explicated; it acquires the certainty possessed by reason rather than by authority, and humans intuit the content of faith. Reason had not the kind of independence from revelation that would permit it to say anything other than faith, not even something less. The notion that the teaching based on faith might have to justify itself relative to an autonomously established reason with a complete account of all that is was both unthinkable and frightening.

The first objection, the first argument in the whole system, proposes that whatever is not above reason is sufficiently treated in the philosophical disciplines. 'Therefore, besides them, there is no need of any further knowledge.' The philosophical sciences providing this complete account are usually attributed to Aristotle, and indeed, the 'Philosopher' is spoken of in the second objection, where his *Metaphysics* is cited to the effect that there is a philosophical science of God. In fact, however, the philosophical disciplines with a complete account of reality are established over and against what revelation might know because of the systematization of philosophical sciences in the Peripatetic and Neoplatonic schools of later Antiquity, on the one hand, and, because of the Islamic Arabic mediation of Aristotle to the Latins, on the other. Arabic philosophy assumed this systematization and added to it an opposition between the whole content of intellect as known conceptually to the faculty of reason and that same content apprehended by representation, the power which enabled prophecy and imaginative persuasion. As Alain de Libera puts it, the Arabs mediated the texts of Aristotle to the Latins as 'a total philosophic corpus, into which the whole of Hellenistic thought, profoundly neoplatonised, had surreptitiously crept' (de Libera 1991: 20).

Within the Islamic Arabic world the last great defender of the need for and certainty of a complete philosophical knowledge of what is was Ibn Rushd, known by Aquinas as Averroes. He called him 'The Commentator' because of the authority of his commentaries on the works of Aristotle. The corpus of the Arabic Aristotle as he was received by the comparatively ignorant Latin Christians was capped by works of theology confected by the Arabs out of elements taken from Plotinus and Proclus. It was not until after 1268 (i.e., during the last six years of his life) that Aquinas was provided with a Latin translation of the *Elements of Theology*, from which he detected the Proclean character of his Aristotle, a discovery which does not seem to have disturbed him. During the 1260s and until his death, Aquinas used newly done translations from the Greek of works of Aristotle and of the ancient Neoplatonic commentators on him. These enabled him to get back behind the Averroist Aristotle he had received and which was entrenched in the Faculty of Arts in Paris and assisted his struggle against some features of its Aristotelianism. Nonetheless, his most authoritative source of philosophical and theological ideas apart from the Scriptures was Dionysius the pseudo-Areopagite, a sixth-century mystical theologian writing in Greek, who portrayed himself as converted in Athens by the Apostle Paul and as the heir to his mystical knowledge but who was in fact a conduit of the Neoplatonism of Plotinus, Proclus, and Damascius. Aquinas was convinced throughout his life that Dionysius and Aristotle had much conceptual ground in common (Hankey 2002a:

161–5). Thomas' Neoplatonic Aristotle was more theological than the original and thus both more easily assimilated to Christianity and more the rival to its revelation.

If Averroes comes to mind in the objections of the first article, Moses Maimonides, his Jewish twelfth-century contemporary also from Cordoba in Spain, appears in Thomas' response. Maimonides' *Guide of the Perplexed* was known to Aquinas from the beginning of his systematic writing. Accepting both orientations, it aimed to deal with what was opposing in the demands on a Jew who was simultaneously a conscientious follower of the Law and excelled at philosophy (Maimonides 1963: intro.). The problems of the Maimonides' disciple resemble those of the Latin theologian most authoritative for Aquinas, Augustine (he and Dionysius share the prizes for his most numerous citations of Christian theologians). Augustine found himself with two undeniable allegiances after he was converted to philosophy, and was only able to come to true Christian faith after he had completed his journey to what Aquinas recognized was Platonism (Augustine 1993: 3. 4–7; 5. 14; 7. 1–2, 10). Significantly, Plotinus supplied Augustine both with a positive conception of immaterial substance and with the way to get it – interior self-knowledge. Aquinas, in contrast, adopts his way for arriving at the same end from Aristotle and from what is Proclean in Dionysius; for all four – Aristotle, Proclus, Dionysius, and Aquinas – the human soul was turned by nature to the sensible and was not capable of immediate self-knowledge (Hankey 2001: 336–41).

The necessity of philosophy for true religion

With Aquinas, for the first time in the Latin Middle Ages, a theologian engaged the philosophers on their own terrain as a separate, limited, subordinate sphere, with its own proper methods and autonomy. Thomas, in opposition both to the Aristotle of Averroes and to the Augustinians, made a humbled but quasi-autonomous philosophy into the servant of revealed theology. Agreeing with Maimonides that what philosophy demonstrated with certainty revelation could not contradict, he agreed equally that, where reason left matters open, Scripture revealed things necessary to reaching the happiness for which God created us (see Aquinas, *Super Sententiis*, lib. 2, dist. 1, q.1, a.5. co. and ad s.c. 6; Maimonides 1963: 2: 15). He adopted the approach taken by Maimonides, who faced the same kind of adversaries to his left and his right: on the one hand, Arabic philosophy, and on the other, the Islam and Jewish dialectical theology which Maimonides identified as shared by and originating with the Christians (Maimonides 1963: 1: 71). Aquinas judged the demand of his Augustinian adversaries that things only faith could know (e.g., the temporal beginning of the world; a universal, individual, and immediate providence; the Trinity; and the Incarnation – the first two items on this list are also on Maimonides') be rationally proved only brought destructive disrepute to both theology and philosophy.

Thomas learns from Dionysius and the Platonists that revelation is normally given in sensible symbols, images, and signs wherein sacred intelligible and super-intelligible realities are adapted to the form of our knowing by being veiled (*Summa Theologiae* (*ST*) I. 1. 9 and I. 3. 1 ad 1). Thus, revelation comes to believers in scriptural images and narratives, which, uncorrected, deceive them into believing divinity to be multiple, corporeal, composite, subject to passions. Maimonides and Aquinas both inherit the tradition of philosophical theology coming from the pre-Socratic and Platonic criticism of mythic accounts of the gods (for a *locus classicus*, see Plato, *Republic* 379b–381c). Plato's standards for purifying poetic theology were radically intensified by his Neoplatonic successors, of whom Aquinas is an heir; thus the corporeality, division, mutability, potentiality, causing of evil ascribed to God in Scripture must be understood as signifying their opposites. In consequence, the philosophical climb by which we can see the truth about spiritual substance which Scripture reveals is both necessary and meritorious. The power of mind is increased corporately and individually by reaching higher levels of abstraction, by our rising to and becoming one with higher levels of reality.

For Aquinas it belongs to our 'natural perfection' not to know God except from creatures and by abstraction from sensible things (*De Veritate* 18. 2). The ladder of the philosophical sciences constitutes them as preambles by which the human mind gains the strength for proving with irrefutable certainty the existence of God (*De Veritate* 10. 12), for knowing both his negative attributes – simplicity, infinity, eternity, etc. – and (in the very limited measure of which it is capable) the divine mysteries standing both above scientific reason and even beyond the metaphysical wisdom toward which reason ascends (*ST* I. 2 to I. 11; *De Veritate* 14. 10). He wonders how we shall understand the words of Scripture from and about separate simple incorporeal substance. Revealed theology based on God's own self-knowledge needs philosophy, not because of what God's knowledge lacks, but because of our human deficiency. Like his Neoplatonic predecessors, Thomas is always aware that our theology, though valid because it participates in higher forms of knowledge, nonetheless belongs to human reason. By its labor of abstraction, human science exercises our minds in the knowledge theology needs of intellectual objects separated from matter. Without philosophy, we would not understand divine speech (*ST* I. 1. 5 ad 2). When arguing against Anselm and the Augustinians that God's existence is not self-evident, he reminds us that humans have even thought that God was a body (*ST* I. 2. 1 ad 2). He begins his treatment of the divine names or attributes with the question about whether God is a body, and uses the knowledge of God at which he has just arrived in his Five Ways to show that he is not (*ST* I. 3. 1).

Given that philosophy is necessary for our right understanding of God and that knowing God is proper to him alone, it is not surprising that Aquinas supposes that philosophy is a kind of revelation: 'the study of philosophy is in its own right allowable and praiseworthy, because God revealed to the philosophers the truth which they perceive, as Romans 1.19 says' (*ST* II–II. 167. 1 ad 3). He understands Aristotle and Plato to teach this so far as they maintain that our knowledge of God is a participation in the divine self-knowing. This doctrine Aquinas finds in the *Metaphysics* as well in as the *Nicomachean Ethics*, and he takes it to be the condition of metaphysics as knowledge of divinity (*In Metaphysicorum* 1. 3, 18–20; *Sententia Libri Ethicorum* 10. 11).

Preserving nature within grace

In *ST* I. 1. 1, Aquinas is concerned with the reasons we need instruction by divine revelation 'even in respect to those things about God which human reason is able to investigate.' In the *De Veritate*, when he is considering whether it is necessary to have faith, he acknowledges his debt to 'the five reasons which Rabbi Moses [Maimonides] gives' (Maimonides 1963: 1. 34; *De Veritate*, 14. 10; *Summa contra Gentiles* (*SCG*) I. 4). In their common judgments about the difficulty of theology and about the necessity of keeping it from all except mature students with long preparation both moral and intellectual, Aquinas and Maimonides were following Plato, Aristotle, the curricula of the Neoplatonic schools, and their predecessors in the Arabic philosophical tradition. The abstractness of philosophy generally, and of metaphysics particularly, the weakness of our minds which must be strengthened by mathematical and other studies, the extent of the ground which must be covered to reach it, the length of time traversing this takes, the need for developed moral virtues and the proper temperament, are all reasons why we require the gift of supernatural revelation.

Nonetheless, in the course of showing the inadequacies of natural reason for attaining the ultimate human happiness, Aquinas actually strengthens it. As against Augustinians (*ST* I. 1. 4, I. 1. 7), for him sacred doctrine is not fundamentally practical or affective but theoretical, and we are saved by knowing truths which philosophical reason unaided by grace cannot know: 'We must know an end before we direct our intentions and actions towards that end. Therefore, it is necessary for human salvation that some truths which exceed human reason be known through divine revelation' (*ST* I. 1. 1). We are related to an end beyond reason in such a way as to strengthen our reason and will by giving to them truths to know and goods to love higher than their natural capacities reach. The infusion of grace perfects the rational power: 'The gifts of grace are added to nature in such a way that nature is not destroyed but is greatly perfected. Hence, even the light of faith, which flows into us by grace, does not destroy the light of the natural reason divinely bestowed on us' (*Super De Trinitate* 2. 3; *ST* I. 1. 8. ad 2). The light of nature is divinely given to us.

The massive *Second Part* of the *Summa Theologiae*, which describes the human in its desire for happiness, both in terms of what nature understands, seeks, and does, and in terms of what grace might give, is set under the idea of the human as 'principle of its own works' because it is 'image of God' (*ST* II–1, prologue). Aquinas places here the foundation on which humans construct their own world, fall away from God, and need a human-divine savior to draw them back to God.

Aquinas places moral virtue and philosophical reason within systematic structures derived by way of lengthy mediation from Porphyry and Iamblichus. In consequence, although the overarching theological and religious framework is for the sake of what philosophy cannot attain, for Thomas as well as for pagan Neoplatonists, philosophy 'is still a way of life which transforms us towards deiformity' (Hankey 2003: 223). Iamblichus introduces the notion of the supernatural into theology; supernature presupposes nature (Iamblichus, *De Mysteriis* 3. 25). Like Aquinas, the 'divine' Iamblichus is all at once a ritualistic priest, a theologian, and a philosopher. Working within the tradition of Neoplatonic systematic theology, Aquinas shares the aim of maintaining the difference, the integrity, and the connection of (1) sacramental practices in which the divine and humans cooperate, (2) human moral discipline, (3) the rational and human work of philosophy culminating in contemplation of God, and (4) our passive yielding to the gracious activity of the divine toward us (Saffrey 1997; Hankey 2003: 211–17).

The final word in *ST* I. 1. 1 continues to provide for revealed knowledge without negating the truth and completeness of the human sciences as human, and by further establishing them. First, it grants that the same things can be treated from two different perspectives without one of them cancelling the other; thus there can be two different sciences of God. Second, it provides the basis for the two sciences: one functions through the power of the light of natural reason, the other through the light of divine revelation. Moreover, they can, at least to some extent, keep out of each other's way because they differ 'according to genus.' Sacred doctrine is a fundamentally different kind of thing from the theology which is part of philosophy (*ST* I. 1. 1 ad 2).

Aquinas preserves the human to the last. Controversially but correctly, Timothy Smith writes about the continuity between the way we know in this life and in the next: building on the way we know now, our intellect will become a '"glorified faculty," made more "potent" for seeing the divine essence' (Smith 2003: 51). In *ST* I. 12, when treating how we know God, Aquinas begins by arguing that both philosophy and faith demand human vision of the divine essence. Without face-to-face knowledge, faith would be nullified because its purpose is human beatitude. Reason, in its turn, would also be denied. It is fulfilled in the knowledge of the principles and causes. This demand being frustrated, man's natural desire would be vain. Thus both faith and reason require that 'the blessed see the essence of God' (*ST* I. 12. 1). Later in this question, we find Thomas' notorious doctrine of created grace, which he developed in order to explain how we can have the demanded knowledge of God's essence. Much criticized, it is, nonetheless, determined by Thomas' desire to preserve the integrity of human nature until the end even when we are united to God. This he does by connecting our final state to the form of knowing peculiar to us, that by abstraction.

Aquinas confronts grave problems in arguing for human knowledge of the divine essence. These ultimately reduce to the incapacity of the finite creature for the infinite creator – a gulf widened by his Neoplatonic authorities – and the inadequacy of the human mind belonging to an embodied soul for the knowledge of divine and angelic subsistent substances existing separately from both matter and motion. Because of the incapacity of the finite to contain or convey the infinite, God cannot be adequately known through an intermediating likeness: no concept, by nature finite, can convey the uncreated infinity. Beatifying union must be immediate. However, humans have some capacity for knowing separate substance and to this a gracious addition can be made:

> Since the created intellect has an innate natural capacity for apprehending individualized form and the concrete act of being in abstraction by means of

a certain power to separate out, it is able through grace to be raised so that it can know subsisting separated substance and the separated subsistent act of being. (ST I. 12. 4. ad 3)

Divine grace gives a higher light to the creature in order, by an addition to its power to know, to raise its natural created capacity beyond its natural scope which, in humans, is forms in matter. Grace continues – even at this absolute limit of creaturely existence – to conform itself to the specific nature of the creature. Put another way, the knowledge of God given by the light of glory far beyond our natural limits adapts itself to the way humans naturally participate in God's uncreated light so that, in accord with a law of mediation (which Aquinas says applies to both nature and grace and which is owed to Iamblichus), every difference is maintained and every extreme is mediated (Hankey 1997: 59–60). We shall be made like God without ceasing to be human.

Proving God's existence

The 'Five Ways' (ST I. 2. 3), which provide the foundation for the rational side of his philosophical and revealed theology, are roughly based in Aristotle's four causes; however, they do not conform closely, and the individual proofs have many sources, including Aristotle's *Physics* and Avicenna's metaphysics (Hankey 2000: 37–56, 139–42). The literature contains endless discussions about their validity and purpose, and no summary is possible here. Three points are worth making.

First, it is important that there are proofs. Some Neoplatonists thought that God was too immediately given to need proving, and that both submitting the divine to proof and placing its highest level within being was a diminution of God (e.g., Iamblichus, *De Mysteriis* 1. 3). Aquinas is dealing with similar attitudes when he confronts both Augustinian theologians who think that God's existence is self-evident and Dionysius, Eriugena, and other thinkers strongly under the influence of apophatic Neoplatonism.

Second, the proofs must be evident to humans, and, in consequence, Thomas' view on what proofs will work depends upon his understanding of the human, and especially of how we know. When he is comparing the Platonic way and Aristotle's way, he writes that Aristotle's reasoning 'by way of motion' is the 'more manifest and certain' when dealing with the existence of intellectual beings (*De Substantiis Separatis* 2. 8). This matches what he says in the *ST* at the beginning of the Five Ways and explains why he begins with the proof from motion there. He discovered the comparison between Plato and Aristotle in the great Neoplatonic commentator Simplicius, who had also judged the Aristotelian way to have a more persuasive necessity in virtue of its relation to sense (Simplicius *Prologus*, 8, lines 74–9). It is essential to this 'way of motion' that it starts with sensibly known corporeal existence, the knowing of which Aquinas judges us to be naturally suited (Hankey 2002a: 169, 173–4).

Third, Thomas' sense of the limits of the human capacity for knowing separate substance, of the inadequacy of the effects by which we know God to be their cause, and of the excess of the divine infinity in respect to all creatures means that he is fundamentally an apophatic theologian. The demonstration of God's existence takes place in the context of a Neoplatonic opposition between the knowledge that God exists and the knowledge of what God is (*ST* I. 2. 2). After the Five Ways and as he is about to begin treating the attributes, Aquinas reminds us that we do not know what God is but what he is not (*ST* I. 3, prologue). The first circle of questions on the unity of the divine, which in imitation of Dionysius is separated from and prior to the treatment of the divine Trinity, begins with simplicity, revealing again the strength of the Neoplatonic influence on his theology. Simplicity is for him a negative characteristic, the denial of all composition. Nonetheless, the very simplicity of God requires that we cannot know God's existence without some apprehension of his nature. It turns out that the Five Ways produce a considerable knowledge of God in what follows.

God's being

Not only the *Summa* as a whole, but also particular treatises within it, describe the Neoplatonic structure of remaining, *exitus*, and *reditus* by which all things except the One return upon their principle (*ST* I. 2 prologue; Hankey 2000 *passim*). The first circle (Questions 3–11) is constructed when, beginning with simplicity, we arrive back at unity by way of the existence of God in all things. The circles succeeding it (i.e., those described by the internal operations, by the Trinity, by the creation, and, ultimately, by salvation) return back to the principle by way of more and more differentiated processions. We have a unification of the Platonic dialectic of the one and the many with Aristotle's logic of activity as *entelecheia* in a Neoplatonic hierarchy (Hankey 1999: 397-408). Moreover, the Neoplatonic figures determine content as well as form.

For example, a concept taken from Proclus, that incorporeal substances have complete return upon themselves, enables the *Summa*'s progress from the circle described by simple *esse* returning to itself as unity in the questions on the divine activities of knowledge, will, and power. These activities determine the emergence of the trinitarian processions (which Aquinas also calls emanations) within the essence, and the emanation outside it, creation. From Aristotle, by way of a profound transformation among the Arabs, especially al-Farabi and Ibn Sina, Aquinas takes the law of spiritual emanation, 'from the one, nothing except a one can come.' It determines how the processions of the divine Word and Spirit occur; they are distinguished as necessary, natural, and prior *vis-à-vis* the voluntary emanation of creation. Another figure, by which the Neoplatonists reconciled Plato and Aristotle – the idea of motionless motion as characterizing the activity of the perfect – enables Aquinas to call God living, and is manifest in the Trinitarian circumincession. Another such figure, taken from Proclus via Dionysius and the *Liber de causis*, provides the structure for the consideration of all spiritual substances from the soul to the divine: they have essence, power, and activity.

It is within the divine simplicity that the identity of existence and essence appears for Thomas. This identity belongs to God who 'is essentially form' and 'form subsisting through itself' (*ST* I. 3. 2). The identity with existence is therefore not an exclusion of essence. The divine *esse* is dynamic so that the diverse predicates emerge out of the plenitude of the simplicity. God is 'essentially good' (*ST* I. 3. 2), a goodness by its nature infinitely diffused within the existence of things. Yet the divine *esse* is also immutable, eternal, and one. It is both the unity essential to beings and one in itself (*ST* I. 11). This doctrine descends to Aquinas by way of the Neoplatonic notion of God as pure being, which probably has its origins in Porphyry's modification of the Plotinian One (Hankey 2000: 3–6; 2005: 49–50; Narbonne 2001: 41–70, 222–44).

God is unknown to us in this present life and, crucially, philosophy understands its own ignorance. Combining two Neoplatonic strategies: (1) the relation between the grade of a substance in the hierarchy and its way of knowing, and (2) the systematic analogy between the ways of knowing and the grades of being, Aquinas develops his particular doctrine of analogy in order to prevent all our judgments about God being false. As against both Moses Maimonides and Dionysius, who may be taken to stand for an extreme negative theology, Aquinas argues that we rightly make affirmative and proper predications of God. Because God possesses the qualities predicated most properly, the qualities are not ascribed to God only as the cause of what is in creatures (*ST* I. 12. 4; *ST* I. 13. 1 *co.*, ad 2 and ad 3; *ST* I. 13 articles 2, 3, 5, 6, 12; see Hankey 2000: 88–95). The correction of the mode of our knowing of God by comparing it to the mode of his own being requires that we are simultaneously looking at reality in a human way and also looking at our place in the cosmos from the divine perspective. This capacity to look at ourselves from beyond ourselves is consequent on our participation in the higher knowing of separate substances. This participation is as much a fact about the psychological and ontological structure of the cosmos – and thus about the constitution of our nature and how it functions within its hierarchically situated place – as it is something vouchsafed by revelation. The distinction, meeting, and fundamental interpenetration of two movements, one up from creatures which constitutes the theology which is for Aquinas a part of philosophy, the other down from God which constitutes for him revealed theology, is from beginning to the end what characterizes Aquinas' teaching.

See also Christianity (Chapter 6), Islam (Chapter 7), Augustine (Chapter 8), Ibn Sina/Avicenna (Chapter 10), Moses Maimonides/Rambam (Chapter 11), The cosmological argument (Chapter 32), The problem of religious language (Chapter 39), Catholic philosophical theology (Chapter 43), Theology and religious language (Chapter 48).

References

Augustine (1993) *Confessions*, trans. F. Sheed, Indianapolis, IN: Hackett.
Hankey, W. J. (2000) [1987] *God in Himself, Aquinas' Doctrine of God as Expounded in the Summa Theologiae*, Oxford Theological Monographs Oxford Scholarly Classics, Oxford: Oxford University Press.
—— (1997) 'Aquinas, Pseudo-Denys, Proclus and Isaiah VI.6,' *Archives d'histoire doctrinale et littéraire du Moyen Âge* 64: 59–93.

—— (1999) '*Theoria versus Poesis*: Neoplatonism and Trinitarian difference in Aquinas,' *Modern Theology* 15: 387–415.

—— (2001) 'Why philosophy abides for Aquinas,' *The Heythrop Journal* 42/3: 329–48.

—— (2002a) 'Thomas' Neoplatonic histories: his following of Simplicius,' *Dionysiu*, 20: 153–78.

—— (2003) 'Philosophy as a way of life for Christians? Iamblichan and Porphyrian reflections on religion, virtue, and philosophy in Thomas Aquinas,' *Laval Théologique et Philosophique* 59/2: 193–224.

—— (2005) 'Self and cosmos in becoming deiform: Neoplatonic paradigms for reform by self-knowledge from Augustine to Aquinas,' in C. M. Bellitto and L. I. Hamilton (eds) *Reforming the Church Before Modernity: Patterns, Problems and Approaches*, Aldershot: Ashgate.

Kerr, F. (2002) *After Aquinas: Versions of Thomism*, Oxford: Blackwell.

de Libera, A. (1991) *Penser au Moyen Âge*, Paris: Seuil.

Maimonides, M. (1963) *Guide of the Perplexed*, trans. S. Pines, Chicago: University of Chicago Press.

Narbonne, J.-M. (2001) *Hénologie, ontologie et Ereignis (Plotin-Proclus-Heidegger)*, L'âne d'or, Paris: Belles Lettres.

Saffrey, H.-D. (1997) 'Theology as science (3rd–6th centuries),' in E. A. Livingstone (ed.) *Studia Patristica*, vol. 29, Leuven: Peeters.

Simplicius (1971) *Commentaire sur les Catégories d'Aristote, Traduction de Guillaume de Moerbeke*, 2 vols., Corpus Latinorum commentariorum in Aristotelem Graecorum 1–2, vol. 1, ed. A. Pattin, Louvain and Paris: Publications universitaires de Louvain; vol. 2, ed. A. Pattin, Leiden: Brill.

Smith, T. L. (2003) *Thomas Aquinas' Trinitarian Theology: A Study in Theological Method*, Washington, DC: Catholic University of America Press.

Further reading

Hankey, W. J. (2000) [1987] *God in Himself, Aquinas' Doctrine of God as Expounded in the Summa Theologiae*, Oxford Theological Monographs/ Oxford Scholarly Classics, Oxford: Oxford University Press. (How Aristotelian and Neoplatonic logics meet in the first forty-five questions of the *Summa Theologiae*.)

—— (2002b) 'Aquinas and the Platonists,' in S. Gersh and M. J. F. M. Hoenen (eds), *The Platonic Tradition in the Middle Ages: A Doxographic Approach*, Berlin: Walter de Gruyter. (An account of Thomas' relation to Platonism in its multiple forms.)

—— (2005) 'Self and cosmos in becoming deiform: Neoplatonic paradigms for reform by self-knowledge from Augustine to Aquinas,' in C. M. Bellitto and L. I. Hamilton (eds) *Reforming the Church Before Modernity: Patterns, Problems and Approaches*, Aldershot: Ashgate. (How Thomas' religious subjectivity derives from later Neoplatonism.)

Kerr, F. (2002) *After Aquinas: Versions of Thomism*, Oxford: Blackwell. (Insightful, wise, hugely knowledgeable, and endlessly charitable.)

Saffrey, H.-D. (1997) 'Theology as science (3rd–6th centuries),' in E. A. Livingstone (ed.) *Studia Patristica*, vol. 29, Leuven: Peeters. (A summary of how the unification of philosophy and religion in late antiquity bears its fruit in Aquinas.)

Velde, R. A. te (1995) *Participation and Substantiality in Thomas Aquinas*, Studien und Texte zur Geistesgeschichte des Mittelalters xlvi, Leiden: Brill. (What Thomas took from Dionysius and how he transformed it.)

13

DAVID HUME

Terence Penelhum

Religion in Hume's career

David Hume (1711–76) is generally considered to be the greatest philosopher to have written in English. He is also the most formidable critic of religion in modern times. In his own time his anti-religious opinions caused him real professional damage, in spite of the general recognition of his personal charm and goodness; and the pride that his native Scotland now takes in him as their greatest Enlightenment figure is quite recent.

The religious environment into which Hume was born was one in which the national church was dominated by a stern form of Calvinism inculcated during the Reformation by John Knox. Hume seems to have reasoned himself away from this tradition during his adolescent years, and to have been devoid of religious sentiment for the rest of his life.

During his student years at Edinburgh University, Hume decided upon a literary career rather than the legal one that his family had wished for him. He went to France for further study, and to write his first and greatest work, A *Treatise of Human Nature*, which appeared in London in 1739 and 1740 (Hume 2000). It did not gain as much attention as Hume had hoped, and he famously said that it 'fell dead-born from the press.' He did, however, gain from it a reputation as an irreligious and atheistic thinker, even though he had removed material on religion from it before it was published. This reputation prevented him from being appointed to the chair of Ethics and Pneumatical (mental) Philosophy at Edinburgh University in 1745 (Mossner 1970: 153–62). Hume felt he had been the victim of superstitious prejudice, and when his next philosophical work came out, it contained material on religion that he had previously excised from the *Treatise*. The work in question is the one now known as the *Enquiry Concerning Human Understanding* (Hume 1999), and the recycled material is Section X, 'Of miracles,' which is still his best-known essay on a religious subject. It is followed by the less well-known but equally important section, 'Of a particular providence and of a future state' in which Hume argues that the popular 'Design' argument for God's existence, which alleges that the order of nature revealed by modern science shows our world to be the work of a divine mind, does not have any more practical implications than a wholly godless naturalism (Hume 1999).

In 1755 and 1756 Hume was once more the target of public criticism for his anti-religious views, and there was an attempt to have him publicly censured at the General Assembly of the Church of Scotland (Mossner 1970: 336–55). By this time the Edinburgh religious establishment contained a group of more liberal figures, known as the Moderates, who included some of Hume's closest friends, and the attempt failed. It is important in judging Hume's detailed intentions to bear in mind that some of his closest associates were clerics, and that he was fully aware of the fact that it was in their urbane hands that Edinburgh became a renowned center of scientific and literary activity (Sher 1985). They were the representatives of what he was subsequently to refer to as 'true religion.' It was they who persuaded Hume not to publish the *Dialogues Concerning Natural Religion*, which he had begun at about this time but which did not see print until after his death (Hume 1980).

The other major work on religion that Hume did publish, in 1757, was *The Natural History of Religion*, which is generally agreed to be the first work of comparative religion in English (Hume 1957). In it Hume turns aside from discussion of philosophical arguments in favor of religious belief to a historical analysis of its origins and psychological sources.

Hume is a very systematic thinker. Not only do his views about religion reflect other themes in his philosophical system; they also form a unitary whole within themselves. I shall attempt in what follows to indicate very briefly, first, those elements in his wider philosophy that are reflected in his philosophy of religion, and then proceed to describe in outline the arguments of his writings on religion, showing as far as I can how they relate to each other (Penelhum 1992).

Hume's system and religion

Hume bases his philosophical system upon an analysis of human nature. We are beings who should understand what our nature is and accept it as it is. His famous skepticism is the result of the fact that he thinks such an understanding shows our reason to be far more limited than most philosophers are prepared to acknowledge. He follows the skeptics of antiquity in considering it beyond our powers to justify the fundamental beliefs on which our life depends: the regularity of nature, the reliability of our senses, and the unity of the self. He departs from them in holding that our natures are saved from despair and inaction by the fact that our passions and instincts commit us to these beliefs in spite of reason's limits. Within these commitments, however, reason does have the power to attain probable conclusions about the world of our common life, and to organize our understanding of that world in the sciences. But grander issues of life's meaning and the origin of all things are beyond our faculties. Hume calls this position 'mitigated scepticism' (Hume 1999: 207).

A natural reaction to this position is to wonder why he does not consider religious beliefs, equally, to be instinctive human commitments. Hume is very aware of this response, which requires him to give an alternative account of why so many of us believe what he does not. He is also intensely aware of the fact that his skepticism has to face the challenge of those who have argued, both in his time and since, that the observation and reflection that gives us science can also show us that the world science describes to us shows indubitable signs of God's intelligent design. He tries to answer the first problem in the *Natural History of Religion*, and the second in the *Dialogues*.

Miracles

Hume's essay 'Of miracles' is perhaps his most famous work, and has generated great controversy. It appeared as Section X of the *Enquiry Concerning Human Understanding*, but it is generally believed that its key argument was developed by Hume during his years in France, and was originally intended to be included in the *Treatise of Human Nature*. By the time of the *Enquiry's* publication, there had been a considerable amount of printed controversy on miracles, and Hume came quite late to the English debate (Burns 1981). Much of that debate had been generated by the Deists, who believed that the order of the world revealed by Newtonian science showed it to be the work of a divine mind, but that such a mind would not need to disturb the order it had created by indulging in miraculous interventions (Byrne 1989). The Deists' orthodox opponents had held that the historical evidence for the miracles of the New Testament showed the truth of the Christian claim that God had intervened in history in the life and resurrection of Jesus. Hume's essay comes down on the side of the Deists in this controversy, although this is as far as his sympathy with them extends.

Hume does not deal with the broad issue of whether there are miracles or not. His agreement with the Deists is over how we ought to respond to the *evidence* for them. That evidence, of course, consists of testimony, and Hume's conclusion about it is that 'no human testimony can have such force as to prove a miracle, and make it a just foundation for any ... system of religion' (Hume 1999: 184).

Hume's argument for his negative conclusion is in two parts, both of them essential to his case. The first (and more original) part is wholly general. A wise man, Hume says, proportions his belief to the evidence. When we are told that some event of importance has taken place, a wise decision requires us to consider both the sort of event that is reported, and the quality of the testimony we have for it. The alleged event may be commonplace, unusual, or unheard-of. The testimony may be recent or old, expert or uninformed, and it may come from persons who are honest and impartial, or biased and gullible. In assessing these factors, we have to depend on our own experience, both experience of comparable events and experience of these and other witnesses. Our resulting assessment may lead to a conflict: the event may be likely enough, but the testimony weak; or the testimony may be impressive but the event highly unlikely. When such conflicts arise, we should suspend judgment.

If the event we are told of is truly miraculous, there is a special factor to consider. A miracle is not merely marvelous, but a 'violation of the laws of nature.' (In a footnote Hume adds 'by a particular volition of the Deity, or by the interposition of some invisible agent.' However necessary this addition is, it does not contribute to Hume's core argument.) In such a case there is uniform past experience against it. Nothing like it has ever happened before. This constitutes a complete 'proof' that any report of it must be untrue. But if the testimony we have for it were impeccably strong, this would amount to a contrary 'proof' that it must have happened! The only wise response to such a 'counterpoise' is suspense of judgment – not acceptance.

The essay continues with a second part in which Hume offers some less original comments on the quality of the miracle testimony that we actually have. It has never approached impeccability. Instead of being impartial and critical, people commonly have a longing for the marvelous and exciting and are happy to pass on stories of wondrous happenings. Miracle stories come from 'ignorant and barbarous' nations. And the miracle tales of one religion cancel out those of another. In these circumstances, the only wise course is not suspense of judgment but denial.

Hume's key contention is that the uniform past experience that lies behind our prior knowledge of the natural law that a miracle would violate, has to be weighed against the testimony that such a miracle has happened. But since this still leaves open the theoretical possibility that this could be balanced by perfect testimony, the arguments of the second part are necessary to complete the case for his negative verdict.

Hume's numerous critics have pointed to the fact that all our learning requires us to accept some testimony that is not put to the test of our own experience; that his argument leaves no room for the cumulative effect of repeated testimony to phenomena we are reluctant to recognize; that the likelihood of a miracle is partly a result of the prior likelihood of the world's being due to the creation of a God who might wish to intervene in it on rare occasions to instruct us; and that some of our actual miracle testimony is better than he says (Swinburne 1970; Fogelin 2003).

Design and providence

Hume clearly believed that his case against miracle testimony was decisive, whatever one thought about God's likely inclination to intervene in his creation. So in making his case, he does not discuss the popular 'Design' argument that both sides in the long miracle debate agreed was a conclusive proof of God's existence. In 'Of a particular providence and of a future state,' he argues against that argument in a way that foreshadows the much more detailed examination in the *Dialogues* (Hume 1999: 187–98). His style is far more indirect and cautious than it is in Section X.

He first presents a lengthy case for holding that even if the Design argument is accepted, it has no practical implications. He invents an imaginary friend who tells of a supposed debate between Epicurus and the citizens of Athens, who are supposed to think that his doubts about the gods are morally dangerous. Epicurus defends himself by saying that even if the workings of nature do show that 'Jupiter' has designed them, this only establishes that Jupiter has the power to bring about the world we see around us. It cannot show that he has the power to produce a better one, or that the one he has produced is a mere porch of entry to another beyond it. To conclude either of these things one has to exceed all available evidence. Hence the calculation of the wisest and most virtuous form of life cannot be rationally founded on suppositions about Jupiter's wishes or future rewards and punishments, but only on the observation of the observable effects of our choices in the present world. So a sober estimate of the value of the Design argument shows it has no practical importance.

Hume then, in his own person, asks his friend whether it is not common for us to ascribe greater powers to agents than to the products we see they have made – as when we suppose a builder capable of completing the unfinished house we see before us. The friend replies that this inference is justified only because we have prior experience of artificers who have completed tasks they have begun. In the case of the world, no such prior experience is available to us.

The essay concludes with a more fundamental criticism of the Design argument, which Hume presents in his own person. It depends on Hume's revolutionary analysis of the nature of causal relationships in Sections IV to VII of the *Enquiry*. On that analysis, to say that one event or agent is the cause of another is to say that phenomena of the first kind have been regularly followed by phenomena of the second kind. For every causal relationship there is a law connecting one *species* of event with another. But the universe is unique. So how can our normal mode of causal reasoning help us to determine how the world has come to be?

Hume's critics have argued that the uniqueness of the universe is not in fact a barrier to speculation about its origin, any more than it prevents our forming theories like that of 'Big Bang' cosmology.

The natural history of religion

If the inference from the world's order to the existence of God is not sound, why has it always seemed so natural? Hume attempts to answer this in the *Natural History*, in which he gives a historical account of how the idea of the Judeo-Christian God is ready to hand in our minds when we engage in philosophical reflection (Hume 1957). He begins by distinguishing between religion's 'foundation in reason' and its 'origin in human nature.' From time to time Hume pays manifestly insincere lip service to the received view that the 'frame of nature' makes it clear to us that it is the work of a single deity. The present work, he says, is not about such philosophical foundations, but about religion's actual origins. He makes two claims at the outset. First, religion is not a universal phenomenon. Hence its widespread presence cannot be due to an 'original instinct.' 'The first religious principles must be secondary' (Hume 1957: 21). They are due to circumstances that may sometimes be absent. Second, religious beliefs originate not in human recognition of natural order, but in response to striking and mysterious natural events like storms and sicknesses. Humans ascribe these to hidden personal causes. These causes are powerful, but still finite, spirits whom we feel we have to propitiate. Hence primitive religion is polytheistic, not monotheistic. Hume here rejects, by an appeal to evidence, the view held both by orthodox thinkers and by the Deists, that humanity was originally aware of one almighty creator, and that this awareness was later corrupted into idolatry. Idolatry, in his view, was where all religion began.

Polytheism, however, has the seeds of monotheism built into it, Hume says. Devotees of restricted and local deities naturally tend to accord pre-eminence to leading gods among them, and then to ascribe qualities to their favored candidates that guarantee their unique status. The intrinsic logic of worship inflates the conception of its object. Even in the loyalty given to princes, there is sometimes the ultimate flattery found in calling them gods. 'How much more natural, therefore, is it, that a limited deity ... should in the end be represented as sovereign maker and modifier of the universe?' (Hume 1957: 43). Religious life in consequence involves an oscillation between adoration of an ultimate God who is altogether transcendent and beyond our capacity to reach, and forms of worship that give him a more intimate and human character that is more in keeping with a limited and familiar spirit. This instability in advanced religion is combined with a corruption of reason in which the faithful are obliged to praise and defend the cosmic policies of a being in whom they have come to believe because of primal fears.

Hume's portrait of religion in the *Natural History* is a dark one that he uses to suggest that it is an inevitable source of intolerance and hypocrisy, and to explain that the key concept of the almighty God of monotheism has evolved from sources that make it the natural beneficiary of the arguments of philosophers who seek ultimate explanations. But although this idea is ready to hand for them, he does not think orthodox theism (or deism) is justified by their arguments. This negative judgment on natural theology is the theme of the *Dialogues* (Hume 1980).

Dialogues Concerning Natural Religion

This great work defies adequate summary. Hume went to great pains on its revision at the close of his life, and in spite of the clarity of its individual arguments, there are some well-known ambiguities in it that stand in the way of any confident interpretation of its overall intent.

The subject, natural religion, is that set of supposed truths about God's being and nature that can be established, or shown to be probable, by human reason alone. The argument that is intended to establish these truths is the Argument from Design. This argument, held in common by both the orthodox and the Deists of that age, was an attempt to ground belief in God on the same sort of reasoning one might use to establish a scientific conclusion. It was therefore the one form of theistic argument that Hume's theory of knowledge would make it reasonable to consider. The use of such argument is sometimes called 'empirical theism.'

There are three characters in the debate. The proponent of empirical theism is Cleanthes, whose pupil, Pamphilus, describes the day's discussions to his friend Hermippus. Cleanthes' two respondents are Philo, said to be a 'careless' skeptic, and Demea, whose responses manifest 'rigid inflexible orthodoxy' and a preference for a priori argument like the Cosmological Proof. Most readers today incline to identify Hume with Philo, in spite of the fact that Pamphilus says at the end that he thinks Cleanthes has won; but we have to approach such identifications with caution. Hume makes ingenious use of the dialogue form to bring out tensions in philosophical

143

theism: for example, Philo joins with Demea in stressing the depths of evil in the cosmos, leaving Cleanthes to appear facilely optimistic, and it is Cleanthes, not Philo, who attacks Demea's attempt to prove God's existence a priori rather than from evidence, thus demonstrating the divisions in the theistic camp.

The work is in twelve Parts. Part One is a discussion of the role and limits of skepticism. Cleanthes suggests that skeptical arguments undermine common sense and science and would paralyze humans into inactivity. Philo agrees that life requires commitment, but says that our faculties are not great enough to determine such lofty matters as the nature of God. Cleanthes, however, has an argument that he presents, in Part Two, to show that God's being, intelligence and goodness can be shown by an appeal to the evidence. So the *Dialogues* does not begin by assuming the correctness of Hume's mitigated skepticism; it is better understood as a lengthy attempt to determine whether it is true.

Cleanthes' argument is as follows. The world is one vast machine, divided into a vast number of lesser machines. Experience teaches us that machines are made by human minds. By analogy, therefore, we should conclude that the world is made by a mind like ours, but infinitely greater.

Philo attacks at once. He uses arguments reminiscent of Section XI of the *Enquiry*. The analogy between the world and a machine is very imprecise, and is based on a comparison between the whole of the universe and some small parts of it. Furthermore, the order we find in machines may be due to human intelligence, but the order and adaptation we find elsewhere in nature is not observed to be due to intelligence, but to other factors, such as animal or vegetable reproduction. (To say these cannot be the real causes is to assume the argument's conclusion in its premises.) And causal inferences require us to observe phenomena of one kind being followed by phenomena of another kind, whereas the universe is (necessarily) unique.

This set of counterarguments is followed by another. Both Demea and Philo see difficulty in Cleanthes' likening of the divine mind to human minds – Demea because this detracts from the infinity and otherness of God, Philo because the human analogy would suggest that God's mind depends (as ours do) upon a body that houses it, and might in its turn have external causes. Furthermore, the anthropomorphism to which Cleanthes is prone would also suggest that the creator's mind has limitations that explain defects in its product, as human limitations explain defects in machines; it suggests that the creation, like human artifacts, is the result of trial and error; and it even suggests that the world might be the handiwork of a number of minds, rather than of one. Perhaps, also, the creator is mortal, as we are.

If the analogy with human intelligence has awkward implications, other analogies that are equally plausible have even more heterodox consequences. The world is as similar to an organism as it is to a machine, so perhaps God is the soul of the world, not outside it; or perhaps the world is the result of some analogue of animal or vegetable generation. And Philo now, in Part Eight, revives the theory of the ancient Atomists, that the motion of ultimate particles initially gave rise to combinations that held together by pure chance, and that some of these continued in being because their structures accidentally had survival value, whereas the others were destroyed, thus leaving us with a cosmos that was accidental in origin but looks designed – an intriguing anticipation of the doctrine of natural selection. Philo's purpose in all these suggestions is not to urge their truth but to emphasize that they have as much intrinsic plausibility as Cleanthes' hypothesis does.

Wearied by these alternatives, Demea interrupts in Part Nine with a version of the classic Cosmological Argument, which is dismissed (by Cleanthes) in one paragraph, whose main burden is that no matter of fact can be demonstrated by an argument that does not lean on evidence.

Parts Ten and Eleven contain two subtle and intricate discussions of evil. Philo and Demea both say, each with his own motive, that the evils in the world are deep and widespread. Cleanthes, in response, agrees that his religious purpose requires him to show that God is benevolent as well as powerful and intelligent. So he insists that their estimate of the gravity of the world's evils is exaggerated, and that the good in the world greatly outweighs its evils. Philo responds to this not by questioning its truth, but by pointing out the implication of Cleanthes' tacit admission that the world, however good overall, still has much evil in it. Here, he says, he triumphs over Cleanthes. For Cleanthes (unlike Demea) has to prove God's goodness *from the evidence*; and while it may be possible to *reconcile* the evils in the world with the perfect goodness of God, the evidence as we find it does not of itself *suggest* it. In Part Eleven Cleanthes responds by abandoning the claim that God's power and goodness are infinite – they are merely very great. He then has to listen while Philo says what he thinks the evidence actually shows. Pain is of great biological importance, when it surely need not be. A deity who retained the appearances of natural law while adjusting its details to spare us calamities could avoid many of the evils we experience. Nature indeed gives her creatures useful powers, but often bestows them in inadequate amounts. And it also provides some benefits in quantities that are far too great for anyone's good, as we see in droughts and floods. In such a mixed world, the most plausible thesis is that the mind or minds that cause the world are a mixture of good and bad, or, more likely still, 'have neither goodness nor malice.'

Part Twelve has puzzled many readers. Demea, exasperated, has left the company, and Philo hints that he can now speak to Cleanthes with greater candor. But he then appears to pay surprising lip service to the very argument he has been attacking for the last ten Parts. He and Cleanthes proceed to have a lengthy discussion about the differences between 'true' and 'false' religion. They debate, in fact, many of the issues that Hume has addressed previously in the *Natural History*. Philo stresses the evils of popular religiosity, and Cleanthes warns him of the risks of abandoning even true religion in his zeal to avoid the defects of the false kind. One interpretation of this final Part (and it is not the only one) is that Philo, more or less representing Hume himself, is prepared to accept Cleanthes' natural religion because the prior discussions have by this time emptied it of all significant content, and that the most human reason can show us is (as Philo puts it in the conclusion) that 'the cause or causes of order in the universe probably bear some remote analogy to human intelligence.' This conclusion is so vague that it has no specific practical implications. But this toothless theism (or deism) is equivalent in practice to the liberal theology of Hume's clerical friends, and although it is doubtful whether Hume believed even this much, it is not a theism that would have caused him anxiety in practice. 'True religion' is not *true*; it is rather too vague to matter. As Philo says to Cleanthes in conclusion, a 'sound, believing Christian' must first be a philosophical skeptic and avoid all dogmatism.

If this reading of the import of the conclusion of the *Dialogues* is the right one, Hume's position at the end of his life is identical to that which we find in Section XI of the *Enquiry*. Human reason has been shown to have no power to establish the reality of the God of orthodox theism on the basis of empirical evidence; but the bland and empty religion to which Cleanthes' position has been reduced is socially and personally acceptable to Hume, precisely because it has no significant content, and therefore no practical implications. Those who wish to resist such a conclusion (if this is indeed what Hume intends) must either attempt to answer his critique of the arguments of empirical theism, or seek a different route to theism, perhaps through a direct appeal to religious experience.

See also The cosmological argument (Chapter 32), The teleological argument (Chapter 33), The problem of evil (Chapter 37), Miracles (Chapter 55).

References

Burns, R. M. (1981) *The Great Debate on Miracles: From Joseph Glanvil to David Hume*, Lewisburg, PA: Bucknell University Press.

Byrne, P. (1989) *Natural Religion and the Nature of Religion: The Legacy of Deism*, London: Routledge.

Fogelin, R. (2003) *A Defense of Hume on Miracles*, Princeton, NJ: Princeton University Press.

Hume, D. (2000) [1739–40] *A Treatise of Human Nature*, ed. D. F. Norton and M. J. Norton, New York: Oxford University Press.

—— (1999) [1748] *An Enquiry Concerning Human Understanding*, ed. T. Beauchamp, Oxford: Clarendon Press.

—— (1980) [1779] *Dialogues Concerning Natural Religion*, ed. N. K. Smith, Indianapolis, IN: Bobbs-Merrill.

—— (1957) [1757] *The Natural History of Religion*, ed. H. E. Root, Stanford, CA: Stanford University Press.

Mossner, E. C. (1970) *The Life of David Hume*, Oxford: Clarendon Press.

Penelhum, T. (1992) *David Hume: An Introduction to his Philosophical System*, Lafayette, IN: Purdue University Press.

Sher, R. B. (1985) *Church and University in the Scottish Enlightenment*, Edinburgh: Edinburgh University Press.

Swinburne, R. (1970) *The Concept of Miracle*, London: Macmillan.

Further reading

Flew, A. G. N. (1961) *Hume's Philosophy of Belief: A Study of his First Enquiry*, London: Routledge & Kegan Paul. (Classic examination of this work, with valuable chapters on Sections X and XI.)

Gaskin, J. C. A. (1988) *Hume's Philosophy of Religion*, 2nd edn, London: Macmillan. (The standard work; comprehensive, sympathetic, accurate.)

Hurlbutt, R. H. (1965) *Hume, Newton, and the Design Argument*, Lincoln, NE: University of Nebraska Press. (See Hume's critique of the Design Argument in its full historical context.)

Sessions, W. L. (2002) *Reading Hume's Dialogues: A Veneration for True Religion*, Bloomington, IN: Indiana University Press. (An elegant and meticulous commentary.)

Sennett, J. F. and D. Groothuis, (eds) (2005) *In Defense of Natural Theology: A Post-Humean Assessment*, Downers Grove, IL: InterVarsity Press. (Contemporary answers to Hume's criticisms.)

Swinburne, R. (1979) *The Existence of God*, Oxford: Clarendon Press. (An impressive attempt to reinstate natural theology in the face of Hume's objections.)

Yandell, K. E. (1990) *Hume's 'Inexplicable Mystery': His Views on Religion*, Philadelphia: Temple University Press. (A critical and sophisticated study, giving due prominence to the *Natural History*.)

14

IMMANUEL KANT

Paul Abela

Introduction

The work of the late eighteenth-century German philosopher Immanuel Kant (1724–1804) is emblematic of the Enlightenment's attempt to square the authority of unfettered reason with the inherited tradition of Christian belief. Although Kant offers no separable 'philosophy of religion' in the modern sense, religious themes are rarely distant from his thought. In the field of knowledge, Kant claims that reason is incapable of supplying any possible proof for God's existence or supporting evidence for his existence. In the domain of moral judgment, Kant contends that belief in God, the soul, and an afterlife are necessary postulates of practical reason. In the sphere of religious belief proper, Kant locates the relevance of revealed religion in the context of its moral dimension, coordinating these moral claims in the architecture of a distilled pure rational religion.

Although these themes are present in many of Kant's texts, in his mature work the central texts are the *Critique of Pure Reason* (1781, 1787) the *Critique of Practical Reason* (1788), and concerning the relation of pure rational religion with ecclesiastical faith, *Religion within the Boundaries of Mere Reason* (1793) and *The Conflict of the Faculties* (1798).

If there is an abiding meta-commitment that unites all of Kant's writings, it is his unswerving commitment to the authority, autonomy, and boundaries of human judgment. Kant's unique mix of rationalist and empiricist concerns, forged in his new transcendental idealist model, places great emphasis on (1) determining the limits and preconditions of cognition and (2) grounding empirical claims within the boundaries of possible experience. Given the complex relation between religious belief and reason, and the equally intricate relation existing between commitments of faith and evidenced empirical belief, Kant's unique treatment of religious themes is of particular contemporary urgency.

God's existence: knowledge and its limits

Kant famously claimed in the *Critique of Pure Reason* that he had to deny knowledge in order to make room for faith (B xxx). Unlike philosophers such as Pascal, who challenged the suitability of reason as a vehicle for religious commitment, Kant's negative claim is directed only to reason in its theoretical employment – as it concerns knowledge claims – not to reason per se. Reason in its practical employment bears the entire weight of the positive Kantian program. Understanding the Kantian shift away from affirming religious belief in terms of knowledge is crucial for an adequate appreciation of the link he forges between practical reason and religious belief.

Whatever standing one may grant to contemporary arguments for God's existence, reason-based proofs occupied a privileged position in early modern philosophy. Rationalist philosophers ranging from dualists like Descartes, to monists such as Spinoza, to essentialists like Leibniz, all devoted considerable energy to offering demonstrations for God's existence that appealed strictly to the conceptual resources of reason. Even some empiricists, Locke for example, granted a role to reason-based proof as a legitimate means for affirming belief in God. Kant's denial of the possibility of such knowledge is aptly described by the German Enlightenment figure Moses Mendelssohn as an 'all-crushing' (*Allzermalmer*) outcome.

The Kantian rejection of a role for theoretical reason in the field of religious belief is motivated by two considerations: (1) the limits of what *pure* reason can in principle deliver concerning ontological commitment, and (2) the broadly empiricist claim that nothing within experience can provide a sufficient evidential basis for the existence of transcendent objects (God, the soul).

Concerning the limited reach of pure reason, Kant claims that all such arguments for God's existence fail. His analysis frames the issue in terms of three generic proof-types – ontological, cosmological, or physico-theological (design) – claiming that all possible proofs fall under one of these types. He directs his most withering critique against the ontological argument. While challenging the remaining two, he asserts that the physico-theological reduces ultimately to the cosmological, and the cosmological in its turn to the ontological.

Although the details of these proofs are well beyond the bounds of this essay, the following can serve as a thumbnail sketch of the general strategy, beginning with the dominant argument against the ontological argument.

The ontological proof identifies arguments that attempt to affirm God's existence on entirely a priori grounds, from mere concepts alone. The example that occupies much of Kant's attention is Descartes's argument of the Fifth Meditation, but Kant's argument applies to the whole class (Anselm, etc.). What these arguments share is the thought that existence can operate as a predicate, and that the concept of a highest being must, by definition alone, contain this predicate. In the same manner as when one thinks of a triangle such that one cannot deny the property that it contains three angles, so too, when one entertains the concept of a highest being – designating an object that contains all predicates within itself – we are caught in a contradiction if we deny this predicate. Hence we can extract, as an analytical truth, the proposition that God exists.

Kant's challenge goes to the heart of the proof strategy:

> If I cancel the predicate in an identical judgment and keep the subject, then a contradiction arises; hence I say that the former necessarily pertains to the latter. But if I cancel the subject together with the predicate, then no contradiction arises; for there is *no longer anything* that could be contradicted. To posit a triangle and cancel its three angles is contradictory; but to cancel the triangle together with its three angles is not a contradiction. It is exactly the same thing with the concept of an absolutely necessary being. If you cancel its existence, then you cancel the thing itself with all its predicates; where then is the contradiction supposed to come from? (B 622–3, emphasis in original, here and throughout)

We can register the force of Kant's response in the general thought that the determination of the existence of an object – any object including the highest being – is a matter that stands outside the merely discursive domain. The attempt to derive existence by means of mere concepts is a kind of category mistake. Conceptual analysis can offer no more than an exhaustive description of the discursive marks (*Merkmal*) that identify the function of a given concept. In other words, by means of conceptual analysis we can make self-conscious the individuating activity of the function expressed by a concept (allowing us ever more fine-grained knowledge of what objects, if any, fall under the concept), but we garner no knowledge of whether there *are* objects that fall under the expressed concept.

The cosmological and design arguments are perhaps more familiar in popular literature. The family of proofs Kant identifies with the cosmological argument asserts the reality of a necessary being on the basis of the need to logically ground the existence of contingent beings. This necessary being is then conceptually linked to the idea of a highest being. The cosmological argument thus has one foot in the empirical domain in so far as it begins with the empirical claim that something exists (usually taken as no more than the thought that 'I am'). Kant claims that the final move in the argument, from a necessary being to a highest being, is no more than a camouflaged appeal to the ontological strategy. Moreover he claims that, even on its own ground, the argument fails insofar as it surreptitiously invokes the category of causality as the necessary bridge between contingent existence and necessary existence. As causal judgments, on the Kantian reading, have significance only within the bounds of possible experience, invoking a cause for all the causes of the world constitutes a leap from the meaningful use of the concept *within* the temporally structured world to a senseless notion of causation *outside* the conditions of temporal structure.

The design argument is the most empirical of the three argument strategies. As we find with modern 'intelligent design' hypotheses, the design argument begins with the empirical reality of nature as a system, reflecting on its intelligible structure and asserting the existence of a creative intelligence as cause. While granting this argument a special place among the three – '[t]his proof always deserves to be named with respect. It is the oldest, clearest and most appropriate to common human reason' (B 651) – Kant maintains that at best, on its own terms, it delivers no more than the idea of an architect working 'who would always be limited by the suitability of the material on which he works, but not *a creator of the world*' (B 655). The attempt to move beyond this limited analogical conclusion invariably reintroduces the cosmological argument (as necessary cause of the contingent status of matter) and once again collapses into the ontological.

While the above sketch offers only a crude outline of Kant's position, the force of the approach, and the extraordinary break with tradition signaled by it, is apparent. After the *Critique of Pure Reason*, the idea that knowledge of the existence of God could be secured by means of a priori proofs is never again a driving force in the Enlightenment's engagement with religious belief.

It is also important to note that the priority Kant attaches to possible experience as the ultimate ground for evidenced belief leaves no room for the possibility that experiential assertions can stand in evidential relations to statements that assert the existence of transcendent objects (God, the soul). Knowledge claims, according to Kant, can never transcend the experiential domain of objects given in space and time subject to the conditions of human judgment (Kant's categories). As the 'conditions of the *possibility of experience* in general are at the same time conditions of the *possibility of the objects of experience*' (B 197), putative knowledge claims that invoke transcendental objects as their cause, or support transcendental objects as effect, are necessarily illegitimate as *claims of knowledge*.

A final implication that should be drawn from Kant's strategy of locating religious belief outside the sphere of knowledge is the immediate inference that while it is impossible to support belief in God (or the soul or an afterlife) by means of theoretical proof or experiential belief, it is also not possible for theoretical reason to disprove commitments of faith. Although this may appear to be of little significance, it occupies an important place in the Kantian account. For example, in response to J. G. Sulzer's expressed hope that the weaknesses of the proofs in God's existence might one day be overcome, Kant claims

> this will never happen. For whence will reason derive the ground for such synthetic assertions, which are not related to objects of experience and their inner possibility? But it is also apodictically certain that no human being will ever step forward who could assert the *opposite* with the least plausibility … whence will he derive the knowledge that would justify him in judging synthetically about things beyond all possible experience? (B 770)

Kant's denial that religious commitments are within the purview of knowledge assertions is thus a two-edged sword. It severs all a priori and empirical support for transcendent claims while at the same time extinguishing all possible arguments for atheism based on a priori and empirical grounds. While closing the door to all such knowledge claims, Kant simultaneously chokes off the possibility that reason in its practical employment might be challenged by disconfirming arguments or evidence from the side of theoretical reason. This effectively sequesters the contribution of practical reason, and secures, negatively, the possibility of affirming religious belief from the practical standpoint.

Practical reason: morality and pure rational religion

It is the determining role of practical reason that stands center stage for understanding Kant's treatment of religion. Emblematic claims such as 'So far as practical reason has the right to lead us, we will not hold actions to be obligatory because they are God's commands, but will rather regard them as divine commands because we are internally obligated to them' (B 847), and 'on its own behalf morality in no way needs religion ... but is rather self-sufficient by virtue of pure practical reason' (R 3) speak directly to the priority Kant attaches to the self-determining character of the moral sphere. On the other hand, claims like 'Morality thus inevitably leads to religion' (R 6) suggest a more complex relationship. The relation of ecclesiastical faith to practical reason is considered in the following section. To get there we must first introduce the architecture Kant deploys in his account of the aims of practical reason. It is in this context that Kant first introduces the defining religious concepts of God and the immortality of the soul.

While Kant's moral philosophy is known for many things, the categorical imperative, the importance of pure rational incentives (duty) for action, and perhaps a deserved sense of things largely ignored (emotion, social solidarity, weakness of the will, etc.), what is most relevant in the immediate context is the teleological character of Kant's account of the aims of action. Not unlike philosophers such as Aristotle, Kant endorses the view that all action has a final aim that is itself not in need of further justification: a highest good. Kant claims that the goal of making ourselves worthy of happiness constitutes this ultimate end (CPrR 110-111).

Kant locates the concept of the highest good in the synthetic unity of virtue and happiness: virtue as an unconditioned requirement, happiness given in proportion to virtue. Unlike happiness-driven accounts of the good life, the Kantian treatment asserts that a life of happiness unconditioned by virtue would be an unworthy life, empty of moral significance. This is a reflection of Kant's well-known commitment to situating moral value exclusively within the activity of moral deliberation itself: the categorical imperative offering a criterion for identifying actions that meet the demands of universality and autonomy. Although Kant offers a number of slightly different glosses on the categorical imperative, the abiding thought is that when we act, we do so on the basis of some aim or purpose, constituted by a reason for the action. Kant claims that the reason we cite for any prospective morally valuable action must be valid for all similarly situated individuals. In acting on a maxim that can be universalized without contradiction, I express my moral agency through a principle that is necessarily impartial and universal in scope. As such, I treat others as ends in themselves rather than as mere means for the realization of my own interests, and I locate my moral projects in a manner that respects their self-determined interests and aims.

This does not entail, as is sometimes thought, an insular conception of moral agency. The relevant Kantian point is simply that the demands of morality speak to us in the voice of duty, transcending the idiosyncratic push and pull of our psychological propensities or cultural proclivities. Moving in the other direction, a life of virtue that is without happiness would be, according to Kant, an incomplete life: 'For, to need happiness, to be also worthy of it, and yet not to participate in it cannot be consistent with the perfect volition of a rational being' (CPrR 110). The need for happiness is man's ineliminable natural end.

Kant maintains that practical reason requires, for the possibility of representing its own efficacy, that the realization of the highest good be regarded as *achievable*:

> to promote the practically possible highest good, nevertheless presupposes at least that the latter is *possible*; in the contrary case it would be practically impossible to strive for the object of a concept that would be, at bottom, empty and without an object. (CPrR 143)

Short of this goal, practical reason would be involved in an *ad absurdum practicum*: seeking to actualize an aim that it cannot represent as reachable. Without adequate grounds for securing this requirement, practical reason becomes self-nullifying.

Kant's response to this worry is deceptively simple. From the practical standpoint, ought implies can. The necessity expressed by an 'ought' directly implies that there *must* be some way that we can discharge our duty. As Kant suggests: 'in the practical task of pure reason, that is, in the necessary pursuit of the highest good, such a connection is postulated as necessary: we *ought* to strive to promote the highest good (which must therefore be possible)' (CPrR 125).

Sadly, even the briefest survey of the mundane or grand features of the human condition demonstrates that no such assurance can be found with the empirical resources at hand. The shattering effect of the Lisbon earthquake on the imagination of the Enlightenment squelched forever the idea that the empirical arrangement of nature offered a purely natural relation to humanity's moral needs. The satirical charm of Voltaire's *Candide* pushed the point forever beyond reason's reach. As Kant registers the general lesson: 'it is not always within our power to provide ourselves with happiness, and the course of nature does not of itself conform to merit … [that our] good fortune in life (our welfare in general) depends, rather, on circumstances that are far from all being in our control' (MM 482). Nonetheless, while such an empirically contingent misalignment is unthreatening in itself, it cannot be the case, on pain of the *ad absurdum practicum*, that there exists a *real* gap between virtue and proportionate happiness.

It is the practical commitment to the existence of God (as the creator of a moral order), and the notion of the immortality of the soul that bridges this chasm. We are able to conceive of how God, as creator and as a moral judge, calibrates virtue with proportionate happiness: 'the existence of a cause of all nature, distinct from nature, which contains the ground of this connection; namely the exact correspondence of happiness with morality, is also *postulated*' (CPrR 125), if not in this world, then in the afterlife. Moreover, as the struggle to realize the highest good is set for us as an unending task, belief in the immortality of the soul is a precondition for representing the enduring struggle toward moral perfection (see *CPrR* 122–4).

These practical commitments, what Kant calls 'practical postulates,' have a different epistemic status from knowledge claims. Where knowledge claims fall somewhere between opinion and truth, necessary practical commitments fall under the category of rational belief or faith (*Glaube*). Rational belief operates in the context where we have complete subjective conviction in the concept, but where we also know that we cannot assert the objective reality of the object (which would be a knowledge claim): 'believing is a holding true which is subjectively sufficient, but *consciously* regarded as objectively insufficient; thus it is contrasted with *knowing*' (*WOT* 141). In this way, a firewall is maintained between the deliverances of reason in its practical employment and the negative results of reason in its theoretical use. Belief in God and the soul is sustained from the standpoint of the conditions of human action, while no knowledge claims are implicated.

It is important to note that while Kant's strategy for affirming belief in God is usefully described as a 'moral proof' to contrast it with theoretical proofs, 'transcendental proof' is more apt since the approach is rooted in an analysis of the preconditions necessary for the possibility of consciously determined activity.

Religious commitment: pure rational faith and revealed religion

Given that moral value is determined entirely within the architecture of practical reason, and that commitments to God and the immortality of the soul are rooted in the a priori demands of the highest good, one could be excused for thinking that revealed religion would have no place in Kant's approach. Instead, Kant devotes substantial attention in his work of the 1790s toward explicating the relation of the practical postulates and the deliverances of revealed religion. Unfortunately, Kant offers conflicting signals on this matter. In this section I canvass a core set of commitments and comment on two competing trajectories that emerge.

These core commitments involve: (1) the claim that the significance of religious belief is located entirely within the drive to cultivate one's moral disposition, (2) a subordinate role assigned to ecclesiastical faith, (3) an argument that identifies the relevant ecclesiastical faith(s) that meet the conditions of pure rational faith. Beyond this core set, a fourth element is also relevant: (4) the expectation that ecclesiastical faith gradually falls away as self-critical forms of culture develop. An assessment of the cogency of (4) separates reductive from non-reductive interpretations of the relation of rational faith and revealed religion.

(1) Kant's position begins with the assertion that the bearing of religious belief is expressed exclusively in terms of its connection to one's moral disposition. It is only along this axis that ecclesiastical observance can have any significance:

> I accept the following proposition as a principle requiring no proof: *Apart from a good life-conduct, anything which the human being supposes that he can do*

> to become well-pleasing to God is mere religious delusion and counterfeit service of
> God. (R 170–1)

Absent its role in the cultivation of moral character, all ecclesiastical articles of faith and practices are no more than forms of religious enthusiasm (*Schwärmerei*) and superstition:

> For the final purpose of even the reading of these holy books, or the investigation of their content, is to make better human beings; whereas their historical element, which contributes nothing to this end, is something in itself quite indifferent, and one can do with it what one wills. (R 111)

In addition to the entirely practical character of religious observance, Kant, as we have seen, grants to religion no expansion of moral content:

> As far as its matter i.e. object is concerned, religion does not differ in any point from morality, for it is concerned with duties as such. Its distinction from morality is a merely formal one; that reason in its legislation uses the Idea of God which is derived from morality itself, to give morality influence on man's will to fulfill all his duties. (CF 36)

(2) Kant does not flinch from the obvious inference entailed by this privileging of the autonomy of the moral domain. Should moral concepts come into conflict with the dictates of religious tradition or articles of ecclesiastical faith, it is the dictates of revealed religion that must give way. The commands of ecclesiastical faith are subordinate to the demands of morality. More than simply challenging the authority of command theories of the good – that a principle or action is good because God commands it – Kant leverages the independence and priority of moral value to infer further that, should we find a religious moral claim to be contrary to our moral duties, we have legitimate grounds to deny divine authorship for such command:

> For if God should really speak to a human being, the latter could still never *know* that it was God speaking. It is quite impossible for a human being to apprehend the infinite by his senses, distinguish it from sensible beings, and *be acquainted with* it as such. – But in some cases the human being can be sure that the voice he hears is *not* God's; for if the voice commands him to do something contrary to the moral law, then no matter how majestic the apparition may be, and no matter how it may seem to surpass the whole of nature, he must consider it an illusion. (CF 63)

Given the weight Kierkegaard was to grant to the account of the sacrifice of Isaac, Kant's example is prescient and throws into sharp relief the enormous separation of the mature eighteenth-century Kantian treatment from the rejection-of-reason approaches characteristic of romantic and post-romantic philosophy of the nineteenth. For Kant there is no gap between moral commitment and the religious impulse, hence no need for the Kierkegaardian leap.

The subordinate status of revealed religion underwrites its role as a vehicle for the demands of rational faith:

> The canon of religion can be called *pure religious faith* (which has no statutes and is based on mere reason); its vehicle can be called *ecclesiastical faith*, which is based entirely on statutes that need to be revealed in order to hold as sacred doctrines and precepts for conduct. (CF 37)

(3) The justification Kant offers for identifying Christianity as the historical embodiment of the demands of practical reason is a topic to itself, well beyond the bounds of this survey. Although Kant offers a good deal by way of justification, including introducing the competing traditions of Abrahamic religion as well as non-monotheistic traditions, it is difficult for the modern reader to view these arguments without some sense of special pleading. The following passage is representative:

> Yet Christianity has the great advantage over Judaism of being represented as coming *from the mouth of the first teacher* not as a statutory but as a moral religion. And since it treads in the closest proximity to reason, it was capable through reason to propagate with the greatest assuredness by itself, even without historical scholarship, at all times and among all people. (R 167)

Kant identifies Christianity as uniquely manifesting the inward demands of the moral life. He interprets the ecclesiastical expression of this demand for inwardness in ways that capture the self-determination and respect for humanity that is consonant with the requirements of practical reason itself. Hence Kant interprets the teachings and statutory expressions of Christianity as if, on x-ray, they illuminate the underlying moral structure enforced by practical reason. The following is but one of many examples of scriptural exegesis offered in this vein:

> First, he [the Christ] maintains that not the observance of external civil or statutory ecclesiastical duties but only the pure moral disposition of the heart can make a human being well-pleasing to God (Matthew, 5.20–48); that sins in thought are regarded in the eyes of God as equivalent to deed (5.8) … Finally, he sums up all duties (1) into one *universal* rule … namely, Do your duty from no other incentive except the unmediated appreciation of duty itself, i.e. love God (the Legislator of all duties) above all else; (2) and into a *particular* rule, one namely that concerns the human being's external relation to other human beings as universal duty, Love everyone as yourself. (R 159–61)

(4) Advancing an interpretation that successfully arbitrates between reductive and non-reductive readings of Christianity within the Kantian model is a difficult task.

Owing to the trouble Kant encountered with Prussian censorship – his 'voluntary' agreement to cease publishing in matters of religion ended only with the death of Frederick William II – it is tempting to interpret the presence of conflicting signals as itself evidence for the (at the time) officially unpopular reductive strategy. Moreover, in terms of the Enlightenment, it is plausible to think that Kant, like Lessing and many other thinkers of the period, was leaving the door open – perhaps wedging the door open – to eventually displacing the increasingly vulnerable aspects of the historical narrative of Christianity with the demands of pure rational faith. Passages such as the following tend to support this view:

> Thus, even though … a historical faith attaches itself to pure religion as its vehicle, yet, if there is consciousness that this faith is merely such and if, as the faith of a church, it carries a principle for continually coming closer to pure religious faith until finally we can dispense of that vehicle, the church in question can always be taken as the *true* one. (R 115)

Given the autonomy of the moral domain, and the fact that religious belief adds no new content to morality, this reductivist trajectory is unmistakable and not without substantial merit.

Notwithstanding, it is also clear that Kant invests a good deal of philosophical capital, in the 1790s, defending the relevance of religious commitment, suggesting a picture of mutual support between the demands of practical reason and Christianity.

This alternative image centers upon the notion that Christianity, building upon its uniquely suited historical narrative, offers an enduring empirically rooted instantiation condition for the dictates of pure practical reason. Christianity sustains the prospect of orienting moral commitment in a recognizably empirical manner. One might think of this on a parallel with Kant's arguments, drawn from his political works, against the possibility of cultivating a single world political culture. Although a committed cosmopolitan, Kant argued against the idea of world government. The driving intuition supporting this constraint is the thought that civil societies garner their character and animating identity in an environment that is capable of expressing their particular interests, organizing their unique projects, and structuring their distinctive modes of civic engagement. The republican virtues of free expression, association, etc., take on significance in these empirical settings.

On similar lines, it is possible to conceive of revealed religion operating as the historically expressed moral environment that breathes life into the a priori moral requirements of practical reason. Granted, it does not independently ground moral value. What it does supply is a moral/religious particularized context for commitment to God and the soul, rendering localized significance to otherwise abstract postulates. In this sense it serves properly not for augmenting psychological categories of commitment – a mere affect eternally hostage to the vagaries of its historical claims – but instead serves to empirically situate the task of making ourselves worthy of happiness.

Rather than seeing revealed religion as occupying a vanishing point outside the space of moral community – a segue from historical expressions to pure religion – one might instead regard ecclesiastical faith as orienting the demands for moral community in the tangled, all-too-human, field of cultural development. When Kant notes that there is a 'natural need of all human beings to demand for even the highest concepts and grounds of reason something that *the senses can hold on to*, some confirmation from experience' (R 109), he is not making a reluctant concession. We are not angels, but embodied social beings. Moral deliberation, and the task of realizing the final aim of practical reason, is not informed *sub species aeternitatis*. As such, ecclesiastical faith may, on this reading, occupy a place of lasting importance in the Kantian approach.

Conclusion

The Kantian strategy of denying knowledge to make room for faith constitutes a radical break with the received rationalist philosophical tradition. Kant locates the bearing of religious commitment entirely within the demands of practical reason. The relation of revealed religion (Christianity) to the postulates of practical reason takes the form of an instantiation condition. Whether the trajectory of Kant's approach is consonant with the general reductivist trend of other late Enlightenment thinkers, or whether revealed religion occupies an enduring position, remains an open, and pressing, contemporary question.

See also David Hume (Chapter 13), Søren Kierkegaard (Chapter 15), The ontological argument (Chapter 31), The cosmological argument (Chapter 32), The teleological argument (Chapter 33), The moral argument (Chapter 34).

References

English translations of Kant's works. Embedded citations follow standard reference protocols for the Academy Edition of (1902–) *Kants gesammelte Schriften*, Berlin: Walter de Gruyter.
Kant, I. (1781, 2nd edn, 1787) *Critique of Pure Reason* ['A,' 'B'], trans. P. Guyer and A. Wood (1996) *Immanuel Kant: Critique of Pure Reason*, New York: Cambridge University Press.
—— (1786) (WOT) *What Does it Mean to Orient Oneself in Thinking?*, trans. A. Wood (1996) *Immanuel Kant: Religion and Rational Theology*, New York: Cambridge University Press.
—— (1788) (CPrR) *Critique of Practical Reason*, trans. M. Gregor (1996) *Immanuel Kant: Practical Philosophy*, New York: Cambridge University Press.
—— (1793) (R) *Religion Within the Boundaries of Mere Reason*, trans. G. di Giovanni (1996) *Immanuel Kant: Religion and Rational Theology*, New York: Cambridge University Press.
—— (1797) (MM) *Metaphysics of Morals*, trans. M. Gregor (1996) *Immanuel Kant: Practical Philosophy*, New York: Cambridge University Press.
—— (1798) (CF) *The Conflict of the Faculties*, trans. M. Gregor and R. Anchor (1996) *Immanuel Kant: Religion and Rational Theology*, New York: Cambridge University Press.

Further reading

Guyer, P. (2000) *Kant on Freedom, Law, and Happiness*, Cambridge: Cambridge University Press, ch. 10. (Concerns the status of the practical postulates.)
Neiman, S. (1994) *The Unity of Reason: Re-reading Kant*, Oxford: Oxford University Press, ch. 4. (A useful integration of religious belief in the larger context of Kant's philosophy.)

Reardon, B. (1988) *Kant as Philosophical Theologian*, Totowa, NJ: Barnes & Noble. (Emphasizes the theological perspective.)

Rossi, P. J. and M. Wreen (eds) (1991) *Kant's Philosophy of Religion Reconsidered*, Bloomington, IN: Indiana University Press. (A relevant collection of important essays.)

—— (2005) *Kant's Philosophy of Religion, Stanford Encyclopedia of Philosophy*, Available: <http://plato.stanford.edu/entries/kant-religion>. (An instructive online survey.)

Wood, A. (1970) *Kant's Moral Religion*, Ithaca, NY: Cornell University Press. (A classic book-length treatment of the relation of morality and religion.)

15

SØREN KIERKEGAARD

Robert C. Roberts

Introduction

Philosophers sometimes apply their skills to religions. They devise arguments for or against one or another of the beliefs that a religion promotes; they clarify the concepts on which religious beliefs and practices turn; they compare the beliefs or concepts of one religion with those of another; they sometimes try to figure out what sort of thing religions are, why they exist, and why people are drawn to them.

Søren Kierkegaard is a philosopher of religion, or more precisely a philosopher of Christianity or a Christian philosopher. In his own peculiar ways he does most of the things I have mentioned. He is preoccupied with Christianity, and according to his own testimony, all of his writings, including the ones he wrote under pseudonyms and the ones that seem to have least to do with religion, were written in the service of Christianity.

Kierkegaard seldom refers to himself as a 'philosopher,' and outwardly much of what he wrote does not look very much like philosophy as most of us know it. His early book *Either/Or* (vol. I) consists of essays of literary and music criticism, a set of romantic-like aphorisms, a whimsical essay on how to avoid boredom, a panegyric on the unhappiest possible human being, a diary recounting a supposed seduction, and (vol. II) two enormous didactic and hortatory ethical letters and a sermon. Many of the books that he wrote in the first half of his literary career are attributed to such pseudonymous authors as A (an otherwise unnamed aesthete), Victor the Hermit, Hilarius Bookbinder, the Watchman of Copenhagen, Constantine the Constant, Nicolas Takenote, Brother Taciturn, John of the Silence, and John the Climber. Some of these pseudonymous authors are fairly well developed characters in their own right, lending the books a character of literary fiction.

In the second half of his career Kierkegaard signed most works with his own name, and most of these writings are in the form of scriptural expositions which he declined to call sermons because he wrote without clerical authority. However, these edifying discourses and Christian deliberations are more akin to sermons than they are to any other literary form. He also wrote a number of such discourses during the period of the pseudonymous writings, and to these, like the later discourses, he also affixed his own name.

Some of Kierkegaard's writings do look a bit like philosophy of religion. *Fear and Trembling*, which examines the story in which the biblical patriarch Abraham undertakes obediently to sacrifice his son Isaac, is a critique of a Hegelian construal of faith. *The Concept of Anxiety* is a rather philosophical and psychological examination of the background for original sin. *Philosophical Fragments* is a (largely covert) comparison of Socrates as a teacher with Christ as a 'teacher,' and is a critique of philosophically influenced accounts of faith like Friedrich Schleiermacher's. It even contains brief discussions of two of the classical arguments for the existence of God, a staple topic in the philosophy of religion. The *Concluding Unscientific Postscript* (postscript to the *Philosophical Fragments*) continues the critique of the Hegelians and indulges in a mouth-filling vocabulary worthy of the opponents who provoked it to arms. But even these most philosophy-like productions are written in styles that are rare in the history of philosophy. (The works of Plato and Nietzsche diverge in somewhat similar ways from the historical norms.)

Owing to Kierkegaard's unconventional styles, the diversity of his pseudonymous personae, the prominence of his pseudonymous works, the sheer volume of writing, and his sometimes impenetrable prose, Kierkegaard has made interpretation difficult. Because of particular comments that he puts in the mouths of some of his personae, he came to be associated, early in the twentieth century, with such existentialists as Jean-Paul Sartre and Martin Heidegger. He was regularly designated 'the father of existentialism,' and interpreted as holding that we human beings have no normative nature but must create our own values by an act resembling choice. Serious Kierkegaard scholars no longer promote this idea, but it persists in textbooks and classrooms, partly under the potent influence of Alasdair MacIntyre. More recently, Kierkegaard has been co-opted by the postmodern deconstructionists and taken to be a thoroughgoing ironist, a writer who simply plays with viewpoints without having one of his own, taking back what he says in one place by what he writes in another and in the final analysis *saying* nothing at all: he is the unsubstantial, indeterminate, forever disappearing ghost behind the pseudonymous writings. Others have interpreted Kierkegaard as a demythologizer or Wittgensteinian fideist. Partially in reaction to the existentialists, deconstructionists, and fideists, some Christian philosophers have tried to assimilate Kierkegaard's work to more traditional theories. Some have read him as proposing a divine command theory of obligation, a 'reformed' view in the epistemology of religion, or a virtue theory in ethics. Such interpretations are, in my view, preferable to the existentialist and deconstructionist ones, because they do pick up substantive themes to which Kierkegaard would assent.

But the assimilations of Kierkegaard to the kinds of theories that are the usual stock-in-trade of philosophers of religion are also misleading, inasmuch as they translate Kierkegaard's practices and ideas into an academic world that is not their natural habitat, and reflect concerns that diverge significantly from his own. In the present essay I explore in what sense Kierkegaard is a philosopher of religion.

Kierkegaard's own account of his activity as a writer

In *The Point of View for My Work as an Author*, published posthumously in 1859, Kierkegaard says that while he was writing under a diversity of pseudonyms (from 1842 on) that expressed a wide variety of life-styles and views of life, he himself was already a religious author. He proves the point by noting that within days or weeks of the publication of each of the pseudonymous books, he published overtly religious discourses under his own name. Though he does not call these Christian discourses, most are expositions of biblical texts. He admits that he was not, at the beginning, entirely clear how this combination of writings was to work as a communication strategy, and he attributes the design to God's guidance, about which he became clearer as his life-project unfolded.

His activity as a writer, he says, was essentially missionary activity on behalf of Christianity. His mission work, unlike that of missionaries to unchurched regions, was entirely a work of reflection designed to take account of the fact that the pagans in his mission field thought they were Christians. The work had first to surmount the 'monstrous illusion' of Christendom: the supposition that all it took to qualify as a Christian was to be born in a Christian country, to be on the church rolls by virtue of a baptismal certificate, and perhaps to show up for church services now and then. Only if this illusion of Christianity was dispelled could one get down to the business of converting people to Christianity. Since the illusion had the character of *misconception*, *misunderstanding*, confusion of *categories*, and the like, the mission work had to be conceptual: in a broad sense, it had to be philosophical work.

The pseudonymous works were to dispel the illusion by depicting, in a fetching and profound way, the life-styles and life-outlooks that constituted more or less real possibilities for Kierkegaard's contemporaries. Their fictional-literary and pseudonymous character made these depictions first-personal: the personae *occupy* the life-styles and -views (stages, existence-spheres) that they represent and discuss, though they often discuss other life-styles and -views – sometimes ones they regard as inferior to their own (Judge William on the aesthetic life) and sometimes higher ones that they profess themselves unable to occupy (especially Johannes de Silentio, *Fear and Trembling*, on Abraham's faith and Johannes Climacus, *Fragments* and *Postscript*, on Christianity). Thus, these works are designed as a sort of depth-mirror in which Kierkegaard's contemporaries might look, so as to see themselves, in their actual lives or the lives to which they might aspire, more clearly and deeply and from a greater diversity of directions than they could or would ever do on their own reflective resources. In a journal entry from 1850 (1967: 213 (X³ A 209)), Kierkegaard says that the aim of his writing was so 'to nail down the Christian qualifications' that no amount of rationalizing could evade them; it was 'like locking the door and throwing away the key' on such mitigating 'reflection.' If one were to read well from both the pseudonymous and the religious works, one would get a clear impression of where one stood 'existentially' *vis-à-vis* Christianity, as well as *vis-à-vis* other life-views located above and below where one currently lives.

The title of Kierkegaard's first book, *Either/Or*, indicates a general character of his goal in writing. The self-clarification that his works aimed to precipitate in his reader would involve a crisis of self-understanding in which one needed *either* to remain in one's current life-style (-understanding) but to do so in a clear understanding of its inadequacy, *or* to 'move up' – say, from the aesthetic to the ethical, or from the ethical to the religious, or from Socratic religiousness to Christianity. Since Christianity, as the ultimate goal of such life-style changes, is a historical phenomenon, a tradition with a rich past that goes back to its origins in the Bible, Kierkegaard's project is a kind of archeology. As he comments in a late journal entry (1852),

> Like the unfortunate madman who says he'll climb down into Dovrefjell to blow up the whole world with a syllogism, what was needed was someone who could, to everyone's knowledge, climb really deep down into the whole world of mediation, mediocrity, and spiritlessness to plant there, for all to see, the explosive either/or. (1951: 476 (X4, A665))

The explosive that Kierkegaard plants in that world of Christendom is his thought, in the form of his writings, both pseudonymous and signed. The pseudonymous works are hidden explosives, designed for ambush, while the signed works are set to explode 'for all to see.' The illusion of Christendom obscures the terms of choice, thus preventing people from having to confront it. So two things need to be understood: (1) where the reader stands in human existence – what her character is – and (2) what Christianity is. Kierkegaard devotes his writings to increasing both self-understanding and understanding of Christianity because this combination of epistemic accomplishments constitutes the crisis that he seeks to precipitate in the individual lives of his contemporaries.

Kierkegaard as a poet-dialectician

Johannes Climacus describes the task of becoming a Christian as 'pathetic-dialectic': a matter of both conceptual clarity and proper passion (concerns and emotions). Being a Christian is not merely correct thinking about Christian topics (say, the ability to give unimpeachable lectures on church dogmatics); conversely, passions that do not integrate distinctively Christian thoughts do not amount to being a Christian either.

In accordance with the character of the pathetic-dialectic task that Kierkegaard set for himself (or rather, God set for him), he often describes himself as a poet-dialectician. 'Poet' here just means that he writes in a strongly literary style; in his work as a dialectician, he is a rhetorician. Like the corresponding aspects of his task, these aspects of his writing are not separable. In his brilliant use of narrative, metaphor and simile, humor and irony, he is always clarifying concepts as part of his larger task. In his capacity as a conceptual analyst, in making distinctions and connections among concepts, he deploys skills in persuading, moving, inciting people with words. In a journal entry from 1845 he says,

> A new science must be introduced: the Christian art of speaking, to be constructed *admodum* Aristotle's *Rhetoric*. Dogmatics as a whole is a misunderstanding, especially as it now has been developed. (1967: 257 (VI A 17))

An expositor who attempted to abstract merely the logical or doctrinal points embodied in Kierkegaard's writings, removing the 'poetic' or rhetorical aspect, *would fail to convey the concepts* that Kierkegaard wishes to convey. The reason is that concept and understanding are correlative. To have a concept is to understand something. But to understand ethical and religious concepts is not just dialectical, but *pathetic*-dialectical, and the communication of pathos is rhetorical.

For example, in the sixth discourse of 'The gospel of sufferings' (Part Three of *Upbuilding Discourses in Various Spirits*), Kierkegaard has a brief discussion (1993: 306–11) of the ethical-religious concepts of deliberation and choice (they come up frequently in his writings). He points out that before people decide what to do, they deliberate, and deliberation is a matter of 'weighing' the options. But a human being does not weigh her options with an initial indifference to the result, the way a balance-scale weighs a piece of cheese relative to the weight on the other side of the balance. No, the human being approaches her deliberations with prior preference-dispositions. And, he says, given human nature as 'composed of temporality and eternity[,]... properly understood the eternal already has a certain overweight and the person who refuses to understand this can never begin really to deliberate' (1993: 307). Thus our human nature prescribes that the eternal be given more weight in our choices than the temporal. However, in Christendom (and no doubt among human beings more generally) this is not the tendency. Some people even 'forget' that there is an eternal dimension at all, and do all their 'deliberating' between options conceived in purely worldly terms. Kierkegaard illuminates the situation of such people with 'a simple picture.'

> When the well-to-do person is riding comfortably in his carriage on a dark but starlit night and has the lanterns lit – well, then he feels safe and fears no difficulty; he himself is carrying along the light, and it is not dark right around him. But just because he has the lanterns lit and has a strong light close by, he cannot see the stars at all. His lanterns darken the stars, which the poor peasant, who drives without lanterns, can see gloriously in the dark but starlit night. The deceived live this way in temporality: busily engaged with the necessities of life, they are either too busy to gain the extensive view, or in their prosperity and pleasant days they have, as it were, the lanterns lit, have everything around them and close to them so safe, so bright, so comfortable – but the extensive view is lacking, the extensive view, the view of the stars. (1993: 310)

This beautiful simile speaks to the heart of someone who may have 'forgotten what it means to exist' (see 1992: 249) and is as much a part of Kierkegaard's analysis of deliberation and choice as the more obviously conceptual remarks that dot these six pages. In the serious reader it tends to awaken the kind of concerned self-reflection without which he would not have a full-blooded understanding of these concepts – which is to say, would not have the concepts of deliberation and choice that fit the Christian way of life.

Consider another concept. The concept of duty belongs to the sphere that Kierkegaard calls ethical. The ethical sphere is inhabited by people who live ethically. And this living, with respect to duty, is characterized not just by the ability to pick out the duties from among the various possible actions one might perform (say, to distinguish duties from actions that are permitted and actions that are prohibited). Such a distinction-making ability is a presupposition of the possession of the concept, but it is also essential to the concept that duty is something important, that a proper orientation to one's duty involves caring about doing it, feeling a compulsion to do one's duty, taking a certain joy in doing one's duty because it is one's duty. This is because duty *is* compulsory and excellent. One who does not see (conceive) duty as something compulsory and excellent *for oneself* does not understand duty as it is understood within the ethical sphere. That is, one does not have the whole ethical concept of duty. The fact that one cannot appreciate duty as compulsory and excellent unless one has an appropriate 'pathos' or feeling attitude toward it implies that discourse aimed at fostering understanding of it will need – as a *conceptual* matter – to have an appropriate rhetorical character. The discourse in which the concept is conveyed must have an ethical mood, rather than, say, the purely 'objective' mood that often characterizes ethical 'theory.' We see such a mood, such discourse as from within the sphere, such passionate ethical seriousness, when we read those passages of *Either/Or*, vol. II, in which Judge William discusses the concept of duty, or those pages in Kierkegaard's *Works of Love*, in which he discusses duty. This rhetorical character of Kierkegaard's conceptual analysis is one of the most important ways in which his writing differs from 'standard' philosophical writing about ethics. But if he is right about the nature of ethical concepts and the understanding of them, it is his way of writing that should be standard, rather than the 'disinterested,' mock-scientific fare that often counts as philosophical ethics.

The concept of faith is a major virtue in the Jewish and Christian traditions, and Kierkegaard was preoccupied with it from the beginning to the end of his writing career. Between 'The expectancy of faith,' which accompanied the publication of *Either/Or* in 1843, and *For Self-Examination* (written in 1853), Kierkegaard wrote voluminously about faith in such works as *Fear and Trembling*, *The Concept of Anxiety*, *Philosophical Fragments*, *Concluding Unscientific Postscript*, *Sickness Unto Death*, and *Practice in Christianity*. All of these writings analyze the concept of faith, on the supposition that if people are confused about faith, as Kierkegaard thought the inhabitants of Christendom were, they will not be in a position to develop the virtue. Faith is a matter of reflection in the sense that one cannot have the virtue unless one has the concept of the virtue – or at any rate the concepts that govern faith's understanding of self, world, and God.

In these writings, Kierkegaard and his personae make and elaborate such conceptual points as the following: faith is not 'the immediate' (an unreflective, effortless, universally instantiated attitude) as Hegel held, but an enormously challenging spiritual goal; faith presupposes an attitude of 'infinite resignation' of worldly prospects; the object of faith must be such as possibly to offend rather than elicit faith; faith has a historical presupposition, that is, it is directed at a historical fact (the incarnation of the Son of God as Jesus of Nazareth); faith is against understanding; faith is a gift of God; faith is an ongoing personal dependency on its historical object; faith is rest in God; faith is a happy passion; faith is a resolution of fundamental dispositional despair and anxiety. Different pseudonyms make these various points, and the pseudonyms do not all have a complete Christian conception of faith. The pseudonyms that are closer to Christianity, or Kierkegaard himself, make the more distinctively Christian points. But all the remarks belong in a Christian conception of faith. So the identification of this trait, among people who are inclined to be confused about its nature, is an important part of the reintroduction of Christianity to Christendom. But it is not the whole.

A piece of discourse (say, an academic lecture) that expounded all the above points in a passionless and personally uninvolved way, making the conceptual points with great logical precision and carefully correcting all dissenting opinion and contrary arguments in a disinterestedly objective way, would be incongruous with its own subject matter. As the dialectic of faith itself points out, that subject matter is one of the most momentous issues in any human life and constitutes a form of *living* a human life. Despite the conceptual accuracy and precision (of a sort) that it displayed, such an exposition would risk inducing a *misunderstanding* of the subject matter in anyone who was not already independently well formed in his understanding of faith. Kierkegaard's and his pseudonyms' writings about faith offer conceptual analyses that are embodied in an appropriately personal rhetoric.

Johannes de Silentio expresses boundless admiration for Abraham in the course of his conceptual analysis and interprets the Abraham narrative, as well as the various narratives with which he compares and contrasts the Abraham narrative, in affecting ways. His own repeatedly avowed inability to understand Abraham conveys to the reader the 'high' character of faith. In *Philosophical Fragments*, Johannes Climacus presents his analysis of faith under a cloak of irony, in the form of a puzzling mock-Hegelian 'deduction' of Christianity from the (supposedly abstract) idea of a teacher who is in every respect unlike Socrates. This rhetorical form is designed to lure the 'speculative' thinker, one who enjoys mounting up on syllogisms to see what conceptual heights he can reach. But this pamphlet is also poetic in the more usual sense. In chapter 2, Climacus tells a touching story of a king in love with a humble maiden to illustrate the sacrificial love of God in becoming incarnate for the sake of the 'learner.'

Two paragraphs ago I gave a quick run-down of some of Kierkegaard's main points about the Christian concept of faith. It was a rough summary drawing on the discussions of faith found in a variety of Kierkegaard's pseudonymous works. As far as I know, Kierkegaard himself never gives us a 'systematic' account of faith. Had he thought that it would serve some purpose in his philosophical mission work, he could easily have done so. Instead, we get the various pseudonymous treatments, highlighting one or another aspect of the dialectic of faith in the form of Kierkegaardian 'poetry,' or we get some aspect of the concept of faith highlighted in the form of a scriptural exposition by Kierkegaard himself, also employing the various devices of narrative, character-sketch, metaphor, simile, irony, and humor. In either case, the writing is a concentrated aspectual treatment tailored to some particular pathology or interest that he takes to be characteristic of his potential readership. In light of the fact that a systematic treatment of the concept of faith could be done, we might wonder why Kierkegaard remained a resolute 'philosophical fragmentist.' He himself frequently makes nasty remarks about Hegel's 'system,' perhaps the most pretentious effort in human history to give an 'overview,' not just of particular topics such as faith, but of everything. But even on more modest topics, Kierkegaard does not give us a 'system,' but instead dialectical 'poetry.' Why?

We can distinguish two senses of 'system.' In the preceding paragraph I mentioned the possibility of assembling all the conceptual remarks about a given topic, such as faith, and arranging them in some systematic order; and I said that Kierkegaard shows no interest in a system even in this modest sense. The Hegelian system was much more ambitious, a deductive system that pretended to show that each concept derived, with something like logical necessity, from each preceding concept, so that the concepts were not just complete and felicitously ordered, but *necessarily* complete and *necessarily* ordered. Kierkegaard belongs to a strand of philosophical tradition that makes the aim of reflection something like therapy, character-transformation, or the inculcation of wisdom, rather than the production of a discursive product that purports to give a complete account. He may even think that 'system,' as a form of discourse, is existentially indigestible: not intellectual fare well designed to make people wise, to help them live their lives more fully, faithfully, dutifully, or virtuously. This would go not only for the Promethean kind of system that Hegel aspired to, but even the more modest sort of 'theory' of faith that might be proposed by some analytic philosopher. The kind of discourse that is well adapted to Kierkegaard's therapeutic project of reintroducing Christianity to Christendom is fragmental discourse, discourse from an angle, discourse adapted to particular human needs and troubles rather than to the rather parochial professorial desire to tie up all the intellectual loose ends.

Leading concepts in Kierkegaard's philosophy of religion

Let me end with brief comments about some of the main concepts Kierkegaard deploys in the pursuit of his missionary-philosophical program. We have looked at the concepts of deliberation and choice, which are activity-concepts that belong to moral psychology, and at the concept of duty. I have also mentioned the concepts of the existence-spheres: the aesthetic, the ethical, religiousness A, and Christianity.

Virtues. Faith is one of the two most important traditional virtue concepts treated in Kierkegaard's writings, both signed and pseudonymous. The other is *love*, which is treated in many places: extensively in *Either/Or* and *Works of Love*, but also in *Eighteen Upbuilding Discourses*, *Repetition*, *Stages on Life's Way*, and *Three Discourses on Imagined Occasions*. This is the concept most naturally distributed across the whole range of the spheres of existence, from the aesthetic to Christianity. Sprinkled throughout Kierkegaard's writings are shorter treatments of other traditional virtues such as *patience*, *perseverance*, *gratitude*, *hope*, *trust*, *courage*, *bold confidence*, and *humility*. Often his discussions of these virtues, as well as of faith and love, connect them to one another; the dialectic of one virtue-concept involves its interconnections with others. From the way the discussion of any virtue brings forth other virtue concepts, as well as concepts like choice and duty, it is clear that for Kierkegaard, as for the classical tradition, the virtues are very much an interdependent *set* of traits, expressed in an interdependent set of activities. Together, they constitute a complete, integrated, healthy character. Virtue concepts are at the center of Kierkegaard's work, because for Christianity to be introduced into Christendom would *be* for the single individuals in Christendom to begin to exemplify the Christian virtues – for them to have the passions and emotions, the patterns of thought, and the dispositions to action characteristic of genuine Christians. Kierkegaard's word 'upbuilding' refers to building up his reader's character. Concepts such as *the single individual, earnestness,* and *purity of heart* identify highly general aspects of the virtues. Being a single individual is not a trait of the same order as courage or patience or faith, but a characteristic without which one cannot properly or deeply exemplify any of the other virtues.

Dimensions. Subjectivity, inwardness, existence, passion, and *character* are concepts that Kierkegaard uses, with variable frequency, in both his pseudonymous and his signed works. In principle, they are moral-spiritual dimension-concepts: not names of personal traits, but rather of the dimensions of reality that need to be attended to by anyone who would undertake the spiritual and moral tasks that his works describe. They specify where the virtues are located, what has to undergo formation for the virtues to emerge. When Climacus avers that Hegelian speculative philosophy has caused the intellectual part of Christendom to 'forget what it means to exist,' and that 'truth is subjectivity,' he is not saying that these unfortunates have become unable to understand sentences that employ the existential quantifier, or that all truth is subjective. He means that these people are paying insufficient attention to an eminently important dimension of human living, namely, the moral and spiritual cultivation of their consciousness, their emotions and passions, the territory of inwardness or subjectivity.

Diagnostic emotions. Many of Kierkegaard's works discuss unhealthy emotions: chiefly *despair, anxiety* and *envy.* These emotions are symptoms of deeper character dysfunctions that can be healed, finally, only by acquiring Christian faith and love. Kierkegaard distinguishes felt despair from a despair that may be unconscious and is compatible with feeling good. Emotional despair is a feeling of intense frustration, of hating what one currently is, and being without hope of relief. Character-despair is a fundamental dispositional orientation of the self to itself, the world, and God, a state of the self such that, in circumstances that might well occur, the individual *would be* cast into emotional despair. Only the self that 'rests transparently in the Power that posited it' (1980a: 14) is proof against emotional despair, and thus free of dispositional despair. But this 'resting' in God is faith.

See also Christianity (Chapter 6), Hiddenness (Chapter 29), The wager argument (Chapter 36), The Incarnation (Chapter 51), Faith (Chapter 56).

References

Kierkegaard, S. (1951) *The Journals of Søren Kierkegaard*, ed. and trans. A. Dru, Oxford: Oxford University Press.

—— (1967) *Søren Kierkegaard's Journals and Papers*, vol. 1, ed. and trans. H. and E. Hong, Bloomington, IN: Indiana University Press.

—— (1980a) *Sickness Unto Death*, trans. H. and E. Hong, Princeton, NJ: Princeton University Press.

—— (1980b) *The Concept of Anxiety*, trans. R. Thomte, Princeton, NJ: Princeton University Press.

—— (1983) *Fear and Trembling; Repetition*, trans. H. and E. Hong, Princeton, NJ: Princeton University Press.

—— (1985) *Philosophical Fragments; Johannes Climacus*, trans. H. and E. Hong, Princeton, NJ: Princeton University Press.

—— (1987) *Either/Or*, 2 vols., trans. H. and E. Hong, Princeton, NJ: Princeton University Press.

—— (1988) *Stages on Life's Way*, trans. H. and E. Hong, Princeton, NJ: Princeton University Press.

—— (1990a) *Eighteen Upbuilding Discourses*, trans. H. and E. Hong, Princeton, NJ: Princeton University Press.

—— (1990b) *For Self-Examination; Judge For Yourself!*, trans. H. and E. Hong, Princeton, NJ: Princeton University Press.

—— (1990c) *Three Discourses on Imagined Occasions*, trans. H. and E. Hong, Princeton, NJ: Princeton University Press.

—— (1991) *Practice in Christianity*, trans. H. and E. Hong, Princeton, NJ: Princeton University Press.

—— (1992) *Concluding Unscientific Postscript*, 2 vols., trans. H. and E. Hong, Princeton, NJ: Princeton University Press.

—— (1993) *Upbuilding Discourses in Various Spirits*, trans. H. and E. Hong, Princeton, NJ: Princeton University Press.

—— (1995) *Works of Love*, trans. H. and E. Hong, Princeton, NJ: Princeton University Press.

—— (1998) *The Point of View: On My Work as an Author; The Point of View for My Work as an Author; Armed Neutrality*, trans. H. and E. Hong, Princeton, NJ: Princeton University Press.

Further reading

Davenport, J. and A. Rudd (eds) (2001) *Kierkegaard After MacIntyre: Essays on Freedom, Narrative, and Virtue*, Chicago: Open Court. (Essays address Alasdair MacIntyre's interpretation of Kierkegaard as a Sartrean existentialist; many of them reject that 'traditional' reading, stressing ways Kierkegaard can help resolve the very issues that preoccupy MacIntyre.)

Evans, C. S. (2006) *Kierkegaard on Faith and the Self: Collected Essays*, Waco, TX: Baylor University Press. (Argues that Kierkegaard is not an irrationalist, and that he traces the problems of faith not to lack of evidence or the rise of science, but to the loss of personhood, emotions, and imagination.)

Hannay, A. and G. Marino (eds) (1997) *Cambridge Companion to Kierkegaard*, Cambridge: Cambridge University Press. (Diverse collection of essays on representative topics within Kierkegaard scholarship by leading scholars.)

16
FRIEDRICH NIETZSCHE
Gary Shapiro

Friedrich Nietzsche's declaration 'God is dead' made him notorious as a stringent critic of Christianity and all forms of otherworldly religion. His criticisms are part of a more general philosophical rejection, on both metaphysical and ethical grounds, of all ideas of transcendence (such as classical Platonism). Nietzsche (1844–1900), born into a family of Lutheran ministers, became a professor of classical philology while young, and wrote a series of polemical books against much traditional religious and philosophical culture; he sharply criticized many nineteenth-century attempts to reconcile science and religion. Philological scholarship involved intense study of deconstructive readings of the Jewish and Christian Scriptures by higher critics such as Strauss and Wellhausen. Many nineteenth-century philosophers and scientists were atheists or agnostics because they accepted Kant's denial of knowledge of things in themselves and saw the consistency of a scientific naturalism that could be expanded with Darwinian explanations of human behavior and culture. Yet Nietzsche dismissed the naive 'enlightenment' view that people would abandon religion simply because of rational argument, and warned that an enlightened scientific culture, having marginalized religion, would be faced with a total crisis of meaning or nihilism.

While Nietzsche's antipathy to western monotheism is obvious, it is necessary to attend to the strategy and rhetoric of his attacks, which are frequently deployed against disguised forms of religion (including the scientific way of life and modern atheism). Nietzsche's judgments about Christianity are typically directed to specific figures, events, and movements; so he is surprisingly sympathetic to Jesus, but a fierce critic of Paul and Luther and of the German idealism which he saw as their heirs. At the same time, Nietzsche's conception of the human (or posthuman) good is related to Plato's conception of the philosopher as ultimate legislator of values, a role envisioned as involving a wise use of religion as communal bond and ground of culture. In this perspective some of Nietzsche's own distinctive ideas, like that of the posthuman (*Übermensch*) and eternal recurrence can be seen as elements of a naturalistic religion. In the late twentieth century some attention has been focused on Nietzsche's complex assessments of a number of non-Christian religions, including Islam, Hinduism, and Buddhism.

The death of God

Nietzsche's signature declaration 'God is dead' is voiced by several figures in his polyphonic texts. In the allegorical aphorism 125 of *Gay Science*, a 'madman' bursts into the marketplace one morning with a lantern, seeking God. The smug non-believers ridicule his quest; they see theism as a quaint, discarded superstition. The madman replies: God is not simply a fictional personage who can be ignored; human culture, in murdering or sacrificing its central organizing principle, now faces the consequences. The smug atheists of the marketplace (secular European society focused on economic goods) don't yet see that God's murder effectively eliminates any analogous principle of meaning (such as economic progress, nationalism, or other substitutes for theism): the madman says, 'Is there any up or down left? Are we not straying as through an infinite nothing?' The death of God is an *event*, in a strong sense, the greatest deed done so far, and it may take humans a very long time to acknowledge their deed. It is a sacrifice in which humans unknowingly surrendered their guiding thought for the possibility of 'a higher history than all history hitherto.' Describing this as a sacrificial act which the agents have yet to own, the madman asks 'what festivals of atonement, what sacred games shall we have to invent?' and visits diverse churches to sing a '*requiem aeternam deo*.' As he asks for new festivals and rites and mourns the dead God, it is far from clear that the madman's 'higher history' will be devoid of all religion, even if it involves acknowledging the absence of a single transcendent God.

This allegory poses two sets of questions: (1) How did monotheism (especially Christianity) gain and maintain its power, and how did it acquire its ability to transform its otherworldly orientation into the disguised forms ('God's shadow') that bewitch modern thought? (Is it its own virtue, its truthfulness, that kills it?) (2) What role is there for religion (e.g., as communal meaning-giving 'festivals' and other practices) in a post-theistic world? How can the philosophical legislator deploy religion in pursuit of a 'higher history?'

Nietzsche's genealogy of Christianity

Traditional Christianity and many other philosophical and religious movements maintain a 'two worlds' conception of reality, one level being that of actual and possible experience of embodied human beings ('this world') and the 'other world' of the eternal, divine, and heavenly. Nietzsche's challenge to otherworldliness is that it involves a denigration of life in this world. Practices of self-denial, belief in eternal divine commands, contempt for ordinary reason and experience, accepting the direction of religious authorities ('priests'), and promises of reward and threats of punishment after death are all targets of Nietzsche's criticisms. In *Thus Spoke Zarathustra*, Nietzsche's eponymous hero takes his name from the Persian Zoroaster, who invented dualistic religion. In Nietzsche's extravagant parody of Luther's Bible, Zarathustra returns to rectify his earlier teaching. We must recognize that all thoughts of another world are based on wishful thinking, and on the desire to escape from a world of change and suffering. Otherworldly religion and philosophy are reaction formations of weakness, sickness, and despair: 'It was suffering and incapacity that created all afterworlds – this and that brief madness of bliss which is experienced only by those who suffer most deeply . . . it was the body that despaired of the earth and heard the belly of being speak to it' (Nietzsche 1982: 143). One might reply that even if a belief arises from pressing psychological needs, it may nevertheless be true. Nietzsche responds that those who would keep belief in transcendence (or its possibility) alive through such skepticism are committed to worshiping the question mark (Nietzsche 1998: 113).

This psychological account may be a plausible explanation of why some individuals find otherworldy religion attractive, but Nietzsche needs a more powerful analysis to understand why ascetic, otherworldly religions play major roles in human history. On the Genealogy of Morality offers a complex account of the development, expansion, and effects of Judaism and Christianity. Nietzsche calls his study 'genealogy' rather than 'history' because it abandons any conception of a single origin for morality and religion, focusing instead on multiple and contingent factors that contribute to these beliefs, practices, and institutions. His analysis is naturalistic, supposing the post-Darwinian discussion of the history of human morality, customs, and institutions (Moore 2002).

As a biologist would ascribe a change in a species to random variation conditioned by various factors (e.g., hereditary character, climate, prey and predators, sudden change of external circumstances), Nietzsche explains Christianity in terms of initial inheritance (Judaism), social and historical matrix (Roman empire), and 'chance' events like the emergence of civilization. The latter is the unintended result of random variations in which aggressive, nomadic groups suddenly find themselves confined and impelled to construct a world of psychological interiority.

Christianity, on his view, inherited a contemporary Jewish culture of ressentiment; it was the religion (at that time, but not before the Babylonian exile in 586/7 BCE) of a conquered people whose values were reactive rather than self-affirming. Christianity was positioned for success by appealing to the lower orders of the Roman empire, thus carrying on the 'slave revolt in morality' on a world-historical scale. Christianity's predecessor religions, on this account, were tribally specific. They presupposed a notion of communal debt to divine figures (originally tribal ancestors), payable typically by sacrifice. The more powerful the community, the greater the debt. Once the community sees itself as universal (like Rome), with a single god corresponding to unified empire, the debt exceeds the possibility of human repayment. In the meantime, urbanized subjects forced into an internalized life transform mere debt into 'bad conscience'; in feeling themselves subject to divine judgment they become their own watchdogs and tormentors. Christianity's solution is that God sacrifices himself for his debtors, but this doctrine of the 'Redeemer' is unsatisfactory because it leaves Christians with the sense of their own unworthiness and impotence.

In his last book, The Antichrist, Nietzsche distinguishes Jesus from what Christianity made of him in terms of doctrine and practice: 'in truth there was one Christian, and he died on the cross' (Nietzsche 1982: 612). Nietzsche's Jesus did not present himself as a 'redeemer;' his 'glad tidings' – exemplified by 'resist not evil' and 'the kingdom of God is within you' – were simply that all could lead a blissful life in the present by surrendering enmity (1982: 600–2). Such a faith, like Buddha's, says Nietzsche, understands itself as being beyond all opposites (like this world/other world) and is 'at every moment its own miracle, its own reward, its own proof, its "kingdom of God"' (1982: 605). The small community around Jesus misunderstood his death as a sacrifice for them, blamed it on the Jewish upper class, incorporated popular messianic expectations, and formulated doctrines of judgment, resurrection, and the beyond totally foreign to the naive and blissful figure they claimed as their inspiration (1982: 614–16). Jesus was a *tabula rasa* on which the Church inscribed its desire for revenge against the powers of the world, the Jewish ruling class, and the Roman empire (Shapiro 1988).

Nietzsche supplements this genealogy of Christianity with a social and psychological account of its ability to dominate the European sphere of meaning. For Nietzsche this requires explanation because of the enormous paradox presented by the prevalence of ascetic religions (and their ascetic secular substitutes). The problem (in quasi-Darwinian terms) is: humans, sharing the fundamental drive of all life to acquire and expend power, appear to be in contradiction to this same drive so far as their beliefs and practices seem directed at suppressing typical expressions of life, designating them as sinful and devaluing them in contrast to 'higher' aims. Nietzsche's response is that the 'priests' (religious leaders) are in fact conservators of the lives of their flocks. They provide them with a totalizing schema of meaning that saves them from the depths of pessimism and despair that they would otherwise experience (Nietzsche 1998: pt. III). The priest is a conscious or unconscious psychologist who shapes and refines human drives. Here Nietzsche draws on his theory of *ressentiment*. In the absence of religious, ideological, or priestly intervention, the weak, sick, or unhappy blame their troubles on those who are healthy, powerful, and successful. Their values are reactive: they see the strong as 'evil'; so they themselves must be 'good' (contrasting with the strong's value system, who happily think themselves 'good' and as an afterthought name the weaker as 'bad'). Priestly technique alters the direction of *ressentiment*: priests teach their flocks to blame themselves for their unhappiness, a step prepared by the internalization of affects called 'bad conscience.' While Christianity is Nietzsche's paradigmatic version of religious bad conscience, the analysis could be applied to any religion, such as Shia Islam, that involves bad conscience, practices of repentance, and an infinite deity.

There are ironic dimensions to this critique of ascetic religion. Nietzsche draws on classical (and so non-Christian) rhetorical forms in his attempt to dislodge monotheistic ways of thought and their transforms. For example, the *Genealogy* begins with a sharp contrast between life-denying Jews and life-affirming Greeks and Romans, thus enlisting the sympathy of his presumed anti-Semitic readers. As the analysis progresses, it becomes clear that, on this view, Christianity is Judaism magnified to a higher power. Going further, Nietzsche attempts to show that presumed alternatives to religious asceticism, such as the scientific way of life or modern atheism, are simply secular variations on this model. According to him, scientists sacrifice their present for the sake of an ultimate truth that recedes into the infinite future, and modern atheists are still in thrall to the notion of a final, unitary truth. Science and atheism reintroduce notions of transcendence in sublimated forms. It was Christian truthfulness that inspired the enlightened inquiries that led to doubting Christian dogma. But it can go one step further: 'Now that Christian truthfulness has drawn one conclusion after the other, in the end it draws its *strongest conclusion*, its conclusion *against* itself: this occurs, however, when it poses the question, "*what does all will to truth mean?*"' (Nietzsche 1998: 117).

Without Christianity, European culture would not have become committed to truthfulness in the form of scientific inquiry and philosophical reflection. Inquiry and reflection first cast religious claims to truth into doubt, but when turned back on the project of truthfulness itself, they unmask it as a form of the ascetic ideal. This self-destruction is an instance of what Nietzsche calls 'the law of life': 'All great things perish through themselves, through an act of self-cancellation' (1998: 117). The possibility of such a development is not limited to Christianity; Nietzsche observes the dynamic carried further among the Assassins (the Nizari sect of Shia Islam based in Alamut, Iran which was powerful around 1100–1250). Religion here becomes not only the basis for a thoroughgoing skepticism, but draws active conclusions which Nietzsche apparently approves:

> When the Christian Crusaders ... came across that invincible order of Assassins, that order of free spirits *par excellence* whose lowest degree lived in an obedience the like of which no order of monks has attained, they also received ... a hint about that symbol and tally-word reserved for the upper degrees alone, as their secretum: 'nothing is true, everything is permitted.' (1998: 109)

Did Nietzsche reject all religion? It is true that the writings of his so-called positivist or enlightenment period (about 1877–80) echo many of the modern skeptical discussions of religion, e.g., he contradicts Schopenhauer by claiming that religion preceded metaphysics in positing the existence of 'another world' and that it did so not because of a religious or metaphysical 'drive' but because of 'an *error* in the interpretation of certain natural events, a confusion of intellect' (Nietzsche 1974: 196). Nevertheless, Nietzsche's examples and references in these texts are overwhelmingly Christian. Even with respect to Christianity, Nietzsche marks significant distinctions between Protestantism and Catholicism. He argues that the Catholic Church was 'the last Roman building,' destroyed by men like Luther who failed to understand what was structurally required for a Church to maintain itself as a living cultural institution. Luther 'handed the holy books to everybody – until they finally got into the hands of the philologists, who are the destroyers of every faith that rests on books' (1974: 311). By rejecting the authority of church councils and encouraging priests to marry (which led to eliminating the confessional), Luther abandoned the idea of the Church as an inspired living body and stripped the priest of the exceptional aura required for maintaining its mystique.

To the extent that Luther reduced religion to an individual relationship with God and unwittingly laid the foundation for critical analysis of sacred texts, he helped to destroy the Church. A Church is above all a structure for ruling that secures the highest rank for the *more spiritual* human beings and that believes in the power of spirituality to the extent of forbidding itself the use of all the cruder instruments of force: and on this score alone the church is under all circumstances a nobler institution than the state. (1974: 313)

Only if religion is equated with a Protestant-oriented notion of individual faith in the transcendent can Nietzsche be said to reject all religion. Since Nietzsche views religions as human institutions, they must be understood in terms of their actual development and operations, not in terms of an eternalistic theology, in accordance with his lapidary genealogical principle that 'only that which has no history is definable' (Nietzsche 1998: 53).

Religion and the philosophical legislator

Nietzsche respects the ascetic ideal, since it is the most powerful system of giving and interpreting meaning yet devised (1998: 106–7). Needing above all to give a meaning to suffering, 'humans would much rather will nothingness than not will' (p. 118). Surely, Nietzsche suggests in *The Antichrist*, human imagination is long overdue in creating new systems of meaning: 'Almost two thousand years – and not a single new god!' (1982: 586). If an alternative construction of meaning is possible, he declares in *Twilight of the Idols*, it will not be grounded in the self-destructive will to truth that emerged from what he sometimes calls 'monotonotheism' (1982: 480), but in a powerful act of creation. Nietzsche calls for a this-worldly, affirmative orientation to life. Is there a place for religion in this affirmation? Beginning with some of his earliest commentators and popularizers, it has been widely assumed that Nietzsche's thought was a form of 'aristocratic radicalism' or extreme individualism.

More recently philosophers have questioned whether Nietzsche ought to be seen as an individualist in any ultimate ontological or ethical sense. Some, including Foucault, Derrida, and Deleuze, emphasize that Nietzsche questions the identity and integrity of the individual ego, and that he describes the self as a political community of drives that cooperate or compete with one another by turns (Schrift 1995). In this vein, Nietzsche (in *Beyond Good and Evil*) says that modern philosophy is a demonstration of the 'merely apparent existence of the subject'; this thought in the form of the Vedanta philosophy was once one of the great religious powers on earth, showing that modern epistemological skepticism is effectively anti-Christian but not antireligious (Nietzsche 2000: 257).

Others point out that Nietzsche, like others of the post-Darwinian generation, treats humans as social animals, analyzable in terms of their complex history of adaptations, unconscious experiments, and (in Nietzsche's view in particular) their will to meaning (Moore 2002; Richardson 2004). As he argues in *Thus Spoke Zarathustra*, values like 'good' and 'evil' are the names given to the habits and practices that a people (*Volk*) has developed in relation to its geographical conditions and its competition with its neighbors (Nietzsche 1982: 170–2). In the twenty-first century it has been argued that Nietzsche was consistent in his dedication to the German romantic and anti-modernist *Völkisch* tradition that values religion as a form of communal solidarity and communication (Young 2006). Nietzsche rejected many of the views that later became central to Nazism (anti-Semitism, belief in German superiority); nevertheless, discussion continues whether and to what extent his thought concerning collective values leaves itself dangerously open to being filled with such reprehensible content or if it can be adapted by a variety of religious and political programs (Golomb 2004).

Nietzsche admired many forms of religion. In *The Birth of Tragedy*, he praises the communal myths, rituals, and festivals of the Greeks; these provide a model not so much in terms of their content but as a splendid example of the poetic imagination making sense of becoming and suffering. Nietzsche often compares Greeks and Christians. For example, in *Beyond Good and Evil: Prelude to a Philosophy of the Future*, he writes 'what is amazing about the religiosity of the ancient Greeks is the enormous abundance of gratitude that it exudes: it is a very noble type of human being that confronts nature and life in this way' (2000: 49). This is more than an aesthetic judgment of defunct cultures, for Nietzsche sees the philosopher making use of religion for the sake of 'higher history.'

In this same work, Nietzsche devotes a chapter to the topic 'What is religious.' Religion is seen from the standpoint of the philosophical legislator who thinks of the future in the broadest terms.

> The philosopher as we understand him, we free spirits – as the human being of the most comprehensive responsibility who has the conscience for the over-all development of the human – this philosopher will make use of religions for his project of cultivation and education, just as he will make use of whatever political and economic states are at hand. (2000: 262)

Nietzsche goes on to detail the importance of religion for the philosophical legislator. (1) Religion can be both a means for a 'governing race' to rule and a refuge for the more spiritual or contemplative. (2) It provides means of self-cultivation (asceticism and puritanism) that aid in the improvement of 'slowly ascending classes.' (3) For the vast majority, religion contributes enormously to the possibility of their being content and at peace.

Yet religion is dangerous, Nietzsche continues, when it sets itself up as 'sovereign' without regard to the philosopher's project of cultivation and education (2000: 264–6). Specifically, Christianity and Buddhism, 'the *sovereign* religions we have had so far,' have been religions for the suffering; they help to preserve the weaker and less-promising members of the species, contributing in the case of Christianity to the formation of the mediocre European 'herd animal' (a judgment Nietzsche would doubtless have extended to western adaptations of Buddhism). Nietzsche is a 'perfec-tionist' in evaluating religions, like other human institutions and pursuits, in terms of how they contribute to the flourishing of individuals and groups (Cavell 1990: 33–63). Cavell claims Nietzsche's perfectionism was inspired by his reading of Ralph Waldo Emerson; Emerson too was a religious pluralist who recognized the value for life of a variety of religious traditions. In Nietzsche's case, flourishing involves the creative expression of power, understood not simply as raw force (*Kraft*) but as shaping authority (*Macht*). 'The will to power,' often misunderstood as a blind admiration for tyranny, is better seen in terms of the artistic and cultural expressions that he explicitly praises: individuals, artists, and civilizations that succeed in attaining 'the grand style.'

Nietzsche and world religions

Nietzsche describes himself as a global thinker, looking at religions and philosophies with 'an Asiatic and supra-Asiatic eye' (2000: 258), and so comments on Hinduism, Buddhism, the religion of the ancient Greeks and Romans, pre-exilic Judaism, and Islam. All of these, in his view, are better ways of managing human life than Christianity (especially Protestantism). Polytheistic religions, like those of Greece and Rome, exhibit first of all 'the wonderful art and gift of creating gods': they are collective manifestations of exuberant imagination. Their plurality of gods recognizes a *'plurality of norms'*: polytheism is one of the earliest and paradigmatic expressions of individuality. Monotheism is 'the greatest danger that has yet confronted humanity,' promulgating a single normal type for the species, thus leading to 'the premature stagnation that most other species have reached' (1974: 191–2).

In *The Antichrist*, Nietzsche sums up his condemnation of Christianity, in part by comparing and contrasting it with Hinduism, Buddhism, early Judaism, and Islam. Religions, in this perspective, are much more than individual sets of beliefs and practices. They are ways of shaping and directing fundamental drives and organizing populations. One text that impressed him was a version of the Hindu Law of Manu (the first lawgiver in that tradition), in Jacolliot's questionable French translation (Bonfiglio 2005/2006). In Manu's prescriptions for a segregation of castes, and total exclusion of untouchables (*chandala*), Nietzsche found confirmation for his idea that cultivating and educating (the main value of religion) was best provided for in a strongly hierarchical society. He was attracted to Jacolliot's attempt to justify Manu on generally Darwinian grounds, the argument being both that the strongest and most spiritual group (the Brahmins) would flourish in these conditions and that such a coherent socio-religious order would also promote the development of other licit groups.

Nietzsche seems to have been susceptible to Jacolliot's claim that Manu's law was the archetype for Moses and Muhammad. Nietzsche expanded his argument that Christianity was a 'slave revolt in morality,' accepting Jacolliot's premise that Jews were descendants of the Indian *chandala* and that the Jews of the lower class in Roman times were *chandala* of the *chandala*. In spring 1888, Nietzsche sketched this theological-political schema in his notebooks:

What a yes-saying Aryan religion, the product of the *ruling* class looks like:
the Lawbook of Manu

What a yes-saying semitic religion, the product of the *ruling* class looks like:
the Lawbook of Muhammad. The Old Testament, in its earlier parts.

What a no-saying semitic religion, the product of the *oppressed* class looks like:
according to Indian-Aryan concepts:
the New Testament – a *chandala* religion.

What a no-saying Aryan religion looks like, having developed among the ruling class:
Buddhism

It is completely understandable that there is no religion of the oppressed Aryan races: for that is a contradiction: a master race is either in charge or goes to ruin. (Nietzsche 1980: 13.380–1)

This schema is operative in Nietzsche's assessments of various religions in his late writings such as *Twilight of the Idols* and *The Antichrist*. In the latter, Nietzsche denounces Christianity for having robbed humanity of the cultural riches of Greco-Roman antiquity and Islam. While religions all depend upon the 'holy lie' (cf. Plato's 'noble lie'), what matters is the end toward which the lie is directed: that is, is it 'yes-saying' or 'no-saying' (1982: 639–43)? From this perspective Nietzsche revalues history's clash of civilizations, as in his anger at the Crusades, whose armies 'fought something before which they might more properly have prostrated themselves in the dust,' and he notes the crucial role of the Germans in this enterprise (1982: 652). In the 'Decree against Christianity,' which Nietzsche's sister removed when she published the book (and which his editors restored), Nietzsche condemns by name only one of the great monotheisms and signs himself 'The Antichrist' (1980: 6.254).

Nietzsche, Dionysus, and the renewal of religion

In *Beyond Good and Evil*, Nietzsche diagnoses the modern condition as one in which the 'religious instinct' is growing powerfully, even though it denies itself 'the theistic satisfaction' (2000: 256). His self-appointed philosophical task is to find ways of shaping this religious instinct. We approach Nietzsche's adumbration of a new (or reformed) philosophical religion by focusing on two elements of religion that Nietzsche praises, when properly understood and directed: sacrifice and spirituality. Nietzsche's Zarathustra calls on his listeners to sacrifice themselves for the sake of the *Übermensch* and the future direction of the earth; and Nietzsche's valuations of human beings and institutions are regularly predicated upon the degree of spirituality that he sees them as promoting. Sacrifice manifests the overflowing power Nietzsche sees throughout the human and natural world; the highest power consists finally in squandering, not accumulating.

Religion can be a provocation to 'higher spirituality (*Geistigkeit*), to test the feelings of great self-overcoming, of silence and solitude' (2000: 263). It involves 'surveying from above, arranging and forcing into formulas this swarm of dangerous and painful experiences' with which religions have been concerned (p. 249). Spirituality is exemplified in genuine philosophical activity, which is a combination 'of a bold and exuberant spirituality that runs *presto* and a dialectical severity and necessity that takes no false step' (p. 329; see also pp. 337, 380, 423). While Nietzsche denounces the fictions of a 'pure spirituality' and of an immaterial, immortal soul, he reinterprets both soul and spirituality in terms of immanence. In another vocabulary, they are fruits of natural autopoiesis, emergent modes of thought and action that develop from complex organic and cultural assemblages of drives and conditions. In several notebook entries Nietzsche describes spirituality as an emergent natural characteristic, suggesting that there is an impersonal spirituality in the inorganic world. For example: 'the world is not at all an organism, but chaos: the development of "spirituality" is a means to the relative continuance of organization' (1980: 13.37; cf. 11.157, 11.255).

In this context Nietzsche's self-identification as the last disciple of Dionysus takes on a more specific sense (2000: 425). Dionysian mysteries celebrate 'the eternal return of life … the triumphant Yes to life beyond all death and change; true life as the over-all continuation of life through procreation, through the mysteries of sexuality' (1982: 561). Expenditure of life in the creation of life is sacrificial. Dionysian gods philosophize, and so engage in a complex form of spirituality. The Platonic Socrates had denied that gods philosophize, because they already possess wisdom. For Nietzsche there is no such totalizing and absolute wisdom in a world of immanence and becoming. So his sketch of Dionysian religion humanizes the gods and divinizes human thought, as it constructs meaning in a world of gendered and multiple gods (Lampert 2006).

While Nietzsche is not so naive as to expect an unmediated return to Greek religion, he calls for a renewal of this-worldly sacrifice and spirituality. The madman saw God's death as a sacrifice for the sake of a 'higher history.' While Nietzsche declared in *Ecce Homo* that he should not be mistaken for the founder of a religion, we might ask why he thought it necessary to issue this precaution. The 'last disciple of Dionysus' was indeed not a 'founder' (like Manu, Moses, and Muhammad), but his 'philosopher of the future' has the task of using and directing religions. Nietzsche's Dionysianism is the diagram of a sacrificial and spiritual religion of immanence.

See also Christianity (Chapter 6), Immanuel Kant (Chapter 14), Truth in religion (Chapter 18), The moral argument (Chapter 34), Problems with the concept of God (Chapter 38), Why is there a universe at all, rather than just nothing? (Chapter 41), The sociobiological account of religious belief (Chapter 42), Sin and salvation (Chapter 53), Continental philosophy (Chapter 60), Phenomenology of religion (Chapter 61).

References

Bonfiglio, T. (2005/2006) 'Toward a genealogy of Aryan morality: Nietzsche and Jacolliot,' *New Nietzsche Studies* 6/3–4 and 7/1–2: 170–84.

Cavell, S. (1990) *Conditions Handsome and Unhandsome*, Chicago: University of Chicago Press.

Golomb, J. (2004) *Nietzsche and Zion*, Ithaca, NY: Cornell University Press.

Lampert, L. (2006) 'Nietzsche's philosophy and true religion,' in K. A. Pearson (ed.) *A Companion to Nietzsche*, New York: Blackwell.

Moore, G. (2002) *Nietzsche, Biology, and Metaphor*, Cambridge: Cambridge University Press.

Nietzsche, F. (1974) *The Gay Science*, trans. W. Kaufmann, New York: Random House.

—— (1980) *Kritische Studienausgabe*, ed. G. Colli and M. Montinari, Berlin: Walter de Gruyter.

—— (1982) *The Portable Nietzsche*, ed. W. Kaufmann, New York: Penguin Books.

—— (1998) *On the Genealogy of Morality*, trans. M. Clark and A. Swensen, Indianapolis, IN: Hackett.

—— (2000) *Basic Writings of Nietzsche*, ed. W. Kaufmann, New York: Random House.

Richardson, J. (2004) *Nietzsche's New Darwinism*, New York: Oxford University Press.

Schrift, A. (1995) *Nietzsche's French Legacy*, New York: Routledge.

Shapiro, G. (1988) 'The writing on the wall: the antichrist and the semiotics of history,' in R. Solomon and K. Higgins (eds) *Reading Nietzsche*, New York: Oxford University Press.

Young, J. (2006) *Nietzsche's Philosophy of Religion*, Cambridge: Cambridge University Press.

Further reading

Conway, D. (ed.) (1998) *Nietzsche: Critical Assessments*, 4 vols., New York: Routledge. (A comprehensive, well-chosen, and extensive collection of critical essays on many topics.)

Fink, E. (2003) *Nietzsche's Philosophy*, trans. G. Richter, New York: Continuum. (A lucid philosophical guide to Nietzsche's thought, following his writings from first to last.)

Jaspers, K. (1961) *Nietzsche and Christianity*, trans. E. B. Ashton, New York: Henry Regnery. (Explores Nietzsche's ambiguity.)

Kaufmann, W. (1974) *Nietzsche: Philosopher, Psychologist, Antichrist*, 4th edn, Princeton, NJ: Princeton University Press. (A standard guide.)

Pearson, K. A. (ed.) (2006) *A Companion to Nietzsche*, New York: Blackwell. (An excellent set of essays, with bibliographies and references.)

Solomon, R. and K. Higgins (2000) *What Nietzsche Really Said*, New York: Schocken. (Corrects many misinterpretations; a contemporary introduction.)

17

WILLIAM JAMES

Ruth Anna Putnam

Preliminary remarks

William James's (1842–1910) philosophy of religion is deeply embedded in his radical empiricism and in his pragmatism. I cannot present James's arguments for these views here; I shall state some of the key elements as they become relevant to James's developing views in the philosophy of religion. At the turn of the twentieth century, as again at the turn of the twenty-first, science and religion – beliefs resulting from empirical methods of inquiry and faith – appeared to be in conflict, especially for philosophers and other reflective persons. For James this conflict is illusory; he will attempt to show that empiricism as he understands it is compatible with religion as he understands that.

Relatively early in his philosophical career James argued repeatedly for the intellectual legitimacy of religious belief. Later, in his best known, most widely read book, *The Varieties of Religious Experience* (delivered as the Gifford Lectures in 1901-2), he offered accounts of religious experiences as evidence for the existence of the divine and ends with some philosophical reflections. Some years later, in *Pragmatism* (delivered as Lowell Lectures in 1906), he offered Pragmatism as a pluralistic and melioristic (philosophy of) religion, but, as in *Varieties*, he devotes only one lecture to this subject. Only late in his life, in *A Pluralistic Universe* (delivered as Hibbert Lectures in 1908), did he develop his philosophy of religion in detail, arguing specifically against the reigning Absolute Idealism of his time but rejecting also conventional theism.

I shall take up these issues in historical sequence. Some additional preliminary remarks are, however, in order. In 1870, James experienced a severe psychological crisis from which he recovered when the writings of the French philosopher Renouvier persuaded him that humans have free will. Henceforth any metaphysical conception and a fortiori any philosophy of religion that James can accept must be compatible with our having free will. Free will would not exist in a purely material world, and it would be meaningless in a world whose future (or whose ultimate salvation, to use James's language) is guaranteed. James often uses such traditional Christian, specifically Protestant, expressions, although he stated explicitly that he was not a Christian. Finally, James distinguished between the religion of common people and the philosophy of religion without ever saying how these relate, but he mentions his interpretation of the former when it seems to agree with his own philosophical religious views.

A defense of faith

In one of his earliest philosophical writings, 'The sentiment of rationality,' James considers what one wants from a worldview (James 1979). One wants it to enable one to go on thinking, living, and acting in the face of confusion, suffering, and other evil; in short, to make sense of our experiences. When it does so, we feel that the world is rational, that we are at home in the universe. Later, in *A Pluralistic Universe*, he found rationality to be too ambiguous a concept and spoke instead of a feeling of intimacy with the universe.

In 'Reflex action and theism' James sets himself the task of 'showing that a God, whether existent or not, is at all events the kind of being which, if he did exist, would form *the most adequate possible object* for minds framed like our own to conceive as lying at the root of the universe. … *Anything short of God is not rational, anything more than God is not possible …*' (1979: 93). God, to put it very simply, is put forward as the answer to the most general, most universal question, the final answer to our incessant 'Why?' But what was James's concept of God in the 1890s?

He writes, 'First, it is essential that God be conceived as the deepest power in the universe, and, second, he must be conceived under the form of a mental personality.' James claims that the divine personality and ours resemble each other in this, 'that both have purposes for which they care, and each can hear the other's call.' This conception of the deity leaves room for free will and provides an active role for us (James 1979: 97, 98).

James's most famous early essay in the philosophy of religion is his mis-titled essay, 'The will to believe' (1979) – *mis*-titled because what he defends, in opposition to religious skeptics, is not our will but our right to believe in 'the religious hypothesis' in advance of the evidence. James begins by pointing out that there are many common situations in which we are forced to choose between two hypotheses, both of which have a certain appeal for us and in which the consequences of our choice are serious. For example, one meets a person who makes friendly overtures. One can either assume (believe) that this person is worth knowing and respond accordingly, or one can be suspicious, afraid of finding, on closer acquaintance, that the person is boring or rude, and refuse to respond to the overtures. Choosing in such a situation is unavoidable and certainly intellectually respectable, and one's choice will have far-reaching consequences. Moreover, acting on one's choice may produce the evidence one now lacks (e.g., one may end up with a wonderful new friend). James maintains that those of us tempted by the 'religious hypothesis' find ourselves in just such a situation. Just as there is nothing intellectually disreputable in responding positively to friendly overtures, so, says James, there is nothing disreputable in affirming the religious hypothesis.

That hypothesis, according to James, affirms, first, that good will triumph over evil (or, at least, that it may if we and the divine powers cooperate) and, second, that 'we are better off even now if we believe her first affirmation to be true,' that is, if we act so as to contribute to the triumph of good over evil (1979: 29–30). So formulated, the religious hypothesis seems clearly to be preferred over the agnostic alternative, but I wonder whether agnostics would formulate it that way. In any case, while James ignored religious experiences in these early writings, he was soon to consider their evidentiary status.

The evidence

Writing to his friend Frances Morse, James described his task in *Varieties of Religious Experience* as follows.

> The problem I have set myself is a hard one: first to defend (against all the prejudices of my 'class') 'experience' against 'philosophy' as being the real backbone of the world's religious life – I mean prayer, guidance, and all that sort of thing immediately and privately felt ... and second, to make the hearer or reader believe, what I myself invincibly do believe, that, although all the special manifestations of religion may have been absurd ... yet the life of it as a whole is mankind's most important function. (James, H. 1920, II: 127)

The first task, then, is a task for a psychologist of religion, and as such James sets before us numerous accounts of the conversion experiences of twice-born Protestants and of mystical experiences by members of various faith communities. James has been criticized for giving a distorted picture of religious life, leaving out all social and ritual aspects as well as the religious lives of ordinary believers. But James doesn't claim to paint a complete picture; he is interested only in those aspects of the religious life that might be evidentiary for religious hypotheses. Of course, it remains an open question whether those experiences are veridical.

James points to numerous similarities between religious experiences and certain other experiences, between religious ideas and other ideas, between religious feelings and other feelings. Thus he points out that insofar as religious belief is belief in an unseen order, it is just like our belief in any other abstraction. We find our way in the universe of concrete objects by the help of such abstract concepts as space, time, causality, thing, etc.; just so we find our way morally by the help of such concepts as God, freedom, soul, justice, etc. These similarities serve to show that religious beliefs are, at any rate, beliefs like other beliefs, and religious concepts are concepts like other concepts serving the same sort of function.

Next, James will show how religious experiences fit into a general psychological account of our mental lives. We are at any moment bombarded by a multitude of sensations, a multitude that would be utterly confusing were we to pay attention to all of them equally; fortunately, our interests will focus our attention, and our concepts will impose an order on the objects of our attention. We are, then, at every moment conscious of a 'field.' Its center is the center of our attention, but we are aware, though less clearly, of what surrounds that center. The field shades off toward its margins, and these are not clearly demarcated. The field at any given time flows out of its predecessor and into its successor; what is marginal at one moment may determine the center of attention for the next, and so on.

James remarks that psychology took a giant step forward in 1886 with the discovery that, in some subjects, there are signs of the influence on consciousness of extra-marginal memories, thoughts, and feelings. Hypnotic suggestion and hysteria (in the technical sense) are explained by reference to incursions of the trans-marginal into the conscious field, and James believes that the idea of irruptions of subliminal material into the conscious field will also explain certain phenomena of religious life such as sudden conversions. Just as in a wide-awake state our senses are a condition of our apprehending physical objects, writes James, 'so it is logically conceivable that *if there be* higher spiritual agencies that can directly touch us, the psychological condition of their doing so *might be* our possession of a subconscious region which alone should yield access to them' (1985: 197; emphasis in original). Noticing similarities between mystic states and states of intoxication by alcohol or nitrous oxide, James concludes,

> our normal waking consciousness, rational consciousness as we call it, is but one special type of consciousness, whilst all about it, parted from it by the filmiest of screens, there lie potential forms of consciousness entirely different. ... No account of the universe in its totality can be final which leaves these other forms of consciousness quite disregarded. (1985: 307–8)

In fact James imagines the conscious self as surrounded by a sea of the subconscious, a 'MORE' as he calls it. That image invites speculation concerning the farther shore, what James calls over-beliefs, the details of the various religions (ibid.).

James has no interest in theologies; he takes himself to have established only this:

> Disregarding the over-beliefs, and confining ourselves to what is common and generic, we have in *the fact that the conscious person is continuous with a wider self through which saving experiences come*, a positive content of religious experience which, it seems to me, *is literally and objectively true as far as it goes*. (1985: 405, emphasis in original)

But surely this claims too much. James has indeed suggested a mechanism by which a higher being *could* influence the self *if there is such a being*, but the 'wider self' might indeed be no more than the conscious self plus its subconscious. However, James took himself to have done more, for, referring to *Varieties*, he wrote some years later that the book 'on the whole has been taken to make for the reality of God' (1978: 143). Before moving on to James's final and carefully worked out over-beliefs, let us take a brief look at pragmatism as a philosophy of religion.

Pragmatism as a meliorism

The years after the publication of *Varieties* were extraordinarily productive. James developed his theory of pure experience in a series of papers published in the *Journal of Philosophy* and posthumously in the volume *Essays in Radical Empiricism*. He presented and published the lectures on *Pragmatism*. He left voluminous manuscripts testifying to his attempts to formulate his philosophy and to meet objections. Finally, he gave the Hibbert Lectures on 'The present situation in philosophy' and published them under the title *A Pluralistic Universe*. Out of this wealth of material, I can only select what bears directly on James's understanding of the divine and our relation to it.

In the first lecture on *Pragmatism*, James offers pragmatism as a solution to a dilemma that he thought was faced by anyone interested in philosophy at the beginning of the twentieth century. Philosophy offers a choice, he said, between an empiricism that leaves no room for religion, that is, materialism, and a rationalism that leaves no room for experience, that is, absolute idealism. James finds both views unacceptable because neither allows for the intimacy he seeks; neither, however logical and even beautiful it may be, lets loose our moral energy; neither leaves room for free will. In contrast, an empiricism that includes religious experiences under the rubric 'experience,' as pragmatism does, leaves room for a religion that is compatible with free will.

James generally dismisses materialism without argument; he wrestles intellectually as well as, I suspect, emotionally with absolute idealism, so ably defended by his colleague and friend Josiah Royce as well as by numerous others. In order to weaken the claims of absolute idealism, James devoted one of the *Pragmatism* lectures to the problem of the 'One and the many,' of which he said that it is the most central problem in philosophy. Thus he asks what might be meant by the claim that the world is one. Of the many interpretations he considers I shall mention only unity of purpose. Clearly, there are examples of unity of purpose: people, organizations, even nations cooperate to achieve common goals, but just as often they have conflicting goals and work against each other. James hopes, as one must, that there will be more cooperation and less strife in the future. But when theologians speak of unity of purpose, James claims, they mean that God has one great purpose that everything in the world serves. It should come as no surprise that James is outraged. 'The scale of evil actually in sight defies all human tolerance,' but idealist philosophers can do no better than finding God's ways mysterious. James adds, 'A God who can relish such superfluities of horror is no God for human beings to appeal to. … In other words the 'Absolute' with his one purpose, is not the man-like God of common people' (1978: 70). The Absolute of the philosophers is the all-Knower. James quotes his colleague Josiah Royce, 'God's consciousness forms in its wholeness one luminous transparent conscious moment.' Empiricists, in contrast, hold that while anything that gets known by someone gets known together with something else, there may be many knowers, and even the greatest knowledge may not be of everything (James 1978: 72, quoting Royce 1987: 292).

What then is the upshot of *Pragmatism*? It is a ringing affirmation of pluralism. It is the view, which he also calls moralistic, that the 'salvation' of the universe, the ultimate triumph of good over evil is not a foregone conclusion; it depends on what each of us contributes to that cause. Against the monotheistic affirmations of Christianity, and I may add here Judaism and Islam, James asserts,

> Their words may have sounded monistic when they said, 'there is no God but God'; but the original polytheism of mankind has only imperfectly and vaguely sublimated itself into monotheism, and monotheism itself, so far as it was religious and not a scheme of class-room instruction for the metaphysicians, has always viewed God as but one helper, *primus inter pares*, in the midst of all the shapers of the great world's fate.

We may, I think take this to be a confession of faith, for a few lines later he wrote, 'I firmly disbelieve, myself, that our human experience is the highest form of experience extant in the universe' (1978: 143).

Over-beliefs

James's goal in A *Pluralistic Universe* is to defend an empiricist, pluralistic pantheism. He rejects materialism virtually without argument. Pantheism makes intimacy with the universe impossible. But he rejects conventional theism, the idea of a God who is wholly other than us for the same reason; there can be no two-way relation between us and such a being. Surprisingly, James assumes that his audience agrees with him up to this point. He and they are left, then, with just two alternatives: Absolute Idealism and James's own pluralism. For both there is a superhuman consciousness or there are superhuman consciousnesses of which human consciousnesses are parts. But for the Absolute Idealists there is one all-enveloping consciousness, and it alone and its total thought are fully real. The finite entities we know and our finite thoughts exist only because they are thought by the Absolute. In James's language, for Absolute Idealism reality exists fully only in the 'all-form.' In contrast, James rejects the idea of the Absolute and prefers to think of reality as existing in the 'each-form.' His most important reason, I believe, is this. From an Absolutist point of view, what we experience as evil – for example, human suffering – is in the larger picture a good. For James, on the other hand, there are real evils, and it is our task to get rid of them. To put it another way, since the Absolute is perfect and what it thinks is alone real, and since the Absolute does not suffer, suffering is not real for Absolute Idealists. James takes it that Absolute Idealism gives us a permanent moral vacation: since suffering is not real, we are under no obligation to alleviate it. James, speaking as a psychologist, recognizes the need for occasional moral holidays, but does not need Absolutism to authorize them, and he has overwhelming reasons to reject it.

Let us then turn to James's views concerning superhuman forms of consciousness. In one of his unpublished and unfinished manuscripts, James defends panpsychism and points out its affinity for pantheism.

> As my body has a conscious soul, I am willing to assume that a conscious soul is connected with other bodies, even down to the smallest material

things which I suppose to exist. I am willing also to believe that there exist larger souls than my own, whether connected or disconnected with the larger material aggregations. The existence of such larger souls may be called a theological question. ... But I do not believe, picturing the whole as I do, that even if a supreme soul exists, it embraces all the details of the universe in a single absolute act either of thought or of will. In other words, I disbelieve in the omniscience of the deity and in his omnipotence as well. The facts of struggle seem too deeply characteristic of the whole frame of things for me not to suspect that hindrance & experiment go all the way through. (James 1988: 5)

James is, of course, right in thinking that once one accepts panpsychism, there is no reason to stop with the human body as the location of consciousness. If molecules can have a rudimentary consciousness, may not the earth have a larger consciousness? This was in fact the view of James's contemporary Gustav Theodor Fechner, a view James found attractive. Finally, by insisting on the finitude of even the highest, most enveloping consciousness, James announces, once again, his opposition to Absolute Idealism as well as to scholastic theism. He thought, however, that the 'common man' shares his belief that God is finite, and insists, 'If it should prove probable that the absolute does not exist, it will not follow in the slightest degree that a God like that of David, Isaiah and Jesus may not exist, or may not be the most important existence in the universe for us to acknowledge' (1977: 54).

James's panpsychism and his pantheism fit well with his ontology of pure experience. According to James, the ultimate elements of reality, the pure experiences, are neutral, neither physical nor mental, but capable of relating to one another in such a way as to form streams of consciousness or to relate in different ways to form physical objects. A pure experience can be part of more than one stream, and of both physical and mental streams at the same time. Thus my seeing a pen is the pen's being seen by me – an event in both streams. More immediately relevant is the possibility of one stream of consciousness being part of another larger one. This possibility corresponds to James's version of pantheism. Let us recall his conclusion at the end of *Varieties*: '*the conscious person is continuous with a wider self through which saving experiences come*' (1985: 405). He ascribes to Fechner the view that each of us is a sense organ of the earth soul and that 'it absorbs our perceptions, just as they occur, into its larger sphere of knowledge, and combines them with the other data there' (1977: 79). Yet, while James wants to argue for what I shall call, for short, an over-soul, he also wants to retain his own individuality and autonomy. Thus arises the problem of the compounding of consciousness, the question whether 'states of consciousness, so called, can separate and combine themselves freely, and keep their own identity unchanged while forming parts of simultaneous fields of experience of wider scope' (1977: 83).

Suppose then you are aware of a bird in a tree. Upon moving your head, you no longer have the bird in your field of vision, but you are now aware of a cat under the same tree. Stepping back a bit, you enlarge your field of vision, and now are aware of a bird in a tree and a cat sitting under the tree. Obviously this is a third awareness, different from either of the preceding two, but how is it related to them? In his monumental *Principles of Psychology*, James held that the bird-in-a-tree awareness and the cat-under-a-tree awareness are not part of the bird-in-a-tree-and-cat-under-the-tree awareness, that the latter is, so to speak, entirely new, though of the same objects: the cat, the tree, and the bird. The alternative view holds that the cat-under-the tree awareness and the bird-in-the tree awareness are literally parts of the cat-under-the-tree-and-bird-in-the-tree awareness just as the cat and the bird and the tree are parts of the scene of which you are aware; call this compounding of consciousness. A theistic God, James holds, would be aware of us in the first way, but Absolute Idealism requires our thoughts to be literally parts of the Absolute. But that leaves open the question how such compounding of consciousness is possible. How can the Absolute compound our several finite consciousnesses of small parts of the universe and vast ignorance into its consciousness of the whole universe as one fact? How can it compound itself out of us? Unfortunately, James's inability to answer this question is an objection not only to Absolute Idealism but also, alas, to any higher enveloping consciousness (e.g., Fechner's earth soul). It leaves us with the god of theism.

But the view that complex psychic states succeed upon the simpler states that we *erroneously* call their parts seems now also untenable. For, according to that view the later, more-complex states have the same function (know the same bird, cat, and tree) as the earlier simpler states, and that seems to James an unintelligible miracle. Thus he finds himself confronted by a trilemma: (a) give up his life-long opposition to a mental substance, in other words, 'bring back scholasticism and common sense' or (b) 'confess the solution of the problem impossible' and then either (i) 'give up my intellectualistic logic' or (ii) 'face the fact that life is logically irrational.' But talk of souls, James claims, does not explain anything. So, facing the dilemma (b), he finds himself 'compelled to give up the logic.' I cannot here explain this rather mysterious assertion. Suffice it to say that James does not abandon ordinary logic for every day or scientific purposes; he rejects certain 'logical' principles that were said, in his day, to give insight into reality (James 1977: 95, 96).

Here we need to remember that James is an empiricist; he will appeal to experience, and he will speak only of probabilities. The religious experiences that he studied in *The Varieties of Religious Experience*, he points out, could not have been predicted from ordinary experience. Thus they 'suggest' (this is James's cautious expression) that our ordinary natural experience is only a part of human experience. Those who have religious experiences are inclined to believe that their consciousness is continuous with a 'wider self from which saving experiences flow in' (1977: 139). And repeated experiences will for them transform belief into certainty. For James, the experiences, that is, the reports of them, count as empirical verification of Fechner's idea, mentioned above, of an earth soul.

But why stop with an earth soul? Why not a soul of the galaxy? Why not a soul of the cosmos, that is, the Absolute? Because all the difficulties, paradoxes, and perplexities already considered would still hold, in particular, the problem of evil and the denial of free will. The only escape, says James, is to affirm pluralism: 'to accept, along with the superhuman consciousness, the notion that it is not all-embracing – the notion, in other words, that there is a God, but that he is finite, either in power or knowledge, or in both at once' (1977: 141). This, James claims, has been the view of the common man all along.

All along James has pointed out that there is a difference between religion, that is the common person's faith, and philosophy of religion. So, when he now claims that his own philosophy of religion is the view of the common believer, he is saying at least this: whatever speaks for his philosophical position speaks also for the common faith, while the arguments against the Absolute leave the common faith undisturbed.

James concludes,

> Thus does foreignness get banished from the world, and far more so when we take the system pluralistically than when we take it monistically. We are indeed internal parts of God and not external creations, on any reading of the panpsychic system. Yet because God is not the absolute, but is himself a part when the system is conceived pluralistically, his functions can be taken as not wholly dissimilar to those of other smaller parts – as similar to our functions consequently. (1977: 143–4)

James admits that he has done no more than to show that pluralism is 'a fully coordinate hypothesis with monism.' He has returned where he began in 'The sentiment of rationality' and in 'The will to believe.' He is faced with two live hypotheses, he must choose between them, and his choice will be determined by which hypothesis will feel more rational and allow for more intimacy.

James assumes that we too are confronted by the same momentous alternative. But are we? For some of us atheism is surely a live hypothesis and for others the alternative is what he calls 'dualistic theism.' In acknowledging that both monistic and pluralistic pantheism are only hypotheses, he leaves room for atheism and dualistic theism as rival hypotheses.

See also Religious pluralism (Chapter 20), The problem of evil (Chapter 37), Naturalistic rejoinders to theistic arguments (Chapter 40), Religious naturalism (Chapter 62), Religious experience (Chapter 63).

References

James, H. (1920) *The Letters of William James*, 2 vols, Boston, MA: Atlantic Monthly Press.
James, W. (1977) A *Pluralistic Universe*, Cambridge, MA: Harvard University Press.
—— (1978) *Pragmatism* and *The Meaning of Truth* (in one volume), Cambridge, MA: Harvard University Press.
—— (1979) *The Will to Believe*, Cambridge, MA: Harvard University Press.
—— (1985) *The Varieties of Religious Experience*, Cambridge, MA: Harvard University Press.
—— (1988) *Manuscript Essays and Notes*, Cambridge, MA: Harvard University Press.
Royce, J. (1987) *The Conception of God*, New York: Macmillan.

Further reading

Carrette, J. (2005) *William James and The Varieties of Religious Experience*, London: Routledge. (Philosophers and psychologists reflect on *Varieties*.)

Lamberth, D. (1999) *William James and the Metaphysics of Experience*, Cambridge: Cambridge University Press. (Situates James's philosophy of religion in the wider context of his philosophy.)

Putnam, R. (ed.) (1997) *The Cambridge Companion to William James*, Cambridge: Cambridge University Press. (Essays on all aspects of James's philosophy, several specifically on his philosophy of religion.)

Part III
RELIGIOUS DIVERSITY

18
TRUTH IN RELIGION
Ian S. Markham

Does truth matter?

For Geivett and Sweetman, 'whether or not it is rational to believe in the existence of God' is 'one of the most important of all human concerns' (Geivett and Sweetman 1992: 3). This assumes that the truth of religion is central: it matters more than anything else. And the use of human rationality to determine its rationality is therefore of vital importance. As Grace Jantzen observes, Geivett and Sweetman might have overstated the case: 'Taken at face value, this statement is a shocking illustration of the blinkered privilege of western philosophers of religion: there are many millions of people for whom just getting enough to eat is of much more pressing concern' (Jantzen 1998: 79). Jantzen wants philosophy reconnected to life. And most normal people do not sit around determining the rationality of their beliefs.

This question posed by Jantzen is a modern version of the famous debate between William Clifford and William James. Clifford's famous essay 'The ethics of belief' insists that all beliefs need to be justified by the evidence. He starts his essay with a shipowner who decides not to investigate or confirm whether the ship is seaworthy. Instead, the owner has a sincere trust and belief that the ship is fine. Because of this untested (and as events subsequently showed, unfounded) belief, the ship sinks. Clifford is harsh: the shipowner 'had no right to believe on such evidence as was before him' (Clifford in Rowe and Wainwright 1998: 458). He then establishes this as a fundamental principle and axiom. Nothing can be taken on trust or authority; everything should be subject to argument and the evaluation of evidence. He sums up: 'it is wrong always, everywhere, and for any one, to believe anything upon insufficient evidence' (ibid.: 460).

It was William James who wrote the reply ('The will to believe'). For James, there are countless moments when the decision is made in the action. To live life denying oneself the possibility of seeing the world in certain ways because of insufficient evidence is unfair. Belief, for James, should be seen in terms of choices. Certain options present themselves as 'live' options (i.e., something that you could imagine yourself believing), 'forced' (i.e., where you have no option but to decide), and 'momentous' (it is not trivial). James then argues that psychologically indecision (because of insufficient evidence) runs the risk of 'losing the truth' (James in Rowe and Wainwright

1998: 466). For James, Clifford overstates the problem of error. He sums up Clifford thus:

> Believe nothing, he tells us, keep your mind in suspense forever, rather than by closing it on insufficient evidence incur the awful risk of believing lies. You, on the other hand, may think that the risk of being in error is a very small matter when compared with the blessings of real knowledge, and be ready to be duped many times in your investigation rather than postpone indefinitely the chance of guessing true. (ibid.)

For James, taking the risk and believing that religion is true opens up all the advantages of such belief. For those for whom a religious belief is a live option (i.e., temperamentally predisposed to the possibility that religion is true), one has a momentous option (being religious is life-transforming) and a forced option (if you opt for agnosticism, then one does not practice the religion, thereby missing out on the benefits).

One interesting feature of this exchange is the following assumption: Clifford presumes that there is insufficient evidence to provide a certain foundation for belief in God; James accepts this assumption, but then argues that evidence is not the only consideration. At the very least this shows that both men, ostensibly on opposite sides of a debate about the nature of belief, agree that the truth about the existence of God is difficult to determine.

Clifford and James, writing in the latter part of the nineteenth century, demonstrate an emerging cultural attitude to truth in religion (one also found in Jantzen), which shaped much of the modernist project. This short essay will outline briefly the history behind different accounts of truth. However, before doing so, it is helpful to identify some of the major accounts of truth you find in the literature.

Different accounts of truth

Most introductions to philosophy offer four main options (see Hospers 1990: 182–8; also Brümmer 1981: 169–78). The first is the correspondence theory of truth. This is probably closest to what most people mean by truth in ordinary speech. Truth is the property of corresponding to reality. So 'it is raining' is true, if, when looking out of the window, I see rain falling. However, the problem with this account is the precise relation between my perception of rain and the reality of rain. How do we bridge the gap between my belief that it is raining and the fact in reality that it is raining? Several standard arguments for skepticism can be introduced at this point: at the most extreme, it is possible we might be dreaming. More interestingly, we all know that a stick placed in water appears bent; so we know that our senses can be misled. This gap between reality and the mental interpretations of reality is, for many philosophers, too difficult for the correspondence theory to bridge.

The second and third options both eliminate the need for a correspondence with reality. Thus, the second theory stresses instead the importance of coherence. Truth is linked to statements. Statements are part of a system. The statements within the system must cohere with each other. The language of untruth is used when one offers a statement that does not fit in with others within the system. Internal consistency within a system is the only possible requirement for truth that one can set. This means that a tribal culture which explains illness in terms of spirits, and a scientific culture which offers molecular explanations are both coherent options and therefore both true (e.g., Bradley 1914).

The third theory seeks to supplement coherence with 'utility.' What is required is not only an internally consistent world view, but one that 'works' in a pragmatic sense.

The fourth view has a variety of names: the disquotational notion, the redundancy view, or (the one preferred by the most capable recent defender, Paul Horwich) the minimalist theory. This account simplifies matters considerably: truth is a synonym for that which is true. It is a way of saying: consider x, x is true means x (see Horwich 1990).

It is odd how these options are often set out without any historical setting. All too frequently the philosopher's preoccupation with ideas disregards the historical context. This entire approach to philosophy has been challenged by the work of Alasdair MacIntyre. The achievement of his *A Short History of Ethics* was that he located and attempted to explicate why some of the apparently 'timeless' theories he was describing emerged at certain points in history (see MacIntyre 1966). So the emotivist theories of ethics advocated by the logical positivists reflected a certain historical and cultural shift: namely, the modern turn to the subject and the inability to understand how to defend the objectivity of moral assertions. Since *A Short History of Ethics*, MacIntyre has developed further narratives to explain changing attitudes to both ethics and rationality.

This essay began by reflecting on the debate between Clifford and James. We noted the shared assumption that the rational justification of the truth of God's existence is very difficult. So inspired by MacIntyre, we shall now attempt a brief narrative that explains the debate surrounding truth.

History of different accounts of truth

In the western tradition, it was Aristotle, perhaps developing Plato's reflections in the *Sophist*, who offered the basic form of the correspondence theory of truth. With significant variations, the basic insight was affirmed throughout the medieval period. Both Augustine and Thomas Aquinas formulate fairly sophisticated versions of the theory.

It was the Enlightenment that created the problems. Kant, building on Hume and Descartes, is responsible for the perceived difficulties with correspondence. Where Augustine had felt that the problems of perception do not undermine the possibility of correspondence with reality, Kant saw the unbridgeable gap (see Augustine 1955: 93f). Kant is best understood in the light of Descartes and Hume. Descartes had created the impossible standard, that knowledge requires complete certainty. Descartes wrote, 'Reason now leads me to think that I should hold back my assent from opinions which are not completely certain and indubitable just as carefully as I do from those which are patently false' (Descartes 1985: 12). Hume had shown that any attempt to meet that condition is doomed to failure (Hume 1978: bk. 1). Kant's solution was to distinguish between the noumenal and the phenomenal. The noumenal is the way things are in themselves; the phenomenal is the way things appear to the mind. Despite the fact that much of Kant reads as if he is suggesting two separate worlds, most contemporary Kantian scholars believe that in fact he sees the noumenal and the phenomenal as part of the same world (see Alison 1983). Kant is, to use Devitt's terminology, holding a minimal doctrine of 'weak, or Fig-Leaf, Realism' (Devitt 1984: 22, 59–61). So it is not that the noumenal causes the phenomenal (two worlds), but that the phenomenal is the only way we can know the noumenal (one world). For Kant, the act of knowing involves both the actual object and the mental imposition of a priori categories along with the spatio-temporal setting. The problem when it comes to truth is that the mental in a very significant way is actually creating the world in which we live. Once this was seen, then consistency with the rational interpretative scheme became much more important. And if consistency matters, then coherence becomes central.

The pragmatist adjustment reflects a concern to explain change. Why adjust from one coherent scheme into another? The pragmatism of William James stresses the expedience of truth (see James 1978). On this view, science and, for James, religion, are true because they work. They reap benefits in terms of quality of life. This is at the heart of his response to Clifford.

This historical sensitivity creates the awareness that philosophical decisions about truth are not simply judgments about the plausibility of each account (in itself a very difficult exercise), but raise the question whether the cultural presuppositions of each account are justified. So the attractiveness of a coherence or pragmatist account of truth depends on the legitimacy of Kant, which in turn depends on the standard set by Descartes. This was MacIntyre's discovery in *Whose Justice? Which Rationality?*, where he shows brilliantly that the modern tendency towards relativism is a result of unreasonable requirements for knowledge.

A central divide, then, in the contemporary debate about truth in religion is over the legitimacy of modernist assumptions about the problem of discovering that truth. Some, inspired by Continental philosophy, believe that Truth (with a capital T, as Richard Rorty puts it) is completely inaccessible. Others seek to challenge these modernist and, in a slightly different variant, postmodern assumptions; they want to continue to affirm the value and centrality of natural theology in their philosophical method.

Truth in religion is inaccessible

It is perhaps the rather enigmatic philosopher Ludwig Wittgenstein who relocates the debates around religious language from truth to meaning. The problem with Wittgenstein is that he can be read in a variety of different ways. However, it is D. Z. Phillips who has offered a very distinctive and influential reading of Wittgenstein.

A key text for Phillips is Wittgenstein's observation in his 'Lectures on religious belief.' Wittgenstein makes the following observation:

> Suppose someone were a believer and said: 'I believe in a Last Judgement', and I said, 'Well, I'm not so sure. Possibly.' You would say that there is an enormous gulf between us. If he said 'There is a German aeroplane overhead', and I said 'Possibly. I'm not so sure', you'd say we were fairly near.
> (Wittgenstein in Rowe and Wainwright: 1998: 293)

Now Phillips reads this in the following way. Wittgenstein argued that human discourse is a multifaceted entity, and no single rationality can embrace its diversity. Instead of searching for one meta-rationality that provides rules of meaningfulness for all human discourse, one should concede that there are many different rationalities with different rules. Wittgenstein (followed by Phillips) offers the analogy of language games. Consider soccer, cricket, patience, and chess: each game has a different set of rules. It would be absurd to ask a goalkeeper to checkmate the forward or to instruct a chess player to use the bishop to bowl an over. The mistake in both cases is that each game has its own set of rules and its own 'language.' You can only judge an activity within a game by the rules of that particular game. So by analogy, science and religion are separate language games. Within science one constructs a hypothesis and provides evidence for and against; in religion one does not do this. To ask the question 'Does God exist?' within the rules of the scientific language game is as inappropriate as asking whether a knight is off-side in chess.

For Phillips, to understand God-talk, one needs to learn the language of religious communities. According to Phillips, as one does this, one discovers that religious people are not making straightforward claims about reality; instead, religious language is a way of coping with the difficulties in life. So a prayer for a sick relative, for example, is not supposed to bring healing to the patient. If one does pray with that expectation, then one is guilty of superstition, and this would not be authentic religion. It would be a case of misapplying quasi-scientific procedures as if religious dealings were comparable to asking the appropriate human benefactor to intervene in one's situation of need. For Phillips, when one understands the language of prayer from within the language game of religion, then one sees that it is really a way of coping with the contingencies of being human.

It is for this reason that Phillips is frequently described as an 'anti-realist' in religion. Does God objectively exist? Phillips' answer is exasperating; he seems to say 'yes' if you are asking the question within the language game of religion, and 'no' if you are asking it within the language game of science.

For Don Cupitt, the issue is clearer. In *Taking Leave of God*, the proofs for God's existence no longer work and faith needs a symbol, not a reality. He insists that with an objective God, worship is grotesque (no objective supreme being should require humans to grovel and offer praise); but once God is turned into a symbol 'that represents to us everything that spirituality requires of us and promises to us' (Cupitt 1980: 14), then worship makes sense. In *Creation out of Nothing*, the inaccessibility of any form of 'Final Truth' is made central. He writes,

For realism to be true there must be a way things really are that is at last articulable in language. But Final Truth is never reached, because the nature of language is such that there is no sentence whose meaning and interpretation are so clear as to be beyond any possibility of further dispute. The consequence is that reality never gets fully closed or fixed, but goes on being contested endlessly. The world is an argument that never gets settled. So there is no objectively-determinate real world that could ever be finally fixed in language. (Cupitt 1990: 60)

Hidden in this passage is the Cartesian standard for knowledge. If one cannot provide an uncontestable description of the world, then the claim that there are better and worse ways of describing the world cannot be justified. Knowledge of the external world requires uncontestable descriptions. The description of the world must be one that others cannot challenge. It must be a description about which one is completely certain and no doubts are entertained. It is these assumptions that others want to challenge.

Truth in religion is possible

Perhaps the clearest opponent of the Phillips and Cupitt approach is Richard Swinburne. Swinburne's initial trilogy set out his basic position. In *The Coherence of Theism* he delivers his account of religious language and defends the coherence of the idea of God. In *The Existence of God* he argues that there are good inductive arguments for the existence of this God. In *Faith and Reason* he argues that belief in the creed of Christianity, which he sees as having probability on its side, is sufficient for the practice of religion.

On religious language, Swinburne is impatient with the complicated accounts formulated by other theologians. He follows the thirteenth-century philosopher and theologian John Duns Scotus. Religious assertions take certain human concepts from mundane situations and stretch them out to apply to God. So the assertion 'God is love' takes the same basic human quality of 'concern for others' and stretches it out to apply to God. There is no need for St Thomas's tortured 'analogy' or Ian Ramsey's 'models and qualifiers.' God has certain qualities to a much greater degree than is possible in humans beings. Just occasionally one finds oneself forced to the use of words in an analogical rather than direct way, but he stresses that this must be the last resort. Swinburne writes,

[C]learly we ought to assume that theists are using words in their ordinary mundane senses.... When the theist says that God is 'good', 'good' is, I suggest, being used in a perfectly ordinary sense. The only extraordinary thing being suggested is that it exists to a degree in which it does not exist in mundane objects. But when theists say that God is a 'person' who is 'necessarily' able to 'bring about' any state of affairs and 'knows' all things, I shall suggest that if what they say is to be coherent some of these words must be being used in somewhat analogical senses. (Swinburne 1977: 71)

Swinburne's intention is to stress the intelligibility of God-talk. Once we start creating unique rules for our language about God, which in principle humans are too finite to understand, then it becomes very difficult to distinguish gobbledygook from coherent talk; and religious talk becomes simply a creation of the imagination. And anyway, argues Swinburne, since it is possible to construct a metaphysic without too much analogy, then let us avoid needless complexity.

With this view of religious language, he then begins to formulate his definition of God. God is, explains Swinburne, 'like a person without a body (i.e. a spirit) who is eternal, free, able to do anything, knows everything, is perfectly good, is the proper object of human worship and obedience, the creator and sustainer of the universe' (1977: 1). Swinburne clearly feels that he is defending the traditional picture of God. Certainly he wants to affirm all the traditional attributes, which also includes God's omnipotence and omniscience. Although he modifies the traditional relation of God and time, he feels that this is a fairly minimalist adjustment for the sake of coherence.

Having sorted out religious language and offered an account of God, which is coherent, Swinburne is ready to demonstrate the existence of God. He is selective about the arguments that he is willing to endorse. Among the traditional arguments, he dismisses the ontological argument completely, while only providing a very weak version of the cosmological argument. Instead, he concentrates on the design argument and the argument from religious experience. On design, Swinburne is struck by the amazing consistency of the natural order: the fact that the laws of nature continue to operate from moment to moment to moment. Clearly this fundamental consistency cannot be explained by science because science is only possible because natural laws are stable; therefore we need an alternative level of explanation. And this alternative explanation is a personal explanation (see Swinburne 1979: ch. 8). On religious experience, he simply draws attention to the many millions of sane, well-balanced individuals who are totally convinced that they have experienced God. If these people were telling us of some everyday experience (such as seeing a mutual friend in the high street), we would be inclined to accept their report. They are not drunk; they don't take drugs; they are not given to spectacular story-telling; and they lack any motive to mislead. Yet when it comes to a metaphysical experience, we suddenly become so much more skeptical. This is unreasonable. We ought to concede that the widespread phenomenon of religious experience is good evidence for the reality of God (see 1979: ch. 13). In both cases – the arguments from design and religious experience – Swinburne wants us to accept them as good inductive arguments for the existence of God.

For Richard Swinburne, philosophy can now step outside the shadow of Kantian epistemology. Unlike Continental philosophy, analytic philosophy provides the tools to rescue religious discourse. He writes:

Other philosophies of the western world, many of which are often lumped together as 'continental philosophy', have in common an allegiance to Kant's claim that investigation of the nature of the world can discover only patterns in phenomena, not their unobservable causes, and hence 'ultimate questions' are beyond theoretical resolution. Kant lived before the establishment of the atomic theory of chemistry, the first scientific theory to purport to show in precise detail some of the unobservable causes of phenomena – the atoms whose combinations give rise to observable chemical phenomena. No one in the twenty-first century can seriously doubt that, what chemistry purported to show, it really did show, and that we now know a very great deal about the unobservable causes of things and the framework of the universe far beyond observation by the naked eye. The Kantian doctrine about the limits of human knowledge was a big mistake; and analytic philosophy, unlike Continental philosophy, has liberated itself from that doctrine. (Swinburne in Harris and Insole 2005: 39)

For Swinburne, truth in religion is possible. There are good arguments for theism (and, as he later argued, for other Christian doctrines), which ought to persuade the skeptic.

Truth issues in religion

Thus far this discussion has concentrated on the underlying character of religious discourse, namely, the extent to which the discourse is grounded in a quest for truth (beyond human projection or linguistic constructions). This essay will conclude by looking at some of the other issues surrounding truth in religion.

The first is the extent to which truth is either grounded in religion or alternatively distinctively shaped by religion. The argument that truth is grounded in religion was made by Brian Hebblethwaite in *The Ocean of Truth*. This connection has an ancient pedigree, perhaps originally made by Augustine of Hippo in *On the Freedom of the Will*. For Hebblethwaite, there is an 'argument from objectivity and truth to God' (Hebblethwaite 1988: 109). I have developed his argument in *Truth and the Reality of God* (Markham 1998). The idea that truth is distinctively shaped by religion was formulated by Bruce Marshall. Marshall, who is building on George Lindbeck's *The Nature of Doctrine*, wants to argue that 'a genuinely theological account of truth and epistemic justification needs to be robustly Trinitarian. It ought to subject whatever ideas it may find useful to the formative discipline of the Christian community's convictions about the triune God' (Marshall 1999: xi–xii). Marshall goes on to argue that the ritual practice of the church is the key to understanding the core commitments of the Christian community and that this practice is firmly Trinitarian. Andrew Moore takes a similar approach and argues for a 'Christian realism' where 'ontology and epistemology [are] shaped in the context of the covenant consummated in Christ' (Moore 2003: 183).

The second issue is the area of religious diversity. When John Hick offered his pluralist hypothesis, his debt to Kant was explicit. Hick explains that the pluralistic

hypothesis is that 'the great world faiths embody different perceptions and conceptions of, and correspondingly different responses to, the Real from within the major
variant ways of being human; and that within each of them the transformation of
human existence from self-centredness to Reality-centredness is taking place' (Hick
1989: 240). He then goes on to say:

> In developing this thesis our chief philosophical resource will be one of Kant's
> most basic epistemological insights, namely that the mind actively interprets
> sensory information in terms of concepts, so that the environment as we
> consciously perceive and inhabit it is our familiar three-dimensional world of
> objects interacting in space. (1989: 240)

For Hick, each culture is experiencing the 'Real' (his preferred inclusive term for 'God'
or the 'Transcendent') through a particular lens. When Christians name the religious
experience 'the triune God,' this is simply their cultural linguistic imposition on the
experience. Meanwhile Buddhists are talking about 'nirvana,' which is a Buddhist
imposition. The great advantage is that no religion is any better or worse than any of
the alternatives.

Opponents of John Hick's pluralist hypothesis have concentrated on his account of
truth. Harold Netland's argument for a version of exclusivism is grounded in a defense
of 'propositional truth,' which means that 'truth is a property of propositions such
that a proposition is true if and only if the state of affairs to which it refers is as the
proposition asserts it to be; otherwise it is false' (Netland 1991: 114–15). For Netland,
God is either triune or not; it makes no sense to talk about God as being neither, nor
beyond any resolution. For Netland, Hick's pluralism is tantamount to agnosticism.

Related to this debate over the Christian theology of other religions, we have
the challenge to relativism. Both Catholic and evangelical theologians have been
challenging the relativist culture of modernity. Pope John Paul II wrote an encyclical
in 1993 called *Veritatis Splendor* ('The Splendor of Truth'). For Pope John Paul II, true
freedom depends on a concept of 'universal truth' (John Paul II 1993: 53). We do not
want a freedom where the Nazi's ethic is the epistemological equivalent of the ethic
advocated by the great civil rights leader, Martin Luther King.

For the evangelicals, Brad Stetson and Joseph Conti argue that true toleration
needs to be grounded in truth. They argue that the Judeo-Christian tradition 'uniquely
has the resources to uphold true tolerance and prevent its collapse into an antitradi-
tional, secular intolerance based on an arbitrary selection of untested and ultimately
incoherent assertions about human rights and purposes' (Stetson and Conti 2005:
173).

So then the concept of truth in religion is a key battleground for the shape of one's
theology. Much is dependent on how one understands truth. Modernity has created
options about the understanding of truth. However, for those who want to continue
to affirm natural theology and an objective God, coupled with a robust account of
freedom and tolerance, modernity has taken a wrong turn.

See also David Hume (Chapter 13), Immanuel Kant (Chapter 14), William James (Chapter 17), Religious traditions and rational assessments (Chapter 19), Religious pluralism (Chapter 20), Inclusivism and exclusivism (Chapter 21), Non-theistic conceptions of God (Chapter 22), Goodness (Chapter 28), The cosmological argument (Chapter 32), The teleological argument (Chapter 33), The moral argument (Chapter 34), The problem of religious language (Chapter 39), Naturalistic rejoinders to theistic arguments (Chapter 40), Why is there a universe at all, rather than just nothing? (Chapter 41), Postmodern theology (Chapter 47), Theology and religious language (Chapter 48), Continental philosophy (Chapter 60), Religious naturalism (Chapter 62), Religion and science (Chapter 64).

References

Alison, H. (1983) *Kant's Transcendental Idealism: An Interpretation and Defense*, New Haven, CT: Yale University Press.

Augustine (1955) *The Problem of Free Choice*, trans. M. Pontifex, London: Longmans.

Brümmer, V. (1981) *Theology and Philosophical Inquiry*, Basingstoke: Macmillan.

Bradley, F. H. (1914) *Essays on Truth and Reality*, Oxford: Clarendon Press.

Cupitt, D. (1980) *Taking Leave of God*, London: SCM Press.

—— (1990) *Creation out of Nothing*, London: SCM Press.

Descartes, R. (1985) *The Philosophical Writings of Descartes*, trans. J. Cottingham, R. Stoothoff, and D. Murdoch, Cambridge: Cambridge University Press.

Devitt, M. (1984) *Realism and Truth*, Princeton, NJ: Princeton University Press.

Geivett, R. D. and B. Sweetman (eds) (1992) *Contemporary Perspectives on Religious Epistemology*, Oxford: Oxford University Press.

Harris, H. A. and C. J. Insole (eds) (2005) *Faith and Philosophical Analysis: The Impact of Analytical Philosophy on the Philosophy of Religion*, Aldershot: Ashgate.

Hebblethwaite, B. (1988) *The Ocean of Truth: A Defence of Objective Theism*, Cambridge: Cambridge University Press.

Hick, J. (1989) *An Interpretation of Religion*, Basingstoke: Macmillan.

Horwich, P. (1990) *Truth*, Oxford: Blackwell.

Hospers, J. (1990) *An Introduction to Philosophical Analysis*, 3rd edn, London: Routledge.

Hume, D. (1978) *A Treatise of Human Nature*, ed. L. A. Selby-Bigge, 2nd edn, Oxford: Clarendon Press.

James, W. (1978) *Pragmatism: A New Name for Some Old Ways of Thinking [and] The Meaning of Truth: A Sequel to 'Pragmatism,'* Cambridge, MA: Harvard University Press.

Jantzen, G. (1998) *Becoming Divine: Towards a Feminist Philosophy of Religion*, Manchester: Manchester University Press.

John Paul II (1993) *Veritatis Splendor*, Encyclical Letter, Washington, DC: United States Catholic Conference.

MacIntyre A. (1966) *A Short History of Ethics*, New York: Macmillan.

Markham, I. (1998) *Truth and the Reality of God*, Edinburgh: T. & T. Clark.

Marshall, B. D. (1999) *Trinity and Truth*, Cambridge: Cambridge University Press.

Moore, A. (2003) *Realism and Christian Faith*, Cambridge: Cambridge University Press.

Netland, H. (1991) *Dissonant Voices: Religious Pluralism and the Question of Truth*, Grand Rapids, MI: Eerdmans; Leicester: Apollos.

Plato (1993) *Sophist*, trans. N. White, Indianapolis, IN: Hackett.

Rowe, W. L. and W. J. Wainwright (1998) *Philosophy of Religion: Selected Readings*, Oxford: Oxford University Press.

Stetson, B. and J. G. Conti (2005) *The Truth about Tolerance: Pluralism, Diversity and the Culture Wars*, Downers Grove, IL: InterVarsity Press.

Swinburne, R. (1977) *The Coherence of Theism*, Oxford: Clarendon Press.

—— (1979) *The Existence of God*, Oxford: Clarendon Press.

Further reading

Blackburn, S. (2005) *Truth: A Guide*, Oxford: Oxford University Press. (A helpful, informed survey of the key debates.)

Cupitt, D. (2002) *Is Nothing Sacred? The Non-Realist Philosophy of Religion*, New York: Fordham University Press. (A clear exposition of non-realism in religion.)

Kirkham, R. L. (1992) *Theories of Truth*, Cambridge, MA: MIT Press. (Probably the best summary of different accounts of truth.)

19

RELIGIOUS TRADITIONS AND RATIONAL ASSESSMENTS

Keith Yandell

Introduction

The structure of this essay is simple. First, we consider what rational assessment of religious traditions means and the current status of the idea that it is possible. Second, beliefs that are philosophical as well as religious will be noted. Third, a particular argument in favor of a typical Buddhist claim is assessed. Fourth, arguments against that claim are assessed. Fifth, some conclusions are drawn.

I note, at the outset, two things. (1) I am not trying to establish or refute any particular religious tradition. Any religious tradition worth considering will involve much more simply in terms of explaining what there is in it to try to establish or refute than I can do here, let alone taking a careful run at assessing it. I am arguing that rational assessment – consideration of arguments and evidence for and against the propositions that comprise the core doctrines of a religious tradition – is possible. (2) In discussing some of the complex Buddhist tradition, I ignore the fact that earlier Buddhism is not, and much of later Buddhism is, idealistic. This has its importance, but it does not matter for my argument here.

The idea of rational assessment of religions

Some major religions (e.g., the varieties of Semitic monotheism, Hinduism, and Buddhism, as well as Jainism) offer diagnoses of a deep disease from which we all suffer and propose a cure. The diagnoses and cures make metaphysical and epistemological assumptions that underlie or constitute central religious doctrines.

The idea of a doctrineless religion has no purchase on any reasonably representative version of the religions just mentioned. Claims that doctrines are useless once one becomes enlightened are balanced by claims that becoming enlightened requires religious knowledge. While not all rational assessment of religious belief is philosophical – e.g., the orthodox Semitic monotheisms require certain historical claims – my concern here is with philosophy. Rational assessment of a single religious tradition is a matter of discovering and stating its core metaphysical, epistemological, and ethical assumptions and doctrines, and considering reasons for and against them. Rational assessment across traditions requires comparative judgments regarding the results of single tradition assessments though one can engage in both simultaneously. Only recently have the details of various traditions and sub-traditions become reliably accessible through competent translations and insightful discussion. It is ironic that this situation, which brightens the prospect of rational assessment of the now better understood traditions and sub-traditions, has been influential in promoting the idea that their rational assessment is impossible by contributing to the view that religions provide a smorgasbord of belief and practice, all of the same quality, among which one picks what suits one's tastes.

Typical rejections of cross-cultural rational assessment note that there are

> people who hold that philosophy as a body of truths ... like mathematics and sciences ought not to differ from people to people. This is not, however, a correct view. Mathematics and sciences are not humanistic studies and may not, therefore, differ from people to people. But not so studies that are humanistic. For any particular people, humanist studies have perforce to be coloured, circumscribed, and motivated by certain basic, though evidently local (because not common to all people of the world) ideas and attitudes and also by how the 'truths' ... have to be utilized in particular historico-geographical circumstances. (Bhattacharya 1975: 174)

Also: 'Mathematical calculations and geometrical theorems hold good universally in all cultures and countries, but such is not the case with philosophical doctrines and theories' (Upadhyaya 1975: 149). In other words, the former is not culture-bound, while the latter is. These claims, obviously not scientific or mathematical, are the very sorts of claims that their authors assert cannot be made; they express propositions that, if true, are cross-culturally true independent of their social, cultural, and historical context. They are true or false, and if true, they are false on their own terms. So they are false. As another Indian philosopher notes:

> the possibility of common or diverse approaches cannot be denied or avoided – common between the same cultural or historically unconnected peoples and times, diverse between the same cultural or historical groups at simultaneous or different times. Agnosticism, atheism, idealism, realism, monism, pluralism, empiricism, transcendentalism, positivism, or even existentialism are [sic] features of philosophy the world over. (Ramakrishna Rao 1975: 102) [Presumably 'transcendentalism' includes theism.]

There are endeavors rationally to assess religious beliefs within the boundaries of India. There are Buddhist arguments against monotheism and monotheistic arguments against Buddhism. There are articulate Jain–Buddhist polemics. Critiques of one Buddhist school or sub-tradition by another are common. Hindu religious thinkers reject other Hindu religious ideas, and there are mutual Hindu–Buddhist critiques. The history of Semitic monotheisms includes argument back and forth. The observations about closed domains simply do not reflect the actual historical situation. Very often the inter-traditional critiques argue from premises accepted by only one group, although there is no necessity to this. Intra-traditional critiques, of course, are more likely to argue from common or closer perspectives. While many of the disputes have concerned the interpretation of sacred texts, many have not. Criticism need not be negative. Two facts are salient here. One is that there are rigorous endeavors in rational assessment of religious doctrines within religious traditions. The other is that there are rigorous endeavors in rational assessment of religious doctrines between religious traditions. Though they often are, such endeavors need not be polemical. They can even occur among friends.

Perhaps the clearest case of powerful assessment of religious doctrine occurs within Hinduism in the case of the monotheistic critique of the monistic absolutism held by Advaita Vedanta. We will pursue a more complex case.

Some religio-philosophical or philosophico-religious doctrines

We begin by stating some conflicting positions held by contemporary philosophers.

Presentism: for any time T, what exists is what exists at T, and nothing else.

Conservative Indexicalism: for any time T, what exists at T is what exists at T as well as what existed at any time before T, and nothing else.

Liberal Indexicalism: for any time T, what exists at T is what exists at T, any time before T, and any time after T.

These views, obviously incompatible, are intended to apply to concrete items. Two other incompatible views are relevant:

Endurantism: there are things that exist for successive periods of time, remaining numerically identical over that period; change is a matter of some enduring item coming to have a property it lacked or to lack a property that it had (or both).

Perdurantism: there is nothing that exists for successive periods of time, save in virtue of its composing parts existing without themselves enduring for successive periods of time; change is a matter of one temporal part of a sequence passing out of existence and another temporal part occurring in it.

There is massive literature on these views, and few think they are beyond rational assessment.

At the root of Buddhist thought are four claims: nothing non-composite endures at all; all unenlightened states are unsatisfactory; there is no enduring self; and dependent origination reigns: nirvana aside, everything that ever exists is caused to exist and exists dependent on other items during all of its momentary existence. These claims oppose everyday belief about persons, which seems to be presupposed by reincarnation and karma doctrine. Reincarnation doctrine holds that a person exists beginninglessly and, unless she becomes enlightened, goes through countless bodies in lifetime after lifetime.

Karma doctrine, in non-theistic contexts, holds that by natural necessity good deeds bring good consequences and bad deeds bring bad consequences so that an agent receives due recompense for all morally relevant behavior. Thus nature ensures justice in the long run. This is most easily understood in terms of an enduring conscious subject retaining personal identity over eons, without exception reaping what he sowed. Buddhism does not interpret reincarnation and karma this way. The closest it comes to doing so is Non-reductionist Buddhism, for which what exists that talk of persons refers to is, at a time, a collection of momentary causally related states, and over time a sequence of such collections. In some sense the sequence is an entity on its own, not reducible to its components. Then there is Reductionist Buddhism, for which the sequence made up of collections is just one collection after another, and each collection is just the states that compose it. There is also Absolutist Buddhism, which denies that there really are states, and hence rejects collections and sequences.

Leaving Absolutist Buddhism aside for now, we begin with the Non-reductionist and Reductionist perspectives. The contrasting view, represented by much of Hinduism and Jainism, holds that there is an absolutely permanent and indestructible *Atman* which is, or in some way serves as the basis of, the human self. Leaving aside the part about absolute permanence and indestructibility, the opposing view to Reductive Buddhism is what is known as Endurantism, whereas Reductionist perspectives are what is known as Perdurantism, with Non-reductive Buddhism being a version of Endurantism that is dubiously orthodox. The dispute between these views plays a central role in contemporary philosophy of mind.

There are obvious differences between the Buddhist context and the modern and contemporary Anglo-American (and Australian, Scandinavian, etc.) context. For example, while Hume was a Perdurantist, he viewed each simple perception as an independently existing entity whereas the Buddhist tradition does not. Probably the most important difference relates to Buddhist concerns with soteriology (salvation, liberation), which is lacking in contemporary philosophical circles. There seem to be at least two ways in which soteriological issues are relevant. One is that for the Buddhist tradition, enlightenment is possible only if there is not ontologically too much to what is to become enlightened.

> Given that phenomena are streams of point instances, they are more non-existent than existent. Compared with the period of existence that has elapsed and the future moments of a thing's existence, the present moment, in which the phenomenon is experienced, is practically a nullity. (Shantarakshita 2005: 391, n. 83)

The traveler to enlightenment must be quite light.

The other is that if there is ontologically too much to what is to become enlightened, attachment to what there is, which makes enlightenment unavailable, is very difficult to avoid, since attachment to anything precludes enlightenment. If all that exists is a sequence of collections of instantaneously appearing and disappearing items, then there is little to which informed attachment is possible. The traveler to enlightenment must travel quite lightly. This-life enlightenment comes by having an esoteric religious experience characterized by peace, bliss, and detachment, in which one recognizes the truth of the Buddhist no-self doctrine. Final enlightenment frees the enlightened one from the necessity of returning to the cycle of rebirth and redeath.

The Theravadins hold to the literalness of reincarnation and karma doctrine. They also hold the doctrine of dependent origination which says that, nirvana aside, every existent depends for its origin and brief existence on other items. They also hold to the conventionality of talk of persons, which involves a no-self doctrine to the effect that just as a chariot is nothing more than its parts, a so-called person is nothing more than its parts. They also hold, against the Sarvastivadins, that only present items exist, not being joined by past and future things. So they represent Reductionist Buddhism, agreeing with Perdurantism and Presentism, thus rejecting Endurantism and Indexicalism. The Sarvastivadins are Indexicalists, holding that eternal dharmas exist but bring about momentary manifestations.

The Pudgalada (a group of schools) worry that if the Theravadin doctrine concerning persons is correct, then there is nothing that has continuity in even one life, let alone over many lifetimes. How then is karma to work? How could the item that sought enlightenment be the item that found it? They offer an account on which there are non-permanent, non-impermanent persons. There are persons who are not made up of temporal stages but also are not gifted with inherent immortality. More puzzling is the characterization of a person as non-identical and non-different: not identical to her temporal parts but not different from them. But this can easily be read as affirming the falsehood of Reductionist Buddhism but maintaining that a person cannot exist in the absence of what the Reductionists view as her temporal parts. This appears to be a version of Endurantism, and has been viewed with almost universal suspicion in other Buddhist perspectives, since it seems to deny the no-self doctrine.

The Pudgalavadins are concerned with the protection of the retributive justice of karma doctrine and the attainment of enlightenment by the numerically identical item that sought it, enough to risk holding a doctrine incompatible with the core of Buddhist teaching.

We have, then, representatives of Endurantism, Perdurantism, Presentism, and Indexicalism. These views are part of a general religious perspective meant to be a guidebook to practices that yield enlightenment. Acceptance of a no-self doctrine – acceptance in a manner that colors all of how one thinks and acts – is held to be part of the in-this-lifetime enlightenment experience itself. Contemporary philosophers who argue for or against Endurantism, Perdurantism, Presentism, and Indexicalist do not take any of these positions to be a matter of saving belief. That said, the various

Buddhist views do include positions on these issues. If religious views cannot be rationally assessed, then these views cannot be rationally assessed. If these views can be rationally assessed, then religious views can be rationally assessed.

There is also Madhyamaka or Absolutist Buddhism, the Buddhist Advaita Vedanta. On this view, the very temporal parts of the alleged collections do not exist. Hence there are no sequences either. The background assumption is that all things are 'empty' in the sense of lacking an essence. The doctrine of co-dependent origination holds that all things depend on other things; nothing exists without depending on something else for its existence. (This is one reason why Buddhism is typically atheistic.) Depending on the direction in which these ideas are developed, it is possible to conclude from them that there really exists no multiplicity of things and that nothing has distinct properties (and hence nothing has properties). This is nihilism. The most famous Buddhist philosopher to be identified with this position is Nagarjuna, who rejects the allegation. Nonetheless, the grounds on which he does so appeal to the familiar Buddhist doctrine of two truths, one conventional and one ultimate. Since 'conventional truth' concerns only a 'world' that we are supposed to have 'constructed,' albeit unknowingly, it is not literally true. What is literally true is ultimate truth; 'ultimate truth' is strictly redundant. Nagarjuna's denial is not cogent, and the widespread Buddhist reading of his position as nihilistic, and hence to be rejected, is justified. Nonetheless, the notion of constructions is influential in Buddhist thought. Those who trade in constructions, and their close kin conventions, are by no means limited to the Buddhist traditions, and these views are hotly debated. None of this even suggests that these issues are beyond the range of rational assessment.

An argument for Perdurantism/Buddhist Non-reductivism, and appeal to enlightenment experience as evidence

Here is an argument that nothing concrete can endure.

1 For all X and Y, if X is numerically identical to Y, then [Necessarily, X is numerically identical to Y].
2 If [Necessarily, X is numerically identical to Y], then for all X and Y, if it is false that [Necessarily, X exists if and only if Y exists], then it is false that X is numerically identical to Y.
3 For all X and Y, if it is false that [Necessarily, X exists if and only if Y exists], then it is false that X is numerically identical to Y.

Step 3 follows from steps 1 and 2, and steps 1 and 2 are necessary truths. So far, then, the argument is in fine shape.

4 For any X and Y, if X exists at time t_1 and Y exists at time t_2, it is false that [Necessarily, X exists if and only if Y exists].
5 If for any X and Y, if X exists at time t_1 and Y exists at time t_2, it is false that

[Necessarily, X exists if and only if Y exists], then it is not possible that something that exists at time t_1 be numerically identical to anything that exists at time t_2.

6 It is not possible that something that exists at time t_1 be numerically identical to anything that exists at time t_2.

Step 5 is a necessary truth, and step 6 follows from steps 4 and 5.

7 If it is not possible that something that exists at time t_1 be numerically identical to anything that exists at time t_2, then nothing can endure.

So:

8 Nothing can endure.

Step 7 is a necessary truth, and step 8 follows from steps 6 and 7. The result, then, is that all goes well with the argument provided step 4 is true. This argument, if correct, not only proves that nothing can endure, but also that nothing can exist over time gaps. Since Endurantism is the major (if not only serious) competitor to Perdurantism, this is a significantly pro-Buddhist argument. The crucial issue here is that 4 is ambiguous. It can mean:

4a If X is a concrete item and exists at t_1, it is not a necessary truth that X exists at t_2.

4b If X is a concrete item and exists at t_1, it is a necessary truth that nothing that exists at t_2 is numerically identical to X.

While 4a is true, it does not help the argument. While 4b would help the argument, it is false unless Perdurantism is true, and hence has no place in an argument for Perdurantism.

The argument just discussed concerns the diachronic identity of persons. There is a different approach to the issue of the synchronic identity of persons. The typical Buddhist claim is that at any given time a person is simply a set of momentary states. It is claimed that this can be discerned by having an esoteric meditative experience in which one directly observes the full contents of what composes oneself (if that word be allowed here) – strictly, what there is at the time to which talk of oneself misleadingly refers – and those contents are discerned to be simply a collection of momentary states. I waive here all appeal to the claim that in this experience one achieves omniscience. One can defend any claim one likes by claiming that some being who is omniscient believes that the proposition that one favors is true, and since omniscient beings have no false beliefs, it is true. Jainism maintains that Jain achievers of enlightenment are omniscient in principle all along, but having an esoteric experience of the proper sort unmasks to the subject himself an omniscience hitherto latent and hidden. The enlightened Jain believes that persons are enduring mental (thinking) substances, and since what an omniscient being believes is true, a person is an enduring mental substance. Buddhism makes analogous claims.

The experiences appealed to may be described as at least quasi-introspective in that they are held to occur typically at the end a long series of meditative states that involve 'looking inward,' and to justify claims about what is ordinarily referred to as the subject of the experience.

There are deep problems with the claim that such experiences confirm the no-self doctrine. One is that, as we have noted, Buddhist meditators and Jain meditators report opposite, or at least contrary, results. A more significant problem is that the Buddhist appeal to such experiences will yield the desired results only on some such assumption as A: *All that makes up what person-at-a-time talk refers to is what is discerned in the right sort of quasi-introspective experience.* This proposition is not itself even possibly confirmed by quasi-introspective experience, nor is it at all clear that it is true. Further, appeal to experience here requires that there be something that discerns the collection of causally interacting momentary states, including observing that they are momentary. So there at least must be some second-order state to which the first-order states are evident. How is this second-order state, which is not identical to a collection of momentary conscious states, but instead is aware of them, and which has properties and causal powers, not a very short-lived substance? But if there are short-lived substances, how do we know that all substances are *short*-lived? Experientially discerning that the collections of states that compose 'oneself' at a time are only momentary, because the members of the collection are only momentary, can't be observed by anything that does not endure long enough to see them arrive and depart. On the doctrine that is supposed to be established by appeal to quasi-introspective experience nothing does endure, but how is this to be experientially confirmed if nothing does endure?

If appeal to memory is made, the memory appealed to must be of a certain sort; it must be a matter of an earlier collection C_1 at time t_1 causing a later collection C2 at t_2 to contain a representation of C_1 that C_2 recognizes as a memory. Such collections, on the no-self theory, must have all sorts of dispositional properties that are passed from one collection to another if what there is of truth in talk about persons is to be true. Beliefs, habits, preferences, and so on, remain stable for more than an instant and they can be stable on a no-self view only by numerically distinct temporal stages passing along the beliefs, habits, preferences, and so on. Earlier stages cause the belief-relevant, habit-relevant, preference-relevant, and so on, properties to be copied from one temporal stage to another. The reliability of such memory states is not itself something that can be established by appeal to quasi-introspective experience, but must be assumed in order for the desired conclusion concerning momentariness to be inferred. So the reliability of memory, where 'memory' must have the particular technical sense, is required as well as appeal to the metaphysical proposition A above. That there is memory in that technical sense will be true only if the doctrine of no-self is assumed. But appeal to quasi-introspective experience was supposed to establish the doctrine that one must assume in order to read the experience as establishing the doctrine. In addition, surely the reliability of memory cannot be assumed, given how mistaken ordinary beliefs based in part on memory are said by Buddhism to be.

An argument against Reductive, Non-reductive, and Absolutist Buddhism

Either there is a minimal unit of time or there is not. If there is, it is the analogue of a spatial point lacking extension, namely a temporal point lacking duration. Suppose there is, and call the briefest time that does involve duration a temporal atom. Either a temporal atom is composed of temporal points or it is not. If it is, then it has an emergent property – a property that none of its members has that is not merely additive. It is impossible that there be temporal atoms that are not composed of temporal points, just as it is impossible that there be lines that are not composed of spatial points. So if there are temporal minima, temporal atoms are items over and above their temporal parts. According to Perdurantism, anything that endures is made up of successive momentary items that exist for a minimal unit of time. Any enduring item, then, is composed of items that occupy only a temporal point. The enduring thing that they compose thus has a non-additive property that its components lack, namely being of temporal extent. So the enduring thing is something more than just its parts. Hence, it is not reducible to those parts, and Reductive Buddhism is false. Non-reductive Buddhism is right.

A response is that what the Reductive Buddhist requires is not that there be a minimal unit like a point, but that there be nothing that lasts very long. In this respect, the Reductive Buddhist is better off if time is atomistic, where atoms are temporally minimal but are not entirely temporally unextended; they have a tiny duration. This escapes the above argument. Nothing endures as long as two temporal atoms, save by having numerically distinct temporal parts that exist in succession. But time probably is not atomistic, and if it is not, then this move is unavailable.

Another response is that what is crucial to the Buddhist doctrine of impermanence is that nothing that has more than instantaneous existence can ever be fully present at any one time. A sequence of temporal stages never exists fully at any time, and time holds only instantaneous items and sequences thereof. There may be no minimal temporal unit, but a universe that contains nothing that lasts longer than the amount of time it takes a strong man to snap his fingers will do nicely. This has the disadvantage of *How long does a temporal stage last?* having no answer. Suppose there is a person, or what person-talk refers to, that is composed of temporal stages. How many stages is she composed of? Any answer is arbitrary. The point is not the epistemological one that we can't tell. The relevant point is metaphysical: there is no fact of the matter as to how many stages compose her. But then it is merely conventional that there are temporal stages, and we are left with Buddhist Absolutism, which most Buddhists reject.

Further, Absolutist Buddhism holds that 'the world' is composed of just conventional items; so there really aren't any temporal stages, hence no collections of temporal stages, hence no sequences of collections. So there is nothing to have any disease to be diagnosed, no one to diagnose them, and no one to be cured. Buddhism itself is only conventionally true, and so is ultimately false. But things can't be conventional all the way down; someone must create the conventions, even if they cannot help doing so. So Absolutist Buddhism is not only false, but self-refuting.

Then Non-Reductionist Buddhism must be right; so sequences are something non-conventional over and above their composing parts. But then a sequence is an enduring being distinct from its parts, though it must have parts in order to exist. So long as a sequence continues, this something else continues and collects karmic credits and debits and achieves enlightenment in this life. This something over and above its 'parts,' that cannot exist without its 'parts,' and is not identical to its 'parts,' is a non-composite enduring being. So Non-reductive Buddhism rejects a core Buddhist tenet, and the Personalists are at the verge, if not in the midst, of heresy.

Conclusion

My point here is not that the previous section refutes Buddhism and we can go on to other religions. The Buddhist tradition is nothing if not subtle, and requires vastly more discussion than it can receive here. My point is rather that Perdurantism versus Endurantism, and Idexicalism versus Presentism are *relevant* to core Buddhist claims that the traditions widely take to be soteriologically essential. Further, these matters are subjects of (de facto) rational discussion. It is no argument for the idea that there is no fact of the matter as to which views are true that it is unlikely that there be universal consent or general consensus concerning this matter. There being universal consent or general consensus is not a necessary condition for the truth about anything other than universal content and general consensus. One cannot avoid refutation by stubbornly failing to grant that is has occurred or being ignorant that it has. There are entailment relations between various philosophical claims and diverse Buddhist doctrines. The tradition itself has a host of distinguished members who have not merely granted, but insisted on, this fact.

Rational assessment of religious belief has been present within and between religious traditions within and across religious borders. It is likely to be polemically most successful if it is internal to a sub-tradition or tradition, but being polemical is not an element essential to rational assessment. There have been many discussions of religious doctrine by parties who disagreed about which doctrines were true, and given the present state of increase of knowledge of what the doctrines are, the degree of de facto possibility for this is greater now than before, so long as accepting a religious pluralism that insists that everyone is equally wrong is not a condition of participating in the enterprise. The Buddhist tradition, like any other, has constraints on what can be held consistently within its scope. The attempt to allow inconsistent positions to be embraced at 'different levels,' or to posit conventional truth and ultimate truth includes trying to escape what follows from such distinctions: ultimate truth is simply true and conventional truth is simply false, a report of how things seem to the unenlightened, who are mistaken.

The doctrines of impermanence, co-dependent arising, and no-self are at the core of Buddhist thought. Indexicalism is incompatible with impermanence. Theism is incompatible with co-dependent arising. No-self is incompatible with the view of persons in theistic Hinduism and Jainism, which is atheistic. Presentism is compatible with these Buddhist doctrines, but Endurantism is not. Perdurantism is compatible with these doctrines. Thus Presentism, atheism, and Perdurantism are Buddhistically permissible, and perhaps required, whereas Indexicalism, theism, and Endurantism are Buddhistically excluded. To claim that no rational assessment of these views is possible is a very strong and highly dubious claim. But if rational assessment of these views is possible, a rational assessment of core doctrines in Buddhism is possible. Hence to claim that no rational assessment of core doctrines in Buddhism is possible is to make a very strong and highly dubious claim. Buddhism is not unique in the relevant regards.

See also Buddhism (Chapter 2), Truth in religion (Chapter 18), Religious pluralism (Chapter 20), Inclusivism and exclusivism (Chapter 21), Non-theistic conceptions of God (Chapter 22), Omniscience (Chapter 24), The problem of religious language (Chapter 39), Theology and religious language (Chapter 48), Phenomenology of religion (Chapter 61).

References

Bhattacharya, K. (1975) 'Traditional Indian philosophy as a modern Indian thinker views it,' in N. K. Devaraja (ed.) *Indian Philosophy Today*, Delhi: Macmillan of India.

Ramakrishna Rao, K. B. (1975) 'The relevance of Indian thought to the evolution of world philosophy,' in N. K. Devaraja (ed.) *Indian Philosophy Today*, Delhi: Macmillan of India.

Shantarakshita (2005) *The Adornment of the Middle Way: Shantarakshita's* Madhyamakalankara *with Commentary by Jamgon Mipham*, trans. Padmakara Translation Group, Boston, MA: Shambala.

Upadhyaya, K.N. (1975) 'Some reflections on the Indian view of philosophy,' in N. K. Devaraja (ed.) *Indian Philosophy Today*, Delhi: Macmillan of India.

Further readings

Christian, W. (1972) *Opposition of Religious Doctrine*, New York: Herder & Herder. (A careful discussion of doctrinal difference across traditions.)

Frykenberg, R. E. and P. Kolenda (1985) *Studies of South Asia*, Madras: New Era Publications. (Contains a critique, by the present author, of the view that philosophical and religious claims are culture-bound.)

Griffiths, P. (1991) *An Apology for Apologetics*, Maryknoll, NY: Orbis Books. (A rigorous defense of rational assessment of religious traditions.)

Hudson, H. (2001) *A Materialist Metaphysics of the Human Person*, Ithaca, NY: Cornell University Press. (Gives a sophisticated materialist account of persons that is supposed to be compatible with some religious views.)

Merricks, T. (2001) *Objects and Persons*, Oxford: Oxford University Press. (Offers a clear critique of reductionism, and defence of Endurantism, regarding persons.)

Smart, N. (1964a) *Doctrine and Argument in Indian Philosophy*, London: Allen & Unwin. (A valuable account of doctrinal differences and arguments concerning them in Indian thought.)

—— (1964b) *Philosophers and Religious Truth*, London: SCM Press. (An imaginary dialogue between representatives of different religious traditions.)

Williams, P. (2000) *Buddhist Thought*, London: Routledge. (Offers a clear and philosophically orientated discussion of the varieties of the Mahayana Tradition.)

Wood, T. (1990) *Mind-only*, Honolulu: University of Hawaii Press. (An excellent discussion of Buddhist idealism.)

Yandell, K. E. (1995) *The Epistemology of Religious Experience*, Cambridge: Cambridge University Press.

(Contains assessments of Buddhist (and Jain) Personalist, and Buddhist Impersonalist, accounts of what is behind talk of persons.)

—— (1999) *Philosophy of Religion*, New York: Routledge. (An attempt to provide a basis for cross-cultural assessment of religious belief.)

20
RELIGIOUS PLURALISM
John Hick

In contemporary philosophy of religion it is customary to use the tripartite distinction between exclusivism, inclusivism, and pluralism. And providing we recognize a range of variations within each, this is accurate. We should, however, note that the entire discussion can be conducted in terms of truth claims or salvation claims or both. There are those who see religions as essentially belief systems, with salvation dependent upon right belief, and those who see salvation as essentially a human transformation which can take place under the banner of different and often incompatible belief systems. But most treat the two as going together, though with different weightings between them. There are also different degrees of emphasis upon the eschatological, or afterlife, aspect of religion.

Extreme pluralism

The most extreme version of pluralism treats the different world religions as enclosed and mutually exclusive systems of belief and salvation, different but of equal value. This is the position of Stephen Kaplan, making use of the work of the physicist David Bohm. Kaplan develops a theory according to which there is a plurality of ultimate realities, both personal and non-personal, each religion being related to a different one. In ordinary usage there can by definition only be one truly *ultimate* reality, but Kaplan introduces his own stipulative definition. He says,

> When a religious tradition declares that it has discovered ultimate reality, I understand that declaration in the context of its soteriological position. An ultimate reality is that ontological nature that provides individuals with a soteriological conclusion to existence – with a form of salvation or liberation. (Kaplan 2002: 24)

He then distinguishes the notion of ultimate reality from metaphysics, which is 'a theory about all reality,' so that there can be a variety of ultimate realities within the one metaphysical system.

In dealing with the problem of both personal and non-personal ultimates, Kaplan makes use of David Bohm's proposed holographic model. In very brief summary, a hologram stores the information from which a three-dimensional image of a physical object can be projected. The image can then be viewed from different angles and distances so that it appears differently to different observers. These different appearances are analogous, he suggests, to the different personal deities. Bohm calls this plurality the 'explicate order.' But the holographic film itself is a single unity, which Bohm calls the 'implicate order,' and this, Kaplan suggests, is analogous to the unity of the undivided One, Brahman, Emptiness. And

> in order to devise a model that includes dualistic and nondualistic traditions, we assume that the implicate and explicate domains logically demand each other ... This scenario allows us to envision how different ultimate realities as professed by different religious traditions can be simultaneously existent and equal. (2002: 124, 126)

Although this is for Kaplan a thought experiment, not based on commitment to any of the traditions, he recommends it as a form of 'metaphysical democracy' in which individuals can choose for themselves between the different ultimate realities and paths of salvation/liberation. 'This model calls for individuals to choose. ... This is a proposal for metaphysical democracy. ... [The ultimates] are not metaphysical impositions from a monolithically structured universe' (2002: 161–2). They are equally real, though each is real only for the adherents of that religion. But from the point of view of Kaplan's theory they are all on a par. His proposal is thus a form of religious pluralism.

Various criticisms have been made. On the level of theory, there is a plurality of ultimate realities only because Kaplan redefines the term to make it so. And his assumption that the implicate and explicate domains logically demand each other, when transferred to the religions, is an assumption adopted only to make his theory possible. For the existence of the personal deities and the non-personal absolutes do not logically require each other. And on the level of religion as historical reality, it is fantasy to think that individuals choose their own religion. In the vast majority of cases people are born into a particular tradition, which forms them from childhood, and they have no opportunity or encouragement to study all the religious options and then make a choice among them. Kaplan's 'metaphysical democracy' is purely theoretical, and has no correspondence with real life.

Another version of extreme pluralism, proposed by S. Mark Heim, could alternatively be regarded as a form of inclusivism since, as he presents it, his own Christian religion occupies a uniquely privileged status. But the basic structure of his theory, namely the world faiths as distinct entities, each with its own distinctive way of life which continues into a distinctive postmortem fulfilment (heaven, paradise, rebirth, absorption into the Ultimate, or other), could also be used without any one system occupying such a status. It thus offers a possible form of extreme pluralism. But, for Heim, whilst all the other postmortem states depicted by the non-Christian faiths are equally real, '[t]o realise something other than communion with the triune God and with other creatures through Christ is to achieve a lesser good' (Heim 2001: 44).

Indeed, '[i]nsofar as alternative ends lack or rule out real dimensions of communion with the triune God, they embody some measure of what Christian tradition regards as loss or damnation' (2001: 182). This is Heim's inclusivism, in the special sense of salvation, potentially, for everyone, but with Christian salvation uniquely superior to all others. He defends it by using a principle of plenitude: the triune God aims, in creation, at a maximum variety of kinds of good, which is provided by the variety of human options, and '[postmortem] consummation mirrors creation in this respect, maintaining the same delight in variety' (p. 248). It is required by the justice of this scenario that each individual freely chooses his or her end state. For these ends 'reflect God's "letting be" of what we become by our own choice, the realization of the self-determination of the creature' (p. 262). And he regards 'annihilation and hell as true options' (p. 286).

But, as in the case of Kaplan's theory, this has no correspondence with real life. It is completely unrealistic to suppose that all, or even many, people around the world are informed about the different religions and freely choose among them. The enormous majority are born into a tradition and have no other options genuinely available to them. The result, for Heim, is that only those born within the Christian tradition can attain the highest good, the Christian heaven, whilst the majority of the human race, through no fault of their own, are condemned to their various lesser ends. As Heim himself presents it, his position is a form of Christian inclusivism.

But even without that restriction, his theory has its difficulties. For each of the postmortem end states that he postulates presupposes a different metaphysical structure of the universe. Thus the Christian scheme presupposes an omnipotent and omniscient creator who judges each individual and can assign them to heaven or hell, the Muslim scheme a different God, the Buddhist scheme a different cosmic process. But there can be only one omnipotent creator, or, according to Buddhism, none. Thus whilst Heim's proposal is possible as a theory, it is not one that can be realized in reality.

Aspectual pluralism

Another form of religious pluralism is aspectual, holding that, in the words of one of its proponents, Peter Byrne, 'the different systems of religious discourse are descriptive of one and the same reality because that reality has multiple aspects' (Byrne 1995: 153). He uses the familiar concept of a 'kind,' for example gold. This exhibits different observable qualities in different circumstances (solid and molten). Its real essence lies 'behind' these observable states, and in the case of some kinds the essence may not be known. Transcendence/Divinity/the Sacred, is also a kind, but a unique kind; and in different circumstances – different human traditions with their different conceptualities and spiritual practices – it is manifested in different ways.

> On this view the sacred as personal Lord and as unlimited ocean of being or unbounded, numinous wholly other are manifestations of a real essence of transcendence which lies behind them. ... Just as gold, at normal

temperature, really is yellow, lustrous and hard, so the transcendent reality is personal Lord and impersonal ground of being in appropriate manifestations of its real essence. Yet, just as the nominal essence of gold does not exhaust its nature but points beyond itself to its real essence, so the nominal essence of the transcendent does not exhaust itself but points beyond itself to its real essence. (1995: 159–60)

The religions, then, are each aware of a different aspect of the transcendent. But Byrne adds that all our human descriptions of the ultimate, expressed in our different theologies or philosophies, are metaphorical: 'each set of doctrinal statements is to be understood in metaphorical fashion. They are the workings out of divergent but mutually apt models for understanding a reality which is for the most part beyond all literal, positive statement' (1995: 164). In this respect the unique supernatural kind, the Transcendent, differs from all natural kinds.

If the religions have access to different aspects of the same ultimate reality, it would seem to follow that by putting their different reports together we could attain a much fuller account of the divine nature. There could thus be a global theology which is more adequate than that of any one tradition. But Byrne does not accept this, on the ground that 'only within forms of practice that constitute living in harmony with ultimate reality – that is, in religions – can any worthwhile relationship with the sacred be achieved' (1995: 197). The religions must remain separate, with their different belief-systems, although 'as traditions they may well profit from sharing insights, spiritualities and the like' (p. 200). But it can be asked, is it not possible for people – perhaps particularly in the modern West – who stand outside all religions to be living 'in harmony with ultimate reality?' And again, from a multi-aspectual point of view, why might not new syncretistic faiths, drawing on the truths and practices of several traditions, be permissible?

The pluralistic hypothesis

It is difficult to find an ideal term to describe this form of religious pluralism. In its most widely discussed form (Hick 2004, and other writings) it is presented under this name as a philosophical hypothesis. The hypothesis rests on four premises, two epistemological and two empirical, in the sense of observational.

First premise: This is the epistemological principle of critical realism, first developed by American philosophers in the twentieth century. This is the view (in distinction from idealism) that there is a reality 'out there' beyond our own minds but (in distinction from naive realism) that this reality is never perceived as it is in itself, unobserved, but always and necessarily as filtered and ordered by the categories of our own minds. The principle is generally accepted in contemporary cognitive psychology and the sociology of knowledge. The pluralistic hypothesis is sometimes described as Kantian, because it makes use of Kant's distinction between things in themselves and as phenomenally present to human consciousness. It could, however, be presented without referring to Kant, for the basic epistemological principle was present centuries earlier in Aquinas's dictum that 'Things known are in the knower according to the mode of the knower' (*Summa Theologica* II–II. q.1. art. 2). Further, Kant's own philosophy of religion was quite different, and he himself would presumably not have approved of this use of his fundamental distinction. But Kant's is nevertheless the biggest name in the development of critical realism.

Second premise: This is the principle of 'critical trust,' namely that it is rational to believe that what seems to be so is indeed so, except when we have reason to think otherwise. Given the ambiguity of the universe, which is able to be interpreted both naturalistically and religiously, this means that it is rational – for those who participate in the field of religious experience – to accept it as cognitive of transcendent reality, except when they have reason to doubt it. The discussion then focuses on such reasons, and particularly on the differences between sense perception, where we all follow the principle, and religious experience. Sense experience is compulsory and therefore universal and uniform – nature would eliminate us if we did not practice the principle of critical trust in relation to it. But religious experience is not compulsory, and hence not universal or uniform. This difference is attributed in the pluralistic hypothesis to a main difference between the putative objects of sense and religious experience: the divine is such that its reality must not be compulsorily evident to us if we are to be free beings in our responses to it.

Third premise: This concerns the existing 'major world faiths.' Each is oriented toward what is believed to be the ultimate reality, which the monotheistic faiths identify as a personal God who is the creator of everything other than God, and who is omnipotent, omniscient, good, and just, whilst the non-theistic faiths identify the ultimate as being beyond the distinction between the personal and the impersonal – as Brahman, Tao, Dharmakaya/Buddha nature/nirvana. As a generic term to cover all these possibilities, both theistic and non-theistic, Ultimate Reality, the Ultimate, the Transcendent, the Real, are equally suitable, but the standard presentation of the pluralistic hypothesis uses 'the Real.'

There is a strong strand within all the world faiths which thinks of the Real in its inner nature as ineffable, or transcategorial – beyond the range of our human categories of thought. But this is only one side of a two-sided coin, the other being our human awareness, in our human terms, of that reality as it affects us.

In Christianity God is, in Gregory of Nyssa's words, 'incapable of being grasped by any term, or any idea, or any other device of our apprehension, remaining beyond the reach not only of the human but of the angelic and all supramundane intelligence, unthinkable, unutterable, above all expression in words' (*Against Eunomius* I. 99); whilst Augustine said that 'God transcends even the mind' (*De Vera Religione* 36, 67), and Aquinas that 'by its immensity the divine substance surpasses every form that our intellect reaches' (*Summa contra Gentiles* I. 14. 3). The same theme runs through Christian thought, including such great Christian mystics as Pseudo-Dionysius, St John of the Cross, and Meister Eckhart, who says that 'before there were creatures God was not God, but, rather, he was what he was. When creatures came to be and took on creaturely being, then God was no longer God as he is in himself, but God as he is with his creatures' (Sermon 28, 1981: 200). However, all have of course at the same time, inconsistently, believed that we know God to be a divine trinity, the second person of whom became incarnate as Jesus of Nazareth. This is an inconsistency which the pluralistic hypothesis avoids.

The most influential Jewish thinker, Maimonides, distinguished between the unknown essence and the known manifestations of God; and many of the mystics speak of En Soph, the Infinite, as beyond human description. Within Islam, the Sufi tradition uses the same distinction. For example, Ibn al' Arabi in *The Bezels of Wisdom*, says, that 'The Essence, as being beyond all these relationships, is not a divinity ... it is we who make Him a divinity by being that through which He knows himself as divine. Thus he is not known [as Allah, God] until we are known' (Al' Arabi 1980: 92).

Turning to the eastern religions, the *Tao Te Ching* begins by affirming that 'The Tao that can be expressed is not the eternal Tao' (ch. 1). In eastern literature the equivalent of 'ineffable' is 'formless.' Advaitic Hindu philosophy distinguishes between *nirguna* Brahman, Brahman without attributes, formless, and *saguna* Brahman, which is that same reality humanly known as Ishwara, God, manifested in the realm of the gods. The distinction is strikingly drawn in the paradoxical statement of an ancient Hindu writer, 'Thou art formless: thy only form is our knowledge of thee.' In Mahayana Buddhism there is the distinction among the three 'bodies' of the Buddha between the Dharmakaya, which is the ultimate formless reality, and its manifestation in the Buddhas, in a heavenly realm and as occasionally incarnate on earth.

The distinction between the Real in itself, in Kantian terms the noumenal Real, and the Real as phenomenally experienced by us humans, is thus well established in religious thinking around the world.

This distinction is fundamental to the pluralist hypothesis, according to which the ultimate transcategorial Real affects humanity in the ways made possible by our human conceptualities and spiritual practices. These differ among the different ways of being human which are the great cultures of the earth. The concept of the personal presides over the theistic faiths, producing its worshiped *personae* (Vishnu, Shiva, the Lord of rabbinic Judaism, the Holy Trinity, Allah, etc.), whilst the concept of the transpersonal presides over the non-theistic faiths, producing the *impersonae* of the Real (Brahman, Tao, Dharmakaya, etc.).

How can the ineffable Real-in-itself 'affect' finite human beings? The answer of the pluralistic hypothesis is that there is an aspect or dimension of our being that naturally responds to the universal presence of the Real. This is recognized by the religions as the image of God within us, the Atman, the Buddha nature, the universal Tao, etc. (Thus the use of the Kantian distinction in relation to religion does not raise the problem that Kant himself faced as to how the noumenal can *cause* the phenomenal when, in his epistemology, causality is itself one of the categories of thought which the mind imposes in constructing the phenomenal world.)

Fourth premise: This premise is that the 'great world faiths' are, so far as we can tell, on a par in their spiritual and moral value. That is to say, each seems to be an equally effective (and of course also equally ineffective) historical context within which human beings are helped to move from natural self-centeredness to a new orientation centered in the Real. Putting it negatively, it is not true of any of the religions that its adherents are, in general, better human beings, morally and spiritually, than the rest of the human race. This raises a question: what criterion is being used? According to the pluralistic hypothesis, this is the universal moral insight expressed in the principle of treating others as one would oneself wish to be treated: the Golden Rule, which is found, in positive or negative form, in the teachings of each one of the world faiths (Hick 2004: 313–14). That the religions are indeed on a par in producing (and failing to produce) unselfish kindness – the quality in Christian terms of *agape* (love), in Buddhist terms of *karuna* (compassion) and *metta* (loving kindness), in Jewish terms of moral righteousness, and in Islamic terms of conformity to the divine nature as *rahman* and *rahim* (gracious and merciful) – can of course be disputed. Likewise the record of the religions as agents in history can be disputed. The issue is empirical, observational. According to the pluralistic hypothesis, when we recognize that over the centuries the religions each show times of cultural flourishing and of decline, times of aggression and persecution, and times of tolerance and peaceful co-existence, we cannot elevate any one, as historical totalities, as superior to the rest. Each is open at different times and in different respects to severe criticism, but these dark sides can be found in them all, and so far as we can judge seem to be of equal weight.

Putting all these premises together, the pluralistic hypothesis is that there is a transcendent and immanent Real, or Ultimate Reality, which is universally present to humanity and of which humans are aware, to the extent that they allow themselves to be so, in the various ways made possible by their different conceptual systems and spiritual practices. The practical outcome is that the religions should accept each other as different but equally valid responses to the Ultimate, should engage in mutual dialogue, including tactful criticism of particular practices, and should each gradually modify any elements in its own dogmas which prevent this. It is thus revisionary insofar as it is accepted within each tradition.

Criticisms of the pluralistic hypothesis

The pluralistic hypothesis has been widely discussed and criticized. The basic theological objection is that it is incompatible with the claim to a unique and final revelation of the truth of one's own religion. It is thus not acceptable to orthodoxy within most of the religions as they are. Or, from the pluralistic point of view, it calls for internal theological development which can only occur gradually. But we are concerned here with philosophical criticisms.

One challenges the concept of the transcategorial Real. How can there be a reality that is quality-less, 'formless?' Alvin Plantinga writes, 'I take it that the term 'tricycle' does not apply to the Real. But if the Real is not a tricycle, then, 'is not a tricycle' applies literally to it; it is a non-tricycle' (2000: 45). The reply offered involves a distinction between 'purely formal' properties, such as 'being able to be referred to' and 'substantial' properties which tell us something about the nature of the Real, such as good/bad, personal/impersonal, and it is these latter that do not apply to the Real either positively *or* negatively. They include substantial but religiously irrelevant ones such as being a tricycle. Just as it does not make sense to ask if an atom is or is not green, because it is not the kind of thing that has colors, so the Real is not of a kind to which such concepts as tricycle apply. It is beyond the scope of our (substantial) human concepts, including religiously irrelevant ones such as being a tricycle. The reason for insisting on this is that, whilst it would do no harm religiously to say, trivially, that the Real is not a tricycle, not a teapot, not made of cheese, etc., to apply the same principle – that substantial properties and their contraries must apply to the Real – would be worse than misleading in the case of religiously relevant properties. For to say that the Real is not impersonal, not evil, not unjust, etc. is to imply that the Real is the kind of thing that can be personal or impersonal, good or evil, etc, and that it is in fact personal, good, just, etc., and this would be to deny its ineffability.

But if salvation/liberation consists in a transformation of human existence from natural self-centeredness to a reorientation centred in the Real, and the criterion by which to recognize it is the presence of love/compassion, is this conception of salvation compatible with the total ineffability of the Real? Must not the nature of the Real in itself be good and loving rather than evil and hating? For 'If the Real has no positive properties of which we have a grasp, how could we possibly know or have grounds for believing that some ways of behaving with respect to it are more appropriate than others?' (Plantinga 2000: 56). This is a good question, to which the answer of the pluralistic hypothesis is that *in relation to us* the Real is experienced in our human terms as good, benign, loving, so that the natural response is a self-transcending love and compassion toward others. There could conceivably be other beings (devils?) who experience it in relation to themselves as hostile, threatening, far from benign. But the witness of the world religions, based on the experience of their founders and major figures, is either an awareness, formed by the concept of personality, of the good and loving *personae* of the Real, or one formed by non-theistic concepts of its *impersonae* expressed in structures of the universe such that we can attain to *moksha* or nirvana or life in accordance with the Tao.

Another issue is that the hypothesis speaks of *the* Real, thus assuming that there is not a plurality of ultimate realities. We saw above, in the discussion of Kaplan's theory of multiple ultimates, the difficulty of developing a coherent position along these lines. But strictly speaking, even the concept of 'being one' rather than many does not apply to the Real. 'One' and 'many' are terms used to distinguish quantity, but our conceptual system requires us to speak of either 'the' Real, implying numerical oneness, or 'a' Real, implying numerical plurality, both of which would be misleading in relation to the transcategorial Real. But we have to use the language that we have.

Do we experience the Real? Many critics have been exasperated by the answer of the pluralistic hypothesis, which is both yes and no. Yes, in the sense that in religious experience we can experience the Real as religious phenomenon, jointly formed (in accordance with the principle of critical realism) by the universal presence of the Real and by our human conceptualities and spiritual practices; and No, in the sense that we cannot directly experience the Real *an sich* – not even in mystical experience, the reports of which always bear the imprint of a particular tradition.

Conclusion

The appeal of religious pluralism, whether philosophically developed in the pluralistic hypothesis or some other form, is that the alternatives of exclusivism and inclusivism seem unrealistic except to those who hold that the tradition into which they happen to have been born is uniquely superior to all others. These are very numerous within each faith, although probably a majority of those within each faith who live in multi-faith societies are nevertheless implicit pluralists, in that in practice they treat their neighbors of other faiths as equals. The sense in multi-faith societies that 'we' are not in a superior spiritual state to 'them' comes not so much from philosophical considerations as from experience. Those others do not seem to be morally and spiritually inferior to the people of one's own tradition. But when this implicit pluralism is made explicit by philosophers and theologians, it gives rise to a clash with their inherited beliefs, which most are neither prepared nor equipped to face. The religious leaders and thinkers find this clash equally hard to grapple with, hence the immense volume of discussion and debate today.

But whilst there are better and worse, good and evil, individuals within all traditions, each of the great world faiths seems to produce saintly individuals of equal stature, and to influence their adherents in general toward a generous concern for others and mutual support amid the inevitable hardships, anxieties, suffering and distresses of life. If salvation/liberation (in its progressive degrees) is a reality observable in people's outlook as expressed in their behavior, it seems, so far as we can tell, to be spread pretty evenly around the world. Religious pluralism is a response to this situation.

See also Thomas Aquinas (Chapter 12), Immanuel Kant (Chapter 14), Truth in religion (Chapter 18), Religious traditions and rational assessments (Chapter 19), Inclusivism and exclusivism (Chapter 21), Non-theistic conceptions of God (Chapter 22), Mysticism among the world's religions (Chapter 23), Problems with the concept of God (Chapter 38), The problem of religious language (Chapter 39), Naturalistic rejoinders to theistic arguments (Chapter 40), Theology and religious language (Chapter 48), Phenomenology of religion (Chapter 61), Religious experience (Chapter 63).

References

Al' Arabi, I. (1980) *The Bezels of Wisdom*, trans. R. W. J. Austin, Mahwah, NJ: Paulist Press.

Aquinas, T. (1945) *Summa Theologica*, Dominican translation, in A. Pegis (ed.) *Basic Writings of Saint Thomas Aquinas*, vol. 2, New York: Random House.

—— (1955) *Summa contra Gentiles*, trans. A. Pegis, Garden City, NY: Doubleday.

Augustine (1953) *De Vera Religione*, in *Augustine: Earlier Writings*, trans. J. Burleigh, London: SCM Press; Philadelphia: Westminster Press.

Byrne, P. (1995) *Prolegomena to Religious Pluralism*, London: Macmillan; New York: St Martin's Press.

Eckhart, M. (1981) *Meister Eckhart*, trans. E. Colledge and B. McGinn, Mahwah, NJ: Paulist Press.

Gregory of Nyssa (1956) *Against Eunomius*, in P. Schaff and H. Wace (eds) *Nicene and Post-Nicene Fathers*, series 2, vol. 5, Grand Rapids, MI: Eerdmans.

Heim, M. (2001) *The Depth of the Riches*, Grand Rapids, MI: Eerdmans.

Hick, J. (2004) [1989] *An Interpretation of Religion*, 2nd edn, London: Macmillan; New Haven, CT: Yale University Press.

Kaplan, S. (2002) *Different Paths, Different Summits*, Oxford: Rowman & Littlefield.

Plantinga, A. (2000) *Warranted Christian Belief*, Oxford: Oxford University Press.

Further reading

D'Costa, G. (ed.) (1990) *Christian Uniqueness Reconsidered*, New York: Orbis. (Essays by Rowan Williams, M. M. Thomas, John Cobb, Wolfhart Pannenberg, J. A. DiNoia, Lesslie Newbigin, Jürgen Moltmann, Paul Griffiths, John Millbank, and others, criticizing the pluralist position.)

Hick, J. (1997) 'The epistemological challenge of religious pluralism' (with responses by William Alston, George Mavrodes, Alvin Plantinga, and Peter van Inwagen), *Faith and Philosophy* 14/3: 277–302. (Essay by Hick with critical responses by some major contemporary philosophers.)

—— (1985) *Problems of Religious Pluralism*, London: Macmillan; New York: St Martin's Press. (Articles on various aspects of religious pluralism.)

Kellenbeger, J. (ed.) (1993) *Inter-Religious Models and Criteria*, London: Macmillan. (Essays by Ninian Smart, John Cobb, John Hick, William Wainwright, William Christian, Keith Yandell, and others.)

Knitter, P. (ed.) (2005) *The Myth of Religious Superiority: A Multifaith Exploration*, New York: Orbis. (Essays by Christian, Jewish, Muslim, Hindu, and Buddhist pluralists.)

Panikkar, R. (1978) *The Intra-Religious Dialogue*, New York: Paulist Press. (The distinctive approach of a famous Catholic thinker.)

Schuon, F. (1975) *The Transcendent Unity of Religions*, New York: Harper & Row. (Expounding the 'transcendental unity of religions' approach.)

21
INCLUSIVISM AND EXCLUSIVISM

Harold A. Netland

Religious diversity and disagreement

As a result of the globalization of the past century we are today much more aware of religious diversity than were earlier generations. This in turn has prompted fresh and urgent questions about the relation between the religions and the implications of religious disagreement for one's own religious commitments.

Religious diversity involves not only differences in rituals or dress but, more significantly, basic differences in ways in which religions understand and respond to reality. The major religions maintain that humankind, and in some cases, the cosmos at large, is in some undesirable state and that there is a way to overcome this predicament. Each religion offers its own remedy for what is afflicting humankind, its own vision of the soteriological goal and how this can be attained. 'A religion proposes a diagnosis of a deep, crippling spiritual disease universal to non-divine sentience and offers a cure. A particular religion is true if its diagnosis is correct and its cure is efficacious' (Yandell 2004: 191). Christian, Islamic, Hindu, and Buddhist traditions maintain that accepting certain truths is essential to attaining the soteriological goal.

But the religions disagree on the nature of the religious ultimate, the human predicament and the way to overcome this predicament. Judaism, Islam, and Christianity, for example, claim that the universe was created by an everlasting, all-powerful God, although they disagree over the nature of this Creator. Non-theistic traditions of Hinduism, Buddhism, Jainism, and Shintoism deny that there is such a God. Both Islam and Christianity maintain that Jesus is to be esteemed, but they disagree sharply over his identity and nature. Christians accept Jesus as the unique incarnation of God: fully God and fully man. Muslims reject this as blasphemous, insisting that although a great prophet, Jesus was only a man. Christianity teaches that the root problem confronting humankind is sin against a holy and righteous God. Hindu, Buddhist, and Jain traditions typically regard the problem as deeply embedded ignorance about reality, although they disagree among themselves over whether enduring souls actually exist. Given such competing claims, it has generally been accepted that not all of the central assertions made by the religions can be true; at least some are false.

Approaches to other religions

There are five basic approaches one might adopt with respect to religious disagreement:

1 All religions are false; there is no religion whose central claims are true.
2 There is no way to determine which, if any, of the religions is most likely to be true, and thus the best response is to remain agnostic about the claims of any religion.
3 While each religion can be regarded as 'true' and 'effective' for its adherents, there is no objective or tradition transcending sense in which we can speak of religious truth.
4 In spite of real disagreements among the religions, we can nevertheless accept each of the religions as partial, historically conditioned responses to the one religious ultimate; no single religious tradition is privileged with respect to truth or soteri-ological effectiveness.
5 There is one religion which is true and soteriologically effective in ways that others are not.

Atheism, reflected in (1), has become influential in the West in recent decades, although it remains a minority perspective. Agnosticism, option (2), is attractive to many today and can be compatible with religious practice. Many remain agnostic about matters of religious truth while nevertheless participating in a religious tradition for pragmatic or social reasons. (3) expresses religious relativism; religious pluralism, which is distinct from relativism, is found in (4). The views expressed in (1), (3), and (4) would be rejected by most devout religious believers. Most religious believers would accept some version of (5), since they regard their own religious perspective to be true in a way that makes it superior to other religions.

It has become customary in the literature to distinguish three broad paradigms for understanding the relation of Christian faith to other religions: exclusivism, inclusivism, and pluralism. Exclusivism and inclusivism both maintain in some sense the superiority of Jesus Christ and Christian faith to other alternatives, whereas pluralism denies this.

Before looking more carefully at exclusivism and inclusivism, we should say something about religious pluralism. Although there has been some diversity on particular issues, until the mid-twentieth century the clear consensus among Christian thinkers was that there is something distinctive, superior, and normative about Jesus Christ and the Christian faith that set it apart from other religions. God has been present and active for humankind's salvation in Jesus of Nazareth in a way not found in other religions. But by the 1970s and 1980s a growing number of western theologians were explicitly rejecting this assumption. *Religious pluralism* maintains that the major religions should be regarded as more or less equally effective and legitimate alternative ways of responding to the one divine reality. All religions are in their own ways complex historically and culturally conditioned human responses to the one divine reality. Salvation, liberation, or enlightenment can be found in all religions. Variations of this view have become widespread in the West and have been vigorously defended by John Hick (Hick 2004). Exclusivism and inclusivism reject religious pluralism for both theological and philosophical reasons. The major philosophical problem confronting pluralism is constructing a plausible and coherent model which (1) reflects accurately the diversity among religions and (2) shows how the major religions are all appropriate responses to the religious ultimate without privileging any particular religious perspective.

Christian exclusivism, as typically understood, maintains that religious truth and salvation are restricted primarily, if not exclusively, to Christianity. It holds that (1) the Bible comprises God's distinctive written revelation, and where the claims of Scripture are incompatible with those of other faiths the latter are to be rejected; (2) Jesus Christ is the unique incarnation of God and only through the person and work of Christ is there the possibility of salvation; and (3) God's saving grace is not mediated through other religions. With some modifications, exclusivism can be said to reflect the dominant position of the Church, Protestant and Roman Catholic, until the twentieth century. It is today primarily identified with evangelical Protestants.

In the nineteenth and twentieth centuries more open perspectives on other religions became widespread, first among theologically more liberal Protestants and then, with Vatican II (1962–5), in Roman Catholicism. *Inclusivism* refers to a broad spectrum of views which embrace the following somewhat ambiguous principles: (1) There is a sense in which Jesus Christ is unique, normative, or superior to other religious figures, and in some sense it is through Christ that salvation is made available; (2) God's grace and salvation, which are somehow based upon Jesus Christ, are also available and efficacious through other religions; and thus (3) other religions should be regarded positively as part of God's purposes for humankind. There is enormous diversity among inclusivists over how these principles are to be understood and applied. Some develop an inclusivist theology of religions within a traditional Trinitarian framework; others modify traditional doctrines, especially in Christology. But the core of inclusivism is the desire to maintain in some sense the uniqueness and normativity of Jesus Christ while simultaneously acknowledging that God's saving grace is present and effective in other religions. Versions of inclusivism are now dominant within mainline Protestant traditions and Roman Catholicism, and can also be found among some evangelicals.

The taxonomy of exclusivism, inclusivism, and pluralism was developed by western thinkers in the debate over Christianity and other religions. While similar discussions have not been as prominent within other religions, analogues to the three approaches can be found there as well. Many traditions in Islam, Hinduism, and Buddhism, for example, are exclusivist in restricting truth and soteriological effectiveness to their own traditions. But there are also more inclusivist or even pluralist perspectives on other religions found among some Muslims, Hindus, and Buddhists.

Different aspects of religious exclusivism

The term 'exclusivist' can be used in various ways, and thus different meanings should be distinguished. *Theological exclusivism*, in line with the previous definition of Christian exclusivism, holds that religious truth and attainment of the soteriological goal are primarily restricted to a particular religion. Many traditions within Islam, Hinduism, Buddhism, and Christianity are theologically exclusive in this sense.

Formal exclusivism refers to the fact that any claim about the way things are which is intended to be true in a non-relative sense excludes something. Thus, to affirm that p is implicitly to deny that $-p$. To claim, for example, that desire results in rebirth is to deny that desire does *not* result in rebirth. Any meaningful affirmation, however trivial or ambiguous, excludes something. In this formal sense, all religious and non-religious worldviews, insofar as they include claims about reality intended to be true, are exclusive.

Consequently, Gavin D'Costa has argued that inclusivist or pluralist perspectives on other religions are really variations of exclusivism (D'Costa 1996); there cannot be a genuinely pluralistic perspective since pluralism 'is always some or other form of explicit or implicit exclusivist tradition-specific narrative' (D'Costa 2000: 90). By maintaining that their own perspective is correct and incompatible alternatives should be rejected, pluralism and inclusivism ultimately collapse into exclusivism. Now there is a legitimate point here. Pluralists and inclusivists, like exclusivists, reject perspectives incompatible with their own and they are exclusive in that sense. But it hardly follows that as substantive perspectives on other religions, inclusivism and pluralism reduce to theological exclusivism. To claim this is to conflate distinct meanings of 'exclusivism' and to ignore very real differences between the three positions in their respective understandings of the relation between Christianity and other religions (Hick 1997). Although Hick's pluralism is formally exclusive, its thesis about the relation among the religions, and the epistemological and ontological commitments this entails, are radically different from exclusivism or inclusivism.

Finally, *social exclusivism* refers to assumptions or practices associated with a religious tradition which are exclusive with respect to social or interpersonal relations. A particular tradition, for example, might restrict membership to believers, or prohibit marriage with those outside the group, or otherwise regulate association with certain groups of people. Some such practices might be uncontroversial, such as the restriction of the office of Baptist pastor to Baptist Christians or of Islamic mullah to Muslims. Others might be morally repugnant but nevertheless protected by law, such as the exclusion of Jews or African Americans from membership in white supremacist groups on racial grounds. The practice of social exclusivism might involve arrogant or elitist attitudes toward those who are different, but it need not do so. One can, for example, maintain that only believing Baptist Christians should pastor Baptist churches and still be humble, gracious and irenic with religious others.

Exclusivism and inclusivism

Both exclusivism and inclusivism are formally exclusivist and maintain that Christian faith is somehow preferable to other religious alternatives. Differences between them arise from theological disputes over just how the superiority of Jesus Christ and Christian faith are to be understood and the implications of this for other religions. Such issues are to be settled primarily by appeal to criteria and methods internal to the Christian tradition, including the interpretation of Scripture and the theological heritage of the Church. While philosophical analysis and the phenomenology of religion might be helpful in such matters, they are not determinative.

Theological exclusivists typically maintain that Scripture and responsible theological reflection do not allow for the more optimistic perspectives of inclusivism (Carson 1996; Edwards 2005). Many exclusivists focus upon the question of salvation, insisting that salvation is restricted to those with an appropriate relationship to Jesus Christ. But even here there can be disagreement. Some maintain that only those who hear the gospel of Jesus Christ in this life and respond explicitly in faith to Christ prior to death can be saved. Others reject this as theologically untenable and adopt mediating positions between such 'restrictivism' and theological inclusivism. Critics charge that an implication of exclusivism is that large numbers of people, perhaps the vast majority of humankind, who have not had the opportunity to hear the gospel and respond to Christ, will not be saved and that this is incompatible with God's justice and goodness. This gives fresh poignancy to the classical issue of theodicy. While a variety of theological responses have been offered by exclusivists, the philosopher William Lane Craig draws upon the notion of God's middle knowledge and the counterfactuals of freedom in arguing that there is no inconsistency between God's omniscience, omnipotence, and omnibenevolence and the fact that people do not hear the gospel and thus are damned. Craig claims that it is possible that there are no persons who, although they in fact did not hear the gospel, would have responded in faith had they been presented with the gospel 'and been sufficiently well informed concerning it' (Craig 2000: 50). Similarly, Alvin Plantinga has argued that accepting Christian exclusivism does not violate any moral or epistemic obligations (Plantinga 2000a).

Inclusivists, by contrast, typically maintain that biblical themes of God's love, justice, and mercy provide ample grounds for concluding that God is present and active even among other religions. Accordingly, we should expect that many who have not encountered the gospel will nevertheless experience God's salvation while remaining within their own religions. Karl Rahner, an early and influential proponent of inclusivism, introduced the notion of 'anonymous Christianity,' which suggests that under certain conditions sincere Hindus or Buddhists can be regarded as 'anonymous' or implicit Christians, and thus be saved, even though they have not had any contact with the gospel or the Church (Rahner 2001). For Rahner, other religions are 'lawful' and potentially salvific only up to the point when an adherent of that religion encounters and really understands the Christian gospel; at that point acceptance of the Christian faith becomes obligatory. Other inclusivists affirm that God's saving grace can be efficacious within non-Christian religions even when adherents choose to remain within their own religions. Hans Küng goes even further, asserting that while the Church is the 'extraordinary' way of salvation, the various religions are the 'ordinary' way of salvation for non-Christian humanity (Küng 1967). Mark Heim, in a creative proposal that defies easy categorization, suggests that there are multiple soteriological ends, multiple 'salvations,' which can actually be experienced by adherents of the various religions (Heim 1995). Thus Buddhists can actually experience nirvana; Muslims can enter Paradise; and so on. But the various ends are all rooted in the triune God of Christian theism and thus the Christian soteriological goal – 'communion with God and God's creatures' – remains ultimate (Heim 2001: 19).

Although use of the categories is now widespread, the taxonomy of exclusivism, inclusivism, and pluralism was introduced only in the 1980s. The extensive discussions of other religions by nineteenth- and twentieth-century Christians were not constrained by the categories, and thus the issues often were formulated in different ways. While the categories can be helpful, adhering rigidly to them results in distorting issues and the views of various thinkers.

The three categories are usually defined in terms of salvation, but doing so makes it difficult to address other questions also demanding attention. Paul Griffiths (2001) suggests that we distinguish questions of truth from those of salvation and that the exclusivist/inclusivist distinction be construed in terms of each. With respect to truth, then, exclusivism holds that true religious claims are found only among the teachings of one's own religion, whereas inclusivism maintains that it is possible that both one's own and other religions teach truth. Open inclusivism acknowledges that some other religions might teach truths not already contained within one's own religion; closed inclusivism denies this (Griffiths 2001: xiv–xv). This is a helpful reminder that categories like exclusivism and inclusivism must be interpreted in light of the particular questions they are meant to address.

But religions involve much more than just truth claims and teachings about salvation. Thus, perspectives on other religions should also address the ritual, social, ethical, and political dimensions of religion. In religiously diverse and democratic societies committed to the free expression of religion, complex questions about religion and public policy also need to be considered. Comprehensive Christian perspectives on other religions should address at least four kinds of issues:

1 Can adherents of other religions be saved by God's grace apart from explicitly embracing Christian faith?
2 Is there any truth in the teachings of other religions?
3 Are there positive values – goodness, beauty, individual or collective benefits for adherents – in other religions?
4 In religiously diverse societies which are committed to religious freedom, how should we treat religious others? What are the implications of such diversity for public policy?

Discussions of exclusivism and inclusivism have, to this point, focused primarily upon (1) and (2), with exclusivists proposing more negative and inclusivists more positive responses. But issues stemming from (3) and (4) are also significant and should be included in a comprehensive perspective on other religions.

Given the range of issues and the many possible answers to each question, it is difficult to define the categories in such a way that exclusivism and inclusivism remain consistent and distinct categories. Moreover, it becomes very difficult to identify particular thinkers as simply exclusivist or inclusivist without qualification, for one might be exclusive in some senses but not in others. One might, for example, be theologically exclusive in maintaining that only those with an explicit relationship to Jesus Christ can be saved while also being an open inclusivist in acknowledging that other religions contain truths not explicitly found within Christianity. Or one might be theologically exclusive but not socially exclusive in the sense of restricting association with those outside the group. Theological exclusivists might also be aggressive in protecting the full rights of religious others to practice their faiths in our diverse societies. One might acknowledge that there is much truth, goodness, and value in non-Christian religions but also insist that salvation is restricted to those with explicit faith in Christ. Conversely, someone might be exclusive with respect to truth but not salvation (a soteriological universalist might also be a theological exclusivist). Karl Barth is an interesting example, as he is often identified as an exclusivist because of his contention that religion is 'unbelief' and that the revelation of God in Christ is the 'abolition' (Aufhebung) of religion (Barth 2001). But Barth's soteriology has also been understood as implying an incipient universalism in which all are saved because all are elect in Christ – something clearly rejected by traditional exclusivists.

It is difficult to see how exclusivism and inclusivism can be defined so that they reflect accurately the very diverse responses we can expect from such widely ranging questions. Thus, while the standard taxonomy can be helpful, the two positions should not be understood as tidy, mutually exclusive categories so much as distinct points on a continuum of perspectives, with particular thinkers falling into one or another category depending upon the particular issue under consideration.

Tolerance and religious diversity

There is a common assumption that exclusivists are least tolerant of religious diversity, inclusivists somewhat more so, and pluralists most tolerant. Exclusivists are regarded as least accepting socially or culturally of religious diversity and inclusivists and pluralists more so. While there is some truth to this, some qualifications are also necessary. We should distinguish at least three senses in which religious others might be accepted.

1 Acceptance of the legal right of diverse religious communities to practice their faith freely.
2 Social acceptance of religious others, so that adherents of other religions are encouraged to participate fully in the social, economic, cultural, and political life of the community and nation.
3 Enthusiastic affirmation and celebration of religious diversity as something good, healthy, and beneficial for individual and community life.

Exclusivism or inclusivism could be compatible with any of the three, although exclusivism is usually linked with (1) and (2), and (3) is typically identified with inclusivism and pluralism.

Furthermore, although exclusivism is often identified with intolerance, the two concepts should be distinguished. Theological exclusivists are frequently dismissed as intolerant for rejecting the beliefs of other religions, whereas inclusivists are regarded as tolerant since they are more accepting of such beliefs. But it is not accepting or rejecting a particular belief that marks one as tolerant or intolerant. For if this were the case, then any time one disagreed with someone's beliefs one would be intolerant; the only way to be tolerant would be to accept all beliefs or withhold judgment about competing beliefs. If theological exclusivism is necessarily intolerant for the Christian exclusivist, then it follows that anyone – Buddhist, Wiccan, atheist, or religious pluralist – who maintains that her beliefs about religious matters are true and rejects incompatible beliefs as false is also similarly morally blameworthy. But surely this is intellectual suicide, not tolerance.

John Horton reminds us that tolerance involves 'the deliberate decision to refrain from prohibiting, hindering, or otherwise coercively interfering with conduct of which one disapproves, although one has the power to do so' (Horton 1998). It is one's behavior toward that of which one disapproves that marks one as tolerant or intolerant. One can believe that religious truth and salvation are largely restricted to one's own tradition and still be appropriately tolerant of others, respecting their freedom of conscience and religious expression. Tolerance of religious diversity – respecting the freedom of religious or non-religious expression – is a recent phenomenon and was largely unknown prior to the modern era (Zagorin 2003). It is undeniable that institutional Christianity from the fifth through seventeenth centuries was often highly intolerant in its treatment of Jews, Muslims, and Christian dissenters. Whether such intolerance was greater than that found in Islam, Hinduism, or Buddhism throughout their histories, or than the intolerance of atheistic totalitarian regimes of the twentieth centuries, is an empirical question for social historians. The point here is simply that there is no necessary connection between theological exclusivism and intolerance.

Since inclusivists typically are more willing to acknowledge goodness, beauty, and truth in other religions than are exclusivists, it is often assumed that they are more tolerant in treatment of religious others than are exclusivists. This may well be the case, although this is an empirical question to be settled by observing behavior of the two groups and not merely by analyzing the categories themselves. It is sometimes assumed that adherents of other religions are likely to appreciate inclusivists more than exclusivists since the former are more accepting of other perspectives. While this might be the case, we should remember that even the most generous forms of Christian inclusivism still regard other religions as somehow less satisfactory than Christianity. Although a Buddhist might appreciate an inclusivist who speaks of the many virtues of Buddhism and acknowledges Buddhists as recipients of God's salvation more than an exclusivist who simply dismisses Buddhism as false, he will still reject the inclusivist's claims about the reality of God and salvation through Christ. Moreover, given the problem of conflicting truth claims, inclusivism – just as exclusivism, pluralism, and atheism – has the unhappy consequence that large numbers of sincere, morally good, and intelligent people are mistaken in some of their fundamental beliefs about reality.

The question of justification

Both exclusivism and inclusivism maintain that, whatever truth, beauty, and goodness they might have, other religions are not on a par with Christian theism. God's revelatory and saving activity is identified with Jesus Christ and the Christian faith in ways not found elsewhere. But is it reasonable to accept this? In particular, given our awareness of religious diversity and disagreement, can one reasonably hold that Christianity is distinctively true? Full discussion of these questions is impossible here, but we can make several brief comments.

Whether a particular theological perspective on other religions is justified depends upon two sets of issues. First, there is the question whether particular doctrinal beliefs (e.g., God revealed himself to the biblical prophets in ways unparalleled in other religions; sincere followers of other religions can be saved by God's grace in Christ) should be accepted. Disputes between exclusivists and inclusivists are largely over how these questions ought to be answered. Since these are issues internal to the Christian faith, they are settled by appeal to authoritative sources and criteria set by the Christian faith itself.

There is, however, a second, more basic, issue: Should one accept Christian theism in the first place? Christian exclusivism or inclusivism is justifiable only if the broader framework within which it is embedded – Christian theism – is itself worthy of acceptance.

But does Christian belief in general need justification? Recently many, following Alvin Plantinga and other Reformed epistemologists, have claimed that Christians can be entirely justified or warranted or 'within their epistemic rights' in believing as they do apart from providing any argument or evidence to justify their beliefs (Plantinga 2000b). This, of course, is controversial and is disputed by many philosophers. But even if one agrees with Plantinga, it seems that parallel claims can be made by followers of other religions so that, in principle, Christians, Buddhists, Hindus, and Confucians can all be epistemically entitled to their respective beliefs even though some of these beliefs are contradictory (Tien 2004). Accordingly, many contend that in contexts in which one is aware of religious disagreement and alien religious beliefs that seem to challenge one's own convictions, some justification for maintaining one's religious beliefs is in order (Griffiths 2001; Basinger 2002). Saying just when this is required and what would constitute adequate justification is notoriously difficult and takes us to the heart of contemporary disputes in epistemology.

Those who claim that it is not reasonable to hold that Christian theism (or any other religion) is distinctively true often accept the epistemic parity thesis, which maintains that evidential and rational considerations relevant to religious belief are such that no particular religious tradition can be said to be rationally superior to others. The evidential data are sufficiently ambiguous that the major religions enjoy more or less epistemic parity. The parity thesis can be used to support either a general agnosticism about all religions or religious pluralism.

But should the epistemic parity thesis be accepted simply because of religious disagreement? Deeply rooted disagreement by itself does not entail that there is no single perspective more likely to be true than others, or that all religious perspectives have roughly the same epistemic support. If, as many philosophers maintain, central beliefs of the religions can be assessed in terms of rationality and truth and some perspectives have much stronger epistemic support than others, then the epistemic parity thesis should be rejected.

Whether a particular form of Christian exclusivism or inclusivism is justified, then, depends upon not only theological considerations internal to the Christian faith but also broader questions about whether acceptance of Christian theism itself needs justification and, if so, whether Christian faith meets the test. And settling the latter issue will involve some assessment of the implications of awareness of religious disagreement for the rationality of one's own religious commitments.

See also Chapters 1–7 on particular religions, Truth in religion (Chapter 18), Religious traditions and rational assessments (Chapter 19), and Religious pluralism (Chapter 20).

References

Barth, K. (2001) [1956] 'The revelation of God as the abolition of religion,' in J. Hick and B. Hebblethwaite (eds) *Christianity and Other Religions: Selected Readings*, rev. edn, Oxford: Oneworld.

Basinger, D. (2002) *Religious Diversity: A Philosophical Assessment*, Burlington, VT: Ashgate.

Carson, D. A. (1996) *The Gagging of God: Christianity Confronts Pluralism*, Grand Rapids, MI: Zondervan.

Craig, W. L. (2000) [1989] '"No other name": a middle knowledge perspective on the exclusivity of salvation through Christ,' in P. L. Quinn and K. Meeker (eds) *The Philosophical Challenge of Religious Diversity*, New York: Oxford University Press.

D'Costa, G. (1996) 'The impossibility of a pluralist view of religions,' *Religious Studies* 32: 223–32.

—— (2000) *The Meeting of Religions and the Trinity*, Maryknoll, NY: Orbis.

Edwards, J. (2005) *Is Jesus the Only Savior?*, Grand Rapids, MI: Eerdmans.

Griffiths, P. (2001) *Problems of Religious Diversity*, Oxford: Blackwell.

Heim, S. M. (1995) *Salvations: Truth and Difference in Religion*, Maryknoll, NY: Orbis.

—— (2001) *The Depth of the Riches: A Trinitarian Theology of Religious Ends*, Grand Rapids, MI: Eerdmans.

Hick, J. (1997) 'The possibility of religious pluralism: a reply to Gavin D'Costa,' *Religious Studies* 33: 161–6.

—— (2004) *An Interpretation of Religion: Human Responses to the Transcendent*, 2nd edn, New Haven, CT: Yale University Press.

Horton, J. (1998) 'Toleration,' in E. Craig (ed.) *Routledge Encyclopedia of Philosophy*, vol. 9, London: Routledge.

Küng, H. (1967) 'The world religions in God's plan of salvation,' in J. Neusner (ed.) *Christian Revelation and World Religions*, London: Burns & Oates.

Plantinga, A. (2000a) [1995] 'Pluralism: a defense of religious exclusivism,' in P. L. Quinn and K. Meeker (eds) *The Philosophical Challenge of Religious Diversity*, New York: Oxford University Press.

—— (2000b) *Warranted Christian Belief*, New York: Oxford University Press.

Rahner, K. (2001) [1966] 'Christianity and non-Christian religions,' in J. Hick and B. Hebblethwaite (eds) *Christianity and Other Religions: Selected Readings*, rev. edn, Oxford: Oneworld.

Tien, D. W. (2004) 'Warranted neo-Confucian belief: religious pluralism and the affections in the epistemologies of Wang Yangming (1472–1529) and Alvin Plantinga,' *International Journal for Philosophy of Religion* 55: 31–55.

Yandell, K. (2004) 'How to sink in cognitive quicksand: nuancing religious pluralism,' in M. L. Peterson and R. J. VanArragon (eds) *Contemporary Debates in Philosophy of Religion*, Oxford: Blackwell.

Zagorin, P. (2003) *How the Idea of Religious Toleration Came to the West*, Princeton, NJ: Princeton University Press.

Further reading

Dupuis, J. (1997) *Toward a Christian Theology of Religious Pluralism*, Maryknoll, NY: Orbis. (A helpful historical survey of Christian thinking about other religions along with a Christian inclusivist theology of religions.)

Kärkkäinen, V. (2003) *An Introduction to the Theology of Religions*, Downers Grove, IL: InterVarsity Press. (A concise overview of the major perspectives on other religions offered by Christian theologians.)

Netland, H. (2001) *Encountering Religious Pluralism*, Downers Grove, IL: InterVarsity Press. (An introduction to the theological and philosophical issues as well as a defense of a moderate Christian exclusivism.)

Quinn, P. L. and K. Meeker (eds) (2000) *The Philosophical Challenge of Religious Diversity*, New York: Oxford University Press. (A collection of some of the more significant articles on epistemological and ontological issues of religious pluralism.)

22

NON-THEISTIC
CONCEPTIONS OF GOD

Michael Levine

Introduction

Talk of 'non-theistic concepts of deity' is meant to provide a framework for thinking about ideas of God that are, in varying degrees, non-theistic – that is, non-personal and not ontologically distinct from and transcendent to the world. At least since the rise of monotheism (theism for short) in the West, any notion of deity conceived non-theistically has been explicated in contrast to some version of theism. Aside from illustrating Foucault's contention that those in power control the ways in which discourse and even truth conditions operate, it indicates that those concerned with articulating a non-theistic concept of deity have been motivated by dissatisfaction with theism to examine alternatives. Non-theistic concepts of deity are seen as alternatives to theistic notions regarded as unacceptable on religious, as well as affective and rational, grounds.

The relation between theistic and non-theistic concepts of deity in early Greek (pre-Socratic) philosophy is far from clear. For one thing, it is difficult to know just what the early Greeks really did believe (see Veyne 1988). On some accounts, theistic (even monotheistic) and non-theistic notions of deity in early Greek thought were regarded as philosophically and religiously compatible. Whatever the relation between theistic and non-theistic notions of deity was in early Greek, Indian, or Chinese thought, it does not seem to be the case that they were, or are, regarded as antithetical to or reactively played off against one another as in western theism. They are more often seen as complementary. Virtually all eastern traditions have non-theistic or atheistic aspects to them, although even allegedly atheistic traditions such as Buddhism or Taoism have theistic, usually polytheistic, practices and beliefs associated with them. Hinduism, an umbrella term for a variety of Vedic Indian traditions, is rightly viewed as polytheistic, non-theistic or atheistic depending on which aspect or tradition one is focusing on, and whether one is attending to religious practice or accompanying philosophies. Their philosophies are often concerned to account for such diversity and compatibility.

Panentheism – the other form of theistic cross-dressing – may be seen as a way of combining theism and pantheism (a non-theistic concept of deity). Like deism and pantheism, it too is best seen, from a western perspective, as a response to theism: a way of overcoming allegedly unacceptable aspects. It can also be seen this way in the Vedantic theology of Ramanuja (1017–1137 CE) (Lipner 1985).

The historical tendency to regard non-theistic concepts of deity in terms of, and in the West, as alternatives to, theism continued into the mid-twentieth century. This is roughly when accounts of non-theistic concepts of deity (e.g., Whitehead's process theology, Tillich's notion of God as 'ultimate concern,' Hartshorne's 'dipolar theism,' and Christian existentialist notions like John Macquarrie's) peaked. There was also much discussion of Freud's psychoanalytic account of religion, Sartre's existentialist and Marxist critiques, and A. J. Ayer's logical positivistic challenge to the meaningfulness of religion assertions. Socio-scientific and comparative approaches to the study of religion generally were also more widely introduced. Though not often considered as such, there is a sense in which some of these critiques, Freudian and Marxist for example, constitute radical accounts (not just critiques) of theism in their own right. They are, after all, concerned with articulating the origins of, and motivations for, belief in a theistic God and thus give some account of theism itself. They are not, however, non-theistic but atheistic – and certainly the Marxist and Freudian critiques of theism can *mutatis mutandis* be leveled similarly at non-theistic conceptions. This was a time, and there has been no time since, when academic discussion about the nature of deity and religion flourished.

Although in journals devoted to process thought, Tillich's views (God as 'the ground of being'), etc. remain, discussion of non-theistic views has waned greatly since Tillich, Whitehead, and Hartshorne were in vogue. The case with figures such as Spinoza and Plotinus is different. However, these discussions of Spinoza and Plotinus are considered largely in the context of history of philosophy and generally not as a plausible metaphysic, or a source of a viable non-theistic concept of deity in their own right. With the ascendency of analytical philosophy of religion with a Christian fundamentalist bent, discussion of non-theistic concepts of deity rarely appears. Although some self-servingly argue that philosophy of religion is again mainstream in contemporary analytic philosophy, the accurate view is that even its dominant Christian strain has been sidelined. This coincides with the fading of any promulgation of alternatives to classical theism.

Non-theistic concepts of deity are best understood not only as resulting from many of the same kinds of theoretical dissatisfactions with theism that theists may have – with the idea, for example, that a theistic God would (or could) allow the kinds and scope of evil there is in the world for the purpose of an allegedly greater good. Related to such disbelief, they are also motivated by a profoundly different ethos and way of seeing things. The deist or pantheist may, for example, think of theodicies based on free will or 'soul making' as not just bad arguments, but as desperate or even question-begging attempts to vindicate the theistic worldview. The situation is little different in the religious case than in the political case – where those of vastly different political views not only see and feel differently about the world; they also cannot understand how the others can believe what they do.

The differences between the worldviews and ethos of those who hold theistic versus non-theistic concepts of deity is manifest by differences in practice. Those with a non-theistic conception of deity, for example, will generally not pray or worship. Thus, in comparing theistic and non-theistic conceptions of deity, their associated practices are as revealing as an elucidation of them solely in terms of beliefs. If you want to know what someone believes or what it means to believe something, it is necessary, though rarely sufficient, to look at what she does – what she practices.

Pantheism

Pantheism is a metaphysical and religious position. Broadly defined it is the view that (1) 'God is everything and everything is God … the world is either identical with God or in some way a self-expression of his nature' (Owen 1971: 74). Similarly, it is the view that (2) everything that exists constitutes a 'unity,' and this all-inclusive unity is in some sense divine (MacIntyre 1967: 34). Aside from Spinoza, other possible pantheists include some of the pre-Socratics, Plato, Lao-Tzu, Plotinus, Eriugena, Schelling, Hegel, Bruno, and Tillich. Possible pantheists among literary figures include R. W. Emerson, Walt Whitman, D. H. Lawrence, and Robinson Jeffers. A popularly identifiable pantheist is Obi-Wan Kenobi of *Star Wars* fame. Indeed, for a ready notion of just what pantheism is, the 'Force' ('may the Force be with you') in *Star Wars*, while very different from Spinoza's singular but fecund substance, is as good a popularization as one is likely to find. Spinoza's *Ethics*, finished in 1675 (two years before his death), is generally regarded as the most thoroughgoing account of a particular pantheistic position. Pantheism is the traditional religious alternative to theism, and many profess pantheistic beliefs – often obscurely. The central claims of pantheism are prima facie no more fantastic than those of theism, and probably less so.

Unity and divinity

Different versions of pantheism offer different accounts of 'unity' and 'divinity.' Perhaps the central problem of pantheism is to determine just how to understand these central terms. For example, philosophical Taoism (sometimes spelled 'Daoism') is one of the best articulated and thoroughly pantheistic positions there is. The *Tao* is the central unifying feature, but just what is meant by the Tao, and understanding how it operates and its implications, require a great deal of interpretation. What kind of unity is (or should be) claimed by pantheists and which, if any, is plausible? There may be acceptable alternative criteria. Like theism, pantheism is by no means a univocal view.

Attributing unity simply on the basis of all-inclusiveness is irrelevant to pantheism. To understand the world as 'everything' is to attribute a sense of unity to the world, but there is no reason to suppose this is pantheistically relevant. Similarly, unity as mere numerical, class, or categorical unity is irrelevant, since just about anything (and everything) can be 'one' or a 'unity' in these senses. Formal unity neither entails or is entailed by types of unity (e.g., substantial unity) sometimes taken to be Unity. Hegel's

Geist, Lao-tzu's *Tao*, Plotinus' *One*, and arguably Spinoza's *substance* are independent of this kind of formal unity.

Unity may also be explained in terms of divinity. The all-inclusive whole may be a unity because it is divine, either in itself (Spinoza's substance), or because of a divine power informing it. This is the case with some pre-Socratics for whom the unifying principle is divine because it is immortal and indestructible. But this does not satisfactorily explain the relation between unity and divinity, or why divinity might be seen as a basis of unity. One cannot decide a priori that the possession of divinity requires personhood without ruling out the possibility of typical types of pantheism (i.e., non-personal types).

Pantheism, theism, and atheism

Where pantheism is considered as an alternative to theism, it involves a denial of at least one, and usually both, central theistic claims. Theism is the belief in a personal God which in some sense transcends the world. Pantheists usually deny the existence of a personal God – a 'minded' Being that possesses the properties of a 'person,' such as having intentional states. There can be a number of reasons for this denial. For example, although pantheists are not atheists, they may, like some atheists (and some theists) think that, given the evil in the world, it makes little if any sense to suppose that such an omnipotent, omniscient, and perfectly good deity exists. Pantheism being a rejection of theism and atheism, pantheists deny that what they mean by God is completely transcendent. They deny that God is 'totally other' than the world or ontologically distinct from it. The dichotomy between transcendence and immanence has been a source of philosophical and religious concern in western and non-western traditions, and all major traditions have at times turned to pantheism as a way of resolving difficulties with the theistic notion of a transcendent deity.

Not all of the problems generated by the theistic notion of God are also problems for pantheism. But given a suitable reformulation, some of them will be. Pantheism will also generate difficulties peculiar to itself. Thus, although evil and creation do not present identical problems for pantheism and theism, it may be possible to reformulate them in a way that makes them applicable to pantheism. Perhaps, too, they can be resolved by pantheism.

Like 'atheism,' the term 'pantheism' was used in the eighteenth century as a term of 'theological abuse,' and it often still is (Tapper 1987). A. H. Armstrong says the term 'pantheistic' is a 'large, vague term of theological abuse' (Armstrong 1976: 187). With some exceptions, pantheism is non-theistic, but it is not atheistic. It is a form of non-theistic monotheism, or even non-personal theism. The primary reason for equating pantheism with atheism is the assumption that belief in any kind of 'god' must be belief in a personalistic God, because God must be a person (or personal being). Schopenhauer said that 'to call the world God is not to explain it; it is only to enrich our language with a superfluous synonym for the word "world"' (Schopenhauer 1951: 40). If what Schopenhauer, Coleridge, Owen, etc. want to show is that believing in a pantheistic God is a confused way of believing in something that can adequately be described apart from any notion of deity, they are mistaken.

Evil

The problem of evil is a product of theism and not directly pertinent to pantheism. It is not, as Owen (1971: 72) claims, 'an embarrassment' intellectually speaking, to pantheists, nor can it be. This reiterates the common view among Spinoza's earliest critics that pantheism, unlike theism, can neither account for evil nor offer any resolution to the problem of evil. The theistic 'problem of evil' cannot be relevant to pantheism since, with the possible exception of acknowledging the presence of evil, pantheism rejects all aspects of theism that generate the problem. Pantheism does not claim that its divine Unity is a morally perfect, omniscient, and omnipotent being.

However, pantheism, as a worldview and religion, needs to address evil and associated moral issues. It offers its own formulations of a 'problem of evil' and its own responses. However, the very idea of evil may be something the pantheist wishes to eschew. 'Evil' is a metaphysical rather than a moral concept; or it is moral concept with a theistic metaphysical commitment. The pantheist may prefer, as many contemporary ethical theorists do, to talk of what is moral.

Immortality

The denial of personal immortality is one of pantheism's most distinctive features, and it may have implications for one's choices in life. Some pantheists believe in types of non-personal immortality (e.g., Spinoza and Robinson Jeffers), and reject the view that personal immortality is more valuable than impersonal immortality. Jeffers suggests that what is significant for the pantheist is the denial of personal immortality and recognition of the individual as a part of the 'one organic whole ... this one God.' He says, the

> parts change and pass, or die, people and races and rocks and stars ... [but the whole remains] ... all its parts are different expressions of the same energy, and they are all in communication with each other, influencing each other, [and are] therefore parts of one organic whole.... [T]his whole alone is worthy of the deeper sort of love; and ... there is peace, freedom, I might say a kind of salvation, in turning one's affections outward toward this one God, rather than inwards on one's self, or on humanity. (Sessions 1977: 481-528)

Jeffers suggests that 'salvation' or immortality is not a matter of life after death, but consists in the recognition, when alive, of the oneness or Unity of everything. It involves a this-worldly utopian vision to which a striving for justice and well-being is essential.

Deism

Deism, according to the *Oxford English Dictionary*, is the 'distinctive doctrine or belief of a deist; usually, belief in the existence of a Supreme Being as the source of finite existence, with rejection of revelation and the supernatural doctrines of Christianity; "natural religion."'

Deism is theism shaken and stirred – but it is theism nonetheless. It defines itself *vis-à-vis* theism by denying, in varying degrees, the supernatural and revelatory aspects of theism. Deists see true religion as based on reason, as fundamentally ethical or equivalent to morality, and as available to all people (even the very stupid and very intelligent?) at all times with no need for divine intervention in history – which in any case they deny. Deism bluntly denies that justice or God's goodness is compatible with a religion that makes salvation or well-being dependent upon any revelation in history which would thereby exclude some people from its very possibility. Some deists, such as Immanuel Kant (1724–1804) – if he is a deist – do allow a role, even a necessary one, for particular manifestations of religion. Many get into the old game of rating religions – a game where Christianity always comes out on top – the perfect historical embodiment of the ideal rational (ethical) religion. Like pantheists, deists were often regarded as atheists (see Gay 1968: 11–12), a situation no different today. Putting the ecumenical (Janus) mask aside, the religious often accuse those of other faiths as being atheists or infidels.

Although Gay (1968: 13) says that the deists 'were powerful agents of modernity' (p. 13), he sees them primarily as polemicists rather than philosophers, historians, or theologians (pp. 9–13). Peter Byrne has a different opinion. He says, for example, 'A great deal … of what we understand by the "historical approach" to Scripture and Christian origins can be traced back to the deists' (Byrne 1989: 94). However, much of what Byrne sees as the English deists' legacy – natural religion, an emphasis on reason, proper socio-scientific and historical approaches to religion – is better attributed to the social, political, and cultural milieu that gave rise to the deists. This includes the corruption and superstition of western religious traditions, the rise of science, as well as the thought of Feuerbach, Marx, Freud, and Darwin. It is more likely that deism, natural religion, religious skepticism, and *some* contemporary approaches to the study of religion, share common causes rather than deism being the cause of religion within the limits of reason. An intellectual pedigree is not the same as a causal one. The sea change in approaches to biblical scholarship and the study of religion is complex and over-determined. Some religious thought after deism (e.g., Schleiermacher's and Hegel's) was in part a reaction to deism. But to see the contemporary study of religion as motivated by such reactions is to see such study as itself religiously motivated. Not surprisingly, much of it is.

If Byrne overestimates the contribution of English deists' to the contemporary study of religion by neglecting other contributing factors, then Gay underestimates it: 'Deism … produced great debate, and a debate that the deists were bound to lose; the opposing side engrossed most of the talent' (Gay 1968: 10). Talent aside, Gay may be mistaking the battle for the war. The deists were more than polemicists, and arguably all of their major skeptical contentions and arguments for those views are correct. Issues relating to God's justice and claims to religious exclusivity that the deists raised by way of rejecting revelation and Christianity's uniqueness are formidable. They are not much discussed in the early twenty-first century ultra-Christian climate of philosophy of religion, but they are not forgotten.

Deism thus denies the interactive features of a transcendent God and immanent creation that are central to traditional revelatory theism. It also attacks, with virulence, institutions like the clergy seen as essential to revelatory religion and on which such religions rely – institutions regarded as largely opposed to all they purport to be. It sees the clergy as destructive progenitors of intolerance, with hypocrisy as underlying its *modus operandi*. It views their tools-in-trade as superstition, fear, power, prejudices, cruelty, and deception, motivated by greed and self-interest. Important differences notwithstanding, as critics of non-natural religion, deists have much in common with Marx and Freud.

Voltaire (1694-1778) was an influential deist, and fledgling America had its share as well (e.g., Thomas Jefferson, Thomas Paine, Benjamin Franklin). But the strongest and most articulate forms of deism came about in eighteenth-century England. Deism, however, comes in varieties and degrees. There is a certain pathos in following Locke's (1632-1704) thoughts, driven by a sense of justice and logic, toward deism and a rejection of supernatural religion, while never quite getting there, resorting instead to intellectual gymnastics if not inconsistency. The same was true with other deists who insisted on reason manifesting itself in progress in history and in an afterlife and personal immortality – all the while rejecting irrationality, superstition, and beliefs generated by fear. On the other hand, 'pathos' may be too strong. It may be that they were simply protecting themselves from the religious bigots of the day. Hume (1711-76), remember, was denied a professorship at both Edinburgh and Glasgow on account of his religious views.

Two kinds of deism: *Deus absconditus* and *deus ex machina* – or *Pas de deux dieux*

Being parasitic on theism, as well as symbiotic with it, deism may be the least interesting of all historically prominent alternative concepts of deity. Although deists generally deny it, deism appears to regard religion – considered as anything other than morality – as otiose. They acknowledge a creator but see religion as basically reducible to morality and morality as accessible only to collective human reason. If deists allow that historical religious traditions express the moral core of religion in particular ways (Christianity always seen as the best), the force of the reduction of religion to morality is mitigated but not removed.

One strand of deism makes religion doubly unnecessary. It sees God as *deus absconditus*, God is not merely hidden but absent. It entertains the notion of God as creator, but rejecting divine intervention in history, revelation, and other supernaturalisms, such deism denies God any further role in creation. It denies that much about God can be ascertained by contemplating creation. Deism in this vein does little to explore its implications other than to claim that ordinary theistic practice like prayer is misguided. The notion of a *deus absconditus* is raised by Hume in his attack on the argument of design. It is one of the best paragraphs in the greatest work on natural theology, Hume's *Dialogues Concerning Natural Religion*:

> In a word, Cleanthes, a man who follows your hypothesis is able perhaps to assert, or conjecture, that the universe, sometime, arose from something like design: but ... [t]his world, for aught he knows, is very faulty and imperfect ... and was only the first rude essay of some infant deity, who afterwards abandoned it, ashamed of his lame performance. (Hume 1947: 168)

This idea that God abandoned his creation may seem negative and on some interpretations it is. If God abandoned creation so that one no longer has recourse to God through religion, then what can the role of religion be for enlightening humankind? Answers vary, but one general deistic response takes the bull by the horns and turns to humanism. There is no role for religion in any traditional sense. People and nations cannot rely on divine guidance (there is none). They must rely on reason (including truths of human nature revealed by novelists, dramatists, and poets), science, moral sentiment and ethics generally, for guidance on how to live well and justly. These are the essential ingredients to a worldview and ethos consonant with the idea that God is not active in human affairs. Leaving issues of creation and immortality aside, this deistic view is barely, if at all, different than thoroughgoing humanism, or the views of Hume, Freud, Marx, or Darwinians on religion.

The majority of deists, however, turn the notion of a *deus absconditus* into a *deus ex machina* (god of the machine), where God has providentially done his work in creation by providing humans with reason, which is all that is necessary to working out their own salvation. Some deists (Kant) also believe that historically grounded religions may play a role in symbolically and approximately representing the deeper truths of religion based solely on reason. Historical religions are more readily accessible to the majority and so have a crucial, even necessary, role to play as reason gains the upper hand in history. And many deists are unwilling to give up theism's promise of personal immortality, which they regard as a demand of reason and justice.

Belief in immortality, and what some deists see as the role of historical religions for human well-being, may separate the latter kind of deism (God as providentially present) from the former (God merely as creator) – though there is no hard line. The latter kind of deist may see the former in largely negative terms, even as atheistic. From one perspective, however, there is little that separates the two. Deists who believe that a creator God abandoned creation see more or less the same role and need for reason and ethics in the governance of human affairs as do the latter kind of deists, who abstractly connect reason to divine providence. Deism may be a form of theism, but to a far greater extent, it is a form of humanism. Nevertheless, there is something inconsonant in the majority view of deists who wish to eschew supernaturalism of any kind in favor of reason, and yet maintain a divine manifestation in reason itself as well as an assumed progress in history via the providential character of the *deus ex machina*.

They want to eat their cake and have it too. Humanists are truer to the word and spirit of deism. In the end, many of the English deists, and Kant, cannot tear themselves from theism and believe solely in a reliance on reason and human ability for progress as they profess to do. Byrne (1989) appears to regard the fundamental religiosity of the deists as at least as significant, if not more so, for religious thought and the study of religion that followed, than whatever influence they have had on the role of reason and critical history in such study. But this tells us more about Byrne than about the deists.

Byrne's thesis is that the contemporary study of religion, the kind found in many religious studies departments and the social sciences generally, is a legacy of deism and the Enlightenment's turn toward natural religion, that is, religion independent of revelation. In terms of an intellectual history some of it is, although there are also independent factors, such as education, literacy, a 'shrinking world,' and the influence of the natural and social sciences. But Byrne does not draw enough of, or the right kind of, distinction between the study of religion on the one hand and contemporary philosophy of religion on the other. Byrne is using philosophy of religion to mean a rational reflection on the nature of religion in relation to humankind and history. But this is not at all what contemporary analytic philosophy of religion does. What Byrne means – this reflection on the nature of religion, its universality or lack thereof, etc. – is taken up in the history of religious thought (as Byrne himself does), or else in theology, speculative history (elsewhere eschewed as archaic) and the history of religions. But it is not part of philosophy of religion now practiced – not even in religious studies.

The idea that philosophy of religion reflects deism's turn toward rationality and natural religion is mistaken. Contemporary philosophy of religion is not merely at odds with the study of religion in the humanities and social sciences, but much of the time ignores or contests it. Exceptions aside, contemporary philosophy of religion is, heart and soul, apologetics. Its agenda and substance are dominated by Christian philosophers less connected to Humean natural theology or deism than to Scholasticism. Rooted in inviolable assumptions and revelation, reason serves faith and the 'truth' of Scripture, which is often literally interpreted. Hence, reason and argument are often distorted in a classic wish-fulfilling manner. Such philosophy of religion is anything but deistic in spirit or practice. It rejects, ignores, misrepresents, or is ignorant of, biblical scholarship; progressive theology; much of religious studies (including relevant aspects of history, sociology, anthropology); as well as critical history and theory of religions. Some Christian philosophers of religion have a take on science in relation to religion that is often suspect, and some even deny evolution (see Levine 1998; 1999; 2000). They are at odds with the intellectual traditions that Bryne argues are the legacy of deism and the Enlightenment. Incidentally, this is why one rarely finds an analytic philosopher of religion in a sophisticated religious studies department. The discomfort on both sides is too great.

Conclusion

We have been considering standard non-theistic conceptions of deity. However, it is worth asking (mischievously) whether theism as conceived by Anselm, Aquinas, Augustine, and Maimonides – theism blended with Aristotelianism and taken up in contemporary philosophy of religion where it is mixed with elements of possible worlds, quantum mechanics, or string theory – is itself theistic.

It took imagination and wishful thinking for Church and medieval Scholastic philosophers – Christian, Arabic and Jewish – to see a theistic God in Aristotle's account of the 'unmoved mover,' and to develop it in line with his account of potentiality, actuality, substance, form, and causation. Aristotle, after all, believed the universe to be eternal. God is not the creator of the universe, as in Scripture, but is its final cause, the reason behind its existence. In his *Summa Theologiae* (1267–73) Aquinas develops Aristotle's thought into a more complete theology. It is not obvious, however, how or why Aquinas and others could use Aristotle's work, notably the *Metaphysics*, as a basis for developing a theistic account of God compatible with Scripture. The notion of God based on Aristotelianism is not merely different from, but at odds with God as depicted in Scripture. This adaptation of Aristotle's philosophy for their own purposes is one of the oddest yet most significant developments in the history of philosophy. It is a legacy that, while dominant, is also, according to many non-theists, religiously and philosophically peculiar. The influence of the Enlightenment, Humean natural theology, and deism casts a shadow over much contemporary analytic philosophy of religion, but is not taken up by it. Indeed, though John Haldane, Nicholas Wolterstorff, and Peter van Inwagen, for example, deny it, they remain hostile to the influence. It is aspects of religious studies and socio-scientific, scientific and contemporary biblical ('excavative') scholarship whose approaches to the study of religion constitute the intellectual, or at least academic, heir to the Enlightenment.

The reason there has been relatively little interest in non-theistic concepts of deity in the twenty-first century is at least twofold. First, contemporary analytic philosophy of religion is dominated by fundamentalist approaches to theism. Examples are Plantinga's and Wolterstorff's (1983) 'properly basic belief'; Wolterstorff's (1995) account of divine discourse; Alston's (1991) epistemology of religious belief; and creationist doctrines and treatments of the problem of evil by Haldane (Smart and Haldane 1996) and van Inwagen (1995). While there is anachronistic debate about whether creationism should be taught alongside evolution in public schools, that creationism doctrine is argued for by prominent Christian analytic philosophers of religion, or that contemporary biblical scholarship is twisted, remains largely unnoticed (see Levine 1998; 1999; 2000). This milieu leaves little room for progressive notions of *theism*, let alone non-theistic concepts of deity.

Secondly, while non-western and comparative approaches to philosophy of religion, the other arena in which pantheism is likely to be discussed, are no longer as concerned with a rapprochement to western theism as they once were (their *raison d'être* since the 1950s), their agenda remains largely religious. Philosophers working in Buddhist and other traditions are engaged in first-order philosophical speculation, analytic expositions, and philosophical/religious reconstructions of their own. As with the case of contemporary analytic philosophy of religion, much of this is religiously motivated, to prove, for example, that aspects of Buddhist doctrine are true. If the investigation of non-theistic concepts of deity is to advance, it must distance itself from philosophy, East and West, in which revealed religion and Scripture, rather than Humean natural theology, informs inquiry.

Additionally, politics and religion are never far removed from one another. Inquiry into non-theistic concepts of deity has always been bound up with issues of social and political justice. Given that much religion today may be seen as a force for the moral, social, and political status quo – at least from the perspective of many religious outsiders – the time may seem hardly ripe for progressive religious thought of any kind. For example, it could be argued that the Roman Catholic Church has not been sufficiently forceful in its response to pedophilia, apparently rewarding those like Cardinal Law (who moved from Boston to Rome), and appearing directly responsible for allowing such practices to continue. Other such objections include the Catholic Church's prohibition of condoms in light of the AIDS crisis, the ban on women priests (often endorsed by gay priests), and the general opposition to gay and women's rights. Rather than religion being at the forefront of moral enlightenment, to many it seems rather to lag behind. Hypocrisy and religion have always had a special (though not necessarily exclusive) relationship. And while the current religious and political climate may not appear to be conducive to progressive religious or political thinking, it may yet lead to a resurgence of meaningful philosophy of religion and practice bound up with a different – and enlightened – vision of social progress and justice.

A study of non-theistic concepts of deity provides reason to deny that the idea of God discussed among philosophers is robustly theistic or religiously relevant. It bears little resemblance to God as depicted in Scripture and plays little or no role in practice. The God of the philosophers is often conceived of as impassible, devoid of emotion and other characteristics, in ways arguably incompatible with notions of personhood. Facile – or worse than merely facile – solutions to the problem of evil are also offered rather than seeing evil as fundamental and mysterious (Levine 2000). The religious view of a theistic God is utterly different. God is seen as active in the world in ways that, arguably, the philosophically conceived God never could be. If so, then the most prominent non-theistic concept of deity is not the pantheistic, panentheistic, or deistic variety, but one from the philosopher's own garden. Can it be that neither Richard Swinburne nor Alvin Plantinga is a theist after all? Good Lord!

See also Hinduism (Chapter 1), Buddhism (Chapter 2), Chinese religions (Chapter 4), Judaism (Chapter 5), Christianity (Chapter 6), Islam (Chapter 7), David Hume (Chapter 13), Truth in religion (Chapter 18), Religious traditions and rational assessments (Chapter 19), The problem of evil (Chapter 37), Problems with the concept of God (Chapter 38), Why is there a universe at all, rather than just nothing? (Chapter 41), Process theology (Chapter 46), Reformed epistemology (Chapter 58), Phenomenology of religion (Chapter 61), Religious naturalism (Chapter 62), Religion and science (Chapter 64).

References

Alston, W. (1991) *Perceiving God*, Ithaca, NY: Cornell University Press.

Armstrong, A. H. (1976) [1940] *The Architecture of the Intelligible Universe in the Philosophy of Plotinus*, Cambridge: Cambridge University Press.

Byrne, P. (1989) *Natural Religion and the Nature of Religion: The Legacy of Deism*, London: Routledge.

Gay, P. (1968) *Deism: An Anthology*, Princeton, NJ: Van Nostrand.

Hume, D. (1947) [1779] *Dialogues Concerning Natural Religion*, 2nd edn, ed. N. K. Smith, London: Nelson.

—— (1976) *The Natural History of Religion* [1757] and *Dialogues Concerning Natural Religion* [1779], 2nd edn, eds A. W. Colver and J. V. Price, Oxford: Clarendon Press.

Levine, M. P. (1998) 'God speak,' *Religious Studies* 34: 1–16.

—— (1999) 'Atheism and theism: J. J. C. Smart and J. J. Haldane,' *Canadian Journal of Philosophy* 29: 157–70.

—— (2000) 'Contemporary Christian analytic philosophy of religion: biblical fundamentalism; terrible solutions to a horrible problem; and hearing God,' *International Journal for Philosophy of Religion* 48: 89–119.

Lipner, J. J. (1985) *Ramanuja: The Face of Truth*, London: Macmillan.

MacIntyre, A. (1967) 'Pantheism,' in P. Edwards (ed.) *Encyclopedia of Philosophy*, New York: Macmillan/Free Press.

Owen, H. P. (1971) *Concepts of Deity*, London: Macmillan.

Plantinga, A. and N. Wolterstorff (eds) (1983) *Faith and Rationality*, Notre Dame, IN: University of Notre Dame Press.

Schopenhauer, A. (1951) 'A few words on pantheism,' in *Essays from the Parerga and Paralipomena*, trans. T. B. Saunders, London: Allen & Unwin.

Sessions, G. (1977) 'Spinoza and Jeffers on man in nature,' *Inquiry* 20: 481–528.

Smart, J. J. C. and J. J. Haldane (1996) *Atheism and Theism*, Oxford: Blackwell.

Tapper, A. (1987) 'Priestley's Metaphysics,' Ph.D. dissertation, University of Western Australia.

van Inwagen, P. (1995) 'The problem of evil, the problem of air, and the problem of silence,' in *God, Knowledge and Mystery: Essays in Philosophical Theology*, Ithaca, NY: Cornell University Press.

Veyne, P. (1988) [1983] *Did the Greeks Believe in their Myths? An Essay on the Constitutive Imagination*, trans. P. Wissing, Chicago: University of Chicago Press.

Wolterstorff, N. (1995) *Divine Discourse: Philosophical Reflections on the Claim that God Speaks*, Cambridge: Cambridge University Press.

Further reading

Hartshorne, C. and W. L. Reese (1953) *Philosophers Speak of God*, London: Chicago University Press. (Wide-ranging discussion of concepts of deity against which Hartshorne's own di-polar (panentheistic) view is defended.)

Levine, M. P. (1994) *Pantheism: A Non-theistic Concept of Deity*, London: Routledge. (An account of pantheism as compared and contrasted with theism.)

Macquarrie, J. (1984) *In Search of Deity*, Gifford Lectures 1983, London: SCM Press. (Examines various concepts of deity.)

McFarland, T. (1969), *Coleridge and the Pantheist Tradition*, Oxford: Oxford University Press. (Study of Coleridge and others who held pantheistic or quasi-pantheistic views.)

Spinoza, B. (1985) *Ethics*, in *The Collected Works of Spinoza*, vol. 1, trans. and ed. E. Curley, Princeton, NJ: Princeton University Press. (The *locus classicus* for pantheism.)

23

MYSTICISM AMONG THE WORLD'S RELIGIONS

Louis Dupré

Mysticism in monotheist religion

The substantive 'mysticism' (in French, *mystique*) did not exist before the seventeenth century. The root verb *muo* ('close [lips and/or eyes]'), from which the adjective *mystikos* was derived, refers to the ancient Greek mysteries, probably to the secrecy of their rituals and teachings. With Philo (first century CE) the word *mystikos* assumed a loosely scriptural meaning, which the Alexandrian church fathers Clement and Origen applied to the Christian, allegorical interpretation of the Bible. In a similar way it came to refer to the symbolic meaning of washing, eating, and drinking in the sacraments of baptism and Eucharist. Gradually the term acquired a spiritual connotation, which eventually led to its modern usage.

None of the preceding meanings refers to a private experience. Not even those Christian writers whom we now regard as having initiated the so-called mystical theology mention such an experience. The late origin of the connotation of private, exceptional experience in Judaism and Islam as well as in Christianity indicates that for the longest time neither religious authorities nor ordinary faithful considered such an experience essential to the faith. Early Christians appear to have regarded an awareness of God's presence as naturally following their religious conversion. But there was nothing private or exceptional about it. They did attribute a continuous awareness of such a presence to Jesus. Paul in his letters to the various Christian communities developed an idea of life in the Spirit, which included some insight in the 'mystery of Christ.' It enabled Christians to understand Scriptures in a deeper, 'revealed' sense, which led to the scriptural meaning of the term 'mystical.'

The Greek Fathers from the third to the ninth century, to whom Christians commonly ascribe the development of a mystical spirituality, hardly mention any but a cognitive experience. The weight of their teaching was intellectual more than affective. Nor did the Neoplatonic philosophy, which they had started to accept in the fourth century, encourage a different outlook. Even Dionysius the Areopagite, a sixth-century Syrian(?) monk, asserted in his *Mystical Theology* (which many now consider the first 'Christian' treatise on the subject), that it consisted in a direct, albeit purely negative knowledge of God. The author had in fact derived much of its content from the Neoplatonic philosopher Proclus.

This trend of interpretation changed at the dawn of the modern age, partly as a result of a different reading some contemplatives (Cistercians and Carthusians) began to propose of Dionysius. Since the awareness of God surpassed all concepts and ideas, the question arose whether mystical theology could still be assumed to consist in a cognitive act. Was it not rather an affective experience? The idea that it was rapidly gained acceptance in the West, without, however, excluding a cognitive component altogether. Moreover, as a subjective experience it became quite naturally a private one. Thus Jean Gerson (1363-1429), the chancellor of the Sorbonne, defined it as 'experiential knowledge of God' (experimentalis Dei cognitio), a knowledge that could be acquired only through an affective union with God. Around the same time, Christian spirituality also began to stress the extraordinary nature of the mystical experience.

Privacy and extraordinariness of experience are, even today, less apparent in the two other monotheistic religions. To be sure, Jews had, long before Christians, developed private as well as public forms of devotion. Yet they continued to refer to them by terms of ordinary devotion, rather than by specifically mystical ones. Thus, the Hebrew term mitzvoth (commandments) had neither the experiential nor the exceptional connotation of the term mysticism. The reasons for the commandments remain hidden in God, but their subject matter concerns all religious Jews and is by no means the privilege of some. Even the esoteric Kabbalah continues in some respects the common halakha tradition of the commandments. In fact, kaballistic writers use a term of common devotion, devekut (cleaving to God), that in the Talmud refers to good works. As that term gradually assumed a more explicitly spiritual denotation, the emphasis increasingly shifted to a hidden knowledge. This was particularly the case in the highly esoteric form of Kabbalah initiated by the Zohar (The Book of Splendor), written in thirteenth-century Spain, but not printed before the sixteenth century. But it was never the exclusive privilege of a closed group, not even in Isaac Luria's theosophical school in Safed (Palestine).

In Islam also, the experience of God's presence long preceded the birth of particular, mystical sects. We may trace that experience to Muhammad himself, who expressed it in the Qur'ān. It consisted in an unconditional surrender to the all-compassionate, all-loving God. As a young man Muhammad (d. 632 CE) frequently withdrew to a cave near Mecca to be alone with God. There, during his fortieth year, an angel appeared to him and recited the first verses of the Qur'ān. A sage acquainted with the Christian writings confirmed that the voice had indeed come from God. Ostracized from Mecca, he was comforted in his trials by a nocturnal vision. He found himself transferred to the temple rock in Jerusalem and from there ascending through the hierarchies of being, up to the presence of God. Ever since that rapture, he appears to have remained conscious of God's presence.

The Qur'ān has preserved his experience of revelations that continued until shortly before his death. In Seyyed Hossein Nasr's (1987) beautiful expression, 'The Muslim lives in a space defined by the sound of the Qur'ān.' The sacred book directs the spiritual life of the faithful to the love of an all-loving God. It instructs all Muslims to 'remember God' and to become interiorly united with him. 'Invoke in remembrance the name of thy Lord and devote thyself to Him with utter devotion' (Q. 73: 8). Even the Sharia, 'the way of the faithful,' must be viewed as an attempt to remain constantly in God's presence by submitting all aspects of life to divine law.

Muhammad's successors, Abu Bakr, Umar, Uthman, and the prophet's younger cousin Ali, whom he himself had taught, were deeply spiritual men. But when the Umayad dynasty came to an end and the Abassids ruled in Baghdad, all emphasis came to be placed on strict observation of the law. Sufism, which had existed since the eighth century, became a separate movement and the imams began to eye the followers of the spiritual path (*tariqa*) with suspicion. In 922 the great Sufi mystic, al-Hallaj, was executed for blasphemy. Others, beginning with his early contemporary Junayd, were more careful. Sufi mysticism – even as medieval Christian spirituality, and the Jewish Kabbalah movement – was influenced by Neoplatonic philosophy. Yet the Sufi brotherhood never separated itself from the common faith; it remained open to all Muslims.

The possibility of a general discussion of mysticism in monotheist religion presupposes that monotheist mystics share at least some common experience. Does it imply that religious mysticism is identical regardless of the tradition in which it appears? As late as the middle of the twentieth century some well-known writers still assumed that a single, homogeneous model of interpretation applied to all cases. That position, advocated by Aldous Huxley (1954) and W. T. Stace (1960), has now almost generally been abandoned. R. C. Zaehner (1956), a respected scholar of comparative religion, qualified it by distinguishing three essentially different kinds of mysticism. Yet he continued to maintain that, despite those differences, the experience of theist, monist, and natural mystics remains essentially identical *within* each of those three varieties. Ninian Smart (1975) claimed that not the experience but only the interpretations (including the mystics' own) differ along doctrinal lines. Those who describe the mystical experience as a state of pure, empty consciousness unmediated by any idea, go even further. F. C. Forman, its principal advocate in America, described it as a gap in consciousness, of which the subject does not become aware until the 'experience' is past. But how does such a gap differ from a dreamless sleep – to which, indeed, one of the Upanishads (*Mandukya*) compared it?

On the opposite side are those who insist that experience and interpretation cannot be separated. For them, the interpretation forms part of the experience. According to Steven T. Katz (1978), no state of mind can ever be wholly unconditioned. Doctrines feed into the experience so much that one cannot exist without the other. This causes him to deny the possibility of a so-called *unio mystica*, which abolishes all distinctness between a perceiving subject and a perceived object, as a Neoplatonic idea adventitiously introduced into the Christian concept of contemplation. In his view, Judaism did not undergo this Neoplatonic influence, at least not to the point of justifying any concept of a *unio mystica*. Both these claims have been contested, as we shall see later.

Today we appear to have moved closer to a consensus that the mystical experience, despite a strong similarity in different religions, remains an analogous notion. Each form of mysticism intrinsically depends on the doctrinal context in which it appears. The question is, however, how far this distinctness can go without altogether destroying the idea of an experience that has a common name. A first point to consider here is that the mystical awareness (taken in the modern sense of a somewhat exceptional state) remains integrated with less intense modes of religious experience, from which it differs in degree of intensity, but not in essence. Because we have unaccountably detached the mystical from ordinary religious experience, the question of the presence of mysticism in any particular religion has attained an unwarranted significance.

To avoid further confusion, I shall follow modern western usage in distinguishing ordinary from mystical experience, but restrict the distinction to the degree of intensity, not to the *nature* of the experience. At every level, religious experience is marked by the awareness of a mysterious and fascinating transcendent presence. Even those religions or branches of religion which attach less importance to experience than to prophetic or moral factors are inspired by the felt presence of God. Now, all religious experiences differ from each other either in content or in context. Part of the context consists in the significance a particular religious tradition attaches to ecstatic or peak experiences. In Vedantic Hinduism, the mystical experience comes close to coinciding with the essence of the religion. In Buddhism also it occupies a primary place, though that place widely differs from one school to another. Because of that difference from the three monotheistic religions, I have not included them in the present essay. The essays on Hinduism and in Buddhism contain ample information on the mystical character of those religions. But within monotheistic faiths the difference between the mystically inclined and others can be considerable.

For Sufis, the religious experience is far more important than it is for more legalistically oriented Muslims. All religious Jews strive for some experiential awareness of God's presence. But groups and individuals considerably differ on the significance of the experience and on the means of attaining it. Among the Christian churches, the Catholic ones (Orthodox, Roman, and Anglican) as well as some Lutherans used to attach greater importance to it than the more prophetically oriented Calvinists or Baptists. But in recent years those differences have become less pronounced.

The place of mysticism in monotheist religion

This raises the question: How important is the place of mysticism in monotheist religion? We first notice that a strong awareness of divine presence has inspired every single founder and all major figures of each faith. That intense awareness tends to weaken in the mass of their followers. Yet spiritual men and women intermittently attempt to revive the original fervor. Insofar as mysticism consists in an awareness of divine presence, it belongs to the *core* of all religions. They could neither begin nor survive without it. Some mode of experience forms an essential component of religion. Its role has become particularly important in the West today, where a growing secularization has practically eliminated the social pressure, which until the recent past still kept many unmotivated people within churches, synagogues, and mosques.

Does this universal presence of at least an inchoately mystical element in religion imply that all mysticism is religious? The answer depends on how one defines religion. In his famous *Discourses on Religion* (1799), Friedrich Schleiermacher considered any merging of the mind with the totality of nature religious. Most experts today would hesitate to consider a feeling of unity with nature actually 'religious,' even though it might potentially be part of a religious experience. Still, few would altogether deny it a mystical character. Even R. C. Zaehner, who regards only theistic mysticism as fully authentic, concedes that the experience of the self expanding beyond its finite borders and merging with nature possesses a mystical quality.

In *The Story of My Heart*, the British writer Richard Jefferies (1848–87) has left a striking example of such nature mysticism. Jefferies rejected the faith in which he was raised and never replaced it with another one. Yet he was obviously endowed with a refined sensitivity for experiencing the unity of all things in nature. His beautiful description of being embraced by this totality now appears in almost any anthology of mystical writers. Everyone remembers the famous lines of Wordsworth's 'Tintern Abbey':

> a sense sublime
> Of something far more deeply interfused,
> Whose dwelling is the light of setting suns ...
> A motion and a spirit, that impels
> All thinking things, all objects of all thought,
> And rolls through all things.

Throughout these verses the reader senses the presence of an all-encompassing reality to which the poet feels united. Many poets have expressed similar mystical or quasi-mystical feelings, among them Jean-Paul Rilke (especially *Duineser Elegien*, Eighth Elegy), Robert Musil, perhaps even Mark Twain in some descriptions of the river in *Huckleberry Finn*. Can we sharply separate the feelings formulated in this secular poetry from the religious mystical experience? If we cannot, how is that experience distinct from the intense aesthetic one?

To answer the question we ought to be clear about the characteristics of the mystical experience in religion. In *The Varieties of Religious Experience* (1902), William James mentioned four of them: ineffability, a noetic quality, passivity, and transiency. *Ineffability* refers to the incommunicable quality of an experience, which words can never describe. Nonetheless, James also categorizes the experience as *noetic*, suggesting that somehow a person feels mentally enriched by it. Ignatius of Loyola describes the life-transforming enlightenment he experienced near Manresa as teaching him more than all the knowledge he had ever gathered before or after the vision. Similarly, Muhammad's *miraj* rapture, which transported him to the temple rock in Jerusalem, illuminated his entire future life.

How are ineffability and cognoscibility, the apophatic and cataphatic aspects of the mystical experience, to be reconciled? Indeed, how can an experience ever be without being 'intentional,' and hence not wholly ineffable? Hans Urs von Balthasar (1982) attempted to justify this paradox by describing it as an experience of non-experience. 'In mysticism every deeper experience of God will be a deeper entering into the "non-experience" of faith, into the living renunciation of experience, all the way into the depths of the "Dark Nights" of John of the Cross – But these nights are precisely an "experience of non-experience" or an experience of the negative, privative mode of experience' (von Balthasar 1982, I: 412–13). In such moments the mystic exchanges experience for openness to the void beyond actual experience. The powers of perception remain alert and awake. But their common objects have left them, and in their place has come a sense of endless expansion. Sensed or known objects, if they appear at all, merely function as heavily charged symbols of a much wider, previously unknown and still-unknowable reality. The mystic abandons the direction of his mind to another Force. He surrenders his sense of reality to a virtual infinity, an endless possibility of being, and thereby transforms his attitude in a way that will determine his entire future. Not only is the mystic *passive*, in the sense that this change surpasses his power: in fact, the mystic abandons the very power of acting through his own power.

Because of the lasting effect this change has on consciousness, it appears incorrect to call such an experience *transient*, as James does. Of course, visions, even the so-called intellectual visions (whereby nothing is seen or imagined, but a new insight in the nature of the real is conveyed) do indeed come and go. Yet advanced mystics have been known to remain for years, in some cases permanently, in a quiet but nonetheless altered state of consciousness. In her *Interior Castle* (1577) Teresa of Avila describes this permanent state as the real goal of the mystical journey, the 'spiritual marriage' (1961: 7, 2). After the Manresa vision, Ignatius constantly remained in God's presence. Muhammad also spent most of his adult life in that enduring awareness of God's proximity. Nor can we doubt that Gautama, the historical Buddha, after his illumination definitively reached a higher state of consciousness. Not only they, yet also many unknown Hasidic Jews and pious Christians may have spent their lives in the aura of a divine light. Their quiet feeling of presence should caution us against drawing too sharp a line between the less sensational but enduring state of piety and the more exalted ones of an al-Hallaj, an Isaac Luria, or a Teresa of Avila.

Mysticism and psychology

Ever since modern spiritual literature came to define mysticism as an exceptional mode of experiencing, it became a special object of psychology. The psychologist takes a legitimate interest in the question of how this particular experience fits within the complex network of the human psyche and how it depends on the support of other, more common acts. In the course of studying this process, however, it is easy to lose sight of the unique nature of the mystical experience and to reduce it to another, more familiar one. All through the twentieth century a number of psychological studies appeared, which 'explained' the mystical state as a more or less pathological one. The allegedly 'hysterical' temperament of Teresa of Avila, of Marguerite-Marie Alacoque, and of Jeanne Guyon, as well as the so-called demonic possessions of Father

Jean-Joseph Surin, and of the nuns of Loudun, appear to confirm their interpretation. James Leuba's *The Psychology of Religious Mysticism* (1925) may count as an early model of psychological reductionism. One need not deny the hysterical inclinations of Marguerite-Marie to consider the way in which Leuba dismisses her visions as too easy.

Freud's approach was more sophisticated. Having defined the entire affective field as moved by the sexual drive, he could not but describe mystical phenomena as expressions of a libido charged with erotic power. In his *Civilization and Its Discontents* (1930), he attributes the so-called 'oceanic feeling' to the ego's relation to an unconscious id. This may occasionally cause the boundaries between self and external world to melt away. The problem with such causal interpretations is that they fail to consider the mystical phenomenon's unique identity, before incorporating it within a pre-existing psychological frame. That the mystical experience is, like all experience, a psychic phenomenon is obvious. That it is entirely explicable through immanent psychological concepts is an unproved prejudice.

William James, still our greatest American psychologist, refuted such reductionist claims even before they were explicitly expressed. Since then, others have taken up the challenge of describing the mystical experience as it actually appears. Rather than exhaustively 'explaining' the phenomenon through psychology, they have attempted to find the psychic structure which makes it possible. A model of such cautious research is Joseph Maréchal's monograph 'On the feeling of presence in mystics and non-mystics' (1908–9) subsequently published in *Studies in the Psychology of the Mystics* (1927). In it, he shows that the feeling of presence, central in most mystical experiences, remains related to, but is not explained by, analogous states of consciousness, in which such a feeling is likewise evoked without any external stimulus. Briefly, it consists in a feeling of presence, in which no sensation appears to support it. Many persons know the odd feeling that someone stands near to them, even though they hear or see nothing. We tend to dismiss such experiences as 'hallucinations' and that is what they are, if we call a vague sensation without external stimulus a hallucination. But there is nothing per se pathological about such experiences. James as well as Maréchal denies that only the ordinary state of consciousness is non-pathological. That state is only one kind; 'while all around it, separated from it by the flimsiest screens,' there are potential forms of consciousness of a completely different nature. Instead of reducing the unknown to the known, they expand the known by the unknown, revealing deeper layers of the self, which psychology has rarely explored.

In the same spirit, the Belgian psychoanalyst Antoine Vergote (1988) has subjected mystical visions and voices to a careful scrutiny. Describing them as 'hallucinosic ideations,' he refuses to accept the common assumption that they are 'pathological,' while admitting that pathological factors may enter into them. But he does not consider them a sufficient reason for dismissing the phenomena as being merely 'the return of the repressed.' Unconscious beliefs may convert an imaginary vision or voice into a real one, but unlike psychotic hallucinations, they do not cause a general breakdown of the common perception of reality. They are hallucinatory only to the extent that their content is dissociated from an actual perception. The power of their impact may render everyday things insignificant or symbolic of a higher reality, but the subject remains critically aware of the vision or voice as occurring within a common environment.

Perhaps even weightier than the psychological question is the metaphysical one. What drives the mind to seek, or at least to desire and to welcome, states of consciousness that add nothing to our theoretical or practical knowledge? Let us first recognize that some persons are more prone to have intense spiritual experiences than others. But speaking in general terms, we may assert that the educated mind experiences a natural desire for contemplation. In *The Life of the Mind*, Hannah Arendt reminded us that, for Plato and Aristotle, active 'thinking,' the inner discourse we carry on with ourselves, counted as no more than a preparation for that passive 'seeing' of truth, which we call contemplation. The term 'contemplation' may well be the most appropriate for rendering the cognitive side of the mystical experience. It establishes a common ground between the highest goal of philosophy and the highest religious aspirations. Besides, it avoids the connotation of extraordinary experiences, inherent in the term 'mysticism' as we use it today.

Thomas Aquinas, together with other medieval thinkers such as Bonaventure, John Duns Scotus, and Nicholas of Cusa, was aware of the religious significance of the ancient notion of contemplation. According to Aquinas, the mind is naturally attracted to contemplation of the highest possible object of thinking, the ultimate cause of all things. Incapable of attaining that First Cause in itself and limited to a contemplation of its presence in creation, the mind nevertheless entertains a natural desire to contemplate what it is unable to reach by its own powers. Believers hope to satisfy this in a beatific vision after death. Some privileged individuals receive a glimpse of this vision in the present life.

Aquinas's presentation is tied to a doctrine of afterlife that many religious-minded do not share. But other thinkers have, without introducing the notion of an afterlife, asserted that an intense noetic desire drives the mind beyond what it is able to comprehend. So did Eric Voegelin in his multi-volume *Order and History*. Neoplatonic philosophy, which shaped much of Arabic, Jewish, and Christian mystical thought, played a major role in the historical awareness of this desire. Indeed, until the eighteenth century the mind's inclination to move beyond the limits of the knowable remained the philosophical justification of mystical desire. In the twentieth century a school of French and French-Belgian philosophers (their leading thinkers were Rousselot, Blondel, and Maréchal) considered the mind's internal dynamism to move beyond the finite object of knowledge the very basis of philosophy. The least we may conclude from these speculations is that philosophical contemplation presents an attitude analogous to the mystical one and a natural justification of its possibility.

Mysticism and love

Yet mysticism is not only contemplative in the cognitive sense. It is also – and foremost – love. Indeed, in all cases we have discussed, love has been the very driving power of mystical contemplation. Evelyn Underhill, in 1911, called mysticism 'a union with the absolute' (Underhill 1968). Do distinctions still apply in that state of mystical union, which alleges to attain that goal? If not, does a state which suspends all distinctness between God and the soul not conflict with all three of the Abrahamic faiths? Is the concept of *unio mystica*, then, after all a Neoplatonic intrusion into all three faiths? Monotheistic religions are, by their very nature, mediated religions – through Moses, Jesus, and Muhammad. For that reason, extreme mystical movements have encountered resistance in all three. How deeply the idea of *fana*, the passing of the soul into the divine Being, offended some Muslims appeared in al-Hallaj's condemnation for blasphemously identifying himself with God. Nor was the Islam alone in this rejection. In the fourteenth century, the Christian Margaretha Porete was burned at the stake for making a claim similar to al-Hallaj's: 'I am the Truth,' meaning, 'I am totally one with God.' For the same reason, the Bishop of Cologne condemned Meister Eckhart. He died while awaiting Pope John XXII's verdict (having beforehand subjected himself to the Pope's judgment). Numerous other troubles haunted even those who held less radical views, among them the late seventeenth century French Quietists, who merely pursued a total union of the will with God's will. Jews proved to be more tolerant of extreme utterances than Christians. Yet even among them, a traditional respect for Kabbalists and Hasidics was often accompanied by a great deal of suspicion of what many considered Neoplatonic or Gnostic deviations from sound doctrine.

Denials of the possibility of a total union in Jewish mysticism have continued until our own time. Still, I think that Moshe Idel, a prominent scholar of Kabbalah, has recently proven its existence. But Jewish mystics, even the extreme ones, kept using the traditional terminology for common religious attitudes, such as *mitzvoth* (commandments) or *devekut* (devotion, cleaving to God). Does the *unio mystica* suppress all distinction? Abraham Abulafia (thirteenth century), one of the earliest Kabbalists to present a total merging with God in mystical union, appears not to have thought so. His technique of combining the Hebrew letters of the divine name aims not at a swoon but at a *revelation* (Idel 1987). Isaac d'Acre, another radical Kabbalist, aiming at mystical union, explicitly cautions against the danger of 'drowning' in the divine ocean.

Early Muslim mystics, Rabia al-Adawiya (d. 801), a former slave girl, Junayd (d. 910), and al-Hallaj (d. 922), all pursued the ideal of a mystical union with God, which they, even as Christian mystics had after the fifteenth century, conceived as an *affective union*, but by no means as a blind, unconscious one. The entire Sufi movement, which in eastern Persia blossomed into the splendid poetry of Said ibn Abi Khaye (d. 1049) and Jalal al Din Rumi (d. 1273), has so much in common with later Christian love mysticism that the expressions are hardly distinguishable from each other.

The sixteenth-century Spanish mystics – Teresa of Avila, John of the Cross, and Ignatius of Loyola – considered the affective *unio mystica* the goal of spiritual life. To them, mysticism consisted in a state of love, which was at the same time an illumination of the mind. Ignatius interpreted his experience near Manresa as an 'illumination.' Teresa of Avila refers to her supreme raptures as 'intellectual visions' distinct from 'imaginary' or 'sensuous' ones. She describes one in her *Relations* (1575) and, like Ignatius, she stresses its cognitive content: 'I came to understand things, which I shall never be able to describe' (1967: 157. 36 and 44).' John of the Cross, in 1586, justified the term 'intellectual vision' as consisting in an (intuitive) understanding of truths about God (1958: II. 23, 2). Yet he adds that such a vision belongs to the state of union and occurs 'in the deepest center of the soul where God Himself dwells.' In this spiritual night, a *substantial union* with God takes place (II. 24, 4). The unitive state is a permanent condition in which God 'touches the substance of the soul.' Here then is the locus of the *unio mystica*, the *theosis* or divinization of the mind, of which also the great Sufi mystics and the ecstatic Kabbalists wrote.

See also Chapters 1–7 on particular religions, William James (Chapter 17), Religious traditions and rational assessments (Chapter 19), Hiddenness (Chapter 29), The problem of religious language (Chapter 39), Theology and religious language (Chapter 48), Prayer (Chapter 57), Religious experience (Chapter 63).

References

Arendt, H. (1977) *The Life of the Mind*, London: Harcourt Brace.
Huxley, A. (1954) *The Doors of Perception*, New York: Harper & Row.
Idel, M. (1987) *Studies in Ecstatic Kabbalah*, Albany, NY: State University of New York Press.
James, W. (1999) [1902] *The Varieties of Religious Experience*, New York: Modern Library.
John of the Cross (1958) *Ascent of Mount Carmel*, Garden City, NY: Doubleday.
—— (1972) [1586] *Subida del Monte Carmelo* in *Obras Completas*, Autores Cristianos, Madrid: Biblioteca de Autores Cristianos.
Katz, S. T. (1978) *Mysticism and Philosophical Analysis*, New York: Oxford University Press.
Maréchal, J. (1927) *Studies in the Psychology of the Mystics*, Whitefish, MT: Kessinger Publishing. Reprinted 2003.
Smart, N. (1975) 'Interpretation and mystical experience,' in *Religious Studies* 1/1.
Stace, W. T. (1960) *Mysticism and Philosophy*, New York: Macmillan.
Teresa of Avila (1961) [1577] *The Interior Castle*, trans. A. Peers, Garden City, NY: Doubleday.
—— (1967) *Cuentas de conciencia* [1575] in *Obras Completas*, Madrid: Autores Cristianos.
Underhill, E. (1968) *Mysticism*, New York: Dutton.
Vergote, A. (1988) *Guilt and Desire*, New Haven, CT: Yale University Press.
Voegelin, E. (2000) *Order and History*, Columbia, MO: University of Missouri Press.
von Balthasar, H. U. (1982–91) *The Glory of the Lord*, 7 vols., San Francisco, CA: Ignatius Press.
Zaehner, R. C. (1956) *Mysticism: Sacred and Profane*, New York: Oxford University Press.

Further reading

Idel, M. (1987) *Kabbalah: New Perspectives*, New Haven, CT: Yale University Press. (A necessary complement and occasional correction of Scholem 1973.)
Maréchal, J. (1964) *Psychology of the Mystics*, Albany, NY: Magi Books. (Still the best psychological study, especially the essay 'On the feeling of presence.')
McGinn, B. (1991–8) *The Presence of God: A History of Western Christian Mysticism*, New York: Crossroad. (By far the best history of western Christian mysticism; four volumes have appeared.)
Schimmel, A. (1975) *Mystical Dimensions of Islam*, Chapel Hill, NC: University of North Carolina Press. (A perceptive, beautiful introduction to Islamic mysticism.)
Scholem, G. (1973) *Major Trends in Jewish Mysticism*, New York: Schocken Books. (The standard work on Jewish mysticism.)
von Hügel, F. (1999) [1923] *The Mystical Element of Religion*, New York: Crossroad. (An excellent description of mysticism in Christian life as a whole.)

Part IV

THE THEISTIC CONCEPT OF GOD

24
OMNISCIENCE
Linda Zagzebski

Introduction and overview

Omniscience is one of the primary traditional attributes of God. In common parlance, God is 'all-knowing,' a being who knows everything there is to know, past, present, and future. Omniscience is one element of intellectual perfection, but an especially interesting element because it raises a number of questions and puzzles.

One set of problems is that omniscience seems to conflict with other divine attributes such as timelessness, perfection, and immateriality. For example, it appears that a timeless being could not know that the test is over since a timeless being would never be later in time than the test. A perfect being could not know that something is frightening since he would never feel fear. An immaterial being could not know that the fabric is scratchy since he has no skin to feel the scratchiness of the material.

These considerations lead to another problem. It is not clear that it is possible for *any* being to be omniscient if knowers in different positions in time or space know different things, each of which differs from what is knowable by a being outside of time and space. Further, some things may be possible objects of knowledge only for a certain person, such as knowing what it is like to be me.

A third problem arises if divine omniscience includes infallible foreknowledge: knowing the future in a way that cannot be mistaken. Infallible foreknowledge appears to make it impossible for the future to be otherwise than the way God knows it to be, thereby conflicting with human free will.

The puzzles above might pressure us to narrow the scope of knowledge of a maximally perfect being, such as eliminating knowledge of the contingent future, or eliminating knowledge that is temporally or spatially relative or relative to beings with the dispositions of finite creatures. But there are other considerations that might lead us to expand the scope of what an omniscient being knows. Knowing the entire past, present, and future might not be sufficient for omniscience. Possibly, an omniscient being not only knows what *did* happen, but also what *would have* happened if certain other things had happened instead, and an omniscient being not only knows what *will* happen, but also what *would* happen if certain other things happen first. So omniscience might not be limited to knowing the actual path of the history of the world, but might include knowing the paths of the other histories that might have occurred, including those paths that branch off at any time in the future. If the omniscient being is also the creator of the world, he would know the entire history of each world he could have created.

We think a perfect being is omniscient because omniscience is a cognitive perfection, but omniscience is not the only cognitive perfection. Whatever reasons we may have to think that God is omniscient may also lead us to think that God has the perfection of other states of intellect such as understanding and wisdom. These features of the divine intellect get very little attention in the contemporary literature because they do not lead to the puzzles that arise from the idea of knowing everything, but they are arguably even more important than omniscience.

Defining omniscience

According to a standard definition of omniscience, a being A is omniscient just in case A knows the truth value of every proposition. Assuming that every proposition is either true or false, then for every proposition p, either A knows p is true or A knows p is false. Curiously, the perennial philosophical problem of defining knowledge is usually not brought up in discussions of omniscience. Few philosophers of religion go on to propose that an omniscient being has true justified beliefs regarding every proposition p, or alternatively, believes each true proposition p according to a reliable belief-producing mechanism, or in some intellectually virtuous manner. Instead, almost all the attention is focused on the scope of divine knowledge: what God knows and does not know, rather than on the conditions for God's epistemic states to count as knowledge. It is taken for granted that, unlike human epistemic states, divine epistemic states never fall short of knowledge, and God does not have to combat skeptical worries. If God has epistemic states, everyone agrees that those states constitute knowledge, and if there are degrees of knowledge, then it is knowledge in the highest degree.

But why think that God has epistemic states at all? The traditional concept of God as a knower like us, only more perfect, is associated with the biblical view of God as personal. Persons have intellects, and if God is perfect, then God has a perfect intellect. One function of the intellect, although not the only function, is to grasp reality. So God perfectly grasps reality. *How* God grasps reality is generally passed over in silence. Aquinas thought that God grasps all of reality through his grasp of his own essence (SCG I. 48). But the divine essence is necessary, and it is difficult to make sense out of grasping something contingent by knowing something necessary. An alternative is to argue that God's will is contingent and to explain the contingency of everything in the world by the contingency of God's will. But reference to the divine will does not explain why the way things are is to some extent up to us. What is up to us does not look like something God can know by grasping either his essence or his will.

If we want to avoid Aquinas's view that God knows everything outside himself by grasping something about himself, it is virtually impossible to avoid metaphors of *looking* at reality all at once, as from the outside. Aquinas himself uses the metaphor of a person on top of a hill looking down upon travelers moving along a road beneath him (*ST* Ia. q.14. a.13 reply obj. 3). All events in time move along like the travelers on the road, and God is fixed outside of time, able to see all temporal reality at one glance.

This metaphor has serious limitations, but at least it has the advantage of describing God as grasping concrete reality directly rather than seeing reality through something else, such as his own essence. The contemporary habit of describing the objects of knowledge as abstract propositions has the same defect. In discussing omniscience, philosophers of religion usually accept the view that when one knows, the object of knowledge is a proposition, an abstract object that corresponds to a grammatically complete declarative sentence. When one knows, one assents to a true proposition. When an omniscient being knows, that being assents to all and only true propositions. According to this view, then, God 'reads off' true propositions in an abstract book of propositions. The book might be in his metaphorical head, but wherever it is, God's contact with the world the propositions are about is not direct. Furthermore, if the objects of God's knowledge are propositions, then God's contact with the world he knows is splintered into discrete units.

Both of these features – the indirectness and the fragmentation – seem to me to be less than ideal ways to know. Admittedly, it is difficult to avoid discussing the range of divine knowledge without treating it as propositional, on the model of human knowledge, but it is helpful to keep in mind that the propositional approach probably distorts divine knowledge. It might also hide some puzzles about omniscience, as we will see in the next section.

Is omniscience compatible with other divine attributes?

Omniscience has traditionally been construed as necessary for divinity for at least two reasons: (1) Ignorance is a defect, and there is no defect in God; (2) God is the creator of everything outside himself and continues to keep everything in existence, governing the entire universe providentially. But to keep everything in existence from moment to moment requires knowing what one is keeping in existence, and governing everything providentially requires knowing every detail of what one is governing. Hence, omniscience is required by the attribute of perfect goodness, and by the doctrine of creation and conservation.

If omniscience is understood as knowing the truth value of every proposition, however, there are some problems with the combination of omniscience and some other divine attributes. Consider the two propositions expressed by the sentences, 'The test is tomorrow,' and 'The test was yesterday.' Both of these sentences could be about the same concrete event – the same test, but some philosophers think that they express different propositions (Prior 1959). That is because it is tempting to build the temporal relationship between the knower and the test into the proposition known. A timeless being could grasp the occurrence of a test on September 1, 2006, but could not know whether the test is past, present, or future. So, if what you know when you know that the test is tomorrow differs from what you know when you know that the test is on September 1, 2006, then a timeless being cannot be omniscient.

Similar problems arise with the attribute of immateriality. Sometimes we express judgments in terms for qualities that seem to be detectable only by beings with a body and the human senses. There are important disputes about the nature of colors, tastes, odors, sounds, and tactile properties, and it is disputable whether there are true propositions attributing these properties to objects in the world. But if there are, how can a being without the relevant sensory faculties know them? Can an immaterial being know that something is blue, fuzzy, or sweet? Certainly he could know in the sense in which a color-blind person can know that the stoplight is red because of its position on the light post, or someone who does not get a joke can see that it is funny because other people are laughing. But even the person who does not get a joke usually has experienced humor and understands it even if she does not experience it on a certain occasion. But what if she had never laughed at anything in her life? Would she even understand the proposition, *That is funny*? The same problem arises for a disembodied being who has never experienced the sensations of blue, fuzziness, or sweetness. There might be a sense in which that being can know that the chocolate is sweet, but there seems to be another, more important sense in which he cannot. Like the person who does not get a joke, he does not really 'get' taste, color, and other sensory qualities.

There may be other properties that can only be perceived by beings with the ability to feel certain emotions such as fear, envy, hate, guilt, or resentment. Whether or not these emotions require a body, they can only be experienced by a defective being, one whose imperfections are intrinsically connected to the ability to have the emotions. Does a being who can experience these emotions know something that a more perfect being cannot know? This is a difficult question to answer. Perhaps there is no proposition that one can know and the other cannot. But there does seem to be a kind of understanding that the being who cannot experience a given emotion lacks. At a minimum, such a being does not understand *what it is like* to feel fear, envy, hate, and so on. If omniscience is not simply the property of knowing all true propositions, but includes knowing what it is like to be in certain subjective states, then if a perfect being lacks the ability to have certain subjective states, a perfect being cannot be omniscient.

This leads to an even more serious problem. There might be subjective states that are limited to beings of a certain kind, as Thomas Nagel (1974) made famous. There might even be subjective states that only a single being can have. Can anyone but you know, really know, what it is like to be you? If not, nobody can be omniscient because nobody can know what it is like to be all the conscious beings in the world.

But perhaps there can be such a being. Suppose God does not simply view the world as from a height, nor does he read off the truth of all propositions in his Book of the World. Suppose God can know everything in as direct a way as it is possible for any being to know anything. I think that means God would have to have the ability to know through the eyes of each conscious being that has ever existed. In a delightful paper criticizing Descartes's Evil Genius hypothesis, O. K. Bouwsma (1949) imagined a conversation between a human being called Tom and the Cartesian Evil

Genius (EG), who sees through Tom's eyes and smells through Tom's nose, whispering skeptical doubts in his ear all the while. For the purposes of Cartesian doubt, the Evil Genius hypothesis works just as well if the EG is really Tom talking to himself, but as long as what Bouwsma describes is imaginable, then it is imaginable that another being, perhaps vastly more powerful and perfect than myself, can enter into my consciousness, experiencing with me all that I experience. Suppose also that this same being can enter into the consciousness of every conscious being in the same way. Such a being would have the property I call omnisubjectivity.

Problems of knowing things like *The test is going on here and now* can be solved if God is omnitemporal and omnipresent. Problems of knowing what it is like to be a bat, to be human, to fear, to see blue, and to be me can be solved if omnisubjectivity is possible. I am not maintaining that omniscience requires omnitemporality, omnipresence, and omnisubjectivity, but if a being with those properties is possible, many of the objections to the possibility of omniscience are avoided. I think more work should be done on the question of whether omnisubjectivity is possible.

Is infallible foreknowledge compatible with human freedom?

If there are true propositions about the contingent future, an omniscient being knows these propositions. However, according to an ancient argument, a true proposition about the future entails the necessity of the future. So if there are now true propositions about the entire future just as there are true propositions about the entire past, we have no more control over the future than over the past. This is the position of logical fatalism. Those philosophers who think the logical fatalist argument is valid almost always deny that there are true propositions about the contingent future. There are not many philosophers who conclude on the basis of truth about the future that the future is necessary.

Foreknowledge per se is not a problem either. Even human beings can know the contingent future in the ordinary sense of 'know,' and nobody worries that that is any more problematic than logical fatalism. For example, suppose I believe that classes begin at my university on a certain date because that is the date announced on the calendar, I have heard the same date mentioned by many people, and there is no evidence to the contrary. Suppose also that when the day arrives, classes do begin. Most of us would not hesitate in saying that I 'knew' beforehand that classes would begin that day because I had a true belief for the right reasons, and nobody would think that my knowledge in any way imposed necessity on the starting day of classes. That is because it was possible that classes would *not* begin that day until the very day they began. If they did not begin that day after all, we would say that I did not know the date beforehand. It is significant that I could have been wrong.

Infallible foreknowledge is different. Suppose that God (or any being) knows the future infallibly. That appears to be sufficient to deprive human beings of free will according to the following simple 'theological fatalist' argument:

1   Suppose that God infallibly believed a hundred years ago that classes will begin next fall on day x.

2   Necessarily, if God believed a hundred years ago that classes begin on day x, then classes will begin on day x.

3   It is unpreventable that God believed a hundred years ago that classes will begin on day x.

4   If it is unpreventable that p, and necessarily (if p then q), then it is unpreventable that q.

5   Therefore, it is unpreventable that classes will begin on day x.

6   If it is unpreventable that classes begin on day x, then the beginning of classes is not brought about by free human choices.

7   Therefore, the beginning of classes is not brought about by free human choices.

Notice that (2) simply follows from the assumption of the first premise that God believes in an infallible way. When you or I believe that classes begin on day x, we might believe something that is true, but there is no necessity that what we believe is true. That is, there is no necessity that the state we are in is a state of knowledge, no matter how good our justification may be. So the parallel to (2) for us is false. In contrast, an infallible believer believes in such a way that necessarily, whatever he believes is true. It is necessary that if he has a belief, that belief constitutes knowledge.

Premise (3) is a form of the principle of the necessity of the past. There are many ways to formulate this principle, but the version I have chosen is one of the strongest because the idea that the past is unpreventable is both intuitively sound and yields a transfer of unpreventability principle (4) that has been defended (Rice 2005). Transfer of necessity or non-causability principles have received a lot of attention in the literature. Some of these principles have been used in arguments that causal determinism leads to fatalism (van Inwagen 1983).

The notion of unpreventability is somewhat vague, but for the argument to work, all that is required is that there is some sense in which the past is unpreventable, and in that same sense the future is unpreventable. That sense is enough to preclude our power over it. We have no more power over the future than over the past. So we have no free will in any sense that includes power to bring about alternate courses of events.

Incompatibilists about infallible foreknowledge and human free will maintain that this argument successfully demonstrates that either God does not have infallible foreknowledge or human beings do not have free will. Compatibilists maintain that the argument is unsuccessful. Since it is formally valid, compatibilists must show that there is a problem with one of the premises.

One well-known compatibilist response goes back to Boethius (1973: bk. V. vi) and Aquinas, who maintained that since God is timeless, God does not literally know anything in the past; so premise (1) is false. God knows everything there is to know, including everything in *our* past, present, and future, and God knows everything infallibly, but God did not know *a hundred years ago*. The first premise is simply mistaken in its assumption about the relationship about God and time, although not mistaken about God's infallibility.

I have argued elsewhere (1991: ch. 2) that the problem with this response is that it simply shifts the problem from a dilemma of foreknowledge and free will to a dilemma of timeless knowledge and free will. The argument can be recast in terms of timeless knowledge and premise (3) would then become

3* It is unpreventable that God timelessly believes that classes begin on day x.

If the past is out of our control, surely the timeless realm is out of our control also. We can't prevent the past from being what it was, but neither can we prevent the timeless realm from being what it timelessly is. Of course, there may be a way out of the new dilemma generated from this premise, but it is not enough to simply replace one dilemma with another.

Another well-known way out of the argument focuses on premise (3). This is the solution of William of Ockham, and it was brought back into the contemporary literature by Marilyn Adams (1967). Ockham thought that what counts as the past is not as clear as we might think. Many propositions are verbally about the past, but are partly about the future. For example, when the logical fatalist argues that truth about the contingent future entails the necessity of the future, a key premise is that we can't do anything about the past truth of the proposition *Classes will begin on day x* because we can't do anything about the past. But the fact that it was true in the past that something would happen in the future is not a fact in the 'hard' past. It is a fact that is partly in the past and partly in the future. That is because the actual beginning of classes on a certain day in the future makes it the case that a certain proposition was true in the past. In that sense something that happens in the future affects something that is true about the past. Similarly, according to Ockham, the fact that God infallibly believed in the past that classes will begin on a certain day in the future is a fact that is partly about the future.

It can be argued, then, that if (a) human beings can affect the fact that a certain proposition p was true in the past, and (b) p's being true in the past is a necessary condition for God's infallibly believing p in the past, then (c) human beings can affect the fact the God infallibly believed p in the past. Both past truth and past infallible belief are not wholly in the past, which is to say, they are not in the hard past.

It is difficult for many philosophers to swallow this approach both because attempts to precisely distinguish the hard past from the soft past have been unsuccessful, and because the approach is intuitively peculiar (Zagzebski 1991: ch. 3). Perhaps a dialectically more successful approach is to throw the burden of proof back on the fatalist. What, exactly, is the sense of unpreventable used in premise (3) which is supposed to be transferred to the future via a principle like (4)? For the fatalist argument to work there has to be a form of the necessity (or unpreventability or non-causability) of the past which both applies to God's past beliefs and has a valid transfer principle of the form of (4). I have raised doubts that there is such a form of necessity (1991; 2002), and Rice has replied (2005).

Another objection to the fatalist argument is that premise (6) is false. Compatibilists about causal determinism and free will already have a view of free will according to which human beings can perform an act freely even though the act is unpreventable, given the causal history of the world and the causal laws; so infallible foreknowledge is no greater problem for them than causal determinism. A more interesting way of denying (6) for the purposes of this essay is to reject both determinism and the principle that free will requires alternate possibilities (Zagzebski 1991; Stump 1996; Hunt 1999).

Suppose that someone concludes from the dilemma of theological fatalism that God does not have infallible foreknowledge. It does not immediately follow that God is not omniscient. There are at least three ways one could maintain the omniscience of God but deny infallible foreknowledge. (1) Suppose that an omniscient being is one who knows the truth value of all propositions that have a truth value. If contingent propositions about the future have no truth value, God would lack foreknowledge but could still be omniscient. (2) Suppose that an omniscient being is one who knows all propositions that are knowable. If future contingent propositions are not knowable, a God without foreknowledge could still be omniscient. (3) An omniscient being knows the truth value of all propositions; so an omniscient being is not mistaken in any of his beliefs, but there is nothing in the definition of omniscience that says that an omniscient being *cannot* be mistaken. God could be omniscient even though there is some other possible world in which he has a false belief. If God is *essentially* omniscient, then God not only has complete foreknowledge, but God infallibly believes each of his beliefs about the future. On the other hand, if God does not have foreknowledge infallibly, then God is not essentially omniscient, although God could still be omniscient.

Cognitive perfection

In a previous section we considered one way in which the doctrine of omniscience should be expanded if it is to capture the idea of knowing everything. An omniscient being not only knows all true propositions, but also knows what it is like to be each kind of creature, and possibly each individual creature. A more traditional way omniscience has been expanded is the sixteenth-century doctrine of middle knowledge, according to which God knows counterfactual propositions of the form:

CF: If creature C were in circumstances S, C would freely do X.

According to the doctrine of middle knowledge, there are true counterfactuals of this form for each possible free creature and each circumstance possible for that creature. If there are true propositions of the form CF, an omniscient being would know them. Some philosophers argue that such knowledge would be much more important for guiding God's providential care than foreknowledge (e.g., Flint 2006), but there are also well-known objections to the doctrine (Hasker 1989; R. Adams 1991).

Even if omniscience includes middle knowledge, however, omniscience is not sufficient for cognitive perfection. Even essential omniscience is not sufficient. That is because the intellect does more than to believe and know. What is understanding? When we say that someone understands a work of art or literature, a philosophical theory, or another person's soul, I think we mean more than that the person knows a lot of propositions about the object understood. I suspect that understanding includes a deeper cognitive grasp than knowledge. The person who understands something sees connections between the parts of the object of understanding, like seeing the way pieces of a jigsaw puzzle fit together. Understanding may also have practical import: knowing how, not just knowing that. If understanding is a good thing to have cognitively and differs from knowledge, a cognitively perfect being would have perfect understanding as well as perfect knowledge.

Wisdom is another divine attribute that is rarely discussed by philosophers because most of us do not pretend to know what it is. Wisdom no doubt is not wholly intellectual, but it presumably does have something to do with the intellect since we would never call anyone wise who is stupid or ignorant. The wisdom of God is an attribute that forces us to acknowledge that the perfection of the intellect is not independent of moral perfection.

See also Christianity (Chapter 6), Augustine (Chapter 8), Thomas Aquinas (Chapter 12), Omnipotence (Chapter 25), Omnipresence (Chapter 26), Eternity (Chapter 27), Goodness (Chapter 28), Creation and divine action (Chapter 30), Problems with the concept of God (Chapter 38).

References

Adams, M. (1967) 'Is the existence of God a "hard" fact?,' *Philosophical Review* 76: 492–503.

Adams, R. M. (1991) 'An anti-Molinist argument,' in J. Tomberlin (ed.) *Philosophical Perspectives 5* (Philosophy of Religion), Atascadero, CA: Ridgeview Publishing.

Aquinas, T. (1997a) *Summa contra Gentiles: God* (SCG), ed. A. C. Pegis, Notre Dame, IN: University of Notre Dame Press.

—— (1997b) *Summa Theologica, Part I* (ST), in A. C. Pegis (ed.) *Basic Writings of Saint Thomas Aquinas*, vol. 1, Indianapolis, IN: Hackett.

Boethius (1973) 'The Consolation of Philosophy,' in *The Theological Tractates and the Consolation of Philosophy*, Loeb Classical Library, London: Heinemann.

Bouwsma, O. K. (1949) 'Descartes' Evil Genius,' *Philosophical Review* 58: 141–51.

Flint, T. P. (2006) *Divine Providence: The Molinist Account*, Ithaca, NY: Cornell University Press.

Hasker, W. (1989) *God, Time, and Knowledge*, Ithaca, NY: Cornell University Press.

Hunt, D. (1999) 'On Augustine's way out,' *Faith and Philosophy* 16/1: 3–26.

Nagel, T. (1974) 'What is it like to be a bat?' *Philosophical Review* 83/4: 435–50.

Prior, A. (1959) 'Thank Goodness that's over,' *Philosophy* 34: 12–17.

Rice, H. (2005) 'Zagzebski on the arrow of time,' *Faith and Philosophy* 22/3: 363–9.

Stump, E. (1996) 'Libertarian freedom and the principle of alternate possibilities,' in J. Jordan and D. Howard-Snyder (eds) *Faith, Freedom, and Rationality*, Lanham, MD: Rowman & Littlefield.

van Inwagen, P. (1983) *An Essay on Free Will*, Oxford: Clarendon Press.

Zagzebski, L. (1991) *The Dilemma of Freedom and Foreknowledge*, New York: Oxford University Press.

—— (2002) 'Omniscience and the arrow of time,' *Faith and Philosophy* 19/4: 503–19.

Further reading

Alston, W. (1986) 'Does God have beliefs?' *Religious Studies* 22/3–4: 287-306. (Alston argues that God's knowledge does not have belief as a component, whether or not God's knowledge is propositional.)

Molina, L. de (1988) [1588] *On Divine Foreknowledge: Part IV of the Concordia*, trans. and ed. A. Freddoso, Ithaca, NY: Cornell University Press. (This translation of the key text by Molina on middle knowledge stimulated work on Molinism in contemporary philosophy.)

Wierenga, E. (1989) *The Nature of God: An Inquiry into Divine Attributes*, Ithaca, NY: Cornell University Press. (An excellent analysis of the traditional divine attributes, with particular focus on omnipotence, omniscience, and perfect goodness.)

Zagzebski, L. (2002) 'Recent work on divine foreknowledge and free will,' in R. Kane (ed.) *Oxford Handbook on Free Will*, Oxford: Oxford University Press. (This essay surveys the contemporary work on the dilemma of freedom and foreknowledge, concentrating on work published in the last two decades of the twentieth century.)

25

OMNIPOTENCE

Joshua Hoffman and Gary Rosenkrantz

Omnipotence, rational theology, and God

According to traditional western theism, classically expressed by Anselm and others, God is the greatest being possible. Included among the attributes of such a being is omnipotence, or maximal power. In other words, God is conceived of as being as powerful as any being could be.

Our approach to understanding omnipotence presupposes the canons of rational theology, where by rational theology we mean a theology that conforms to the principles of rationality. The latter include the laws of logic, both deductive and non-deductive, as well as principles covering the use of evidence from sense perception, introspection, and memory. Hence, we would not accept, for example, an account of omnipotence that entails a contradiction.

This rational approach to God's omnipotence is faced with several challenges, including concerns about the coherence of omnipotence, related questions about what limits, if any, there are to the power of an omnipotent agent, and the issue of the compatibility of omnipotence with God's other attributes. First, the famous 'paradox' of the stone challenges the coherence of omnipotence: could an omnipotent being make a stone so massive that such a being could not move it? It has seemed to some that because this question cannot be answered coherently, the notion of omnipotence is self-contradictory. Second, some have held that an omnipotent agent has the power to bring about or change what is necessarily true. Is such an understanding of omnipotence coherent? Third, it might be thought that since many past occurrences are contingent, an omnipotent being can now bring about or change the past. Such a view is highly controversial, in that many philosophers regard the past as fixed and backwards causation as impossible. A coherent account of omnipotence should address this controversy. Fourth, there is the issue of whether the notion of an omnipotent being other than God is coherent. For example, could there be a single, non-divine omnipotent agent? Could there be two or more omnipotent beings at the same time? Finally, are two of the defining characteristics of God, namely, omnipotence and moral perfection, compatible? More specifically, if God is powerless to do evil, then how can God be omnipotent?

The meaning of 'omnipotence'

It might be thought that omnipotence should be understood in terms of the power to perform some set of tasks. Examples of tasks are to create a stone too massive for oneself to lift, to do evil, or to make oneself non-omnipotent. However, more recently, several philosophers have sought to analyze omnipotence in terms of the power to bring about an appropriately defined set of states of affairs (where a state of affairs must either obtain or fail to obtain) (Rosenkrantz and Hoffman 1980b; Flint and Freddoso 1983; Wierenga 1989: 12–35).

There are at least four senses of 'omnipotence' that deserve consideration. First, there is the notion of having the power to bring it about that any state of affairs obtains. One might say that in this sense, to be omnipotent is to be literally all-powerful. Henceforth, for simplicity's sake, we abbreviate 'bring it about that a state of affairs obtains' as 'bring about a state of affairs.' By 'power' we mean ability plus opportunity, or the 'all-in' sense of power, as opposed to the mere ability sense of power. Clearly, a being who is omnipotent cannot be prevented by circumstances from exercising whatever abilities that being possesses: nothing could prevent an omnipotent being from exercising its powers.

According to the first notion of omnipotence, an omnipotent agent has the power to bring about necessary, impossible, and contingent states of affairs. Descartes appears to have employed such a notion (Frankfurt 1977; Curley 1984; Descartes 1984: Meditation I). Necessarily, if an agent has the power to bring about a state of affairs, then possibly, that agent brings about that state of affairs. Hence, according to this notion, an omnipotent agent could bring about impossible states of affairs such as *that a horse is not an animal*, and *that there is a round square*. This would violate the laws of deductive logic, in particular, the law of non-contradiction. Moreover, if an agent could bring about a necessary state of affairs, such as *that 1+1=2*, then it would be possible, if that agent had not acted, for the necessary state of affairs in question not to have obtained, which is absurd. For both these reasons, the first sense of omnipotence is incoherent. Thus, we conclude that it is not possible for any agent to have the power to bring about all states of affairs (Maimonides 1904; Aquinas 1948).

According to a second notion, omnipotence is the power to bring about any state of affairs which possibly obtains at some time. However, since necessary states of affairs are possible states of affairs, but, as has been argued, are not possibly brought about, this second notion is also incoherent.

According to a third notion, omnipotence is the power to bring about any contingent state of affairs. Our earlier criticisms do not apply to this notion. However, the following contingent state of affairs, namely, *that a ball rolls at t*, where *t* is a past time, illustrates the sort of difficulty confronting this notion of omnipotence. Intuitively, if a ball has *already* rolled at *t*, then it is no longer within the power of an agent to bring it about that a ball rolls at *t*. Such an act would involve backward causation, something of highly dubious coherence. Moreover, intuitively, if a ball has *not* rolled at *t*, then it is not within the power of an agent to bring it about that a ball rolls at t. This would involve changing the past, something that appears to be impossible.

According to the fourth, and final, notion, omnipotence is *maximal power*: overall power that no being could exceed. As we have seen, such power is not the power to bring about either impossible or necessary states of affairs, nor the power to bring about all contingent states of affairs. Furthermore, a being with maximal power need not have the power to bring about whatever any other agent has the power to bring about. If a certain being, a, can bring about some state of affairs, and another being, b, cannot, it may nevertheless be true that b is overall more powerful than a, for it could be that b has more states of affairs within its power than does a. Hence, it is possible that for any agent other than b, b is more powerful than that other agent is, even though such an agent has it within its power to bring about certain states of affairs that b cannot. Given our earlier arguments, this fourth, and weakest, notion of omnipotence appears to have the best chance of being coherent.

Given this conception of omnipotence, could there be two or more omnipotent agents who exist at the same time? (Here we assume that the two agents are in time. Since many theologians think that God would be outside of time, we note that if one or both posited omnipotent agents are outside of time, then the argument below can be rephrased in terms of the contrary states of affairs that they are attempting to bring about being at the same time.) If there could be, then it appears that possibly, omnipotent agent 1 attempts to make a blade of grass move at time t (when agent 1 exists) and omnipotent agent 2 endeavors to bring it about that the blade of grass does not move at time t (when agent 2 exists). Intuitively, in such a case, neither agent would affect the blade of grass as to its motion or rest. Hence, omnipotent agent 1 would be powerless to move the blade of grass, and omnipotent agent 2 would be powerless to keep the blade of grass from moving. Their two endeavors would cancel each other out, leaving the motion or rest of the blade of grass to be determined by other factors. But it is absurd to suppose that an omnipotent agent could lack the power to move or the power to prevent the motion of a blade of grass. Hence, neither agent 1 nor agent 2 is after all omnipotent.

A first reply that might be made is that while neither agent 1 nor agent 2 brings about what he attempts to bring about, each of them *can* do so, since each possesses the *ability* to do so. Granted, neither has the *opportunity* to do so. In response, we remind the reader that the sense of 'can' in terms of which omnipotence is to be understood is the ability *plus* opportunity sense. It is in that sense that neither agent 1 nor agent 2 *can* do what he endeavors to do. It might also be replied that there could be two omnipotent agents, just as long as *necessarily*, each never tries to do anything that thwarts what the other seeks to do. However, since it is highly dubious that it is possible for there to be two such omnipotent agents, who *by nature*, cooperate in this sense, it appears that there could not be two such omnipotent agents.

Given this fourth sense of omnipotence, could there be a contingently omnipotent agent? One's first reaction is that this is possible, but there is the following argument to consider. Given that God exists, God necessarily exists, God either necessarily exists at all times or necessarily exists outside of time, and God is necessarily omnipotent.

However, as we have seen, there cannot be two omnipotent agents at the same time, or one in time and one outside of time, or two outside of time. If God exists, a contingently omnipotent agent would have to be other than God. Hence, if God exists, it is not possible for there to be a contingently omnipotent agent. On the other hand, if neither God nor any other necessarily existing, necessarily omnipotent agent exists, then it does seem possible for there to be a contingently omnipotent agent.

The alleged paradox of the stone

A well-known challenge to the coherence of omnipotence is the so-called paradox of the stone. The challenge starts with a question: can an omnipotent agent, a, make a stone, s, too heavy for a to lift? If one answers that a can do this, then there is something that a cannot do, namely, bring it about that a lifts s. If one answers that a cannot make a stone, s, that is too heavy for a to lift, then there is again something a cannot do, namely, bring it about that s is a stone too heavy for a to lift. Thus, it appears that omnipotence is paradoxical, for it seems to lead to the conclusion that there is something an omnipotent agent cannot do that it should have the power to do. The defense of omnipotence against this charge of incoherence is in two stages.

First, assume that a is necessarily omnipotent. On that assumption, since it is *impossible* for a to be non-omnipotent, a cannot bring it about that a is non-omnipotent. Because, necessarily, an omnipotent agent can move any stone, the state of affairs, *that there is a stone too heavy for a to lift*, is impossible. Because an omnipotent agent is not required to have the power to bring about an impossible state of affairs (and, indeed, cannot have such a power), a's being omnipotent is compatible with a's lacking the power to bring it about that there is a stone too heavy for a to lift.

Second, suppose that a is contingently omnipotent. On that supposition, it is possible for a to bring it about that there is a stone, s, too heavy for a to lift. a could bring this about by bringing it about both that a ceases to be omnipotent, and that there is such a stone, s, in that temporal order. Once a ceases to be omnipotent, then there can be a stone too heavy for a to lift. Hence, on the supposition that a is contingently omnipotent, it is possible for a to bring it about that there is a stone too heavy for a to lift, just as long as the time at which this stone is too heavy for a to lift is other than a time at which a is omnipotent. The appearance of paradox disappears when one realizes that the case of a necessarily omnipotent agent and the case of a contingently omnipotent agent need to be considered separately (Rosenkrantz and Hoffman 1980a).

Contingent states of affairs an omnipotent agent cannot bring about

We have already argued that no omnipotent agent can have the power to bring it about that an impossible or necessary state of affairs obtains. Moreover, we have noted that there are even some contingent states of affairs that an omnipotent agent cannot have the power to bring about. The following is a list of states of affairs of the latter sort:

(a) A cloud moved.
(b) A cloud moves at time t (where t is a past time).
(c) Aristotle writes for the first time.
(d) The earth spins on its axis an odd number of times less than six.
(e) A cloud moves and there is never an omnipotent agent.
(f) Smith freely decides to run.

(a) and (b) are past states of affairs. As we argued earlier, necessarily, no agent can bring about a past state of affairs. Hence, for example, if it is true that a cloud moved, then no agent has it within its power now either to bring it about that a cloud moved or bring about that it is not the case that a cloud moved. Some have called this the 'necessity of the past.'

(c) also involves the necessity of the past, but in a less direct way. There *are* times when an omnipotent agent can bring about (c), but such times precede the time when Aristotle writes for the first time. Once Aristotle writes, then (c) can no longer be brought about by an omnipotent agent, owing to the necessity of the past.

Similarly, prior to the earth's fifth rotation on its axis, (d) can be brought about. After that fifth rotation, an omnipotent agent cannot bring about (d). Clearly, (e) cannot be brought about by an omnipotent agent. Yet, it can be argued plausibly that a non-omnipotent agent can bring about (e) by causing a cloud to move, when there is never an omnipotent agent. The first premise of such an argument is a plausible form of the principle of the *diffusiveness of power*. According to this principle, for any agent, A, and for any states of affairs, p & q, if A brings about p, q obtains, and q is not within the power of any agent other than A, then A brings about (p & q). The second premise is that the following conjunctive state of affairs is possible: a non-omnipotent agent brings it about that a cloud moves & no omnipotent agent ever exists & it is not within the power of any agent to bring it about that an omnipotent agent never exists. It appears that while this conjunction is not compatible with the existence of God, it is compatible with the existence of a contingently omnipotent agent (Hoffman and Rosenkrantz 1988).

Finally, if libertarianism with respect to free actions and decisions is true, then an omnipotent agent (who is other than Smith) lacks the power to bring about (f). However, it appears that a non-omnipotent agent, i.e., Smith, *does* have the power to bring about (f). As we argued earlier, it is not required that an omnipotent agent have the power to bring about every state of affairs that any other agent has the power to bring about. (e) and (f) illustrate this general fact.

As examples (a) through (e) show, an adequate analysis of omnipotence should not require that an omnipotent agent have the power to bring about states of affairs like (a) through (e). Nor should it require such an agent to have the power to bring about states of affairs like (f), on the assumption that libertarianism is true. It is desirable for an analysis of omnipotence to be neutral about such an assumption, especially since discussions about omnipotence often occur in the context of theism, and theists often assume that God and some of God's creations have libertarian free will.

Given the disparate nature of (a) through (f), it is by no means obvious how one can appropriately restrict the powers of an omnipotent agent when formulating an analysis of omnipotence. We believe that we provide such a formulation in what follows.

The analysis of omnipotence

Our analysis of omnipotence is in terms of the concept of a state of affairs being *unrestricted repeatable*. According to this approach, by identifying certain features of (a)–(f), we can find a feature that none of them possesses, related to unrestricted repeatability, and in terms of which an analysis of omnipotence can be stated (Hoffman and Rosenkrantz 2002: ch. 8)

First, unless it is *possible for some* agent to bring about a state of affairs, an omnipotent agent should not be required to be able to bring about that state of affairs. However, (a) is not possibly brought about by any agent. Since (a) is not possibly brought about by someone, an omnipotent agent is not required to be able to bring about (a). For the same reason, such an agent is also not required to be able to bring about impossible or necessary states of affairs.

Next, while (b) and (c) are possibly brought about by some agent, they are not *repeatable*: that is, it is not possible for either one of them to obtain, subsequently fail to obtain, and then obtain again.

Third, while (d) *is* repeatable, it is *not unrestrictedly* repeatable; that is, it cannot obtain, then fail to obtain, then obtain again, and so on, forever after.

Fourth, although (e) *is* unrestrictedly repeatable, (e) is a *logically* complex state of affairs, namely, a *conjunctive* state of affairs whose second conjunct is *unrepeatable*. These examples suggest a theory about how power and repeatability are related to one another – namely, that no possible agent be required, regardless of circumstances, to have the power to bring about *either* a state of affairs that is not unrestrictedly repeatable, *or* a conjunctive state of affairs one of whose conjuncts is not unrestrictedly repeatable.

Lastly, even though (f) is unrestrictedly repeatable, (f) is another type of complex state of affairs. Specifically, it is *identifiable with or analyzable as* a conjunctive state of affairs. The latter of state of affairs has three conjuncts, the second of which is not possibly brought about by anyone. This conjunctive state of affairs may be expressed as the conjunction of the following three states of affairs: (1) Smith decides to run; & (2) there is no *antecedent* sufficient causal condition of Smith's deciding to run; & (3) there is no concurrent sufficient causal condition of Smith's deciding to run. Note that necessarily, if (2) is true, then no one other than Smith brings about (1), since someone other than Smith's bringing about (1) entails that there *is* a sufficient causal condition for (1). Because it is impossible for an agent to have power over what is *past*, (2) is not possibly brought about by anyone. Thus, an omnipotent agent ought not to be required to have the power to bring about a state of affairs that is identifiable with or analyzable as a conjunctive state of affairs one of whose conjuncts is not possibly brought about by anyone.

On the basis of these ideas, omnipotence is analyzable in terms of the following three definitions.

(*D1*) The period of time t is a sufficient interval for s $=_{df}$ s is a state of affairs such that: it is possible that s obtains at a time-period which has the duration of t. For example, any period of time with a duration of 1 minute is a sufficient interval for the state of affairs *that a top spins for 1 minute*.

(*D2*) A state of affairs, s, is unrestrictedly repeatable $=_{df}$ s is possibly such that: $(n)(\exists t_1)\,(\exists t_2)\,(\exists t_3) \ldots (\exists t_n)[(t_1 < t_2 < t_3 < \ldots < t_n$ are periods of time which are sufficient intervals for s & s obtains at t_1 & s doesn't obtain at t_2 & s obtains at t_3 & $\ldots$ & s obtains at t_n) if and only if n is odd]. In *D2*, 'n' ranges over all natural numbers, and $t_{1 \ldots n}$ are non-overlapping. Moreover, *D2* presupposed that either possibly, time is without beginning, or possibly, time is endless (or both). For instance, the state of affairs *that a top spins for 1 minute* is unrestrictedly repeatable.

(*D3*) x is omnipotent at $t =_{df}$ (s) (if it is possible for some agent to bring about s then at t x has it within his power to bring about s). In *D3*, x ranges over agents, and s over states of affairs satisfying the following condition: (C) (i) s is unrestrictedly repeatable, and of the form 'in n minutes, p', & (p is a complex state of affairs $\rightarrow$ (each of the parts of p is unrestrictedly repeatable & possibly brought about by someone)), or (ii) s is of the form 'q forever after,' where q is a state of affairs which satisfies (i). In (C) (ii), we speak of a state of affairs of the form 'q forever after,' where q is a state of affairs which satisfies (i). The sort of state of affairs we have in mind is one such as *in one minute, a top spins forever after*. There are two sorts of situations in which this state of affairs could obtain. The first is that the top will begin to spin *in one minute*, and then continue to spin forever after. The second is that the top will begin to spin *earlier than that*, for example, one minute earlier, will be spinning in one minute, and will continue to spin forever after. Note that in (C), 'n' ranges over real numbers, and p is not equivalent to a state of affairs of the form 'in n minutes, r,' where n is not equal to zero.

In applying *D3* to states of affairs like (e) and (f) it should be observed that a *conjunct* of a conjunctive state of affairs is a *part* of such a complex state of affairs. A complex state of affairs is one that is either constructible out of other states of affairs via the logical apparatus of first-order logic enriched with whatever modalities one chooses to employ, or else analyzable (in the sense of a philosophical analysis) into a state of affairs which is so constructible. Thus, a (logical) *part* of a complex state of affairs, s, is one of those states of affairs out of which s, or an analysis of s, is constructed.

We note that *D3* satisfies our *desideratum* that an omnipotent agent not be required to have the power to bring about either impossible or necessary states of affairs, or states of affairs such as (a)–(f). Furthermore, *D3* does not overly limit the power of an omnipotent agent, since an agent's bringing about a state of affairs can always be 'cashed out' in terms of that agent's bringing about an unrestrictedly repeatable state of affairs that it is possible for some agent to bring about. In other words, necessarily, for any state of affairs, s, if an agent, a, brings about s, then either s is an unrestrictedly repeatable state of affairs which it is possible for some agent to bring about, or else a brings about s by bringing about q, where q is an unrestrictedly repeatable state of affairs which it is possible for some agent to bring about. For example, an omnipotent agent can bring about the state of affairs, *that in one hour, Aristotle observes a squid for the first time*, by bringing about the state of affairs, *that in one hour, Aristotle observes a squid*, when this observation of a squid is Aristotle's first. And although the former state of affairs is a non-repeatable one that D3 does *not* require an omnipotent agent to have the power to bring about, the latter state of affairs *is* an unrestrictedly repeatable state of affairs that D3 *does* require an omnipotent agent to have the power to bring about.

Divine omnipotence and divine moral perfection

It has been argued that the traditional God has incompatible attributes, namely, necessary existence, omnipotence, omniscience, and moral perfection (Pike 1969; Hoffman 1979). The argument has been that it is impossible for God to have the power to bring about evil, while non-omnipotent (and morally imperfect) beings may have this power. While the precise form of such an argument varies depending on what exactly the relation between God and evil is thought to be, generally speaking it is argued that divine moral perfection and omnipotence are incompatible because God's being omnipotent entails that God has the power to bring about evil, but God's being morally perfect entails that God is powerless to bring about evil.

One possible response to an argument of this kind assumes that, necessarily, if God exists, then the actual world is a best possible world (Hoffman 1979). Assume that this response is neutral with respect to whether divine moral perfection is to be understood as perfect goodness, perfect virtue, or some combination of goodness and virtue. The notion of a best possible world should be understood in light of this neutrality, namely, as a world either of unsurpassable goodness, as a world governed by a being of unsurpassable virtue, or as a world with an optimal balance of goodness and virtuous governance (Hoffman and Rosenkrantz 2002: ch. 7).

On the assumption that the actual world is a best possible world, and that God necessarily creates a best possible world, the existence of God entails that there could not be an evil unless it were necessary for some greater good, in which case any state of affairs, s, containing any evil incompatible with a best possible world is *impossible*. Hence, if God exists, any moral evil, that is, any evil brought about by an agent, and any natural evil, or any evil which has an impersonal, natural cause, must be necessary for some greater good. But it has been shown that it is not possible for *any* agent, including God, to bring about an impossible state of affairs.

With respect to any state of affairs, s, containing an evil incompatible with a best possible world, God would lack the power to bring about s because of his moral perfection, and any created agent would lack the power to bring about s either because

(i) God would not create an agent who had the power to bring about *s*, or (ii) God would not permit any created agent to bring about *s*. Thus, to the extent indicated, if God's attributes impose moral restrictions on the nature of the universe and on what he can bring about, then they impose parallel restrictions on what any other agents can bring about. The foregoing line of reasoning implies that God's moral perfection and omnipotence are not incompatible.

This argument about God and the possibility of evil has been disputed by theists such as Plantinga, who do not hold that God's existence implies the existence of a maximally good world, but do hold that God seeks to create as good a world as he can (Plantinga 1974). Plantinga allows for there to be evil that is *unnecessary* for any greater good that outweighs it. Such an evil involves libertarian free decisions of non-divine agents, which God does not prevent, but which these other agents can prevent. Plantinga contends that God is not wrong to permit an evil of this kind, since God cannot bring about a vital good, the existence of free human agents, without there being an evil of this kind. Alternatively, it might be argued that God does no wrong in this sort of case, because he does not know how to do better (knowledge of the future free actions of created agents being impossible). However, because an omnipotent God is not required to have power over the libertarian free decisions of non-divine agents, it follows that on these views, his omnipotence and moral perfection are compatible, roughly to the extent indicated earlier in our discussion of the view that God's existence implies a maximally good world.

See also Christianity (Chapter 6), Omniscience (Chapter 24), Omnipresence (Chapter 26), Eternity (Chapter 27), Goodness (Chapter 28), The moral argument (Chapter 34), Problems with the concept of God (Chapter 38), Process theology (Chapter 46).

References

Aquinas, T. (1948) *Summa Theologiae*, New York: Benziger Brothers.

Curley, E. M. (1984) 'Descartes on the creation of the eternal truths,' *Philosophical Review* 93: 569–97.

Descartes, R. (1984) *Meditations on First Philosophy*, in *The Philosophical Writings of Descartes*, vol. 2, trans. J. Cottingham, R. Stoothoff, and D. Murdoch, Cambridge: Cambridge University Press.

Flint, T. and A. Freddoso (1983) 'Maximal power,' in A. Freddoso (ed.) *The Existence and Nature of God*, Notre Dame, IN: University of Notre Dame Press.

Frankfurt, H. (1977) 'Descartes on the creation of the eternal truths,' *Philosophical Review* 86: 36–57.

Hoffman, J. (1979) 'Can God do evil?' *Southern Journal of Philosophy* 17: 213–20.

Hoffman, J. and G. S. Rosenkrantz (1988) 'Omnipotence redux,' *Philosophy and Phenomenological Research* 49: 283–301.

—— (2002) *The Divine Attributes*, Oxford: Blackwell.

Maimonides (1904) *Guide for the Perplexed*, trans. M. Friedlander, London: George Routledge & Sons.

Pike, N. (1969) 'Omnipotence and God's ability to sin,' *American Philosophical Quarterly* 6: 208–16.

Plantinga, A. (1974) *God, Freedom, and Evil*, New York: Harper & Row.

Rosenkrantz, G. S. and J. Hoffman (1980a) 'The omnipotence paradox, modality, and time,' *Southern Journal of Philosophy* 18: 473–9.

—— (1980b) 'What an omnipotent agent can do,' *International Journal for Philosophy of Religion* 11: 1–19.

Wierenga, E. (1989) *The Nature of God: An Inquiry into Divine Attributes*, Ithaca, NY: Cornell University Press.

Further reading

Craig, E. (ed.) (1998) *Routledge Encyclopedia of Philosophy*, London: Routledge. (Contains many articles on topics discussed in this chapter as well as extensive bibliographies. Also available in an online version at http://www.rep.routledge.com/.)

Quinn, P. L. and C. Taliaferro (eds) (1997) *A Companion to Philosophy of Religion*, London: Blackwell. (Offers chapters on relevant topics with bibliographies.)

Zalta, E. N. (ed.) (2006) *Stanford Encyclopedia of Philosophy*, http://plato.stanford.edu/. (An online encyclopedia, although not yet completed, that offers resources similar to those in the *Routledge Encyclopedia of Philosophy*.)

26
OMNIPRESENCE
Edward Wierenga

Introduction

In a familiar passage, often cited when the topic is omnipresence, the psalmist asks God,

> Where can I go from your spirit?
> Or where can I flee from your presence?
> If I ascend to heaven, you are there;
> If I make my bed in Sheol, you are there.
>   (Psalm 139: 7–8, NRSV)

The idea seems to be that, for any place one chooses, God is there. There are two suppositions lurking here. The first is that God really is *present* at or *located* at various places. The second is that he is present in this way *everywhere*. The latter is the thesis that God is *omnipresent*. There is a hint of a third idea in this passage, however, which makes the claim that God is omnipresent problematic. The psalmist asks about the location of God's spirit; but God *is* a spirit. How can we understand a spirit, something immaterial, being present in space? Perhaps we have an intuitive idea of what it is for a physical object to be present or to be located at a place or in a region of space. But what sense can be made of something non-physical, something that neither is nor has a body, being present at a place?

Anselm

Anselm (1033–1109) noticed that there was something puzzling here. In chapter 20 of his *Monologion* he argued that '[the supreme essence] exists everywhere and always.' In the next chapter, however, he argued that 'it is quite impossible for it to exist everywhere and always.' Finally, he tried to reconcile this 'contradictory language – but ineluctable logic' by distinguishing two senses of 'existing as a whole in a place.' In one sense a thing 'X has a place if that place contains the extent of X by circumscribing it and circumscribes it by containing it.' In this sense, ordinary physical objects are contained in regions of place. These things obey a law that applies to created substances: if they are wholly present at a place, then they are contained in that place and cannot simultaneously be wholly contained in some other place. But God is not thus contained in space, for 'Supreme Truth does not admit at all of the big and small, the long and the short, which belong to spatial and temporal distention.' Instead, God is in every place in a sense according to which he is wholly present at every place. Anselm holds that 'it is necessary that [God] be present as a whole simultaneously to all places and times.'

But exactly does it mean to say that God is present as a whole in every place? I have proposed (Wierenga 1988) interpreting Anselm's second sense of 'presence' by appealing to what Anselm says about the location of created souls in chapter 13 of his *Proslogion*, namely, that they can be wholly present in more than one place in virtue of *sensing* wholly in more than one place (say, in places occupied by different parts of the soul's body). Although God does not have sense organs by which he could sense, Anselm thinks that he is 'supremely perceptive' in that he knows what is happening, directly and without inference or intermediaries. On this account, God's omnipresence would consist in his having this kind of direct knowledge of what is happening everywhere.

Leftow (1989), however, has called attention to other passages in Anselm in which he appeals to God's sustaining things in existence (and, therefore, to the extent of God's *power*) in his discussion of omnipresence. Emphasizing God's power in attempting to give an account of omnipresence makes Anselm's treatment more like that of Aquinas, the topic of the next section.

Thomas Aquinas: knowledge, power, and essence

Thomas Aquinas (1225–74) held that God's presence is to be understood in terms of God's power, knowledge, and essence. He writes, 'God is in all things by his power, inasmuch as all things are subject to his power; he is by his presence in all things, inasmuch as all things are bare and open to his eyes; he is in all things by his essence, inasmuch as he is present to all as the cause of their being' (*ST* I. 8. 3). Aquinas attempts to motivate this claim with some illustrations:

> But how [God] is in other things created by him may be considered from human affairs. A king, for example, is said to be in the whole kingdom by his power, although he is not everywhere present. Again, a thing is said to be by its presence in other things which are subject to its inspection; as things in a house are said to be present to anyone, who nevertheless may not be in substance in every part of the house. Lastly, a thing is said to be substantially or essentially in that place in which its substance is. (*ST* I. 8. 3)

Aquinas distinguished between being in place by 'contact of dimensive quantity, as bodies are, [and] contact of power' (*ST* I. 8. 2, ad 1). A king is thus supposedly present in his kingdom not by dimensive quantity but by contact of power. In the *Summa contra Gentiles*, Aquinas wrote that 'an incorporeal thing is related to its presence in something by its power, in the same way that a corporeal thing is related to its presence in something by dimensive quantity,' and he added that 'if there were any body possessed of infinite dimensive quantity, it would have to be everywhere. So if there were an incorporeal being possessed of infinite power, it must be everywhere' (SCG III. 68. 3). So the first aspect of God's presence in things is by having power over them. The second aspect noted in the passage above is that God is present in everything, which Aquinas glosses as everything being 'bare and open to his eyes' or being known to him. The third feature, that God is present to things by his essence, is understood as his being the cause of their being.

Aquinas's understanding of omnipresence can thus be summarized as the thesis that God is present at a place just in case there is a physical object that is at that place and God has power over that object, knows what is going on in that object, and God is the cause of that object's existence. (In this opinion he followed a formula put forth by Peter Lombard (late eleventh century to 1160) in his *Sentences* I. xxxvii. 1.)

This account of omnipresence has the consequence that, strictly speaking, God is present everywhere that some physical thing is located. Perhaps, however, this is exactly what the medievals had intended. Anselm had said, for example, that '"Everywhere," then, in the sense of "in everything that exists" is, as regards the truth, the more appropriate thing to say of the supreme nature' (*Monologion* 23).

A recent account

Richard Swinburne (Swinburne 1993) begins his discussion of omnipresence by asking what it is for a person to have a body. He thus assumes that the way in which a person is related to her body will provide us with an analogy for the way God is related to the world. Although Swinburne insists that God is an immaterial spirit, he supposes this claim to be compatible with a certain 'limited embodiment.' Swinburne develops his account by appeal to the notions of a 'basic action' (an action one performs, perhaps raising one's arm, without having to perform another action in order to do it) and of 'direct knowledge' (knowledge that is neither inferential nor dependent on causal interaction). He then says that 'the claim that God controls all things directly and knows about all things without the information coming to him through some causal chain, e.g., without light rays from a distance needing to stimulate his eyes, has often been expressed as the doctrine of God's omnipresence' (Swinburne 1993: 106). Swinburne's account is thus, as he notes, very much in the spirit of that of Aquinas.

The world as God's body

Swinburne is willing to concede that, at least in a 'limited embodiment' way, the world is God's body. (Charles Hartshorne (1941) had explicitly accepted as a consequence of omnipresence that the world is God's body.) But this conclusion is controversial. Charles Taliaferro, for example, while endorsing this overall account of omnipresence as knowledge, power, and essence, notes that the basic actions human beings perform 'can involve highly complex physical factors … [including] many neural events and muscle movements, whereas with God there is no such physical complexity' (Taliaferro 1994: 277). Taliaferro then adds that this immediacy in the case of God's action is precisely a reason to say that 'the world does not function as God's body the way material bodies function as our own.'

I add a second objection. I hold that as Hartshorne and Swinburne develop accounts of God's power and knowledge, God would have the same knowledge of and control over what happens in empty regions of space as he does with respect to those regions occupied by material objects (Wierenga 1997). (For a more sympathetic treatment of the suggestion that the world is God's body, but without an explicit application to divine omnipresence, see the careful discussion by Wainwright (1987).) In other words, Hartshorne's and Swinburne's accounts of omnipresence, unlike that of Aquinas, do not interpret God's presence as presence *in things*. But it would be implausible to count a thing as part of God's body on the basis of his knowledge of and power over the region of space that thing occupies, when God's knowledge and power would extend in the same way to that region if it were unoccupied. So it seems as though one could accept the traditional account of divine omnipresence without having to conclude that the world is God's body.

A related suggestion sometimes made is that, rather than the universe being God's body, the totality of material things which make up the universe just *is* God. This is the doctrine of *pantheism*, of which Spinoza (1632–77) is usually thought to be a leading proponent (1985: pt. I, *Ethics*). Pantheism seems to provide a poor account of divine omnipresence, however, for at least two reasons. First, it is not at all plausible to think that the material universe or the totality of all material objects is itself the kind of thing which could be a person or an agent of any kind. So claiming that it is God seems to be fundamentally mistaken. Even if this objection could be avoided, however, the totality of material things obviously has parts at different places. So if it were God, God would have parts at different places – a thesis that is incompatible with the traditional if controversial claim that God is simple – and God would not be *wholly* present at any of these places. But the claim that God is omnipresent, as we saw above, is usually taken to require that he be wholly present at every place.

It might be asked, however, whether the claim that God is omnipresent leads to pantheism. If God really is everywhere, how could there be anything distinct from him? Anselm's answer is that God is present in space in a way that does not rule out the presence of physical things in the same place. Robert Oakes has proposed an account of omnipresence intended to show that God's omnipresence is actually incompatible with pantheism (Oakes 2006). According to Oakes, space is 'constituted' by God's omnipresence, and things located in space are therefore distinct from God. Oakes's central idea seems in need of additional explication, however, and his account has the controversial consequence that space exists necessarily (if God does), even if it is contingent that the universe exists.

Future directions

There seem to be two emerging trends in discussions of divine omnipresence. One is to take the insights of recent work in analytic metaphysics, especially work on the nature of physical objects and their existence through time, and to apply these ideas to God's existence. An especially rich account in this vein is given by Hud Hudson (forthcoming), who specifies four different ways in which a physical object can be related to a region of space, and then argues that one of them can apply to God, as well.

A second approach is more theological. It tries to find what is theologically important about omnipresence. One treatment along these lines is Brom (1993). More recently, Eleonore Stump, in her Wilde Lectures (forthcoming), develops accounts of closeness and personal presence which she applies to divine omnipresence. In particular, she requires an openness to a kind of second-person experience, which she explains as an availability for shared experience, for full presence. Stump develops these ideas as part of her exploration of the kind of union to be desired in love. The root idea, then, on Stump's view, is that God is omnipresent in virtue of his offer to love his creatures. This is no doubt a theologically important idea, but it is not clear how it applies to God's presence in places in which there are no creatures and it seems not to allow the possibility that God be present at a place without an offer to love.

See also Thomas Aquinas (Chapter 12), Non-theistic conceptions of God (Chapter 22), Omniscience (Chapter 24), Eternity (Chapter 27), Hiddenness (Chapter 29), Creation and divine action (Chapter 30).

References

Anselm (1988) *Monologion* and *Proslogion*, in B. Davies and G. R. Evans (eds) *Anselm of Canterbury: The Major Works*, Oxford: Oxford University Press.

Aquinas, T. (1945) (ST) *Summa Theologica*, 2 vols., in A. Pegis (ed.) *Basic Writings of Saint Thomas Aquinas*, New York: Random House.

—— (1975) (SCG) *Summa contra Gentiles*, trans. J. F. Anderson, Notre Dame, IN: University of Notre Dame Press.

Brom, R. (1993) *Divine Presence in the World*, Kampen, The Netherlands: Kok Pharos Publishing House.

Hartshorne, C. (1941) *Man's Vision of God and the Logic of Theism*, New York: Harper & Brothers.

Hudson, H. (forthcoming) 'Omnipresence,' in M. Rea and T. Flint (eds) *Oxford Handbook of Philosophical Theology*, Oxford: Oxford University Press.

Leftow, B. (1989) 'Anselm on omnipresence,' *New Scholasticism* 63: 326–57.

Lombard, P. (1971–81) *Sententiae in IV libris distinctae* (*Four Books of Sentences*), 2 vols., ed. I. C. Brady, OFM., Grottaferrate: Editiones Collegii S. Bonaventurae Ad Claras Aquas.

Oakes, R. (2006) 'Divine omnipresence and maximal immanence,' *American Philosophical Quarterly* 43: 171–9.

Spinoza, B. (1985) *Ethics*, in *The Collected Works of Spinoza*, vol. 1, ed. and trans. E. Curley, Princeton, NJ: Princeton University Press.

Stump, E. (forthcoming) 'Closeness, presence, and internal integration,' Wilde Lecture 3, May 9, 2006, Oxford University.

Swinburne, R. (1993) [1977] *The Coherence of Theism*, rev. edn, Oxford: Oxford University Press.

Taliaferro, C. (1994) *Consciousness and the Mind of God*, Cambridge: Cambridge University Press.

Wainwright, W. (1987) 'God's world, God's body,' in T. V. Morris (ed.) *The Concept of God*, Oxford: Oxford University Press.

Wierenga, E. (1988) 'Anselm on Omnipresence,' *New Scholasticism* 62: 30–41.

—— (1997) 'Omnipresence,' in P. L. Quinn and C. Taliaferro (eds) *A Companion to the Philosophy of Religion*, Oxford: Blackwell.

Further reading

Brom, R. (1993) *Divine Presence in the World*, Kampen, The Netherlands: Kok Pharos Publishing House. (Philosophically and scientifically informed theological treatment of omnipresence.)

Hudson, H. (forthcoming) 'Omnipresence,' in M. Rea and T. Flint (eds) *Oxford Handbook of Philosophical Theology*, Oxford: Oxford University Press. (Philosophically sophisticated application of work in metaphysics to the topic of omnipresence.)

Swinburne, R. (1993) *The Coherence of Theism*, rev. edn, Oxford: Oxford University Press. (Important contribution to many issues in philosophical theology by the former Nolloth Professor of the Philosophy of the Christian Religion at Oxford University.)

Wierenga, E. (1988) 'Anselm on omnipresence,' *New Scholasticism* 62: 30–41. (One of the first discussions of omnipresence.)

27
ETERNITY
Alan G. Padgett

In philosophical theology the topic of eternity deals with the relationship between God and time, broadly conceived. Although this topic does come up to some extent in eastern religion and philosophy, the most serious and sustained discussions take place in the western tradition, which is where our focus will be. We must limit this contribution to the long philosophical and theological tradition dating back to the early Greeks and the Bible. Our question will be: how is this God related to time? Although this seems to be a rather abstract question, in fact it reaches deep into our understanding of God and the relationship between creation and the Creator.

Two views of eternity

As with many issues in western philosophical theology, the historical roots of this debate go back to Christian Scripture and Greek philosophy. Tracing this issue back to these earliest sources, we discover the two main views of divine eternity in western tradition: (a) God exists forever 'in' time, and (b) God exists 'outside of' time. On either viewpoint God is eternal; the question is how we best understand this attribute. Let us call the first viewpoint 'everlastingness' (sometimes called sempiternity) and the second viewpoint 'timelessness' or atemporal eternity. Later we will canvass some recent attempts to split the difference between these alternatives with some kind of third option. On both of these traditional understandings, God's life is not temporally limited: God exists forever without coming into being or passing out of being. With respect to change, a timeless God cannot change in any way, while a God who is everlasting may or may not be strictly immutable.

The Christian Bible presents a God who is everlasting. Psalm 90: 2 is a good example: 'Before the mountains were born, and You gave birth to the earth and world, from eternity to eternity You are God.' The Hebrew word for 'eternity' here means a long period of time (not a timeless eternity) and is often translated as 'everlasting' in many English Bibles. This is consistent with the narratives concerning God and Israel or the Church. For example, the prophet Isaiah (speaking for God) proclaims: 'I the LORD, the first and to the last of them I am He' (Isa. 41: 4). A God who exists from the first to the last is an everlasting Lord, not a timeless one. Again, at the opening of Scripture, even though God creates the heavens and the earth 'in the beginning,'

Genesis 1: 1–3 says nothing at all concerning a beginning to time itself. It is plausible to understand the phrase 'there was evening and there was morning, Day One' as only the first day in the week of God's creation, not a beginning to time itself (Gen. 1: 5; see Barr 1962: 145–9). Yet another example comes from wisdom literature. Proverbs personifies Wisdom as being with God before all ages and before the beginning of the creation of the earth (Prov. 8: 22–6). However, this does not have to suggest a beginning to time itself, but only that Wisdom was with God even before the act of creation commenced. Finally, some New Testament passages speak of God's grace or promise existing 'before the ages began' (Titus 1: 2), even 'before the time of the ages' (2 Tim. 1: 9), but language like this is an expansive way of claiming that God's promises are eternal without prejudice to either understanding of eternity. The Greek word for ages or eternity in these New Testament passages means a very long period of time, not a timeless eternity.

God in the texts of the Christian Bible (and especially the narratives) is an everlasting God, not absolutely timeless. Another way of saying this is that the God of the Bible has a history, a story, and so must be temporal to some degree. Passages like the ones we have just mentioned can be made compatible with an already established philosophical notion of divine timelessness; but they do not teach nor imply such a perspective (contra Craig 2001: 3–8). If God is everlasting, then he exists forever as a temporal being. God's eternity is infinite, and his life is unlimited by time, yet God does undergo temporal passage from past, to present, to future. God lives with us in our history. This implies that there are episodes in God's life which no longer exist, and equally there must be future episodes which have not yet come into being. This point is an important one in the debate concerning divine eternity.

With respect to timelessness, the pre-Socratic philosopher Parmenides was the first in recorded history to articulate the rather difficult concept of a being 'beyond' time. Philosophers debate the exact meaning of the fragments we have left from his philosophical poem, *The Way of Truth* (an extended meditation on Being itself, not God), but his approach was influential. Plato picked up this notion of a complete, perfect, and unchanging eternity, applying it to the Forms. The middle Platonist philosopher Plutarch is the first to apply this idea to God: 'Single, he [God] has completed "always" in a single now, and that which really is in this manner only "is," without having come into being, without being in the future, without having begun, and without being due to end' (1936: 393B). The metaphor of God being 'outside' of time is difficult to spell out with precision in literal language, but Plutarch is getting close. A timeless God has no temporal attributes, including change, becoming, past, present, or future. Such a God exists only in a kind of 'present,' a very different kind of 'now' from our temporal one: one which never changes, never becomes, is never past nor future but always a timeless presence. A timeless God has no temporal location and no temporal duration. Words indicating time can only apply to this God in a very limited and analogical sense; such sentences are not literally true.

Boethius gave a famous definition of this concept: 'the whole, simultaneous and perfect possession of unlimited life' (*Consolation of Philosophy* 5. 6). A timeless God (unlike an everlasting one) lives all of his life in a timeless, unchanging presence: a 'whole, simultaneous and perfect' life without any episode ceasing to exist. Origen of Alexandria is the first Christian theologian to apply this notion to God, and later Augustine developed the idea quite fully. Passing through Boethius and Anselm to Aquinas, it became the standard viewpoint in Greek and Latin philosophy and theology. To sum up: a timeless God exists in one, whole, unlimited, and complete life, which is timeless and unchanging. Temporal language for such a God cannot apply with literal predication, but must be analogous or metaphorical. God's timeless 'present' is an unchanging presence throughout time and space.

Timeless eternity

Why did this viewpoint, this notion of timeless eternity, become so dominant? The impulse here lies in a perfect being theology with strong Platonic roots (Rogers 2000: 54–70). For most of the tradition, since God is the greatest possible being (or 'the being than which none greater can be conceived'), he must be timeless. From this viewpoint, time and change were seen as imperfections. A temporal being must be a finite being, one which comes into existence and passes away, a changing thing like all the other things around us. As the uncreated and infinite source of all other being, God must be perfect Being Itself, and beyond both change and time. Any change in God implies an imperfection, a moving away from absolute perfection toward some lesser state; or at least this is assumed to be the case for Perfect Being theology. For example, an everlasting God has episodes of his life that are past, and so do not exist. So even if an everlasting God does not come into being or pass out of being, since God interacts with creation in the biblical tradition (for example, creating the world out of nothing or sustaining all things in being through time), an everlasting God must be a changing God. But such a God is not Perfect Being. So the true God, to be a perfect being, must be both immutable and wholly timeless. These are the fundamental instincts behind the traditional understanding of God as timeless.

Two important arguments in favor of timeless eternity come from contemporary physics and astronomy. In relativity theory, time and space are understood to be intertwined. Physicists will speak of 'spacetime' for this reason, rather than time or space as separate dimensions. Since God is beyond space, does this not imply that God must also be beyond time? Furthermore, there is abundant evidence that the spacetime universe we inhabit has a beginning, the so-called Big Bang. If time has a beginning, and God is eternal, then God must be timeless. The spacetime universe is God's creature, including all the spatial and temporal things within it. God will need to be beyond both time and space to be the eternal and infinite Creator of the universe of spacetime. This conclusion was anticipated by Augustine, who argued that God brings time itself into existence in the beginning, when he first creates temporal things (*Confessions* 11. 12–13). This also answers the question for an everlasting God (mentioned by Augustine) of what God was up to for the infinite time which passed before creation. A timeless God does not wait for anything, but does all things at once, timelessly. God acts 'outside of' time, but the effects of this timeless action take place within time and history. God's actions in history only *appear* to be stretched out in time because *we* are temporal beings.

Everlastingness

The greatest virtue of a theory of everlasting eternity is this: it is clear, uncompli- cated, and devoid of philosophical conundrums, at least prima facie (Swinburne 1977: 210–22). While it may be difficult to imagine an unending, infinite past or future life, it does not seem to have any obvious conceptual difficulties. Most of the arguments in favor of everlasting divine eternity are in fact problems with timelessness. We will thus consider some of the problems with a timeless view of eternity here, because they are in fact arguments in favor of the proposition that God is, in some way, a temporal being. If God is temporal in some way, then timelessness must be false.

Arguments in favor of temporality in God usually turn on more deeply held beliefs. That is, more centrally important truths about God and the world are assumed in order to put forth a particular view of eternity (namely everlastingness). Divine omniscience is one such deeply held belief. That God is omniscient is generally accepted by theists of all types. Among analytic philosophers of religion, omniscience has normally been defined in terms of propositions. God knows the truth-value of all propositions, so that God knows for all true propositions that they are true, and for all false ones that they are false. If God is timelessly eternal, however, there seem to be some things God cannot know. To a timeless God, all moments of 'now' must all be alike. But then God does not seem to know what time it is – a very basic fact of our ordinary world. And thus a timeless God does not appear to be fully omniscient (Prior 1962; Hasker 1989). Put in terms of sentences, God would not know the truth of a simple statement like 'It is 8.00 a.m.' (spoken at 8.00 a.m.) or 'Today is Monday' (spoken on Monday) because for a timeless God there is no (literal) now or today. One response to this problem is to claim that indexical sentences like these (that is, sentences with terms that point to a here or a now or an individual speaker) can be understood by those who do not share that particular point of view, and still known to be true or false (Castañeda 1967). Take the indexical term 'my' in English. If you claim 'My name is Hector,' I can know that is true without actually being Hector. Even if God knows all of time from eternity, God can still know that 'Today is Monday' is true when I speak it, because God also knows that *for me today is Monday*. It does not have to be Monday for God in order for God to know this sentence to be true for that speaker in that context of utterance. More complex problems in the philosophy of language usually emerge at this point; we must press on, but the general terms of the debate should be clear.

We now come to a difficult problem in the philosophy of time, however. In the long run, this cannot be avoided. It is impossible to decide rationally between everlasting and timeless notions of eternity without considering the issues of the nature of tempo- rality, especially the reality of temporal passage (Padgett 1992; Craig 2001; DeWeese 2004). By 'temporal passage' here, we mean the difference between past, present, and future: is this difference real and objective, or subjective and purely a mental phenomenon? Despite the powerful impression we all have of the reality of temporal passage, writers and philosophers for many long years have supposed (or argued) that temporal passage is subjective or mind-dependent. All stories of time travel, for example, whether by human technology or the magic of Merlin, suppose that the past and future are just as real in their own way as our present. Idealist philosophers and modern philosophers of physics have also argued for such a notion. On this view, all of history is spread out, like a road seen from a very high mountain, stretching before the eye of eternity, all of it equally real. This understanding of time has been called the 'B-Theory,' the block theory, and the tenseless theory of time. I prefer to call it the stasis theory of time. The opposite view, which is sometimes called the 'A-Theory,' the tensed theory or the dynamic theory of time, we will call the process theory of time (Craig 2000a; 2000b). Among the many issues in the philosophy of time, this debate is only about one: whether temporal passage from past to present to future is ontologically genuine or mind-dependent.

Those philosophers who defend a timeless divine eternity often imply a stasis theory of time in their arguments, even when they deny it at face value. Consider, for example, two metaphors taken from the work of Eleonore Stump, Norman Kretzmann, and Brian Leftow (well-known defenders of atemporal eternity). Drawing upon the work of Aquinas, Stump and Kretzmann use the explanatory metaphor of a circle (time) with a center point (eternity). The center is not on the circumference, and yet it is present to every point on the circumference of the circle (Stump and Kretzmann 1981: 441). To take another example, in a metaphor drawn from relativity theory, Brian Leftow suggests that divine timelessness is a kind of 'frame of reference' that embraces and includes, all at once in eternity, the whole of time past, present, and future (Leftow 1991: 217–45; also Stump and Kretzmann 1992). Both of these analogies or metaphors actually assume a stasis theory of time (even though their authors claim otherwise). In the circle metaphor, the whole of the circle *is* (tenselessly) so that every point on the circumference can be 'present' (timelessly) to the center. Likewise in Leftow's analogy, in timeless eternity God 'sees' the whole of time past, present, and future at once within his timeless 'frame of reference.'

However, in the physics of relativity, a frame of reference is an abstract system of uniform measure created by objects/observers moving but at rest relative to each other. On Leftow's account the cosmos and the Creator are not moving at rest relative to each other, and so this is quite a bad analogy. Since a frame of reference established (among other things) a uniform measure for temporal units, how can it be timeless (see Padgett 1993)? This bad analogy forces Leftow to the incoherent claim that before-after relations are (in eternity) logical relations, not really temporal ones. The arguments are long and complex, but it does seem that despite themselves, defenders of timeless divine eternity are forced to embrace some kind of stasis theory of time on pain of incoherence (Padgett 1992; Craig 2001).

A second argument for some kind of temporality in God is similar to this first one. This argument focuses on God's action in the world as the one who creates and sustains all things in being (Padgett 1992: 55–81). Assuming a process or dynamic theory of temporal passage, how can a God who is absolutely timeless and changeless sustain in being something which comes into being within time and then passes away? Imagine three episodes in the life of a changing thing or person (by an episode we mean a short phase in the life or history of a person or thing). Let us call them episode A at (time) t_1, episode B at t_2, and episode C at t_3. Since a timeless God cannot be simultaneous with anything in time (given the definition of 'simultaneous' as 'at the same time'), we will invent the 'no-time relation' or NTR to speak of God and the world. Further, we stipulate that time t_2 is the present time. Now, given divine timelessness, there is one eternal and unchanging act by which God sustains the whole of temporal reality. If the stasis theory of time is true, this picture makes sense since the whole of time is equally real. God's timeless act is in NTR to every event and episode within time because all of them are equally real. But on the standard process theory of time, only present episodes are fully real (past episodes used to be real, and future episodes will be real, but these are versions of unreality for the present). God's timeless immutable act of creation/sustaining now holds in being episode B of our person/thing. Because God is directly causing the being of that episode, God's eternal act is NTR to B and t_2. But since time t_1 is past, episode A does not exist. God is not now sustaining in being episode A, even though God's eternal act is equally NTR to time t_1. Remember: God's act from eternity must be completely unchanging! Equally, episode C is future and so not now real even though God's eternal act of creation/sustaining is in NTR to time t_3.

Something is wrong with this picture. If God is the ground of all being, whose power and activity sustain everything in being by a direct, immutable, and eternal act, God's activity must (on the process theory) change over time if God is truly active within a dynamic historical process of becoming. Of course the process theory may be incorrect, but there are powerful reasons to prefer it to the stasis theory, including our everyday experience of time which in no way is undermined by modern physics and philosophy (but we cannot here enter into this debate). If God is understood as the absolute ground of all being, who sustains all things by a direct, NTR act of creative/sustaining power, then the above argument (assuming a process theory of time) presents a real problem for traditional conceptions of divine timelessness. Thus, it is a powerful argument for some kind of temporality in God.

A third way?

It would be nice if we could combine somehow these two theories of eternity in a way which did justice to the different theological-*cum*-philosophical intuitions they embody. Can *both* of these theories be true somehow, perhaps from different points of view? Some modern theologians have, in fact, drawn concepts from both traditions: but the resulting theology of eternity has problems with coherence. For example, Karl Barth wrote that 'Time has nothing to do with God' (*CD* II/1, 608) and yet also claims in the same work 'Even the eternal God does not live without time. He is supremely temporal' (III/2, 437; contra Barth, see Padgett 1992: 141–5). Since theology seeks after the truth about God, it must avoid incoherence like this.

There are three quite similar viewpoints today which seek to find a middle way between everlastingness and timelessness for God. All of them draw upon modern physics and philosophy for their understanding of time. All three accept a difference between a bare metaphysical passage of time and a robust physical time. While each view is somewhat different, there are many similarities. There may be enough similarity to speak of three varieties of a new doctrine of eternity, a third way between the two traditional ones.

We begin with the beginning of time. Physical or measured time has an absolute beginning at the Big Bang, or whenever all of cosmic reality first began. But what about before the First Change, that is, before the absolute beginning of all cosmo-logical time and all changes? The scholar who has published the most on time and eternity in the twentieth century, William Lane Craig, defends a view in which God is *timeless* without creation, and *becomes temporal* with creation (Craig 2001).

Now this looks a bit incoherent at first glance. Craig claims for this logically prior timeless existence that there are 'no intervals of time prior to creation' and that 'there would be no earlier and later, no enduring through successive intervals and, hence, no waiting, no temporal becoming, nothing but the eternal "now"' (Craig 2001: 270). And yet Craig cannot really mean that God is fully timeless without creation. Even as God is in this 'timeless' state, God is *capable of changing* (otherwise God could not become temporal with creation). Now a fully timeless being cannot change, because time and change are interconnected. Change takes time, and so nothing that is fully timeless can ever change. Any time a change occurs for an object, a duration (a bit of time) also occurs for that object. A fully timeless being does not change from being timeless to being temporal, because a fully timeless being does not change.

Further, there is a simple argument which can show that Craig's view must be modified to be coherent. I will start with the claim that if a change is *possible* for a thing, then that thing is temporal in some way. Call this claim C. We can prove that C must be true through indirect proof, that is, we deny it to show that it cannot be false (and so must be true). So we deny C: it is not the case that if an object X can change, it does undergo duration (i.e., go through some kind of temporal passage). By the logical of conditionals, this is equivalent to: X can change and X does not undergo duration. But as we know from the previous paragraph, if X does not undergo duration then it cannot change, because change takes time. So the denial of C must be false, ergo C must be true (Padgett 1992: 12–17, 147–8). From this simple argument, we have to think of a bare metaphysical temporality which is nothing more than the dimension of the possibility of change. Anything that is capable of change, therefore, undergoes some kind of minimal temporal passage even if there are no changing things in existence (yet) to measure that passage. This implies that Craig cannot really mean that without creation God is wholly timeless, but with creation God is temporal, because even without creation it is *possible* for God to change.

Making this needed correction in Craig's viewpoint yields the revised view of Richard Swinburne (Swinburne 1993). Swinburne now holds that God is everlasting once creating begins, but argues that prior to the first change God was only minimally temporal. Before the first change, God existed in an undifferentiated, amorphous and unchanging single, infinite event. During this non-finite period without measure or change, it is wrong to think that God exists for days, hours, or years. Measured-time words like these would not really apply to eternity before creation because there would be no changing thing, and so no time as we know it in our everyday world (no spacetime and no physical time).

I call such an understanding of eternity 'relative timelessness.' This infinite, single, and unchanging duration has many of the properties of timeless eternity (but is still capable of change in the future). In other words, if we are forced to give a 'geometry' to this relative timeless eternity, it would have to be a line *without any possibility of division into intervals or distinct points* (contra Craig 2001: 269) – that is, a line which is one undifferentiated event. Of course in geometry any line is made up of points (an infinite number!), but the reader must allow, *per impossibile*, a 'line' without such divisions and points in order to grasp this eternity concept properly. If one sticks to a normal geometrical understanding of lines and points, the analogy simply breaks down and is unhelpful.

A third viewpoint, which I myself hold, adds the notion that God's eternity is *always* relatively timeless to some degree. I argue that (a) God's time is unchanging and relatively timeless before the first change and (b) relatively timeless and changing in relationship to creation after the first change (Padgett 1992; 2001). My viewpoint is different from the revised view of Swinburne and the corrected view of Craig in arguing that even after the first change and the beginning of creation, measured time words do not literally apply to God. This is because I affirm a metric conventionalism for ordinary, created time, in which temporal metrics require regulation by the laws of nature, choice of inertial reference frames, and associated choice of a 'clock.' None of these makes any sense applied to God's infinite and eternal being, and so I reject the idea that history provides us with a metric for eternity. Furthermore, since God is spaceless and omnipresent, God does not exist in spacetime but transcends it. Finally, only God is infinite in temporal existence: our time occurs only within God's infinite and immeasurable temporality. God's being/becoming is thus the ground of our ordinary, physical time. Thus God and creation are in the same time, but not all the properties of temporal creatures apply to God. Thus I argue against Craig and Swinburne that some aspects of God's relative timelessness before creation continue to apply even when God changes with a dynamic creation. We might say that God becomes more robustly temporal after creation by becoming a changing being. But God for eternity past was *always* temporal in a bare metaphysical sense, since God was always capable of change.

What then do these three versions of a third view of eternity have in common? Is there enough similarity to speak of a third viewpoint on divine eternity? One might suggest something like this: on this more recent theory of eternity, God is a temporal being in a minimalist sense of the word, while still transcending the negative aspects we associate with ordinary, finite temporal beings. God is both temporal and yet also relatively timeless.

See also Augustine (Chapter 8), Thomas Aquinas (Chapter 12), Omniscience (Chapter 24), Omnipresence (Chapter 26), Creation and divine action (Chapter 30), The cosmological argument (Chapter 32).

References

Augustine (1912) *Confessions*, Loeb Classical Library, London: Heinemann.

Barr, J. (1962) *Biblical Words for Time*, London: SCM Press.

Barth, K. (1932–75) (CD) *Church Dogmatics*, 4 vols, 13 pts, Edinburgh: T. & T. Clark.

Boethius (1973) 'The consolation of philosophy,' in *The Theological Tractates and the Consolation of Philosophy*, Loeb Classical Library, London: Heinemann.

Castañeda, H.-N (1967) 'Omniscience and indexical reference,' *Journal of Philosophy* 64: 203–10.

Craig, W. L. (2000a) *The Tensed Theory of Time*, Dordrecht: Kluwer Academic.

—— (2000b) *The Tenseless Theory of Time*, Dordrecht: Kluwer.

—— (2001) *God, Time and Eternity*, Dordrecht: Kluwer.

DeWeese, G. (2004) *God and the Nature of Time*, Aldershot: Ashgate.

Hasker, W. (1989) *God, Time and Knowledge*, Ithaca, NY: Cornell University Press.

Leftow, B. (1991) *Time and Eternity*, Ithaca, NY: Cornell University Press.

Padgett, A. G. (1992) *God, Eternity and the Nature of Time*, London: Macmillan.

—— (1993) 'Eternity and the Special Theory of Relativity,' *International Philosophical Quarterly* 33: 219–23.

—— (2001) 'Eternity as relative timelessness,' in G. Ganssle (ed.) *God and Time: Four Views*, Downers Grove, IL: InterVarsity Press.

Plutarch (1936) 'On the E at Delphi,' in *Moralia*, vol. 5, Loeb Classical Library, London: Heinemann.

Prior, A. N. (1962) 'The formalities of omniscience,' *Philosophy* 37: 119–29.

Rogers, K. A. (2000) *Perfect Being Theology*, Edinburgh: Edinburgh University Press.

Stump, E. and N. Kretzmann (1981) 'Eternity,' *Journal of Philosophy* 78: 429–58.

—— (1992) 'Eternity, awareness and action,' *Faith and Philosophy* 9: 463–82.

Swinburne, R. (1977) *The Coherence of Theism*, Oxford: Oxford University Press, rev. edn 1993.

—— (1993) 'God and time,' in E. Stump (ed.) *Reasoned Faith*, Ithaca, NY: Cornell University Press.

Further reading

Brabant, F. H. (1937) *Time and Eternity in Christian Thought*, London: Longman & Green. (A fine historical overview of issues and authors, although somewhat dated now.)

Craig, W. L. (2001) *Time and Eternity: Exploring God's Relationship to Time*, Wheaton, IL: Crossway Books. (A readable presentation of Craig's point of view in a single volume; a good textbook for students.)

Ganssle, G. E. and D. Woodruff (eds) (2002) *God and Time: Essays on the Divine Nature*, New York: Oxford University Press. (An important collection of advanced essays by major figures in the field today.)

Helm, P. (1988) *Eternal God*, Oxford: Oxford University Press. (An important exposition of the timeless eternity position.)

Pike, N. (1970) *God and Timelessness*, London: Routledge. (The most important volume on this topic from the earlier generation of philosophers of religion.)

Swinburne, R. (2001) *The Christian God*, Oxford: Oxford University Press. (An important volume which updates some of his earlier views and discusses many attributes of God in philosophical terms.)

Yates, J. (1991) *The Timelessness of God*, Lanham, MD: University Press of America. (An often overlooked defense of God's timelessness which is worth reading.)

28

GOODNESS

Michael Beaty

Introduction

For theists, Divine Goodness is both a fundamental confession and a problematic concept. I identify two affirmations that provide criteria for a satisfactory concept of divine goodness, and briefly discuss divine transcendence and its apparent implications for conceiving divine goodness. Then I present a Thomistic account of divine goodness and compare it to the most familiar account among contemporary analytic philosophers of religion, a neo-Anselmian position. I also discuss critically some of the problems for each perspective.

Two affirmations

God is good. God's goodness is affirmed by Christians, Jews, and Muslims, the three major Abrahamic traditions. Their sacred texts and practices depict God as making covenants with his people, promising his fidelity to their welfare in return for their obedience and trust. Their confessions and liturgies present God as having qualities we admire in ourselves (being benevolent, just, and merciful) and presume that God responds to prayers and shares in the grief and suffering of his people. Such affirmations of divine goodness appear to affirm God's *moral goodness* and presume a *personal* understanding of God: that God is a person or is like a person. Other affirmations appear to affirm God's goodness on the basis of principally metaphysical considerations: that God is the most real being or a maximally perfect being. Sometimes the affirmation of divine goodness is based on the belief that God must be worthy of worship and that only a being of unsurpassable *metaphysical goodness* could satisfy this condition.

God is transcendent. God's metaphysical status or 'greatness is of a different order from that of his creatures' (Plantinga 1980: 1). Transcendence includes, at a minimum, God's qualitative difference from created objects, though the concept of transcendence is puzzling and difficult to formulate (Kvanvig 1984: 379). The qualitative difference is typically explicated as God's aseity, simplicity, and sovereignty (Plantinga 1980: 1–2).

Language and divine transcendence

The two affirmations when taken together and located in a broader framework of reasonable beliefs generate a number of philosophically perplexing puzzles for theists. Two questions frame my discussion: (1) How can we speak of God's goodness? (2) What can we say about God's goodness?

Transcendence and theological predicates

The problem of transcendence. Can we speak of God's goodness at all, given God's exalted metaphysical status as a being qualitatively different from the ordinary objects of our experience? Since human words get their meanings from naming and describing ordinary objects, why think we can speak of God at all? If we can, how so? Call this perplexity the *problem of divine transcendence.*

The *problem of anthropomorphism.* Theists apparently face a dilemma. Either divine goodness is completely different in kind from the goodness we admire in ourselves or in other objects or it is the same kind. If divine goodness is entirely different, then divine goodness is unintelligible to us. If we construe divine goodness as more of the same stuff as human goodness, then it is intelligible but surely is not divine goodness and, so, is idolatrous (Martin 1960: 17–18, 58). Call the latter horn of the dilemma the *problem of anthropomorphism.* So, theists seem to be faced with a choice between transcendence and unintelligibility or intelligibility and anthropomorphism.

Three alternatives

Some words may be used *equivocally*, with different meanings, such as 'he killed a fly (a winged insect)' and 'she caught a fly (a baseball/softball caught in the air properly).' Some words are used *univocally*, with the same meaning. 'Dog' univocally refers to the same kind of animal nature in 'Bear is Becca's dog' and 'Paisley is Zack's dog.' Some words are used analogically. I use 'courage' analogously in speaking of the courage of a valued dog in saving her mistress from a bear attack and the courage of Martin Luther King Jr. during civil rights marches. The behavior of both the dog and Dr King are similar, but, plausibly, courage as a character trait in human beings is different from what directs the behavior in the dog.

Equivocity and transcendence. If 'good' in 'God is good' and 'Socrates is good' have different meanings and its meaning when applied to God is unknown to us, then *equivocity* preserves God's transcendence, but entails that divine goodness is incomprehensible to us. If we generalize to all predicates, then apparently God's nature is incomprehensible to us and we can say nothing true of God.

Univocity and human goodness. If 'good' is applied to both God and Socrates with the same meaning, then *univocity* suggests that divine and human goodness are qualitatively the same, even if we say that God is perfectly good. The worry is that while divine goodness is comprehensible, it may imply that God is merely a super human being.

Analogy and theological predicates. If we speak of a dog's courage and Martin Luther King's courage, then we presume enough similarity for a common conceptual content while enough difference makes us resist thinking that we are speaking univocally. If God's goodness is enough like human goodness that we can identify a common conceptual content but different enough, metaphysically, then perhaps language used *analogically* may preserve both intelligibility and divine transcendence.

A Thomistic account of divine goodness

Classical Thomism

Aquinas, like Avicenna and Maimonides, insisted that we can know *that* God exists, but we cannot know *what* God is; we cannot know God's *nature as it really is* (*ST* Ia. 13. 1; *SCG* I. 14). Unlike them, Aquinas does not restrict the use of the theological predicates to *via negativa*, the way of negation, recognizing that preserving God's transcendence in this way makes it impossible to provide a positive construal of divine goodness, for it makes 'good' applied to human beings and God equivocal. Instead, Aquinas seized on Anselm's notion that 'all good things are good through some one thing that is good through itself' (Anselm *Monologion*, ch. 1). Rather than relying only on a Platonic and univocal account of goodness, Aquinas developed a complex doctrine of analogy, a form of predication that intends to preserve the incomprehensibility of God, avoid mere anthropomorphism, and undergird a more robust understanding of divine goodness and its relation to creaturely goods.

Analogy in Aquinas. Compare 'Socrates is good' and 'God is good.' Because God is simple and not a member of any genus or species, by 'God is good,' according to Aquinas, we cannot mean the same thing as when we say 'Socrates is good' because typically 'good' is a kind-relative term (Geach 1956: 33–42; Davies 1993: 85–6). Socrates' benevolence, his knowledge, and his power are distinct from one another, from his existence, and from other qualities of Socrates that are acquired over time. But God's benevolence and knowledge and power are neither distinct from one another, from God's existence, nor from God's essence. God's goodness (his benevolence, knowledge, and power) are not qualities that are acquired over time. Thus, while the goodness of Socrates and God are similar (both can be counted on to act benevolently and justly), which is included in what 'good' signifies or means, the manner (mode of signifying) in which Socrates and God are good are radically different. Since the mode of signifying is radically different in each, 'good' is used analogously, when said of Socrates and God, rather than univocally or equivocally.

Aquinas affirms God's transcendence by insisting that 'good' in 'God is good' is used analogously; so the affirmation of God's goodness is not only meaningful but provides positive knowledge about God. Indeed, Aquinas affirms that our knowledge of the goodness of created things not only provides knowledge of divine goodness but also that philosophical reflection affirms the dependence of creaturely goods on God.

Aquinas on Being and Goodness. Aquinas's account of divine goodness begins with the claim that 'Goodness and being are really the same, and differ only in idea' (*ST*

Ia. 5. 1). 'Good' means 'what is desirable' and always refers to being under the aspect of desirability, while 'being' means 'what is' or 'what actually exists,' without including in its meaning any reference to desirability (ST Ia. 5. 1). Each individual desires its own perfection as the kind of thing it is (ST Ia. 5. 1). Since perfection consists in the actualization of one's potential being as a kind of thing, goodness refers to the process of something becoming completely actual. So, 'good' and 'being' have different meanings, but when used properly, each has the same referent.

As a member of a species, an individual has a set of characteristics that are essential to members of that species. Among a species' *differentia* are the potential powers that are specific to it. When these specific powers are fully actualized, they are perfections, and the individual in question realizes the end which is peculiar to a kind of thing, K. So, to be a perfectly good K is to be a K whose potential being as a K has been actualized completely. What is desirable as a K is to perfect its specific powers. The goodness of K refers to the being of K, and 'good' links desirability and perfection with the being of a certain kind of thing. When a K's potential powers are stymied so they cannot be developed, then it is defective. Its powers are thwarted so it cannot be fully what it ought to be as a K. Because it lacks being as a K, it also lack goodness. Its lack of goodness is a privation of being (Davies 1993: 89–92; Stump 2003: 68).

'Good' said of God: Aquinas's positive account

Aquinas's account of the goodness of mundane objects poses initial difficulties for thinking and speaking about God's goodness since God is not a member of any kind, genus or species. Nonetheless, Aquinas defends 'God is good' as intelligible and provides the following positive account.

God is good. First, 'good belongs to God pre-eminently' because God is desirable (ST Ia. 6. 1). He is desirable because everything seeks its own perfection and an effect is similar to the cause of the effect. Since God is the first cause of all things, he is the first cause of all perfections. So, all things desire God insofar as they desire their perfection. Since goodness consists in desirability, we may say that God is good (ST I. q.2. a.3).

God is perfectly good. Aquinas notes that 'we call that perfect which lacks nothing of the mode of its perfection.' So, 'God is good' signifies that God lacks nothing in the way of being and thus lacks nothing in the way of goodness (ST Ia. 4. 1). Additionally, since all the perfections of creatures are effects of God, all these perfections are in God. Finally, according to Aquinas, 'everything good is called good by its perfection' (ST Ia. 6. 3). The perfection of any individual is a function of (1) the perfection of its own being, (2) the respect in which accidents must be added for its perfection, and (3) the extent to which its perfection consists in attaining something outside itself as its end. Only God is such that his perfection is pure act and not the unfolding of potential being into actuality. Only God is perfect without accidents and without reference to an end other than itself. So, God is *perfectly good*.

God is the highest good. Aquinas distinguishes God as equivocal cause from univocal causes. A univocal cause produces one kind of effect. An equivocal cause produces many kinds of effects and is similar to the effects, but in a superlative fashion. All created perfections have God as their equivocal cause, but they exist in God in a superlative way (*ST* Ia. 4. 2; Ia. 6). Since what is desired in God is found in God in a more excellent way, in the most perfect way possible (as pure act), then God is the *highest good* (*ST* Ia. 6. 2; Davies 1993: 89).

God is essentially good and Goodness itself. Only God is identical with his essence. God's essence is his actuality but the actuality of created things is separate from their essence. The specific powers are accidents which are necessary for creaturely perfection but are not a part of creaturely essences. Finally, since God is absolutely simple, all creaturely perfections exist in God, not as a multiplicity of distinct qualities or properties, but as one undifferentiated unity. What is accidental to creatures (wisdom, justice, and power) are identical in God. So, only God is *essentially good*. Since God is essentially good, we may speak of God as *goodness itself* (*ST* I. 5. a.1; *ST* I. 6a. 3). All other things are good by participation (*ST* Ia. 6. 3).

Aquinas's account of divine goodness preserves God's transcendence because God's nature as it really is remains incomprehensible to human beings. Yet we may speaking truthfully and positively of God's goodness by analogical extensions of our ordinary ways of speaking of creaturely goods, a way of speaking that explains and highlights the dependency of creaturely goods on God.

Questions about a Thomistic account of divine goodness

The appeal to analogy cannot work. How does one determine the way in which God and human beings are similar enough to ground the use of language analogously, since the emphasis is on (1) the difference between God and human beings and (2) that God's nature as it is in itself is incomprehensible to us? What makes it possible to use the analogous language truthfully and prevents it from being disanalogy? If God's nature is really unknown to us, then we can have no confidence that human language picks out similarities between God and creaturely goodness.

God is personal and morally good. Aquinas's richly metaphysical account of Divine Goodness supports the claim that God is the source and exemplar of human goodness. Does it satisfy the theistic convictions that God is personal, a good God who is not merely a kind of Platonic cause and exemplar of justice, prudence, courage, temperance, and the like, but that God is himself just and benevolent?

According to Brian Davies, Aquinas teaches that 'God's goodness is not moral goodness' (Davies 1993: 97) because God does not belong in the same class as persons (Davies 2000: 135–6, 561–4). Presumably, Davies is denying that God possesses the analogues to any of the human moral virtues.

Divine simplicity is incoherent. Neo-Anselmian philosophers respond to the doctrine of divine simplicity with incredulity, and for several reasons. First, we speak as if God has many qualities. He is omnipotent, omniscient, and perfectly good, for example. Isn't it incoherent to claim that omnipotence is identical to omniscience and both to perfect goodness? Isn't it incoherent to claim that God just is identical to each and all of these? Isn't it incoherent to claim that God is a quality or a property (Plantinga 1980: 47, 140–6; Hoffman and Rosenkrantz 2002: 68)?

A neo-Anselmian conception of divine goodness

Most analytic philosophers of religion have followed a particular and peculiarly modern reading of Anselm rather than Aquinas in discussing divine goodness. I briefly compare Classical Perfect Being Theology as expressed in Anselm to a Neo-Anselmian account of Perfect Being Theology.

Classical Anselmianism

The positive account. Anselm's core ideas are (1) God is 'that which a greater cannot be thought' and (2) God is whatever 'it is better to be than not' (Anselm *Proslogion*, ch. 5). On the basis of this method, Anselm claims that God cannot not be; he exists through, and only through himself or is *a se*, is simple (having no parts), is just, truthful, happy, omniscient, omnipotent, impassible, merciful, eternal, omnipresent, etc. However, later Anselm acknowledges that his method implies a multiplicity in God, but that such a multiplicity cannot be true of God's nature, given God's simplicity and unity – a unity which entails that all the divine attributes 'are one. Each of them is all of what you are, and each is what the rest are' (ibid.: ch. 18), which helps explain Anselm's earlier remark, 'Therefore, Lord, you are not merely that than which a greater cannot be thought; you are something greater than can be thought' (ibid: ch. 15).

It is natural to read Anselm as committed to univocity in speaking of divine and human or creaturely goodness (Rogers 2000: 16). However, Anselm's confession of God's incomprehensibility suggests that our human understanding of good or great-making qualities (as perfections) may not be applied to God univocally because to do so suggests a composition in God that cannot be true, a composition made evident by the compossibility problems (e.g., being both just and merciful) which Anselm himself discusses. Anselm identifies a problem, but he is unable to resolve it. This is because the Aristotelian distinctions between univocal, equivocal, and analogical meanings are not yet available to him. In contrast, neo-Anselmians affirm Anselm's core ideas but are dismissive of his concerns about the latter's implications for multiplicity in God and proceed as if the development of an adequate construal of divine goodness is relatively unproblematic.

Neo-Anselmians and perfect being theology: the positive construal

Neo-Anselmians accept the two core ideas of Anselm, which they regard as having great power and simplicity, for all the divine attributes are generated from them and then they are unified under the single notion of maximal perfection or maximal goodness. Perfect being theology also offers other apparent advantages (Morris 1987: 13). Its method allows us to move from ordinary judgments about good or great-making properties to judgments about the nature of God as a perfect being. Perfect Being Theology underscores the common theistic conviction that God is like a person (Plantinga 1990: 29; Taliaferro 1998: 95–105; Hoffman and Rosenkrantz 2002: 13).

It provides an account of divine goodness that fits well with human moral goodness, for essential to our conception of ourselves as persons is the appropriateness of moral assessments of our actions and character traits. However, neo-Anselmians apparently accept univocity with respect to the theological predicates but reject divine simplicity.

God is a perfect being. Neo-Anselmians identify God as the greatest possible being, a maximally perfect or maximally great being. God's *metaphysical goodness* consists in his exemplifying necessarily a maximal set of compossible great-making properties. A great-making property is a property it is intrinsically better to have than to lack (Morris 1987: 12). Since it is better to be knowledgeable, powerful, and good than not, omniscience, omnipotence, and perfect goodness are among God's divine attributes.

God is morally good. God's perfect goodness includes moral goodness, since being morally good is a property it is intrinsically better to posses than to lack. Some neo-Anselmians construe being morally good as a function of fulfilling one's moral duties by acting in accord with universal moral principles, such as truth-telling and promise-keeping. 'Divine moral goodness is basically understood on the model of human moral goodness' (Morris 1987: 26).

God is perfectly morally good. While God is not thought to have 'all and only those duties human beings' have, God, unlike us, satisfies his moral duties perfectly and engages in gracious acts of supererogation (Morris 1987: 26). Thus, God is perfectly morally good. Because God is perfectly morally good, God not only can be relied upon to keep his promises and covenants, but also he can be expected to act graciously with humankind in ways that go beyond the mere fulfillment of duty.

God is maximally morally good. Neo-Anselmians articulate the divine attributes in terms of modal properties and possible worlds. A property is something that is possibly exemplified such as being red, having knowledge, doing one's duty, or being just. A maximally perfect being has the property of being perfectly morally good essentially – there is no possible world in which God exists and lacks perfect moral goodness. It is a part of the Anselmian conception of God that God exists necessarily. That is, God not only exists in the actual world, but in every possible world. Thus, as a maximally perfect being, he possesses perfect moral goodness in every possible world. Call this 'being maximally morally good.' It follows that it is not possible that God fail to exhibit the property of being morally good. God cannot do evil.

Questions about neo-Anselmianism and divine goodness

Perfect being theology and anthropomorphism. Since it is intrinsically better to be perfectly morally good than not, divine goodness includes being maximally morally good. Whether it is construed as principally a function of duty or of virtue, divine moral goodness is understood qualitatively as the same kind of goodness as human moral goodness. This prompts the 'not only false but idolatrous' objection, for it implies that our conceptions are adequate to the nature of God.

One way neo-Anselmians may handle this objection is to insist that univocity is about the meaning or conceptual content of the relevant theological predicates, not about their metaphysical reference. If 'being morally good' is given a functional analysis, then the meaning makes no reference to the intrinsic nature of the thing named. A loudspeaker is anything with the function of converting electronic signals into sound, a function compatible with many different types of material or internal structures, and one may recognize something as a loudspeaker without being able to comprehend its internal structure (Alston 1989: 68). If moral duty is principally performing or not performing certain actions, and moral virtue is principally behaving or not behaving in certain characteristic ways, then a functional analysis of moral goodness seems possible. The affirmation that God is good need neither treat God and human beings as metaphysically in the same class nor need it imply that human beings grasp God's nature as it is in itself. In short, God and human moral goodness may be qualitatively the same, understood functionally, without being metaphysically the same. So, divine transcendence is not threatened but an illuminating account of divine goodness is available, so a contemporary Anselmian may claim.

Perfect Being Theology, Properties, and Multiplicity. A deeper issue for theists is the extent to which the neo-Anselmians are willing to reject divine simplicity and accept divine multiplicity. According to both Anselm and Aquinas, the absolute simplicity of God consists in an undifferentiated metaphysical unity within which there are no real distinctions. In contrast, many neo-Anselmians insist that God's power is really distinct from God's knowledge and both are distinct from God's goodness, concluding that the doctrine of divine simplicity is 'an utter mistake,' 'totally unsatisfactory,' or 'patently false' (Plantinga 1980: 47, 51; Moreland and Craig 2003: 524). However, the neo-Anselmian acceptance of divine multiplicity raises the question of whether the various great-making properties are logically compossible. Some critics charge that the idea of maximal greatness is self-contradictory, which implies that at least one of the allegedly great-making properties is itself incoherent or inconsistent with other divine perfections.

Maximal moral goodness and omnipotence. If God is maximally morally good, God does what moral duty requires not only in the actual world, but in every possible world (Wierenga 1989: 9–11). So, if God is maximally morally good, then God cannot refrain from doing what is morally required. Finitely powerful human creatures have the power to violate their duty; so an essentially omnipotent being is able to resist his duties. If God is both maximally omnipotent and maximally morally good, then God does and does not have the power to refrain from doing what is morally required. Apparently, these attributes are not jointly compossible. Either God is contingently omnipotent and maximally morally good or contingently perfectly morally good and maximally omnipotent. Some neo-Anselmians accept that there are possible worlds in which God acts morally badly. In the actual world, God is perfectly morally good, but he is able to act morally badly and should God do so, he would vacate the office of being God (Pike 1969: 208–16).

The assertion that God can do what is morally wrong will fall harshly on most theists' ears. A more familiar move, especially among Thomists, is to insist that being able to sin indicates a lack of power. Hence, there is no incompatibility in being both maximally omnipotent and maximally morally good. Indeed, given a commitment to divine simplicity, Thomists can claim that these two expressions are merely different ways of referring to the same metaphysical condition of God. So, moral failure is a privation or lack of power. That God cannot act morally badly is an expression of both perfect power and perfect moral goodness because they are merely different descriptions which refer to the same thing.

Some neo-Anselmians make a similar point by claiming that omnipotence must be compatible with the other divine properties, especially maximal moral goodness, so whatever the correct analysis of omnipotence is, it will not be incompatible with divine goodness (Wierenga 1989: 17, 205). But how does this response avoid being a version of 'God can do all the things he has the power to do' and, thus, explanatorily impotent? Why does maximal moral goodness get the pride of place rather than omnipotence? How are neo-Anselmians to answer these questions, especially if maximal omnipotence and maximal moral goodness are really metaphysically distinct properties?

Maximal moral goodness and morally significant freedom. Neo-Anselmian greatness includes being maximally morally good. Suppose also that a necessary condition of being morally good is that the person or agent is significantly morally free. Suppose some person, S, is *significantly morally free*, if and only if, with respect to some morally required action A, it is possible for S to do, or to refrain from doing A. But if some person S, is maximally morally good, and if A is morally required, then S will be unable to refrain from doing A. So, if S is maximally morally good, then S is not significantly morally free. No being can be both maximally morally good and morally free (Morriston 1985: 258). In short, the concept of maximal moral goodness is incoherent.

For some, the argument shows that the domain of divine moral goodness is smaller than human moral goodness. For example, some argue that God has no moral duties because moral rules have no regulative force for a being that is maximally morally good, since such a being cannot do what is evil. When theists read in their sacred Scriptures that God has made promises to Abraham, God is not actually making promises but expressing his intentions (Alston 1990: 316). This response raises two important questions. First, can theists accept that their Scriptures speak so misleadingly about God (Stump 1992)? Second, can the proponent of this view provide some other positive construal of divine goodness that does not include morally significant freedom as a necessary condition (Wierenga 1989: 208; Stump 1990: 277–8)? Can this be done without abandoning univocity for analogy or equivocity in speaking of both maximal moral goodness and human moral goodness?

Maximal perfection and the existence of evil. Is the Anselmian conception of a maximally perfect God compatible with the existence of evil? It seems intuitively plausible that a maximally perfect being, possessing maximal omniscience, omnipotence, and moral goodness, would create a world with no evil in it. Some have claimed that the existence of evil logically entails that a maximally perfect being does not exist (Mackie 1992: 25–6). Call this the deductive argument from evil (Gale 1991: 98).

The deductive problem of evil can be successfully refuted, but the typical refutation prompts two worries for the neo-Anselmian position. Plantinga argues that 'God, a being who is omnipotent, omniscient, and perfectly morally good, exists' is compatible with 'Evil exists' because 'It is possible that a world with morally significantly free creatures is better than a world without such free creatures' (Plantinga 1974: 30). If being morally significantly free is essential to the concept of moral goodness, then, once again, being maximally morally good appears incoherent. Second, why is such a world better than a world without morally significantly free creatures? Plausibly, the reason is that such a world contains human beings who image God's goodness and participate in it. Yet, if God is maximally morally good, then human beings do not image the kind of moral goodness God possesses, for human beings have morally significant freedom and God does not. Thus, the world is not better because some of its inhabitants image and participate in divine goodness, but for some other, yet unknown reason.

Concluding remarks

This essay canvasses two basic ways of understanding divine goodness: classical Thomism and neo-Anselmianism. Aquinas provided a robust understanding of divine goodness. Some theists worry that (1) its conception of full actuality cannot account for God as personal and as morally good and that (2) divine simplicity is incoherent and unbiblical. Some impressive efforts have been made to defend divine simplicity (Rogers 2000: 24–38; Stump 2003: 91–130). Neo-Anselmians provide an intuitively simple conception of God as a maximally great being and an easily accessible and appealing account of divine goodness. Some neo-Anselmians praise Perfect Being Theology precisely because it generates many philosophically interesting problems about the perfections of God (Hoffman and Rosenkrantz 2002: 13). Yet, theists may regard this compliment as faint praise. Critics worry that it diminishes the distance between God and human beings in an unacceptable manner and that it fails to provide, despite its promises, an adequate account of divine goodness, or more generally, a coherent account of God as a maximally perfect being. For some defenders of the conception of God as a maximally perfect being defend a conception which rejects key features of the classical conception of God (e.g., omnipresence, atemporal eternity, self-existence, immutability, or simplicity). At the deepest level, the dispute between Thomists and neo-Anselmians may turn on whether divine simplicity is an essential feature of a maximally perfect being or not and the extent to which divine simplicity is consistent with a Platonic view of properties (Bergmann and Brower 2006: 2).

See also Judaism (Chapter 5), Christianity (Chapter 6), Islam (Chapter 7), Augustine (Chapter 8), Ibn Sina/Avicenna (Chapter 10), Moses Maimonides/Rambam (Chapter 11), Thomas Aquinas (Chapter 12), Omnipotence (Chapter 25), The moral argument (Chapter 34), The problem of evil (Chapter 37), Problems with the concept of God (Chapter 38), The problem of religious language (Chapter 39), and Theology and religious language (Chapter 48).

References

Alston, W. (1989) *Divine Nature and Human Language*, Ithaca, NY: Cornell University Press.

—— (1990) 'Some suggestions for divine command theorists,' in M. Beaty (ed.) *Christian Theism and the Problems of Philosophy*, Notre Dame, IN: University of Notre Dame Press.

Anselm (1996) *Monologion* and *Proslogion*, trans. T. Williams, Indianapolis, IN: Hackett.

Aquinas (1997a) (SCG) *Summa contra Gentiles: God*, ed. A. C. Pegis, Notre Dame, IN: University of Notre Dame Press.

—— (1997b) (ST) *Summa Theologica, Part I*, in A. C. Pegis (ed.) *Basic Writings of Saint Thomas Aquinas*, vol. 1, Indianapolis, IN: Hackett.

Bergmann, M. and J. Brower (2006) 'A theistic argument against Platonism (and in support of truthmakers and divine simplicity),' unpublished manuscript.

Davies, B. (1993) *The Thought of Thomas Aquinas*, Oxford: Clarendon Press.

—— (2000) *Philosophy of Religion: A Guide and Anthology*, Oxford: Oxford University Press.

Gale, R. (1991) *On the Nature and Existence of God*, Cambridge: Cambridge University Press.

Geach, P. (1956) 'Good and evil,' *Analysis* 17: 33–42.

Hoffman, J. and G. Rosenkrantz (2002) *The Divine Attributes*, Oxford: Blackwell.

Kvanvig, J. (1984) 'Divine transcendence,' *Religious Studies* 20: 377–87.

Mackie, J. L. (1992) 'Evil and omnipotence,' in M. Adams and R. Adams (eds) *The Problem of Evil*, Oxford: Oxford University Press.

Martin, C. B. (1960) *Religious Beliefs*, Ithaca, NY: Cornell University Press.

Moreland, J. P. and W. L. Craig (2003) *Philosophical Foundations for a Christian Worldview*, Downers Grove, IL: InterVarsity Press.

Morris, T. (1987) *Anselmian Explorations: Essays in Philosophical Theology*, Notre Dame, IN: Notre Dame Press.

Morriston, W. (1985) 'Is God significantly free?,' *Faith and Philosophy* 2: 257–64.

Pike, N. (1969) 'Omnipotence and God's ability to sin,' *American Philosophical Quarterly* 6: 208–16.

Plantinga, A. (1974) *God, Freedom and Evil*, Grand Rapids, MI: Eerdmans.

—— (1980) *Does God have a nature?*, Milwaukee, WI: Marquette University Press.

—— (1990) 'Advice to Christian philosophers,' in M. Beaty (ed.) *Christian Theism and the Problems of Philosophy*, Notre Dame, IN: University of Notre Dame Press.

Rogers, K. (2000) *Perfect Being Theology*, Edinburgh: Edinburgh University Press.

Stump, E. (1990) 'Intellect, will, and the principle of alternate possibilities,' in M. Beaty (ed.) *Christian Theism and the Problems of Philosophy*, Notre Dame, IN: University of Notre Dame Press.

—— (1992) 'God's obligations,' *Philosophical Perspectives* 6: 457–91.

—— (2003) *Aquinas*, London: Routledge.

Taliaferro, C. (1998) 'Personal,' in B. Davies (ed.) *Philosophy of Religion: A Guide to the Subject*, Washington, DC: Georgetown University Press.

Wierenga, E. (1989) *The Nature of God: An Inquiry into Divine Attributes*, Ithaca, NY: Cornell University Press.

Further reading

Adams, R. (1999) *Finite and Infinite Goods: A Framework for Ethics*, Oxford: Oxford University Press. (Defends a Platonic account of the good in which God is the Supreme Good – the good exemplified by God is intrinsic excellence and the goodness of finite things consists in their resemblance to God.)

Burrell, D. (1986) *Knowing the Unknowable God: Ibn-Sina, Maimonides, Aquinas*, Notre Dame, IN: University of Notre Dame Press. (A helpful discussion of the problem of divine transcendence as articulated in the works of three important figures in Islamic, Jewish and Christian religious traditions.)

Flint, T. and A. Freddoso (1983) 'Maximal power,' in A. Freddoso (ed.) *The Existence and Nature of God*, Notre Dame, IN: University of Notre Dame Press. (A seminal essay defending the view that a being can be both omnipotent and impeccable, as well as almighty.)

MacDonald, S. (1991) *Being and Goodness: The Concept of the Good in Metaphysics and Philosophy*, Ithaca, NY: Cornell University Press. (A fine set of essays on being and goodness in medieval philosophy.)

Rowe, W. (2004) *Can God Be Free?* Oxford: Clarendon Press. (Interesting discussion of the problems concerning the relation of freedom, and praiseworthiness in relation to divine or perfect goodness.)

Zagzebski, L. (2004) *Divine Motivation Theory*, Cambridge: Cambridge University Press. (An innovative theory that identifies God as the Good, and the exemplar and source of all creaturely goodness. The ultimate explanation of human moral goodness is its resemblance to God's motivations and God's virtues.)

29
HIDDENNESS
Michael J. Murray and David E. Taylor

The problem of hiddenness

Very few people will claim that God's existence is an obvious feature of reality. Not only atheists and agnostics, but theists too generally acknowledge that God is, at least to some extent, hidden. The psalmist, for example, exclaims in apparent frustration, using words later uttered by Jesus on the cross: 'My God, my God, why have you forsaken me? Why are you so far from saving me, so far from the words of my groaning? O my God, I cry out by day but you do not answer' (Psalm 22: 1–2).

For theists divine hiddenness can be a source of anxiety or despair. Some atheists, on the other hand, view hiddenness as fodder for an argument against the existence of God. Recently, the Argument (for atheism) from Hiddenness has taken a new, more rigorous form, most notably in the works of philosopher John Schellenberg. The simplest version of Schellenberg's argument looks like this:

1 If there is a God, he is perfectly loving.
2 If a perfectly loving God exists, reasonable non-belief in the existence of God does not occur.
3 Reasonable non-belief in the existence of God does occur.
4 No perfectly loving God exists.
5 There is no God.

(Schellenberg 1993: 83).

Schellenberg argues that since premise (1) is true by definition and premises (4) and (5) follow from the earlier ones, the only controversial claims in the argument are (2) and (3). Schellenberg accepts premise (3) because he takes it to be obvious that at least some non-belief, his own at any rate, is indeed reasonable.

What about (2)? Schellenberg claims that theists should be attracted to this premise. Most theistic traditions argue that ultimate human fulfillment is found by entering into a deep, personal relationship with God. Therefore, if God is truly loving, it is reasonable to think that he will seek to do whatever is necessary to bring his creatures into a position where such a relationship is possible. There are numerous conditions that are necessary to do this, but only one need concern us here, namely that God *make his existence known* to creatures in such a way that they could not reasonably fail to see it. It seems indubitable that person A cannot enter into a deep and personal loving relationship with person B unless person A knows that person B exists. Hence it is a minimally necessary condition of God's entering into such a relationship with *us* that he make his existence known to us. For this reason, we should expect that God would reveal himself to us in a way that rules out the possibility of reasonable non-belief.

But even if our expectations here are warranted, perhaps our acceptance of (2) is premature. What if God has good reason to withhold evidence for the truth of theism in spite of his similarly good reason to prevent reasonable non-belief? Since there might be such reason, premise (2) should be rejected in favor of the more cautious:

2* If a perfectly loving God exists, reasonable non-belief does not occur, unless God has a morally sufficient reason to permit the occurrence of such reasonable non-belief.

Were we to revise the argument in this way, Schellenberg would need to adjust premise (3) of his argument as well to read:

3* (a) Reasonable non-belief occurs, and (b) at least some of it occurs for no good reason.

Now the crux of the argument lies in (3*) alone.

Objections to (3*a)

One way to argue against (3*) is to attack its first conjunct and deny that reasonable non-belief actually occurs. There is a great deal of non-belief in the world, of course. Some of this non-belief occurs in the form of atheism and agnosticism. But even more of it occurs in the form of what religious believers are likely to regard as erroneous beliefs concerning the nature or identity of God. Many Christians, for example, regard Hindu belief in God as a form of non-belief since, by the Christian's lights, the god of Hinduism does not in fact exist. Could one reasonably take all such non-belief to be unreasonable or culpable? Some critics of the argument have argued that the answer is yes.

Taking inspiration from Jonathan Edwards, William Wainwright (2002) claims that God has provided us with sufficient objective evidence of his existence, and that it is only because of certain corrupt, faulty dispositions that we are blind to it. Furthermore, since we are ultimately responsible for these corrupt dispositions, our non-belief is *culpably unreasonable*. According to Schellenberg (1993: 62), A's belief that *p* is inculpable (reasonable) if and only if 'his evidence, inductive standards, and belief as to *p*'s probability on the evidence have been, in his own view at the time, adequately investigated.' Wainwright agrees that these conditions are necessary for inculpable belief, but denies their sufficiency since there are situations in which one can meet all the above conditions and yet still *culpably* believe (or fail to believe). This can happen in one of two ways. First, *if* one can be held responsible for being in an epistemic environment in which relevant evidence is unavailable, or in which it is difficult to cultivate the appropriate epistemic capacities, one can be culpable for one's belief (or non-belief) despite meeting Schellenberg's conditions. Second, Wainwright claims, *if* one can be held responsible for one's 'passional nature,' one can be held responsible for judgments about the relative weight of evidence, and hence will be culpable for beliefs based on that evidence, despite meeting Schellenberg's conditions. Hence, according to Wainwright, insofar as we can be culpable for the epistemic circumstances or passional nature that contributes to our non-belief, we can reasonably be held responsible for that non-belief. If each instance of what Schellenberg takes to be reasonable non-belief were to fall into one or both of these categories, then all theistic non-belief would be culpable.

Before we can assess Wainwright's position, we need to know more about the notions of 'epistemic situation' and 'passional nature' at work in this argument. Generally, one's epistemic situation consists of the totality of the external circumstances relevant to the formation of belief in a certain domain. If I am a detective investigating the murder of Jones down by the river, it behooves me to examine the crime scene and other related sites near the river. These would be the appropriate epistemic circumstances in which to form beliefs about the murder. If I decided to investigate the crime by examining the restroom at the McDonald's across town instead, I would have put myself in epistemic circumstances that make it impossible for me to come to hold appropriate beliefs about the crime and its perpetrator. Wainwright's point is that we can, like a wayward detective, culpably place ourselves in epistemic circumstances that lead us to non-belief in the existence of God.

The phrase 'passional nature' is adapted from William James, who uses it to refer (roughly) to a person's fundamental intuitions, desires, and dispositions concerning an issue under scrutiny prior to the evaluation of any objective evidence (Wainwright 1995: 96–107; 2002: 111). We all know people who, for example, are quick to attribute vicious motives to others. When they see someone cut them off in traffic, they immediately conclude that the action was done with malicious intent. Perhaps they readily form such judgments because of past ill-treatment from others or because of their general uncharitable temperament. Whatever their explanation, they come to the world with a bias that leads them to assess evidence in a way that favors one explanation or conclusion over other equally (or more) plausible explanations. Insofar as we have control over our having these intuitions, desires and dispositions, we are responsible and thus potentially culpable for the beliefs they might yield, including non-belief in theism.

Wainwright thus holds that the non-belief which Schellenberg regards as reasonable is in fact a result of one's culpable epistemic situation or passional nature, and hence is itself culpable. It may seem reasonable to hold that at least *some* non-belief is culpably unreasonable in this way. But is it reasonable to believe that possibly *all* non-belief is of this sort? Critics will likely think that there are many non-believers whose epistemic environment and passional nature are both appropriate for the acquisition of religious belief, thus undercutting this criticism of (3*a). It is difficult to know how the question can be confidently settled. Non-believers who take themselves to be properly situated and disposed to the evidence might be self-deceived or otherwise mistaken. And yet, there do seem to be honest, well-intentioned, and fully informed non-believers.

Objections to (3*b): invalid 'noseeum' inference?

Even if the theist grants (3*a), Schellenberg must provide us with reason for thinking that some of the reasonable non-belief occurs *for no good reason*. Initially it seems that this burden will be easy to satisfy. For consider the agnostic who deeply wants to believe, and happily would believe if God would only provide him with a tiny bit more evidence, maybe even just a vague religious experience. Now the question is: What *possible* good could come out of God's permitting *this* person's continuing reasonable non-belief? It seems that in this case, and others like it, there simply is no greater good that could justify such reasonable non-belief. And in light of this, the reasonable conclusion to draw is that cases like this are, after all, instances of reasonable non-belief occurring for no good reason.

The defender of the Argument from Hiddenness is here arguing that she has looked long and hard for some possible greater good to which this non-belief might contribute, but has ultimately come up empty-handed. She sees no reason that God would permit such suffering, and so it is reasonable for her to conclude that there is none. Arguments of this general sort have been labeled 'noseeum arguments.'

Are 'noseeum arguments' good arguments? Sometimes they are. For a noseeum inference to be good, two conditions must be met. First, it must be the case that I am looking in the right place for the thing in question. If my wife asks me if we have any milk and I look in the oven, I am looking in the wrong place. My failing to see it *there* would not be good evidence that we don't have any milk. Second, it must be the case that I would see the thing in question if it really were there. If my wife asks me if we have ants in our lawn and I look out the window and say, 'Nope – I don't see any,' I have made a bad noseeum inference. I am looking in the right place, but ants are too small to be seen by me from this location even if they are there.

Is Schellenberg well positioned to make a noseeum inference to the claim that at least some instances of reasonable non-belief occur for no good reason? Some have argued that the answer is no (McKim 2001: 87–91, 104). Consider the first test. When looking for greater goods to justify reasonable non-belief, are we looking in the right place? Maybe we are, but we can't say for sure. We might well consider all the types of goods we can think of to see if any of them would justify reasonable non-belief. But how do we know that there are not many different types of goods that we either do not or cannot understand with our limited, creaturely intellectual and moral capacities? If there are such goods, perhaps we have been looking in the wrong place. So it is not clear that this noseeum inference meets the first condition. This also shows us why this noseeum inference does not clearly meet the second condition either. If there are some potentially justifying goods that we cannot fathom at all, then we will not come to know them even when looking in 'the right places.'

Schellenberg has offered three responses to the charge that he has deployed a fallacious noseeum inference. First, he argues that, contrary to the claims made above, his noseeum inferences *do* pass the tests. On Schellenberg's view, if the permission of divine hiddenness serves any sort of good at all, those goods would be (or would likely be) goods for *human beings*. Consequently, it is 'unlikely that they, or their relation to [hiddenness], should be impossible for us to grasp' (Schellenberg 1993: 90). If this is right, then if we can see no connection between divine hiddenness and certain greater goods for human beings, we can conclude that there is no good reason for hiddenness. We have, after all, looked in the right place, and we would have seen the goods we were looking for if they were there.

Unfortunately, this reply contains three undefended and highly controversial assumptions. We can unearth these by considering three questions. First, is it right to say that the goods at which hiddenness aims would have to be human goods? Why couldn't the outweighing goods be of another sort, say goods that contribute to an overall better universe? Schellenberg does not say. Second, why should we think that even if hiddenness does aim at human goods, that we would be aware of all *human* goods that God wants for us to enjoy? Some of these goods might, for example, be presently unimaginable goods that we are able to experience only in a postmortem state of existence. Finally, why does Schellenberg think that if hiddenness is aimed at securing known goods, that it would be obvious to us what the connection between hiddenness and those goods would be? For all we know, certain painful experiences we undergo at one point or another contribute to the formation of a character of outweighing virtue in the distant future. If so, perhaps the connection between those experiences and that virtue would be impossible for us to understand before (or even after) the fact. The same, it seems, is true, for all we know, with the evil of hiddenness.

Schellenberg's second response is to claim that any good that would be secured through divine hiddenness could be equally secured by God's choosing to *relationally withdraw* from his creatures. Such withdrawal would serve to bring about any goods that hiddenness would be thought to achieve, and it could do this while still ruling out any reasonable non-belief. Thus, no unknown goods would justify hiddenness. Schellenberg puts the point this way:

> What I have in mind here is analogous to what has traditionally been called 'the dark night of the soul' – a state in which there is evidence for God's existence on which the believer may rely, but in which God is not felt as directly present to her experience, and may indeed feel absent. ... this sort of hiddenness can produce the goods in question and is compatible with God being revealed to all who do not resist God. (1993: 299–300)

Can withdrawal bring about the same goods as hiddenness? It seems impossible to say in the abstract. To know, we would have to consider each good individually. But of course, if there are inscrutable goods, we have no way of considering *them* on a case-by-case basis, and hence cannot determine if withdrawal could bring them about.

In his final response Schellenberg (2005b: 300–1) claims that the noseeum objection is question-begging. According to Schellenberg, anyone who holds that it is possible that there exist inscrutable goods for the sake of which God would permit reasonable non-belief is committed to the following: The possibility that such inscrutable goods exist is *not ruled out by anything we know or justifiably believe*. But accepting this claim assumes that (2) from the original formulation of the argument is false. For (2) clearly *rules out* the possibility of there being *any* goods for the sake of which God would permit reasonable non-belief (for if there were any such goods, God might permit reasonable non-belief on behalf of them, and so (2) would be false). Hence, to claim that it is possible that there exist hidden goods of the sort in question is to assume that the crucial premise (2) is false, and this is to beg the question.

However, begging the question against (2) is not problematic since, as we saw earlier, one should not be moved to accept (2) in the first place, but rather only the more modest (2*). Appeals to the possibility of inscrutable goods to explain hiddenness are unproblematic given (2*), since (2*) clearly leaves open this possibility. Schellenberg might object that such critics have altered his original argument to better their purposes. But this reply fails since, as we saw, we should have never accepted (2) in the first place; only belief in (2*) is warranted.

Objections to (3*b): good reasons for hiddenness

Rather than taking refuge in the possibility of inscrutable goods as a way of undermining (3*b), some theists have instead argued that we can see at least some of the goods that constitute justifying reasons for hiddenness. We turn to the two most important such explanations in what follows.

The good of filial knowledge

Paul Moser (2002; 2004) argues that God remains hidden to some creatures because failure to so hide would prevent those creatures from coming to know God in the proper way. Moser's argument hinges on a distinction between two types of knowledge of God: (1) *propositional* knowledge that God exists, and (2) *filial* knowledge of God. The first is simply the belief that God exists. The second is a much deeper knowledge that consists of one's 'humbly, faithfully, and lovingly standing in a relationship to God as our righteously gracious Father' (Moser 2004: 49). According to Moser, God's perfectly loving character requires that he promote and facilitate not just our propositional knowledge of God, but also our filial knowledge of God.

Propositional knowledge is a necessary condition for filial knowledge, but alone it can prove detrimental to one's relationship with the divine. Simply knowing 'that God exists' in the way that we know any other true proposition about the world objectifies and trivializes God and his purposes. Not only is this an evil in itself, but those with mere propositional knowledge might respond to God with an indifferent, hateful, impersonal, or presumptuous attitude. Since God wants nothing more than for us to lovingly respond to him, he will not promote propositional knowledge except insofar as this is a component of our filial knowledge of him.

So why hasn't God bestowed upon us the means to know him *filially*? That is, why does he remain hidden with respect to *this* type of knowledge? Moser claims that in order for one to know God filially, one must turn toward God in a 'morally serious' manner. We cannot respond to God in the appropriate loving manner unless we are open to moral transformation, distancing ourselves from our material and selfish values. Further, we cannot know God in a filial way unless we recognize him as Lord and Father. According to Moser, if we open our hearts to God in this way, then God will make himself known to us through his morally transforming love. This love is the '*cognitive* foundation for genuine filial knowledge of God,' and when one possesses it, one is unable to deny God's existence and all-loving character.

Schellenberg (2004: 55–6) argues that this response fails since there are clearly individuals who fully seek God in the way that is required for filial knowledge and yet have neither it nor propositional knowledge. One might, of course, raise doubts about how Schellenberg could know that there are such individuals. Moser further responds that even if there are such cases, we can presume that God is waiting for his 'appointed time' to bestow the grace of filial knowledge in such cases, and that there is no way to show that this filial knowledge will not be forthcoming.

The good of morally significant freedom

Some philosophers (Swinburne 1979; Murray 2002) have argued that hiddenness is rather a necessary condition for a world containing human creatures that enjoy morally significant free choice. Such a world must meet certain conditions: it must contain human beings, endowed with the power of free choice, who are presented with alternative courses of action between which it is genuinely possible for them to select. For a world to meet these conditions, it must be configured in particular ways. Most relevant among these ways in this context is this: the world must be set up in such a way that the free creatures in it often have genuine incentives for doing both good and bad actions. In order for one to be free, one must be able to choose between alternative courses of action, and in order to have such an ability, one must possess incentives or desires for each of the alternatives.

The claim that genuine 'dual incentives' are a necessary condition for morally significant freedom rests on a certain plausible though controversial principle: in order for it to be possible for me voluntarily to perform an action, it must be that I have some significant desire or other positive attitude toward performing that action. If I have absolutely no desire (or a desire that is overwhelmed by contrary desires) to perform a certain action, say pull out my favorite dahlias from my garden, and furthermore have desires to leave them right where they are, then it is psychologically *impossible* for me to choose to pull them. Part of the reason this principle seems right is that it is hard to imagine what I would say to explain my pulling the dahlias after the fact if I did in fact do it. I would have to say something like: 'Although I had no (or a negligible) desire to pull the dahlias and strong desires to leave them in place, I pulled them nonetheless.' If we heard someone say something like this, we would conclude that he was confused, deluded, or deranged. We just can't bring ourselves to perform an act of will when we have no (or a negligible) desire to perform that action and strong desires to refrain from performing it. We can take a more general lesson from this, namely, that if the world does not contain incentives for us to choose both good and evil actions, then we will not be truly free to choose between them.

There is more than one way that such dual incentives can be eliminated from our world. One way would be for God to set up the world so that we are subjected to coercive threats to behave in accordance with the dictates of morality at all times. We can imagine God setting up the world in such a way that we are followed around by moral 'highway patrolmen,' ready to punish us whenever we make a morally evil choice. In this case, any incentives for doing evil would be eliminated or at least overwhelmed by the presence of the moral patrolman, and we would be psychologically unable to choose evil.

Such freedom-removing conditions could be established in other ways as well. For example, if God were to make his existence clearly and powerfully known to us, the impact would be no less than the moral patrolmen. If we knew that God was there, watching over us continuously, all incentives to choose evil would be lost along with our ability to choose between good and evil actions. Our moral free choice would have been eliminated. Some have argued that this need to prevent pervasive coercion is one reason why God must remain hidden, at least to the extent that his existence is not as obvious as a patrol car following us on the highway.

Critics of this explanation of hiddenness have argued that it fails for three reasons. First, Schellenberg (2002: 37) argues that there are no implications for freedom or incentives for choosing evil if God merely makes his *existence* known to us. Such implications would follow only if God were also to reveal his *moral will*. Hence God could eliminate reasonable non-belief while safeguarding moral freedom. Second, defenders of the Argument from Hiddenness (Schellenberg 1993: 129) note that there are many religious individuals who are completely convinced of the existence of a God watching over their every move, perhaps because of powerful religious experiences, and who still seem to be capable of doing both good and evil. Given this, it is hard to believe that God's becoming evident to someone undermines the possibility of genuine freedom. Finally, Schellenberg (2005b: 293–6) argues that even if human beings were subject to coercive pressure of this sort, they would still be able to choose between two morally significant alternatives: doing good *out of a sense of duty* or *merely out of a sense of fear* of divine punishment. Doing the first would be morally good and indeed vastly morally superior to the second. Thus human beings in these circumstances would face genuinely distinct and morally significant alternatives.

It is not clear, however, that any of these replies succeeds. We have already seen that Moser argues that the first does not. On his view, providing creatures with evidence sufficient to generate 'propositional knowledge' alone is indeed *harmful* to creatures. As a result, God's love entails that were God to make himself known to us, he would reveal something beyond his mere existence. In addition or instead, God would make known those things necessary for 'filial knowledge,' including his moral will. Thus, the content of what a loving God would reveal to us would indeed have the potentially freedom-compromising practical implications.

The second criticism points to cases which show that powerful divine manifestations do not always undermine the possibility of morally significant freedom. But this alone is not a problem for this explanation of hiddenness. One can grant that different people will have different levels of 'threat indifference.' Some individuals are coerced by the slightest perceived threat while others seem to resist nearly all attempts at coercion. To preserve creaturely freedom God must remain largely hidden to individuals of the former type, though he can present powerful evidence of his existence to those of the latter type. For all we know, those individuals who believe in the existence of God because of these powerful religious experiences and who yet retain morally significant freedom are all of this latter sort.

With regard to the third criticism, it is not at all clear that we can choose between acting on the different sorts of motives that Schellenberg imagines, or if we could, know that we have. Imagine that in a spirit of holiday good will I decide to go drop a one hundred dollar bill in the bucket of the Salvation Army volunteer standing outside of my local Wal-Mart. As I step out of my car with the bill in my hand, the Salvation Army worker sees me coming and assumes I am another self-indulgent Wal-Mart customer about to go into the store and blow another hundred dollars on senseless trinkets. As I arrive at his bucket his anger finally boils over. He pulls out a gun and says, 'Hand me the money!' Stunned, I quickly drop the bill in the bucket and run.

Why did I hand him the bill? At that moment I had two possible motives on which I could have acted: charity and fear. But which one did I actually choose to act on? The concern for my own safety ran so high at that moment that I don't see how I could have decided to act merely on the motive of charity. But even if it were possible for me to have acted on charity alone, I am not sure I could know after the fact which motive was actually the one acted on. In light of this, it is doubtful that morally significant freedom, even of the sort Schellenberg proposes here, would survive in a world in which God makes his existence plain and obvious to us.

See also William James (Chapter 17), The problem of evil (Chapter 37), Faith (Chapter 56).

References

McKim, R. (2001) *Religious Ambiguity and Religious Diversity*, New York: Oxford University Press.

Moser, P. K. (2002) 'Cognitive idolatry and divine hiding,' in D. Howard-Snyder and P. K. Moser (eds) *Divine Hiddenness: New Essays*, Cambridge: Cambridge University Press.

—— (2004) 'Divine hiddenness does not justify atheism,' in M. Peterson and R. VanArragon (eds) *Contemporary Debates in Philosophy of Religion*, Malden, MA: Blackwell.

Murray, M. (2002) 'Deus absconditus,' in D. Howard-Snyder and P. K. Moser (eds) *Divine Hiddenness: New Essays*, Cambridge: Cambridge University Press.

Schellenberg, J. (1993) *Divine Hiddenness and Human Reason*, Ithaca, NY: Cornell University Press.

—— (2002) 'What the hiddenness of God reveals,' in D. Howard-Snyder and P. K. Moser (eds) *Divine Hiddenness: New Essays*, Cambridge: Cambridge University Press.

—— (2004) 'Reply to Moser,' in M. Peterson and R. VanArragon (eds) *Contemporary Debates in Philosophy of Religion*, Malden, MA: Blackwell Publishing.

—— (2005b) 'The hiddenness argument revisited (II),' *Religious Studies* 41/3: 287–303.

Swinburne, R. (1979) *The Existence of God*, Oxford: Clarendon Press.

Wainwright, W. (1995) *Reason and the Heart*, Ithaca, NY: Cornell University Press.

—— (2002) 'Jonathan Edwards and the hiddenness of God,' in D. Howard-Snyder and P. K. Moser (eds) *Divine Hiddenness: New Essays*, Cambridge: Cambridge University Press.

Further reading

Adams, R. (1985) 'Involuntary Sins,' *Philosophical Review* 94/1: 3–31. (Explores culpability for various involuntary states including the holding of certain beliefs.)

Howard-Snyder, D. (1996) 'The Argument from Divine Hiddenness,' *The Canadian Journal of Philosophy* 26/3: 433–54. (Presents an alternative objection to (3*b).)

Howard-Snyder, D. and P. K. Moser (eds) (2002) *Divine Hiddenness: New Essays*, Cambridge: Cambridge University Press. (Eleven essays in response to Schellenberg's *Divine Hiddenness and Human Reason*.)

Schellenberg, J. (2005a) 'The hiddenness argument revisited (I),' *Religious Studies* 41/2: 201–15. (The first of two essays in response to Howard-Snyder and Moser's *Divine Hiddenness*.)

30
CREATION AND DIVINE ACTION
William Lane Craig

Creation

God is conceived in traditional western theology to be the cause of the world both in his initial act of bringing the universe into being and in his ongoing conservation of the world in being. These two actions have been traditionally classed as species of *creatio ex nihilo*, namely, *creatio originans* (originating creation) and *creatio continuans* (continuing creation). The latter notion was further subdivided into divine *conservatio* (preservation of the world) and divine *concursus* (God's causing everything that happens in the world).

While this is a handy rubric, it unfortunately quickly becomes problematic if pressed to technical precision. For if we say, as it seems we should, that a thing is created at a time *t* only if *t* is the first moment of the thing's existence, then the doctrine of *creatio continuans* implies that at each moment God creates a new individual, numerically distinct from its chronological predecessor. We are thus landed in the bizarre doctrine of occasionalism, according to which no persisting individuals exist, so that personal agency and identity over time are precluded. On the other hand, if we try to elude this problem by reinterpreting creation in such a way that it does not involve a thing's first beginning to exist at the time of its creation, then something important about the concept of creation would seem to be lost. It is therefore preferable to take 'continuing creation' as but a *façon de parler* and to distinguish conservation from creation.

We may distinguish conservation from creation, not in terms of a difference in God's power or action, but in terms of the object of his action. Intuitively, creation involves God's bringing something into being. Thus, if God creates some entity *e* at a time *t*, then *e* comes into being at *t*. We can analyze this notion as follows:

E₁. *e* comes into being at *t* if and only if (i) *e* exists at *t*, (ii) *t* is the first time at which *e* exists, and (iii) *e*'s existing at *t* is a tensed fact.

Accordingly,

E₂. God creates *e* at *t* if and only if God brings it about that *e* comes into being at *t*.

God's creating e involves e's coming into being, which is an absolute beginning of existence, not a transition of e from non-being into being. In creation there is no entity on which the agent acts to bring about its effect. It follows that creation is not a type of change, since there is no enduring subject which persists from one state to another.

It is precisely for this reason that conservation cannot be properly thought of as essentially the same as creation. For conservation does presuppose a subject which is made to persist from one state to another. In creation God does not act on a subject, but constitutes the subject by his action. In contrast, in conservation God acts on an existing subject to perpetuate its existence. Conservation ought therefore to be understood in terms of God's preserving some entity e from one moment of its existence to another. We may therefore provide the following analysis of divine conservation:

E_3. God conserves e if and only if God acts upon e to bring about e's existing from t until some $t^* > t$ through every sub-interval of the interval $t \rightarrow t^*$.

The divine action itself (the causing of existence) may be the same in both cases, but in one case it may be instantaneous and presupposes no prior object, whereas in the other case it occurs over an interval and does involve a prior object.

The doctrine of creation involves an important metaphysical feature which is under-appreciated: it commits one to a tensed or A-Theory of time. For if one adopts a tenseless or B-Theory of time, then things do not literally come into existence. Things are four-dimensional objects which tenselessly subsist and begin to exist only in the sense that their extension along their temporal dimension is finite in the *earlier than* direction. The universe thus does not come into being on a B-Theory of time, regardless of whether it has a finite or an infinite past relative to any time. Hence, clause (iii) in E_2 represents a necessary feature of creation. In the absence of (iii) God's creation of the universe, *ex nihilo* could be interpreted along tenseless lines to postulate merely the universe's ontological dependence on God and its finitude in the *earlier than* direction.

What about conservation? At first blush this notion would seem to be much more amenable to a tenseless construal. God can be conceived to act tenselessly on e to sustain it from t_1 to t_2. But a moment's reflection reveals this construal to be problematic. What if e exists only at t? Or what if e is the whole, four-dimensional space-time block? In neither case can God be said to conserve e, since the entities do not persist from one time to another. Yet on a tenseless view of time, God is the source of being for such entities and therefore in some sense sustains them. Similarly, if we allow timeless entities into our ontology, such as abstract objects, then God must be the source of their being as well. In their case there is properly speaking no conservation, no preserving them in existence from one moment to another. The existence of such entities would seem to necessitate a third category of creation not contemplated by the classical theologians, a sort of static creation, which is the relation appropriate to a tenseless theory of time. We can use 'sustenance' as the technical term for such divine action and explicate it as follows:

E_4. God sustains e if and only if either e exists tenselessly at t or e exists timelessly, and God brings it about that e exists.

The very idea of the need for conservation in being thus also implies an A-Theory of time. Conservation of an entity is necessary if that entity is to endure from one moment to another and not to lapse into non-being. On a B-Theory of time, no lapse of time occurs, and so conservation is unnecessary, indeed, excluded. Rather, God is engaged in sustaining the four-dimensional universe as a whole and every entity in it, whether that entity has a temporal extension or exists merely at an instant. Thus, even conservation is compromised if definitions of it are given which are compatible with a B-Theory of time.

The second aspect of what was traditionally called *creatio continuans* was divine *concursus*. According to this doctrine God is the cause of everything that happens in the world. That is not to say that God is the only cause, as occasionalists claim; rather, God concurs with the action of every cause, and in the absence of this concurrence, no effects would be produced by them. This remarkable doctrine has been almost totally eclipsed in contemporary discussions of God-world relations. Yet it seems to follow from divine conservation, which is the only doctrine of creation that many contemporary theologians are willing to embrace. For if God conserves e from t to t^*, then he must not only conserve e in abstraction, but in its concrete particularity with all its properties. Suppose that e is a piece of cotton that is at t brought into proximity with a flame and so becomes black and smoldering at t^*. God does not simply conserve the piece of cotton from t to t^*, but the cotton in its particularity. For the cotton to exist in all its particularity from t to t^*, God must bring about its existing with its properties. Therefore, conservation requires God to be a cause of e's being F at t and e's being G at t^*.

It might be suggested that while God wills that e is F at t, he does not bring about e's being F at t. This suggestion, however, is incompatible with divine providence. For either God wills that e is F at t or he does not. If not, then God is utterly indifferent to what happens in the world, conserving it in being but not caring what happens in it, which denies God's providence. Suppose, then, that God does will that e is F at t. Then his will is either directive or permissive. If his will is directive, then God is impotent, since e's being F at t is not brought about by God's willing that e is F at t. But if God's will is merely permissive, then divine providence is again denied, since God does not directly will anything to happen. Conservation therefore plausibly entails concurrence.

Since the rise of modern theology with Schleiermacher, the doctrine of *creatio originans* has been allowed to atrophy, while the doctrine of *creatio continuans* has assumed supremacy. Undoubtedly this was largely due to theologians' fear of a conflict with science. But the discovery in the early twentieth century of the expansion of the universe, coupled with the Hawking–Penrose singularity theorems of 1968, which demonstrated the inevitability under very general conditions of a past, cosmic singularity as an initial boundary to space-time, forced the doctrine of *creatio originans* back into the spotlight. As physicists Barrow and Tipler observe, 'At this singularity, space and time came into existence; literally nothing existed before the singularity, so, if the Universe originated at such a singularity, we would truly have a creation *ex nihilo*' (Barrow and Tipler 1986: 442).

Of course, various and sometimes heroic attempts have been made to avert the beginning of the universe posited in the standard Big Bang model and to regain an infinite past. But none of these alternatives has commended itself as more plausible than the standard model (see Craig forthcoming). The old Steady State model, the Oscillating model, and Vacuum Fluctuation models are now generally recognized among cosmologists to have failed as plausible attempts to avoid the beginning of the universe. Attempts to extend inflationary models infinitely into the past, as well as attempts to employ so-called M-Theory to envision higher dimensional scenarios involving no past boundary, have been invalidated by the Borde–Vilenkin–Guth theorem. This theorem proves that any universe which has on average been globally expanding at a positive rate is geodesically incomplete in the past and therefore has a past boundary. Most cosmologists believe that a final theory of the origin of the universe must await the as-yet undiscovered quantum theory of gravity. Such quantum gravity models may or may not involve an initial singularity, although attention has tended to focus on those that do not. But even those that eliminate the initial singularity, such as the Hartle–Hawking model, still involve a merely finite past and, on any physically realistic interpretation of such models, imply a beginning of the universe. Such theories, if successful, thus enable us to model the origin of the universe without an initial cosmological singularity and, by positing a finite past time on a closed geometrical surface of space-time rather than an infinite time on an open surface, support temporal *creatio ex nihilo*.

Divine action

Theologians traditionally distinguished two sorts of divine providence: *providentia ordinaria*, which describes God's non-miraculous activity in the world, and *providentia extraordinaria*, which handles God's miraculous acts in the world. The degree to which the doctrine of divine providence has atrophied in contemporary theology is striking, leaving many thinkers with little more than a doctrine of divine *conservatio*.

The principal challenge facing any account of God's ordinary providential governance of the world concerns how to reconcile divine sovereignty with creaturely freedom. A startling solution to this enigma emerges from Luis de Molina's (1535–1600) doctrine of divine middle knowledge. Opposed to Luther and Calvin's denial of human freedom, Molina would have been equally averse to recent revisionist views of divine providence which deny divine foreknowledge and celebrate God's taking risks.

Molina defines providence as God's ordering of things to their ends, either directly or mediately through secondary agents. Middle knowledge, together with Molina's doctrine of simultaneous concurrence, supplies the underpinnings of his doctrine of providence. According to the doctrine of middle knowledge, logically prior to his decree to create a world, God knows what any free creature he could create would freely do in any freedom-permitting circumstances God might place him in. Because the relevant subjunctive conditionals of the form *If some agent S were placed in circumstances C, then S would freely perform action A* are true or false logically prior to God's decree, even God in his omnipotence cannot bring it about that S would freely refrain from A if he were placed in C. By his middle knowledge God knows, in effect, what is the proper subclass of all logically possible worlds which it is feasible for him to actualize. By a free decision, God decrees to actualize one of those worlds which he knows to be feasible through his middle knowledge. In so doing he also decrees how he himself would act in any set of circumstances, so that subjunctive conditionals concerning divine free decisions become true coincidentally with the divine decree. Given God's free decision to actualize a world, God then possesses knowledge of all remaining propositions that are in fact true in the actual world, including future contingent propositions. God then concurs with the free decisions of creatures to bring about their effects in the world.

Aquinas had interpreted the notion of divine concurrence to mean that God acts on secondary causes in order to produce their actual operations, a view that came to be known as the doctrine of pre-motion. With regard to contingent acts of the will, this doctrine implied that the free decisions of creatures are produced by God's causing a person's will to turn itself this way or that. Molina rejects this interpretation of divine concurrence as utterly deterministic and incompatible with the existence of sin. Instead, he proposes to regard divine concurrence as simultaneous concurrence; that is to say, God acts, not *on*, but *with* the secondary cause to produce its effect. Thus, when a person freely wills to produce some effect, God concurs with that person's decision by also acting to produce that effect; but he does not act on the person's will to move it to its decision. In sinful decisions, God concurs by acting to produce the effect, but he is not responsible for the sinfulness of the act, since he did not move the creature's will to do it. Rather, out of his determination to allow human freedom, he merely permitted the decision to be made. In thus either willing or permitting everything that happens, God acts to produce every event in the actual world. Molinism thus effects a dramatic reconciliation between divine sovereignty and human freedom.

What objections might be raised against a Molinist account? Surveying the literature, one discovers that the detractors of Molinism tend not so much to criticize the Molinist doctrine of providence as to attack the concept of middle knowledge upon which it is predicated. These objections, however, have been repeatedly answered by defenders of middle knowledge. The most prominent of these is the so-called grounding objection, (on which see Craig 2001). What objection, then, might be raised, not to middle knowledge per se, but to a Molinist account of providence?

Perhaps the most serious objection to a Molinist theory of providence is that it is *too* successful in showing how God could sovereignly control a world of free creatures. For given that the circumstances C are non-determining, it must be a brute, contingent fact how S would choose in C. But then it is plausible that there are an indefinite number of circumstances C* which differ from C in imperceptible or causally irrelevant ways (for example, a stellar event in Alpha Centauri at the time of S's decision) in which S would choose differently than in C. So God, by placing S in one of these circumstances C*, could bring it about that S choose freely whatever God wishes without any deleterious impact upon God's providential plan.

What is the significance of this objection? It does nothing to undermine the Molinist account of providence as such. In particular it does not in any way undermine the freedom of the creatures in whatever circumstances they find themselves, for their choices are in every case causally undetermined. If a choice is freely made in C, then it would be freely made in C* which includes some causally irrelevant event not included in C. If God places S in C, then S's freedom is not compromised by the mere fact that had God placed S in C* instead, S would have chosen differently.

Rather, what the objection threatens to undermine is the theological utility of the doctrine of middle knowledge. For the distinction between broadly logically possible and feasible worlds becomes insignificant, since God can bring about whatever free creaturely choices he desires without detriment to his plan. The Molinist account of providence would be useless in explaining why apparently less than optimal states of affairs obtain; like the Calvinist, the Molinist would have to ascribe them to God's perfect will. The Molinist account would still enjoy the advantage of making room for creaturely freedom; but it would be of little help in explaining, for example, why evil exists.

The objection, however, is predicated upon a number of questionable assumptions. First, the argument seems to assume that one is dealing with events distributed by blind chance. But it is not by chance that S chooses A in C. So one must not think of S's free choices as distributed by chance across the class of circumstances. Quite the contrary, free choices are made for reasons. And that gives grounds for thinking that S's choices would not vary wildly in various C*, namely, the C* are indistinguishable from C, so that one's reasons for choosing A in C also hold for C*. (Empirical evidence for constancy across C*: just ask the relevant person whether he would have chosen differently had C* rather than C been his circumstances.)

Second, it assumes that the circumstances C mentioned in the counterfactual's antecedent are unlimited. But this is far from obvious. It is universally agreed that events later than the time of S's choice ought not to be included in C. Why not? The most evident answer is because events which are future at t can have no influence on S's situation at t and, hence, are just irrelevant to S's decision. But events which are sufficiently distant from S are just as irrelevant as future events even if those events are simultaneous with or even earlier than t. Only events which are connectable via a light signal to the event of S's decision seem to be relevant to S's choice. Events having a space-like separation from that event are as irrelevant as future events; indeed, special relativity theory holds that for some observers at S's location (those moving at near light speeds) these events *are* future at the time of S's choice. This suggests that only events in or on S's past light cone are properly part of C. Thus, the substitution of circumstances C* for C, where $C \subseteq C^*$, will not affect the truth of the counterfactual in question, since only C is relevant to its truth value.

Third, the objection assumes that imperceptible events included in S's past light cone can be altered without significant effect upon S's situation at t. But the lessons of both quantum theory and chaos theory have taught us that such an assumption is false. The imperceptible indeterminacy in the position of a cue ball on a billiard table is such that after only a dozen shots the indeterminacy in the ball's location has been magnified to the size of the entire table. Chaotic systems vary unpredictably with the tiniest perturbation. Certainly some events, say, in the very recent past far from S's location, might be alterable without significant impact on S's situation at t; but these will be finite in number, and it will be anybody's guess whether S would freely choose differently were one of them to be altered. The available alterations may fall far short of what is necessary for God's bringing about any desired free choice on S's part.

Finally, the objection assumes that God's concern is with S's choice alone. But God's concern is with a whole history of free creatures on into eternity future. Even if substituting C^* for C were sufficient for bringing about any free choice of S at t, that says nothing about the feasibility of actualizing a whole world of free creatures, a task which plausibly involves infinite complexity. It is then not at all implausible that the difference between broadly logically possible worlds and feasible worlds should become significant and dramatic.

Theologians have traditionally identified God's *providentia extraordinaria* with miracles. But a Molinist account of divine providence based on God's middle knowledge suggests a category of non-miraculous, special providence, which it will be helpful to distinguish. One has in mind here events which are the product of natural causes but whose context is such as to suggest a special divine intention with regard to their occurrence. For example, as the Israelites approach the Jordan River, a rockslide upstream blocks temporarily the water's flow, enabling them to cross into the Promised Land (Josh. 3: 14–17). By means of his middle knowledge, God can providentially order the world so that the natural causes of such events are, as it were, ready and waiting to produce such events at the propitious time, perhaps in answer to prayers which God knew would be offered. Of course, if such prayers were not to be offered, then God would have known this and so not arranged the natural causes, including human free volitions, to produce the special providential event. Events wrought by special providence are no more outside the course and capacity of nature than are events produced by God's ordinary providence, but the context of such events – such as their timing, their coincidental nature, and so forth – points to a special divine intention to bring them about. Such events seem to deserve more appropriately than miracles the appellation *providentia extraordinaria*.

If, then, we distinguish miracles from both God's *providentia ordinaria* and *extraordinaria*, how should we characterize miracles? Since the dawning of modernity, miracles have been widely understood to be 'violations of the laws of nature.' In his *Philosophical Dictionary* article 'Miracles,' for example, Voltaire states that according to accepted usage, 'A miracle is the violation of mathematical, divine, immutable, eternal laws' and is therefore a contradiction. Voltaire is in fact quite right that such a definition is a contradiction, but this ought to have led him to conclude, not that miracles can thus be defined out of existence, but that the customary definition is defective. Indeed, an examination of the chief competing schools of thought concerning the notion of a natural law in fact reveals that on each theory the concept of a violation of a natural law is incoherent (Bilynskyj 1982).

Rather, a miracle – in distinction from both God's ordinary and special providence – involves God's acting to cause an event in the sequence of natural events in the absence of any secondary cause of that event. A miracle would thus seem to be an event which would not have been produced by the natural causes operative at a certain time and place. Whether an event is a miracle is therefore relative to a time and place. Given the natural causes operative at a certain time and place, for example, rain may be naturally inevitable but on another occasion miraculous. Of course, some events, say, the resurrection of Jesus, may be absolutely miraculous in that they are at every time and place beyond the productive capacity of natural causes. Since blind natural causes at a specific time and place would have produced an event if they could have, we may speak of miracles, not as violations of the laws of nature, but as naturally impossible events, events which at certain times and places cannot be produced by the relevant natural causes.

A difficulty for such a conception is raised by certain proponents of so-called Intelligent Design who insist that if miracles are so defined in terms of 'counterfactual substitution,' then divine action to cause events in the series of natural causes need not involve miracles. William Dembski argues that an unembodied intelligence may inject information into the natural world with a zero input of energy by exploiting quantum indeterminacy, leading in turn through various means of amplification to massive effects on the macroscopic level which would bear unmistakable evidence of intelligent action (Dembski 2004: 147, cf. 179, 185, 264). For example, a quantum mechanical device might spit out indeterministically a sequence composed of zeroes and ones; were the bit string produced by this device to yield an English text-file in ASCII code that delineates the cure for cancer, we should have undeniable evidence of intelligent action. Every bit can be accounted for in terms of an irreducibly chance-driven process, and yet the arrangement of the bits leaves no doubt about the input of intelligence. There is no counterfactual substitution involved – no disposition or tendency of natural causes which has been overridden by divine intervention – and, hence, no miracle. Yet were God so to act, he would be the cause of certain events in the series of natural events for which there are no secondary causes.

Even on this scenario, however, counterfactual substitution is still involved on the macroscopic level. For the macroscopic event would not, in all probability, have occurred were the natural causes left alone. Indeed, given Dembski's bound on small probabilities, one can truly say that the event could not have occurred. That makes it a naturally impossible event, or a miracle. Thus, for example, Jesus' turning water into wine would still count as a miracle in the sense of counterfactual substitution, even if no counterfactual substitution took place on the microscopic level. Moreover, Dembski presupposes without justification that quantum indeterminacy is ontic rather than epistemic. On a Bohmian interpretation, indeterminacy may prevent our knowledge of the causal conditions determining some event, but those conditions are present nonetheless, so that divine action in the sequence of quantum events would involve counterfactual substitution. Given the obscurity of the traditional

Copenhagen interpretation of quantum mechanics, a comprehensively deterministic account may well be preferable.

Now the question is, what could conceivably transform an event that is naturally impossible into a real historical event? Clearly, the answer is the personal God of theism. For if a transcendent, personal God exists, then he could cause events in the universe that could not be produced by causes within the universe. Given a God who created the universe, who conserves the world in being, and who is capable of acting freely, miracles are evidently possible. Only to the extent that one has good grounds for believing atheism to be true could one be rationally justified in denying the possibility of miracles. In this light, arguments for the impossibility of miracles based upon defining them as violations of the laws of nature are vacuous.

Nonetheless, contemporary theologians, particularly those engaged in the dialogue between science and theology, have displayed a puzzling antipathy toward the view that God has acted miraculously in nature. Their favored view tends to be theistic complementarianism, according to which science is in principle capable of providing a complete and adequate explanation of everything that happens in the world solely in terms of natural causes. Such thinkers are eager to affirm God's action as a primary cause in conserving the universe in being but reject his interposition in the series of secondary causes in the universe. If they do admit God's interposition in the series of secondary events, they limit God's action to the production of quantum effects permitted by the Uncertainty Principle. Theirs is a discreet deity, a sort of God-of-the-(quantum)-gaps who covers himself with indeterminacy.

Theistic complementarians do not seem to realize, however, the degree to which they have rendered themselves vulnerable to the full force of atheistic arguments offered by scientific naturalists such as Adolf Grünbaum to the effect that conservation laws alone serve to explain the enduring existence of the universe from one moment to the next, so that divine conservation is not just unnecessary but precluded (see Vaughan and Dacey 2003: 152; Grünbaum 2004; cf. Larmer 2005). Divine creation and conservation require the rejection of theistic complementarianism, thereby opening the door for miracles as well. Moreover, Dembski's scenario remains a serious problem for complementarians' *deus absconditus*, for, as Dembski illustrates, divine actions on the quantum level can yield effects which will be unmistakable evidence of intelligent action on God's part. In such a case nothing has been gained by trying to confine divine action to quantum gaps.

The more interesting question is whether the identification of any event as a miracle is possible. Hume's celebrated argument against miracles is now widely recognized as demonstrably fallacious (see decisive critique by Earman 2000). The key to detecting a genuine miracle will be the religio-historical context in which the event occurs. Bilynskyj (1982: 222) provides the following criteria for identifying some event E as a miracle:

1 The evidence for the occurrence of E is at least as good as it is for other acceptable but unusual events similarly distant in time and space from the point of the inquiry.

2 An account of the natures and/or powers of the causally relevant natural agents, such that they could account for E, would be clumsy and ad hoc.

3 There is no evidence except the inexplicability of E for one or more natural agents which could produce E.

4 There is some justification for a supernatural explanation of E, independent of the inexplicability of E.

The availability of adequate criteria shifts the discussion to the historical question of whether sufficient evidence for any particular miracle exists. This question can be answered only on a case-by-case basis.

See also Thomas Aquinas (Chapter 12), Omniscience (Chapter 24), Omnipotence (Chapter 25), The cosmological argument (Chapter 32), The teleological argument (Chapter 33), Resurrection (Chapter 52), Miracles (Chapter 55), Prayer (Chapter 57).

References

Barrow, J. and F. Tipler (1986) *The Anthropic Cosmological Principle*, Oxford: Clarendon Press.

Bilynskyj, S. (1982) 'God, nature, and the concept of miracle,' Ph.D. dissertation, University of Notre Dame, Notre Dame, IN.

Craig, W. L. (2001) 'Middle knowledge, truth-makers, and the grounding objection,' *Faith and Philosophy* 18: 337–52.

—— (forthcoming) 'Cosmology and naturalism,' in B. Gordon and W. Dembski (eds) *The Nature of Nature: Examining the Role of Naturalism in Science*.

Dembski, W. (2004) *The Design Revolution*, Downers Grove, IL: InterVarsity.

Earman, J. (2000) *Hume's Abject Failure: The Argument against Miracles*, Oxford: Oxford University Press.

Grünbaum, A. (2004) 'The poverty of theistic cosmology,' *British Journal for the Philosophy of Science* 55: 561–614.

Larmer, R. (2005) 'Theistic complementarianism and Ockham's Razor,' *Philosophia Christi* ns 7: 501–12.

Vaughn, L. and A. Dacey (2003) *The Case for Humanism*, Lanham, MD: Rowman & Littlefield.

Further reading

Copan, P. and W. L. Craig (2004) *Creation out of Nothing: A Biblical, Philosophical, and Scientific Exploration*, Grand Rapids, MI; Leicester: Baker Academic/Apollos. (A thorough defense of the doctrine of *creatio ex nihilo*; includes detailed exegesis of biblical and extra-biblical texts, along with discussion of metaphysical arguments for the past's finitude and a summary of the physical evidence for the beginning of the universe.)

Dembski, W. (2004) *The Design Revolution*, Downers Grove, IL: InterVarsity. (A defense of the inference to a Designer of the universe which includes a very nuanced treatment of various ways in which God's action in the world might be construed.)

Earman, J. (2000) *Hume's Abject Failure: The Argument against Miracles*, Oxford: Oxford University Press. (A devastating critique of Hume's famous argument against miracles from a leading philosopher of science; includes excerpts from largely forgotten critiques by Hume's contemporaries which reveal that they already understood where the fallacies in Hume's objection lay.)

Flint, T. (1998) *Divine Providence*, Ithaca, NY: Cornell University Press. (One of the foremost philosophical defenders of Molinism compares different accounts of God's control of the world and argues for the superiority of an account based on divine middle knowledge.)

Larmer, R. (2005) 'Theistic complementarianism and Ockham's Razor,' *Philosophia Christi* ns 7: 501–12. (Incisive critique of the easy complementarianism that dominates theological thought about God's action in the world.)

von Wachter, D. (2003) 'Modality, causality, and God,' D.Phil. thesis, University of Oxford. (A doctoral thesis supervised by Richard Swinburne by a rising German philosopher and theologian exploring the nature of God's causal relations with the world, including creation, conservation, and intervention.)

Part V
ARGUMENTS FOR GOD'S EXISTENCE

31
THE ONTOLOGICAL ARGUMENT

E. J. Lowe

The ontological argument is an a priori argument for God's existence which was first formulated in the eleventh century by St Anselm, was famously defended by René Descartes in the seventeenth century, and still has important modern advocates, such as Alvin Plantinga. It has also had equally famous critics, such as Immanuel Kant in the eighteenth century and Gottlob Frege and Bertrand Russell in the nineteenth to twentieth centuries. To say that the argument is an a priori one is just to say that it is a deductive argument from premises whose truth is deemed to be knowable without recourse to empirical evidence of any kind. The argument has received many different formulations in the course of its long history, but St Anselm's original version in his *Proslogion* of 1077/8 (chs. 2 and 3: see Charlesworth 1965) can be reconstructed in something like the following way:

1 God is, by definition, a being than which none greater can be conceived.
2 A being than which none greater can be conceived exists at least in the mind.
3 It is greater to exist in reality than to exist only in the mind.
4 Therefore, God – a being than which none greater can be conceived – exists not only in the mind but also in reality.

The premises here need some elucidation. Premise (1) is supposed to be a conceptual truth. It tells us that the concept of God is the concept of a greatest possible being – a being so great that it is impossible to conceive of a greater being, or, in other words, a being of maximal greatness. This is a plausible claim, certainly concerning the traditional Christian conception of God as a being who is omnipotent, omniscient, omnibenevolent, and the creator of all things. Even so, the idea of maximal greatness may appear a little puzzling to the modern mind, because it seems to imply that there are *degrees of being*, as though being lies on a scale with a maximum at one end and a minimum at the other. And yet modern philosophers tend to assume that being is simply an all-or-nothing affair: either something exists, or it does not, and 'exists' means exactly the same as it applies to any sort of entity.

However, this modern view is not incontrovertible, and for many centuries philosophers have thought differently about existence. In particular, traditional metaphysics, with its roots in the thought of Aristotle and his medieval followers, the Scholastics, holds that entities belonging to different ontological categories do not all exist in exactly the same way. For example, it holds that entities in the category of *substance* have a more basic kind of existence than entities in the category of *quality* or *mode*, because entities of the latter sort depend for their existence on substances, whereas the reverse is not the case (see Lowe 1998: ch. 6). Thus it would be said that the shape and color of an individual substance – of an individual animal, let us say, such as a horse – depend for their existence on that individual, precisely because they are essentially *its* qualities and so cannot exist separately from it. But it would also be said that even within the most fundamental category of substance, there are degrees of being, because there are degrees of existential dependence. Consider, for instance, something such as a pile or heap of rocks. This is clearly an individual thing or substance, rather than a quality or mode of any such thing. Even so, the pile evidently depends for its existence on the individual rocks that make it up – whereas they do not, conversely, depend for their existence on it. In that sense, the pile is a more dependent being than is any of the rocks that compose it. However, the rocks in turn depend for *their* existence on other things, most obviously the various mineral particles of which they themselves are composed.

It would seem that *all* material substances are, very plausibly, dependent beings in this sense, even if some should turn out to be simple substances, not composed of anything further. For it seems that they are all *contingent* beings, where a contingent being is one that does not exist of necessity. Consider, for example, a single elementary particle of physics, such as a certain individual electron, e, which is, according to current physical theory, not composed of anything more fundamental. Surely, e might not have existed at all. But could e have been the only thing to exist? We might think that we can imagine a world in which all that exists is this single electron, e. But, in fact, modern physics would repudiate this idea as nonsensical. Electrons are not really to be thought of as being 'particles' in a commonsense way, but are, rather, best thought of as quantized states of a space-permeating field; and according to this way of thinking of them, it really makes no sense to envisage one of them as having an existence that is wholly independent of anything else.

However, even though it makes no sense to think of an electron, or indeed any 'material substance,' as having such a wholly independent existence, we clearly *can* make sense of the idea of a being that does have such an existence: a being that depends for its existence, in any sense whatever, on absolutely nothing other than itself. This, indeed, would seem to be the core of the idea of a *maximally great* being. Without presuming that such a being does exist, we can surely affirm that such a being *could* exist. And this, in effect, is what premise (2) of the argument is affirming. So let us turn to that premise.

Premise (2) states that 'A being than which none greater can be conceived exists at least in the mind.' In other words, we can coherently think of there existing such a being, one which has an absolutely independent existence. A corollary seems to be, as I have just remarked, that such a being *could* exist: it has at least possible existence, even if it does not actually exist. The reference to 'the mind' in premise (2) suggests that something of a purely psychological nature is being affirmed by it, but this is misleading. The ontological argument is not supposed to be about our powers of thought or imagination, but about whether a being of a certain kind could and indeed does exist. Understood in this way, premise (2) seems to be fairly compelling. That being so, the cogency of the ontological argument in its present formulation turns on the status of premise (3), which affirms that 'It is greater to exist in reality than to exist only in the mind.' This premise, too, needs some unpacking. The idea behind it can be cashed out in the following way. I have already said that it seems plausible to suppose, in line with premise (2), that a maximally great being could exist. But suppose that such a being is a merely possible being, that is to say, a being that could exist, but does not actually exist, and therefore does not exist *of necessity*. To suppose this is to suppose that a maximally great being could be a *contingent* being.

However, expressed this way, the supposition looks decidedly suspect. For we have already seen that it is very plausible to suppose that all contingent beings are, in one way or another, dependent beings, and hence not 'maximally great,' in the sense of having an absolutely independent existence. In other words, a supposedly maximally great being that did not exist of necessity and so also *in actuality* ('in reality') would not really be a maximally great being. This, in effect, is what premise (3) can be construed as saying.

Of course, this is not the only possible way of construing (3): it could be construed instead as saying, merely, that anything that actually exists is, for that reason alone, a 'greater' being than anything that does not actually exist but merely could exist. Indeed, that is what (3) more literally seems to be saying. But understood in that way (3) is not at all plausible. Clearly, given that we are now interpreting the notion of degrees of being in terms of degrees of existential *dependency*, it is rather implausible to contend that no merely possible being is less dependent in nature than any actually existent being. Consider, for instance, some merely possible material substance, such as an individual horse that might have existed but does not in fact exist, and contrast this with an actually existing quality or mode of an actually existing horse. Surely, the actually existing quality is an entity that is more of a dependent being in its nature than is the merely possible horse: for the latter is (or would be) a *substance* whereas the former is merely a *quality*, and all qualities are subordinate to substances in their degree of dependency.

Of course, if one thought of possible existence as being a lesser (because, presumably, more dependent) kind of *existence* than actual existence, then indeed one might suppose that even the most dependent actually existing entity is less dependent than the least dependent merely possible entity. But that way of thinking is very arguably confused. To say that something could exist ('has possible existence') is, plausibly, not to assign to it a kind of existence, but merely to qualify or modify, in a certain manner, a claim concerning the existence of that thing. For example, when I say that the golden mountain could exist, I am not assigning to it a shadowy sort of existence: indeed, I am not affirming that it does exist at all, in any sense whatever. Rather, I am retreating from any such existence claim to a weaker claim: one that is entailed by, but does not entail, the claim that it exists.

Let me now try to reformulate the ontological argument, as it was set out earlier, with the foregoing elucidations in mind. It now comes out as follows:

1* God is, by definition, a maximally great being – that is, a being that is absolutely independent of anything else for its existence.

2* A maximally great being *could* exist.

3* A maximally great being could not have merely possible existence – it would have to exist of necessity and so also in actuality.

4* Therefore, God – a maximally great being – does actually exist.

Is this a sound argument? That is to say, are its premises true and does its conclusion follow deductively from those premises? On the face of it, it would seem so. Of course, one might have doubts as to whether the being whose existence is affirmed in the conclusion, (4*), must have *all* of the various divine attributes traditionally assigned to God, such as omniscience and omnibenevolence. But let's set aside that difficulty for present purposes. Even without assuming that the argument establishes the existence of the traditional Christian God in this sense, it is a remarkable enough argument.

Before I proceed, let me say something concerning Descartes's version of the ontological argument, which appears in his *Fifth Meditation* of 1641 (see Descartes 1984). Although Descartes did not formulate the argument in anything much like the way that Anselm did, he did formulate it in a way that seems reasonably close to the version that I have just presented above. Descartes maintained that, because God is by definition a 'perfect' being, *eternal and necessary existence* belongs to the nature or 'essence' of God, just as, for example, having internal angles whose sum is equal to that of two right angles belongs to the nature of a Euclidean triangle. From this Descartes inferred that God must indeed *exist*, just as we may infer, with regard to any (Euclidean) triangle, that its internal angles add up to two right angles.

He anticipated the objection that, in the case of a triangle, we can only infer from the nature of the triangle that its internal angles have this sum on the supposition that the triangle does indeed *exist*, and thus that, likewise, we can only infer from the nature of God that God exists, on the supposition that *he* exists – thereby making the ontological argument implicitly circular. But Descartes rejected this objection as spurious, apparently with good reason. For a triangle is only a contingent being: it is something which, given its nature, *could* fail to exist, and which consequently only has any properties at all on the supposition that it *does* exist; for, or so it would clearly seem, a non-existent thing cannot actually possess any properties. But what is being claimed concerning God is that he is, by nature, a *necessary* being; one 'whose essence includes its existence.'

This is a good point to consider some of the other well-known objections to the ontological argument in its various formulations. One of the oldest is the 'perfect island' objection that is due to the monk Gaunilo, an early critic of Anselm to whom Anselm himself replied. The idea is this. The ontological argument looks suspiciously like a formula to 'define into existence' pretty well anything we like. Consider the perfect island. This would not only have, let us say, exactly the right amount of sun and shady palm trees, cool running streams of fresh water, delightful breezes, green pastures, and so forth, but also, of course, it would *exist*: for it is surely more perfect ('greater') to exist in reality than merely to exist in the mind. Who would not rate an *existent* island of the above description more highly than a merely imagined island of that description? But it is plainly absurd, wishful thinking to suppose, on these grounds, that such an island really does exist. The same, it will be said, applies to the ontological argument: it is merely an exercise in wishful thinking.

However, the objection is clearly spurious and unfair. When we talk about God as being, by nature, a 'perfect' or 'maximally great' being, we are using these terms in a quite specific technical sense, to imply that God is, by definition, a being whose existence is absolutely independent of anything else. By contrast, in talking of a 'perfect' island, we are talking about a purely contingent being of a certain kind – for all islands, being material objects, are by their nature contingent beings – which has certain humanly pleasing features in the highest possible degree. Clearly, from the mere fact that such an island could exist, we cannot infer that it does exist. But the whole point about God, according to the ontological argument, is that he is conceived – and coherently *can* be conceived – to be a being who, in virtue of being maximally great by nature, has *necessary* existence and who consequently *does* exist.

But perhaps the best-known objection of all to the ontological argument – an objection that is commonly thought to deal it the killer blow – is the Kantian objection that 'existence is not a predicate' (*Kantian* because it first appears in Kant's *Critique of Pure Reason* of 1781; see Kant 1933: 500–7). This objection is usually cashed out in the following way. It is an error, or so it is claimed, to suppose that the verb 'exist' functions, as many other verbs and verb phrases do – for example, the verbs 'run' and 'eat' and the verb phrases 'is red' and 'is square' – to attribute some special *property* to an object or objects. Accordingly, when we list the properties of anything, we should certainly not include *existence* among them. As one of the original critics – Pierre Gassendi – of Descartes's version of the ontological argument urged, existence is not so much a *property* of any thing as it is that without which something cannot have *any* properties. And as Kant himself put it, the notion of existence adds nothing to the concept of a thing: to conceive of an *existent* table of a certain color, shape, size, and weight is no different from merely conceiving of a table with just those properties. After all, if the concept of *an existent F* were different from that simply of *an F*, then it seems that I could not conceive of *an F* and bring *just such a thing* into existence: for what I would bring into existence would have to be *an existent F*; and this, allegedly, is not precisely the sort of thing that I was conceiving of when I was merely conceiving of *an F*. But that is surely absurd: I can, surely, conceive of an (as yet nonexistent) table and bring *exactly such a thing* into existence.

In modern times, in the hands of such logicians as Frege and Russell, this sort of point has been made in terms of the proper way to translate talk about existence into the formal language of first-order predicate logic, namely, by means of the so-called *existential quantifier*, '∃' (see, e.g., Frege 1953: par. 53 and Russell 1919: 203). In this language, 'Dogs exist,' for instance, is translated as '$(\exists x)(x$ is a dog),' which can be re-expressed in logician's English as 'There is something, x, such that x is a dog.' According to the Frege–Russell view of existence, 'There is something, x, such that $x \ldots$' is, technically speaking, a *second-level predicate*, used not to predicate a property of any object or objects, but rather to predicate a rather special second-level property of first-level properties – where a first-level property is a property that can be had by objects, such as redness or squareness. Thus, on this view, to say that dogs exist is just to say that the first-level property of *doghood*, or *being a dog*, has the second-level property of *having at least one instance*, that is, of being possessed by at least one object. Of course, 'Dogs exist' is a general proposition, as opposed to the singular proposition 'God exists.' However, there is a standard way of translating a singular proposition of the form 'a exists,' where 'a' is a singular term (such as a proper name), into the formal language of first-order predicate logic; namely, as '$(\exists x)(x = a)$,' that is, in logician's English, as 'There is something, x, such that x is identical with a.' So, on this view, to say that *God exists* is just to say that *the property of being identical with God has at least one (and, of course, only one) instance.*

But how is all this, even supposing that it is correct, supposed to bear upon the ontological argument? Well, it does so in the following way. In one version of the ontological argument (one that is very close to Descartes's), it may be expressed thus:

5 God is, by definition, a perfect being and thus a being that possesses all the divine perfections.
6 One of the divine perfections is eternal and necessary existence.
7 Hence, God possesses eternal and necessary existence and so, *a fortiori*, possesses existence.
8 Therefore, God exists.

The error in the argument is then supposed to be that it treats eternal and necessary existence, and thus also existence *simpliciter*, as being one of the divine attributes or properties, alongside such properties as omniscience, omnipotence, and omnibenevolence. But, according to the Frege–Russell account of existence, existence is not a first-level property – a property of objects – but only a second-level property: it is a property of first-level properties.

Thus, on this view, what we affirm, effectively, when we affirm that God exists is that all of the divine attributes are in fact instantiated, indeed, that collectively they are uniquely instantiated, by just one object. But we cannot regard eternal and necessary existence as one of these attributes, because to do so is to make a *logical* error: the error of treating a second-level property as if it were a first-level property. Hence, there is no sound logical argument from a definition of God as a perfect being, together with a list of the divine perfections, to the conclusion that God does in fact exist. We can no more 'define God into existence' than we can define *anything* into existence.

However, it may be objected that nothing in the foregoing formulation of the ontological argument implies that either existence or eternal and necessary existence is a 'first-level property.' For nothing in that formulation of the argument presumes that a 'divine perfection' must be a divine *attribute* or *property*, in the way that omniscience or omnipotence are. It is true that line (7) speaks of God 'possessing' eternal and necessary existence, and indeed of 'possessing' existence. But it needn't be presumed that 'possession' in this sense has to be thought of as a relation between an object and a 'first-level' property. In short, it is far from clear that the Frege–Russell account of existence does anything to undermine the ontological argument if it is carefully and appropriately formulated. Furthermore, it is in any case very much open to question whether Frege and Russell were in fact correct in their account of existence (see McGinn 2000: ch. 2). On the face of it, their account is really rather counterintuitive and not altogether easy to comprehend. Suppose, with Frege and Russell, we take the statement 'Dogs exist' to be expressing the proposition that *the property of doghood has at least one instance*. What, exactly, are we to understand by the notion of a (first-level) property's having at least one instance? Isn't this really just to say that at least one object exists that possesses the property in question? In other words, isn't it the case that the logician's notion of a property's having at least one instance, far from serving to explain the notion of existence, needs to be explained by appeal to that very notion?

There is much to be said in favor of the view that the notion of existence is a basic or primitive one, which cannot be explained in terms of any more fundamental notion or notions. This is not to say that we should regard existence as being a 'first-level property.' Maybe we shouldn't regard it as a property at all. After all, properties themselves are entities that do, or at least can, exist: but do we seriously and literally want to say that existence itself exists? Very arguably, we should not reify existence, that is, treat it as being, itself, an entity of any kind. But, in any case – as I have already indicated – in formulating the ontological argument, we do not have to presume a particular view regarding what existence is, or is not. Contrary to the followers of Frege and Russell, we do not need to presume that it is a first-level property. Indeed, we do not need to presume that existence itself *is* anything at all, in the sense of being an entity belonging to some specific ontological category. The Frege–Russell objection – and the Kantian objection from which it descends – is just a red herring with no real bearing on the soundness of the ontological argument.

As for the charge that the ontological argument illicitly attempts to 'define God into existence,' perhaps we should reflect on the following fact. No one objects to the claim that the *nonexistence* of certain things follows from their definition: that, for example, the nonexistence of *squircles* follows from the definition of a squircle as *a plane figure that is both square and circular*. If definitions can have implications regarding nonexistence, why should they not have implications regarding existence too? The worry might be that, if we allowed this, a priori existence claims would be just too easy to make. But why should that be supposed? Only if one thought that definitions are just arbitrary concoctions of the human mind. Some definitions might be like that, perhaps – and it would certainly be dangerous to suppose that these could have positive existential implications. But, very arguably, the definition of God is far from being an arbitrary concoction of the human mind, any more than the definition of a circle is.

We need to distinguish, in this context, between *real* definitions and purely *verbal* definitions (see Fine 1994). A purely verbal definition is typically stipulative or conventional in character, consisting in a rule which allows us to substitute one word or phrase for another, as, for example, 'bachelor' may be defined as 'unmarried man.' A *real* definition, by contrast, attempts to characterize, as perspicuously as possible, the nature or essence of some actual or possible being. 'Essence' is simply a word standardly used to translate a phrase of Aristotle's whose more literal translation is something like 'the what it is to be' or 'the what it would be to be.' Thus, a characterization of the essence of a geometrical figure, such as a circle, is a perspicuous way of saying *what it is, or would be, for something to be a circle*. Here is one such way, standardly found in textbooks of geometry: to be a circle is to be a closed line all of the points in which are equidistant from another given point (the centre of the circle). Here is another: to be a circle is to be the locus or path of a point moving continuously at a fixed distance around another point. These 'real' definitions tell us what circles are or, at least, would be. Similarly, a real definition of God tells us what God is or would be.

But according to Anselm, Descartes, and other adherents of the ontological argument, the real definition of God is distinctive and remarkable, in that it tells us that what God is or would be is something that could not fail to exist. And that, in their view, is why we are rationally compelled to conclude that, indeed, he does exist. All we need to come to this conclusion rationally is to grasp the real definition of God, that is, understand what God is or would be. Actually, we do not even need to *fully* grasp what God is or would be – which is just as well, since this is probably beyond the capabilities of finite intelligences like ours – but just to grasp that, at the very least, he is or would be a maximally great being. This is why Anselm, quoting the biblical text (Ps. 14: 1; 53: 1), remarks that 'The fool has said in his heart that God does not exist.' His point would seem to be this. Either the Fool does grasp, to a sufficient extent, the real definition of God, but nonetheless denies that God exists, in which case he is indeed a fool, for he thereby displays a failure of rationality. Or else the Fool does not grasp, to a sufficient extent, the real definition of God, in which case he is likewise a fool; he thinks that he understands what he is saying in denying that God exists and that he is justified in that denial, but does not really understand it and so is not really justified, so that in this case too he displays a failure of rationality.

If, as I am suggesting, the ontological argument is a sound one, how can we formulate it most perspicuously for a modern audience? Here we may usefully draw upon Alvin Plantinga's way of presenting the argument (Plantinga 1974: ch. 10), using the language of 'possible worlds' and modern modal logic: the logic of possibility and necessity. Here is how it may be done along these lines.

9 God is, by definition, a maximally great being and thus a being whose existence is necessary rather than merely contingent.

10 God, so defined, *could* exist; in other words, he *does* exist in *some* possible world.

11 Suppose that *w* is a possible world in which God, so defined, exists: then it is true in *w*, at least, that God exists there and, being God, exists there as a *necessary* being.

12 But a necessary being is one which, by definition, exists in *every* possible world if it exists in *any* possible world.

13 Hence, the God who exists as a necessary being in *w* is a being that exists in *every* possible world, including *this*, the actual world.

14 Therefore, God exists in the actual world; he actually exists.

There are, of course, various queries that one could raise about this version of the argument. Are we, for example, really entitled to suppose that God, so defined, *could* exist – that he exists in at least some possible world? Might it not be the case that the real definition of God harbors some deep-seated contradiction, rendering his existence impossible? Perhaps so: after all, we should not be dogmatic in matters of fundamental metaphysics, but should always be prepared to acknowledge, if need be, the fallibility of our rational intellects. On the other hand, there does not appear to be any such contradiction; so the burden of proof surely lies with the opponent of the ontological argument to try to show that there is. Although we should not be dogmatic, neither should we be unduly skeptical. We should put trust in our rational capacities unless and until we find good reason to doubt them; and even then, of course, we cannot abandon trust in them altogether, for we must at least be confident that we have indeed found a good reason to doubt them.

Another worry might be this: are we really entitled to suppose that, even if there could be a maximally great being – a being that depended on absolutely nothing else for its existence – there could be only one such being? This is a worry about the provable *uniqueness* of God. To this worry it is less easy to find a simple and compelling answer. Even so, if this were the only weakness in the ontological argument, it would still be a remarkably important argument.

Finally, what are we to say in answer to those – let us call them the 'metaphysical nihilists' – who claim that *there might have been nothing rather than something*? If they are correct, then, of course, God cannot possibly exist. But then, doesn't this mean that the burden of proof lies with the metaphysical nihilists to show that God – a maximally great being – cannot possibly exist? For unless they can show this, what entitles them to be so confident that, indeed, nothing at all need have existed – that *there might have been absolutely nothing*?

See also Immanuel Kant (Chapter 14), Eternity (Chapter 27), Goodness (Chapter 28), The cosmological argument (Chapter 32), Problems with the concept of God (Chapter 38).

References

Charlesworth, M. J. (1965) *St Anselm's Proslogion*, Oxford: Clarendon Press.

Descartes, R. (1984) [1641] *The Philosophical Writings of Descartes*, Vol. II, trans. J. Cottingham, R. Stoothoof and D. Murdoch, Cambridge: Cambridge University Press.

Fine, K. (1994) 'Essence and modality,' in J. E. Tomberlin (ed.) *Philosophical Perspectives, 8: Logic and Language*, Atascadero, CA: Ridgeview Publishing.

Frege, G. (1953) *The Foundations of Arithmetic* [*Die Grundlagen der Arithmetik*, 1884], trans. J. L. Austin, 2nd edn, Oxford: Blackwell.

Kant, I. (1933) [1781] *Critique of Pure Reason*, trans. N. K. Smith, corrected edn, London: Macmillan.

Lowe, E. J. (1998) *The Possibility of Metaphysics: Substance, Identity, and Time*, Oxford: Clarendon Press.

McGinn, C. (2000) *Logical Properties: Identity, Existence, Predication, Necessity, Truth*, Oxford: Clarendon Press.

Plantinga, A. (1974) *The Nature of Necessity*, Oxford: Clarendon Press.

Russell, B. (1919) *Introduction to Mathematical Philosophy*, London: Allen & Unwin.

Further reading

Millican, P. (2004) 'The one fatal flaw in Anselm's argument,' *Mind* 113: 437–76. (An overview of Anselm's version of the ontological argument and the many objections that have been raised against it.)

Nolan, L. (2005) 'The Ontological Argument as an exercise in Cartesian therapy,' *Canadian Journal of Philosophy* 35: 521–62. (A well-informed and original interpretation of Descartes's conception of the purpose of the ontological argument.)

32

THE COSMOLOGICAL ARGUMENT

David S. Oderberg

A brief history of cosmological arguments

There is no such thing as *the* cosmological argument. Rather, there are several arguments that all proceed from facts or alleged facts concerning causation, change, motion, contingency, or finitude in respect of the universe as a whole or processes within it. From them, and from general principles said to govern them, one is led to deduce or infer as highly probable the existence of a *cause* of the universe (as opposed, say, to a *designer* or a *source of value*). Such arguments have a venerable history. A cosmological argument from heavenly motion to a 'world soul' is found in Plato's *Laws*, bk. 10. This kind of argument is given extended elaboration and defense by Aristotle, both in the *Physics* (bks. 7–8) and the *Metaphysics* (bk. 12/lambda), where he argues for an 'unmoved mover' from the existence of motion within the cosmos (again, primarily astronomical).

Cosmological arguments abound in medieval Arabic philosophy. There are arguments to the existence of a necessary cause of the universe from the existence of contingent beings (due to the *falsafa* ('philosophy') scholars, a school heavily influenced by Greek thought) and arguments to the existence of a first cause of the universe from the temporal finitude of the universe (due to the *kalam* ('discourse') scholars, a rival school of more traditional Qur'ānic theology) (Craig 1980: ch. 3). Defenders of the contingency argument include al-Farabi/Abu Nasr (*c*.870–950), Ibn Sina/Avicenna (980–1037), and Ibn Rushd/Averroes (1126–98). Supporters of what is now known as the kalam cosmological argument include al-Kindi (*c*.801/5–873) and al-Ghazālī/Algazel (1058–1111).

In Jewish philosophy, the figure standing head and shoulders above the rest is Rabbi Moses ben Maimon/Maimonides/Rambam (1135/8–1204). He proposed an elaborate form of Aristotle's unmoved or 'prime' mover argument, based on an Aristotelian conception of the motion of the heavens, concluding: 'This Prime Motor of the sphere is God, praised be His name!' (Maimonides 1956: pt. II, ch. I). He also gave arguments from the existence of change and from contingency, among others.

Both Maimonides and the Islamic philosophers (and, needless to say, Aristotle) had a profound influence on Thomas Aquinas (1224/5–74). Of his celebrated Five Ways of proving the existence of God, the first three are cosmological: the first is based on the observation of motion or change; the second on that of causation; and the third on contingency (Aquinas 1920a: q.2; 1955: ch. 13). Whilst Aquinas, ever faithful to Aristotle, followed Maimonides in criticizing the kalam argument for the temporal finitude of the universe, his great contemporary Bonaventure (1221–74) supported it in his *Commentary on the Sentences* (bk. 2, 1. 1. 1. 2. 1–6).

Cosmological arguments, like all arguments for the existence of God, suffered their vicissitudes from the early modern period and on into contemporary thought. John Locke (1632-1704) gave a brief statement and defense of the kalam argument in his *Essay Concerning Human Understanding* (1689) (Locke 1975: 620; IV. 10.3). Samuel Clarke (1705) famously defended the argument from contingency in his *Discourse Concerning the Being and Attributes of God* (Clarke 1998). On the other hand, both David Hume (in 1779) and Immanuel Kant (in 1781-7) launched fierce attacks on cosmological arguments in general, from which even now most philosophers do not think they have recovered (Hume 1948: IX; Kant 1933: 507–14, A603/B631–A614/B642).

Modern defenders of the argument from contingency have included Richard Taylor (1992), Robert Koons (1997), Richard Gale and Alexander Pruss (1999), and Richard Swinburne (2004). William Rowe (1998), though a critic, is sympathetic. By far the most prominent defender of the kalam argument has been William Lane Craig (Craig 1979; Craig and Smith 1993). Opponents of one or more varieties of cosmological argument have included: Bertrand Russell (especially contingency; see Hick 1964); J. L. Mackie (all versions: see Mackie 1982, ch. 5); Paul Edwards (contingency and causation: in Burrill 1967: I, sect. C); and Quentin Smith (for the kalam argument, see Craig and Smith 1993).

Thomistic arguments from motion and causation

The First and Second Ways of Aquinas encapsulate the kinds of argument against infinite causal regresses that go back to Aristotle. What is remarkable about them is that they *assume* the infinite temporal duration of the universe. Aquinas echoes Maimonides' statement that 'even if we were to admit the eternity of the universe, we could by any of these methods prove the existence of God' (Maimonides 1956: II. 1). Dialectically the point is very important, since many objectors to cosmological arguments claim that if the universe is temporally infinite, this obviates the need for a first mover.

We observe the existence of objects that move, change, and come into existence. But whatever is changed is changed by another (let us, for simplicity, include motion within change). And whatever is caused to exist is caused to exist by another. But this series of changes or causes cannot be infinite. Hence there must be a first source of change, a first cause, that is itself not changed by anything else or caused by anything else. We can amalgamate the First and Second Ways into a master argument: even if the universe extends infinitely into the past, the causal processes within it cannot themselves be infinite but must terminate in an uncaused cause of everything else.

One of the key premises of the master argument is the Aristotelian claim that whatever is caused or changed is caused or changed by something else. Aquinas gives various arguments for this principle. For example, nothing is self-caused because then it would have to be prior to itself, which is impossible. The assumption is that causes are prior to their effects, and objectors point to simultaneous causation (e.g., a head resting on a pillow) to refute it. But it is by no means clear that Aquinas is talking about *temporal* priority; rather, he seems to be saying that causes are logically or at least *metaphysically* prior their effects, in the sense that the cause has a separate existence from its effect, just as the head is separate from the pillow although it causes the indentation at the same time as the indentation exists.

It might be objected that this is merely to presuppose that whatever is caused is caused by another, not to prove it. Thomas goes further, however. He argues that if a thing were self-caused (i.e., it brought itself into existence) – remember that we are talking about concrete material objects – then it would *have* to exist by virtue of the very kind of thing it was; in Scholastic terminology, its essence would have to include its existence. For how else could it bring itself into existence other than by being a certain kind of thing with a certain essence? But its essence has no reality, hence no actual effects, apart from the realization of that essence in the existing thing itself. (Aquinas is no Platonist about essences.) So in order to have any real effects – including the effect of bringing into existence the thing whose essence it is – the object would already have to exist (i.e., to have a metaphysically prior or separate reality). So it really would have to exist separately from – 'prior' to – itself, which is incoherent.

The objector might accept that no object can be self-caused in this sense, but surely an object can be self-changing or self-moving? Anthony Kenny, in his critique of the Five Ways, attacks the premise that nothing can move or change itself (Kenny 1969: 21–3). He focuses on Aquinas's argument from actuality and potentiality in defense of the premise. The defense goes, it seems, that an object x that changes from F to G must, before becoming G, be *potentially* G. But whatever changes x from F to G must itself be *actually* G. Yet no object can be both actually and potentially G at the same time and in the same respect; hence x can only be changed by some other object y that is itself *actually* G and can turn x's potential G-ness into actual G-ness. As Kenny wryly objects, 'a kingmaker need not himself be king, and it is not dead men who commit murders' (1969: 21).

This reading of Aquinas is uncharitable (Craig 1980: 173). True, Thomas uses the unfortunate example of wood being heated by something already hot, but the context (see, e.g., Aquinas 1920a: q.2 a.3) makes it clear that all he is committed to is the thought that no potentiality can be made actual except by something itself already actual: dead men do not commit murders, but living men do. Hence nothing can actualize itself. But don't at least some living things *change* and *move* themselves? For Aquinas, following Aristotle, the idea is that while, in a manner of speaking, animals are self-changers (and self-movers), they are not so in such a way as to violate the principle that everything is changed by another. Animals possess a spontaneity of internal instinct, but their instinctive responses are either to external stimuli or are cases of a part of the animal (say, a rumbling stomach) moving the whole (say, by causing a feeling of hunger). Humans have free will as well as instinct, but their free actions, while not *determined* by things other than themselves, are at least causally influenced and moved by such things, or else by humans' own parts. Even taking account of the logical role of reasons in human action, the fact is that my smacking my lips is to some degree caused by the plate of pizza in front of me; and my telephoning my friend is to some degree caused by my memory of her – yet the memory is not me, only a mental episode that moves me.

Yet, says Aquinas, the regress of causes cannot go on forever: it must terminate in a prime mover. One way to understand this thought is via the familiar analogy of the train with an endless series of carriages. If you are told, in response to the question 'What moves the carriages?', that 'it's carriages all the way along,' you will – one hopes – be more than a little incredulous. *What* moves any carriage if it's just carriages into infinity? There has to be an engine *somewhere*! No carriage pulls any other carriage by itself; they are all *instruments* of the first member of the series that pulls them all; with no engine, no carriage can move. Kenny accuses Aquinas of basing this premise on an outmoded cosmology relying on heavenly spheres within spheres, like some gigantic clock mechanism requiring someone to wind it up, rather than on what we now know to be the laws of physics governing planetary motion (and motion in general). Yet it is not clear that the antiquated cosmology or physics is essential to Aquinas's argument. For even if the series of contemporaneous causes operative in the world right now is *said* to terminate in laws, it is hard to know what it means to say that the laws *cause* anything. They govern motion, but do they cause it?

Remember that Aquinas is talking about the contemporaneous causes operative in the universe now, not about causes operative in the past. He accepts that reason cannot disprove that the universe is infinite in the past. This is why the opponent's appeal to inertia as a counterexample to the principle that what moves is moved by another is held by the defender to be beside the point. Aquinas's position is consistent with the existence of an object that has been moving uniformly for eternity past; what he does not allow is that anything could right now be part of an infinite series of contemporaneous causes and effects. But why shouldn't he equally accept that such a series might be infinite?

Aquinas distinguishes between so-called 'essential' and 'accidental' causal series (Aquinas 1920b: q.46 a.2), claiming that the universe in its temporal extent involves only an accidental causal series, where for three things x, y, and z following one another in time, y's causing z does not depend upon x's causing y. Human A begets human B who begets human C, but B's begetting C does not depend causally on A's begetting B; and this could go on forever into the past. But when it comes to the causal series operative right now, there is a relation of instrumental dependence between the members: the sun illuminates the moon which illuminates the earth, all of this happening simultaneously; again, the sun heats the earth, the earth nourishes the plant *by means of* being heated by the sun, the plant grows by means of being heated by the earth, and so on. And what causes the sun right now to do what it does – something else? But this, says Aquinas, cannot go on forever – *something* has to get the chain of causes going, something that is not itself caused by anything lest the same question be asked again.

This sort of argument is not the most popular among supporters of cosmological arguments, probably because of the persistent suspicion that it is somehow tied up with an outdated cosmology. Yet it deserves reviving: it does not obviously depend on outmoded science, whatever the latter's influence on Aquinas at the time. Moreover, the argument, if at all plausible, would be a sharp weapon against the many opponents who think that an eternal universe precludes the possibility of a first cause.

The argument from contingency

The argument from contingency is not so much about causal processes but the contingent nature of the universe and everything within it: nothing that does exist in the universe *has* to exist. There might have been no universe at all. Yet doesn't the existence of a contingent thing require an explanation, moreover an explanation in terms of something other than itself? The explanation for the existence of a necessary being, if there were one, would be in terms of its own nature, in virtue of which it *had* to exist. Contingent beings, however, are just that: contingent or dependent on something else for their existence. Just as I owe my existence to my parents, and they to theirs, so the series extends back in time.

The defender of the argument allows that this series might be infinite just as in the case of the First and Second Ways, but still demands an explanation for the existence of the entire series, infinite or not – for it too must be contingent given that all its members are. So it too, like every one of its members, cannot have an explanation in terms of itself but only of another. Yet that other could not be one or more members of the series, since then we would argue circularly in purporting to explain the existence of the whole in terms of that of its parts – and the sum of its parts is what we wanted to explain in the first place! Therefore we have to go *outside* the sum of contingent beings, which is the universe, to some other entity that explains it. And this explainer must itself be necessary, since if it were contingent, the demand for an explanation would merely be pushed a stage further back.

Again, temporal considerations are not essential to the argument. Whether or not it is temporally finite, the defender claims our contingent universe must have an explanation outside itself. Contingency, as it were, cries out for an explanation. Hume, for one, thought this demand otiose: 'In such a chain, too, or succession of objects, each part is caused by that which preceded it, and causes that which succeeds it. Where then is the difficulty? But the *whole*, you say, wants a cause.... Did I show you the particular causes of each individual in a collection of twenty particles of matter, I should think it very unreasonable should you afterwards ask me what was the cause of the whole twenty. This is sufficiently explained in explaining the cause of the parts' (Hume 1948: 59–60). Russell concurs, going so far as to accuse the defender of the fallacy of composition: 'Every man who exists has a mother, and it seems to me your argument is that therefore the human race must have a mother, but obviously the human race hasn't a mother – that's a different logical sphere' (Hick 1964: 175).

Yet not all inferences from parts to wholes are fallacious: every part of Fido is physical, so Fido is physical; every part of this patch of grass is green, so this patch of grass is green. It depends on what one is talking about, in particular what 'logical spheres,' or better 'categories,' are involved. Now it may be that the universe as a whole is greater than the sum of its parts, in the sense that it can survive the loss or change of some of them; but does that put it into a different category? If everything within the universe is contingent, then how could the universe, taken as a whole, be anything other than contingent? Take away each contingent thing in it and there is no universe. If contingent things require an explanation outside themselves, on what logical or ontological grounds would the universe be exempt?

The two most common rejoinders by opponents at this point are: (1) insist, with Hume, that we have all the explanation we need as long as we can explain each contingent thing in terms of another (without, of course, going round in a circle) (Edwards, in Burrill 1967: 119); (2) maintain, following Russell (Hick 1964: 175) that 'the universe is just there, and that's all' (Mackie 1982: 84–6). As to (1), says the defender, one cannot explain the entire universe simply by explaining the existence of each element in terms of another. For one does not thereby explain why there is anything at all. Rowe puts the reply in terms of an infinite succession of human beings, each one begotten by the previous one: 'if *all* we know is that there always have been men and that every man's existence is explained by the causal efficacy of some other man, we do not know *why* there always have been men rather than none at all' (Rowe 1998: 154–5).

But how could this be, rejoins the opponent, if the defender has already supported the contingency of the universe on the ground that the universe just is the collection of all the contingent things? If each contingent member of the collection has an explanation, doesn't the whole collection *ipso facto* have an explanation? Yet it is not clear why, if contingency carries over from parts to whole, the whole must be *explained* in terms of the individual parts – especially since the universe as a whole can survive variation or loss of parts.

Returning to Rowe's analogy, even if we can explain why there are *these* men by saying that Jacob was begotten by Isaac, and Isaac by Abraham, and so on to infinity, we do not thereby explain why there are *any* human beings at all. Similarly, we might be able to explain why *these* things in the universe exist element by element, but we do not thereby explain why there is a universe at all, especially given that every element in the universe could have been different.

Now if the universe were spatio-temporally finite, it might be that the existence of the whole would be explained in terms of an explanation of each element. But this, says the defender, will not help, since we have to go outside them all in order to explain at least one of them – in a temporal series, the first. This notion is sharpened by Taylor's thought that the universe *could* have consisted of a single object: being contingent, it would need an explanation, and the explanation certainly could not appeal to the object itself.

As to rejoinder (2), the 'brute fact' claim, defenders of the contingency argument appeal to the Principle of Sufficient Reason. For Leibniz (*Monadology*, 1714), 'no fact can be real or existent, no statement true, unless there be a sufficient reason why it is so and not otherwise' (Leibniz 1951: § 32); for Clarke, writing in 1717, '[u]ndoubtedly] nothing is, without a sufficient reason why it is, rather than not; and why it is thus, rather than otherwise' (Leibniz-Clarke 1956: 30 (Third Reply)). Opponents invariably see the principle as anything but obvious, though finding counterexamples that do not beg the question is difficult. Moreover, in order to refute the principle, one would have to show that there is something (of the relevant kind, say, some state of affairs) that does not have an explanation, not merely that there is something whose explanation it might be, at least to some degree, beyond our intellectual powers to discern.

There is a persistent clash of intuitions when it comes to the Principle of Sufficient Reason, as well as much debate over exactly how to formulate it (Rowe 1998: xii–ix, 144–51.) The defender of the contingency argument, however, will insist on at least this: that if *anything* cries out for an explanation, contingent existents do. The universe is contingent. So it too requires an explanation, moreover one that does not appeal to itself or any of its parts on pain of circularity.

The kalam cosmological argument

This argument differs from the preceding ones inasmuch as its defenders insist one *can* prove on metaphysical grounds that the universe is temporally finite. The argument holds that the universe had a beginning of its existence; but whatever begins to exist must have a cause of the beginning of its existence; hence the universe must have a cause. Now Kant, in his First Antinomy (Kant 1933: 396–402), attempted to show that reason cannot demonstrate one way or the other whether the universe had a beginning in time. Nonetheless, defenders such as William Lane Craig have maintained that reason can in fact do this job. That the universe had a beginning they defend on the ground that if it were infinite in time, it would be an *actual* infinite, a collection of things each of which actually existed. It would not be a mere *potential* infinite, that is to say a collection that was finite at any moment in past time but that could be enlarged by adding one more element.

Craig (Craig and Smith 1993: ch. 1) gives several examples of how postulating an actual infinity leads to highly counterintuitive results, many of them deriving from the well-known fact that an infinite collection has parts that are equal in size to the whole. Now we *may* not regard as troubling the fact that the set of even numbers is of exactly the same size as the set of natural numbers, of which the former is but a subset; that's just how infinite collections behave, as mathematician Georg Cantor maintained. But can we apply this to the real world? Consider an actually infinite library: can it be seriously asserted that by adding a book to it, we do *not* increase the size of the library? Or that if we were to take every second book off the shelves, we would not have *reduced* the size of the library? Or that we could iterate the process, removing every second book in the remaining collection, and so on forever, without reducing the size of the library by a *single* book, since it remains infinite?

Turning to spatially infinite collections, were we to say that a wooden ruler one foot long consisted of an actual infinity of segments – rather than simply accepting that it could *potentially* be divided into an infinite number of segments (for every segment you could cut it in half, and so on without end) – it seems we would be forced to assert that it was composed of an actual infinity of points of zero dimension. But how can any physical object like a wooden ruler literally be composed of *dimensionless* points? Doesn't Zeno still hold sway here, inasmuch as no amount of nothing (even an infinite amount!) can make up something? These and related considerations lead the kalam defender to cast doubt on the very idea that anything could be actually infinite, the universe being no exception. Moreover, he also appeals to empirical confirmation of the beginning of the universe in observations concerning the 'Big Bang' (Craig and Smith 1993: 35–57).

Further, defenders agree with one half of Kant's antinomy, namely that no infinite series can be formed by successive addition; in other words, that one cannot 'traverse the infinite.' How exactly this applies to the argument is controversial. The general idea is that no infinite totality can be formed by the successive addition of objects. Since one cannot complete an infinite totality, it has to come into existence all at once or not at all. But the series of states of the universe has not come into existence all at once, since it involves the temporal succession of state upon state. Wittgenstein thought it ridiculous that one might come across a person saying, '-5, -4, -3, -2, -1, 0!' and who, when asked what he was doing, claimed that he had just finished reciting the series of negative numbers backwards from infinity. I have argued (2002) that this sort of scenario would violate the Principle of Sufficient Reason: if the reciter claimed to have finished his job on April 9, 2006, surely we would be entitled to ask why he had finished *then* rather than, say, on April 8, or April 10, or November 30, 1363 or January 12, 5041. The very date of completion requires an explanation, yet if the scenario were real, an explanation would be in principle impossible. So for the universe, considered as a temporally infinite series formed by successive addition: event succeeds event, one state of the universe is added to by another, and the whole series of prior states of the universe is added to every time a new state of the universe, consisting of a collection of newly occurring events, comes into existence. At any point of time the cosmos has a certain configuration and distribution of objects and qualities. If it has existed forever, why are things *just* as they are at *this* point in time?

As to the universe's having a cause of its beginning to exist, defenders rely on the proposition what whatever begins to exist must have a cause of the beginning of its existence. To put it more popularly, nothing can come from nothing: things do not just pop into existence without a cause. Now Hume, writing in 1739–40, did not think such a proposition demonstrable (Hume 1978: I. iii. 3) since he thought it *conceivable* that something might just pop into existence without a cause. But can we really conceive it? And how would we know we were conceiving an object's coming into existence *uncaused* as opposed to its coming into existence with an *unknown* cause, or that we were not merely conceiving an object's coming into existence without at the same time conceiving of its cause (Anscombe 1974)? More importantly, what does 'conceive' mean in such a context? Maybe we can *imagine* it, but it is less clear that we can form a conception of such an event in a rational sense (i.e., in a sense schooled by rational reflection). The defender maintains that we never observe such a thing happening in the world around us. (Even so-called quantum fluctuations are supposed to involve particles emerging from a pre-existing space-time structure, not a genuine vacuum.) Why should the universe, if it began to exist, be any different? Craig takes the principle that nothing can come into existence uncaused to be self-evident. Perhaps it is indeed indemonstrable (though we might appeal to observation and common sense, adding that to try to prove it would involve appealing to premises that were less evident than the conclusion itself); but that does not mean we should follow Hume in taking belief in it to be somehow non-rational.

Conclusion

The flourishing contemporary debates over the kalam cosmological argument and the argument from contingency show that the epitaph of cosmological arguments is far from being written. Moreover, the neglected First and Second Ways are ripe for reinvestigation. In addition, there is vigorous discussion of whether the first cause at which such arguments are directed must be the traditional God of monotheism as opposed to an impersonal, blind force. There are reasons for thinking one can deduce or plausibly infer at least some of the qualities of the monotheistic God (e.g., God as a personal cause) from cosmological arguments (on this, see Craig in Craig and Smith 1993: 64–7), but this would take us too far afield.

See also Creation and divine action (Chapter 30), Naturalistic rejoinders to theistic arguments (Chapter 40), Why is there a universe at all, rather than just nothing? (Chapter 41), Catholic philosophical theology (Chapter 43), Religion and science (Chapter 64).

References

Anscombe, G. E. M. (1974) '"Whatever has a beginning of existence must have a cause": Hume's argument exposed,' *Analysis* 34: 145–51. Reprinted in G. E. M. Anscombe (1981) *Collected Philosophical Papers*, vol. 1, Oxford: Blackwell.

Aquinas (1920a) *Summa Theologica*, Part 1, QQ I–XXVI; vol. 1 of *The 'Summa Theologica' of St Thomas Aquinas¸ literally translated by the Fathers of the English Dominican Province*, London: Burns, Oates & Washbourne.

—— (1920b) *Summa Theologica*, Part 1, QQ XXVII–XLIX; vol. 2 of *The 'Summa Theologica' of St Thomas Aquinas¸ literally translated by the Fathers of the English Dominican Province*, London: Burns, Oates & Washbourne.

—— (1955) *Summa contra Gentiles*, Book 1: God; bk. 1 of *On the Truth of the Catholic Faith (Summa Contra Gentiles)*, Garden City, NY: Image/Doubleday.

Burrill, D. (ed.) (1967) *The Cosmological Arguments: A Spectrum of Opinion*, Garden City, NY: Anchor/Doubleday.

Clarke, S. (1998) *A Demonstration of the Being and Attributes of God and Other Writings*, ed. E. Vailati, Cambridge: Cambridge University Press.

Craig, W. L. (1979) *The Kalam Cosmological Argument*, London: Macmillan.

—— (1980) *The Cosmological Argument from Plato to Leibniz*, London: Macmillan. Reprinted 2001, Eugene, OR: Wipf & Stock.

Craig, W. L. and Q. Smith (1993) *Theism, Atheism, and Big Bang Cosmology*, Oxford: Clarendon Press.

Hick, J. (ed.) (1964) *The Existence of God*, New York: Macmillan.

Hume, D. (1948) *Dialogues Concerning Natural Religion*, ed. H. D. Aiken, New York: Hafner Press.

—— (1978) *A Treatise of Human Nature*, eds L. A. Selby-Bigge and P. H. Nidditch, Oxford: Clarendon Press.

Kant, I. (1933) *Critique of Pure Reason*, trans. N. K. Smith, London: Macmillan.

Kenny, A. (1969) *The Five Ways*, London: Routledge & Kegan Paul.

Leibniz, G. W. (1951) *Leibniz: Selections*, ed. P. R. Wiener, New York: Charles Scribner's Sons.

Leibniz–Clarke (1956) *The Leibniz–Clarke Correspondence*, ed. H. G. Alexander, Manchester: Manchester University Press.

Locke, J. (1975) *An Essay Concerning Human Understanding*, ed. P. H. Nidditch, Oxford: Clarendon Press.

Mackie, J. L. (1982) *The Miracle of Theism*, Oxford: Clarendon Press.

Maimonides, M. (1956) *The Guide for the Perplexed*, trans. M. Friedländer, New York: Dover (reprint of 2nd rev. edn, 1904).

Oderberg, D. S. (2002) 'Traversal of the Infinite, the "Big Bang" and the Kalam Cosmological Argument,' *Philosophia Christi* NS 4: 305–36.

Rowe, W. (1998) *The Cosmological Argument*, New York: Fordham University Press (reprint of 1975 edn, with new preface).

Taylor, R. (1992) *Metaphysics*, 4th edn, Englewood Cliffs, NJ: Prentice-Hall.

Further reading

Brown, P. (1966) 'Infinite causal regression,' *Philosophical Review* 75: 510–25. (Important explanation of Aquinas on types of causal series.)

Gale, R. and A. Pruss (1999) 'A new Cosmological Argument,' *Religious Studies* 35: 461–76. (Defends the argument from contingency using a weaker version of the Principle of Sufficient Reason than traditionally appealed to.)

Koons, R. C. (1997) 'A new look at the Cosmological Argument,' *American Philosophical Quarterly* 34: 193–211. (Defends a version of the argument from contingency using modal logic and the Lesniewski–Goodman–Leonard calculus of individuals.)

Reichenbach, B. (2004) 'Cosmological Argument,' in E. N. Zalta (ed.) *The Stanford Encyclopedia of Philosophy* (Fall 2004 edn), available at: http://plato.stanford.edu/archives/fall2004/entries/cosmological-argument/ (accessed 10 April 2006). (A useful survey.)

Swinburne, R. (2004) *The Existence of God*, 2nd edn, Oxford: Clarendon Press. (His inductive version of the cosmological argument is in chapter 7.)

Vallicella, W. F. (1997) 'On an insufficient argument against Sufficient Reason,' *Ratio* 10: 76–81. (A brief but noteworthy defense of the Principle of Sufficient Reason.)

Vollert, C., L. H. Kendzierski, and P. M. Byrne (eds) (1964) *On the Eternity of the World*, Milwaukee, WI: Marquette University Press. (A selection of key texts from Aquinas, Bonaventure, and Siger of Brabant.)

33
THE TELEOLOGICAL ARGUMENT
Robin Collins

Introduction

Design arguments have a long history, probably being the most commonly cited argument for believing in a deity. In ancient India, for instance, the argument from design was advanced by the so-called Nyaya (or logical-atomist) school (100–1000 CE), which argued for the existence of a deity based on the order of the world, which they compared both to human artifacts and to the human body (Smart 1964: 153–4). In the West, the design argument goes back to at least Heraclitus (500 BCE). It reached its highpoint with the publication of Paley's *Natural Theology* (1802), which primarily appealed to the intricate structure of plants and animals as evidence for design. With the advent of Darwin's theory of evolution, this version of the argument underwent an almost fatal blow, although it has gained a small following since the 1990s among advocates of the so-called intelligent design movement. By far the most widely cited evidence for design, however, is that from findings in physics and cosmology during the twentieth century. In this essay we will mainly focus on the evidence from the so-called fine-tuning of the cosmos for conscious, embodied life (CEL), although we will briefly look at other evidence from the beauty and elegance of the laws of nature.

The evidence of fine-tuning

Many examples of this fine-tuning can be given, a few of which we will briefly recount here. One particularly important category of fine-tuning is that of the *constants* of physics. The constants of physics are a set of fundamental numbers that, when plugged into the laws of physics, determine the basic structure of the universe. An example of such a constant is the gravitational constant G that is part of Newton's law of gravity, $F = GM_1M_2/r^2$. G essentially determines the strength of gravity between two masses. If one were to double the value of G, for instance, then the force of gravity between any two masses would double.

So far, physicists have discovered four forces in nature: gravity, the weak nuclear force, electromagnetism, and the strong nuclear force that binds protons and neutrons together in an atom. As measured in a certain set of standard dimensionless units (Barrow and Tipler 1986: 292–5), gravity is the least strong of the four forces, and the strong nuclear force is the strongest, being a factor of 10^{40} – or ten thousand billion, billion, billion, billion – times stronger than gravity.

Various calculations show that the strength of each of the forces of nature must fall into a very small CEL-permitting region for CEL to exist. As just one example, consider gravity. Compared to the total range of forces, the strength of gravity must fall in a relatively narrow range in order for CEL to exist. If we increased the strength of gravity a billion-fold, for instance, the force of gravity on a planet with the mass and size of the earth would be so great that organisms anywhere near the size of human beings, whether land-based or aquatic, would be crushed. (The strength of materials depends on the electromagnetic force via the fine-structure constant, which would not be affected by a change in gravity.) Even a much smaller planet of only 40 feet in diameter – which is not large enough to sustain organisms of our size – would have a gravitational pull of one thousand times that of earth, still too strong for organisms of our brain size, and hence level of intelligence, to exist. As astrophysicist Martin Rees notes, 'In an imaginary strong gravity world, even insects would need thick legs to support them, and no animals could get much larger' (Rees 2000: 30). Other calculations show that if the gravitational force were increased by more than a factor of 3000, the maximum lifetime of a star would be a billion years, thus severely inhibiting the probability of CEL evolving (Collins 2003). Of course, a three-thousand-fold increase in the strength of gravity is a lot, but compared to the total range of the strengths of the forces in nature (which span a range of 10^{40}, as we saw above), it is very small, being one part in a billion, billion, billion, billion.

There are other cases of the fine-tuning of the constants of physics besides the strength of the forces, however. Probably the most widely discussed (and esoteric) among physicists and cosmologists is the fine-tuning of what is known as the *cosmological constant*. This is a number in Einstein's theory of general relativity that influences the expansion rate of the universe. If the cosmological constant were not fine-tuned to within an extremely narrow range – one part in 10^{53} or even 10^{120} of its 'theoretically possible' range of values – the universe would expand so rapidly that all matter would quickly disperse, and thus galaxies, stars, and even small aggregates of matter could never form (see, e.g., Rees 2000: 95–102, 154–5; Collins 2003).

Besides the constants of physics, however, there is also the fine-tuning of the laws. If the laws of nature were not just right, CEL would probably be impossible. For example, consider again the four forces of nature. If gravity (or a force like it) did not exist, masses would not clump together to form stars or planets and hence the existence of complex CEL would be seriously inhibited, if not rendered impossible; if the electromagnetic force didn't exist, there would be no chemistry; if the strong force didn't exist, protons and neutrons could not bind together and hence no atoms with atomic numbers greater than hydrogen would exist; and if the strong force were a long-range force (like gravity and electromagnetism) instead of a short-range force that only acts between protons and neutrons in the nucleus, all matter would either almost instantaneously undergo nuclear fusion and explode or be sucked together forming a black hole.

Similarly, other laws and principles are necessary for CEL. As the prominent Princeton physicist Freeman Dyson points out (1979: 251), if the Pauli-exclusion principle did not exist, which dictates that no two fermions can occupy the same quantum state, all electrons would occupy the lowest atomic orbit, eliminating complex chemistry; and if there were no quantization principle, which dictates that particles can only occupy certain discrete allowed quantum states, there would be no atomic orbits and hence no chemistry since all electrons would be sucked into the nucleus.

Finally, in his book *Nature's Destiny*, the biochemist Michael Denton extensively discusses various higher-level features of the natural world, such as the many unique properties of carbon, oxygen, water, and the electromagnetic spectrum, that are conducive to the existence of complex biochemical systems. As one of many examples Denton presents, both the atmosphere and water are transparent to electromagnetic radiation in a thin band in the visible region, but are transparent nowhere else except to radio waves. If, instead, either of them absorbed electromagnetic radiation in the visible region, the existence of terrestrial CEL would be seriously inhibited, if not rendered impossible (Denton 1998: 56–7). These higher-level coincidences indicate a deeper level fine-tuning of the fundamental laws and constants of physics.

As the above examples indicate, the evidence for fine-tuning is extensive, even if one has doubts about some individual cases. As the philosopher John Leslie has pointed out, 'clues heaped upon clues can constitute weighty evidence despite doubts about each element in the pile' (Leslie 1988: 300). At the very least, these cases of fine-tuning show the truth of Freeman Dyson's observation that there are many 'lucky accidents in physics' (1979: 251) without which CEL would be impossible.

The argument formulated

Now it is time to consider the way in which the existence of a fine-tuned universe supports theism. In this section, I will argue that the evidence of fine-tuning primarily gives us a reason for preferring theism over what could be called the naturalistic single-universe hypothesis (NSU): the hypothesis that there is only one universe, and it exists as a brute fact. (We will examine the typical alternative explanation of the fine-tuning offered by many atheists – what I call the 'many-universes hypothesis' – in a section below.) We will present our argument for the case of the fine-tuning of the constants, but with some modifications it will apply to the other types of fine-tuning for CEL mentioned above.

Although the fine-tuning argument against the NSU can be cast in several different forms – such as inference to the best explanation – I believe the most rigorous way of formulating the argument is in terms of what is often called the *likelihood principle*, a standard principle of confirmation theory (e.g., see Sober 2002). Simply put, the principle says that *whenever we are considering two competing hypotheses, an observation counts as evidence in favor of the hypothesis under which the observation has the highest probability (or is the least improbable).* Since the type of probability in the likelihood principle is what is known as *epistemic probability* (see below), the likelihood principle can be reworded more intuitively in terms of what could be called the *surprise principle*: namely, whenever we are considering two competing hypotheses, an observation counts as evidence in favor of the hypothesis under which it is least surprising. Moreover, the degree to which the observation counts in favor of one hypothesis over another is proportional to the degree to which the observation is more probable (or less surprising) under the one hypothesis than the other.

Using this principle, we can develop the fine-tuning argument in a two-step form as follows:

> Premise (1) The existence of a fine-tuned universe with CEL is not highly improbable (or surprising) under theism.
>
> Premise (2) The existence of a fine-tuned universe with CEL is very improbable (surprising) under the NSU.
>
> Conclusion: From premises (1) and (2) and the likelihood principle, it follows that the fine-tuning data provides significant evidence to favor of the design hypothesis over the NSU.

At this point, we should pause to note two features of this argument. First, the argument does not say that the fine-tuning evidence proves that the universe was designed, or even that it is likely that the universe was designed. Indeed, of itself it does not even show that we are epistemically warranted in believing in theism over the NSU. In order to justify these sorts of claims, we would have to look at the full range of evidence both for and against the design hypothesis – something I am *not* doing in this essay. Rather, the argument merely concludes that the fine-tuning significantly *supports* theism *over* the NSU. (I say 'significantly supports' because presumably the ratio of probabilities for the fine-tuning under theism versus the NSU is quite large.)

In this way, the evidence of the fine-tuning argument is much like a defendant's DNA being found on the murder weapon, in a trial. By the 'likelihood' or 'surprise principle,' the DNA on the murder weapon provides significant evidence that the defendant is guilty because its existence would be much more surprising if the defendant were innocent than if he were guilty. Yet one could not conclude merely from the DNA alone that the defendant is guilty, for there could be other counter-vailing evidence, such as the testimony of reliable witnesses that he was not at the scene of the crime. The DNA would still count as significant evidence of guilt, but this evidence would be counterbalanced by the testimony of the witnesses. Similarly the evidence of fine-tuning significantly supports theism over the NSU, though it does not itself show that, everything considered, theism is the most plausible explanation of the existence of a universe with CEL.

Support for the premises

Support for Premise (1): Premise (1) is easy to support and somewhat less controversial than premise (2). The argument in support of it can be simply stated as follows: *since God is an all-good being, and in and of itself it is good for intelligent, conscious beings to exist, it not highly surprising or highly improbable that God would create a world that could support CEL.* Thus, the fine-tuning is not highly improbable under theism.

Support for Premise (2): Upon looking at the data, many people find it very obvious that the fine-tuning is highly improbable under the NSU. And it is easy to see why when we think of the fine-tuning in terms of various analogies. In the 'dart-board analogy,' for example, the theoretically possible values for fundamental constants of physics can be represented as a dart-board that fills the whole galaxy, and the conditions necessary for CEL to exist as a small inch-wide target. Accordingly, from this analogy it seems obvious that it would be highly improbable for the fine-tuning to occur under the NSU – that is, for the dart to hit the target by chance.

Now some philosophers, such as Keith Parsons (1990: 182), object to the claim that the fine-tuning is highly improbable under the NSU by arguing that since we only have one universe, the notion of the fine-tuning of the universe being probable or improbable is meaningless.

Although I do not have space to provide a full-scale response to this objection, I will briefly sketch an answer. The first is to note that the relevant notion of probability occurring in the fine-tuning argument is a widely recognized type of probability called *epistemic probability* (e.g., see Hacking 1975; Plantinga 1993: chs. 8 and 9). Roughly, the epistemic probability of a proposition can be thought of as the degree of confidence or belief we rationally should have in the proposition. Further, the conditional epistemic probability of a proposition R on another proposition S – written as $P(R/S)$ – can be defined as the degree to which the proposition S *of itself* should rationally lead us to expect that R is true. Under the epistemic conception of probability, therefore, the statement that *the fine-tuning of the cosmos is very improbable under the NSU* is to be understood as making a statement about the degree to which the NSU would or should, *of itself*, rationally lead us to expect cosmic fine-tuning.

The notion *of itself* is important here. The rational degree of expectation should not be confused with the degree to which one should expect the constants of physics to fall within the CEL range if one believed the NSU. For even those who believe in this hypothesis should expect the constants of physics to be CEL-permitting since this follows from the fact that we are alive. Rather, the conditional epistemic probability in this case is the degree to which the NSU *of itself* should lead us to expect constants of physics to be CEL-permitting. This means that in assessing the conditional epistemic probability in this and other similar cases, one must exclude contributions to our expectations arising from other information we have, such as that we are alive. In the case at hand, one way of doing this is by means of the following sort of thought experiment. Imagine a disembodied being with mental capacities and a knowledge of physics comparable to that of the most intelligent physicists alive today, except that the being does not know whether the values of the constants of physics allow for CEL to arise. Further, suppose that this disembodied being believed in the NSU. Then, the degree that being should rationally expect the constants of physics to be CEL-permitting will be equal to our conditional epistemic probability, since its expectation is solely a result of its belief in the NSU, not other factors such as its awareness of its own existence.

Given this understanding of the notion of conditional epistemic probability, it is not difficult to see that the conditional epistemic probability of a constant of physics having a CEL-permitting value under the NSU will be much smaller than under theism. The reason is simple when we think about our imaginary disembodied being. If such a being were a theist, it would have some reason to believe that the values of constants would fall into the CEL-permitting region (see the argument in support of premise (1) above). On the other hand, if the being were a subscriber to the NSU, it would have no reason to think the value would be in the CEL-permitting region instead of any other part of the 'theoretically possible' region R. Thus, the being has more reason to believe the constants would fall into the CEL-permitting region under theism than the NSU; that is, the epistemic probability under theism is larger than under the NSU, or put differently, the existence of a CEL-permitting universe is more surprising under the NSU than theism. How much more surprising? That depends on the degree of fine-tuning. Here, I will simply note that it seems obvious that in general the higher the degree of fine-tuning – that is, the smaller the width of the CEL-permitting range is to the 'theoretically possible' range – the greater the surprise under the NSU, and hence the greater the ratio of the two probabilities. To go beyond these statements and to assign actual epistemic probabilities (or degrees of surprise) under the NSU – or to further justify these claims of improbability – would require defending a version of the probabilistic principle of indifference, which is beyond the scope of this essay.

Objections to the argument

As powerful as the fine-tuning argument against the NSU is, several major objections have been raised to it by both atheists and theists. In this section, we will consider some of these objections in turn.

Objection 1: more fundamental law objection

One criticism of the fine-tuning argument is that, as far as we know, there could be a more fundamental law under which the constants of physics *must* have the values they do. Thus, given such a law, it is not improbable that the known constants of physics fall within the CEL-permitting range. Besides being entirely speculative, the problem with postulating such a law is that it simply moves the improbability of the fine-tuning up one level, to that of the postulated physical law itself. As the astrophysicists Bernard Carr and Martin Rees note, 'even if all apparently anthropic coincidences could be explained [in terms of some grand unified theory], it would still be remarkable . that the relationships dictated by physical theory happened also to be those propitious for CEL' (Carr and Rees 1979: 612).

For the theist, then, the development of a grand unified theory would not undercut the case for design, but would only serve to deepen our appreciation of the ingenuity of the creator. Instead of separately fine-tuning each individual parameter, in this view, the designer simply carefully chose those laws that would yield CEL-permitting values for each parameter.

Objection 2: other forms of CEL objection

Another objection commonly raised against the fine-tuning argument is that as far as we know, other forms of CEL could exist even if the constants of physics were different. So, it is claimed, the fine-tuning argument ends up presupposing that all forms of CEL must be like us. One answer to this objection is that many cases of fine-tuning do not make this presupposition. If, for example, the cosmological constant were much larger than it is, matter would disperse so rapidly that no planets, and indeed no stars, could exist. Without stars, however, there would exist no stable energy sources for complex material systems of any sort to evolve. So, all the fine-tuning argument presupposes in this case is that the evolution of CEL requires some stable energy source. This is certainly a very reasonable assumption.

Objection 3: the 'Who Designed God?' objection

Perhaps the most common objection that atheists raise to the argument from design, of which the fine-tuning argument is one instance, is that postulating the existence of God does not solve the problem of design but merely transfers it up one level, to the question of who designed God. One response to the above argument is that it only relies on comparison of the epistemic probabilities of fine-tuning under the two different hypotheses, not on whether the new hypothesis reduces the overall complexity of one's worldview. As an analogy, if complex, intricate structures (such as aqueducts and buildings) existed on Mars, one could conclude that their existence would support the hypothesis that intelligent, extraterrestrial beings existed on Mars in the past, even if such beings are much more complex than the structures to be explained.

Second, however, for reasons entirely independent of the argument from design, God has been thought to have little, if any internal complexity. Indeed, medieval philosophers and theologians often went as far as advocating the doctrine of divine simplicity, according to which God is claimed to be absolutely simple, without any internal complexity. So, atheists who push this objection have a lot of arguing to do to make it stick. (For a more detailed treatment of the 'Who Designed God Objection,' see Collins 2005.)

The many-universes hypothesis

Another objection to considering fine-tuning as evidence for design is one that takes us almost into the realm of science fiction: the proposal that there are a very large number of universes, each with different values for the fundamental parameters of physics. If such multiple universes exist, it would be no surprise that the parameters in one of them would have just the right values for the existence of CEL, just as in the case where if enough lottery tickets were generated, it would be no surprise that one of them turned out to be the winning number.

How did these universes come into existence? Typically, the answer is to postulate some kind of physical process, what I will call a 'universe generator.' Against the naturalistic version of the universe-generator hypothesis, one could argue that the universe generator itself must be 'well designed' to produce even one CEL-sustaining universe. After all, even a mundane item such as a bread-making machine, which only produces loaves of bread instead of universes, must be well-designed as an appliance *and* have just the right ingredients (flour, yeast, gluten, and so on) in just the right amounts to produce decent loaves of bread. Indeed, as I have shown in detail elsewhere (Collins forthcoming), if one carefully examines the most popular, and most well-developed universe-generator hypothesis – that arising out of inflationary cosmology – one finds that it contains just the right fields and laws to generate CEL-permitting universes. Eliminate or modify one of the fields or laws by just a little bit, and no CEL-sustaining universes would be produced. If this is right, then invoking some sort of universe generator as an explanation of fine-tuning only pushes the issue of design up one level to the question of who or what designed it.

Besides the universe generator hypothesis, a very small minority of scientists and philosophers have proposed what could be called a *metaphysical* many-universe hypothesis, according to which universes are thought to exist on their own without being generated by any physical process. Typically, advocates of this view – such as the late Princeton University philosopher David Lewis (1986) and the University of Pennsylvania astrophysicist Max Tegmark (1998) – claim that every possible set of laws is instantiated in some universe or another. One problem with this hypothesis is that it cannot explain why we inhabit a universe that is so orderly and has such low initial entropy: it is much more likely for there to exist local islands with the sort of order necessary for CEL than for the entire universe to have such an ordered arrangement. Thus, their hypothesis cannot explain the highly ordered character of the universe as a whole.

Among others, George Schlesinger has raised this objection against Lewis's hypothesis (1984). This sort of objection was raised against a similar explanation of the high degree of order in our universe offered by the famous physicist Ludwig Boltzmann, and has generally been considered fatal to Boltzmann's explanation (Davies 1974: 103).

Despite these objections and the fact that the multiple-universe hypothesis typically has been advanced by naturalists as an alternative explanation to design, I am not objecting to the notion of many universes itself. I actually believe that theists should be open to the idea that God created our universe by means of a universe generator. It makes some sense that an infinitely creative deity would create other universes, not just our own.

Other evidences for design

Besides the fine-tuning for CEL, there are other significant evidences for design based on the findings of physics and cosmology, such as the extraordinary degree of beauty, elegance, harmony, and ingenuity exhibited by the fundamental mathematical structure of the universe. For instance, Nobel Prize-winning physicist Steven Weinberg, himself an atheist, devotes a whole chapter of his book, *Dreams of a Final Theory* (ch. 6, 'Beautiful theories'), to explaining how the criteria of beauty and elegance are commonly used to guide physicists in formulating the right laws. Because this beauty and elegance has been so successful in guiding physicists in developing highly successful theories, it is difficult to claim that this beauty and elegance is merely in the eye of the beholder. Today, this use of beauty and elegance as a guide is particularly evident in the popularity of superstring theory, which is widely considered the most feasible candidate for a truly fundamental theory in physics. Yet, it is almost entirely motivated by considerations of elegance, having no direct experimental support in its favor (Greene 1999: 214).

Now such beauty, elegance, and ingenuity make sense if the universe was designed by God. I would contend, however, that apart from some sort of design hypothesis, there is no reason to expect the fundamental laws to be elegant or beautiful. The metaphysical many-universes hypothesis, for example, cannot in any obvious way explain why our universe has such an elegant and beautiful fundamental structure, since under this hypothesis there would be many, many universes that contained observers in which the underlying mathematical structure would not be beautiful. Thus theism makes more sense of this aspect of the world than atheism, whether that atheism is of the single-universe or many-universe variety (see Collins forthcoming). Similar things could be said about the fact that the world is arranged in just the right way so that we can understand its underlying structure, something which could be called the 'discoverability' of the laws of physics, as for example discussed by Eugene Wigner (1960) and Mark Steiner (1998).

Conclusion

In this essay, I have argued that the fine-tuning of the cosmos for CEL provides strong evidence for preferring theism over the NSU. I then argued that although one can partially explain the fine-tuning of the constants of physics by invoking some sort of many-universes generator, we have good reasons to believe that the many-universe generator itself would need to be well designed, and hence that hypothesizing some sort of many-universes generator only pushes the case for design up one level. I further argued that other features of the structure of the universe, such as the beauty and elegance of the laws of nature, also suggest design. When all the evidence is considered, I believe, one has a good cumulative case argument for a designer – that is, an argument in which many lines of evidence point to the same conclusion. Of course, one would need additional arguments, such as those offered by Richard Swinburne (2004: ch. 5), to conclude that the designer is the theistic God.

See also David Hume (Chapter 13), Immanuel Kant (Chapter 14), Creation and divine action (Chapter 30), The cosmological argument (Chapter 32), Naturalistic rejoinders to theistic arguments (Chapter 40), Why is there a universe at all, rather than just nothing? (Chapter 41), Religion and science (Chapter 64).

References

Barrow, J. and F. Tipler (1986) *The Anthropic Cosmological Principle*, Oxford: Oxford University Press.

Carr, B. J. and M. J. Rees (1979) 'The Anthropic Cosmological Principle and the structure of the physical world,' *Nature* 278 (12 April): 605–12.

Collins, R. (2003) 'The evidence for fine-tuning,' in N. Manson (ed.) *God and Design*, London: Routledge.

—— (2005) 'Hume, fine-tuning and the Who Designed God? Objection,' in J. Sennett and D. Groothius (eds) *In Defense of Natural Theology: A Post-Humean Assessment*, Downers Grove, IL: InterVarsity Press.

—— (forthcoming) 'A theistic perspective on the Multiverse Hypothesis,' in B. Carr (ed.) *Universe or Multiverse?*, Cambridge: Cambridge University Press.

Davies, P. (1974) *The Physics of Time Asymmetry*, Berkeley, CA: University of California Press.

Denton, M. (1998) *Nature's Destiny: How the Laws of Biology Reveal Purpose in the Universe*, New York: Free Press.

Dyson, F. (1979) *Disturbing the Universe*, New York: Harper & Row.

Greene, B. (1999) *The Elegant Universe: Superstrings, Hidden Dimensions, and the Quest for the Ultimate Theory*, New York: W. W. Norton.

Hacking, I. (1975) *The Emergence of Probability: A Philosophical Study of Early Ideas About Probability, Induction and Statistical Inference*, Cambridge: Cambridge University Press.

Leslie, J. (1988) 'How to draw conclusions from a fine-tuned cosmos,' in R. Russell, W. R. Stoeger, and G. V. Coyne (eds) *Physics, Philosophy and Theology: A Common Quest for Understanding*, Vatican City State: Vatican Observatory Press.

Lewis, D. (1986) *On the Plurality of Worlds*, New York: Blackwell.

Parsons, K. (1990) 'Is there a case for Christian theism?', in J. P. Moreland and K. Nielsen (eds) *Does God Exist? The Great Debate*, Nashville, TN: Thomas Nelson.

Plantinga, A. (1993) *Warrant and Proper Function*, Oxford: Oxford University Press.

Rees, M. (2000) *Just Six Numbers: The Deep Forces that Shape the Universe*, New York: Basic Books.

Schlesinger, G. (1984) 'Possible worlds and the mystery of existence,' *Ratio* 26: 1–18.

Smart, N. (1964) *Doctrine and Argument in Indian Philosophy*, London: Allen & Unwin.

Sober, E. (2002) 'Bayesianism – its scope and limits,' in R. Swinburne (ed.) *Bayes's Theorem*, Oxford: Oxford University Press.

Steiner, M. (1998) *The Applicability of Mathematics as a Philosophical Problem*, Cambridge, MA: Harvard University Press.

Swinburne, R. (2004) *The Existence of God*, 2nd edn, Oxford: Clarendon Press.

Tegmark, M. (1998) 'Is "the theory of everything" merely the ultimate ensemble theory?', *Annals of Physics* 270: 1–51. Preprint at http://arxiv.org/abs/gr-qc/9704009.

Weinberg, S. (1992) *Dreams of a Final Theory*, New York: Vintage Books.

Wigner, E. (1960) 'The unreasonable effectiveness of mathematics in the natural sciences,' *Communications on Pure and Applied Mathematics* 13: 1–14. Available at http://www.dartmouth.edu/~matc/MathDrama/reading/Wigner.html.

Further reading

Holder, R. (2004) *God, the Multiverse, and Everything: Modern Cosmology and the Argument from Design*, Aldershot, and Burlington, VT: Ashgate. (Argues that the evidence of fine-tuning supports theism.)

Leslie, J. (1989) *Universes*, London: Routledge. (Explores the question of multiple universes as an alternative to a design explanation of fine-tuning.)

—— (ed.) (1998) *Modern Cosmology and Philosophy*, Amherst, NY: Prometheus. (Articles exploring the implications of modern cosmology for philosophy and teleology.)

Manson, N. (ed.) (2003) *God and Design: The Teleological Argument and Modern Science*, New York: Routledge. (Twenty-one authors vigorously debate the merits of divine teleology, from the realm of biology to cosmology.)

Manson, N. and J. Richards (eds) (2005) *Philosophical Issues in Intelligent Design*, Special Issue of Philosophia Christi NS 7/2 (December). (Contains a debate about whether the fine-tuning can be considered improbable.)

Robson, J. (ed.) (1987) *Origin and Evolution of the Universe: Evidence for Design?* Montreal: McGill Queen's University Press. (Explores whether biology and cosmology provide evidence for design.)

Susskind, L. (2005) *The Cosmic Landscape: String Theory and the Illusion of Intelligent Design*, New York: Little, Brown & Co. (A leading physicist presents the many-universes hypothesis based on superstring theory, claiming that it eliminates the need to appeal to a design explanation of the fine-tuning.)

34

THE MORAL ARGUMENT

Paul Copan

During the Peloponnesian War (431–404 BCE, including a six-year truce), the inhabitants of the island of Melos tried to remain neutral in the war between Athens and Sparta. Unfortunately, Melos couldn't hold out. Athens demanded tribute payment, offering peace in exchange. The Melians tried to negotiate, appealing to their right to their own empire. The Athenians rejected the Melians' 'fine phrases' of duty and morality. The Athenians asked the Melians

> not to imagine that you will influence us by saying … that you have never done us any harm … since you know as well as we do that, when these matters are discussed by practical people, the standard of justice depends upon the equality of power to compel and that in fact the strong do what they have the power to do and the weak accept what they have to accept. (cited in Glover 1999: 28–30)

The Melians claimed the Athenians' interests would best be served by preserving the principles of justice and fair play; after all, *they* too might be attacked one day. They appealed to a transcultural morality. Athens replied to Melos:

> It is a general and necessary law of nature to rule wherever one can. This is not a law we made for ourselves, nor were we the first to act upon it when it was made. We found it already in existence, and we shall leave it to exist forever among those who come after us. We are merely acting in accordance with it, and we know that you or anybody else with the same power as ours would be acting in precisely the same way. (ibid.)

In the end, the Melians refused to submit to Athens, and Athens besieged the city, killed the military-aged men, and sold the women and children into slavery.

Thrasymachus in Plato's *Republic* used the same sort of argument as the Athenians. He defined the 'just' as the 'advantage of the stronger' (*Republic* 338c; 339a; 340a; 341a; 344c). The 'just' person praised by Socrates only gets taken advantage of. Thrasymachus thus prefers the might-makes-right approach: the strong person rules rightly when she rules to her advantage, but rules wrongly when to her disadvantage (339a).

Were the Melians and Socrates correct, or were the Athenians and Thrasymachus? Do objective moral values such as justice and goodness exist? If they do, then on what basis: naturalism, an eastern monism or pantheism, some version of Platonism where moral values are part of the furniture of reality, theism? Many theistic thinkers have suggested that a connection exists between a personal good God and objective moral values: if such values do exist, then it is likely that a personal, good God exists.

This chapter explores some themes related to the moral argument for God's existence. If objective moral values exist, then God's existence is probable. This essay addresses the proper basicality of objective moral values, the is–ought problem (the naturalistic fallacy), theism's greater explanatory power regarding objective moral values, and the unlikelihood of moral values in a God-less universe, and the Euthyphro dilemma. While this essay responds more directly to naturalism, much of its argumentation would apply to other non-theistic perspectives, whether 'religious' or not.

The proper basicality of moral belief

We are wiser to assume that our senses, not to mention our powers of reasoning, are functioning reasonably well, unless we have good reason to doubt them, think them unreliable, or believe they are systematically deceiving us. Even the most radical skeptic assumes this 'principle of credulity' by taking for granted the reliability of his reasoning powers so that he can confidently draw skeptical conclusions. The skeptic will likely appropriate a host of logical laws to prove his point that we ought to share his inferences, and no doubt think we're in error to question his assessment. Though we may misperceive or make logical mis-steps, such mistakes in no way call into question the general reliability of our senses or reasoning powers.

In much the same way, there are certain *moral* truths that we can't *not* know (Budziszewski 2003). Even though we make faulty moral judgments, we should take these truths as givens, unless we have been suppressing our conscience or engaging in self-deception. We possess an inbuilt 'yuck factor': basic moral intuitions about the wrongness of torturing babies for fun, raping, murdering, or abusing children. Beyond this, we can readily recognize that kindness is a virtue and not a vice, that we ought to treat others as we would want to be treated, and that there is a moral difference between Mother Theresa and Pol Pot or Joseph Stalin. Those not recognizing the proper basicality of these truths are simply wrong, not functioning properly. Apart from and prior to any agreed-upon 'social contract,' we can intuitively recognize that all human beings have certain rights before the law or that racism is immoral.

Nicholas Rescher observes that if members of a particular tribe think that sacrificing first-born children is acceptable, 'then their grasp on the conception of morality is somewhere between inadequate and nonexistent' (1989: 43). Such a moral awareness is basic or 'bedrock,' as Kai Nielsen puts it:

> It is more reasonable to believe such elemental things [as wife-beating and
> child abuse] to be evil than to believe any skeptical theory that tells us we

cannot know or reasonably believe any of these things to be evil. ... I firmly believe that this is bedrock and right and that anyone who does not believe it cannot have probed deeply enough into the grounds of his moral beliefs. (1990: 10–11)

Affirming human rights and human value – and certain duties in light of them – is something we would readily expect if God exists (Porter 1999). As St Paul affirms, all people can know right from wrong apart from special revelation from God; the rightness of basic moral laws and the wrongness of their violation can be known by anyone not suppressing his conscience or hardening his heart (Lewis 1965):

> For when Gentiles who do not have the Law [of Moses] do instinctively the things of the Law, these, not having the Law, are a law to themselves, in that they show the work of the Law written in their hearts, their conscience bearing witness and their thoughts alternately accusing or else defending them. (Rom. 2: 14–15, NASB)

Robert Audi offers a description of how such moral intuitions function. They are (1) *non-inferential* or *directly apprehended*; (2) *firm* (they must be believed as propositions); (3) *comprehensible* (intuitions are formed in the light of an adequate understanding of their propositional objects); (4) *pre-theoretical* (not dependent on theories nor are they themselves theoretical hypotheses). Such moral knowledge emerges not from reflection on abstract principles but from reflecting on particular cases (particularism). Moreover, these prima facie intuitions are *not* indefeasible. That is, they may be adjusted or refined in light of other considerations or overriding circumstances. For instance, keeping a promise may be overridden by circumstances preventing me from keeping it, but I still have a duty to explain to my friend why I could not keep the promise (Audi 1997: 32–65).

Thus, even if human beings make faulty moral judgments and can be misguided at points, we would be wrong to abandon the quest for goodness or become moral skeptics: 'we cannot always or even usually be totally mistaken about goodness' (Adams 1999: 20). As with our senses or our rational faculties, we are wise to trust our basic moral intuitions even though modification or further reflection may be necessary. As with our sense perception and rational powers, we ought to take our moral intuitions seriously unless there is good reason to doubt them.

Morality and the naturalistic fallacy

David Hume claimed that one cannot logically move from the (scientific) description 'is' (or 'is not') to the (moral) prescription 'ought' (or 'ought not') without smuggling in some hidden premises (Hume 1888: 469; I. III. i). With certain differences, G. E. Moore argued in his *Principia Ethica* that we cannot move from *is* to *ought*, a move known as the naturalistic fallacy; nor, he added, can *ought* be reduced to *is*. That is, naturalistic definitions such as 'goodness = what is desirable or pleasurable' or 'goodness = what maximizes utility' do not sufficiently capture the essence of goodness. Goodness – that which is to be valued in and of itself – is irreducible to natural properties. We 'intuit' simple or irreducible non-natural properties just as we 'see' colors as simple and unanalyzable. Morality cannot be defined in natural terms. There is something 'non-natural' to goodness (Moore 1903: 6).

Some naturalistic moral realists believe that twentieth-century developments in the philosophy of science – together with 'naturalistic' developments in epistemology and philosophy of language – can help in the articulation and defense of moral realism: 'moral realism can be shown to be a more attractive and plausible position if recent developments in realist philosophy of science are brought to bear in its defense' (Boyd 1997: 106; cf. Brink 1989; Martin 2002; Shafer-Landau 2005). Theists allegedly cannot, without question begging, charge naturalistic moral realists as guilty of committing the naturalistic fallacy when moving from *is* to *ought* (Frankena 1970; 1976; 1981).

However, objective moral values rooted in naturalism with its purported 'scientific' support are actually undermined by the naturalistic worldview itself. For one thing, naturalists increasingly take their worldview to involve a strict materialism. However, material or physical properties such as extension, color, shape, or size are far different from moral values, which are not blue or orange and about two meters across, of an oblong shape, rough to the touch, and somewhat elastic. No physics textbook will include 'moral value' in its attempted description of matter. There is a *background* or *contextual* problem for the naturalist who believes in objective moral values: how do we move from a universe that originates from no prior matter into a universe of valueless matter and energy, eventually arriving at moral values, including human rights, human dignity, and moral obligation? It is hard to see how the naturalist could bridge this chasm.

Furthermore, let's say that valuable, morally responsible human beings have evolved after billions and billions of years of mindless planetary and biological evolution, *and* that objective moral values exist as a pre-existent part of the (Platonic) furniture of the universe. This would mean there exists a fantastic cosmic coincidence: namely, a correspondence between these pre-existent objective values and objectively valuable human beings

Theism – not naturalism or other non-theistic worldviews – offers both the appropriate context for affirming objective moral values as well as human dignity and worth. There is no remarkable cosmic coincidence between the existence of rights-bearing humans and the existence of objective moral values to which humans are obligated. A more suitable context for such values is the very character of a supremely valuable and good God, in whose image or likeness humans have been made, not naturalism (not to mention other non-theistic worldviews). This *imago Dei* would include possession of moral capacities, value, and obligations.

George Mavrodes comments on the place of moral values in a naturalistic worldview like that of Bertrand Russell's: 'Values and obligations cannot be deep in such a world. They have a grip only upon surface phenomena, probably only upon a man. What is deep in a Russellian world must be such things as matter and energy, or perhaps natural law[s], chance, or chaos' (Mavrodes 1986: 225). On the other hand, theism 'gives morality a deeper place in the world than does a Russellian view and thus permits it to "make sense"' (p. 226).

Furthermore, contrary to what naturalistic moral realists claim, 'scientific explanation' seems to call for rejecting the existence of objective moral values instead of unnecessarily bloating their ontology. More precisely, why insert objective moral values when bare scientific descriptions may be all that is required? Why not use *non*-moral terms and explanations of certain events that naturalistic moral realists typically take as morally weighted? Why not eliminate objective morality in the name of simplicity? Naturalistic moral realists claim that moral facts help explain certain actions performed by individuals, for example, 'Hitler killed millions of Jews because he was morally depraved.' But it is questionable whether the naturalistic moral realist has adequately made his case for the explanatory *necessity* of moral facts. Perhaps a 'strictly scientific response' would look like this:

> Hitler was a very bitter and angry person. Because of various false beliefs about Jews (most importantly his belief that Jews were responsible for Germany's defeat in World War I), he found hatred for the Jews to be a satisfying way of releasing his pent-up hostility and anger. His moral beliefs did not place any bounds or restraints on his expression of that hatred. (Carson 2000: 194)

While the moral realist may argue that moral facts are perhaps *relevant* to explain Hitler's behavior, he generally fails to refute the charge that moral facts are *necessary* to explain Hitler's behavior. That is, 'moral properties seem to be dispensable for explanatory purposes. Natural properties seem to be doing all of the work in the explanations in question' (p. 198). Further, nothing is *explained* by assuming that moral properties are constituted by natural facts: 'The best explanations of human behavior available to us at the present time do not make use of claims to the effect that moral facts are constituted by natural facts ... and it is a mystery how those properties cause or explain observable phenomena' (pp. 198–9). Simply to *posit* that moral properties have been instantiated by nature – that they have emerged from (or 'supervened upon') natural ones – is a far cry from *explaining* how this is so. It is difficult to see why the naturalist must resort to moral explanations when parsimony suggests another course: the 'scientific' one. If we are going the route of description and science, then why resort to the prescriptive? The is–ought problem still seems difficult for the naturalist to overcome.

Naturalists typically support their scientific account of moral realism by appeal to *epistemological* methodology (e.g., Martin 2002; Shafer-Landau 2005; but see Rea 2004), but they lack the proper *ontological* basis for morality. There is a confusion of *knowing* and *being*. Claiming to be able to recognize moral values and to make or refine moral judgments seems inadequate; what is lacking is the foundation or basis for affirming the value, dignity, and moral responsibility of human beings and the existence of moral obligations. Given a valueless, impersonal, materialistic metaphysical backdrop, why think that valuable, personal, responsible moral agents should ever appear on the scene? If, on the other hand, a personal God exists who has made humans – theists and non-theists alike – in his image, then we should not be surprised that atheists can recognize the same objective moral values theists can. We function properly, according to our design, when we think and act morally.

Though naturalistic moral realists claim that the necessity of moral truths renders God's existence irrelevant, their necessity would *still* require grounding in the character of a good, personal God: he necessarily exists in all possible worlds, is the source of all necessary moral truths, and is explanatorily prior to these moral values, which stand in asymmetrical relation to his necessity. We could compare this to a pendulum, whose period (completed swing) can be deduced from the pendulum's length, but not vice versa. That is, the pendulum's length explains its period, not the reverse (Mann 1997). And even if a moral standard existed independently of God, the question still remains of how morally valuable and morally responsible beings could emerge from the cause-and-effect processes of valueless matter. That mindless naturalistic evolution could produce beings obligated to moral laws 'anticipating' their arrival is a massive cosmic coincidence indeed! The existence of a good personal God, who created humans in his image, offers a simpler and less ad hoc connection.

In the words of Thomas Carson: '[naturalistic] moral realists have not yet proffered theories developed in sufficient detail to be very useful in explaining or predicting the relevant (moral) phenomena' (Carson 2000: 199). To date, 'no [naturalistic] moralist-realist theory has anything like the explanatory or predictive power of atomic theory' (ibid.; also, Audi 1993: 111).

The connection between God and objective morality

As suggested above, the contextual fit between naturalism and moral realism is not a good one. Michael Martin claims that there is 'no a priori reason why objective moral values could not be constituted by matter' (Martin 2002: 45). But again, one would be hard-pressed to find a physics textbook that features 'possessing objective moral values' as a description or definition of 'matter.' Whether constituted by matter or supervening upon it, objective moral values along with moral obligations and human dignity prove to be an ill-fit in a naturalistic setting. A more 'natural' context for moral values and human dignity is the *theistic* one. We have been made by a personal, self-aware, purposeful, good God to resemble him in certain important ways. We should prefer a context that offers a better match or fit for affirming human dignity, worth, rights, and objective moral values. Theism offers just such a match-up. A supremely valuable, personal, good Creator offers the context for affirming that human beings have value, dignity, and moral responsibility/obligations. Naturalism, on the other hand, requires that we move from *valueless* processes to *valuable* beings, scientific *description* to moral *prescription*, from *is* to *ought*. Theism suggests a superior explanatory context (Rea 2004).

Furthermore, naturalism's affirmation of morality seems more ad hoc and contrived given its rootedness in valueless, mindless processes. Theism is much more basic an explanation, offering a smoother transition between a good God and human dignity and rights. No background-defying assumptions are needed. The personal value of human beings derives naturally from being created by a supremely valuable divine personal Being. Consider a parallel scenario: it is no surprise that many naturalists acknowledge the difficulty of accounting for the emergence of thought, consciousness, or technicolor subjective (first-person) experience from non-thinking matter (McGinn 1990: 10-11). Here too, theism offers a smooth transition between a supremely conscious Being to the existence of consciousness within the universe. Apart from the existence of this supremely aware Being, consciousness would not exist at all. Similarly, apart from a supremely good personal Being, moral values and dignity or rights would not be instantiated in the world; therefore there would be no objective moral values.

Just as consciousness makes better sense in a world in which a supremely self-aware Being exists, so objective moral values make better sense in a world in which a supremely good Being exists. The deeper, more basic, unified, and less ad hoc explanation is to be preferred.

To further reinforce this theism-morality connection, a number of naturalists have acknowledged the likelihood of mere subjective moral values if nature is all there is. Some explicitly acknowledge that if moral values exist, this would furnish us with good evidence that God exists. Atheist J. L. Mackie asserted that objective morality in a naturalistic world is a 'queer' or odd phenomenon; a theistic world would better accommodate it: if objective moral values exist, 'they make the existence of a god more probable than it would have been without them. Thus we have … a defensible argument from morality to the existence of a god' (Mackie 1982: 115–16).

It is not difficult to find naturalists who consider ethics to be nothing more than a human invention or a biological adaptation for survival and reproduction. Russell avers that 'the whole subject of ethics arises from the pressure of the community on the individual' (Russell 1954: 124). As another naturalist puts it, morality is simply the 'ephemeral product of the evolutionary process, just as are our other adaptations' – our hands and feet and teeth. 'Morality is just an aid to survival and reproduction, and has no being beyond this' (Ruse 1989: 268). Our awareness of morality is simply one of 'biological worth' (p. 262). In light of the twentieth-century's moral horrors and the subsequent moral crisis, Jonathan Glover suggests that morality may survive 'when seen to be a human creation' (Glover 1999: 41). His advice is that humans 're-create ethics' (p. 42).

The problem with such a construal of morality as subjective is that naturalistic evolution appears to undermine confidence not only in our moral intuitions and basic convictions, but in reason and the thought-process itself. If we are simply organisms wired to survive and reproduce, then we may end up believing many *falsehoods* that help us to survive. Naturalistic evolution is not interested in true belief, but in fighting, fleeing, feeding, and reproducing. We may believe human beings have moral value and that we really have moral obligations, and these beliefs may help us as a species to survive, but they may be completely false. We can take no confidence in our reasoning process. If we happen to be correct in our skepticism, it is purely accidental rather than rational.

However, if a trustworthy God has created our noetic structure, then we can have confidence in our rational faculties and moral intuitions rather than constantly doubting their reliability. If we have been designed to trust our faculties, constantly failing or refusing to trust them is a sign of cognitive malfunction (Plantinga 2000: 185).

The theist can maintain that because the source of the cosmos is ultimately personal and morally good, human dignity and objective moral values find themselves at home here. Intrinsic value must be given at the outset; otherwise, it doesn't matter how many non-personal and non-valuable components we happen to stack up. From valuelessness valuelessness comes, but value produces value.

A *personal* Creator, who made human *persons* in his image, thus serves as the ontological basis for the existence of objective moral values, moral obligation, human dignity and rights. Without the existence of a personal God, there would be no persons at all; and if no persons existed, then no moral properties would be instantiated in our world. God is the necessary ground for the realization of moral properties. Moral values and personhood are deeply intertwined.

The atheistic moral realist claims that the statement 'Murder is wrong' would hold true even if God does not exist. A few responses are in order. First, even if we grant that moral facts are just brute givens and necessarily true (just as logical laws are), the huge cosmic coincidence of or correspondence between these *moral facts* and the eventual evolutionary development of self-reflective moral beings who are obligated to them and recognize them demands explanation. These moral facts, it appears, were *anticipating* our emergence. A less ad hoc explanation is that a good God made valuable human beings in his image. Second, the necessity of moral truths does not diminish their need for grounding in the character of a personal God. God necessarily exists in all possible worlds, and God can be the source of necessary moral truths that stand in asymmetrical relation to God's necessity. So God would still be explanatorily prior to these moral values.

The Euthyphro dilemma

Some have suggested, following Plato's *Euthyphro* dialogue, that goodness ('what is holy') is either what God happens to command – in which case it is arbitrary – *or* what God must conform to, in which case an independent standard of morality exists (*Euthyphro* 10a). Writes naturalist David Brink: 'if God were to exist, she [sic] would command all and only good or morally correct actions *because* these actions are good or right prior to and independently of God's will and because God herself [sic] is good'; on the other hand, moral properties do not 'consist in properties of divine will' (Brink 1989: 158).

This dilemma is more apparent than real. It is ultimately resolved by rooting objective moral values in the non-arbitrary, essentially good *character* of God who has made us in his image; even if divine commands offer instructive and particular direction, they are reflective of God's good nature.

Here are further considerations. (1) If the naturalistic moral realist adheres to a moral standard herself, we can ask the question: 'Are these moral values good simply because they are good, or is there an independent standard of goodness to which they conform?' Posing the Euthyphro argument offers her no actual advantage over a theistic perspective. (2) The naturalist's query is pointless since we must eventually arrive at some self-sufficient and self-explanatory stopping point beyond which the discussion can go no further. (3) God, who is essentially perfect, does not have obligations to some external moral standard; God simply acts, and it is good and he naturally does what is good. (4) The idea that God could be evil or command evil is utterly contrary to the very definition of God; otherwise, such a being would not be God and would not be worthy of worship. (5) The acceptance of objective values assumes a kind of ultimate goal or cosmic design plan for human beings, which would make no sense given naturalism, but makes much sense given theism, which assumes a plan (Copan 2003).

Conclusion

Human dignity, moral responsibility, and moral obligations are properly basic. We constantly take these for granted in our personal lives and in the public square (e.g., our judicial and penal system). Rightly functioning human beings will recognize these bedrock intuitive moral principles. And if moral values, human dignity, and personal responsibility exist, it seems that theism has ample resources to account for these facts – namely, being made in the image of a good, personal God. Without such a personal, good God, there would be no moral values because there would be no persons in whom value resides (Copan 2003; 2004; 2007).

Of course, a successful moral argument does not fully reveal that the God of Abraham, Isaac, Jacob, and Jesus exists, which would constitute a full-blown or robust theism. The moral argument can be supplemented with other successful theistic arguments, for example, or by considering possible special revelation that further clarifies the identity of this God. Perhaps this God has made some provision to rescue us from our desperate plight in a world of evil and suffering. This argument does, however, strongly suggest a supreme personal moral Being who is worthy of worship, who has made us with dignity and worth, to whom we are personally accountable, and who may reasonably be called 'God.'

See also Goodness (Chapter 28), The argument from consciousness (Chapter 35), The problem of evil (Chapter 37), Sin and salvation (Chapter 53).

References

Adams, R. M. (1999) *Finite and Infinite Goods: A Framework for Ethics*, Oxford: Oxford University Press.
Audi, R. (1993) 'Ethical naturalism and the explanatory power of moral concepts,' in S. J. Wagner and R. Warner (eds) *Naturalism: A Critical Appraisal*, Notre Dame, IN: University of Notre Dame Press.
—— (1997) *Moral Knowledge and Ethical Character*, New York: Oxford University Press.
Boyd, R. (1997) 'How to be a moral realist,' in S. Darwall, A. Gibbard, and P. Railton (eds) *Moral Discourse and Practice: Some Philosophical Approaches*, New York: Oxford University Press.
Brink, D. O. (1989) *Moral Realism and the Foundations of Ethics*, New York: Cambridge University Press.

Budziszewski, J. (2003) *What We Can't Not Know*, Dallas, TX: Spence.

Carson, T. L. (2000) *Value and the Good Life*, Notre Dame, IN: University of Notre Dame Press.

Copan, P. (2003) 'The moral argument,' in P. Copan and P. K. Moser (eds) *The Rationality of Theism*, London: Routledge.

—— (2004) 'Morality and meaning without God: another failed attempt,' *Philosophia Christi* NS 6: 295–304.

—— (2007) 'The moral argument,' in P. Copan and C. Meister (eds) *Philosophy of Religion: Classic and Contemporary Issues*, Oxford: Blackwell.

Frankena, W. K. (1970) 'The naturalistic fallacy,' in W. Sellars and J. Hospers (eds) *Readings in Ethical Theory*, 2nd edn, New York: Appleton-Century-Crofts.

—— (1976) 'Obligation and motivation in recent moral philosophy,' in K. E. Goodpaster (ed.) *Perspectives on Morality: Essays by William K. Frankena*, Notre Dame, IN: University of Notre Dame Press.

—— (1981) 'Is morality logically dependent upon religion?', in P. Helm (ed.) *Divine Commands and Morality*, Oxford: Oxford University Press.

Glover, J. (1999) *Humanity: A Moral History of the Twentieth Century*, London: Jonathan Cape.

Hume, D. (1888) [1739–40] *A Treatise of Human Nature*, ed. L. A. Selby-Bigge, Oxford: Clarendon Press.

Lewis, C. S. (1965) *The Abolition of Man*, New York: Macmillan.

Mackie, J. L. (1982) *The Miracle of Theism*, Oxford: Clarendon Press.

Mann, W. E. (1997) 'Necessity,' in P. L. Quinn and C. Taliaferro (eds) *Companion to Philosophy of Religion*, Malden, MA: Blackwell.

Martin, M. (2002) *Atheism: Morality, and Meaning*, Amherst, NY: Prometheus.

Mavrodes, G. (1986) 'Religion and the queerness of morality,' in R. Audi and W. J. Wainwright (eds) *Rationality, Religious Belief, and Moral Commitment: New Essays in the Philosophy of Religion*, Ithaca, NY: Cornell University Press.

McGinn, C. (1990) *The Problem of Consciousness*, Oxford: Blackwell.

Moore, G. E. (1903) *Principia Ethica*, Cambridge: Cambridge University Press.

Nielsen, K. (1990) *Ethics Without God*, rev. edn, Buffalo, NY: Prometheus.

Plantinga, A. (2000) *Warranted Christian Belief*, New York: Oxford University Press.

Plato (1989) *The Collected Dialogues of Plato*, ed. E. Hamilton and H. Cairns, Princeton, NJ: Princeton University Press.

Porter, J. (1999) *Natural and Divine Law*, Grand Rapids, MI: Eerdmans.

Rea, M. (2004) 'Naturalism and moral realism,' in T. Crisp, D. VanderLaan, and M. Davidson (eds) *Knowledge and Reality*, Dordrecht: Kluwer.

Rescher, N. (1989) *Moral Absolutes: An Essay on the Nature and Rationale of Morality*, Studies in Moral Philosophy, vol. 2, New York: Peter Lang.

Ruse, M. (1989) *The Darwinian Paradigm*, London: Routledge.

Russell, B. (1954) *Human Society in Ethics and Politics*, London: Allen & Unwin.

Shafer-Landau, R. (2005) *Moral Realism: A Defence*, New York: Oxford University Press.

Further reading

Adams, R. M. (1999) *Finite and Infinite Goods: A Framework for Ethics*, Oxford: Oxford University Press. (A detailed exposition on the deep connection between God and goodness.)

Copan, P. (2003) 'The moral argument,' in P. Copan and P. K. Moser (eds) *The Rationality of Theism*, London: Routledge. (An overview of the moral argument for God's existence.)

Graham, G. (2001) *Evil and Christian Ethics*, Cambridge: Cambridge University Press. (A discussion of goodness and evil, which can be more plausibly understood given theism; naturalistic attempts to explain the existence of evil prove to be quite disappointing.)

Hare, J. (1997) *The Moral Gap: Kantian Ethics, Human Limits, and God's Assistance*, Oxford Studies in Theological Ethics, Oxford: Oxford University Press. (Points us to God's existence and divine assistance in light of moral ideals and our failure to live up to them.)

Kirkpatrick, F. G. (2003) *A Moral Ontology for a Theistic Ethic*, Burlington, VT: Ashgate. (A wide-ranging discussion of the needed personal theistic metaphysic to ground ethics.)

Rist, J. (2003) *Real Ethics: Rethinking the Foundations of Morality*, Cambridge: Cambridge University Press. (An excellent introduction to the history of western ethical discussion and a presentation of the only two ethical alternative views: Nietzschean nihilism or transcendent theism, the latter offering the more solid ontological grounding.)

Sorley, W. R. (1921) *Moral Values and the Idea of God*, 2nd edn, New York: Macmillan. (A classic defense of the moral argument, showing the close connection between personhood and objective moral values.)

Wainwright, W. J. (2005) *Religion and Morality*. Burlington, VT: Ashgate. (An excellent discussion that focuses on the Euthyphro argument and aspects of the divine command theory.)

35

THE ARGUMENT FROM CONSCIOUSNESS

J. P. Moreland

Consciousness is among the most mystifying features of the cosmos. Colin McGinn claims that its arrival borders on sheer magic because there seems to be no naturalistic explanation for it: 'How can mere matter originate consciousness? How did evolution convert the water of biological tissue into the wine of consciousness? Consciousness seems like a radical novelty in the universe, not prefigured by the aftereffects of the Big Bang; so how did it contrive to spring into being from what preceded it?' (McGinn 1999: 13–14). Accordingly some argue that, while finite mental entities may be inexplicable on a naturalist worldview, they may be best explained by theism, thereby furnishing evidence for God's existence. This chapter will attempt to clarify the argument for God's existence from finite consciousness (hereafter, AC) and evaluate three alternatives to it.

Two preliminaries

Two preliminary assumptions should be made explicit. First, premise (1) of AC (below) posits a commonsense understanding of mental states such as sensations, thoughts, beliefs, desires, and volitions. So understood, mental states are in no sense physical since they possess features, e.g., an intrinsic feel such as the hurtfulness of pain, and intentionality (ofness or aboutness directed toward an object; for example, a particular thought is of or about the moon), which are not owned by physical states. One way to reject AC is to reject this assumption. Since most rivals to AC assume with its advocates a dualist construal of consciousness, we shall grant this dualist assumption in what follows.

Second, causal explanations in the natural sciences should exhibit a kind of causal necessity; physical causal explanations must show why an effect must follow given the relevant causal conditions. At least five reasons have been proffered for this assumption:

(a) Causal necessitation unpacks the deepest, core realist notion of causation, namely, causal production according to which a cause 'brings about' or 'produces' its effect.

(b) Causal necessitation fits the paradigm cases of causal explanation (e.g., macro-solidity/impenetrability in terms of micro-lattice structures, repulsive forces; mass proportions in chemical reactions in terms of atomic models of atoms/molecules, bonding orbitals, energy stability, charge distribution) central to the core theories (e.g., the atomic theory of matter) that constitute a naturalist worldview and in terms of which it is purported to have explanatory superiority to rival worldviews.

(c) Causal necessitation provides a way of distinguishing accidental generalizations (e.g., plants grow when exposed to the sun's heat) from true causal laws (plants grow when exposed to the sun's light).

(d) Causal necessitation supports the derivation of counterfactuals (e.g., if that chunk of gold had been placed in aqua regia, then it would have dissolved) from causal laws (gold dissolves in aqua regia).

(e) Causal necessitation clarifies the direction of causality and rules out the attempt to explain a cause by its effect.

The argument from consciousness

AC may be expressed in inductive or deductive form. As an inductive argument, AC may be construed as claiming that given theism and naturalism as the live options fixed by our background beliefs, theism provides a better explanation of consciousness than naturalism and, thus, receives some confirmation from the existence of consciousness.

AC may also be expressed in deductive form. Here is one deductive version of AC:

1 Genuinely non-physical mental states exist.
2 There is an explanation for the existence of mental states.
3 Personal explanation is different from natural scientific explanation.
4 The explanation for the existence of mental states is either a personal or natural scientific explanation.
5 The explanation is not a natural scientific one.
6 Therefore, the explanation is a personal one.
7 If the explanation is personal, then it is theistic.
8 Therefore, the explanation is theistic.

Theists such as Robert Adams (1992) and Richard Swinburne (Swinburne 1997: 174–99; 2004: 192–212) have advanced a slightly different version of AC which focuses on mental/physical correlations and not merely on the existence of mental states. Either way, AC may be construed as a deductive argument.

Premises (2), (4), and (5) are the ones most likely to come under attack. We are granting (1) for the sake of argument. Premise (3) turns on the fact that personal explanation differs from event-causal covering-law explanations employed in natural science. Associated with *event* causation is a covering law model of explanation according to which some event (the *explanandum*) is explained by giving a correct deductive or inductive argument for that event. Such an argument contains two features in its *explanans*: a (universal or statistical) law of nature *and* initial causal conditions.

By contrast, a *personal* explanation (divine or otherwise) of some state of affairs brought about intentionally by a person will employ notions such as the intention of the agent, the relevant power of the agent that was exercised in causing the state of affairs, and the means used to accomplish the intention.

Advocates of AC employ the difference between these two modes of explanation to justify premise (2). Briefly, the argument is that given a defense of premises (4) and (5), there is no natural scientific explanation of mental entities. Thus the phenomena cited in (1) may not be taken as unique facts that can be explained naturalistically. Moreover, the appearance of mental entities and their regular correlation with physical entities are puzzling phenomena that cry out for explanation. Since personal explanation is something people use all the time, this distinctive form of explanation is available, and its employment regarding the phenomena cited in (1) removes our legitimate puzzlement regarding them.

Premise (7) seems fairly uncontroversial. To be sure, Humean-style arguments about the type and number of deities involved could be raised at this point, but these issues would be intramural theistic problems of small comfort to naturalists. That is, if the explanation for finite conscious minds is supernatural, then naturalism is false.

Premise (4) will be examined in conjunction with two alternatives to AC that reject it: Colin McGinn's position and panpsychism.

That leaves (5). At least four reasons have been offered for why there is no natural scientific explanation for the existence of mental states (or their regular correlation with physical states):

(a) *The uniformity of nature.* Prior to the emergence of consciousness, the universe contained nothing but aggregates of particles/waves standing in fields of forces relative to each other. The story of the development of the cosmos is told in terms of the rearrangement of micro-parts into increasingly more complex structures according to natural law. On a naturalist depiction of matter, it is brute mechanical, physical stuff. The emergence of consciousness seems to be a case of getting something from nothing. In general, physico-chemical reactions do not generate consciousness, but they do in the brain. Yet brains seem similar to other parts of organisms' bodies (e.g., both are collections of cells completely describable in physical terms). How can like causes produce radically different effects? The appearance of mind is utterly unpredictable and inexplicable. This radical discontinuity seems like an inhomogeneous rupture in the natural world. Similarly, physical states have spatial extension and location but mental states seem to lack spatial features. Space and consciousness sit oddly together. How did spatially arranged matter conspire to produce non-spatial mental states? From a naturalist point of view, this seems utterly inexplicable.

(b) *Contingency of the mind/body correlation.* The regular correlation between types of mental states and physical states seems radically contingent. Why do pains instead of itches, and thoughts or feelings of love, get correlated with specific brain states? On the basis of strong conceivability, zombie worlds (worlds physically like ours in which creatures' bodies move like ours do but in which there is no consciousness) and inverted qualia worlds (worlds where people discriminate red objects from other objects and use the word 'red' while pointing to them, but do so on the basis of having a sensation of blue while looking at red objects and who have a sensation of red while looking at blue objects) are possible. No amount of knowledge of the brain state will help to answer emergentist questions about the existence and precise nature of mental–physical correlations. Given the requirement of causal necessitation for naturalistic causal explanations, there is *in principle* no naturalistic explanation for either the existence of mental states or their regular correlation with physical states. For the naturalist, the regularity of mind/body correlations must be taken as contingent brute facts. But these facts are inexplicable from a naturalistic standpoint, and they are radically unique compared to all other entities in the naturalist ontology. Thus, it begs the question simply to announce that mental states and their regular correlations with certain brain states is a natural fact.

(c) *Epiphenomenalism and causal closure*. Most naturalists believe that their worldview requires that all entities whatever are either physical or depend on the physical for their existence and behavior. One implication of this belief is commitment to the causal closure of the physical. On this principle, when one is tracing the causal antecedents of any physical event, one will never have to leave the level of the physical. Physical effects have only physical causes. Rejection of the causal closure principle would imply a rejection of the possibility of a complete and comprehensive physical theory of all physical phenomena, something that no naturalist should reject. Thus, if mental phenomena are genuinely non-physical, then they must be epiphenomena: effects caused by the physical that do not themselves have causal powers. But epiphenomenalism is false. Mental causation seems undeniable. The admission of epiphenomenal non-physical mental entities may be taken as a refutation of naturalism. Why? Because if a form of naturalism implies epiphenomenalism and epiphenomenalism is false, then that form of naturalism is false.

(d) *The inadequacy of evolutionary explanations*. Naturalists are committed to the view that, in principle, evolutionary explanations can be offered for the appearance of all organisms and their parts. It is not hard to see how an evolutionary account could be given for new and increasingly complex physical structures that constitute different organisms. However, organisms are black boxes as far as evolution is concerned. As long as an organism, when receiving certain inputs, generates the correct behavioral outputs under the demands of fighting, fleeing, reproducing, and feeding, the organism will survive. What goes on inside the organism is irrelevant and only becomes significant for the processes of evolution when an output is produced. Strictly speaking, it is the output, not what caused it, which bears on the struggle for reproductive advantage. Moreover, the functions organisms carry out consciously *could just as well have been done unconsciously*. Thus, both the sheer existence of conscious states, the precise mental content that constitutes them, and their regular correlation with types of physical states is outside the pale of evolutionary explanation.

We have looked at four reasons why many scholars, including many naturalists, hold that naturalism requires the rejection of consciousness construed along dualist lines.

The naturalistic worldview

At this point, it may be wise to look briefly at the nature of naturalism as a worldview to gain further insight into why consciousness is such a problem for naturalists. Naturalism usually includes the following:

1 different aspects of a naturalist epistemic attitude (e.g., a rejection of so-called 'first philosophy' in which there is no philosophical knowledge or justified beliefs that are independent of and more basic than scientific knowledge), along with an acceptance of either strong or weak scientism (either science provides justified beliefs or science is vastly better than other disciplines in providing justified beliefs);
2 a Grand Story which amounts to a causal account of how all entities whatsoever have come to be, told in terms of an event causal story described in natural scientific terms with a central role given to the atomic theory of matter and evolutionary biology;
3 a general ontology in which the only entities allowed are those that either (i) bear a relevant similarity to those thought to characterize a completed form of physics or (ii) can be explained according to the causal necessitation requirement in terms of the Grand Story and the naturalist epistemic attitude.

For our purposes, it is important to say a bit more about naturalist ontological commitments. A good place to start is with what Frank Jackson calls the location problem (Jackson 1998: 1–5). According to Jackson, given that naturalists are committed to a fairly widely accepted physical story about how things came to be and what they are, the location problem is the task of locating or finding a place for some entity (e.g., semantic contents, mind, agency) in that story. As an illustration, Jackson shows how the solidity of macro-objects can be located within a naturalist worldview. If solidity is taken as impenetrability, then given the lattice structure of atoms composing, say, a table and chair, it becomes obvious why they cannot penetrate each other. Given the naturalist micro-story, the macro-world could not have been different: the table could not penetrate the chair. Location requires showing how the troublesome entity had to arise given the Grand Story.

There are three constraints for developing a naturalist ontology and locating entities within it:

(a) Entities should be knowable by empirical, scientific means.
(b) The origin of those entities should be necessitated by physical entities and processes according to the Grand Story.

(c) Entities should bear a relevant similarity to those found in chemistry and physics or be shown to depend necessarily on entities in chemistry and physics.

Given theism and naturalism as rivals, theists who employ the argument from consciousness seek to capitalize on the naturalistic failure to come to terms with consciousness by offering a rival explanation for its appearance. That failure is why most prominent naturalists (e.g., David Papineau 1993) reject premise (1) of AC ('Genuinely non-physical mental states exist.') and either eliminate or, in one way or another, identify conscious states with physical ones.

Unfortunately for naturalists, consciousness has stubbornly resisted treatment in physical terms. Consciousness has been recalcitrant for naturalists, and premise (1) is hard to dismiss. Aware of this problem, various naturalists who accept premise (1) have proposed certain alternatives to theism and AC. In the next section, we shall look at three representative options.

Alternatives to AC

John Searle's biological naturalism

John Searle has developed a naturalistic account of consciousness which would, if successful, provide justification for rejecting premise (5) of AC (Searle 1992). According to Searle, since about the 1940s philosophy of mind has been dominated by strict physicalism because it was seen as a crucial implication of taking the naturalistic turn. For these naturalists, if one abandons strict physicalism, one has rejected a scientific naturalist approach to the mind/body problem and opened oneself up to the intrusion of religious concepts and arguments about the mental.

By contrast, Searle's own solution to the mind/body problem is biological naturalism: while mental states are exactly what dualists describe them to be, nevertheless, they are merely emergent biological states and processes that causally supervene upon a suitably structured, functioning brain. Brain processes cause mental processes, which are not ontologically reducible to the former. Consciousness is just an ordinary (i.e., physical) feature of the brain and, as such, is merely an ordinary feature of the natural world.

Given that he characterizes consciousness as dualists do, why does Searle claim that biological naturalism does not represent a rejection of scientific naturalism which, in turn, opens the door for religious concepts about and explanations for the mental? Searle's answer to this question is developed in three steps.

In step one, he cites several examples of emergence (liquidity, solidity, features of digestion) that he takes to be unproblematic for naturalists and claims that emergent consciousness is analogous to the unproblematic cases.

In step two, he formulates two reasons why consciousness is not a problem for naturalists: (i) The emergence of consciousness is not a problem if we stop trying to picture or image consciousness. (ii) In standard cases (heat, color), an ontological reduction (e.g., identifying a specific color with a wavelength) is based on a causal reduction (e.g., claiming that a specific color is caused by a wavelength) because our pragmatic interests are in reality, not appearance.

In these cases we can distinguish the *appearance* of heat and color from the *reality*, place the former in consciousness, leave the latter in the objective world, and go on to define the phenomenon itself in terms of its causes. We can do this because our interests are in the reality and not the appearance. The ontological reduction of heat to its causes leaves the appearance of heat the same. Regarding consciousness, we are interested in the appearances, and thus the irreducibility of consciousness is merely due to pragmatic considerations, not to some deep metaphysical problem.

In step three, Searle claims that an adequate scientific explanation of the emergence of consciousness consists in a detailed, lawlike set of correlations between mental and physical state tokens.

Several things may be said in response to Searle's position. Regarding steps one and two, his cases of emergence (rigidity, fluidity) are not good analogies to consciousness since the former are *easy* to locate in the naturalist epistemology and ontology, but consciousness is *not*. Given a widely accepted physicalist description of atoms, molecules, lattice structure, and the like, the rigidity or fluidity of macro-objects follows necessarily. But there is no clear necessary connection between any physical state and any mental state. For example, given a specific brain state normally 'associated' with the mental state of being appeared to redly, inverted qualia worlds (worlds with that physical state but radically different mental states 'associated' with it), zombie worlds (worlds with that physical state and no mental states at all) and disembodied worlds (worlds with beings possessing mental states with no physical entities at all) are still metaphysically possible. It is easy to locate solidity in a naturalist framework but the same cannot be said for consciousness.

Further, the emergence of genuinely new properties in macro-objects that are not part of the micro-world (e.g., heat construed as warmth, color construed commonsensically as a quality) presents problems for naturalists in the same way consciousness does and, historically, that is why they were placed in consciousness. Contrary to Searle, they were not so placed because of the pragmatics of our interests. For example, historically, the problem was that if so-called secondary qualities (tastes, smells, colors, sounds, textures) were kept in the mind-independent world, there was no naturalistic explanation for why they emerged on the occasion of a mere rearrangement in micro-parts exhaustively characterized in terms of primary qualities (primary qualities are those features taken to exhaust the nature of matter, e.g., mass, size, shape, location, being in motion or at rest, having such and such forces of attraction or repulsion, vibrating at a certain frequency). Secondary qualities construed along commonsense lines are not among the primary qualities employed to characterize the micro-world and, indeed, seem contingently linked to the micro-world. It is this straightforward ontological problem, not the pragmatics of reduction or the attempt to image consciousness, that presents difficulties for naturalism.

In fact, the emergence of mental properties is more like the emergence of normative (e.g., moral) properties than the properties of solidity or digestion. Even the atheist J. L. Mackie admitted that the emergence of moral properties provided evidence for a moral argument for God's existence analogous to AC: 'Moral properties constitute so odd a cluster of properties and relations that they are most unlikely to have arisen in the ordinary course of events without an all-powerful god to create them' (Mackie 1982: 115). Mackie is right on this point. Given theism, if a naturalist were simply to claim that the emergence of moral properties was a basic naturalistic fact, this would be an ad hoc, question-begging ploy of assuming a point not congruent with a naturalistic worldview. Searle's 'explanation' of consciousness is guilty of the same charge.

Regarding step three, 'explanations' in science that do not express the sort of necessity we have been discussing are better taken as *descriptions*, not *explanations*. For example, the ideal gas equation is a description of the behavior of gases. An explanation of that behavior is provided by the atomic theory of gas. Further, given theism and AC, it is question-begging and ad hoc for Searle to assert that mental entities and mental/physical correlations are basic, since such entities are natural in light of theism but unnatural given philosophical naturalism. As naturalist Jaegwon Kim notes, the correlations are not explanations (Kim 1996: 8). They are the very things that need explaining and, given a proper understanding of the real questions, no naturalistic explanation seems to be forthcoming. By misconstruing the problem, Searle fails to address the real issue and, weighed against AC, his position is inadequate.

Colin McGinn's agnostic 'naturalism'

Naturalist Colin McGinn has offered a different solution (McGinn 1999). Given the radical difference between mind and matter as it is depicted by current or even an ideal future physics, there is no naturalistic solution that stays within the widely accepted naturalist epistemology and ontology. Darwinian explanations fail as well because they cannot account for why consciousness appeared in the first place. What is needed is a radically different kind of solution to the origin of mind, one that must meet two conditions: (i) it must be a naturalistic solution, and (ii) it must depict the emergence of consciousness and its regular correlation with matter as necessary and not contingent facts.

McGinn claims that there must be two kinds of unknowable natural properties that solve the problem. There must be some general properties of matter that enter into the production of consciousness when assembled into a brain. Thus, all matter has the potentiality to underlie consciousness. Further, there must be some natural property of the brain he calls C* that unleashes these general properties.

The temptation to take the origin of consciousness as a mystery, indeed, a mystery that is best explained theistically, is due to our ignorance of these properties. However, given C* and the general properties of matter, the unknowable link between mind and matter is ordinary, commonplace, and necessitates the emergence of consciousness. Unfortunately, evolution did not give humans the faculties needed to know these properties and, thus, they are in principle beyond our grasp. We will forever be agnostic about their nature. However, they must be there since there must be some naturalistic explanation of mind as all other solutions have failed.

McGinn offers two further descriptions of these unknowable yet ordinary properties that link matter and mind: (i) they are not sense perceptible, and (ii) since matter is spatial and mind non-spatial, they are either in some sense pre-spatial or are spatial in a way that is itself unknowable to our faculties. In this way, these unknowable properties contain at least the potentiality for both ordinary spatial features of matter and the non-spatial features of consciousness as judged by our usual concept of space.

In sum, the mind/matter link is an unknowable mystery due to our cognitive limitations resulting from our evolution. And since the link is quite ordinary, we should not be puzzled by the origin of mind, and no theistic explanation is required.

Critics have offered at least three criticisms of McGinn's position. First, given McGinn's agnosticism about the properties that link mind and matter, how can he confidently assert some of their features? How does he know they are non-sensory, pre-spatial, or spatial in an unknowable way? How does he know some of these properties underlie all matter? Indeed, what possible justification can he give for their reality? The only one he suggests is that we must provide a naturalistic solution and all ordinary naturalistic ones either deny consciousness or fail to solve the problem. But given the presence of AC, McGinn's claims are simply question-begging. Indeed, his agnosticism seems to be a convenient way of hiding behind naturalism and avoiding a theistic explanation. Given that theism enjoys a positive degree of justification prior to the problem of consciousness, he should avail himself of the explanatory resources of theism.

Second, it is not clear that his solution is a version of naturalism, except in name only. In contrast to other entities in the naturalist ontology, McGinn's linking properties cannot be known scientifically, nor are they relevantly similar to the rest of the naturalist ontology. Thus, it becomes vacuous to call these properties 'naturalistic.' McGinn's own speculations strike one as ad hoc in light of the inadequacies of naturalistic explanations. In fact, McGinn's solution is actually closer to an agnostic form of panpsychism (see below) than to naturalism. Given AC, McGinn's solution is an ad hoc readjustment of naturalism.

Third, McGinn does not solve the problem of consciousness; he merely relocates it. Rather than having two radically different entities (unlocated mind and located matter, that seem to be contingently connected), he offers us unknowable properties with two radically different aspects. For example, his links contain the potentiality for ordinary spatiality and non-spatiality, for ordinary materiality and mentality. Moreover, these radically different aspects of the linking properties are just as contingently related (the capacity for spatiality and non-spatiality do not require each other to exist and, indeed, seem to contingently connected; the same may be said for the capacities for materiality and mentality). And these contingently related features seem to be without a linking intermediary to connect them every bit as much as non-spatial mental and spatial physical properties fail to have an intermediary connecting link on a dualist perspective. The contingency comes from the nature of mind and matter as naturalists conceive it. It does not solve the problem of the contingency of a connecting link to remove it from mind and matter directly and to relocate the contingent connection by characterizing it as two aspects (potential for spatiality and for non-spatiality; potential for materiality and for non-materiality) of some unknowable entity.

Panpsychism

For the vast majority of philosophers, there are few serious advocates of panpsychism, though it has been suggested by Thomas Nagel (Nagel 1986) and David Chalmers (Chalmers 1996). The main exception to this generalization is panpsychist David Skrbina (Skrbina 2005). Roughly, panpsychism is the view that all matter has consciousness within it. Since each parcel of matter has its own consciousness, the brain is conscious since it is just a collection of those parcels. Consciousness is pervasive in nature; so its apparent emergence in particular cases is not something that requires special explanation. One can distinguish two forms of panpsychism. According to the strong version, all matter has conscious states in it in the same sense that organisms such as dogs and humans do. According to the weak form, regular matter has consciousness in a degraded, attenuated way in the form of proto-mental states that, under the right circumstances, yield conscious mental states without themselves being conscious.

The strong form is quite implausible. For one thing, regular matter gives no evidence whatever of possessing consciousness. Further, if all matter has consciousness, why does it emerge in special ways only when certain configurations of matter are present? And if conscious human beings are in some sense merely combinations of little bits of consciousness, how are we to account for the unity of consciousness and why do people have no memory of the conscious careers of the bits of matter prior to their combination to form humans? There is no answer to these questions and few, if any, hold to strong panpsychism.

What about the weak version? Given the current intellectual climate, a personal theistic or a naturalistic explanation would exhaust at least the live – if not the logical – options. It is widely thought that weak panpsychism has serious problems in its own right (e.g., explaining what an incipient or proto-mental entity is; how the type of unity that appears to characterize the self could emerge from a mere system of parts standing together in various causal and spatio-temporal relations; and why certain physical conditions are regularly correlated with the actualization of consciousness when the connection between consciousness and those conditions seems to be utterly contingent).

Moreover, panpsychism is arguably less reasonable than theism on other grounds. Given justification for this claim, theism enjoys greater positive epistemic justification than does panpsychism prior to consideration of the issue of consciousness, and all things being equal, the appeal to panpsychism to explain consciousness is undermotivated.

Finally, panpsychism is merely a label for and not an explanation of the phenomena to be explained. As Geoffrey Madell notes, 'the sense that the mental and the physical are just inexplicably and gratuitously slapped together is hardly allayed by adopting ... a pan-psychist ... view of the mind, for [it does not] have any explanation to offer as to why or how mental properties cohere with physical' (Madell 1988: 3).

Conclusion

Prominent naturalist Jaegwon Kim has observed that 'if a whole system of phenomena that are prima facie not among basic physical phenomena resists physical explanation, and especially if we don't even know where or how to begin, it would be time to reexamine one's physicalist commitments' (Kim 1998: 96). For Kim, genuinely non-physical mental entities are the paradigm case of such a system of phenomena. Kim's advice to fellow naturalists is that they must simply admit the irreality of the mental and recognize that naturalism exacts a steep price and cannot be had on the cheap. However, if feigning anesthesia – denying that consciousness construed along commonsense lines is real – is the price to be paid to retain naturalism, then the price is too high. Fortunately, the theistic argument from consciousness reminds us that it is a price that does not need to be paid.

See also The moral argument (Chapter 34), Naturalistic rejoinders to theistic arguments (Chapter 40), Why is there a universe at all, rather than just nothing? (Chapter 41), The sociobiological account of religious belief (Chapter 42), Miracles (Chapter 55), Religious naturalism (62), and Religion and science (64).

References

Adams, R. (1992) 'Flavors, colors and God,' reprinted in R. D. Geivett and B. Sweetman (eds) *Contemporary Perspectives in Religious Epistemology*, New York: Oxford University Press.
Chalmers, D. (1996) *The Conscious Mind*, New York: Oxford University Press.
Jackson, F. (1998) *From Metaphysics to Ethics*, Oxford: Clarendon Press.
Kim, J. (1996) *Philosophy of Mind*, Boulder, CO: Westview Press.
—— (1998) *Mind in a Physical World*, Cambridge, MA: MIT Press.
McGinn, C. (1999) *The Mysterious Flame*, New York: Basic Books.
Mackie, J. L. (1982) *The Miracle of Theism*, Oxford: Clarendon Press.
Maddell, G. (1988) *Mind and Materialism*, Edinburgh: Edinburgh University Press.
Nagel, T. (1986) *The View from Nowhere*, New York: Oxford University Press.
Papineau, D. (1993) *Philosophical Naturalism*, Oxford: Blackwell.
Searle, J. (1992) *The Rediscovery of the Mind*, Cambridge, MA: MIT Press.
Skrbina, D. (2005) *Panpsychism in the West*, Notre Dame, IN: University of Notre Dame Press.
Swinburne, R. (1997) *The Evolution of the Soul*, Oxford: Clarendon Press.
—— (2004) *The Existence of God*, Oxford: Clarendon Press.

Further reading

Hasker, W. (1999) *The Emergent Self*, Ithaca, NY: Cornell University Press. (Contains a rigorous defense of property and substance dualism.)
Kim, J. (2005) *Physicalism or Something Near Enough*, Princeton, NJ: Princeton University Press. (Updates the debate about physicalism and presents Kim's version of epiphenomenal property dualism.)
McGinn, C. (1999) *The Mysterious Flame*, New York: Basic Books. (A readable, creative attempt to preserve naturalism while admitting there is no naturalist explanation of consciousness.)
Moreland, J. P. (1998) 'Searle's biological naturalism and the argument from consciousness,' *Faith and Philosophy* 15: 1–24. (Offers a critique of Searle's position and defends the argument from consciousness.)
Searle, J. (1992) *The Rediscovery of the Mind*, Cambridge, MA: MIT Press. (Defends a commonsense view

of consciousness and argues that all a naturalist needs to do to explain it is to correlate it with various brain states.)

Swinburne, R. (1997) *The Evolution of the Soul*, Oxford: Clarendon Press. (Presents a careful case for property and substance dualism, and defends the argument from consciousness.)

36

THE WAGER ARGUMENT

Joshua L. Golding

Pascal's Wager

Traditional arguments for the rationality of religious belief such as the ontological, cosmological, and teleological arguments seek to demonstrate that God exists or to show that God's existence is probable on the basis of the evidence of the senses. These may be referred to as *cognitive* arguments since they aim to show that we can know with certainty or probability that God exists. In contrast, the argument known as 'Pascal's Wager' (Pascal 1973: 92–6) aims to show that it is rational to believe in God, through consideration of the potential value of having this belief. Hence, the Wager may be referred to as a *pragmatic* argument for belief in God.

A summary of Pascal's Wager is as follows. We are faced with a decision about whether or not to believe in God. Since God is conceived as infinite and the human mind is finite, it is impossible for us to assess whether or not God exists. Using our cognitive capacities alone, we cannot make this decision rationally. But the decision is forced. Therefore, we should base our decision on consideration of what possible effect belief (or disbelief) in God will have on our welfare or happiness. At first glance, it seems we have everything to gain and nothing to lose if we choose to believe in God. For, if God exists and we believe in him, we shall attain great happiness in the afterlife. If God does not exist, and we believe in him, we haven't lost much. (Momentarily, Pascal will refine this last step.) On the other hand, if we choose not to believe in God, we shall not attain great happiness under any circumstance. The diagram or 'matrix' from Hacking 1972 represents the features of this decision problem.

Relevant possible states of affairs

	God exists	God does not exist	
Options { (1) Believe in God	great gain	no great gain	} Outcomes
(2) Do not believe in God	no great gain	no great gain	

Under the assumptions set out in the diagram, Pascal claims the rational choice is to believe in God. Using modern terminology, the option of belief in God 'dominates' over the option of disbelief, since it has a better result if God exists and no worse result if God does not exist. However, Pascal reconsiders the hasty assumption that one has nothing to lose by being a believer. For, if it turns out God does not exist, the believer will have believed in vain and perhaps lost many goods he would have enjoyed otherwise. So, Pascal refines the argument by introducing the notion that if God exists, the gain in the next world for the believer is not merely great but infinite. Pascal holds fast to the assumption that one has no chance of attaining the infinite gain if God does not exist, nor if one opts for disbelief. (Interestingly, Pascal does *not* claim that the disbeliever will suffer great harm if God exists; he claims only that the disbeliever will *lose* the infinite gain.) The following matrix represents this refined version of the decision problem.

Relevant possible states of affairs

Options		God exists	God does not exist	Outcomes
	(1) Believe in God	infinite gain	some finite loss	
	(2) Do not believe in God	some finite gain	some finite gain	

Given these assumptions, Pascal argues again that it is more rational to choose belief rather than disbelief. For, an option which has even a small probability of gaining infinite value is a more rational choice than an option which has a high probability of gaining a very large finite gain. Using modern terminology, the option of belief in God has a higher *expected value* than the option of disbelief. The expected value of an option is computed by (1) multiplying the probability of each possible state of affairs by the value of the outcome on that option, and (2) summing all the products obtained, for all possible states of affairs on that option. The rationale behind the expected value principle is that it provides a sensible procedure for taking into account both the probabilities and the potential values of available options. Thus, if (as Pascal assumes) the probability of God's existence is ½, the expected value of belief in God may be computed as follows:

½ × infinite gain + ½ × some finite loss = infinite gain.

Note that the same result would be attained even if the probability of God's existence is less than ½, so long as it is assumed to be a real probability greater than zero. Furthermore, given Pascal's assumptions, the expected value for not believing in God is computed as follows:

½ × some finite gain + ½ × some finite gain = some finite gain.

The result is that the expected value of belief in God is infinite, and the expected value of disbelief is finite. Hence, belief in God is the rational choice.

At this stage, Pascal considers one final objection. Having been shown that it is pragmatically rational to believe in God, the atheist may complain that he can't help himself; the fact is that he does not believe in God. What's an atheist to do? Pascal responds by recommending that if a person acts and speaks like a religious believer, sooner or later he will become one. While we may not be able to choose to believe in some proposition, we can choose to do certain things which are likely to induce that belief. In closing, Pascal intimates that a person who follows this route will ultimately arrive at a devout and sincere belief in God, in which the calculation of the Wager is left behind.

Critical discussion of the Wager

So much for a summary of Pascal's Wager. Since its publication, the argument has been criticized on several grounds. While many philosophers regard the Wager as woefully unsuccessful, since the late twentieth century a number of philosophers have come to its defense. We may group the standard objections into four categories. We shall also discuss defenses and revisions of the Wager.

(1) One set of objections concerns Pascal's claims at the outset regarding the cognitive features of the decision problem. Pascal claims that our cognitive capacities are unable to make the decision about whether to believe in God. The only ground Pascal supplies for this claim is that the idea of God is infinite and the human mind is finite. It is a non sequitur to infer that one cannot cognitively assess whether or not God exists. After all, we are able to form some conception of an infinite being; otherwise we would not be having this discussion. Moreover, infinity is not the only feature of our concept of God. Pascal himself conceives of God as intelligent, powerful, benevolent, and yet also as a judge, since God rewards those who believe in him. These features of our concept of God may be (and indeed have been) used in cognitive arguments for, or against, God's existence. At the very least, Pascal needs to defend more substantively the claim that cognitive reason is unable to assess whether God exists.

A related objection concerns Pascal's apparent assumption that the probability of God's existence should be assigned ½. Pascal uses this assumption as a basis for saying that the decision to believe should be settled on pragmatic grounds. If God's existence (or nonexistence) had a probability of greater than ½, the move to pragmatic considerations would not be justified. (The notion that Pascal advocates throwing cognitive reason to the winds and making the decision solely on pragmatic grounds is a misreading of the Wager.) It may be argued that if our cognitive capacities cannot decide whether or not to believe in God, under such circumstances the cognitively rational choice is either to (a) leave the probability of God's existence unassigned, or (b) adopt the metaphysically more parsimonious hypothesis that God does not exist. A defense or reformulation of the Wager needs to show why these options are misguided, or why the argument succeeds in spite of these options.

Defenders of the Wager might respond that the argument is addressed to a specific audience, namely, those who find the cognitive arguments for and against God's existence inconclusive (Rescher 1985: 25), or those who find themselves in the predicament of believing that God's existence and nonexistence have roughly the same probability. However, even if the Wager can be salvaged in this manner, still another objection concerns Pascal's claim that the choice between belief in God and disbelief is 'forced.' If the decision is whether to *believe that God exists* or to believe *that God does not exist*, there seems to be a third option, namely, to *believe neither hypothesis*. There is a genuine cognitive difference between *believing that not-p*, and *not believing p*. An analogy is helpful here. Some people believe that there exists life on other planets, and some people believe it is not the case that there exists life on other planets. But it seems quite possible to suspend belief, that is, to believe neither of these propositions. It is sometimes thought that Pascal can easily respond by saying that suspension of belief in God's existence is tantamount to believing that God does not exist, since God will not reward agnostics any more than he will reward atheists. But, aside from the problem of how Pascal can justify this theological claim, the objection remains that so long as suspension of belief is a genuine option, it is arguably the most cognitively rational choice, even if it does involve losing infinite bliss. By Pascal's own lights, if suspension of belief is a real possibility, the move to pragmatic considerations is blocked.

Still another possible revision is to recast the Wager as an argument in support of some religious commitment other than belief, such as the *assumption for practical purpose that God exists* (see Golding 1990). It is a common occurrence that it may be pragmatically rational to assume some proposition is true, even if it is cognitively rational to suspend belief in that proposition. For example, a scientist might not know whether a cure for cancer is attainable. However, it may be pragmatically rational to assume for practical purpose that such a cure is attainable. A similar strategy might work in the case of religion. Even if there is insufficient cognitive proof for God's existence, it might very well be the case that there is pragmatic justification for assuming that God exists for practical purposes, if it can be shown that the only way or the best way of attaining some very valuable good is by making that assumption. This strategy escapes several criticisms of the Wager which focus on its attempt to provide a pragmatic justification of *belief*. We shall return later to this last suggestion.

(2) A second class of objections involves technical worries concerning the notion of an infinite value, and especially concerning the use of an infinite value in an expected value calculation. First, in what sense can a finite creature attain an infinite good? The notion of an infinite good needs to be explicated and defended. One natural way Pascal might begin to do this is by using the notion of God. God is conceived as the infinitely good being, and the infinite value is to be conceived as consisting in some kind of relationship with God in which a person participates or partakes of God's infinite goodness (see Golding 2003: 55–66). Whether this can be done successfully is beyond our scope here. But, as we shall see later, such a strategy would strengthen the Wager Argument in other ways as well.

Still, even on the assumption that an infinite value makes sense, it seems one should be wary of using an infinite value in an expected value calculation. In the course of his argument, Pascal claims that a tiny probability of attaining an infinite value always outstrips any large chance of gaining any large finite value. However, it also seems (absurdly) that an option that has a tiny probability of attaining an infinite value has the same expected value as an option with a large probability of resulting in an infinite value. For example, suppose that on one bet I have a ½ chance of winning an infinite value, and on a second bet I have a $\frac{1}{20}$ chance of winning an infinite value. Common sense would say that it is rational to choose the first bet over the second bet. Yet if we employ the expected value calculus, the expected value of *both* bets turns out to be infinite! Perhaps the lesson to be derived is that one should not use infinite value in any expected value calculation at all.

One way in which proponents of the Wager might respond is to concede that in cases where an infinite value is at stake, one should not apply the expected value calculation directly, but rather one should treat that infinite value as *no worse than some astronomically high finite value*. Suppose that on bet (a) I have a ½ chance of attaining infinite value, and on bet (b) I have a $\frac{1}{20}$ chance of attaining infinite value. If I apply the expected value in the standard way, I will indeed attain the counterintuitive result that both choices are equally rational. But if I treat the infinite value as *no worse than some very high finite value*, then the expected value of the first option will be higher than that of the second one. For, a ½ chance of attaining some very high finite value is obviously higher than a $\frac{1}{20}$ chance of attaining that same value. On the other hand, suppose that on bet (c), I have a $\frac{1}{20}$ chance of attaining an infinite value, whereas on bet (d) I have a ½ chance of winning a large finite value, call it z. I should indeed hesitate to apply the expected value directly to this case. However, I know that there is some finite value high enough – call it h – such that a $\frac{1}{20}$ chance of winning h would be preferable to a ½ chance of winning z. In particular, so long as h is more than 10 times z, the expected value of bet (c) would be higher than that of bet (d). But I know that an infinite value is no worse (indeed it is much better!) than h. Hence, I can safely conclude that (c) is the better bet.

Still another possible revision is to replace the notion of an infinite value with the notion of a supreme good that is *finite but qualitatively superior to any other competing good* (Golding 2003: 79–81). One kind of good is qualitatively superior to another kind of good if any tiny bit of that first good is better than any large amount of the second kind of good, and any incremental increase in that first good is better than any large increase in that second kind of good. Using the expected value principle, even a tiny probability of attaining the first kind of good would be higher than a large probability of attaining any amount of a lesser kind of good. Yet, since that good is finite, a higher chance of attaining that superior good would be preferable to a lower chance of attaining that same kind of good. The strategy would then be to argue that the kind of good one might attain by having a certain kind of relationship with God is qualitatively superior to any other competing good. Since that good is conceived as finite, it would follow that any course of action which is deemed to have a higher chance of attaining that good would be more rational than any course of action which has a lesser chance of attaining that same good. We shall return to this strategy shortly.

(3) A third set of objections concerns Pascal's assumptions regarding the link between having certain specific religious beliefs and the attainment of an infinite gain (if it is attainable at all). Pascal assumes without argument that the only possibility of

attaining an infinite gain is that a God (of a certain sort) exists and one believes in him. This raises what is probably the most widely discussed objection to the Wager, namely, the 'problem of other gods.' Pascal seems blithely to ignore several possible states of affairs. Just to list a few, perhaps God is all-forgiving, and he rewards everyone with infinite bliss in the afterlife, regardless of their beliefs. Alternatively, perhaps God rewards only those whose belief in him is *not* motivated by pragmatic considerations. Still another possibility is that God rewards only certain theists, say for example, Muslims, but not Christians. Or perhaps he rewards only those who engage in some arbitrary or absurd action, such as jumping up and down three times every Tuesday. Alternatively, perhaps God will reward all and only atheists. Indeed, some critics of Pascal have attempted to use the Wager strategy as an argument for atheism as the safest choice under the circumstances (see Martin 1983). Finally, although this is less commonly suggested, Pascal ignores the possibility that some infinite gain might be attainable even if there is no God at all. If any of these possibilities are considered, Pascal's Wager fails to establish its conclusion that it pragmatically rational to believe in (a certain kind of) God.

Clearly, it would help Pascal's argument if there were some way of taking into account the relative probabilities of various hypotheses concerning what is the most plausible and/or probable way in which one might attain the ultimate gain. However, the present objection is exacerbated when taken together with the previous objection. As noted above, if Pascal relies on the strategy of trying to show that the expected value of belief in God is infinite, the problem arises that an option that has even a *tiny* chance of attaining infinite value is also infinite. Hence, it seems that so long as there is even some tiny probability that one can attain infinite value *without* believing in (a certain kind of) God, Pascal's argument fails.

By the same token, if the objection described previously can be met in either one of the two ways described above, then the present objection is mitigated, if not completely dissolved. Suppose we do not treat the ultimate gain of having a certain relationship with God as infinite but rather as *no worse than some very astronomically high finite value*. Or suppose we conceive of it as *finite but qualitatively superior to all other non-religious goods*. On either of these strategies, it turns out that an option which has a higher probability of resulting in that supreme (but finite) value has a higher expected value than any option which has a lower probability of resulting in that value. In this way, the relative probabilities of various hypotheses about how one might attain the supreme value become relevant.

With this in hand, defenders of the Wager could respond to the 'problem of other gods' by arguing that it is more likely that the supreme gain will be attained if (a traditional sort of) God exists than if not. The strategy here is to establish a conceptual link between the traditional monotheistic conception of God and the conception of a supreme value. For example, it could be argued that only a supremely good and powerful being could supply a kind of good that is either astronomically high or qualitatively superior to any other competing good. Alternatively, it could be argued that the ultimate gain is best conceived as a relationship in which one partakes or participates in the goodness of a supremely good being, who is qualitatively superior to any other possible being. If this is correct, the kind of God who would reward all and only those who jump up and down three times every Tuesday is not the kind of God which can supply the best kind of good. In this way, it could be argued that it is more plausible that one will attain the supreme value if a certain traditional sort of God exists than if not. This in turn implies that it is more probable that one will succeed in attaining the supreme value if one casts one's lot with traditional theism rather than agnosticism or atheism.

Even if this strategy works, two problems still linger. First, how does one know which theistic religion to choose? Differently stated, why should one be a Christian rather than a Jew or a Muslim (or vice versa)? However, once the supreme value is no longer conceived as infinite, defenders of the Wager may respond that (1) one should choose the religion which seems most probably true on other grounds, or (2) one should at least choose some version of theism over non-theism. For, if there are equally plausible ways of attaining the supreme value, then they are all equally rational to choose. But one should choose at least *one* of those ways over none at all.

Still, a second lingering problem concerns the assumption that a *belief* in God is necessary or even conducive to the attainment of the supreme good. Suppose it is true that I will attain the supreme good only if a God of a certain sort exists. Why should I think that belief in God is necessary or conducive to the attainment of that supreme good? One possible response is that the doctrine that belief is necessary for attaining the ultimate value happens to be taught by the religion which seems over all to be the most probable of all available candidates. Of course, this response will only work if indeed it can be shown that the religion in question is more probably true than others. Another possible response is that if the good is conceived as a relationship with God, then I can only have that relationship if I believe in God. However, that does not in itself show that having the belief is itself conducive to attaining the relationship. Once again, a convenient strategy is to replace the attempt to justify a belief in God with the attempt to justify a *pragmatic assumption* that God exists, for the purpose of pursuing a good relationship with God (Golding 2003). If indeed one can attain the supreme value only if there is a God, then it is rational to guide one's actions on the assumption that there is a God, for the purpose of pursing that relationship. We shall return to this strategy shortly.

(4) The fourth set of objections claims that the Wager recommends that we do something immoral or religiously inappropriate. Suppose one could show that belief in God is our 'best bet.' Still, is it morally proper to believe in something through self-interest? Is it religiously pious to do so, even if God does exist? Moreover, Pascal's closing recommendation that one should get oneself to believe by acting as a believer seems to constitute a form of self-brainwashing.

Pascal might very well respond as follows. Surely there is nothing wrong with pursuing one's own self-interest, so long as one is not doing anything immoral in the process. The question is whether *believing* something on the basis of self-interest is somehow immoral or inappropriate. Now, Pascal has already argued that in this particular case, (a) cognitive reason cannot make the decision about whether or not to believe in God, and (b) we are forced to make a decision. If Pascal is right about these claims, then we have no choice but to make the decision on non-cognitive grounds. Since we are forced to make the decision on non-cognitive grounds, we might as well do what is in our best interest.

The same point applies in defense of his closing recommendation that one act as a believer. By Pascal's lights, the atheist's belief is just as cognitively unfounded as the theist's belief. Both are in the position of believing as a result of non-cognitive considerations. Perhaps the atheist's belief is a result of habit, or upbringing, or simply the desire to avoid the inconveniences of church. Arguably, the claim that it is immoral to 'get oneself to believe' a proposition is valid only if one has the option of cognitively adjudicating whether or not to believe that proposition. Pascal has already argued that in this case, cognitive adjudication is not possible. To claim that he is wrong about that is to revert to other criticisms discussed above.

Moreover, with the regard to the worry about 'self-interest,' Pascal can easily reformulate the argument as an appeal to consideration of what is the best possible condition for a person to attain. The traditional conception of the afterlife is not merely one of *subjective* pleasure or bliss. It is also conceived as the *objectively* best possible state. Nothing could be better than having the best possible relationship with the best possible being (i.e., God). The only reason Pascal repeatedly uses the term 'happiness' in the Wager is because he assumes his audience is (crassly?) self-interested. But for those who are interested in pursuing the best possible life, Pascal could also argue that taking a shot at beatitude is the best possible choice from a moral point of view. In fact, it has been argued that Pascal's strategy can be used to show that one has the obligation to help *others* become believers, since by doing so one furthers their chances of attaining what is best for *them* (see Morris 1986). In short, the appeal to self-interest does not exclude an appeal to moral considerations as well.

The objection that a pragmatically based belief is *religiously* inappropriate can only be made from some religious standpoint. From a Christian point of view, there is arguably nothing wrong with believing in God as a means to personal gain. On the contrary, the Bible often exhorts us to believe and to worship because it is in our best interest to do so. The same is true for Judaism and Islam. Of course, this may not be the ideal or the only reason to believe in God, but it is certainly a common theme in many world religions. Pascal himself intimates toward the end of the argument that the Wager may be viewed as a stepping stone toward a more mature form of belief in God, to be developed later on in the believer's life or perhaps in some future state after death.

Alternatively, the Wager might be revised as a justification for some form of religious commitment other than belief, such as an assumption for practical purpose that God exists (Golding 1990). Suppose we grant that it is morally and intellectually problematic to *believe* some cognitively dubious proposition on pragmatic grounds. Surely, it need not be morally or intellectually problematic to assume that same proposition for practical purposes. It will be pragmatically rational to make that assumption, if the potential value of making that assumption is higher than that of not doing so. If that value is conceived as the best possible objective state for a person to be in, it may even be morally obligatory to make that assumption.

Concluding remarks

We have discussed several objections to the Wager and various ways in which defenders of the Wager might respond. Criticisms concern Pascal's claims that reason is unable to assess whether God exists and that the choice is forced; technical worries concerning the notion of infinite value; Pascal's assumptions linking a belief in (a certain sort of) God with the attainment of infinite value; and finally, moral and intellectual qualms about pragmatic justification of belief. We have discussed different strategies for defending and of revising the Wager. For many philosophers, the Wager is hopelessly flawed.

In my opinion, the most promising strategy is to (1) replace the notion of an infinite value with a value that is finite but qualitatively superior to any other kind of good, and (2) replace the attempt to justify a belief in God with the attempt to pragmatically justify the assumption for practical purpose that God exists. The burden would then be to show why it is plausible to conceive of a certain relationship with God as qualitatively superior to any other kind of good, and why it is plausible to think that some theistic way of life is more probable than any non-theistic way of life to result in that good relationship with God. If these tasks can be carried out, the Wager strategy may be successfully used as a pragmatic justification for the assumption that there is a God.

See also Søren Kierkegaard (Chapter 15), Hiddenness (Chapter 29), Heaven and hell (Chapter 54), Faith (Chapter 56).

References

Golding, J. L. (1990) 'Toward a pragmatic conception of faith,' *Faith and Philosophy* 7 (October): 486–503.
—— (2003) *Rationality and Religious Theism*, Aldershot: Ashgate.
Hacking, I. (1972) 'The logic of Pascal's Wager,' *American Philosophical Quarterly* 9: 186–92.
Martin, M. (1983) 'Pascal's Wager as an argument for not believing in God,' *Religious Studies* 19: 57–64.
Morris, T. (1986) 'Pascalian Wagering,' *Canadian Journal of Philosophy* (September): 437–54.
Pascal, B. (1973) [1670] *Pensées*, trans. J. Warrington, London: J. M. Dent.
Rescher, N. (1985) *Pascal's Wager: A Study of Practical Reasoning in Philosophical Theology*, Notre Dame, IN: University of Notre Dame Press.

Further reading

Jordan, J. (1994) *Gambling on God*, Lanham, MD: Rowman & Littlefield. (A collection of critical essays on Pascal's Wager.)
Lycan, W. and G. Shlesinger (2002) 'You bet your life: Pascal's Wager defended,' in D. Shatz (ed.) *Philosophy and Faith*, New York: McGraw Hill. (Presents a lively and forceful defense of the Wager.)
Rescher, N. (1985) *Pascal's Wager: A Study of Practical Reasoning in Philosophical Theology*, Notre Dame, IN: University of Notre Dame Press. (A full-length exposition and defense of the Wager.)
Sobel, J. H. (2003) *Logic and Theism: Arguments For and Against Beliefs in God*, Cambridge: Cambridge University Press. (See chapter 13, devoted mainly to the Wager.)

Part VI
ARGUMENTS AGAINST GOD'S EXISTENCE

37

THE PROBLEM OF EVIL

Richard M. Gale

The widespread existence of evil is the greatest challenge to the rationality of belief in the God of traditional theism, who has every perfection to an unlimited extent, among which are being omnipotent (all-powerful), omniscient (all-knowing), omni-benevolent (all-good), and sovereign (all-determining). One form that this challenge takes is an argument that attempts to deduce a contradiction from the existence of both God and evil, but the more popular form is an inductive argument that infers from the known evils of the world that it is improbable that God exists or, more weakly, that the probability of his existence is lowered by these evils. The theist responds to the deductive argument by offering a defense in which it is shown how it is possible for God to have a morally exonerating excuse for permitting or causing these evils. There are two ways in which the theist counters the inductive argument. One is to give a *theodicy*, which is a defense coupled with some evidence that the possible excusing condition articulated in the defense actually obtains. The other is *theistic skepticism*, which holds that we humans are incapable of understanding God's reasons for permitting evil.

The deductive argument

The aim of this argument, which was first given by J. L. Mackie (1982: 150–76), is to hang the theist by her own rope. From an initial set of premises accepted by the theist, namely, that there exists an omnipotent and omnibenevolent God and that evil exists, it is deduced that evil does not exist, thereby resulting in the contradiction that evil exists and that evil does not exist. In order to deduce that evil does not exist, it must be assumed that an omnipotent being can bring about anything and that an omni-benevolent being will prevent and eliminate every evil it can. The theist challenges both of these assumptions. An omnipotent God can bring about only everything that it is consistent for him to bring about and an omnibenevolent being prevents and eliminates every *unjustified* evil, that is, every evil for which there is not a morally exonerating excuse. Thus, from the initial set of premises it can be deduced only that unjustified evil does not exist. But that evil exists and that unjustified evil does not exist is not a contradiction.

This manner of rebutting Mackie's argument, however, leaves us with the resident problem of explaining how a being who has all of God's unlimited perfections could be morally justified in bringing about or permitting an evil. The excuses that we are familiar with do not seem applicable to God, given that he is omni-competent. The lack-of-power excuse for failing to eliminate or prevent an evil ('I wasn't strong enough to lift the car that you were pinned under') cannot be available to an omnipotent being. And the excusable-ignorance excuse ('How could I have known that saying "Niagara Falls" would send him into a homicidal rage?') could not apply to an omniscient being. And since God is sovereign over everything, he cannot be excused because of a lack of opportunity ('I couldn't have saved him from dying from the rattler's bite because I did not have the needed anti-venom serum or I wasn't there').

The theist is prepared to offer a number of possible excuses for God's causing or permitting evil. There is the cover-all compensation-in-an-afterlife defense. It is essential that the worldly suffering and afterlife compensation form an integral unity. It won't do for God to say, 'I caused you five units of worldly suffering; so I will give you ten units of pleasure in an afterlife.' For why didn't he just create the pleasures *sans* the suffering? A number of responses make use of creedal doctrines of different theistic religions, an example of which is the merited-punishment defense according to which the evils that befall us result from the first generation of humans freely rebelling against God, with their ruin being inherited by all of their descendants. Peter van Inwagen has extended this defense so that it covers chance, gratuitous evils: those that are necessary neither for the realization of an outweighing good nor the prevention of an even greater evil (in Howard-Snyder 1996). Through these evils God makes it clear that man cannot live apart from him. Eleonore Stump has espoused a defense that is a close cousin to van Inwagen's in that it too is based on original sin (Stump 1985). Natural evils, that is, those that cannot be attributed to the improper use of free will by finite persons, help to realign our wills so that they will again be directed toward serving God by reminding us that we are unable to make it on our own. Marilyn McCord Adams has developed a redemptive suffering defense that is based upon the value of martyrdom, which then is extrapolatable to some, but not all, other types of suffering (Adams 1989). Through being successfully tested in her faith, the martyr builds a closer relation of trust with her God. Furthermore, through suffering she gets a vision into the inner life of God incarnate on the cross. This defense, as well as Stump's, has a limited application since it does not apply to the suffering of animals and the very young.

Many who give these creedal-based defenses take them to be theodicies as well, since they are prepared to argue that the Scriptures upon which they are based are true revelations, which is a matter that falls outside the purview of this essay. A major challenge to these strained defenses is that they seem to depict God as petty, wrathful, and vindictive, which is inconsistent with his being a God of love, a God that is eminently worthy of worship and adoration. Such a God, it is contended, is worthy only of a prudence-based fear and obedience.

The free will defense

The most important defense is the free will defense (FWD), whose aim is to articulate a possible justification for God's creating persons who sometimes freely go morally wrong, thereby resulting in moral evil. There are several different versions of it (e.g., Plantinga 1974). The following is a generic brand FWD that captures what is common to them.

1 It is God's intention to create the best overall situation or the best world that he can. Intention premise
2 A world containing free persons who freely perform both right and wrong actions, but for the most part go right, is better than any possible world devoid of free persons. Normative premise
3 God cannot cause or determine in any way what a created person freely does. Incompatibilist premise
4 It is logically possible that God is contingently unable to create free persons who always go right.
God-could-be-unlucky premise

Premise (1) results from God's being omnibenevolent. A consequence of the normative premise, (2), is that God is morally excused from permitting some moral evil if this is the price that he must pay for there to exist any free persons at all. The incompatibilist premise, (3), requires that a free action be determined wholly by the agent and thus not by something external to the agent, such as prior causes or even the will of God, which can be explicitly formulated as:

L. A free act is not sufficiently caused by anything external to the agent.

Without this premise the proponent of the FWD would have no response to the objection of the causal or theological compatibilist, such as Augustine and Leibniz, who contend that God could have determined that every created free person always freely goes right by either, respectively, a suitable determination of the initial state of the universe and the causal laws or simply willing in his own inimitable supernatural way that they do.

Each version of the FWD will tell a different story about how the God-could-be-unlucky premise, (4), could be realized, of how it is possible that God be frustrated in his endeavor to create a universe containing moral good (good that results from the use of creaturely free will) *sans* moral evil. They differ with respect to whether God has *middle knowledge*, that is, foreknowledge of what would result from his creating various types of free persons in this or that possible world. Alvin Plantinga's version gives God middle knowledge but has created free persons who, not God, determine what they freely do (Plantinga 1974). The created free persons alone take 'the fall,' the blame, for the moral evil they wrought. Although God is responsible for the moral evils wrought by the free persons he creates, since he could have prevented these evils simply by not creating any free persons, he is not blameworthy for them, since he, unlike the created free persons, has a morally exonerating excuse for permitting these evils based on the great value of there being free persons.

The other two versions of the FWD deny God middle knowledge, having him create free person without knowing what will result. Herein God's benevolence is exonerated because of excusable ignorance. And, if it is charged that he acts recklessly in creating free persons without knowing in advance what will result, the answer is that it is well worth the gamble, given the great value of free will. The Robert M. Adams's version bases God's ignorance on there not being any fact of the matter, and therefore nothing to be known, about what would result from his creating various kinds of free persons (1979). The Richard Swinburne version holds that there are such facts but denies that God can access them (Swinburne 1979). Each of these three versions will be discussed in turn.

According to Plantinga's version, God cannot both create free beings and determine what they freely do, since this would violate L. What he must do, therefore, is to create persons who are free with respect to certain actions and then leave it up to them what they freely do. This requires that God creates incomplete or diminished persons. To see how this works, we must begin with a *possible free person*, which is a maximal and compossible set of abstract properties and contains the property of being free with respect to at least one morally significant action, A, that is, the property of either freely doing A or freely refraining from doing A. Alternatively, you can think of a possible free person as a compossible set of abstract propositions that completely describes the life of such a free person, everything that she does and undergoes, including her free actions. The set of properties is compossible in that it is logically possible that a single person instantiates all of them, and it is maximal because for every property that could be possessed by a person either it or its complement is included in the set, the complement of the property P being non-P.

Each possible free person contains a *diminished possible free person*, which is its largest proper subset of properties that is such that for any action A, it neither includes or entails freely doing A; nor does it include or entail freely refraining from doing A. A property H includes or entails another property G just in case it is logically impossible that H be instantiated and G not be. The property of being red, for example, includes or entails the property of being colored since it is impossible for an object to be red but not be colored. A diminished possible free person is a 'freedom-neutral' set of properties.

For every possible free person containing the property of freely doing A, there is a numerically distinct possible person that includes all of the same properties save for its including the property of freely refraining from doing A instead. Let us call such a pair of possible free persons an 'incompatible pair.' Whenever you freely perform an action, you instantiate one member of such a pair to the exclusion of the other. For any incompatible pair, God will be contingently unable to actualize one person in the pair. Let our specimen incompatible pair be P and P_1, who include all of the same properties save for P's including freely doing A and P_1's instead including freely refraining from doing A.

The question is: What would result if God were to instantiate diminished person, DP, that is common to P and P_1? Would the concrete instantiator of this diminished person or set of freedom-neutral properties freely do A or freely refrain? Plainly, it must do one or the other, since it has the disjunctive property of either freely doing A or freely refraining from doing A. Thus, it is either true that

F. If DP were instantiated, the instantiator would freely do A.

or true that

F*. If DP were instantiated, the instantiator would freely refrain from doing A.

Let us call these free will subjunctive conditional propositions 'F-conditionals.' An F-conditional has an antecedent that reports the instantiation of a diminished possible free person and consequent that reports the performance of a free action by the instantiator. If F is true, then were God to instantiate DP, it would result in P being actualized; whereas, if F* is true, were God to actualize DP, it would result in P_1 being actualized. Since F and F* are logically incompatible, it follows that if F is true, God is unable to actualize P_1, and if F* is true, God is unable to actualize P. But necessarily one of them is true and therefore necessarily true that God cannot actualize P or cannot actualize P_1.

At the outset let us confine ourselves to possible persons that include the property of being free with respect to only one action, such as persons P and P_1 above. What we establish then can be generalized to more complex possible persons. Any incompatible pair of such simplified persons is a Dr Jekyll and Mr Hyde pair, the former being the one that contains the property of freely doing A (which we'll suppose is the morally right thing to do), the latter the property of freely refraining from doing A (which is the morally wrong thing to do). God might not be able to actualize P, the Dr Jekyll member of the pair, since F could be false. But what could be true for this particular Dr Jekyll and Mr Hyde pair could be true for all of them. Every incompatible pair of this sort could be such that it is true that if God were to instantiate the diminished possible person common to both, the instantiator would freely do the morally wrong alternative. Under such unfortunate circumstances, God can actualize only Hydes, and therefore will not attempt to instantiate any of these simple possible free persons, assuming that his brand of benevolence requires that there be a favorable balance of moral good over moral evil.

The result can be generalized so as to apply to more rich possible persons that contain the property of being free in respect to more than one action. It could still be the case for every such person that it is true that if God were to actualize its diminished person, the instantiator would freely go wrong with respect to at least one of these actions, which shows that it is possible that God cannot actualize a possible world in which all free persons always freely go right.

At this point, Plantinga can complete his FWD by claiming that in the possible world in which the truth-values of the F-conditionals preclude God from actualizing any Dr Jekylls or, more generally, possible persons containing the property of always freely doing what is right, he is excused for creating persons who sometimes freely go wrong provided that for the most part they freely go right. The F-conditionals are God's kryptonite. They have brute, contingent truth-values that are not determined by God and limit his power in a similar way to that in which fate limits the powers of the Greek gods. In both cases there is a force or power above and beyond the control of the individual that limits its powers to do what it wants. The idea that God must be lucky, that he must be dealt a favorable poker hand of F-conditional facts, if he is to be able to create a universe containing moral good *sans* moral evil, strikes some as blasphemous, as a radical distortion of the orthodox concept of God's omnipotence. While Plantinga's account of omnipotence is not every theist's cup of tea, certainly not that of the great medieval theists, it might be the cup of tea that will prove most digestible and healthy for theism in its effort to construct an adequate defense for God's permitting moral evil.

Numerous objections have been made to Plantinga's FWD, but each one admits of a response. The first claims, contra the normative premise, that it would be better for God to create a world containing conscious automata who are programmed by God always to go morally right than a world containing persons who freely perform both right and wrong actions. Plainly, this is not the normative intuition of the theist, who places a much greater value upon free will than does this objection. And since it is the internal consistency of theism that is challenged by the deductive argument from evil, it should be the theist's normative intuition that is operative.

There are a number of objections to the 'God-can-do-more' variety that have been advanced by Robert M. Adams (1979). All of them are subject to the following dilemma. If God goes so far as to ensure that all created persons always go right, he negates their freedom; and, if he doesn't go this far, he leaves it open that he will be thwarted by the contingent truth-values of the relevant F-conditionals. Yet another objection is based on God's having the power to step in just in the nick of time when he foresees, on the basis of his middle knowledge, that someone will freely go wrong, by either preventing this wrong choice or causally quarantining the culprit from the surrounding world after she has made her wrong choice so that no innocent persons are harmed. But, if he does the former, he negates the culprit's free will by denying her the power to choose other than the right alternative; and, if he does the latter, he has failed to bestow significant freedom on her since she lacks the freedom to act.

There is an opposite objection to the God-can-do-more variety, namely, that God cannot consistently do as much as is required by Plantinga's FWD. It could be argued that God, in virtue of having middle knowledge, has a freedom-canceling control over created persons; and, therefore, the buck of moral blame for moral evils cannot stop with them but must reach through to God, which destroys the FWD's attempt to show how God can escape blame, although not responsibility, for these evils. The reason for this is that if a person foreknows what will result from his doing something, he causes this result. Thus, God, in virtue of having middle knowledge of what will result from his actualizing a diminished possible person, causes the actions of the created persons.

And, since God causally determines all of this person's actions, he has a freedom-canceling control over her.

This objection can be overcome by going with either one of the other two versions of the FWD, since each denies that God has such foreknowledge. On the Adams version, God lacks this foreknowledge because the F-conditionals are neither true nor false, since there is nothing in reality that could make them true. Thus, there is no fact of the matter to be known by God in advance. For the Swinburne version, the F-conditionals are either true or false, but God lacks middle knowledge of them. This seems to be a blatant violation of God's omniscience, since he does not know every true proposition. Swinburne models God's omniscience on his omnipotence. Just as God can bring about anything that it is consistent for him to bring about, he knows every true proposition that it is consistent for him to know. The reason why it would be inconsistent for God to know the truth of F-conditionals in advance of his creative choices is that this would preclude his being able to create free persons, but it is essential to God that he can create free persons.

The inductive argument

The inductive argument, which has been championed by William Rowe, begins with the fact that there are numerous terrible evils, E, for which we are unable to find any good that would justify God, were he to exist, in permitting E (in Howard-Snyder 1996). From this failure to find such goods it is inductively inferred that there probably are no goods that would justify God's permitting E. And, since God cannot coexist with unjustified evil, it follows that probably God does not exist. A weaker version of the inductive argument holds that E lowers the probability that God exists over what it is relative to our background knowledge, K, alone; that is

$$P \text{ (God exists/There are evils } E \text{ and } K) < P \text{ (God exists/}K).$$

K includes everything that we know that is not relevant to determining the truth of either that God exists or that there are evils E.

There also is an *abductive* or inference to the best explanation version of the inductive argument that goes back to Hume and finds a contemporary defender in Paul Draper (in Howard-Snyder 1996). It contends that the known evils and goods of the world are more probable, more to be expected, on the hypothesis that God does not exist than it is by the hypothesis that God exists.

The theist has a battery of responses to these inductive arguments. One is to point out that a proposition's probability can vary across different reference classes. The probability that Feike can swim relative to the proposition that he is Frisian is quite low but can be much higher relative to the proposition that many people believe that they have seen him swim. Similarly, the proposition that God exists relative to the conjunction of K and that there are evils E could be quite low but be quite high when all of the arguments for the existence of God are added to this conjunction. And, if it is probable that God exists relative to the agglomeration of these arguments, then it also is probable that for each evil specified in E, there is a God-justifying reason. In fact, if among them is a knock-down ontological argument, we can be certain that there is and thus that there are evils E does not even lower the probability that God exists. It was because Leibniz thought he had such an argument that he confined himself in his misnamed book, *The Theodicy* (1952), to sketching some possible *defenses* for God's allowing evil without making any effort to give evidence for their actually obtaining. Augustine did likewise.

Another response is to give a theodicy for E, the most impressive of which is John Hick's free-will-cum-soul-building one (Hick 1966). It is based on the reasonable axiological intuition that it is better to achieve some desirable state through one's own free endeavoring than to be in this state from the very beginning or have it imposed on one by some external power. God could have created human beings in a state of perfection, but it is better that he created them in an imperfect state so that they could freely bring about their own moral progress in approximating this ideal state, which, for the Christian, is union or a communal relation with God. God does not merely allow but actually causes natural evils so as to give persons the opportunity to freely develop certain desirable character traits, such as sympathy, charity, courage, patience, and the like. If it be objected that this would license a finite father breaking his son's legs so as to afford him an opportunity for soul-building, the reply is that this confounds the role of God as the designer of the entire scheme of things with that of created person, which is that of promoting good and fighting evil. Thus, the fact that God is permitted to do things that a human being is not does not result from his being subject to a different moral code than are humans but to the different roles they play.

Hick's theodicy does not apply to all known cases of evil. The baby who succumbs to leukemia or the deer that dies painfully in a forest fire is not afforded an opportunity by these evils to engage in soul building. To handle these recalcitrant cases Hick has supplemented his theodicy with a compensation-in-an-afterlife one. But the latter is nothing more than a defense, since the evidential credentials for it are very thin.

But by far the most favored response among sophisticated contemporary theorists, most notably Alston, Plantinga, Wykstra, and van Inwagen, is that of theistic skepticism (in Howard-Snyder 1996). Because our imaginative and cognitive powers are so radically limited, we are not warranted in inferring that there are not or probably are not God-justifying reasons for evils E. Theistic skepticism involves our inability, first, to access the divine mind so as to determine the different sorts of reasons that God could have for permitting evil and, second, to determine whether some purported God-justifying reason applies to a given case of evil. The former will be called 'reason skepticism' and the latter 'application skepticism.' Defenders of theistic skepticism invariably supplement it with some speculation about possible defenses or theodicies for E. This is fitting, since the believer must have some target for her faith, however sketchy and evidentially unsupported it is.

Rowe's argument mistakenly assumes that we are up to divining every possible God-justifying reason for permitting evil. As Stephen Wykstra has put it, God's reasons are 'noseeums' for us (in Russell and Wykstra 1988). If you carefully inspect a room and fail to detect a zebra, it is reasonable for you inductively to infer that there is no zebra in the room. But if you were trying to detect an ammonia molecule in the room, your failure to find it by unaided observation would not justify your inference that no ammonia molecule is in the room. The divine mind is the ultimate noseeum for us, regardless of what instruments of detection we employ. Our minds are to God's as a one-month-old baby's is to an adult's mind.

Many objections have been lodged against theistic skepticism. One is that it precludes the theist from employing teleological arguments, although not ontological and cosmological arguments; for, if the bad things about the world should not be evidence against the existence of God, the good things should not count in favor of his existence. Teleological arguments turn into two-edge swords. Maybe the good aspects of the world that these arguments appeal to are produced by a malevolent deity so as to highlight evil or because they are necessary for the realization of an outweighing evil, and so on for all the other demonodicies.

The most serious problem for theistic skepticism, which is raised by Bruce Russell, is that it seems to require that we become complete moral skeptics (Russell and Wykstra 1988). Should we be horrified at a child being brutally tortured and raped? Should we have tried to prevent it or take steps to prevent similar incidents in the future? Who knows?! For all we can tell, it might be a blessing in disguise or serve some God-justifying reason that is too deep for us to access. The result of this moral skepticism is paralysis of the will, since we can have no reason for acting, given that we are completely in the dark whether the consequences of our action is good or bad.

Another objection concerns whether theistic skepticism allows for there to be a meaningful personal love relation with God. The problem is whether we humans can have such a relation with a being whose mind so completely transcends ours, who is so inscrutable with respect to his values, reasons, and intentions.

Making God so inscrutable also raises a threat that theism thereby will turn out to be falsified or, if not falsified, rendered meaningless. Several atheists, including Michael Scriven and Theodore Drange, have used the hiddenness of God as the basis for an argument against his existence (Scriven 1966; Drange 1998). There is, they say, a presumption of atheism so that no news is bad news. Numerous quotations from the Bible are assembled in which it is said that God's intention in creating men was so that they would come to know of his existence and worship, obey, and enter into a communal loving relation with him. Thus, if we do not have good evidence that God exists because he has chosen to remain hidden, this constitutes good evidence against his existence.

By not allowing known evils E to count against God's existence, not even allowing it to lower the probability that he exists, the skeptical theist might be draining the theistic hypothesis of all meaning. E is itself a staggering array of evils, many of the most horrifying sort. If E is not the least bit probability-lowering, then it would appear that for theistic skeptics no amount of evil would be. Even if the world were a living hell in which each sentient being's life was one of unrelenting suffering of the worst sort, it would not count as evidence against God's existence; it would not lower the probability of his existence one bit. This seems highly implausible and calls into question the very meaningfulness of the claim that God exists. And this is so whether or not we accept the notorious verifiability theory of meaningfulness, which Plantinga likes to have die the death of self-reference by pointedly asking whether it is applicable to itself. We can recognize that something has gone wrong even if we cannot come up with a good theoretical explanation of why it is wrong.

We have yet to consider one rather obvious way for theists to meet the challenge of evil: settle for a finite God, as do process theologians like Alfred North Whitehead (1979) and Charles Hartshorne (1964a; 1964b). There are many ways to achieve this, since God has many omni-perfections that can be tinkered with. No theist wants to downgrade his omnibenevolence, since this would preclude God from playing the role of an eminently worship-worthy being.

The most obvious omni-perfection to downgrade is omnipotence, which brings us back to the Demiurge of Plato's *Timaeus*. Like a sculptor who is given a block of marble to work with that limits what he can create because it has a nature of its own, this god is given stuff to work with that limits what he can create. But if God is not all-powerful, how powerful is he? Does not this account of God's excuse for allowing evil run into the same unfalsifiability-in-principle problem as did theistic skepticism? No matter how much evil there is, the response is that he is just not *that* powerful, which resembles the punch-line of the famous shaggy dog joke, 'Yes, he was a shaggy dog, but he wasn't *that* shaggy.'

See also Omniscience (Chapter 24), Omnipotence (Chapter 25), Goodness (Chapter 28), Hiddenness (Chapter 29), The ontological argument (Chapter 31), The teleological argument (Chapter 33), The moral argument (Chapter 34), Problems with the concept of God (Chapter 38), Natural rejoinders to theistic arguments (Chapter 40), Process theology (Chapter 46), Heaven and hell (Chapter 54).

References

Adams, M. M. (1989) 'Horrendous suffering and the goodness of God,' *Aristotelian Society Supplementary Volume* 63: 297–310.

Adams, R. M. (1979) 'Middle knowledge and the problem of evil,' *American Philosophical Quarterly* 14: 109–17.

Drange, T. M. (1998) *Nonbelief and Evil: Two Arguments for the Nonexistence of God*, Amherst, NY: Prometheus.

Hartshorne, C. (1964a) *Man's Vision of God and the Logic of Theism*, Hamden, CT: Archon.

—— (1964b) *The Divine Relativity: A Social Conception of God*, New Haven, CT: Yale University Press.

Hick, J. (1966) *Evil and the God of Love*, New York: Harper & Row.

Howard-Snyder, D. (ed.) (1996) *The Evidential Argument from Evil*, Bloomington, IN: Indiana University Press.

Leibniz, G. F. W. (1952) *Theodicy*, ed. A. Farrer, trans. E. M. Huggard, New Haven, CT: Yale University Press.

Mackie, J. L. (1982) *The Miracle of Theism: Arguments For and Against the Existence of God*, Oxford: Clarendon Press.

Plantinga, A. (1974) *God, Freedom and Evil*, Grand Rapids, MI: Eerdmans.

—— (1979) 'The probabilistic argument from evil,' *Philosophical Studies* 35: 1–53.

Russell, B. and S. Wykstra (1988) 'The inductive argument from evil: a dialogue,' *Philosophical Topics* 16: 133–60.

Scriven, M. (1966) *Primary Philosophy*, New York: McGraw Hill.

Stump, E. (1985) 'The problem of evil,' *Faith and Philosophy* 2: 392–424.

Swinburne, R. (1979) *The Existence of God*, Oxford: Clarendon Press.

Whitehead, A. N. (1979) *Process and Reality*, corr. edn, New York: Free Press.

Further reading

Gale, R. M. (2007) *On the Philosophy of Religion*, Belmont, CA: Wadsworth. (A full and balanced discussion of the problem of evil.)

Howard-Snyder, D. (ed.) (1996) *The Evidential Argument from Evil*, Bloomington, IN: Indiana University Press. (This volume contains important essays by Alston, Draper, Plantinga, Rowe, Russell, van Inwagen, and Wykstra.)

Lewis, C. S. (1940) *The Problem of Pain*, London: Geoffrey Bles. (An especially good book for the novice because it is clearly and cogently written.)

38
PROBLEMS WITH THE CONCEPT OF GOD
Bede Rundle

There are gods, and there is God. The question of the existence of gods, such as those of the ancient Greeks or Romans, is nowadays unlikely to engage western philosophers or theologians seriously. Insofar as a god is thought of on the model of man or beast, it has a corporeal dimension, and the question of its existence is much as with more familiar beings: while of greater anatomical interest, whether there is a god with the head of a horse and the body of a man is comparable with the question of the existence of the abominable snowman. The supposition that Helios and his flaming chariot is responsible for the rising and setting of the sun no longer commands great respect among astrologers, let alone astronomers, and even those little versed in science can do better than appeal to the wrath of Poseidon in accounting for earthquakes, or thank Zeus Xenios when their guests come to no harm. Gods, it may be said, belong with elves, leprechauns, fairies, and trolls, being of little more theological interest than garden gnomes.

Or would that be an overhasty verdict? After all, while many gods have a corporeal nature, they have also been credited with superhuman powers and, indeed, with immortality. But would this testify to an otherworldly existence, rather than show merely that there are more beings in *this* world than we might have dreamed of? Would not a god who could act upon material things, perhaps possessing powers quite beyond those of any human agent, still be a denizen of our universe? Certainly, anything which can make its presence felt will thereby show itself to have at least a physical side to its nature. So, a being which can be imagined to manipulate material bodies may be imagined to act upon us, and we could become aware of that action by trying to resist its efforts: we learn that we are being pushed or pulled, say, when we experience pressure being exerted upon our bodies. If there is no such experience when we try to resist, what becomes of the idea that we are being acted upon? The agent imagined would, I am supposing, be invisible, but nonetheless capable of a spatial location, as well as possessing other physical attributes. There would, of course, be mystery here, but nothing which attested to a non-terrestrial existence, a further life in a purely supernatural domain, let alone an existence outside space and time, as God is customarily thought to enjoy. The difficulty of making sense of a non-physical agent, coupled with that of conceiving of its interaction with the physical, takes us to the heart of our problem, but before tackling this issue, we shall look at difficulties centering on verification.

Problems of verification

The major challenge to theology in the twentieth century came from logical positivism and its principle of verification. According to that principle, meaningful hypotheses fall into one of two categories, that of logical and mathematical propositions, or that of propositions which can be found to be true by observation and experimentation. Anything which falls outside these categories, as with many propositions relating to God, is to be dismissed as meaningless, or at least as lacking the character of a factual claim. It is of interest that, on the matter of gods, theists and atheists alike may invoke considerations having to do broadly with verification: gods are the sort of being that, if they existed, you would expect to find, and they are simply not to be found. However, when we turn from gods to God, we turn to a very different concept, and therewith a much more contested role for verification.

Positivism is generally held to have been discredited, one of the commonest objections being that, since it falls foul of its own requirements for meaningfulness, it can hardly claim to lay down necessary conditions for meaningfulness elsewhere. We may wonder whether this is perhaps too swift a rejection. True, it does not appear that an empirical verification can be sought for the principle, but it is less clear that it lacks standing as a conceptual truth. Perhaps, if we had a clearer conception of what meaning and verification involve, we should perceive the intimate relation which the positivist alleges. However, just as much to the point is the consideration that certain kinds of proposition, including some we have just been touching upon, invite verificationist challenges. It is precisely because beings thought real by the ancients are never encountered that we regard claims for their existence as gratuitous. Wittgenstein's identification of meaning with use appears to be a liberating move: a form of words may fail to present a testable hypothesis, but enjoy a use nonetheless. However, it could be that certain kinds of use are possible only if verifiability is assured. For instance, it would seem that A could not be regarded as inductive evidence for B unless B had been found to be so when A obtained; so a condition requiring verifiability is implicit in the characterization of A as evidence of this kind.

How do matters stand when we turn from gods to God? Does the verificationist still have a case to be answered? We may approach this issue via a consideration of the parable of the garden in John Wisdom's celebrated paper, 'Gods' (Wisdom 1944–5: 191–2). After a prolonged absence, two people return to their garden to find both signs of neglect and apparent evidence of a gardener's attention. One of them is disposed to play down the disorder, insisting that a gardener has been at work and, as the days pass, explaining the lack of more direct evidence for a gardener by saying that he is invisible to mortal eyes. The other, more impressed by the neglect, refuses to allow that there has been a gardener. Each cites evidence in favor of his case, but eventually the hypothesis of a gardener ceases to be experimental, each party having the same expectations as to what may be found.

Clearly, such a parable is of relevance only to a limited range of religious beliefs; most notably, those which affirm an intervention by a god or God in the course of events, an action which will make a difference in what is to be found. To the extent that the hypothesis of such intervention may be likened to an experimental hypothesis, it will be to the point to criticize someone who fails to treat it as such, introducing on an ad hoc basis saving qualifications whenever the hypothesis threatens being overturned by the evidence. The charge is not 'meaningless because unverifiable,' but 'vacuous because consistent with every possible state of affairs' – a status which would appear to be ruled out for propositions which are other than a priori. On the other hand, many propositions about God, and particularly propositions affirming his existence, will more cogently be held by the theist to be true, however the world may be. No ad hoc adjustments are needed to bring into line with empirical findings the proposition that an all-powerful being outside space and time exists, since nothing we might observe *could* count against it. It is noteworthy that Wisdom vacillates between talking of God and talking of gods, his argument being more immediately applicable to the latter.

Transcendence problems related to prayer

The proposition that God exists is pre-eminent among propositions that theists have held to be necessary, a status which has led to its dismissal by many. Necessary truths, it is said, cannot extend to matters of existence since they merely reflect the arbitrary conventions of our language. However, a basis in linguistic usage cannot tell you that a mathematical proposition is not existential, and it is not clear that a proposition to the effect that reality has to include a deity can be ruled out just because it is putatively both necessary and existential. There is a sense, familiar from discussions of existence and predication, in which 'God necessarily exists' is not *about* God in the way 'God became man' or 'God is just' purports to be, as is shown by the paraphrase of the former as 'At least one being must be divine,' which has as its subject matter reality in general rather than a particular individual. Ironically, those who refuse to allow that the existential statement could be necessary may well be guilty of assimilating these two forms to one another. If God exists, this surely does not just *happen* to be so, but the real threat is that nothing could satisfy the descriptions which divinity requires, that God is impossible. If God does not exist, this, too, surely does not just *happen* to be the case.

Propositions about minor deities do not enjoy the necessity which is argued for these more sophisticated claims, but, of course, not everything that is said about the Christian God is immune from verificationist considerations, since God is commonly supposed to have intervened in the natural world, as when acting in answer to prayers, becoming man, and working miracles. However, verificationist appeals may be problematic here, and it is not clear that this is where the real problem arises. One of the main obstacles to pressing such appeals derives from the supposition that divine acts flow from a being endowed with a will and intellect. Consider the belief in the efficacy of petitionary prayer. Many still hold to this belief in the face of unanswered prayers, and it would be reasonable for them to draw a comparison with requests to human agents. In either case, we are not dealing with a phenomenon subject to exceptionless law, but it is for the agent petitioned to judge whether a request should be granted or not. That it should sometimes be turned down is not a reason for never making a request, though repeated disappointments on matters of importance may lead us to conclude that there is little benefit to be derived from calling upon God's help.

But suppose it is insisted that God always answers our prayers, even when what we pray for patently does not come about. Faced with this difficulty, the apologist may make more than one move. He may simply concede that not all our prayers are answered, but he may continue to hold that the claim remains intact: God does indeed answer our prayers, but on some occasions by giving us something other than what we had prayed for. We asked for fine weather for the village fete, but since it rained continuously that day, perhaps he was waiting for the more important church bazaar to gladden our heart. The weather that day also proving inclement, perhaps some other function is going to be favored. Or perhaps some benefit of much greater significance will be forthcoming as a result of our prayer.

We may object to this salvaging attempt on the grounds that conferring these other benefits does not count as answering the prayer actually offered and so does not save the claim, strictly understood. We may also protest that if just any desirable turn of events is welcomed as God's answer to our prayers, we shall have no reason to infer a peculiarly divine intervention rather than put the happening down to the natural course of events, which, even without prayer, are often in accordance with our wishes. Compare the claim of those who hold that God will punish people who act in a certain way and who take any of the ills which befall the latter as showing the rightness of that judgment, even though they are ills only to be expected for human beings generally.

The following is worth noting. However ad hoc the apologist's attempts at saving his hypothesis from refutation, it is his unprincipled manner of handling the apparent refutations that is to be questioned, rather than the hypothesis itself. That is, the hypothesis may at each stage have some determinate content, but in the face of a threatened refutation, an ad hoc amendment is made. That, too, proving to be unfulfilled, another qualification is introduced, with no relaxation of this procedure until something in accordance with the claim is found to take place. Compare a claim that all As are B. When it is pointed out that As which are F are not B, the claim may be modified to 'All As which are not F are B', a move which may be repeated in the face of the apparent truth that As which are G are not B, and so on. At each stage we may have a definite hypothesis; the culprit, if any, is its inconstant proponent. I say 'if any' since it may be possible to say quite reasonably that the hypothesis had not been intended to extend to As which are F. To pursue this point, even if the only reason for qualifications is to avoid refutation, that does not necessarily disqualify a form of words from making a serious claim. An arithmetical formula may be successively qualified to protect it from refutation, as when we refuse to allow '5 + 3 = 8' to be falsified by the possibility that the objects counted should coalesce or disappear. The objection in the theological case is that this strategy changes the character of the proposition, making it a conceptual truth that God answers our prayers when it had been supposed to enjoy a quasi-factual standing, something in part learned by the experience of mankind.

While there are these undoubted complexities, I would suggest that the question of verification does not get to the heart of the difficulty, which lies in making sense of God's intervention in our lives. And that is a difficulty because God, along with other supernatural agents, is thought to transcend the physical world in a way that is at odds with having what it takes to impinge upon its occupants.

Consider the example of prayer to a deceased saint. So, St Anthony is said to be the saint to whom to pray if you wish to find something you have lost. How is the saint's assistance realized? How does he direct your steps, your gaze, your rummagings, in such a way that you come across the lost article? You have no evidence of your body being moved by unfamiliar powers, no reason to suppose that your thoughts and movements proceed from different causal antecedents from those obtaining on normal occasions. More important, you have no idea *how* the novel causation is effected. St Anthony is long dead, out of touch with the instruments of change in this world, lacking the wherewithal to redirect, modify, or in any other way manipulate physical bodies and processes. Given how much is lacking in what we know to be necessary for action of the relevant kind, what is left of the hypothesis that St Anthony is behind our successful searches? And the situation is no better if we invoke God rather than the saint. Not only do we have the problem of making sense of the intervention of a non-physical being in the physical world, a being who is outside space and time, but we have the further problem of making sense of a subject of the peculiarly divine attributes.

It is worth stressing the gap between our conception of causation and what it is required to do when God, angels, souls, or other incorporeal beings are the relevant agents. Causation is often made out to be a puzzling metaphysical notion, but it is one that is familiar through the numerous causal verbs in our language, such as *lift, steer, burn, squeeze, tear, bend, dissolve, shake,* and so forth. These are verbs which describe the action of one thing on another: instances of causation which can be readily observed, which do not in general require knowledge of scientific laws, and whose application in countless cases is not open to serious doubt. In philosophical parlance, the relation of cause and effect is taken to be central, but this formula risks omitting a key factor apparent in our homely examples – namely, the presence of something which is acted upon by the agent in producing the effect, as when we heat something and it melts or when we stretch something and it snaps. The notion of acting upon something is an extension of the notion of coming into physical contact with something. Straightforward enough with such acts as cutting, bending, and breaking, less apparent visually with acts such as heating or freezing, and yet more elusive with the causation involved in, say, the action of an electronic device that unlocks your car door from a distance, as also with other transactions at a submicroscopic level. Puzzling though some of the latter phenomena may be, they are events in the physical world; there is no exit from our space and time, no appeal to anything transcendent. A physicist can explain to us what passes from the electronic device to the lock, even though we see nothing in this space. The saint's help in finding something does not make use of any such devices, whether familiar or understood only by scientists. How can it be anything but empty verbiage to cling to the idea of causal action when nothing whatsoever of a cause as we understand the notion is in evidence? And, as already indicated, this difficulty is in no way lessened by supposing that God himself is the agent. Attributing unlimited powers to him does not address the question of intelligibility just outlined.

A similar dilemma is encountered when appeal is made to *mind* to explain God's nature. God does not have a body; he is not physical. What, then, is there left for him to be? Not an abstraction – that does not fit in with his creative power – but the only remaining category of relevance would appear to be that of mind. But what use of 'mind' is intended? The number of choices is daunting, the term figuring in such diverse idioms as 'make up one's mind,' 'change one's mind,' 'have an original mind,' 'have one's mind on one's work,' and so forth. Fortunately, there are identifiable themes which take us through this motley. So is it mind as involving intention ('I've got a good mind to complain,' 'She made up her mind to speak out'), or is it mind as this relates to opinion ('He's changed his mind,' 'We are of the same mind on this matter')? Then again, we have 'mind' as involved in awareness of or attention to something ('Bear his advice in mind,' 'Cast your mind back to those events'), and also 'mind' as this connects with abilities involving thought and reasoning ('He has a highly original turn of mind,' 'He is one of the great minds of our time'). This final category appears to be the most relevant for us, with the last example of the right general shape. However, while a person may be described as, say, a great mind, this is a matter of focusing on a particular human capacity rather than on something detachable from the person – no more than with 'change one's mind' and all the others. Compare the free-floating use of 'intelligence' as in 'A cosmic intelligence rules the world.' This may focus on a key attribute of the putative ruler, but the question remains as to the nature of the subject of that attribute. Is there any sense in which God could be *just* a mind or an intelligence, any more than he could be just a memory, a mood, an intention, a decision, an opinion?

Is *spirit* perhaps the notion we are searching for? There is nothing amiss with *mind* in terms of its meaningfulness; it is just that it does not appear to bear the right meaning for the theist's purposes. *Spirit* – and *soul* – are more problematic in this respect. We are trying to make sense of the notion of an intelligent incorporeal agent of change in the material world. These terms may have a use in which such agency is part of what it is to be a spirit, but this does not make the exercise of that agency any more perspicuous. Our conception of a causal transaction is so much wedded to notions implying spatial extension and occupancy that we can ring the changes for as long as we wish on words supposedly denominating beings having this role without moving a step nearer to understanding how that role is possible.

Spirit and soul may be part of a primitive picture now seen to be no more than that, but is there not a modern replacement in the form of *energy*? Some speak of energy, especially 'pure' energy, as if it were some kind of stuff, and indeed it is true that the notion, so understood, has been enlisted by some in trying to make sense of an incorporeal force or agent. But energy belongs to a wholly different category. It is a capacity for work, and as a capacity compares with abilities, propensities, liabilities, and so forth, terms all far removed from names of stuffs or agents, such as 'magnet,' 'fire,' or 'acid.'

Similar observations apply to *force*. We use the term with respect to agents, whether personal or impersonal, as with 'the armed forces' and 'the forces of nature,' and it also has a more complex use illustrated by such phrases as 'exert a force.' Transferring the term in the first use to supposed non-physical agents presents just the problems of intelligibility which we have found with respect to such agents, and uses of the second kind appear to depend on the availability of verbs of action such as *pull*, *lift*, or *squeeze* relating to interactions between physical subjects and objects. Squeezing an orange is a matter of exerting a force, an action which can be readily redescribed by means of such verbs.

Problems of transcendence relating to miracles

We saw that the fundamental difficulty raised by petitionary prayer was how anything could count as God answering the prayer when this involves intervention in the world. The same difficulty arises with respect to miracles, although, as with prayer, attention is often focused upon other aspects of the problem. In Hume's celebrated discussion, for instance, the question of the reliability of testimony is to the fore, along with that of the likelihood of events which run counter to human experience (Hume 1902). It is no doubt in place to question human testimony when presented with a seemingly far-fetched tale, but this risks ignoring the central issue. We are not necessarily interested only in historical fact; we should like to know what the best case could prove, whether the believer's case could in principle be established if the possibility of error and deception in reports of wondrous happenings could be discounted.

We have here two difficult steps. First, the step to saying that only some out-of-the-ordinary power could be responsible for certain happenings. Second, the step to saying that, beyond this, a divine or supernatural agent is behind them. So, we are familiar with the seemingly inexplicable feats performed by entertainers who make a convincing show of reading minds, predicting future events, making objects vanish and reappear and so forth – feats in comparison with which seemingly walking on water or changing it into wine is a relatively minor accomplishment. We may not have the remotest idea as to how such things are achieved, but we have good reason to suppose that a mundane explanation is at hand, as indeed the practitioners are often happy to admit. But let us suppose that strange powers unknown to science are genuinely at work. Where does that take us? We shall assuredly have to allow that the universe is less well understood than we had appreciated, but how could the extraordinary feats give testimony to a supernatural, let alone a divine, power? What could we encounter which would demand the agency, not of some quite exceptionally powerful natural agent, but of a being outside space and time who created the universe? Stay within our world and there is at least a chance that an extension of our knowledge will eventually encompass what we have witnessed; exit that domain altogether and we leave behind the very possibility of an eventual understanding, the appeal to non-physical agency making for the breakdown of our notions of causation and explanation.

The problem of what counts as a genuine explanation, highlighted with the question of miracles, is also to the fore with attempts at proving the existence of God. Consider the argument for his existence based on the apparent design to be found in the universe. Prior to Darwin, it would seem remarkable that anyone should have resisted the claim that an intelligent being was responsible for the existence of living things with their extraordinarily complex and exquisitely adapted organs and faculties. However, even in the absence of any naturalistic explanation, it could reasonably be said that the theistic alternative was wanting. If animals, and human beings in particular, pose a problem through their possession of all the organs and faculties which make their lives possible, how much more problematic will a being be who has what it takes to create such creatures? There is no real advance in having one datum in need of explanation give way to an even more intractable variant of the same problem. The alternative – an appeal to evolution by natural selection – may well present its own unresolved difficulties, but it at least offers hope of avoiding a repetition of the initial problem. Creationists protest that, given difficulties faced by the theory of evolution, divine agency should be admitted as at least a possible explanation. However, whatever the objections that evolution has to face, they do nothing to support divine creation as a coherent, let alone explanatory, theory.

The problem which we have identified as central extends to the doctrine of analogy, although, as with the notion of God as a necessary being, it is important not to overstate the difficulties. The view that terms used of God can enjoy at best a use analogous to that with which we are familiar may rest on a misconception of either use. Virtues attributable to God, as with his justice, love, knowledge, and wisdom, could be explicated in much the same way as when they are attributed to human subjects, even if the degree of the virtue is that much greater in his case. Our understanding of such virtues is an understanding of the way they may be manifested in just and loving actions and wise and knowledgeable judgments. There is nothing in the subject, whether human or divine, that has in addition somehow to be penetrated. The difficulty lies in knowing what would count as a manifestation by God of these traits, the key notions which this would involve, as those relating to agency, seemingly being beyond rescue by an appeal to analogy if anything like our account of causation is on target.

This is not so say that, even with respect to the more amenable names of virtues, there are not difficulties in making sense of descriptions used of God. There are questions of the mutual consistency of God's attributes, and the notion of the divine simplicity – according to which there is in God no distinction between his justice, say, and his knowledge and which would have God identified with an abstraction such as truth – poses a seemingly insuperable problem of intelligibility.

Theism as theory?

It may be objected that our general approach has not taken into account one important possibility. If we consider hypotheses concerning God in piecemeal fashion, we may find answers to individual questions elusive, but should we not be thinking in terms of a *theory* which stands or falls for more general reasons? There are numerous objections to this approach, one of the more notable being the way the appeal to theory is abused in avoiding refutation, but the major consideration is that saying that one is putting forward a theory does not address questions of meaning. So, a theist might say: 'Your objections may have some force, but they do not have the strength to overturn the general picture I have; they can at most motivate peripheral emendations.' But our objections have largely to do with the very intelligibility of theism. Just as creationism and intelligent design fail as genuine explanations, so they are wanting even as theories. More generally, dignifying theism with the title of 'theory' does nothing to make it easier to grasp the relations between the supernatural and the natural which we have found to be at the heart of the difficulties in making sense of theism.

See also The problem of religious language (Chapter 39), Naturalistic rejoinders to theistic arguments (Chapter 40), Why is there a universe at all, rather than just nothing? (Chapter 41).

References

Hume, D. (1902) [1777] *An Enquiry Concerning Human Understanding*, ed. L. A. Selby-Bigge, Oxford: Clarendon Press.

Wisdom, J. (1944–5) 'Gods,' *Proceedings of the Aristotelian Society* 45: 185–206.

Further reading

Cahn, S. M. and D. Shatz (eds) (1982) *Contemporary Philosophy of Religion*, Oxford: Oxford University Press. (A wide range of readings.)

Kenny, A. J. P. (1986) *The God of the Philosophers*, Oxford: Clarendon Press. (A critique of the coherence of traditional divine attributes.)

Mackie, J. L. (1982) *The Miracle of Theism*, Oxford: Clarendon Press. (A critique of arguments for and against the existence of God.)

Martin M. (1990) *Atheism: A Philosophical Justification*, Philadelphia: Temple University Press. (A comprehensive critique of theism.)

Rundle, B. (2004) *Why there is Something rather than Nothing*, Oxford: Clarendon Press. (A fuller treatment of the present topic.)

39

THE PROBLEM OF RELIGIOUS LANGUAGE

Kai Nielsen

I shall limit myself to discussing the role of language in philosophy concerning religion (more specifically Judeo-Christian and Islamic traditions) during the twentieth and twenty-first centuries. But it should not be forgotten that well before the linguistic turn with twentieth-century analytical philosophy, there was also concern with linguistic and conceptual issues. The astute and complicated discussion of predication concerning God during the Middle Ages is a prominent example. Moreover, there is a concentrated concern with language during much of the histories of world religions (Soskice 1984; 1997). But it is with the rise of analytic philosophy that such attention moves to center stage.

I shall start by discussing the verificationism that became central with the emergence of logical positivism, moving to the metaphysical realism that rose in reaction to verificationism, then turning to the Wittgensteinian reaction as an alternative to both of the above, and ending with the neo-pragmatist reaction to all this characteristic of Richard Rorty and Jeffrey Stout (Rorty 2002; Stout 2002).

Verificationism

Logical positivists (in some basic respects following David Hume) maintained that cognitively meaningful language is either analytic (true by definition or by what follows from a definition, e.g., 'Tadpoles are young frogs' or 'Tadpoles are frogs'), or factual (when they are construed as empirical and verifiable). There are, of course, expressive, evocative, and ceremonial uses of language, but sentences when they are not, or are not also descriptive uses of language are not, according to them, cognitively meaningful and have no truth-conditions: they can tell us nothing about what is the case. All sentences that are neither analytic nor factual (i.e., empirical) are alleged to be devoid of cognitive significance.

Twentieth-century verificationists have been led to eschew both *decisive* verification and falsification. Plenty of perfectly meaningful scientific statements are not decisively verifiable and plenty are not decisively falsifiable. Moreover, some are neither decisively verifiable nor decisively falsifiable (e.g., 'Every substance has some solvent'). But verificationists have moved to a weaker verifiability criterion, namely that for a sentence to be *factually* meaningful, it must be directly or indirectly confirmable or infirmable at least in principle (it must be logically possible to confirm or disconfirm it). This is an empirical *testability* criterion. Abstract physical laws are almost never – perhaps never – *directly* confirmable or disconfirmable. We can, of course, in an indirect way either give evidence for or against them showing in that indirect way they are confirmable or disconfirmable. But both direct and indirect confirmation or disconfirmation as a test for factual intelligibility is always fallible. Data may be variously interpreted; mistakes in observation can always be made; and inferences from observation to theories can always go awry.

Moreover, it is not obvious that even for de-anthropomorphized developed theistic beliefs that we can rule out some indirect confirmation or disconfirmation of them in principle. We may not have even the slightest idea of how to confirm or disconfirm 'God created the heavens and the earth,' 'God loves his creation,' or 'The providential order of God reigns in the world' (Nielsen 1982: 140–70). But that does not entail that they are notions that are not in some way in principle confirmable or disconfirmable, though the burden of proof is on the believer to indicate how this could be so.

The same is true for certain postulations of physics or biology. Moreover, it will be claimed that the very verifiability criterion (in any form) is self-refuting. 'That all meaningful statements are either analytic or empirically testable' is itself neither analytic nor empirically testable and thus should be rejected as cognitively meaningless on those very grounds. However, if we do not take testability as a general criterion of meaning but as a criterion of *factual* meaningfulness and regard, as Martin and I do, the criterion as a *proposal* justified on pragmatic grounds and not itself as a putative statement of fact, we get something that is not self-refuting and is more plausible (Nielsen 1982; Martin 1997). Proposals are not themselves analytic or empirical claims to truth or falsity any more than imperatives or questions are, but they, like them, can be pragmatically meaningful and have a point. However, theists can make their quite different proposals too: proposals which run against verificationism. But then the issue would shift to various social and moral as well as pragmatic considerations and cannot be settled from a consideration concerning intelligibility or meaningfulness.

Logical positivists typically, after accepting that, go on to claim that when we are talking about the facts we are talking *evidential empirical data*. 'Empirical fact' is taken by them to be a pleonasm. It will in turn be replied that this rests on pure unwitting stipulation on the empiricist's part and hardly fits with the way physics has developed: the fundamental particles of physics are not empirically identifiable data. A fact *au contraire* is just what a true proposition (or statement) states. It is not an event, process, or thing in the world (or 'out of the world'). Moreover, there are mathematical, logical, moral, legal, and normative political facts, none of which are baldly empirical data. Why then can't there be religious facts? It is just as important that we not reify (objectify) these facts so as to try to regard them as objects or entities (things) in the world or 'beyond the world' in some allegedly 'supernatural world.' If we do something like that (trying to treat them as 'non-natural facts'), then we get human projections rooted in illusion. But we do not have to, and should not, so reify.

However, in making positive assertions of whatever type, we are claiming that certain propositions are true. How we *establish* something to be true is often a difficult business and varies with the discourse we are engaging in and is sometimes very tenuous and inconclusive. It may in some instances even be altogether impossible. But the sense of 'true' in saying anything is true remains importantly unproblematic. A proposition (sentence, if you will) is true if what it says is so. But all such sayings that something is so do not even purport to be empirical sayings so (i.e., saying so need not be saying that something empirically identifiable is so). A proposition of whatever type expressed by an indicative sentence is either true or false (has a truth-value) when 'p' (an indicative sentence) is used to assert p. When we take the quotation marks off 'p,' we get p: '"$2 + 2 = 4$" is true if and only if $2 + 2 = 4$'; '"Killing is wrong" is true if and only if killing is wrong'; '"If p then p or q" is true if and only if p then p or q'; '"Same sex marriage is illegal in the United States" is true if and only if same sex marriage is illegal in the United States'; '"Empires are evil" if and only if empires are evil'; and '"God created the heavens and the earth" is true if and only if God created the heavens and the earth.' If a fact is just what a true proposition (statement or sentence) states, then there are *all kinds of facts*: logical, mathematical, legal, moral, political, and religious. Truth is not an *epistemological* notion.

In speaking of the *meaning* (*use*) of 'true,' we are not speaking of how a truth claim is confirmed, warranted, established, or legitimized; we are not even necessarily asserting that it is establishable or legitimizable. It may even be verification-transcendent. To say something is true is to say that if it really is true, it is time-independent; if p is true it has always been true and will always be true (e.g., if there were rocks some places at the bottom of the Mississippi in 1592 then it was, is, and will always be true that there were rocks at the bottom of the Mississippi in 1592). In this way truth is time-independent – eternal, if you want to reify things. But this says nothing about how we confirm, establish, legitimatize, or in any way ascertain the truth of a proposition. That, unlike truth itself, is time- and domain-specific. *Taking* or establishing something to be true is always time-dependent and what we take to be true, no matter how carefully justified, how well warranted, or even ideally rationally acceptable, may always turn out to be false. That is just a matter of how we use 'true' and 'warrantedly assertable' and 'rationally acceptable.' It always makes sense to say 'rationally acceptable but still possibly false.' This is why I (along with many others) say that truth is not an epistemic notion. In one way truth is not very important for it is not a means of establishing anything (Rorty 1991: 126–50).

What is crucial in religion (as elsewhere) is how we *warrant* or *establish* (if we can warrant or establish) a religious claim to be true. Perhaps we cannot do so. Perhaps we can articulate neither truth-conditions nor assertability-conditions for religious claims. We have in effect seen above that indicative religious utterances have a truth-value. But it does not seem at least that they – more accurately the non-anthropomorphic ones – have either truth-conditions or assertability-conditions. But it remains the case, and trivially so, that 'God exists' is true if and only if God exists.

It will be said of empiricists and some pragmatists that they have a vanishingly poor conception of fact. But it will in turn be replied that that will be so only if we say an 'empirical fact' is a pleonasm. But that for the above reasons is a mistake. To ask for 'the facts and only for the facts' (Charles Dickens's Mr Gradgrind to the contrary notwithstanding) *need* not be to ask for 'the empirical data' (or even 'the statistical data'). We have seen that this is not true; it is not even true that this is all that remains relevant for empiricism. Moreover, religious claims are not empirical claims. But then what kind of claims are they? Some religious utterances are analytic (e.g., 'God is eternal'). But not all of them are (e.g., 'There are eternal things,' 'There is eternal Being,' or 'God created the heavens and the earth'). There seems to be no way we could justify such putative claims. We certainly cannot empirically confirm them or, for that matter, disconfirm them.

Should we, perhaps, take them on faith, completely on trust? This is increasingly difficult for people with modern sensibilities, or does this just come to having empiricist prejudices? But is that just because of unexamined empiricist dogmas? Perhaps. But that is increasingly difficult to accept when we see that indicative religious utterances or at least the fundamental ones are without truth-conditions or assertability-conditions. It is very difficult, given that, to see what sense (if any) they have. And so the debate around verificationism and its implications goes around and around. And it should be added that we have touched on only some of the considerations that are crucial (see Putnam 2002; 2004).

Metaphysical realism in religion

Metaphysical realism (including theistic metaphysical realism) enters here with its revival of things away from the linguistic turn: away from a fixation on how language is used. It capitalizes on the type of considerations that we have raised in the last part of the previous section concerning what it means to speak of facts and the narrowness of empiricist treatments of 'fact.' Fact is a many-splendored thing.

The empiricist tradition took a fact to be something that corresponds to a sense impression (something that a sense impression depicts) or sometimes even more reductively (unconsciously flirting with linguistic idealism) to identifying a fact with what a sense impression or possible sense impression is. The verificationists (principally logical positivists), having taken the linguistic turn, expressed much the same thing as did the classical empiricists, only in linguistic terms. They spoke of an 'empiricist language' and of observation sentences and observation terms. However, they succumbed to criticisms of the type articulated in the previous section. By 1938 leading logical positivists, Rudolf Carnap and Carl Hempel, had completely abandoned verificationism for *individual* statements (sentences) or for meaningful scientific predicates. It was no longer held that a predicate to be factually meaningful must be either an observation predicate or reducible to an observation predicate. They came to realize that such terms as 'charge' and 'electron' do not enter physics through definitions or even reductions. Rather they are simply taken as *primitives* (Carnap 1938: 139–214; Putnam 2002). As Putnam put it, 'On the revised logical positivist criterion of cognitive significance, it is the system of *scientific statements as a whole* that has factual content' (2002: 23–4). It is no longer individual statements or predicates allegedly confronting sense experience that must be testable but the whole of the scientific system.

Physics – for them, the veritable paradigm of the cognitively meaningful – was replete with theoretical terms: not only 'charge' and 'electron' but 'protons,' 'neutrons,' 'neutrinos,' 'quarks,' 'curved space-time,' and 'gravitational field.' That there are such entities is neither directly or indirectly testable nor observationally or operationally definable. But they are integral to present-day physics. Carnap and Hempel, followed by Quine, took such abstract and theoretical terms to be 'empirically meaningful' as long as *the system in which they occur as a whole* enables us to predict more successfully what we experience with them than we could without them.

Theistic metaphysical realists (as well as others) were quick to realize that if physics could utilize such abstract and theoretical terms, sometimes introduced as undefined primitives into a scientific system, there was no reason (or at least no apparent reason) that we could not have 'God' entering the category of cognitively meaningful terms as well as 'proton.' Judaism, Christianity, and Islam could introduce their (in positivist jargon) 'theoretical terms' as undefined primitives as well as physics. True, religion, unlike physics or biology, isn't in the prediction business but has different ends in view: different purposes. Religions are concerned with making sense of life and with providing guidance for how we should live our lives or, depending on the religion, with salvation or enlightenment. But why should this make a difference? Religion just has different purposes or ends in view. Both religion and science can introduce their central abstract terms into their systems in the same way. These terms can be *postulated* and taken as undefined primitives. Religion and science serve different purposes with diverse rationales. So why should only the scientific purposes be legitimate? Only the blindest scientistic-oriented philosopher would think that all purposes or even all rational or reasonable purposes are scientific.

However, it will be replied, religion – traditionally at least – has served *cosmological* purposes as well. And it is characteristically claimed by traditional religious people that without the cosmology, the meaning of life, ethical, salvation, and enlightenment functions of religious discourse would be quite groundless indeed, not only that, but eviscerated. Religion, in effect, would be reduced to something like morality touched with emotion. So, it is claimed, the metaphysical realist side of religion is essential: religion, that is, makes *verification-transcendent* claims and postulates realities – entities, or Being if you will – which are not in any way empirically establishable and its claims are not *synthetic a priori* claims either. But physics does so as well; so why is it not legitimate for religion to do so?

It in turn will be responded that more and more contemporary people remain religious without that cosmology. The cosmological for them is just a bit of mythology that is really not important to their religious belief. We are justified, they claim, in accepting Judaism, Christianity, and Islam if they more than any other alternatives help us make sense of our lives and yield a better understanding, weak though it may remain, of how to order our lives. But this has repeatedly and powerfully been challenged by many utterly secular thinkers such as Hobbes, Mill, Feuerbach, Marx, and Dewey and, in our time, by Richard Rorty (1998; 2006). We can, perhaps, make sense of our lives and morality more adequately in utterly secular terms (Nielsen 1996: 557–99; 2001: 56–76).

Religion backed up by metaphysical realism may not be vulnerable to verificationist arguments, and metaphysical realists may be justified in setting aside the linguistic turn. But such metaphysical realists defending a religious point of view are challengeable, and deeply so, *normatively*; they and the religions they defend are challengeable for being something that does not answer to modern (or if you will postmodern) sensibilities. Have these secularists just been enculturated (brainwashed, to put it crudely) into the typical ways of construing or reacting to things of contemporary educated life? Is it (as has sometimes been said of liberalism) a form of cultural imperialism? Richard Rorty remarks, with reference to his exchange with Gianno Vattino concerning religion, that Vattino finds the whole issue between atheism and theism interesting while he (Rorty) finds it uninteresting. Rorty remarks, 'Considering that he [Vattino] was raised a Catholic and I was raised in no religion at all, this is not surprising' (Rorty 2003a: 144). Does finding personal significance in religion or not just come down to having been exposed to different forms of conditioning? Does rationality or reasonability or conceptual sophistication or careful moral thought and disciplined reflection have nothing to do with it (Rorty and Vattino 2004)?

The Wittgensteinian turn concerning religious discourse

Enter Wittgenstein's, or at least a putatively Wittgensteinian, way of looking at religion and religious discourse. Wittgenstein would have scorned the idea that he had a *philosophy* of language or a philosophy of anything else (including religion). He – or so he viewed himself – was not in the business of constructing either a philosophical system or a point of view. In this respect he was with Kierkegaard. Philosophy was for him an *activity* and his aims in engaging in it were largely conceptually therapeutic: to help, as he put it, the fly out of the fly-bottle.

However, he did attend carefully to our language as it was used in context and was remarkably finely attuned to it. For him philosophical nonsense emerged largely from not properly understanding the workings of our language, particularly when we reflect about it in specific contexts. He saw language as an activity; we play various and diverse language-games (characteristic things we do with words) for various purposes. None of these language-games has priority over others, and there is no super-language or cluster of basic language-games on which all others depend; there is no foundational base which gives the rest their legitimacy or insures their rationality. Wittgenstein utterly rejects such rationalism or foundationalism whether it is thought to be metaphysical or scientific. Such approaches do not attend to how language actually functions, but impose a picture on it. Our actual languages are constituted by language-games. These language-games are embedded in practices (ways of acting and being) that humans in a society characteristically engage in and that deeply form them. Forms of life – religions, science, and witchcraft in some societies (e.g., the Azande), views of the world and ethical stances – have embedded in them practices.

(On the pervasiveness of the belief in witchcraft in West Africa, see Appiah 2006: 35–55.)

Within a language-game there is typically justification and lack of justification, evidence and proof as well as mistaken and groundless opinion. But we can't say this for language-games, practices, and forms of life (modes of social life) themselves taken as a whole. We cannot, that is, intelligibly say of a language-game or practice (or a whole cluster of language-games or a form of life) that we have something that is justified or unjustified, something that is reasonable or unreasonable, something we have evidence for, proof for and the like. And we cannot say we lack any of these things either, for we do not understand what it would be like to have them. There is no coherent way even of saying they are reasonable or unreasonable. These appraisive terms have no grip here. There can be proof or justification *within* a practice – using the built-in norms of the practice – but not *of* them or *of* all the practices of a society taken together. This has led many philosophers (e.g., Saul Kripke and Hilary Putnam) to think that Wittgenstein was a relativist (Putnam 1992: 168–79).

Beliefs, utterances, conceptions, concepts 'are only intelligible in the context of ways of living or modes of social life as such' (Winch 1995: 100–1). Science is one such mode, morality another, and religion still another or perhaps they are each distinctive clusters of language-games and practices *in* a form of life. 'Each,' Peter Winch tells us, 'has criteria of intelligibility peculiar to itself ... [W]ithin science or religion actions can be logical or illogical,' rational or irrational, justified or lacking in justification, reasonable or unreasonable, worthy of acceptance or not (ibid.). There is, Winch has it, no bringing these clusters of practices constituting a mode of life themselves before 'the bar of reason' such that we could coherently say they are *true or false* or that religion as such a mode of social life is an illusion or is just a human projection.

Judaism, Christianity, Islam, Buddhism, Hinduism are themselves either forms of life or *in* forms of life (depending on how we take Wittgenstein). Still, religious language-games with their practices, along with other language-games, are not balkanized. How they are taken depends on their connections with other language-games. However, the religious language-games, as we have seen, still have their distinctive criteria and distinctive point. Standing outside all our religious practices, we cannot, it is claimed, reasonably assess them, for they are just there like our lives and they either mean something to us – have some importance to us – or they do not (Rhees 1997). Indeed, we cannot stand outside *all* practices and criticize anything; there is no practice-free perspective on anything (Nielsen and Phillips 2005). But using one practice or cluster of practices, we can sometimes relevantly criticize another practice or cluster of practices (ibid.).

However, from this Wittgensteinian point of view at least, there is no showing that they must have some significance for us. They are just there (to repeat) like our lives and they are either of significance for us or they are not, or we remain ambivalent about this. But there is no reason they *must* have significance or lack significance for us or that, if we are clearheaded, we must be ambivalent. For them to have significance for us or for us to reject the idea that they can have such significance, we must of

423

course have some *minimal understanding* of the use of religious terms or sentences. But for this it is enough for us, believers or not, to have grown up and been encultured in a social world that has a religious form of life. There is no showing they *must* or even should mean something to us (have some significance for us or value to us) if we are to be reasonable, not self-deceived or in bad faith.

This Wittgensteinian conception of things has generally been taken as bad news by both traditional theistic philosophers *and* by those naturalistically and secularly rooted. For it challenges root and branch how both of them conceive of things and of the common grounds of their disputes with one another. If we see religion as at all a *normative* issue, it challenges our respective stances. Moreover, it seems to give us grounds for setting aside the verificationist disputes between verificationists and their metaphysical realist opponents discussed in the previous section. (A useful introduction to these disputes includes the debates between Bertrand Russell and Frederick Copleston S. J., and between A. J. Ayer and Copleston: Russell and Copleston 1964; Ayer and Copleston 1957.)

I shall simply note two kinds of objection to such Wittgensteinianisms in religion, the second of which has to do more with the above characterization of it.

First kind

First, Anthony Kenny, someone well-versed in Wittgenstein, has remarked that Wittgenstein's influence on the philosophy of religion has been disastrous. The concept of language-games, he argued, and as we have seen, has a central place in Wittgenstein's thought concerning religion (as well as in everything else). But Kenny also remarks that 'the concept of language-game is an obscure and ambiguous one in Wittgenstein's writings: *in the hands of some of his religious admirers it has become a stonewall defense against any demand for a justification of belief in God*' (Kenny 1975: 245 my italics). Kenny goes on to add that one unfortunate effect of that is that it shuts down the very possibility of any fruitful dialogue between religious belief and critical philosophy.

Second, some early Wittgensteinian accounts of religion tended to see Wittgenstein as dividing his account of religious language-games from other language-games, but that was quickly seen to be neither a good Wittgenstein reading nor, quite independently of that, good philosophy (Nielsen and Phillips 2005). But once the various language-games and practices across the board were seen, an interconnected space was opened up to question their *individual* autonomy. There is, however, no way of either transcending all these interconnected practices and looking, *without benefit of a practice*, at the whole ensemble or assessing an individual practice as a whole, judging its reasonableness or coherence or rationality. Such notions are unintelligible. We can – and sometimes relevantly – criticize one practice by another one (e.g., the practice of religion criticizing ethics, science criticizing religion, ethics criticizing religion, science criticizing ethics and ethics critizing science). Often this has been done irrelevantly, as with, for example, 'Creation *science*' or religious opposition to Darwin, but it has been done relevantly as well.

Moreover, it is often important to juxtapose practices. Most fundamentally it is important, if we can, perspicuously to arrange them into a coherent whole. Wittgenstein has given us reason to be suspicious of that but no good reason to think it is impossible and, where reasonably possible, not desirable. We perhaps can get our various practices into a wide reflective equilibrium, and in that way put them into a coherent whole so that we would not see them as just a jumble (Nielsen 1996: 169–206). Our sense of 'reasonable' is contextual, but not so contextual as to be impossible for us to speak appropriately of the reasonability or lack thereof of one or another such putting of our practices together. We might, in the course of such putting together, sometimes modify a practice or even abandon one in light of its lack of fit with other practices; sometimes we may even abandon whole clusters of practices for not squaring with the ensemble of other practices, as in the case of some strata of some West African societies giving up belief in witches. This does not require us, or indeed enable us, to use one cluster of practices – say science – as a critical fulcrum with which to criticize and judge all the others. (That is a crucial error of scientism.)

But we perhaps can, by reflecting and using rather minimal common notions of what is reasonable, come to see how our various practices could best fit together. (Though the elements constitutive of reasonability will themselves be involved and it will be necessary to ask about their ethnocentricity and to see how they all fit together with the things of which they are said to be reasonable.) Our various practices with their forms of life are not just there to be accepted or rejected for no reason. In societies such as ours, we can – and perhaps should – ask if people can reasonably be religious or not and, if so, how and in which of the religions and even which sect. (Or is that simply a matter of where you happen to have been brought up?) Or can – I think improbably – religious belief and commitment float free of any doctrinal allegiance at all? But religious belief need not be, and should not be, like the first language one learns, just the result of a historical contingency simply drilled into us. It will be partly that – typically initially that – but it need not be *solely* so. In some parts of the world one can make, and often there one feels inwardly the pressure to make, such choices; where some of us are luckily enough situated, we can make it a matter of reflective, and hopefully of reasonable, choice and resolve, and thus we can choose with better or worse reasons and alignments of sentiments.

Third, in the Judaic-Christian-Islamic religions, the concept of God, while not being the sole important thing in these religions, is of central importance. If we, considering these religious strands, approach these matters in a Wittgensteinian way, we will attend to the use of 'God' in our religious language-games, and how this discourse functions in our religious practices. Religions – particularly Judaism and Islam – have (and not without reason) been reluctant to 'name God.' But to have faith in God, to be able to worship God, we have to have *some* understanding of who or what we are to worship or who or what we are to have faith in (Nielsen 1963; 1965). Indeed belief *in* God presupposes a belief *that*: a belief that God exists (Nielsen 1982: 92–100). Though the God of these religions is a mystery – a 'non-mysterious God,' clear to the light of reason, would not be the God of these faiths – God cannot be so mysterious that we cannot understand 'God' at all, or we would not be able to believe in him, worship him, have faith in him.

But when we look at how we characterize God in our de-anthropomorphized religions (as all have come to be with their development), we find he is characterized inconsistently (incompatible predicates are attributed to him). God is said to be a pure spirit, a person without body or parts and to be an individual (a person – or a tri-personal unity, as within the Christian tradition). He is also said to be infinite and utterly transcendent to the world, yet someone who responds to our prayers (sometimes in ways that come as a shock to our expectations). However, even if we can make sense of a 'bodiless person' (some task in itself), we have a plain contradiction in speaking of 'an infinite individual' and of 'God who is utterly transcendent to the world and who sometimes responds to our prayers and thus in some way enters into the world.' We are not just (or perhaps not at all) speaking here of the God of the philosophers but the God of our sacred religious Scriptures, the God of the ordinary worshiper engaging in the religious language-games of his Jewish, Christian, or Islamic culture. It is not enough, as Wittgenstein would have it, to recognize this language-game is played and with that acknowledgment simply accept as in order that language-game.

Second kind

There is a kind of objection to the above Wittgensteinian account that has sometimes been made. It contends that, whatever its intrinsic merits or lack thereof, it is neither genuinely Wittgensteinian nor accurate of the Wittgensteinians who have extensively discussed religion from a Wittgensteinian point of view (Malcolm 1977 and 1994; Bouwsma 1984; Phillips 1993; Winch 1994; Rhees 1997). This has been contested, in our extensive exchanges, by myself and D. Z. Phillips, and has in turn been defended by Phillips (Nielsen and Phillips 2005).

Wittgenstein wrote little directly on religion. The view given above in the text is my own and like any other, given the paucity of material, it is a reconstruction. It is closest, I believe, to those of the avowed Wittgensteinians Norman Malcolm and Peter Winch (Malcolm 1977; 1994; Winch 1994; 1995). But my concern is not that it is the most faithful interpretation of Wittgenstein, or even whether we could ascertain what that is, but with the fact that it is in itself a powerful, and perhaps compelling, account, in the spirit of Wittgenstein's views on philosophy, language, and of religion; and, it is plausibly arguable, the least vulnerable to secular critique. If we are concerned with how religious discourse functions in our lives, it is a crucial view with which to come to grips.

A neo-pragmatist turn on religious discourse

The view we are setting out here is reflected in Robert Brandon, Richard Rorty and Jeffrey Stout (Brandon 1994; Rorty 2002; Stout 2002). I shall utilize principally Rorty's way of articulating it. It is more explicitly historicist than Wittgensteinian views and more clearly sets aside a *representationalist* view of language for an anti-representation-alist *coping* one: language is being viewed (including, of course, religious language) not as a tool for representation but as a tool for coping with various life situations into which we are thrown. Although Wittgenstein speaks of giving perspicuous representations of the workings of our language for particular purposes, he could as well be read, in spite of that, as generally taking a coping view. However, along with 'tool,' both 'representation' and 'coping' with respect to language are metaphorical. I think the pragmatists make a good case that generally 'coping' is a more useful metaphor than 'representing,' but it could be the case that in some situations 'representing' is a better metaphor than 'coping.' In any event, it is important to keep in mind that they, along with 'tool,' both are metaphors and that in some situations it may be worthwhile to ask what they are metaphors of.

Wittgenstein aside, let us look at this neo-pragmatist view. These pragmatists believe (as do Wittgensteinians) that philosophy, and indeed religion or even science, cannot rise above the relevant social practices of its time and judge their desirability by reference to something that is not itself an alternative social practice. They are with Hegel on this one. When asked, as Rorty puts it, '"Are these desirable norms?" or "Is this a good social practice?" all ... [pragmatists] can do is ask [in turn] "by reference to what encompassing social practice are we supposed to judge desirability?" or, more usefully, "by comparison to the norms of what proposed alternative, to norms of what alternative social practice?"' (Rorty 2002: 74). We can have no sense of who we are and who we should strive to be that swings free of these social practices that constitute the way of life of which we are a part. There is, again as Rorty puts it, no 'goal of inquiry which is what it is apart from those practices, and [no] foreknowledge ... which can help us decide which practices to have' (2002: 73). This is as true of religious practices and discourses and of atheist practices and discourses as any other. Rorty goes on to add, 'We should stop trying to put our discursive practices within a larger context, one which forms the background of all possible social practices' (2002: 73).

We can, of course, be reflective about our social practices but this consists in nothing more than contrasting them 'with alternative past or proposed practices' (2002: 75). (Here Rorty's account strengthens the Wittgensteinian account I gave.) This is what it is to hold in thought our time. There is no expert culture – philosophy or theology or religion or science – whose task is to determine 'the future direction of the conversation of Humankind' (ibid.). This just goes on, without direction, as various human beings in various conditions converse. And the more inclusive the group the better.

This is at a great distance from 'Christ is the Way, the Truth, and the Life' or from Aquinas, Maimonides, or Ibn Rushd (Averroes) as it is from Calvin, Luther, or Kierkegaard and almost equally from d'Holbach, Hume, Spinoza, and Nietzsche. It is even a considerable distance from Putnam's Third Enlightenment, the way of thinking developed by John Dewey (Putnam 2004: 96–108). Putnam and Kripke would again cry 'relativism.' Rorty would respond 'No! Only *historicism, contextualism* and a rejection of *Absolutism*' (Mendicta 2006: 126). He is trying to make clear what it is firmly to come to accept our contingency, eschewing unequivocally the ambition of transcendence. Does any religion do so? Can any religion suitably interpreted do so? Religions have, of course, changed over time, Catholicism's claims about the 'Eternal Church' notwithstanding. Can they change so much as to eschew ambitions of transcendence? Should they do so? Would that mean the end of any religious point of view? But could religion come to an end? Would that be a good thing? Can we be non-evasive and eschew these questions?

See also Christianity (Chapter 6), Islam (Chapter 7), Ibn Sina/Avicenna (Chapter 10), Moses Maimonides/Rambam (Chapter 11), Thomas Aquinas (Chapter 12), David Hume (Chapter 13), Immanuel Kant (Chapter 14), Søren Kierkegaard (Chapter 15), Friedrich Nietzsche (Chapter 16), William James (Chapter 17), Mysticism among the world's religions (Chapter 23), Problems with the concept of God (Chapter 38), Natural rejoinders to theistic arguments (Chapter 40), Why is there a universe at all, rather than just nothing? (Chapter 41), The sociobiological account of religious belief (Chapter 42), Postmodern theology (Chapter 47), Theology and religious language (Chapter 48), Phenomenology of religion (Chapter 61), Religious naturalism (Chapter 62), Religious experience (Chapter 63), Religion and science (Chapter 64).

References

Appiah, K. A. (2006) *Cosmopolitanism: Ethics in a World of Strangers*, New York: W. W. Norton.

Ayer, A. J. and F. C. Copleston (1957) 'Logical Positivism: a debate,' in P. Edwards and A. Pap (eds) *A Modern Introduction to Philosophy*, New York: Free Press.

Bouwsma, O. K. (1984) *Without Proof or Evidence: Essays of O. K. Bouwsma*, ed. J. L. Craft and R.E. Hustwit, Lincoln, NE: University of Nebraska Press.

Brandon, R. (1994) *Making It Explicit*, Cambridge, MA: Harvard University Press.

Carnap, R. (1938) 'The foundations of logic and mathematics,' in the *International Encyclopedia of Unified Science*, vol. 1, pt. 1, Chicago: Chicago University Press.

Kenny, A. (1975) 'In defense of God,' *Times Literary Supplement* (February 7): 145.

Malcolm, N. (1977) 'The groundlessness of belief,' in S. C. Brown (ed.) *Reason and Religion*, Ithaca, NY: Cornell University Press.

—— (1994) *Wittgenstein: A Religious Point of View?* Edited with a response by P. Winch, Ithaca, NY: Cornell University Press.

Martin, M. (1997) 'The verificationist challenge,' in P. L. Quinn and C. Taliaferro (eds) *A Companion to Philosophy of Religion*, Oxford: Blackwell.

Mendicta, E. (ed.) (2006) *Take Care of Freedom and Truth Will Take Care of Itself: Interviews with Richard Rorty*, Stanford, CA: Stanford University Press.

Nielsen, K. (1963) 'Can faith validate God-talk?' *Theology Today* 20: 173–84.

—— (1965) 'Religious perplexity and faith,' *Crane Review* 8/1: 1–17.

—— (1982) *An Introduction to the Philosophy of Religion*, London: Macmillan.

—— (1996) *Naturalism without Foundations*, Amherst, NY: Prometheus.

—— (2001) *Naturalism and Religion*, Amherst, NY: Prometheus.

Nielsen, K. and D. Z. Phillips (2005) *Wittgensteinian Fideism?*, London: SCM Press.

Phillips, D. Z. (1993) *Wittgenstein and Religion*, Basingstoke: Macmillan.

Putnam, H. (1992) *Renewing Philosophy*, Cambridge, MA: Harvard University Press.

—— (2002) *The Collapse of the Fact/Value Dichotomy and Other Essays*, Cambridge, MA: Harvard University Press.

—— (2004) *Ethics without Ontology*, Cambridge, MA: Harvard University Press.

Rhees, R. (1997) *Rush Rhees on Religion and Philosophy*, ed. D. Z. Phillips, Cambridge: Cambridge University Press.

Rorty, R. (1991) *Objectivity, Relativism and Truth*, Cambridge: Cambridge University Press.

—— (1998) 'Pragmatism as romantic polytheism,' in M. Dickstein (ed.) *The Revival of Pragmatism*, Durham, NC: Duke University Press.

—— (2002) 'Cultural politics and the question of the existence of God,' in N. Frankenberry (ed.) *Radical Interpretations in Religion*, New York: Cambridge University Press.

—— (2003a) 'Religion in the public square: a reconsideration,' *Journal of Religious Ethics* 33: 141–9.

—— (2006) 'Pragmatism as anti-authoritarianism,' in J. Shook and J. Margolis (eds) *A Companion to Pragmatism*, Malden, MA: Blackwell.

Rorty R. and G. Vattino (2004) *The Future of Religion: Richard Rorty and Gianni Vattino*, ed. S. Zabala, New York: Columbia University Press.

Russell, B. and F. C. Copleston (1964) 'A debate on the existence of God', in J. Hick (ed.) *The Existence of God*, New York: Macmillan.

Soskice, J. M. (1984) *Metaphor and Religious Language*, Oxford: Oxford University Press.

—— (1997) 'Religious language,' in P. Quinn and C. Taliaferro (eds) *A Companion to Philosophy of Religion*, Oxford: Blackwell.

Stout, J. (2002) 'Radical interpretation and pragmatism: Davidson, Rorty, and Brandon on truth,' in N. Frankenberry (ed.) *Radical Interpretation in Religion*, New York: Cambridge University Press.

Winch, P. (1994) 'Discussion of Malcolm's essay,' in N. Malcom, *Wittgenstein: A Religious Point of View?*, edited with a response by P. Winch, Ithaca, NY: Cornell University Press.

—— (1995) *The Idea of a Social Science*, 2nd edn, London: Routledge.

Further reading

Diamond, M. and T. V. Litzenburg, Jr. (eds) (1953) *The Logic of God/Theology and Verification*, Indianapolis, IN: Bobbs-Merrill. (Classic discussions on verification.)

Hägerström, A. (1964) *Philosophy and Religion*, London: Allen & Unwin. (By a major Swedish philosopher of the early twentieth century who developed an intricate and penetrating non-cognitivist and projectionist account of religious discourse.)

Hart, H., R. A. Kuipers and K. Nielsen (eds) (1999) *Walking the Tightrope of Faith*, Amsterdam: Rodolpi. (Essays on fideism, Wittgensteinianism and religion, and atheism.)

Nielsen, K. (1962) 'On speaking of God,' *Theoria* 28: 110–37. (An account of a basically Hägeströmian conception of religious discourse but in a more contemporary and analytic idiom.)

—— (1989) *God, Scepticism and Modernity*, Ottawa, ON: University of Ottawa Press. (A collection of essays on central issues of religious discourse.)

Rorty, R. (1997) 'Religious faith, intellectual responsibility and romance,' in R. A. Putnam (ed.) *The Cambridge Companion to William James*, Cambridge: Cambridge University Press. (A critique of the standard intellectualist accounts of religious discourse.)

—— (2003b) 'Anti-clericalism and atheism,' in M. A. Wrathall (ed.) *Religion after Metaphysics*, Cambridge: Cambridge University Press. (An argument that is anti-clericalism and not atheism that is essential in considering the viability of religion.)

Wrathall, M. (ed.) (2003) *Religion after Metaphysics*, Cambridge: Cambridge University Press. (Essays on neo-pragmatism, postmodernism and deconstructionism on religion.)

40
NATURALISTIC REJOINDERS TO THEISTIC ARGUMENTS

Keith M. Parsons

The Humean strategy

Let us call a 'theistic argument' any argument intended to support the claim that God exists. In this essay I propose a strategy for rebutting theistic arguments based upon David Hume's paradigmatic demolition of the argument from analogy. I show that Hume's plan of attack can be generalized and made applicable to many different kinds of theistic arguments. To illustrate, I employ the Humean strategy to two theistic arguments: Richard Swinburne's inductive version of the cosmological argument and William Lane Craig's defense of the 'fine-tuning' design argument.

In Hume's day, the leading theistic argument inferred an analogy between nature and human artifacts. According to this argument, we find throughout the natural world an arrangement of means-to-ends relationships exactly resembling, though vastly exceeding in scale, accuracy, and intricacy, the objects produced by human contrivance. For instance, just as a watch is designed to tell time, so an eye is apparently designed to see. It ostensibly follows that nature is the product of an intelligent designer whose mind resembles the human mind, though of vastly greater power and creativity.

Hume deployed three tactics in his refutation. First, he extended the analogy, that is, for the sake of argument, he conceded the analogy between nature and human design. However, he drew conclusions that were highly uncongenial to the proponents of the argument. For instance, just as we blame the architect if the building is poorly designed, so nature's flaws should lead us to infer incompetence in its designer. Hume contends that the pain, waste, and ugliness in the natural world points to an incompetent designer. Further, even a competent designer might not be eternal, infinite, all-powerful, all-knowing, or good, which are all essential properties of the God of theism.

Hume's second tactic was to question the assumed analogy at the heart of the design argument. Proponents of the design argument compared the universe to a great machine. But the universe is not really much like a watch, or any other product of human craft. For instance, there is a difference of materials. We know that bits of glass and metal will not spontaneously come together to form a watch, but can we be sure that natural materials will not self-organize into complex and orderly arrangements? In fact, we know that they do. We frequently observe order, even means-to-end order, spontaneously arising in natural systems. The best-known process of natural self-organization is, of course, natural selection (a process unknown to Hume, though he comes tantalizingly close to stating it in some passages). Natural selection is an observable process whereby successive populations of organisms improve their means-to-ends adaptations to their environments. However, natural selection is only one of many observable processes of self-organization in nature (see Shanks 2004).

We can generalize: the means-to-end organization of something like a watch is *always* imposed from outside by an extrinsic designing and manufacturing process. In nature, on the other hand, so far as we can observe, we see that such order *always* arises from spontaneous self-organization brought about by impersonal causes intrinsic to nature itself. A watch and an eye are therefore crucially different. Each is a highly ordered system exhibiting means-to-end organization. But insofar as we have observed the origins of order in natural things, we see that this order comes about in a radically different manner than with artificial things.

Prima facie, therefore, and despite superficial similarities of organization, orderly natural systems appear to originate in a very different way than manufactured items. At this point, defenders of design will likely admit that nature is full of self-organizing and self-maintaining systems, but they will insist that explaining *this* is precisely what requires a designer. Suppose we come to a clearing in a jungle and find a fully automated and self-maintaining factory. Obviously, an intelligent designer set up this factory. By analogy, the universe with all of its self-organizing and self-maintaining systems – much like those our imagined factory, only immeasurably grander and more complex – must have been set up by a stupendously intelligent designer.

Hume would reply that we cannot know a priori that order, even means-to-ends order, requires an intelligent designer. We can support the designer inference only when we encounter the particular kinds of orderly systems that experience has shown us are likely to result from design. Experience shows that factories are set up by intelligent designers and do not originate in any other way. However, a factory is just not sufficiently like the universe to justify a similar inference about origins. For one thing, an essential feature of a factory is that it has an identifiable purpose: the manufacture of a given product. The universe has no apparent overall purpose. If, as some suggest, the aim of the universe is to produce intelligent life, it seems a remarkably inefficient, roundabout, and risky means of achieving that end.

How, then, did order originate in the universe? Hume notes that the way that ideas originate and organize themselves in a mind is a process at least as mysterious as the way order arises in material systems. Therefore, it explains nothing to trace the order in matter back to a mind. We simply replace one particular mystery with another equally singular one. We save an unnecessary step if we just say that the physical universe originally contained intrinsic orderliness, which, through the operation of lawful but impersonal physical processes and interactions, developed into the many orderly natural systems we currently see. If we must use an analogy, the universe developed like a mighty oak growing from an acorn. Hume's final tactic, therefore, is to propose a counter-analogy: it is more reasonable to compare the origin of order in the universe to the generation and development of an organism, which occurs automatically and is guided by the organism's innate organization, than to compare it to the imposition of extrinsic order on an artifact.

This was Hume's strategy, to extend the analogy, question the analogy, and propose a counter-analogy. (The account of Hume's critique of the argument from analogy as employing these three tactics is given in Moore 1986.) As a response to the design argument of his day, these arguments were very cogent. However, Hume's riposte did more than rebut a particular argument; it made a permanent contribution to the art of philosophical polemics: Hume gave us a generalizable strategy for refuting theistic arguments. We may generalize Hume's strategy as follows:

1 Concede the argument. And then show that it falls far short of establishing the existence of the theistic God.
2 Expose the unwarranted assumption. At the heart of each theistic argument is an unjustifiable assumption, or, at least, an assumption that can be, and in fact is, reasonably rejected by many people.
3 Propose an alternative. When the theistic argument offers a particular explanation or analogy, propose one that is more, or at least equally reasonable.

Each of these tactics may not apply to every theistic argument, but they apply to many of them. To illustrate, I shall apply the generalized strategy to two theistic arguments: Richard Swinburne's cosmological argument and William Lane Craig's fine-tuning argument.

Swinburne's cosmological argument

Swinburne is an expert in the field of confirmation theory, the study of how hypotheses are supported by evidence, and he treats the existence of God as a hypothesis that can be confirmed by evidence. For evidence to confirm a hypothesis, it must meet a certain condition: the evidence must be more likely to exist given that the hypothesis is true than that hypothesis is false. For instance, for the fingerprints on the murder weapon to count as evidence against the accused, it must be more likely that the fingerprints will be on the weapon if the accused is guilty than if the accused is not guilty. If, on the other hand, the fingerprints are just as likely to be on the weapon whether or not the accused is guilty, the fingerprints obviously cannot be evidence of guilt.

Swinburne proposes a version of the cosmological argument. He claims that the existence of a complex physical universe is evidence for the existence of God. As with the fingerprint evidence mentioned above, the existence of a complex physical universe is evidence for God's existence if and only if such a universe is more likely to exist given that God exists than if God does not exist. Swinburne must therefore argue that a complex physical universe is more likely to exist if there is a God than if there is not.

One possibility is that there is no God and the universe simply exists as an ultimate, unconditioned, irreducible, uncaused, inexplicable (i.e., 'brute') fact. Swinburne must therefore show that the universe is more likely to exist given that God exists than given that it is a brute fact. How could one argue this? Swinburne appeals to the criterion of simplicity. When scientists must select between two rival theories, then, all other things being equal, they consistently choose the simpler theory. Suppose that T and T* are empirically equivalent theories; that is, each explains the relevant data equally well, and has passed equally rigorous tests. However, T is simpler than T* because it postulates fewer logically independent entities or entities of fewer different kinds or entities with fewer properties, and so forth. In this case, scientists will prefer T to T*. Swinburne argues that theism, the hypothesis that God exists, is much simpler than naturalism, the hypothesis that the universe exists as a brute fact:

> To start with, theism postulates a God with capacities as great as they logically can be. He is infinitely powerful, omnipotent. That there is an omnipotent God is a simpler hypothesis than that there is a God who has such-and-such limited power (e.g. the power to rearrange matter, but not the power to create it). (Swinburne 2004: 97)

So, theism postulates a single very simple being, whereas naturalism must postulate a complex multitude of entities:

> A complex physical universe (existing over time or beginning to exist at some finite time) is indeed a rather complex thing. ... consider the vast diversity of galaxies, stars, plants, and pebbles on the seashore. ... There is a complexity, particularity, and finitude about the universe which cries out for explanation. (2004: 150)

Swinburne argues that because theism is so much simpler than naturalism, it is far more probable that the universe exists given that God exists than that the universe exists as a brute fact. If Swinburne's argument succeeds, he shows that the existence of a complex physical universe supports theism over naturalism.

However, our three Humean tactics can be applied to Swinburne's argument. First, let's concede the argument so far. That is, for the sake of argument, let's suppose that the existence of a complex physical universe is more probable given that God exists than that such a universe is a brute fact. The problem is that, as Swinburne recognizes, there are *two* ways the universe could exist even if there is no God. First, the universe could be a brute fact, as we have noted. Second, the universe could have been caused by something other than God. For Swinburne's cosmological argument to work, the probability that a complex physical universe exists given that God exists must be higher than the sum of *two* other probabilities: the probability that the universe exists as a brute fact *plus* the probability that it is caused by something other than God (recall that you figure the probability of one thing *or* a mutually exclusive alternative by simply summing their individual probabilities).

Further, there are indefinitely many possible hypotheses about beings or entities other than God that might have created the universe. Now it may be that *each* of these alternative hypotheses postulates a less plausible creator than God. But Swinburne has given no very good reason for thinking that the probability that God created the universe is higher than the *sum* of the individual probabilities of all those indefinitely many alternative hypotheses *plus* the probability that the universe is just a brute, uncaused fact. It is just not clear that appeal to the allegedly greater simplicity of theism will do the job here.

Moving on, Swinburne's argument turns on the claim that theism is simpler than naturalism: 'The intrinsic probability of theism is, relative to other hypotheses about what there is, very high because of the great simplicity of theism' (2004: 109). The second Humean point to make against Swinburne is to question the assumption. The present universe *is* enormously complex, but cosmologists tell us that the present universe has developed from an initially very simple state. Nevertheless, Swinburne asserts that God's unlimited attributes, such as omniscience and omnipotence, possess a simplicity that no finite, limited properties can match. Let us suppose that every naturalistic cosmology must postulate, as an irreducible brute fact, some finite property of the initial state of the universe. Swinburne will then say that theism is necessarily simpler than any such naturalistic cosmology because finite quantities have a definiteness and a particularity that infinite quantities lack: 'A finite limitation cries out for explanation of why there is just that particular limit in a way that limitlessness does not' (2004: 97).

However, omnipotence, defined as the maximum logically possible degree of power, seems to be just as definite, distinct, determinate, and particular a degree of power as any other amount of power. There is no clear reason to expect, a priori, that omnipotence will more likely exist as a brute, uncaused fact than power of any other degree. Further, God's omnipotence is, prima facie, a rather complex property. Divine omnipotence entails not simply the ability to deploy unlimited amounts of energy, but the logically independent abilities to create, arrange, sustain, or annihilate matter and energy, or, indeed, to actualize all sorts of possible worlds that contain nothing like the matter and energy that constitute our universe.

In fact, the hypothesis of theism seems to add considerable complexity to our overall view of reality. God is traditionally conceived as omnipotent, omniscient, omnipresent, immutable, infinite, transcendent, eternal (or everlasting), and incorporeal (indeed, the Christian God, if you accept the identity of the Son and the Father and the doctrine of the Incarnation, had to be at one time both corporeal *and* incorporeal). In other words, theism postulates a being with powers and properties utterly without parallel to anything in the physical universe. Even if we assume that all of these postulated divine properties are intelligible – a very big assumption – theism clearly is a hypothesis that carries a large amount of weighty metaphysical baggage. A worldview that carries such baggage appears *ipso facto* less simple than naturalism, which simply discards the baggage.

Finally, why suppose that a simpler entity is more likely to exist as an ultimate, uncaused brute fact than a more complex one? Unless we could discover a metaphysical principle that entailed that simpler worlds are more likely to exist uncaused than more complex ones, it is hard to see what justification such a supposition could be given. Swinburne argues that the fact that we always choose the simpler of two empirically equivalent hypotheses as more likely to be true shows that we are betting that reality will turn out simpler than more complex: 'In holding simpler theories to be more probable than complex theories, the inquirer is holding it to be more probable that the world as a whole is simple than that it is complex' (Swinburne 1997: 42). Therefore, either our practice of preferring the simpler of two empirically equivalent theories is just irrational, or it must be true a priori that reality is ultimately more likely to be simple than complex.

But is there a more reasonable, alternative, explanation of why we rationally prefer the simpler of two empirically equivalent hypotheses, and even consider it more likely to be true, than that we are making a sort of metaphysical bet about how ultimate reality will turn out? Our third Humean tactic against Swinburne is to offer an alternative. We have to remember that every hypothesis is *our* postulation, and that nature is under no obligation to honor any of our posits. We don't make our hypotheses any more complex than we have to, not because we bet that reality is ultimately simple, but, on the contrary, because we recognize that we have no a priori assurance of what nature is like. Nature might be simple at bottom, or it might be complex. We have no way of knowing ahead of time. Further, if nature is complex, it is surely unlikely to be complex in just the ways that *we* might antecedently stipulate. By adding gratuitous postulations to our hypotheses, we merely increase the number of ways we are likely to be wrong (we give more 'hostages to fortune,' as it is frequently expressed). The only way to proceed is to start with simple hypotheses – recognizing that they might well be too simple – and to complicate our hypotheses when, and only when, *nature* requires it. Further, if the history of science is any guide, nature has often required us to complicate our initially simple hypotheses.

The upshot is that Swinburne's cosmological argument fails to provide any reason to regard the existence of a complex physical universe as evidence for the existence of God. There is no reason to think that the existence of a complex physical universe is less probable given that there is no God than given that there is. Theism is not obviously a simpler hypothesis than naturalism, and, even if it is, the criterion of simplicity gives us no grounds to expect that ultimate brute facts will be simple rather than complex.

Craig's fine-tuning argument

William Lane Craig's argument picks up where the analogy argument, criticized so effectively by Hume, leaves off. The basis of Craig's argument is that the very possibility of the development of certain types of complex systems, such as carbon-based intelligent life-forms (e.g., *Homo sapiens*), is highly dependent upon initial conditions that had to be present in the Big Bang itself:

During the last 30 years scientists have discovered that the existence of intelligent life depends on a delicate and complex balance of initial conditions simply given in the Big Bang itself. We now know that life-*prohibiting* universes are vastly more probable than any life-*permitting* universe like ours. How much more probable? Well, the answer is that the chances that the universe should be life-permitting are so infinitesimal as to be incomprehensible and incalculable. (Craig and Flew 2003: 20; emphasis in original)

Craig claims that if the initial conditions of the universe or the fundamental constants of nature had differed by an infinitesimal degree, conditions necessary for the development of intelligent life would never have been realized (2003: 20–1). Further:

it's not just each quantity which must be finely tuned. Their ratios to one another must also be exquisitely fine-tuned. So, improbability is multiplied by improbability by improbability, until our minds are reeling with incomprehensible numbers. (2003: 21)

So, it is inconceivable that this fine-tuning could be due to chance, and there is, Craig asserts, no physical reason, no law of nature, that specifies these particular values of the physical quantities. Craig therefore offers the following argument:

1 The fine-tuning of the initial conditions of the universe is due either to law, chance or design.
2 It is not due to either law or chance.
3 Therefore, it is due to design. (ibid.)

It makes no difference if there are natural self-organizing processes like natural selection if the very possibility of the existence of self-organizing complex systems is thus wholly dependent upon conditions that *themselves* must have been finely tuned by a designer. Nevertheless, we can apply the three Humean sorts of critique to this argument also.

First, let's follow Hume's lead and concede the argument to see what follows. Suppose that the universe did have a designer. What kind of designer? Maybe the designer is now dead, or has moved on to the creation of other universes and forgotten all about us. Maybe the designer was a completely evil being who wished to create complex intelligent life to torment. We certainly have no grounds for ascribing to the designer the attributes of the theistic God (omniscience, etc.). It is far from clear that such a designer even designed with anything like humans in mind. Maybe, in the spirit of Douglas Adams's *Hitchhiker's Guide to the Galaxy*, what the designer really wanted were turtles, but the conditions necessary to get turtles got humans as a by-product. On the other hand, if the designer *did* want humans, trying to get them by setting up the necessary initial conditions and hoping that they would eventually evolve would be about as clear an instance of *unintelligent* design as you could imagine. Now these speculations may sound flippant, but the point is entirely serious. Given only that the initial conditions of the universe were finely tuned, we are left almost totally in the dark about the nature or intentions of the designer. As an argument for the *theistic* God, the fine-tuning argument is very weak. Of course, Craig thinks that other theistic arguments can make up for the deficiencies of the fine-tuning argument, but the appeal to fine-tuning leaves us so far from the theistic God that those arguments have a lot of proving to do – and each of those other arguments has been subjected to powerful criticisms (see Oppy 2006).

Turning now to the second sort of Humean critique, we question Craig's use of the concepts of chance and probability. In his statement of the fine-tuning argument, Craig blithely invokes the concepts of probability and chance in claiming that life-prohibiting universes are vastly more probable than life-permitting ones and indeed that the chances of getting the latter are 'infinitesimal' (Craig and Flew 2003: 20). But what do concepts such as 'chance' and 'probability' even *mean* here, and how do we apply them in the context of the fine-tuning argument? It seems to me that defenders of fine-tuning arguments intend to assert that the universe is improbable either in an epistemic sense or in an objective, metaphysical sense. That is, they are saying either (a) the proposition that the universal constants are life-friendly is highly unlikely to be true given everything that we know, or (b) that it is a metaphysical truth that it is a priori extremely unlikely that a possible universe with life-friendly constant values would be the actual universe. Let's take the epistemic claim first.

In our ordinary assessments of epistemic probability we draw upon empirical background information (i.e., information that we take as given). We make the following sorts of judgments: The chance of getting heads is 50 percent *given* that we are tossing a fair coin and that the usual laws of nature are in effect. The probability of drawing an ace is $1/13$ *given* that it is drawn from a well-shuffled deck of fifty-two playing cards. The probability that Sue will develop influenza within the next 48 hours is 20 percent to 40 percent *given* that she is unvaccinated and has just inhaled live virus particles. Now compare: the probability that the charge on the proton would be 1.602×10^{-19} coulomb is (allegedly) infinitesimal *given* ... what? Against what background could we possibly make such a judgment? As Robin Le Poidevin points out, if the laws of physics are our background, they will either be irrelevant or imply that the charge on the proton is exactly what it is (Le Poidevin 1996: 49–50). If the laws of physics are not our background, what is? The point is this: we can sensibly say that some proposition is likely or unlikely to be true if we have some relevant background information, like the laws of physics, as a basis for our estimates. But what is the background when we are asked to judge that the laws of physics *themselves* are likely or unlikely? There just doesn't seem to be anything more basic to appeal to than the laws of physics.

Well, perhaps metaphysics is more basic than physics, and we can ascertain some a priori metaphysical sense in which the laws of nature are improbable. This is what Craig seems to be getting at when he offers an illustration that supposedly explains the sense in which life-permitting universes are improbable:

> Take a sheet of paper and place on it a red dot. That dot represents our universe. Now slightly alter one or more of the finely-tuned constants and

physical quantities ... As a result we have a description of another universe, which we may represent as a new dot in the proximity of the first. If that new set of constants and quantities describes a life-permitting universe, make it a red dot; if it describes a universe which is life-prohibiting, make it a blue dot. Now repeat that procedure arbitrarily many times until the sheet is filled with dots. What one winds up with is a sea of blue with only a few pinpoints of red. (Craig and Flew 2003: 164–5)

Unfortunately, this illustration merely highlights the problem. What do the dots represent? Craig says that they stand for possible universes. *Possible universes*. Does it even make sense to say that a possible universe *has* some objective, purely a priori probability of being actualized? Assuming, for the sake of argument, that it does, how do we decide, even approximately, what that value is? What weights of probability would we assign to the subintervals that partition our sample space of possible universes? A priori, wouldn't an infinite number of ways of making such assignments be equally valid? I don't know the answers to these questions, and, for all that Craig has told us, he doesn't either. Craig has often asserted, as a deep metaphysical truth, that universes cannot pop into existence *ex nihilo*. Shouldn't we say the same about probabilities? And again, the most basic problem here is deciding what sense it could make to say that one proposed set of ultimate brute facts has a greater chance of being actualized than some other. Immanuel Kant, in the *The Critique of Pure Reason*, argued that concepts, like probability, that we meaningfully apply in empirical contexts become hopelessly muddled when we try to apply them to metaphysical conundrums, such as asking which possible universes are likely to be actualized. I think writers like Swinburne and Craig show how right he was.

Finally, suppose that the initial conditions of our universe really are incomprehensibly improbable, and cry out for explanation. Wouldn't the designer hypothesis be only one possibility for getting an explanation, and maybe not the most reasonable one? Might there be an alternative explanation? After all, cosmology is a work in progress, and physicists are still searching for the Theory of Everything (TOE). Might it not be more reasonable to wait and observe the progress of science before leaping to a design hypothesis? When I made this suggestion in an earlier exchange, Craig responded as follows:

Parsons holds out hope for a Theory of Everything (TOE) that would show a life-permitting universe like ours to be physically necessary. ... If this alternative is to be more than an 'atheism of the gaps,' appealing to ignorance in hopes of that some unknown naturalistic possibility might be found to explain the data, then there must be evidence for this alternative. ... (Craig and Flew 2003: 164)

Actually, this is not so much an argument as an attempt to seize the rhetorical high ground. The 'atheism of the gaps' comment is clearly an attempt to pre-empt and deflect on to critics the obvious charge that defenders of fine-tuning arguments are merely pursuing the latest effort in the long, discreditable history of 'God of the gaps' strategies. 'Gap' apologists have many times sought to insert God's creative activity into the gaps in scientific explanations. Naturally, as science progresses and the gaps close, gap-apologists must beat a hasty and undignified retreat. Why not regard fine-tuning arguments as merely the latest effort to locate a gap for God? Craig responds that the best current candidates for a TOE would not solve the fine-tuning problem, but would only relocate it to another level (2003: 164). For instance, super-string theory or M-theory, the current best candidate for a TOE, must simply postulate that space-time has a particular number of dimensions. But why wouldn't a designer hypothesis similarly relocate the fine-tuning enigma to the purported designer? Why a life-friendly designer rather than one of indefinitely many other metaphysical possibilities (i.e., possible transcendent life-indifferent entities)? Unless this question has a satisfactory answer, there is no reason why a life-friendly supernatural designer would be a more likely ultimate brute fact than a set of life-friendly universal constants.

In conclusion, Craig's argument is no more successful than Swinburne's. Perhaps these arguments legitimately serve to reinforce the beliefs of those already committed to theism. However, as a tool of apologetics, a weapon to bludgeon unbelievers into submission, these arguments are far too frail to do the job.

See also David Hume (Chapter 13), Immanuel Kant (Chapter 14), Non-theistic conceptions of God (Chapter 22), Hiddenness (Chapter 29), Creation and divine action (Chapter 30), The cosmological argument (Chapter 32), The teleological argument (Chapter 33), Problems with the concept of God (Chapter 38), Why is there a universe at all, rather than nothing? (Chapter 41). Religion and science (Chapter 64).

References

Craig, W. L. and A. G. N. Flew (2003) *Does God Exist? The Craig/Flew Debate*, ed. S. W. Wallace, Burlington, VT: Ashgate.

Le Poidevin, R. (1996) *Arguing for Atheism: An Introduction to the Philosophy of Religion*, New York: Routledge.

Moore, K. D. (1986) *A Field Guide to Inductive Arguments*, Dubuque, IA: Kendall/Hunt.

Oppy, G. (2006) *Arguing About Gods*, Cambridge: Cambridge University Press.

Shanks, N. (2004) *God, the Devil, and Darwin: A Critique of Intelligent Design Theory*, Oxford: Oxford University Press.

Swinburne, R. (2004) *The Existence of God*, 2nd edn, Oxford: Oxford University Press.

—— (1997) *Simplicity as Evidence of Truth*, Milwaukee, WI: Marquette University Press.

Further reading

Everitt, N. (2004) *The Non-Existence of God*, New York: Routledge. (A succinct but comprehensive defense of atheism.)

Martin, M. (1990) *Atheism: A Philosophical Justification*, Philadelphia: Temple University Press. (A comprehensive, detailed defense of atheism which includes responses to theistic arguments by a leading atheistic philosopher.)

Parsons, K. M. (1989) *God and the Burden of Proof: Plantinga, Swinburne, and the Analytic Defense of Theism*, Buffalo, NY: Prometheus. (A readable analysis and critique of recent analytic defenses of theism with a focus on who bears the burden of proof.)

41

WHY IS THERE A UNIVERSE AT ALL, RATHER THAN JUST NOTHING?

Adolf Grünbaum

Introduction

In a well-known essay of 1714, the philosopher G. F. W. Leibniz raised, in effect, the following question: 'Why is there a universe *at all*, rather than just nothing?' He actually put this question somewhat differently by asking: 'Why is there *something* rather than nothing?' But since the 'something' that actually exists is indeed the universe, I have preferred to recast Leibniz's question taking that into account. I shall refer to this Leibnizian question as 'The Primordial Existential Question,' and I shall use the acronym 'PEQ' to denote it for brevity.

Let us note at the outset that PEQ rests on important presuppositions. If one or more of these presuppositions is either ill-founded or demonstrably false, then PEQ is aborted as a non-starter, because it would be posing a non-issue (pseudo-problem). And, in that case, the very existence of something, rather than nothing, does *not* require explanation. PEQ will indeed turn out to be a non-starter, because one of its crucial presuppositions is demonstrably ill-founded. As we shall see in due course, that presupposition is a corollary of a distinctly Christian doctrine, which originated in the second century CE.

What are the most important presuppositions of PEQ? Clearly, one of them is that the notion of a state of affairs in which absolutely nothing exists is both *intelligible* (meaningful) and *free from contradiction*. Let us call such a supposed state of affairs 'the Null Possibility,' as the British philosopher Derek Parfit does (Parfit 1998: 420). And let us refer to a supposed world in which there is nothing as 'the Null World.'

Parfit gives the following version of PEQ:

why is there a Universe at all? It might have been true that nothing ever existed: no living beings, no stars, no atoms, not even space or time. When we think about this ['Null'] possibility, it can seem astonishing that anything exists. (1998: 420)

Evidently, in this statement Parfit inferred the 'Null Possibility' without ado, declaring: 'It might have been true that nothing ever existed.' But he gave no cogent justification for avowing this logical possibility to be genuine. He just assumed peremptorily that the nihilistic proposition 'There is nothing,' or 'The Null World obtains,' is both intelligible and free from contradiction. Instead of providing a conceptual *explication* of the Null Possibility, Parfit has evidently offered a mere open-ended enumeration of the absence of familiar furniture from the Null World: 'no living beings, no stars, no atoms, not even space or time.' Thereupon, he enthrones PEQ on a pedestal: 'No question is more sublime than why there is a Universe [i.e., some world or other]: why there is anything rather than nothing' (ibid.). Besides presupposing that the Null Possibility is logically robust, Parfit's motivation for PEQ tacitly *pivots* on the supposition that, *de jure*, there should be nothing contingent.

Is it imperative to explain why there *isn't* just nothing contingent?

Parfit has told us that 'When we think about this ['null'] possibility, it can seem astonishing that anything exists.' And assuming such an astonished response, he feels entitled to ask why the Null Possibility does not obtain, i.e., why there is something after all, rather than just nothing. But I must ask: Why should the mere contemplation of the Null Possibility reasonably make it 'seem astonishing that anything exists'?

If some of us were to consider the logical possibility that a person might conceivably metamorphose spontaneously into an elephant, for example, I doubt strongly that we would feel even the slightest temptation to ask why that mere logical possibility is not realized. Why then, I put it to Parfit, should anyone reasonably feel astonished at all that the Null Possibility, if genuine, has remained a mere logical possibility and that something does exist instead? *In short, why should there be just nothing, merely because it is logically possible?* This mere logical possibility of the Null World, I claim, does not suffice to legitimate Parfit's demand for an explanation of why the Null World does not obtain, an explanation he seeks as a philosophical anodyne for his misguided astonishment that anything at all exists. As a matter of terminology, note that I shall refer to the existence of an object as 'logically contingent' if its *non*existence is *logically* possible (i.e., if it *might* not exist).

Must we explain why any and every *de facto unrealized* logical possibility is not actualized?

To justify a negative answer to this question, let us inquire quite generally: for any and every de facto unrealized logical possibility, is it well conceived to demand an explanation of the fact that it is *not* actualized? As we know, Leibniz's Principle of Sufficient Reason (PSR) has been used to answer affirmatively that every fact has an explanation. Yet, as we shall see, Leibniz himself did not regard that principle as itself an adequate justification for his PEQ, because he also relies on the presupposition of PEQ that the existence of something contingent is not to be expected at all, and therefore calls for explanation. But even his PSR is demonstrably unsound.

To appraise his Principle of Sufficient Reason, consider within our universe the grounds for the demise in recent quantum theory of the universal causation familiar from Newton's physics, as codified in the Pierre-Simon Laplace's so-called 'determinism.' This empirically well-founded quantum theory features merely probabilistic rather than universal causal laws governing such phenomena as the spontaneous radioactive disintegration of atomic nuclei, yielding emissions of alpha or beta particles, and/or gamma rays. In this domain of phenomena, there are not only logically but also physically possible particular events that *could* but do not actually occur under specified initial conditions. Yet it is impermissibly legislative to insist that merely because these events are thus *possible*, there *must* be an explanation entailing their specific non-occurrence, and similarly, of course, for probabilistically governed actually occurring events. This lesson was not heeded by Richard Swinburne, who avowed entitlement to *pan*-explainability, declaring: 'We expect all things to have explanations' (Swinburne 1991: 287). In our exegesis of Leibniz below, we shall deal further with his PSR.

The case of quantum theory shows that an empirically well-grounded theory can warrantedly discredit the tenacious demand for the satisfaction of a previously held ideal of explanation, such as Leibniz's PSR. To discover that the universe does not accommodate rigid prescriptions for explanatory understanding is not tantamount to scientific failure; instead, it is to discover positive reasons for identifying certain coveted explanations as phantom.

To prepare the ground for our challenge to the legitimacy of PEQ, we need to ask how we are to understand more deeply the *tenacity* with which PEQ has been asked, not only by some philosophers but even in our culture at large. An illuminating set of answers is afforded, it seems, by delving critically into two sorts of impetus for the question PEQ as follows:

1 historically based assumptions going back to the second century of the Christian era, which served to inspire PEQ;
2 explicitly a priori justifications of PEQ put forward by Leibniz, Swinburne and others.

Christian doctrine as an inspiration of PEQ

One possible interpretation of Genesis is that God's creation of heaven and earth out of nothing (Gen. 1:1) is the first stage of creation, and in the second stage he shapes what is desolate and uninhabitable into an ordered, habitable environment for humankind. This was, indeed, Moses Maimonides' reading of the opening passage of the book of Genesis. Yet there is some biblical exegesis contending that this doctrine of creation *ex nihilo* was not avowed in the book of Genesis at all. Though the doctrine may have had a prehistory, it was first widely held by Christian theologians, beginning in the second century CE as a distinctly Christian precept (May 1994). Thus, in an exegetical essay, 'Genesis's account of creation,' the Jewish scholar Norbert Samuelson wrote more recently: 'this [Hebraic] cosmology presupposes that initially God is not alone. Prior to God's act of creation . . . [t]he earth, [and] water are the stuff from which God creates' (Samuelson 2000: 128).

But Christian writers regarded their specific conception of divine creation *ex nihilo* as a philosophical advance over the account in the book of Genesis, if only because they held that an omnipotent God had no need for pre-existing materials to create the universe. Thus, as one such Christian writer noted rather patronizingly, 'The abstract notion of "nothing" does not seem to have been reached by the Israelite mind at that time' (Loveley 1967: 419). And, evidently, the notion of nothingness was essential to generate PEQ.

According to traditional Christian existential doctrine, the very existence of any and every contingent entity other than God himself is utterly dependent on God at any and all times. Let us denote this fundamental Christian axiom of total existential dependence on God by the acronym DA for 'Dependency Axiom.' Clearly, DA entails the following cardinal maxim: 'without God's [constant creative] support [or perpetual creation],' the world 'would instantly collapse into nothingness' (Hasker 1998: 695; cf. Edwards 1967: 176). As we shall see, this assumption most unfortunately and perennially played a very influential role in western philosophy, as illustrated by the writings of Thomas Aquinas and René Descartes.

Evidently, the Christian DA, in turn, entails that *in the absence of an external cause, the spontaneous, natural, or normal state of affairs is one in which nothing contingent exists at all*. In earlier writings, I have denoted the assertion of this *existential spontaneity of nothingness* by the acronym 'SoN,' which is short for 'the spontaneity of nothingness' (Grünbaum 2000: 5). As before, we shall usually refer to the putative state of affairs in which no contingent objects exist at all as 'the Null World,' a locution that is preferable to the term 'nothingness.' In that parlance, SoN asserts the *existential spontaneity* of the Null World.

As we can see, the fundamental Christian existential axiom DA of total existential dependence on God entails SoN. In other words, logically the truth of SoN is a *necessary condition* for the truth of the fundamental existential tenet of Christian theism. In this clear sense, SoN is a *presupposition* of DA, which will turn out to be a heavy doctrinal burden indeed. SoN is 'a heavy doctrinal burden,' because, as we shall see, it is completely baseless.

According to SoN, the actual existence of something contingent – qua deviation from the supposedly spontaneous and natural state of nothingness – automatically requires a creative external cause out of nothing, an existential cause. And such a supposed *creative* cause must be distinguished, as Aquinas emphasized, from a merely *transformative* cause: transformative causes produce changes of state in contingent things that already exist in some form, *or* the transformative causes generate new entities from previously existing objects, such as in the building of a house from raw materials.

444

Furthermore, in accord with the traditional Christian commitment to SoN, divine creation out of nothing is required at every instant at which the world exists in some state or other, whether it began to exist at some moment having no temporal predecessor in the finite past, or has existed forever. More precisely, having presupposed SoN, traditional Christian theism makes the following major claim: in the case of any contingent entity E other than God himself, if E exists, or begins to exist without having a transformative cause, then its existence must have a creative cause out of nothing, *rather than being externally uncaused.*

Yet, as some scholars have pointed out, 'To the ancient Indian and Greek thinker, the notion of *creatio* [out of nothing] is unthinkable' (Bertocci 1973: 571). Thus, in Plato's *Timaeus*, there is no creation out of nothing by the Demiurge, who is held to transform chaos into cosmos, although that notion is very vague. Indeed, as John Leslie has informatively pointed out: 'To the general run of Greek thinkers the mere existence of things [or of the world] was nothing remarkable. Only their *changing* patterns provoked [causal] inquisitiveness' (Leslie 1978: 185, italics added). And he mentions Aristotle's views as countenancing the acceptance of 'reasonless existence' (ibid.).

It is a sobering fact that, before Christianity molded the philosophical intuitions of our culture, those of the Greeks and of many other world cultures were basically different existentially (Eliade 1992). No wonder that Aristotle regarded the material universe as uncreated and eternal. In striking contrast, SoN is deeply ingrained in the traditional Christian heritage, even among a good many of those who reject Christianity in other respects. In effect, we all grew up with SoN at our mother's knee, as it were. And we then internalized it as quasi-common sense. Thus, the Christian climate lends poignancy to Leslie's conjecture that 'When modern Westerners have a tendency to ask *why there is anything at all*, rather than nothing, possibly this is *only* because they are heirs to centuries of Judeao-Christian thought' (1978: 185, italics added). So much for the Christian historical contribution to PEQ via its SoN doctrine.

Henri Bergson

Early in the twentieth century, Henri Bergson was alert to the often beguiling, if not insidious, role of SoN in metaphysics, and he aptly articulated that assumption as inherent in PEQ. In 1935, speaking of occidental philosophy, Bergson lucidly wrote disapprovingly about PEQ as follows:

> part of metaphysics moves, consciously or not, around the question of knowing why anything exists – why matter, or spirit, or God, rather than nothing at all? But the question presupposes that *reality fills a void*, that underneath Being lies nothingness, that *de jure* there should be nothing, that we must *therefore explain* why there is *de facto* something. (Bergson 1974: 239-40)

Bergson's concise formulation of SoN as a presupposition of (PEQ) is that '*de jure* there should be nothing.' But as a rendition of this cardinal presupposition of PEQ, his formulation that *de jure* there *should* be nothing is significantly incomplete: It needs to be amplified by the further claim that there indeed *would* be nothing in the absence of an overriding external cause or reason!

Thus, let us bear in mind hereafter that SoN makes the following very strong existential assertion: De jure, *there should be nothing contingent at all rather than something contingent, and indeed, there would be just nothing contingent in the absence of an overriding external cause (reason).*

Importantly, SoN can be challenged by the counter-question: 'But why *should* there be nothing contingent, rather than something contingent?' And, indeed, why *would* there be nothing contingent in the absence of an overriding external cause (reason)? In effect, Leibniz endeavored to disarm this challenge, as we are about to see, when he tried to legitimate SoN – albeit unsuccessfully – as part of a twofold a priori justification of PEQ (Leibniz 1973: 199).

Since PEQ is predicated on SoN, PEQ will be undermined in due course by the failure of a priori defenses of SoN, and, furthermore, by the unavailability of any empirical support for it.

Therefore, I now turn to some attempts at a priori justifications of PEQ.

A priori justifications of PEQ by Leibniz, Swinburne and others

A number of writers have appealed to the supposed a priori simplicity of the Null World to argue that *de jure* there should be nothing and that therefore the actual existence of our world makes an answer to PEQ imperative.

In stark contrast to Bergson, both Leibniz (1973: 199) and the Oxford theist Richard Swinburne (1991: 283-4) maintained that SoN is a priori true. And their reason was that the Null World is simpler, both existentially and conceptually, than a world containing something contingent or other. This very ambitious assertion poses two immediate questions: (a) Is the Null World really a priori simpler, and indeed the simplest world existentially as well as conceptually? And (b) even assuming that the Null World is thus doubly simpler, does its supposed maximum dual simplicity *mandate existentially* that there should be just nothing *de jure*, and, furthermore, does it mandate that there *would* be just nothing in the absence of an overriding cause (reason), as claimed by SoN?

Let us assume, just for the sake of argument, that Leibniz and Swinburne could warrant a priori the maximum conceptual and existential simplicity of the Null World, as avowed by Leibniz, when he declared: '"nothingness" is simpler and easier than "something"' (1973: 199). It is of decisive importance, I contend, that *even if the supposed maximum existential simplicity of the Null World were warranted a priori, that presumed simplicity would not mandate the claim of SoN that de jure the thus simplest Null World must be spontaneously realized existentially in the absence of an overriding cause.* Yet, to my knowledge, neither Leibniz nor Swinburne, nor any other author, has offered any cogent reason at all to posit such an existential imperative.

To clarify Leibniz's reasoning, let us comment on the context in which Leibniz formulates his PEQ, and then seeks to justify it at once, by relying carefully on both of the following two premises: (a) his PSR, and (b) an a priori argument from simplicity for the presupposition SoN inherent in PEQ. Leibniz does so in two crucial paragraphs (7 and 8) of his 1714 essay, in which he declares in part:

> the great principle of sufficient reason [PSR] holds that *nothing takes place without sufficient reason* . . . [that is] a reason sufficient to determine why it is thus and not otherwise. This principle having been laid down, the first question we are entitled to ask will be: *Why is there something rather than nothing?* For 'nothing' [the Null World] is simpler and easier than 'something.' Further supposing that things must exist, it must be possible to give a reason *why they must exist just as they do* and not otherwise. (1973: 199)

These avowals by Leibniz invite the following array of comments:

(1) Right after enunciating his PSR, Leibniz poses PEQ 'Why is there something rather than nothing?' as 'the first question we are entitled to ask.' However, immediately after raising this question, he relies on simplicity *to justify* its presupposition SoN that *de jure*, there should be nothing contingent at all, rather than something contingent: 'For "nothing" [the Null World] is simpler and easier than "something."' Thus, Leibniz is telling us here, in effect, that the Null World is the a priori simplest of all, besides being 'the easiest.' But, alas, he does not tell us here in just what sense the Null World is 'the easiest.'

(2) It is vital to appreciate that Leibniz explicitly went beyond his PSR to justify his PEQ on the heels of enunciating PSR and posing PEQ: Fully aware that PEQ presupposes SoN, he clearly did not regard PEQ to be justified by PSR alone, since he explicitly offered a simplicity argument to justify the presupposed SoN immediately after posing PEQ. Most significantly, he is not content to rely on PSR to ask just the truncated question 'Why is there something contingent?' without the accompanying clause 'rather than nothing.' Instead, he uses SoN in his PEQ to convey his dual thesis that (a) the existence of something contingent *is not to be expected at all*, and (b) its actual existence therefore cries out for explanation.

Thus, the soundness of Leibniz's justification of his PEQ evidently turns on the cogency of his PSR as well as of his a priori argument for SoN. As for the correctness of his PSR, please recall our objections to it, which were prompted by Parfit's illegitimate reliance on PSR to demand an explanation of why there isn't just nothing, rather than something. More fundamentally, the modern history of quantum physics teaches that PSR, which Leibniz avowedly saw as metaphysical (1973: sec. 7), cannot be warranted a priori and indeed is untenable on empirical grounds. The principle asserts that every event – in Leibniz's parlance, anything that 'takes place' or 'happens' – has an explanatory 'reason [cause] sufficient to determine why it is thus and not otherwise.'

As we saw, Leibniz and Swinburne offered an unsuccessful simplicity argument, claiming that SoN is true a priori. Recall that, according to the SoN doctrine, *de jure*, there *should* be nothing contingent at all, rather than something contingent, and indeed, there *would* be just nothing contingent in the absence of an overriding external cause (or reason).

Since the a priori defense of SoN has failed, we need to inquire whether it might possibly be warranted empirically. But it will turn out as an induction from various episodes in the history of science that SoN is altogether ill-founded empirically. To examine the empirical status of SoN, it will be useful to reformulate it in Richard Swinburne's words as follows: 'Surely the most natural state of affairs is simply nothing: no universe, no God, nothing' (1996: 48).

Let us denote our own universe by 'U_0.' And now consider the corollary of SoN that pertains to our world U_0. This corollary asserts that it is natural or spontaneous for *our* universe U_0 not to exist, rather than to exist. As against any a priori dictum on what is the 'natural' status of our world, the verdict on that status will now be seen to depend crucially on *empirical* evidence. Two cosmological examples will now spell out this empirical moral:

First, the natural evolution of one of the Big Bang models of the universe countenanced by general relativistic cosmology is a clear cosmological case in point. This model, the so-called Friedmann universe, is named after the Russian mathematician Alexander Friedmann. In the context of Einstein's general theory of relativity, the Big Bang 'Friedmann universe' has the following features:

1 It is a spatially closed, so-called spherical universe (a '3-sphere'), which expands from a point-like Big Bang to a maximum finite size, and then contracts into a point-like crunch (Wald 1984: 100–1).
2 That universe exists altogether for only a finite span of time, such that no instants of time existed prior to its finite duration or exist afterward (Grünbaum 1998: 25–6).
3 As a matter of natural law, its total rest-mass is conserved for the entire time period of its existence (Wald, ibid), so that, during that entire time, there is no need for a supernatural agency to prevent it from lapsing into nothingness, as envisioned by Aquinas and Descartes (Grünbaum, ibid.).

Evidently, the 'natural' dynamical evolution of the Friedmann Big Bang universe *as a whole* is specified by the empirically supported general relativistic theory of cosmology. Thus, the 'natural,' spontaneous behavior of Big Bang worlds is not vouchsafed a priori.

Second, the same epistemic moral concerning the empirical status of cosmological naturalness is spelled out by the illuminating case of the now largely defunct Bondi and Gold so-called steady-state cosmology of 1948.

Their 1948 steady-state theory features a spatially and temporally infinite universe in which the following steady-state cosmological principle holds: as a matter of natural law, there is large-scale conservation of matter-density (Bondi 1960). Note that this conservation is not of matter, but of the density of matter over time. The conjunction of this constancy of the density with the mutual recession of the galaxies from one another then entails a rather shocking consequence. Throughout space-time, and without any matter-generating agency, new matter (in the form of hydrogen) pops into existence completely naturally in violation of *matter-energy* conservation (Bondi 1960:

73–4, 140, 152). Hence the steady-state world features the accretion or formation of new matter as its natural, normal, spontaneous behavior. And although this accretive formation is indeed out of nothing, it is clearly not 'creation' by an external agency. Apparently, if the steady-state world were actual, it would discredit the doctrine of the medieval Latin epigram, *Ex nihilo, nihil fit* ('From nothing, nothing comes'), which freely translated says that 'you cannot get blood out of a stone.'

The spontaneous matter-accretion in the steady-state world occurs at the rate required by the constancy of the matter-density amid the rate of the mutual galactic recession, and it populates the spaces vacated by the mutual galactic recession. Thus, in the hypothesized Bondi and Gold world, the spontaneous accretion of matter would be explained deductively as entirely natural by the conjunction of two of its fundamental physical postulates. But the rate of this spontaneous cosmic debut of new matter is small enough to leave the traditional, received matter-energy conservation law essentially intact locally (terrestrially).

The steady-state theory owes its demise to the failure of its predictions and retro-dictions to pass observational muster in its competition with the Big Bang cosmology. This episode again teaches us that empirically based scientific theories are our sole epistemic avenue to the "natural' behavior of the universe at large, though only fallibly so, of course, since such theories are liable to be replaced by others in the light of further empirical findings.

Thus it is fitting that we should ask: What is the empirical verdict on the corollary of SoN, which asserts that 'it is natural for our universe *not* to exist, rather than to exist'? Its proponents have offered no empirical evidence for it from cosmology, let alone for SoN itself, believing mistakenly, as we saw, that it can be vouchsafed a priori *à la* Leibniz.

PEQ as a *failed* springboard for creationist theism: the collapse of Leibniz's and Swinburne's theistic cosmological arguments

Probably everyone of us has wondered at some time in our lives: 'Where did every-thing come from?' This question is not a demand for a statement of the earlier physical history of our existing universe. Instead, this question is based on the deeply ingrained, largely unconscious assumption of SoN, a question that is simply another version of Leibniz's PEQ. But I have been at pains to argue that SoN has neither a priori nor empirical credentials. And SoN is a crucial presupposition of PEQ. Thus, by resting on an ill-founded premise, the cosmic existential PEQ is an ill-conceived non-starter, which poses a pseudo-issue. By the same token, the inveterate college bull-session question 'Where did everything come from?' is fundamentally misguided, and should therefore be forsaken. Indeed, this unfortunately time-honored question is as much a pseudo-question as the question 'When did you stop beating your wife?' if addressed to a man who never beat his wife at all.

As we saw, both Leibniz and Swinburne took PEQ seriously, having endorsed its presupposition SoN. And then they argued that the answer to PEQ calls for divine creation, thereby offering a so-called 'first cause' or cosmological argument for the existence of God. The core of Leibniz's and Swinburne's cosmological arguments can be encapsulated as follows:

1 The Null world, which is devoid of all contingent existents, is the simplest (existentially).
2 The claim made by SoN is true: namely, *de jure*, the Null World should obtain qua being the simplest, and indeed it *would* obtain as the most 'natural' or normal state of affairs in the absence of an external cause (or 'reason').
3 But the *de facto* existence of our universe of contingent objects is a massive deviation from the Null World mandated by SoN.
4 This colossal existential deviation from the supposed existential 'normalcy' of nothingness cries out for explanation by a suitably potent cosmic cause, which makes an answer to PEQ imperative. The required cause is a creator out of nothing. Hence the God of theism exists.

But, as we saw very explicitly, the primordial existential PEQ is fundamentally misguided by resting on the baseless presupposition SoN, and thereby poses a pseudo-issue. Yet the purported imperative to answer precisely this misguided question is the basis for Leibniz's (1973: secs. 7 and 8) and Swinburne's (1991: ch. 7) cosmological arguments for the existence of God. Thus, *PEQ cannot serve as a springboard for creationist theism.* Hence Leibniz's and Swinburne's cosmological arguments are fundamentally unsuccessful.

Conclusion

We began with Leibniz's PEQ: Why is there something, such as our universe, rather than nothing? This question is reminiscent of a question that we all recall from our college bull sessions, namely, 'Where did everything come from?' However, as I argued in detail, these questions are not innocent but assume the Christian doctrine SoN, which claims that, in the absence of an external cause, there should be and would be just nothing.

Furthermore, I contended in detail that SoN is seriously ill-founded both conceptually and empirically, so that PEQ is aborted as posing a non-issue. Yet Leibniz and Swinburne relied on PEQ and SoN to argue for divine creation out of nothing. Hence Leibniz's and Swinburne's creationist argument fails completely.

See also Creation and divine action (Chapter 30), The cosmological argument (Chapter 32), The teleological argument (Chapter 33), Naturalistic rejoinders to theistic arguments (Chapter 40), Religion and science (Chapter 64).

Note

This is the featured lecture of the Dan and Carole Burack President's Distinguished Lecture Series, delivered at the University of Vermont on Thursday, April 20, 2006.

References

Bergson, H. (1974) *The Two Sources of Morality and Religion*, trans. R. A. Audra and C. Brereton with W. Carter, Westport, CT: Greenwood Press.

Bertocci, P. (1973) 'Creation in religion,' in P. Wiener (ed.) *Dictionary of the History of Ideas: Studies of Selected Pivotal Ideas*, vol. 1: *Abstraction in the Formation of Concepts to Design Argument*, New York: Scribner.

Bondi, H. (1960) *Cosmology*, 2nd edn, Cambridge Monographs on Physics Series, Cambridge: Cambridge University Press.

Edwards, P. (1967) 'Atheism,' *The Encyclopedia of Philosophy*, vol. 1, New York: Macmillan/Free Press.

Eliade, M. (1992) *Essential Sacred Writings from Around the World*, San Francisco, CA: HarperCollins.

Grünbaum, A. (1998) 'Theological misinterpretations of current physical cosmology,' *Philo* 1/1: 15-34.

—— (2000) 'A new critique of rheological interpretations of physical cosmology,' *The British Journal for the Philosophy of Science* 51: 1–43.

Hasker, W. (1998) 'Religious doctrine of creation and conservation,' in E. Craig (ed.) *Routledge Encyclopedia of Philosophy*, vol. 2, London: Routledge.

Leibniz, G. F. W. (1973) 'Principles of nature and of grace founded on reason,' in G. H. R. Parkinson (ed.) *Leibniz: Philosophical Writings*, trans. G. H. R. Parkinson and M. Morris, London: J. M. Dent.

Leslie, J. (1978) 'Efforts to explain all existence,' *Mind* 87: 181–94.

Loveley, E. (1967) 'Creation,' *The New Catholic Encyclopedia*, vol. 4, New York: McGraw Hill.

May, G. (1994) *Creatio ex Nihilo*, trans. A. S. Worrall, Edinburgh: T. & T. Clark.

Parfit, D. (1998) 'The puzzle of reality. Why does the universe exist?,' in P. van Inwagen and D. Zimmerman (eds) *Metaphysics: The Big Questions*, Malden, MA: Blackwell.

Samuelson, N. (2000) 'Judaic theories of cosmology', in J. Neusner, A. Avery-Peck, and W. Green (eds) *The Encyclopedia of Judaism*, vol. 1, Leiden and Boston: Brill.

Swinburne, R. (1991) *The Existence of God*, rev. edn, Oxford: Clarendon Press.

—— (1996) *Is There a God?*, Oxford and New York: Oxford University Press.

Wald, R. M. (1984) *General Relativity*, Chicago: University of Chicago Press.

Further reading

Edwards, P. (1967) 'Why?' *The Encyclopedia of Philosophy*, vol. 8, New York: Macmillan/Free Press. (A very lucid digest of the views of various philosophers on 'The Super-Ultimate "Why".' But Edwards argues that this question is meaningless, whereas I contend above that it rests on a baseless presupposition, and is therefore a pseudo-problem.)

Grünbaum, A. (1998) 'Theological misinterpretations of current physical cosmology,' *Philo* 11: 15–34. (This article undermines the attempt to enlist the Big Bang cosmogony to give a creationist theological answer to Leibniz's Primordial Existential Question.)

—— (2004) 'The poverty of theistic cosmology,' *British Journal for the Philosophy of Science* 51: 561–614. (An in-depth treatment of the issues in my 1998 essay above.)

Leibniz, G. F. W. (1973) 'Principles of nature and of grace founded on reason,' in G. H. R. Parkinson (ed.) *Leibniz: Philosophical Writings*, trans. G. H. R. Parkinson and M. Morris, London; J. M. Dent. (This is the *locus classicus* of the historic PEQ.)

42
THE SOCIOBIOLOGICAL ACCOUNT OF RELIGIOUS BELIEF

Michael Ruse

Sociobiology is the study of the evolution of behavior, including human behavior. Today, evolutionists are almost all Darwinians, meaning that natural selection is considered the key causal factor. The important thing about selection is that it does not merely lead to change but to change of a particular kind, namely in the direction of adaptation or contrivance. Selection produces things that function toward desired ends, such as the eye being used for seeing and the teeth being used for biting and chewing. Not all features of the living world are necessarily adaptive. Some occur by chance and some are byproducts of selection. So a major part of the evolutionist's task, a major part of the sociobiologist's task, is determining if something is adaptive and hence probably produced by selection, or if something is not adaptive and in which case what did cause it, if indeed there was an identifiable cause.

Religion is a major factor in human behavior and culture, and naturally it has attracted considerable sociobiological attention. The big problem is whether or not it is adaptive and if so in what way, and if not why then does it exist. Although the name 'sociobiology' dates from the 1970s – being popularized by Edward O. Wilson's magnificent book, *Sociobiology: The New Synthesis* (1975) – it is best to start with Charles Darwin himself to set the background.

Darwin on religion

Darwin turns to the question of religion in his *Descent of Man* (1871). Thinking that the most primitive form of religion occurs when savages believe in spirit forces, he asks about its origins. Apparently it is all a question of seeing spirits in inanimate objects, feeling or pretending or mistakenly believing that they are truly alive.

> The tendency in savages to imagine that natural objects and agencies are animated by spiritual or living essences, is perhaps illustrated by a little fact

which I once noticed: my dog, a full-grown and very sensible animal, was lying on the lawn during a hot and still day; but at a little distance a slight breeze occasionally moved an open parasol, which would have been wholly disregarded by the dog, had any one stood near it. As it was, every time that the parasol slightly moved, the dog growled fiercely and barked. He must, I think, have reasoned to himself in a rapid and unconscious manner, that movement without any apparent cause indicated the presence of some strange living agent, and that no stranger had a right to be on his territory. (1871, I: 67)

Darwin did not think that explanations of religious belief bore on the truth or falsity of religion. Whether true or false, the important point is that religion as considered by the scientist be considered a natural phenomenon. He stressed this point again and again.

I am aware that the assumed instinctive belief in God has been used by many persons as an argument for His existence. But this is a rash argument, as we should thus be compelled to believe in the existence of many cruel and malignant spirits, only a little more powerful than man; for the belief in them is far more general than in a beneficent Deity. The idea of a universal and beneficent Creator does not seem to arise in the mind of man, until he has been elevated by long-continued culture. (1871, II: 394–5)

Darwin's position, therefore, was that religion is a natural phenomenon – or rather a phenomenon that can be treated naturally – and he saw it as something that had evolved. It is noteworthy that Darwin said little about religion and its relationship to natural selection. Here there is a major break from Darwin's parallel discussion of morality, which did get linked firmly to selection. He claimed not to be addressing the truth status of religion. By this time in his life Darwin had become an agnostic; certainly he thought that Christianity is not proven in its essentials and was false in many details, and he did not think that religion could be directly promoted by selection. For Darwin, religion seems to be almost accidental, and brought about by animal features or powers that are simply misdirected. When we see something moving, it normally makes sense to think that it is living. We make mistakes and ultimately this leads into religion. The one concession that Darwin was prepared to make to the value of religion is that, in the case of civilized people, religion does help reinforce morality: 'With the more civilised races, the conviction of the existence of an all-seeing Deity has had a potent influence on the advance of morality' (Darwin 1871, II: 394). But even here, Darwin did not want to explore the matter in more detail.

Religion as adaptive

In the hundred years after Darwin's *On the Origin of Species* (1859), there was much interest in putative natural origins of religion. But most discussion came from the newly developing social sciences rather than from biology. The growth of sociobiology has changed all of that. As always in discussions of evolution, it is natural selection that drives the course of the investigation. Hence, let us be guided by biological categories, Darwinian categories, that is. Most importantly, we will expect a division between those who think that religion is something brought about directly by natural selection, and those (like Darwin) who think that religion is something of a by-product. Then, among those who suppose selection as the cause, there will be division between those who think that religion is of direct adaptive advantage to humans and those who think that it might not be such a good thing to have, and that it's perhaps a product of something like sexual selection or is perhaps adaptive for someone or thing other than humans (like parasites). There is also the possibility of division between individual and group selectionists, that is, between those who think that religion must be for the benefit of the individual and those who think that religion is of group worth, perhaps even to the detriment of the individual. Finally, there is the possibility of division between those who think that religion is essentially biological and those who think that culture is causally significant in the development of religion if not all-important.

Starting with those who think that religion is selection-produced and of value to humans, we find Edward O. Wilson himself. It is apparently all a matter of group identity and sticking together.

> The highest form of religious practice, when examined more closely, can be seen to confer biological advantage. Above all, they [*sic*] congeal identity. In the midst of the chaotic and potentially disorienting experiences each person undergoes daily, religion classifies him, provides him with unquestioned membership in a group claiming great powers, and by this means gives him a driving purpose in life compatible with his self interest. (Wilson 1978: 188)

Wilson does allow that there can be cultural selection between sects, but essentially we start with the biology and all else is on the surface.

> Because religious practices are remote from the genes during the development of individual human beings, they may vary widely during cultural development. It is even possible for groups, such as the Shakers, to adopt conventions that reduce genetic fitness for as long as one or a few generations. But over many generations, the underlying genes will pay for their permissiveness by declining in the population as a whole. Other genes governing mechanisms that resist decline of fitness produced by cultural evolution will prevail, and the deviant practices will disappear. Thus culture relentlessly tests the controlling genes, but the most it can do is replace one set of genes with another. (1978: 178)

Wilson has always been ambivalent about the comparative significances of individual- and group-selective processes. On the religion issue, he rather divides, thinking that it is something brought on by a group process, but surely with individual benefits also. More robustly individualistic are the physical anthropologist Vernon Reynolds and the scholar of religion Ralph Tanner (1983). They are quite accepting of hypotheses such as that circumcision of males, something central to religious practices of Jews and others, is something that prevents disease. This is a practice that benefits individuals. Somewhat ingeniously, Reynolds and Tanner suggest that religions tend to divide into those that promote high reproductive rates – many Semitic religions— and those that do not – North European Calvinism, for instance. This is something echoing interests and concerns of Darwin in the *Descent*. There, the great evolutionist worried that the worthless Catholic Irish seemed to have lots of children whereas the hardworking Presbyterian Scots had but few. This was a horrific reflection, seemingly negating the upward, progressive nature of the evolutionary process, a picture so dear to the heart of Darwin and his fellow Victorians. Darwin consoled himself with the reflection that the Irish do not look after their children, whereas the Scots do, and so on balance the Scots, if anything, do better than the Irish.

Reynolds and Tanner pick up on this insight, drawing on its modern equivalent, so-called r and K selection theory. The herring is an r-selectionist, having many offspring but not caring for them. The elephant is a K-selectionist, having but few offspring and investing a great deal of parental care. As part of this theory, today's evolutionists suggest that if conditions are highly variable, then a good reproductive strategy helps one to have lots of offspring, albeit with little individual attention (r-selection), whereas if conditions are stable, the better strategy is few children and much care (K-selection). Variable conditions mean that sometimes you might strike it rich whereas with few offspring you might never do that well; and conversely with stable conditions you can guarantee that some will generally do well, but that having huge numbers will overtax your resourses. In the case of male circumcision, acknowledging that there are questions about the evidence, Reynolds and Tanner nevertheless write:

> Despite the confused state of the data, it is not unreasonable to put the question: If circumcision does reduce the risk of penile or cervical carcinoma, what effects would this have on reproductive success? The answer is that such success should be increased (all other things being equal) in families or groups practising circumcision. ... In the case of Judaism it represents part of Abraham's Covenant with God, the covenant in which God called him to leave Ur and to found a new nation; also in the Covenant was the promise from God that his 'seed' would inherit the land. (1983: 240)

The idea seems to be that by moving to Israel, Abraham was moving to a land where the chances of raising children moved from very variable to more certain (albeit within restricted limits), and hence there was a move from r-selection-type practices to K-selection-type practices, one of the latter being circumcision.

455

Groups and memes as units of selection

Showing just how different people's thinking can be and yet still (in the eyes of advocates) be under the banner of Darwinism – that is, in the sociobiological mode – are the biologist David Sloan Wilson (2002) and the philosopher Daniel Dennett (2006). Wilson is openly committed to a group-selective analysis of religion, wanting to regard societies as akin to organisms and as strengthened by a sincere commitment to a religious doctrine. He ties this thesis strongly to morality, which he speaks of as having 'both a genetically evolved component and an open-ended cultural component' (Wilson 2002: 119). Wilson analyses the society that John Calvin founded in Geneva in the sixteenth century, listing the rules that governed this group: 'Obey parents'; 'Obey magistrates'; 'Obey pastors'; and on down the list to 'No lewdness, and sex only in marriage'; 'No theft, either by violence or cunning'; and so forth. Of this Wilson writes:

> To summarize, the God–people relationship can be interpreted as a belief system that is designed to motivate . . . behaviors. . . . Those who regard religious belief as senseless superstition may need to revise their own beliefs. Those who regard supernatural agents as imaginary providers of imaginary services may have underestimated the functionality of the God–person relationship in generating real services that can be achieved only by communal effort. Those who already think about religion in functional terms may be on the right track, but they may have underestimated the sophistication of the 'motivational physiology' that goes far beyond the use of kinship terms and fear of hell. Indeed, it is hard for me to imagine a belief system better designed to motivate group-adaptive behavior for those who accept it as true. When it comes to turning a group into a societal organism, scarcely a word of Calvin's catechism is out of place. (2002: 105)

Although he thinks that culture is crucial, ultimately D. S. Wilson sees real change as genetic. Coming in a very different direction, the philosopher Daniel Dennett (2006) agrees entirely that religion is promoted by selection; but he is not at all convinced that this selection is necessarily for the benefit of humans, nor is it essentially (or truly in any way) genetic. Dennett has adopted a theory of Richard Dawkins (1976) that posits the existence of 'memes,' units of culture akin to genes, that compete for people's allegiances. Rival memes, as it were, invade people's minds, and those that win are those that are selected to continue. Winning is not random, but a function of the features – the adaptations – that the memes have or promote. Successful advertising obviously is a paradigmatic example of memes at work, one of which is: smoking Marlborough cigarettes makes you a real man; this meme overrides the knowledge that doing so is in fact highly detrimental to your health and well-being.

For Dennett, religion is a meme parasite that has features that make it attractive even if it is not necessarily very good for the possessor. So that no one miss this point, he begins his book, *Breaking the Spell: Religion as a Natural Phenomenon*, by introducing the reader to the lancet fluke (*Dicrocelium dendriticum*), a parasite that corrupts the brain of an ant, causing it to strive to climb blades of grass. It then gets eaten by a sheep or cow, and thus the fluke can complete its life cycle before its offspring are excreted and taken up again by ants.

> Does anything like this ever happen with human beings? Yes indeed. We often find human beings setting aside their personal interests, their health, their chances to have children, and devoting their entire lives to furthering the interests of an *idea* that has lodged in their brains. The Arabic word *islam* means 'submission,' and every good Muslim bears witness, prays five times a day, gives alms, fasts during Ramadan, and tries to make the pilgrimage, or *hajj*, to Mecca, all on behalf of the idea of Allah, and Muhammad, the messenger of Allah. Christians and Jews do likewise, of course, devoting their lives to spreading the Word, making huge sacrifices, suffering bravely, risking their lives for an idea. So do Hindus and Buddhists. (2006: 4)

To be fair, Dennett adds that secular humanists are often not much better in this regard.

Religion as byproduct

What of those who think religion falls more into the by-product category? The late Stephen Jay Gould (2002) himself was one who thought along these lines. The whole of human culture came under this category for him. But most would not be this sweeping. Apart from anything else, religion with its costs – devotion to others, celibacy, ritual physical disfigurement, sacrifice, and so forth – simply does not seem to be the sort of thing that just happened as a by-product. It is too costly. More likely is the idea that religion, as it were, parasitically comes into existence and power on the backs of other things – real, powerful adaptations – and manages to exist because it cannot be stopped or because ultimately its costs are simply not that great. Student of culture Pascal Boyer (2002) inclines to the first option. For him, religion simply subverts or borrows features that our biology has put in place for good adaptive reasons, and for whatever reason it cannot be eradicated.

> The building of religious concepts requires mental systems and capacities that are there anyway, religious concepts or not. Religious morality uses moral intuitions, religious notions of supernatural agents recruit our intuitions about agency in general, and so on. This is why I said that religious concepts are parasitic upon other mental capacities. Our capacities to play music, paint pictures or even make sense of printed ink-patterns on a page are also parasitic in this sense. This means that we can explain how people play music, paint pictures and learn to read by examining how mental capacities are recruited by these activities. The same goes for religion. Because the concepts require all sorts of specific human capacities (an intuitive psychology, a tendency

to attend to some counterintuitive concepts, as well as various social mind adaptations), we can explain religion by describing how these various mind capacities get recruited, how they contribute to the features of religion we find in so many different cultures. We do not need to assume that there is a *special* way of functioning that occurs only when processing religious thoughts. (Boyer 2002: 311)

But what is it that allows religion to get its hold in the first place? Anthropologist Scott Atran (2004) inclines to the second option, that religion grabs something adaptively useful and exploits it. For him, the big threat facing organisms such as humans is other living beings, above all, other living beings as threats. In an argument reminiscent of Darwin and his dog, Atran suggests that what we have is a somewhat overeager projection of the living on to the inanimate. It used to be thought that the baroque nasal appendages of the titanotheres were a case of sensible evolution having taken a step too far. Perhaps the same is true of religion. Cuckoos exploit the innate mechanisms that their host birds have for raising their young. Religion does much the same for humans.

Supernatural agent concepts critically involve minimal triggering of evolved agency-detection schema, which are a part of folk psychology. Agency is a complex sort of 'innate releasing mechanism.' Natural selection designs the agency-detection system to deal rapidly and economically with stimulus situations involving people and animals as predators, protectors, and prey. This results in the system's being trip-wired to respond to fragmentary information under conditions of uncertainty, inciting perception of figures in the clouds, voices in the wind, lurking movements in the leaves, and emotions among interacting dots on a computer screen. This hair-triggering of the agency-detection mechanism readily lends itself to supernatural interpretation of uncertain or anxiety-provoking events.

People interactively manipulate this universal cognitive susceptibility so as to scare or soothe themselves and others for varied ends. They do so consciously or unconsciously and in causally complex and distributed ways, in pursuit of war or love, to thwart calamity or renew serendipity, or to otherwise control or incite imagination. The result provides a united and ordered sense for cosmic, cultural, and personal existence (Atran 2004: 78).

Serious science?

What can we say about these various ideas and hypotheses? One thing is for certain. They can't all be true! For every action there is an equal and opposite reaction. For every idea about the evolution of religion, there is an idea that takes exactly the opposite tack. Science can break down for two basic reasons: the theories are no good or the evidence is not supportive. Both of these reasons come into play with the socio-biological accounts of religion.

With respect to theory, straight Darwinism goes from strength to strength. The same cannot always be said of the ideas used to explain religion. Take the theory of memes. It really is crude to the point of non-being, certainly to the point of the non-helpful. What is a meme? It is a chunk of culture analogous to a gene. As it happens, genes are hard enough to define, but we do have some idea of them as the smallest functioning length of DNA. But what is the smallest functioning length of culture? Is Catholicism a meme? Is the authority of the pope a meme? Is transubstantiation a meme? Why the authority of the pope, for example, rather than each and every one of the dogmas that he endorses? And what kind of theory do you have as memes clash and come together and sometimes fuse and sometimes break apart? How is Mormonism a meme unto itself as compared to evangelical Christianity, which is part of the Protestant Christianity meme? Does Mormonism somehow include a lot of the evangelical Christianity meme, or are they separate memes? And so on and so forth. The point is not that Dennett is necessarily wrong in arguing that ideas sometimes have lives of their own, or that religions can be dreadful things that take over people's minds to their own detriment – if not about Catholicism, then most of us think this way about cults such as Scientology – but that memetics is not very helpful in understanding what is going on. One is really just taking regular language and putting it in fancy terms. No new insights. No new predictions. No astounding claims that turn out to be true.

There are analogous weaknesses with evidence. One might praise David Sloan Wilson for wanting to turn to real examples to articulate and flesh out his thinking. But his discussion of Calvinism really will not do. If Calvinism was such a terrific booster of societies and helped them work so well, why did it so frequently fail to convince? Take the English in the sixteenth century (MacCulloch 2004). Henry VIII broke from the Catholic Church because he wanted to take a new wife and the pope forbade it. His son, Edward VI was ultra-Protestant, more Lutheran than anything else. But when Edward died as a teenager his older sister Mary came to the throne and, as an ardent Catholic, persecuted Protestants, many of whom fled to the continent. By that time, the middle of the sixteenth century, the German Lutheran areas were often violent and torn by war and strife, and so these exiles headed for safer, quieter, Reformed (Calvinist) areas. When Mary died and her younger Protestant sister Elizabeth came to the throne, the now-convinced Calvinists all flooded back. But generally, the English were not keen on what they had to offer. They did not want the repressive morality and life-style of those who later came to be known as Puritans. So we had the Elizabethan compromise, an Anglican Church, to this day a bricolage of Catholic style and Protestant theology. And it was certainly not unsuccessful. Given the new-found stability under the compromise, the English saw off the Spanish and their armada. It is true that in the seventeenth century the Roundheads, the Puritans, won the Civil War and lopped off the head of King Charles I, but within twelve years the Royalists, the more central Anglicans, were restored and the Puritans were out again.

More generally, sociobiologists are far too given to isolating one bit of history, one place in time and space, and thinking you have the basis for a whole theory. This comment applies particularly to Americans – Edward O. Wilson and Daniel Dennett come at once to mind – who start with assumptions about the universal appeal and force of religion. By any measure, given its anti-Enlightenment obsession with religion, America is a very peculiar country, at least compared to the rest of the First World. It is very dangerous to argue about the need that humans have of religion if in fact a lot of humans really do not seem to need much religion at all. England is a case in point. Most young couples want a church wedding. But that is about the limit to their involvement with religion until the time comes to travel to the crematorium. Generally, religion in the lives of the average person in England is about as relevant as the royal family. Significantly, the Queen and her family are expected to observe the ritual practices as a proxy for the rest of the population. Not all writers on the biology of religion are totally provincial in thinking that their home society is the norm – not even that all American writers on the biology of religion are equally provincial in thinking that their home society is the norm – but it is an issue inadequately addressed.

God?

Suppose that there is something to the naturalistic Darwinian approach to religion, its history and its nature. How does this cash out philosophically? What does this tell us about God, his nature, and his existence? You might flip the argument entirely on its head, showing on non-Darwinian grounds that God does not exist and then setting forth on a naturalistic journey to explain why nevertheless so many people persist in believing that he is real. This is the tack taken by Dennett. He trots through the various arguments for the existence of God, following through with the standard objections. Then, with God dismissed, Dennett is ready to give an argument about why we are deceived. It is hardly surprising that for Dennett religion is a parasite like the lancet fluke.

What if you do not want to go down that path? Ask the basic question about God and his existence: not the question about whether God exists, but whether a Darwinian account of origins shows that God exists or not. Was Darwin right in thinking that the reality or not of God is irrelevant to a naturalistic account of religion? Edward O. Wilson goes entirely the other way. He says that Darwinism gives a naturalistic account of religion and that is an end to religion as a true description of how things are. As it happens, Wilson thinks that the human psyche demands religion, and thus he sees the place to move in with a kind of evolutionary humanism. But this is because Darwinism has already done its corrosive work.

But make no mistake about the power of scientific materialism. It presents the human mind with an alternative mythology that until now has always, point for point in zones of conflict, defeated traditional religion. Its narrative form is the epic: the evolution of the universe from the Big Bang of fifteen billion years ago through the origin of the elements and celestial bodies to the beginnings of life on earth. The evolutionary epic is mythology in the sense that the laws it adduces here and now are believed but can never be definitively proved to form a cause-and-effect continuum from physics to the social sciences, from this world to all other worlds in the visible universe, and backward through time to the beginning of the universe. Every part of existence is considered to be obedient to physical laws requiring no external control. The scientist's devotion to parsimony in explanation excludes the divine spirit and other extraneous agents. Most importantly, we have come to the crucial stage in the history of biology when religion itself is subject to the explanations of the natural sciences. As I have tried to show, sociobiology can account for the very origin of mythology by the principle of natural selection acting on the genetically evolving material structure of the human brain.

If this interpretation is correct, the final decisive edge enjoyed by scientific naturalism will come from its capacity to explain traditional religion, its chief competition, as a wholly material phenomenon. Theology is not likely to survive as an independent intellectual discipline (Wilson 1978: 192).

I suspect that Wilson is wrong and Darwin was right. The fact that you can give a naturalistic explanation of religion does not at once imply that religion is false. I can give a naturalistic explanation of my belief that the truck is bearing down on me, but it does not follow that the truck is not bearing down on me. It is true that if all you have is a naturalistic explanation, then (Dennett-like) you will probably not be eager to embrace religion. If you can show that religion is indeed a parasite on the mind, why take it any more seriously than the hucksters' email claims that their client has left millions of dollars for the taking? But for the traditional religious person – at least, for the traditional Christian religious person – religion has another source of epistemic power that email spam does not have. Faith. This being so, then far from a naturalistic account being threatening, many expect such a naturalistic explanation of origins. God had to impart the information to humankind in some way, and why not through evolution? Nor would it be a counterargument that the explanation might make the arrival of religion rather less than edifying – like a dog barking at a parasol blowing in the wind. The job is done.

What about something that often comes up in naturalistic discussions of the origins of religion, namely the comparative issue? The Christians believe one thing, the Jews another, and the Muslims a third. Now, you might think that this is a pretty good argument against all of them. How can the Christian God be so loving and insist that we acknowledge and worship him, condemning to eternal damnation all of those Asians who grew up in ignorance? But even if you do accept the argument against God based on comparative religion, note that this has nothing whatsoever to do with evolution. It was an argument that moved the deists at the end of the seventeenth century. Moreover, evolution or not, the believer can continue to believe in the face of religious diversity: the Christians (or whoever) got it right and the others did not, and that is the end of matters.

Conclusion

If evolution is true, and it is, and if natural selection is the main mechanism, and it is, then the sociobiological approach to religion cannot be without merit. But it has far to go before it can command assent and respect.

See also Truth in religion (Chapter 18), The moral argument (Chapter 34), Why is there a universe at all, rather than just nothing? (Chapter 41), Religious naturalism (Chapter 62), Religion and science (Chapter 64).

References

Atran, S. (2004) *In Gods We Trust: The Evolutionary Landscape of Religion*, New York: Oxford University Press.
Boyer, P. (2002) *Religion Explained: The Evolutionary Origins of Religious Thought*, New York: Basic Books.
Darwin, C. (1859) *On the Origin of Species*, London: John Murray.
—— (1871) *The Descent of Man*, London: John Murray.
Dawkins, R. (1976) *The Selfish Gene*, Oxford: Oxford University Press.
Dennett, D. C. (2006) *Breaking the Spell: Religion as a Natural Phenomenon*, New York: Viking.
Gould, S. J. (2002) *The Structure of Evolutionary Theory*, Cambridge, MA: Harvard University Press.
MacCulloch, D. (2004) *The Reformation: A History*, New York: Viking.
Reynolds, V. and R. Tanner (1983) *The Biology of Religion*, London: Longman.
Wilson, D. S. (2002) *Darwin's Cathedral*, Chicago: University of Chicago Press.
Wilson, E. O. (1975) *Sociobiology: The New Synthesis*, Cambridge, MA: Harvard University Press.
—— (1978) *On Human Nature*, Cambridge, MA: Harvard University Press.

Further reading

Atran, S. (2004) *In Gods We Trust: The Evolutionary Landscape of Religion*, New York: Oxford University Press. (A well-written book by an anthropologist who seems to have a solid grasp of the real nature of religion.)
Boyer, P. (2002) *Religion Explained: The Evolutionary Origins of Religious Thought*, New York: Basic Books. (Another interesting book on the natural origins of religion.)
Dennett, D. (2006) *Breaking the Spell: Religion as a Natural Phenomenon*, New York: Viking. (A controversial account of religion using meme theory.)
Wilson, D. S. (2002) *Darwin's Cathedral*, Chicago: University of Chicago Press. (Although I have been rather critical of it in my essay, it is recommended reading for being well written and certainly provocative.)
Wilson, E. O. (1978) *On Human Nature*, Cambridge, MA: Harvard University Press. (The place to start your own reading on this topic: a Pulitzer Prize-winning work, covering most of the basic ideas of human sociobiology, including implications for religion, in a style as fresh today as when it was written.)

Part VII

PHILOSOPHICAL THEOLOGY

43
CATHOLIC PHILOSOPHICAL THEOLOGY

Laura L. Garcia

Catholic philosophers are officially committed to the capacity of human reason to know some truths about God, as the *Catechism of the Catholic Church* clearly states.

> Created in God's image and called to know and love him, the person who seeks God discovers certain ways of coming to know him. These are also called proofs for the existence of God, not in the sense of proofs in the natural sciences, but rather in the sense of 'converging and convincing arguments,' which allow us to attain certainty about the truth. … Without this capacity [for natural knowledge of God], man would not be able to welcome God's revelation. (paragraphs 31, 36)

Some truths about God and his nature belong within the set of Christian doctrines known as the *preambles of faith*. While the preambles are included in what has been revealed, it is possible to come to know them independently of special revelation. There is no official list of preambles, though the existence and unity of God would surely appear on any such list. Writing to the church in Rome, the apostle Paul insists that God's existence and power are evident in his creation (Rom. 1: 19–20; all scriptural quotations are from the *New Revised Standard Version*). The pre-eminent Catholic philosopher and theologian Thomas Aquinas finds Aristotle's Cosmological Argument for a First Cause (Unmoved Mover) cogent and convincing. Since Aristotle had no access to sacred Scripture, Thomas concludes that God's existence is knowable by the natural light of reason. What has been done is, of course, possible.

Christian moral principles that are accessible to reason also belong among the preambles of faith. Faced with the impressive virtue theory elaborated in Aristotle's *Nicomachean Ethics*, Aquinas concludes that moral principles can be discovered by human minds. The only exceptions here might be specific supererogatory precepts in the teaching of Jesus, such as the injunction to bless those who curse you. Aquinas's natural law theory of ethics draws heavily from Aristotle, but is also influenced by Augustine, Stoicism, and Roman legal theory. An abridged form of natural law ethics animates modern British political philosophy by way of John Locke and others, influencing the United States Constitution and the UN Declaration of Human Rights. Moral philosophers continuing the tradition of Thomistic ethics include Russell Hittinger (2003) and Ralph McInerny (1997). Germaine Grisez (1983; 1993; and 1997) proposes a 'new natural law theory' which bypasses the empirical foundations of Aristotle's moral theory, appealing to an intuitive grasp of basic goods such as life, learning, and friendship. John Finnis (1991, 1998), Robert George (2001), and Joseph Boyle (in Lawler et al. 1998) further explicate and defend the new natural law theory, applying it to issues in moral and political philosophy.

Preambles of faith

Here we focus on preambles that belong specifically to theology, the science of God. Natural theology, in spite of its name, is really a philosophical enterprise, one of discovering what human reason can know about God independently of revelation. While Thomas Aquinas believes there are successful deductive proofs for God's existence which begin from what is self-evident or evident to sense experience, he does not restrict natural theology to deductive arguments or to those with such stellar epistemic credentials. 'Converging and convincing arguments' are also included, appealing to a broad range of generally accepted claims and experiences.

Natural theology is practiced mainly (though not exclusively) by theists and religious believers. It includes arguments *against* as well as *for* theistic claims concerning the existence and nature of God, the compatibility of divine foreknowledge with human freedom, of perfect goodness with human suffering, and so on. In addition, it falls to natural theology to provide an account of faith and to explain faith's relationship to reason and the other sciences. To the extent that natural theology assumes there are true propositions about God, it must give an account of the meaning of religious language. Thomas treats these topics and many others in Books I–III of the *Summa contra Gentiles*, committing himself to the search for wisdom about the highest things, a journey that begins in philosophy but ultimately points beyond it.

Although Thomas emphasizes the importance of natural theology, he does not claim that belief in God is rational only when it is held on the basis of objective philosophical proofs. Rather, given the weakness and fallibility of human minds, it is appropriate for God to include even the preambles of faith within revelation, making them more certain, more widely accessible, and unmixed with errors. Optimism about the human search for wisdom comports with the Catholic theological principle that *grace builds upon nature*. This principle is neither a restriction on God's actions nor an epistemic requirement on the faithful; rather it is arrived at inductively on the basis of divine actions in creation and salvation.

The beginning of Thomas's *Summa contra Gentiles* (SCG) might serve as the charter of natural theology:

So, in the name of the divine Mercy, I have the confidence to embark upon the work of a wise man, even though this may surpass my powers, and I have set myself the task of making known, as far as my limited powers will allow, the truth that the Catholic faith professes, and of setting aside the errors that are opposed to it. (SCG I. 2)

Natural theologians may find consolation from the next paragraph, which begins: 'To proceed against individual errors, however, is a difficult business.'

Mysteries of faith

As we have seen, Catholic theology distinguishes two ways of knowing theological truths, by the light of reason and by faith in God's word. Doctrinal claims that are knowable only if God reveals them are called *mysteries of faith*. While preambles *may* be accepted by faith, mysteries *must* be accepted by faith. The *Catholic Catechism* defines faith as follows:

> Faith is first of all a personal adherence of man to God. At the same time, and inseparably, it is a *free assent to the whole truth that God has revealed.* . . . In faith, the human intellect and will cooperate with divine grace: 'Believing is an act of the intellect assenting to the divine truth by command of the will moved by God through grace.' (paragraphs 150, 155)

Revelation is indispensable to Christianity, a faith grounded on particular historical events and an understanding of their theological significance. Major mysteries of the Christian faith include the Trinity, the Incarnation, and the Atonement. Reason has three tasks with respect to these revealed doctrines. First, one can assent to a doctrine only if one understands it, having at least a basic grasp of its meaning. This cannot be complete comprehension, as that would turn faith into sight. Nor must each believer consciously entertain and assent to each and every doctrine taught by Scripture or the Magisterium of the Church. While there is some minimal content required here (the Apostles' Creed perhaps), anyone who accepts the truth of all that God reveals implicitly accepts the whole content of revelation.

Reason also investigates apparent conflicts between revealed doctrines and truths gained from other sources, operating from the assumption that truth is one, and that all truth is God's truth. Reconciling initially inconsistent claims may call for surrendering one of them or, more often, reinterpreting one or both. Finally, Christian philosophers can defend doctrines of the faith against attempts to prove their impossibility. For this defense, it suffices to locate logical flaws in the argument or to show that one or more premises is possibly false (not necessarily true). Premises that are possibly false can be rationally rejected on the basis of divine authority.

Natural theology traditionally operates within an empiricist theory of knowledge that grounds all knowledge about the contingent features of the world in experience. For Aristotle and Thomas, claims with the highest epistemic credentials are either self-evident or evident to sense experience, with immediate logical implications of these a close second. Natural theology aims high, but also includes some probable arguments. The strategy is to begin from premises accepted by almost everyone, using these to provide rational support for claims about God. Historically speaking, the 'big three' arguments for God's existence are the ontological argument, the cosmological argument, and the teleological (or design) argument. Thomas presents a version of Aristotle's cosmological argument in his *Summa contra Gentiles*, urging that a being whose essence is existence is necessary to account for the existence of contingent beings, whose nature or essence is distinct from their existence.

The ontological argument, adumbrated by Augustine and developed into a formal proof by Anselm in the eleventh century, rests on no empirical claims. It begins with a definition of God common to theists and atheists alike: God is the being than which none greater can be conceived. Adding only self-evident premises, Anselm claims to show that God (so defined) must actually exist. This proof is something of a philosophical Rubik's cube, attracting the scrutiny of philosophers of every persuasion. Thomas declared it unsound in principle, on the grounds that no being's existence is knowable simply by definition. While granting this principle as a general rule, Anselm held that it admits of at least one exception. The ontological argument resurfaced in the 1970s primarily owing to the work of Alvin Plantinga (1974), who employs principles of modal logic to construct a version of the proof that is manifestly valid and that has only one premise. That premise, while very plausible, is not one that it would be irrational to reject. Hence, Plantinga claims only to have shown that belief in God is rational, not that unbelief is irrational, as Anselm had hoped to prove.

The teleological argument appeals to evidence of purpose or rational design in the universe as explained only by positing a personal cause of the world, a Maker with a Mind. Prior to Darwin, philosophers such as William Paley often drew examples from organisms with parts perfectly adapted for their function or with capacities perfectly suited to their environment. While these are (purportedly) explained by the theory of evolution, other examples have taken their place. These include cases of what is called 'irreducible complexity' in organisms, which confer an evolutionary advantage only when present in their complete form. Another example comes from Big Bang cosmology, which includes an initial singularity at the beginning of the universe that has no scientific explanation from within that universe, rendering a theistic cause plausible or perhaps even probable. Also, various scientists, mathematicians, and philosophers have pointed to evidences of Intelligent Design in the finely tuned structures of the universe.

Speaking to first-century Athenian citizens, the Apostle Paul undermines the credentials of the local pagan deities: 'The God who made the world and everything in it, he who is Lord of heaven and earth, does not live in shrines made by human hands, nor is he served by human hands, as though he needed anything, since he himself gives to all mortals life and breath and all things' (Acts 17: 24–5). A popular strategy in recent years posits God as the best (or only) explanation for such data as the existence and law-like regularity of the universe (Swinburne 2004); the temporal beginning of the universe (Craig 1979); the nature and capacities of human minds

(Haldane 2002); the compatibility of self-interest and the moral law (see Kant 1956); the voice of conscience (Newman 1985); and many others.

Confidence in reason is at low tide on academic shores, but the Catholic philosophical tradition defends human reason as naturally ordered to truth and able to reach some knowledge even of divine things. As Paul tells the Athenians, God created humans with a mind that thirsts for truth, 'so that they would search for God and perhaps grope for him and find him, though indeed he is not far from each one of us' (Acts 17: 27).

Objections to natural theology

Some critics of natural theology are hostile to all metaphysical claims. Global anathemas of this sort appear in the work of David Hume, Immanuel Kant, Karl Marx, logical positivists, anti-realists, social constructionists, and Wittgensteinian fideists. But not all objections to natural theology are inspired by metaphysical skepticism. Some claim natural theology has failed, at least in the positive project of supporting truths about God on grounds accessible to reason and experience. The negative project of defusing objections to faith may still be viable, but proofs for God produce few converts. Of course the goal of natural theology is to see what can be known about God apart from revelation, not to force every rational person into theism. Even supposing that every argument in the history of positive natural theology is flawed, it does not follow that no better arguments exist. Still, given the track record of natural theology in converting skeptics, the wise course of action might be politely to set it aside. This prudential objection to natural theology is compelling only if philosophical success requires convincing all inquiring minds, but few philosophical arguments are successful in those terms.

Within Christian philosophy, disagreements about the nature of faith fuel an ongoing intramural debate about the appropriateness of arguments for God. Christians generally agree that faith involves a firm and unwavering trust in God and a confidence in revealed doctrines that borders on certitude. Some infer from this that a belief in God's existence arrived at on the basis of rational arguments inevitably lacks the strength of conviction proper to religious belief. Even if positive natural theology succeeds, it produces at best a tentative, conditional belief in God liable to evaporate at the next meeting of the American Philosophical Association.

Thomas accepts both that faith requires certitude and that philosophical arguments rarely yield such certitude. Those who judge a philosophical argument to have demonstrated its conclusion are likely to say that they *know* it and do not merely believe it. But such judgments are fallible, and the certitude of faith rests on another basis. In faith the mind chooses to accept a claim because that acceptance is bound up with a perceived good. In knowledge the intellect's acceptance is compelled by the evidence presented, with little or no role for the will. Faith rests on revelation, but a philosopher convinced by a proof for God still has the virtue of faith if she would continue to believe in God in the absence of proof. Similarly, a rationally induced belief in God that falls short of faith may still be a prelude to faith.

Christianity and tolerance

Christians propose specific doctrines as objectively true, addressed to persons in every culture and at every historical moment, and this scandalizes many in the academy and outside it. Such religious 'exclusivism' runs counter to the popular assumption that all religions are historically conditioned and socially constructed, revealing more about the religious than about the God they worship. Josef Ratzinger (Pope Benedict XVI) unmasks the shallow thinking behind this assumption in *Truth and Tolerance* (2003). Christianity proposes truths about God, humankind, and salvation as received from God himself and addressed to every human being, whose origin and destiny is in God. By their very nature, truths like these cannot belong to any one culture or time; rather, whoever hears the gospel proclaimed is personally addressed by God.

Some religions make few propositional claims, focusing instead on deep religious experiences and means to arrive at them. Such an emphasis characterizes certain eastern religious traditions, but its influence can be discerned in western theologies such as that of Paul Tillich and in popular culture phenomena like transcendental meditation, some forms of yoga, and the Forum (formerly known as 'EST'). While these movements often claim to enhance physical and emotional well-being, they make few specific claims about life's meaning or purpose.

The cooperation of reason and faith in this search for meaning is eloquently defended by Pope John Paul II in *Fides et ratio* (*Faith and Reason*). He rejects the Enlightenment dogma of evidentialism, that whatever is not supported by acceptable rational evidence should be rejected as mere superstition. Revealed theology fared poorly under that dogma, though some evidentialist Christians obligingly began sifting through the Scriptures, trying to separate the rational wheat from the superstitious chaff. Ultimately suspicion fell on any belief, sacred or mundane, held more firmly than public evidence warranted. Evidentialism has fared poorly itself in recent years, owing to the inverse relationship between epistemic certitude and empirical content.

Religious language

From the 1920s to the 1960s, large tracts of English-speaking philosophy labored under the shadow of logical positivism and its verification criterion of meaning. Positivism is evidentialism for the twentieth century; empirical certitude extends only to what is immediately presented in sense experience (sense-data), and statements that cannot be verified or falsified by such evidence are not just rationally suspect but meaningless. Some philosophers friendly to religious belief struggled to find a linguistic role for God-talk other than the obvious one, that of saying things about God. But logical positivism began to unravel in the 1950s and 1960s, under assault from foes who accused it of being hoist on its own petard and even from friends (such as W. V. O. Quine) who questioned the independence and certitude of its basic empirical statements. As the twentieth century drew to a close, natural theology and philosophy of religion reappeared on the philosophical menu, along with a smorgasbord of metaphysical options from anti-realism to Zoroastrianism.

Assuming that statements about God are at least meaningful, a different problem arises within what is cheerfully called 'the community of religious language users.' If human concepts derive from sense experience, it seems they cannot be ascribed to God with exactly the same meaning they have when applied to creatures. Thomas proposes that they express a relation between creatures and God, either one of negation (God is immutable) or one of analogy (God is good). This theory of analogy is explicated in much depth and clarity by Ralph McInerny (1996).

The sentence 'God is good' captures a truth about God in a way tailored or adjusted to human understanding. Goodness exists in God in a mode that is qualitatively distinct from the way it exists in creatures. The absolute unity of the divine essence precludes any division into subject and properties, a fact imperfectly captured in assertions such as 'God is Beauty,' or 'God is Goodness Itself.' But these formulations are misleading if understood to characterize God as a property or as a Platonic Form. The best course is to begin with standard-issue goodness, remove all defects attributable to the finitude of its creaturely instances and stretch it to its maximum extent. When attributed to God, the resulting concept captures a truth about him in a mode we can understand. But human language and human thought cannot represent the divine nature as it is in itself.

Mysteries of faith are based on divine revelation, which raises the question of how such a claim could be authenticated. Defending the divine origin of the Scriptures is the positive task of Christian apologetics. The negative task responds to attempted disproofs of doctrines specific to Christianity. Apologetics can also incorporate analogies or parallels that shed greater light and intelligibility on specific dogmas, though here the goal is not refuting the skeptical but 'the training and consolation of the faithful' (SCG I. 9).

Systematic theology

A bolder philosophical project suggests itself at this point, one that Scott MacDonald (1998) calls *clarificatory theology*. It is like natural theology in using standard philosophical techniques of reasoning (definition, conceptual analysis, examination of supporting arguments) but differs from natural theology in applying these methods to specifically Christian doctrines. MacDonald notes that while philosophers cannot simply assume the *truth* of, for instance, the doctrine of the Incarnation, they can 'engage in philosophical clarification and explication of that notion,' setting aside or bracketing questions about its truth. This is standard procedure for evaluating philosophical theories about the nature of knowledge or the ground of moral truths. MacDonald adds, '[Often] the successful completion of some of these clarificatory tasks is in some ways a prerequisite for assessing the truth of a theory' (1998).

In this spirit, Christian philosophers have recently turned their attention toward such doctrinal heavyweights as the Trinity, the Incarnation, the Atonement, Sin, and Sanctification (see Part VIII of this volume). In a time when many theologians are eager to distance themselves from theology – defined as a discipline that assumes the truth of the articles of faith – philosophers have stepped into the resulting vacuum, making clarificatory theology the popular cutting edge of philosophy of religion. While clarificatory (or systematic) theology obviously needs doing, philosophical forays in the field meet with mixed reviews. In order to explicate a Christian doctrine, it must first be spelled out in propositional form, relying on a theological and hermeneutical tradition. Such traditions are in turn constrained by the set of propositions held to be fixed and authoritative. Since philosophers rarely disclose the theological tradition presupposed in their work, clarificatory theology risks becoming anything but.

Major currents

The Thomistic synthesis of Christianity and Aristotelian philosophy provides a model for Catholic philosophers and theologians seeking to engage the intellectual currents of the day. That engagement has produced the richness and variety found within Catholic philosophy since the mid-twentieth century. What follows is a brief (and non-canonical) overview of this wealth of thought and of some who made important contributions to it, whatever their personal religious beliefs.

The thought of Thomas Aquinas occupies pride of place in Catholic philosophy, having received several papal recommendations including that of John Paul II. Philosophers inspired by Thomism have made the greatest impact on the philosophy profession as a whole. Well-known examples are Etienne Gilson (1993; 2002) and Jacques Maritain (1995; 1996), with further contributions by Anthony Kenny (1969, 2002), Norman Kretzmann (1999), Kretzmann and Eleonore Stump (1999) Scott MacDonald (1991), Ralph McInerny (1997), Mark McLeod (1993), John O'Callahan (2003), Eleonore Stump (2003), and John Wippel (2000). Alasdair MacIntyre's work in moral philosophy (1990) finds much of value in the virtue ethics of Aristotle and Thomas. Catholic scholars have also found importance in the work of later medieval thinkers; see William of Ockham 1991 (Adams 1990; Spade 2005); Luis de Molina 1988; and Francisco Suárez 1994; 2002 (Gracia 1989).

The analytic philosophical method has been employed in natural theology by Elizabeth Anscombe (1981; and in Geach and Gormally 2005), Michael Dummett (1991; 2004), Peter Geach (1969; 2001), John Haldane (2002; 2004), Richard Swinburne (2004) and Linda Zagzebski (1996). Gabriel Marcel constructed a postwar philosophy of hope that is sometimes called Catholic Existentialism (1977). Phenomenological realism and personalism are developed in forms congenial to Christianity by Edith Stein (2002) and Dietrich von Hildebrand (1991), and defended by John Crosby (1996), David Schindler (1996), Robert Sokolowski (1995), and Karol Wojtyla (1979).

Philosophers today have instant access to the riches of their theological and philosophical tradition and colleagues around the globe. This wealth of resources makes it likely that Catholic philosophical theology of the coming years will be synthetic, bringing together schools of thought formerly thought to have little in common. Versions of Thomism have ongoing appeal as viable alternatives to such current intellectual trends as skepticism, anti-realism, and relativism. Particularly promising new research programs are Thomistic personalism, popularized by Pope John Paul II, and analytic Thomism, defined by John Haldane and holding appeal for religiously serious philosophers trained in the methods of analytic philosophy.

See also Christianity (Chapter 6), Augustine (Chapter 8), Thomas Aquinas (Chapter 12), Creation and divine action (Chapter 30), The ontological argument (Chapter 31), The cosmological argument (Chapter 32), The argument from consciousness (Chapter 35), The problem of religious language (Chapter 39), Protestant theology (Chapter 45), and Reformed epistemology (Chapter 58).

References

Adams, M. M. (1990) *William Ockham*, 2 vols., Notre Dame, IN: University of Notre Dame Press.

Anscombe, E. (1981) *The Collected Philosophical Papers of G. E. M. Anscombe*, vol. 1: *From Parmenides to Wittgenstein*, Minneapolis, MN: University of Minnesota; vol. 2: *Metaphysics and the Philosophy of Mind*, Minneapolis, MN: University of Minnesota; vol. 3: *Ethics, Religion and Politics*, Minneapolis, MN: University of Minnesota.

Aquinas, T. (1975) *Summa contra Gentiles*, Notre Dame, IN: University of Notre Dame Press.

Catechism of the Catholic Church, 2nd edn (1997) Washington, DC: United States Catholic Conference.

Craig, W. L. (1979) *The Kalam Cosmological Argument*, New York: Barnes & Noble.

Crosby, J. (1996) *The Selfhood of the Human Person*, Washington, DC: Catholic University of America Press.

Dummett, M. (1991) *The Logical Basis of Metaphysics*, Cambridge, MA: Harvard University Press.

—— (2004) *Truth and the Past*, New York: Columbia University Press.

Finnis, J. (ed.) (1991) *Natural Law*, 2 vols, New York: New York University Press.

—— (1998) *Aquinas: Moral, Political, and Legal Theory*, New York: Oxford University Press.

Geach, M. and L. Gormally (eds) (2005) *Human Life, Action and Ethics: Essays by G. E. M. Anscombe*, Exeter: Academic.

Geach, P. (1969) *God and the Soul*, London: Routledge.

—— (2001) *Truth and Hope*, The Fürst Franz Josef und Fürsten Gina Lectures, delivered at the International Academy of Philosophy in the Principality of Liechtenstein, Notre Dame, IN: University of Notre Dame Press.

George, R. P. (2001) *A Defense of Natural Law*, New York: Oxford University Press.

Gilson, E. (1993) *Christian Philosophy: An Introduction*, 2nd edn, trans. A. Maurer, Toronto: Pontifical Institute of Medieval Studies.

—— (2002) *Thomism: The Philosophy of Thomas Aquinas*, 6th edn, trans. L. K. Shook and A. Maurer, Toronto: Pontifical Institute of Medieval Studies.

Gracia, J. J. E. (1989) *The Metaphysics of Good and Evil According to Suárez: Metaphysical Disputations 10, 11 and 23*, Munich: Philosophia Verlag.

Grisez, G, (1983, 1993, 1997) *Way of the Lord Jesus*, 3 vols, Quincy, IL: Franciscan Press, vol. 1: *Christian Moral Principles*, vol. 2: *Living a Christian Life*, vol. 3: *Difficult Moral Questions*.

Haldane, J. (ed.) (2002) *Mind, Metaphysics, and Value in the Thomistic and Analytical Traditions*, Notre Dame, IN: University of Notre Dame Press.

—— (2004) *Faithful Reason: Essays Catholic and Philosophical*, New York: Routledge.

Hittinger, R. (2003) *The First Grace: Rediscovering the Natural Law in a Post-Christian World*, Wilmington, DE: ISI Books.

Kant, I. (1956) 'The existence of God as a postulate of pure practical reason,' in *Critique of Practical Reason*, trans. L. W. Beck, New York: Liberal Arts Press.

Kenny, A. (1969) *The Five Ways*, New York: Schocken Books.

—— (2002) *Aquinas on Being*, Oxford: Clarendon Press.

Kretzmann, N. (1999) *The Metaphysics of Creation: Aquinas's Natural Theology in Summa contra Gentiles*, 2 vols, Oxford: Clarendon Press.

Kretzmann, N. and E. Stump (eds) (1999) *The Cambridge Companion to Aquinas*, New York: Cambridge University Press.

Lawler, R., J. Boyle, and W. E. May (1998) *Catholic Sexual Ethics: A Summary, Explanation and Defense*, 2nd edn, Huntington, IN: Our Sunday Visitor.

MacDonald, S. (ed.) (1991) *Being and Goodness: The Concept of the Good in Metaphysics and Philosophical Theology*, Ithaca, NY: Cornell University Press.

—— (1998) 'Natural theology,' in E. Craig (ed.) *Routledge Encyclopedia of Philosophy*, London: Routledge. Retrieved on July 26, 2006 from http://www.rep.routledge.com/article/K107.

McInerny, R. (1996) *Aquinas and Analogy*, Washington, DC: Catholic University of America Press.

—— (1997) *Ethica Thomistica*, rev. edn, Washington, DC: Catholic University of America Press.

MacIntyre, A. (1990) *Three Rival Versions of Moral Inquiry*, London: Duckworth.

McLeod, M. (1993) *Rationality and Theistic Belief: An Essay on Reformed Epistemology*, Ithaca, NY: Cornell University Press.

Marcel, G. (1977) *The Mystery of Being*, presented in Aberdeen, Scotland as the Gifford Lectures, 1949–50, South Bend, IN: Gateway Editions.

Maritain, J. (1995) *Degrees of Knowledge*, ed. R. McInerny, translated from the fourth French edition under the supervision of G. B. Phelan, Notre Dame, IN: University of Notre Dame Press (Collected Works of Jacques Maritain, vol. 7).

—— (1996) *Integral Humanism, Freedom in the Modern World and A Letter on Independence*, ed. O. Bird, J. Evans, R. O'Sullivan, trans. O. Bird, Notre Dame, IN: University of Notre Dame Press (Collected Works of Jacques Maritain, vol. 11).

Molina, L. de (1988) [1588] *On Divine Foreknowledge, Part IV of the Concordia*, trans. A. Freddoso, Ithaca, NY: Cornell University Press.

Newman, J. H. (1985) *An Essay in Aid of a Grammar of Assent*, ed. I. Ker, Oxford: Clarendon Press.

O'Callahan, J. (2003) *Thomist Realism and the Linguistic Turn: Toward a More Perfect Form of Existence*, Notre Dame, IN: University of Notre Dame Press.

Plantinga, A. (1974) *The Nature of Necessity*, Oxford: Clarendon Press.

Ratzinger, J. (Pope Benedict XVI) (2003) *Truth and Tolerance: Christian Belief and World Religions*, Fort Collins, CO: Ignatius Press.

Schindler, D. (1996) *Heart of the World, Center of the Church: Communio Ecclesiology, Liberalism, and Liberation*, Grand Rapids, MI: Eerdmans.

Sokolowski, R. (1995) *The God of Faith and Reason: Foundations of Christian Theology*, Washington, DC: Catholic University of America Press.

Spade, P. V. (ed.) (2005) *The Cambridge Companion to Ockham*, New York: Cambridge University Press.

Stein, E. (2002) *Finite and Eternal Being: An Attempt at an Ascent to the Meaning of Being*, trans. K. F. Reinhardt, Washington, DC: ICS Publications.

Stump, E. (2003) *Aquinas*, New York: Routledge.

Suárez, F. (1994) [1597] *On Efficient Causality: Metaphysical Disputations 17, 18 and 19*, trans. A. Freddoso, New Haven, CT: Yale University Press.

—— (2002) [1597] *On Creation, Conservation and Concurrence: Metaphysical Disputations 20, 21, and 22*, trans. A. Freddoso, South Bend, IN: St Augustine's Press.

Swinburne, R. (2004) *The Existence of God*, Oxford: Clarendon Press.

von Hildebrand, D. (1991) *What is Philosophy?* New York: Routledge.

William of Ockham (1991) [c. 1327] *Quodlibetal Questions*, trans. A. Freddoso and F. E. Kelley, New Haven, CT: Yale University Press.

Wippel, J. (2000) *The Metaphysical Thought of Thomas Aquinas: From Finite Being to Uncreated Being*, Washington, DC: Catholic University of America Press.

Wojtyla, K. (Pope John Paul II) (1979) *The Acting Person*, trans. A. Potocki, Dordrecht: Reidel.

Zagzebski, L. (1996) *Virtues of the Mind: An Inquiry into the Nature of Virtue and the Ethical Foundations of Knowledge*, New York: Cambridge University Press.

Further reading

Aquinas, T. (1948) *Summa Theologica*, New York: Benziger Brothers. (Christian Classics Ethereal Library: http://www.ccel.org. Works by Aquinas and a host of classical texts in philosophy and theology available on this website.)

Haldane, J. and J. J. C. Smart (1996) *Atheism and Theism*, Oxford: Blackwell. (Debate between an analytical Thomist and a convinced naturalist. Haldane argues that certain empirical phenomena defy scientific explanation in principle. Smart hypothesizes a wildly bloated ontology in order to preserve his position that the 'fine-tuning' of our universe is unsurprising.)

Kreeft, P. and R. Tacelli, S. J. (1994) *Handbook of Christian Apologetics*, Downers Grove, IL: InterVarsity Press. (A helpful overview of natural theology and a defense of doctrines specific to Christianity.)

Maritain, J. (electronic): Website of the Jacques Maritain Center at the University of Notre Dame: http://www2.nd.edu/Departments//Maritain/aristotl.htm. (Online resources include works by Aristotle, Maritain, and others.)

McInerny, R. (2001) *Characters in Search of Their Author*, Gifford Lectures, delivered at Glasgow, Scotland 1999–2000, Notre Dame, IN: University of Notre Dame Press. (Thomistic diagnosis of philosophy's ills and their source in the Cartesian turn to the subject, with Aristotelian realism as the cure.)

44
EASTERN ORTHODOXY
Paul L. Gavrilyuk

The beginnings of philosophical theology in early Christianity may be traced to the works of the Apologists of the second century CE. Justin Martyr (*c*.100–*c*.165) and Athenagoras (second century) defended the Christian worldview by appealing to reason and revelation. The attitudes of the early Fathers towards Greek and Hellenistic philosophies ranged from outright rejection (e.g., Tertullian, Hippolytus, Jerome) to selective integration (e.g., Justin, Clement of Alexandria and the Origenist tradition). It is indisputable that the categories and presuppositions of later Platonism, Stoicism and to a lesser degree other philosophical schools of late antiquity played a significant role in the development of early Christian theology. However, the normative assessment of this influence continues to be a subject of lively debate among the theologians and historians of doctrine.

In contrast to largely critical assessments of Hellenism that prevailed in German historiography of the twentieth century, Georges Florovsky (1893–1979) saw 'Christian Hellenism' (i.e., the synthesis of revelation and Hellenistic philosophies which came to its fruition in Byzantium) as constitutive of Orthodox teaching. Florovsky went so far as to claim that Russian theologians, notably Vladimir Soloviev (1853–1900), Nikolai Berdiaev (1874–1948), and Sergius Bulgakov (1871–1944), took the wrong turn by abandoning the normativity of Hellenism and embracing modern metaphysical and epistemological projects, especially German Idealism (Florovsky 1937). Other Orthodox theologians, such as John Meyendorff (1926–92) and Alexander Schmemann (1921–83), unlike Florovsky, did not stake as much upon the purist retention of Christian Hellenism. Rather, they saw the categories of Greek philosophy as neutral tools that in principle could find their functional equivalents in contemporary philosophical conceptuality. It may be useful to compare this debate among Orthodox patristics scholars to the one on the status of Aristotelian philosophy among the neo-Thomists.

The debate about the status of Hellenism in Orthodox theology has more than purely historical interest. Most present-day Eastern Orthodox theologians work with the tacit assumption of enduring continuity between patristic and contemporary Orthodox modes of theologizing. This assumption is reinforced by the fact that the Eastern Orthodox tradition has not suffered from two crises that disrupted the intellectual history of the western Church: the barbarian invasions of the early Middle

Ages and the Reformation. The intellectual shift associated with the transition from the age of the Fathers to the age of the Schoolmen in the West was, comparatively speaking, inconsequential for the East. Its politically tumultuous past notwithstanding, the Christian East experienced no crisis of authority comparable in depth to the one endured by the Christian West during the Reformation and Enlightenment. Strikingly, neither the political dominance of Muslims in the Middle East, nor even the confrontation with militant atheism during the twentieth century, had precipitated equally dramatic changes in the dominant patristic paradigm of Orthodox theology.

The Eastern Orthodox Church is commonly described as the Church of the seven Ecumenical Councils (Ware 1993). This statement means that all Eastern Orthodox theologians take the core teachings of these councils – the Nicene Creed, the Chalcedonian definition, the definition about the two wills in Christ, and the definition concerning the veneration of icons – as supremely authoritative (although they may disagree on the meaning and function of these statements in the modern context). More broadly, the description 'the Church of the seven Ecumenical Councils' implies that the tacit epistemic commitments of the Orthodox theology are pre-modern: the appeal to the tradition (or, more precisely, to the divine revelation as enshrined in the tradition of the Church) has priority over the appeals to reason and experience. It is the conciliar mind of the Church, not the autonomous mind of an individual theologian, nor the Bible, nor the pope, that is the final court of appeal in doctrinal matters. The principle of *sobornost'* (conciliarity) plays a pivotal role in resolving doctrinal disputes (Khomiakov 1907).

The Orthodox theology also reveals its pre-modern character in that most Orthodox theologians assume the supernaturalist view of the world to be true without offering any formal arguments in support of this assumption. It is revealing that natural theology has never gained in Eastern Orthodox thought the distinctive, if contested, place that it came to occupy in the philosophical theology of the West since Scholasticism.

Negatively, the pre-modern character of Eastern Orthodox theology may be viewed as a sign of its backwardness. It is telling, for example, that the Russian Orthodox Church in more than a thousand years of its existence did not put forth a single dogmatic statement. This is a sign of a remarkable resilience to change, especially when compared to an impressive doctrinal fecundity of western Christian communions in the same period.

One could object, however, that the progress in theology and philosophy, unlike that in natural sciences, is not measured by the number of new theories that are put forth in a given historical period. Hence, the Orthodox Church's reluctance to endorse new dogmas as universally binding upon all faithful – what one might call its dogmatic reserve – far from being an indicator of the Church's theological infertility, may be attractive for several reasons. One advantage of such dogmatic minimalism is that it provides a broader range of acceptable theological options and offers new opportunities for seeking doctrinal unity in ecumenical dialogue. Furthermore, given the postmodern disillusionment with the Enlightenment project, many western theologians have turned to the Eastern Fathers and contemporary Orthodox theology, seeking remedies for the intellectual wounds inflicted by modernity. Some western thinkers – for example, the representatives of the *resourcement* movement – are compelled by the unapologetic supernaturalism of the Fathers. Others appeal to the patristic paradigm in order to free contemporary theology from its captivity to the Enlightenment epistemologies (Abraham 1998; Milbank et al. 1999).

Given the high status accorded to patristic heritage by the Orthodox, it is useful to map the types of Eastern Orthodox philosophical theology according to their engagement with the intellectual and spiritual heritage of the fathers. Narrowing this survey to the developments since the mid-nineteenth century, one may distinguish two main patterns of such an engagement: retrieval and modernization. The retrievalist project, commonly referred to as neopatristic synthesis, has a unified set of assumptions (discussed below). In the modernizing project the questions raised by the Enlightenment and German Idealism determined the extent and the manner in which the thought of the Fathers was engaged.

Neopatristic synthesis

Neopatristic synthesis is a dominant key in which modern Eastern Orthodox theology is done. While the expression 'neopatristic synthesis' is associated with the names of Vladimir Lossky and Georges Florovsky, these Russian theologians did not invent a new approach, but rather captured a well-established one. Indeed, for most Eastern Orthodox theologians throughout the centuries, to theologize was to enter into the mind of the Fathers. Such a theological enterprise was not merely an exercise in repetition of what the authoritative theologians of the past had said. Unlike rigid traditionalism, the neopatristic synthesis is not a mechanical summary of isolated propositions from patristic writings. On the contrary, to enter into the mind of the Fathers is to understand the inner logic of patristic thought; to learn how to think with the Fathers; to acquire a scriptural mind, i.e., to grasp the inner connections and the overarching purpose of Scripture following patristic examples (Florovsky 1972).

According to this view, philosophical theology cannot be separated entirely from the study of the historical development of doctrine. Christian teaching has been formulated as the mind of the Church struggled to express the content of historically given divine revelation. There is a broad consensus among the neopatristic theologians that the theistic vision of the Nicene Creed, with its ontology of the triune God infinitely surpassing everything in creation, is a necessary metaphysical foundation of any theological speculation. The neopatristic project may be viewed as an informal cumulative case for Trinitarian theism. In this version of theism, rational considerations do not function in isolation from tradition, but are planted in a network of communal practices, including rites of initiation, liturgy, prayer, asceticism and other forms of spiritual discipline. The appeal is also made to the authority of the saints and the Fathers of the Church, whose testimony is given a privileged epistemic status. Patristic writings are mined not only as sources of authoritative theological claims, as they tended to be in Scholasticism, but also as containing valuable epistemic resources and paradigms of theologizing, in particular, the connection that the Fathers make between speculative theology and the transformation of the self.

On the one hand, the approach to theology proposed by the neopatristic school has the following advantages: (1) it vindicates the grounding of theological truth-claims in historical revelation by giving priority to tradition, not to reason or experience; (2) it calls modern theology to return to a robustly supernaturalist and theocentric vision of the world; (3) by focusing on the ontology of the reality of God, it overcomes the Enlightenment's prioritization of epistemology; (4) it offers unique points of contact with postmodern modes of theologizing, especially in the emphasis upon the role of the believing community in formulating religious beliefs.

On the other hand, the critics of this approach may object that (1) somewhat one-sided reliance upon tradition to resolve deep theological dilemmas is question-begging and retrograde; (2) the failure to provide formal arguments for traditional theism and supernaturalism verges on unarticulated fideism; (3) neopatristic synthesis is an exercise in purely descriptive history of ideas that leaves most normative questions of philosophical theology unresolved; (4) the exclusive concentration on the patristic period does not allow one adequately to address contemporary questions, and often ignores them. While these objections are considerable, there is a growing number of theologians who are attracted to the Trinitarian theism of the Fathers because it is not defined by the Enlightenment patterns of rationality. Influential modern scholars, whose work draws heavily upon patristic heritage in this fashion, include: Hilarion Alfeyev, John Behr, Andrew Louth, John Meyendorff, Jaroslav Pelikan, Alexander Schmemann, Dimitru Staniloae, Kallistos Ware, and John Zizioulas.

While the neopatristic school dominates much of contemporary Orthodox thinking in both the Church and the academy, other ways of engaging religious questions came to be explored by Russian religious thinkers from the second half of the nineteenth century onwards. Many of these figures were writers, poets, and public intellectuals, not professional philosophers or theologians (Berdiaev 2002: 157). They were intellectually and spiritually dissatisfied with academic theology offered at the Orthodox seminaries of pre-revolutionary Russia. What united this group of religious thinkers was the pursuit of ultimate questions, such as the existence of God, the meaning of life, theodicy, social justice, and the ultimate destiny of humankind. Their quite discordant answers are not readily classifiable according to conventional modes of western philosophical theology. In the absence of a better umbrella term, I have earlier referred to their mode of theologizing as modernizing, because they departed from the prevailing Scholastic and neopatristic paradigms.

Considerations of space will allow giving more than a cursory treatment only to two influential trajectories and to briefly mention other developments. The main representatives of the first trajectory, Fyodor Dostoevsky (1821–81) and N. Berdiaev, brought new existential depth to the understanding of freedom, suffering, and personhood. The second trajectory, sophiology, and attendant metaphysical questions, was pursued in the writings of Vladimir Soloviev, Pavel Florensky (1882–1937), and Sergius Bulgakov. I will also briefly discuss the onomatodoxic controversy which stimulated a deeply original discussion of religious language. Finally, the critique of Marxism and Communism in Russian political theology also deserves to be mentioned.

Freedom, personhood, and the problem of evil

The tragic vision of Dostoevsky is predicated upon the central conviction that all limiting questions of human existence have inescapably religious answers. In order to become existentially gripping, even the denial of God – and Dostoevsky's heroes are capable of a profound revolt against God – has to acquire quasi-religious features. Prince Myshkin, the protagonist of *The Idiot* (1868), observes that atheism is wrong not because it is intellectually indefensible, but because it does not do justice to the limiting questions of human existence. The main characters of *The Brothers Karamazov* (1879–80) and *Crime and Punishment* (1866) come to the full realization of this point when confronted either with the tragedy of undeserved suffering or with the guilt of their own sinfulness.

The hero of the first novel, Ivan Karamazov, is morally disgusted with the superfluous suffering of children present in the world. He rejects the rationalist ways of doing theodicy, saying that the amount of the good does not balance out the amount of evil; the eternal bliss of afterlife cannot make one oblivious to the injustice in this life. Ivan famously captures this point by saying that the entire eternal harmony of heaven is not worth a tear of one innocently tortured child. Anticipating Sartre and Camus, Dostoevsky's hero rejects the world as absurd and revolts against God. However, Ivan is equally convinced that no version of secular humanism is capable of deterring humans from evil: 'If there is no God, then everything is permitted.' A Godless world, as Ivan will come to realize, is even more absurd than the world with God. The claim that everything is permitted in a world without God drives Ivan's alter ego, Smerdiakov, who is described as a 'village atheist,' to commit the atrocious crime of parricide. The tragic chain of coincidences leads another brother, Mitya Karamazov, to be condemned for the crime that he has not committed and be sent to Siberia. Ivan is profoundly shaken and tortured by guilt. On the verge of insanity, Ivan comes to see all participants of the drama as sharing in the crime, an insight that Dostoevsky expresses in the maxim 'everyone is guilty for everyone else.' For Alyosha, the youngest of the Karamazov brothers, who is a novice in a monastery, God's embracing of innocent suffering on the cross is the only answer to theodicy that does not trivialize the mystery of human suffering.

The tragic hero of *Crime and Punishment*, Rodion Raskolnikov, aspires to become a superman by committing a superfluous murder and thereby rising above the conventional moral norms of society. He chooses a victim whom he considers worthless: a greedy old woman who is a pawnbroker. He ends up killing both the woman and her mentally impaired half-sister. Despite the fact that his crime is undetected, Raskolnikov discovers to his dismay that his act has failed to transform him into a superman. On the contrary, he is tortured by guilt and feels a compelling need to atone for his crime. At the end of the novel, he reports himself voluntarily to the police and feels a relief only when he is given a harsh prison sentence. For Raskolnikov, crime begins a process of self-discovery; punishment becomes the means of healing his conscience. When guilt and shame break the barriers of pride and self-reliance, the heart becomes more open to the intuitive grasp of God's presence.

Dostoevsky's approach to theodicy is both unsettling and illuminating. On the one hand, he rejects all rationalist solutions to the problem of evil. The Russian novelist was convinced that the ultimate questions, such as the existence of evil, had to be resolved existentially, not just intellectually. On the other hand, his works are shot through with the conviction that human beings draw closer to the mystery of God's absence and presence when their lives are profoundly shaken by evil and suffering. In such circumstances, turning toward or away from God becomes inescapable. Berdiaev formulated this truth in the following way: evil exists; therefore there must be a God.

Berdiaev shared Dostoevsky's tragic vision of the human condition. Human freedom has a dark and irrational side. To be free means to be capable of self-destruction and terrible evil. But freedom also has the opposite side. Freedom is constitutive of personhood. For human persons to exist is to be free. Drawing upon the German mystic Jakob Boehme, Berdiaev speculates that freedom is the *Ungrund* (or *Urgrund*), the metaphysical ground of God's being. As such, the uncreated freedom is above the distinction between good and evil. The uncreated freedom is a primal creative act of differentiation between a (theistic) God – who is perfectly good – and nothingness. God cannot be blamed for causing or even permitting evil, because God is not the ultimate ontological source of human freedom. Berdiaev parts with traditional theism when he insists that freedom is ontologically prior to God himself. For him, human persons are both created and uncreated, since they all share in the uncreated freedom. This freedom may become a source of terrible wickedness, the ontological limit of which is the realm of the demonic. However, uncreated freedom is also a source of human creativity.

Berdiaev undertakes a systematic vindication of creative act, an anthropodicy. For him there are two equally fulfilling paths to God: the repentance of a saint and the creative act of a genius. Berdiaev observes that the Church has historically recognized only the way of self-purification as valid, and has been reluctant to approve of the way of human creativity. It may be objected that not all creative acts ought to be thus sanctified. One's inspiration may also come from the realm of the demonic. Berdiaev counters this objection by insisting that all human acts of repentance are bedeviled by similar ambiguities. Hence we distinguish between genuine repentance and a super-ficial or hypocritical one. Berdiaev argues that a genuine creative act is utterly selfless and offers a way of becoming God-like by imitating the Creator (Berdiaev 1955). He saw the alienation of art and culture from the Church as a result of the Church's failure to recognize the value of creativity.

For Berdiaev, religious philosophy was adogmatic. The ecclesiastical dogma stood in the way of free philosophical inquiry into the nature of reality. However, Berdiaev turned this Enlightenment cliché on its head, when he insisted upon the priority of revelation, mystical experience, and intuition over reason and everyday experience.

He was as critical of dogmatism as he was of narrow rationalism, empiricism, and positivism. Narrow rationalists refuse to acknowledge the foundational, paradigm-setting character of revelation and mystical experience. They operate with the artificial division between the natural and supernatural, typically offering arguments from certain features of nature to the existence of God who is beyond nature. Berdiaev rejects this approach. The purpose of philosophical theology is not to defend Christianity against secular culture, but to build a new culture on Christian foundations. For him, as for Dostoevsky, the reality of God is grasped existentially when one comes to recognize that the non-religious answers to the ultimate questions of human existence are unsatisfactory. The denial of God leads to the denial of the divine in human beings, to dehumanization (Berdiaev 1996).

Although Berdiaev acknowledged his debt to the spiritual sources of patristic tradition, he saw himself as a religious philosopher, not an Orthodox theologian. He never sought the endorsement of his controversial religious ideas by the Orthodox Church.

Sophiology

The metaphysical idealism of V. Soloviev inspired a generation of early twentieth-century Russian writers, poets, and public intellectuals. Soloviev's system of Christian philosophy retained the centrality of the doctrines of the Trinity and Incarnation which is characteristic of Eastern Orthodox theology. In response to the Enlightenment critique of traditional Christian beliefs, Soloviev offered a complex synthesis in which Christian Platonism, Spinoza's and Schelling's pantheism, as well as Hegel's dialectical method played a constructive role. In his works *The Crisis of Western Philosophy* (1874) and *A Critique of Abstract Principles* (1880), Soloviev criticized the limitations of Enlightenment rationalism, empiricism, and positivism. In *Philosophical Principles of Integral Knowledge* (1877), he provided his own theory of the development of human knowledge in three stages: the early stage when all fields of knowledge were undifferentiated and subordinated to religion; the present stage, represented mostly by western Europe, is characterized by progressive secularization and atomization of learning in which different spheres of knowledge vie for dominance over each other; and the final stage in which all spheres of human existence will be organically reunited.

Metaphysically, Soloviev backed this scheme by his philosophy of All-Unity (*vseed-instvo*). Following Hegel, he pointed out that the ultimate reality cannot be limited by any finite reality and therefore has to include all things. Soloviev departed from pantheism when he refused to identify God simply with everything there is. Soloviev drew many of his ideas from later Platonism, including the insight that God is beyond being as the source of all being, the power that holds everything in existence. However, if for Plotinus the unity of the supreme divine principle, the One, excluded all multiplicity, for Soloviev God was both one and all. Soloviev's metaphysical idealism is a version of panentheism (everything is in some sense included in God, but God is not everything) which takes into account the concern to maintain divine transcendence (God is distinct from creatures as their metaphysical ground and as the power of being) and divine unity (God is the interrelatedness of all things).

Soloviev argued that panentheism offered the most satisfactory solution to the metaphysical problem of relationship between the Absolute and the relative, the Infinite and the finite, the Creator and the created. Some metaphysical rivals of panentheism, such as monism, pantheism, and materialism, dissolved the problem by denying the existence of the ontological gulf between God and the world. Other ontologies, such as dualism and traditional theism, recognized the existence of the gulf, but failed to provide an adequate solution to how the gulf can be bridged. Panentheism was free from such limitations, since it both safeguarded the divine otherness and affirmed the world's ideal unity with God.

Soloviev drew upon the biblical concept of divine wisdom, Sophia, to capture this insight. For Soloviev, Sophia was the ideal humanity, eternally united and existing in God. Sophia was both created and uncreated: ontologically united with God and at the same time the living organic unity of all humanity. As such she is Divine-humanity, or Godmanhood (*Bogochelovechestvo*). Soloviev also identified Sophia with the World Soul and with the Body of Christ. Inspired by later Platonism, Soloviev located the origin of evil in the fall of the World Soul from the union with the divine principle. The purpose of history was to restore the unity between God and humanity. Soloviev argued that all core doctrines of the Church were reducible to a single foundational dogma of Godmanhood. Hence, sophiology came to bear upon all loci of systematic theology, including cosmology, Trinity, Incarnation, anthropology, ecclesiology, and eschatology. For Soloviev, Sophia was not only an abstract metaphysical entity, but also a personal being.

In his memoirs the Russian philosopher recalled having three quasi-erotic mystical encounters with Sophia, who manifested herself as the eternal feminine, a motif that had precedents in German mysticism and Romanticism. Soloviev found artistic expressions of his philosophical insight in the iconography of the Orthodox churches dedicated to St Sophia in Constantinople, Kiev, Novgorod, and elsewhere.

Bulgakov considered Soloviev his 'philosophical guide to Christ' and developed his sophiology by introducing a distinction between two modes of Sophia: creaturely and divine. Somewhat misleadingly, Bulgakov identified divine Sophia with the essence (*ousia*) of God (Bulgakov 1993). He located the ontological basis of the ideal humanity in the divine essence. Bulgakov reinterprets the act of creation out of nothing as the ontological separation of divine and creaturely aspects of Sophia. While historically redemption is associated with the work of Christ, metaphysically it corresponds to the return of creaturely Sophia to the unity with the divine Sophia. This reunion is to take place in the Church, which Bulgakov, following Soloviev and Florensky, saw as the most significant manifestation of Sophia. Another instantiation of creaturely Sophia reconciled to God was Mary, the Theotokos ('God-bearer'), in her deified, heavenly state.

Bulgakov was unapologetic about the highly speculative character of sophiology and saw it as an antidote against anti-dogmatic rationalism and historicism that prevailed in the West. Some of his Orthodox contemporaries, including Florovsky and Lossky, were not persuaded and regarded sophiology as a dead-end of Orthodox dogmatics. The church officials accused Bulgakov of introducing the fourth entity into the triune Godhead. More to the point, his opponents argued that Sophia was a superfluous metaphysical construct whose functions could be entirely subsumed by Christ, who as the Logos incarnate was Godman and the Wisdom of God. They observed that by identifying Sophia with the quasi-personal dimension of divine essence, rather than with the second person of the Trinity, Bulgakov introduced metaphysical assumptions that threatened to overshadow the soteriological centrality of the historical divine incarnation. In response to these objections Bulgakov insisted that the main intent of sophiology had been to give the fullest elucidation and the foundation of the central dogma of Godmanhood. While sophiology is unlikely to become a part of the future Orthodox dogmatics, there has been a resurgence of interest in this topic among contemporary theologians and historians (e.g., Kornblatt and Gustafson 1997; Valliere 2000). The permanent contribution of Soloviev and Bulgakov lies in making Godmanhood the conceptual framework for Christian anthropology, ecclesiology, eschatology, and political theory.

The onomatodoxic controversy

In the second decade of the twentieth century a controversy broke out in one of the Russian monasteries on Mount Athos in Greece. The subject of debate was the theology of the so-called Jesus prayer, the most common version of which reads: 'Jesus Christ, Son of God, have mercy upon me, a sinner.' The practitioners of this prayer, led by hieromonk Antonii Bulatovich (1870–1919), asserted that 'the name of God is God Himself' (Alfeyev 2002). Their intention was to establish a close ontological link between the uncreated divine energies on the one hand, and the act of naming God on the other hand. They claimed that the name of God participated in the reality of God. For this reason, they were called 'name-glorifiers.' Their opponents objected that such a close linking of God and his name verged on idolatry. The theological debate deteriorated into a violent confrontation between the monks and church hierarchy, which led to the forceful expulsion of more than a thousand 'name-glorifiers' from their monastery. Several Russian philosophers, including Pavel Florensky and Aleksei Losev, developed highly sophisticated theories of religious language in defense of the 'name-glorifiers.' The onomatodoxic controversy is the most important theological debate to emerge out of the spiritual experience of the Orthodox Church after the Palamite controversy of the fourteenth century. For this reason, the theology of prayer will continue to be of interest to the Orthodox theologians of the twenty-first century (Alfeyev 2002).

Orthodox political theology

Decades before the Bolshevik Revolution of 1917, Russian religious philosophers produced a devastating critique of Russian Marxism and Communism, unmasking their quasi-religious nature. Dostoevsky was the first to expose the demonic and dehumanizing character of atheistic socialism and terrorism in *The Demons* (1872). In the minds of Russian revolutionaries the socialist vision of justice became a powerful utopia fueled by millenarian hope to establish a Godless paradise of classless society on earth. As Bulgakov, Berdiaev, and others warned in a highly controversial collection of essays, *Landmarks* (1909), the fulfillment of this apocalyptic vision would require terrible sacrifices of human lives and freedom. They rightly foresaw that revolutionary socialism would lead to the personality cult of revolutionary leaders and idolatrous divinization of the power of the totalitarian state. Instead of leading humanity on the path of deification, Godless socialism will bring about man-god, a prophecy that became a tragic reality when Stalin came to power in the Soviet Union. It is regrettable that liberation theologians have largely ignored this criticism of Marxism in their work.

After the collapse of the Soviet Union, the Orthodox Church gradually rebuilt its educational institutions. The confrontation with the western culture of radical pluralism and postmodernity provoked a largely negative, conservative and anti-western reaction from the Church. The engagement of postmodern challenges has only begun, as evidenced by the work of David Hart in Orthodox theological aesthetics (Hart 2005). While the ideas of modernizing Orthodox theologians are being gradually rediscovered in the West, the neopatristic synthesis remains the dominant mode of theologizing.

See also The problem of evil (Chapter 37), The Trinity (Chapter 49), The Incarnation (Chapter 51).

References

Abraham, W. (1998) *Canon and Criterion in Christian Theology*, Oxford: Clarendon Press.

Alfeyev, H. (2002) *Sviashchennaia taina tserkvi: vvedenie v istoriiu i problematiku imiaslavskikh sporov*, 2 vols, St Petersburg: Aleteia.

Berdiaev, N. (1955) *The Meaning of the Creative Act*, trans. D. A. Lowrie, New York: Harper.

—— (1996) *Istina i otkrovenie*, St-Petersburg: Izdatel'stvo Russkogo Hristianskogo gumanitarnogo instituta.

—— (2002) *Russkaia ideia*, Moscow: AST.

Bulgakov, S. (1993) *Sophia: The Wisdom of God*, Hudson, NY: Lindisfarne Press.

Florovsky, G. (1937) *Puti russkogo bogosloviia*, 3rd edn, Paris: YMCA Press; English translation (1979) *Ways of Russian Theology*, trans. R. L. Nichols, Belmont, MA: Nordland Publishing Company.

—— (1972) *Bible, Church, Tradition: An Eastern Orthodox View*, Belmont, MA: Nordland Publishing Company.

Hart, D. B. (2005) *The Beauty of the Infinite: The Aesthetics of Christian Truth*, Grand Rapids, MI: Eerdmans.

Khomiakov, A. (1907) *Sochineniia bogoslovskiia*, Moscow: Kushnerev. Repr. 1995.

Kornblatt, J. D. and R. F. Gustafson (eds) (1997) *Russian Religious Thought*, Madison, WI: University of Wisconsin Press.

Milbank, J., C. Pickstock and G. Ward (eds) (1999) *Radical Orthodoxy: A New Theology*, London: Routledge.

Valliere, P. (2000) *Modern Russian Theology: Bukharev, Soloviev, Bulgakov*, Grand Rapids, MI: Eerdmans.

Ware, T. (1993) *The Orthodox Church*, Harmondsworth: Penguin.

Further reading

Lossky, V. (2002) *The Mystical Theology of the Eastern Church*, trans. members of the Fellowship of St Alban and St Sergius, Crestwood, NY: St Vladimir's Seminary Press. (An influential exposition of apophatic theology and Palamism by a leading neopatristic theologian of the twentieth century.)

Soloviev, V. (2005) *The Justification of the Good: An Essay on Moral Philosophy*, trans. B. Jakim, Grand Rapids, MI: Eerdmans. (The first systematic presentation of religious ethics in modern Russian religious thought.)

Staniloae, D. (1998) *The Experience of God*, trans. and ed. I. Ionita and R. Barringer, Brookline, MA: Holy Cross Orthodox Press. (The first volume of a multi-volume systematic theology, covering religious epistemology and the doctrine of the Trinity, by a prominent Romanian theologian who writes within the framework of neopatristic synthesis.)

Zizioulas, J. (1997) *Being as Communion: Studies in Personhood and the Church*, Crestwood, NY: St Vladimir's Seminary Press. (An influential account of Orthodox anthropology that develops relational ontology by synthesizing patristic thought and existentialism.)

45
PROTESTANT THEOLOGY

Daniel von Wachter

The Apostle Paul warned Christians: 'Beware lest any man spoil you through philosophy and vain deceit' (Col. 2: 8) and that the message of the cross is 'foolishness' (1 Cor. 1: 18) to non-Christians. However, in most Christian traditions this was taken to mean, not that Christian doctrine is really contrary to reason and that Christians should not cultivate thinking and argument, but only that there are philosophers whose teachings are contrary to Christianity and who consider Christianity to be foolish. As Christians have answers to the questions about the meaning of life already, they do not look for these answers in philosophy. But they can nevertheless pursue philosophy, as they can pursue any science, and they can use philosophy to spell out Christian doctrines and to consider arguments for and against their truth.

The philosophical discipline in which this is done today is called 'philosophy of religion,' or 'philosophical theology.' Often the former term is used for any philosophical investigaton of matters concerning God or religion, and the latter term for the philosophical analysis of specific doctrines or practices within a particular religion. (There is, however, as we shall see, another discipline that is also called 'philosophy of religion,' whose main founder was Friedrich Schleiermacher. It tends to presuppose the falsity of traditional Christian doctrine and is concerned not with doctrines but with religion as a human phenomenon.) The term 'philosophical theology' is the translation of *theologia rationalis*. Traditionally, metaphysics is divided into *metaphysica generalis*, which is ontology, and *metaphysica specialis*, which consists of philosophical theology, philosophy of mind (*psychologia rationalis*), and philosophical cosmology (*cosmologia rationalis*). Philosophical theology is thus a part of metaphysics.

Until relatively recently, there was not the division between theology and philosophy that there is now in many departments of theology. The philosophical method of analysis and argument is also the method of theology, and being a theologian entails therefore being a philosopher. This is also true for a large part of Protestant Christianity.

The Reformers

Martin Luther (1483–1546) sometimes spoke derogatorily about reason (*Vernunft*), even calling it a 'whore' of the devil, meaning that the devil has some power over it. Replying to Erasmus of Rotterdam's (1469–1536) defense of free will, he wrote that such delusions arise if reason is employed in order to understand God. He opposed the Scholastic theology of his day and its Aristotelian assumptions, but he did not hold that reason is entirely defunct. In his *Disputations about Man* (1536) he states: 'Even after Adam's fall God has not taken from reason its sovereignty but has rather confirmed it.' And we should keep in mind that at the Diet of Worms, when he was summoned to renounce his views, he famously answered that he cannot recant a word unless he is convicted by Scripture *and plain reason.*

Other reformers affirmed the value of philosophy and reason unambiguously. Philipp Melanchthon (1497–1560), for example, defended the harmony of reason and Christian revelation and endorsed parts of Aristotle's philosophy. Melanchthon's work in natural theology (i.e., the pursuit of knowledge of God through reason), inspired later Protestant work in this field, e.g., by Johann Gerhard (1582–1637). Also Erasmus of Rotterdam, although he endorsed the Reformation only partly, contributed to the development of Protestant philosophical theology. It was he who coined the term 'philosophia Christi.'

John Calvin (1509–64) sometimes defended his claims explicitly through 'natural reason.' Reason, he writes, 'could not be entirely destroyed; but being partly weakened and partly corrupted, a shapeless ruin is all that remains' (Calvin 1960: 2.2.12). Especially its ability to know God is corrupted: 'To the great truths, what God is in himself, and what he is in relation to us, human reason makes not the least approach' (ibid.) Karl Barth (1886–1968) later took this thought further and rejected natural theology and the use of philosophical method in theology in general. Calvin's main point is that reason cannot deliver knowledge of God that is as 'sure and firm' as is required by Christian faith, which entails an unwavering commitment to God. But apart from that, reason is still a God-given guide to truth. 'To charge the intellect with perpetual blindness, so as to leave it no intelligence of any description whatever, is repugnant not only to the Word of God, but to common experience' (Calvin 1960: 2.2.12).

The Reformation did not introduce a fundamentally new view about the relationship between faith and reason and about philosophy into Christianity. Like earlier theologians, the Reformers took the harmony between reason and Christian faith to be desirable and achievable. Like earlier theologians, they recognized, and perhaps emphasized relatively strongly, that reason is limited and debilitated through the Fall, and they acknowledged that philosophy can contribute to clarifying and defending Christian doctrine.

Protestant Scholasticism

Protestants continued to teach philosophy, for example Melanchthon at Wittenberg, Peter Martyr Vermigli (1500–62) at Oxford, Jerome Zanchi at Strassburg (1516–90), Conrad Gesner (1516–65) at Zurich, and Theodore Beza (1519–1605) at Geneva. There was a need and a desire to spell out Christian doctrine with the insights of the Reformation, and philosophy and logic were needed for this. As the type of philosophy pursued resembled medieval Scholastic philosophy, in its emphasis on logic but also its reliance on Aristotle, the theology of that period until around 1700 is called 'Protestant Scholasticism.'

The theologian, philosopher, and physicist Rudolph Goclenius (1547–1628) in Marburg was called 'Christian Artistotle,' 'Teacher of Germany,' and 'Light of Europe.' Goclenius's *Lexicon philosophicum* (1613) explains concepts from metaphysics, logic, and ethics. Here we find one of the first occurrences of the term 'ontology'! As with Melanchthon, philosophy for Goclenius was indispensable for theology, although it should always be a servant of theology. That does not mean that reason is defunct or that philosophy is not a guide to truth, but only that some truths about God are available only through revelation. Goclenius is also remarkable because of his defense of freedom of opinion, which is the object of his work *Conciliator philosophicus* (1609). He argued that freedom of opinion is essential for science (including theology and philosophy).

Johann Gerhard in Jena (1582–1637) developed, on the basis of the Lutheran doctrine of justification, a sophisticated theory of conversion. He uses Aristotelian philosophy to spell out the biblical doctrine. His nine volume *Loci theologici* is the most comprehensive and influential Lutheran work of theology at this time. Gerhard also developed a theory of verbal inspiration of Scripture. He ascribed to the Bible *auctoritas* (i.e., the Bible is the source and norm for Christian doctrine), *perfectio et sufficientia* (i.e., the Bible does not need any additions), *perspicuitas* (i.e., the Bible is understandable and explains itself), and *efficacia* (i.e., the Bible induces faith). There were disagreements among Protestants at that time about issues such as whether the vowels in the Hebrew Bible are inspired, but all – Lutherans as well as Calvinists – agreed that the Bible is inspired by God verbally. Philosophy is used to spell out the doctrines contained in the Bible.

Christoph Scheibler (1589–1653), a Lutheran theologian who taught mainly in Dortmund, presented in his *Opus metaphysicum* a metaphysical theory that was inspired by Francisco Suárez. He also adopted Suárez's method to discuss all possible objections thoroughly. Among Scheibler's numerous works there is a major work in natural theology, *Theologia naturalis et angelographia*, and writings on logic in which he develops Melanchthon's logic further.

Like the Lutheran Scholastics (and, we may say, virtually all Christian theologians until Kant) the Reformed Scholastics also used metaphysics in theology. A particularly able philosopher was Francis Turretin (1623–87), who taught at the theological academy in Geneva. His main work, *Institutio Theologiae Electicae*, was widely used as a textbook, by later Calvinist scholars also. For Turretin 'scriptural exegesis and metaphysical argumentation are compatible' (Rehnman 2002: 168); he spells out and investigates doctrines he takes from the Bible with the methods of metaphysics and relates them to other metaphysical claims. Reason is also a presupposition of revelation: in order to understand a revelation, the nature of the revealer has to be known at least rudimentarily. 'Turretin, therefore, talks of the presupposed object of the articles of saving faith which is known from natural theology and sound reason, and which teaches, among other things, the existence of a just, wise, and good God, and the immortality of the soul' (Rehnman 2002: 170).

Cambridge Platonism

In England the harmony between faith and reason was particularly strongly emphasized by a group of Protestant philosophers called the 'Cambridge Platonists,' who were 'the first philosophers to write primarily and consistently in the English language' (Hutton 2001). Among them were Ralph Cudworth (1617–88), Henry More (1614–87), and Benjamin Whichcote (1609–83). They often called reason 'the Candle of the Lord.' For More, the 'intellect of man is as it were a small compendious transcript of the divine intellect' (Taliaferro 2005: 26).

In his *Antidote against Atheism* (1652), Henry More presents an ontological argument as well as an argument from design for the existence of God. He points out, however, that although theism deserves 'full assent from any unprejudiced mind,' we are of course fallible. It is epistemically *possible* that the evidence there is for the existence of God is misleading. He illustrates this with the story that two men go to the top of Mount Athos where they find an altar with ashes on it which exhibit the words *Deo Optimo Maximo*. This is very good evidence that some humans have written these words into the ashes, but there is a *possibility* that some wind has moved the ashes thus. Nevertheless we are justified in assuming that the ashes were moved by human beings: 'we may give full assent to that which notwithstanding may possibly be otherwise' (in Taliaferro 2005: 17). One should keep this in mind when one evaluates Immanuel Kant's arguments against the possibility of metaphysics, because Kant assumed and postulated that metaphysics must bring apodictic certainty. It is a matter of debate which metaphysicians in the history of philosophy assumed or hoped for apodictic certainty for their claims, or whether any did.

Against their Calvinist contemporaries, the Cambridge Platonists affirmed human freedom, which we have as we are created in the image of God. Cudworth explains in his *Treatise of Freewill* that it is not perfect freedom, but we 'seem clearly to be led by the instincts of nature to think that there is something … in our own power (though dependently upon God Almighty), and that we are not altogether passive in our actings, nor determined by inevitable necessity in whatever we do' (in Taliaferro 2005: 33). It was perhaps their affirmation of free will that led them to call for freedom of opinion. Whichcote writes: 'A man has as much right to use his own understanding in judging of truth as he has a right to use his own eyes to see his way. There it is no offense to another that any man uses his own right' (Taliaferro 2005: 36). They were criticized for this, even though the freedom of opinion they called for was limited: atheism was not to be tolerated.

British Protestant philosophy of religion continued

The philosophical defense of freedom of opinion and of religion was pursued further by John Locke (1632–1704) in his *Letter Concerning Toleration* (1685). (We may take Locke to be a Protestant, although there are some reasons for saying that he was a Unitarian.) Like the Cambridge Platonists, he emphasized fallibilism: reason is a guide to truth and we do have knowledge, but it is based on evidence that supports our beliefs more or less strongly and does not make error strictly impossible. Locke writes: 'In the greatest part of our concernment, he [God] has afforded us only the twilight, as I may so say, of probability, suitable, I presume, to that state of mediocrity and probationership, he has been pleased to place us in here, wherein to check our over-confidence and presumption' (*An Essay Concerning Human Understanding*, IV. 14. 2). That reason, within these limits, is also a guide to truths about God, Locke argues in his book *The Reasonableness of Christianity as Delivered in the Scriptures* (1695). He explicates the essential Christian doctrines through exposition of the Bible and defends them. That Jesus is the Messiah, he argues, is confirmed by, among other things, a 'multitude of miracles' and in particular by Jesus' resurrection. He affirms that there is reasonable support for belief in the existence of God: 'The works of nature, in every part of them, sufficiently evidence a deity.' There can be, for Locke, truths that we cannot know through reason but only through revelation, but we should never believe something that contradicts reason. Revelation can be above reason but not against reason.

Locke's epistemology in which all knowledge was a matter of degrees of probability was developed further and applied in natural theology by the Anglican Bishop Joseph Butler (1692–1752). He came from a Presbyterian family but entered the Church of England in 1714, when he moved to Oxford and became a student at Oriel College. In 1738 he became Bishop of Bristol, in 1750 Bishop of Durham. His main work, *The Analogy of Religion, Natural and Revealed* (1736), constitutes the most thorough criticism of deism of his time. Butler admired Samuel Clarke (1675–1729), who was the leading apologist for the Christian religion in his generation. But he found that Clarke's arguments for the existence of God and against deism and Spinozism were too rigid. 'If they succeed they are incontrovertible: but if they fail, they are simply fallacies, and carry no weight at all' (Lucas 1978). In response, Butler developed 'very probable arguments' (he synonymously calls them 'probable proofs') by which he meant arguments that make it more reasonable to believe the thesis in question. In the beginning of his main work, *The Analogy of Religion, Natural and Revealed*, he writes: '*Probable* evidence is essentially distinguished from demonstrative by this, that it admits of degrees; and of all variety of them, from the highest moral certainty, to the very lowest presumption' (ibid.). His endeavor is to weigh the evidence concerning the existence of God and concerning the truth of Christianity. The best arguments available are not deductive arguments, where the premises contradict the denial of the conclusion, but inductive arguments, where the premises raise the probability of the conclusion. He makes a cumulative case for Christianity, emphasizing that we must take all available evidence into account. Skeptics of Christianity often make the mistake of confusing the claim that a thesis can be doubted or criticized with the claim that the thesis is false or irrational to believe:

> Yet there are people absurd enough to take the supposed doubtfulness of religion for the same thing as proof of its falsehood, after they have concluded it doubtful from hearing it often called in question. This shews how infinitely unreasonable sceptical men are, with regard to religion, and that they really lay aside their reason on this subject as much as the most extravagant enthusiasts. (ibid.)

Butler's project of a cumulative case for theism using inductive arguments was taken up more than 250 years later by another member of Oriel College: Richard Swinburne. We will come back to his work.

Around this time in British colonial America, the preacher, theologian, philosopher, and missionary Jonathan Edwards (1703–58) was writing significant, rich treatises and essays in philosophical theology that are being carefully studied today. Particularly influential was his defense of Calvinist theology. Edwards was fascinated by science and saw no conflict between science and his faith. William Paley (1743–1805), another promoter of natural theology in Britain, in the generation after Butler, was an Anglican priest. In his book *Natural Theology, or Evidences of the Existence and Attributes of the Deity collected from the Appearances of Nature* (1802), he presents the famous watchmaker argument for the existence of God. He asks the reader to imagine that he finds a watch somewhere in nature, in which case he would surely rightly assume that somebody made the watch. By analogy, he explains, it is rational to assume that a sufficiently powerful personal being – namely God – made the universe. In *A View of the Evidences of Christianity* (1794), Paley presupposes the existence of God and provides evidence for other Christian doctrines.

The tradition of Protestant natural theology was continued, for example, by Thomas Chalmers (1780–1847) and William Cunningham (1805–61), both Scottish evangelicals. Chalmers wrote the first 'Bridgewater treatise.' Francis Henry Egerton, Eighth Earl of Bridgewater (1756–1829) had left £8,000 to be paid to authors who wrote 'On the Power, Wisdom and Goodness of God, as manifested in the Creation.' The eight books that were awarded a prize were called 'Bridgewater Treatises.' In Scotland at that time there was a particularly lively debate about miracles. As George Campbell (1719–96) had already done, he extensively criticized David Hume's essay 'On miracles.'

Adam Lord Gifford bequeathed £80,000 to the four Scottish universities for the establishment of a series of lectures to 'promote and diffuse the study of Natural Theology in the widest sense of the term – in other words, the knowledge of God.' These 'Gifford Lectures' began in 1885 and have been delivered continuously since then.

German philosophy of religion until Kant

In Germany after the Protestant Scholastics mentioned earlier, two Protestants who contributed to the philosophy of religion were Christian Thomasius (1655–1724) and Christian von Wolff (1679–1754). Thomasius is best known for his defense of natural law theory, where he followed Hugo Grotius (1583–1645) and Samuel von Pufendorf (1632–97). At the University of Leipzig he was the first to lecture in German. Under Philipp Jakob Spener's (1635–1705) influence, he became sympathetic to pietism. He emphasized that man's will is evil and that revealed religion and salvation through Christ are necessary.

Wolff sought to make philosophy and theology more rigorous. He emphasized the need to give clear and precise definitions, to defend the premises of one's arguments, and to give valid arguments. Kant later called this 'dogmatic.' Wolff found revelation and reason to be compatible and gave arguments for the existence of God. God is, according to Wolff, a perfect being, a being without limits and without any change, who exists necessarily. He has the source of his existence in his own essence; he is an *ens a se*. God's perfection is mirrored by the world. Wolff was expelled from the University of Halle when some Thomasians and some pietists charged him of denial of free will and of deism.

While the pietists in Halle tended to hold that reason must be subordinated to revelation, the pietists in Königsberg did not share these worries. Martin Knutzen (1713–51), for example, was a pietist too in that he emphasized the need of conversion and sanctification (i.e., the progressive spiritual transformation of the soul following conversion), but he employed Wolff's philosophical method to produce a *Philosophical Proof of the Truth of the Christian Religion*, published in German (*Philosophischer Beweis von der Wahrheit der christlichen Religion*) in 1747 in Königsberg. It is a remarkably comprehensive philosophical defense of Christianity.

A new conception of 'reason'

In the eighteenth century a new movement developed, abandoning philosophical theology and the traditional idea that there is a harmony between faith and reason, and this led to what today is called 'liberal theology' in Protestant churches. The two main features of this movement are as follows: first, it is said that miracles and traditional Christian doctrine are contrary to reason and that one cannot believe in them anymore. Second, nevertheless it is not said that Christian doctrine is false or that atheism is true, but instead Christianity is modified so that it fits with the denial of miracles.

This movement is a part of the 'Enlightenment.' The term 'Enlightenment' is usually used so that it includes Thomasius and Wolff, and its main defining feature is taken to be a strong reliance on reason. The problem with this usage is that Protestant Scholasticism (as well as most earlier European philosophy) also strongly relied on reason but is not taken to be a part of the Enlightenment. The history of philosophy here perhaps could be carved up more adequately by defining

'Enlightenment' through the claim that miracles and traditional Christian doctrine are incompatible with reason. Thomasius and Wolff then would not be part of the Enlightenment. The Enlightenment in this narrower sense can be called 'anti-super-naturalist Enlightenment.' Sometimes the term 'modernism' is used to refer to the claim that traditional Christian doctrine is incompatible with reason and 'modern thinking,' and the term 'revisionism' to refer to attempts to revise Christianity so that it accords with reason.

One can see the Jewish philosopher Baruch Spinoza (1632–77) as a forerunner of this movement. Certainly Herman Samuel Reimarus (1694–1768) was one. He held that Jesus taught a 'natural' and 'practical' religion whereas the disciples taught a supernatural religion. Jesus preached the kingdom of God but recognized his illusion when he was crucified. The disciples stole Jesus' body and invented the resurrection, the ascension, and the message of salvation through Christ. Despite his views, Reimarus stayed in the Protestant Church. He sought to change the Church so that it would adhere to 'natural religion' and give up belief in miracles and revelation.

Many theologians in the nineteenth and twentieth centuries based their rejection of traditional Christian doctrine and their turn to revisionist forms of Christianity on the philosophy of Immanuel Kant (1724–1804) and the alleged 'end of traditional metaphysics.' In particular, Kant is taken to have refuted all traditional arguments for the existence of God; he developed a conception of religion in which morality is the essence of religion; and he gave a moral argument for the existence of God in a revised sense.

The most influential proponent of revisionist theology was the Prussian theologian Friedrich Schleiermacher (1768–1834). He claimed that 'religion is not, as one usually thinks, knowledge or acting, metaphysics or morality, or a combination of both. But it is contemplating and feeling the universe, the infinite, the eternal within the temporal' (Schleiermacher 1958: 277). This is a radically new idea. Christianity, traditionally conceived, contains doctrines about God, Jesus Christ, Jesus' resurrection, sin, judgment, life after death, atonement, etc. Christians believe them to be true and take them to be *reasons* to live and act in certain ways; for example, to repent and pray and ask God for forgiveness, to help the sick, to endure persecution, or to rejoice.

So, on the one hand, there are the doctrines; on the other hand, there are the actions that Christians choose because they believe the doctrines to be true. Schleiermacher, convinced that one cannot believe traditional Christian doctrine anymore, abandons exactly this combination. While others who, likewise, could no longer believe in Christian doctrine gave up religion or reduced it to morality, Schleiermacher held that religion is, or is to be replaced by, a feeling (of dependence). Schleiermacher can be seen as the founder of the discipline that in German is also called 'philosophy of religion' (*Religionsphilosophie*), but he is concerned with religion as a human phenomenon without investigating the truth of religious doctrines.

The idea that traditional Christian doctrine is contrary to reason has prevailed in German Protestant theology ever since Kant. Georg Wilhelm Friedrich Hegel (1770–1831), although he professed to be an orthodox Lutheran, held that 'the aim and essence of all true religion,' including the Christian religion, is human morality.

Albrecht Ritschl (1822–89) identified the 'kingdom of God' with the moral ideals of which Jesus gave an example. Justification, for him, is not liberation from guilt but liberation from the feeling of guilt. Rudolf Bultmann (1884–1976) famously wrote:

> It is impossible to use electric light and the wireless and to avail ourselves of modern medical and surgical discoveries, and at the same time to believe in the New Testament world of spirits and miracles. (Bultmann 1961: 4–5)

Instead of giving up Christianity, however, Bultmann sought to 'demythologize' it (i.e., to give new meanings to the Christian doctrines so that they do not claim anything supernatural anymore but only express 'existential' attitudes such as hope). Karl Barth (1886–1968) objected to this attempt to make Christianity palatable to reason (or to what Bultmann and Barth took to be reason) and claimed that theology should not attempt to make Christian faith reasonable. Consequently he rejected all natural theology.

German post-Kantian Protestant theology in all its major strands holds that traditional Christian doctrine is not in harmony with reason, and it rejects philosophy of religion in the sense of philosophical theology as we find it, for example, in Protestant Scholasticism, in Martin Knutzen, or in pre-Reformation theology.

The renaissance of philosophy of religion and philosophical theology

Today, however, philosophy of religion and the more specific discipline of philosophical theology are as strong as they have ever been. Christians as well as atheists participate in the debate and defend their metaphysical views. In the first half of the twentieth century, logical positivism prevailed in Anglo-Saxon philosophy and declared all religious claims and all metaphysical claims in general to be meaningless. But in the 1970s philosophers who were Christians and were convinced neither by positivism nor by Kant, Schleiermacher, or Bultmann began to occupy themselves with metaphysical questions about God and religion. This movement took shape when in 1977 the Society of Christian Philosophers (SCP) was founded on the initiative of William Alston, who is an Episcopalian, together with, among others, Alvin Plantinga, Nicholas Wolterstorff, and George Mavrodes. Its journal *Faith and Philosophy* soon became the leading journal for the philosophy of religion. Besides the SCP, where anyone can become a member who considers himself a Christian and a philosopher, the Evangelical Philosophical Society, whose members have to affirm the full trustworthiness of the Bible, was formed in 1974. It re-launched its journal *Philosophia Christi*, 'for the scholarly discussion of philosophy and philosophical issues in the fields of ethics, theology, and religion' in 1999, which since then has been growing steadily in reputation and numbers of subscriptions.

Also beginning in the 1970s, in Britain, Richard Swinburne, who was the Nolloth Professor for the Philosophy of the Christian Religion at Oriel College, Oxford (1985-2002), began to produce the most comprehensive and thorough philosophical explication and defense of theism and Christianity of our time. Originally he was an

Anglican but is now Russian Orthodox. In *The Coherence of Theism* (1977) Swinburne discusses how the attributes of God are best spelled out, and he defends the coherence of the claim 'There is a God.' In *The Existence of God* (1979) he makes a cumulative case for the existence of God using Bayes's Theorem and taking into account modern science. The nature of faith, and the question of under which conditions a religious belief and a religious commitment are rational are investigated in *Faith and Reason* (1986). In *Responsibility and Atonement* (1989) Swinburne first pursues general questions concerning goodness and guilt and then considers how and under which conditions God might forgive or punish. *Revelation* (1992) investigates what would show that some book or creed conveys revealed truth and considers in particular the Bible and the Christian Creeds. The doctrines of the Trinity and of the Incarnation Swinburne explores in *The Christian God* (1994). Why God might allow evil to occur is discussed in *Providence and the Problem of Evil* (1998). More recently, Swinburne presented arguments for the resurrection of Jesus in *The Resurrection of God Incarnate* (2003).

While Swinburne seeks to give positive arguments for the truth of Christianity, Alvin Plantinga, who is from the Reformed Christian tradition, rather defends the rationality of Christian beliefs without giving arguments for their truth. He argues that belief in God can be 'properly basic' (i.e., rational without being supported through evidence). In *Warranted Christian Belief* (2000) Plantinga argues that Christian beliefs probably are knowledge if they are true. Another influential contribution to the new debate about the epistemology of religious belief is William Alston's book, *Perceiving God* (1991), in which he first presents a general account of justification through perception and then argues that perception of God is possible and would make belief in God rational.

The philosophy of religion has become so lively that it is impossible to survey it in a few paragraphs. Generally today's philosophers of religion do not share Kant's or Schleiermacher's sentiment that nowadays one cannot believe in miracles and in traditional Christian doctrine. Neither theistic analytic philosophers nor atheist philosophers of religion find the Schleiermacherian approach convincing. Commenting on the Bultmann passage above, the Christian philosopher Peter van Inwagen observes: 'If Bultmann knew of some reason for believing this assertion, he did not share it with his readers' (van Inwagen 1995: 3). He then points out that analytic philosophers tend to be straightforward atheists or else 'religious in a very old-fashioned way,' having belief in a personal God and miracles.

> Any sort of 'liberal' or 'secularized' or 'modernist' religion (religion of Bultmann's sort) tends to be regarded with disdain by philosophers, who view modernist versions of Christianity or Judaism as irreligion wearing a disguise that they are professionally incapable of not seeing through. (1995: 6)

Thus there is a great divide today between Schleiermacherian theologians and analytic philosophers of religion. The Schleiermacherians consider the analytic philosophers to be naive, and the analytic philosophers consider the Schleiermacherians' hostility to the supernatural irrational and think that the Schleiermacherians do not have any arguments.

See also Christianity (Chapter 6), David Hume (Chapter 13), Immanuel Kant (Chapter 14), Truth in religion (Chapter 18), Religious traditions and rational assessments (Chapter 19), Revelation (Chapter 50), Sin and salvation (Chapter 53), Reformed epistemology (Chapter 58), Continental philosophy (Chapter 60).

References

Bultmann, R. (1961) *Kerygma and Myth*, ed. H. W. Bartsch, New York: Harper.

Calvin, J. (1960) *Institutes of the Christian Religion*, trans. F. L. Battles, Philadelphia: Westminster Press.

Edwards, J. (1980) *The Works of Jonathan Edwards: Scientific and Philosophical Writings*, ed. W. E. Anderson, New Haven, CT: Yale University Press.

Hutton, S. (2001) 'Cambridge Platonists,' in E. N. Zalta (ed.) *The Stanford Encyclopedia of Philosophy*. Online at: <http://plato.stanford.edu/archives/win2001/entries/cambridge-platonists/>.

Lucas, J. R. (1978) *Butler's Philosophy of Religion Vindicated (Durham Cathedral Lecture)*, Durham: Dean & Chapter. Online at: <http://users.ox.ac.uk/~jrlucas/theology/butler.html>.

Rehnman, S. (2002) 'Theistic metaphysics and biblical exegesis: Francis Turretin on the concept of God,' *Religious Studies* 38: 167–86.

Schleiermacher, F. (1958) *On Religion, Speeches to its Cultured Despisers*, trans. J. Oman, New York: Harper & Row.

Taliaferro, C. (2005) *Evidence and Faith: Philosophy and Religion since the Seventeenth Century*, Cambridge: Cambridge University Press.

van Inwagen, P. (1995) *God, Knowledge, and Mystery*, Ithaca, NY: Cornell University Press.

Further reading

Butler, J. (2005) *The Analogy of Religion, Natural and Revealed*, Ann Arbor, MI: Scholarly Publishing Office/University of Michigan Library. (Presents a cumulative case for the existence of God.)

Clark, K. J. (ed.) (1993) *Philosophers Who Believe*, Downers Grove, IL: InterVarsity Press. (Eleven analytic philosophers' descriptions of their spiritual journeys.)

Moreland, J. P. and W. L. Craig (2003) *Philosophical Foundations for a Christian Worldview*, Downers Grove, IL: InterVarsity Press. (A comprehensive introduction to the main disciplines of philosophy from a Christian perspective.)

Plantinga, A. (1984) 'Advice to Christian philosophers,' *Faith and Philosophy* 1/3: 253–71. Also online at: <http://leaderu.com>. (Plantinga's suggestions to Christian philosophers to do their work in a distinctively Christian way.)

46
PROCESS THEOLOGY
John B. Cobb, Jr.

History

Process thought has been part of the western philosophical tradition since Heraclitus. However, it played little role in philosophy of religion prior to Hegel. Hegel contributed to the fully historical thinking about religion that is a necessary element in any processive philosophy of religion or theology.

Process theology emerged in the Divinity School of the University of Chicago. Toward the end of the nineteenth century, the Chicago school developed the processive understanding of religion and theology by the socio-historical method. It understood Christianity as a socio-historical movement whose formulations of belief and projects of action reflected the conditions and thought forms of successive historical epochs.

The distinctiveness of Christianity is its historical rise in Israel around the person and teaching of Jesus and the response he evoked. Through all the subsequent changes many people attempted to follow him. How to do this responsibly depended on analysis of the situation. In the late nineteenth and early twentieth centuries, Shirley Jackson Case and Shailer Matthews at the University of Chicago identified democracy and science as the crucial features of their situation, which shaped the form Christianity should take.

The interest in science was particularly important for the development of this school of thought. Evolutionary theory supported a radically processive view of the coming into being of living creatures and of the explosion of species. Whereas previously, science had treated its subject matter in primarily static ways, evolutionary thought spread beyond biology so that the universe as a whole came to be conceived as the result of a process and as now in process. Evolutionary theory also brought human beings fully into this processive physical nature.

There was much fresh thinking about the assumptions of physics and its relation to human self-understanding. Earlier, physics had treated the natural world as matter in motion, and for some the inclusion of human beings within nature meant that we are exhaustively explainable in this way. However, new developments in physics suggested that the quanta that make up the world are not little bits of matter. Perhaps they are better understood as events or processes.

The Chicago school was keenly interested in the new thinking developing among scientists. It was convinced that this provided possibilities for rethinking the implications of Jesus for our time in a non-reductive, non-deterministic, scientific context. Whereas theologians elsewhere generally favored a dualism, based on Kantian philosophy, the Chicago school wanted an integrated understanding of scientific knowledge and human meaning.

A promising philosopher-scientist was Alfred North Whitehead, who moved from England to Harvard in 1924. His thinking was remarkably congenial to such American philosophers as William James, John Dewey, and Charles Saunders Peirce. In 1925 he published *Science and the Modern World* (Whitehead 1925) which included discussion of the nature and role of religion. This was followed the next year by *Religion in the Making* (Whitehead 1927).

The Chicago theologians were startled by this book by a mathematical physicist who, until shortly before this time, was a professed atheist. In his effort to understand the cosmos, Whitehead concluded that the order in the world, apart from which there could be no definite things, derived from a prior order in the sphere of potentiality. This order, which at once limits and provides novelty, could not occur or affect the world except through a cosmic actuality. The theologians were not accustomed to this degree of realism. They invited a philosopher of religion, Henry Nelson Wieman, to explain the book to them, and they subsequently invited him to join the faculty. Shortly thereafter, in 1928, Charles Hartshorne, an assistant of Whitehead at Harvard, joined the Department of Philosophy and accepted a joint appointment in the Divinity School.

Wieman and Hartshorne drew from Whitehead in different ways. Wieman was a radical empiricist, that is, one who wanted to stay close to experience understood as including much more than sensation and thought. For him the deepest religious need is to have confidence in the reality in which we place our trust. He undertook so to describe that process in which human good grows that its reality could not be doubted, and to show that we can trust it without knowing what the outcome will be. He called for faith in 'creative transformation,' which he sometimes called 'God' (Wieman 1946).

Hartshorne was a rationalistic metaphysician preoccupied with the nature of God. For him, process thinking corrected traditional misconceptions and thereby removed obstacles to belief. The main problem with traditional arguments for God was the incoherence of the idea of God. Given a coherent idea, one that fitted well with what we know of a processive universe, valid arguments could be formulated (Hartshorne 1941). Hartshorne devoted special attention to a form of the ontological argument (Hartshorne 1965).

Both thinkers could draw on Whitehead's philosophy. Whitehead had developed a conceptually rigorous understanding of relational experience that supported radical empiricism. He emphasized that all thinking arises in experience and that all ideas must be tested against it. He also believed that most experience is not human. There are electronic occasions of experience on the one side and divine experience on the other. His theoretical development of the nature and role of the divine experience provided much of the grist that Hartshorne refined and elaborated in his metaphysics.

Whitehead's own program had been quite different from both. For him religious issues were part of a broad cosmological reconstruction (Whitehead 1929). This required the extension of the hypothetical or speculative method from the sciences to a comprehensive theory that includes metaphysical elements. His method was to propose hypotheses, draw forth their implications, and then test them. His most general hypothesis is that events or experiences are more fundamental than enduring substances and objects. This requires testing in all the natural sciences as well as socio-historical and humanistic fields. Religious experience and beliefs are among these.

Employment of the speculative method does not depend on any fixed foundation, and it does not build to certain conclusions. Everything is open to correction in the light of new evidence. This is true of the sciences, and certainly also of the cosmology. But this tentativeness does not lead to skepticism. There is a vast body of knowledge that, for most practical purposes, is well established and reliable. Change in science and in cosmology usually consists in incorporating into a larger context that can explain new data as well as what was previously known. A process cosmology does not require abandonment of all that has been learned by those who have understood the world to be composed of matter in motion.

Whitehead's cosmology depicts a world in which everything is so interrelated that academic approaches that divide up the data already distort them. Philosophy should not be separated from other fields, and religious thinking cannot be separated from other forms. Philosophy of religion is integrated into process philosophy as a whole, as in the three-volume work of Frederick Ferré (Ferré 1996; 1998; 2001).

Insofar as the faculty at Chicago used a term for what they shared it was 'neo-naturalism.' In addition to the radical empiricists, the rationalistic metaphysicians, and the speculative cosmologists, there were other neo-naturalists who drew on multiple naturalist traditions. Bernard Meland represents this stance. He continued the historical emphasis of the earlier Chicago school, enriching it with cultural and aesthetic motifs. Bernard Loomer moved across all these boundaries, but is best located here.

The Chicago school broke up in the 1950s and 1960s with key faculty going to Harvard, Union, Princeton, Emory, and the Graduate Theological Union. The heirs of neo-naturalism have continued to express their commonality and differences in the Highland Institute and the *Journal of American Philosophy and Theology*. They are now more likely to call themselves naturalists, pragmatists, radical empiricists, or histori-cists than neo-naturalists.

During the 1950s, Loomer spoke of 'process theology,' and this term rapidly came into general use. All branches of the Chicago school thought in processual terms, but 'process theology' has tended to name the work of those who followed Whitehead and Hartshorne most closely. This tradition has been promoted by the Center for Process Studies, which I founded in 1973 with David Griffin at the Claremont School of Theology, and by its journal, *Process Studies*, established and long edited by Lewis Ford.

At Chicago, instead of a department of 'systematic theology' there was a department of 'constructive theology.' The idea was that recent intellectual changes in the nineteenth and twentieth centuries were so drastic that students needed to rethink religious beliefs for themselves. The results were generally at the periphery of church theology. This kind of process thinking continues to this day.

However, as the conceptualities of Whitehead and Hartshorne were more fully appropriated, their fruitfulness for broader use in mainstream theology was recognized. In the 1960s, a Chicago graduate, Schubert Ogden, synthesized a Hartshornian understanding of God with a Bultmannian understanding of human existence and Christology (Ogden 1961; 1963). Daniel Day Williams wrote *The Spirit and the Forms of Love*, which remains the best Whiteheadian systematic theology (Williams 1968). Since then process categories have been applied to many traditional theological topics. William Beardslee developed the connection between process thought and biblical studies. Chalice Press is publishing a commentary series on the Beardslee model (Beardslee 1994) written from this perspective. There is extensive process writing also on preaching, Christian education, and pastoral counseling.

Whitehead influenced William Temple and Lionel Thornton in England and, in the United States, Norman Pittenger, who adopted the 'process' label (Pittenger 1968). The context for these thinkers was Anglicanism rather than American naturalism. After Vatican II, Catholic followers of Teilhard recognized affinities with Whitehead. The first book to bear the title 'Process Theology' was edited by Ewert Cousins, a leading Catholic theologian, and consisted of essays by Whiteheadians and Teilhardians (Cousins 1971). Although the openness of Catholics to process theology has decreased, close relations between Teilhardians and Whiteheadians continue. For a while there was a strong Whiteheadian influence at Yale.

The movement of process thinking was further broadened by Griffin's labeling his SUNY Series 'Constructive Postmodernism,' which includes several volumes by Griffin himself (Griffin 2001). The term 'postmodern' had been used sporadically by process thinkers since the 1960s. The later French movement that gave 'postmodernism' wide currency reinforced many Whiteheadian criticisms of modernity, but it concluded on a 'deconstructive' note. Whiteheadians joined with other constructive critics of modernity in emphasizing *re*construction.

Standard teaching

The greatest contribution of Whitehead to philosophy may be his doctrine of 'physical prehension.' A prehension is the way one occasion of experience participates in the constitution of another, most effectively in its immediate successor. Each occasion feels the feelings of preceding occasions. A physical prehension is also called a 'causal feeling,' since it is the way causality works in the world. Each new occasion is a creative synthesis of prehensions of past occasions, because just how it constitutes itself out of these prehensions is decided only in its act of becoming. Viewing the world in terms of these prehensive integrations changes everything, including the way we think of God.

The best-known feature of process theology is, accordingly, its proposal of an alternative theism. Theism has long been identified with the idea that there is an absolute, timeless, impassible, and immutable being. Whitehead and Hartshorne do not deny that in some respects these characteristics apply to God, but they regard this aspect of deity as abstract. What is concretely actual is a universal prehensive unification, enduring through time, and, therefore, in some respects, changing.

Consider the New Testament emphasis on God's love. This character of God is unchanging. But precisely this unchanging character of God involves God's feelings of the feelings in the world that God loves. God as unchanging love rejoices in human joy and sorrows with human misery. As time passes and the world changes, so does God's experience of the world. It grows as new events occur.

Hartshorne argues this partly in terms of the nature of perfection. The Greeks thought of perfection as invulnerability. To be vulnerable is to be subject to being hurt by others. That was seen as an imperfect condition. Hence, if God is perfect, God is not subject to being affected by others. Under the influence of Greek values, the Church projected invulnerability on God. However, the supreme biblical value is love, and the lover in affected by what happens to the loved one. Accordingly, perfection is total empathy or compassion. Process theologians believe they are releasing biblical wisdom from imprisonment by Greek ideals.

The view that God suffers in and with the suffering world has gained considerable currency among Christians. Process theologians may be alone, however, in holding that this teaching makes more sense philosophically as well as theologically than the traditional one it replaces. For both Whitehead and Hartshorne, since all actualities feel, experience, empathize with, or 'prehend' other actualities, God as an actuality does so in an unlimited or perfect way.

Process theologians also offer distinctive views of God's knowledge and power. They join the tradition in affirming omniscience. God knows all actuality as actuality and all possibility as possibility, but they oppose the traditional view that omniscience implies exact foreknowledge of future events. Because events include an element of self-determination, perfect knowledge includes knowledge of what *may* be decided but not of exactly what *will* happen.

Process theologians affirm that God has ideal power. This power is God's causal efficacy in the world. That means that all occasions in the world experience or prehend God, thereby incorporating God into their own becoming. But this ideal power is not a monopoly of power. Optimum power can be exercised only where there are other powers. It is the ability, not to control or destroy, but to empower and influence.

Many Christians and Jews suppose that the idea that God does or could determine everything is biblical. However, process theologians argue that there is little basis for it in the Bible. The doctrine of creation out of nothing, with which its history is closely connected, is not biblical. The word 'almighty,' frequently used in translations of Genesis, Exodus, and Job replaces a proper name of a deity, *Shaddai*, which has no such connotation. In short, almightiness or omnipotence has been read into the Bible from outside by those who worshiped controlling power. The Bible depicts God much more as interacting with free agents than as controlling puppets. Here, too, process theologians believe they are releasing the Bible from alien interpretation.

Since most process theologians come from the tradition of socio-historical understanding of the Bible, they need not suppose that the ideas they reject have no grounding whatsoever in biblical texts. The Christians among them emphasize the prophetic tradition and want to be faithful to Jesus. If Jesus is like God, as they believe, then God is not an absolute, immutable, omnipotent being controlling all events. God is much better imaged as a loving parent whom Jesus called *Abba*, who knows and understands what people are experiencing, feels with them, and encourages, empowers, and liberates them.

This shift in the understanding of divine power is a major emphasis of process theologians. It supports, and has been enriched and deepened by, the feminist critique of patriarchy. Most process theologians have also supported liberation movements generally and resist the American imperial project.

Process theologians believe that the traditional view of divine control over all things distorts the revelation in Jesus and the theology of Paul and has also done great harm. It leads to contradictions that are misnamed paradoxes. In this model the more power is attributed to God, the more humans are disempowered. If everything happens as God wills it to happen, then God is responsible for all sin, yet nothing is more central to biblical thinking than human responsibility. No wonder thoughtful humanists often become atheists! This kind of God must 'die' if humans are to live. Otherwise people are required to believe nonsense or be charged with heresy.

Those who believe that controlling power is godlike are likely to seek to exercise this 'godlike' control over others: husbands over wives, parents over children, rulers over subjects. A tradition that arose as a protest against Roman imperialism lends itself to use by new imperial powers. Those who are militarily defeated and easily controlled are viewed as inferior, even subhuman. In the name of God so understood, Jesus' message is reversed.

Further, if God is in control of everything, then the course of events must express God's intentions. When unjust suffering strikes those who believe in such a God, what are their options? Some may insist that there is a hidden purpose in the evil. Some may decide that God is unjust and cruel. Others may reject belief in God altogether. Just at the point when people most need the comfort and assurance of God's love, it becomes impossible to reconcile that love with actual experience.

Adopting a process perspective does not do away with the evil. Nor are all intellectual puzzles about how God's role relates to this evil immediately resolved. Nevertheless, the existential and theoretical question of evil is transformed. Much that happens is no longer seen as expressing God's intentions. God is on the side of the sufferers, suffering with them and working for the absent justice.

Many cling to the idea of God's total control in order to be assured that all will come out right in the end. Process theology offers no certainty about the outcome of history – only hope that as people work with God, a better world is possible. The assurance that gives meaning is that in God all that has been attained in the world lives on. The deepest meaning of our lives is that we contribute them to God. Process theologians are divided over whether persons will have new experiences after death, but they agree that, in any case, the ultimate fulfillment is found, not in endlessly existing as individuals, but in God.

Central to any Christian theology is the understanding of Jesus. For process theologians, more important than doctrines about Jesus is faithfulness to him in personal and communal life. Hence the historical study of Jesus is important. But doctrine is important, too, and that doctrine should be informed by what we know historically. Although there are different accents among process theologians here, most affirm that it is through Jesus that believers gain their fullest understanding of God – that is, Jesus is revealer. It is in participation in Jesus' faithfulness even in suffering and death that Christians are most open to the forgiving, healing, and empowering love of God – that is, Jesus is savior. It is in loyally following Jesus in service of others that they find the most fulfilling lives – that is, Jesus is Lord.

Process theologians affirm unhesitatingly that God was incarnate in Jesus. They are unhesitating because for them God is incarnate in everything. The Christian affirmation of incarnation is profoundly important, but it does not distinguish Jesus from other people. Incarnation has been paradoxical because for substantialist metaphysics one substance, the divine, cannot occupy the same space as another, the human. Process theologians reject that way of thinking. Instead, without the participation of the divine reality no event would occur. The more fully God is present in the event, the greater is its own creativity.

God's presence in every human experience is directing that experience toward the fullest potential of that moment, a potential itself given by God. But in every human experience there is a decision that often 'misses the mark' toward which God calls. Some process theologians distinguish Jesus from others in terms of the fullness of his response to God. Others emphasize the uniqueness of what God called Jesus to do and be. Still others argue that the very selfhood of Jesus was co-constituted by God's presence within him.

On this topic, as on many others, the basic vision of God and the world provided by Whitehead and Hartshorne offers multiple ways of appropriating the biblical message in our time. What are excluded are views of supernatural intervention, on the one hand, or the absence of God from any event in the world, on the other. What remain are diverse emphases and insights shaped by different traditions and personal experience.

This diversity characterizes thinking by process theologians also with regard to the Church. However, there are common assumptions influencing their thought. Human beings are not separated individuals relating to one another externally. Hence notions of churches as voluntary associations of individuals are not adequate. To enter the Church is to become part of an ongoing community in which the re-enactment of Jesus' life and death strengthens their field of force. The Church is where participants are repeatedly confronted with the life and teaching of Jesus and other aspects of the biblical message. It is also where their efforts to live in faithfulness to Jesus are supported by a community. In this community God is able to work redemptively in especially powerful ways.

Emphases and contributions

Virtually all modern western thought has been informed by the assumption of an underlying substantial world. The mind or self is supposed to underlie experience. Matter is supposed to underlie the objects of sight and touch. Even though philosophical analysis has long exposed the difficulties in this conceptuality, its hold on most scholarship has remained intact. Accordingly, the claim of process thought to provide a different and better basic conceptuality has implications for all fields. The project of process thinkers is vast, and progress is slow.

Process theologians have seen the pursuit of some portions of this project as part of their responsibility. Of central importance for them are theological issues of the sort illustrated above. However, they understand the theological task as quite broad. They have been empowered by Whitehead's vision to give significant leadership in the areas of (1) science and religion, (2) religious pluralism, and (3) ecology and economics.

(1)Liberal theologians recognized the need to revise theology in light of the knowledge gained from science. However, most dealt with the problem by distinguishing the spheres of science and theology in such a way that each could pursue its work with little attention to the other. The Chicago faculty, in contrast, sought Whitehead's help in the integration of science and theology.

Still more distinctive of the process theologians who are heirs of the Chicago school is their aim to contribute to the Whiteheadian effort to revise science as well as theology. Most of the dominant formulations by scientists in their various fields are still couched in terms of the old and, process thinkers believe, outdated vision of matter in motion. Whitehead himself offered a theory of relativity based on a conceptuality different from Einstein's. A number of quantum theorists have found his ideas fruitful for new interpretations.

Process theologians work with those scientists who see the need for change in how to view the world, that is, to view it as composed of interrelated events. This work has continued Whitehead's contribution to physics and also extended it to chemistry, biology, and physiological psychology. Ian Barbour has led in providing an overall view of how the sciences can be understood in a coherent way that also fits with a revised Christian theology (Barbour 1990).

(2) Whitehead also led the way into reflection about religious pluralism. His knowledge of religious traditions outside of Christianity was in no way comparable with his knowledge of science, but the idea that the various traditions could benefit from interaction with one another was part of his vision. He especially favored the mutual fructification of Buddhism and Christianity, and this is a dialogue to which process theologians have contributed. They find in Buddhism a basic understanding of reality much like that of Whitehead. Process theologians have also engaged in dialogue with other traditions and have sought to rethink Christian affirmations in light of what they learn. Jews, Muslims, Hindus, Buddhists, and Chinese religionists influenced by Whitehead have also advanced dialogue, and together they have contributed to a

deeper pluralism than what is usually called by that name. This deeper pluralism is one in which the full distinctiveness of each tradition can be maintained and affirmed in ways that do not derogate from the basic convictions of others (Griffin 2005).

(3) Some process thinkers were concerned about ecological problems long before the ecological crisis attracted public concern. Hartshorne, as a bird lover and student of bird song, had developed keen sensitivity in this area. Others were alerted only in the late 1960s and 1970s. However, all were philosophically committed to the intrinsic value of all things and especially of all living things, and all understood the interconnections among all things. Hence they quickly embraced the new emphases and incorporated them into their theological formulations. Charles Birch, a process theologian and biologist from Australia, gave the leading speech on sustainability at the Word Council of Churches meeting in Nairobi in 1975, when the WCC adopted sustainability as an essential part of the vision of the good society.

Process theologians thus participated in the widespread repentance of the Protestant churches for the neglect of the natural context that had been supported by much Protestant theology especially since Kant. As they recognized that improvements in church teaching had little effect on the policies that shaped the actual course of events, some turned to economics. Economic theory is based on the older scientific worldview which treats individuals as self-enclosed beings related to one another only externally. It values everything other than human beings by the price it brings in the market. Process theologians criticize both this individualism and this anthropocentrism and propose economic theories and global practices markedly different from those that now obtain (Daly and Cobb 1994).

Status and prospects

Process thought does not fit well into an academia that channels study and research into separated academic disciplines, including philosophy as one such discipline. Partly for this reason, it survives only at the fringes of these disciplines. It fares a little better in professional schools, where practical concerns require more flexible approaches. It has played some role, for example, in schools of education where Whitehead's own writings on the subject belong to a larger family that also includes the writings of John Dewey. There has been some interest in schools of management. And process theology has survived in a number of schools of theology.

Some of the ideas that were once distinctive of process theology are now widespread. These include the idea that God suffers with us in our suffering, an emphasis on inter-relationality, and a rejection of dualism and anthropocentrism. Ecofeminism (Christ 2003) and process theology are mutually supportive. The ideas of those conservative evangelicals who have become 'open theologians' are remarkably similar. Many lay people in old-line churches respond quickly to process theology, often saying that they have always thought this way and now have a label for their ideas.

On the other hand, specific adherence to a distinct school of thought called process theology has declined in academia in the United States. This is even more true of process philosophy. Whereas Whitehead's influence is gaining ground in Europe and growing rapidly in East Asia, the religious dimension is prominent in only a few of the countries involved.

Given the likelihood of growing global interest in Whiteheadian thought, the future of process theology now seems to depend on whether theologians will want to seek integration with thought in other fields or continue to define theology as one academic discipline among others. If the former choice becomes important, process theology will have a continuing role to play.

See also Christianity (Chapter 6), Omniscience (Chapter 24), Omnipotence (Chapter 25), Eternity (Chapter 27), Creation and divine action (Chapter 30), Religion and science (Chapter 64).

References

Barbour, I. (1990) *Religion in an Age of Science: The Gifford Lectures 1989–1991* vol. 1, New York: Harper & Row.

Beardslee, W. (1994) *First Corinthians: A Commentary for Today*, St Louis, MO: Chalice Press.

Christ, C. (2003) *She Who Changes: Reimagining the Divine in the World*, New York: Palgrave Macmillan.

Cousins, E. (ed.) (1971) *Process Theology: Basic Writings of a Major Modern Movement*, New York: Newman Press.

Daly, H. and J. Cobb (1994) *For the Common Good: Redirecting the Economy toward Community, the Environment, and a Sustainable Future*, updated and expanded edition, Boston, MA: Beacon Press.

Ferré, F. (1996) *Being and Value: Toward a Constructive Postmodern Metaphysics*, Albany, NY: State University of New York Press.

—— (1998) *Knowing and Value: Toward a Constructive Postmodern Epistemology*, Albany, NY: State University of New York Press.

—— (2001) *Living and Value: Toward a Constructive Postmodern Ethics*, Albany, NY: State University of New York Press.

Griffin, D. (2001) *Reenchantment without Supernaturalism: A Process Philosophy of Religion*, Ithaca, NY: Cornell University Press.

Griffin, D. (ed.) (2005) *Deep Religious Pluralism*, Louisville, KY: Westminster John Knox.

Hartshorne, C. (1941) *Man's Vision of God and the Logic of Theism*, New York: Harper & Brothers.

—— (1965) *Anselm's Discovery*, LaSalle, IL: Open Court Press.

Ogden, S. (1961) *Christ without Myth*, New York: Harper & Brothers.

—— (1963) *The Reality of God and Other Essays*, New York: Harper & Row.

Pittenger, N. (1968) *Process Thought and Christian Faith*, New York: Macmillan.

Whitehead, A. N. (1925) *Science and the Modern World*, New York: Free Press.

—— (1927) *Religion in the Making*, New York: Macmillan.

—— (1929) *Process and Reality: An Essay in Cosmology*, New York: Macmillan. Corrected edition (1978) eds D. Griffin and D. Sherburne, New York: Free Press.

Wieman, H. N. (1946) *The Source of Human Good*, Chicago: University of Chicago Press.

Williams, D. D. (1968) *The Spirit and the Forms of Love*, New York: Harper & Row.

Further reading

Cobb, J. and D. Griffin (1976) *Process Theology: An Introductory Exposition*, Philadelphia: Westminster Press. (Still used to introduce theological students to process theology although written in a different theological context.)

Hartshorne, C. (1970) *Creative Synthesis and Scientific Method*, London: SCM Press. (The best overview of Hartshorne's philosophy including his philosophy of religion.)

Keller, C. (2003) *Face of the Deep: A Theology of Becoming*, London: Routledge. (An important theological study by one who synthesizes French deconstructive postmodernism with process theology.)

McDaniel, J. and D. Bowman (eds) (2006) *Handbook of Process Theology*, St Louis, MO: Chalice Press. (Essays by twenty contemporary process thinkers on theological topics.)

Suchocki, M. (1993) *God-Christ-Church: A Practical Guide to Process Theology*, rev. edn, New York: Crossroad. (An accessible introduction to process theology.)

Whitehead, A. N. (1933) *Adventures of Ideas*, New York: Macmillan. (An especially good entrée to Whitehead's philosophy.)

47

POSTMODERN THEOLOGY

Pamela Sue Anderson

Jean-François Lyotard attributed 'postmodern' to the fundamental condition of twentieth-century thinking in a manner which made the prefix stick. *The Postmodern Condition* is known to have been prophetic in calling forth 'an incredulity towards metanarratives' which applies equally to all of the sciences as forms of knowledge (Lyotard 1979: xxvi). As a result, no account of any kind of knowledge could have a definite beginning, development, and ending. Systematic theology suffers a serious blow from a general recognition of this postmodern condition. Yet certain theologians and some philosophers of religion continue with ambitious narratives about orthodox Christianity (Milbank 1992; Milbank et al. 1999; Plantinga 2000).

Postmodern theologians will agree that the metanarrative of modern philosophy as consistently rational progress has failed. As the Enlightenment narrative goes, the world is rational insofar as it is shaped by a particular sense of reason. This sense renders an agreement of both the secular and the religious sciences as long as they remain consistent with the norms of reason: each human character has been given a rational faculty with which the subjects of this story will eventually achieve universal certainty, peace, and prosperity. This grand story portrays a march of progress which has become incredible in light of the global reality of our lives today. The story's picture of reality is no longer compatible with either secular or religious views of the world as we understand the present, past, or future.

Lyotard seems right about knowledge, but also about moral progress. There is no universally recognized narrative about progress toward peace; at a minimum, the moral development of humanity is not linear. So, the grand narrative of Enlightenment history and rational self-development would appear to be false. One reading of this condition restricts 'the postmodern' to the end of Enlightenment hope. Yet another reading intends to hold on to a strong thread of hope for making sense of things. Reason, history, and metaphysics – including metaphysical accounts of the self and of God – are the central casualties of a failure of twentieth-century progress. Metaphorical description of 'the death' of these victims is, at times, thought premature. If postmodern theology refers to a condition at the end of the twentieth century, then are we moving toward new life in post-postmodernism with significant stories about God?

There is little concrete evidence that either theologians or philosophers have begun with a new Enlightenment narrative. Skeptics continue to employ the attribute 'postmodern.' In the late 1970s the 'post' before 'modern' might have been thought to herald an ending to one grand story with a view to another story. Today both academic and non-academic writers appear stuck with no end, no new start, and no progressive change. The use of the prefix 'post'- persists not only before modern, but before Christian: a theologian can avowedly be 'post-Christian' (see Hampson 1996). Instead of an end or a new start, post-Christian implies a loss of belief in a Christian God.

We live after what has been, but is no longer fully, trusted as rational and certain. To clarify earlier comments Lyotard claims, 'Postmodernism ... is not modernism at its end but in the nascent state, and this state is constant' (2001: 369). It is fair to say that postmodern theology remains in a state out of which various movements emerge. But is every movement of theology to be called postmodern? If so, how is the distinctiveness of the postmodern defined? A distinctive quality of the postmodern state of theology could be its formative nature as multiple, partial stories about God. Another characteristic of the postmodern condition seems to distinguish itself as a pursuit of a general story in which faith as the condition for truth still shapes human corporate living, acting, and thinking.

Well before Lyotard, Friedrich Nietzsche (1844–1900) ushered in twentieth-century atheism from a critical standpoint at the end of the nineteenth-century. Nietzsche's aphorisms have been profoundly prophetic. His words from *The Gay Science* retain a clear ring of truthfulness: 'even we devotees of knowledge today, we godless ones and anti-metaphysicians, still take our fire too from the flame which a faith thousands of years old has kindled: that Christian faith, which was also Plato's faith, that God is truth, that truth is divine' (Nietzsche 2001: 201, sect. 344).

The most extreme atheists, the most anti-metaphysical of thinkers, including postmodern theologians – who, if not explicitly 'anti-metaphysical,' are often 'anti-realist' – still take their cognitive and conative inspiration from the flame of a faith that God is truth. In a book whose title resonates with the postmodern in articulating themes and variations on an Enlightenment philosopher, *Noble in Reason, Infinite in Faculty: Themes and Variations on Kant's Moral and Religious Philosophy* (2003), A. W. Moore captures the spirit of Nietzsche's fire and of Lyotard's incredulity. His post-Kantian account is compelling:

> It is frequently urged nowadays that there is no 'metanarrative.' ... there is no preordained story about the human condition to which all our own individual stories must be subordinated: things, to that extent, do not make sense.
>
> Perhaps not. But we must hope that there is whatever enables *us* to make sense *of things*. We must hope that there is whatever enables us to carry on telling our own individual stories. (Moore 2003: 195–6)

The flame of faith continues in active hope. This is alive in postmodern philosophers who want to believe that God's existence is either certain or possible and in those who literally believe in the impossible when it comes to God. Theological activity is bound to be weak at times. Nevertheless, its spark survives after a century haunted by a confusing array of postmodern polemics. Nietzsche's 'flame which a faith thousands of years old has kindled' remains the bottom line for both metaphysicians and anti-metaphysicians in the twenty-first century.

Systematic theology: new master narratives

To systematize all of reality under a single Christian frame of reference is the sort of overarching narrative which has been the target of the twentieth-century postmodern critics who claim incredulity toward metanarratives. Yet the rejection of one grand story is not so simple: there are different versions of postmodernism in theology. One version makes sense of a new theology named 'Radical Orthodoxy' (Milbank et al. 1999). Radical Orthodox theologians embrace Lyotard's incredulity toward a grand narrative as a critique of a secular account of reality. This critique identifies a decisive theological problem with secular philosophy in the role given to reason as universal in the Enlightenment story (Milbank 1992: 30–44). Admittedly, not even those theologians who call themselves, or are called, 'Radical Orthodox' think alike. Their individual positions are each too complex for an adequate summary. But generally they replace the narrative of secular philosophy with a new story about 'post-secular philosophy' (Blond 1998). In not giving up all metanarratives, they assume a weak incredulity. Their disbelief is directed toward secularism, not a radically sacred narrative.

Radical Orthodoxy as a postmodern theology is a strong response to the loss of optimism in the face of the failure of all forms of knowledge that sought indubitable certainty. The ground for this rejection of secularism is that historical progress cannot be made as long as reason depends upon humanity's ability to find truth without God. Yet Radical Orthodoxy depends on its own master narrative as a framework which is to be genuinely universal, since it is based upon Christian truth under which all of reality fits (see Milbank et al. 1999).

Radical Orthodox theology is compatible with an idea of a post-secular philosophy rather than a modern conception of a secular epistemology; the latter is dismissed for wrongly claiming to be the universal truth. The bias of Radical Orthodoxy asserts that Christianity provides the truth. On a positive note, the postmodern claim to dethrone human reason opens the way to the faith of Christianity. Postmodern fluidity and uncertainty are thought preferable, in protecting the faith of Christian orthodoxy, to the fixed but thin certainties of modern secularism. Such postmodern theology finds no loss in giving up an autonomous reasoning which has failed to achieve moral progress in history.

However, not all philosophers or theologians are persuaded by 'the truth' of an orthodox reading of Christian doctrine. It is ironical to claim that this master narrative is postmodern, and self-defeating to call it universal when not even every Christian theist would accept Radical Orthodoxy as a true account of reality. A similar problem of an exclusive theistic narrative remains implicit in Alvin Plantinga's Christian philosophy of religion. Plantinga conceives a warrant theory of belief which makes his position more in keeping with the postmodern turn in its rejection of classical Cartesian foundationalism – yet without rejecting foundationalism entirely (Plantinga 2000).

Plantinga asks whether Christian belief is acceptable for intelligent people living in a postmodern world. His answer tells a story about Christian beliefs being warranted to the extent that they are formed by properly functioning cognitive faculties. Human knowers not only have natural cognitive faculties such as perception, memory, and reasoning that enables knowledge of things, but humans also have a natural cognitive faculty that enables them to form basic beliefs about God. Plantinga's Reformed epistemology demonstrates that *warrant* distinguishes knowledge from true belief. His postmodern narrative of creation, sin, and salvation tells a Calvinist theological story about how the human natural cognitive faculty is dulled or damaged by sin; but this damage can be repaired by faith, which restores this cognitive faculty of belief-formation and enables every Christian to defend herself with warranted belief.

Radical Orthodoxy and Reformed epistemology offer their respective master narratives as positive postmodern alternatives to modern secular or anti-intellectual narratives concerning God, man and woman. However, there are serious worries with these alternatives. Ambivalence between Enlightenment and postmodern conceptions of reason worries certain feminist philosophers of religion, especially when it comes to women's identity-formation, their rationality and autonomy (see Anderson 1998: 31–66; Filipczak 2004: 198, 210–22).

The master narratives of postmodern theology undermine positive advances made by Enlightenment reason. Even if women and non-European men have been marginalized by certain applications of Enlightenment conceptions, they may be loath to give up modern, secular values for pre-modern, theological orthodoxy. Steps taken against medieval social institutions by Enlightenment reasoning in past centuries, in order to recognize and protect the intrinsic worth of human subjects as rational and moral agents within communities, remain significant for addressing theological forms of sexual, racial, ethnic, social, material, and economic oppression. The strong theological critiques of Enlightenment philosophy which do away completely with rational agency, and dimensions of the Enlightenment story which actually support communal and individual autonomy, undermine social equality and various concrete freedoms. It is, then, difficult to see how the narratives of Radical Orthodoxy and Reformed Epistemology, insofar as their authority is 'a mastery over' secular reason, can avoid pre-modern styles of teaching, which are not only dogmatic, but perniciously oppressive toward women and all of those non-Christians on the margins of socially and economically privileged theological circles. Ambivalence toward practices and beliefs with exclusive assumptions concerning human identity characterizes feminist debates about postmodern theories, more widely, in philosophy and the social sciences (see Anderson 1998; 2004).

Post-enlightenment stories and morality

A postmodern response to the Enlightenment philosophy of Immanuel Kant different from that of Moore's philosophical variations on Kantian themes is worth mentioning. There exists a theological conception of love which has been articulated in direct reaction to a strict reading of Kant's moral law. This conception is 'the gift' from God which creates an excessive form of love. In turn, this generates a theological alternative which seeks to replace Enlightenment morality with a humanly impossible gift of incomprehensible love. A Kantian philosopher would doubtlessly warn that this theological alternative risks heteronomy, mystification, and the threat of a pernicious illusion. Yet the postmodern theorist Kevin Hart describes this as 'a robust postmodern faith' which 'would be oriented entirely to the love of God'; this excessive love cannot be achieved by human subjects, but 'overflows their actions and words' (Hart 2004: 135).

To the ears of modern philosophers, this postmodern faith is dangerously close to an anti-intellectual fideism – reminiscent of certain pre-modern theology. Yet, to be fair, not all postmodern theology pictures the excessive love of God replacing human morality. The opposite is true in the notable case of postmodern philosopher-theologian Edith Wyschogrod, who revisions moral philosophy with a new conception of saintly altruism. Drawing from a unique range of literature and philosophy, Wyschogrod puts together a 'postmodern' account of the saint's excessive desire 'for the other' which does not end in unethical extremes of either masochism or sadomasochism. Her balancing of desire and altruism, love and moral philosophy, is fine-tuned and depends upon highly nuanced readings of, in particular, Martin Heidegger, Emmanuel Levinas, and Julia Kristeva (Wyschogrod 1990; Wyschogrod in Ward 1997: 341–55). The crucial point is that postmodern theology can be morally brilliant and innovative, not merely complicated or regressive.

Postmodern theology and morality are not alone in seeking to learn from modern literature and move forward into new, non-oppressive stories. 'The postmodern' does not have one simple definition in any contemporary field of knowledge or practice. Its definitions continue to vary with the subject matter, with time and place. Often its definition varies within any one discipline. So theology is no exception. To assess postmodern theology further, it is useful to describe its context as shaped by the loss of modern belief in (1) the moral progress of humankind in history, (2) a conception of reason as ushering in universal agreement, or certainty, and (3) a grand narrative account of being created human as persons who are equal. In fact, this threefold loss has had a decisive impact upon twenty-first century religions, and not only (Christian) theology.

An extreme reading of the postmodern loss of belief also undermines the essence, and so any definition, of religion as literally *religio* (bond) (see Mandair 2003: 87–100). Assume that 'belief' means basically any thought passed down or acquired and held to be true. Then, along with its own definitions, the postmodern displaces the modern epistemological task of philosophy of religion. While undermining religion conceived as a body of commonly held beliefs binding individuals together, postmodern theories have little room for a philosopher's concern to justify religious belief rationally as true. Postmodern theory is, then, anti-foundationalist. At times, belief is displaced by a new conception of religion in terms of its bodily and ritual practices. While knowledge as justified true belief is, more or less, the epistemological focus of modern western philosophy, postmodern philosophy shifts the focus of religion away from the epistemology of belief. Certain 'postmodern feminist' (if the two adjectives are not self-contradictory) philosophers energetically urge practitioners of philosophy of religion to move beyond any preoccupation with epistemology; in shorthand, to move 'beyond belief' (Armour 2002: 212–26; Hollywood 2004: 225–40; cf. Anderson 1998: 39, 53–4).

There may not be agreement on this question of belief or practice. Postmodern theologians are keen to differ. If the rational justification of belief as true no longer forms the foundation for theological knowledge, then philosophy of religion could appear redundant; but Plantinga offers an argument against this. Nevertheless, the epistemic practices of philosophy of religion might generate a western distortion of the lived experiences of religious communities. What is thought to be a postmodern move beyond belief replaces philosophy with a social anthropology of religion and, at times, with a postcolonial political insistence that theology should give up its exclusive position of privilege in western academic discourse in order to enable the study of cultural forms of global mysticism (see King 1999). Whereas postmodernism undermines moral, cognitive, and biological certainties, a traditional religion such as Christianity has rested on these very certainties. A simplified, postmodern story about the God of Christianity records the denial of the solid foundation of the past as a disruption of a stable world – and its theology. God as the central character of some postmodern narrative changes from a fixed point to fluid imagery. The implications of this change in conceptions of God are not only significant for Christianity and Islam, but for Orthodox Judaism and Oriental religions.

A sociologist might argue that the popularity of fundamentalism in world religions is a reaction to the loss of any rational foundation for knowledge. Contemporary forms of religious fundamentalism are offshoots of postmodern theology insofar as the fundamentalists seek unequivocal beliefs, working each belief point by point in a dependent yet oppositional relationship to postmodern uncertainties. The worst extreme of fundamentalism – the religious believer who justifies terrorist tactics globally on the grounds of 'their God' – is identified as one of the conditions which haunts postmodern theology and (im)morality.

A condition which accompanies the postmodern rise in religious fundamentalism is moral relativism. The flip side of asserting the absolute values of any fundamentalist position is a relativist account explaining the coexistence of opposing values. Moral relativism is raised in the context of conceiving theology with local narratives and practices, whether sustained by universal claims or not. The nature of this moral relativism emerges as one of the earliest indications of postmodernism. In stark contrast, as seen already, Wyschogrod creates a new vision in a postmodern saintly ethics, which transcends strictly local perspectives.

Postmodern theorists who are sensitive to ethics of difference or alterity in religious practices have shifted both academic and popular concern toward comparative religions. In turn, this has a knock-on effect upon how morality is conceived. Nevertheless, it is common for westerners to think of other religions in terms derived from their own values and moral concepts within a Christian tradition. The implicit westernized Christian morality is the object of cultural critiques. Belief is claimed, by some theorists, to be an example of a modern, immoral imposition on to the study of religions. Postmodernism admits that Christianity is not the one true religion. And yet postmodern theology has an uncertain relationship with a multiplicity of religious narratives which raises a question about the 'end' of theology.

Theology: end or transformation?

Postmodern tensions threaten theology as a systematic study of Christianity with the uncertainties of its own future. It is unfair to reduce theology to an elite or exclusive frame of reference on reality. Yet a real issue is whether the postmodern incredulity toward metanarratives calls for an end or a transformation of theology. The perspectives of Christian theologians might become displaced by 'the study of religions.' The reality of an unstable academic scene (e.g., indiscriminate disruption of university departments of theology and of religions) provides ready evidence for questioning the value of postmodern fluidity.

In terms of its content, theology cannot be assessed fairly if all things postmodern reject reason, epistemology, and autonomous agency. For example, it is contentious to claim that non-western religions in the world are concerned with disciplinary practices rather than the belief which dominates theology. Discussions of belief are *not* necessarily incompatible with bodily rituals. Quite the reverse: religious rituals as disciplinary practices are not separable from, or do not make sense, without beliefs. The question whether belief or practice is the proper focus for philosophy of religion exposes a false opposition. The difference between belief and practice is better understood as a descriptive distinction between an epistemological-ethical focus and a human anthropological-psychological focus on God or religion. Perhaps the former is thought compatible with Enlightenment philosophy, the latter with postmodern theology. There is a considerable difference between asking how we justify our beliefs as true – or, how we justify our actions on the basis of this knowledge – and what dispositions are actually formed by religious practices – or what ought to form and re-form our cognitive virtues. But it does not follow that these two sets of questions are incompatible with each other. Instead, each can recognize the concrete differences which determine religious practices and inform theological doctrines.

bell hooks is not afraid to be up front about what has been a postmodern exclusion of the presence of black women. But, instead of an oppositional stance, she gives concrete advice:

> The failure to recognize a critical black presence in the culture and in [most] scholarship and writing on postmodernism compels a black reader, particularly a black female reader, to interrogate her interest in [this] subject. (hooks 1990: 24)

She adds:

> If radical postmodernist thinking is to have a transformative impact, then a critical break with the notion of 'authority' as 'mastery over' must not simply be a rhetorical device. It must be reflected in habits of being, including styles of writing as well as chosen subject matter. (p. 25)

The feminist theologian and philosopher of religion Amy Hollywood is equally bold in her insistence that Christian theologians and postmodern philosophers can and should give their attention to religious *habitus* (Hollywood 2004: 229–33). The question is, how does a new focus on 'habits of being' (hooks) and *habitus*, as corporal dispositions or disciplinary practice, tackle concrete theological questions of liberation related to race and class differences, alongside differences of sexual orientation and mystical experiences?

Postmodern theologians who discuss whether belief or practice has priority could be caught up in western abstractions. Yet these postmodern debates lend support to the actual subversion by postcolonial theorists of the epistemological practices of modern philosophy for genealogical studies of ritual action. The social anthropologist Talal Asad, writing on Islam and Christianity, persuades some philosophical theologians to focus upon genealogies of religions which re-conceive ritual (Asad 1993: 57–58, 131; cf. Hollywood 2004). Ritual is, then, no longer a symbolic action, expressing some psychological or sociological function whose real field of meaning is in the mind or the realm of a social group, but is a disciplinary practice, or apt performance, forming and re-forming religious dispositions – and as such becomes central to postmodern theology.

Postmodern critiques of analytical reason and symbolic action challenge modern philosophy and, especially, the equation of religion with belief. If decisive, such critiques will have forced the fields of theology and religious studies to recognize the wider cultural issues of gender, sexuality, class, race, and bodily practices as tools for forming religious subjectivities, embodying beliefs, shaping cognitive dispositions and re-forming virtues. Yet there are problems with these genealogical critiques of reason, ritual, and symbolic action, notably the limited nature of any resistance to or re-formation of disciplinary practices. The more abstract and conceptual dimensions of the philosophical theologian cannot be merely jettisoned for a postmodern play of multiple narratives of difference – insofar as the content of theology has an integral relationship to the reality of people's lives.

Responses to postmodern critiques of modern philosophy of religion still draw upon aspects in the fields of both religious studies and Christian theology. One major response to the threefold postmodern loss of belief focuses upon religious experience understood as outside of the limits of possible knowledge. These terms are compatible with modern philosophy; this postmodern study of religions becomes an exercise in finding new possibilities in experiencing the impossible. In particular, Kant moves philosophy to the limits of human knowledge, and this postmodern response picks up the idea that religion lies outside the possible, outside of language, in the realm of mystery and gift.

Postmodern discussions of 'the gift' reflect ways in which the instability of this concept results in experiencing the impossible. As soon as a donor gives someone a gift, the recipient is put into debt. This adds to the donor, not to the recipient; but this is exactly the opposite of what the gift is supposed to do. Philosopher Jacques Derrida and theologian Jean-Luc Marion attempt to discuss the impossible give-and-take interchange concerning the gift (Marion and Derrida 1999: 20–53). Marion elucidates the desire to experience the impossible, or to recognize the inscrutable, as the defining element for a postmodern, however mystical, conception of theology.

Lyotard supports the desire and the possibility of experiencing the impossible in terms of the Kantian sublime. The sublime is an experience of the absolute greatness, which cannot be capped by reason, understanding or imagination (Lyotard 1994). But this sublime also constitutes a barrier to any search for totality; the postmodern movement resists all totalizing accounts of ultimate reality. Postmodern readings of mystical experience which are shaped by the sublime, its greatness and its inexpressibility, avoid the problems with limiting God, or the subject of religious experience, to the realm of the possible. Advocates of a mystically inclined, postmodern theology make post-Kantian moves to avoid the problem of conceiving God in anthropomorphic or gynecological terms – each of which might be exclusive of an opposite sex. Certain feminist theologians and philosophers of religion have found this mystical alternative attractive for debates about the nature both of the divine and of bodily practices. Yet there remains the danger of illusion and mystification, especially in associating God with the impossible and ineffable. These are dangers which modern philosophical conceptions of God and religious experience aim to avoid.

The various problems and possibilities in accounts of the limits of the human relationship to the divine, mystical, or the unsayable are debated by contemporary continental philosophers. Does the response of postmodern theologians to genealogical critiques support a philosophy of ineffable religious ritual? What would happen to postmodern theology if its main focus turned to ritual performances? Modern philosophy's focus on the justification of belief may be undermined by this postmodern focus, but then the nature of religion would remain unsayable and indefinite. It would be only as stable as the practices forming its dispositions, only as strong as the power shaping each ritual and only as fixed as the gender of each construction.

Postmodern theology: truth and truthfulness

Theologians and philosophers continue to think that truth matters – or, if not truth, then truthfulness. The concern for truth about Christian belief and its morality has led theologians to take a postmodern stance, and, at times, to assert a post-Christian stance. There is significance in the truthfulness of those who are self-avowedly post-Christians who directly challenge those postmodern theologians who fail to see the self-contradictory nature of their own master narratives.

The master narratives of Radical Orthodoxy and Reformed Epistemology are compatible with a weak form of the postmodern critique of metanarratives. The weakness of these critiques rests in universalizing their own partial perspectives on reality in a grand story. The new theological narratives may have initially constituted the hoped-for alternative to secular reason's failures where modern skepticism had seemed to replace religious belief. Yet insofar as not everyone assents to a Christian narrative, its universality is undermined. The insistence that a failure to assent to what is universal results from sin, or from some lack of faith, or grace, or of the gift of God, is an inadequate response for postmodern theologians aware of their global contexts.

A large question looms for postmodern theology, whether sense can be made theologically of a postmodern world caught up in inexpressible experiences of the humanly impossible. These experiences are constructed out of the postmodern fluidity and uncertainty which replaces reason and its certainty. One answer refers to the post-Kantian sublime as the ungraspable heart of religious experience – that is, experience of a subject who remains tied to God. For postmodern believers such greatness gives a sense of God who is not available to reason or language. Further questions arise about the content of this postmodern theology, including the nature of God. Mystery, saintly humility, and sensible ecstasy sound exciting notions which could be rich with theological possibility. Yet these postmodern notions suffer from a dramatic loss of particularity and concreteness. To what precisely do the disciplinary practices related to ineffability and religion aspire? Consider postmodern debates about the possibility of apophatic theology (see Marion and Derrida 1999: 21–53; Turner 2002).

To attribute 'postmodern' to theology assumes an unstable position in the recognition of multiple narratives, embodying concrete material and social differences. A differential theology of people, places, perspectives, and practices which is postmodern cannot remain static if it is to keep its edge on the modern. Instead, postmodern theology maintains a transformation, or conversion from an old to a new direction. A conversion from one place to another captures the unstable positioning which characterizes the postmodern relation to the modern; the present to the past and future. Care is taken to ensure that the energy of the novel does not become the inertia of old assurances (Lyotard 2001: 363–70).

The upshot of postmodern theology is an ethical displacement of Christian beliefs which have been blindly Eurocentric. In the nascent state of postmodern theology, there exist the *possibilities* of generating ground for the formation of non-patriarchal, non-sexist, non-racist, and yet vibrant perspectives on God. Postmodern theology exhibits a willingness to create a future. With the possibility of constructive change, contemporary theologians and philosophers can move in a direction which neither forgets nor returns to its past. Detours and mistakes remain inevitable owing to the finite nature of human knowledge and to the limited grasp of truth. Hope springs from a common fire lit by the flame of more than two thousand years of faith in truth, a truth that is divine.

See also Christianity (Chapter 6), Immanuel Kant (Chapter 14), Friedrich Nietzsche (Chapter 16), Truth in religion (Chapter 18), Religious traditions and rational assessments (Chapter 19), Religious pluralism (Chapter 20), Inclusivism and exclusivism (Chapter 21), Mysticism among the world's religions (Chapter 23), Reformed epistemology (Chapter 58), Continental philosophy (Chapter 60), Phenomenology of religion (Chapter 61).

References

Anderson, P. S. (1998) *A Feminist Philosophy of Religion: The Rationality and Myths of Religious Belief*, Oxford: Blackwell.

—— (2004) 'Postmodernism and religion,' in S. Sim (ed.) *The Routledge Companion to Postmodernism*, 2nd edn, London: Routledge.

Armour, E. (2002) 'Beyond belief: sexual difference and religion after onto-theology,' in J. Caputo (ed.) *The Religious*, Oxford: Blackwell.

Asad, T. (1993) *Genealogies of Religion: Discipline and Reasons of Power in Christianity and Islam*, Baltimore, MD: Johns Hopkins University Press.

Blond, P. (ed.) (1998) *Post-secular Philosophy: Between Philosophy and Theology*, London: Routledge.

Filipczak, D. (2004) 'Autonomy and female spirituality in a Polish context: divining a self,' in P. S. Anderson and B. Clack (eds) *Feminist Philosophy of Religion: Critical Readings*, London: Routledge.

Hampson, D. (1996) *After Christianity*, London: SCM Press.

Hart, K. (2004) *Postmodernism: A Beginner's Guide*, Oxford: Oneworld Publications.

Hollywood, A. (2004) 'Practice, belief and feminist philosophy of religion,' in P. S. Anderson and B. Clack (eds) *Feminist Philosophy of Religion: Critical Readings*, London: Routledge.

hooks, bell (1990) 'Postmodern blackness,' *Yearning: Race, Gender, and Cultural Politics*, Boston, MA: South End Press.

King, R. (1999) *Orientalism and Religion: Postcolonial Theory, India and 'The Mystic East,'* London: Routledge.

Lyotard, J.-F. (1979) *The Postmodern Condition: A Report on Knowledge*, trans. G. Bennington and B. Massumi, Minneapolis, MN; Minnesota University Press.

—— (1994) *Lessons on the Anayltic of the Sublime*, trans. E. Rottenberg, Berkeley, CA: Stanford University Press.

—— (2001) 'Note on the meaning of the word "post" and answering the question "What is postmodernism?"' in R. Kearney and D. Rasmussen (eds) *Continental Aesthetics, Romanticism to Postmodernism: An Anthology*, Oxford: Blackwell.

Mandair, A.-P. S. (2003) 'What if *religio* remained untranslatable?', in P. Goodchild (ed.) *Difference in Philosophy of Religion*, Aldershot: Ashgate.

Marion, J-L. and J. Derrida (1999) 'In the name: how to avoid speaking of "negative theology"' and 'Response by Jacques Derrida,' in J. D. Caputo and M. J. Scanlon (eds) *God, The Gift and Postmodernism*, Bloomington, IN: Indiana University Press.

Milbank, J. (1992) 'Problematizing the secular,' in P. Berry and A. Wernick (eds) *Shadow of Spirit: Postmodernism and Religion*, London: Routledge.

Milbank, J., C. Pickstock and G. Ward (1999) *Radical Orthodoxy: A New Theology*, London: Routledge.

Moore, A. W. (2003) *Noble in Reason, Infinite in Faculty: Themes and Variations on Kant's Moral and Religious Philosophy*, London: Routledge.

Nietzsche, F. (2001) *The Gay Science*, trans. J. Nauckhoff, Cambridge: Cambridge University Press.

Plantinga, A. (2000) *Warranted Christian Belief*, New York: Oxford University Press.

Turner, D. (2002) 'Apophaticism, idolatry and the claims of reason,' in O. Davies and D. Turner (eds) *Silence and the Word: Negative Theology and Incarnation*, Cambridge: Cambridge University Press.

Ward, G. (ed.) (1997) *The Postmodern God*, Oxford: Blackwell.

Wyschogrod, E. (1990) *Saints and Postmodernism: Revisioning Moral Philosophy*, Chicago: University of Chicago Press.

Further reading

Caputo, J. (ed.) (2002) *The Religious*, Oxford: Blackwell. (This timely volume of essays in continental philosophy rethinks religion after the postmodern critique of the God of traditional metaphysics, reinvigorating classical debates with contemporary accounts of transcendence, otherness and becoming divine.)

Hollywood, A. (2002) *Sensible Ecstasy: Mysticism, Sexual Difference and the Demands of History*, Chicago: University of Chicago Press. (This erudite monograph is essential reading for postmodern theologians seeking to connect action and contemplation, emotion and reason, body and soul, secular and sacred.)

Kearney, R. (1984) *Dialogues with Contemporary Continental Thinkers: The Phenomenological Heritage*, Manchester: Manchester University Press. (This brilliant set of highly accessible dialogues introducing the hermeneutics of Ricoeur, the post-structuralism of Derrida, the ethics of Levinas, the critical theory of Marcuse, and the religious poetics of Breton, has become a highly significant milestone in bridging continental and Anglo-American thinkers on topics which are today at the heart of postmodern theology.)

Ward. G. (ed.) (2001) *The Blackwell Companion to Postmodern Theology*, Oxford: Blackwell. (This lively collection of essays written for a new millennium is prefaced by Ward's original introduction, situating the contributors in the cultural and international context in which their contributions to postmodern theology are understood.)

48
THEOLOGY AND RELIGIOUS LANGUAGE

Peter Byrne

Problems in religious language

Over a long period philosophers and theologians in the West have reflected on a range of issues concerning how human beings can talk of God. The underlying problem they address arises from the assumption that God is a transcendent entity. If God is transcendent, how can human language be fit for describing and identifying the divine? This root problem branches into more specific ones, as can be illustrated if we take a sample statement about God.

Consider 'God is wise.' This statement appears to attribute the property wisdom to God. Given that God, if he exists, is a transcendent entity and quite unlike the normal, everyday things that we could intelligibly call wise, does 'wise' retain any meaning when used of God? If so, how might that meaning be fixed? These questions relate to what I shall call 'the problem of predication.' Answers to the questions within the problem of predication have included appeals to negative theology, to analogical meaning, and to metaphor. Within 'God is wise' there is a subject term and we might ask how that subject term serves to identify what we want to attribute wisdom to. This is 'the problem of reference.' Consider the whole statement: we may wonder how it can be anchored in evidence. What, if anything, might show such statements to be true or false? The anchoring of such statements in evidence seems problematic, given that their putative subject is remote from experience. If we accept that knowing the meaning of a statement involves knowing what would show it to be true or false, then this worry about the anchorage of God-statements generates a further worry about how they can be understood. This is 'the problem of verification.'

So far we have three broad problems in religious language: those of predication, reference, and verification. All three, but particularly the last, give rise to a fourth set of issues: those to do with realist versus anti-realist interpretations of religious language. We may wonder if the intent and function of 'God is wise' are analogous to those of 'Pluto is a planet.' The latter statement, whether true or false, is an attempt to state what is the case about a mind-independent reality. Whether it is true or false depends on what is the case quite independently of human concepts and beliefs. We can interpret it realistically. Debates in philosophy of religion since the 1960s have raised the question of whether statements about God can be interpreted in the same fashion.

The problem of predication

The problem of predication concerning statements about divinity is as old as philosophical reflection on God. It arises out of two conflicting tendencies in human thought about God. One is to stress God's transcendence, and the other is to stress God's similarity to human beings.

The stress upon transcendence is rooted in the needs of worship and the needs of natural theology. Worship looks to be degrading, if not utterly superstitious, if directed to an object that is not qualitatively different from, and immeasurably superior to, anything remotely like a creature. Monotheistic worship brings an emphasis upon the qualitative gap between God and creatures. Natural theology has also led to a stress on divine transcendence. From the Greeks onward, it has appealed to God to answer fundamental questions about the nature and existence of empirical reality. For example, God has been invoked as the explanation of why there is a world of things that come to be and pass away at all. For the invocation of God to work in this context, he cannot be another thing that comes to be and passes away. He must be a necessary being. He must have a mode of being different from that of finite things.

The logic of both worship and natural theology thus points toward a God who is qualitatively different from human beings. Yet philosophical theology also tends to describe God as having versions of human attributes and perfections such as knowledge, life, wisdom, and justice. The religious life leads in this direction. The worshipful God of monotheism must also be something that human beings can relate to. God must be concerned with human well-being. God must be capable of 'hearing' human prayers and willing and able to respond to them. Moreover, the God of natural theology must have some human-like attributes. God serves to explain order in the world because God has something like intelligence. God creates not in the way in which the rain creates rust in my car, but in the way in which a potter creates a pot. God must have versions of some key human attributes. God is worthy of worship because the human-like attributes he has correspond to human perfections, not defects, and he has these perfections in a degree or a mode that makes him infinitely superior to even the best human being.

The problem of predication is the problem that philosophical theology both wants to describe God as having versions of human perfections, but also to say that God is utterly unlike anything finite and creaturely, such as a human being. In the discussions of this problem in the Middle Ages, God's transcendence was fixed through the inheritance of Hellenistic philosophical theology. Through a variety of indirect sources, the Neoplatonic account of a first being as immutable, eternal (timeless), incorporeal, perfect, and possessed of aseity played a major role in the thought of Maimonides, Aquinas, and others. These 'metaphysical attributes' of God served to highlight the otherness of the divine. They are ways of pointing to the qualitatively different mode of being enjoyed by the divine. They were held to entail a further, crucial metaphysical attribute: simplicity. An absolutely fundamental way in which God's mode of existence is other than ours is that, like all creatures, we are compounded beings, whereas God is an absolutely simple being. In writers such as Maimonides and Aquinas, for whom the problem of predication looms large, divine simplicity brings with it a number of respects in which God is not like us. There is in him no difference between essential and accidental attributes. He has no accidental attributes. In God all attributes are one. His goodness is his power, which is his wisdom, and so on. In God there is no distinction between essence and existence. This means God does not exist by being one exemplification of a kind (divinity). God is his nature and his nature is his existence. Simplicity, so characterized, rapidly leads to the conclusion that God has no properties. If it is true to say that God is wise, it is not so because God possesses the property wisdom. The surface meaning of 'God is wise' hides a different logic.

The above entails that, for Maimonides and Aquinas, the logic of the statement 'God is wise' is fundamentally different from that of 'Socrates is wise.' The latter serves to ascribe a property to a subject; the former does not. Both agree therefore that there is a form of equivocation in the two uses of 'wise'; the word cannot have the same sense when used of God and of creatures. To think that 'wise' bears its 'creaturely sense' when used of God is to lapse into anthropomorphism and to fail to acknowledge the divine transcendence. For Maimonides, a word like 'wise' is used of God either in a negative sense – that is, to exclude God from the class of foolish, ignorant things – or as an 'attribute of action' – that is, to describe one of God's operations or effects rather than his essence (Maimonides 1963: 111–47).

Aquinas's view appears to be radically different. Words like 'wise' are used of God in an extended but related sense, as when one says of both Peter Byrne and the muesli he eats that they are healthy. Aquinas is none too clear on what this analogous sense of human perfection terms might be. This gloss is typical: '"Living" in "God is living" does not mean the same as "causes life"; the sentence is used to say that life does pre-exist in the source of all things, although in a higher way than we can understand or signify' (Summa Theologiae Ia. 13. 2, ad 2). Aquinas's account of talk about God (in the Summa Theologiae Ia. 13) relies on a distinction between what words like 'wise' signify in God and how they signify it. We signify such divine perfections as life and wisdom by using predicates drawn from the human case. These are utterly misleading when used of the absolutely simple source of all. For us, their sense is given by their referring to properties different from each other and different from our essence and existence. But we use them to refer to something in God that is their surpassing cause. As surpassing life in humanity, divine life is not something different from any other 'properties' God has and not distinct from his essence and his existence. The mode of signification of these predicates is thus inadequate to the thing we use them to signify.

There is an important respect in which both the negative account of Maimonides and the analogical account of Aquinas are alike (despite the fact that Aquinas explicitly criticizes Maimonides in Ia. 13. 2). Both regard the problem of predication as so immense that they agree we cannot use human perfection terms to penetrate the veil of ignorance that separates us from the divine essence. In a passage introducing question 3 of the *prima pars* of the *Summa*, Aquinas states, 'Now we cannot know what God is, but only what he is not.' This is a sentiment he shares with Maimonides.

It must be said that the problem of predication undergoes a major transformation as we move away from medieval philosophical theology toward twenty-first century debates about God. A striking feature of philosophical theology since the Enlightenment is the widespread abandonment of the earlier view of God as an absolutely simple first cause. Many twenty-first century philosophers begin from the position that God is a personal being. This being has distinct attributes. His aseity and simplicity are in consequence understood in much attenuated ways. His simplicity, for example, may be understood as consisting in no more than the mutual connectedness of the divine attributes (for example, they are all entailments of the super-attribute 'perfect being'). Gone, then, are the strictures against ascribing positive properties to God. God's mode of being may still transcend the human and the creaturely, but not in the radical way it does for Aquinas. It will be accepted that God cannot be wise in quite the way Socrates is wise. Thus Socrates' wisdom is acquired over time and is compatible with a degree of ignorance and error. But these differences can be catered for by distinguishing between the property of wisdom per se and the way this property is manifested in this or that entity.

To this distinction can be added another: between the core meaning of 'wise' and the associations the term acquires through the contexts we normally use it in. Thus we come to think of wisdom as something that is learned through experience, but that feature is not part of the core meaning of 'wisdom.' In talking about God we need to strip away such peripheral associations of perfection terms. That does not involve giving 'wise' a new sense, but it does allow us to form a picture of wisdom per se, which can then guide us in ascribing wisdom to God.

Using the above apparatus, a number of writers have contended that human perfection terms can be used univocally of God and creatures, while not at the same time getting rid of divine transcendence (Swinburne 1977: ch. 5; Alston 1989a).

If the theism of Swinburne and others has a muted stress on divine transcendence, there are influences on other modern writers that lead them to the conclusion that God's nature is unknown and unknowable, and thus to radical doctrines of divine predication. For example, such radical agnosticism about God is preached in Kant's mature writings and leads to the conclusion that positive descriptions of God cannot serve to ascribe properties to him (Kant 1997: A695–8/B723–6). The influence of Kant and empiricism combined in modern philosophy to produce a powerful sense that talk of a transcendent God is deeply problematic. One result of this has been an appeal to metaphor to explain the meaning of positive descriptions of God. This appeal has taken many forms, not least because there are different accounts of the logic of metaphor. In general, metaphor is that figure of speech whereby we speak of one thing in terms that are more appropriate of another. To see the distinctiveness of a metaphorical approach to descriptions of God, it is essential to realize that metaphor does not involve extending or changing the senses of words. If we say, in the language of Psalm 23, that 'The LORD is my shepherd,' we speak about God in terms that are more appropriate of a distinctively human activity. For the metaphor in the psalm to work, it is vital that terms like 'shepherd' retain their original sense, for we need the customary associations of the word to create the network of understanding that orients us in our thinking of God under the model of a shepherd. Thinkers like Aquinas had recognized that some words were used metaphorically of God. 'Lion' in 'God is a lion' is one of his examples (Ia. 13. 3). The point at issue in metaphorical accounts of religious language is whether *all* positive descriptions of God are to be understood metaphorically.

Such a pan-metaphor view is to be found in McFague (1982; 1987). On her account, even a statement such as 'God is wise' is at root metaphorical since it is no more than part of the working out of what is merely a model of God (God as a personal ruler of the universe). Writing from a post-Kantian, post-empiricist outlook, McFague states that the only sure item of religious faith is that there is a personal power in the universe which is on the side of life and its fulfillment. We then use different models of this power in the construction of theologies. The specific statements about God made within any one of these models are but metaphors.

McFague's metaphor theory of divine descriptions is deemed to be non-cognitive by her critics. She contends that the criteria of model choice determining our descriptions of God are fundamentally pragmatic. Models of God are to be recommended on the basis of the attitudes and practical policies they encourage. Thus, 'God is wise' cannot be deemed true/false in the naive way we might think 'Socrates is wise' is true/false. Other metaphor theorists in religious language regard (successful) metaphors as truth-apt and cognitive in function. They claim that recognizing the metaphorical function of descriptions of God is a way of both paying due respects to divine transcendence and of seeing descriptions of the divine as information-bearing. (A full account along these lines is worked out in Soskice 1985.) From the standpoint of defenders of the literal and univocal interpretation of predications of God, these metaphorical approaches to divine descriptions are betrayals of the need for religious statements to have truth-values and clear entailments. It has been argued that there can be no irreducible metaphors in theology because any metaphor that claims to be true must have a literal core that can be stated in principle. Thus pan-metaphoricism is false: if any metaphorical statements about God are true, some literal statements about him must also be true (Alston 1989b; reply in Byrne 1995b: 144–8).

The problem of reference

The problem of reference covers a range of issues surrounding how 'God' and equivalent terms function as referring expressions. The issues intersect with discussions in general philosophy of language about reference and proper names.

Some see proper names as shorthand for descriptions. Consonant with that, one may see 'God' as a title-term, with a sense such as 'the one and only perfect creator of all that is' (Pike 1970). The problem of how the reference of 'God' is fixed then collapses into the problems of predication and verification. Some follow Kripke in viewing proper names as rigid designators and as in no way shorthand for descriptions. For these thinkers, 'God' would get a reference through some initial act of 'dubbing' in a divine–human encounter and through an unbroken sequence of subsequent uses of the name that was causally indebted to this initial act. The problem of fixing the reference of 'God' is then bound up with discussions of religious experience (Miller 1986; Alston 1989c). The debate between these rival theories of the reference of 'God' has implications for discussions of religious diversity. Crudely, it is easier to see how different faiths with conflicting theologies might nonetheless worship the same divine ultimate if we take a non-descriptive approach to the reference of proper names (Byrne 1995b: 39–53.).

The problems surrounding how the reference of 'God' can be fixed can be taken further. Some philosophers consider that they are so serious as to provide a strong case for skepticism about the very possibility of 'God' functioning as a successful referring expression. It has been argued that the fundamental distinction in our language and metaphysics between qualities and abstract entities, on the one hand, and particulars and substances, on the other, depends on our ability to locate particulars within the spatio-temporal framework. The idea of a unique individual, something that has numerical identity, is bound up with the idea of something that is at least temporally related to the spatio-temporal things around us that we can indicate through ostension. The putative referent of 'God' cannot be so related and cannot thus be conceived as a particular. (It can be seen from the above discussion of divine simplicity that God in classical theism occupies an uncomfortable half-way position between a substance and a quality.) This particular problem of reference links with verificationism as another source of skepticism about the meaninglessness of talk of God (Le Poidevin 1995: 498; in reply, see Byrne 2003: 95).

The problem of verification

The question 'How, if it all, may statements about God be verified?' became the source of skepticism about the meaning of religious language with the influence of logical positivism in the 1930s and 1940s. Positivists had a theory of meaning that tied meaning to experience and an associated criterion of the meaningful that claimed that sentences that could not be verified by experiential data lacked meaning. More precisely, they lacked cognitive meaning; they did not express true/false statements and thus had no information-bearing content. In works such as A. J. Ayer's Language, Truth, and Logic (esp. ch. 6), the case was mounted from this verificationism that talk about God could not be cognitively meaningful because no attempt to talk about transcendent, non-empirical entities could be meaningful in this way. Such attacks were part and parcel of a long-standing attempt to debunk religion from a standpoint that took science as the paradigm of knowledge, rationality, and, in this case, meaning. The statements and concepts of natural science, it was claimed, have a cognitive function because they are anchored in experience. 'Metaphysical' modes of thought, such as religion, were compared with this paradigm and found wanting.

The verificationist critique of religion produced an enormous literature in philosophy of religion in the second half of the twentieth century. It is possible to divide responses to the critique into a number of strategic types. A broad division must be made between strategies of acceptance and rejection. Acceptance strategies depend on seeing a verificationist criterion of the meaningful as valid (in some formulation or other). Rejectionist strategies deny the validity of verificationist conceptions of the meaningful.

Acceptance strategies that avoid the stark, skeptical conclusion that religious language is devoid of any meaning can pursue the search for non-cognitive functions of religious language. It is granted that sentences about God do not express truth-valued statements, but perhaps they serve to express and vivify our practical commitments (Braithwaite 1971).

Acceptance strategies may take the form of trying to show that statements about God can meet the challenge of a suitable version of the verification principle. Hick's well-known paper 'Theology and verification' (1971) offers an instance of this strategy. Hick sets out what is, in his view, an acceptable version of the verification principle and argues that postmortem experiences could in principle provide unambiguous evidence of an experiential kind to anchor claims about God. Hick's response to verificationism has generated its own subliterature through the attacks on it by Nielsen (1971) and defenses of Hick against Nielsen (such as Penelhum 1971).

Rejection strategies take heart from the fact that verificationist ideas about meaning in particular, and the logical positivist program in general, have come under enormous criticism in their home territory: the philosophy of science. It has proved notoriously difficult to find a formulation of the verification principle that allows in all the standard statements of natural science (see Hempel 1952). This difficulty is due to two underlying commitments of science: the commitment both to statements with universal force and to statements about theoretical, unobservable entities. These commitments signal a drive in science to make statements that cannot be translated into ones about experiential data and that cannot be conclusively proved by reliance on such data. These commitments cast doubt on the underlying theory behind the postivists' criterion of meaning.

Verificationist criteria of meaning depend on two links. One is between testability and meaning (statements that cannot be tested are without cognitive meaning). One is between testability and experience (*the* way to test truth-claims is by way of observation). The two links are separate from each other. Thus there are empiricist philosophers such as Russell who accept the link between testability and experience, but deny that untestable claims are meaningless; they are simply unknowable (see Russell 1962: 271). Both links can and have been questioned. Many scientific hypotheses are untestable when first formulated and advanced. They may nonetheless have a clear enough sense, one that guides further theoretical and empirical inquiry that might, in the future, yield tests for them. Moreover, many scientific hypotheses are very remote from observation, and only highly abstract and theoretical considerations decide on their ultimate worth. (Good cases against verificationist criteria of meaning can be found in Heimbeck 1969 and Swinburne 1977.)

The rejection of either or both of the two elements within the verifiability criterion of meaning can be taken further. It can be argued that the criterion lacks a rationale unless it is seen to flow from an appropriate theory of meaning. The theory from which it originally flowed was an empiricist one. Such a theory makes the meaning of a word stem from its one-to-one correspondence to something in sense experience (ignoring terms with purely syntactic meaning). Meaningful sentences can then be translated into talk about observables. Thus it follows that their truth-value can be determined by reference to observation. This empiricist theory of meaning fits in ill with examples of apparently meaningful terms and statements in many areas of inquiry (including science – see above). If it is rejected, it is hard to see why anyone would want to accept the criterion of the meaningful that it has spawned (see Brown 1976; Byrne 2003: 83–6).

Realism and anti-realism

Many of the issues arising from positivist critiques of religion have migrated to new-style discussions of the realist interpretation of religious language. Realism versus anti-realism in the interpretation of a mode of discourse relates to whether we can take the statements in that mode of discourse to be true or false of the appropriate mind-independent entities. Thus a realist interpretation of discourse about theoretical entities in science will take the statements of such discourse to be true or false insofar as they correspond to facts about genuine, unobservable features of nature. It is evident that non-cognitivist interpretations of religion, such as those offered by Braithwaite, are anti-realist. For they deny that religious sentences are expressive of truth-valued statements at all. Interpretations of religious discourse that take statements about God to be roundabout ways of talking of human nature (as is suggested by some themes in Feuerbach's *The Essence of Christianity*) can also be seen to be anti-realist insofar as they make religious statements to be about an inappropriate (because non-transcendent) entity.

Many complexities surround the issue of realism versus anti-realism in the interpretation of religious discourse. They are hidden in the notion of 'taking religious statements to be about an appropriate mind-independent entity.' Atheists hold that religious statements are not successfully about such an entity. They are metaphysical anti-realists. They may re-interpret religious discourse in a consciously revisionist way. Thus Huxley thinks the statements of Christian theism as ordinarily understood are false. Yet there is some truth to be redeemed in statements about God if they are re-cast as statements about aspects of the natural world (Huxley 1957: 188). Anti-realists of a different stripe may argue that religious statements are not even *in intent* about a mind-independent entity. They may favor a version of the view that all reality is constructed, in some manner, by our conceptual schemes. They may think that all modes of discourse are about mind-dependent entities. (They are then global anti-realists, according to Byrne 2003: ch. 2.) Anti-realists may be commenting neither on the success nor on the intent of religious discourse, but on its function and explanation. Thus they may argue that, although religious believers intend to speak of a mind-independent transcendent entity, and although we cannot show that such an entity does not exist, it is clear that religious discourse is not controlled by cognitive contact with this postulated transcendent entity. It is obvious, they contend, that religious discourse is caused and shaped by truth-blind forces, such as human needs and desires. It does not arise out of discovery, proof, awareness of evidence and reason, or anything of the sort. So, in terms of its function, origin, and explanation, religion is not a realist enterprise. (See Zamulinski 2003 for a case along these lines.)

Realism and its opposing anti-realism thus take various forms in the interpretation of religious discourse. Metaphysical realism/anti-realism is just the old debate about the reality of God in a new guise. Realism/anti-realism stances on the intent of theistic discourse relate to whether the apparently referential, propositional character of theistic statements is to be taken seriously. Global views about the interpretation of language and human cognition affect this particular debate, as do concerns expressed by some in, for example, the Wittgensteinian tradition, that a so-called realist interpretation of religious discourse masks the intimate connections between religious language and action (or value). Anti-realism that focuses on the function and explanation of religious language draws upon a long tradition of wholly anthropological interpretations of religion whose notable modern representatives are Feuerbach, Marx, and Freud.

Feminism and religious language

Feminist critiques of religious language have added powerfully to debates on theology and religious language from the 1970s onwards (as will be evident from the separate essay on feminism and religion in this volume). In very general terms, radical feminists writing on this subject can be seen as judging that the attempt by traditional theology to give a non-anthropomorphic sense to descriptions of God have failed. Traditional descriptions of God are irredeemably anthropomorphic – and androcentric at that. By reference to McFague's model-based interpretation of religious discourse, we may see feminist critics of religious discourse as claiming that theistic discourse has been no more than an adumbration of male-based and male-serving models of the divine. There is here an implicit critique of classical doctrines of analogy and negative predication. Feminists on religious language are also drawing upon the aforementioned anti-realist, anthropological critiques of the function and cause of religion and religious discourse. In so doing, they give special emphasis to the alleged way religious discourse has been moved by, and has served to express, typically male needs and desires. They think that religious discourse, while purporting to be about a transcendent God, has been the projection of male needs and thought-forms for the purpose of male domination. They are very much on the side of the anti-realists. Many are not simply critics of religious language, but – once again, like many anti-realists – want to produce reconstructed forms of talk about the divine that will enable such talk to survive, albeit in a radically new guise (Jantzen 1998; in reply to the general feminist perspective, see Byrne 1995a).

It will be seen that feminist anti-realism reflects the underlying source of problems in talk about God: how can human language, if at all, serve as a means of putting human beings in touch with a radically transcendent reality?

See also Moses Maimonides/Rambam (Chapter 11), Thomas Aquinas (Chapter 12), The problem of religious language (Chapter 39), Feminism (Chapter 59).

References

Alston, W. P. (1989a) 'Functionalism and theological language,' in *Divine Nature and Human Language*, Ithaca, NY: Cornell University Press.

—— (1989b) 'Irreducible metaphors in theology,' in *Divine Nature and Human Language*, Ithaca, NY: Cornell University Press.

—— (1989c) 'Referring to God,' in *Divine Nature and Human Language*, Ithaca, NY: Cornell University Press.

Aquinas, T. (1964) *Summa Theologiae*, vol. 3, trans. H. McCabe, London: Blackfriars/Eyre and Spottiswoode.

Ayer, A. J. (1971) *Language, Truth, and Logic*, 2nd edn, Harmondsworth: Penguin.

Braithwaite, R. B. (1971) 'An empiricist's view of the nature of religious belief,' in B. Mitchell (ed.) *The Philosophy of Religion*, Oxford: Oxford University Press.

Brown, S. (1976) 'What is the verifiability criterion a criterion of?', in G. Vesey (ed.) *Impressions of Empiricism*, London: Macmillan.

Byrne, P. (1995a) 'Omnipotence, feminism, and God,' *International Journal for the Philosophy of Religion* 37: 145–66.

—— (1995b) *Prolegomena to Religious Pluralism*, London and Basingstoke: Macmillan.

—— (2003) *Religion and Realism*, Aldershot: Ashgate.

Feuerbach, L. (1957) *The Essence of Christianity*, trans. M. Evans, New York: Harper & Row.

Heimbeck, P. (1969) *Theology and Meaning*, Stanford, CA: Stanford University Press.

Hempel, C. G. (1952) 'Problems and changes in the empiricist criterion of meaning,' in L. Linski (ed.) *Semantics and the Philosophy of Language*, Urbana, IL: University of Illinois Press.

Hick, J. (1971) 'Theology and verification,' in B. Mitchell (ed.) *The Philosophy of Religion*, Oxford: Oxford University Press.

Huxley, J. S. (1957) *Religion without Revelation*, London: Parrish.

Jantzen, G. (1998) *Becoming Divine*, Manchester: University of Manchester Press.

Kant, I. (1997) *Critique of Pure Reason*, trans. P. Guyer and A. Wood, Cambridge: Cambridge University Press.

Le Poidevin, R. (1995) 'Internal and external questions about God,' *Religious Studies* 31: 485–500.

Maimonides, M. (1963) *The Guide of the Perplexed*, trans. S. Pines, Chicago: University of Chicago Press.

McFague, S. (1982) *Metaphorical Theology*, Philadelphia: Fortress Press.

—— (1987) *Models of God*, Philadelphia: Fortress Press.

Miller, R. B. (1986) 'The reference of "God,"' *Faith and Philosophy* 3: 3–15.

Nielsen, K. (1971) *Contemporary Critiques of Religion*, London: Macmillan.

Penelhum, T. (1971) *Problems of Religious Knowledge*, London: Macmillan.

Pike, N. (1970) *God and Timelessness*, London: Routledge.

Russell, B. (1962) *An Enquiry into Meaning and Truth*, Harmondsworth: Penguin.

Soskice, J. M. (1985) *Metaphor and Religious Language*, Oxford: Clarendon Press.

Swinburne, R. G. (1977) *The Coherence of Theism*, Oxford: Clarendon Press.

Zamulinski, B. (2003) 'Religion and the pursuit of truth,' *Religious Studies* 39: 43–60.

Further reading

Burrell, D. (1973) *Analogy and Philosophical Language*, New Haven, CT: Yale University Press. (A radical interpretation of Aquinas on analogy.)

Hughes, G. (1987) 'Aquinas and the limits of agnosticism,' in G. Hughes (ed.) *The Philosophical Assessment of Theology*, Tunbridge Wells: Search Press. (A good survey of issues about Aquinas and the problem of predication.)

Phillips, D. Z. (1970) *Faith and Philosophical Enquiry*, London: Routledge. (Displays a Wittgensteinian understanding of religious language.)

Runzo, R. (ed.) (1992) *Is God Real?*, London and Basingstoke: Macmillan. (Essays showing a variety of issues in realist/anti-realist debates.)

Part VIII
CHRISTIAN THEISM

49
THE TRINITY
Ronald J. Feenstra

Introduction

The Christian doctrine of the Trinity holds that there is one God who is also three persons. This doctrine, although rooted in Scripture, was not explicitly stated or developed until the early Church began reflecting both on its sacred writings, including the writings of the apostles, and on its worship of Jesus Christ. Two basic ways of understanding the Trinity have developed and persisted from the early Church to the present. A renaissance of Trinitarian theology began in the twentieth century.

Biblical roots

By the end of the first century, Jesus' followers faced a difficult conceptual problem. On the one hand, they affirmed one of the central teachings of the Hebrew Scriptures: that there is but one God, Yahweh (Deut. 6: 4; Mark 12: 29). On the other hand, they regarded Jesus not only as Messiah (Christ) and Son of God, but also as God. They then faced questions such as these: how could God be one if both Father and Son are God? What is the relationship between the Father and the Son? Is God's Spirit also God? Although the New Testament includes brief glimpses into the relationship between Father and Son, as in Jesus' prayer to the Father (John 17: 1–26), it focuses on God's activity rather than on the nature of, or relationships among, the Father, Son, and Spirit (Wainwright 1962: 6).

The New Testament frequently ascribes divine titles and functions to both the Father and the Son. Accordingly, the New Testament identifies God as one, as Father, or as God and Father: 'one God and Father of all' (Eph. 4: 6; cf. Rom. 3: 30; 1 Cor. 8: 4–6). Yet the New Testament also speaks of Jesus Christ as Lord (Acts 7: 59; Rom. 10: 9; 1 Cor. 8: 6; 16: 22; Phil. 2: 11) and as God (John 1: 1–2, 18; 20: 28). Since several of these and other passages are thought to echo liturgical material, it appears that early Christian worship spoke of Jesus Christ as Lord and God. The New Testament also indicates that early Christians prayed to Jesus Christ (Acts 7: 59–60; 1 Cor. 16: 22; Rev. 22: 20) and described him as executing the divine functions of creating, saving, and judging (Col. 1: 16; John 3: 16–17; 5: 21–7). Thus the Son, like the Father, has life in himself and should be honored as the Father is honored (John 5: 23, 26).

Biblical descriptions of Jesus Christ's relationship to God the Father also raise important and complicated issues. On the one hand, the New Testament describes Jesus as having existed with the Father prior to his birth and as the 'exact imprint' of God's being (John 8: 58; 17: 5; Heb. 1: 2–3). On the other hand, the Bible suggests Jesus' subordination to the Father as the one sent by the Father and as one who will be subordinate to the Father at the eschaton (John 5: 30; 14: 28; 1 Cor. 15: 24–8). The complexity of biblical descriptions of Jesus Christ can be seen in a single passage that describes Jesus as 'the firstborn of all creation' (suggesting creaturely subordination), but also as the one who is 'before all things,' and in whom 'all things in heaven and on earth were created' and 'all the fullness of God was pleased to dwell' (Col. 1: 15–20). Early Christian theologians grappled with passages such as these in their struggle to understand and articulate Jesus Christ's status and relationship to the Father.

New Testament references to the Spirit also include important material for the doctrine of the Trinity. Despite some passages that might not suggest that the Spirit is personal, other passages seem to imply that the Spirit is a person (Wainwright 1962: 200–4, 223). Thus Jesus describes the Spirit as guiding his disciples' speech when they are brought to trial (Mark 13: 11) and as one against whom blasphemy is not forgivable – implying personal status as one who can be blasphemed (Mark 3: 29; Matt. 12: 31; Luke 12: 10).

Although the work of the Spirit is closely associated with the work of Christ, the relationship between the two is not always clear in Scripture. Jesus promises his disciples that when he leaves them, he will send the Spirit, who will be their advocate (John 16: 7). But he sometimes speaks of himself and sometimes of the Spirit as coming to his disciples after he leaves them (John 14: 18, 26). And Paul speaks of both the Spirit and of Christ dwelling in and making intercession for believers (Rom. 8: 9–11, 26–7, 34). Curiously, Paul even seems to identify Christ and the Spirit: 'the Lord is the Spirit' (2 Cor. 3: 17–18).

Despite ambiguous biblical evidence regarding whether the Spirit is personal, as well as suggestions that the Spirit may be (rather than stand in for) the ascended Christ, Christians did not become binitarians. Some important passages led Christians to speak of a divine triad rather than a dyad. All four New Testament Gospels describe Jesus' baptism, where Jesus is present as the one being baptized, the Spirit descends on him, and a voice from heaven speaks of Jesus as 'my Son' (Mark 1: 9–11 and parallels). By noting the presence and activity of all three divine figures, these baptismal passages provide important grounds for the doctrine of the Trinity. The New Testament also includes statements that suggest three who are equal. Perhaps best-known are the baptismal formula ('baptizing them in the name of the Father and of the Son and of the Holy Spirit' (Matt. 28: 19) and the closing benediction of 2 Corinthians ('The grace of the Lord Jesus Christ, the love of God, and the communion of the Holy Spirit be with all of you' (13: 14)). Other passages also include threefold references to Father (sometimes simply called 'God'), Son, and Spirit (1 Cor. 12: 4–6; 2 Thess. 2: 13–14;

Titus 3: 4–6; 1 Pet. 1: 2). Taken together, the descriptions of Jesus' baptism and these triadic statements suggest that Father, Son, and Spirit are distinct in certain functions, yet equal in status. These passages do not, however, clarify the relationships among these three.

In short, although the Christian doctrine of the Trinity is rooted in, and would not have been developed apart from, biblical affirmations of the divinity of Jesus Christ and the Spirit, as well as key triadic texts, Scripture does not clarify the relationships among the three. In particular, Scripture's statements about the Son's equality with, yet subordination to, the Father led the early Church to struggle to understand the relationship between the Father and the Son.

The early Church

Given the exalted claims made in the New Testament about Jesus Christ and his relationship to the Father, combined with the threefold affirmations about Father, Son, and Spirit, the early Church wrestled with difficult issues in its understanding of Father, Son, and Spirit. Already in the second century, the Christian Apologists such as Justin Martyr and Theophilus spoke about the unity of God as well as about the divine pre-existence of the Logos and the Triad (*trias*) of Father, Word, and Wisdom (Kelly 1978: 109; Fortman 1982: 50–1). Although the second-century Apologists were vague about the Spirit's status and function, nevertheless they articulated the beginnings of the doctrine of the Trinity (Kelly 1978: 102-3).

By the third century, two currents of thought had developed: one, largely associated with Rome in the West, emphasized divine unity; the other, initially associated with Alexandria in the East, emphasized the threeness within God (Kelly 1978: 109–10). Among the former, belief in the oneness of God and the deity of Christ led the modalistic monarchians (notably, Sabellius) to speak of God as one being who appears first as Father and then as Son in the work of creation and redemption (pp. 121–2). Among the latter, Origen spoke of Father, Son, and Spirit as three persons or *hypostases*, distinct eternally and not just as manifested in their work. Origen also spoke of the Son and Spirit as possessing divine characteristics derivatively from the Father and therefore as subordinate to the Father (pp. 129–32).

As the fourth century opened, the Christian Church had not yet settled on either the limits of acceptable thought on, or a common vocabulary about, the divine threeness and oneness (Hanson 1989: 143-44). Arius, a presbyter in Alexandria, provoked the Church into doing so when he proposed that God the Father is the unique, transcendent, unoriginate source of everything that exists – including the Son, who was created out of nothing by the Father's will or decision and therefore had a beginning (Kelly 1978: 227–8). Arius also held that, as a finite being whose essence was dissimilar to the Father's, the Word or Son 'can neither see nor know the Father perfectly and accurately' (pp. 228–9). Arians spoke of the divine Triad as three *hypostases* who did not share the same essence or nature (p. 229).

In response to the controversy generated by Arius's proposals, the Council of Nicea in 325 composed a creed that affirms belief in 'one Lord Jesus Christ, the Son of

God, begotten from the Father, ... begotten not made, of one substance [*homoousion*] with the Father' and anathematizes those who 'assert that the Son of God is from a different hypostasis or substance' than the Father (Kelly 1972: 215). Although it seems clear that Nicaea used the term *homoousion* at least in part because Arians found it unacceptable, it is less clear what Nicea meant by the terms *homoousion* and *hypostasis* (Hanson 1988: 181–202; Stead 1994: 160–72). For example, the term *ousia* could refer either to an individual thing or entity (primary substance) or to an essence or substance common to several individuals (secondary substance). During half a century of further debate, affirming 'three hypostases' as distinct but consubstantial persons became accepted despite concerns by some western theologians that it suggested three hypostases that were alien from one another and thus three gods (Kelly 1978: 253–4). Debate during this period also clarified the Spirit's status as fully divine and equal with the Father and Son (such that some referred to the Spirit as *homoousion* with the Father and the Son) (pp. 255–63).

In 381, the Council of Constantinople issued a new creed, sometimes known as the Nicene-Constantinopolitan Creed, both reaffirming and revising important teachings of Nicaea. Significantly, it drops the anathemas from Nicea (including the anathema against saying the Son is of a different hypostasis than the Father), and it adds to Nicea's bare assertion, 'and in the Holy Spirit,' affirmations that the Spirit is Lord and life-giver, proceeds from the Father, is worshiped and glorified together with the Father and the Son, and has spoken through the prophets (Hanson 1988: 816–19). The following year, a group of bishops in Constantinople wrote a synodical letter summarizing the true faith as belief in 'one divinity, power, and substance of the Father and Son and Holy Spirit; and in their equal honor, dignity, and co-eternal majesty; in three most perfect hypostases or three perfect prosopa' (Fortman 1982: 85).

Among the major figures engaged in the fourth-century discussions were Athanasius of Alexandria (*c*.296–373) and the three Cappadocians: Basil of Caesarea (*c*.330–79), Gregory of Nazianzus (329/30–389/90), and Gregory of Nyssa (*c*.330–*c*.395). The Cappadocians describe the Trinity as three divine hypostases sharing one divine *ousia* and therefore as *homoousios* with one another (Stead 1994: 162). Accordingly, Gregory of Nyssa says Father, Son, and Holy Spirit are analogous to Peter, James, and John – three distinct persons who share one nature. Recognizing that some might consider this tritheism, Gregory offers two responses. First, appealing to Platonism, he says that just as three persons who share divinity are one God, so too three persons who share humanity should be called 'one human,' although we customarily abuse language by speaking of 'many humans' (Gregory 1979: 331, 336). Second, he argues that the unity of operations or works of God underlies the unity of the three divine persons as one God. So the Father does not do anything by himself 'in which the Son does not work conjointly'; nor does the Son have 'any special operation apart from the Holy Spirit'; and therefore the 'unity existing in the action' of the three divine persons prevents speaking in the plural of three gods (pp. 334–5). In sum, Gregory argues, 'The Father is God: the Son is God: and yet by the same proclamation God is One, because no difference either of nature or of operation is contemplated in the Godhead' (p. 336).

The views of Gregory and the other Cappadocians have been especially influential in Eastern Christian thought.

Augustine's (354-430) views on the Trinity have dominated Western Christian theology. Like the Cappadocians, Augustine emphasizes the unity of will and work of Father, Son, and Spirit, who have 'but one will and are indivisible in their working' (Augustine 1991: II.9). Similarly, Augustine rejects any suggestion that the sending of the Son and Spirit implies 'any inequality or disparity or dissimilarity of substance between the divine persons' (IV. 32). Augustine's discussion of the Trinity is influenced by his understanding of divine simplicity (VI. 8, VII. 1–3, XIV. 22). Noting the difficulty of translating concepts from Greek to Latin theology, he says that the Greek formula of one *ousia*, three *hypostases* sounds to him like one being, three substances; so he prefers to speak of one being or substance, three persons (V. 10, VII. 10–11).

Augustine's difference with the Cappadocians over terminology comes to expression in his discussion of analogies for the Trinity. Augustine rejects the 'three human' analogy, noting both the disanalogy that other humans could emerge with the same nature and that, if the image of the Trinity is realized in three human beings, then humans would not have been in God's image until there was a man, woman, and their child (VII. 11, XII. 5–9). He offers instead a variety of 'psychological' or unipersonal analogies for the Trinity. Thus the triad of the human mind, its self-knowledge, and its love are an image of the one substance of the Trinity (IX. 2–18). Alternatively, a person's memory, understanding, and will are distinct, yet one mind and one substance (X. 17–18).

Still, Augustine does not completely avoid social analogies; and he sharply qualifies his commitment to unipersonal analogies for the Trinity. In discussing Jesus' claim that he and the Father are one (John 10: 30) and his prayer that his disciples will be one as he and the Father are one (John 17: 22), Augustine employs a social analogy: 'just as Father and Son are one not only by equality of substance but also by identity of will, so these men … might be one not only by being of the same nature, but also by being bound in the fellowship of the same love' (IV. 12). Then, in the concluding book of his work on the Trinity, Augustine notes that all images of the Trinity are inadequate: 'So the trinity as a thing in itself is quite different from the image of the trinity in another thing' (XV. 42). In particular, both social and psychological analogies ultimately falter: 'while a triad of men cannot be called a man, that triad is called, and is, one God. … Nor is that triad like this image, man, which is one person *having* those three things; on the contrary, it *is* three persons, the Father of the Son and the Son of the Father and the Spirit of the Father and the Son' (XV. 43).

The similarities between the Cappadocians and Augustine on the Trinity show broad areas of agreement and commitment to the language of the Nicene-Constantinopolitan Creed. Still, the differences between them indicate two distinct schools of thought on the Trinity, one primarily associated with Eastern, the other primarily with Western, Christianity.

Medieval thought

The doctrine of the Trinity became the main theological point at issue in the eleventh-century schism between Eastern and Western Christianity. Although the Nicene-Constantinopolitan Creed says only that the Holy Spirit 'proceeds from the Father,' by the fifth and sixth centuries – under the influence of Augustine's thought – western Christian theologians added that the Holy Spirit proceeds from the Father *and the Son* (*filioque*) (Kelly 1972: 358–9). Asserting the Spirit's procession from the Son as well as the Father became an important means for western theologians to affirm the Son's full equality with the Father (Pelikan 1974: 185). In contrast, Eastern Christian thinkers held that 'the Spirit proceeded *from* the Father *through* the Son,' but insisted that 'the Father was the source or fountain-head of Deity' (Kelly 1972: 359). For the East, 'there could be no procession also from the Son, for whatever was common to two hypostases had to be common to all three, and then the Holy Spirit would proceed also from himself' (Pelikan 1974: 194). Although the Church of Rome for a time resisted tampering with the creed, eventually it added the *filioque*, thereby provoking a dispute with the East (Kelly 1972: 366–7).

Medieval western thought on the Trinity was influenced by Boethius' (*c.*480–*c.*524) definition of a person as 'The individual substance of a rational nature,' which he takes to be equivalent to the Greek term *hypostasis* (Boethius 1973: 85–7). Boethius speaks of divine persons as 'predicates of relation' (p. 27). Building on Boethius' thought, Thomas Aquinas (*c.*1225–74) says, 'a divine person signifies a relation as subsisting … and such a relation is a hypostasis subsisting in the divine nature, although in truth that which subsists in the divine nature is the divine nature itself' (Aquinas 1948: I. q.29. a.4). So Aquinas defines a Trinitarian person as a *subsistent* relation. Aquinas sees his position as occupying a middle ground between two opposite errors: Arianism and Sabellianism. To avoid Arianism, Aquinas speaks of a *distinction* between divine persons, but not of a separation or division; to avoid Sabellianism, he rejects both the phrase, 'the only God,' since 'Deity is common to several,' and the word 'solitary,' 'lest we take away the society of the three persons' (I. q.31. a.2). Reflecting western views, Aquinas holds that, if the Spirit did not proceed from the Son as well as the Father, he could not be distinguished from the Son, since his relation to the Father would be identical to the Son's relation to the Father (I. q.36. a.2).

Proposals since the nineteenth century

Standing in the background of discussions of the Trinity since the nineteenth century is the work of Friedrich Schleiermacher (1768–1834), who considers the Trinity only in the conclusion of his major work, *The Christian Faith*. Schleiermacher gives several reasons for putting the doctrine of the Trinity in what is essentially an appendix to this theology. First, on the basis of his method of working from an analysis of religious consciousness, Schleiermacher argues that this consciousness could never give rise to 'the assumption of an eternal distinction in the Supreme Being' (Schleiermacher 1928: 739). Raising an issue that would become important in twentieth-century theology, Schleiermacher, working from his analysis of God-consciousness, says, 'we have no formula for the being of God in Himself as distinct from the being of God in the world' (p. 748). Second, he finds the Church's doctrine inconsistent, affirming the equality of the persons while also making the Father superior to the other two (pp. 742–4). Finally, on the grounds that the Protestant Reformation offered no new treatment of this doctrine, but left the Church vacillating between tritheism and Unitarianism, he sees a doctrine due for 'reconstruction' (pp. 747–9).

The 'reconstruction' of the doctrine of the Trinity began in the first half of the twentieth century, initiated by Karl Barth but joined in by theologians of every theological and confessional stripe, including Karl Rahner, Leonard Hodgson, Jürgen Moltmann, Leonardo Boff, Catherine LaCugna, and John Zizioulas. Since the 1980s, Christian philosophers as well as theologians have addressed important issues in the doctrine of the Trinity.

Writing in 1932, Barth develops the doctrine of the Trinity from his analysis of the event of divine revelation. In revelation, says Barth, 'God, the Revealer, is identical with His act in revelation and also identical with its effect'; this is a threefold reality that Barth describes as 'Revealer, Revelation, and Revealedness' (1975: 295–6).

Barth argues that in modern thought 'person' has a different meaning than it did in the patristic and medieval periods, having acquired 'the attribute of self-consciousness' (1975: 357). As a result, on the one hand, speaking of three divine persons using this new concept of person, with the Trinity composed of 'three independently thinking and willing subjects,' seems inescapably tritheist; but, on the other hand, speaking of divine 'persons' as if the modern concept of personality did not exist is obsolete and unintelligible today (pp. 357–8). So, replacing the term 'person' with 'mode (or way) of being,' Barth restates the doctrine of the Trinity as follows: 'the one God, i.e. the one Lord, the one personal God, is what He is not just in one mode but … in the mode of the Father, in the mode of the Son, and in the mode of the Holy Ghost' (p. 359). This is not modalism, argues Barth, because the three modes are not manifestations that are foreign to God's essence and beyond which God is not Father, Son, and Spirit (p. 382). Rather, just as 'fatherhood is an eternal mode of being of the divine essence,' so too Jesus Christ 'does not first become God's Son or Word' and the Holy Spirit 'does not first become the … Spirit of God, in the event of revelation' (pp. 390, 414, 466). 'Down to the very depths of deity … as the ultimate thing that is to be said about God,' God is Father, Son, and Spirit (p. 414).

Contemporary theologians have wrestled with a question at the heart of the doctrine of the Trinity: how can we move from God's presence and action in Jesus Christ and the Spirit (that is, the divine 'economy') to speaking of what God is in himself? Defending a position similar to Barth's, Rahner states a thesis that has become axiomatic for many: 'The "economic" Trinity is the "immanent" Trinity and the "immanent" Trinity is the "economic" Trinity' (Rahner 1974: 22). Catherine LaCugna notes one implication of this identification of the economic and immanent Trinity: 'God has given Godself to us in Jesus Christ and the Spirit, and this self-revelation or self-communication is nothing less than what God is as God. Creation, redemption, and consummation are thus anchored in God's eternity' (LaCugna 1991: 209).

In contrast to Barth and Rahner, who favor unipersonal models, Moltmann defends a social view of the Trinity. Moltmann argues that, if there is just one divine subject, 'then the three Persons are bound to be degraded to modes of being, or modes of subsistence, of the one identical subject,' which would not merely revive 'Sabellian modalism,' but also 'transfer the subjectivity of action to a deity concealed "behind" the three Persons' (Moltmann 1981: 139). He argues that, on Barth's view, the 'one divine personality' must be ascribed either to the Father or, like Sabellius, to 'a subject for whom all three trinitarian persons are objective' (p. 143). On Moltmann's view, 'The unity of the divine tri-unity lies in the *union* of the Father, the Son and the Spirit, not in their numerical unity. It lies in their *fellowship*, not in the identity of a single subject' (p. 95). On the basis of Jesus' prayer for his disciples in John 17: 21, Moltmann concludes that, since the disciples are not only to have fellowship with one another that resembles the union of the Son and the Father, but also to have '*fellowship with God* and, beyond that, a *fellowship in God*,' the unity of the Trinity implies the soteriological uniting of creation in God (pp. 95–6).

Among more recent scholars, Cornelius Plantinga, Jr. and Brian Leftow represent two main alternatives for understanding the Trinity. Plantinga develops and defends a social Trinitarian view. He presents the Trinity as 'a divine, transcendent society or community of three fully personal and fully divine entities: the Father, the Son, and the Holy Spirit,' who are unified by sharing the divine essence and by 'their joint redemptive purpose, revelation, and work.' On this view, each member is 'a distinct person, but scarcely an *individual* or *separate* or *independent* person,' and each has 'penetrating, inside knowledge of the other as other, but as co-other, loved other, fellow' (Plantinga 1989: 27–8). Plantinga offers three reasons that this does not constitute tritheism: important strands in the Christian tradition speak of three distinct persons; the pluralist Christian heresy is Arianism, which posits 'three *ontologically graded* distinct persons'; and social Trinitarianism does not affirm three autonomous or independent persons (Plantinga 1989: 32–7).

Leftow articulates and defends 'Latin Trinitarianism.' Employing the concept of a trope as 'an individualized case of an attribute,' he notes that, although Cain and Abel 'had the same nature, they had distinct tropes of that nature,' such that when Abel's humanity perished, Cain's did not. Leftow argues that 'both Father and Son instance the divine nature (deity),' but, unlike Cain and Abel, 'they have but one trope of deity between them' (Leftow 2004: 305). Recognizing that this view seems to suggest that there is just one divine person, Leftow imagines a situation in which time-travel allows three distinct segments of one person's life to appear simultaneously (to us) as three persons side-by-side (p. 307). Analogously, 'God's life runs in three streams,' with God as Father in one, as Son in another, and as Spirit in the third (p. 319). Leftow argues that this account avoids modalism because it can affirm a 'Trinity of being' by saying that 'the Persons' distinction is an eternal, necessary, non-successive and intrinsic feature of God's life, one which would be there even if there were no creatures,' and because, although 'the God who is the Father is crucified,' he is crucified 'at the point in His life at which He is not the Father, but the Son' (p. 327).

The doctrine of the Trinity, 'which is the specifically Christian way of speaking about God,' has important implications for the Christian life: it 'summarizes what it means to participate in the life of God through Jesus Christ in the Spirit' (LaCugna 1991: 1). As LaCugna observes, we cannot enter into the divine life without also entering into 'a life of love and communion with others' (p. 382).

See also Christianity (Chapter 6), Augustine (Chapter 8), Thomas Aquinas (Chapter 12), Eastern Orthodoxy (Chapter 44), The Incarnation (Chapter 51).

References

Aquinas, T. (1948) *Summa Theologica*, trans. Fathers of the English Dominican Province, rev. edn, New York: Benziger Bros.

Augustine (1991) *The Trinity*, trans. E. Hill, New York: New City Press.

Barth, K. (1975) *Church Dogmatics*, I/1, eds G. W. Bromiley and T. F. Torrance, Edinburgh: T. & T. Clark.

Boethius (1973) *The Theological Tractates* and *The Consolation of Philosophy*, trans. H. F. Stewart, E. K. Rand, and S. J. Tester, Loeb Classical Library, Cambridge, MA: Harvard University Press; London: William Heinemann.

Fortman, E. (1982) *The Triune God: A Historical Study of the Doctrine of the Trinity*, Grand Rapids, MI: Baker.

Gregory of Nyssa (1979) 'On "not three Gods": to Ablabius,' in P. Schaff and H. Wace (eds) *A Select Library of Nicene and Post-Nicene Fathers of the Christian Church*, 2nd series, vol. V, Grand Rapids, MI: Eerdmans.

Hanson, R. (1988) *The Search for the Christian Doctrine of God: The Arian Controversy 318–381*, Edinburgh: T. & T. Clark.

—— (1989) 'The Achievement of Orthodoxy in the fourth century AD,' in R. Williams (ed.) *The Making of Orthodoxy*, Cambridge: Cambridge University Press.

Kelly, J. (1972) *Early Christian Creeds*, 3rd edn, New York: Longman.

—— (1978) *Early Christian Doctrines*, rev. edn, New York: Harper & Row.

LaCugna, C. (1991) *God for Us: The Trinity and the Christian Life*, San Francisco: HarperCollins.

Leftow, B. (2004) 'A Latin Trinity,' *Faith and Philosophy* 21: 304–33.

Moltmann, J. (1981) *The Trinity and the Kingdom*, trans. M. Kohl, San Francisco, CA: Harper & Row.

Pelikan, J. (1974) *The Spirit of Eastern Christendom (600–1700)*, vol. 2 of *The Christian Tradition*, Chicago: University of Chicago Press.

Plantinga, C. (1989) 'Social Trinity and Tritheism,' in R. J. Feenstra and C. Plantinga, Jr. (eds), *Trinity, Incarnation, and Atonement: Philosophical and Theological Essays*, Notre Dame, IN: University of Notre Dame Press.

Rahner, K. (1974) *The Trinity*, trans. J. Donceel, New York: Seabury Press.

Schleiermacher, F. (1928) *The Christian Faith*, ed. H. R. Mackintosh and J. S. Stewart, Edinburgh: T. & T. Clark.

Stead, C. (1994) *Philosophy in Christian Antiquity*, Cambridge: Cambridge University Press.

Wainwright, A. (1962) *The Trinity in the New Testament*, London: SPCK.

Further reading

Boff, L. (1988) *Trinity and Society*, trans. P. Burns, Maryknoll, NY: Orbis. (A social Trinitarian view emphasizing liberation themes.)

Brower, J. and M. Rea (2005) 'Material constitution and the Trinity,' *Faith and Philosophy* 22: 57-76. (Uses Aristotle's concepts of form and matter to describe the divine essence as like matter that is individuated into three persons by three distinct forms or properties.)

Davis, S., D. Kendall, and G. O'Collins (eds) (1999) *The Trinity: An Interdisciplinary Symposium on the Trinity*, Oxford: Oxford University Press. (Articles on biblical, patristic, and systematic issues.)

Hodgson, L. (1943) *The Doctrine of the Trinity*, London: Nisbet. (A significant statement of social Trinitarianism.)

Olson, R. and C. Hall (2002) *The Trinity*, Grand Rapids, MI: Eerdmans. (A summary of biblical and historical material, plus an extended annotated bibliography.)

Rusch, W. (ed.) (1980) *The Trinitarian Controversy*, Philadelphia: Fortress. (A collection of important early documents.)

Stead, C. (1977) *Divine Substance*, Oxford: Clarendon Press. (A study of the concept of substance in the early Church's understanding of the Trinity.)

Zizioulas, J. (1985) *Being as Communion*, Crestwood, NY: St Vladimir's Seminary Press. (An Eastern Orthodox statement of the Trinity.)

50
REVELATION
Ellen T. Charry

Revelation is the truth disclosed by or about God. Christians assume, and sometimes try to argue, that God exists and freely and lovingly communicates with human beings publicly and perhaps privately for the sake of their well-being. Beyond that, questions rapidly scurry about. Does God disclose himself or a set of ideas? How can we rely on what we think is the truth disclosed or communicated by God? In responding to these questions, revelation is variously presented as Scripture as a bulk literary deposit, or Scripture as the history of God's dealings with the world. Quite separate is the claim that revelation is knowledge of God, not necessarily or only disclosed in Scripture, but also from sense experience or disclosed to the mind itself. Underlying the several discussions all along the line is the epistemological dimension of the problem of revelation: how is it that we know God and his intentions for us?

While some of these questions go back to the fourth century with the incisive questioning of Augustine of Hippo, whose huge output is shot through with episte-mological anxiety, they all became far more pressing with the modern understanding of knowledge defined by empirical evidence as the sole criterion of knowledge and one of its offshoots, historical biblical scholarship. The positivist vision of knowledge triumphed, and Christian theology was sent into a tailspin about whether we reliably know God at all and whether the traditional sources for doing so (Scripture, tradition, reason) are reliable. A new view of the possibility and nature of revelation now tied to experience emerged from this struggle. Here we will first briefly review the traditional view behind the modern crisis. Then we will examine recent discussion on the human capacity by means of which we know God experientially. Finally, we will point out some recent suggestions regarding the content of revelation.

Background

The central Christian belief about revelation is, of course, that it is the Christian Bible or is contained in it. The Bible has two forms, Catholic / Anglican and Protestant, the Protestant version lacking the apocryphal or deutero-canonical books. The bulk of the canon was received from the Jews, along with their doctrine of plenary inspiration, with other books of distinctly Christian orientation gradually added in. The whole was adopted as the authoritative list of the holy books of the Christian Church in the mid-fourth century. These became the epistemic criterion for preaching, argument, and teaching especially to define the parameters of the community's identity: the Church is that community defined by the teachings of these books deemed to be divinely inspired in authorship and content. Frank Kermode describes 'the mythical or magical view of the canon,' a 'text [that] is held to be eternally fixed, unalterable, and of such immeasurable interpretative potential that it remains, despite its unaltered state, sufficient for all future times' (Kermode 1987: 605). The Bible is the foundational set of books of the Christian tradition.

Yet Scripture was not the only source of revelation. Because it was unwieldy, for missionary purposes it became necessary to try to boil it down into a relatively simple summary statement of belief for new recruits. Thus, the Creed became the interpretive guide to Scripture. Yet even simple creedal statements did not stop the questions about how we know God. The Bible said that we know the history of God's interaction with the world. Creeds identified a simple summary of the content of Christian belief (a rule of faith). Yet, epistemic questions persisted.

Augustine of Hippo was the first to focus on the epistemological question of how we can (be expected to) love God unless we know him and correctly so. For, although the tradition had claimed that we know God's works through Scripture, it is another matter entirely to know God himself, a goal toward which Christians often pressed, even at times against their own advice. This question of the relationship between love and knowledge marbles Augustine's enormous output. To put the matter as succinctly as possible, Augustine argued that we cannot love what we do not know. And loving God is essential to conforming ourselves to him that we may be happy. In two of his major works, the *Confessions* and the *Trinity* (Augustine 1991a: bk. 9; Augustine 1991b: bk. 9), he struggles with the problem and offers an answer. Knowing God is not unlike knowing other things. Some things we know from experience, and we use memory and imagination to expand that base until it can be corroborated by further experience. We extrapolate from what we do know, using our imagination analogically, to things that we do not yet know but want to or long to know because we have some intuition or hunch about their beauty and value and so want to know them. For example, a student wants to study astronomy because he loves looking at the stars and imagines that to know them better would bring him further joy and satisfaction. So it is with God. We see and know good things and we want (to know) the very goodness that makes them so appealing, and that goodness is God. So, we want (to know) God even if we do not realize that it is God that we want to know. Thus Augustine is responsible for the notion that whether we understand it correctly or not, all souls long for God who communicates himself to them through material goods to lead them to the prime spiritual one – himself. Why would God create us unable to know him if he is the source of our life and salvation? It would be self-defeating on God's part to create humanity unable to know him, since knowing him is essential to our well-being. Thus, for Augustine, while the Bible is divine revelation, its testimony is so varied that other measures are needed to tell us the truth(s) of and about God. Since its early centuries, Christians were not content with scriptural testimony but wanted to press beyond to God himself. Thus the question of revelation became entwined with the human ability to discern God either directly through rational exercise or indirectly by extrapolating from what we do know.

Although Augustine often wrote as if all humans have this capacity to extrapolate from sensate to abstract things, he sometimes suggested that we do not always or necessarily know God through sensate things. Rather, knowing God is a matter of divine illumination that is spontaneous and unpredictable. God reveals his very being through material things; those persons whom he illuminates with knowledge of himself grasp this and ascend to the joy of seeing and tasting God, even if only incompletely in this life.

This view remained unchallenged until the twelfth century when the translation of Aristotle into Latin introduced a new standard of truth that threatened the Augustinian synthesis. Scholastic method divided theology from philosophy as separate sources of knowledge of the truth. Thomas Aquinas brokered this gap in his treatise on faith in the *Summa Theologiae* (Aquinas 1954: ST II. 2 qq.1, 2, 3, 11; Penelhum 1997). Here we have a rather new interpretation of revelation. It is no longer insight into the divine nature grasped by divine illumination but several sources of written knowledge that call for harmonization in order to arrive at the truth about God and what we need to know of him. Thus the science of theology (sacred doctrine) becomes the preserve of a professional class.

The distinction between Augustine and Aquinas on revelation is pivotal. For Augustine, revelation is the truth of and about God extrapolated from Scripture that is confirmed by the individual experientially. For Thomas, revelation appears in various trustworthy written sources of truth that the professional theologian distills as a body of ecclesiastically approved information. This deposit of faith contains propositions both about God himself and about other things that relate to God. It is compiled to be assented to by the Christian masses through the 'cognitive habit' of faith. Assent to this body of doctrine assures the obedient believer of acceptance into the community of the faithful. Thus, revelation was transformed from being a moral and spiritual encounter with God to being the background to doctrine: eternally valid propositions constructed by professionals for mass consumption.

Protestantism trimmed down the medieval model, admitting but one revelatory source, scripture. Protestant Scholasticism, which synthesized Scripture into a set of now Protestant doctrines, emerged in the seventeenth century, precisely the same time that the authority of Scripture began to give way under the penetrating gaze of moderns, especially Baruch Spinoza (Spinoza 1998) and the eighteenth-century English deists, John Toland (Toland 1995) and Matthew Tindal (Tindal 1730). Bishop Joseph Butler (Butler 1900) and Peter Browne (Browne 1697) responded to deism to defend the older view of revelation. When controversies broke out in earnest over the historicity of miracles recorded in the Bible, revelation was thrown into crisis. David Hume (Hume 1988) responded to John Tillotson (Tillotson 1684). William Paley offered the strongest response to Hume (Paley 1952), but Hume's skepticism seemed to carry the day. Modern skepticism threatened revelation and thereby the entire Christian edifice.

The final word on our ability to know God rationally was spoken by Immanuel Kant (Kant 1965). In the great *Critique of Pure Reason* he argued persuasively that pure reason cannot penetrate beyond sensate things. It can know nothing of the noumenal or intelligible world. That is the preserve of practical or moral reasoning. We must postulate God and the moral law in order to sustain civil society. With Scripture's authority undermined, this show-stopping judgment that reason cannot know God on its own, Kant threw the discussion of revelation back to the theologians, now unaided by either Scripture or reason.

In the twentieth century, revelation continued to be a contentious issue, with theologians challenged by rational and scientific interpretations of events that would undermine claims that God exists and consequently that he communicates with humans for their well-being. The overwhelming characteristic of these late modern 'takes' on revelation is that they all reject the Scholastic notion that revelation undergirds a set of propositional truth-claims derived from Scripture, or Scripture and tradition, and in one way or another embrace the notion of revelation as divine self-disclosure or self-communication. Facing the modern pressure that all knowledge is historically conditioned, theologians turned to the idea that revelation is an encounter or experience that sends one to the theistic hypothesis. Now we turn to three experiential interpretations of revelation.

How we know God

As noted above, Augustine of Hippo expended enormous energy on the human capacity to know God. He assumed that we extrapolate divine creativity by reflecting on our experience of the world, and the experience of our own mind. And when we do both we are able to know God – as Trinity – and ourselves in the divine image. That is, for Augustine, God discloses himself to us both in history (Scripture) and experience.

Despite Augustine's intriguing integration of Scripture, philosophy of mind, and moral psychology in order to know God and ourselves properly, later theology failed to explore the inner life until the prompt of modern existentialism. In the twentieth century, there emerged a growing interest in revelation as experience, with a concomitant lack of interest in revelation as a set of doctrinal statements propositionally stated apart from experience. Here we will note three twentieth-century theologians who turned to revelation as encounter but differed on the epistemic capacities by means of which it is received: Karl Rahner, Karl Barth through Christoph Schwöbel, and the American, H. R. Niebuhr.

Trained in neo-Thomism and well read in Martin Heidegger, Karl Rahner was a modern liberal Roman Catholic theologian. He picked up the Augustinian emphasis on revelation as knowledge of God as a supplement to revelation as the report of theologians on doctrines (that he calls transcendental revelation) in addition to Scripture (that he calls categorical revelation), thus presenting a far more open and broader understanding of revelation and the human capacity to receive it than probably anyone before him.

He begins from the assertion that human beings are spiritual, that is, capable of interpreting experience and history abstractly, apart from themselves, and with an anticipatory openness to the future, or being, as Heidegger puts it. Rahner's metaphysical anthropology bases itself on the absolute openness of man to the other, his ability to receive divine revelation (McCool 1975: 20). He further insists that this universally given transcendent openness to the supramundane means that God can communicate with us through human words that promote inner growth. Since we are meant for this openness to God and are free to attend to his self-communication, Rahner argues that we exercise our human freedom properly when we interpret the world and its past, ourselves and our lives as they take place in history as a continuous interaction with God (ibid.: 59–65).

Rahner's experiential focus departs from, or, perhaps more precisely, expansively reinterprets the standard theological conversation about revelation, stemming from medieval Scholasticism that identified two types of revelation: general and special. General revelation, which serves as a basis for natural theology, in turn has two types: one connected with observing nature and one with thought. A standard classic Christian argument for knowing God argued that the existence of and knowledge about God is available by looking at the orderliness and power and beauty of the natural world. Inference of this sort is often the tack of the psalmists, Psalm 19: 1 ('the heavens declare the glory of God; and the firmament proclaims his handiwork') being perhaps the most oft-quoted example. Inferring a cause from observable effects was widespread in Christian arguments for the existence of God and revelation until David Hume demolished the argument (Hume 1970).

The second form of natural theology is rational argument. Anselm of Canterbury's invention of the ontological argument in his *Proslogion* is the earliest example of this approach to general revelation. It, along with other arguments for the existence of God, was felled by Kant who set limits to what pure reason can know. In short, general revelation (and natural theological arguments derived from it) did not weather the storms of modernity any better than did special revelation, as miracles, prophecy, and the doctrine of scriptural inspiration were assailed.

The second type of revelation, called 'special' or 'supernatural' to distinguish it from the first type, is also often called divine revelation proper. It is usually identified with the Christian Bible, although Catholics and Protestants have different versions of the canon as noted earlier. At present, the identification of revelation exclusively with the Bible is also being challenged, as we see with Rahner.

Rahner argues that his thematization of transcendental revelation is not natural theology, even though it is universally available to all persons, because it is not natural but supernatural. Some would dispute this, however, raising another whole set of questions. Divine self-communication is divine revelation proper even though it is co-extensive with the whole history of the world's freedom, including the various religions that have been produced (Rahner 1978). He puts it this way, 'As we understand it, when God comes to us in his freedom, in his absolutely and radically supernatural grace in what we have called the offer of God's self-communication, the God of supernatural salvation and of grace is already at work' (pp. 145–6). His basic point is that human beings are created open to the future/reality/being, and God freely comes to meet them in that openness. Transcendental revelation is not then something that we do on our own, but is the result of our interaction with God's coming to meet us in the historical reality of our life. Scripture cannot be construed any other way.

While Rahner gave the widest possible range to revelation, his contemporary, also attentive to the historical nature of all reality, saw it in a quite narrow range. For Karl Barth, revelation is the event of the Incarnation. There is no experience that enables God to be known outside this singular objective historical event. While Rahner operates at the top of a funnel, Barth operates at the bottom.

By the 1970s, the notion of experience, deriving from Locke's account of empirical evidence, had so subjectivized the notion of revelation that it was nearly emptied of content. Christoph Schwöbel undertook an analysis of experience to support Barth's insistence that revelation is personal divine self-communication as Jesus Christ (Schwöbel 1992: ch. 4). It is the foundation and orientation of all human relationships and self-understanding.

Schwöbel argues that experience is more complex than is generally assumed because it depends on perception, and perception is attending to certain sensory stimuli that are responded to, and so is always individual (1992: 104). Simple perception is a component of experience, which is more complex because it involves interpreting the perceptions 'as something,' using a general interpretive framework that relies upon rules (p. 105). Experience is the synthesis of perceptions into more general structures of meaning that is always historically concrete. That is, all experience is culturally and historically conditioned. This is a commonplace in contemporary epistemology.

He then turns to the role of the subject. Such interpretation requires cognitive competence because synthesizing experience is a creative and selective art. Here Schwöbel returns to Augustine's reflections on knowledge that is shaped by memory and expectation. Understanding experience requires becoming an interpretive artist of sorts to interact freely and personally with the environment. This is a self-conscious process in which we understand ourselves as interpretive agents who enter freely into social communication (1992: 108). Echoing Rahner and behind him Heidegger, Schwöbel points to the openness of reality for interpretation by means of experience.

At this point, Schwöbel makes a Barthian turn by noting tension between what is constituted for the experiencing subject and what is constituted by it. The former means that the latter is not entirely free but receives the former passively. Constitution of experience and self-constitution by means of interpreting experience are limited, fallible, and relative. There is really no free act of synthesis, for experience is finally not self-produced but at least partially given. Experience becomes an ontological concept (1992: 109).

When the limits and fallibility of experience are recognized by the subject of experience, it becomes 'the determination of reality as an object of experience and certainty by interpreting and organizing subjects on the basis of the disclosedness of reality' (1992: 111). The active ordering of reality is seen to be dependent upon the 'objective order of reality, but [God's] activity is not in itself accessible to human knowledge' but is given to it (p. 112). And so Schwöbel arrives at the Barthian point: 'the concept of revelation (as the basic concept of a theory of divine agency) expresses the event of disclosure which is the condition of the possibility of experience (as the basic concept of a theory of human agency)' (p. 112). Revelation makes experience possible, and that revelation is the event of the Incarnation.

The difference between Rahner and Schwöbel/Barth is small but significant. They agree that revelation is divine self-disclosure and that human knowing is creative and interactively interprets reality freely and imaginatively. The primary difference between them is that Rahner does not foreclose interpretation of experience by revelation but sought to open up the closed windows of the Catholic Church to human creativity and imagination. He posits far more freedom within fallibility to human agency in receiving and interpreting divine self-communication. He was reacting against a closed and restrictive tradition of Roman Catholic fundamental theology that presented revelation based on biblical accounts of miracles and prophecies as unambiguous (Daly 1997: 32–3).

Barth was going in the other direction. He was protesting liberal Protestant's loosening of revelation from the objective content of the faith in the name of instinctive human ability to know God apart from special revelation. And, as Schwöbel puts it, he posited revelation as the presupposition of human experience passively received by the subject of experience. Rahner was championing creativity; Barth was championing humility.

Another contemporary of Rahner and Barth was H. R. Niebuhr who took a position between them, arguing that revelation is a function of faith understood through a community's imagination (Niebuhr 1960). Like Barth, Niebuhr begins not from any assumption of universal experience but from Christian Scriptures. Yet revelation is not simply given there. It occurs when the individual is about to read and interpret the Scripture from the point of view and in the context of church history (1960: 37). In saying that revelation is a moral encounter with God interpreted through the tradition, Neibuhr makes an interesting and important foray into the inner experience of revelation, a rather different tack from that taken by Schwöbel, who started with experience in general.

Niebuhr distinguished external history that deals with objects from internal history that processes them. Internal history is the internalization of external history whose events become our own past. The issues of Scripture and church history become our own and come to constitute our identity as participants in the life of the community. Revelation is soteriological (as it is for Rahner) in that we come to see ourselves through the identity of the community and its practices and beliefs. As a moral experience, revelation is transformative as it is for Augustine because it is ballast for self-interpretation. For a participant in the values, practices, and beliefs of the community, all historical events are events of divine self-disclosure. Revelation provides an interpretive grid through which personal experience and the past take on larger meaning than either could on their own, because it takes into itself other people's lives as transmitted over time (1960: 80). Revelation is the foundation of a rational moral life (p. 96). Like Augustine, Niebuhr views revelation as the source of spiritual maturation. When the values and principles of life are well internalized, they so reshape one's character that deviation from them causes inner conflict. He is moving from traditionally Protestant deontological ethics to character or virtue ethics based on his revision of revelation.

Revelation is only possible in faith as a meeting between the self-disclosing God that happens over and over and grows as it reconstructs natural knowledge about God that may also be available from nature or other religions. Niebuhr, like many other liberal Protestants, was influenced by Martin Buber's stunning work *I and Thou* (Buber 1937).

Like the others, Niebuhr was rejecting the notion that revelation is located in or perhaps limited to propositions, and putting forth the Augustinian idea that revelation is an encounter between the person who is open to God and the self-disclosure of God through events and material objects – again notably but apparently not exclusively the Incarnation, as Barth has it. Nor is the Incarnation the foundation of all human experience as Schwöbel has it quite strongly, so that coming to faith is coming to the condition of the possibility of experience altogether. Niebuhr realizes that the Christian story may not be revelatory for some and that non-Christian stories and the practices of other religious communities can also be revelation for others. In this he agrees with Rahner. Thus Niebuhr, although he undertakes confessional theology that begins from and takes place within the Christian household, ends up providing a framework whereby Christians can analogize from the salvific power of Christian revelation to that of other traditions.

Content of revelation

In sum, the long Christian discussion of revelation has had two foci: although Scripture is revelation proper, knowledge of God is extrapolated from experience; further, we extrapolate a set of beliefs about God and moral guidelines from God from the material world and written sources deemed reliable for this purpose. These have often been integrated in various ways. Both foci are involved in contemporary construals of revelation even when these interpret experience differently and highlight the content of revelation differently. We will exemplify the various ways in which construals of experience and interpretations of Christian source material are sometimes integrated with three offerings that highlight the content of revelation differently.

God is known in the Beautiful

The first example is that the content of revelation is God himself, here refracted as the attribute of beauty extracted from the Incarnation. Hans Urs von Balthasar followed Augustine's path that God created us able to know him through material things. In an essay entitled 'Revelation and the Beautiful,' he seeks to reclaim the theological dimension of beauty after the perilous modern divorce between the good and the beautiful that released the beautiful to commercial interests (von Balthasar 1964). Knowing God comes in experiencing the beautiful in the holy and this, for

Christians, is not an aesthetic attitude, but the beauty of the human form spilled out in the repugnant sight of the crucified Christ.

God is the beauty in the drama of suffering, including its grotesque cruelty that acquires a kind of sacramental image that emits a moral summons to the beholder. In that experience we encounter the indigence of human life to which Christ surrenders and with which individuals and peoples continuously grapple. The beauty of God revealed in Christ's exquisite suffering returns beauty to us from positivism as a great gift. The humiliation of Christ makes God's beauty the more resplendent and accessible to the one contemplating it.

Christ, von Balthasar suggests, is God's greatest work of art in which creation arrives at its zenith. Here we see human helplessness carried to its deepest point. The viewer has no choice but to follow it into hell for the release of those who await the promise of release and there to be overwhelmed yet again at a deeper level. To see that such suffering brings release is to be confronted with the redeeming power of the divine beauty and caught up in its jaws.

God is revealed in the doctrinal witness of the Church

Balthasar presents revelation as the contorted beauty of God seen exceptionally clearly in the Incarnation. Less poetically, but with deep resonances, William J. Abraham argues that acceptance of revelation depends upon the discerning eye of the beholder (Abraham 2006). It is useless to continue trying to find a foundational epistemic principle on which to ground Christian doctrine. He appeals to the inner testimony of the Holy Spirit that John's gospel, say, will guide the Church into all truth. Instead of insisting on a single locus of epistemic authority like Scripture or the papal magisterium, it suffices to acknowledge that the order and beauty of the world themselves arouse an experience of knowing God and justify a theistic orientation toward reality. Formal reasoning has failed to provide a strong epistemic foundation for belief and is not needed to be persuaded of revelation.

Because epistemizing a single locus of power that authenticates revelation is unfeasible, Abraham urges instead trust that the discerning eye that enables individuals to adopt a theistic outlook also operates in the Church in its formulation of doctrine. The Holy Spirit leads toward doctrinal truth through the sacramental and liturgical life of the Church, various teachers, Scriptures, and institutional developments that give rise to doctrines, most notably the Incarnation and the Trinity. This extends the theme that we are 'wired' to recognize God on the individual level to trust that that wiring, along with other cognitive and imaginative capacities, suffices to yield true doctrine over a long period of time and in many, informal and indirect ways.

God's commitment to humanity is revealed in a Person

While von Balthasar trusts that we know God in the beautiful and Abraham trusts the canonical heritage as the intellectual content of the faith, for Karl Barth the content of revelation is the disclosure of God's electing love of humanity in Jesus Christ (Barth

1956). Recognition of this fact may itself be miraculous, for it is not the result of any human capacities, even God-given ones. Disclosure of God's electing love may take a beautiful or grotesque form, but that is finally irrelevant, perhaps even dangerous, according to Barth. The commitment is ensconced in canonical doctrines carefully transmitted, but these are not indebted to interpretive ingenuity by centuries of devotees, for these may distort the message. For Barth, the content of revelation is the tangible promise of God's embrace of humanity in Jesus Christ.

Here, somewhat oddly, the content of revelation is the realization of a promise in the form of a person. It is not experienced as it is for von Balthasar and Abraham, but noetic; it is an idea to be accepted as the source of self-understanding on the pain of radical self-misunderstanding.

See also Christianity (Chapter 6), Augustine (Chapter 8), Thomas Aquinas (Chapter 12), The problem of religious language (Chapter 39), Catholic philosophical theology (Chapter 43), Protestant theology (Chapter 45), Theology and religious language (Chapter 48), Religious experience (Chapter 63).

References

Abraham, W. J. (2006) *Crossing the Threshold of Divine Revelation*, Grand Rapids, MI: Eerdmans.
Aquinas, T. (1954) *Nature and Grace*, Philadelphia: Westminster Press.
Augustine (1991a) *Confessions*, Oxford: Oxford University Press.
—— (1991b) *The Trinity*, Brooklyn, NY: New City Press.
Barth, K. (1956) *Church Dogmatics I.2: The Doctrine of the Word of God*, trans. G. Bromiley, Edinburgh: T. & T. Clark.
Browne, P. (1697) *A letter in answer to a book entitled, Christianity not mysterious, as also to all those who set up for reason and evidence in opposition to revelation and mysteries*, London: Printed for R. Clavell.
Buber, M. (1937) *I and Thou*, trans. R. G. Smith, Edinburgh: T. & T. Clark.
Butler, J. (1900 [1736]) *Analogy of Religion*, Philadelphia: Lippincott.
Daly, G. (1997) *Divine Revelation*, Grand Rapids, MI: Eerdmans.
Hume, D. (1970) [1779] *Dialogues Concerning Natural Religion*, Indianapolis, IN: Bobbs Merrill.
—— (1988) [1748] *An Enquiry Concerning Human Understanding*, LaSalle, IL: Open Court.
Kant, I. (1965) [1781] *Critique of Pure Reason*, New York: St Martin's Press.
Kermode, F. (1987) *Literary Guide to the Bible*, Cambridge, MA: Belknap/Harvard University Press.
McCool, G. A. (ed.) (1975) *A Rahner Reader*, New York: Crossroad.
Niebuhr, H. R. (1960) *The Meaning of Revelation*, New York: Collier Books.
Paley, W. (1952) [1794] *A View of the Evidences of Christianity*, Murfreesboro, TN: Dehoff Publications.
Penelhum, T. (1997) 'Revelation and philosophy,' in P. Avis (ed.) *Divine Revelation*, Grand Rapids, MI: Eerdmans.
Rahner, K. (1978) *Foundations of Christian Faith: An Introduction to the Idea of Christianity*, New York: Seabury Press.
Schwöbel, C. (1992) *God: Action and Revelation*, Kampen: Pharos.
Spinoza, B. D. (1998) [1670] *Theological-political Treatise*, Gebhardt edn, trans. S. Shirley with introduction by S. Feldman, Indianapolis, IN: Hackett.
Tillotson, J. (1684) *A Discourse against Transubstantiation*, London: Printed by M. Flesher for B. Aylmer and W. Rogers.
Tindal, M. (1730) *Christianity as Old as the Creation: Or, the Gospel, a Republication of the Religion of Nature*, London: n.p.
Toland, J. (1995 [1696]) *Christianity Not Mysterious*, London: Thoemmes.
von Balthasar, H. U. (1964) *Word and Revelation: Essays in Theology I*, Montreal: Palm Publishers.

Further reading

Avis, P. D. L. (ed.) (1997) *Divine Revelation*, London: Darton, Longman & Todd. (Eleven excellent essays on various perspectives on Christian revelation: biblical, Roman Catholic, Protestant, philosophical, critical theory, divine action, world religions, the Gospels, feminist theology, Jesus as revelation, and 'reaffirmed.')

Dulles, A. R. (1983) *Models of Revelation*, Garden City, NY: Doubleday. (Introductory overview of prominent Christian understandings of revelation.)

Pramuk, C. (2006) '"Strange fruit": black suffering/white revelation,' *Theological Studies* 67/2 (June): 346–77. (A pungent call from black theology for white conversion to the black experience as revelatory.)

Samuelson, N. (2002) *Revelation and the God of Israel*, Cambridge: Cambridge University Press. (A Jewish perspective on revelation as communication of divine presence that eludes defined content.)

51

THE INCARNATION

Thomas D. Senor

The Christian doctrine of the Incarnation is, at bottom, the claim that Jesus Christ was God incarnate. As traditionally understood, this does not mean that Jesus was a specially appointed prophet or that he was adopted by God or even that he was pre-existent and existentially unique. No, the doctrine of the Incarnation is more radical that any of that. Its claim is that the human being Jesus of Nazareth was and is God.

Not surprisingly, Jesus' identity claims assumed divine prerogatives (i.e., having the ability to forgive sin; being the Lord of the Sabbath; being God's unique Son and the Son of Man of Daniel 7; asserting authority over the Torah). Such assertions implying that he stood in the place of God didn't go over well with either the Jewish community in which Jesus had lived or in the larger Hellenistic and Greek worlds. How could God be born? How could the divine being literally walk the earth as a human who ate, drank, and slept? The very idea was, to borrow a phrase used in a similar context by the Apostle Paul in First Corinthians, 'a stumbling block to Jews and foolishness to Gentiles' (1: 23 NRSV). Nevertheless, that is the doctrine that became the received view in the traditional Christian Church.

This essay will consider the nature of this essential Christian doctrine, examine a particularly thorny philosophical problem to which it gives rise, and discuss three potential responses proposed by its defenders.

The doctrine

In the third century CE, the Christian Church expended its collective theological energy coming to terms with the relationship of Jesus Christ to God the Father. It was in the fourth century that the focus switched to the humanity of Christ. Orthodox Christianity had always affirmed Jesus' physical reality. Although some Gnostic sects had taught that Christ, while divine (indeed, *because* divine) was not physically embodied, early church theologians as far back as at least the writer of the letters of John (generally believed to have been written at the very end of the first century) stressed that Jesus Christ had a physical body.

The meat of the doctrine of the Incarnation can be found in the Nicene Creed and the 'Chalcedonian Definition.' Here is the relevant section of the former:

We believe in one Lord, Jesus Christ,
the only Son of God,
eternally begotten of the Father,
God from God, Light from Light,
true God from true God,
begotten, not made,
of one Being with the Father.
Through him all things were made.
For us and for our salvation
he came down from heaven:
by the power of the Holy Spirit
he became incarnate from the Virgin Mary,
and was made man.

The emphasis here is clearly on the divinity of Christ. During the early fourth century the Christian Church was divided over the nature of Christ. Arius and his followers argued that Jesus Christ was pre-existent but was not eternal; rather, the Son had been God's first creation. He was thought unique and in many ways vastly superior to other created entities, but he was not of the same substance as God the Father. Although the vote was hotly contested, in 325 the bishops at the Council of Nicea explicitly rejected Arianism and embraced the doctrine that the Son was not only pre-existent but was also 'begotten not made', that is, consubstantial with the Father.

While the Nicene Creed made explicit Christ's divinity and asserted his humanity, it wasn't until almost 130 years later that a more fully developed account of the relationship of Christ's humanity to his divinity was hammered out at the Council of Chaceldon in 451. The key Christological claim is that Jesus Christ is 'fully God and fully human.' The humanity that Christ exemplifies is like ours except that his is not stained with sin. Importantly, this implies that while the incarnate God is the Word made flesh, he is not *simply* the Word made flesh. The statement endorsed at this council (known as the 'Chalcedonian Definition') insists that Christ not only had a human body but a human 'rational soul.' In other words, he was not just the soul of God the Son housed in a human body: he had a human mind as well. Had he not had the conative and cognitive aspects of humanity, he would have not been 'fully human.'

The chief philosophical objection

There are various objections that can be raised against the doctrine of the Incarnation. Some are epistemological. For example, it might be thought that even if the accounts of the life of Christ in the Gospels are presumed to be accurate, there is nothing there (or in any other records) that could justify the claim that Christ is literally God. This may or may not be a good objection to belief in the Incarnation, but it will not be the subject of our focus here. Instead, the objection that will occupy us is metaphysical in nature. In the most straightforward of terms, it goes like this:

It is a necessary truth that God is omnipotent and omniscient. This truth stems from the very concept of God: no being that lacked these properties would qualify as divine. Furthermore, it is also a necessary truth that no human being can have infinite knowledge and power; to be human is to be finite. And now we can see why it is impossible for there to be a being who is both fully divine and fully human. To be fully divine is to meet all of those conditions necessary for divinity. Such a person will then be omnipotent, and omniscient. To be fully human, on the other hand, requires a person to be limited in power and knowledge. So a person who is fully divine and fully human will be an omnipotent, omniscient being who is limited in power and knowledge. But that is a logically inconsistent description. Therefore, the doctrine of the Incarnation is not even possibly true: it represents a metaphysical impossibility.

Let's try to be a bit more formal in our presentation of the problem. The argument intends to show

[C] It is not possible that Jesus Christ is fully God and fully human.

Here's a more explicit formulation of the argument:

1 Necessarily, anything that is God (i.e., divine) is omnipotent. (premise)
2 Necessarily, anything that is human is not omnipotent. (premise)
3 Suppose: It is possible that Jesus Christ is both divine and human. (supposition for reductio)
4 It is possible that Jesus is both omnipotent and human. (from 1, 3)
5 It is possible that Jesus is both omnipotent and not omnipotent. (from 2, 4)
6 But it is not possible that Jesus is both omnipotent and not omnipotent. (premise)

[C] Therefore, it is not possible that Jesus Christ is both divine and human.

Because the heart of this objection to the classical understanding of the Incarnation is a claim of logical inconsistency, let's dub the argument above the 'Inconsistency Argument.' Actually, what we have here is an instance of a more general argument type. I've selected omnipotence to represent all those divine qualities that, on the face of it, would seem to be inconsistent with essential human qualities.

Before trying to figure out how the defender of traditional Christology can best respond, let's make sure we fully appreciate the argument. There are three premises among its seven steps. The first two are alleged necessary truths that derive from the concepts of God and humanity, respectively. The rationale for them was discussed above, and we will have reason to come back to them later. For now we can grant that they have at least a certain prima facie plausibility. The only other genuine premise is step 6, which claims that it is not possible that Jesus Christ be both omnipotent and not omnipotent. The justification for this premise is none other than the Law of Non-contradiction which says that nothing can be both true and false. So if Jesus Christ is fully God and fully human, and if being the former entails being omnipotent and being the latter entails being not omnipotent, then traditional Christology is committed to both the truth and the falsity of the claim that Jesus Christ was omnipotent, and thus to denying the Law of Non-contradiction.

The argument is logically valid, and so the other steps will be true if our premises are true. There are, then, only three ways of rationally avoiding the conclusion: one of the premises must go. Either something can fail to be omnipotent and yet be divine, or something can be omnipotent and yet be human, or something can both have and lack the same property. As we will see, the denial of each one of these premises lines up with a traditional response to this Christological objection.

Denying step 1: the kenotic solution

The first premise of the Inconsistency Argument is that, necessarily, anything that is divine is omnipotent. The traditional concept of the Christian God includes the concept of a being who created the universe *ex nihilo*, and whose power is unlimited. To affirm these things would seem to be nothing other than to affirm God's omnipotence. So in denying the first step does the Christian also deny that God has unlimited power? Not necessarily. Peter Geach (1977) famously argued that Christians should give up the concept of omnipotence in favor of what he termed 'almightiness.' Being 'almighty' would entail that there could be nothing more powerful than God, even if (for technical philosophical and theological reasons we don't have time to get into) God is not omnipotent per se. However, giving up the ascription of omnipotence for these reasons will not help with the Inconsistency Argument, as steps 1 and 2 could easily be recast with 'almighty' in place of omnipotence.

The grounds for a more robust denial of the first step of the Inconsistency Argument can be found in the New Testament itself. The Apostle Paul, writing to the church at Philippi, had this to say about the Incarnation:

> Let the same mind be in you that was in Christ Jesus,
> Who, though he was in the form of God, did not regard equality with God as something to be exploited,
> But emptied himself, taking the form of a slave, being born in human likeness.
> (Phil. 2: 5–7 (NRSV)).

The later kenotic tradition (the name of which derives from the Greek word *kenosis* which means 'emptying') interprets this text as claiming that, in some metaphysically serious way, the second person of the Trinity gave up, or emptied himself of, some aspects of his divinity in order to take on humanity. The implication is that the point of the Inconsistency Argument is recognized even here: in order to become human, God the Son had to empty himself of those aspects of his divine nature that were inconsistent with his becoming incarnate as a human being. Omnipotence and omniscience are prime candidates for what the Son surrendered, although there may have been others as well. Therefore, the kenoticist will say, it's not true that in order to be God a being must be omnipotent because Jesus Christ was both fully God and fully human. Not only do we have a possible counterexample – we have an actual one! (See Feenstra 1989 for a robust defense of kenoticism.)

The problem with this approach is that it appears to gut our concept of God. That is, step 1 is grounded in a widespread and plausible account of the divine nature. According to this view, what it is to be God is to be a being with attributes such as omnipotence, omniscience, perfect goodness, etc. The worry with the kenotic account of the Incarnation is that in divesting himself of divine properties like omnipotence and omniscience, God the Son thereby ceases to be God. For in order for kenoticism to be of help to the Christological traditionalist, it must not imply that God the Son gave up *divinity* in order to take on humanity.

Notice also that the problem for the Chalcedonian isn't just that omnipotence is apparently inconsistent with genuine humanity, but that so many of the other attributes are too. God is not only all-powerful, but omniscient, necessarily good, eternal, etc. So even if it were possible for a divine being to give up some of his infinite attributes, how could it be that God the Son emptied himself of all of these qualities and yet *remained divine?* It is tempting to understand the kenotic position as implying that the Son gave up his divinity to become human. If the kenoticist insists that the Son's divinity was maintained while many of its distinctive attributes were given up, she will then owe us an account of divinity on which it is possible that God is not omnipotent, omniscient, necessarily good, eternal, etc. (See Senor 1991 for a proposal along these lines.)

Thorny though the aforementioned problem is, it does not represent the most serious objection to the kenotic solution. As noted above, the grounds for kenoticism would seem to be a tacit recognition of the philosophical problem made explicit in the Inconsistency Argument: in order to become human, God the Son had to abandon (at least temporarily) those qualities of divinity that are inconsistent with his human incarnation. Once the Son is suitably emptied, there is no barrier to taking on a human nature. This method of getting around the Inconsistency Argument will work as long as (a) giving up paradigmatic divine qualities is consistent with remaining divine and (b) all the divine qualities that are inconsistent with human nature can be set aside. The first objection we discussed concerns (a). We are now setting our sights on (b).

As we begin to consider (b), note that there is nothing inherently mysterious in the idea of property divestment. You have the ability to divest yourself of some of your current qualities. Suppose you are a married professor of philosophy who lives in New York City. Get divorced, quit your job, and move to Texas and you'll have changed some of your rather important properties. But you've got other properties that you aren't in a position to do anything about (e.g., having been born in the twentieth century). Call properties of this latter sort 'stable properties.' The kenotic strategy depends on the non-stability of all the divine properties that are inconsistent with humanity. For if any of those attributes turn out to be stable, then there will be a property that the incarnate God the Son will both have and lack. And one such instance is all the Inconsistency Argument needs to show the logical incoherence of the doctrine of the Incarnation.

There are, it would seem, any number of stable divine properties that are apparently inconsistent with human nature. For example, on standard theism, God is the uncreated, necessarily existing creator of all that is other than himself. Yet these qualities, one and all, are both stable and yet apparently inconsistent with a person's having a human nature. Since the kenotic approach leaves us with a human being who is the uncreated, necessarily existing creator of all that is other than himself, one may be excused for thinking that rather little ground has been made against the Inconsistency Argument.

So even if kenoticism can provide grounds for denying step 1 of this particular version of the Inconsistency Argument, it is far from clear that it is a successful strategy for dealing with all such arguments.

Denying step 2: Thomas Morris's 'two minds' reply

Since there will be instances of the Inconsistency Argument that have an unassailable first premise, we must look elsewhere if we are to defend orthodox Christology. Working through the argument's steps in order, let us now consider step 2. What is our ground for thinking that, necessarily, all human beings lack omnipotence?

We might think that the answer to this is rather simple and directly parallel to what we had to say earlier about the divine qualities: it is part of our concept of humanity that humans are finite creatures with fairly limited capacities. We are of a rather small size even when measured by terrestrial standards, and our powers are thus circumscribed by what a being weighing at most a few hundred pounds is capable of. So in the same way that our concept of divinity necessitates that only an omnipotent being counts as divine, our concept of humanity requires that only a being with limited powers (and who thus lacks omnipotence) could be human.

Thomas Morris (1986) has challenged this claim about the concept of humanity (Richard Swinburne 1994 gives a similar defense). Making a distinction between cluster concepts and natural kind concepts, Morris argues that it is only the former whose essence can be known by simple a priori reflection and which will consist of other concepts knowable by reflection. So, for example, our concept of a bachelor is a cluster concept par excellence. By reflection, we can come to know that no one who is married can be a bachelor. However, we do not find out the essence of a natural kind in the same way. Take, for example, our concept of an orange. We might think we could say that an orange is a sweet, orange-colored fruit with a peel. While this is a fair description of a standard orange, we must acknowledge that those of us who are not horticulturists lack the expertise to say that these are necessary conditions of something's falling under the botanical kind *orange*. That is, we could possibly learn that there are types of oranges that are green and sour when ripe. If our concept of an orange were a cluster concept, we'd be in a position to tell the horticulturists, 'No, you apparently don't understand what an orange is: nothing that is green when ripe could *possibly* be an orange.' But we are not in a position to say that. Being an orange is to be a member of a certain natural kind, and the essences of natural kinds are discovered by empirical investigation rather than conceptual reflection.

What does all this have to do with the Incarnation? Morris thinks that once we understand that our notion of humanity is a natural kind rather than a cluster concept, we will see that many of the convictions we might have about the essence of humanity may, in principle, be overridden in the same way that our conviction that being orange when ripe may be shown to be wrong by botany. Just as being orange in color might be very *common* amongst oranges even if it is not essential for being an orange, so the objector to the Inconsistency Argument can say that while lacking omnipotence might be extremely *common* among humans, it is not an *essential* property of humanity.

Whereas the first response to the Inconsistency Argument held fast to the standard human kind properties, and gave ground on the Son's divine attributes, the current reply does just the reverse. To be fully human, in this sense, is to have a properly functioning human body and mind. Precisely what that consists in will be determined by a complete science of the human person, and not by a priori reflection on our nonscientific concept of humanity. What we currently know of the humankind nature might not obviously preclude the possibility of that nature's becoming intimately associated with a divine nature and all that that involves.

So far we've said nothing about the 'Two Minds' aspect of Morris's position. There are two reasons for appealing to the duality of minds. First, the New Testament contains passages which seem to suggest, for example, that there are things Jesus Christ does not know (see Matthew 24: 36). The second reason for insisting on the Two Minds view is that without it, the defender of orthodoxy may seem to have won the battle but lost the war. By dropping all the relevant features of humanity that were incompatible with the standard divine properties, the Christian is in danger of being left with a picture of Jesus Christ as perhaps technically human but rather little like us.

What makes Morris's Two Minds view distinct from just any orthodox position (as we've seen, the Chalcedonian definition insists that Jesus Christ had both human body and rational soul in addition to the mind of God the Son) is its insistence that during the Son's time on earth, it was the human mind that was primarily that through which God incarnate consciously operated. Taking on and functioning through the consciousness of a human mind can explain how Christ could be both ignorant of some things and yet omniscient: the ignorance is a function of the conscious human mind while omniscience is had in the divine mind. Furthermore, we can suppose that the human mind came to know most things in much the same way that any typical human mind would come to know them. We needn't think of the infant Christ consciously pondering the thoughts of the Godhead if it is the human mind that was the primary vehicle in which conscious thought occurred.

The main problem for the Two Minds view is squaring it with the Chalcedonian Definition's insistence that there is but a single person in the Incarnation. Morris himself sees this difficulty and attempts to make plausible his claim that two minds can be had by a single person. Yet as John Hick (1989) points out, there is a dilemma here for Morris: if there are two distinct minds in the Incarnation, and if the human mind has access to the divine mind only inasmuch as the divine mind allows it to have (which is Morris's view), then it would seem that the relationship between the mind of God the Son and the human mind of Christ is in principle no different from God the Son's relationship with any other human mind. None of us (including Jesus Christ) has unrestricted access to God the Son's mind; all of us (including Jesus Christ) know just as much of the divine mind as the divine mind chooses to reveal. Morris sees this part of the dilemma as a potential problem and tries to solve it by maintaining that the human and divine minds of God incarnate have a single, shared set of *cognitive and causal powers*. The distinction in the two minds is in their accompanying belief systems, and not in the faculties that produce (or are associated with) them. But if we say there is but one set of causal and cognitive powers, and that these powers are the cognitive and causal powers of God the Son, then it is highly questionable if a genuine human mind, or 'rational soul,' has been taken on at all. So the dilemma is this: either there are two distinct sets of cognitive and causal powers, or there are not. If there are, then the unity of the Incarnation is threatened (and the heresy known as Nestorianism looms), and there is apparently, in principle, no unique relation between the human mind of Christ and the mind of God the Son. If there are not two distinct sets of powers, then it is hard to see that God incarnate had a genuine human mind (and the heresy known as Apollinarianism looms).

One final point in defense of the Two Minds view: it is clear that orthodoxy insists that God the Son took on a complete human nature and that includes taking on a complete human mind or 'rational soul.' So Morris might claim that, to some degree at least, all defenders of the Chalcedon Definition will have to face Hick's dilemma.

Denying step 6: The compositional model

The final premise of the argument comes at step 6, and it asserts that it is not possible that Jesus Christ be both omnipotent and not omnipotent. As claimed above, this is really grounded in what might just be the single most important rule of logic and of rational thought: the Law of Non-contradiction. How, one might reasonably ask, could the believer deny something so basic?

The key, the defender of orthodoxy will say, is that one can affirm the Law of Non-contradiction and yet deny step 6. For Jesus Christ differs from the rest of humanity in one very important respect: he has two natures, one divine and one human. So property ascriptions to him are ambiguous in a way that property ascriptions to the rest of us aren't. When we say that Jesus is omnipotent, what we are really asserting is that Jesus Christ, qua divine nature, is omnipotent. And when we say that Jesus Christ lacks omnipotence, what we are asserting is that Jesus Christ, qua human, lacks omnipotence. Had Christ a single nature, then the claim that he is both omnipotent and not omnipotent would violate the Law of Non-contradiction. But as it is, there is no contradiction in saying that, qua his divine nature Christ is omnipotent and qua his human nature he is not.

Eleonore Stump (2004) and Brian Leftow (2004) offer independent, although strikingly similar accounts of the metaphysics of the Incarnation that they find in the writings of Thomas Aquinas. The fundamental idea is that God incarnate is a compositional entity composed of God the Son and the human body and mind of Jesus Christ. On this account, the properties that God incarnate has qua divinity are properties that are had by his divine part; similarly, his human properties are had by his human part. This approach puts some flesh on the bones of the qua claim above. The apparent inconsistency is resolved by assigning the properties in question to distinct parts of God incarnate. Just as there are no logical difficulties in saying of an apple that it is red qua its skin and not red qua its core, so there is no logical problem with the claim that Jesus Christ is omnipotent qua his divine part and not omnipotent qua his human part.

The difficulty with this view can be seen if we keep squarely in mind that the doctrine asserts that although there are two natures, there is but one person and hence a single subject of predication. So even if we grant that the divine part is omnipotent and the human part is not omnipotent, we must ask if the compositional God incarnate is omnipotent. If we say that having an omnipotent part, God incarnate himself is omnipotent, then we would seem to be right back where we started: Jesus Christ (who is God incarnate) is a human who is yet omnipotent. But if we go the other way and say that the human part trumps the divine part where omnipotence is concerned, and hence that God incarnate is not omnipotent, then we have a divine being who is not omnipotent. So one might be excused for wondering how the compositional account cuts ice against the Inconsistency Argument. For in the final analysis, it doesn't seem to offer us a way of seeing how Jesus Christ could be both omnipotent and not omnipotent; instead, it shows only how he could have an omnipotent part and a non-omnipotent part. But these things were never in doubt. No one ever thought that, say, his left eye brow was omnipotent. And the Christological traditionalist has always claimed that he was omnipotent in his divine nature. The point at issue is whether the person who is God incarnate can be said to be omnipotent, not whether he has an omnipotent part.

There is another difficulty inherent in the compositional picture. Orthodoxy is clear that there is only a single person in the Incarnation. The person who is God the Son and the person who is Jesus Christ are the same person. However, the friend of the compositional picture cannot assert this. For God the Son is, on the compositional view, but a proper part of the whole that is God incarnate. The conclusion must be either that God incarnate is a person too, and so there are two persons in the Incarnation (but this is the heresy of Nestorianism pure and simple), or God incarnate has a person as a part (i.e., God the Son) but is not a person himself. But then Jesus Christ, who the tradition tells us just *is* God incarnate, is an impersonal conglomerate with a personal part. Yet surely this is not theologically acceptable to the Chalcedonian tradition that claims that the two natures are joined in such a way that they are 'concurring in one Person' and that the incarnate God, Jesus Christ, is 'in all things like unto us.' The compositional view would seem to have trouble with both of these claims: the God incarnate has a person as a part but *is* not a person, and hence seems to be not much like us at all.

Conclusion

In a brief essay such as this, it is not possible to explore the philosophical difficulties and attempted solutions in anything like the detail they deserve. Nor is it possible to so much as mention all the issues that should have a hearing. What can be said by way conclusion is simply this: what the doctrine of the Incarnation proposes is deeply mysterious, and while a good prima facie case can be made for its being logically inconsistent, the defender of the tradition is not without resources in attempting to cast doubt on the Inconsistency Argument.

See also Christianity (Chapter 6), Religious pluralism (Chapter 20), Inclusivism and exclusivism (Chapter 21), Omniscience (Chapter 24), Omnipotence (Chapter 25), Creation and divine action (Chapter 30), The Trinity (Chapter 49), Revelation (Chapter 50), Resurrection (Chapter 52), Sin and salvation (Chapter 53), Miracles (Chapter 55).

References

Feenstra, R. (1989) 'Reconsidering kenotic Christology,' in R. J. Feenstra and C. Plantinga (eds) *Trinity, Incarnation, and Atonement*, Notre Dame, IN: University of Notre Dame Press.

Geach, P. (1977) *Providence and Evil*, Cambridge: Cambridge University Press, chapter 1, previously published as 'Omnipotence,' *Philosophy* 48 (1973): 7–20.

Hick, J. (1989) 'The logic of God incarnate,' *Religious Studies* 25: 409–23.

Leftow, B. (2004) 'A timeless God incarnate,' in S. T. Davis, D. Kendall, and G. O'Collins (eds) *The Incarnation: An Interdisciplinary Symposium on the Incarnation of the Son of God*, New York: Oxford University Press.

Morris, T. (1986) *The Logic of God Incarnate*, Ithaca, NY: Cornell University Press.

Senor, T. (1991) 'God, supernatural kinds, and the Incarnation,' *Religious Studies* 27: 353–70.

Stump, E. (2004) 'Aquinas' metaphysics of the Incarnation,' in S. T. Davis, D. Kendall, and G. O'Collins (eds) *The Incarnation: An Interdisciplinary Symposium on the Incarnation of the Son of God*, New York: Oxford University Press.

Swinburne, R. (1994) *The Christian God*, New York: Oxford University Press.

Further Reading

Collins, G. (1995) *A Biblical, Historical, and Systematic Study of Jesus Christ*, New York: Oxford University Press. (A study of general issues of Christology.)

Hebblethwaite, B. (1987) *The Incarnation: Collected Essays in Christology*, Cambridge: Cambridge University Press. (A philosophically sophisticated theologian's defense of the orthodox doctrine.)

Hick, J. (2006) *The Metaphor of God Incarnate: Christology in a Pluralistic Age*, Louisville, KY: Westminster John Knox Press. (A critical look at the traditional doctrine.)

Norris, R. (1980) *The Christological Controversy*, Minneapolis, MN: Augsburg Fortress. (Readings in early development of the doctrine of the Incarnation.)

52

RESURRECTION

Craig A. Evans

Beliefs in forms of postmortem survival, immortality of the soul, reincarnation, and other forms of transformation from this life to the next circulated in late antiquity and came to diversity of expression, even within a given religious system (Davis 1997). The idea of resurrection, whereby the dead are restored to life (and by this is meant a life superior to the previous life and almost always understood as everlasting life), appears to be distinctive of early Judaism and Christianity. Approximate parallels have been put forward, but on closer examination they really are not the same.

Many Jews in late antiquity came to believe in resurrection, though others believed only in the immortality of the soul, while yet others believed that physical death terminates the human being. These perspectives will be surveyed in what follows. The Christian perspective on resurrection will be shown to be different from Jewish ideas, in that the Christian understanding relies less on speculation and biblical interpretation but more on the dramatic event of the resurrection of Jesus. Thus, the Christian doctrine of resurrection has a distinctly historical orientation.

Resurrection and postmortem life ideas in ancient Israel and the Hebrew Scriptures

The oldest portions of Hebrew Scripture say nothing about resurrection (Tromp 1969). Death is understood as the termination of physical life: 'you are dust, and to dust you shall return' (Gen. 3: 19 (biblical quotations from RSV); cf. Ps. 90: 2–3). The description of the human being as 'dust' recalls the story of creation (Gen. 2: 7: 'the LORD God formed man of dust from the ground, and breathed into his nostrils the breath of life; and man became a living being'). The implication is that when the living breath is gone, the physical being disintegrates into the dust from which it had originally been taken. God's life-giving breath has been taken back (Ps. 104: 29–30; Eccles. 12: 7). The dead descend into Sheol (e.g., Gen. 37: 35; 42: 38; 44: 29, 31). Some Hebrew Scriptures declare that once descended into Sheol, there remains no hope of escape: 'As the cloud fades and vanishes, so he who goes down to Sheol does not come up' (Job 7: 9). Accordingly, those in Sheol cannot praise God or give thanks (e.g., Isa. 38: 18; Ps. 6: 5; 88: 10 – but see opposite).

Nevertheless, there are some indications in Hebrew Scripture that death is not necessarily the end of human existence. One text apparently contradicts the passage from Job cited opposite: 'The Lord kills and brings to life; he brings down to Sheol and raises up' (1 Sam. 2: 6; and perhaps Ps. 89: 48). Indeed, in the story of Saul's attempt to contact Samuel through a medium (1 Sam. 28: 3, 11–19), we are left with the impression that those in Sheol sleep and can be aroused: 'Then Samuel said to Saul, "Why have you disturbed me by bringing me up?"' (28: 15). The dead are sometimes described as 'shades,' perhaps in the sense of those who sleep and still have a shadow-like existence (e.g., Isa. 14: 9; Jer. 51: 39; Prov. 2: 18; Job 26: 5). And finally, Ps. 16: 9–11 could be taken to imply that Sheol is not the end ('you do not give up to Sheol' (adapted from RSV)), but the original meaning may only have been the hope that the righteous one will not die before his time.

Other texts suggest that the dead, though greatly weakened and diminished, still exist and still have some awareness. Accordingly, the dead tremble (Ps. 6: 3; Job 4: 14); they rejoice (Ps. 1: 10); they praise God (Ps. 35: 10); they mutter (Isa. 8: 19; 29: 4); and they can even feel the worms gnawing at them (Job 14: 22; Isa. 66: 24). 'Hence, even in death the soul maintains a very intimate relation to what is left of the body' (Meyers 1971: 12–13, quotation from 13).

In an oracle (or psalm) of uncertain date, found in Isaiah (at 26: 7–19 (adapted from RSV)), a contrast is made between the wicked dead, who 'will not live; they are shades, they will not arise' (26: 14), and the righteous dead: They 'shall live, their bodies shall rise. O dwellers in the dust, awake and sing for joy! For your dew is a dew of light, and on the land of the shades you will let it fall' (26: 19). The anticipation of awaking and rising from the 'dust' recalls the older traditions of dying and returning to the dust. Although the oracle of Isaiah is probably metaphorical, it may well testify to a third- or fourth-century BCE belief in the resurrection of the righteous.

The clearest expression of resurrection hope is found in an eschatological vision in Daniel 12: 1–3:

> At that time shall arise Michael, the great prince who has charge of your people. And there shall be a time of trouble, such as never has been since there was a nation till that time; but at that time your people shall be delivered, every one whose name shall be found written in the book. And many of those who sleep in the dust of the earth shall awake, some to everlasting life, and some to shame and everlasting contempt. And those who are wise shall shine like the brightness of the firmament; and those who turn many to righteousness, like the stars forever and ever.

The prophecy appears to be based on Isaiah 26. Those who awake from their sleep in the dust shall awaken 'to everlasting life,' while others will awaken 'to shame and everlasting contempt' (26: 2). Although it is disputed, this interesting passage may well be an early expression of resurrection hope (c.165 BCE), however limited in scope it is.

There are three other passages from Hebrew Scripture that should be mentioned briefly, which have sometimes been adduced as evidence of early resurrection ideas. The first is Hosea 6, where in verse 2 the eighth-century BCE prophet promises a beleaguered northern kingdom: 'After two days he will revive us; on the third day he will raise us up, that we may live before him.' But the primary reference here – notwithstanding Jesus' later allusion to this passage, as well as its paraphrase in the targum – is to national restoration: God will someday restore apostate and judged Israel. The second passage is found in Job, where the sufferer proclaims his faith: 'After my skin has been thus destroyed, then in my flesh I shall see God' (19: 26 (NRSV)). Job has not implied that after his *death* he will see God, but that even after severe torment – even to the point of being 'skinned alive' – he still anticipates witnessing God's vindication *before he dies* (i.e., while still 'in my flesh'). The third passage is the famous vision of the dry bones in Ezekiel 37: 1–14, especially verse 13: 'And you shall know that I am the Lord, when I open your graves, and raise you from your graves, O my people.' This passage may well have contributed to ideas of resurrection in later thinking (and may also reflect the ancient belief that a small residue of life clings to bones), but the highly metaphorical vision concerns the restoration of Israel, not the literal resurrection of individual humans.

Resurrection ideas in Judaism prior to Christianity

In the intertestamental period (i.e., the last two to three centuries BC), the Jewish people began to give explicit expression to the concept of personal resurrection, whether bodily or only in reference to one's spirit. The idea appears in a variety of writings, including apocalyptic, wisdom, and romance (Nickelsburg 1972).

The oldest material is found the Book of the Watchers (i.e., *Enoch* 1–36), which dates to the third century BCE. In chapter 22 the angel Raphael informs Enoch of the place where 'all the souls of men are gathered,' where they await judgment (22: 3–4). In contrast to the righteous, the wicked will not 'be raised later from' this place (22: 13). Later, Enoch learns that the life span of the righteous will be extended: 'they will live much life on earth, which your fathers lived' (25: 4–6). Resurrection is not explicitly mentioned, nor is eternal life, but the promise of long, healthy life is a step in this direction. In a later section of *Enoch* known as the Epistle of Enoch (i.e., *Enoch* 92–105), which dates to the second century BC, the resurrection of the righteous is promised: 'Be of good cheer, souls of the righteous who have died, the just and the godly ... let them rise up and be saved, and they shall see us eating and drinking forever' (102: 4, 8).

Hope of resurrection for the righteous, who have faithfully kept God's Law, is expressed in 2 Maccabees 7, a work that dates to about 100 BCE, in the gruesome account of the torture and death of the mother and her seven sons. The second brother says to Antiochus IV, the Greek king persecuting the Jewish people: 'You accursed wretch, you dismiss us from this present life, but the King of the universe will raise us up to an everlasting renewal of life, because we have died for his laws' (7: 9). The third brother says: 'I got these (limbs) from Heaven, and because of his laws I disdain them, and from him I hope to get them back again' (7: 11). To this the fourth brother says: 'One cannot but choose to die at the hands of men and to cherish the hope that God gives of being raised again by him. But for you there will be no resurrection to life!' (7: 14). And finally, the brave mother says to her sons: 'Therefore the Creator of the world, who shaped the beginning of humanity and devised the origin of all things, will in his mercy give life and breath back to you again, since you now forget yourselves for the sake of his laws' (7: 23 (quotations of Apocrypha from RSV)).

Two other first century BCE pseudepigraphal texts give expression to hopes of resurrection. According to the *Psalms of Solomon*, 'they that fear the Lord shall rise to life eternal' (3: 12); 'the life of the righteous shall be forever; but sinners shall be taken away into destruction' (13: 11; cf. 14: 9–10). In the *Testament of Judah* we are told that the patriarchs 'Abraham, Isaac and Jacob will arise to life' (25: 1) and 'they who have died in grief will arise in joy ... and they who are put to death for the Lord will arise to life' (25: 4).

And finally we have an intertestamental text from Qumran, in which the advent of the Messiah appears to be linked to resurrection: '[... For the hea]vens and the earth shall obey his Messiah ... For he shall heal the wounded, he shall make alive the dead, he shall send good news to the afflicted' (4Q521 frag. 2, col. 2, lines 1 and 12). Reference to healing the wounded may advert to the final eschatological battle, envisioned at Qumran (e.g., in 1QM and related texts) and in other Jewish traditions. With the battle won, either the Messiah, or God through his Messiah – the antecedents of the pronouns are not clear – will heal the wounded, raise the dead, and announce good news to the oppressed.

Resurrection ideas in Hellenism

In old Greek tradition the souls of the departed were thought to cross over the River Styx, to the Elysian Fields, or, in another manifestation, to the Isle of the Blest (Vergil, *Aeneid* 6. 637–40). Later ideas included the notion of the human spirit ascending (or descending) to be with the gods or perhaps inhabiting the body of an animal (for a recent survey of the opinions, see Porter 1999). One tradition speaks of Isis, who raised her son Horus from the dead and made him immortal (Diodorus Siculus 1. 25. 6); another speaks of Herakles rescuing a man's wife from Hades (Euripides, *Alcestis*). But it is unlikely that these myths were understood as paradigms for mortals. These stories – and they are few – were understood as exceptional. Indeed, Aeschylus the Athenian tragedist has the god Apollo declare:

> When the dust has soaked up a man's blood,
> Once he is dead, there is no resurrection [anastasis]. (Eumenides 647–8)

In view of this opinion, expressed in a popular play widely circulating in Greece, and certainly well known in Athens itself, it is perhaps not surprising that first-century CE Athenians ridiculed Paul's affirmation of the resurrection while speaking on the Areopagus (Acts 17: 31–2). Nevertheless, some Greeks may have entertained ideas somewhat akin to Jewish ideas about resurrection. Indeed, Jewish ideas may have been influenced by Greek conceptions (Porter 1999).

To be sure, many Greeks in late antiquity believed in some form of postmortem existence. We see this in many epitaphs (conveniently assembled in Lattimore 1942), as in the following:

> I have gone to the gods; I am among the immortals. (*Epigrammata Graeca* [*EG*] 340. 7–8)

> The precinct of heavenly Zeus keeps me ... for he took me immortal from the fire. (*Inscriptiones Graecae* [*IG*] 12. 1. 142. 3–4)

> ... you made haste to join the immortals ... Farewell, and be glad in Elysium .... (*Supplementum Epigraphicum Graecu* [*SEG*] 4. 727)

Other epitaphs explicitly deny any form of afterlife, as we see in the following:

> Wayfarer, do not pass by my epitaph, but stand and listen, and then, when you have learned the truth, proceed. There is no boar in Hades, no ferryman Charon ... All of us who have died and gone below are bones and ashes – there is nothing else. What I have told you is true. (*EG* 646. 1–7)

> Death is the final depth to which all things sink, rich and poor, brute and human. (*EG* 459. 7–8)

> We shall never again see you alive. (*IG* 12. 8. 398. 3)

> I grew from earth and I have turned back into earth. (*EG* 75. 3)

> There is nothing left – for nothing awakens the dead – except to afflict the souls of those who pass by. Nothing else remains. (*IG* 9. 2. 640. 8–9)

The polemical nature of these denials of postmortem existence gives the impression of protests against popular beliefs (so Lattimore 1942: 342: the denials 'indicate that there was a belief in the afterlife to combat'). But what we do not encounter in the Greek epitaphs is anticipation of bodily resurrection. That appears to have been primarily a Jewish and Christian hope.

Resurrection ideas in Jesus and his contemporaries

Jesus not only believed in resurrection; he evidently commanded his disciples, whom he sent out as apostles, to proclaim the rule of God and to 'raise the dead' (see Matthew 10: 8), perhaps as adumbrations of the resurrection anticipated in the last age. When asked if he was the awaited Coming One, Jesus responded by saying, 'the blind receive their sight and the lame walk, lepers are cleansed and the deaf hear, and the dead are raised up, and the poor have good news preached to them' (Matt. 11: 5; Luke 7: 22). The declaration 'the dead are raised up' refers to actual resuscitations but also anticipates the resurrection. In another setting, Jesus urged his affluent contemporaries to treat the poor with generosity: 'and you will be blessed, because they cannot repay you. You will be repaid at the resurrection of the just' (Luke 14: 14). Resurrection and eschatological judgment are here combined. In a different tradition found in the fourth Gospel, the resurrection is affirmed by Jesus and his followers (John 5: 29; 11: 24).

Even Herod Antipas, tetrarch of Galilee, wondered if Jesus – about whom he had heard so much – was the beheaded John the Baptist, 'raised from the dead' (Mark 6: 16). We should not infer too much from this third-hand report, but it seems that Herod and perhaps also his advisers believed in the possibility of resurrection and so wondered if the recently executed John had been raised from the dead and had brought back with him amazing power. How else were the deeds of Jesus to be explained?

Some Jewish individuals and groups in the approximate time of Jesus did not believe in resurrection. Best known among them were the Sadducees, a small, aristocratic group, well represented among the ruling priests in the late second temple period. The New Testament gospels tell of an encounter between Jesus and the Sadducees ('who say there is no resurrection'). Appealing to the story of Moses and the burning bush, Jesus defends the doctrine (Matt. 22: 23–33; Mark 12: 18–27; Luke 20: 27–40).

Josephus, the first-century Jewish historian and apologist, describes the views of the Pharisees, Sadducees, and Essenes. He says the Pharisees believed that the human soul is imperishable and 'passes into another body' (*Jewish Wars* [*JW*] 2. 163). It is likely that Josephus is referring to resurrection (cf. ibid.: 3. 374; *Against Apion* 2. 218). In contrast to Pharisaic opinion, the Sadducees did not believe in postmortem judgment or existence of any kind (*JW* 2. 165). This sharp difference of opinion between Pharisees and Sadducees lies behind Paul's provocative declaration, before the Jewish council: 'with respect to the hope and the resurrection of the dead I am on trial' (Acts 23: 6). According to Josephus, the Essenes viewed the soul as trapped in the physical body, from which it is released at death and is 'borne aloft' (*JW* 2. 154–5). One wonders if Josephus here is presenting the Essene view in a Greek light. The book of Daniel and related materials were popular at Qumran, so one would think the resurrection passage in Daniel 12: 2 would have been authoritative in Essene eschatology. Moreover, the already mentioned 4Q521 seems to envision resurrection. Perhaps postmortem ideas at Qumran – Josephus notwithstanding – were not very different from the ideas held by Pharisees.

In the time of Jesus, references to bodily resurrection become more frequent. The pseudepigraphal writings yield many such examples. The *Apocryphon of Ezekiel* prophesies that 'the dead shall arise and those in the tombs shall be raised up' (1: 1–2). According to the *Testament of Job* the righteous person 'shall be raised up in the resurrection' (4: 9). In the Jewish portion of the *Sibylline Oracles*, the seer declares that God 'will raise up mortals once more as they were before' (4: 182). The *Testament of Abraham* declares that 'all flesh shall arise' (7: 16, version B; cf. 18: 9, version A). Several references to resurrection are found in the *Life of Adam and Eve* (Greek version: 10: 2; 13: 3 'then shall all flesh be raised up'; 28: 4; 41: 3; 43: 2). The description 'all flesh' may well have been inspired by the eschatological promise of Isaiah 40: 5, that 'all flesh will see the salvation of God.' There are yet other references to resurrection, all of which should be understood as bodily (cf. 4 Ezra 7: 32, 37; *Lives of the Prophets* 2: 12; *History of the Rechabites* 13: 5; 16: 6). Other passages speak of immortality, though it is not clear that bodily resurrection is in view (cf. *Joseph and Aseneth* 15: 3–4; Wisdom 1–5; 4 Macc. 5: 37; 7: 19; 9: 8; 13: 17; 18: 16–19, 23; *2 Baruch* 21: 23; 30: 2–5).

The Pharisaic belief in the resurrection becomes standard eschatology in the rabbinic tradition. Its earliest witness is preserved in the Mishnah, oral law codified and published by Rabbi Judah the Prince in the early third century CE. The phrase 'resurrection of the dead' becomes idiomatic (cf. *m. 'Abot* 4: 22; *Berakot* 5: 2; *Sanhedrin* 10: 1; *Sota* 9: 15). Failure to believe in the resurrection is heresy and may result in failure to obtain life in the world to come.

The resurrection of Jesus and its early interpretation

There are aspects of the resurrection of Jesus that place it in a category of its own. Although in some ways it is coherent with several of the texts that have been reviewed above, there are features of the resurrection of Jesus that are distinctive and quite unexpected in light of Jewish beliefs expressed in late antiquity. First, those who held to bodily resurrection thought of it in terms of *general* resurrection. All of the Jewish texts above that speak of resurrection envision the judgment of humankind *as a whole*, with rewards for the righteous and punishment for the wicked. This is why Paul speaks of Jesus' resurrection as 'first fruits of those who have fallen asleep' (1 Cor. 15: 20) and the Matthean evangelist – or a later scribe – feels compelled to narrate the strange story of the saints who exited their tombs the first Easter (Matt. 27: 52–3). Second, all of the texts that speak of resurrection envision it as an *eschatological* event. Resurrection was understood to take place at the end of normal human history, not at some mid-point. This likely explains why many early Christians believed that end-times were at hand (2 Thess. 2: 2; Phil. 4: 5). Third, although there was some tradition – notably Isaiah 53 – that may have been understood as hinting at messianic suffering, there is no text or tradition known to us that envisioned the crucifixion of the Messiah, whether subsequently resurrected or not. This is precisely why Trypho the Jew could not be persuaded that Jesus was the Messiah (Justin Martyr, *Dialogue with Trypho* 89.1; 90.1). Therefore, although it is not wrong to see lines of continuity between the resurrection of Jesus and some antecedent eschatological texts and speculations, the actual event of Easter itself can hardly be explained as fulfillment of these texts and speculations. The resurrection of Jesus was both unexpected and difficult to explain.

In view of these discrepancies, why did Jesus' followers interpret his appearances in terms of *resurrection*? Appearances of Jesus would not in themselves necessarily lead to the conclusion that a resurrection had taken place. After all, Jewish speculation also entertained the possibility of postmortem survival of the soul or spirit, quite apart from the question of bodily resurrection. Moreover, Jewish tradition also included belief in ghostly apparitions. Even the disciples on one occasion thought they had seen a spirit or ghost (see Mark 6: 49). Others later thought that Peter – thought to be in prison or perhaps dead – standing at the door was Peter's 'angel' (see Acts 12: 12–16). So why did Jesus' followers speak of the *resurrection* of Jesus and not simply a vision or Jesus, or Jesus' angel, or Jesus' spirit?

The conclusion that Jesus was truly resurrected assumed a heavy burden of proof. Jewish beliefs about resurrection envisioned a 'standing up,' which is the meaning of both the Hebrew and the Greek words that are usually translated 'resurrection' (as in 2 Macc. 7: 14; *Enoch* 102: 8; *T. Judah* 25: 1, 4; *T. Job* 4: 9; *Life of Adam and Eve* 10: 2; 41: 2). Resurrection was thought to be corporeal and therefore passages sometimes refer to the resurrection of the flesh (as in *Life of Adam and Eve* 13: 3; *T. Abraham* B 7: 16). Resurrection also implied exiting the tomb or place of burial (as in *Apoc. Ezek.* 1: 1–2). Resurrection was, in effect, the reversal of burial. Unless these things could be said of Jesus, then his postmortem appearances would have been explained in terms other than resurrection.

What persuaded Jesus' followers to speak of resurrection was their knowledge that Jesus had died, had been buried in a known place, and had exited that place. These facts, which were open to verification, in combination with the appearances convinced his followers that Jesus was indeed resurrected. It is therefore essential to understand the circumstances of Jesus' death and burial, if the resurrection claims of his followers are to be properly assessed.

Much of the critical discussion of the gospel resurrection narratives suffers from a lack of adequate acquaintance with Jewish traditions of death and burial, especially with respect to the burial of executed persons or persons who in some way died dishonorable deaths. It sometimes suffers too from wrong inferences from archaeological evidence and historical records. In a controversial book published in the 1990s, a scholar suggested that Jesus' body – in keeping with general Roman practice – probably was not taken down from the cross and given customary Jewish burial. It was further suggested that Jesus' corpse was either left hanging on the cross, or, at best, was cast into a ditch and covered with lime. In either case, his corpse was left exposed to birds and animals. Jesus was not properly buried. Therefore, the story of the empty tomb is no more than theology and apologetic legend.

It needs to be emphasized that in the Jewish world burial was absolutely necessary. Burial of all persons, including executed criminals, was to take place the day of death. No body was to be left unburied over night. This was in part due to compassion, but it was primarily due to the wish to avoid defilement of the land (as commanded in Scripture; see Deut. 21: 22–3). This understanding of Scripture was current in the time of Jesus (see 11QTemple 64: 7–13a, a passage in an important Qumran scroll where Deut. 21: 22–3 is interpreted in reference to crucifixion). The tradition is attested in the Mishnah, where in the discussion of the rules pertaining to execution, the sages teach that one hanged must not be left overnight, lest the command in Deuteronomy 21: 22–3 be violated (*m. Sanh.* 6: 4). The discussion continues, noting that the executed person was not to be buried in the 'burying-place of his fathers,' but in one of the places reserved for the burial of criminals (*m. Sanh.* 6: 5). And finally, the discussion concludes by recalling that after the flesh of the executed criminal had decomposed, his bones could then be gathered and taken to the family burial place, but no public lamentation was permitted (*m. Sanh.* 6: 6). Josephus remarks: 'Jews are so careful about funeral rites that even malefactors who have been sentenced to cruci-fixion are taken down and buried before sunset' (*JW* 4. 5. 2 §317). Roman authorities were expected to comply with Jewish customs, sometimes outside the land of Israel, as Philo attests: 'I have known cases when on the eve of a holiday of this kind, people who have been crucified have been taken down and their bodies delivered to their kinsfolk, because it was thought well to give them burial and allow them the ordinary rites' (*Flaccus* 10 §83). Philo speaks here in reference to Roman authority in Egypt.

This was the practice during the time of Jesus, in Palestine, as the skeletal remains of Yehohanan attest. This man was crucified in the late 20s, during the administration of Pontius Pilate, and was buried according to Jewish customs. One year after death, his bones were gathered and placed in an ossuary (or bone box). We know that Yehohanan was crucified, because his right heel bone was still transfixed by an iron spike that the executioners evidently had been unable to extract. The properly buried remains of one or two other persons who probably had been executed have also been discovered in Jerusalem.

Only during time of insurrection and war were Jewish burial practices and sensi-tivities not respected by the Roman authorities. For example, during the siege of Jerusalem (69–70 CE) General Titus crucified Jewish captives and fugitives opposite the walls of the city and left their bodies to rot in the sun, to demoralize the rebels (*JW* 5. 6. 5 §289; 5. 11. 1 §449). Titus did not permit burial, because he knew how important it was to the Jewish people.

In view of the evidence it is virtually a certainty that arrangements would have been made to bury Jesus and the other men crucified with him. Joseph of Arimathea either volunteered or was assigned the task of seeing to the prompt and unceremo-nious burial of Jesus and, probably, the other two men. Jesus was not buried honorably – no executed criminal was – but he was buried properly. Jewish law required it; and in peacetime, Roman authority permitted it.

It also is highly probable that the story of the discovery of the empty tomb is also historical. This is so because it is women who make the discovery. Surely a fictional account would have Peter and other disciples discover the empty tomb, not relatively unknown women. The women went to the tomb to mourn privately, as Jewish law and custom allowed, and, even more importantly, to note the precise location of Jesus' tomb, so that the later gathering of his remains for reburial in his family tomb would be possible.

All the details in the gospel accounts of the burial of Jesus and the subsequent discovery of the empty tomb are in keeping with Jewish burial customs. The unexpected discovery of the empty tomb proved to be a major factor in the interpre-tation of the appearances of Jesus in terms of resurrection, even though it was not in step with current ideas (as in Paul, in 1 Cor. 15: 3–10: 'Christ died ... he was buried ... he was raised ... he appeared'). (For important studies, see Allison 2005; Craig 1989; Wright 2003.)

See also Judaism (Chapter 5), Christianity (Chapter 6), David Hume (Chapter 13),

Inclusivism and exclusivism (Chapter 21), Creation and divine action (Chapter 30), The Incarnation (Chapter 51), Sin and salvation (Chapter 53), Heaven and hell (Chapter 54), Miracles (Chapter 55).

References

Allison, D. C., Jr. (2005) *Resurrecting Jesus: The Earliest Christian Tradition and its Interpreters*, London: T. & T. Clark International.

Craig, W. L. (1989) *Assessing the New Testament Evidence for the Historicity of the Resurrection of Jesus*, Studies in the Bible and Early Christianity 16, Lewiston, NY: Edwin Mellen.

Davis, S. T. (1997) 'Survival of death,' in P. L. Quinn and C. Taliaferro (eds) *A Companion to Philosophy of Religion*, Malden, MA: Blackwell.

Lattimore, R. A. (1942) *Themes in Greek and Latin Epitaphs*, Illinois Studies in Language and Literature 28.1–2, Urbana, IL: University of Illinois Press.

Meyers, E. M. (1971) *Jewish Ossuaries: Reburial and Rebirth*, Biblica et orientalia 24, Rome: Pontifical Biblical Institute Press.

Nickelsburg, G. W. E. (1972) *Resurrection, Immortality and Eternal Life in Intertestamental Judaism*, Harvard Theological Studies 26, Cambridge, MA: Harvard University Press.

Porter, S. E. (1999) 'Resurrection, the Greeks and the New Testament,' in S. Porter, M. A. Hayes, and D. Tombs (eds) *Resurrection*, Journal for the Study of the New Testament, Supplements 186 (Roehampton Institute, London Papers 5), Sheffield: Sheffield Academic Press.

Tromp, N. J. (1969) *Primitive Conceptions of Death and the Nether World in the Old Testament*, Biblica orientalia 21, Rome: Pontifical Biblical Institute Press.

Wright, N. T. (2003) *The Resurrection of the Son of God*, vol. 3 of *Christian Origins and the Question of God*, Minneapolis, MN: Fortress Press.

Further reading

Allison, D. C., Jr. (2005) *Resurrecting Jesus: The Earliest Christian Tradition and its Interpreters*, London: T. & T. Clark International. (An excellent study that carefully assesses all of the relevant data, concluding that the resurrection of Jesus, though not provable, is probable.)

Meyers, E. M. (1971) *Jewish Ossuaries: Reburial and Rebirth*, Biblica et orientalia 24, Rome: Pontifical Biblical Institute Press. (A very important study of Jewish burial traditions and ideas of death and postmortem survival, arguing that these traditions must be taken into account if the New Testament gospel resurrection narratives are to be properly understood.)

Nickelsburg, G. W. E. (1972) *Resurrection, Immortality and Eternal Life in Intertestamental Judaism*, Harvard Theological Studies 26, Cambridge, MA: Harvard University Press. (The classic study of Jewish ideas concerning resurrection and immortality in the period leading up to Jesus and the New Testament era, essential material for understanding early Christianity's proclamation of the resurrection of Jesus.)

Porter, S. E. (1999) 'Resurrection, the Greeks and the New Testament,' in S. Porter, M. A. Hayes, and D. Tombs (eds) *Resurrection*, Journal for the Study of the New Testament, Supplements 186 (Roehampton Institute, London Papers 5), Sheffield: Sheffield Academic Press. (Suggests that bodily resurrection may have been entertained in Greek thought, and perhaps influenced Judaism.)

Wright, N. T. (2003) *The Resurrection of the Son of God*, vol. 3 of *Christian Origins and the Question of God*, Minneapolis, MN: Fortress Press. (Offers an important assessment of the relevant scriptural background for Jewish and Christian hopes of resurrection and immortality.)

53

SIN AND SALVATION

Gordon Graham

The philosophical treatment of sin and salvation

Sin and salvation are central concepts in many, though not all, of the major religions of the world. They have figured especially prominently in Judeo-Christianity, with the result that the development of doctrines relating to them has been a notable feature of theological reflection in that tradition. By contrast, there has been relatively little strictly *philosophical* reflection on sin and salvation. Of major philosophers in the modern period, only Immanuel Kant (1724–1804) gives the subject of sin sustained attention, and even then not in one of his major works (Kant 1998). On the other hand, since the most influential theological doctrines deploy alternative (though not necessarily contradictory) conceptions of sin and salvation, the philosophical analysis and clarification of these can offer a valuable and distinctive way of understanding them.

Sin and salvation may be said to be interrelated in the following way. Salvation is the remedy for sin, and sin is the cause of our need for salvation. However, we can distinguish three broad conceptions of sin – sin as wrongdoing, sin as bondage, and sin as alienation – to which there are three corresponding conceptions of salvation: salvation as pardon, salvation as rescue, and salvation as reconciliation. These conceptions are often interrelated, but for the purposes of analysis it is useful to distinguish them in this way. The clarification that results may offer a better understanding of how the relation between sin and salvation is best understood.

Conceptions of sin

A very common conception of sin is that of wrongdoing. On this conception, sin falls into the same broad category as crime, that is to say, an illicit or improper kind of action. Understood in this way, 'sin' is really a collective noun equivalent to the plural 'sins,' actions that an individual may perform. Sin differs from crime in being contrary to the law of God rather than the law of the state, and commonly both are further distinguished from moral wrongdoing, that is to say, action contrary to the principles of morality. The three classifications are not to be regarded as mutually exclusive; a given action – theft, say – can be criminal, sinful and morally wrong. Nor are they coextensive, however. Many religions prescribe dietary restrictions, yet even within those religions failure to observe them is not thought of as immoral, and modern legal jurisdictions very rarely make religious observation obligatory. Conversely, in many countries there are actions that have been made legal – abortion, for instance – which continue to be quite widely regarded as both sinful and immoral.

The conception of sin as wrongdoing has a long history. Perhaps its most ancient and influential manifestation is to be found in the Ten Commandments, the rules delivered by God to Moses as those by which anyone faithful to the covenant must live. In pre-Reformation Christianity, and subsequently in Catholicism, it is this quasi-legal conception that is central to the identification of the 'seven deadly sins' and to the important distinction between 'mortal' and 'venial' sins, the former being of a much greater significance than the latter. It is also a conception that is deeply consonant with a long-standing approach to the question of religious conduct, namely casuistry, or the refinement of principles of conduct to provide ever closer guidance on how we should live. Such casuistry is a notable feature of Catholicism, but it has a counterpart in any variety of Judaism that lays great store by the biblical book of Leviticus, which sets out rules of conduct in great detail. Where religion has declined, as it has in much of western Europe, it is this conception of sin that has continued to dominate contemporary secular thought, since 'sin' has come to mean those actions of which religious people disapprove, but which are to be regarded as 'really' wrong only insofar as they are also immoral or illegal.

The conception of sin as wrongdoing, however, faces an important difficulty. Almost all religions are animated by the idea that human beings *as such* stand in need of salvation. But this could not be the case if sin consists simply in wrongful actions performed. If it were, then it would follow that there are some human beings – those who have never acted wrongly – who are not in need of salvation and to whom, accordingly, the religion in question is irrelevant. One such obvious class is infants. Very young children are almost never held responsible at law and cannot plausibly have immoral actions imputed to them. Why should the position be any different with respect to sinful action? It is difficult to see that it could be, and yet the common Christian practice of baptizing infants (like similarly sacramental practices in other religions) suggests that even 'innocent' children stand in need of some sort of divine redemption. Moreover, such a practice has been widely endorsed where infant mortality is high, carrying the implication that even children who will *never* commit wrongful acts need saving grace.

It is reflection on this fact that has led to a different conception of sin, not as action at all, but as a condition of some sort, a condition that every human being is in, independently of their freely chosen actions. What is this condition? Early Judaism was in large part 'this-worldly,' and the bondage into which sinfulness cast the Jewish people was their vulnerability to natural and political disasters, and especially their subjection to foreign rulers. But within this tangible conception, there is the suggestion of a deeper, less earthly conception of bondage, namely our *mortality*. 'A human being,' the Hebrew psalmist says, 'however firm he stands, is but a puff of wind, his life but a passing shadow' (Ps. 39: 5–6). However, human mortality is a conception of bondage more obvious to the religions of the West than of the East. For (later)

Judaism, Christianity, and Islam, the major problem to confront human beings is the inescapability of death; for Buddhism, Hinduism, and Sikhism, all of which believe in reincarnation, the problem is precisely the opposite. It is the endless round of birth and rebirth that holds us captive, and from our *immortality* that we need to escape.

It may be that the religions of the East and West are so fundamentally different in this regard that there is no way of conceiving the human condition that is true to both. Yet it is difficult not to understand the eastern concept of *moksha* or liberation as a kind of salvation, and hence tempting to try to find some overarching conception of sin that can illuminate the religious aspiration of the East as well as the West. If there *is* such a conception, then it is to be found in the perception that by the nature of things human beings have hopes that their very own nature frustrates. We can think of this as a kind of imprisonment, and it is this conception that fits best with the Christian doctrine of 'original sin.' People who are imprisoned (or indeed constricted by ailments and illnesses) have desires which, by the nature of the case, they are unable to satisfy. So too, the condition of original sin is one in which our spiritual aspirations outstrip our spiritual powers.

The conception of sin as bondage can be combined with the conception of sin as wrongdoing. Famously, the Apostle Paul connects the two when he speaks of the 'unspiritual self' in which 'the will to do good is there, but the ability to effect it is not' (Rom. 7: 9). Here the idea is that some background condition – freedom from innate impulses, perhaps – has to be supplied if wrongdoing is to be avoided. But more importantly, once that condition *is* supplied, then the individual can be freed even of consciousness of sin. A 'law' of right and wrong becomes unnecessary for anyone who has left behind any desire to break it. In a not wholly dissimilar way, the Buddhist who relinquishes the life-sustaining activity of desiring itself is freed from the inevitable frustration of unsatisfied desires.

But why does it matter if the 'unspiritual self' sins? Why does it matter if we seek desires that will ultimately be frustrated? In asking this question, it is important to remember the threefold distinction between sinfulness, immorality, and criminality. Many answers have been given as to why people should respect the law and act morally, and though there is continuing disagreement about the adequacy of these answers, no one is in much doubt that in some way effective appeal can be made to human welfare and the rights of others. But why is it important (say) for Jews and Muslims to observe the prohibition on eating pork, or for Christians to take Holy Communion on a regular basis? It is at this point that the third conception of sin comes into play, namely, sin as the condition of alienation from God or the divine.

This conception is graphically illustrated by the biblical story of the Fall. On the face of it, eating the fruit of the Tree of Knowledge seems innocent enough. But, as Augustine (354–430) remarks, this should not lead us to think of the act as 'light and trivial' because the act, however innocent, had been forbidden. 'God's command required obedience, and this virtue is, in a certain sense, the mother and guardian of all other virtues in a rational creature' (*City of God* XIV. 12). This is what makes it a dramatic rupture in the relationship between Creator and created. The great western religions, including Islam, can all be thought of as attempts to diagnose and to overcome this rupture. Once more, this is a conception of sin that can be connected with the other two; human limitations lead to sinful acts that deepen humanity's alienation from its spiritual root and home. It is this third conception of sin that the poet and Anglican divine John Donne (1572–1631) had in mind when he wrote

> when we shall have given to those words, by which hell is expressed in the Scriptures, the heaviest significations ... *fire*, and *brimstone*, and *weeping*, and *gnashing*, and *darkness*, and *the worme* ... the hell of hells, the torment of torments is the everlasting absence of God, and the everlasting impossibility of returning to his presence. (1953–62: *Sermons* V, emphasis original)

Conceptions of salvation

If we think of sin as a distinctive type of wrongdoing, this has a natural association with an equally common conception of salvation as its remedy, namely, salvation as divine pardon. The idea that God forgives the sins of those who truly repent of them is probably as ancient as the idea of sin itself, and one way to explicate it more fully is to explore the legal model on which it is conceived. When people break the law of the land, through their actions they have, in a sense, forfeited their citizenship, which is to say the rights and privileges that citizenship gives them. That is why just punishment is possible; the state that fines a criminal removes her property against her will, but this does not imply that the state is also a thief and is itself stealing property. A fine is not a theft, because it is in accordance with justice. There are a number of competing philosophical theories of punishment. Deterrence, retribution, and reformation are the three main ones, but it is a fourth – the reparative theory – that is most likely to illuminate the religious parallel. According to this theory, the essence of crime is that it does damage to the community to which the criminal belongs and to the relationship of the criminal to that community. The function of punishing people, and the only adequate justification for doing so, is that it repairs the damage done. Punishing criminals to deter others from crime, or just because they deserve it, can only be justified insofar as deterrence and retribution can be combined with the reparative theory; criminals deserve no more than the level of punishment required to repair the damage they have done.

Applied to the idea of sin, the parallel would appear to be this. Sinful actions damage the sinner's relationship to God; God's just retribution repairs that damage. There are several important problems with this parallel, however. First, it leaves no room for pardon. The administration of punishment is a requirement of justice; the prerogative of mercy sets punishment, and thus justice, aside. The person who is pardoned is not punished, and if punishment is a necessary part of repairing a damaged relationship, pardon will prevent that repair. Yet all the major religions of the West emphasize the necessity of divine mercy. The Qur'ān opens with the declaration 'In the Name of God, the Merciful'; Judaism's major book of prophecy, Isaiah, promises that God will freely forgive; the Christian New Testament tells us that 'through

Christ's sacrificial death, we shall be … *saved* … from final retribution.' (Rom. 5: 9, emphasis added). Kant struggles with this doctrine (1998: VII) since it so obviously flies in the face of the requirements of justice and undermines individual responsibility. Nevertheless, divine forgiveness is unquestionably a central part of the religions of the West, and especially of the Lutheranism that dominated Kant's Germany. Nor is it hard to see why it should be central. If just punishment can repair our damaged relationship with God, no special act on God's part is required. Humanity can itself enforce the principles of right and wrong.

But in any case, viewed from another perspective, even a world in which crime and punishment, sin and retribution are perfectly matched, must fall importantly far short of what is required. This is the perspective of those eastern religions that subscribe to the doctrine of 'karma,' a doctrine usefully thought of as a moral equivalent of the law of the conservation of energy. According to the doctrine of karma, there is built into the world a guarantee that the ill effects of every evil deed will at some point be counterbalanced; whatever the immediate appearances, no one ultimately escapes retribution. But far from the law of karma constituting a promise of salvation, it is precisely one of the main factors tying human beings to the endless round of birth and rebirth from which the enlightened seek liberation.

Just as the Hindu seeks freedom from karma, so too Pauline Christianity seeks freedom from the law. 'I delight in the law of God,' says St Paul, 'but I perceive in my outward actions a different law that my mind approves, and making me a prisoner under the law of sin which controls my conduct. Wretched creature that I am, who is there to rescue me from this state of death? Who but God?' (Rom. 7: 22–4). The conception of salvation as the reparation of sin through retribution is unsatisfactory. We are, as Cranmer's *Book of Common Prayer* puts it, 'tied and bound by the chain of our sins' and only 'the pitifulness of [God's] great mercy [can] loose us' (Post-Communion prayer for Ash Wednesday). In short, it is not the justice of God that is required, but his grace.

The concept of grace as God's response to sin generates a conception of salvation more fitted to the conception of sin as bondage than sin as wrongdoing. It is this concept that most naturally generates the idea of a Savior, some external, divine, or supernatural being through whose agency human salvation is made possible. This is how the figure of Jesus Christ is perceived in almost all versions of the Christian religion, but in this respect Christianity is simply perpetuating one of the principal Jewish ideas out of which it grew; namely, a Messiah that would save and restore Israel to its rightful place as God's chosen people. At the time of Jesus, the Jewish concept of Messiah was that of a quasi-military/political figure. But in light of biblical references to God himself coming and intervening to save his people (e.g., Isa. 60: 1–2; Zechariah 2: 10–11; Mal. 3: 1–3), Christianity reinterpreted this idea in a powerfully supernatural direction when it conceived of the historical Jesus as God incarnate. By contrast, Islam stresses the humanity of its Prophet, and yet Muhammad may also be said to be a savior since it is only through the revelation embodied in the Qur'ān that the Muslim can know 'the Straight Path,' the 'path of the Blessed' and avoid the path of 'those who have gone astray' (Sura 1).

Concepts of 'bondage' and 'liberation' are to be found in the religions of both East and West, but if 'salvation as liberation' is taken to imply a savior then a difference opens up between the monotheistic religions and some of the religions of the East. Though Sikhs hold their ten 'gurus' in veneration, it is the Adi Granth or Guru Granth Sahib, the holy scriptures themselves that provide the means of salvation. And while the monotheists say with Paul that there is none but God to rescue us from the state of eternal death, the Buddha tells his followers to 'free *yourselves* from the tangled net of sorrow' (in Carus 1998; emphasis mine) and remarks in another place that if there are gods, they have their own salvation to work out.

Buddhism ought not to be taken as characterizing the religions of the East, however, because it differs from Hinduism and Sikhism in a significant respect. For the Buddhist the goal of liberation is not the salvation of souls but the achievement of release or extinction, nirvana. The outcome of sin (or desire) is the perpetuation of bondage, but there is no further underlying account as there is in other religions. Buddhists have no use for the third conception of sin identified above: sin as alienation. The position in the other eastern religions is different. Just as monotheists think that sin separates us from God both collectively and as individuals, a recurrent theme in Hinduism is the false separation of Atman (the individual soul) and Brahman (the soul or spirit that pervades all things). At the deepest level, Hinduism holds, Atman and Brahman are one, despite appearances, and the knowledge of Brahman is the supreme goal of human life, since it brings release from the endless round of suffering and rebirth which results from mistaking appearance for reality. In this way, the end of bondage (*moksha*) is the end of alienation, so that despite many deep differences, the Hindu's ultimate aspiration comes close to that of monotheism. This is true even with respect to the variety of western monotheisms that might seem to lie farthest from the mysticism of the East. Thus the *Shorter Catechism* of the Protestant Westminster Assembly declares that 'the chief end of man' is 'to glorify God, and enjoy him for ever.' The absorption of Atman in Brahman is even more strikingly at one with the hope expressed in 'The Christian Year' by John Keble, an influential figure in the nineteenth-century Anglo-Catholic revival, that in the end 'we lose ourselves in heaven above.' There is some reason to think, then, that the most widespread conception of sin is that of alienation, and of salvation as the overcoming of that alienation.

It is with the concept of alienation that theological and philosophical reflection comes closest, most strikingly in the works of G. W. F. Hegel (1770–1831). Hegel understood the task of philosophy to be that of tracing the development of Mind as it overcomes a series of ultimately false distinctions, chiefly the distinctions we naturally draw between Mind and Nature, Self and Other, the Individual and the Absolute. He held that the philosophical understanding which results from this endeavor constitutes a rationalization of the truth embodied in the Christian religion, thereby allying the spiritual and the intellectual. Hegel's conception of the 'Absolute' was hugely influential for a time and led to a movement known as 'Absolute Idealism.' Among the philosophers to take it up was the English philosopher F. H. Bradley (1846–1924). No doubt because of the British presence there, Bradleyan Idealism spread to India where it uncovered a deep consonance with Hindu theology and in this way revealed unexpected common metaphysical ground between European philosophy and eastern religion.

When sin and salvation have been adequately conceived, there remains the question of how sin is to be overcome and salvation secured. Here too we can detect three recurrent themes at work in many of the world's religions, each of which very broadly correlates with the three conceptions of sin and salvation we have identified. This threefold classification is most evident in Hinduism perhaps, where the first is the 'way of works' (roughly, the ethical life given to good deeds), the second the 'way of knowledge' (philosophical or theological contemplation of reality), and the third the 'way of devotion' (spiritual exercises and observances). Arguably, all the major religions of the world can be interpreted as seeking an adequate understanding of how these three 'ways' can be integrated, and the divisions within them can be construed as arising from different emphases on each. In Christianity, for instance, 'liberal' denominations such as the Quakers and Unitarians have emphasized the first, Calvinistic Protestantism has focused chiefly on the second, while Roman Catholicism has laid greater store by the third. Within Islam, the 'Five Pillars' place both ethical and spiritual obligations on the believer, but a passionate commitment to *ilm*, knowledge, was a notable mark of Islam in the medieval period, a tendency which the great prophet al-Ghazālī (1058/9–1111 CE), in turn, sought to correct.

Against sin and salvation

Conceptions of sin and salvation are intrinsic to a religious understanding of human experience. Given the prevalence of religion in human culture, it is not enough for those who reject religion simply to repudiate these conceptions along with it. Humanists have to explain what is wrong with the ideas of sin and salvation, and how, in their more enlightened world, these concepts are to be replaced. The most notable philosophical figure in the rejection of religion is Friedrich Nietzsche (1844–1900). Nietzsche takes it for granted that the basis of religion is a belief in the existence of God and a divine order, and that the development of the sciences has shown this belief to be false. Accordingly, no educated person can seriously continue to believe it. Yet religion persists, even among the educated classes. Why so? Nietzsche's explanation is that there are residual aspects of religion which the European psyche, given its history, is reluctant to abandon, and the larger part of his writing is thus devoted to a historical and psychological analysis of the roots of religion, an analysis whose purpose is to expose and thus exorcise the continuing hold that religion has upon us.

One of the most important targets in this endeavor is otherworldliness, which Nietzsche interprets as a life-denying attitude that amounts to self-hatred on the part of human beings. Accordingly, an important part of his task is to depict human life in ways that make it possible to celebrate being human – *Human, All Too Human* being the title Nietzsche gave to a collection of aphoristic paragraphs gathered together in chapters. In the chapter 'On the history of moral feelings,' Nietzsche identifies the idea of sin as a useful starting point for human reflection, but one which must be left behind.

The man who wants to gain wisdom profits greatly from having thought for a time that man is basically evil and degenerate: this idea is wrong . . . but its roots have sunk deep into us and our world. To understand ourselves we must understand it; but to climb higher, we must then climb over and beyond it. (1994: 56)

It is certainly true that a sense of sin can come uncomfortably close to pathological self-hatred. Some intensely religious lines by the Christian poet Phineas Fletcher run, 'See, I am black as night./See, I am darkness: dark as hell,' and it is difficult to think that these could be said sincerely without self-hatred. At the same time, Nietzsche's own image of 'climbing over and beyond' the understanding that human beings have hitherto achieved itself suggests that the conceptual structure of sin and salvation is not so easy to escape. The author of the book of Ecclesiastes advises us that 'there is nothing good for anyone to do here under the sun but to eat and drink and enjoy himself' (Eccl. 8: 15), and it is indeed possible to combine metaphysical fatalism with ethical hedonism in this way. This is not such an easy attitude to adopt, however. More natural is the belief that human limitation often results in error, that by means of insight (our own or other people's) we can overcome the limitation and correct that error, and that the resulting wisdom will enhance, even transform, our lives. This is a general picture that Nietzsche subscribes to as much as any of the religious figures he condemns. He even uses the concept of sin to make his point about the need to affirm life. 'The preaching of chastity amounts to a public incitement to anti-nature. Every kind of contempt for sex ... is the real sin against the holy spirit of life' (1979: 5). What Nietzsche commends differs greatly from the life that Christianity prescribes, obviously, but in its way it nonetheless offers an analysis of sin, and a prospect of salvation if only we can avoid it.

See also Chapters 1–7 on individual religions, Friedrich Nietzsche (Chapter 16), Protestant theology (Chapter 45), Phenomenology of religion (Chapter 61), Religious experience (Chapter 63).

References

Augustine (1998) *City of God against the Pagans*, trans. and ed. R. W. Dyson Cambridge: Cambridge University Press.
Book of Common Prayer (1662), Cambridge: Cambridge University Press
Carus, P. (1998) [1894] 'Entering into nirvana' in *Buddha, the Gospel*, Chicago: Open Court. Excerpted from: http://www.sacred-texts.com/bud/btg/btg98.htm (accessed 15 May 2006).
Donne, J. (1953–62) *The Sermons of John Donne*, ed. E. V. Simpson and G. R. Potter, Berkeley, CA: University of California Press.
Kant, I. (1998) [1793] *Religion within the Boundaries of Mere Reason*, trans. and ed. A. Wood and G. Di Giovanni, Cambridge: Cambridge University Press.
Nietzsche, F. (1979) [1888] *Ecce Homo*, trans. R. J. Hollingdale, Harmondsworth: Penguin.
—— (1994) [1878] *Human, All Too Human*, trans. M. Farber and S. Lehmann, Harmondsworth: Penguin.

Further reading

Adams, M. M. (1991) 'Sin as uncleanness,' in J. E. Tomberlin (ed.), *Philosophical Perspective 5: Philosophy of Religion*, Ridgeview, CA: Ridgeview Publishing Company. (Another recent treatment of the topic of sin in contemporary philosophy.)

Craig, E. (ed.) (1998) 'Sin' and 'Salvation,' in *Routledge Encyclopedia of Philosophy*, London: Routledge. (Both articles written by philosophers in the analytic tradition; article on salvation includes extensive reference to world religions.)

Hastings, J. (ed.) (1908) 'Sin' and 'Salvation,' in *Encyclopedia of Religion and Ethics*, Edinburgh: T. & T. Clark. (A monumental work, still available in print, with comprehensive treatments of the concepts of sin and salvation within the world's major religions; the former article includes an account of sin in Native American religion.)

Ricoeur, P. (1967) *The Symbolism of Evil*, New York: Harper & Row. (A related work from a different philosophical tradition.)

Wainwright, W. (1988) 'Original Sin' in T. V. Morris (ed.) *Philosophy and the Christian Faith*, Notre Dame, IN: University of Notre Dame Press. (A treatment of the subject of sin by a contemporary philosopher.)

54

HEAVEN AND HELL

Jerry L. Walls

The doctrines of heaven and hell are among the most intellectually fascinating as well as existentially engaging claims made by historic Christianity. For the better part of two millennia, heaven and hell have been vivid realities that have provided moral and spiritual orientation for western culture. The truth was never so beautiful, nor the stakes ever so high in the quest to find and follow the truth. Eternal joy of unimaginable glory and delight could be gained, and eternal misery of unspeakable horror could be suffered. With the prospects for happiness and misery so magnified, the meaning of our lives and the significance of our choices are both elevated to dramatic proportions.

This dramatic picture of our lives is entailed by the Christian doctrine of God and its remarkable account of salvation. Of course, the other great theistic religions, Judaism and Islam, have their own doctrines of salvation and corresponding accounts of heaven and hell. But the distinctively Christian doctrine that God is a Trinity of persons who exists in an eternal relationship of love, and has created us in his image, gives a distinctive shape to how Christians conceive of heaven and hell. Whereas the essence of heaven is a perfected relationship of love with the Trinitarian God that fulfills our nature, hell is the loss of this relationship and of all the good things we were created to enjoy. Both heaven and hell must be understood in light of the Christian conception that final salvation includes the redemption and restoration of the larger created order. The God of Christian revelation, who created this world and became incarnate in a real body of flesh and blood in order to redeem it, promises a final salvation in a resurrected body on a renewed earth. As N. T. Wright puts it, 'the ultimate future, as chapters 21 and 22 [of Revelation] make clear is not about people leaving 'earth' and going to 'heaven', but rather about the life of 'heaven', more specifically the New Jerusalem, coming down *from* heaven to earth – exactly in line with the Lord's Prayer' (Wright 2003: 59-60). This conception of salvation is profoundly at odds with notions of salvation that are exclusively spiritual in any sense that would demean or trivialize material creation, including our bodies.

Hell: traditional and contemporary views

As traditionally conceived, at least among western theologians, eternal hell has been defended primarily as a matter of divine justice imposed upon deserving sinners who reject the grace of God and the salvation that he offers. Augustine, Aquinas, Anselm, and Jonathan Edwards are among the notable figures who have formulated influential arguments in favor of this conception of hell. Anselm formulated his version of this argument in his famous account of the purpose of the atonement of Christ. We owe God total and perfect honor, Anselm argued; so any sin against him puts us in infinite debt to him that accordingly deserves infinite punishment. Edwards developed a similar argument by appealing to God's infinite nature. Since God is infinite in his loveliness, honor, and authority, our obligation to love and honor him is likewise infinite. To fail in this obligation is to merit infinite consequences. Moreover, traditional theologians typically held that repentance after death is impossible, and consequently, no one can escape from hell.

In elaborating the punishment view of hell, traditional theologians often distinguished between the 'pains of sense' and the 'pain of loss.' The former of these was typically understood to include literal fire of agonizing intensity, while the latter emphasized the unhappiness that naturally results from being separated from God, the true source of all joy and happiness.

To summarize then, the traditional view of hell includes three claims:

1 Some persons will never accept the grace of God and therefore will not be saved.
2 Those who reject the grace of God will be consigned to hell, a place of great misery that is the just punishment for the sin they commit in this life.
3 There is no escape from hell, either by repentance or by suicide or annihilation.

Much of the contemporary discussion of hell has centered on the traditional arguments defending the claim that eternal torment is the just punishment for human sin (the combination of 2 and 3 above). Among those who have subjected these arguments to searching critical scrutiny are Marilyn Adams, Jonathan Kvanvig, and Charles Seymour. This critique begins by contesting the claim that human sin could ever be infinitely serious. Even the most notorious of sinners, such as Hitler, have done only finite evil and caused finite harm, however enormous it is. Next, it is contended that a just punishment should fit the crime, or be proportionate to it. An infinite punishment would be disproportionate to finite sins; so a just God could not employ such punishment. There is a general consensus among contemporary philosophers that the traditional view cannot overcome this 'proportionality problem'; so those who affirm the doctrine of eternal hell have turned to other arguments to make moral sense of it.

The most common strategy is to appeal to libertarian freedom to show how eternal hell can be compatible with God's perfect love and power. That is, it is contended that we have the freedom to reject God, even to the point of being forever separated from him. C. S. Lewis famously summed up the essence of this view in his remark that the doors of hell are 'locked on the *inside*' (Lewis 1962: 127). In the same vein, Richard Swinburne has defended the doctrine of hell on the grounds that we may, over time, form the sort of character that can no longer choose God and the good (Swinburne 1983: 48–9). Those who take this position thus typically affirm the pain of loss, but downplay or deny the pains of sense.

Kvanvig has defended a variation on this position that he calls the 'issuant conception of hell' (Kvanvig 1993: 112). His position is so called because he believes the doctrine of hell should issue from the same character of God as the doctrine of heaven, namely, his love. It is a mistake, he thinks, to stress love only with reference to heaven, while emphasizing justice in connection with hell. The final choice all of us face, according to Kvanvig, is either a relationship with God or annihilation, for to choose to live independently of God is in fact to choose annihilation, since living independently of God is actually impossible. However, not all who reject God choose annihilation in a clear and settled way. It is precisely because of his love that he allows them to remain in existence. Kvanvig's view is accordingly a 'composite' view since it allows for both eternal separation as well as annihilation (1993: 151–9).

Seymour has focused on human choice in developing a defense of eternal hell that he calls 'the freedom view.' His fundamental definition of hell is that it is 'an eternal existence, all of whose moments are on the whole bad' (Seymour 2000: 161). For this to be true of hell, he thinks it is not enough for hell to have the pain of loss; it must also include pains of sense. His appeal to freedom is crucial, for he rejects the traditional arguments for the claim that sins committed in this life could be sufficiently serious to warrant eternal punishment. Rather, it is the continuing choice to sin that keeps sinners in the perpetual pains of hell.

Seymour believes that sinners can in principle repent and would be accepted by God if they did; so if they remain in hell, it is due to their choice to persist in sin. Both Kvanvig and Seymour, then, deny the third claim of the traditional view listed above, namely, that there is no escape from hell. The notion that sinners in hell choose to persist in their sin forever thus represents a solution to the 'proportionality problem' that plagues more traditional views of hell.

The universalist option

A growing number of Christian philosophers and theologians are challenging the first claim of the traditional view of hell in favor of the view that all persons eventually will be saved. Not surprisingly, those who take this line typically focus on libertarian freedom and the crucial role it plays in the contemporary defense of the doctrine that not all will be saved.

Marilyn Adams has argued that those who rely on libertarian freedom in defending eternal hell exaggerate the dignity of human nature as something so sacrosanct that not even God may legitimately interfere with it. She sees this tendency particularly in 'mild' versions of the doctrine which hold that hell is simply the natural consequence of freely choosing to reject God and the love he offers. Adams complains that advocates of mild hell tend to assume that God and human adults are moral peers in their insistence that we have the right to resist God and choose evil instead. As she sees it, this is not the appropriate sort of respect for God to pay to the likes of us.

Indeed, the deeper difficulty here is that free will approaches underestimate what she calls the 'size gap' between divine and created persons. Whereas free will approaches picture the relationship between God and human persons with the analogy of parents and adolescent or adult children, Adams thinks it is better modeled by the relationship between a mother and an infant or a toddler. In the latter relationship, there is little if any sense that the child is free and responsible and that it would be wrong to interfere with his choices. This nicely serves Adams's view that God can save everyone in the end, and relieves her of the worry of how God can accomplish this without violating our freedom. If God needs to causally determine some things in order to prevent the everlasting ruin of some of his children, Adams colorfully comments, this is 'no more an insult to our dignity than a mother's changing a diaper is to the baby' (Adams 1999: 157).

Thomas Talbott has also mounted a sustained attack on the doctrine of eternal hell, building his case on both biblical and philosophical grounds (Talbott 2003). Talbott's philosophical case against eternal hell largely focuses on his claim that the idea of choosing hell is finally incoherent. The reason for this is that there is no intelligible motive for choosing hell. One may temporarily choose evil under the illusion that so choosing will make one happy. But God will eventually shatter this illusion by making one ever more miserable until the point is reached that one must repent and turn to God. Thus Talbott affirms the view that universalism is necessarily true, in contrast to the more common claims that universalism is possibly true or very probably true.

His argument for this claim hinges crucially on his account of what is involved in freely choosing an eternal destiny. In short, such a choice must be fully informed, and once the person making the choice gets what she wants, then it must be the case that she never regrets her choice. This means that the person must be free from ignorance and illusion both in her initial choice as well as later. She must fully understand what she has chosen while freely persisting in that choice.

Given these conditions, Talbott thinks there is an obvious and important asymmetry between choosing fellowship with God as an eternal destiny, on the one hand, and choosing hell as an eternal destiny, on the other. Whereas the first of these obviously is possible, the latter is not because it simply makes no sense to say someone could knowingly persist in the choice of eternal misery.

Obviously, the philosophical credibility of the doctrine of hell will largely depend on one's judgments about the nature and value of freedom as well as one's views of moral psychology. Those who disagree with Adams will argue that freedom is of sufficient value itself, or is the means to other goods of sufficient value, that God will not override it to save us. In a similar vein, Talbott's critics will need to make the case that there are, contrary to his claims, intelligible motives for the choice of eternal damnation.

Freedom and the coherence of eternal hell

As already noted, Talbott's view hinges crucially on a particular view of freedom. In addition to his view of what is involved in freely choosing an eternal destiny, his argument also relies heavily on his view that hell is pictured in the New Testament 'as a forcibly imposed punishment rather than as a freely embraced condition' (2001: 417). In terms of the three claims of the traditional view of hell listed earlier, Talbott denies (1) and (3) but affirms (2). This view of hell is what underwrites his claim that it is unintelligible that anyone could freely choose it forever. As Talbott sees it then, the forcibly imposed misery of hell will eventually move even the most hardened sinners to repent and gladly and freely – in the non-determined sense – choose heaven for their eternal destiny.

A third important component of his argument is a distinction he has drawn between having the power to do something, on the one hand, and being psychologically capable of doing it, on the other. To illustrate the difference, he cites Augustine's view that the redeemed in heaven will no longer even be tempted to disobey God. Indeed, they will see with perfect clarity that God is the source of happiness and sin is the source of misery, so that sin and disobedience will no longer be psychologically possible for them. But surely they will not be less free as a result of this, nor will it be the case that they lack the power to sin, despite the fact that sin is no longer a psychological possibility for them (Talbott 1988: 13).

Talbott's distinction between power and psychological ability may be granted as a helpful one. However, even with this distinction granted, there are serious problems with his claim that persons who repent under forcibly imposed punishment are free in a non-determined sense. First, the notion of ever increasing misery, misery without a distinct limit, destroys the very notion of a free choice. The reason for this is that finite beings like ourselves are simply not constituted in such a way that we can absorb ever-increasing misery. At some point, we would either be coerced to submit, or we would go insane, or we would perish. In short, we have neither the *power* nor the *psychological ability* to withstand constantly increasing misery, regardless of whether that misery is physical or emotional in nature. To put it another way, our freedom can only take so much pressure. Where exactly the limit lies is perhaps not easy to say, but clearly there is such a limit (Walls 1992: 129–33; 2004a: 206–13).

For punishment to elicit a truly free choice that is morally significant, on the other hand, the person receiving the punishment must come to see the truth about himself and his actions and genuinely want to change. He must achieve moral insight in the process and come genuinely to own that insight in the sense that he desires to act on it and implement it into his life. He must want to change because of the truth he has seen, not merely to escape or avoid the punishment that is being forced upon him. In short, the insight and understanding that truly transforms cannot be coerced or instilled by forcibly imposed punishment.

Interestingly, Talbott recognizes this point, as is apparent from the fact that he draws a distinction between two kinds of compulsion, one of which he defends and other of which he repudiates. As an example of the 'right' kind of compulsion, he appeals to dramatic conversions like those of St Paul, or more recently, C. S. Lewis, who reports that he had a sense of God closing in on him in such a way that it seemed impossible to do otherwise than to submit to God. The 'wrong' sort of compulsion, which Talbott repudiates, is that defended by the likes of Augustine, who was willing to employ the sword to persuade the Donatists to come back to the Church. He contrasts the two kinds of compulsion in the following: 'A stunning revelation such as Paul reportedly received, one that provides clear vision and *compelling evidence*, thereby altering one's beliefs in a perfectly rational way, does not compel behavior in the same way that threatening someone with a sword might' (Talbott 2001: 427). Now Talbott is surely right that there is an important difference between these two kinds of compulsion, and that the latter is not only morally objectionable, but also incompatible with any meaningful sense of freedom.

However, this very distinction poses problems for Talbott, given his view of hell as 'forcibly imposed punishment,' or as he also puts it, 'unbearable suffering' (2001: 417). For those traditional accounts of hell that Talbott claims to endorse surely include intense physical pain. If he does not believe hell includes physical pain and punishment, then he should not pretend to endorse the traditional understanding of what makes the punishment of hell unbearable. If he does in fact endorse the traditional view, then to avoid outright inconsistency here, we need some explanation of how forcibly imposed punishment that produces unbearable misery is not the wrong kind of compulsion that Talbott rejects. Indeed, this point holds even if he thinks the misery of hell is only psychological or spiritual. If it is objectionable to compel repentance by the sword, it is surely objectionable to compel repentance by forcibly imposed misery of the psychological or emotional variety, misery that may be just as painful and coercive.

In response to these criticisms, Talbott has clarified his position in some important respects. First, it is clear that at the end of the day, he believes that sinners who persist in rebellion against God and experience ever-increasing misery as a result, finally have no choice but to submit to God and repent. There is indeed a limit to the amount of misery any finite creature can absorb, so the choice to turn to God if this point is reached is not free in the libertarian sense of the word. The choices we make in arriving at this point are free but, ironically, those choices bring us to a point where the only option that remains is to repent of those very choices (Talbott 2004: 220–3).

Second, and more importantly, he has clarified what he means by 'unbearable suffering' and 'forcibly imposed punishment.' What has emerged is that he does not treat these terms in his 2004 article in the way they are typically understood in traditional accounts of hell, and in some of his other writings. To illustrate the sort of suffering he has in mind, he offers the example of a foolish married man who has an affair with an unstable woman, who, as an act of revenge, later murders his wife and child. Talbott says the man's subsequent guilt, sorrow, and sense of loss would be an unbearable suffering. God could use these to move him to repentance, and 'insofar as God uses the man's suffering as a means of correction, or as a means of encouraging repentance, we can again say that the man has endured a *forcibly imposed punishment* for his sin.' Moreover, he points out 'the good in the worst of sinners – the indestructible image of God if you will – can itself become a source of unbearable torment' (2004: 218).

While this is helpful for understanding his position, these very clarifications produce a dilemma for Talbott that make his case for necessary universalism much less plausible. In short, it appears he must either give up his account of unbearable torment, or he must give up his claim that all sinners must reach a point where they can resist no farther. Talbott's claim that all sinners will reach a point where they cannot but give in to God was persuasive so long as he affirmed that God will forcibly impose punishment that is literally unbearable. But his clarified account of unbearable misery does not seem at all certain to have this effect.

Consider again his example of the foolish philanderer. Granted that his actions and the subsequent course of events would indeed cause him great misery, is repentance *inevitable*? No doubt God could use his suffering as a means of correction to *encourage* repentance, as Talbott notes, but there is nothing in the case as described that makes such a response inevitable. Indeed, we can easily imagine a scenario in which, rather than repenting, he becomes angry and embittered if he believes God allowed the murder of his wife and baby to punish him for his affair.

Consider the incident further in light of Talbott's observation that the good in sinners can become the source of unbearable torment. One way we may choose to deal with our torment is by rationalizing our actions, thereby deadening or suppressing the very good that is causing this torment. Of course, this involves a certain degree of dishonesty, self-deception, and suppression of one's God-given nature – one's conscience and moral sensitivities. Common experience reinforces the observation that we can become desensitized by repeatedly performing precisely those acts that previously caused one to feel pain or remorse.

Of course, God could cause increasing pain to us in other ways as we rationalized our actions and desensitized our consciences. He could forcibly impose greater and greater pain, keep turning up the heat, until we reached the point where resistance would be impossible for us. But presumably Talbott would reject this as the wrong sort of compulsion, given his clarifications.

So again, Talbott has a dilemma on his hands. He can either forthrightly affirm divinely imposed misery that is literally unbearable (which his clarifications seem to repudiate) or he can give up his claim that all sinners will inevitably reach a point where resistance is impossible. This dilemma undermines Talbott's case that the doctrine of eternal hell is incoherent and therefore not possibly true (Walls 2004b: 226–7).

Contemporary challenges to heaven

Let us suppose now that the argument just presented is a sound one and eternal hell is not only a possibility but also a reality. If this is true, it provides grist for an argument that can be used against heaven, ironically. The heart of the argument, which goes back at least to the nineteenth-century theologian Schleiermacher, contends that the eternal *damnation of any* is incompatible with the *salvation of any* for the simple reason

591

that awareness of the sufferings of the lost would undermine the happiness of the saved. The argument assumes not only that the saved would be cognizant of the damned, but also that they would care about them. Anyone who has been fully transformed by the love of God would surely love all persons and desire their salvation. Because eternal happiness assumes being perfected in love, this entails that the saved would care deeply about the lost. In short, heaven and eternal hell are incompatible. If any are to enjoy eternal joy, all must do so. The argument is usually cast as an argument against the doctrine of eternal hell, but the reality is that it can also be cast as an argument against heaven that can only be answered by modifying traditional Christian thought.

There have been attempts to rebut this argument by trying to show that eternal hell is not in fact incompatible with eternal happiness. These arguments typically try to show that the blessed are in such a state of overwhelming bliss that nothing could disturb their happiness, or that they see the nature of evil with sufficient clarity that they can be at peace with the reality of damnation, or even that the blessed in heaven may not be aware of the lost in hell. These arguments have been criticized by Eric Reitan, in favor of the claim that all must be saved if any are to enjoy perfect happiness (Reitan 2002: 432–45). It is worth noting, incidentally, that many traditional theologians would not likely have felt the force of this problem, so keenly felt by many contemporary believers. Indeed, far from seeing eternal hell as a problem for heaven, many traditional theologians believed the punishment and misery of the wicked would glorify the justice of God and thereby actually enhance the joy of the redeemed (Walker 1964: 29).

But even if contemporary believers cannot identify with this sentiment, they may still feel that there is something profoundly wrong with the notion that hell should have any claim against heaven, that hell should have veto power over the joy of the redeemed. Think of Jesus' parable of the prodigal who returns (Luke 15: 25–32). The older brother refuses to come in to celebrate. But why should the party stop simply because some refuse to enter the banquet hall? God cannot be held captive by such party-poopers and spoil sports. While we have the right to sit it out, we don't have the right to hold up the joyous celebration of God's redeeming love by all who have accepted it.

A second challenge to heaven in contemporary thought is by way of historical analysis of the origins of the doctrine. Those who take this approach contend that the doctrine of heaven, as it developed historically, was inspired by dubious motivations, a charge that was advanced with great rhetorical flair by Nietzsche as part of his 'genealogy' of western morality. More recently, historians have written accounts of the origins of belief in heaven that could be used to support Nietzsche's suspicious reading. J. Edward Wright, for instance, argues that the doctrine of heaven has a rather shady historical pedigree, in both its Jewish and its Christian versions. He writes:

> Many people's visions of heaven were prompted by a desire to prove that God favors one group exclusively, their group. True, these visions inspire hope for members of the favored group, but they create a dangerous sense of superiority over outsiders by dehumanizing or demonizing them. (Wright 2000: 202)

As he tells the story of how the doctrine of heaven developed, it was largely motivated by a desire to reinforce certain beliefs and behaviors, often to the point of manipulation and intimidation (2000: 137, 157, 163, 177, 184).

In reply, it is no doubt true that some, if not many, of those who appealed to heaven and the afterlife have done so at least partly for reasons cited by Wright. As he observes, however, at the inception of the idea of the afterlife in Judaism was a concern for the bedrock ideal of justice. In the face of hopeless injustice in this life, faith in a God of ultimate justice can be sustained only if this life is not the final reality (Wright 2000: 158, 191–2). In other words, belief in an afterlife is simply the logical outcome of maintaining faith in a good God while wrestling with the problem of theodicy. It is precisely the goodness of God, a goodness comprised of perfect love as well as justice, that provides the ground for a belief in heaven motivated by our best aspirations and desires, one that also purges us of what falls short of these.

The final contemporary challenge to the doctrine of heaven I shall mention is one that has a distinctly modern/postmodern feel to it. The objection, famously put forward in an article by Bernard Williams (1993), contends that the whole idea of eternal happiness is incoherent because no matter how delightful the joys of heaven, they would eventually inevitably become boring. Whereas previous generations of persons in western culture looked forward to heaven with ardent longing, many in our age are loathe to embrace this hope. There is something more than a little ironic in this fact, as Carol Zaleski has noted. 'Our ancestors were afraid of Hell; we are afraid of Heaven. We think it will be boring' (Zaleski 2000: 42). There is not space here even to sketch the various responses to this objection, but Garth L. Hallett has critically surveyed six proposed solutions to the boredom difficulty, namely: timeless beatitude, heavenly continuation, indefinite progress, subjective timelessness, eternal youthfulness, and creative contentment. Hallett is inclined to think that none of these options is clearly impossible, though he thinks the first poses the most problems. Together, he thinks, the six may form a 'cumulative case' and provide material for us to imagine 'various conceivable ways in which the life to come might surpass all present felicity without a touch of ennui' (Hallett 2001: 288).

If it is true that heaven would inevitably become boring, and is therefore not worthy of the hope and longing it has traditionally inspired, then our lot is unhappy indeed. For it is only heaven that can offer the happiness that all rational creatures can hardly help but desire. Nothing short of this will suffice to give us what we most deeply crave. Clearly, if some partial experience of happiness is desirable, perfect happiness is even more so. Now either we have such happiness or we do not. If we do not, then it is something we want, and if we never get it, our lives will end in some degree of frustration. On the other hand, if we have it, we would not want it to end. If it did, either by coming to an abrupt conclusion or by petering out in boredom, then again, our lives would end in frustration. The only alternative to a frustrating end to our lives is perfect happiness, happiness without an end (Walls 2002: 193–200).

See also Inclusivism and exclusivism (Chapter 21), Goodness (Chapter 28), The problem of evil (Chapter 37), Resurrection (Chapter 52), Sin and salvation (Chapter 53), Miracles (Chapter 55).

References

Adams, M. M. (1999) *Horrendous Evils and the Goodness of God*, Ithaca, NY: Cornell University Press.

Hallett, G. (2001) 'The tedium of immortality,' *Faith and Philosophy* 18: 279–91.

Kvanvig, J. (1993) *The Problem of Hell*, New York: Oxford University Press.

Lewis, C. S. (1962) *The Problem of Pain*, New York: Macmillan.

Reitan, E. (2002) 'Eternal damnation and blessed ignorance: is the damnation of some compatible with the salvation of any?', *Religious Studies* 38: 429–50.

Seymour, C. (2000) *A Theodicy of Hell*, Dordrecht: Kluwer.

Swinburne, R. (1983) 'A theodicy of heaven and hell,' in A. J. Freddoso (ed.) *The Existence and Nature of God*, Notre Dame, IN: University of Notre Dame Press.

Talbott, T. (1988) 'On the divine nature and the nature of divine freedom,' *Faith and Philosophy* 5: 3–24.

—— (2001) 'Freedom, damnation and the power to sin with impunity,' *Religious Studies* 37: 417–34.

—— (2003) 'A case for christian universalism,' in R. A. Parry and C. H. Partridge (eds) *Universal Salvation? The Current Debate*, Grand Rapids, MI: Eerdmans.

—— (2004) 'Misery and freedom: reply to Walls,' *Religious Studies* 40: 217–24.

Walker, D. P. (1964) *The Decline of Hell*, Chicago: University of Chicago Press.

Walls, J. L. (1992) *Hell: The Logic of Damnation*, Notre Dame, IN: University of Notre Dame Press.

—— (2002) *Heaven: The Logic of Eternal Joy*, New York: Oxford University Press.

—— (2004a) 'A hell of a choice: reply to Talbott,' *Religious Studies* 40: 203–16.

—— (2004b) 'A hell of a dilemma: rejoinder to Talbott,' *Religious Studies* 40: 225–7.

Williams, B. (1993) 'The Makropulos case: reflections on the tedium of immortality,' in J. M. Fischer (ed.) *The Metaphysics of Death*, Stanford, CA: Stanford University Press.

Wright, J. E. (2000) *The Early History of Heaven*, New York: Oxford University Press.

Wright, N. T. (2003) *For all the Saints: Remembering the Christian Departed*, Harrisburg, PA: Morehouse.

Zaleski, C. (2000) 'In defense of immortality,' *First Things* 105: 36–42.

Further reading

Crockett, W. (ed.) (1992) *Four Views on Hell*, Grand Rapids, MI: Zondervan. (Explores the literal, the metaphorical, the purgatorial, and the conditional views of hell.)

McGrath, A. E. (2003) *A Brief History of Heaven*, Oxford: Blackwell. (A history that focuses on art and literature rather than theological sources.)

Russell, J. B. (1997) *A History of Heaven*, Princeton, NJ: Princeton University Press. (Culminates in Dante's picture of heaven.)

Segal, A. F. (2004) *Life After Death: A History of the Afterlife in Western Religion*, New York: Doubleday. (Comprehensive volume that discusses virtually every significant ancient text.)

55
MIRACLES
R. Douglas Geivett

Christian theists are supernaturalists. They believe that God – a non-embodied personal being who is omnipotent, omniscient, and omnibenevolent – interacts causally and intentionally with the physical universe in a way that transcends the operation of the laws of nature. On occasions of that sort, God brings about events that otherwise would not happen. Such acts of God are called 'miracles.'

Philosophical interest in miracles has two focal points, one conceptual and the other epistemological. 'What is a miracle?' is the most fundamental conceptual question. Since miracles contrast with events that conform to the laws of nature, philosophers must also address conceptual questions about the laws of nature and their relation to the concept of miracle. The first main part of this chapter explores these conceptual issues. The next section deals, in a general way, with the central epistemological question: is belief that miracles have happened ever justified? This question requires reflection on a cluster of interrelated issues. Alleged miracles are historical events. It would seem that they are therefore subject to historical investigation. This special epistemological issue is treated in the final section of this chapter.

Conceptual issues

David Hume (d. 1776) famously, if not definitively, said that 'a miracle is a violation of the laws of nature' (Hume 1978: 114). Elsewhere in the same passage, he wrote more fully: 'A miracle may be accurately defined, *a transgression of a law of nature by a particular volition of the Deity, or by the interposition of some invisible agent*' (p. 115, n. 1; italics in original). This definition, relegated to a footnote in Hume's essay 'On miracles,' is an improvement in that it refers specifically to the role of the Deity in causing some (if not all) miraculous events.

Many of Hume's skeptical successors, and some of his accusers, have thought that Hume's definition entails that miracles are logically impossible. If they're right, the definition grounds a conveniently swift refutation of miracle claims. Martin Curd (sympathetic with this argument against miracles) has made the supposed implication of Hume's definition clear in the following way:

We can analyze the difficulty in understanding miracles as violations of law by noticing that the following four statements form a logically inconsistent set.

1 E is a miracle.
2 If E is a miracle then there is at least one law of nature, L, such that E violates L.
3 If E violates L then E is a counterinstance of L.
4 If L is a law of nature then L has no counterinstances.

If statements 2, 3, and 4 are true, then there are no miracles. Moreover, if 2, 3, and 4 were necessary truths (because they are conceptual or definitional truths), then this would show not merely that 1 is false, but also that it is logically impossible for any event to be miraculous. This is the core argument against the possibility of miracles as violations of law. (Curd 1996: 175–6)

Statement 3 provides a convenient way of talking about a violation of the laws of nature: it is a *counterinstance* to the laws of nature. (While useful, this language is a mild syntactical blunder, as we can see if we consider the counterparts to miracles understood as counterinstances to the laws of nature. These would be natural events that occur in conformity to the laws of nature. But are natural events *instances* of the laws of nature? Thinking of them that way is odd.) Statement 2 assumes a definition of miracle: it is a violation of the laws of nature. But that is not the only definition presupposed in the argument. Statement 4 assumes that laws of nature have no counterinstances. This presupposes a certain general conception of natural laws. Whatever that conception is, it entails that there can be no miracles. Apparently, it assumes an especially raw version of necessitarianism about the laws of nature. It would seem that miracles have been deemed impossible by definitional fiat. Is this satisfactory?

Curd's shortcut through the thickets of dialectic about miracles is not very promising. It has two spectacular weaknesses. First, the assumed conception of natural laws begs the question against theism, a point to which I'll return. Second, there are competing analyses of the laws of nature that do not beg the question in favor of theism and that do not permit such a tantalizing shortcut. These are deflationary theories that run the gamut from moderate to extreme. In the more moderate category, regularity theories (which have a distinctively Humean cast) hold that laws of nature are merely statements about our observations of past regularities, having no inherent necessity. (Variations on this theme can be found in Braithwaite 1953; D. Lewis 1973; Hesse 1974, 1980; Skyrms 1980.) But the evidence is pretty strong that Hume himself did not consider miracles, as he defined them, to be logically impossible. For one thing, his argument against the rationality of belief in miracles makes no use of the point (see Earman 2000: 12–14). Extreme deflationary theories include skepticism about the reality of natural laws and outright denial of their existence (see Cartwright 1983; van Fraassen 1989).

The concept of miracle we seek to understand presupposes theism, for it is defined as an act of God that bears a certain relation to the laws of nature. It is instructive, then, to consider how theism might construe the laws of nature. I draw attention to two contributions that theistic philosophers have made on this topic.

Speaking of the fundamental laws of nature, Richard Swinburne argues that 'science cannot explain why every object has the same powers and liabilities' (1996: 49). If the laws governing the behavior of the universe in the orderly and intelligible manner presupposed (and confirmed) by science is sheer happenstance, it is 'a most extraordinary coincidence.' In contrast to naturalism, which must regard the laws of nature as 'brute facts' that have no explanation, theism provides a plausible explanation for the existence of natural laws. For 'the hypothesis of theism leads us to expect' such phenomena 'with some reasonable degree of probability. God being omnipotent is able to produce a world orderly in these respects' (1996: 52). Swinburne supplements his argument with reflections on the suitability of this world as a theatre for realizing the goods of embodied human action and animal behavior (see 1996: ch. 4).

C. S. Lewis seems to have believed much the same thing:

> If we admit God, must we admit Miracle? Indeed, indeed, you have no security against it. That is the bargain. Theology says to you in effect, 'Admit God and with Him the risk of a few miracles, and I in return will ratify your faith in uniformity as regards the overwhelming majority of events.' The philosophy which forbids you to make uniformity absolute is also the philosophy which offers you solid grounds for believing it to be general, to be *almost* absolute. (C. S. Lewis 1966: 106)

The attitude here is that if theism is true, then the laws of nature are due to the ordinances of God. It is precisely because of God that there are *laws* of nature.

A second contribution follows directly on the heels of this idea that God the creator has ordained the laws of nature. It, too, is suggested in C. S. Lewis's remark. The nomic necessity of nature's laws allows of exceptions. The laws of nature, as it were, 'dictate' what happens in the natural world. But the 'dictates of nature' are not absolute, because the universe is not a closed system. Because the laws of nature are not absolute, they may be overridden. In the case of miracles they are overridden; the general 'dictates of nature' are overridden by acts of a being whose existence entails that the universe is not a closed system. If the nomic character of the 'laws of nature' is understood in this way, then it may be coherent to speak of a *violation* of nature's laws. To 'violate' the laws of nature is to 'override' their 'dictates.'

The result is a robust conception of natural laws. Realists about the laws of nature should be happy because there is real nomic necessity. At the same time, there is something contingent about the operation of nature's laws. As John Earman has suggested, according to 'the modern conception of determinism … laws allow for contingency in "initial conditions" and necessitate only conditionals of the form "If the initial conditions are such-and-such, then the state at a later time will be so-and-so"' (2000: 9). Theists hold that absolutely initial conditions – on the front-end of the history of the universe – are determined freely by God. So the initial conditions are not the brute facts they would be if naturalism is true.

When it comes to the laws of nature, there is necessity, but not raw necessity. Since God, when creating the universe, determines the laws of nature, they operate at God's mercy. Not only is there contingency in the initial conditions; there is contingency in the law-like behavior of physical objects at any time during the history of the physical universe. The kind of 'conditional necessity' envisioned here ensures that there is both real necessity in the natural behavior of the world, and the real possibility of exceptions, that is to say, miracles.

J. L. Mackie, though he argued against the rationality of belief in miracles, was firm in his conviction that the concept of miracle is coherent:

> there is no obscurity in the notion of intervention. Even in the natural world we have a clear understanding of how there can be for a time a closed system, in which everything that happens results from factors within that system in accordance with its laws of working, but how then something may intrude from outside it, bringing about changes that the system would not have produced of its own accord, so that things go on after this intrusion differently from how they would have gone on if the system had remained closed. All we need do, then, is to regard the whole natural world as being, for most of the time, such a closed system; we can then think of a supernatural intervention as something that intrudes into that system from outside the natural world as a whole. (Mackie 1982: 21)

The obvious point is that the concept of divine intervention – in the form of overriding the laws of nature, to use my language – is coherent. Miracles are not ruled out a priori by definition. Nevertheless, strong nomic necessity is safeguarded, and with it there is a firm basis for contrasting the miraculous and the non-miraculous.

To be sure, this understanding of laws of nature and the concept of miracle is made intelligible within a theistic context. Since that is precisely the context in which miracles would happen *if they occur*, it begs no questions. Analogously, naturalism entails that miracles do not occur. So the coherence of the concept of miracle ultimately depends on which position, theism or naturalism, is true. (If we think of coherence as an *epistemic* notion, then we may remain neutral on the question of theism versus naturalism, and still consider the concept of miracle to be coherent, as long as we consider theism itself to be coherent.) As Richard Purtill writes,

> It comes as no great surprise to discover that a position assuming naturalism leaves no room for miracles and that a position affirming the existence of a creator of the natural order allows for miracles, or that a position that describes natural laws as simply a summary of what happens cannot even make the contrast between miracles and nonmiraculous events. (Purtill 1997: 70)

Epistemological issues

There are varieties of skepticism about miracles. We've seen that one variety is rooted in conceptual assumptions about laws of nature and the kind of universe ours is. This strategy, proposed by Curd and others, must be buttressed with a plausible general argument for naturalism. In critical discussions about miracles, this is seldom forthcoming. In fact, arguments for naturalism as a general conceptual framework are rare in any context.

J. L. Mackie – who agrees that the possibility of miracles is not precluded a priori, by definition – argues that there can never be good reason for believing that miracles have occurred:

> Where there is some plausible testimony about the occurrence of what would appear to be a miracle, those who accept this as a miracle have the double burden of showing both that the event took place and that it violated the laws of nature. But it will be very hard to sustain this double burden. For whatever tends to show that it would have been a violation of natural law tends for that very reason to make it most unlikely that it happened. Correspondingly, those who deny the occurrence of a miracle have two alternative lines of defence. One is to say that the event may have occurred, but in accordance with the laws of nature. Perhaps there are unknown circumstances that made it possible; or perhaps what were thought to be the relevant laws of nature are not strictly laws; there may be as yet unknown kinds of natural causation through which this event might have come about. The other is to say that this event would indeed have violated natural law, but that for this very reason there is a strong presumption against its having happened, which it is most unlikely that any testimony will be able to outweigh. ... The *fork*, the disjunction of these two sorts of explanation, is as a whole a very powerful reply to any claim that a miracle has been performed. (Mackie 1982: 26)

This is as much an a priori argument against miracles as the one Mackie repudiates. When confronted with *any* miracle claim, the skeptic has an out: either deny that the alleged event took place or hold out for a naturalistic explanation. This is Mackie's fork. He believes it's available to the skeptic when confronted with any miracle claim whatsoever, even 'where there is some plausible testimony about the occurrence of what would appear to be a miracle.' What are we to make of this claim?

First, Mackie's thesis applies only in cases where belief that a miracle has occurred relies essentially on testimonial evidence. Presumably, an eyewitness to an event that appears to that person to be miraculous need not be able to *show* that it took place. If I'm driving my car through the California desert on highway 395 and a US Navy jet suddenly drops low in front of me, comes directly at me (at Mach-whatever), and passes a few dozen feet above me, I will almost certainly acquire a justified belief about that event; but there may be nothing I could do to show others that it happened.

Their evidence that it happened would be limited to my testimony. They may or may not believe me. If they believe me, they may or may not be justified. The point is, *I* would be justified by the evidence *I* have.

We're not talking about a miracle in this instance. But we're talking about a very unusual event. (It's only happened once in my experience, and I've never heard of it happening to anyone else under similar circumstances.) In the same way, if a person witnessed an event that fits a certain description, that would, in general, be enough for that person to be justified in believing that the event happened as described, even if it was unusual in the sense implied by the miraculous. The experiential data may be so compelling that the refusal to allow that the event was a miracle may depend on an accompanying belief that there is or must be some perfectly natural explanation for it. This is a situation where denying that the event took place does not seem to be a reasonable option.

It does seem that the second burden stipulated by Mackie applies, *mutatis mutandis*, even in eyewitness cases. Again, an eyewitness need not be able to *show* that a miraculous-seeming event really was a violation of the laws of nature in order to be justified in believing that it was a miracle. But the eyewitness should, one would think, have reason to believe that the event was a miracle. The eyewitness should have adequate evidence that it is an instance of divine intervention. (For a controversial account of how such belief may be warranted without evidence, see Plantinga 2000.) Others hold that membership in a community of believers, some of whom are in possession of the relevant evidence, provides all the justification some believers need to ground their fundamental religious beliefs.

Second, in setting forth the conditions for rational belief that a miracle has occurred, Mackie has us suppose that 'there is some plausible testimony about the occurrence of *what would appear to be a miracle*.' Perhaps we are given a description of an event that nearly everyone would agree would qualify as a miracle, if the event actually happened as described. This kind of agreement is hardly trivial.

Third, Mackie explicitly says that his two lines of defense against miracle claims are available to 'those who *deny* the occurrence of a miracle' (1982: 26, emphasis added). He is not suggesting that his dual strategy warrants mere *agnosticism* about miracles. He is saying that since one or the other defensive move will always be available, one should always deny that miracles are actual. I don't suppose that justified denial requires evidence that guarantees that miracles do not occur. But the evidence against miracles must be strong enough to tip the scales fairly obviously against their occurrence. If there is a zone of rough epistemic parity between the proposition that miracles occur and the proposition that miracles do not occur, and the evidence regarding miracles lies within that zone, then denying the miraculous is not justified.

Fourth, as far as Mackie is concerned, if an event falls under a description that implies that the event is a violation of natural law, then that is a sufficient basis for denying that the event occurred. No other evidence against its occurrence is needed. No mitigating factors are possible. The occurrence of the event can be as strongly attested as you like. It can never be enough to overturn the presumption against miracles. His fork is supposed to ensure that the skeptic always has a way out.

Fifth, there is real potential for tension between the two lines of defense for anyone who would deny miracles. The first line of defense mentioned is to allow that the event occurred, and to hold that its occurrence must have been in accordance with the laws of nature. But why should a skeptic ever adopt this defensive strategy? Presumably, this strategy is preferred when testimonial evidence for an alleged miracle is so strong that it is unreasonable to deny that the event occurred. Many factors determine strength of testimonial evidence. But it is doubtful that the specific character of an alleged event should weigh decisively in assessing the strength of testimonial evidence supporting its occurrence.

Mackie's second line of defense is to claim that the alleged event would, if it occurred, be a violation of the laws of nature. But why should a skeptic ever adopt this strategy? Presumably, this strategy is to be favored when the alleged event falls under a description that makes it unreasonable to suppose that it could have occurred in accordance with the laws of nature. The alleged event may, on the assumption that it happened, be an utterly recalcitrant anomaly. It may be that (a) the alleged event cannot be explained in terms of the laws of nature as they are currently understood; (b) if the alleged event is to be explained naturally (rather than supernaturally), it would have to be in terms that require a radical revision of our current understanding of nature's laws; and (c) our current understanding of nature's laws is so fertile and entrenched that it would be more counterproductive to endorse a revision than to retain it more or less as is. This point is central to Richard Swinburne's position:

> We have to some extent good evidence about what are the laws of nature, and some of them are so well-established and account for so many data that any modifications to them which we could suggest to account for the odd counter-instance would be so clumsy and *ad hoc* as to upset the whole structure of science. In such cases the evidence is strong that if the purported counter-instance occurred it was a violation of the laws of nature. (Swinburne 1968: 323)

Suppose that theism is true. Then miracles are possible, for the reasons described earlier. This adds an important proviso to the principle that a violation of nature's laws is 'most unlikely.' There is, even on theistic assumptions, a strong presumption in favor of a natural explanation for any physical event. But theism does not underwrite, as naturalism does, a resolute refusal to allow that a bona fide miracle has occurred. Theism implies that miracle is a meaningful category for classifying events.

Bringing the considerations of the last three paragraphs together, it appears that Mackie's counsel may not always be feasible. There may, at least in principle, be exceptionally strong testimonial evidence for the occurrence of an event that qualifies as an utterly recalcitrant anomaly, and the very real possibility that the event is best classified as a miracle. What then?

There's more. *Sixth*, we have been assuming that the only evidence relevant to determining the epistemic status of beliefs that miracles have happened in the past is testimonial evidence. But even if the alleged miracles that lie at the heart of theistic belief happened in the distant past, and testimonial evidence is for that reason crucial for determining whether belief that they happened is justified, there may be more to the total evidential situation than just the testimonial evidence that is available.

Again, suppose that theism is true. It is not beyond imagination that God, being omnipotent, could cause an event that would leave us so utterly stupefied that we would be embarrassed to demand a naturalistic explanation. And it is not beyond hope that God, being omnibenevolent, would have a clear motive to produce an event that was meant to draw attention to God's kind intentions. Some skeptics have argued that if God was in the business of making miracles happen, they would happen with much greater frequency than they do, since God would have sufficient motive and power to solve the world's problems by means of miraculous interventions. There are skeptics who imagine that if they were omnipotent, they would act differently than God appears to have acted. But how many skeptics would act differently than God has (on our current assumption that God exists) if they, like God, were *omniscient*? I'm sure they don't know. But these skeptics may be on to something. If Christian theism is true, God has acted, and acted miraculously, for the good of his creatures in ways that reverberate beyond the limits of human imagination. God's most salient act within the skein of human history is, according to Christianity, the resurrection of Jesus Christ from the dead.

Miracles and historical method

Miracles, as we have been thinking about them, are historical events. Christian theism makes much of the claim that Jesus Christ literally rose bodily from the dead. This alleged event has such fundamental significance for Christianity that if it did not happen, wrote the Apostle Paul, Christian faith is worthless (1 Cor. 15: 17). David Hume alluded to the alleged resurrection of Jesus in his celebrated critique of miracles: 'But it is a miracle, that a dead man should come to life' (Hume 1978: 115). There are two reasons for Hume's reference. First, Hume was deliberately challenging Christian belief. And, as John Earman reminds us, 'for all of the participants in the eighteenth-century debate on miracles, Hume included, a resurrection is the paradigm example of a miracle' (Earman 2000: 12). The resurrection is, to be sure, a fit candidate for what Mackie would call a violation of the laws of nature.

If the resurrection of Jesus is an event that 'would indeed have violated natural law,' then, says Mackie, 'for that very reason there is a very strong presumption against its having happened, which it is most unlikely that any testimony will be able to outweigh' (Mackie 1982: 26). The thing the skeptic must do, then, is deny that it happened.

The reasonableness of denying the occurrence of this alleged event cannot be settled here. But we can set forth some principles that are relevant to determining the rationality of belief in the resurrection.

First, if we are to believe that Jesus rose bodily from the dead, there must be ample evidence for this event. The testimonial evidence must be strong. How strong it must be depends on the availability of other relevant evidence.

Second, much depends on the background evidence for theism. If there is sufficient evidence to justify belief in God, then there is reason to believe that God is interested in the human condition. In particular, God may have certain purposes for human beings and be concerned about their multifaceted predicament: the elusive quest for substantial purpose, moral failure and confusion, the problem of suffering, and end-of-life anxieties. If there is a remedy, God would know that, too. And this remedy would be suited to an accurate diagnosis of the human condition. Any remedy worthy of such a physician must have a good prognosis, as well. So there must be some way to apply the remedy with the expectation of a good result. In short, if we have background evidence that there is a wise and generous God who would intervene on behalf of human persons and enlighten them regarding his intended solution to the human predicament, such evidence will be relevant to the assessment of testimonial evidence that a miracle has happened. Testimonial evidence is no longer isolated from broader theistic evidence (see Geivett 1997).

Third, we should consider what possible motive God might have for bringing about the resurrection of such a person as Jesus. Why this man and not some other? Here, the life and character of Jesus is crucial. What was his background? His message? His role in human history?

Fourth, the specific data in support of a historical resurrection must be handled with historical responsibility. New Testament historians have sifted the details of extant accounts. The focal points of their research concern evidence that the tomb of Jesus was found empty by his disciples, and that Jesus was seen alive again by people who knew him and could easily have recognized him. But the central issue about which historians agree, whether they are believers or skeptics, is that the disciples of Jesus sincerely believed that Jesus had been raised. It has been argued that their belief cannot be explained adequately except on the grounds that they were eyewitnesses of the empty tomb and of the postmortem presence of Jesus alive in their midst. (For the most impressive exploration of these elements in the Christian tradition, see Wright 2003; see also Stewart 2006.)

Fifth, some may object that a supernatural event, even if it is 'historical,' cannot be the proper object of historical investigation. There is a sense in which this seems correct (see Geivett 2003: 56–9; and 2006). But as I've suggested elsewhere (1997: 186–7),

> the phenomena of an empty tomb and the recognition of the physical presence of a familiar person are perfectly natural facts. . . . There is nothing particularly extraordinary about an empty tomb (the tomb was presumably empty before Jesus' body was laid to rest there). And people who believe they have spoken with a person of long and close acquaintance are generally given the benefit of the doubt when they report that they have seen the person again recently. In asserting that the tomb was observed to be empty, or that Jesus was seen alive on such and such a day, no miracle is explicitly affirmed. That a miracle occurred is inferred from these facts

... if facts they are. It seems to me to be within the province of historical research to investigate such claims as these, and to judge how likely it is, on historical principles, that the tomb was empty and that Jesus was seen alive, regardless of the metaphysical implications.

Suppose that there is ample background evidence for theism, and that this theism grounds a reasonable expectation that God would act on behalf of humanity. And suppose that a miracle such as the resurrection of Jesus would be auspicious both to procure the requisite remedy and to corroborate its authenticity as divine. Then how great must the actual historical (testimonial) evidence be to justify belief in the resurrection of Jesus? C. S. Lewis suggested that to admit the existence of God is to risk a few miracles (Lewis 1966). It may be that miracles are to be expected, so that if the best historical evidence for a miracle converges on a single event of singular significance, that is evidence enough (see Geivett 2005). What, then, is so singularly significant about the resurrection of Jesus? (1) If anything is a miracle, this qualifies. (2) The event has superlative credentials as a religiously significant event. (3) No other purported miracle is as widely investigated by historians of religion. (4) This purported miracle is about as well-attested as they come. (5) Miracle stories are not as plentiful in non-theistic religious traditions.

See also Christianity (Chapter 6), David Hume (Chapter 13), Truth in religion (Chapter 18), Religious traditions and rational assessments (Chapter 19), Religious pluralism (Chapter 20), Inclusivism and exclusivism (Chapter 21), Hiddenness (Chapter 29), Creation and divine action (Chapter 30), Why is there a universe at all, rather than just nothing? (Chapter 41), The Incarnation (Chapter 51), Resurrection (Chapter 52), Sin and salvation (Chapter 53), Faith (Chapter 56).

References

Braithwaite, R. B. (1953) *Explanation*, Cambridge: Cambridge University Press.
Cartwright, N. D. (1983) *How the Laws of Physics Lie*, New York: Oxford University Press.
Curd, M. (1996) 'Miracles as violations of laws of nature,' in J. Jordan and D. Howard-Snyder (eds) *Faith, Freedom, and Rationality: Philosophy of Religion Today*, Lanham, MD: Rowman & Littlefield.
Earman, J. (2000) *Hume's Abject Failure: The Argument Against Miracles*, Oxford: Oxford University Press.
Geivett, R. D. (1997) 'The evidential value of miracles,' in R. D. Geivett and G. R. Habermas (eds) *In Defense of Miracles*, Downers Grove, IL: InterVarsity Press.
—— (2003) 'Reflections on theism,' in S. W. Wallace (ed.) *Does God Exist?* Aldershot: Ashgate.
—— (2005) 'David Hume and a cumulative case argument,' in J. F. Sennett and D. Groothuis (eds) *In Defense of Natural Theology: A Post-Humean Assessment*, Downers Grove, IL: InterVarsity Press.
—— (2006) 'The epistemology of resurrection belief,' in R. B. Stewart (ed.) *The Resurrection of Jesus: John Dominic Crossan and N. T. Wright in Dialogue*, Minneapolis, MN: Fortress Press.
Hesse, M. (1974) *The Structure of Scientific Inference*, Berkeley, CA: University of California Press.
—— (1980) 'A revised regularity view of scientific laws,' in D. H. Mellor (ed.) *Science, Belief and Behaviour*, Cambridge: Cambridge University Press.
Hume, D. (1978) [1777] 'On miracles,' section x in J. Selby-Bigge (ed.) *An Enquiry Concerning Human Understanding*, 3rd edn, with textual revisions and notes by P. H. Nidditch, Oxford: Clarendon Press.
Lewis, C. S. (1966) *Miracles*, New York: Macmillan.

Lewis, D. (1973) *Counterfactuals*, Oxford: Blackwell.

Mackie, J. L. (1982) *The Miracle of Theism*, Oxford: Clarendon Press.

Plantinga, A. (2000) *Warranted Christian Belief*, Oxford: Oxford University Press.

Purtill, R. (1997) 'Defining miracles,' in R. D. Geivett and G. R. Habermas (eds) *In Defense of Miracles*, Downers Grove, IL: InterVarsity Press.

Skyrms, B. (1980) *Causal Necessity*, New Haven, CT: Yale University Press.

Stewart, R.B. (ed.) (2006) *The Resurrection of Jesus: John Dominic Crossan and N. T. Wright in Dialogue*, Minneapolis, MN: Fortress Press.

Swinburne, R.G. (1968) 'Miracles,' *Philosophical Quarterly* 18/73: 320–8.

—— (1996) *Is There a God?* Oxford: Oxford University Press.

van Fraassen, B. C. (1989) *Laws and Symmetry*, Oxford: Clarendon Press.

Wright, N. T. (2003) *The Resurrection of the Son of God*, Minneapolis, MN: Fortress Press; London: SPCK.

Further reading

Davis, S. T. (1993) *Risen Indeed: Making Sense of the Resurrection*, Grand Rapids, MI: Eerdmans. (A philosopher's case for rational belief in miracles that responds thoroughly to prevailing objections. Valuable for its philosophical approach.)

Geivett, R. D. and G. R. Habermas (eds) (1997) *In Defense of Miracles*, Downers Grove, IL: InterVarsity Press. (Includes a reprint of David Hume's influential essay 'On miracles,' an original critical essay by Antony Flew, and fourteen original essays by Christian philosophers on such topics as the definition of miracle, criteria for identifying a miracle, the relationship between miracles and scientific investigation, evidence for the existence of God, the possibility of divine action in the world, the intelligibility of the Christian doctrine of Incarnation, the evidence for fulfilled prophecy, and evidence for the resurrection of Jesus.)

Houston, J. (1994) *Reported Miracles: A Critique of Hume*, Cambridge: Cambridge University Press. (A sophisticated response to the Humean critique of miracles that manages somehow to continue to influence critical reflection on the topic.)

Sobel, J. H. (2004) 'Clouds of witnesses – "Of miracles,"' ch. 7 in *Logic and Theism: Arguments for and Against Beliefs in God*, Cambridge: Cambridge University Press. (An elaborate and sophisticated negative assessment of the rationality of belief in miracles.)

Swinburne, R. (1970) *The Concept of Miracle*, London: Macmillan. (The best brief philosophical treatment of the concept of miracle by a widely respected Christian philosopher.)

—— (ed.) (1989) *Miracles*, New York: Macmillan. (The best collection of seminal journal articles (pro and con) on philosophical aspects of the concept of miracle.)

56
FAITH
W. Jay Wood

Introduction

The notion of faith is among the most contested terms in the philosophical and theological lexicon. The term 'faith' can refer, variously, to a specific set of religious doctrines, the trust we place in God, a contrast to knowledge, a deeply anchored theological virtue, or even an attitude or posture in the face of the unknown – to select among its various meanings. Though faith is central to the Abrahamic religions of Judaism, Christianity, and Islam, as well as to some of the other world's religions, the concept also has non-religious uses. Persons are sometimes said to have faith in a political cause, another person, or even their automobile. Because of Christianity's influential role in western philosophy, and since no univocal concept covers everything that writers have had in mind in using the term, I shall focus on faith as articulated in the Christian religion, though many points will be germane to other religious and non-religious uses of the term. I will suggest that religious faith is a complex, multi-dimensional quality of persons that, paradigmatically, involves one's intellect, will, and behavior, in acts of belief or judgment, trust, and obedience. At various moments in the life of faith, one or the other of these elements may be prominent. Writers who emphasize one aspect of faith to the exclusion of others often focus on particular moments in the life of faith, but not on the career of faith throughout a person's life.

Faith and knowledge

While belief in propositions is not the whole of faith, it is an aspect of paradigmatic instances of faith. The manner of believing associated with faith has been traditionally contrasted with knowledge and opinion. Persons have knowledge, according to the Greek gold standard, if they have self-reflective awareness that the object of knowledge is certain. Augustine, with many subsequent thinkers, claims that such self-reflective certainty comes in at least two forms. Understanding (*intellectus*) is the faculty of mind by which one grasps self-evident a priori truths such as mathematical and logical axioms. Knowledge (*scientia*) is the cognitive power to infer truths from self-evident starting points and, by extension, refers to the truths so inferred. John

Locke echoes this distinction by claiming that 'intuition and demonstration are the degrees of knowledge; whatever comes short of one of these, with what assurance soever embraced, is but faith or opinion, but not knowledge' (Locke 1959: 4.2.14). What unites these two forms of knowledge is that the knowing agent acquires them through his own cognitive powers. Upon seeing, the mind assents irresistibly and is subsequently in repose; there is no need for further inquiry into its truth.

The truths of faith and belief, according to traditional lines of demarcation, are not 'seen' through our native intellectual powers, though one may have probabilistic evidence for belief. For Aquinas, belief (*credere*) is a success term, and differs from opinion (*opinio*) in excluding falsehood. Doubt and opinion, unlike faith, come with 'doubt and fear of the opposite side' one thinks it probable to some degree that what one believes might be false. In faith, says Aquinas, 'the intellect assents to something, not through being sufficiently moved by its proper object, but through an act of choice, whereby it turns voluntarily to one side rather than to the other: and if this be accompanied by doubt and fear of the opposite side there will be opinion, while if there be certainty and no fear of the other side, there will be faith' (Aquinas 1981: II–II. q.1. art.4). Belief, or faith, also comes to us chiefly through the testimony of another. If I grasp the axioms of Euclid, and from them derive the Pythagorean theorem, I know the latter to be true. If a mathematician tells me that Euclid's axioms entail the Pythagorean theorem, I take it on the authority of another and merely believe. In the case of religious faith, one's belief rests on the testimony of a prophet, apostle, or the Church, which is ultimately traceable to the say-so of God. The truths of faith having their source in God is what legitimates their being accepted as certain.

Many contemporary epistemologists no longer distinguish sharply between belief and knowledge, making this classical division between faith and knowledge problematic. Knowledge is no longer treated as a separate genus from belief, but is often characterized as adequately grounded or warranted true belief. Nor do most contemporary philosophers think that knowledge must be invincibly certain. Indeed, they are inclined to say that scientists know facts about the world if they are supported to a very high degree of probability. And so-called externalist epistemologists deny that we must have reflective access to the grounds of our knowledge; it can arise simply out of faculties functioning properly in appropriate environments. If, for example, my remembering that I ate breakfast this morning arises out of properly functioning faculties in a suitable environment, then I have memorial knowledge, even though it is neither an instance of *intellectus* or *scientia*. Most contemporary philosophers also think that we can have testimonial knowledge, whereas on the classical understanding this would be an oxymoron.

The content of faith

Aquinas distinguishes between the preambles of faith and the mysteries of faith. The former include propositions such as 'God exists,' 'God is one,' and 'God is powerful,' all of which he thinks can be established by the *scientia* of natural theology. The mysteries of faith, however, contain truths that human reason cannot acquire or see to be true through its own cognitive powers. Truths such as that God is triune and that he created the world *ex nihilo* must be revealed by God in order to be known. Because many people have neither the time, talent, nor training to prove for themselves that God exists, God graciously includes the preambles of faith as part of the revelation of himself given to prophets and apostles, as recorded in Scripture, and as promulgated by the Church. Together, the preambles and mysteries comprise the core of 'The Christian Faith,' as summarized in the Church's creeds and as professed in worship. John Calvin criticized the schoolmen (Scholastics) for having too intellectual a conception of faith that emphasizes assenting to propositions about God. Whichever schoolmen Calvin may have had in mind, this charge can't be leveled at Augustine and Aquinas, who both distinguish between *believing in a God*, which focuses on God as the intellectual object of faith, and *believing in God*, which requires that our wills be directed to the good and moved by grace in a way that requires trust. It is in the former but not the latter sense that the demons are said to believe (ibid.: II–II. 5. 2).

Calvin himself defines faith as 'a sure and firm knowledge of the divine favour toward us, founded on the truth of free promise in Christ, and revealed to our minds, and sealed on our hearts, by the Holy Spirit' (Calvin 1981: 3.2.7). Calvin teaches that knowledge of faith does not include intellectual comprehension, for the content of faith surpasses understanding. And by 'sure and firm,' Calvin does not mean epistemically indubitable in the Cartesian sense; he means to underscore the strength of our confidence and assurance that God will bring about our good. Interestingly, Calvin says such assurance is compatible with episodes of doubt and anxiety about our faith (1981: 3. 2. 17, 21). But how can one have firm knowledge and at the same time harbor doubts? Nicholas Wolterstorff suggests that by 'firmness' Calvin means 'steadfast' or 'persevering.' The person of firm faith, though sometimes assailed by doubt, will be very reluctant to abandon his beliefs and will persevere in them (Wolterstorff 1990: 412–13).

Calvin's definition is instructive for it emphasizes what is perhaps the most important aspect of faith: personal trust (*fiducia*). Here, Calvin follows Martin Luther who says 'it is a further function of faith that it honors him whom it trusts with the most reverent and highest regard, since it considers him truthful and trustworthy. There is no other honor equal to the estimate of truthfulness and righteousness with which we honor him whom we trust' (Luther 1962: 59). Trust is marked by a lack of anxiety and a corresponding confidence that the person trusted can be counted on to act for one's good. While our personally trusting God is indeed the heart of faith, it is nevertheless inseparable from belief and active obedience, the other two facets of faith. Trusting God is obviously connected with believing certain things about God: that he exists, has made promises and will honor them, has the power to bring about our good, and so forth: 'For whoever would draw near to God must believe that he exists and rewards those who seek him' (Heb. 11: 6 (RSV)). It is also connected to obedience since, as Luther himself points out, trusting God is our chief act of obedience, from which other good works follow.

Faith and reason

Greece and Rome hellenized the birthplace of Christianity through conquest; Christianity returned the favor through conversion. Christian faith coexisted uneasily with Greek philosophy, however, giving rise to the famous problem of faith and reason. Tertullian put the question picturesquely: 'What has Jerusalem to do with Athens? What concord is there between the Academy and the Church?' (Tertullian 1966: 39). The question of how faith is to be related to reason masks at least three different questions. First, what are the respective spheres of faith and theoretical reason and what are the beliefs appropriate to each? Second, is faith epistemically rational (i.e., can faith commitments possess whatever sorts of grounds are necessary for the beliefs to be reasonable and not foolish)? Third, is faith practically reasonable (i.e., does faith help us to realize our own and others' flourishing)?

Augustine, and the medieval tradition that followed him, were chiefly concerned with faith's relationship to knowledge (*episteme*). Augustine sought to negotiate a middle path between the extremes of the Manicheans and Neoplatonist philosophers, for whom self-reflective certainty was the sole intellectual standard, and church fathers such as Tertullian, who famously claimed that Christ's resurrection 'is by all means to be believed, because it is absurd ... the fact is certain because it is impossible' (Tertullian 1951: ch. 5). Augustine's elegant solution provided an enduring model: 'Understanding is the reward of faith. Therefore, seek not to understand in order to believe, but believe in order to understand' (Augustine 1953: *Epistula* 120). 'For faith is understanding's step; and understanding faith's attainment' (1953: *Sermons* 76. 1–2). Certainly this is true in order of time; children must begin by trusting the testimony of others before they are mature enough to see some truths for themselves. Even as adults we must trust, among other things, that our cognitive faculties are reliable, that there is an external world to which our faculties direct us, that nature's laws are uniform, and that we are not under malign skeptical influence. For Augustine, the life of faith will one day culminate in faith's reward, knowing God as we have been known, seeing him face to face. This being so, we ought not shrink from what foretastes of this are to be offered in this life. 'Therefore, whatever a man of faith does not yet see he ought to believe in such a way as to hope for and love the seeing of it' (1953: *Epistula* 120).

Although Augustine and Aquinas were chiefly concerned to mark faith and reason's distinctive boundaries, both were also aware that it is possible to believe foolishly, to misplace trust. Aquinas insists, however, 'that to give assent to the truths of faith is not foolishness even though they are above reason' (Aquinas 1975: ch. 6). The truths of faith are accompanied, he says, by 'fitting' or 'likely' arguments that attest to their having come from God. Divine revelation was accompanied by miracles, moral transformation, the rapid spread of the Church, and can be seen as the fulfillment of prophecy, which all serve to authenticate the revelation as coming from God. Aquinas is clear that the signs that attest to the truths of faith as coming from God do not serve as arguments that give us *intellectus* or *scientia* of the truths so revealed. So the believer's certainty concerning the matters of faith rests on their having been revealed by God, not on our possessing independent epistemic grounds for their truth.

Locke's epistemology shifts our focus to the epistemic rationality of faith. It was forged in response to the wars of the Reformation and the social unrest spawned by religious enthusiasts, the strength and confidence of whose religious feelings ran far ahead of good judgment. As noted, Locke thought knowledge is restricted to what is grasped through immediate intuitive insight and demonstration; the rest is but faith and opinion. Faith, says Locke, 'is the assent to any proposition, not thus made out by the deductions of reason, but upon the credit of the proposer, as coming from God, in some extraordinary way of communication. This way of discovering truths to men, we call revelation' (Locke 1959: 4. 18. 2). Yet Locke thinks even faith, as a deliverance of revelation, must be appropriately regulated by reason. He counsels that we adjust the level of confidence we have in any matter of faith so as not to exceed our evidence that God has indeed revealed it. And the evidence most appropriate to ground a particular claim as coming from a divine source is that it be accompanied by a miracle. But many of us have never seen a miracle, and those beneficiaries to whom the faith was first given with miraculous accompaniment are two millennia gone. It follows from Locke's view, then, that the confidence we place in any item of faith cannot exceed the attenuated historical evidences we now have that any such item was miraculously revealed. Most persons, of course, have never attended to the historical credentials of Christian revelation claims, but depend on the say-so of authorities that such events transpired. And testimonial evidence cannot underwrite a level of confidence in claims to faith that puts them on a par with knowledge. Says Locke: 'The floating of other Men's Opinions in our brains makes us not one jot the more knowing, though they happen to be true' (1959: 1. 4. 23). Anthony Kenny has recently criticized faith commitments on grounds similar to Locke's:

> No doubt it may be reasonably believed that Moses and Jesus did and said many of the things ascribed to them in the Bible; but can it reasonably be believed with a degree of certainty resembling that of knowledge? Unless the relevant story can be as certain as the commitment which faith demands of the believer, the commitment is, so far forth as it is faith, irrational. And if the belief is a commitment that is rationally in proportion to the support given by the history, it is, so far forth as it is rational, something less than faith. (Kenny 1992: 56–7)

Kenny poses a dilemma to the believer: since the believer's evidence for something's having been revealed from God falls short of what is needed for knowledge, the believer is irrational to accept it on a par with knowledge. If the believer lowers his confidence in a belief to match his evidence, he fails to embrace it as faith. Kenny thinks that some historical claims can qualify as knowledge; he claims to know, for instance, that Charles I was beheaded in London. He concludes, though, that religious faith is not a virtue, but a vice, unless the historical events constituting the divine revelation can be supported with evidence equal to that enjoyed by his belief about Charles I.

One can respond to Kenny's challenge either by trying to meet his demands for evidence or by denying that evidence is necessary to have the degree of warrant needed for knowledge. Richard Swinburne tries to meet the demand for evidence by offering a traditional two-stage approach that begins by offering arguments for God's existence, then moves to establish the historical reliability of the Bible, especially as it depicts the life and work of Christ (1992). Swinburne's probabilistic case for Christian faith requires him to offer independent arguments for God's existence, the possibility of miracles, the reliability of the biblical record, and for the present-day Christian Church as a reliable continuer of the apostles' teachings. By Swinburne's admission, the evidential case for the truth of the Christian revelation claims is, at best, probabilistic. But Swinburne disagrees with Kenny that faith commitments must be epistemically certain from the outset. When Christians speak of faith's certainty, they often have in mind the firmness of faith, rather than epistemic certainty. And when they do speak of the *episteme* of faith, they acknowledge that it is a mark of mature faith, and must be nurtured through ongoing reflection in the company of the faithful, and aided by the work of the Holy Spirit.

Reformed epistemologists such as Alvin Plantinga, Nicholas Wolterstorff, and William Alston have argued that belief in God can be properly basic, that is to say, epistemically warranted in the absence of argumentative support. Belief in God is thus like belief that there is an external world or that there are other minds. We do not adduce reasons for such beliefs; rather, we simply find ourselves believing them in appropriate experiential circumstances. Clearly, this is an account of warranted belief in the externalist tradition mentioned above; one needn't have reflective access to the grounds of a belief to be warranted in believing it. Plantinga explains that our taking belief in God as basic is the outworking of what John Calvin called the *sensus divinitatis*, a disposition or capacity of reason that disposes us to form beliefs about God and the things of God in appropriate circumstances. Plantinga extends this idea of beliefs arising out of warrant-producing processes to include the central claims of the gospel. In what he calls the 'Extended Aquinas–Calvin Model,' Plantinga proposes a model to explain how our accepting the central claims of the gospel, such as that Jesus Christ is God Incarnate, are warranted because they are instigated in us by the reliable direction of the Holy Spirit. '[On] this model,' says Plantinga,

> faith is a belief-producing process or activity, like perception or memory. It is a cognitive device, a means by which belief, and belief on a certain set of topics, is regularly produced in regular ways. In this it resembles memory, perception, reason, sympathy, induction, and other more standard belief-producing processes. It differs from them in that it also involves the direct action of the Holy Spirit, so that the immediate cause of belief is not to be found just in her [the believer's] natural epistemic equipment. (Plantinga 2000: 256)

Critics point out that the same strategy for justifying faith commitments might be employed by devotees of Krishna or of some other deity. Plantinga acknowledges this point, and doesn't try to provide argument for the truth of his model. He rests content to say that if his model is true, then the beliefs comprising Christian faith are warranted.

To relate faith to practical as well as epistemic reason requires that we explore further some of the dimensions of trust: whether it is practically reasonable to trust another person must be assessed in the light of one's *context* (who is being trusted, in what circumstances, and with what degree of evidential support?), the *content* being entrusted (what are you trusting the other to do?), and the structure and strength of one's *concern* regarding both (how strong is one's desire for the good one hopes the other will help to bring about?). Suppose you are leading a band of pioneers westward into California during the gold rush. You reach the Rocky Mountains but your maps do not make clear the exact location of the pass that will lead your party through the mountains. Your party does not have time for trial and error in negotiating the mountains as supplies are tight, winter is approaching, and error could prove disastrous for all. A man presents himself to your party as a guide and offers to lead you through mountains for what seems a reasonable fee. The man seems to speak knowledgeably of the terrain, the number of days it will take to reach the other side of the mountains, the various streams and other obstacles one will encounter and so forth. You have also heard stories of unscrupulous guides having led unwary parties into ambushes where they were robbed. Is it practically reasonable to entrust the welfare of your party to the guide?

Obviously the strength of concern is very high; it is very important to the entire party to reach California. What is being entrusted is nothing less than the livelihood and perhaps the lives of the travelers. And the context includes entrusting the welfare of the group to a stranger in circumstances that could potentially be dangerous. This scenario makes for permutations. Suppose what is being entrusted to the guide is a packet of letters of no great importance. Suppose that the travelers have ample supplies to postpone their trek through the mountains till spring, or that the guide is well known to many in the party as reliable. The practical wisdom of trusting the guide must delicately balance all of these elements. Here faith may also be rewarded with direct acquaintance. If one trusts the guide, one will have increasing confirmation with each passing day that what the guide said was true, until one knows for oneself information for which one was formerly dependent on the say-so of another.

Paul Helm qualifies his evidentialist approach to religious faith to acknowledge the demands of practical reason. Trusting God, he writes, is no different than trusting a bridge to bear one's weight; both demand evidence if they are to be instances of reasonable faith. All else being equal, he says, the strength with which we trust God should be proportioned to the evidence we have for God's existence and trustworthiness. Helm admits, however, that sometimes all else is not equal. Sometimes our personal needs are so pressing that we have to act in the absence of evidence. Here considerations of prudential rationality predominate. 'In faith over the long term, belief ought to be proportioned to evidence, and desire to belief. But in the short term, and where desire is stronger than belief, it may nevertheless be rational to have a belief whose strength is greater than present evidence warrants' (Helm 2000: 157).

I would go further than Helm to claim that things are seldom – if ever – equal, and that considerations of practical reason are always in place in matters of religious faith. Whether one is trusting another for directions across town, to repair one's appliance, to take care of one's children, or to guide one's eternal destiny, the evidence of the other's trustworthiness is always balanced with and interpreted through the strength of one's concerns. The presence of one's concerns helps to explain Calvin's stead-fastness when faith is assailed by doubt. Seeing the world through the eyes of faith involves more than believing propositions on the strength of evidence one takes to be adequate; it also includes orienting the whole of life by these beliefs and the concerns that accompany them. To withdraw faith is no mere matter of revising a belief or two, but a matter of revising a way of life. Moreover, as I will claim below, the concerns of the will influence the way we assess the evidence for trusting God, so that trusting God is not strictly a matter of pure epistemic reason.

The role of the will in faith

The faculty of the will is traditionally divided into its conative and executive aspects. The former is the seat of one's cares, concerns, loves, passions, and emotions, what we refer to collectively as one's affections. The executive will is the motive power by which we orient ourselves toward that which we love. We have just noted how the affections bear on the practical rationality of faith. Not only does the practical ration-ality of faith, in part, turn on the strength of our various concerns, but the evidential assessment of another's trustworthiness also involves the will.

Locke, along with Enlightenment thinkers in general, feared enthusiasm and saw the emotions as impeders of proper intellectual function. But a contrary theme that runs through the history of western philosophy, as early as Plato's *Symposium*, notes the way the structure of our loves (i.e., the will) coordinates with reason to attain the highest and hardest won knowledge, such as moral, religious, interpersonal knowledge, and self-knowledge. Aristotle said that all men by nature desire to know, but also that the desire must be trained in virtue to gain moral knowledge. Augustine claims that 'the bringing forth of the mind is preceded by some desire, by which, through seeking and finding what we wish to know, the off-spring, viz. knowledge itself is born' (1890: 9. 12. 18). Augustine too acknowledges that this natural desire for knowledge itself needs to be tutored and refined, and that an undisciplined, undiscriminating appetite for knowledge can lead to our seeking knowledge of the trivial and perverse. Aquinas lists as among the gifts of wisdom imparted by the Holy Spirit a sympathetic 'attunement' or 'connaturality' with moral and divine matters (1981: II–II. 45. 2). Similarly, Jonathan Edwards suggests that special grace confers upon its recipients a new 'sense of the heart' that assists reason to discern the clear evidence of divine activity, giving rise to religious knowledge. He writes that spiritual understanding

> consists in a sense of the heart, of the supreme beauty and sweetness of
> the holiness or moral perfection of divine things, together with all that

discerning and knowledge of things of religion, that depend upon, and flow from such a sense. ... I say, a sense of heart; for it is not speculation merely that is concerned in this kind of understanding; nor can there be a clear distinction made between the two faculties of understanding and will, as acting distinctly and separately, in this matter. When the mind is sensible of the sweet beauty and amiableness of a thing, that implies a sensibleness of sweetness and delight in the presence of the idea of it; and this sensibleness of the amiableness or delightfulness of beauty, carries in the very nature of it, the sense of the heart; or an effect and impression the soul is the subject of, as a substance possessed of taste, inclination and will. (Edwards 1959: 272)

Although they differ in the details, the Christian thinkers mentioned above insist that emotions and the concerns characteristic of the will combine with intellect to produce the knowledge distinctive of faith. A passion for knowledge of God is likely to promote our pursuit of it and heighten our attentiveness to matters that bear on religious faith. According to Edwards, dispositions of the heart help us to recognize and properly assess the force of evidence bearing on the truths of faith. Moreover, emotions of charity and humility may make one more open to instruction and correction regarding divine matters.

Faith as a virtue

A virtue is an acquired disposition to excellent functioning in some generically human sphere of activity that is difficult and important. Virtues, so defined, range over intellectual, moral, and theological matters, disposing us to right thinking, right emotions and action, and true faith, all of which in the Christian scheme are indispensable to our final flourishing. To call faith a disposition is to say that it is a deeply anchored habit, a default rather than an occasional trait of the personality. As already noted, faith is partly an epistemic process that directs us to beliefs about God that are above human reason, but it is a process whose success requires the operation of the Holy Spirit and the cooperation of the human will. Unlike natural virtues, such as justice and courage, which we acquire through imitation and repetition, the theological virtue of faith is given by grace. Faith is thus a polyconsequential disposition, issuing in action, emotion, and judgments or beliefs. Since faith comes in degrees, the more faith one has, the better (by Christian standards) will be the actions, emotions, and judgments that issue from faith. It is also easy to see how these facets of faith mutually reinforce one another. To engage in prayer, worship, service, and other practices associated with the Christian life tend to deepen one's affections for the persons or matters prayed for. Deepened affections, in turn, tend to focus one's attention, make salient features of one's experience that bear on one's faith, reinforce inclinations to further prayer, make one more sensitive to the promptings of the Holy Spirit, and perhaps even situate one well to begin understanding what one has accepted on faith. Faith is both formed in and contributes to these practices. So the life begun in faith receives experiential confirmation in the form of moral transformation, a heightened sensitivity to the divine presence, and emotional dispositions to hope, contentment, and peace, all of which contribute to growth in understanding.

Persons who by grace continue to grow in faith simultaneously see their growth in the other theological virtues of hope and charity. Persons disposed to faith are disposed to hope, to rest confident that God will strengthen them to endure the trials of this life and that he will successfully guide them to the life hereafter. And the life to which we are drawing ever nearer is that of charity, or friendship with God, now and in the life to come. Alfred Freddoso writes:

> In short, believers with the right affections who strive to live in accord with the theoretical object proposed by divine revelation will undergo a profound cognitive transformation as they become more and more adept at seeing their lives and the world in general from the perspective of their heavenly Father. (Freddoso 2005: 181)

See also Christianity (Chapter 6), Augustine (Chapter 8), Thomas Aquinas (Chapter 12), Truth in religion (Chapter 18), Religious traditions and rational assessments (Chapter 19), Hiddenness (Chapter 29), The wager argument (Chapter 36), Catholic philosophical theology (Chapter 43), Revelation (Chapter 50), Prayer (Chapter 57), Reformed epistemology (Chapter 58), Phenomenology of religion (Chapter 61), Religious experience (Chapter 63).

References

Aquinas, T. (1975) [1259–60] *Summa contra Gentiles: Book I: God*, Notre Dame, IN: University of Notre Dame Press.
—— (1981) [1266–73] *Summa Theologica*, vol. 3, trans. the Fathers of the English Dominican Province, Westminster, MD: Christian Classics.
Augustine (1953) *Letters*, vol. II (83–130), in *Fathers of the Church*, trans. W. Parsons, Washington, DC: Catholic University Press of America.
—— (1890) *On the Trinity*, in P. Schaff (ed.) *Nicene and Post-Nicene Fathers*, vol. 3, trans. A. W. Haddan, New York: Christian Literature Publishing. Online at: http://www.newadvent.org/fathers/130109.htm.
Calvin, J. (1981) [1559] *Institutes of the Christian Religion*, vol. 1, trans. H. Beveridge, Grand Rapids, MI: Eerdmans.
Edwards, J. (1959) [1746] *Religious Affections*, ed. J. Smith, New Haven, CT: Yale University Press.
Freddoso, A. (2005) 'Christian faith as a way of life,' in W. E. Mann (ed.), *The Blackwell Guide to the Philosophy of Religion*, Malden, MA: Blackwell.
Helm, P. (2000) *Faith with Reason*, Oxford: Oxford University Press.
Kenny, A. (1992) *What Is Faith?*, Oxford: Oxford University Press.
Locke, J. (1959) [1690] *An Essay Concerning Human Understanding*, vol. 2, New York: Dover Publications.
Luther, M. (1962) [1520] *The Freedom of a Christian*, in J. Dillenberger (ed.) *Martin Luther: Selections from his writings*, New York: Anchor Doubleday.
Plantinga, A. (2000) *Warranted Christian Belief*, Oxford: Oxford University Press.
Swinburne, R. (1992) *Revelation, From Metaphor to Analogy*, Oxford: Oxford University Press.
Tertullian (1951) [early third century] *On the Flesh of Christ*, in A. Roberts and J. Donaldson, *The Ante-Nicene Fathers*, vol. 3, Grand Rapids, MI: Eerdmans.

—— (1966) *The Prescriptions Against the Heretics* 7, in H. T. Kerr (ed.) *Readings in Christian Thought*, Nashville, TN: Abingdon Press.

Wolterstorff, N. (1990) 'The assurance of faith,' *Faith and Philosophy* 7/4 (October): 412–13.

Futher reading

Evans, C.S. (1996) *The Historical Christ and the Jesus of Faith: The Incarnational Narrative as History*, Oxford: Oxford University Press. (Proposes a view that combines evidentialist and Reformed epistemological concerns in accepting the central claims of the gospel.)

—— (1998) *Faith Beyond Reason: A Kierkegaardian Account*, Grand Rapids, MI: Eerdmans. (A nuanced and reasonable presentation and defense of some of Kierkegaard's main points regarding faith and the limits of reason.)

Penelhum, T. (1995) *Reason and Religious Faith*, Boulder, CO: Westview Press. (Clearly written, philosophically engaging treatment of the main philosophical issues surrounding faith.)

Swinburne, R. (2005) *Faith and Reason*, 2nd edn, Oxford: Oxford University Press. (A sophisticated, thorough account of an evidentialist approach to faith that considers major currents in epistemology and theology.)

57
PRAYER
Charles Taliaferro

There are many forms of prayer in many religious traditions. *The Oxford Book of Prayer* includes prayers from Jewish, Christian, and Islamic sources as well as from Hinduism, Buddhism, Taoism, Baha'i, and Zoroastrianism. This collection also includes indigenous African, Native American, and other sources (Appleton 1988). Because prayer forms a fundamental feature of many religions, philosophy of religion needs to take prayer seriously.

This chapter will consider first whether religious prayer should best be understood as addressed to a sacred, divine, or supernatural reality. It will then focus on the nature and value of petitionary prayer. The term 'prayer' is derived from the Latin *precari* ('to ask earnestly'), and considerable philosophical work has gone into articulating and challenging the idea that an all-good God would respond to human petitions. Not all prayer is petitionary (there are prayers of adoration and confession, for example), but the practice of beseeching God to respond to human requests has generated the deepest debates. A further section addresses prayers of praise. Why has theistic tradition emphasized the value, and even the religious duty, of praising God? Praising a ruler might make sense in the world of ancient Mesopotamia, but today the practice may well seem to reveal a crude anthropomorphism. At the end of this chapter I raise eight questions to provoke further philosophical reflection.

Prayer and realism

Some philosophers and theologians hold that prayer to God need not involve any belief or hope that there is a God. This may well seem obviously right; it makes sense to cry out for human help, for example, even if you believe you are in peril and no one is around for, after all, you may be wrong and assistance is just around the corner. Don Cupitt, however, takes the further step in claiming that prayer to God makes sense even when one is correct in the conviction that God is a myth. 'I continue to pray to God. God is the mythical embodiment of all one is concerned with in the spiritual life. He is the religious demand and idea ... the enshriner of values. He is indeed – but as a myth' (Cupitt 1981: 167). This kind of 'prayer' seems more like a meditation on values than the widespread act of worship and petition that we find in the great world religions. Such meditation or contemplation of values might take the form of prayer and have immense value, but still not resemble the central cases of prayer. It is very difficult, for example, *not* to interpret Muslim prayers as directed to Allah, the transcendent creator, sustainer, and merciful judge of the cosmos. But consider the position of D. Z. Phillips. He maintains that the practice of prayer is intelligible; it makes sense to pray to God. However, he believes that the current philosophical investigation into the nature of God (the object of prayer) is based on a confusion.

Phillips's position rests on his views of meaning and language. Phillips is a leading exponent of the view that the meaning of religious language invoking 'God' is firmly implanted in religious practice. 'To see what is meant by the reality of God, we must take note of the concept formation by which the notion of the divine is rooted in the reactions of praise and worship' (Phillips 1986: 25). Phillips argues, further, that 'God' and other religious terms such as 'grace' and 'soul' are not properly seen by philosophers as referring to a transcendent reality that may be conceived of independent of religious practice. On Phillips's view, it would be a mistake for philosophers to infer that religious believers (Phillips's central cases are usually Christian) are addressing a God who is conscious of the cosmos or who is gracious in showing mercy:

> It is not 'consciousness,' metaphysically conceived, that shows us what is meant by 'the mind of God,' but the religious practice in which that notion has its application. But do not be drawn into the old confusion: if one finds out what is meant by 'the mind of God' and gives heed to it, *that* is what one is heeding, not the practice! ... It is a misunderstanding to try to get 'behind' grace to God, since 'grace' is a synonym for 'God.' As with 'generosity is good,' so with 'the grace of God': we are not attributing a predicate to an indefinable subject. We are being given a rule for *one* use of 'good' and 'God,' respectively. God's reality and God's divinity, that is, his grace and love, come to the same thing. God is not 'real' in any other sense. (Phillips 2005: 457, 459)

One benefit of Phillips's strategy is that he makes the field of philosophy of religion focus on *religion*, just as a philosophy of science or art is all the better for being focused on science or art.

While Phillips may be right, I suggest that, historically and today, religious practitioners in Christianity and the other religions where one prays to God or Allah or Brahman, there is an abiding assumption that the prayers are not addressed to the practice of praying or just to fellow human beings. There is, rather, the assumption that there truly is a God of grace (not just language or practice in which these terms have meaning) and the reality of this Creator God is not contingent on the activity of any creature. W. D. Hudson offers this general portrait of a divine reality that is the object of prayer:

> Whatever is god is *aware* of the believer. Such awareness may be differently conceived in different religions. When, for example, the animist owner of

a fetish beats it in order to secure the compliance of the spirit within, the awareness which he conceives the spirit to have is vastly different from that attributed by the author of Psalm 139 to the god who had searched him and known him. But for all such variation in the nature of the awareness, whatever is god is conceived to be in some manner and degree aware of the believer. Even in the most mystical of religions communion, rather than merely contemplation, is conceived ultimately to exist between the believer and the object of his belief; and communion is logically impossible without awareness of each other in all parties to it. Awareness, then, is a universal defining characteristic of god. (Hudson 2003: 9)

The supposition that the divine is conscious or is consciousness is also borne out in traditions within Hinduism and Buddhism. The *Upanishads* contain this prayer: 'Thou art consciousness itself, Thou art creator of time, All-knowing art thou' (Prabhavananda 1957: 126). Buddhists similarly have characterized the Buddha as a supreme, omniscient reality. The Buddha has *sarvanjna*, awareness of everything. 'Buddha is aware of all possible objects of awareness and is aware of them without error or distortion of any kind' (Griffiths 1994: 72).

Phillips's position also seems to be challenged by the case of outstanding philosophers who speculate on God's power, goodness, grace, and 'consciousness' (or 'mind') in the context of prayers. Augustine and Anselm stand out as first-rate thinkers who articulated their philosophy of God – taking up such issues as God's relation to time or God's perfection in knowing creation – in the context of their prayers (Anselm 1979; Augustine 1997).

The view that religious language can be taken to be *referential* ('God' refers to God) is often called *realism*, whereas the denial of this is termed non-realism or anti-realism. Adopting realism, alone, does not mean adopting a belief that there *is* a God or Brahman. Atheists, as well as theists, are realists. Being a realist about prayer, for example, simply means that you think that either there is or is not a divine or sacred reality being referred to. Realists can certainly disagree about the precision of terms used to refer to God (how much religious language involves metaphors? analogies? allegory?), and they can similarly disagree about when different sets of religious terms refer to the same sacred reality. (When, for example does it make sense to affirm that Jews, Christians, and Muslims pray to the same God?) So, simply adopting realism does not, alone, address the many fascinating philosophical issues raised by prayer.

Petitionary prayer

Some philosophers have worried about the practice of petitioning God in theistic tradition. Is petitionary prayer at odds with the belief that God is essentially good? Why should God's action rest on whether someone requests the action? If the divine act is good (imagine this involves the healing of an ill child), wouldn't God simply do the act? David Basinger claims: 'With respect to our basic needs (goods), it is never justifiable for God to withhold that which he can and would like to give us until petitioned' (Basinger 2004: 267). Basinger uses an analogy with ordinary parental duties:

> just as I don't think that a parent could justifiably withhold basic health care or minimum shelter from a child until requested in order to foster appreciation of the parent as a provider, so I don't believe that God could justifiably withhold life-saving or life-sustaining intervention until requested primarily to foster better appreciation of God's role as provider or to teach us something about his nature or to keep from spoiling us. (2004: 266)

Basinger thereby sets aside the idea that petitionary prayer is defensible because it fosters a valuable appreciation for our dependency upon God or it creates some other good.

Replies to this challenge often situate prayer in the context of the overall theistic affirmation of human freedom and responsibility. Assuming God created persons with freedom, and in circumstances in which persons are responsible for each other, why wouldn't God allow for ways in which persons can benefit others through God's action? The case of the ill child is part of the overall problem of evil: Why is the life of *any* child cut short? Perhaps the suffering or premature death of even a single child suffices to show that there is no God, that God is not all-good or is not a moral agent, and so on. But if one believes that it is not wrong for an all-good God to create and sustain our cosmos, presumably one thereby recognizes that in our world children do have different levels of care, and parents have different resources in healing their children. I have argued elsewhere that theists who hold that God loves created persons have reason for thinking that physical death is not the end; there is a ground for hoping, if not believing, that there are opportunities for redemption beyond this life (Taliaferro 2003).

In this enlarged perspective, God does provide an ultimate life-sustaining intervention for all (whether requested or not). Given this background, might it not be permissible for some goods, even basic ones, to be brought about through petition? Consider the case of twin brothers named Cain and Abel, both of whom are addicted to heroin. Imagine they are identical in all respects, including their shared belief that there is a 'Higher Power' who can give them strength to overcome their addiction. Imagine further that Abel petitions this Higher Power and is given such strength, but Cain refuses on the grounds that he will not seek help from anyone. If the Higher Power aids Abel, assisting him to a moral regeneration and healing, but not Cain, is the Higher Power blameworthy? Arguably not, especially if one believes that this Higher Power will seek Cain's regeneration at another time in another context.

Comparing cases like Cain's and Abel's has some plausibility, I believe, because the petition itself may be seen as instrumental in Abel's healing. The bare fact that he might petition a Higher Power could be a first step toward being receptive to the assistance of others. But what about Basinger's complaint in the case of prayers for an innocent child's recovery? In reply, I suggest that the introduction of another party may not be any more problematic (and also no less problematic) than when innocent children are dependent upon other people for ordinary care. Imagine, for example, that Cain and Abel are single parents and Abel, by the grace of the Higher Power, is able to nurse his child to health, while Cain refuses any help of a Higher Power or even ordinary assistance and the child remains ill. Clearly this is all part of the problem of evil, and it is not possible to settle that debate over theism here. But if one believes it is possible for an all-good God to create a world where the well-being of children depends upon others, it is not clear that petitionary prayer should create an additional problem. There is, however, one factor that complicates Basinger's case of the ill child or the subsequent Cain and Abel parable.

The matter of comparing two cases – where one case involves an ill child being prayed for and another when the ill child is not prayed for – is problematic, for all children and practitioners everywhere, and all of creation, are prayed for by monks and nuns, and the religious orders in many religions. The Cain and Abel case reflects a difference in what might be considered intimate, directed prayer, but from a wider perspective even the children in secular countries are prayed for by others. *The Book of Common Prayer* contains prayers for all that is created and, if there is extraterrestrial life, presumably any remote ETs are prayed for as well. There are prayers now for future generations, so even if all religions were to cease praying, these future generations have been prayed for. But while we cannot formulate problem-free thought experiments that compare people who are and who are not prayed for, we can imagine two cases that are relevant.

First, consider what may be called *The Petitionary World*. In this world – which is precisely like ours in all its main features – imagine that some of the good that occurs and some evil avoided is due to petitionary prayer. In this world, imagine that, in May and June of 1940, the successful evacuation of 300,000 troops from Dunkirk was brought about, in part, by God in response to petitionary prayer. In this scenario, the event was truly what Winston Churchill called a 'miracle.' Now, consider *The Non-Petitionary World*. In this world, imagine conditions that are just like the Petitionary World – there is the same amount of good and evil, but none of the good that occurs or evil that is prevented is due to petitionary prayer. So, in this world, imagine that there was also a successful evacuation of the same number of troops, but this was not due to God's response to petitionary prayer. I suggest that the first world has an additional value that the second world lacks; this value may be called *a mediatory good*. By a mediatory good I mean the valuable mediation of a good agent.

Not all mediation is good. The overbearing parent who insists on mediating *all* interactions between her children may well undermine their freedom, sense of self-worth, and confidence. But some mediation can be of great value because it is part of a greater good of friendship or respectful love. Imagine two cases. In one, you are reflecting about whether to adopt a child. You consider your resources, do the proper research, and proceed to adopt a wonderful child. In a different scenario, you are reflecting about the adoption, undertaking the research but cannot, by yourself, reach a conclusion. You then discuss this with a friend who gently, respectfully, and lovingly points to all the benefits of adoption, goes with you to the relevant agencies, and takes pleasure with you when you adopt a wonderful child. Both cases may have equal value on so many fronts, and the first may even have greater worth insofar as we can imagine it required more courage to undertake the adoption solo rather than in the company of a friend. Even so, the second case has great value in the loving mediation. In the case of Dunkirk, I suggest that the Petitionary World includes the value of many people cooperating and contributing to the miracle. Given that the evacuation is good, then the well-intentioned seeking to participate and help facilitate the evacuation through God's aid is (I suggest) a further good.

Obviously, more work needs to be done in a fuller defense of petitionary prayer. It may be objected that what I am calling the Non-Petitionary World contains a good (God's absolute, all-determining sovereignty, for example) missing in the Petitionary World. I have elsewhere defended the goodness of acting in concord with God (Taliaferro 1992), but clearly a sustained defense of the case for petitionary prayer would need to offer reasons for thinking that such divine–human concordant mediation is not trumped or overshadowed by some other value (Mann 2005).

The problem of praise

Some philosophers have charged that the very idea that God should command or desire praise reflects a crude anthropomorphism. Isn't there something vain in the portrait of God requiring prayers of adoration? Thomas Hobbes once complained about philosophers who seek to give God compliments. Perhaps some of the prayers of worship are an attempt to flatter God (Rundle 2004: 18).

One way to avoid this objection would be to treat God as a property like goodness. Taking pleasure in goodness itself could well be seen as good. But for better or for worse, this route seems unavailable to theistic world religions in which God is described in personal or person-like terms (God loves, knows, creates, and so on). There might be an interesting middle position in Hinduism when God is describable in personal and impersonal terms. Consider, for example, the prayers of Mahatma Gandhi in his autobiography. On the one hand, God is described as Truth: 'I worship God as Truth only' (Gandhi 1927: xi). And yet God is also addressed here as a person: 'I am seeking after Him' (p. xii) and as a reality that may lead and guide us. Gandhi ends his book this way: 'In bidding farewell to the reader, I ask him to join with me in prayer to the God of Truth that He may grant me the boon of Ahimsa in mind, word, and deed' (p. 383).

What might be called the problem of divine vanity seems sharpest when God is conceived of in terms of absolute power, as Hobbes did. If God's claim or right to be worshiped is grounded on the sheer awesomeness of divine power, one may rightly worry that this unleashes religious values (service to God's glory) that may radically conflict with ethics or improperly overshadow human values. A better theistic response to the problem may stem from an alternative concept of God (found in Augustine, Anselm, Aquinas, and others) that God is essentially good. Worship of God may then be seen as directed upon the goodness of God's nature and the goodness of divine acts. On this model, praise (worship, awe, delight, pleasure) is directed upon God's good act of creating and conserving the cosmos and the excellence of God's properties. In theism, the praise is still directed toward a reality that is described in personal terms (or, for Christians, a tri-unity of persons), but one is some distance away from the Hobbesian notion of God as pure unbridled power (Taliaferro 1989; Copan 2006).

There may remain a related problem of vanity with respect to prayer. Might it be the case that prayer in theistic religions reflects the vanity of the believer? Why suppose God, the Creator of the cosmos, would be at all concerned with prayers of supplication or praise? Such a supposition may well reflect vanity, just as much as it would if one were to pray that God would promote one's self-aggrandizement. But the supposition that one's welfare and the very existence of the cosmos rest on an external, transcendent power may also reflect and promote humility. Praising an all-good Creator may help impede disproportionate self-preoccupation and self-praise.

The scope of a philosophy of prayer

There are abundant, additional philosophical concerns raised by prayer. Here are eight questions about prayer that are addressed by contemporary philosophers:

1 If God brings about an event in response to a petitionary prayer, would that event have to be a miracle? (Holland 1965)
2 Does it make sense to pray for God to change the past? (Dummett 1964)
3 Does petitionary prayer that God would bring about an event make sense if God, from the standpoint of eternity, providentially determined every aspect of creation? (Alston 1985)
4 If God is eternal (or non-temporal or transcendent over time); or changeless (immutable); or impassable (not subject to emotions like sorrow), does petitionary prayer make sense? (Alston 1985; Stump 1997).
5 To what extent should a philosophy of prayer be shaped by the portrait of prayer in Scripture? If it is plausible to see petitionary prayer in the Vedas, the Hebrew Bible, the New Testament, and the Qur'ān, would this be a compelling reason for Hindu, Jewish, Christian, and Muslim philosophers to accept the coherence and credibility of petitionary prayer? (Morris 1987)
6 Even if one is not sure there is a God who answers petitionary prayer, might it not be that one still has an obligation to pray for those in need because, in case there is such a God, one may thereby be assisting others? (Lemos 1998)
7 What is the scope and restraint of petitionary prayer? It is one thing to pray for the healing of a sick child, but what about praying for illness to befall an enemy or for victory in battle or for the outcome of a sporting event? (Kreider 2003)
8 The practice of prayer raises questions that concern a philosophy of ritual. In Shakespeare's *Hamlet*, there is the line 'Words without thoughts never to heaven go' (III. iii). But can't saying the words of a prayer – which one routinely rattles off thoughtlessly – still count as a prayer? Some manuals on prayer focus on bodily posture, breathing, the use of icons, silence, and music. There is ample opportunity here for developing a philosophy of prayer that involves aesthetics and a philosophy of human nature. (Schilbrack 2004)

See also Problem of evil (Chapter 37), Problems with the concept of God (Chapter 38), The problem of religious language (Chapter 39).

References

Alston, W. P. (1985) 'Divine-human dialogue and the nature of God,' *Faith and Philosophy* 2: 5–20.
Anselm (1979) *The Proslogion*, trans. M. J. Charlesworth, Oxford: Clarendon Press.
Appleton, G. (ed.) (1988) *The Oxford Book of Prayer*, Oxford: Oxford University Press.
Augustine (1997) *The Confessions*, Cambridge: Cambridge University Press.
Basinger, D. (2004) 'God does not necessarily respond to prayer,' in M. Peterson and R. Van Arragon (eds) *Contemporary Debates in Philosophy of Religion*, Oxford: Blackwell.
Copan, P. (2006) 'Divine narcissism: a further defense of divine humility,' *Philosophia Christi* NS 8/2 (Winter): 313–25.
Cupitt, D. (1981) *Taking Leave of God*, New York: Crossroad.
Dummett, M. (1964) 'Bringing about the past,' *Philosophical Review* 73: 338–59.
Gandhi, M. K. (1927) *The Story of My Experiments with Truth*, trans. M. Desai, Ahmedabad: Navajivan Publishing House.
Griffiths, P. (1994) *On Being Buddha*, Albany, NY: State University of New York Press.
Holland, R. F. (1965) 'The miraculous,' *American Philosophical Quarterly* 2: 43-51.
Hudson, W. D. (2003) 'What makes religions' views religious?,' in C. Taliaferro and P. Griffiths (eds) *Philosophy of Religion: A Reader*, Oxford: Blackwell.
Kreider, A. (2003) 'Prayers for assistance as unsporting behavior,' *Journal of Philosophy of Sport* 30: 17–25.
Lemos, J. (1998) 'An agnostic defense of obligatory prayer,' *Sophia* 37: 70–87.
Mann, W. (2005) 'Divine sovereignty and aseity,' in W. Wainwright (ed.) *The Oxford Handbook of Philosophy of Religion*, Oxford: Oxford University Press.
Morris, T. V. (1987) *Anselmian Explorations: Essays in Philosophical Theology*, Notre Dame, IN: University of Notre Dame Press.
Phillips, D. Z. (1986) *Belief, Change and Forms of Life*, Atlantic Highlands, NJ: Humanities Press.
—— (2005) 'Wittgensteinianism: logic, reality, and God,' in W. J. Wainwright (ed.) *The Oxford Handbook of Philosophy of Religion*, Oxford: Oxford University Press.
Prabhavananda, S. (1957) *The Upanishads*, trans. F. Manchester, New York: New American Library.
Rundle, B. (2004) *Why Is There Something Rather Than Nothing?* Oxford: Clarendon Press.
Schilbrack, K. (2004) *Ritual and Philosophy*, London: Routledge.
Stump, E. (1997) 'Petitionary prayer,' in P. Quinn and C. Taliaferro (eds) *A Companion to Philosophy of Religion*, Oxford: Blackwell.
Taliaferro, C. (1989) 'The vanity of God,' *Faith and Philosophy* 6: 140–55.
—— (1992) 'God's estate,' *Journal of Religious Ethics* 20: 69–92.
—— (2003) 'Why we need immortality,' C. Taliaferro and P. Griffiths (eds) *Philosophy of Religion: A Reader*, Oxford: Blackwell.
Walls, J. (2002) *Heaven: The Logic of Eternal Joy*, Oxford: Oxford University Press.

Further reading

Basinger, D. (1995) 'Petitionary prayer,' *Religious Studies* 31: 475–84. (A strong case against the efficacy of petitionary prayer.)
Brümmer, V. (1984) *What Are We Doing When We Pray?* London: SCM Press. (A comprehensive exploration of the intelligibility of prayer.)
Davis, C. F. (1986) 'The devotional experiment,' *Religious Studies* 22: 15–28. (Davis argues that through prayer and other devotional exercises an agnostic may obtain experiential evidence for theism.)
Hebblethwaite, B. (1978) 'Providence and divine action,' *Religious Studies* 14: 223–36. (A theistic case for

seeing petitionary prayer in terms of seeking to impact God's action in and through created causes, but not as a request for miracles.)

Issler, K. (2001) 'Divine providence and impetratory prayer,' *Philosophia Christi* NS 3/2: 533–41. (A good overview of different accounts of prayer.)

Moore, G. (1988) *Believing in God: A Philosophical Essay*, Edinburgh: T. & T. Clark. (An acute argument that the God of Christianity is personal. Moore's analysis of prayer locates it as a part of a religious form of life rather than as a plea for changing the mind of a divine personal reality.)

Murray, M. (2004) 'God responds to prayer,' in M. Peterson and R. Van Arragon (eds) *Contemporary Debates in the Philosophy of Religion*, Malden, MA: Blackwell. (A defense of petitionary prayer.)

Phillips, D. Z. (1965) *The Concept of Prayer*, London: Routledge. (A case against petitionary prayer.)

Stump, E. (1979) 'Petitionary prayer,' *American Philosophical Quarterly* 16: 81–91. (A much-discussed defense of the efficacy of petitionary prayer in light of a robust understanding of the divine attributes. Stump's positive case for prayer rests on the conviction that God is personal or a person-like reality.)

Ward, K. (1990) *Divine Action*, London: Collins. (An elegant portrait of theism and prayer.)

Part IX

RECENT TOPICS IN PHILOSOPHY OF RELIGION

58

REFORMED EPISTEMOLOGY

John Greco

Reformed epistemology is an approach to issues about faith and rationality organized around a central thesis: that beliefs about God can be rational or reasonable even if they are not based on supporting evidence or reasons. The *locus classicus* for Reformed epistemology is *Faith and Rationality* by Alvin Plantinga and Nicholas Wolterstorff (1983). There Wolterstorff tells us that these views 'bear a close affinity to positions long held on the relation of faith to reason by the Continental Reformed (Calvinist) tradition' (Plantinga and Wolterstorff 1983: 7). Specifically, Reformed epistemology is 'anti-evidentialist' in rejecting the need for, or even the appropriateness of, arguments for God's existence. Moreover, beliefs about God can nevertheless be rational, or reasonable, or respectable from an intellectual point of view. Put another way, beliefs about God can be 'properly basic.' That is, they can be held independently of supporting evidence or reasons, and properly so.

Two clarifications of the position are immediately necessary. First, Reformed epistemology does not hold that beliefs about God are groundless, or based on nothing at all. Rather, the idea is that beliefs about God need not be based on a particular sort of grounds – the sort involved in giving reasons or arguments for one's beliefs. On the contrary, beliefs about God are appropriately grounded in one's personal experience of God. Second, the thesis is not that *all* beliefs about God are properly basic. Rather, the idea is that *some* beliefs about God *can* be. This way of understanding the thesis is in keeping with Reformed epistemology's rejection of 'the evidentialist objection' to religious belief, which says that *no* belief about God can be rational unless it is based on good reasons.

The central thesis of Reformed epistemology, then, is that some beliefs about God can be properly basic, and therefore need not be based on reasons or arguments to be rational. It will be helpful to divide arguments in favor of this central thesis into two phases. In a merely negative phase, Reformed epistemologists have criticized the evidentialist objection to belief in God. That is, they have examined arguments for thinking that belief in God must be based on evidence to be rational, and they have found these arguments wanting. In a more positive phase, Reformed epistemologists have developed theories of rationality and knowledge that support the contention that belief in God can be properly basic. That is, they have developed general theories about what makes a belief properly basic, and they have offered reasons for thinking that beliefs about God can be put in that category.

The negative phase

The Reformed objection to natural theology

The Reformed tradition has always been wary of arguments in favor of God and Christianity. In particular, the tradition has taken a dim view of 'natural theology,' or the practice of giving arguments or proofs for God's existence. According to the Reformed theologian Herman Bavinck, 'Scripture does not reason in the abstract. It does not make God the conclusion of a syllogism, leaving it to us whether we think the argument holds or not' (Bavinck 1951: 78–9, in Plantinga 1983: 64). According to John Calvin, 'The prophets and apostles do not ... dwell upon rational proofs' (Calvin 1960: 78; in Plantinga 1983: 67).

One way to interpret these passages is that they are endorsing a strong sort of fideism, one that opposes faith to reason and that chooses faith over reason. However, Plantinga suggests that a different position is being expressed here, if only implicitly and inchoately. Rather than opposing faith to reason, Plantinga argues, the Reformers were challenging a particular conception of reason. Specifically, they were challenging a conception of reason on which only a very few things can be known without proof, and where the rest, including belief in God, must be proven in order to be intellectually respectable. The Reformed theologians were rejecting this view, Plantinga argues, and rightfully so. Belief in God can be rational even if it is not based on arguments or proofs.

This explains why the Reformed tradition has taken a dim view of natural theology, and of any sort of evidentialist apologetics. In particular, people who try to provide arguments for God's existence seem to share an assumption with the people who demand them: that such arguments are needed in the first place. The Reformed idea, according to Plantinga, was to reject this shared assumption about what it takes for belief in God to be rational or reasonable.

The evidentialist objection and classical foundationalism

Let us state the evidentialist objection to belief in God more formally:

1 Beliefs about God are rational only if they are based on good reasons that serve for their evidence.
2 But there are no good reasons for believing that God exists. Beliefs about God are not based on good evidence.

Therefore,

3 Beliefs about God are not rational.

One way to respond to this objection is to challenge premise (2). In that case one might go about trying to provide the reasons in question by way of an argument or proof. Another way to respond to the objection, however, is to challenge premise (1). Why should we think that beliefs about God are rational only if they are based on good reasons or evidence? As Plantinga points out, we do not typically think that *all* beliefs must be based on reasons in order to be rational. That would imply an infinite regress of reasons. So the evidentialist objection must assume that there is something special about beliefs about God. It must assume that beliefs about God in particular are in need of good reasons. But why so?

According to a number of Reformed epistemologists, the evidentialist objection assumes a general view about reason and knowledge that has come to be known as 'classical foundationalism' (see Plantinga 1983; Wolterstorff 1983). Specifically, classical foundationalism lays down strict criteria regarding which beliefs can be properly basic and which cannot. According to ancient and medieval versions of the view, only beliefs that are 'self-evident' or 'evident to the senses' can be properly basic. According to modern versions of the view, only beliefs that are self-evident or 'incorrigible' can be properly basic, where an incorrigible belief is one that is impossible to be wrong about. Clearly, if classical foundationalism is true, then beliefs about God are not properly basic. This is because beliefs about God are neither self-evident, evident to the senses, nor incorrigible. Put another way, if classical foundationalism is true, then beliefs about God are rational only if they are based on good reasons or evidence, presumably reasons that are themselves self-evident, evident to the senses, or incorrigible.

But *is* classical foundationalism true? Reformed epistemologists, and many other epistemologists with them, have argued that it is not. One problem with the view, Plantinga has argued, is that it is 'self-referentially incoherent'; that is, the view lays down conditions for rationality that it does not satisfy itself. Another problem, perhaps more telling, is that the view seems to be too strict in the conditions that it lays down. In sum, the view entails that many beliefs that we think are rational are not.

> One crucial lesson to be learned from the development of modern philosophy – Descartes through Hume, roughly – is just this: relative to propositions that are self-evident and incorrigible, most of the beliefs that form the stock in trade of ordinary life are not probable. ... Consider all those propositions that entail, say, that there are physical objects, or that there are persons distinct from myself, or that the world has existed for more than five minutes. (Plantinga 1983: 59–60)

Ancient and medieval foundationalism fares better, since it allows perceptual beliefs about physical objects to be properly basic. Nevertheless, Plantinga argues, these positions continue to make beliefs about the past and beliefs about other persons irrational (Plantinga 1983: 60).

Notice that this response does not beg the question against the evidentialist objector. That is, the response does not assume that beliefs about God can be properly basic, or even that they can be rational at all. Rather, it insists that the conditions for rationality laid down by classical foundationalism are too strict by almost anyone's lights, because they discredit *non*-religious beliefs that almost anyone thinks are rational. Here we witness a common dialectic in the Reformed epistemology literature: it is argued that, if a particular objection against the rationality of religious beliefs were sound, it would make other, non-religious beliefs irrational as well. And therefore, if one is to conclude that religious beliefs are irrational on the basis of the objection in question, then one must conclude that the other beliefs are irrational as well. Of course, one might accept that result, embracing a kind of skepticism that goes well beyond beliefs about God. But that would be a hollow victory against the rationality of religious beliefs in particular.

Objections to the claim that belief in God can be properly basic

Several objections have been raised against the idea that beliefs about God can be properly basic. The most natural, perhaps, is that if beliefs about God can be basic then any belief can be. This has been labeled 'The Great Pumpkin Objection,' for obvious reasons (Plantinga 1983: 74–8). Reformed epistemologists have responded that the objection is mistaken. Specifically, the claim that classical foundationalism is too strict does not imply that anything goes.

A second objection to Reformed epistemology is that it embraces fideism. But as we have already seen, this kind of worry misunderstands the position. The central thesis of Reformed epistemology is that belief in God *is* rational, or at least that it can be, even if it is not based on arguments or reasons. This can hardly be fideism, which opposes faith to rationality. As explained above, Reformed epistemology does not reject rationality but rather a particular conception of rationality, which it argues is inadequate on independent grounds.

These responses to the objections are sound as far as they go. Nevertheless, one might find them unsatisfying. One might think that the real worry behind the objections has not been addressed. Perhaps that real worry is this: for all that has been said so far, we have no reason for thinking that beliefs about God *are* properly basic. That is, all we have so far is a negative point: a critique of the evidentialist assumption that beliefs about God cannot be properly basic. Here we must move to Reformed epistemology's positive phase: arguments in favor of theories of rationality and knowledge that replace classical foundationalism, and that explain how beliefs about God can be properly basic. These arguments were already present in the earliest literature articulating a Reformed epistemology, but became more developed later on.

The positive phase

Plantinga's proper function account

Perhaps the most influential theory in this regard has been Alvin Plantinga's proper function view (Plantinga 1993b). He defends a general theory of rationality and knowledge along the following lines. First, he makes clear that cognition has a normative dimension: when we say that a belief is rational or that a person is reasonable, for example, we are making value judgments. We are using value-laden language to ascribe normative properties to beliefs and believers. Accordingly, one task of epistemology is to investigate the sort of normative property that distinguishes mere opinion from reasonable belief and knowledge. Plantinga's preferred terms for this property are 'positive epistemic status' and 'warrant.' His substantive position is that what gives a belief positive epistemic status, and therefore converts it into knowledge, is that it is the result of one's cognitive faculties functioning properly: 'in the paradigm cases of warrant, a belief B has warrant for S if and only if that belief is produced in S by his epistemic faculties working properly in a appropriate environment' (Plantinga 1993b: 9).

Plantinga qualifies this basic position in several ways. First, a cognitive faculty might be functioning properly even if does not function infallibly. Second, a faculty functions properly to the extent that it functions as it was designed to function. From a theistic point of view such design will be by God, but non-theists can also make use of the concept of design. Even non-theists think that, in some relevant sense, a bird's wings are designed for flying.

The reason this second refinement is important is that it distinguishes cognitive processes that are reliable by design from cognitive processes that are reliable *by accident*. Thus consider a counterexample raised against 'process reliabilism,' or the view that knowledge is true belief that is formed by a reliable process. By cruel coincidence, S has a brain lesion that reliably causes him to believe that he has a brain lesion. Imagine also, however, that S has no evidence in favor of this belief, or even that he has evidence against it. Obviously, S's belief that he has a brain lesion does not have positive epistemic status even though, by hypothesis, it is caused by a reliable process. The reason for this, Plantinga tells us, is that S's belief is reliable by accident. Although the cognitive processes giving rise to S's belief are functioning reliably, they are not functioning in the way they were designed to function (Plantinga 1993a: 195).

Plantinga's proper function account has much to recommend it. First, it nicely explains why knowledge arises from normal uses of perception, memory, introspection, and deduction, but not by wishful thinking, neurotic worrying, or hasty generalization. As was noted above, the theory also constitutes an advance over simple versions of reliabilism, avoiding counterexamples such as that of the person with the brain tumor.

Moreover, Plantinga's theory supports the central claim of Reformed epistemology: that beliefs about God can be properly basic. The relevant idea is that we are endowed with a properly functioning faculty for knowing God directly. One way to conceive such a faculty is as a kind of religious perception. According to this model, beliefs about God can be grounded by a religious experience of God or God's creations. Looking at the stars, the believer *feels* the presence of the Creator. While praying in the pew, the believer *senses* that she is in communion with her Lord. Such perceptions then act as grounds for a belief that the Creator is present in his creation, or that one is communing with one's Lord. Alternatively, the faculty could be conceived on the analogy of logical intuition. Upon contemplating certain propositions about God, the believer simply 'sees' that they are true. In either case, the relevant beliefs qualify as properly basic: such beliefs have positive epistemic status, but do not owe this status to any inference or argument.

If such a faculty exists, and if Plantinga's conditions for positive epistemic status are correct, then the relevant beliefs about God will have positive epistemic status. Insofar as those beliefs are grounded in experience rather than arguments or proofs, they will be properly basic as well.

Alston's perceptual model

Within the context of Plantinga's proper function account, it is natural to think of our awareness of God on an analogy with perception. In each case, beliefs of the relevant sort are formed directly on the basis of experience, rather than on the basis of some inference in an argument or proof. A perceptual model has also been defended by William Alston, in the context of what he calls a 'doxastic practices' approach to positive epistemic status (Alston 1983; 1991). Alston's view is that positive epistemic status in general is the result of relevant doxastic practices, or practices for forming, revising, and maintaining beliefs in response to various sorts of evidence. Some of these practices are reasoning practices – they take us from presently held beliefs to new beliefs on the basis of licensed inferences. Other practices, however, are what Alston calls 'perceptual practices.' For example, normal human beings engage in the practice of forming beliefs about physical objects directly on the basis of sensory experience. Alston's idea is that beliefs about God might arise from an analogous practice. That is, in the context of some doxastic practices, it is appropriate to form beliefs about God directly on the basis of 'religious' or 'mystical' experience.

Here again we see a kind of argument by analogy: just as it is possible for some non-religious beliefs to be appropriately grounded in experience rather than reasoning, so it is possible for some religious beliefs to be so grounded. Of course, someone who is unsympathetic with this sort of argument will insist that the analogy is no good: that there are important differences between beliefs about physical objects grounded in sensory experience and beliefs about God grounded in religious experience. That is exactly where disagreement is likely to focus.

Along these lines, it is important to consider two claims that an objection to Alston's perceptual model must make. First, the objection must claim that there is some *difference* between beliefs about physical objects grounded in sensory experience and beliefs about God grounded in religious experience. Second, the objection must claim that the difference is a *relevant* difference. That is, it must claim that the difference in question should make a difference to the epistemic status of the beliefs in question. For example, it might be objected that we know that sensory experience is reliable, whereas we have no such guarantee about the reliability of religious experience. In response to this sort of objection, Alston points out that there is in fact no *non-circular* guarantee that sensory experience is reliable. In fact, all our reasons for thinking that sensory experience is reliable involve the use of sensory experience, and so the two kinds of practice are in the same boat in this respect. On the other hand, neither practice is such that we have good reasons for thinking that it is *unreliable*. Again, the two are in the same boat – the analogy holds.

In the course of defending his perceptual model, Alston considers four additional objections (Alston 1983: 121–30). Again, each is supposed to mark a relevant difference between our practice of employing sensory experience to form beliefs about physical objects (call this 'SP') and the practice of employing religious experience to form beliefs about God (call this 'RP').

1 Within SP there are standard ways of checking the accuracy of any particular perceptual belief.
2 By engaging in SP we can discover regularities in the behavior of objects and make predictions about future behavior on this basis.
3 The capacity for SP and its practice is found universally among human beings.
4 All normal adult human beings use basically the same conceptual scheme when using SP.

In responding to these objections, Alston concedes that each identifies a real difference between the two kinds of practice. What he argues, however, is that none of these constitute a *relevant* difference. More specifically, none of these give us good reason for thinking that RP is unreliable, or less reliable than SP. Alston's idea is that the objects of SP are supposed to be physical objects. As such, it is to be expected that SP would be widespread and would reveal regularities in their behavior. The object of RP, however, is supposed to be God. Accordingly, it is unreasonable to expect that RP would have the features listed in (1) to (4), even if it is reliable. That is because, in part, God is so 'wholly other.' In particular, he is wholly other from physical objects, and so can't be expected to act like physical objects.

One might question whether Alston should have conceded even that (1) to (4) mark differences between sensory practice and religious practice. It is not obvious, for example, that RP identifies no regularities at all in God's behavior. Neither is it obvious that a capacity for SP is found universally among all adult human beings (some people are blind or deaf), or that all human beings use the same conceptual scheme to form beliefs about physical objects.

Either way, it is not obvious that there are relevant differences between SP and RP.

How 'Reformed' is Reformed epistemology? Plantinga's A/C model

Early on Plantinga saw Aquinas as an evidentialist. More specifically, he saw him as engaged in evidentialist apologetics, or as trying to provide the sort of arguments for belief in God that the evidentialist objection demands (e.g., Plantinga 1983: esp. 39–63). In more recent work Plantinga sees Aquinas as an ally. Although the arguments of natural theology might have various uses, they are not required to ground knowledge of God or to make belief in God rational. On this point Plantinga now sees Aquinas and Calvin to be in agreement, noting Aquinas's view: 'To know in a general and confused way that God exists is implanted in us by nature' (*Summa Theologiae* I. q.2. a.1. ad 1; in Plantinga 2000: 170).

The 'Aquinas/Calvin model' or 'A/C model' takes over much of Plantinga's earlier view: human beings are fitted with a special faculty for knowing God, a *sensus divinitatis* by which, in a wide variety of circumstances, we are made aware of God's existence, presence, love, or work. The view is now broadened, however, so as to apply to Christian beliefs specifically, and this requires adding some new ideas. Again, the project is to explain how Christian beliefs might be warranted or properly basic, as opposed to *showing* that they are. Accordingly, it is appropriate to add ideas to which Christians are already committed for the purposes of constructing the new model. The A/C model is therefore extended as follows.

According to the Christian tradition, human beings have fallen into sin and are therefore in need of salvation. Moreover, God intends to inform us of his plan for our salvation. He could have done so in any number of ways, says Plantinga, but in fact chose to do so through a 'three-tiered cognitive process' (Plantinga 2000: 243). First, God arranged for the production of Scripture, written by men but inspired in such a way that God is the principal author. Second, the Holy Spirit works in the hearts of the faithful so as to repair the damages of sin, including its cognitive and affective damages. It is by virtue of this activity that our natural awareness of God is repaired and restored. Moreover, it is by virtue of the activity of the Holy Spirit that Christians come to accept the great teachings of the gospel. This Christian faith is the third element of the process. Hence Calvin characterizes such faith as 'a firm and certain knowledge of God's benevolence towards us, founded upon the truth of the freely given promise in Christ, both revealed to our minds and sealed upon our hearts through the Holy Spirit' (Calvin 1960: 551; in Plantinga 2000: 244). According to Aquinas, 'The believer has sufficient motive for believing, for he is moved by the authority of divine teaching confirmed by miracles and, what is more, by the inward instigation of the divine invitation' (*Summa Theologiae* II–II. q.2. a.9, resp.; in Plantinga 2000: 249).

Since the model is consistent, it successfully shows how Christian beliefs might be warranted and properly basic. That is, it demonstrates the possibility. Moreover, if the Christian faith is true, then the A/C model or something like it is true, and therefore Christian beliefs *are* warranted and properly basic for many believers. This is because, according to Plantinga, such beliefs will often satisfy the conditions for warrant and proper basicality in general. He writes,

> when these beliefs are accepted by faith and result from the internal insti-
> gation of the Holy Spirit, they are produced by cognitive processes working
> properly; they are not produced by way of some cognitive malfunction. Faith,
> the whole process that produces them, is specifically designed by God himself
> to produce this very effect – just as vision, say, is designed by God to produce
> a certain kind of perceptual beliefs. (Plantinga 2000: 257)

The careful reader will note that Plantinga's account of warrant has changed from his earlier work to the later. Specifically, the earlier account made warrant the result of properly functioning *faculties*, whereas now warrant is said to result from properly functioning *processes* in general. The reason for the change is that the new A/C model is designed to accommodate the rationality of Christian beliefs, and for this Plantinga finds it necessary to refer to the 'three-tiered cognitive process' involving the testimony of Scripture and the work of the Holy Spirit. On the face of it, this new source of warrant cannot be accommodated by the older faculty view.

Unfortunately, this change in Plantinga's general account of warrant threatens to make that position implausible. To see this, recall the case of the brain lesion raised above. We can change the story so as to make it a counterexample to Plantinga's new account. Suppose that S's brain lesion did not occur naturally. Rather, S is the patient of a benevolent and reliable brain surgeon, one who manipulates S's brain so as to implant various true beliefs. If S knows nothing about the manipulation, then clearly the beliefs in question do not have warrant. And yet the beliefs are the result of a cognitive process that is both reliable and designed to produce true beliefs.

One strategy for avoiding this counterexample readily suggests itself: go back to Plantinga's original account, which makes the believer's cognitive abilities or faculties the seat of reliability and proper function. Can Plantinga do this, and still use the A/C model to account for the rationality of Christian beliefs inspired by Scripture and the Holy Spirit? I will end by suggesting how he can.

When applying the A/C model to Christian beliefs, Plantinga often emphasizes the special activity of the Holy Spirit, as when he writes that faith 'differs from [other warrant-producing processes] in that it also involves the direct action of the Holy Spirit, so that the immediate cause of belief is not to be found just in [the believer's] natural epistemic equipment' (2000: 256). In other places, however, Plantinga emphasizes that belief results from a kind of testimony: 'But then this just is a special case of the pervasive process of testimony, by which, as a matter of fact, we learn most of what we know' (p. 251). So sometimes Plantinga says that the immediate cause of belief is the Holy Spirit, whereas other times he says that belief is a response to testimony, implying that our faculties for receiving and responding to testimony are the cause of belief.

There is a tension here but no contradiction – not if the Holy Spirit causes belief by means of the believer's own faculties for receiving and responding to testimony. We may even continue to say that the Holy Spirit is the 'immediate' cause of belief, so long as immediacy is consistent with a role for those faculties. We might say with Aquinas that, 'The act of believing is an act of the intellect assenting to the Divine truth at the command of the will moved by the grace of God' (*Summa Theologiae* II–II. q.2. a.9, resp.). This model supports the view that Christian belief can be warranted and even properly basic, and it is consistent with Plantinga's earlier faculty account of warrant.

At this point we may return to the case of the benevolent brain surgeon. If the brain surgeon simply implants true beliefs in his patient, bypassing the patient's own cognitive and affective faculties, then these cannot have warrant even if they result from a process designed to produce true beliefs. But suppose that the surgeon merely enables belief, either by repairing a natural faculty or by creating a new faculty. Suppose, for example, that the surgeon repairs a natural faculty for receiving testimony, or creates a faculty that makes receiving a new kind of testimony possible. If the resulting faculty is sufficiently reliable and well enough integrated with the rest of the person's cognitive architecture, then I see no reason not to count the resulting beliefs as warranted.

This model for warranted Christian belief continues to emphasize the role of grace. First, warranted Christian belief still depends on the divine testimony itself. Second, the activity of the Holy Spirit is still required for the repair or creation of the relevant faculties of intellect and will. Finally, the activity of the Holy Spirit might be needed to move those faculties in a specific act of faith. Nevertheless, the present model understands faith as essentially grounded in the intellect and will of the believer, however dependent those faculties are on the grace of God for their creation and proper functioning, or for their exercise in a particular instance.

See also Christianity (Chapter 6), Thomas Aquinas (Chapter 12), Mysticism among the world's religions (Chapter 23), Naturalistic rejoinders to theistic arguments (Chapter 40), Catholic philosophical theology (Chapter 43), Protestant theology (Chapter 45), Revelation (Chapter 50), Religious experience (Chapter 63).

References

Alston, W. P. (1983) 'Christian experience and Christian belief,' in A. Plantinga and N. Wolterstorff (eds), *Faith and Rationality*, Notre Dame, IN: University of Notre Dame Press.
—— (1991) *Perceiving God: The Epistemology of Religious Experience*, Ithaca, NY: Cornell University Press.
Bavinck, H. (1951) *The Doctrine of God*, trans. W. Hendriksen, Grand Rapids, MI: Eerdmans.
Calvin, J. (1960) *Institutes of the Christian Religion*, trans. F. L. Battles, Philadelphia: Westminster Press.
Plantinga, A. (1983) 'Reason and belief in God,' in A. Plantinga and N. Wolterstorff (eds) *Faith and Rationality*, Notre Dame, IN: University of Notre Dame Press.
—— (1993a) *Warrant: The Current Debate*, Oxford: Oxford University Press.
—— (1993b) *Warrant and Proper Function*, Oxford: Oxford University Press.
—— (2000) *Warranted Christian Belief*, Oxford: Oxford University Press.
Plantinga, A. and N. Wolterstorff (eds) (1983) *Faith and Rationality*, Notre Dame, IN: University of Notre Dame Press.
Wolterstorff, N. (1983) 'Can belief in God be rational if it has no foundations?' in A. Plantinga and N. Wolterstorff (eds) *Faith and Rationality*, Notre Dame, IN: University of Notre Dame Press.

Further reading

Audi, R. and W. Wainwright (eds) (1986) *Rationality, Religious Belief, and Moral Commitment*, Ithaca, NY: Cornell University Press. (A collection of essays, some of which extend or critique Reformed epistemology.)
Greco, J. (1997) 'Catholics vs. Calvinists on religious knowledge,' *American Catholic Philosophical Quarterly* 71/1: 13–34. (Argues for affinities between Alvin Plantinga's and Linda Zagzebski's epistemologies, taking them as representatives of the Reformed and Catholic traditions, respectively.)
Plantinga, A. (1991) 'The prospects for natural theology,' in J. Tomberlin (ed.) *Philosophical Perspectives*

vol. 5: *Philosophy of Religion*, Atascadero, CA: Ridgeview Publishing. (Explores various ways in which natural theology might contribute to the rationality of religious beliefs.)

Stump, E. (1992) 'Aquinas on the foundations of knowledge,' *Canadian Journal of Philosophy*, suppl. vol. 17: 125–58. (Responds to Plantinga's earlier criticisms of Aquinas, and argues for affinities between Plantinga's and Aquinas's epistemologies.)

Wolterstorff, N. (1986) 'The migration of the theistic arguments: from natural theology to evidentialist apologetics,' in R. Audi and W. Wainwright (eds) *Rationality, Religious Belief, and Moral Commitment*, Ithaca, NY: Cornell University Press. (Explores the different purposes of arguments for God's existence, and how these changed from the medieval to the modern period.)

Zagzebski, L. (ed.) (1993) *Rational Faith: Catholic Responses to Reformed Epistemology*, Notre Dame, IN: University of Notre Dame Press. (A collection of essays by Catholic philosophers responding to various aspects of Reformed epistemology.)

59
FEMINISM
Harriet A. Harris

The philosophy of religion has been slower than theology and some of her other sister disciplines, notably moral philosophy and philosophy of science, to attract the scrutiny of feminists or to engage with feminist critique. It was a volume of the American philosophy of religion journal, *Hypatia* (1994), that most directly opened the discussion. Two monographs in feminist philosophy of religion followed in 1998: Pamela Sue Anderson's *A Feminist Philosophy of Religion: The Rationality and Myths of Religious Belief*, and, a few months later, Grace Jantzen's *Becoming Divine: Towards a Feminist Philosophy of Religion*.

It is in the area of religious epistemology that feminist thought is having its largest impact, either in questioning constructions of rationality, or in challenging the very focus on epistemology that has come to dominate Anglo-American philosophy of religion.

Anderson and Jantzen differ on this matter. Anderson remains epistemologically focused in her work, whilst Jantzen, who died in 2006, argues that we should sideline epistemological questions and engage primarily instead in ethical concerns. Both authors have been influenced by francophone philosophy, especially that of Irigaray and Kristeva, and behind them, Lacan and Derrida. Anderson also draws heavily on the thought of Michèle Le Doeuff. The francophone assessments of patriarchal rationality (cf. Joy et al. 2002) have informed their characterizations of Anglo-American philosophy of religion as 'male-neutral' (Anderson 1998: 13; 2004: 94) or 'masculinist' (Jantzen 1998; 2000; 2002), and influenced their endeavors to operate outside the usual boundaries of the discipline. Irigaray's dialectical insistence upon the divine as that which stresses continuity (whether between mind and body, nature and culture), informs Jantzen's critique of binary oppositions. That said, Jantzen bases her challenge to philosophy of religion on an unsustainable binary opposition between epistemology and ethics, whereas Anderson overcomes this binary in developing a virtue-style epistemology.

Despite their deep disagreements with one another, they have been jointly criticized by Amy Hollywood for remaining within 'the mainstream of analytic and continental philosophy of religion in focussing on belief' (Hollywood 2004: 225). Hollywood studies the place of ritual, by which she means embodied practice, in religion. Following the work of Marcel Mauss and Talal Asad (1993), she argues that our beliefs and emotions are themselves shaped by 'the learned nature of one's *habitus*' (2004: 237).

Anderson and Jantzen have also been jointly criticized by Sarah Coakley, seemingly in the opposite direction, for being unduly pessimistic about epistemological developments in Anglo-American philosophy of religion. Coakley (2005: 516-21) argues that various philosophical trends are already 'feminizing' analytical philosophy of religion, including interest in: desire in relation to claims of an immediate contact with the divine; apophatic discourse; and the effects of religious experience on religious epistemology.

Coakley and Hollywood may seem to occupy opposite ends of a spectrum regarding epistemology, but both endeavor to write into their philosophy ways that religious practice informs thought and belief. Coakley's specific interest is contemplative prayer (2002). Moreover, they both share with Jantzen and Anderson concern that philosophy of religion be practiced in ways that acknowledge rather than screen out our embodiment. This concern may be seen as the hallmark of feminist philosophy of religion, but not as its special preserve. The question arises (cf. Coakley 2005) whether there is specific work for feminists to perform that is not also being carried out by virtue epistemologists and by philosophers of religion such as Michael McGhee (1992; 2000) and Mark Wynn (2002; 2003), who are interested in the spiritual and emotional life.

Dismantling and reconfiguring the discipline

Because their focus is epistemological (even if to question that very focus), Anderson and Jantzen call for such extensive reconstruction of philosophy of religion that their work is best understood as prolegomena to the discipline. They problematize not only contextual values, such as conceiving God as omnipotent, immutable, omnipresent Father, but also constitutive values of philosophical method. The question of how to dismantle and rebuild is always a vexed one for feminists. Anderson (1998: 12) employs, via W. V. O. Quine, Otto Neurath's image of the philosopher rebuilding the ship of philosophy whilst it is out at sea. Her method of rebuilding involves two key moves, by which she would bridge the worlds of Anglo-American and Continental philosophy. First, drawing on feminist standpoint epistemology (FSE), she asks philosophers to reflect critically on their own embodied standpoint (e.g., 1998: 227), and to attempt to think from the various vantage points of the variously less privileged, so as to yield less exclusive and distorted representations of reality. Second, inspired by Le Doeuff's work on the philosophical imaginary (Le Doeuff (1989), she probes the symbolic in order to reclaim reason for women and to explore the potential of myth and imagery.

Jantzen also holds that we are in flux: 'The skills and methods of the philosophy of religion are ... dominated by the phallus. ... There is no pure place for a woman to stand, no unambiguous subject-position already available' (1998: 211). The two key elements in her method are psychoanalytical and pragmatic. She uses psychoanalysis to bring to consciousness the 'resistances and repressions' of the masculinist position.

She then proposes employing practical tests for what promotes flourishing: 'Through ongoing work and play with and for one another, some symbols, myths, and practices will be found to be nourishing and others will not; some will open up to divine horizons and others will need to be modified or discarded' (1998: 211–12).

Anderson's commitment to objectivity

Anderson rejects many principles of formal reasoning used by analytical philosophers, including simplicity, consistency, and coherence, but retains the principle of objectivity. FSE aims to supplant weak objectivity, in which 'certain biases allow subjects to claim knowledge of the world as it is while excluding from that world the lives of women, of nondominant races, of nonprivileged classes' (1998: 73; cf. 2001), by strong objectivity.

Strong objectivity is formed by working with insights from multiple standpoints, including, most significantly, standpoints from the margins rather than the center of power. The feminist contention, Anderson says, 'is that this privileged perspective narrows and distorts the subject's knowledge not only of social life but of scientific "facts"' (1998: 73). What counts as fact is shaped by the knowers and their processes of coming to knowledge. Here FSE differs from feminist empiricism, and Anderson may be undermining her project by having insufficient recourse to evidences or realist truth, by which to claim privilege for particular standpoints (cf. Coakley 2005: 514–15). In more recent articles, Anderson describes standpoint in terms of ethical achievement: gaining an epistemically informed perspective through struggle (2001: 145; cf. Harris 2004a; 2004b). She is then less able to claim privilege for a 'feminist' standpoint, but her priority becomes the struggle to arrive at fuller understanding, of which feminists may need less convincing than many others.

Anderson's specific concern is to include desire and sexual difference in an account of rationality, rather than intuition or emotion, which have been the focus of some feminist works (1998: 23–4, n. 11), although she has become interested in cognitive emotion, such as 'care-knowing' (2004). She draws on the poststructuralist influence of the francophone 'feminists' in order to accommodate difference whilst remaining committed to epistemology, and to realism, despite these poststructuralists being prima facie anti-epistemological in regarding rationality as inherently male. She allies them with FSE insofar as both reflect Kant's insight on the limits of our reason, and understand these limits in a Hegelian sense as imposed by our historical situatedness.

Through the work of Kristeva and Irigaray, she seeks to recover sexually specific discourse: following Kristeva in pointing out the debt that patriarchy owes to femininity; and drawing on Irigaray's mimetic recollection of ancient patriarchal-matriarchal battles which resulted in the exclusion of women from the divine. The idea of divine women allows women to become subjects (1998: 116–17), displacing the dominant male-neutral disembodied subject who constructs the male-neutral disembodied God. Anderson replaces the formal reasoning of the disembodied subject with 'substantive' reasoning which, feminists insist, must include the specificity of embodied life (1998: 213). Substantive reasoning embraces desire as the passionate yearning for justice and freedom. Yearning is a rational passion, such as the desire for social change, which is linked to embodied experiences. So it makes sense of the pursuit of Enlightenment goals of practical reason whilst being true to specificity (1998: 174). This notion of yearning, informed by bell hooks' African-American perspective and Hindu women's *bhakti* (cf. Dalamiya 2004), unites desire and reason, spiritual goals and the struggle for justice.

Jantzen's psychoanalytic and pragmatic focus

Jantzen rejects FSE's quest for fuller knowledge. She finds the quest for knowledge oppressive because wherever 'norms' are established, all sorts of people and experiences are rendered 'abnormal.' Jantzen believes that philosophy of religion, as practiced in Britain and North America, has itself set norms and disregarded other ways of thinking (1998: 18–26). In particular, it manifests an obsession with a type of perfection that involves bodily transcendence. Jantzen finds debates over the impassibility, self-sufficiency, and perfection of God a distraction from more important questions about the kind of resources religion can provide for our transformation. Jantzen's proposal, most fully stated in *Becoming Divine*, is that feminist philosophy of religion is radically discontinuous with a masculinist tradition.

Jantzen nowhere strictly defines 'masculinism,' but her critique of it is at least six-fold. First, it is a critique of the binary oppositions operative in the entire western symbolic, including the modernist binary between theism and atheism which has philosophers of religion transfixed (1998: 64–8, 97, 128, 266–7). These oppositions determine the issues and shape of philosophical debate, and result in repression of one half of the binary: for example, belief is debated and configured in opposition to desire, and desire is repressed (1998: 86). Similarly, obsession with immortality opposes and represses birth, embodiment, nature, woman (1998: 131).

Second, the obsession with immortality affects the construction of rationality, and of rational agents as unaffected by personal history, psychoanalytic forces, or socioeconomic context. For example, debates about free will typically overlook psychological and social factors that shape people's wills and affect the extent of their choice. In tandem, the divine subject is idealized as totally disconnected, unaffected, and all-seeing, as in Richard Swinburne's thought experiment about what it must be like to be an omnipresent spirit (Swinburne 1977: 104–5; Jantzen 1998: 28–9, 36–7). Jantzen's key question is whether women can become divine, given that God is modelled on the male, rational subject. If, as she proposes, becoming divine means becoming fully human – rather than becoming limitless or infinite – our primary task is to 'develop our own identities' (1998: 26), which are bounded by birth and eradicate the valorization of infinity.

Mortality is a third aspect of masculinism; the preoccupation with death and the consequent development of theologies built around salvation. Jantzen deconstructs the 'text' of death (i.e., the western philosophical and theological tradition), by showing it to be built on an unacknowledged foundation of birth (1998: 135). Religion, Jantzen argues, should not be about our being rescued from death but about our birth and coming to fruition. Philosophy of religion ought to be adequate to these life-enhancing projects. To this end she builds on the work of Hannah Arendt in giving full theoretical seriousness to the fact of our natality, rather than to the fact that we will die. (She edited an issue of *The Scottish Journal of Religious Studies* 19/1 (1998), entitled *Beginning with Birth*, in order to explore this possibility.) She refers to human beings as 'natals' rather than 'mortals,' and works to reconfigure and reclaim desire in terms of plenitude and creativity. She draws on the spiritual *Showings* of Julian of Norwich to reveal desire that is not premised in lack but in God's desire for her. God's love and grace are overflowing, and the divine desire finds its mimesis in Julian's desire for God (2002).

Ironically, she operates with a strong binary of life and death, despite her critique of binary oppositions. Beverley Clack (2002) argues that Jantzen's focus on natality is itself repressive, in denying painful and mortal aspects of human reality. Coakley (2002: 156) asks whether the postmodern intellectual obsession with the body is an evasive ploy, 'fuelling, as well as feeding off, more "popular" manifestations of death-denial, and screening us from political and social horrors that we otherwise cannot face?' Jantzen argues that she is not creating a binary of mortality/natality, but is recovering a repressed natality through the practice of double-reading, or deconstruction, and that thereby an obsession with mortality comes to light (2000).

Preoccupation with justifying beliefs is a fourth aspect of masculinism. Jantzen believes that a focus on the rationality of beliefs distorts the activity of religious believing, and fails to comprehend that practical and moral struggles necessarily take precedence for most people. She contends that philosophy of religion ought to be about our becoming little 'godlings.' She calls her book, *Becoming Divine*, instead of something like 'The Being of God,' which would invite us to focus, as philosophers of religion usually do, on the existence and nature of God (1998: 257–8). She expresses our becoming divine by the term 'flourishing,' rather than by such traditional theological terms as 'rebirth,' 'regeneration,' and 'salvation,' which suggest to her a masculinist appropriation of birth (the need to be born again, of spirit not of flesh) (1998: 141–3).

Her positive assessment of a Feuerbachian projection theory is crucial for understanding these first four elements of her critique: human characteristics are projected on to the divine because human beings wish to become divine (1998: 88–95). She disregards Feuerbach's understanding that the desire that motivates projection also insists on the ontological independence of that which is projected (cf. Hollywood 2004: 228). She believes that a projection theory of religion moves us away from questions of realism and non-realism, and invites us to ask questions about adequacy instead: 'Are the characteristics thus projected really the ones that will best facilitate human becoming? ... Or are they partial, distorting, or inimical to the flourishing of some groups of people?' (Jantzen 1998: 89).

Thus she attacks the prioritizing of ontology and epistemology in the philosophy of religion. For example, she takes up process theology's notion of a changing, suffering God, whilst criticizing process theologians for expressing this ontologically: 'For all that process thinkers talk of Becoming rather than Being, God in their writings is still an entity ... ; and it is this onto-theological reality on which process theologians are focused' (1998: 257). Jantzen argues that 'such onto-theology prior to an ethics in the face of the other constitutes "religion adrift"' (ibid.). She follows Emmanuel Levinas, who describes relationship with the other as attentiveness to particularity. Identifying the other as a being who is a member of a universal is a gesture of violence. It subsumes the individual under an ontological category, and is blasphemous in the case of God (1998: 235–6, 250).

The desire for determinative meaning is a fifth masculinist trait, and therefore Jantzen favors metaphorical over analogical attempts to speak of the divine. Analogies, which invite us to measure the extent of their adequacy, are used by modern philosophers of religion not to open up the divine horizon but to tie down meaning (1998: 178–9). So she explores the power of metaphors to work in ways that are more than intellectual, that are psychological and cultural, striking at the level of the symbolic (1998: 174–93).

Finally, Jantzen's critique of masculinism is a critique of phallocentrism, following, but also subverting, Lacan. Lacan holds the phallus to be the universal signifier and hence claims that language is masculine. His focus on the phallus as the designator of desire (rather than, say, breasts) seems to him to supply evidence that women do not have a language. To Irigaray and Jantzen, Lacan's theory is itself suggestive of male usurpation: it is not that women aren't talking, but that men aren't listening (1998: 51–3). Hence, Jantzen takes issue with Kristeva's adoption of a Lacanian perspective, wherein Kristeva argues that by entering into the linguistic realm a child's primal 'feminine' creativity is repressed.

Jantzen's critique is a multifaceted assault on the intended and supposed neutrality of the philosophy of religion as practiced by British and North American analytical philosophers. The various strands come together, for example, in a strong critique of theodicy (1998: 259–64): as preoccupied with solving an intellectual problem, as working with a western, masculinist concept of God, as failing to ask who is suffering and who is making progress, as paying insufficient attention to human agency, and as manifesting a necrophiliac concern with the transcendent realm.

Jantzen acknowledges that she does not address any of the usual topics in a philosophy of religion syllabus. Her principle aim is to recover the symbolically feminine. This means that not everyone will recognize her project as philosophy, but will instead see it as, perhaps a psychoanalytical, surrogate for philosophy (cf. Almond 1992; Fricker and Hornsby 2000: 3).

Embodiment and the ideal agent

The image of the soul ascending toward God leaving behind all that is earthly and bodily looms large in the Christian cultural psyche. As Martha Nussbaum writes: 'The very metaphor of ascent suggests to us that there is something low about where we usually live and are' (2001: 681). One might imagine that since Christianity is the religion of the Incarnation, of God becoming enfleshed, locating the divine amongst our bodily selves ought to be straightforward. Yet the Christian tradition has created ambivalence about the flesh, even while celebrating the sanctification of base, material elements. Nussbaum traces numerous accounts from western philosophers, novelists, poets, and composers all of which 'wish to rise above … the everyday functions of life and everyday objects, from mud hair and dirt, as the Platonist would say.' This means, Nussbaum goes on to say, that:

> despite a general agreement in the Christian and post-Christian accounts that a truly adequate love will embrace the flaws and imperfections of a human being as well as the goodness – all of these ascents in a real sense repudiate us. Nobody has a menstrual period in Plato. Nobody excretes in Spinoza. Nobody masturbates in Proust. … Augustine and Dante record such moments, but leave them behind in hell. (2001: 681)

Such a heritage leads to skepticism about resources in religion, and specifically within Christianity, that can be put to transformative, liberative purposes. For example, Catherine Clément asks Julia Kristeva (2001: 88) whether waste, with its feminine and bodily associations, finds a place within the divine universe of the western world, given Christianity's preoccupation with healing the unclean. The post-Christian, philosophical theologian Daphne Hampson sees the very idea of Incarnation as yet another spirit-flesh or Word–flesh binary that implies the lower status of material creation (2002: 95). Sarah Coakley finds a 'dearth of literature in analytical philosophy of religion on the concept of 'self' in *all* its dimensions' (2002: 99, original emphasis), finding instead a focus on the mind–body problem, which can exacerbate the very problem of abstracted selves.

What happens to embodiment when philosophers practise abstraction as part of their discipline? A central issue in feminist philosophy of religion is that of the 'God's-eye point of view' (Soskice 1992; Anderson 1998; 2004; 2005; Jantzen 1998; Harris 2004a). The key question here is whether the notion of a God's-eye view, even in its most sophisticated and percipient forms, such as Charles Taliaferro's Ideal Observer (IO) theory (1998; 2005), is pedalling an unhelpful abstraction. If God provides the model of ideal observation, as is Taliaferro's proposal (1998: 206), does this imply disembodiment as an aspect of ideal observation, and if so can this aid us, as embodied, contextualized beings, in providing a model for thought or moral judgment?

IO theory finds a ready home in philosophy of religion because it has so much in common with, indeed a heritage in, classical conceptions of God, as all-seeing, all-knowing, disembodied, immutable, impassible, and impartial: 'a theistic view of God,' Taliaferro writes, 'would more accurately be described as the portrait of what is believed to be an ideal agent' (Taliaferro 1998: 210). But IO theory is vulnerable to the point made by feminist empiricist Lorraine Code, that 'only people with the resources and power to believe that they can transcend and control their circumstances would see the detachment that the ideal demands as even a theoretical option' (Code 1992: 141). If all inquiry comes out of, and is intricately bound up with, human purposes, then these purposes have to be evaluated. Can the necessary evaluative task be written into an IO theory?

Janet Martin Soskice attributes the omni-everything conception of God to one, albeit dominant, strand of Christian tradition that has sought to disengage the self from the disenchanted universe. In a well-known essay called 'Love and attention,' she pitches this construct against other strands of Christian tradition that call us to attentiveness to the physical needs of those around us. The strands of tradition upon which she draws configure God as one who directs 'a just and loving gaze ... upon an individual reality' (1992: 200). This has been a seminal essay undergirding feminist and other attempts to modify constructions of God and rationality. It has influenced both Taliaferro's highly developed IO theory and Anderson's ongoing critique of that theory.

Taliaferro builds into his account of the God's-eye point of view a significant affective element, so that he is not presenting a God who is detached and aloof, but one who is affectively apprised of the position and feelings of all involved parties. The moral agent must attempt, like God, to know what it is like to be the agents, victims, and bystanders in any given situation. He thereby acknowledges a key concern that Anderson raises: that subjects operate with biases by which they 'claim knowledge of the world as it is while excluding from that world the lives of women, of nondominant races, or nonprivileged classes' (Anderson 1998: 73). Against Anderson, Taliaferro (2005) defends the claim that there are such things as facts, and not only points of view. He presents his ethic as a view from everywhere rather than an attempted ahistorical and impersonal view from nowhere. He promotes impartiality as able to involve passion and desire, and he denies that impartiality is always unattainable. Even where it is unattainable, he insists that it functions constructively as a regulating ideal, not unlike the way that strong objectivity functions as a regulating ideal in Anderson's work. He proposes that shedding your own point of view, or rather, discovering your authentic point of view through having grappled with the points of view of others, is not a threat to moral integrity but rather part and parcel of moral development.

He is most in tune with Soskice's ideal of total attentiveness when he draws on a meditation on the gaze of God by the fifteenth-century German philosopher and cardinal, Nicholas of Cusa (Taliaferro 2005). Nicholas understands God's Absolute Sight as embracing all modes of seeing. Rather than overriding our subjectivity, the loving gaze of God apprehends our lives within God's broader vision. Moreover, God's apprehension enables us to transcend our limitations and become our authentic selves.

Anderson (2005) engages with Taliaferro's Cusanian version of IO theory. She likes the Cusanian image of the loving embrace, and argues that we should use Cusa's insights to replace IO theories with a theory of ideal discourse. She argues that the desire to know all relevant facts whilst also remaining impartial implies a fact–value distinction that Taliaferro himself wishes to override. If one must know all relevant facts, one must also know social and personal 'facts,' which are less stable than empirical or natural facts. Knowledge of social and personal facts involves inside awareness of how context and status affect interpretation. Such knowledge would help toward omnipercipience but would threaten one's impartiality. Taliaferro believes, and Anderson denies, that impartiality can be made compatible with personal values and affections. How, Anderson asks, could an impartial assessment resolve differences between two people with conflicting, deeply held religious beliefs?

Anderson argues that an ideal observer theory, even as modified by Taliaferro, is inadequate for resolving moral disputes. She holds that two parties (such as a husband and wife talking through the wife's extramarital affair, or two women disagreeing about the ethics of abortion) might really share all nonmoral facts, and sympathetically understand each other's feelings, values and attitudes, and seek to be impartial, and yet still disagree. Taliaferro insists that such disagreement could be explained within the terms of his theory: perhaps both sides are right, each picking out good or bad aspects of the situation; perhaps the matter over which judgment is to be reached is morally neutral; or perhaps the parties are in fact clouded in their judgment without realizing it. Anderson says that the two parties might not agree even over what constitutes genuine understanding. Moreover, the manner of discourse affects the degree to which others are understood. She is suggesting that the purposes of each party, the power dynamics with which they interact with one another, the ways in which each is used to acting or being acted upon in the world, and numerous other subtle and difficult to categorize factors affect our judgments not only about whether something is good or reasonable, but what counts as good or reasonable. She suspects that these various factors are likely to be screened out or smoothed over in any theory that promotes an all-knowing and impartial ideal.

Anderson proposes instead a model of collective discourse, in which the fact of people's different points of view is taken on board in the need to arrive at a collective stage of decision-making. Here, agents are partial but may also be aware of their partiality and limitations. Carefully thought-out, committed positions are recognized as rational and potentially insightful, rather than cast as lesser stages on the way to a transcendent ideal. The goal is to reach a moral outcome that each party agrees 'incorporates better than any other outcome what each regards as ethically significant' (2005: 92), rather than to achieve a comprehensive view from everywhere. Her case against Taliaferro turns largely on her finding inadequate his account of how partiality (such as attention to the personal and passionate) relates to impartiality.

Amy Hollywood raises the stakes still further. While not directly discussing IO theory, she presents an argument that fundamentally undermines its aspirations to impartial judgment. In discussing differences between feminists and non-feminist evangelical women, she argues:

> These differences are not simply the result of conflicting propositions about the world and women's place within it, but reflect deeply embodied dispositions, emotions, and beliefs. Appeals to reason will never be able fully to overcome the divide – a divide that tends toward an absolute refusal of debate. (Hollywood 2004: 237)

Hollywood's point is that we are all shaped by learned dispositions and beliefs that are grounded in emotions and desires, which are themselves shaped by cultural bodily practice, including gait, manners of sleeping and eating, clothes, birth, and nursery patterns (2004: 230). IO theory has grown up with the epistemological and political assumptions of liberalism, which 'refuse to recognise the embodied nature of the *habitus*' (p. 237).

Turning this dilemma into a strength, feminist philosophers of religion are promoting the question of how a deepening specificity is related to better or best judgment – in particular, how embodiment, which includes moral and spiritual formation, affects us as religious knowers. Ideal observation may not be a matter of being everywhere (or nowhere), but of being very much somewhere, shaped and developed by particular practices. This discussion is broader than a specifically feminist epistemological debate, and concerns the strengths and weaknesses of a virtue-style religious epistemology that incorporates spiritual, alongside moral and intellectual, virtues (see Harris 2004a; 2004b; 2005; Coakley 2005).

See also Christianity (Chapter 6), Omniscience (Chapter 24), Omnipresence (Chapter 26), Problems with the concept of God (Chapter 38), The problem of religious language (Chapter 39), The sociobiological account of religious belief (Chapter 42), Postmodern theology (Chapter 47), Theology and religious language (Chapter 48), Prayer (Chapter 57), Continental philosophy (Chapter 60), Religious experience (Chapter 63).

References

Almond, B. (1992) 'Philosophy and the cult of irrationalism,' in A. P. Griffiths (ed.) *The Impulse to Philosophise*, Oxford: Oxford University Press.

Anderson, P. S. (1998) *A Feminist Philosophy of Religion: The Rationality and Myths of Religious Belief*, Oxford: Blackwell.

—— (2001) 'Standpoint: its proper place in a realist epistemology,' *Journal of Philosophical Research*: 131–53.

—— (2004) 'An epistemological-ethical approach to philosophy of religion: learning to listen,' in P. S. Anderson and B. Clack (eds) *Feminist Philosophy of Religion: Critical Readings*, London: Routledge.

—— (2005) 'What's wrong with the God's eye point of view? A constructive feminist critique of the Ideal Observer theory,' in H. A. Harris and C. J. Insole (eds) *Faith and Philosophical Analysis: The Impact of Analytical Philosophy on Philosophy of Religion*, Aldershot: Ashgate.

Asad, T. (1993) *Genealogies of Religion: Disciplines and Reasons of Power in Christianity and Islam*, Baltimore, MD: Johns Hopkins University Press.

Clack, B. (2002) 'Embodiment and feminist philosophy of religion,' *Women's Philosophy Review* 29: 46–63.

Clément, C. and J. Kristeva (2001) *The Feminine and the Sacred*, trans. J. M. Todd, Basingstoke: Palgrave.

Coakley, S. (2002) *Powers and Submissions: Spirituality, Philosophy and Gender*, Oxford: Blackwell.

—(2005) 'Feminism and analytical philosophy of religion,' in W. J. Wainwright (ed.) *The Oxford Handbook of Philosophy of Religion*, Oxford: Oxford University Press.

Code, L. (1992) 'Feminist epistemology,' in J. Dancy and E. Sosa (eds) *A Companion to Epistemology*, Oxford: Blackwell.

Dalamiya, V. (2004) 'Loving paradoxes: a feminist reclamation of the Goddess Kali,' in P. S. Anderson and B. Clack (eds) *Feminist Philosophy of Religion: Critical Readings*, London: Routledge.

Fricker, M. and J. Hornsby (eds) (2000) 'Introduction,' in *The Cambridge Companion to Feminism in Philosophy*, Cambridge: Cambridge University Press.

Hampson, D. (2002) 'Review of Susan Parson's *The Ethics of Gender*,' *Women's Philosophy Review* 29: 92–6.

Harris, H. A. (2004a) 'On understanding that the struggle for truth is moral and spiritual,' in U. M. King and T. Beattie (eds) *Gender, Religion and Diversity: Cross-Cultural Perspectives*, London: Continuum.

—— (2004b) 'Struggling for truth,' in P. S. Anderson and B. Clack (eds) *Feminist Philosophy of Religion: Critical Readings*, London: Routledge.

—— (2005) 'Is analytical philosophy clipping our wings? Reformed epistemology as a test-case,' in H. A. Harris and C. J. Insole (eds) *Faith and Philosophical Analysis: The Impact of Analytical Philosophy on Philosophy of Religion*, Aldershot: Ashgate.

Hollywood, A. (2004) 'Practice, belief and feminist philosophy of religion,' in P. S. Anderson and B. Clack (eds) *Feminist Philosophy of Religion: Critical Readings*, London: Routledge.

Hypatia 9 (1994) ed. N. Frankenberry and M. Thei.

Jantzen, G. M. (1998) *Becoming Divine: Towards a Feminist Philosophy of Religion*, Manchester: Manchester University Press.

—— (2000) 'Response to Harriet Harris,' *Feminist Theology* 23: 119–20.

—— (2002) 'A Reconfiguration of Desire: Reading Medieval Mystics in Postmodernity,' *Women's Philosophy Review* 29: 23–45.

Joy, M., K. O'Grady and J. L. Poxon (eds) (2002) *French Feminists on Religion: A Reader*, London: Routledge.

Le Doeuff, M. (1989) 'Long hair, short ideas,' in *The Philosophical Imaginary*, trans. C. Gordon, London: Athlone. Repri, 2002, London: Continuum.

McGhee, M. (ed.) (1992) *Philosophy of Religion and Spiritual Life*, Cambridge: Cambridge University Press.

—— (2000) *Transformations of Mind: Philosophy as Spiritual Practice*, Cambridge: Cambridge University Press.

Nussbaum, M. C. (2001) *Upheavals of Thought: The Intelligence of Emotions*, Cambridge: Cambridge University Press.

Soskice, J. M. (1992) 'Love and attention,' in M. McGhee (ed.) *Philosophy of Religion and Spiritual Life*, Cambridge: Cambridge University Press. Repr. in P. S. Anderson and B. Clack (2004) *Feminist Philosophy of Religion: Critical Readings*, London: Routledge.

Swinburne, R. (1977) *The Coherence of Theism*, Oxford: Clarendon Press.

Taliaferro, C. (1998) *Contemporary Philosophy of Religion*, Oxford: Blackwell.

—— (2005) 'The God's eye point of view: a divine ethic,' in H. A. Harris and C. J. Insole (eds) (2005) *Faith and Philosophical Analysis: The Impact of Analytical Philosophy on Philosophy of Religion*, Aldershot: Ashgate.

Wynn, M. (2002) 'Valuing the world: the emotions as data for the philosophy of religion,' *International Journal for Philosophy of Religion* 52: 97–113.

—— (2003) 'Saintliness and the moral life: Gaita as a source for Christian ethics,' *Journal of Religious Ethics* 31/3: 463–86.

Further reading

Anderson, P. S. (1998) *A Feminist Philosophy of Religion: The Rationality and Myths of Religious Belief*, Oxford: Blackwell. (The first monograph to be published in feminist philosophy of religion.)

Anderson, P. S. and B. Clack (2004) *Feminist Philosophy of Religion: Critical Readings*, London: Routledge. (A selection of critical readings.)

Jantzen, G. M. (1998) *Becoming Divine: Towards a Feminist Philosophy of Religion*, Manchester: Manchester University Press. (Attacks 'masculinist' features of Anglo-American philosophy of religion, and seeks to recover emphases upon natality and life that the author believes have been repressed in the western philosophical tradition.)

60

CONTINENTAL PHILOSOPHY

Jean-Yves Lacoste

From the end of the Enlightenment to the First World War

Modern Continental philosophy of religions began very obviously in 1799, when F. D. E. Schleiermacher (1768–1834) published his *Speeches on Religion*. The work aimed at putting an end to Enlightened skepticism toward 'religion' – not Christianity – and therefore provides the (cultured) reader with an apologetic of religious *feeling* with slight pantheistic overtones. When man does not feel the world religiously, his perception of reality is mutilated. All sense of infinity disappears. The cultural context of the *Speeches* is clear: they are written in the age of Schiller and Goethe. The theological context, however, is not that clear. Though one must not forget that Schleiermacher, then a young parson in Berlin, was preaching the Christian gospel in church at the time he was writing the *Speeches*, they are a plea for 'religion' and for no definite religion. One must add, though, that Schleiermacher envisages a very specific religion: a pietistic religion with a God (or an Absolute) the heart can feel.

The same feature is to be found in Schleiermacher's *magnum opus*, his *Christian Faith*. Here again, feeling is the arch-concept. Man's relation to God is lived in a 'feeling of absolute dependence,' and the content of Christian theology is interpreted according to this feeling – with the awkward consequence that a doctrine which cannot be felt (e.g., the doctrine of the Trinity) will only find its niche in the book's appendix. The anthropological reduction is clear. The concept of 'feeling of absolute dependence' is not derived from the specificity of Christian experience (even if it may mean 'knowing oneself as a creature'). Therefore, a philosophical a priori governs Schleiermacher's dogmatics.

Because of his cultural and anthropocentric emphasis, the nineteenth century was to become Schleiermacher's century. Opposition came very soon nonetheless. It came first from within German idealism. J. G. Fichte (1762–1814), who had published *An Attempt at a Critique of All Revelation* in 1792, where revelation, in Kantian fashion, is restricted to its moral content, would later state that 'the metaphysical only, and not the historical, gives beatitude.' G. W. F. Hegel's (1770–1831) contribution is of paramount importance. Hegel's philosophy of religion is a history of the development of religion from its elementary form to the 'consummate religion', namely, Christianity. Christianity is a religion. But as a religion it is also the unsurpassable religion, the religion in which the Absolute is 'manifest' (*offenbar*). There is more, though. For if Hegel's philosophy of religion ends with the absolute religion, his philosophy doesn't. Religious knowledge is not the last knowledge. And when consciousness has grasped absolute religion, it has still to reach 'absolute knowledge,' that is, a speculative knowledge where the content of religion becomes conceptually translucent. Absolute knowledge is knowledge of the Christian God and no other. (Also, neither absolute religion nor absolute knowledge is a matter of 'feeling.') However, this is theology and not faith, and faith must find its fulfillment in theology.

A former friend of Hegel's, F. W. J. Schelling (1775–1854) opposed in his late philosophy the absorption of 'absolute religion' into 'absolute knowledge.' Schelling's project, after repudiating his earlier so-called 'negative philosophy,' was to develop a 'positive philosophy.' In lectures given at Berlin, Schelling organized this positive philosophy as (a) a philosophy of mythology and (b) a philosophy of revelation (namely Christian revelation). We are dealing here with a speculative description and a teleology: 'mythology' has a philosophical truth of its own, but this truth culminates in Christianity. And as in Hegel, one point is clear: Schelling knows of no boundary between philosophy and theology and deals with theological material without the slightest concern for some 'supernatural' faith. The Christian God, as the mythological gods, stands at the philosopher's disposal.

S. A. Kierkegaard (1813–55) is known for his perpetual polemics against Hegel's 'system' and his frustration as a listener to Schelling's Berlin lectures. It is nonetheless a remarkable fact that he, too, knows of no boundary between philosophy and theology. His *Philosophical Fragments* is devoted to Christology and the theory of faith. His *Concept of Anxiety* deals with the concept of original sin. Here again, the Enlightenment is over, and theology is practiced out of theological ghettos. The originality of Kierkegaard's attempts lies in his almost total lack of interest for the 'content' of the Christian religious experience. Faith, as described in the *Fragments*, faces an 'absolute paradox' (the Incarnation), and the paradox is not to be known except through love ('one does not enter into truth, except through charity,' as Augustine put it). One turns therefore from the *what* of faith to its *how*. There is indeed a 'way' to religious life, insofar as Kierkegaard describes existence as being lived 'aesthetically,' 'ethically,' and 'religiously.' But no dialectic leads to religious life. Furthermore, Christianity is not the 'consummate religion': the Kierkegaardian contrast is between Socrates and Jesus – between Hellenism and Christology, between the presence of a master and the presence of a savior. It is also worth noting that the Kierkegaardian accentuation of the *how* and of decision (a 'leap into faith') allows him to bypass the problems of historical exegesis and of the 'historical Jesus.' Whatever scholarship can teach us, God incarnate will always be the 'absolute paradox,' which is not to be understood objectively before believing in him, but which is known through believing in him. Historical inquiry cannot prove either faith or the absence of it.

It is not surprising that the atheistic answer to a philosophy of religion which had turned into a philosophy of Christianity evoked during Kierkegaard's lifetime an attempted demolition of the Christian experience. L. Feuerbach (1804–72) published his *Essence of Christianity* in 1841. The thesis is clear-cut: the Christian God is a human artifact. No other God is known to Feuerbach, and his atheism is no anti-theism. Where does the secret of Christianity lie? In anthropology. Interpreting God's love is nothing else than interpreting human love and its ambitions. Interpreting Christ's passion is nothing else than interpreting the 'essence of the heart' and of human suffering (and Feuerbach brushes aside the metaphysical God, who is *actus purus* and not *passio pura*). 'The fundamental dogmas of Christianity are realized wishes of the heart.' More precisely, 'the essence of Christianity is the essence of the heart [*Gemüt*].' K. Barth would later remark that Feuerbach's attack is an attack on *religion* and not on the Christian *faith*. Feuerbach's God is undeniably not transcendent (not least because he does not exist): he is the hypostatized sum of human desires. This means that all knowledge becomes secondary.

We are back on classical ground with Karl Marx's (1818–83) critique of religion, which is by no means a critique of Christianity alone. Marx's dissertation was devoted to Greek materialism, his ambition was to develop a materialistic science of history and economy, and religion has no other function in his philosophy than the function of an alienating ideology. Through religion, alienated man does not become conscious of his alienation. Religion, therefore, in a wholly anti-Hegelian fashion, is not knowledge at all, and knowledge of the actual situation of man in history and economics can only be achieved by the materialistic knowledge that can prove how ideology distorts man's relationship to (material) reality. Thus, when the utopian classless society becomes reality, no room will be left for any religious ideology: in such a society, unprecedented production-relations will make materialism the only possible vision of being. E. Bloch (1885–1977) would later give a distinctly religious version of Marx's philosophy of the end of history: Marxism appears as the foundation of an eschatological hope and Marxist praxis as a secularized messianism.

Feuerbach's atheism was directed against the Christian God. So was F. Nietzsche's (1844–1900). As an exaltation of weakness and asceticism, Christianity, according to Nietzsche, is the way to nihilism (to the 'devaluation of the highest values'). Following the Crucified means taking leave of the world. It means refusing 'life' – that is, being-in-the-flesh and will. Platonism, in a way, had refused the world before Christianity did. But even if Christianity may be called 'a Platonism for the people,' Nietzsche's critique is much more anti-Christian than it is anti-Platonic. Nietzsche indeed provides us with an alternative religion of sorts. To the Christian focus on history as salvation-history, he opposes a conception of the 'eternal return of the same.' The 'eternal return' works as a substitute to the eschatological hope in a resurrection. The mythological figure of Dionysus is opposed to the historical figure of Jesus. The anti-messiah Zarathustra eclipses the ascetic priest. And the 'will to power' (i.e., the self-affirmation of life) provides man with a way to overcome Platonic-Christian nihilism. Nietzsche the atheist puts on the lips of a 'fool' the ominous words, 'God is dead.' His philosophy, nonetheless, shelters an alternative gospel. One must add that Nietzsche's 'religion' is a religion of art, where truth has lost all validity ('truth is ugly') and where values are always man-created values.

It has become a commonplace to associate Marx, Nietzsche, and S. Freud (1856–1939), and there is something correct in this association. Freud, though, is no critic of Christianity, and the 'cultural' texts he devotes to religion aim at reconstructing the origins of monotheism as well as at characterizing religion as a collective neurosis. Freud's originality is thus to use the tools of a therapeutic practice to interpret global cultural contexts. The interpretation itself does not hesitate to be mythological: one ought to locate the origin of religion in rites of expiation celebrated after the 'sons' of a primitive family/tribe have murdered their 'father' to have access to the women of the tribe. At any rate, the point at issue is clear. Philosophy of religion traditionally describes man as a 'religious animal.' But is this an essential determination? According to Freud, man becomes religious as a consequence of non-religious events. In its depth structures, his psyche does not oppose to the emergence of religious phenomena. But they are not innate. Religion, therefore, has to be deciphered, and the desires psychoanalysis will discover will not be religious: they will be sexual.

The twentieth century

Twentieth-century philosophy of religion began with two texts, one philosophical and one theological. In his philosophical book on the 'holy,' the neo-Kantian R. Otto (1869–1937) offered a rational approach to the irrational. The 'holy' is irrational, but we can experience it. Epistemology and description coincide in Otto. The 'holy' (or, as Otto coins it, 'the numinous') is conceptualized as a *mysterium tremendum et fascinosum* ('frightening and fascinating mystery'). This mystery is a mystery the disclosure of which fits with our abilities to know. It is also a faceless mystery, with no theistic overtones. Also, this being a mystery we are allowed to feel, Otto is in some way heir to the Schleiermacherian tradition.

Otto's book was published in 1917. The notable *theological* text by K. Barth (1886–1968), *To the Romans*, was published in 1919. These two works seem to have little in common. Unlike Otto, Barth writes from a strictly Christian point of view. Barth, nonetheless, is also concerned with the irrational (his God is the 'Wholly Other'), and his influence would go beyond the frontiers of Christianity. Neoplatonism already knew that the first principle was 'the other [*thateron*].' Augustine knew that God is 'definitely other [*valde aliud*].' Kierkegaard had spoken of an 'infinite qualitative difference' between God and man. Barth came to be the chief exponent of such a difference (i.e., of God's transcendence). As such, God is not known through any human ability to know. And as such, the only rationality he obeys is his. One must also notice that a few years before (1902), the bell had been tolling for the Hegelian interpretation of Christianity as the 'absolute religion' with the publication of E. Troeltsch's (1865–1923) *The Absoluteness of Christianity*. From the perspective of a history of cultures, Christianity is only God's revelation to the West. Therefore, no hierarchy of religions – no evolution of religions which would culminate in Christianity – is thinkable any more. The history of religions has no apologetic value or meaning.

Husserlian phenomenology was not interested in the phenomenon known as 'religion,' although Heidegger (1889–1976) did lecture in 1920–21 on Paul and Augustine. It belonged to the mature and late Heidegger to make decisive contributions. Under the influence of the corpus which he almost used as his Bible (i.e., Hölderlin's works), Heidegger, who had conceptualized in *Being and Time* a 'world' where nothing 'religious' was at home, discovered in the 1930s the existence of an 'earth' he can but describe with numinous accents. Later, the absence of God is compensated for by the proximity of 'divine beings,' and the description becomes one of a sort of pagan experience. This was a consequence of Heidegger's main concern since the late 1930s: to overcome 'metaphysics', namely, all philosophy since Socrates. Metaphysics has been oblivious to 'Being' and interested in 'beings' and their 'beingness.' This interest in beings has led metaphysicians to crown the hierarchy of beings with a supreme being, God (or the One). This supreme being, moreover, is no object of possible worship: one cannot kneel before the *causa sui*. Therefore, retrieving a sense of Being and retrieving a sense of religious behavior cannot be dissociated. If metaphysics is essentially 'onto-theological,' it follows that an onto-theological religious behavior rests on an equivocation. If theology is possible, Heidegger said once, the word 'Being' can have no place in it.

J.-L. Marion (b. 1946) followed vigorously in the footsteps of Heidegger when he argued that divine *agapē* is beyond Being and has no need to 'be', although Heidegger's 'divine entities' are undeniably beings. It was certainly not Heidegger's intention to work out a philosophy of religion. A major question arises nonetheless from his work: is religious life, or experience, concerned with beings? Theologians have tried to give an answer. According to P. Tillich (1886–1965), God is to be thought of as the 'ground of being,' while J. Macquarrie (b. 1919) speaks of 'being itself.' Aquinas had already done his best not to define God as a being: his God is not an *ens* ('being') but *ipsum esse subsistens* ('self-subsistent being'). Coming to terms with the Heideggerian critique of onto-theology has been a major task for philosophers and theologians for half a century.

Heidegger had readers with no posterity worth mentioning. However, original attempts were made in the phenomenological movement after the Heideggerian proposals. E. Levinas's (1906–95) phenomenology is meant to be strictly philosophical, despite all theological additions. Although the phenomena he describes (almost exclusively the encounter with Other Man) are not explicitly religious, his is nonetheless a remarkable contribution to the philosophy of religion. Intersubjectivity is precisely, in Levinas, the 'religious' event. The human face is to be taken as God's 'trace,' and there is no other. Intersubjectivity, therefore, is interpreted as a 'liturgy,' and again there is no other. The goal is to construct ethics as a first philosophy and not to give ethics the status of religious experience. In Levinas, religious experience, feeling, love of God, etc. – all these traditional items – never appear. Levinas's way is nonetheless an alternative philosophy of religion. One ought to add that Levinas claims to owe most of his thought to F. Rosenzweig (1886–1929), whose *Star of Redemption* is the most incisive critique of Hegel from a Jewish point of view. And *a contrario*, one must say that Levinas owes nothing to H. Cohen's (1842–1918) *Religion of Reason*, the first philosophy of religion ever written from such a point of view (but within a neo-Kantian frame of mind). Levinas had been a student of Husserl's. P. Ricoeur (1913–2005) would translate Husserl's *Ideas* into French, but he developed a thoroughly hermeneutical philosophy of religion.

Ricoeur's concerns were first with the interpretation of guilt. Then they were with the working out of a 'general hermeneutics' (i.e., a theory of all interpretation) as such. Within his general hermeneutics, there is room, though, for a 'special hermeneutics,' which is concerned about the interpretation of biblical texts. A few seminal essays propose a concept of the 'world of the text.' The classical text is a text we cannot dissociate from its 'world' (i.e., from the experience of the world it expresses), and this world is a world the reader can make his own. Ricoeur's concept of a 'world of the text' and Gadamer's concept of 'fusion of horizons' are probably the main theoretical tools of hermeneutics since the 1960s.

The biblical text, nonetheless, is not a case among others, and the general tendency of Ricoeurian hermeneutics is to privilege religious documents over all texts, and the biblical text over other religious documents. The ambition is not explicitly theological. Ricoeur's reading of guilt and original sin aims at being a philosophical understanding of a theological object. His theory of interpretation deals with predilection for religious texts and Christian religious texts in particular, but in keeping with philosophical standards, if any. Nothing is more foreign to hermeneutics than 'objective' treatment of texts. Ricoeurian hermeneutics does not fail to notice it: in dealing rationally with religious texts, involvement is a proof of rationality. And as Ricoeur spent a long part of his teaching life in Chicago, one will not be surprised to find in his late work traces of Anglo-Saxon influence. Ricoeur was teaching in the same faculty as D. Tracy (b. 1939) when Tracy wrote his *Analogical Imagination*. J. Greisch (b. 1942) has brilliantly systematized Ricoeur's philosophy of religion.

The merit of another French phenomenologist, M. Henry (1922–2002), has been to come to an original philosophy of religion on the basis of a philosophy of 'life' understood as radical immanence and self-affection. Anything 'religious' is absent in Henry's work, from his *Essence of Manifestation* to a book on the painter Kandinsky, the conclusion of which states that 'art is the resurrection of eternal life.' And if one turns to Henry's later writings, one does not meet with a philosophy of 'religion,' but with a philosophy of Christianity. 'Religion' again fails to acquire a precise status, and the philosopher finds his food in Christian doctrines. The theology of incarnation gives a deeper meaning to a phenomenology of the flesh. Divine pathos illuminates the phenomena of human affection. Indeed, no room is left for a general religious experience with Christian experience being a case of it. But one can easily suspect that Henry's conceptual dealings with 'life' or 'flesh' have a validity of their own outside the boundaries of a description of Christian doctrines. They provide us with a 'religious' interpretation of 'life' or 'flesh' – an interpretation, though, where the Christian experience acquires (again) the status of arch-experience: 'life' and 'flesh' disclose their full reality within such an experience.

No one would accuse J. Derrida (1930–2005) of having developed a keen interest in religious phenomena. His connection to phenomenology, on the other hand, is limited to his first (and perhaps best) book, *Voice and Phenomenon*. But the many obstacles he put in the way of any 'metaphysics' were also put in the way of theology and philosophy of religion, which evoked fruitful discussion. Derrida radicalized Heidegger's phenomenological 'destruction' of philosophical texts and turned it into a 'deconstruction,' the aim of which was to prove the absence of necessity and the pseudo-logics of what has been written. He refused the existence of any 'master-word' (Being, God). He argued that we deal perpetually with traces and not with presences (the text is the trace of his author), and that the chief sin of 'metaphysics' has been to focus on presence. And therefore, any idea of a unitary meaning vanishes: meaning is 'disseminated' in the endless plurality of readings.

Many responses have been offered. J.-L. Chrétien (b. 1952) rightly argues that no primacy of textuality can obfuscate situations where speech-acts cannot be understood as 'traces.' Derrida has challenged sacramental theology (in the Catholic world) to work out a post-metaphysical concept of sacramental presence. A seminal sketch by M. Constantini (b. 1949) suggests that 'the Bible is no text' and that it can only be understood in a dialogical way. Also, J.-L. Marion has shown that Derrida's attack on negative theology as thoroughly metaphysical was wrong and misleading.

One ought probably to add that the twentieth century has been a period when Freud's critique of religion and Christianity has been omnipresent. Though religion was not a major concern for him, he developed in two brilliant books (*The Future of an Illusion*; *Civilization and its Discontents*) an interpretation of religion as collective neurosis and proposed in *Moses and Monotheism* a bizarre genealogy of Judaism. Freud's demolition of religion has been in the background all the time, but one must not forget that psychoanalytic practice is not loaded by no prejudice against religion.

Research between the twentieth and twenty-first century

Dominating philosophies do not exist any more, but one must admit that phenomenology is still the leading influence in Continental philosophy of religion. The influence, once again, involves first of all a philosophy of Christianity. In Marion's early work, the conceptual 'idols' of metaphysics are demolished in such a fashion that the only room left is for the 'icon' – namely, for a Christological knowledge of God without any religious context.

There are other philosophical movements present as well. In Y. Labbé (b. 1943), from a Hegelian perspective, Christ's death and being-dead become again a matter of philosophical inquiry. From the same perspective, C. Bruaire's (1932–86) philosophy of the body tries to think a possible salvation for the body, and philosophical theology becomes definitely Trinitarian in his last texts. Phenomenology, eventually, is also omnipresent in J.-Y. Lacoste (b. 1953), who tries to develop a non-'religious' (i.e., anti-Schleiermacherian and anti-Jamesian) logic of 'liturgy' (not worship!) – that is, of what man does *coram Deo* (before the face of/ in the presence of God), as subverting the Heideggerian logic of being-in-the-world.

That being said, the work of Continental philosophy of religion is not being done by France alone! Among prominent non-French figures, one must pay attention to R. Schaeffler's (b. 1926) work. The author of a general theory of experience culminating in religious experience, Schaeffler has also tried to bypass the problem of 'philosophy of religion' and gives a 'philosophical introduction into theology.' 'Communication', J. Habermas' (b. 1929) chief concept, has also had a noteworthy reception in the philosophy of religion. For Habermas, religions are communal institutions. And J. Taubes's (1923–87) little-known influence has contributed to the bridging of many gaps, for example, between political theology and the philosophy of religion, between hermeneutics and eschatological concerns. H. G. Gadamer's (1900–2002) hermeneutics has also provided theologians with new opportunities to update their concept of tradition.

We can sum up the leading themes of two centuries of continental philosophy. (1) With a few exceptions, the concept of 'religion' has become problematic and so has become the project of a philosophy of religion. (2) The opposition between the 'God of Abraham, Isaac and Jacob' and the 'God of the philosophers and scholars' (Pascal), again with a few exceptions, has become obsolete. (3) Also with a few exceptions, philosophy of religion and history of religions keep being neatly separated. (4) Finally, no philosophy of religions has progressed much beyond the bare fact that there are religions and that religion is an abstraction. Despite this summary, however, we must remember that (Continental) philosophy is still developing.

See also Christianity (Chapter 6), Augustine (Chapter 8), Thomas Aquinas (Chapter 12), Immanuel Kant (Chapter 14), Søren Kierkegaard (Chapter 15), Friedrich Nietzsche (Chapter 16), Problems with the concept of God (Chapter 38), Postmodern theology (Chapter 47), Phenomenology of religion (Chapter 61).

References

Barth, K. (1933) *The Epistle to the Romans*, London: Oxford University Press.
Bloch, E. (1985) *Werkausgabe: Das Prinzip Hoffnung*, vol. 5, Frankfurt-Suhrkamp.
Bruaire, C. (1968) *Philosophie du corps*, Paris: Seuil.
Chrétien, J.-L. (1990), *La voix nue: Phénoménologie de la promesse*, Paris: Minuit.
Cohen, H. (1972) *Religion of Reason out of the Sources of Judaism*, New York: Unger.
Costantini, M. (1976), 'La Bible n'est pas un texte,' *Communio* (Fr) 1/7: 40–54.
Derrida, J. (1967) *La voix et le phénomène*, Paris: Presses Universitaires de France.
Feuerbach, L. (1957) *The Essence of Christianity*, New York: Harper.
Fichte, J. G. (1978) *An Attempt at a Critique of All Revelation*, Cambridge: Cambridge University Press.
Freud, S. (1928) *The Future of an Illusion*, London: Hogarth Press.
—— (1930) *Civilization and its Discontents*, London: Hogarth Press.
—— (1939) *Moses and Monotheism*, London: Hogarth Press.
Greisch, J. (2004) *Le buisson ardent et les lumières de la raison*. In *L'invention de la philosophie de la religion*, vol. 3: *Vers un paradigme herméneutique*, Paris: Cerf.
Gadamer, H.-G. (1994) *Truth and Method*, New York: Continuum
Habermas, J. (1998) *On the Pragmatics of Communication*, ed. M. Cooke, Cambridge, MA: MIT Press.
Hegel, G. W. F. (1984–7) *Lectures on the Philosophy of Religion*, 3 vols, Berkeley, CA: University of California Press.

Heidegger, M. (1974) *Identity and Difference*, New York: Harper & Row.
—— (1977) *The Question Concerning Technology, and Other Essays*, New York: Harper & Row.
—— (1996) *Being and Time*, Albany, NY: State University of New York Press.
Henry, M. (2000) *Incarnation: une philosophie de la chair*, Paris: Seuil.
—— (2003) *I Am the Truth: Toward a Philosophy of Christianity*, Stanford, CA: Stanford University Press.
Kierkegaard, S. (1980) *The Concept of Anxiety*, trans. R. Thomte, Princeton, NJ: Princeton University Press.
—— (1985) *Philosophical Fragments; Johannes Climacus*, trans. H. and E. Hong, Princeton, NJ: Princeton University Press.
Labbé, Y. (1980) *Le sens et le mal*, Paris: Bibliothèque des Archives de Philosophie.
Lacoste, J.-Y. (2004) *Experience and the Absolute*, Bronx, NY: Fordham University Press.
Levinas, E. (1969) *Totality and Infinity: An Essay on Exteriority*, Pittsburgh: Duquesne University Press.
Macquarrie, J. (1967) *Principles of Christian Theology*, London: SCM Press. Rev. edn 1977.
Marion, J.-L. (1991) *God without Being*, Chicago: University of Chicago Press.
—— (2001) *The Idol and Distance*, Bronx, NY: Fordham University Press.
Marx, K. (1983) *The Portable Karl Marx*, ed. E. Kamenka, New York: Penguin Books.
Nietzsche F. (1995) *Philosophical Writings*, German Library 48, New York: Continuum.
Otto, R. (1950) *The Idea of the Holy*, New York: Oxford University Press.
Ricoeur, P. (1981) *Essays on Biblical Interpretation*, London: SPCK.
Rosenzweig, F. (1971) *The Star of Redemption*, London: Routledge & Kegan Paul.
Schaeffler, R. (1995) *Erfahrung als Dialog mit der Wirklichkeit*, Friburg and Munich: Alber.
Schelling, F. W. J. (1983 [1858]) *Philosophie der Offenbarung*, 2 vols, Darmstadt: Wissenschaftliche Buchgesellschaft.
Schleiermacher, F. D. E. (1965) *On Religion: Speeches to its Cultured Despisers*, New York: Harper.
—— (1999) *The Christian Faith*, Edinburgh: T. & T. Clark.
Taubes, J. (1996) *Vom Kult zur Kultur*, Munich-Paderborn: Wilhelm Fink.
Tillich, P. (1951) *Systematic Theology*, vol. 1, Chicago: University of Chicago Press.
Tracy, D. (1981) *The Analogical Imagination. Christian Theology and the Culture of Pluralism*, London: SCM Press.
Troeltsch, E. (1972) *The Absoluteness of Christianity and the History of Religions*, London: SCM Press.

Further reading

Bello, A. A. (1985) *Husserl, Sul problema di Dio*, Rome: Edizione Studium. (The only available book on Husserl and God, it includes the majority of Husserl's texts on the problem.)
Buckley, M. (1987) *At the Origins of Modern Atheism*, New Haven, CT: Yale University Press. (Modern atheism is mostly Continental.)
Caputo, J. (1990) [1978] *The Mystical Element in Heidegger's Thought*, reprinted with corrections, New York: Fordham University Press. (Necessary to anyone interested in the influence of Heidegger on the philosophy of religion.)
Colpe, C. (ed.) (1977) *Die Diskussion um das 'Heilige,'* Darmstadt: Wissenschaftliche Buchgesellschaft. (Important texts by Windelband, Wundt, Söderblom, Cold, Caillois, etc.)
Franck, D. (1998) *Nietzsche et l'ombre de Dieu*, Paris: Presses Universitaires de France. (The best available essay on Nietzsche's atheism.)
Jaeschke, W. (ed.) (1994) *Der Streit um die göttlichen Dinge (1799–1812)*, Hamburg: Meiner. (Important texts by Goethe, Hegel, Jacobi, Novalis, Schlegel, with an excellent commentary.)
Lash, N. (1981) *A Matter of Hope: A Theologian's Reflections on the Thought of Karl Marx*, London: Longman & Todd. (The best book on Marx from a theological point of view.)
Lochman, J. M. (1977) *Encountering Marx*, Philadelphia: Fortress Press. (Probably the best introduction to Marx.)
Lübbe, H. (1986) *Religion nach der Aufklärung*, Graz: Styria. (An innovative book on the room left to religion by the Enlightenment.)

Mattei, J.-F. (ed.) (1992) *Les œuvres philosophiques*, 2 vols, Paris: Presses Universitaires de France. (Useful entries and bibliographies on all authors quoted in the chapter.)

Oelmüller, W. (ed.) (1984–1986) *Religion und Philosophie*, 3 vols, Paderborn: Schöningh. (Interested in more than *Continental* philosophy of religion, but always useful on the topic.)

Splett. J. (1971) *Die Rede vom Heiligen*, Freiburg: Alber. (Still the standard work on the 'holy.')

61

PHENOMENOLOGY OF RELIGION

Merold Westphal

The basic idea of phenomenology

Heidegger says that phenomenology means 'to let that which shows itself be seen from itself in the very way in which it shows itself from itself' (Heidegger 1962: 58). For Merleau-Ponty it means 'relearning to look at the world' (Merleau-Ponty 1962: xx). It is thus better conceived as a virtue akin to attentiveness and openness than as a method. This means that in its broadest sense the phenomenology of religion is a descriptive approach to the philosophy of religion. It assumes that religion is a phenomenon, that it shows itself and can be observed; but rather than try to *evaluate* or *explain* religious beliefs and practices, it seeks to *describe* them carefully so as to help us see them clearly, however we may subsequently seek to evaluate or explain them.

This means that any descriptive approach can be called phenomenological, including the work of scholars such as Eliade (1958; 1959), James (1958), Malinowski (1954), Otto (1958), and Van der Leeuw (1963) along with others whose work is also called the history, sociology, or psychology of religion, comparative religion, and ethnography or cultural anthropology.

A somewhat more restricted sense of phenomenology of religion refers to work done by philosophers working in the tradition whose founding father is Edmund Husserl (see Husserl 1970; 1982). The central idea for Husserlian phenomenology is intentionality. All consciousness is *consciousness of* … . This relation of consciousness to its object or content is taken to define the realm of the mind and to be a unique, non-causal, non-spatial relation. Two further specifications of this notion are important here. First there is the correlation between the intentional act (*noesis*) and the intentional object (*noema*). The 'what' or content of consciousness can only be given in conformity with the 'how' or mode of awareness; in other words, nothing can be *given* to me apart from the way in which I *take* it. This means that phenomenological description can focus either upon the intentional act or, more concretely, the horizon, life-world, or the language-game of the believing soul from which the intentional act emerges; or it can focus on the intentional 'object': God, the gods, the Sacred, or the Holy.

Second, since we can intend or think about objects such as Santa Claus or the unicorn that we do not take to be real, phenomenology brackets or sets aside all questions about the actual existence of intended objects in order to focus on describing them as given to consciousness along with the acts by which they are taken. This is called the phenomenological reduction, restricting noematic analysis to the contents of consciousness whether or not anything corresponds to these representations in the real world.

Hermeneutics as a modification of the phenomenological ideal

The most interesting work in phenomenology of religion in this stricter sense has been done by neither Husserl nor his most faithful disciples. In the best work we normally find a phenomenology at work that has taken the hermeneutical turn to one degree or another. Its basic claim is that the intentional act (taking) is better understood as interpretation than as intuition, as seeing-as rather than as simple or pure seeing, as construal rather than as mirroring. In other words, what appears, what is given, strictly speaking, is sufficiently indeterminate that it can be taken in more than one way. Or, to put it another way, the given underdetermines the taking. Each intentional act renders the intentional object more fully determinate in a way that is contingent rather than necessary. Thus, for example, one believing soul can construe acts of sacrifice as commerce with the gods, while another can see them as unconditional self-donation.

The hermeneutical circle

Three distinct moments within the hermeneutical turn challenge the Platonic and Enlightenment ideal of pure reason, which Husserl calls rigorous science, an objectivity uncontaminated by the contingency and corresponding plurality of perspectival presuppositions. The first is the hermeneutical circle, whose analysis we owe especially to Schleiermacher and Heidegger (Heidegger 1962: 31–3; Westphal 2001: 106–27, 47–74). This is the notion that interpretation is not presuppositionless, that every understanding is guided by pre-understanding, that expectations and anticipations are what enable us to see something as something. Since these a priori conditions of possible interpretation are themselves contingent, they can be revised or replaced in the ongoing process of interpretation, hence the image of the circle to signify the mutual determination of pre-understanding and specific interpretation. The movement from twelve o'clock to six o'clock represents the way construals are determined by presuppositions, while the movement back from six to twelve represents the way in which anomalies in interpretation lead to alteration in the assumptions that originally played the role of the a priori.

The hermeneutical detour

The second specification of the hermeneutical turn is the detour through specific cultural deposits (texts, traditions, practices, institutions) that are themselves already interpretations. A phenomenology of perception can reflect on what it is to see a physical object as such, without reference to any particular object. The phenomenology of religion is not like this. Thus, to repeat an earlier example, a phenomenology of prayer cannot assume that prayer will always have the same structure. It may be construed as a quasi-magical technique for getting the goodies from the gods, or it may be understood as disinterested self-transcendence (Westphal 1984: 138-59). Thus Ricoeur speaks of 'the detour through the contingency of cultures, through an incurably equivocal language, and through the conflict of interpretations' (1970: 42). The phenomenologist of anything as concrete as religion must take 'the long detour of the signs of humanity deposited in cultural works' and 'the detour of understanding the cultural signs in which the self documents and form itself ... [so that] reflection is nothing without the mediation of signs and works ...' (Ricoeur 1981: 143, 158-9). Practicing what he preaches, Ricoeur gives us in a classic study (1967) a phenomenology of the confession of evil in terms of the symbols of defilement, sin, and guilt as found in various texts, and in terms of four culturally specific narratives about the beginning and end of evil.

Since this hermeneutical detour involves paying close attention to the beliefs and practices of one or more specific religious traditions, it has been objected that it is a disguised form of theology, sneaking religion into phenomenology by the back door (Janicaud et al. 2000). But this charge is triply mistaken. Unlike theology, phenomenology does not address itself to any 'church,' any particular community of faith; unlike theology, phenomenology does not appeal to the authority of any scripture, tradition, or institution; and unlike theology, phenomenology leaves open the question of the truth of the beliefs and the appropriateness of the practices described. The phenomenologist as such, whatever personal faith and commitment there may or may not be, describes phenomena that are undeniably there to be described without judging their validity.

The hermeneutics of suspicion

A third hermeneutical challenge to the ideals of pure reason, rigorous science, and neutral objectivity is found in the hermeneutics of suspicion (Ricoeur 1970). It has been defined as '*the deliberate attempt to expose the self-deceptions involved in hiding our actual operative motives from ourselves, individually or collectively, in order not to notice how and how much our behavior and our beliefs are shaped by values we profess to disown*' (Westphal 1998: 13). Ricoeur names Marx, Nietzsche, and Freud as the 'three masters' who 'dominate the school of suspicion' (1970: 32). But one could add such names as the apostle Paul, Augustine, Luther, and Kierkegaard to this list, since for them sin is most definitely an epistemological category insofar as belief is all too often shaped by unholy desire.

It may seem that with suspicion we have crossed the line between description and explanation and thus left phenomenology behind. But perhaps this is just another detour, this time from the manifest content of religious experience to the latent motivation and disguised function of religious beliefs, practices, and institutions. One might appeal to two considerations in support of seeing the hermeneutics of suspicion as an extension of the phenomenological project rather than its abandonment. First, that which self-deception does its best not to notice is sometimes all too plain to be seen, and thus described, by the observer. Second, the observer may be friendly or unfriendly to religion, as the previous paragraph indicates. Since suspicion can be motivated either by hostile unbelief or repentant belief, its work as such can be read as being theologically uncommitted, whatever the identity and interests of the author. What Ricoeur says about psychoanalysis applies to suspicion in general:

> My working hypothesis … is that psychoanalysis is necessarily icono-clastic, regardless of the faith or nonfaith of the psychoanalyst, and that this 'destruction' of religion can be the counterpart of a faith purified of all idolatry. Psychoanalysis as such cannot go beyond the necessity of icono-clasm. This necessity is open to a double possibility, that of faith and that of nonfaith, but the decision about these two possibilities does not rest with psychoanalysis … . The question remains open for every man whether the destruction of idols is without remainder; this question no longer falls within the competency of psychoanalysis. It has been said that Freud does not speak of God, but of god and the gods of men; what is involved is not the truth of the foundation of religious ideas but their function. … (1970: 230, 235)

These three moments, the hermeneutical circle, the hermeneutical detour, and the hermeneutics of suspicion all point to an opacity within human subjectivity. They suggest that we are not given immediately to ourselves and that reflection, whose goal is self-understanding, can neither start nor end with full transparency. While reflection can bring to light aspects of our (in this case, religious) lives that are otherwise unnoticed or even repressed, there will always be presuppositions, cultural deposits, and hidden interests at work in ways of which we are at best dimly aware. Phenomenologists of religion who take the hermeneutical turn seriously will understand that both the religious interpretations of being-in-the-world they seek to describe *and* their own descriptions are caught up within the contingency and opacity that signify the finitude of human understanding. In the hermeneutical turn the phenomenology of religion is at once Kantian and anti-Kantian. It is the former insofar as it articulates the finitude of human understanding in terms of the a priori conditions of possible experience; but it is the latter insofar as it denies universality and necessity to these conditions and sees them as particular and contingent and thus unavoidably plural and changeable.

Jean-Luc Marion

Two of the most interesting and insightful recent phenomenologies of religion come to us from France in the work of Jean-Luc Marion and Jean-Yves Lacoste. A brief look at their work will provide a sampling of a much wider field of inquiry. The two central themes for Marion are the distinction between the idol and the icon and the phenomenology of the saturated phenomenon.

The idol and the icon

In the first instance, the idol and the icon are physical objects of religious significance. The phenomenological distinction Marion draws concerns the nature of the intentional act. When the gaze comes to rest on its object, settles, and freezes there and does not 'transpierce' it to something beyond it, the object is taken as an idol. The physical object, perhaps a statue of some sort, is simply identified with the divine. Moreover, since the intentional object does not exceed the gaze of the believing soul, Marion suggests that it is reduced to being the mirror of the believer, whose perception thereby becomes the measure of the divine. Marion does not call this idolatry because he disapproves of it but because he thinks this (mis)understanding of the object violates the religious sensibility for which the divine always exceeds our gaze and our grasp, is always more than a mirror of our own faculties which, in turn, are never its measure. One might say that in the idol religion reduces itself to magic and makes of its object a talisman. All we have to do is switch from the perceptual to the conceptual field to see that there are conceptual idols as well whenever we think our concepts grasp the divine without remainder and that we need not look beyond them to what exceeds our grasp. In the one case a physical object contains all there is of the divine, and in the other case some conceptual scheme captures the sacred without remainder. What gets lost is the *mysterium* from Otto's formula for the holy: *mysterium tremendum et fascinans* (Otto 1958: 12–40; Marion 1991: 7–17).

By contrast there are perceptual and conceptual icons whenever in seeing a religiously significant physical object or thinking in terms of religiously significant concepts we intend the divine as that which transcends both our look and our language. We do not forget that it is at once invisible and incomprehensible. This, Marion suggests, is how religion understands itself. While the biblical distinction between the true God and the idols of the nations is a theological distinction, this is a phenomenological distinction. For it suggests that the images that were considered idols by the prophets of ancient Israel might well have functioned as icons. That would not make them images of the true God from the standpoint of Israel's theology; but it would make them authentically religious, icons not idols in the phenomenological sense of these terms. The 'object' of religious intentionality is transcendent in an epistemological sense. It exceeds, overflows, and overwhelms the capacities of sense *and* of intellect to receive it, to take it in the same measure as it gives itself.

There is another important element in Marion's concept of the icon. In the case of the idol the believing soul is the only subject and the idol is the object. It does not look back, which is why the gaze of the idolater, whether perceptual or conceptual, becomes the measure of its object. It is understood to be only what it is 'seen' to be. But it is different with the icon. It functions as a subject that looks at us. Marion is here thinking of Christian icons that typically include the faces of the Madonna and Child or some saint. The icon 'opens in a face that gazes at our gaze' (1991: 19–22).

Moreover, as a gaze that emanates from the sacred, this gaze takes priority over our gaze. We look as those already looked upon. Correspondingly, when concepts function iconically, they not only signify that which exceeds our understanding but also that which exceeds our agency, and even our identity. We are called into being by that which puts us in question, which addresses us with commands and promises (Marion 2002a: 263–300). Before we see, we are seen; before we think, we are thought; before we act, we are acted upon; and before we speak, we are spoken to. Here we get the cash value of Heidegger's definition of phenomenology given above. When the phenomenon is that which *shows itself* from itself and we let it show itself *from itself*, the subject is decentered; initiative is shifted from my intentionality activity to the agency of that what gives itself on its own terms.

Here we get a modification of Husserlian phenomenology at least as substantial as the hermeneutical turn: inverted intentionality (Marion 1991: 19; 2002b: 37, 44, 61, 87, 99, 113–19). This is what Levinas calls 'an intentionality of a wholly different type' (1969: 23), an intentionality of which I am the object rather than the subject. My consciousness of … or awareness of … does not originate in the intentional act I direct toward something or other. It rather originates in the gaze or the address of another which defines both me and the situation in which I find myself before I can define them for myself. Here the epistemological transcendence of the sacred expands to an ethical transcendence as my agency and my agenda are superseded by an agency and an agenda not my own. In its character as response, the religious life is always a life of responsibility.

The saturated phenomenon

It is the epistemological transcendence of the sacred that is the focus in Marion's analysis of the saturated phenomenon (2000; 2002a: §§ 19–24). In the events called epiphany or revelation, the invisible renders itself visible, as is the case with the icon. There is thus a phenomenon to be described, but it has a distinctive character.

Husserlian phenomenology takes seeing a physical object as its paradigm. In that case I always intend more than is given to intuition. I intend the sides I cannot see and the internal 'filling' that I could see only by taking the object apart. Changes of perspective can add to my stockpile of intuition, but can never close the gap between what I intend and what I actually see. The saturated phenomenon, by contrast, is saturated with intuition. More is given to intuition than I can intend, so that both the self (the I think, the transcendental ego) and its horizons of expectation are overwhelmed. The visible gives itself as the presence of the invisible, the conceptually comprehended as the incomprehensible. It is not that I need more intuition or better concepts, but rather that what is given to sense or to intellect overflows the capacities of both. Marion develops this excess in detail with the help of Kant's four types of categories: quantity, quality, relation, and modality (Marion 2000; 2002a: 21–2).

This structure is not uniquely religious. Marion describes four non-religious types of phenomena that are saturated in this sense, that give themselves beyond our ability to receive (2002a: §23; 2002b). These are the historical event; the work of art, especially the painting; the flesh or the presence of our own bodies to ourselves; and the human face that presents itself as one to whom and for whom we are responsible. This fourth category has a distinctly Levinasian flavor. (Marion calls the second and fourth categories 'idol' and 'icon' respectively, but this is confusing since the terms have different meanings here from their earlier use (1991)). The epiphany or revelation that Christians call the Incarnation belongs to this general category of phenomena; indeed, it combines all four types of saturation in one (2002a: §24). The subjectivity that corresponds to this kind of 'objectivity' can only be described as gifted to itself and as called to respond (2002a: §§25–30).

Jean-Yves Lacoste

Two key terms in Lacoste's phenomenology of religion are liturgy and place. By liturgy he means the human relation to the Absolute in its entirety. It has a broader meaning than worship, and a fortiori a particular style of worship. Just as Heidegger calls human beings *Dasein* to avoid the conceptual baggage of such standard terms as person, self, soul, subject, and so forth, so Lacoste says 'liturgy' to avoid connotations of 'religious experience' that he does not wish to concede.

World and earth

By place Lacoste means that to ask 'Who?' we are we must ask 'Where?' we are. What is our native habitat? He distinguishes two answers Heidegger gives to that question, one from the *Being and Time* (world) and one from the later writings, especially under inspiration from Hölderlin (earth). As being-in-the world we belong to a place in the strongest sense of the term: we belong to it rather than or at least before it belongs to us. We are decentered by its priority, which we experience as sovereignty. Thus in belonging we do not really belong but experience ourselves as not at home (*unzuhause*) in a world that is uncanny (*unheimlich*). Anxiety is the fundamental mood of this place, revealing to us the underlying unity of all its landscapes (Lacoste 2004: 8–13).

The second scene in which human life takes place is the earth. Earth differs from world in part because it is not the all-encompassing horizon but only one dimension of the Fourfold (*das Geviert*) comprised of earth and sky, mortals and gods. *Dasein* was already mortal as being-in-the-world, whose temporality was being-toward-death. It is the earth and the gods that make this a different place. The earth shelters and protects, so that mortals can find themselves at home (*zuhause*) and experience can have the character of homecoming (*Heimkunft*). Mortals are still mortals, but they are not alone. They live in the presence of the gods, and life consequently has a meaning that arises when the poet sings the sacred (*das Heilige*, the German title of Otto's book (Lacoste 2004: 13–18).

Lacoste makes two important comments on the dialectic of world and earth. First, it is in fact a dialectical relation. Between being displaced or exiled in a godless world and dwelling in the land of the gods there is no neat boundary; nor is either moment more fundamental than the other. 'Before the world reveals to us that we are there without feeling at home, and before the earth offers itself as a shelter, dwelling place, and homeland, world and earth comprise the double secret of place' (2004: 19). Human existence is open to both possibilities, living in the insecurity of godless secularity and living in the sacred security offered to us by poets or preachers so easy to please that they are hard to distinguish from self-help gurus. What is more, we are capable of living in both at once, sliding back and forth between the two without sensing the contradiction between them.

Lacoste's second comment is the key to his entire project. It is that the gods that bring comfort and security within the Fourfold represent an 'immanent sacred ... but not a transcendent God. Just as *Dasein* was without God in the world, mortals live without God in the "Fourfold," and it is by no means certain that the God for which they wait is worthy of the name' (2004: 18). In other words, he wants to do a phenomenology of a possible God who cannot be found in either of Heidegger's places.

So we must ask: In what sense are the gods of romantic poetry and its more recent successors immanent rather than transcendent? Lacoste's answer is that they are subordinate to Being or its equivalent, the sacred. 'The sacred exercises its authority over the gods, and over God (over 'the God') himself. But if it is necessary to speak of God in rigorous terms, then the current subordination of the gods to the sacred, and the potential subordination of God to the sacred, clearly shows that between the Heideggerian concept of the divine and the divinity of God, there is in fact an equivocal relation' (Lacoste 2004: 18). Just as the gods of the Greeks were subject to Fate, so for Heidegger the gods of the past and the God for whom we might wait are subject to a horizon, a prior condition at once ontological and epistemic, into which they must fit. They are the finite furniture of a realm they do not govern. They are not the Ground of Being but rather are grounded in or by Being. In other words, they are not the Absolute, and God is not the Lord of Being. Lacoste is here in full agreement with Marion for whom Heidegger, after seeking to rescue the God of biblical faith from metaphysics in its onto-theological mode (Westphal 2001: 1–28), replaces those a priori constraints with new ones in the form of his own theory of Being (Marion 1991: 25–52).

Transcendence and transgression

Like Marion, Lacoste is trying to think phenomenologically about the possibility of a genuine divine transcendence. To that end he posits that liturgy requires transgression. That is to say that if we are to have a relation to a God who is Absolute we must transgress (subvert, transfigure, contradict, critique, contest, disturb, exceed, break through) the boundaries of the complex place signified by world/earth. Or perhaps the transgression comes from the other direction. For the first thing Lacoste says about the God who is 'an absolute who is someone, and over whom there is no supreme and impersonal authority' and for whom neither the world, nor the difference between earth and world, nor the wedding of earth and sky 'can provide the transcendental conditions' is that this 'Lord of Being' will be 'an Absolute who is someone, and who promises a relation with him.' To try to think this God is 'with all due respect to him, reason enough to take leave of the philosopher' (Lacoste 2004: 21).

This God, for whom phenomenology seeks to reserve a place or non-place of possibility, is (1) a someone, a fully personal God, (2) a someone who speaks, and (3) a someone whose speech is promise. Clearly Lacoste has the God of Abraham, Isaac, and Jacob in mind as he dismisses 'the philosopher' in a Pascalian tone of voice. Liturgy signifies the possibility that 'beyond the historial [*sic*, read historical] play between world and earth, man has for his true *dwelling place* the *relation* he seals with God or that God seals with him' (2004: 98). The name of this site beyond the dialectic of world and earth is Kingdom, and the time of liturgy is eschatological time. Much of Lacoste's book is given over to spelling out the meaning of this eschatological time, what it means to live neither in anxiety nor in comfort but in hope. Without apology he does this in overtly Christian language. No doubt Janicaud would consider Lacoste a theological wolf in the clothing of a phenomenological sheep; and no doubt the Christian believer can read the text as an analysis of the faith shared with the author. But as a phenomenologist, Lacoste is only claiming that there are more possibilities than Heidegger has dreamed of and that while the philosopher can choose to ignore these, that is not a reason why others should as well.

Lacoste's §37 is entitled 'World, earth, and kingdom,' and one of the synonyms for transgression, not included above, is bracketing, a term Husserl uses for the phenomenological reduction. Just as for Husserl this bracketing is not a denial of the reality of the world beyond our thinking of it but a temporary setting that aside in order to focus attention on something else, so for Lacoste there is no denial that we live in Heidegger's world and earth but rather a deliberate directing of our attention beyond their limits – thus transgression. Liturgical existence does not mean that we cease to live in the dialectical tension between world and earth; it rather signifies that these are relativized in a wider horizon whose sovereign neither they nor their grounding principles are. So perhaps a better image than bracketing might be Hegel's notion of *Aufhebung* or Kierkegaard's notion of teleological suspension. In both cases, that which takes itself to be complete and self-sufficient is recontextualized into a larger whole of which it is not the ground or organizing principle. Here the Transcendent and Absolute is not a rival of the immanent and relative but their ground and telos. But the Transcendent/Absolute and the immanent/relative become rivals to each other when the latter takes itself to be absolute.

See also Immanuel Kant (Chapter 14), Søren Kierkegaard (Chapter 15), Postmodern theology (Chapter 47), Continental philosophy (Chapter 60), Religious experience (Chapter 63).

References

Eliade, M. (1958) *Patterns in Comparative Religion*, trans. R. Sheed, New York: New American Library.

—— (1959) *Cosmos and History: The Myth of the Eternal Return*, trans. W. R. Trask, New York: Harper & Row.

Heidegger, M. (1962) *Being and Time*, trans. J. Macquarrie and E. Robinson, New York: Harper & Row.

Husserl, E. (1970) *The Idea of Phenomenology*, trans. W. P. Alston and G. Nakhnikian, The Hague: Martinus Nijhoff.

—— (1982) *Ideas Pertaining to a Pure Phenomenology and to a Phenomenological Philosophy: First Book*, trans. F. Kersten, The Hague: Nijhoff.

James, W. (1958) *The Varieties of Religious Experience*, New York: New American Library.

Janicaud, D., et al. (2000) *The Theological Turn in French Phenomenology* in *Phenomenology and the 'Theological Turn': The French Debate*, trans. B. G. Prusak, New York: Fordham University Press.

Lacoste, J. (2004) *Experience and the Absolute: Disputed Questions on the Humanity of Man*, trans. M. Raftery-Skehan, New York: Fordham University Press.

Levinas, E. (1969) *Totality and Infinity: An Essay on Exteriority*, trans. A. Lingis, Pittsburgh, PA: Duquesne University Press.

Malinowski, B. (1954) *Magic, Science, and Religion and Other Essays*, Garden City, NY: Doubleday.

Marion, J. (1991) *God Without Being*, trans. T. A. Carlson, Chicago: University of Chicago Press.

—— (2000) 'The saturated phenomenon' in D. Janicaud et al., *The Theological Turn in French Phenomenology* in *Phenomenology and the 'Theological Turn': The French Debate*, trans. B. G. Prusak, New York: Fordham University Press.

—— (2002a) *Being Given Toward a Phenomenology of Givenness*, trans. J. L. Kosky, Stanford, CA: Stanford University Press.

—— (2002b) *In Excess: Studies of Saturated Phenomena*, trans. R. Horner and V. Berraud, New York: Fordham University Press.

Merleau-Ponty, M. (1962) *Phenomenology of Perception*, trans. C. Smith, London: Routledge & Kegan Paul.

Otto, R. (1958) *The Idea of the Holy*, trans. J. Harvey, New York: Oxford University Press.

Ricoeur, P. (1967) *The Symbolism of Evil*, trans. E. Buchanan, New York: Harper & Row.

—— (1970) *Freud and Philosophy: An Essay on Interpretation*, trans. D. Savage, New Haven, CT: Yale University Press.

—— (1981) *Hermeneutics and the Human Sciences*, trans. J. B. Thompson, New York: Cambridge University Press.

Van der Leeuw, G. (1963) *Religion in Essence and Manifestation*, 2 vols, New York: Harper & Row.

Westphal, M. (1984) *God, Guilt, and Death: An Existential Phenomenology of Religion*, Bloomington, IN: Indiana University Press.

—— (1998) *Suspicion and Faith: The Religious Uses of Modern Atheism*, New York: Fordham University Press.

—— (2001) *Overcoming Onto-theology: Toward a Postmodern Christian Faith*, New York: Fordham University Press.

Further reading

Benson, B. and N. Wirzba (eds) (2005) *The Phenomenology of Prayer*, New York: Fordham University Press. (Various essays on the stated topic.)

Bloechl, J. (ed.) (2003) *Religious Experience and the End of Metaphysics*, Bloomington, IN: Indiana University Press. (Various essays on the stated topic.)

Faulconer, J. (ed.) (2003) *Transcendence in Philosophy and Religion*, Bloomington, IN: Indiana University Press. (Various essays on the stated topic.)

Gadamer, H.-G. (2004) *Truth and Method*, trans. J. Weinsheimer and D. G. Marshall, New York: Continuum. (Key text for philosophical hermeneutics.)

Guerrière, D. (ed.) (1990) *Phenomenology of the Truth Proper to Religion*, Albany, NY: State University of New York Press. (Essays treating the phenomenology of religious truth from existential, hermeneutic, ethical, deconstructive, and transcendental perspectives.)

Hart, K. and B. Wall (eds) (2005) *The Experience of God*, New York: Fordham University Press. (Various essays on the stated topic.)

62
RELIGIOUS NATURALISM
Donald A. Crosby

Common traits of religious naturalism

Religious naturalists find religious meaning, value, and importance solely in nature or in some aspect of the natural order. The antithesis of religious naturalism is any kind of supernaturalism, i.e., belief in supernatural beings, principles, or powers thought to reside in a supernatural realm. Nature and its ongoing changes are metaphysically ultimate for religious naturalists. Nothing exists beyond nature, and a supernatural ground of nature is unnecessary. Nature in some shape or form is all there is now, ever has been, and ever shall be.

Their rejection of the supernatural also means that religious naturalists make no appeal to supernatural revelations, inspirations, visitations, or commands. For them, all religious knowledge and awareness grow out of endeavors of humans to experience, understand, and respond to religious meanings and values implicit in nature itself. Moreover, there is no supernatural source of transformation, empowerment, forgiveness, or salvation. Many religious naturalists speak with confidence of the reality and importance of such things as transcendence, grace, and spirituality, but they regard these things as operative entirely within the natural order – an order of which human beings and their minds, cultures, and histories are an inseparable part.

Religious naturalists take seriously the methods and findings of the natural sciences. They seek to develop religious outlooks consistent with these methods and findings, and to avoid the sorts of conflict between science and religion that have plagued religious traditions of the West in the past. They are also religiously inspired by the discoveries of science and especially by scientific descriptions of cosmic, terrestrial, and biological evolution. However, they typically resist reductionistic interpretations of the natural sciences, e.g., interpretations that regard as ultimately insignificant and unreal anything other than the descriptions and explanations of physics. Religious naturalists can be materialists, but if so they are generally non-eliminative materialists, a position affirming the irreducible reality and indispensable functions of life, mind, and spirit. Most religious naturalists deny human postmortem survival, regarding it as supernatural in character and as lacking convincing empirical support.

Significant differences among religious naturalists

In addition to these common traits of the outlooks of religious naturalists, there are also significant differences among them. Some seek to incorporate their outlook into existing religious traditions such as those of Judaism or Christianity; others do not. Some retain concepts of 'God' or 'the divine'; others do not. Some religious naturalists affirm the whole of nature as the appropriate focus of religious conviction and commitment; others affirm only a certain aspect of nature in this way. The latter tend to see religious values as melding smoothly into moral values, while the former are more likely to envision a distinctively religious sphere of value. The latter think it essential to affirm a morally unambiguous religious object, i.e., one that is unqualifiedly good in the moral sense of that term, while the former affirm the religious value of the whole of nature as their focus of faith despite nature's admitted amorality or moral ambiguity.

Some religious naturalists insist that science alone, especially as exemplified in the natural sciences, is competent to provide objective and reliable descriptions of nature. Meanings and values, including those of religion, are then conceived as human responses to the established theories of the natural sciences at a given time. Others argue that other perspectives, such as those of the humanities, the arts, and the experiences of daily life, should be called upon to complement the natural sciences and to do justice to the fullness of nature in its multiple aspects.

Some religious naturalists tend to confine the relevant experiences for assessing claims about nature to sensate experiences, thus endorsing in this manner as well as others a narrower meaning of 'scientific.' Others expand the range of relevant experiences to include such things as aesthetic, moral, and religious experiences, as well as the full range of experienced conditions, needs, functions, and aspirations of human life. The latter insist on testing claims about nature and the place of humans in nature on the basis of lived experience in all of its dimensions, not just sensate experiences. This kind of religious naturalist obviously has a broader conception of what it means to reason scientifically and to be a scientific empiricist.

With these characterizations and contrasts in mind, we can now discuss views of some of those who have developed versions of religious naturalism in the twentieth and twenty-first centuries, the period in which this outlook has come to the fore as a significant movement in religious thought in the West. The discussion can serve as a representative sampling of this viewpoint's various forms.

Representative sampling of religious naturalists

Many religious naturalists do not see themselves as espousing religious visions utterly distinct from existing religious traditions but rather as revising these traditions in order to bring them up to date – especially in relation to developments in the natural sciences – and to capture in a more relevant and meaningful way what they deem most important in the traditions. Examples are Henry Nelson Wieman and Bernard Loomer, influential Christian theologians of the mid-twentieth century. A more recent example is Christian theologian Gordon Kaufman of Harvard Divinity School, who prefers to label his outlook 'biohistorical naturalism' (Kaufman 2004: 42–5). Another example of a religious naturalist endeavoring to revise and update an existing religious tradition is Mordecai Kaplan, founder of the Reconstructionist movement in Judaism.

Other religious naturalists prefer to develop versions of religious naturalism not explicitly tied to any particular religious tradition, although they may draw upon features of existing traditions in articulating their positions. They may also exhort proponents of existing traditions to incorporate into their traditions aspects of religious naturalism such as its respect for the methods and findings of the natural sciences. Examples of this type of religious naturalist include Connie Barlow, Robert Corrington, Donald Crosby, John Dewey, Ursula Goodenough, Charley Hardwick, Karl Peters, and Jerome Stone.

Religious naturalists wishing to retain concepts of 'God' or 'the divine' do so either because they are spokespersons for religious traditions in which these concepts are fundamental, or because they regard them as having a powerful, if not indispensable, symbolic religious significance, especially in the West. They do not adhere to traditional theistic conceptions of God but reinterpret God-language and the symbol of God so as to make them consistent with religious naturalism.

For example, Kaufman and Peters interpret the term 'God' to apply to the 'serendipitous creativity' (Kaufman's term) of a cosmos that evolves and changes in surprising and unpredictable ways (Peters 2002: 35–7, 139–40; Kaufman 2004: 42, 45–9). Neither thinker conceives of God as a substantial entity or personal being but views God rather as processes of nature in which creation and destruction are inextricably entwined. Another religious naturalist, Stone, uses the term 'divine' for what he regards as our deepest religious experiences as natural beings: experiences that 'generate and support and *transform* our idea of good *and that provide situationally transcendent resources of renewal*' (Stone 1992: 207, his emphasis). Thus for him, the 'divine' is not a particular being but a particular type of experience.

Other religious naturalists decline to engage in God-talk. For them, the admittedly powerful symbol of God points in the wrong directions. It should be given up because it stubbornly connotes – despite all efforts at revision – a supernatural being that created the world out of nothing and is required to sustain its existence. This symbol is therefore radically misleading and runs counter to the central claims of religious naturalism. Barlow, Crosby, and Goodenough are examples of religious naturalists who do not include reinterpretations of God in their respective viewpoints and accord to nature itself the reverence and commitment assumed to be appropriate only to a supernatural God in theistic religions.

Another significant difference among religious naturalists is whether or not they affirm the whole of nature or only a part of nature as the appropriate focus of religious commitment. Thinkers such as Crosby, Kaufman, Loomer, and Peters view the whole of nature or the entire range of nature's creative and destructive powers in this way, while religious naturalists such as Dewey, Kaplan, and Wieman regard only a part of nature as being worthy of wholehearted religious devotion.

This second group assumes, along with traditional theism, that the religious ultimate must be unqualifiedly good from a moral standpoint and therefore that amoral, evil, or destructive aspects of nature cannot be included in what has positive religious value. The religious object's moral goodness might greatly exceed or be more splendid in its character than what humans can imagine, but it cannot run counter to or fall short of what they recognize as morally good. To qualify as an appropriate focus of religious concern, or so this group supposes, the religious object must be free of any hint of moral ambiguity.

Dewey sees the religious function as the 'working union of the ideal and the actual,' characterizing it as 'natural and moral.' 'Whether one gives the name "God" to this union,' he comments, 'is a matter for individual decision,' but Dewey himself regards it as being 'identical with the force that has in fact been attached to the conception of God in all the religions that have a spiritual content.' He does not restrict the religious function to the single ideal of moral 'righteousness'; he includes within it other ideal ends such as 'beauty, truth, and friendship.' But he is unwilling to associate this function with anything that conflicts with or does not contribute to the attainment of moral ideals (Dewey 1962: 52, 54). Wieman uses the term 'God' to refer to 'the form (structure, character) of actual events which distinguishes the source of all human good so far as this source operates in a way qualitatively different from human operations, and produces values more important for human existence and human improvement than man can produce on his own initiative' (Wieman 1963: 10; see also Wieman 1946). So, as with Dewey, the emphasis is on positive values for human existence and human improvement, not upon anything of a morally ambiguous character.

Similarly, Kaplan conceives of God, the focal point of religious thought and life, not as a supernatural being but as a particular process or function within nature: 'that aspect of reality which elicits the most serviceable traits, the traits that enhance individual human worth and further social utility' (Kaplan 1934: 397). Once again, then, the focus is on the religious object's power to engender and inspire goodness in the lives of human beings, not on anything morally ambiguous in its character or effects. And the religious object is conceived as an aspect of nature, not the whole of nature.

In contrast with religious naturalists who assume the religious object's unqualified moral goodness and identify that object as only an aspect of nature, others readily acknowledge the moral ambiguity of nature and affirm the whole of it as religiously appropriate and valuable despite that ambiguity. Its appropriateness and value are therefore not to be confined to or identified with the moral senses of those terms but have a distinctively religious meaning. This meaning encompasses nature's moral ambiguity as reflected in such things as an evolutionary history riddled with extinctions of species, pervasive predations on beings capable of suffering, rampant starvation and disease, and destructive events such as earthquakes, fires, and floods.

Peters, for example, observes that nature's creativity is correlative with its destructiveness. New species evolve as old species become extinct. Populations are kept in balance by predation, starvation, and death. With the destruction of old ecosystems, new ones come into being. Nature's ongoing changes are made possible not only by its creations but also by its destructions. We can live religiously in the presence of nature's moral ambiguities by 'being open to the possibilities of new life, new truth, new beauty, and new love that emerge in the midst of suffering' (Peters 2002: 112; also ch. 15).

From this perspective, then, the religious value lies in nature's creative processes that have brought into being the human species, the multitude of other species past and present, the earth itself, and the universe as a whole. And these ongoing creative processes necessarily incorporate aspects of destructiveness, pain, and evil. Thus I conclude that what is unqualifiedly right or good from a religious perspective, namely, the whole of nature with all its creative and destructive events and powers, includes what has to be seen as at least partly evil from a moral point of view. Religious goodness and moral goodness are therefore not one and the same. Human moral standards are not directly derivable from nature, although they might be patterned after some aspects of nature, but must be independently fashioned in ways appropriate to the social existence of humans as a distinctive species. My point is not that morality is negligible or unimportant, religiously speaking. It can in some circumstances, for example, serve as a vital check on religious claims' plausibility or acceptability. Religious outlooks, on the other hand, provide contexts and sources of motivation for developing or adhering to moral principles. I argue that the two species of value are not the same and should not be confused with one another (2002: ch. 7; Crosby 2005: 200–4).

Likewise, Kaufman reasons that, while the serendipitous creativity of nature as a whole deserves to be called 'God,' humans must strive to emulate in their moral lives only what is 'productive' – not destructive or hurtful – in that creativity as they strive to live in relation to one another and to the other creatures sharing their planet (Kaufman 2004: 62). Loomer joins religious naturalists who see the whole of nature as the focus of religious faith. He strongly emphasizes the seemingly counterintuitive idea that the moral ambiguity of nature's processes is precisely what helps to qualify them as 'God,' i.e., as the appropriate focus of religious commitment: 'an ambiguous God is of greater stature than an unambiguous deity' (Loomer 1987: 43).

The totality of the world is for Loomer undeniably ambiguous, containing such things as good and evil, creation and destruction, order and disorder, pleasure and pain, while a supposed God of absolute goodness could encompass and account for only one side of such contrasts. Therefore, such a deity is for Loomer hopelessly small, limited, and abstract, in contrast with the vastness, complexity, and concreteness of the world. A fully concrete, 'living, dynamic, and active' God of adequate status or 'size' is what is needed for robust religious faith. Thus God must be identified with the entirety of the world, not just with an aspect of it (ibid.).

An important implication of Loomer's position is that an adequate religious object must not be centered primarily on human beings and their problems and concerns but must encompass the whole of nature. Correspondingly, Kaufman states that a revised symbol of God in today's world must be related not merely or primarily to the lives and existential concerns of humans, but to the 'much more basic matter of the objective conditions that make all life . . . possible' on earth (2004: 38). Both thinkers can be interpreted to mean that humans cannot help but be caught in ambiguities of a world and its creative processes that, in a post-Copernican and post-Darwinian age, are far from being aimed exclusively at them. Loomer and Kaufman gratefully affirm an abundance of sustaining power and goodness in the workings of the world, but they also counsel us not to be demoralized or overcome when we encounter the inevitable amorality or moral ambiguities of these workings.

Corrington's religious naturalism is a special case. While agreeing with the religious naturalists now under discussion that it is 'anthropomorphic hubris' that envisions the sacredness of nature as 'shaped by and to human ends,' including human moral ends (Corrington 1997: 2, 6), he disagrees that the whole of nature is sacred. Instead, the sacred is for him but one of the innumerable orders of nature natured (*natura naturata*) and is itself a product of the potencies of the 'ejective unruly ground' of nature naturing (*natura naturans*) (1997: 10, 100).

Corrington is reluctant even to speak of nature as a conceptual whole: 'strictly speaking, nature is beyond all genera and cannot be located within a higher genus.' It 'is the sheer availability of whatever is.' A fundamental rift or abyss separates 'the attained and emerging orders of nature natured' from 'the potencies of nature naturing,' meaning that there is no way in which the two together can constitute an unproblematic or clear-cut conceptual whole (1997: 2–3). The unruly ground itself 'remains lost in the depths of mystery and gloom. It cannot be gathered up under the arms of reason and brought into a full transparency.' Corrington characterizes this wholly natural, ever-present, turbulent ground of nature's emergent orders, properties, and laws as 'beyond good and evil' (pp. 98–9, 105). Similarly, in what he calls nature's 'sacred folds' or 'numinous folds,' there are manifestations ('epiphanies') of exceptional religious power and significance that 'cannot be moral or immoral per se' (pp. 23, 55). Even if we later apply ethical predicates to such a sacred fold or epiphany as it 'enters into the orbits of individual and communal forms of interpretation ... the reverbera- tions of any given fold are ambiguous and fragmented' (p. 26). Thus for Corrington, the moral and conceptual ambiguities of both nature and the sacred dimensions of nature are ineluctable.

A central issue in all forms of religious naturalism is how nature is to be conceived. This issue leads readily into the problem of what the role of the natural sciences is or ought to be in contributing to or providing this conception. Some religious naturalists tend to leave it to the natural sciences to provide them with an objective or reliable view of nature. They then take this view as their reference point and develop possi- bilities of religious meaning and value they claim to discern within, or to be entitled to base upon, the scientific accounts. Examples of this approach among religious naturalists are Barlow, Goodenough, Hardwick, and Peters.

Barlow, Goodenough, and Peters focus their religious faith upon nature as scien- tifically described and do not attempt to develop an outlook on nature that reaches beyond the physical sciences. Barlow declares that '[s]cientists can tell us what is and what was and perhaps even what will be, but not what it all *means*.' Tracing out religious implications of science's objective descriptions of the world and its processes is something inherently 'subjective.' Hence, 'the way of science' as her preferred route to religious (and ethical) 'meaning-making' requires that we regard 'our interpretations of meaning and value' as 'largely constructions' (Barlow 1997: 16–19, 223, 227). Thus Barlow leaves descriptions of objective reality entirely up to natural scientists while depicting religious thinkers as providing subjective interpretations of what those descriptions can be taken to mean for living our lives. We should rely upon science to tell us what is real, while religious interpretations invite us to brood upon existential meanings of what is real. A problem with Barlow's analysis is that, in driving a wedge between fact and value (or ethical and existential meaning) – and thus between the natural sciences and the humanities – it seems not to take sufficiently into account the fact that humans are an integral part of nature and that their existential needs, concerns, and values ought somehow to be included in a fully adequate, objective understanding of nature, not relegated to a purely subjective realm.

Barlow would seem to be on firmer ground in the last chapter of her *Green Space, Green Time* when she cites with approval Goodenough's allegation that meaning emerges into the cosmos with all forms of life, since all of them strive to maintain themselves in existence. Each of them has a telos or project and must find ways to realize it and to produce more of its kind. Meaning-seeking and meaning-making, then, are integral parts of nature, not distinct from it. Acknowledgment of this fact implies that they need to be given an appropriate place in adequate descriptions of nature (Goodenough 1994; Barlow 1997: 223–5).

Goodenough's position on the relation of the natural sciences to religion seems close to Barlow's, however, when she speaks elsewhere of 'religious emotions' as being 'elicited by natural reality' and takes for granted that the question of 'How things are' is best answered by natural science, while that of 'Which things matter' is the business of valuative enterprises such as ethics and religion (Goodenough 1998: xvii, xiv). So once again, science provides all the facts that are needed, and religion interprets the meanings of those facts. Religious values and meanings are not included in objective descriptions of nature but are emotional and imaginative responses to those descriptions.

Peters does not draw sharp dichotomies between scientific facts and religious values; he rests content with science's descriptions of nature and takes them as his context in developing his religious naturalism. He makes no attempt to construct a philosophical cosmology or metaphysics that includes scientific descriptions but goes beyond them (Peters 2002). Hardwick, drawing on John F. Post's work (Post 1987), asserts 'that only the basic objects of mathematical physics exist and that everything at a higher or more complex level can occur only if there is a corresponding occurrence at the level of physics' (Hardwick 1996: 33). Hardwick is not a reductionist, however, and he does not conceive of values as being merely subjective. Things at higher or more complex levels, such as moral and religious values, are real in their own right and can be thoroughly objective even though they are all attributes of one thing, namely, the physical as described by physics. There are many ways the world is, many different 'faces' it exhibits as its emergent entities, functions, or properties, even though these faces are facets of physical reality and are ultimately dependent upon physical reality. All truth, at whatever level or kind, is determined, fixed, or delimited by physical truth as described by the science of physics (1996: 50, 34–6).

Hardwick goes on to say that God is a real aspect of nature, just as religious truths in general have the capability of being, so long as we do not think of 'God' as having a referent (1996: 63). He contends that God has no ontological status but 'that the very meaning of "God" is valuational rather than ontological' (p. 54). A locution such as 'God exists' (and its associated modes of religious discourse, such as those involving faith, salvation, and grace) is 'a kind of meta-assertion that compactly expresses a valuational matrix, a form of life and an attendant seeing-as' that is not merely subjective (p. 65). Hardwick insists that the natural sciences, especially physics, 'offer the best guide to establish ultimate ontological entities' but that there are other domains of discourse than the ontological one that can lay claim to being true and non-reductively so (p. 77). Valuative discourse such as that we find to be pervasive in religion is amenable to 'a full-fledged physicalist account of value-determination,' i.e., 'the world in the sense of the basic physical entities' as described by physics 'determines value' (p. 59). The essential point of Hardwick's analysis is that religion and its discourse lie solely in the domain of value, but that its commitments and claims are not merely subjective and can be rooted in and meaningfully assessed in terms of the findings of physics. This process of assessment is argued to be non-reductive. So physics has priority in the ontological realm, telling us what the world is ultimately like, but non-ontological realms such as religion can lay claim to objective truths of their own sort.

Other religious naturalists draw upon the disciplines of the natural sciences for their conceptions of nature but strive to go beyond these disciplines in developing their views of nature and its processes, views they regard as more adequate to the fullness and completeness of nature than an exclusively scientific account can be. In doing so, this group tends also to have a more extended notion of the kinds of experience that are needed for an adequate vision of nature, and not to restrict empiricism to sensate experiences. Examples are Dewey, Corrington, Crosby, and Stone.

Experiences of emotion, intentionality, consummation, and value (and many other kinds of non-sensate experiences that figure prominently in everyday life) have for Dewey as fundamental a role in helping us understand the nature of nature as do the sensate experiences and regular causal processes focused upon in the physical sciences' descriptions and explanations of natural processes (Dewey 1958: esp. chs 3 and 4). Corrington, as we saw, directs considerable attention to, among other things, experiences of religious epiphanies or sacred folds putting us in touch with the deep-lying, mysterious presence and power of nature naturing. He does not restrict himself to the nature natured that is the pre-eminent concern of the natural sciences.

I regard the natural sciences as only one important avenue of approach for a full comprehension of nature, arguing that other perspectives – especially the perspectives of thoughtful metaphysical inquiries into how the diverse aspects of lived experience relate to one another and fit together – need also to be brought into play (Crosby 2002: ch. 3). Stone advocates 'a generous empiricism' that 'refuses to restrict observation by the canons of [scientific] precision and measurement.' While respecting the contributions of the natural sciences, his brand of empiricism is keenly receptive to, among other things, appreciations of the 'transforming resources and challenging worth' that for him are also crucial aspects of our experiences of the world (Stone 1992: 113).

Dewey insists that even the term 'scientific' should encompass modes of reasoning appropriate to fields other than those of the natural sciences – fields that include not only the social sciences but the arts, philosophy, and religion. 'Scientific reasoning' is for Dewey synonymous with responsible, empirical, method-directed, fruitful reasoning in general, and he devotes one of his major later writings to explaining how this kind of reasoning can best be explicated and understood (Dewey 1991). So he can claim to be thoroughly scientific in developing his conception of nature and a version of religious naturalism consistent with this conception even as he includes but also reaches beyond the natural sciences in doing so (Dewey 1958, 1962).

Merits of religious naturalism

We can now list some merits of religious naturalism that could be claimed by its proponents. (1) There is no in-principle conflict with scientific interpretations of the physical world and its development. (2) No appeal is needed to a dubious supernatural realm beyond the world; more than enough wonder, grandeur, and mystery exist in the world itself and in the creative forces operating within it. (3) Religious naturalism invites us to come to terms with our finitude as natural beings rather than seeking desperately to deny or overcome that finitude. (4) It is more selfless in that it is not preoccupied with personal salvation beyond the grave. (5) It inspires us to reverence and love the earth, our natural home, and to take responsibility in this life for its continuing well-being. (6) It motivates us to feel at one with the other creatures of earth instead of viewing ourselves as apart from them or lording over them. (7) It encourages us to think for ourselves rather than to rely on putative supernatural revelations claiming to bring saving visions from another world. Readers are invited to reflect upon these alleged merits of religious naturalism and to compare them with supernaturalistic versions of religious faith.

See also Problems with the concept of God (Chapter 38), The problem of religious language (Chapter 39), Naturalistic rejoinders to theistic arguments (Chapter 40), Why is there a universe at all, rather than just nothing? (Chapter 41), The sociobiological account of religious belief (Chapter 42).

References

Barlow, C. (1997) *Green Space, Green Time: The Way of Science*, New York: Copernicus.
Corrington, R. (1997) *Nature's Religion*, Lanham, MD: Rowman & Litttlefield.

Crosby, D. A. (2002) *A Religion of Nature*, Albany, NY: State University of New York Press.

—— (2005) 'The distinctiveness of religion and religious value,' *American Journal of Theology and Philosophy*, 26/3 (September): 199–206.

Dewey, J. (1958) *Experience and Nature*, 2nd edn, New York: Dover Publications.

—— (1962) *A Common Faith*, New Haven, CT: Yale University Press.

—— (1991) *Logic: The Theory of Inquiry*, Carbondale, IL: Southern Illinois University Press.

Goodenough, U. (1994) 'The religious dimensions of the biological narrative,' *Zygon* 29: 603–18.

—— (1998) *The Sacred Depths of Nature*, New York: Oxford University Press.

Hardwick, C. D. (1996) *Events of Grace: Naturalism, Existentialism, and Theology*, Cambridge: Cambridge University Press.

Kaplan, M. (1934) *Judaism as a Civilization*, New York: Macmillan.

Kaufman, G. (2004) *In the Beginning . . . Creativity*, Minneapolis, MN: Augsburg Fortress.

Loomer, B. (1987) 'The size of God,' in W. Dean and L. E. Axel (eds) *The Size of God: The Theology of Bernard Loomer in Context*, Macon, GA: Mercer University Press.

Peters, K. E. (2002) *Dancing with the Sacred: Evolution, Ecology, and God*, Harrisburg, PA: Trinity Press International.

Post, J. F. (1987) *The Faces of Existence: An Essay in Nonreductive Metaphysics*, Ithaca, NY: Cornell University Press.

Stone, J. (1992) *The Minimalist Vision of Transcendence: A Naturalistic Philosophy of Religion*, Albany, NY: State University of New York Press.

Wieman, H. N. (1946) *The Source of Human Good*, Chicago: University of Chicago Press.

—— (1963) 'Intellectual autobiography,' in R. Bretall (ed.) *The Empirical Theology of Henry Nelson Wieman*, New York: Macmillan. Excerpted from: <http://www.harvardsquarelibrary.org/unitarians/wiemanapp.html> (accessed 19 July 2005).

Further reading

Corrington, R. (1997) *Nature's Religion*, Lanham, MD: Rowman & Litttlefield. (Explores the concept of nature naturing.)

Peden, W. C. and L. E. Axel (1993) *New Essays in Religious Naturalism*, Macon, GA: Mercer University Press. (Essays by and about religious naturalists.)

Peters, K. E. (2002) *Dancing with the Sacred: Evolution, Ecology, and God*, Harrisburg, PA: Trinity Press International. (Identifies God with processes of nature.)

Stone, J., D. A. Crosby, V. Goodenough, C. D. Hardwick, and G. Kaufman (2003) 'Symposium-naturalism: varieties and issues,' *Zygon* 38: 85–120. (Five religious naturalists speak.)

63
RELIGIOUS EXPERIENCE
Gwen Griffith-Dickson

A significant number of people claim to have had a religious experience of some kind. Studies conducted in the English-speaking world have put that number between one- and two-thirds of respondents, depending on the methods of questioning used. (Broadly speaking, the more lengthy and confidential the setting, the higher the positive result (Hay 1982; Hood 1995). Many people refer to a spiritual experience of some kind as their grounds for believing in God or in their religion. Religious experience is often put forward as a source of knowledge of God or of religious truths; and many schools of philosophy as well as branches of science take experience as the foundation of knowledge. On that basis it would seem sensible to take religious experience as a source of religious knowledge. However, atheists and skeptics claim that there is good reason to doubt the validity of such experiences; and extensive research has been done in the social sciences, especially psychology, to find alternative explanations for their cause.

Arguments from religious experience

In response to challenges from skeptics, analytic philosophers of religion have put forward arguments that claim that religious experiences can be used as evidence for the existence of God, or at least can be taken as the basis of valid knowledge. Early in the evolution of this discourse Basil Mitchell (Mitchell 1981) suggested that the phenomenon of religious experience could form part of a cumulative case for God's existence; this idea has been taken up by other philosophers such as Richard Swinburne and Caroline Frank Davis (Davis 1989; Swinburne 2004).

The crucial points in Swinburne's case that it is rational to believe the evidence for religious experience are two principles: the Principle of Credulity (PC) and the Principle of Testimony (PT). Unless special considerations are present, it is a principle of rationality that if it seems to someone that x is present, then x probably is present. What we seem to perceive is probably the case. If we accept this as a fundamental 'principle of rationality,' we do not need other justifications to accept the experience as evidential. If we don't, then what faces us is a 'skeptical bog,' in which we are obliged to doubt everything that cannot be proven deductively. This places the onus of proof not on the believer, to demonstrate why an experience is worthy of acceptance, but rather on the skeptic to show why a religious experience should be rejected. But even if we grant that it is rational for people to believe in their own experiences, does that give a reason why the rest of us ought to? Here is where the PT comes in. This suggests that normally people tell the truth. Therefore they are probably accurate in reporting their experiences. If we apply both principles, it is rational to believe that what people tell us they perceived is probably the case.

William Alston examines the way we form beliefs on the basis of experience of other kinds, like sensory perception, and argues that Christian belief in God based on experience is similarly rational because it enjoys the same conditions as other belief-forming practices (Alston 1991). Keith Yandell has devised his version of the argument with criteria that must be met if a religious experience is to be taken as veridical.

> For any subject S and experience E, if S's having E is a matter of its (phenomenologically) seeming to S that S experiences a numinous being N, then if S nonculpably has no reason to think that:
> (i)   S would seem to experience N whether or not there is an N that S experiences, or
> (ii) if E is nonveridical, S could not discover that it was, or
> (iii) if E is of a type T of experience such that every member of T is nonveridical, S could not discover this fact, then E provides S evidence that there is an N, provided that
> (iv) O exists falls within the scope of both collegial and lateral disconfirmation.
> [O = God with attributes of omniscience, omnipotence, etc.]
> (Yandell 1993: 274)

Yandell further adds that there must be no good reason for believing that the person is incapable of telling the difference between a veridical experience and a delusory one, and it must be possible to rule out the existence of the apparent object of experience, should it not exist. If people have numinous experiences under conditions that satisfy all of Yandell's conditions, then there is experiential evidence that God exists (ibid.).

Jerome Gellman has adapted the Swinburnian approach with an argument named BEE (Best Explanation of Experience), supplemented by its companion argument STING (Strength in Number Greatness).

> If a person, S, has an experience, E, which seems (phenomenally) to be of a particular object, O (or of an object of kind, K), then *everything else being equal* the best explanation of S's having E is that S has experienced O (or object of kind, K), rather than something else or nothing at all. (Gellman 1997: 46, emphasis in the original)

As is characteristic of such arguments, Gellman observes that BEE is an indispensable principle of rationality that we put in constant use in other contexts. STING argues that the case for the veridicality of religious experience grows with the number of people having such experiences (Gellman 1997).

The absence of religious experience

Naturally these arguments have been met with criticism on a number of points. Critics of the argument have observed that if reported experiences of God are evidence for the existence of God, the absence of such experiences should be evidence against God's existence. As Michael Martin put is, the absence of a chair is good evidence for there being no chair in the room (Martin 1990: 170). So, should religious experiences and the lack of religious experiences be given equal weight as evidence? There are various considerations to be borne in mind.

Superficially Martin's argument may look fair-minded, but there are good reasons for saying that these two claims are not symmetrical: to conclude that something exists because you perceive it, and to conclude that something does not exist because you failed to perceive it. Using Martin's example, we might conclude that there is no chair in the room at the moment we look in, but would we be justified in concluding that no chairs exist whatsoever? It is difficult not to infer that something exists when you experience it; but when we fail to experience something there could be a number of other reasons for its absence, and we would need further reasons to warrant the inference that no such thing exists.

The atheist might retort that God is understood to be eternal and omnipresent and so ought therefore to be perpetually on view and available for inspection. Few religious believers actually maintain that it works like this. Many put the responsibility for not experiencing God on the human being concerned, rather than on an 'absence' of God. If I cannot access the internet on my laptop, it is not conclusive proof that there is no wireless connection available; it may be that I do not have the right card in my laptop. Spiritual experience could be similar: it requires the right conditions to be present in the human subject and not just the presence or absence of the divine 'object' of experience.

Conflicting reports

Another reason why the idea of religious experience as a form of testimony is challenged is that the witnesses conflict. Flew is the doyen of those who have rejected the credibility of religious experience as grounds for religious belief, on the grounds that what or who is allegedly experienced varies so much that the testimony is unreliable (Flew 1974).

Various arguments have been deployed against his challenge. Others have argued that differences in testimony there may be, but some may be wrong; moreover, one cannot reasonably infer that because *some* conflict, *all* are wrong. There are conflicts in testimony in other areas of research, including science.

Davis argues that while different types of experience cannot all be reduced together, a more complex kind of reconciliation is still possible. She, like others, seeks to identify a common core of mystical experience, stable across different religious traditions, which she describes as 'freedom from all sense of time, space, personal identity, and multiplicity, which leaves them with a blissful, 'naked awareness' of perfect unity and a sense that "this is it," the ultimate level of reality' (Davis 1989: 178). The common core, in my summary of her description, is: mystics generally agree that the ordinary world is not the ultimate reality, nor is the everyday self the deepest self. Ultimate reality is holy, and however it is described, all descriptions are inadequate. Some form of union with ultimate reality is our highest good (1989: 190–2).

Gellman observes that most apparently conflicting testimony arising from people's spiritual experiences does not rest on contradictions in doctrine, but rather on specifically personal details, like God's particular message to the subject of the experience. These do not give rise to logical or indeed theological conflicts so much as the kind of interesting difference that one would expect to see between individuals. God might also will to reveal different things to different people (Gellman 1997: 95).

Confirming or falsifying the evidence

One of the problems with treating religious experience as if it is just like other experiences, or close enough for comfort, is the fact that it is usually impossible to confirm or falsify these experiences as we can with other similar experiences. Bertrand Russell famously complained that while the 'man of science' was able to create repeatable experiences which others could follow and confirm, mystics cannot (Russell 1935: 187–88). Of course not all branches of science are as easy to control as Russell imagined, as cosmologists, vulcanologists and climatologists might observe. In many situations, the data accumulates piecemeal and not in a controlled fashion, and makes for a 'cumulative case' which skeptics can doubt for a considerable length of time; as we can see this in controversial areas such as the nature of AIDS, when it was first observed, or the reality or causes of climate change.

Nevertheless, when there is doubt, religious experiences cannot generally be checked and confirmed as many other kinds of event can be. We usually cannot use one sense to test the first: 'I seem to be hearing God, but can I see him or smell him?' isn't usually a sensible question. Nor can we normally invite a second person to check, although people commonly do go to a more experienced person for counsel. Nor can we repeat the same conditions to see if it happens and draw reliable conclusions if it does not.

Some philosophers have, however, proposed ways of falsifying religious experience. It is widely conceded, for example, that if there are sound reasons for doubting the witnesses' sanity or honesty, or if the experience was self-contradictory in some way, we may deem it to be suspect. Others have sought to provide grounds for confirming the validity of experience. Davis provides four sets of criteria for genuine experiences: internal and external consistency; the moral and spiritual 'fruits' or consequences of the experience; consistency with orthodox doctrine of the religious tradition in question; and the evaluation of the subject's general psychological and mental condition (1989: 71–7). Yandell suggests that comparison of descriptions of experiences from different religions over time can provide a degree of corroboration (1993: 267). Alston points to the practice in long-established religions of looking for the 'fruits' of an experience in a person's life or behavior, testing the 'output' of a religious experience as a way of probing its validity (1991).

I would suggest that we would be more successful in our analysis if we do not view religious experiences as an analogy with sensory experience or information-gathering in the sciences. Perhaps this is just a category mistake. Arguably religious experiences are more like experiences of a relationship than perceptions of a material object (for a saucy analogy, see Griffith-Dickson 2000: 133–44). Many personal experiences, especially those that occur within a relationship, cannot be experienced by another exactly as we do. We can encourage others to have their versions of such experiences, perhaps by describing how we did it, but we must then recognize that their experiences would be unique and personal; and above all, subject also to the will of the other party whom one wishes to experience.

Psychological factors

Some may feel that Swinburne's trust in witnesses is a little too generous when it comes to the case of spiritual or allegedly supernatural experiences. One reason is that spiritual experiences can closely resemble psychotic experiences; how credible is this as 'testimony'? More generally, many have argued that such experiences can be explained – or indeed 'explained away' – by psychology; and therefore they lose their value as evidence for some kind of supernatural entity that supposedly causes such events.

Social sciences have accounted for religious experience in broadly three ways. One is to consider whether these experiences are generated physiologically in some way. Some have investigated the parallels between other vivid and unusual experiences, such as those that occur in schizophrenic or psychotic episodes or after taking drugs, or whether they might be altered states of consciousness that can occur naturally, or the result of mental illness. Others have explored ways in which they might be artificially induced, such as by 'brainwashing,' education, conditioning or indoctrination, social pressure, or the power of suggestion. A group of explanations, finally, has arisen from psychoanalytic or psychodynamic theories which seek the explanation in theories of Oedipal conflict and guilt, fantasies of an idealized father-figure, or the need for psychic integration (for a summary of such studies, see Hood 1995; Griffith-Dickson 2000).

The overall picture emerging from these studies is complex. No single theory or explanation accounts for religious experience as a whole. 'Religious experience' is a very broad notion and difficult to define. Researchers commonly define 'religious experiences' in narrower ways, studying experiences with certain features. They seek explanations or psychological factors that correlate with such experiences; but these explanations apply to those narrow types of experience, and may not adequately account for others. Indeed, reviewing the studies, one wonders sometimes which happened first: the definition of religious experience or the psychological explanation.

Where researchers claim that religious experience resembles psychotic or pathological conditions, they tend to have identified and investigated people who have had dramatic experiences with aspects of quasi-sensory perception, such as visions and voices, featuring demons or other entities. These are precisely the kinds of religious experience that most resemble psychotic episodes. But as it happens, most spiritual experiences reported are not at all like that.

Meanwhile, researchers who investigate whether religious experience is down to suggestion or hysteria investigate people who have dramatic and emotional experiences at revivalist prayer meetings and similar settings which encourage high levels of emotional arousal and have strong currents of social influence or pressure. Sometimes they can indeed find correlations between certain personality types and certain religious experiences. However, when these studies are taken together as a whole, one begins to suspect not so much that a researcher has found the psychological explanation for religious experience as such, but rather that she has discovered something rather more modest: that people with certain kinds of personalities, when they have spiritual experiences, have the experiences that match their personalities. But still, each explanation is only relevant to a comparatively small proportion of cases. No one psychological theory has adequately explained religious experience as a whole. Meanwhile, the various theories come from competing and mutually contradicting schools of psychology; so simply compiling them all to give a composite psychological explanation of religious experience does not provide an intellectually coherent and satisfying answer either.

Psychological explanations don't convincingly 'explain away' all these experiences although they can give enlightening accounts of many of their features. But nevertheless problems still arise if we are asked to follow Swinburne's two principles in order to take all reported experiences at face value.

PC and PT may hold when the experience in question is a simple matter of sense perception. Something must seriously be going wrong if we disagree on whether we see a tree in front of us. But most spiritual experiences are *not* about straightforward sense perception; that is precisely why people call them 'religious,' 'spiritual,' or 'supernatural.' In such cases, it is often not about perceiving something with the senses at all, but about one's inner experience, an insight, a feeling, a communion, a commitment. This means that, more than usual, one is talking about the interpretation of an event, its significance and meaning. When the emphasis is on experience as what is interpreted, the PC and the PT become a little more complex to apply. Interpretations of meaning are highly variable and individual, and not usually a question of just getting the facts and descriptions right. It is not unusual for people to reflect on such experiences over time, and alter their understanding of them. One could ask Swinburne then, *which* testimony we should believe, if someone's report of his experience differs a year later.

Interpretation of a psychologically complex event is also much more difficult and fallible than reporting sensory perceptions. It is easier to come up with an inadequate or distorted report, without being dishonest or mentally unbalanced. Interpretations can also be highly personal and have little meaning for another person. For these reasons, the PC and PT may seem a little simplistic when applied to matters of spirituality. It might be better to say: all things being equal, people are credible witnesses to the fact that they experienced something; and their accounts should be given weight. Nevertheless we have better grounds than usual for begging to differ on the import, impact, significance of that event.

Interpretation

Some have gone on to suggest that religious experience testimony is not credible because it has been heavily 'interpreted,' and is inevitably subjective. This is a suggestion worth considering, because many experiences are not unequivocally of some otherworldly being, but of an otherwise unexceptional percept – a sunset perhaps, a piece of music – which takes on a powerful significance, a deeper meaning, or a sense that God or religious meaning is coming *through* that percept. What that means is that much of the meaning or significance of an experience, and therefore perhaps its testimonial value, is coming from the human subject who experiences it. Does this matter?

Philosophers have approached this question by examining the relationship between 'experience' or 'event' and 'interpretation.' Can there be a 'pure' experience untainted by interpretation? This has been hotly contested. Some say that all experience is inevitably interpreted. Others want to distinguish the 'given,' what is 'out there,' of an experience, from the later subjective, interpretative element. Further questions then are, if there can be a pure description of an experience, is it more useful than one that has been interpreted? Does interpretation compromise evidential value?

Issues to do with the nature of experience and the role of interpretation should be revisited now in the light of the increased understanding we have of the brain and how it operates. We know now that sensory information goes first and fastest to the limbic system, sometimes called 'the emotional brain,' which sorts it swiftly by 'pattern-matching.' If we see a long, very thin object lying across the road, we might pattern-match it to a rope or to a snake, depending on our previous life experiences. It is then emotionally tagged and flagged up as urgent or not; a thing pattern-matched as a rope will have a very different emotional tag from one perceived as a snake. The information arrives more slowly at the neo-cortex, the parts of the brain that engage in logic or in creativity. This allows for more analysis, or more elaboration, at a later stage than the moment of perception.

In a way, this means that both protagonists are right: those who see all perception as inevitably 'interpreted' and those who want to distinguish an unconscious non-volitional 'given' of perception from a later optional task of reflection. There is an immediate 'interpretation' in the limbic system's pattern-matching, which can cognize data and come to the wrong conclusion. And there can be later reflection, which can be as fallible as human musings can often be.

How does this affect our question? It means that there is an initial act of pattern-matching as well as a potential (but not inevitable) rumination: two different moments and ways where our understanding of our own experience may go wrong or right. An extraordinary event, unprecedented in our experience, may not have the 'right' pattern to match it in our minds. The subject may then fall back on similar experiences reported by others, or texts or ideas within familiar religious or other traditions. But the pattern-match is only as good as the resources available to the individual; and here people may well go wrong in labeling or categorizing their experience, or making assumptions about its origin, cause, or purpose.

It should be borne in mind, however, that if this applies to all experience that involves sensory input, it is not a problem uniquely for spirituality. In the dark, when anxious, one can mistake a rope for a snake just as one can mistake an inner voice for the voice of God when feeling distressed and in need of consolation. And this general principle holds both for the arguments in favor of acknowledging religious experience and the objections mounted against them. Much of the force of these arguments, varied as they are, rests on an analogy or claim to parity for religious experiences and other kinds of experience. Much of the force of the objections to them, in turn, comes from rejecting that parity, by claiming that spiritual experience is more suspect than other kinds of perception because certain conditions don't hold. Both are right in some measure. Many other kinds of uncontroversial, but special human experiences would not survive the demands placed on religious experience to prove itself (Griffith-Dickson 2000: 143). On the other hand, it must be acknowledged that spiritual experiences pose these problems for us in a particularly challenging way.

Changing the discussion

One could be a little dissatisfied with the way that spiritual experience has been discussed in the world of English-speaking analytic philosophy. It is ironic that in many religious traditions, experience and spirituality have often been contrasted with the world of argument, logic, and proof rather than being fodder for it. Some might regret the way that the voices of argument have commandeered the terrain of spirituality. Knowledge of God or religious truths is also treated as if it is only inferential, whether deductive or inductive. Again this is in contrast to the way that it has often functioned in the world of spirituality and mysticism. The Muslim scholar Mutahhari, for example, suggests that religious reflection moves back and forth between a 'philosophical' moment of analysis and an existential moment of one's experience and action, or between the 'language of reason' and 'mystic experience' (Mutahhari 2002: 92).

Meanwhile, the assumption – so often unquestioned in these discussions – that religious experience is something like sensory perception exacerbates, or even creates, some of the philosophical problems we have examined in this chapter. Moreover, the focus on 'experience' as 'experiences' – discrete and isolated events – threatens to distort our understanding of the religious or spiritual life. Shouldn't religious or spiritual experience be seen as the whole of the religious or spiritual life? Would that not give rise to a different set of philosophical questions (Griffith-Dickson 2000; 2005)?

See also William James (Chapter 17), Religious traditions and rational assessments (Chapter 19), Religious pluralism (Chapter 20), Mysticism among the world's religions (Chapter 23), Hiddenness (Chapter 29), The problem of religious language (Chapter 39), The sociobiological account of religious belief (Chapter 42), Revelation (Chapter 50), Prayer (Chapter 57), Reformed epistemology (Chapter 58), Phenomenology of religion (Chapter 61).

References

Alston, W. P. (1991) *Perceiving God: The Epistemology of Religious Experience*, Ithaca, NY: Cornell University Press.

Davis, C. F. (1989) *The Evidential Force of Religious Experience*, Oxford: Clarendon Press.

Flew, A. (1974) *God and Philosophy*, London: Hutchinson.

Gellman, J. (1997) *Experience of God and the Rationality of Theistic Belief*, Ithaca, NY: Cornell University Press.

Griffith-Dickson. G. (2000) *Human and Divine: An Introduction to the Philosophy of Religious Experience*, London: Duckworth.

—— (2005) *Philosophy of Religion*, SCM Core Texts, London: SCM Press.

Hay, D. (1982) *Exploring Inner Space*, Harmondsworth: Penguin.

Hood, R. W., Jr. (ed.) (1995) *Handbook of Religious Experience*, Birmingham, AL: Religious Education Press.

Martin, M. (1990) *Atheism: A Philosophical Justification*, Philadelphia: Temple University Press.

Mitchell, B. (1981) *The Justification of Religious Belief*, New York: Oxford University Press.

Mutahhari, M. (2002) *Understanding Islamic Sciences: Philosophy; Theology; Mysticism; Morality; Jurisprudence*, London: ICAS Press.

Russell, B. (1935) *Religion and Science*, Oxford: Oxford University Press.

Swinburne, R. (2004) *The Existence of God*, Oxford: Clarendon Press.

Yandell, K. (1993) *The Epistemology of Religious Experience*, Cambridge: Cambridge University Press.

Further reading

Alston, W. P. (1991) *Perceiving God: The Epistemology of Religious Experience*, Ithaca, NY: Cornell University Press. (The culminating work of many shorter articles and studies, focusing on the rationality of forming a belief in God on the basis of religious experience.)

Davis, C. F. (1989) *The Evidential Force of Religious Experience*, Oxford: Clarendon Press. (A detailed study of the topic, examining the question of whether religious experience provides reliable evidence for the existence of God, with a useful review of psychological aspects of the question.)

Gellman, J. (1997) *Experience of God and the Rationality of Theistic Belief*, Ithaca, NY: Cornell University Press. (A work which constructs his particular argument for the existence of God on the basis of phenomenon of religious experience.)

Griffith-Dickson, G. (2000) *Human and Divine: An Introduction to the Philosophy of Religious Experience*, London: Duckworth. (This focuses on the problem of evil and of religious experience (five chapters on the latter) from an interfaith perspective. It includes a chapter reviewing and assessing contributions from psychology of religion.)

Hood, R. W., Jr. (ed.) (1995) *Handbook of Religious Experience*, Birmingham, AL: Religious Education Press. (An edited volume which contains a number of studies of different issues within the psychological study of religious experience.)

Mitchell, B. (1981) *The Justification of Religious Belief*, New York: Oxford University Press. (An examination of the broader issue of religious belief, which includes a discussion of religious experience.)

Swinburne, R. (1979) *The Existence of God*, Oxford: Clarendon Press. (This presents his 'cumulative argument' for the existence of God, using Bayes's Theorem of probability. Religious experience takes up a chapter in this book. Originally published in 1979, it has been heavily revised in the 2004 edition.)

Yandell, K. (1993) *The Epistemology of Religious Experience*, Cambridge: Cambridge University Press. (An examination of the epistemological questions raised by religious experiences.)

64
RELIGION AND SCIENCE
Mikael Stenmark

One issue of concern for philosophy of religion is the relationship between science and religion. In what way should we understand the relationship between two of the most influential achievements of human culture?

Philosophers have for a long time been interested in this topic, but the broader academic scene within which this discussion has taken place has drastically changed within a few decades. What once was a specialized conversation between small numbers of scholars has now become a topic for scholars from a variety of academic disciplines. This discussion has also burst on to the public scene in ways which would have been almost unthinkablein the 1970s or 1980s. There has been a veritable explosion of books, papers and conferences on science and religion, new courses on science and religion added to the curriculum, and a number of centers (e.g., the Zygon Center for Religion and Science, the Ian Ramsey Centre) and societies (e.g., the European Society for the Study of Science and Theology and the International Society for Science and Religion) have also sprung up. New journals specifically focusing on the science and religion encounter have been released such as *Zygon: Journal of Religion and Science* and *Theology and Science*, and websites launched such as *Metanexus* and *Counterbalance*.

Philosophers have, surprisingly enough, played a minor role in this new emergent interdisciplinary study of science and religion, which has instead been dominated by theologians and natural scientists. Nevertheless, the science–religion debate raises a host of interesting philosophical questions.

How to relate science and religion

One issue of interest concerns precisely how science and religion can be related. How could we, in an illuminating and unbiased way, characterize the main possible ways of relating science and religion?

A first possibility is to maintain that science and religion are rivals. They compete on the same turf and in the end one will emerge as the winner. This *conflict view* has been defended by both philosophers and scientists. John Worrall maintains: 'Science and religion are in irreconcilable conflict. ... There is no way in which you can be *both* properly scientifically minded *and* a true religious believer' (2004: 60). Edward O.

Wilson writes that science will eventually be able 'to explain traditional religion ... as a wholly material phenomenon' (1978: 192).

Conflicts between science and religion can be avoided if they are taken to be inquiries in separate domains. The *independence view* maintains that science and religion are not rivals at all because they have no turf in common. In *Rocks of Ages*, Stephen Jay Gould claims that the idea that there has been and still is a war going on between science and religion is wrong. Instead he maintains that each inquiry frames its own questions and criteria of assessment. Gould writes that 'the net, or magisterium, of science covers the empirical realm. ... The magisterium of religion extends over questions of ultimate meaning and moral value. These two magisteria do not overlap, nor do they encompass all inquiry' (Gould 1999: 6).

Any view in between the conflict view and the independence view would have to presuppose an overlap between science and religion, that is, some area of contact. Hence, the *contact view* says that there is an intersection between science and religion. They are different practices, but science and religion overlap in some respect.

Claiming that there is a *conflict* between science and religion is not, however, a sufficient condition for being a defender of the conflict view. This is so because conflict between science and religion is compatible with both the conflict view and the contact view. Although a necessary condition for being a proponent of the conflict view is to claim that there exists a conflict between the two practices, more is needed, since this is something a spokesperson for the contact view could maintain as well. The additional requirement would, it seems, consist of the idea that religion can never be reconciled with science. One and only one of the two will stand as the winner in the end.

But here we run into problems because when scholars call certain persons advocates of the 'conflict view,' it is because they believe there is a serious and comprehensive clash between religion and science, not necessarily that there is no area of compatibility whatsoever. Ian Barbour (1997) and John Haught (1995), for instance, count not only scientific naturalists or materialists but also religious literalists as advocates of the conflict view. But even if Christian fundamentalists, for instance, see a serious and profound conflict between science and religion, they surely would deny that religion can never be reconciled with science: once scientists get their theories right, they claim, most of the conflict will disappear.

If we accept this description, then we can say that someone maintaining that there is conflict at many intersecting points between science and religion would count as a spokesperson for the conflict view rather than for the contact view. This would mean that a defender of the contact view basically believes that science and religion have different aims, means, and subject matter but that there is nevertheless some area of overlap. What this implies is that probably the most fruitful way of understanding these three science–religion views is to see them as three positions on a scale where the conflict view is located on one end and the independence view on the other with the contact view in the middle, though its boundaries are a bit fuzzy.

Different kinds of contact views

Many who are engaged in the science–religion dialogue today seem to defend some kind of contact view. Even if Barbour's 'theology of nature' entails that the main source of theology lies outside science, scientific theories may nevertheless affect the reformulation of certain religious doctrines, particularly the doctrines of creation and human nature. On these issues there is an overlap between science and religion. Richard Swinburne (1996) and probably most defenders of natural theology would think the traffic goes the other way around. The existence of God is made probable by evidence discovered by science such as the 'fine-tuned' character of the universe, namely that the fundamental parameters of the early universe seem to be fine-tuned for the conditions required for the emergence of life and intelligence.

Others have pointed to the similarities between the methodological structures of science and religion (or theology). Philip Clayton and Steven Knapp (1996) maintain that both science and theology make truth claims about reality, which could be understood in terms of a similar explanatory model, namely inference to the best explanation. Moreover, Nancey Murphy (1990) thinks that Imre Lakatos's notion of a scientific research program, with a hard core and a surrounding protective belt of auxiliary hypothesis, could successfully be applied to theology.

Some of the thinkers who have been more skeptical toward religion can also be classified as proponents of the contact view. Michael Ruse (2001), for instance, believes that there is contact, sometimes tension, and even disagreement between science and religion (more exactly between Darwinism and Christianity), but that although it is not easy for a Darwinian to be a Christian, it is possible.

What is evident, however, is that some scholars think that the overlap between science and religion is fairly limited, and the reformulation of the content of these practices will seldom be called for, whereas others think, for instance, that significant doctrinal reformulation of religion is necessary. It might therefore be fruitful to distinguish between a *weak* and a *strong* contact view. How should one make such a distinction?

One idea is to suggest, as Barbour does, that someone who limits the area of contact to metaphysical presuppositions, methods of inquiry, conceptual tools or models and the like exemplifies the weak contact view, whereas the strong contact view adds to these the theoretical content of science (theories) and religion (beliefs and stories). But suppose that someone claims that the methods of the two practices are or should be the same in the sense that the only evidence that ought to be allowed in both science and religion is observational evidence of the kind that is used in the natural sciences. Such an overlap at the methodological level between science and religion might entail far more radical changes in religion than if we maintain that, for instance, the Christian doctrine of original sin must be modified because of changes in scientific theory. The same results would follow – when it comes to theories of language – if one embraced the positivist idea that the only cognitively meaningful statements are empirical propositions verifiable by sense data. Many religious statements would then lose their cognitive status, failing even to be true or false.

But perhaps we should instead focus on the need to reformulate religion in the light of the development of science. So, whether it has to do with the aims, the means, or the result of using these means to achieve these aims (which include the formation of beliefs, stories or theories), proponents of the weak contact view maintain that substantial reformulation of religion will seldom be called for. Proponents of the strong contact view, on the other hand, claim that substantial reformulation of religious aims, methods or beliefs/doctrines will fairly frequently be called for.

Notice, however, that if we do this, we presuppose that the traffic only goes in one direction, from science to religion. This reflects the general assumption of the science–religion debate, namely that contemporary science is all right as it is; it is religion that needs to change. But the problem is that there is a significant group of scholars who do not think that science is acceptable as it is and who in various ways argue for a science shaped by religion – people who believe that there is a need to develop a 'faith-informed science' (see the last section). We need a typology which also allows for this kind of view. The suggestion is therefore that we define the *weak contact view* as the view that merely minor reformulations or changes of either science or religion are called for in the area of contact and the *strong contact view* as the view that more substantial reformulations or changes of either science or religion are called for in the area of contact.

However, if we define the strong and weak contact view in this way, then both theological conservatives like Alvin Plantinga (1991; 1996) and liberals like Gordon Kaufman (2001) would be identified as defenders of a strong contact view, even though they have radically different views. Kaufman argues that changes in scientific theory make it necessary to reconstruct the conception of God that has traditionally been endorsed by Christians, Muslims, and Jews. There is a conflict between a personal conception of God and scientific theories about cosmic and biological evolution. Plantinga, on the other hand, is ready to question – in the light of his Christian beliefs – parts of evolutionary theory.

It might, in other words, be useful to add another element to the typology. By adding it, we can identify not merely strong and weak versions of the contact view, but also determine whether their advocates tend, when a conflict or tension arises in the area of contact, to give priority to science or to religion. The *science-priority contact view* states that when there is a conflict in the contact area of science and religion, then a reformulation or change of religion is called for unless there are very good reasons to believe otherwise. The *religion-priority contact view* states that when there is a conflict in the contact area of science and religion, then a reformulation or change of science is called for unless there are very good reasons to believe otherwise. Hence, Kaufman has a strong tendency to think that it is something within the practice of religion we should change, whereas Plantinga believes instead that it is something within the practice of science that needs to be altered. When a conflict or tension arises, advocates of these different views place the burden of proof on opposite sides.

A possible objection to the type of typology developed here is that it is too ahistorical, universal, and static to provide a useful map of the relationship between science and religion that people throughout the ages have advocated. This could be avoided if we understand that the characterization of different ways that the science–religion relationship developed are compatible with the idea that they can – and indeed have – changed. If we accept that science and religion are social practices, then like all other social practices, they can change over time. As a result, it is possible that at time t_1 there is no overlap between science and religion; but owing to, say, scientific theory development at time t_2, there is an area of contact between these two practices and perhaps at time t_3 there will be a union between science and religion, or vice versa. Hence there is no immediate risk that the typology proposed would turn out to be too ahistorical and static to provide a useful map of the relationship between science and religion.

It would not be too universal either, because the typology is applicable to not merely variation over time but to different kinds of sciences and different kinds of religions. In other words, science could be explicated in terms of a particular discipline like physics or biology or in terms of all the natural sciences or the natural sciences and the social sciences, and so on. Religion could be explicated not merely in terms of different religions such as Christianity, Islam, and Buddhism, but also in terms of denominations within a religion such as Orthodox, Catholic, and Protestant Christians. Hence the relationship between the natural sciences and Christianity at time t_1 might look quite different from the relationship between the natural sciences and Buddhism at time t_1.

The methodological challenge to religion

Beliefs, theories, and the like are acquired, revised, or rejected in the actual life of both science and religion. These processes involve reasoning of some sort. Do practitioners in both fields endorse the same kinds of reasoning or if not, should they endorse the same kinds of reasoning? Many have seen this as a challenge to religion. All religions face the challenge posed by the successful methodology of science. Science seems to provide a reliable – perhaps even the only reliable – path to knowledge, whereas religion seems to be subjective, emotional, and based on traditions or authorities. This constitutes the *methodological challenge to religion*.

Is it legitimate critically to challenge the way beliefs are formed, rejected, and revised in religion by taking science as the paradigm example of rationality? In the broadest sense, any 'methodology' of science and religion refers to the *means* of different kinds that are developed in these practices to obtain the goals that characterize these activities in question. A subset of these means is the 'epistemic' one dealing with belief formation, justification, and revision. So first, when we have a good grasp of the goals of science and religion, it seems we are in a position to determine whether the means their practitioners have developed to achieve these goals are successful, interchangeable, or movable from one particular practice to another.

Practitioners of religion and science have some aims in mind when they do what they do; so what is it that they are trying to achieve by these activities? What is offered here is an outline of how one can think about the teleology of science and religion. Roughly, we could assume that the overall aim of religion is to help people theoretically understand and practically integrate the divine dimension of reality into their lives and thereby release its capacity or value for their lives and for their existential concerns. The practitioners of religion differ in their accounts of what the appropriate means are for bringing about this change, but they seem to agree that this is a primary aim of religion. We could say that religion has a *soteriological goal.* In Christianity this typically means that salvation lies in a personal relationship with God through Jesus of Nazareth. Science, on the other hand, is generally understood to lack this kind of concern.

Typically religion also has an epistemic goal (that is, it attempts to say something true about reality), but it is subordinated to the soteriological goal. This is true, at least, in the sense that many Christians do not merely affirm the truth of beliefs such as that there is a God, that God is love, or that God created the world. Instead their primary aim is to have an appropriate relationship with God so that they can implement the divine dimension of reality in their lives. For them it is sufficient to know what is necessary for them to live the life they must, in relation to God.

Scientists have the epistemic goal of contributing to the long-term community project of understanding the natural and social world. In a similar fashion, religious practitioners may have the aim of contributing to the religious community's long-term goal of understanding the divine, to the extent that this is understood to be possible for beings in our predicament. Note that even though this formulation parallels that of science, it is a more controversial and slightly misleading characterization in the religious case. This is because in religion, the emphasis is so much on *being* religious, on *living* a life in the presence of the divine. The epistemic goal of religion is shaped by the soteriological agenda. Therefore, it is perhaps more adequate to say that the epistemic goal of Christianity, for instance, is to promote as much knowledge of God as is necessary for people to live a religious life successfully (knowing that God is love, that God wants to redeem us, and how God redeems us, etc.).

A crucial difference between the epistemic goals of the two practices is then that in science the aim is to increase the *general body of knowledge* about the social and natural world, whereas in religion it is to increase the *knowledge of each of its practitioners* to such an extent that they can live a religious life successfully. To contribute to the epistemic goal of religion is first of all to increase, up to a certain level, the religious knowledge (say, at least to the level necessary for salvation) of as many people as possible (although Judaism is one exception to this rule). It is not, as in science, to move the frontiers of knowledge of nature and society forward as much as possible.

To achieve their epistemic goal, scientists work on different problems. They specialize and there is thus a division of labor. Moreover, scientists try to provide individuals belonging to different research groups with access to the data they discover and to the theories they develop. An integrated part of this process is not only cooperation, but also competition among scientists, allowing and encouraging the critical scrutiny of other people's work. In religion, on the other hand, the process of critical evaluation is done in quite a different and less systematic way. The key question in this practice is whether the *means* (or in scientific terminology, the methods) that have been developed by the previous generations of practitioners of Christianity, for example, to allow contact with God, to enable its practitioners to live a Christian life successfully and to help other people become Christians, are still appropriate, or whether instead these means need to be improved or even radically changed in some way.

So whereas the mission of science is not to have all of us give up our old occupations and become scientists, the mission of many religions is something like that; it is to make all non-religious practitioners into religious practitioners and give people the religious knowledge they need to live such lives successfully. The social organization and the process and aim of critical evaluation will then look different if you are principally concerned with the question 'How could we improve our relationship to God and make the path to salvation understandable and compelling to people who are not yet practitioners?' rather than 'How could we improve our understanding of and control over events in the natural and social world?' Therefore, differences in the teleology of scientific and religious practice explain (at least to some extent) why different means are developed to attain the goals of these two practices, and it also shows that what has been a successful means in one practice could not automatically or straightforwardly be assumed to be also a successful means in the other.

The theoretical challenge to religion

For many in the science–religion dialogue, science raises a *theoretical challenge to religion*; that is to say, current scientific theories are understood to have implications for the content of religious beliefs and theological doctrines. It is assumed that at least there is an overlap here so that a reformulation of religious ideas about God, creation, human nature, and so forth might be called for. Some of the topics discussed concern all theistic religions (at least Judaism, Christianity, and Islam); others concern more specifically Christian beliefs and doctrines.

One set of issues focuses on *conceptions of God* and the scientific account of the world. Is a belief in a personal God compatible with scientific theories or must the divine be understood differently in an age of science? Religious skeptics such as Steven Weinberg (1994) maintain that the universe offers no evidence whatsoever that any divine personality underlies the universe and conclude that therefore we should not hold such a belief or any religious belief at all. Religious theists such as John Polkinghorne (1989) would claim such compatibility whereas religious naturalists such as Kaufman (2001) would agree with Weinberg but deny that his rejection of religion is justified. Instead, the divine needs to be reinterpreted as a profound immanent mystery, as serendipitous creativity. A discussion among religious theists in the science–religion debate is whether science supports or is more in consonance with a panentheist than a classic theist conception of God.

Another important question concerns how to understand divine action within a scientifically described universe. Some agree with Paul Davies (1992) that God designed the world as a many-leveled creative process of law and change in which he endowed matter with diverse potentialities and let the world create itself. Others, like George F. R. Ellis (2002), reject this kind of revised deism and maintain that quantum indeterminacy provides the 'gate' through which God can act on the physical universe. Polkinghorne suggests instead that we should see God's action as an input of pure information. In chaos theory an infinitesimally small energy input can produce a very large change in the system. God's selection among the possibilities present in chaotic processes could bring about novel structures, and in this way God could act in the universe.

Another set of issues centers on religious and scientific *conceptions of human nature* and our place in nature. The traditional Judeo-Christian view held that the first humans, Adam and Eve, were created in the Garden of Eden. But evolutionary theory entails that there never was a paradise without conflict, death, and suffering and that we are descendents of earlier pre-human beings. Not only does it seem as if the traditional doctrine of the Fall must go and the category of sin be reinterpreted, but the question must be asked: When and how did evolving hominids become beings created in the image of God? Different solutions have been proposed. For instance, Terence Penelhum (2000) suggests that Christians have to see the doctrine of *imago Dei* not as a statement of what human beings originally were, but as a statement of what they have the capacity to be. What about religious ideas concerning a free will and evolutionary accounts that we are determined by our genes, inherited from more primitive ancestors? How could Mother Teresa's behavior on the streets of Calcutta have been an expression of genuine altruism if, as Richard Dawkins (1989) and others have maintained, she and all of us are the survival machines of selfish genes?

Many biologists in particular seem to think that evolutionary theory implies both a meaningless universe and humanity's (*Homo sapiens*) being the result of a purposeless and natural process that did not have us in mind. This idea undermines the religious belief that there is a purpose or meaning to the existence of the universe and to human life in particular. A possible response is that even if we assume that God's knowledge is limited to everything that is or has been and what follows deterministically from it, it seems as though God's ability to predict with great accuracy the outcome of future natural causes and events is enormous (Stenmark 2001). We cannot, therefore, automatically assume that what is likely given such an amount of knowledge is the same as what is likely given the scientific knowledge that we happen to have. So if God planned to create us and if it is likely that we would actually come into existence, given what God can know about the future of the evolving creation, then we could reasonably claim that we are here for a reason, and that there is a purpose in this sense to our existence. To establish the opposite conclusion seems to require more than basing our calculation of probable outcomes on current scientific theories.

Neuroscientific studies of religious experience have also received a great deal of attention in the science–religion dialogue. Studies of brain activity during religious experiences at the least make it clear that religious experiences have correlates in brain functional states, and at the most that they (or many of them) are the result of abnormal neural activities in the temporal lobes and limbic system. As Jerome Gellman (2001) points out, even if some of these studies seem to be unjustifiably reductionistic, they have relevance for the possibility of an evidential case for the validity of mystical experiences of God.

The value/ideology challenge to science

The level of engagement described so far has typically been understood in terms of the relevance of the content of particular scientific theories for religious belief. If there is any traffic, it is assumed to be one-way: from science to religion. But this third challenge changes the flow of the traffic in an interesting way. Since at least the publication of Thomas Kuhn's *The Structure of Scientific Revolution* (1962), there has been a growing awareness within the philosophy of science, and perhaps even more significantly within the sociology of science, of the role of hidden ideologies and value-commitments within scientific knowledge production. These insights seem to undermine the received conception of science, the *value-free view*, and the self-understanding many scientists have of what they are doing as scientists. This is the *value/ideology challenge to contemporary science*. These philosophers and sociologists have instead maintained that we need a new conception of science in which science and values are explicitly linked. We need a science that is infused with or guided by values, ideology, and by extension, religion. We must develop a *value-directed view* of science because it is excessively naive to think that science is an objective and universal enterprise which does not depend on any creed or ideology.

This opens up a way from religion to science; religion should shape science because realistically all we can have is a science which in fact is an androcentric science, a feminist science, a left-wing science, a faith-informed science, and so on. Science understood in this way will be explicit about the philosophical presuppositions, value commitments, and ideological elements that shape its practitioners and their activities. Plantinga's idea of an Augustinian science and Golshani's idea of an Islamic science would be examples of this way of thinking. Plantinga writes that 'in doing Augustinian science, you start by assuming the deliverances of the [Christian] faith, employing them along with anything else you know in dealing with a given scientific problem or project' (Plantinga 1996: 377). Golshani instead advocates an Islamic science by which he means 'a science that is framed within an Islamic worldview and whose main characteristics are that it considers Allah as the Creator and Sustainer of the universe; does not limit the universe to the material world; attributes a telos to the universe; and accepts a moral order for the universe' (Golshani 2000: 4).

On the one hand, it seems fairly clear that the value-free view is losing its credibility and many engaged in the science–religion debate seem to fail to take this into account. On the other hand, it might be possible to develop a plausible conception of science that is not an example of the value-free view but which nevertheless falls short of being an instance of an Augustinian or Islamic science (e.g., Stenmark 2004; response in Ratzsch 2004).

See also Creation and divine action (Chapter 30), The cosmological argument (Chapter 32), The teleological argument (Chapter 33), The sociobiological account of religious belief (Chapter 42), Miracles (Chapter 55), Religious naturalism (Chapter 62).

References

Barbour, I. (1997) *Religion and Science*, San Francisco, CA: HarperSanFrancisco.

Clayton, P. and S. Knapp (1996) 'Rationality and Christian self-conceptions,' in M. W. Richardson and W. J. Wildman (eds) *Religion and Science*, London: Routledge.

Davies, P. (1992) *The Mind of God*, New York: Simon & Schuster.

Dawkins, R. (1989) *The Selfish Gene*, Oxford: Oxford University Press.

Ellis, G. F. R. (ed.) (2002) *The Far-Future Universe*, Radnor, PA: Templeton Foundation.

Gellman, J. (2001) *Mystical Experience of God*, Aldershot: Ashgate.

Golshani, M. (2000) 'How to make sense of "Islamic Science"?,' *American Journal of Islamic Social Sciences* 17/3 (March): 1–21.

Gould, S. J. (1999) *Rocks of Ages: Science and Religion in the Fullness of Life*, New York: Ballantine.

Haught, J. F. (1995) *Science and Religion*, New York: Paulist Press.

Kaufman, G. (2001) 'On thinking of God as serendipitous creativity,' *Journal of the American Academy of Religion* 69: 409–25.

Murphy, N. (1990) *Theology in the Age of Scientific Reasoning*, Ithaca, NY: Cornell University Press.

Penelhum, T. (2000) *Christian Ethics and Human Nature*, Harrisburg, PA: Trinity Press.

Plantinga, A. (1991) 'When faith and reason clash: evolution and the Bible,' *Christian Scholar's Review* 21: 8–32.

—— (1996) 'Science: Augustinian or Duhemian?' *Faith and Philosophy* 13: 368–94.

Polkinghorne, J. (1989) *Science and Providence*, London: SPCK.

Ratzsch, D. (2004) 'Stenmark, Plantinga, and scientific neutrality,' *Faith and Philosophy* 21: 353–64.

Ruse, M. (2001) *Can a Darwinian be a Christian?*, Cambridge: Cambridge University Press.

Stenmark, M. (2001) *Scientism: Science, Ethics and Religion*, Aldershot: Ashgate.

—— (2004) 'Should religion shape science?,' *Faith and Philosophy* 21: 334–52.

Swinburne, R. (1996) *Is there a God?* Oxford: Oxford University Press.

Weinberg, S. (1994) *Dreams of a Final Theory*, reprint edn, New York: Vintage.

Wilson, E. O. (1978) *On Human Nature*, Cambridge, MA: Harvard University Press.

Worrall, J. (2004) 'Science discredits religion,' in M. L. Peterson and R. J. VanArragon (eds) *Contemporary Debates in Philosophy of Religion*, Oxford: Blackwell.

Further reading

Brooke, J. H. (1991) *Science and Religion*, Cambridge: Cambridge University Press. (A historical survey of the interaction between science and religion.)

Stenmark, M. (2004) *How to Relate Science and Religion*, Grand Rapids, MI: Eerdmans. (Explores different models of how to relate science and religion.)

Van Huyssteen, J. W. V. (2003) *Encyclopedia of Science and Religion*, vols 1-2, New York: Thomson/Gale. (Presents all the key concepts and issues in the science–religion debate.)

INDEX

DATE DUE

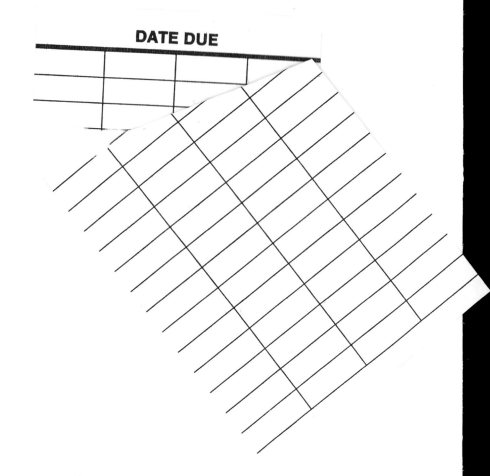